The Official *SCRABBLE*® Players Dictionary

Third Edition

MERRIAM-WEBSTER, INC., PUBLISHERS
SPRINGFIELD, MASSACHUSETTS

The Official SCRABBLE® Players Dictionary
has been endorsed by the
National SCRABBLE® Association.

For information on SCRABBLE® clubs, tournaments, publications,
school programs, and other activities, contact:

National SCRABBLE® Association
Box 700
Greenport, NY 11944
Phone: (516) 477-0033
Fax: (516) 477-0294

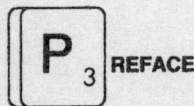

PREFACE

This is the third edition of the enormously popular Official SCRABBLE® Players Dictionary, and it includes more than 1,000 words not included in the previous edition. This dictionary has been prepared especially for lovers of SCRABBLE® Brand crossword games and is endorsed by the National SCRABBLE® Association for recreational and school use.

It is important to remember that The Official SCRABBLE® Players Dictionary was edited solely with this limited purpose in mind. It is not intended to serve as a general dictionary of English; thus, such important features of general dictionaries as definitions of multiple senses, pronunciation respellings, etymologies, and usage labels are omitted.

It is the intention of the makers of SCRABBLE® Brand crossword games that they be enjoyed by children and adults alike. With this consideration in mind, words likely to offend players of the game have been omitted from this edition. The words omitted are those that would qualify for a warning usage note on the basis of standards applied in other Merriam-Webster dictionaries.

The detailed organization and special features of the dictionary are explained in the Introduction which follows. It should be read with care by all who use the dictionary. Now that this new updated work is available, we are confident that it will afford satisfaction and enjoyment to SCRABBLE® Brand crossword game players everywhere.

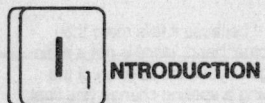

1 INTRODUCTION

MAIN ENTRIES ● Main entries are listed in boldface type and are set flush with the left-hand margin of each column. Except for an occasional cross-reference (such as **MISSPOKEN** past participle of misspeak), main entries contain from two to eight letters, since words within this range are considered to be most useful to SCRABBLE® crossword game players. Words that are not permissible in SCRABBLE® crossword games have not been included in this dictionary. Thus, proper names, words requiring hyphens or apostrophes, words considered foreign, and abbreviations have been omitted. Because dictionaries have different standards for selecting entries, several desk dictionaries were consulted in preparing the list of main entries for this book. Obsolete, archaic, slang, and nonstandard words are included because they are permitted by the rules of the game. All variant forms of a main entry are shown at their own alphabetical places and defined in terms of the principal form. Words that exceed eight letters in length and are not inflected forms of words entered in this dictionary should be looked up in a desk dictionary. The National SCRABBLE® Association recommends Merriam-Webster's Collegiate Dictionary, Tenth Edition, as a source of additional words.

RUN-ON ENTRIES ● A main entry may be followed by one or more derivatives in boldface type with a different part-of-speech label. These are run-on entries. Run-on entries are not defined since their meanings are readily derivable from the meaning of the root word.

FENDER   *n* pl. -S a metal guard over the wheel of a motor vehicle **FENDERED** *adj*

HAMULUS   *n* pl. -LI a small hook **HAMULAR, HAMULATE, HAMULOSE, HAMULOUS** *adj*

No entry has been run on at another if it would fall alphabetically more than three places from the entry. When you do not find a word at its own place, it is always wise to check several entries above and below to see if it is run on.

CROSS-REFERENCES ● A cross-reference is a main entry that is an inflected form (such as the plural form of a noun, the past tense form of a verb, or the comparative form of an adjective) of another word. An inflected form is entered as a main entry if it undergoes a spelling change in addition to or instead of suffixation *and* if it falls alphabetically more than three places away from the root word.

For example, in the entries reproduced below, **DICING** is a main entry because it involves a spelling change (the final -*e* of *dice* is dropped) besides the addition of the -ING ending and because it falls more than three places from the entry DICE. On the other hand, *dices* is not a main entry because it involves no spelling change beyond the addition of the ending -S. The word *diced,* although involving a spelling change (the final -*e* of *dice* is dropped), is not a main entry because it does not fall more than three places from DICE. DICIER and DICIEST are main entries because they involve a spelling change (the -*e* is dropped and the final -*y* is changed to -*i*) besides the addition of the -ER, -EST endings and they fall more than three places from the entry DICEY.

DICE	*v* DICED, DICING, DICES to cut into small cubes
DICENTRA	*n* pl. -S a perennial herb
DICER	*n* pl. -S a device that dices food
DICEY	*adj* DICIER, DICIEST dangerous
DICHASIA	*n/pl* flower clusters
DICHOTIC	*adj* affecting the two ears differently
DICHROIC	*adj* having two colors
DICIER	comparative of dicey
DICIEST	superlative of dicey
DICING	present participle of dice

This policy is intended to make the word desired as easy to find as possible without wasting space. Nevertheless, many inflected forms will appear only at the main entry.

You should always look at several entries above and below the expected place if you do not find the desired word as a main entry.

Cross-reference entries for present tense third person singular forms of verbs use the abbreviation "sing."

PARTS OF SPEECH ● An Italic label indicating a part of speech follows each main entry except cross-references (such as DICIER, DICIEST, DICING), for which the label is given at the root word. The eight traditional parts of speech are indicated as follows:

n	noun	*pron*	pronoun
v	verb	*prep*	preposition
adj	adjective	*conj*	conjunction
adv	adverb	*interj*	interjection

The label *n/pl* is given to two kinds of nouns. One is the plural noun that has no singular form.

KINETICS *n/pl* a branch of science dealing with motion

The other is the plural noun of which the singular is not entered in this dictionary. Singular forms are omitted if they contain more than eight letters.

NUCLEOLI *n/pl* nucleoles

Nucleolus, the singular form, has nine letters and is not entered.

When a word can be used as more than one part of speech, each part of speech is entered separately if the inflected forms are not spelled alike. For example, both the adjective *pale* and the verb *pale* are entered because the inflected forms vary.

PALE   *adj* PALER, PALEST lacking intensity of color

PALE   *v* PALED, PALING, PALES to make or
            become pale

On the other hand, the verb *leg* is entered while the noun *leg* is not because the inflected form *legs* at the verb is spelled the same as the plural form of the noun. In a dictionary for SCRABBLE® crossword game players, entry of the noun is therefore redundant. Homographs (words spelled alike) which may be used as the same part of speech are treated in the same way. For example, *gin* is entered as a verb twice because the inflected forms are spelled differently.

GIN   *v* GINNED, GINNING, GINS to remove seeds
           from cotton

GIN   *v* GAN, GUNNEN, GINNING, GINS to begin

If both sets of inflected forms were spelled alike, only one *gin* would be entered in this dictionary. In this way the dictionary includes as many different spellings as possible yet avoids wasting space with repeated entry of words spelled in the same way. The SCRABBLE® crossword game player, after all, needs only one entry to justify a play.

INFLECTED FORMS   ●   Inflected forms include the past tense, past participle, present participle, and present tense third person singular of verbs, the plural of nouns, and the comparative and superlative of adjectives and adverbs. They are shown in capital letters immediately following the part-of-speech label. Irregular inflected forms are listed as main entries when they fall four or more alphabetical places away from the root word (see **Cross-References** above). All inflected forms are allowable for play in SCRABBLE® crossword games.

The principal parts of the majority of verbs are shown as -ED, -ING, -S (or -ES when applicable). This indicates that the past tense and past participle are formed simply by adding -*ed* to the entry word, that the present participle is formed simply by adding -*ing* to the entry word, and that the present third person singular is formed simply by adding -*s* (or -*es*) to the entry word.

NEATEN   *v* -ED, -ING, -S to make neat

When inflection of an entry word involves any spelling change in addition to the suffixal ending (such as the dropping of a final -*e*, the doubling of a final consonant, or the changing of a final -*y* to -*i*) or when the inflection is irregular, the inflected forms given indicate such changes.

MOVE   *v* MOVED, MOVING, MOVES to change from
           one position to another

SUP   *v* SUPPED, SUPPING, SUPS to eat supper

PLY   *v* PLIED, PLYING, PLIES to supply with or
offer repeatedly PLYINGLY *adv*

EAT   *v* ATE or ET, EATEN, EATING, EATS to
consume food

For verbs of more than one syllable, either the last syllable or the last
two syllables are shown.

MUMBLE   *v* -BLED, -BLING, -BLES to speak unclearly

BENEFIT   *v* -FITED, -FITING, -FITS or -FITTED,
-FITTING, -FITS to be helpful or useful to

The plurals of nouns are preceded by the abbreviation "pl." Most
plurals are shown as -S (or -ES when applicable) to indicate that the
plural is formed simply by adding the given suffix to the entry word.

ACID   *n* pl. -S a type of chemical compound

When pluralizing a noun involves any spelling change in addition to the
suffixal ending (such as the changing of a final -*y* to -*i*- or a final -*f* to
-*v*-) or when the plural is irregular, the plural form shown indicates such
change.

CITY   *n* pl. CITIES a large town

BEEF   *n* pl. BEEFS or BEEVES a steer or cow
fattened for food

ORNIS   *n* pl. ORNITHES avifauna

In such cases involving polysyllabic nouns at least the last syllable is
shown.

EULOGY   *n* pl. -GIES a formal expression of high praise

For the sake of clarity, two groups of nouns that are confusing to many,
those ending in -*o* and those ending in -*y*, are always indicated in this
dictionary by showing at least the last syllable, even though no spelling
change is involved.

MUNGO   *n* pl. -GOS a low-quality wool

NAY   *n* pl. NAYS a negative vote

Variant plurals are shown wherever they add another word permissible
in SCRABBLE® crossword games.

CELLO   *n* pl. -LOS or -LI a stringed musical instrument

Plurals which have the same form as the singular are shown only when
they are the only plural for that entry. This is done to show that for the
entry in question it is not permissible to add -*s* (or -*es*) to the singular to
create a plural.

TAKA   *n* pl. TAKA a monetary unit of Bangladesh

VEG   *n* pl. VEG a vegetable

Otherwise, they are omitted and only the plural with the inflection is
shown.

DEER   *n* pl. -S a ruminant mammal

The comparative and superlative forms of adjectives and adverbs are shown, when applicable, immediately following the part-of-speech label. Any spelling changes are indicated in the forms shown.

JUST   *adj* JUSTER, JUSTEST acting in conformity with what is morally good

FAR   *adv* FARTHER, FARTHEST or FURTHER, FURTHEST at or to a great distance

LACEY   *adj* LACIER, LACIEST lacy

Not all adjectives or adverbs can be inflected, and only those inflected forms shown are acceptable. None of the adjectives and adverbs listed as run-on entries in this dictionary have inflected forms.

DEFINITIONS   ●   In most cases, only one very brief definition is given for each main entry since definitions do not play a significant role in the SCRABBLE® crossword game. This definition serves only to orient the player in a general way to a single meaning of the word. It is not intended to have all the precision and detail of a definition in a good general dictionary.

When a word consisting of eight letters or less appears in a definition but is not an entry in this dictionary, it is glossed in parentheses. For example, at the entry for the verb *hand,* the noun "hand" is used in the definition and is glossed because the noun *hand* is not a separate entry.

HAND   *v* -ED, -ING, -S to present with the hand (the end of the forearm)

A main entry that is a variant form of another entry is defined in terms of the most common form, which is entered and defined at its own alphabetical place.

MATZA   *n* pl. -S matzo

MATZAH   *n* pl. -S matzo

MATZO   *n* pl. -ZOS, -ZOT, or -ZOTH an unleavened bread

SCRABBLE® crossword game players in Canada will be pleased to learn that variant forms such as *honour, centre,* and *cheque,* which are often omitted from general dictionaries, have also been included in this book.

LISTS OF UNDEFINED WORDS   ●   Lists of undefined words appear after the entries of the prefixes RE- and UN-. These words are not defined because they are self-explanatory: their meanings are simply the sum of a meaning of the prefix combined with a meaning of the root word. All of their inflected forms are given, however.

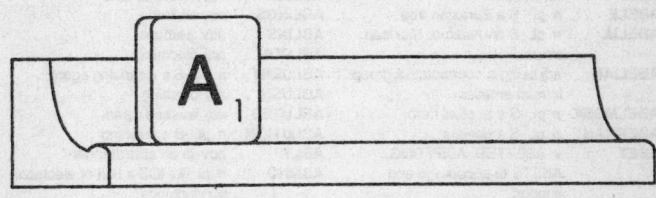

A₁

AA	*n pl.* -S rough, cindery lava
AAH	*v* -ED, -ING, -S to exclaim in amazement, joy, or surprise
AAL	*n pl.* -S an East Indian shrub
AALII	*n pl.* -S a tropical tree
AARDVARK	*n pl.* -S an African mammal
AARDWOLF	*n pl.* -WOLVES an African mammal
AARGH	*interj* — used to express disgust
AARRGH	*interj* aargh
AARRGHH	*interj* aargh
AASVOGEL	*n pl.* -S a vulture
AB	*n pl.* -S an abdominal muscle
ABA	*n pl.* -S a sleeveless garment worn by Arabs
ABACA	*n pl.* -S a Philippine plant
ABACK	*adv* toward the back
ABACUS	*n pl.* -CI or -CUSES a calculating device
ABAFT	*adv* toward the stern
ABAKA	*n pl.* -S abaca
ABALONE	*n pl.* -S an edible shellfish
ABAMP	*n pl.* -S abampere
ABAMPERE	*n pl.* -S a unit of electric current
ABANDON	*v* -ED, -ING, -S to leave or give up completely
ABAPICAL	*adj* directed away from the apex
ABASE	*v* ABASED, ABASING, ABASES to lower in rank, prestige, or esteem **ABASEDLY** *adv*
ABASER	*n pl.* -S one that abases
ABASH	*v* -ED, -ING, -ES to make ashamed or embarrassed
ABASIA	*n pl.* -S a defect in muscular coordination in walking
ABASING	present participle of abase
ABATE	*v* ABATED, ABATING, ABATES to reduce in degree or intensity **ABATABLE** *adj*
ABATER	*n pl.* -S one that abates
ABATIS	*n pl.* -TISES a barrier made of felled trees
ABATOR	*n pl.* -S one that unlawfully seizes an inheritance
ABATTIS	*n pl.* -TISES abatis
ABATTOIR	*n pl.* -S a slaughterhouse
ABAXIAL	*adj* situated away from the axis
ABAXILE	*adj* abaxial
ABBA	*n pl.* -S father — used as a title of honor
ABBACY	*n pl.* -CIES the office of an abbot
ABBATIAL	*adj* pertaining to an abbot
ABBE	*n pl.* -S an abbot
ABBESS	*n pl.* -ES the female superior of a convent of nuns
ABBEY	*n pl.* -BEYS a monastery or convent
ABBOT	*n pl.* -S the superior of a monastery
ABBOTCY	*n pl.* -CIES abbacy
ABDICATE	*v* -CATED, -CATING, -CATES to give up formally
ABDOMEN	*n pl.* -MENS or -MINA the body cavity containing the viscera
ABDUCE	*v* -DUCED, -DUCING, -DUCES to abduct
ABDUCENS	*n pl.* -CENTES a cranial nerve
ABDUCENT	*adj* serving to abduct
ABDUCING	present participle of abduce
ABDUCT	*v* -ED, -ING, -S to draw away from the original position

ABDUCTOR n pl. -ES or -S an abducent muscle

ABEAM adv at right angles to the keel of a ship

ABED adv in bed

ABELE n pl. -S a Eurasian tree

ABELIA n pl. -S an Asian or Mexican shrub

ABELIAN adj being a commutative group in mathematics

ABELMOSK n pl. -S a tropical herb

ABERRANT n pl. -S a deviant

ABET v ABETTED, ABETTING, ABETS to encourage and support

ABETMENT n pl. -S the act of abetting

ABETTAL n pl. -S abetment

ABETTED past tense of abet

ABETTER n pl. -S abettor

ABETTING present participle of abet

ABETTOR n pl. -S one that abets

ABEYANCE n pl. -S temporary inactivity

ABEYANCY n pl. -CIES abeyance

ABEYANT adj marked by abeyance

ABFARAD n pl. -S a unit of capacitance

ABHENRY n pl. -RIES or -RYS a unit of inductance

ABHOR v -HORRED, -HORRING, -HORS to loathe

ABHORRER n pl. -S one that abhors

ABIDANCE n pl. -S the act of abiding

ABIDE v ABODE or ABIDED, ABIDING, ABIDES to accept without objection

ABIDER n pl. -S one that abides

ABIGAIL n pl. -S a lady's maid

ABILITY n pl. -TIES the quality of being able to do something

ABIOSIS n pl. -OSES absence of life **ABIOTIC** adj

ABJECT adj sunk to a low condition **ABJECTLY** adv

ABJURE v -JURED, -JURING, -JURES to renounce under oath

ABJURER n pl. -S one that abjures

ABLATE v -LATED, -LATING, -LATES to remove by cutting

ABLATION n pl. -S surgical removal of a bodily part

ABLATIVE n pl. -S a grammatical case

ABLAUT n pl. -S a patterned change in root vowels of verb forms

ABLAZE adj being on fire

ABLE adj ABLER, ABLEST having sufficient power, skill, or resources

ABLE n pl. -S a communications code word for the letter A

ABLEGATE n pl. -S a papal envoy

ABLER comparative of able

ABLEST superlative of able

ABLINGS adv ablins

ABLINS adv perhaps

ABLOOM adj blooming

ABLUENT n pl. -S a cleansing agent

ABLUSH adj blushing

ABLUTED adj washed clean

ABLUTION n pl. -S a washing

ABLY adv in an able manner

ABMHO n pl. -MHOS a unit of electrical conductance

ABNEGATE v -GATED, -GATING, -GATES to deny to oneself

ABNORMAL n pl. -S a mentally deficient person

ABOARD adv into, in, or on a ship, train, or airplane

ABODE v ABODED, ABODING, ABODES to forebode

ABOHM n pl. -S a unit of electrical resistance

ABOIDEAU n pl. -DEAUS or -DEAUX a type of dike

ABOIL adj boiling

ABOITEAU n pl. -TEAUS or -TEAUX aboideau

ABOLISH v -ED, -ING, -ES to do away with

ABOLLA n pl. -LAE a cloak worn in ancient Rome

ABOMA n pl. -S a South American snake

ABOMASAL adj pertaining to the abomasum

ABOMASUM n pl. -SA the fourth stomach of a ruminant

ABOMASUS n pl. -MASI abomasum

ABOON adv above

ABORAL adj situated away from the mouth **ABORALLY** adv

ABORNING adv while being born

ABORT v -ED, -ING, -S to bring forth a fetus prematurely

ABORTER n pl. -S one that aborts

ABORTION n pl. -S induced expulsion of a nonviable fetus

ABORTIVE adj failing to succeed

ABOUGHT past tense of aby and abye

ABOULIA n pl. -S abulia **ABOULIC** adj

ABOUND v -ED, -ING, -S to have a large number or amount

ABOUT adv approximately

ABOVE	*n pl.* -S something that is above (in a higher place)
ABRACHIA	*n pl.* -S a lack of arms
ABRADANT	*n pl.* -S an abrasive
ABRADE	*v* ABRADED, ABRADING, ABRADES to wear away by friction
ABRADER	*n pl.* -S a tool for abrading
ABRASION	*n pl.* -S the act of abrading
ABRASIVE	*n pl.* -S an abrading substance
ABREACT	*v* -ED, -ING, -S to release repressed emotions by reliving the original traumatic experience
ABREAST	*adv* side by side
ABRI	*n pl.* -S a bomb shelter
ABRIDGE	*v* ABRIDGED, ABRIDGING, ABRIDGES to reduce the length of
ABRIDGER	*n pl.* -S one that abridges
ABROACH	*adj* astir
ABROAD	*adv* out of one's own country
ABROGATE	*v* -GATED, -GATING, -GATES to abolish by authoritative action
ABROSIA	*n pl.* -S a fasting from food
ABRUPT	*adj* -RUPTER, -RUPTEST rudely brief **ABRUPTLY** *adv*
ABSCESS	*v* -ED, -ING, -ES to form an abscess (a localized collection of pus surrounded by inflamed tissue)
ABSCISE	*v* -SCISED, -SCISING, -SCISES to cut off
ABSCISIN	*n pl.* -S a regulatory substance found in plants
ABSCISSA	*n pl.* -SAS or -SAE a particular geometric coordinate
ABSCOND	*v* -ED, -ING, -S to depart suddenly and secretly
ABSEIL	*v* -ED, -ING, -S to rappel
ABSENCE	*n pl.* -S the state of being away
ABSENT	*v* -ED, -ING, -S to take or keep away
ABSENTEE	*n pl.* -S one that is not present
ABSENTER	*n pl.* -S one that absents himself
ABSENTLY	*adv* in an inattentive manner
ABSINTH	*n pl.* -S absinthe
ABSINTHE	*n pl.* -S a bitter liqueur
ABSOLUTE	*adj* -LUTER, -LUTEST free from restriction
ABSOLUTE	*n pl.* -S something that is absolute

ABSOLVE	*v* -SOLVED, -SOLVING, -SOLVES to free from the consequences of an action
ABSOLVER	*n pl.* -S one that absolves
ABSONANT	*adj* unreasonable
ABSORB	*v* -ED, -ING, -S to take up or in
ABSORBER	*n pl.* -S one that absorbs
ABSTAIN	*v* -ED, -ING, -S to refrain voluntarily
ABSTERGE	*v* -STERGED, -STERGING, -STERGES to cleanse by wiping
ABSTRACT	*adj* -STRACTER, -STRACTEST difficult to understand
ABSTRACT	*v* -ED, -ING, -S to take away
ABSTRICT	*v* -ED, -ING, -S to form by cutting off
ABSTRUSE	*adj* -STRUSER, -STRUSEST difficult to understand
ABSURD	*adj* -SURDER, -SURDEST ridiculously incongruous or unreasonable **ABSURDLY** *adv*
ABSURD	*n pl.* -S the condition in which man exists in an irrational and meaningless universe
ABUBBLE	*adj* bubbling
ABULIA	*n pl.* -S loss of will power **ABULIC** *adj*
ABUNDANT	*adj* present in great quantity
ABUSE	*v* ABUSED, ABUSING, ABUSES to use wrongly or improperly **ABUSABLE** *adj*
ABUSER	*n pl.* -S one that abuses
ABUSIVE	*adj* characterized by wrong or improper use
ABUT	*v* ABUTTED, ABUTTING, ABUTS to touch along a border
ABUTILON	*n pl.* -S a flowering plant
ABUTMENT	*n pl.* -S something that abuts
ABUTTAL	*n pl.* -S an abutment
ABUTTED	past tense of abut
ABUTTER	*n pl.* -S one that abuts
ABUTTING	present participle of abut
ABUZZ	*adj* buzzing
ABVOLT	*n pl.* -S a unit of electromotive force
ABWATT	*n pl.* -S a unit of power
ABY	*v* ABOUGHT, ABYING, ABYS to pay the penalty for
ABYE	*v* ABOUGHT, ABYING, ABYES to aby
ABYSM	*n pl.* -S an abyss
ABYSMAL	*adj* immeasurably deep

ABYSS n pl. -ES a bottomless chasm **ABYSSAL** adj

ACACIA n pl. -S a flowering tree or shrub

ACADEME n pl. -S a place of instruction

ACADEMIA n pl. -S scholastic life or environment

ACADEMIC n pl. -S a college student or teacher

ACADEMY n pl. -MIES a secondary school

ACAJOU n pl. -S a tropical tree

ACALEPH n pl. -LEPHAE or -LEPHS a jellyfish

ACALEPHE n pl. -S acaleph

ACANTHUS n pl. -THI or -THUSES a prickly herb

ACAPNIA n pl. -S a lack of carbon dioxide in blood and tissues

ACARI pl. of acarus

ACARID n pl. -S a type of arachnid

ACARIDAN n pl. -S acarid

ACARINE n pl. -S acarid

ACAROID adj resembling an acarid

ACARPOUS adj not producing fruit

ACARUS n pl. -RI a mite

ACAUDAL adj having no tail

ACAUDATE adj acaudal

ACAULINE adj having no stem

ACAULOSE adj acauline

ACAULOUS adj acauline

ACCEDE v -CEDED, -CEDING, -CEDES to consent

ACCEDER n pl. -S one that accedes

ACCENT v -ED, -ING, -S to pronounce with prominence

ACCENTOR n pl. -S a songbird

ACCEPT v -ED, -ING, -S to receive willingly

ACCEPTEE n pl. -S one that is accepted

ACCEPTER n pl. -S one that accepts

ACCEPTOR n pl. -S accepter

ACCESS v -ED, -ING, -ES to get at

ACCIDENT n pl. -S an unexpected or unintentional occurrence

ACCIDIA n pl. -S acedia

ACCIDIE n pl. -S acedia

ACCLAIM v -ED, -ING, -S to shout approval of

ACCOLADE n pl. -S an expression of praise

ACCORD v -ED, -ING, -S to bring into agreement

ACCORDER n pl. -S one that accords

ACCOST v -ED, -ING, -S to approach and speak to first

ACCOUNT v -ED, -ING, -S to give an explanation

ACCOUTER v -ED, -ING, -S to equip

ACCOUTRE v -TRED, -TRING, -TRES to accouter

ACCREDIT v -ED, -ING, -S to give official authorization to

ACCRETE v -CRETED, -CRETING, -CRETES to grow together

ACCRUAL n pl. -S the act of accruing

ACCRUE v -CRUED, -CRUING, -CRUES to come as an increase or addition

ACCURACY n pl. -CIES the quality of being accurate

ACCURATE adj free from error

ACCURSED adj damnable

ACCURST adj accursed

ACCUSAL n pl. -S the act of accusing

ACCUSANT n pl. -S an accuser

ACCUSE v -CUSED, -CUSING, -CUSES to make an assertion against

ACCUSER n pl. -S one that accuses

ACCUSTOM v -ED, -ING, -S to make familiar

ACE v ACED, ACING, ACES to score a point against in a single stroke

ACEDIA n pl. -S apathy

ACELDAMA n pl. -S a place of bloodshed

ACENTRIC adj having no center

ACEQUIA n pl. -S an irrigation ditch or canal

ACERATE adj acerose

ACERATED adj acerose

ACERB adj ACERBER, ACERBEST sour

ACERBATE v -BATED, -BATING, -BATES to make sour

ACERBIC adj acerb

ACERBITY n pl. -TIES sourness

ACEROLA n pl. -S a West Indian shrub

ACEROSE adj needle-shaped

ACEROUS adj acerose

ACERVATE adj growing in compact clusters

ACERVULI n/pl spore-producing organs of certain fungi

ACESCENT n pl. -S something that is slightly sour

ACETA pl. of acetum

ACETAL n pl. -S a flammable liquid

ACETAMID n pl. -S an amide of acetic acid

ACETATE n pl. -S a salt of acetic acid
ACETATED adj

ACETIC adj pertaining to vinegar

ACETIFY v -FIED, -FYING, -FIES to convert into vinegar

ACETIN n pl. -S a chemical compound

ACETONE n pl. -S a flammable liquid
ACETONIC adj

ACETOSE adj acetous

ACETOUS adj tasting like vinegar

ACETOXYL n pl. -S a univalent radical

ACETUM n pl. -TA vinegar

ACETYL n pl. -S a univalent radical
ACETYLIC adj

ACHE v ACHED, ACHING, ACHES to suffer a dull, continuous pain

ACHENE n pl. -S a type of fruit
ACHENIAL adj

ACHIER comparative of achy

ACHIEST superlative of achy

ACHIEVE v ACHIEVED, ACHIEVING, ACHIEVES to carry out successfully

ACHIEVER n pl. -S one that achieves

ACHILLEA n pl. -S yarrow

ACHINESS n pl. -ES the state of being achy

ACHING present participle of ache

ACHINGLY adv in an aching manner

ACHIOTE n pl. -S a yellowish red dye

ACHOLIA n pl. -S a lack of bile

ACHOO interj ahchoo

ACHROMAT n pl. -S a type of lens

ACHROMIC adj having no color

ACHY adj ACHIER, ACHIEST aching

ACICULA n pl. -LAE or -LAS a needlelike part or process
ACICULAR adj

ACICULUM n pl. -LA or -LUMS a bristlelike part

ACID n pl. -S a type of chemical compound

ACIDEMIA n pl. -S a condition of increased acidity of the blood

ACIDHEAD n pl. -S one who uses LSD

ACIDIC adj sour

ACIDIFY v -FIED, -FYING, -FIES to convert into an acid

ACIDITY n pl. -TIES sourness

ACIDLY adv sourly

ACIDNESS n pl. -ES acidity

ACIDOSIS n pl. -DOSES an abnormal condition of the blood
ACIDOTIC adj

ACIDURIA n pl. -S a condition of having excessive amounts of acid in the urine

ACIDY adj sour

ACIERATE v -ATED, -ATING, -ATES to turn into steel

ACIFORM adj needle-shaped

ACING present participle of ace

ACINUS n pl. -NI a small, saclike division of a gland ACINAR, ACINIC, ACINOSE, ACINOUS adj

ACKEE n pl. -S akee

ACLINIC adj having no inclination

ACME n pl. -S the highest point
ACMATIC, ACMIC adj

ACNE n pl. -S a skin disease
ACNED adj

ACNODE n pl. -S an element of a mathematical set that is isolated from the other elements

ACOCK adj cocked

ACOLD adj cold

ACOLYTE n pl. -S an assistant

ACONITE n pl. -S a poisonous herb
ACONITIC adj

ACONITUM n pl. -S aconite

ACORN n pl. -S the fruit of the oak tree

ACOUSTIC n pl. -S a hearing aid

ACQUAINT v -ED, -ING, -S to cause to know

ACQUEST n pl. -S something acquired

ACQUIRE v -QUIRED, -QUIRING, -QUIRES to come into possession of

ACQUIRER n pl. -S one that acquires

ACQUIT v -QUITTED, -QUITTING, -QUITS to free or clear from a charge of fault or crime

ACRASIA n pl. -S a lack of self-control

ACRASIN n pl. -S a substance secreted by the cells of a slime mold

ACRE n pl. -S a unit of area

ACREAGE n pl. -S area in acres

ACRED adj owning many acres

ACRID adj -RIDER, -RIDEST sharp and harsh to the taste or smell

ACRIDINE n pl. -S a chemical compound

ACRIDITY n pl. -TIES the state of being acrid

ACRIDLY adv in an acrid manner

ACRIMONY n pl. -NIES sharpness or bitterness of speech or temper

ACROBAT n pl. -S one skilled in feats of agility and balance

ACRODONT n pl. -S an animal having rootless teeth

ACROGEN n pl. -S a plant growing at the apex only

ACROLECT n pl. -S a high form of a language

ACROLEIN n pl. -S a flammable liquid

ACROLITH n pl. -S a type of statue

ACROMION n pl. -MIA the outward end of the shoulder blade **ACROMIAL** adj

ACRONIC adj occurring at sunset

ACRONYM n pl. -S a word formed from the initials of a compound term or series of words

ACROSOME n pl. -S a thin sac at the head of a sperm

ACROSS prep from one side of to the other

ACROSTIC n pl. -S a poem in which certain letters taken in order form a word or phrase

ACROTISM n pl. -S weakness of the pulse **ACROTIC** adj

ACRYLATE n pl. -S an acrylic

ACRYLIC n pl. -S a type of resin

ACT v -ED, -ING, -S to do something

ACTA n/pl recorded proceedings

ACTABLE adj suitable for performance on the stage

ACTIN n pl. -S a protein in muscle tissue

ACTINAL adj having tentacles

ACTING n pl. -S the occupation of an actor

ACTINIA n pl. -IAE or -IAS a marine animal

ACTINIAN n pl. -S actinia

ACTINIC adj pertaining to actinism

ACTINIDE n pl. -S any of a series of radioactive elements

ACTINISM n pl. -S the property of radiant energy that effects chemical changes

ACTINIUM n pl. -S a radioactive element

ACTINOID n pl. -S an actinide

ACTINON n pl. -S an isotope of radon

ACTION n pl. -S the process of acting

ACTIVATE v -VATED, -VATING, -VATES to set in motion

ACTIVE n pl. -S a participating member of an organization

ACTIVELY adv with activity

ACTIVISM n pl. -S a doctrine that emphasizes direct and decisive action

ACTIVIST n pl. -S an advocate of activism

ACTIVITY n pl. -TIES brisk action or movement

ACTIVIZE v -IZED, -IZING, -IZES to activate

ACTOR n pl. -S a theatrical performer **ACTORISH** adj

ACTRESS n pl. -ES a female actor **ACTRESSY** adj

ACTUAL adj existing in fact **ACTUALLY** adv

ACTUARY n pl. -ARIES a statistician who computes insurance risks and premiums

ACTUATE v -ATED, -ATING, -ATES to set into action or motion

ACTUATOR n pl. -S one that actuates

ACUATE adj sharp

ACUITY n pl. -ITIES sharpness

ACULEATE adj having a sting

ACULEUS n pl. -LEI a sharp-pointed part

ACUMEN n pl. -S mental keenness

ACUTANCE n pl. -S a measure of photographic clarity

ACUTE adj ACUTER, ACUTEST marked by sharpness or severity **ACUTELY** adv

ACUTE n pl. -S a type of accent mark

ACYCLIC adj not cyclic

ACYL n pl. -S a univalent radical

ACYLATE v -ATED, -ATING, -ATES to introduce acyl into

ACYLOIN n pl. -S a type of chemical compound

AD n pl. -S an advertisement

ADAGE n pl. -S a traditional saying expressing a common observation **ADAGIAL** adj

ADAGIO n pl. -GIOS a musical composition or movement played in a slow tempo

ADAMANCE n pl. -S adamancy

ADAMANCY n pl. -CIES unyielding hardness

ADAMANT n pl. -S an extremely hard substance

ADAMSITE n pl. -S a lung-irritating gas

ADAPT v -ED, -ING, -S to make suitable

ADAPTER n pl. -S one that adapts

ADAPTION n pl. -S the act of adapting **ADAPTIVE** adj

ADAPTOR *n* pl. -S adapter

ADAXIAL *adj* situated on the same side as

ADD *v* -ED, -ING, -S to combine or join so as to bring about an increase **ADDABLE** *adj*

ADDAX *n* pl. -ES a large antelope

ADDEDLY *adv* additionally

ADDEND *n* pl. -S a number to be added to another

ADDENDUM *n* pl. -DA something added or to be added

ADDER *n* pl. -S a venomous snake

ADDIBLE *adj* capable of being added

ADDICT *v* -ED, -ING, -S to devote or surrender to something habitually or compulsively

ADDITION *n* pl. -S something added

ADDITIVE *n* pl. -S a substance added to another to impart desirable qualities

ADDITORY *adj* making an addition

ADDLE *v* -DLED, -DLING, -DLES to confuse

ADDRESS *v* -DRESSED or -DREST, -DRESSING, -DRESSES to speak to

ADDUCE *v* -DUCED, -DUCING, -DUCES to bring forward as evidence

ADDUCENT *adj* serving to adduct

ADDUCER *n* pl. -S one that adduces

ADDUCING present participle of adduce

ADDUCT *v* -ED, -ING, -S to draw toward the main axis

ADDUCTOR *n* pl. -S an adducent muscle

ADEEM *v* -ED, -ING, -S to take away

ADENINE *n* pl. -S an alkaloid

ADENITIS *n* pl. -TISES inflammation of a lymph node

ADENOID *n* pl. -S an enlarged lymphoid growth behind the pharynx

ADENOMA *n* pl. -MAS or -MATA a tumor of glandular origin

ADENOSIS *n* pl. -NOSES abnormal growth of glandular tissue

ADENYL *n* pl. -S a univalent radical

ADEPT *adj* ADEPTER, ADEPTEST highly skilled **ADEPTLY** *adv*

ADEPT *n* pl. -S an adept person

ADEQUACY *n* pl. -CIES the state of being adequate

ADEQUATE *adj* sufficient for a specific requirement

ADHERE *v* -HERED, -HERING, -HERES to become or remain attached or close to something

ADHEREND *n* pl. -S the surface to which an adhesive adheres

ADHERENT *n* pl. -S a supporter

ADHERER *n* pl. -S one that adheres

ADHERING present participle of adhere

ADHESION *n* pl. -S the act of adhering

ADHESIVE *n* pl. -S a substance that causes adhesion

ADHIBIT *v* -ED, -ING, -S to take or let in

ADIEU *n* pl. ADIEUS or ADIEUX a farewell

ADIOS *interj* — used to express farewell

ADIPOSE *n* pl. -S animal fat **ADIPIC** *adj*

ADIPOSIS *n* pl. -POSES obesity

ADIPOUS *adj* pertaining to adipose

ADIT *n* pl. -S an entrance

ADJACENT *adj* next to

ADJOIN *v* -ED, -ING, -S to lie next to

ADJOINT *n* pl. -S a type of mathematical matrix

ADJOURN *v* -ED, -ING, -S to suspend until a later time

ADJUDGE *v* -JUDGED, -JUDGING, -JUDGES to determine judicially

ADJUNCT *n* pl. -S something attached in a subordinate position

ADJURE *v* -JURED, -JURING, -JURES to command solemnly

ADJURER *n* pl. -S one that adjures

ADJUROR *n* pl. -S adjurer

ADJUST *v* -ED, -ING, -S to bring to a more satisfactory state

ADJUSTER *n* pl. -S one that adjusts

ADJUSTOR *n* pl. -S adjuster

ADJUTANT *n* pl. -S an assistant

ADJUVANT *n* pl. -S an assistant

ADMAN *n* pl. -MEN a man employed in the advertising business

ADMASS *adj* pertaining to a society strongly influenced by advertising

ADMIRAL *n* pl. -S a high-ranking naval officer

ADMIRE *v* -MIRED, -MIRING, -MIRES to regard with wonder, pleasure, and approval

ADMIRER *n* pl. -S one that admires

ADMIT *v* -MITTED, -MITTING, -MITS to allow to enter

ADMITTER *n* pl. -S one that admits

ADMIX *v* -MIXED or -MIXT, -MIXING, -MIXES to mix

ADMONISH *v* -ED, -ING, -ES to reprove mildly or kindly

ADNATE *adj* joined to another part or organ

ADNATION *n* pl. -S the state of being adnate

ADNEXA *n/pl* conjoined anatomical parts **ADNEXAL** *adj*

ADNOUN *n* pl. -S an adjective when used as a noun

ADO *n* pl. ADOS bustling excitement

ADOBE *n* pl. -S an unburnt, sun-dried brick

ADOBO *n* pl. -BOS a Philippine dish of fish or meat

ADONIS *n* pl. -ISES a handsome young man

ADOPT *v* -ED, -ING, -S to take into one's family by legal means

ADOPTEE *n* pl. -S one that is adopted

ADOPTER *n* pl. -S one that adopts

ADOPTION *n* pl. -S the act of adopting **ADOPTIVE** *adj*

ADORABLE *adj* worthy of being adored **ADORABLY** *adv*

ADORE *v* ADORED, ADORING, ADORES to love deeply

ADORER *n* pl. -S one that adores

ADORN *v* -ED, -ING, -S to add something to for the purpose of making more attractive

ADORNER *n* pl. -S one that adorns

ADOWN *adv* downward

ADOZE *adj* dozing

ADRENAL *n* pl. -S an endocrine gland

ADRIFT *adj* drifting

ADROIT *adj* ADROITER, ADROITEST skillful **ADROITLY** *adv*

ADSCRIPT *n* pl. -S a distinguishing symbol written after another character

ADSORB *v* -ED, -ING, -S to gather on a surface in a condensed layer

ADSORBER *n* pl. -S one that adsorbs

ADULARIA *n* pl. -S a mineral

ADULATE *v* -LATED, -LATING, -LATES to praise excessively

ADULATOR *n* pl. -S one that adulates

ADULT *n* pl. -S a fully developed individual

ADULTERY *n* pl. -TERIES voluntary sexual intercourse between a married person and someone other than his or her spouse

ADULTLY *adv* in a manner typical of an adult

ADUMBRAL *adj* shadowy

ADUNC *adj* bent inward

ADUNCATE *adj* adunc

ADUNCOUS *adj* adunc

ADUST *adj* scorched

ADVANCE *v* -VANCED, -VANCING, -VANCES to move or cause to move ahead

ADVANCER *n* pl. -S one that advances

ADVECT *v* -ED, -ING, -S to convey or transport by the flow of a fluid

ADVENT *n* pl. -S arrival

ADVERB *n* pl. -S a word used to modify the meaning of a verb, adjective, or other adverb

ADVERSE *adj* acting in opposition

ADVERT *v* -ED, -ING, -S to call attention

ADVICE *n* pl. -S counsel regarding a decision or behavior

ADVISE *v* -VISED, -VISING, -VISES to give advice to

ADVISEE *n* pl. -S one that is advised

ADVISER *n* pl. -S one that advises

ADVISING present participle of advise

ADVISOR *n* pl. -S adviser

ADVISORY *n* pl. -RIES a report

ADVOCACY *n* pl. -CIES the act of advocating

ADVOCATE *v* -CATED, -CATING, -CATES to speak in favor of

ADVOWSON *n* pl. -S the right of presenting a nominee to a vacant church office

ADYNAMIA *n* pl. -S lack of physical strength **ADYNAMIC** *adj*

ADYTUM *n* pl. -TA an inner sanctuary in an ancient temple

ADZ *n* pl. -ES a cutting tool

ADZE *n* pl. -S adz

ADZUKI *n* pl. -S the edible seed of an Asian plant

AE *adj* one

AECIA pl. of aecium

AECIAL *adj* pertaining to an aecium

AECIDIAL *adj* pertaining to an aecium

AECIDIUM *n* pl. -IA an aecium

AECIUM *n* pl. -IA a spore-producing organ of certain fungi

AEDES *n pl.* AEDES any of a genus of mosquitoes

AEDILE *n pl.* -S a magistrate of ancient Rome

AEDINE *adj* pertaining to an aedes

AEGIS *n pl.* -GISES protection

AENEOUS *adj* having a greenish gold color

AENEUS *adj* aeneous

AEOLIAN *adj* eolian

AEON *n pl.* -S eon

AEONIAN *adj* eonian

AEONIC *adj* eonian

AEQUORIN *n pl.* -S a protein secreted by jellyfish

AERATE *v* -ATED, -ATING, -ATES to supply with air

AERATION *n pl.* -S the act of aerating

AERATOR *n pl.* -S one that aerates

AERIAL *n pl.* -S an antenna

AERIALLY *adv* in a manner pertaining to the air

AERIE *n pl.* -S a bird's nest built high on a mountain or cliff AERIED *adj*

AERIER comparative of aery

AERIES pl. of aery

AERIEST superlative of aery

AERIFORM *adj* having the form of air

AERIFY *v* -FIED, -FYING, -FIES to aerate

AERILY *adv* in an aery manner

AERO *adj* pertaining to aircraft

AEROBE *n pl.* -S an organism that requires oxygen to live AEROBIC *adj*

AEROBICS *n/pl* exercises for conditioning the heart and lungs by increasing oxygen consumption

AEROBIUM *n pl.* -BIA aerobe

AERODUCT *n pl.* -S a type of jet engine

AERODYNE *n pl.* -S an aircraft that is heavier than air

AEROFOIL *n pl.* -S airfoil

AEROGEL *n pl.* -S a highly porous solid

AEROGRAM *n pl.* -S an airmail letter

AEROLITE *n pl.* -S a meteorite containing more stone than iron

AEROLITH *n pl.* -S aerolite

AEROLOGY *n pl.* -GIES the study of the atmosphere

AERONAUT *n pl.* -S one who operates an airship

AERONOMY *n pl.* -MIES the study of the upper atmosphere

AEROSAT *n pl.* -S a satellite for use in air-traffic control

AEROSOL *n pl.* -S a gaseous suspension of fine solid or liquid particles

AEROSTAT *n pl.* -S an aircraft that is lighter than air

AERUGO *n pl.* -GOS a green film that forms on copper

AERY *adj* AERIER, AERIEST airy

AERY *n pl.* AERIES aerie

AESTHETE *n pl.* -S esthete

AESTIVAL *adj* estival

AETHER *n pl.* -S the upper region of the atmosphere AETHERIC *adj*

AFAR *n pl.* -S a great distance

AFEARD *adj* afraid

AFEARED *adj* afeard

AFEBRILE *adj* having no fever

AFF *adv* off

AFFABLE *adj* easy to talk to AFFABLY *adv*

AFFAIR *n pl.* -S anything done or to be done

AFFAIRE *n pl.* -S a brief amorous relationship

AFFECT *v* -ED, -ING, -S to give a false appearance of

AFFECTER *n pl.* -S one that affects

AFFERENT *n pl.* -S a nerve that conveys impulses toward a nerve center

AFFIANCE *v* -ANCED, -ANCING, -ANCES to betroth

AFFIANT *n pl.* -S one who makes a written declaration under oath

AFFICHE *n pl.* -S a poster

AFFINAL *adj* related by marriage

AFFINE *n pl.* -S a relative by marriage

AFFINED *adj* closely related

AFFINELY *adv* in the manner of a type of mathematical mapping

AFFINITY *n pl.* -TIES a natural attraction or inclination

AFFIRM *v* -ED, -ING, -S to state positively

AFFIRMER *n pl.* -S one that affirms

AFFIX *v* -ED, -ING, -ES to attach

AFFIXAL *adj* pertaining to a prefix or suffix

AFFIXER *n pl.* -S one that affixes

AFFIXIAL *adj* affixal

AFFLATUS *n pl.* -ES a creative inspiration

AFFLICT *v* -ED, -ING, -S to distress with mental or physical pain

AFFLUENT *n pl.* -S a stream that flows into another

AFFLUX n pl. -ES a flowing toward a point

AFFORD v -ED, -ING, -S to have sufficient means for

AFFOREST v -ED, -ING, -S to convert into forest

AFFRAY v -ED, -ING, -S to frighten

AFFRAYER n pl. -S one that affrays

AFFRIGHT v -ED, -ING, -S to frighten

AFFRONT v -ED, -ING, -S to insult openly

AFFUSION n pl. -S an act of pouring a liquid on

AFGHAN n pl. -S a woolen blanket or shawl

AFGHANI n pl. -S a monetary unit of Afghanistan

AFIELD adv in the field

AFIRE adj being on fire

AFLAME adj flaming

AFLOAT adj floating

AFLUTTER adj nervously excited

AFOOT adv on foot

AFORE adv before

AFOUL adj entangled

AFRAID adj filled with apprehension

AFREET n pl. -S an evil spirit in Arabic mythology

AFRESH adv anew

AFRIT n pl. -S afreet

AFT adv toward the stern

AFTER prep behind in place or order

AFTERS n/pl dessert

AFTERTAX adj remaining after payment of taxes

AFTMOST adj nearest the stern

AFTOSA n pl. -S a disease of hoofed mammals

AG adj pertaining to agriculture

AGA n pl. -S a high-ranking Turkish military officer

AGAIN adv once more

AGAINST prep in opposition to

AGALLOCH n pl. -S the fragrant wood of a tropical tree

AGALWOOD n pl. -S agalloch

AGAMA n pl. -S a tropical lizard

AGAMETE n pl. -S an asexual reproductive cell

AGAMIC adj asexual

AGAMOUS adj agamic

AGAPE n pl. -PAE or -PAI the love of God for mankind **AGAPEIC** adj

AGAR n pl. -S a viscous substance obtained from certain seaweeds

AGARIC n pl. -S any of a family of fungi

AGAROSE n pl. -S a sugar obtained from agar

AGATE n pl. -S a variety of quartz **AGATOID** adj

AGATIZE v -IZED, -IZING, -IZES to cause to resemble agate

AGAVE n pl. -S a tropical plant

AGAZE adj gazing

AGE v AGED, AGING or AGEING, AGES to grow old

AGEDLY adv oldly

AGEDNESS n pl. -ES oldness

AGEE adv to one side

AGEING n pl. -S aging

AGEISM n pl. -S discrimination based on age

AGEIST n pl. -S an advocate of ageism

AGELESS adj never growing old

AGELONG adj lasting for a long time

AGENCY n pl. -CIES an organization that does business for others

AGENDA n pl. -S a list of things to be done

AGENDUM n pl. -S an item on an agenda

AGENE n pl. -S a chemical compound used in bleaching flour

AGENESIA n pl. -S agenesis

AGENESIS n pl. AGENESES absence or imperfect development of a bodily part **AGENETIC** adj

AGENIZE v -NIZED, -NIZING, -NIZES to treat with agene

AGENT n pl. -S one who is authorized to act for another **AGENTIAL** adj

AGENTING n pl. -S the business or activities of an agent

AGENTIVE n pl. -S a word part that denotes the doer of an action

AGENTRY n pl. -RIES the office or duties of an agent

AGER n pl. -S one that ages

AGERATUM n pl. -S a flowering plant

AGGADIC adj haggadic

AGGER n pl. -S a mound of earth used as a fortification

AGGIE n pl. -S a type of playing marble

AGGRADE v -GRADED, -GRADING, -GRADES to fill with detrital material

AGGRESS v -ED, -ING, -ES to commit the first act of hostility

AGGRIEVE v -GRIEVED, -GRIEVING, -GRIEVES to distress

AGGRO *n pl.* -GROS a rivalry or grievance

AGHA *n pl.* -S aga

AGHAST *adj* shocked by something horrible

AGILE *adj* able to move quickly and easily **AGILELY** *adv*

AGILITY *n pl.* -TIES the quality of being agile

AGIN *prep* against

AGING *n pl.* -S the process of growing old

AGINNER *n pl.* -S one that is against change

AGIO *n pl.* AGIOS a premium paid for the exchange of one currency for another

AGIOTAGE *n pl.* -S the business of a broker

AGISM *n pl.* -S ageism

AGIST *v* -ED, -ING, -S to feed and take care of for a fee, as livestock

AGITATE *v* -TATED, -TATING, -TATES to move with a violent, irregular action **AGITABLE** *adj*

AGITATO *adj* fast and stirring — used as a musical direction

AGITATOR *n pl.* -S one that agitates

AGITPROP *n pl.* -S pro-Communist propaganda

AGLARE *adj* glaring

AGLEAM *adj* gleaming

AGLEE *adv* agley

AGLET *n pl.* -S a metal sheath at the end of a lace

AGLEY *adv* awry

AGLIMMER *adj* glimmering

AGLITTER *adj* glittering

AGLOW *adj* glowing

AGLY *adv* agley

AGLYCON *n pl.* -S a type of chemical compound

AGLYCONE *n pl.* -S aglycon

AGMA *n pl.* -S eng

AGMINATE *adj* clustered together

AGNAIL *n pl.* -S a piece of loose skin at the base of a fingernail

AGNATE *n pl.* -S a relative on the father's side **AGNATIC** *adj*

AGNATION *n pl.* -S the relationship of agnates

AGNIZE *v* -NIZED, -NIZING, -NIZES to acknowledge

AGNOMEN *n pl.* -MINA or -MENS an additional name given to an ancient Roman

AGNOSIA *n pl.* -S loss of ability to recognize familiar objects

AGNOSTIC *n pl.* -S one who disclaims any knowledge of God

AGO *adv* in the past

AGOG *adv* in a state of eager curiosity

AGON *n pl.* -S or -ES the dramatic conflict between the main characters in a Greek play

AGONAL *adj* pertaining to agony

AGONE *adv* ago

AGONES a pl. of agon

AGONIC *adj* not forming an angle

AGONIES pl. of agony

AGONISE *v* -NISED, -NISING, -NISES to agonize

AGONIST *n pl.* -S one that is engaged in a struggle

AGONIZE *v* -NIZED, -NIZING, -NIZES to suffer extreme pain

AGONY *n pl.* -NIES extreme pain

AGORA *n pl.* -RAS or -RAE a marketplace in ancient Greece

AGORA *n pl.* AGOROT or AGOROTH a monetary unit of Israel

AGOUTI *n pl.* -S or -ES a burrowing rodent

AGOUTY *n pl.* -TIES agouti

AGRAFE *n pl.* -S agraffe

AGRAFFE *n pl.* -S an ornamental clasp

AGRAPHA *n/pl* the sayings of Jesus not found in the Bible

AGRAPHIA *n pl.* -S a mental disorder marked by inability to write **AGRAPHIC** *adj*

AGRARIAN *n pl.* -S one who favors equal distribution of land

AGRAVIC *adj* pertaining to a condition of no gravitation

AGREE *v* AGREED, AGREEING, AGREES to have the same opinion

AGRESTAL *adj* growing wild

AGRESTIC *adj* rural

AGRIA *n pl.* -S severe pustular eruption

AGRIMONY *n pl.* -NIES a perennial herb

AGROLOGY *n pl.* -GIES the science of soils in relation to crops

AGRONOMY *n pl.* -MIES the application of scientific principles to the cultivation of land

AGROUND *adv* on the ground

AGRYPNIA *n* pl. -S insomnia

AGUE *n* pl. -S a malarial fever **AGUELIKE, AGUISH** *adj* **AGUISHLY** *adv*

AGUEWEED *n* pl. -S a flowering plant

AH *interj* — used to express delight, relief, or contempt

AHA *interj* — used to express surprise, triumph, or derision

AHCHOO *interj* — used to represent the sound of a sneeze

AHEAD *adv* at or to the front

AHEM *interj* — used to attract attention

AHIMSA *n* pl. -S the Hindu principle of nonviolence

AHOLD *n* pl. -S a hold or grasp of something

AHORSE *adv* on a horse

AHOY *interj* — used in hailing a ship or person

AHULL *adj* abandoned and flooded, as a ship

AI *n* pl. -S a three-toed sloth

AIBLINS *adv* ablins

AID *v* -ED, -ING, -S to help

AIDE *n* pl. -S an assistant

AIDER *n* pl. -S one that aids

AIDFUL *adj* helpful

AIDLESS *adj* helpless

AIDMAN *n* pl. -MEN a corpsman

AIGLET *n* pl. -S aglet

AIGRET *n* pl. -S aigrette

AIGRETTE *n* pl. -S a tuft of feathers worn as a head ornament

AIGUILLE *n* pl. -S a sharp, pointed mountain peak

AIKIDO *n* pl. -DOS a Japanese art of self-defense

AIL *v* -ED, -ING, -S to cause pain or discomfort to

AILERON *n* pl. -S a movable control surface on an airplane wing

AILMENT *n* pl. -S a physical or mental disorder

AIM *v* -ED, -ING, -S to direct toward a specified object or goal

AIMER *n* pl. -S one that aims

AIMFUL *adj* full of purpose **AIMFULLY** *adv*

AIMLESS *adj* lacking direction or purpose

AIN *n* pl. -S ayin

AINSELL *n* pl. -S own self

AIOLI *n* pl. -S garlic mayonnaise

AIR *v* -ED, -ING, -S to expose to the air (the mixture of gases that surrounds the earth)

AIR *adv* AIRER, AIREST early

AIRBOAT *n* pl. -S a boat used in swampy areas

AIRBORNE *adj* flying

AIRBOUND *adj* stopped up by air

AIRBRUSH *v* -ED, -ING, -ES to apply in a fine spray by compressed air, as paint

AIRBURST *n* pl. -S an explosion in the air

AIRBUS *n* pl. -BUSES or -BUSSES a passenger airplane

AIRCHECK *n* pl. -S a recording made from a radio broadcast

AIRCOACH *n* pl. -ES the cheaper class of accommodations in commercial aircraft

AIRCRAFT *n* pl. AIRCRAFT any machine or device capable of flying

AIRCREW *n* pl. -S the crew of an aircraft

AIRDATE *n* pl. -S the scheduled date of a broadcast

AIRDROME *n* pl. -S an airport

AIRDROP *v* -DROPPED, -DROPPING, -DROPS to drop from an aircraft

AIRER *n* pl. -S a frame on which to dry clothes

AIRFARE *n* pl. -S payment for travel by airplane

AIRFIELD *n* pl. -S an airport

AIRFLOW *n* pl. -S a flow of air

AIRFOIL *n* pl. -S a part of an aircraft designed to provide lift or control

AIRFRAME *n* pl. -S the framework and external covering of an airplane

AIRGLOW *n* pl. -S a glow in the upper atmosphere

AIRHEAD *n* pl. -S a stupid person

AIRHOLE *n* pl. -S a hole to let air in or out

AIRIER comparative of airy

AIRIEST superlative of airy

AIRILY *adv* in an airy manner

AIRINESS *n* pl. -ES the state of being airy

AIRING *n* pl. -S an exposure to the air

AIRLESS *adj* having no air

AIRLIFT *v* -ED, -ING, -S to transport by airplane

AIRLIKE *adj* resembling air

AIRLINE *n pl.* -S an air transportation system

AIRLINER *n pl.* -S a large passenger aircraft

AIRMAIL *v* -ED, -ING, -S to send mail by airplane

AIRMAN *n pl.* -MEN an aviator

AIRN *n pl.* -S iron

AIRPARK *n pl.* -S a small airport

AIRPLANE *n pl.* -S a winged aircraft propelled by jet engines or propellers

AIRPLAY *n pl.* -PLAYS the playing of a record on a radio program

AIRPORT *n pl.* -S a tract of land maintained for the landing and takeoff of aircraft

AIRPOST *n pl.* -S a system of conveying mail by airplane

AIRPOWER *n pl.* -S the military strength of a nation's air force

AIRPROOF *v* -ED, -ING, -S to make impermeable to air

AIRSCAPE *n pl.* -S a view of the earth from an aircraft or a high position

AIRSCREW *n pl.* -S an airplane propeller

AIRSHED *n pl.* -S the air supply of a given region

AIRSHIP *n pl.* -S a lighter-than-air aircraft having propulsion and steering systems

AIRSICK *adj* nauseated from flying in an airplane

AIRSPACE *n pl.* -S the portion of the atmosphere above a particular land area

AIRSPEED *n pl.* -S the speed of an aircraft with relation to the air

AIRSTRIP *n pl.* -S a runway

AIRT *v* -ED, -ING, -S to guide

AIRTH *v* -ED, -ING, -S to airt

AIRTIGHT *adj* not allowing air to escape or enter

AIRTIME *n pl.* -S the time when a broadcast begins

AIRWARD *adv* toward the sky

AIRWAVE *n pl.* -S the medium of radio and television transmission

AIRWAY *n pl.* -WAYS a passageway in which air circulates

AIRWISE *adj* skillful in aviation

AIRWOMAN *n pl.* -WOMEN a female aviator

AIRY *adj* AIRIER, AIRIEST having the nature of air

AISLE *n pl.* -S a passageway between sections of seats **AISLED** *adj*

AISLEWAY *n pl.* -WAYS an aisle

AIT *n pl.* -S a small island

AITCH *n pl.* -ES the letter H

AIVER *n pl.* -S a draft horse

AJAR *adj* partly open

AJEE *adv* agee

AJIVA *n pl.* -S inanimate matter

AJOWAN *n pl.* -S the fruit of an Egyptian plant

AJUGA *n pl.* -S a flowering plant

AKEE *n pl.* -S a tropical tree

AKELA *n pl.* -S a leader of a cub scout pack

AKENE *n pl.* -S achene

AKIMBO *adj* having hands on hips and elbows bent outward

AKIN *adj* related by blood

AKVAVIT *n pl.* -S aquavit

AL *n pl.* -S an East Indian tree

ALA *n pl.* ALAE a wing or winglike part

ALACK *interj* — used to express sorrow or regret

ALACRITY *n pl.* -TIES cheerful promptness

ALAE *pl.* of ala

ALAMEDA *n pl.* -S a shaded walkway

ALAMO *n pl.* -MOS a softwood tree

ALAMODE *n pl.* -S a silk fabric

ALAN *n pl.* -S a large hunting dog

ALAND *n pl.* -S alan

ALANE *adj* alone

ALANG *adv* along

ALANIN *n pl.* -S alanine

ALANINE *n pl.* -S an amino acid

ALANT *n pl.* -S alan

ALANYL *n pl.* -S a univalent radical

ALAR *adj* pertaining to wings

ALARM *v* -ED, -ING, -S to frighten by a sudden revelation of danger

ALARMISM *n pl.* -S the practice of alarming others needlessly

ALARMIST *n pl.* -S one who alarms others needlessly

ALARUM *v* -ED, -ING, -S to alarm

ALARY *adj* alar

ALAS *interj* — used to express sorrow or regret

ALASKA *n pl.* -S a heavy fabric

ALASTOR *n pl.* -S an avenging deity in Greek tragedy

ALATE *n pl.* -S a winged insect

ALATED *adj* having wings

ALATION n pl. -S the state of having wings

ALB n pl. -S a long-sleeved vestment

ALBA n pl. -S the white substance of the brain

ALBACORE n pl. -S a marine food fish

ALBATA n pl. -S an alloy of copper, nickel, and zinc

ALBEDO n pl. -DOS or -DOES the ratio of the light reflected by a planet to that received by it

ALBEIT conj although

ALBICORE n pl. -S albacore

ALBINAL adj albinic

ALBINIC adj pertaining to albinism

ALBINISM n pl. -S the condition of being an albino

ALBINO n pl. -NOS an organism lacking normal pigmentation

ALBITE n pl. -S a mineral **ALBITIC** adj

ALBIZIA n pl. -S a tropical tree

ALBIZZIA n pl. -S albizia

ALBUM n pl. -S a book for preserving photographs or stamps

ALBUMEN n pl. -S the white of an egg

ALBUMIN n pl. -S a simple protein

ALBUMOSE n pl. -S a proteose

ALBURNUM n pl. -S sapwood

ALCADE n pl. -S alcalde

ALCAHEST n pl. -S alkahest

ALCAIC n pl. -S a type of verse form

ALCAIDE n pl. -S the commander of a Spanish fortress

ALCALDE n pl. -S the mayor of a Spanish town

ALCAYDE n pl. -S alcaide

ALCAZAR n pl. -S a Spanish fortress or palace

ALCHEMY n pl. -MIES a medieval form of chemistry **ALCHEMIC** adj

ALCHYMY n pl. -MIES alchemy

ALCID n pl. -S a diving seabird

ALCIDINE adj pertaining to a family of seabirds

ALCOHOL n pl. -S a flammable liquid

ALCOVE n pl. -S a recessed section of a room **ALCOVED** adj

ALDEHYDE n pl. -S a type of chemical compound

ALDER n pl. -S a shrub or small tree

ALDERFLY n pl. -FLIES a winged insect

ALDERMAN n pl. -MEN a member of a municipal legislative body

ALDOL n pl. -S a chemical compound

ALDOLASE n pl. -S an enzyme

ALDOSE n pl. -S a type of sugar

ALDRIN n pl. -S an insecticide

ALE n pl. -S an alcoholic beverage

ALEATORY adj pertaining to luck

ALEC n pl. -S a herring

ALEE adv toward the side of a vessel sheltered from the wind

ALEF n pl. -S aleph

ALEGAR n pl. -S sour ale

ALEHOUSE n pl. -S a tavern where ale is sold

ALEMBIC n pl. -S an apparatus formerly used in distilling

ALENCON n pl. -S a needlepoint lace

ALEPH n pl. -S a Hebrew letter

ALERT adj ALERTER, ALERTEST ready for sudden action **ALERTLY** adv

ALERT v -ED, -ING, -S to warn

ALEURON n pl. -S aleurone

ALEURONE n pl. -S protein matter found in the seeds of certain plants

ALEVIN n pl. -S a young fish

ALEWIFE n pl. -WIVES a marine fish

ALEXIA n pl. -S a cerebral disorder marked by the loss of the ability to read

ALEXIN n pl. -S a substance in the blood that aids in the destruction of bacteria

ALEXINE n pl. -S alexin

ALFA n pl. -S a communications code word for the letter A

ALFAKI n pl. -S alfaqui

ALFALFA n pl. -S a plant cultivated for use as hay and forage

ALFAQUI n pl. -S a teacher of Muslim law

ALFAQUIN n pl. -S alfaqui

ALFORJA n pl. -S a leather bag

ALFRESCO adv outdoors

ALGA n pl. -GAE or -GAS any of a group of primitive aquatic plants **ALGAL** adj

ALGAROBA n pl. -S the mesquite

ALGEBRA n pl. -S a branch of mathematics

ALGERINE n pl. -S a woolen fabric

ALGICIDE n pl. -S a substance used to kill algae

ALGID adj cold

ALGIDITY n pl. -TIES coldness

ALGIN n pl. -S a viscous substance obtained from certain algae

ALGINATE n pl. -S a chemical salt

ALGOID adj resembling algae

ALGOLOGY *n pl.* -GIES the study of algae

ALGOR *n pl.* -S coldness

ALGORISM *n pl.* -S the Arabic system of arithmetic notation

ALGUM *n pl.* -S almug

ALIAS *n pl.* -ES an assumed name

ALIBI *v* -BIED, -BIING, -BIES or -BIS to make excuses for oneself

ALIBLE *adj* nourishing

ALIDAD *n pl.* -S alidade

ALIDADE *n pl.* -S a device used in angular measurement

ALIEN *v* -ED, -ING, -S to transfer to another, as property

ALIENAGE *n pl.* -S the state of being foreign

ALIENATE *v* -ATED, -ATING, -ATES to make indifferent or unfriendly

ALIENEE *n pl.* -S one to whom property is transferred

ALIENER *n pl.* -S alienor

ALIENISM *n pl.* -S alienage

ALIENIST *n pl.* -S a physician who treats mental disorders

ALIENLY *adv* in a foreign manner

ALIENOR *n pl.* -S one that transfers property

ALIF *n pl.* -S an Arabic letter

ALIFORM *adj* shaped like a wing

ALIGHT *v* ALIGHTED or ALIT, ALIGHTING, ALIGHTS to come down from something

ALIGN *v* -ED, -ING, -S to arrange in a straight line

ALIGNER *n pl.* -S one that aligns

ALIKE *adj* having close resemblance

ALIMENT *v* -ED, -ING, -S to nourish

ALIMONY *n pl.* -NIES an allowance paid to a woman by her divorced husband

ALINE *v* ALINED, ALINING, ALINES to align

ALINER *n pl.* -S aligner

ALIPED *n pl.* -S an animal having a membrane connecting the toes

ALIQUANT *adj* not dividing evenly into another number

ALIQUOT *n pl.* -S a number that divides evenly into another

ALIST *adj* leaning to one side

ALIT a past tense of alight

ALIUNDE *adv* from a source extrinsic to the matter at hand

ALIVE *adj* having life

ALIYA *n pl.* -S aliyah

ALIYAH *n pl.* -YAHS or -YOS or -YOT the immigration of Jews to Israel

ALIZARIN *n pl.* -S a red dye

ALKAHEST *n pl.* -S the hypothetical universal solvent sought by alchemists

ALKALI *n pl.* -LIES or -LIS a type of chemical compound **ALKALIC** *adj*

ALKALIFY *v* -FIED, -FYING, -FIES to alkalize

ALKALIN *adj* alkaline

ALKALINE *adj* containing an alkali

ALKALISE *v* -LISED, -LISING, -LISES to alkalize

ALKALIZE *v* -LIZED, -LIZING, -LIZES to convert into an alkali

ALKALOID *n pl.* -S a type of chemical compound

ALKANE *n pl.* -S a type of chemical compound

ALKANET *n pl.* -S a European plant

ALKENE *n pl.* -S a type of chemical compound

ALKIES *pl.* of alky

ALKINE *n pl.* -S alkyne

ALKOXIDE *n pl.* -S a type of chemical salt

ALKOXY *adj* containing a univalent radical composed of alkyl united with oxygen

ALKY *n pl.* -KIES one who is habitually drunk

ALKYD *n pl.* -S a synthetic resin

ALKYL *n pl.* -S a univalent radical **ALKYLIC** *adj*

ALKYLATE *v* -ATED, -ATING, -ATES to combine with alkyl

ALKYNE *n pl.* -S a type of chemical compound

ALL *n pl.* -S everything that one has

ALLANITE *n pl.* -S a mineral

ALLAY *v* -ED, -ING, -S to reduce in intensity or severity

ALLAYER *n pl.* -S one that allays

ALLEE *n pl.* -S a tree-lined walkway

ALLEGE *v* -LEGED, -LEGING, -LEGES to assert without proof or before proving

ALLEGER *n pl.* -S one that alleges

ALLEGORY *n pl.* -RIES a story presenting a moral principle

ALLEGRO *n pl.* -GROS a musical passage played in rapid tempo

ALLELE n pl. -S any of several forms of a gene **ALLELIC** adj

ALLELISM n pl. -S the state of possessing alleles

ALLELUIA n pl. -S a song of praise to God

ALLERGEN n pl. -S a substance capable of inducing an allergy

ALLERGIC adj pertaining to allergy

ALLERGIN n pl. -S allergen

ALLERGY n pl. -GIES a state of hypersensitive reaction to certain things

ALLEY n pl. -LEYS a narrow passageway

ALLEYWAY n pl. -WAYS an alley

ALLHEAL n pl. -S a medicinal herb

ALLIABLE adj capable of being allied

ALLIANCE n pl. -S an association formed to further the common interests of its members

ALLICIN n pl. -S a liquid compound

ALLIED past tense of ally

ALLIES present 3d person sing. of ally

ALLIUM n pl. -S a bulbous herb

ALLOBAR n pl. -S a change in barometric pressure

ALLOCATE v -CATED, -CATING, -CATES to set apart for a particular purpose

ALLOD n pl. -S allodium

ALLODIUM n pl. -DIA land held in absolute ownership **ALLODIAL** adj

ALLOGAMY n pl. -MIES fertilization of a flower by pollen from another

ALLONGE n pl. -S an addition to a document

ALLONYM n pl. -S the name of one person assumed by another

ALLOPATH n pl. -S one who treats diseases by producing effects incompatible with those of the disease

ALLOT v -LOTTED, -LOTTING, -LOTS to give as a share or portion

ALLOTTEE n pl. -S one to whom something is allotted

ALLOTTER n pl. -S one that allots

ALLOTTING present participle of allot

ALLOTYPE n pl. -S a type of antibody

ALLOTYPY n pl. -TYPIES the condition of being an allotype

ALLOVER n pl. -S a fabric having a pattern extending over the entire surface

ALLOW v -ED, -ING, -S to put no obstacle in the way of

ALLOXAN n pl. -S a chemical compound

ALLOY v -ED, -ING, -S to combine to form an alloy (a homogenous mixture of metals)

ALLSEED n pl. -S a plant having many seeds

ALLSPICE n pl. -S a tropical tree

ALLUDE v -LUDED, -LUDING, -LUDES to make an indirect reference

ALLURE v -LURED, -LURING, -LURES to attract with something desirable

ALLURER n pl. -S one that allures

ALLUSION n pl. -S the act of alluding **ALLUSIVE** adj

ALLUVIA a pl. of alluvium

ALLUVIAL n pl. -S soil composed of alluvium

ALLUVION n pl. -S alluvium

ALLUVIUM n pl. -VIA or -VIUMS detrital material deposited by running water

ALLY v -LIED, -LYING, -LIES to unite in a formal relationship

ALLYL n pl. -S a univalent radical **ALLYLIC** adj

ALMA n pl. -S almah

ALMAGEST n pl. -S a medieval treatise on astrology or alchemy

ALMAH n pl. -S an Egyptian girl who sings and dances professionally

ALMANAC n pl. -S an annual publication containing general information

ALME n pl. -S almah

ALMEH n pl. -S almah

ALMEMAR n pl. -S a bema

ALMIGHTY adj having absolute power over all

ALMNER n pl. -S almoner

ALMOND n pl. -S the edible nut of a small tree

ALMONER n pl. -S one that distributes alms

ALMONRY n pl. -RIES a place where alms are distributed

ALMOST adv very nearly

ALMS n pl. ALMS money or goods given to the poor

ALMSMAN n pl. -MEN one who receives alms

ALMUCE *n pl.* -S a hooded cape

ALMUD *n pl.* -S a Spanish unit of capacity

ALMUDE *n pl.* -S almud

ALMUG *n pl.* -S a precious wood mentioned in the Bible

ALNICO *n pl.* -COES a magnetic alloy

ALODIUM *n pl.* -DIA allodium **ALODIAL** *adj*

ALOE *n pl.* -S an African plant **ALOETIC** *adj*

ALOFT *adv* in or into the air

ALOGICAL *adj* being outside the bounds of that to which logic can apply

ALOHA *n pl.* -S love — used as a greeting or farewell

ALOIN *n pl.* -S a laxative

ALONE *adj* apart from others

ALONG *adv* onward

ALOOF *adj* distant in interest or feeling **ALOOFLY** *adv*

ALOPECIA *n pl.* -S baldness **ALOPECIC** *adj*

ALOUD *adv* audibly

ALOW *adv* in or to a lower position

ALP *n pl.* -S a high mountain

ALPACA *n pl.* -S a ruminant mammal

ALPHA *n pl.* -S a Greek letter

ALPHABET *v* -ED, -ING, -S to arrange in the customary order of the letters of a language

ALPHORN *n pl.* -S a wooden horn used by Swiss herdsmen

ALPHOSIS *n pl.* -SISES lack of skin pigmentation

ALPHYL *n pl.* -S a univalent radical

ALPINE *n pl.* -S a plant native to high mountain regions

ALPINELY *adv* in a lofty manner

ALPINISM *n pl.* -S mountain climbing

ALPINIST *n pl.* -S a mountain climber

ALREADY *adv* by this time

ALRIGHT *adj* satisfactory

ALSIKE *n pl.* -S a European clover

ALSO *adv* in addition

ALT *n pl.* -S a high-pitched musical note

ALTAR *n pl.* -S a raised structure used in worship

ALTER *v* -ED, -ING, -S to make different

ALTERANT *n pl.* -S something that alters

ALTERER *n pl.* -S one that alters

ALTHAEA *n pl.* -S althea

ALTHEA *n pl.* -S a flowering plant

ALTHO *conj* although

ALTHORN *n pl.* -S a brass wind instrument

ALTHOUGH *conj* despite the fact that

ALTITUDE *n pl.* -S the vertical elevation of an object above a given level

ALTO *n pl.* -TOS a low female singing voice

ALTOIST *n pl.* -S one who plays the alto saxophone

ALTRUISM *n pl.* -S selfless devotion to the welfare of others

ALTRUIST *n pl.* -S one that practices altruism

ALUDEL *n pl.* -S a pear-shaped vessel

ALULA *n pl.* -LAE a tuft of feathers on the first digit of a bird's wing **ALULAR** *adj*

ALUM *n pl.* -S a chemical compound

ALUMIN *n pl.* -S alumina

ALUMINA *n pl.* -S an oxide of aluminum

ALUMINE *n pl.* -S alumina

ALUMINUM *n pl.* -S a metallic element **ALUMINIC** *adj*

ALUMNA *n pl.* -NAE a female graduate

ALUMNUS *n pl.* -NI a male graduate

ALUMROOT *n pl.* -S a flowering plant

ALUNITE *n pl.* -S a mineral

ALVEOLAR *n pl.* -S a sound produced with the tongue touching a place just behind the front teeth

ALVEOLUS *n pl.* -LI a small anatomical cavity

ALVINE *adj* pertaining to the abdomen and lower intestines

ALWAY *adv* always

ALWAYS *adv* at all times

ALYSSUM *n pl.* -S a flowering plant

AM present 1st person sing. of be

AMA *n pl.* -S amah

AMADAVAT *n pl.* -S an Asian songbird

AMADOU *n pl.* -S a substance prepared from fungi for use as tinder

AMAH *n pl.* -S an Oriental nurse

AMAIN *adv* with full strength

AMALGAM *n pl.* -S an alloy of mercury with another metal

AMANDINE *adj* prepared with almonds

AMANITA *n pl.* -S any of a genus of poisonous fungi

AMANITIN *n pl.* -S a chemical compound

AMARANTH *n pl.* -S a flowering plant

AMARELLE *n pl.* -S a variety of sour cherry

AMARETTI *n/pl* macaroons made with bitter almonds

AMARETTO *n pl.* -TOS a kind of liqueur

AMARNA *adj* pertaining to a certain historical period of ancient Egypt

AMASS *v* -ED, -ING, -ES to gather

AMASSER *n pl.* -S one that amasses

AMATEUR *n pl.* -S one that engages in an activity for pleasure

AMATIVE *adj* amorous

AMATOL *n pl.* -S a powerful explosive

AMATORY *adj* pertaining to sexual love

AMAZE *v* AMAZED, AMAZING, AMAZES to overwhelm with surprise or wonder **AMAZEDLY** *adv*

AMAZON *n pl.* -S a tall, powerful woman

AMBAGE *n pl.* -S a winding path

AMBARI *n pl.* -S ambary

AMBARY *n pl.* -RIES an East Indian plant

AMBEER *n pl.* -S tobacco juice

AMBER *n pl.* -S a fossil resin

AMBERINA *n pl.* -S a type of glassware

AMBEROID *n pl.* -S amboid

AMBERY *n pl.* -BERIES ambry

AMBIANCE *n pl.* -S ambience

AMBIENCE *n pl.* -S the character, mood, or atmosphere of a place or situation

AMBIENT *n pl.* -S ambience

AMBIT *n pl.* -S the external boundary of something

AMBITION *v* -ED, -ING, -S to seek with eagerness

AMBIVERT *n pl.* -S a person whose personality type is intermediate between introvert and extravert

AMBLE *v* -BLED, -BLING, -BLES to saunter

AMBLER *n pl.* -S one that ambles

AMBO *n pl.* AMBOS or AMBONES a pulpit in an early Christian church

AMBOINA *n pl.* -S amboyna

AMBOYNA *n pl.* -S the mottled wood of an Indonesian tree

AMBRIES *pl. of* ambry

AMBROID *n pl.* -S a synthetic amber

AMBROSIA *n pl.* -S the food of the Greek and Roman gods

AMBRY *n pl.* -BRIES a recess in a church wall for sacred vessels

AMBSACE *n pl.* -S bad luck

AMBULANT *adj* ambulating

AMBULATE *v* -LATED, -LATING, -LATES to move or walk about

AMBUSH *v* -ED, -ING, -ES to attack from a concealed place

AMBUSHER *n pl.* -S one that ambushes

AMEBA *n pl.* -BAS or -BAE amoeba **AMEBAN, AMEBIC, AMEBOID** *adj*

AMEBEAN *adj* alternately responding

AMEER *n pl.* -S amir

AMEERATE *n pl.* -S amirate

AMELCORN *n pl.* -S a variety of wheat

AMEN *n pl.* -S a word used at the end of a prayer to express agreement

AMENABLE *adj* capable of being persuaded **AMENABLY** *adv*

AMEND *v* -ED, -ING, -S to improve

AMENDER *n pl.* -S one that amends

AMENITY *n pl.* -TIES the quality of being pleasant or agreeable

AMENT *n pl.* -S a mentally deficient person

AMENTIA *n pl.* -S mental deficiency

AMERCE *v* AMERCED, AMERCING, AMERCES to punish by imposing an arbitrary fine

AMERCER *n pl.* -S one that amerces

AMESACE *n pl.* -S ambsace

AMETHYST *n pl.* -S a variety of quartz

AMI *n pl.* -S a friend

AMIA *n pl.* -S a freshwater fish

AMIABLE *adj* having a pleasant disposition **AMIABLY** *adv*

AMIANTUS *n pl.* -ES a variety of asbestos

AMICABLE *adj* friendly **AMICABLY** *adv*

AMICE *n pl.* -S a vestment worn about the neck and shoulders

AMICUS *n pl.* AMICI one not party to a lawsuit but permitted by the court to advise it

AMID *n pl.* -S amide

AMIDASE *n pl.* -S an enzyme

AMIDE *n pl.* -S a type of chemical compound **AMIDIC** *adj*

AMIDIN *n pl.* -S the soluble matter of starch

AMIDINE *n pl.* -S a type of chemical compound

AMIDO *adj* containing an amide united with an acid radical

AMIDOGEN *n pl.* -S a univalent chemical radical

AMIDOL *n pl.* -S a chemical compound

AMIDONE *n pl.* -S a chemical compound

AMIDSHIP *adv* toward the middle of a ship

AMIDST *prep* in the midst of

AMIE *n* pl. -S a female friend

AMIGA *n* pl. -S a female friend

AMIGO *n* pl. -GOS a friend

AMIN *n* pl. -S amine

AMINE *n* pl. -S a type of chemical compound **AMINIC** *adj*

AMINITY *n* pl. -TIES the state of being an amine

AMINO *adj* containing an amine united with a nonacid radical

AMIR *n* pl. -S a Muslim prince or governor

AMIRATE *n* pl. -S the rank of an amir

AMISS *adj* being out of proper order

AMITIES pl. of amity

AMITOSIS *n* pl. -TOSES a type of cell division **AMITOTIC** *adj*

AMITROLE *n* pl. -S an herbicide

AMITY *n* pl. -TIES friendship

AMMETER *n* pl. -S an instrument for measuring amperage

AMMINE *n* pl. -S a type of chemical compound

AMMINO *adj* pertaining to an ammine

AMMO *n* pl. -MOS ammunition

AMMOCETE *n* pl. -S the larva of a lamprey

AMMONAL *n* pl. -S a powerful explosive

AMMONIA *n* pl. -S a pungent gas

AMMONIAC *n* pl. -S a gum resin

AMMONIC *adj* pertaining to ammonia

AMMONIFY *v* -FIED, -FYING, -FIES to treat with ammonia

AMMONITE *n* pl. -S the coiled shell of an extinct mollusk

AMMONIUM *n* pl. -S a univalent chemical radical

AMMONO *adj* containing ammonia

AMMONOID *n* pl. -S ammonite

AMNESIA *n* pl. -S loss of memory

AMNESIAC *n* pl. -S one suffering from amnesia

AMNESIC *n* pl. -S amnesiac

AMNESTIC *adj* pertaining to amnesia

AMNESTY *v* -TIED, -TYING, -TIES to pardon

AMNION *n* pl. -NIONS or -NIA a membranous sac enclosing an embryo **AMNIC**, **AMNIONIC**, **AMNIOTIC** *adj*

AMNIOTE *n* pl. -S a vertebrate that develops an amnion during the embryonic stage

AMOEBA *n* pl. -BAS or -BAE a unicellular microscopic organism **AMOEBAN**, **AMOEBIC**, **AMOEBOID** *adj*

AMOEBEAN *adj* amebean

AMOK *n* pl. -S a murderous frenzy

AMOLE *n* pl. -S a plant root used as a substitute for soap

AMONG *prep* in the midst of

AMONGST *prep* among

AMORAL *adj* lacking a sense of right and wrong **AMORALLY** *adv*

AMORETTO *n* pl. -TI or -TOS a cupid

AMORINO *n* pl. -NI an amoretto

AMORIST *n* pl. -S a lover

AMOROSO *adv* tenderly — used as a musical direction

AMOROUS *adj* pertaining to love

AMORT *adj* being without life

AMORTISE *v* -TISED, -TISING, -TISES to amortize

AMORTIZE *v* -TIZED, -TIZING, -TIZES to liquidate gradually, as a debt

AMOSITE *n* pl. -S a type of asbestos

AMOTION *n* pl. -S the removal of a corporate officer from his office

AMOUNT *v* -ED, -ING, -S to combine to yield a sum

AMOUR *n* pl. -S a love affair

AMP *n* pl. -S ampere

AMPERAGE *n* pl. -S the strength of an electric current expressed in amperes

AMPERE *n* pl. -S a unit of electric current strength

AMPHIBIA *n/pl* organisms adapted for life both on land and in water

AMPHIOXI *n/pl* lancelets

AMPHIPOD *n* pl. -S a small crustacean

AMPHORA *n* pl. -RAE or -RAS a narrow-necked jar used in ancient Greece **AMPHORAL** *adj*

AMPLE *adj* -PLER, -PLEST abundant **AMPLY** *adv*

AMPLEXUS *n* pl. -ES the mating embrace of frogs

AMPLIFY *v* -FIED, -FYING, -FIES to make larger or more powerful

AMPOULE *n* pl. -S ampule

AMPUL *n* pl. -S ampule

AMPULE *n* pl. -S a small glass vial

AMPULLA *n* pl. -LAE a globular bottle used in ancient Rome **AMPULLAR** *adj*

AMPUTATE *v* -TATED, -TATING, -TATES to cut off by surgical means

AMPUTEE *n* pl. -S one that has had a limb amputated

AMREETA *n* pl. -S amrita

AMRITA n pl. -S a beverage that bestows immortality in Hindu mythology

AMTRAC n pl. -S a military vehicle equipped to move on land and water

AMTRACK n pl. -S amtrac

AMU n pl. -S a unit of mass

AMUCK n pl. -S amok

AMULET n pl. -S an object worn to protect against evil or injury

AMUSE v AMUSED, AMUSING, AMUSES to occupy pleasingly **AMUSABLE** adj **AMUSEDLY** adv

AMUSER n pl. -S one that amuses

AMUSIA n pl. -S the inability to recognize musical sounds

AMUSIVE adj amusing

AMYGDALA n pl. -LAE an almond-shaped anatomical part

AMYGDALE n pl. -S amygdule

AMYGDULE n pl. -S a small gas bubble in lava

AMYL n pl. -S a univalent radical

AMYLASE n pl. -S an enzyme

AMYLENE n pl. -S a flammable liquid

AMYLIC adj pertaining to amyl

AMYLOGEN n pl. -S amylose

AMYLOID n pl. -S a hard protein deposit resulting from degeneration of tissue

AMYLOSE n pl. -S the relatively soluble component of starch

AMYLUM n pl. -S starch

AN indefinite article — used before words beginning with a vowel sound

ANA n pl. -S a collection of miscellaneous information about a particular subject

ANABAENA n pl. -S a freshwater alga

ANABAS n pl. -ES a freshwater fish

ANABASIS n pl. -ASES a military advance

ANABATIC adj pertaining to rising wind currents

ANABLEPS n pl. -ES a freshwater fish

ANABOLIC adj pertaining to a process by which food is built up into protoplasm

ANACONDA n pl. -S a large snake

ANADEM n pl. -S a wreath for the head

ANAEMIA n pl. -S anemia **ANAEMIC** adj

ANAEROBE n pl. -S an organism that does not require oxygen to live

ANAGLYPH n pl. -S a type of carved ornament

ANAGOGE n pl. -S a spiritual interpretation of words **ANAGOGIC** adj

ANAGOGY n pl. -GIES anagoge

ANAGRAM v -GRAMMED, -GRAMMING, -GRAMS to transpose the letters of a word or phrase to form a new one

ANAL adj pertaining to the anus

ANALCIME n pl. -S analcite

ANALCITE n pl. -S a mineral

ANALECTA n/pl analects

ANALECTS n/pl selections from a literary work or group of works

ANALEMMA n pl. -MAS or -MATA a type of graduated scale

ANALGIA n pl. -S inability to feel pain

ANALITY n pl. -TIES a type of psychological state

ANALLY adv at or through the anus

ANALOG n pl. -S analogue

ANALOGIC adj pertaining to an analogy

ANALOGUE n pl. -S something that bears an analogy to something else

ANALOGY n pl. -GIES resemblance in some respects between things otherwise unlike

ANALYSE v -LYSED, -LYSING, -LYSES to analyze

ANALYSER n pl. -S analyzer

ANALYSIS n pl. -YSES the separation of a whole into its parts

ANALYST n pl. -S one that analyzes

ANALYTIC adj pertaining to analysis

ANALYZE v -LYZED, -LYZING, -LYZES to subject to analysis

ANALYZER n pl. -S one that analyzes

ANANKE n pl. -S a compelling necessity in ancient Greek religion

ANAPAEST n pl. -S anapest

ANAPEST n pl. -S a type of metrical foot

ANAPHASE n pl. -S a stage of mitosis

ANAPHOR n pl. -S a word or phrase that takes reference from a preceding word or phrase

ANAPHORA n pl. -S the repetition of a word or phrase at the beginning of several successive verses or sentences

ANARCH n pl. -S an advocate of anarchy

ANARCHY n pl. -CHIES absence of government **ANARCHIC** adj

ANASARCA *n pl.* -S a form of dropsy

ANATASE *n pl.* -S a mineral

ANATHEMA *n pl.* -MAS or -MATA a formal ecclesiastical ban or curse

ANATOMY *n pl.* -MIES the structure of an organism ANATOMIC *adj*

ANATOXIN *n pl.* -S a toxoid

ANATTO *n pl.* -TOS annatto

ANCESTOR *v* -ED, -ING, -S to be an ancestor (a person from whom one is descended) of

ANCESTRY *n pl.* -TRIES a line or body of ancestors

ANCHOR *v* -ED, -ING, -S to secure by means of an anchor (a device for holding a floating vessel in place)

ANCHORET *n pl.* -S a recluse

ANCHOVY *n pl.* -VIES a small food fish

ANCHUSA *n pl.* -S a hairy-stemmed plant

ANCHUSIN *n pl.* -S a red dye

ANCIENT *adj* -CIENTER, -CIENTEST of or pertaining to time long past

ANCIENT *n pl.* -S one who lived in ancient times

ANCILLA *n pl.* -LAE or -LAS a helper

ANCON *n pl.* -ES the elbow ANCONAL, ANCONEAL, ANCONOID *adj*

ANCONE *n pl.* -S ancon

ANCRESS *n pl.* -ES a female recluse

AND *n pl.* -S an added condition or stipulation

ANDANTE *n pl.* -S a moderately slow musical passage

ANDESITE *n pl.* -S a volcanic rock

ANDESYTE *n pl.* -S andesite

ANDIRON *n pl.* -S a metal support for holding wood in a fireplace

ANDROGEN *n pl.* -S a male sex hormone

ANDROID *n pl.* -S a synthetic man

ANE *n pl.* -S one

ANEAR *v* -ED, -ING, -S to approach

ANECDOTE *n pl.* -DOTES or -DOTA a brief story

ANECHOIC *adj* neither having nor producing echoes

ANELE *v* ANELED, ANELING, ANELES to anoint

ANEMIA *n pl.* -S a disorder of the blood ANEMIC *adj*

ANEMONE *n pl.* -S a flowering plant

ANEMOSIS *n pl.* -MOSES separation of rings of growth in timber due to wind

ANENST *prep* anent

ANENT *prep* in regard to

ANERGIA *n pl.* -S anergy

ANERGY *n pl.* -GIES lack of energy ANERGIC *adj*

ANEROID *n pl.* -S a type of barometer

ANESTRUS *n pl.* -TRI a period of sexual dormancy

ANETHOL *n pl.* -S anethole

ANETHOLE *n pl.* -S a chemical compound

ANEURIN *n pl.* -S thiamine

ANEURISM *n pl.* -S aneurysm

ANEURYSM *n pl.* -S an abnormal blood-filled dilation of a blood vessel

ANEW *adv* once more

ANGA *n pl.* -S any of the eight practices of yoga

ANGAKOK *n pl.* -S an Eskimo medicine man

ANGARIA *n pl.* -S angary

ANGARY *n pl.* -RIES the right of a warring state to seize neutral property

ANGEL *v* -ED, -ING, -S to support financially

ANGELIC *adj* pertaining to an angel (a winged celestial being)

ANGELICA *n pl.* -S an aromatic herb

ANGELUS *n pl.* -ES a Roman Catholic prayer

ANGER *v* -ED, -ING, -S to make angry

ANGERLY *adv* in an angry manner

ANGINA *n pl.* -S a disease marked by spasmodic attacks of intense pain ANGINAL, ANGINOSE, ANGINOUS *adj*

ANGIOMA *n pl.* -MAS or -MATA a tumor composed of blood or lymph vessels

ANGLE *v* -GLED, -GLING, -GLES to fish with a hook and line

ANGLEPOD *n pl.* -S a flowering plant

ANGLER *n pl.* -S one that angles

ANGLICE *adv* in readily understood English

ANGLING *n pl.* -S the sport of fishing

ANGORA *n pl.* -S the long, silky hair of a domestic goat

ANGRY *adj* -GRIER, -GRIEST feeling strong displeasure or hostility ANGRILY *adv*

ANGST *n pl.* -S a feeling of anxiety or dread

ANGSTROM *n pl.* -S a unit of length

ANGUINE *adj* resembling a snake

ANGUISH *v* -ED, -ING, -ES to suffer extreme pain

ANGULAR adj having sharp corners

ANGULATE v -LATED, -LATING, -LATES to make angular

ANGULOSE adj angular

ANGULOUS adj angular

ANHINGA n pl. -S an aquatic bird

ANI n pl. -S a tropical American bird

ANIL n pl. -S a West Indian shrub

ANILE adj resembling an old woman

ANILIN n pl. -S aniline

ANILINE n pl. -S a chemical compound

ANILITY n pl. -TIES the state of being anile

ANIMA n pl. -S the soul

ANIMAL n pl. -S a living organism typically capable of voluntary motion and sensation **ANIMALIC** adj

ANIMALLY adv physically

ANIMATE v -MATED, -MATING, -MATES to give life to

ANIMATER n pl. -S animator

ANIMATO adv in a lively manner — used as a musical direction

ANIMATOR n pl. -S one that animates

ANIME n pl. -S a resin obtained from a tropical tree

ANIMI n pl. -S anime

ANIMISM n pl. -S the belief that souls may exist apart from bodies

ANIMIST n pl. -S an adherent of animism

ANIMUS n pl. -ES a feeling of hostility

ANION n pl. -S a negatively charged ion **ANIONIC** adj

ANISE n pl. -S a North African plant

ANISEED n pl. -S the seed of the anise used as a flavoring

ANISETTE n pl. -S a liqueur flavored with aniseed

ANISIC adj pertaining to an anise

ANISOLE n pl. -S a chemical compound

ANKERITE n pl. -S a mineral

ANKH n pl. -S an Egyptian symbol of enduring life

ANKLE v -KLED, -KLING, -KLES to walk

ANKLET n pl. -S an ornament for the ankle

ANKUS n pl. -ES an elephant goad

ANKUSH n pl. -ES ankus

ANKYLOSE v -LOSED, -LOSING, -LOSES to unite or grow together, as the bones of a joint

ANLACE n pl. -S a medieval dagger

ANLAGE n pl. -GEN or -GES the initial cell structure from which an embryonic organ develops

ANLAS n pl. -ES anlace

ANNA n pl. -S a former coin of India and Pakistan

ANNAL n pl. -S a record of a single year

ANNALIST n pl. -S a historian

ANNATES n/pl the first year's revenue of a bishop paid to the pope

ANNATTO n pl. -TOS a yellowish-red dye

ANNEAL v -ED, -ING, -S to toughen

ANNEALER n pl. -S one that anneals

ANNELID n pl. -S any of a phylum of segmented worms

ANNEX v -ED, -ING, -ES to add or attach

ANNEXE n pl. -S something added or attached

ANNOTATE v -TATED, -TATING, -TATES to furnish with critical or explanatory notes

ANNOUNCE v -NOUNCED, -NOUNCING, -NOUNCES to make known publicly

ANNOY v -ED, -ING, -S to be troublesome to

ANNOYER n pl. -S one that annoys

ANNUAL n pl. -S a publication issued once a year

ANNUALLY adv once a year

ANNUITY n pl. -TIES an allowance or income paid at regular intervals

ANNUL v -NULLED, -NULLING, -NULS to make or declare void or invalid

ANNULAR adj shaped like a ring

ANNULATE adj composed of or furnished with rings

ANNULET n pl. -S a small ring

ANNULI a pl. of annulus

ANNULLED past tense of annul

ANNULLING present participle of annul

ANNULUS n pl. -LI or -LUSES a ring or ringlike part **ANNULOSE** adj

ANOA n pl. -S a wild ox

ANODE n pl. -S a positively charged electrode **ANODAL, ANODIC** adj **ANODALLY** adv

ANODIZE v -IZED, -IZING, -IZES to coat with a protective film by chemical means

ANODYNE n pl. -S a medicine that relieves pain **ANODYNIC** adj

ANOINT *v* -ED, -ING, -S to apply oil to as a sacred rite

ANOINTER *n* pl. -S one that anoints

ANOLE *n* pl. -S a tropical lizard

ANOLYTE *n* pl. -S the part of an electricity-conducting solution nearest the anode

ANOMALY *n* pl. -LIES a deviation from the common rule, type, or form

ANOMIE *n* pl. -S a collapse of the social structures governing a given society **ANOMIC** *adj*

ANOMY *n* pl. -MIES anomie

ANON *adv* at another time

ANONYM *n* pl. -S a false or assumed name

ANOOPSIA *n* pl. -S a visual defect

ANOPIA *n* pl. -S anoopsia

ANOPSIA *n* pl. -S anoopsia

ANORAK *n* pl. -S a parka

ANORETIC *n* pl. -S anorexic

ANOREXIA *n* pl. -S a loss of appetite

ANOREXIC *n* pl. -S one affected with anorexia

ANOREXY *n* pl. -OREXIES anorexia

ANORTHIC *adj* denoting a certain type of crystal system

ANOSMIA *n* pl. -S loss of the sense of smell **ANOSMIC** *adj*

ANOTHER *adj* one more

ANOVULAR *adj* not involving ovulation

ANOXEMIA *n* pl. -S a disorder of the blood **ANOXEMIC** *adj*

ANOXIA *n* pl. -S absence of oxygen **ANOXIC** *adj*

ANSA *n* pl. -SAE the projecting part of Saturn's rings

ANSATE *adj* having a handle

ANSATED *adj* ansate

ANSERINE *n* pl. -S a chemical compound

ANSEROUS *adj* silly

ANSWER *v* -ED, -ING, -S to say, write, or act in return

ANSWERER *n* pl. -S one that answers

ANT *n* pl. -S a small insect

ANTA *n* pl. -TAE or -TAS a pilaster formed at the termination of a wall

ANTACID *n* pl. -S a substance that neutralizes acid

ANTALGIC *n* pl. -S an anodyne

ANTBEAR *n* pl. -S an aardvark

ANTE *v* ANTED or ANTEED, ANTEING, ANTES to put a fixed stake into the pot before the cards are dealt in poker

ANTEATER *n* pl. -S any of several mammals that feed on ants

ANTECEDE *v* -CEDED, -CEDING, -CEDES to precede

ANTED a past tense of ante

ANTEDATE *v* -DATED, -DATING, -DATES to be of an earlier date than

ANTEFIX *n* pl. -FIXES or -FIXA an upright ornament at the eaves of a tiled roof

ANTELOPE *n* pl. -S a ruminant mammal

ANTENNA *n* pl. -NAE or -NAS a metallic device for sending or receiving radio waves **ANTENNAL** *adj*

ANTEPAST *n* pl. -S an appetizer

ANTERIOR *adj* situated in or toward the front

ANTEROOM *n* pl. -S a waiting room

ANTETYPE *n* pl. -S an earlier form

ANTEVERT *v* -ED, -ING, -S to displace by tipping forward

ANTHELIA *n/pl* halolike areas seen in the sky opposite the sun

ANTHELIX *n* pl. -LICES or -LIXES the inner curved ridge on the cartilage of the external ear

ANTHEM *v* -ED, -ING, -S to praise in a song

ANTHEMIA *n/pl* decorative floral patterns used in Greek art

ANTHER *n* pl. -S the pollen-bearing part of a stamen **ANTHERAL** *adj*

ANTHERID *n* pl. -S a male reproductive organ of certain plants

ANTHESIS *n* pl. -THESES the full bloom of a flower

ANTHILL *n* pl. -S a mound formed by ants in building their nest

ANTHODIA *n/pl* flower heads of certain plants

ANTHOID *adj* resembling a flower

ANTHRAX *n* pl. -THRACES an infectious disease

ANTI *n* pl. -S one that is opposed

ANTIAIR *adj* directed against attacking aircraft

ANTIAR *n* pl. -S an arrow poison

ANTIARIN *n* pl. -S antiar

ANTIATOM *n* pl. -S an atom comprised of antiparticles

ANTIBIAS *adj* opposed to bias

ANTIBODY *n* pl. -BODIES a body protein that produces immunity against certain microorganisms or toxins

ANTIBOSS *adj* opposed to bosses

ANTIBUG *adj* effective against bugs

ANTIC *v* -TICKED, -TICKING, -TICS to act in a clownish manner

ANTICAR *adj* opposed to cars

ANTICITY *adj* opposed to cities

ANTICK *v* -ED, -ING, -S to antic

ANTICLY *adv* in a clownish manner

ANTICOLD *adj* effective against the common cold

ANTICULT *adj* opposed to cults

ANTIDORA *n/pl* holy breads

ANTIDOTE *v* -DOTED, -DOTING, -DOTES to counteract the effects of a poison with a remedy

ANTIDRUG *adj* opposed to illicit drugs

ANTIFAT *adj* preventing the formation of fat

ANTIFLU *adj* combating the flu

ANTIFOAM *adj* reducing or preventing foam

ANTIFUR *adj* opposed to the wearing of animal furs

ANTIGAY *adj* opposed to homosexuals

ANTIGEN *n* pl. -S a substance that stimulates the production of antibodies

ANTIGENE *n* pl. -S antigen

ANTIGUN *adj* opposed to guns

ANTIHERO *n* pl. -ROES a protagonist who is notably lacking in heroic qualities

ANTIJAM *adj* blocking interfering signals

ANTIKING *n* pl. -S a usurping king

ANTILEAK *adj* preventing leaks

ANTILEFT *adj* opposed to leftism

ANTILIFE *adj* opposed to life

ANTILOCK *adj* designed to prevent the wheels of a vehicle from locking

ANTILOG *n* pl. -S the number corresponding to a given logarithm

ANTILOGY *n* pl. -GIES a contradiction in terms or ideas

ANTIMALE *adj* opposed to men

ANTIMAN *adj* antimale

ANTIMASK *n* pl. -S a comic performance between the acts of a masque

ANTIMERE *n* pl. -S a part of an organism symmetrical with a part on the opposite side of the main axis

ANTIMONY *n* pl. -NIES a metallic element

ANTING *n* pl. -S the deliberate placing, by certain birds, of living ants among the feathers

ANTINODE *n* pl. -S a region between adjacent nodes

ANTINOMY *n* pl. -MIES a contradiction between two seemingly valid principles

ANTINUKE *adj* opposing the use of nuclear power plants or nuclear weapons

ANTIPHON *n* pl. -S a psalm or hymn sung responsively

ANTIPILL *adj* opposing the use of contraceptive pills

ANTIPODE *n* pl. -S an exact opposite

ANTIPOLE *n* pl. -S the opposite pole

ANTIPOPE *n* pl. -S one claiming to be pope in opposition to the one chosen by church law

ANTIPORN *adj* opposed to pornography

ANTIPOT *adj* opposing the use of pot (marijuana)

ANTIPYIC *n* pl. -S a medicine that prevents the formation of pus

ANTIQUE *v* -TIQUED, -TIQUING, -TIQUES to give an appearance of age to

ANTIQUER *n* pl. -S one that antiques

ANTIRAPE *adj* concerned with preventing rape

ANTIRED *adj* opposed to communism

ANTIRIOT *adj* designed to prevent or end riots

ANTIROCK *adj* opposed to rock music

ANTIROLL *adj* designed to reduce roll

ANTIRUST *n* pl. -S something that prevents rust

ANTISAG *adj* designed to prevent sagging

ANTISERA *n/pl* serums that contain antibodies

ANTISEX *adj* opposed to sexual activity

ANTISHIP *adj* designed for use against ships

ANTISKID *adj* designed to prevent skidding

ANTISLIP *adj* designed to prevent slipping

ANTISMOG *adj* designed to reduce pollutants that cause smog

ANTISMUT *adj* opposed to pornography

ANTISNOB *adj* opposed to snobbery

ANTISTAT *adj* designed to prevent the buildup of static electricity

ANTITANK *adj* designed to combat tanks

ANTITAX *adj* opposing taxes

ANTITYPE *n* pl. -S an opposite type

ANTIWAR *adj* opposing war

ANTIWEAR *adj* designed to reduce the effects of long or hard use

ANTIWEED *adj* concerned with the destruction of weeds

ANTLER *n pl.* -S the horn of an animal of the deer family **ANTLERED** *adj*

ANTLIKE *adj* resembling an ant

ANTLION *n pl.* -S a predatory insect

ANTONYM *n pl.* -S a word opposite in meaning to another

ANTONYMY *n pl.* -MIES the state of being an antonym

ANTRA a *pl.* of antrum

ANTRAL *adj* pertaining to an antrum

ANTRE *n pl.* -S a cave

ANTRORSE *adj* directed forward or upward

ANTRUM *n pl.* -TRA or -TRUMS a cavity in a bone

ANTSY *adj* -SIER, -SIEST fidgety

ANURAL *adj* anurous

ANURAN *n pl.* -S a frog or toad

ANURESIS *n pl.* -RESES inability to urinate **ANURETIC** *adj*

ANURIA *n pl.* -S absence of urine **ANURIC** *adj*

ANUROUS *adj* having no tail

ANUS *n pl.* -ES the excretory opening at the end of the alimentary canal

ANVIL *v* -VILED, -VILING, -VILS or -VILLED, -VILLING, -VILS to shape on an anvil (a heavy iron block)

ANVILTOP *n pl.* -S an anvil-shaped cloud mass

ANXIETY *n pl.* -ETIES painful or apprehensive uneasiness of mind

ANXIOUS *adj* full of anxiety

ANY *adj* one, no matter which

ANYBODY *n pl.* -BODIES a person of some importance

ANYHOW *adv* in any way

ANYMORE *adv* at the present time

ANYONE *pron* any person

ANYPLACE *adv* in any place

ANYTHING *n pl.* -S a thing of any kind

ANYTIME *adv* at any time

ANYWAY *adv* in any way

ANYWAYS *adv* anyway

ANYWHERE *n pl.* -S any place

ANYWISE *adv* in any way

AORIST *n pl.* -S a verb tense **AORISTIC** *adj*

AORTA *n pl.* -TAS or -TAE a main artery **AORTAL, AORTIC** *adj*

AOUDAD *n pl.* -S a wild sheep

APACE *adv* swiftly

APACHE *n pl.* -S a Parisian gangster

APAGOGE *n pl.* -S establishment of a thesis by showing its contrary to be absurd **APAGOGIC** *adj*

APANAGE *n pl.* -S appanage

APAREJO *n pl.* -JOS a type of saddle

APART *adv* not together

APATETIC *adj* having coloration serving as natural camouflage

APATHY *n pl.* -THIES lack of emotion

APATITE *n pl.* -S a mineral

APE *v* APED, APING, APES to mimic

APEAK *adv* in a vertical position

APEEK *adv* apeak

APELIKE *adj* resembling an ape (a large, tailless primate)

APER *n pl.* -S one that apes

APERCU *n pl.* -S a brief summary

APERIENT *n pl.* -S a mild laxative

APERITIF *n pl.* -S an alcoholic drink taken before a meal

APERTURE *n pl.* -S an opening

APERY *n pl.* -ERIES the act of aping

APETALY *n pl.* -ALIES the state of having no petals

APEX *n pl.* APEXES or APICES the highest point

APHAGIA *n pl.* -S inability to swallow

APHANITE *n pl.* -S an igneous rock

APHASIA *n pl.* -S loss of the ability to use words

APHASIAC *n pl.* -S one suffering from aphasia

APHASIC *n pl.* -S aphasiac

APHELION *n pl.* -ELIA or -ELIONS the point in a planetary orbit farthest from the sun **APHELIAN** *adj*

APHESIS *n pl.* -ESES the loss of an unstressed vowel from the beginning of a word **APHETIC** *adj*

APHID *n pl.* -S any of a family of small, soft-bodied insects

APHIDIAN *n pl.* -S an aphid

APHIS *n pl.* APHIDES an aphid

APHOLATE *n pl.* -S a chemical used to control houseflies

APHONIA *n pl.* -S loss of voice

APHONIC *n pl.* -S one affected with aphonia

APHORISE v -RISED, -RISING, -RISES to aphorize

APHORISM n pl. -S a brief statement of a truth or principle

APHORIST n pl. -S one that aphorizes

APHORIZE v -RIZED, -RIZING, -RIZES to write or speak in aphorisms

APHOTIC adj lacking light

APHTHA n pl. -THAE a small blister in the mouth or stomach APHTHOUS adj

APHYLLY n pl. -LIES the state of being leafless

APIAN adj pertaining to bees

APIARIAN n pl. -S an apiarist

APIARIST n pl. -S a person who raises bees

APIARY n pl. -ARIES a place where bees are kept

APICAL n pl. -S a sound articulated with the apex (tip) of the tongue

APICALLY adv at or toward the apex

APICES a pl. of apex

APICULUS n pl. -LI a sharp point at the end of a leaf

APIECE adv for each one

APIMANIA n pl. -S an excessive interest in bees

APING present participle of ape

APIOLOGY n pl. -GIES the study of bees

APISH adj slavishly or foolishly imitative APISHLY adv

APLASIA n pl. -S defective development of an organ or part

APLASTIC adj not plastic

APLENTY adj being in sufficient quantity

APLITE n pl. -S a fine-grained rock APLITIC adj

APLOMB n pl. -S self-confidence

APNEA n pl. -S temporary cessation of respiration APNEAL, APNEIC adj

APNOEA n pl. -S apnea APNOEAL, APNOEIC adj

APOAPSIS n pl. -APSIDES the high point in an orbit

APOCARP n pl. -S a fruit having separated carpels

APOCARPY n pl. -PIES the state of being an apocarp

APOCOPE n pl. -S an omission of the last sound of a word APOCOPIC adj

APOCRINE adj pertaining to a type of gland

APOD n pl. -S an apodal animal

APODAL adj having no feet or footlike appendages

APODOSIS n pl. -OSES the main clause of a conditional sentence

APODOUS adj apodal

APOGAMY n pl. -MIES a form of plant reproduction APOGAMIC adj

APOGEE n pl. -S the point in the orbit of a body which is farthest from the earth APOGEAL, APOGEAN, APOGEIC adj

APOLLO n pl. -LOS a handsome young man

APOLOG n pl. -S apologue

APOLOGAL adj pertaining to an apologue

APOLOGIA n pl. -GIAS or -GIAE a formal justification or defense

APOLOGUE n pl. -S an allegory

APOLOGY n pl. -GIES an expression of regret for some error or offense

APOLUNE n pl. -S the point in the orbit of a body which is farthest from the moon

APOMICT n pl. -S an organism produced by apomixis

APOMIXIS n pl. -MIXES a type of reproductive process

APOPHONY n pl. -NIES ablaut

APOPHYGE n pl. -S a concave curve in a column

APOPLEXY n pl. -PLEXIES a sudden loss of sensation and muscular control

APORT adv on or toward the left side of a ship

APOSPORY n pl. -RIES a type of reproduction without spore formation

APOSTACY n pl. -CIES apostasy

APOSTASY n pl. -SIES an abandonment of one's faith or principles

APOSTATE n pl. -S one who commits apostasy

APOSTIL n pl. -S a marginal note

APOSTLE n pl. -S a disciple sent forth by Christ to preach the gospel

APOTHECE n pl. -S a spore-producing organ of certain fungi

APOTHEGM n pl. -S a maxim

APOTHEM n pl. -S the perpendicular from the center to any side of a regular polygon

APPAL v -PALLED, -PALLING, -PALS to appall

APPALL v -ED, -ING, -S to fill with horror or dismay

APPANAGE n pl. -S land or revenue granted to a member of a royal family

APPARAT n pl. -S a political organization

APPAREL v -ELED, -ELING, -ELS or -ELLED, -ELLING, -ELS to provide with outer garments

APPARENT adj easily seen

APPEAL v -ED, -ING, -S to make an earnest request

APPEALER n pl. -S one that appeals

APPEAR v -ED, -ING, -S to come into view

APPEASE v -PEASED, -PEASING, -PEASES to bring to a state of peace or contentment

APPEASER n pl. -S one that appeases

APPEL n pl. -S a feint in fencing

APPELLEE n pl. -S the defendant in a type of judicial proceeding

APPELLOR n pl. -S a confessed criminal who accuses an accomplice

APPEND v -ED, -ING, -S to add as a supplement

APPENDIX n pl. -DIXES or -DICES a collection of supplementary material at the end of a book

APPESTAT n pl. -S the mechanism in the central nervous system that regulates appetite

APPETENT adj marked by strong desire

APPETITE n pl. -S a desire for food or drink

APPLAUD v -ED, -ING, -S to express approval by clapping the hands

APPLAUSE n pl. -S the sound made by persons applauding

APPLE n pl. -S an edible fruit

APPLIED past tense of apply

APPLIER n pl. -S one that applies

APPLIQUE v -QUED, -QUEING, -QUES to apply as a decoration to a larger surface

APPLY v -PLIED, -PLYING, -PLIES to bring into contact with something

APPOINT v -ED, -ING, -S to name or assign to a position or office

APPOSE v -POSED, -POSING, -POSES to place side by side

APPOSER n pl. -S one that apposes

APPOSITE adj relevant

APPRAISE v -PRAISED, -PRAISING, -PRAISES to set a value on

APPRISE v -PRISED, -PRISING, -PRISES to notify

APPRISER n pl. -S one that apprises

APPRIZE v -PRIZED, -PRIZING, -PRIZES to appraise

APPRIZER n pl. -S one that apprizes

APPROACH v -ED, -ING, -ES to come near or nearer to

APPROVAL n pl. -S the act of approving

APPROVE v -PROVED, -PROVING, -PROVES to regard favorably

APPROVER n pl. -S one that approves

APPULSE n pl. -S the approach of one moving body toward another

APRAXIA n pl. -S loss of the ability to perform coordinated movements **APRACTIC, APRAXIC** adj

APRES prep after

APRICOT n pl. -S an edible fruit

APRON v -ED, -ING, -S to provide with an apron (a garment worn to protect one's clothing)

APROPOS adj relevant

APROTIC adj being a type of solvent

APSE n pl. -S a domed, semicircular projection of a building **APSIDAL** adj

APSIS n pl. -SIDES an apse

APT adj APTER, APTEST suitable

APTERAL adj apterous

APTERIUM n pl. -RIA a bare area of skin between feathers

APTEROUS adj having no wings

APTERYX n pl. -ES the kiwi

APTITUDE n pl. -S an ability

APTLY adv in an apt manner

APTNESS n pl. -ES the quality of being apt

APYRASE n pl. -S an enzyme

APYRETIC adj having no fever

AQUA n pl. AQUAE or AQUAS water

AQUACADE n pl. -S a swimming and diving exhibition

AQUANAUT n pl. -S a scuba diver trained to live in underwater installations

AQUARIA a pl. of aquarium

AQUARIAL adj pertaining to an aquarium

AQUARIAN n pl. -S a member of the old sects that used water rather than wine in religious ceremonies

AQUARIST n pl. -S one who keeps an aquarium

AQUARIUM n pl. -IUMS or -IA a water-filled enclosure in which aquatic animals are kept

AQUATIC n pl. -S an organism living or growing in or near water

AQUATINT v -ED, -ING, -S to etch, using a certain process

AQUATONE n pl. -S a type of printing process

AQUAVIT n pl. -S a Scandinavian liquor

AQUEDUCT n pl. -S a water conduit

AQUEOUS adj pertaining to water

AQUIFER n pl. -S a water-bearing rock formation

AQUILINE adj curving like an eagle's beak

AQUIVER adj quivering

AR n pl. -S the letter R

ARABESK n pl. -S a design of intertwined floral figures

ARABIC adj derived from gum arabic

ARABICA n pl. -S an evergreen shrub that produces coffee beans

ARABIZE v -IZED, -IZING, -IZES to cause to acquire Arabic customs

ARABLE n pl. -S land suitable for cultivation

ARACEOUS adj belonging to the arum family of plants

ARACHNID n pl. -S any of a class of segmented invertebrate animals

ARAK n pl. -S arrack

ARAMID n pl. -S a type of chemical compound

ARANEID n pl. -S a spider

ARAPAIMA n pl. -S a large food fish

ARAROBA n pl. -S a Brazilian tree

ARB n pl. -S a type of stock trader

ARBALEST n pl. -S a type of crossbow

ARBALIST n pl. -S arbalest

ARBELEST n pl. -S arbalest

ARBITER n pl. -S one chosen or appointed to judge a disputed issue ARBITRAL adj

ARBOR n pl. -S a shady garden shelter

ARBOR n pl. -ES a tree

ARBOREAL adj living in trees

ARBORED adj having trees

ARBORETA n/pl places for the study and exhibition of trees

ARBORIST n pl. -S a tree specialist

ARBORIZE v -IZED, -IZING, -IZES to form many branches

ARBOROUS adj pertaining to trees

ARBOUR n pl. -S a shady garden shelter ARBOURED adj

ARBUSCLE n pl. -S a dwarf tree

ARBUTE n pl. -S an evergreen tree ARBUTEAN adj

ARBUTUS n pl. -ES an evergreen tree

ARC v ARCED, ARCING, ARCS or ARCKED, ARCKING, ARCS to move in a curved course

ARCADE v -CADED, -CADING, -CADES to provide with an arcade (a series of arches)

ARCADIA n pl. -S a region of simple pleasure and quiet

ARCADIAN n pl. -S one who lives in an arcadia

ARCADING n pl. -S an arcade

ARCANE adj mysterious

ARCANUM n pl. -NA or -NUMS a mystery

ARCATURE n pl. -S a small arcade

ARCH v -ED, -ING, -ES to bend like an arch (a curved structure spanning an opening)

ARCHAIC adj pertaining to an earlier time

ARCHAISE v -ISED, -ISING, -ISES to archaize

ARCHAISM n pl. -S an archaic word, idiom, or expression

ARCHAIST n pl. -S one that archaizes

ARCHAIZE v -IZED, -IZING, -IZES to use archaisms

ARCHDUKE n pl. -S an Austrian prince

ARCHER n pl. -S one that shoots with a bow and arrow

ARCHERY n pl. -CHERIES the sport of shooting with a bow and arrow

ARCHIL n pl. -S orchil

ARCHINE n pl. -S a Russian unit of linear measure

ARCHING n pl. -S a series of arches

ARCHIVE v -CHIVED, -CHIVING, -CHIVES to file in an archive (a place where records are kept) ARCHIVAL adj

ARCHLY adv slyly

ARCHNESS n pl. -ES slyness

ARCHON n pl. -S a magistrate of ancient Athens

ARCHWAY n pl. -WAYS a passageway under an arch

ARCIFORM adj having the form of an arch

ARCKED a past tense of arc

ARCKING a present participle of arc

ARCO *adv* with the bow — used as a direction to players of stringed instruments

ARCSINE *n pl.* -S the inverse function to the sine

ARCTIC *n pl.* -S a warm, waterproof overshoe

ARCUATE *adj* curved like a bow

ARCUATED *adj* arcuate

ARCUS *n pl.* -ES an arch-shaped cloud

ARDEB *n pl.* -S an Egyptian unit of capacity

ARDENCY *n pl.* -CIES ardor

ARDENT *adj* characterized by intense emotion **ARDENTLY** *adv*

ARDOR *n pl.* -S intensity of emotion

ARDOUR *n pl.* -S ardor

ARDUOUS *adj* involving great labor or hardship

ARE *n pl.* -S a unit of surface measure

AREA *n pl.* AREAE a section of the cerebral cortex having a specific function

AREA *n pl.* -S a particular extent of space or surface **AREAL** *adj* **AREALLY** *adv*

AREAWAY *n pl.* -WAYS a sunken area leading to a basement entrance

ARECA *n pl.* -S a tropical tree

AREIC *adj* pertaining to a region of the earth contributing little surface drainage

ARENA *n pl.* -S an enclosed area for contests

ARENITE *n pl.* -S rock made up chiefly of sand grains

ARENOSE *adj* sandy

ARENOUS *adj* arenose

AREOLA *n pl.* -LAE or -LAS a small space in a network of leaf veins **AREOLAR, AREOLATE** *adj*

AREOLE *n pl.* -S areola

AREOLOGY *n pl.* -GIES the study of the planet Mars

ARETE *n pl.* -S a sharp mountain ridge

ARETHUSA *n pl.* -S a flowering plant

ARF *n pl.* -S a barking sound

ARGAL *n pl.* -S argol

ARGALA *n pl.* -S a type of stork

ARGALI *n pl.* -S a wild sheep

ARGENT *n pl.* -S silver **ARGENTAL, ARGENTIC** *adj*

ARGENTUM *n pl.* -S silver

ARGIL *n pl.* -S a white clay

ARGINASE *n pl.* -S an enzyme

ARGININE *n pl.* -S an amino acid

ARGLE *v* -GLED, -GLING, -GLES to argue

ARGOL *n pl.* -S a crust deposited in wine casks during aging

ARGON *n pl.* -S a gaseous element

ARGONAUT *n pl.* -S a marine mollusk

ARGOSY *n pl.* -SIES a large merchant ship

ARGOT *n pl.* -S a specialized vocabulary **ARGOTIC** *adj*

ARGUABLE *adj* capable of being argued about **ARGUABLY** *adv*

ARGUE *v* -GUED, -GUING, -GUES to present reasons for or against

ARGUER *n pl.* -S one that argues

ARGUFIER *n pl.* -S one that argufies

ARGUFY *v* -FIED, -FYING, -FIES to argue stubbornly

ARGUING present participle of argue

ARGUMENT *n pl.* -S a discussion involving differing points of view

ARGUS *n pl.* -ES an East Indian pheasant

ARGYLE *n pl.* -S a knitting pattern

ARGYLL *n pl.* -S argyle

ARHAT *n pl.* -S a Buddhist who has attained nirvana

ARIA *n pl.* -S an elaborate melody for a single voice

ARID *adj* -IDER, -IDEST extremely dry **ARIDLY** *adv*

ARIDITY *n pl.* -TIES the state of being arid

ARIDNESS *n pl.* -ES aridity

ARIEL *n pl.* -S an African gazelle

ARIETTA *n pl.* -S a short aria

ARIETTE *n pl.* -S arietta

ARIGHT *adv* rightly; correctly

ARIL *n pl.* -S an outer covering of certain seeds **ARILED, ARILLATE, ARILLOID** *adj*

ARILLODE *n pl.* -S a type of aril

ARIOSE *adj* characterized by melody

ARIOSO *n pl.* -SOS or -SI a musical passage resembling an aria

ARISE *v* AROSE, ARISEN, ARISING, ARISES to get up

ARISTA *n pl.* -TAE or -TAS a bristlelike structure or appendage **ARISTATE** *adj*

ARISTO *n* pl. -TOS an aristocrat

ARK *n* pl. -S a large boat

ARKOSE *n* pl. -S a type of sandstone **ARKOSIC** *adj*

ARLES *n/pl* money paid to bind a bargain

ARM *v* -ED, -ING, -S to supply with weapons

ARMADA *n* pl. -S a fleet of warships

ARMAGNAC *n* pl. -S a French brandy

ARMAMENT *n* pl. -S a military force equipped for war

ARMATURE *v* -TURED, -TURING, -TURES to furnish with armor

ARMBAND *n* pl. -S a band worn around an arm (an upper appendage of the human body)

ARMCHAIR *n* pl. -S a chair with armrests

ARMER *n* pl. -S one that arms

ARMET *n* pl. -S a medieval helmet

ARMFUL *n* pl. ARMFULS or ARMSFUL as much as the arm can hold

ARMHOLE *n* pl. -S an opening for the arm in a garment

ARMIES pl. of army

ARMIGER *n* pl. -S one who carries the armor of a knight

ARMIGERO *n* pl. -GEROS armiger

ARMILLA *n* pl. -LAE or -LAS a thin membrane around the stem of certain fungi

ARMING *n* pl. -S the act of one that arms

ARMLESS *adj* having no arms

ARMLET *n* pl. -S an armband

ARMLIKE *adj* resembling an arm

ARMLOAD *n* pl. -S an armful

ARMLOCK *n* pl. -S a hold in wrestling

ARMOIRE *n* pl. -S a large, ornate cabinet

ARMONICA *n* pl. -S a type of musical instrument

ARMOR *v* -ED, -ING, -S to furnish with armor (a defensive covering)

ARMORER *n* pl. -S one that makes or repairs armor

ARMORIAL *n* pl. -S a treatise on heraldry

ARMORY *n* pl. -MORIES a place where weapons are stored

ARMOUR *v* -ED, -ING, -S to armor

ARMOURER *n* pl. -S armorer

ARMOURY *n* pl. -MOURIES armory

ARMPIT *n* pl. -S the hollow under the arm at the shoulder

ARMREST *n* pl. -S a support for the arm

ARMSFUL a pl. of armful

ARMURE *n* pl. -S a woven fabric

ARMY *n* pl. -MIES a large body of men trained and armed for war

ARMYWORM *n* pl. -S a destructive moth larva

ARNATTO *n* pl. -TOS annatto

ARNICA *n* pl. -S a perennial herb

ARNOTTO *n* pl. -TOS a tropical tree

AROID *n* pl. -S a flowering plant

AROINT *v* -ED, -ING, -S to drive away

AROMA *n* pl. -S a pleasant odor

AROMATIC *n* pl. -S a fragrant plant or substance

AROSE past tense of arise

AROUND *prep* on all sides of

AROUSAL *n* pl. -S the act of arousing

AROUSE *v* AROUSED, AROUSING, AROUSES to stimulate

AROUSER *n* pl. -S one that arouses

AROYNT *v* -ED, -ING, -S to aroint

ARPEGGIO *n* pl. -GIOS a technique of playing a musical chord

ARPEN *n* pl. -S arpent

ARPENT *n* pl. -S an old French unit of area

ARQUEBUS *n* pl. -ES an early portable firearm

ARRACK *n* pl. -S an Oriental liquor

ARRAIGN *v* -ED, -ING, -S to call before a court of law to answer an indictment

ARRANGE *v* -RANGED, -RANGING, -RANGES to put in definite or proper order

ARRANGER *n* pl. -S one that arranges

ARRANT *adj* outright **ARRANTLY** *adv*

ARRAS *n* pl. ARRAS a tapestry **ARRASED** *adj*

ARRAY *v* -ED, -ING, -S to place in proper or desired order

ARRAYAL *n* pl. -S the act of arraying

ARRAYER *n* pl. -S one that arrays

ARREAR *n* pl. -S an unpaid and overdue debt

ARREST *v* -ED, -ING, -S to seize and hold by legal authority

ARRESTEE *n* pl. -S one that is arrested

ARRESTER *n* pl. -S one that arrests

ARRESTOR *n* pl. -S arrester

ARRHIZAL *adj* rootless

ARRIS *n* pl. -RISES a ridge formed by the meeting of two surfaces

ARRIVAL *n* pl. -S the act of arriving

ARRIVE *v* -RIVED, -RIVING, -RIVES to reach a destination

ARRIVER *n* pl. -S one that arrives

ARROBA *n* pl. -S a Spanish unit of weight

ARROGANT *adj* overly convinced of one's own worth or importance

ARROGATE *v* -GATED, -GATING, -GATES to claim or take without right

ARROW *v* -ED, -ING, -S to indicate the proper position of with an arrow (a linear figure with a wedge-shaped end)

ARROWY *adj* moving swiftly

ARROYO *n* pl. -ROYOS a brook or creek

ARSENAL *n* pl. -S a collection or supply of weapons

ARSENATE *n* pl. -S a chemical salt

ARSENIC *n* pl. -S a metallic element

ARSENIDE *n* pl. -S an arsenic compound

ARSENITE *n* pl. -S a chemical salt

ARSENO *adj* containing a certain bivalent chemical radical

ARSENOUS *adj* pertaining to arsenic

ARSES pl. of arsis

ARSHIN *n* pl. -S archine

ARSINE *n* pl. -S a poisonous gas

ARSINO *adj* containing a certain univalent chemical radical

ARSIS *n* pl. ARSES the unaccented part of a musical measure

ARSON *n* pl. -S the malicious or fraudulent burning of property ARSONOUS *adj*

ARSONIST *n* pl. -S one that commits arson

ART *n* pl. -S an esthetically pleasing and meaningful arrangement of elements

ARTAL a pl. of rotl

ARTEFACT *n* pl. -S an artifact

ARTEL *n* pl. -S a collective farm in Russia

ARTERIAL *n* pl. -S a type of highway

ARTERY *n* pl. -TERIES a vessel that carries blood away from the heart

ARTFUL *adj* crafty ARTFULLY *adv*

ARTICLE *v* -CLED, -CLING, -CLES to charge with specific offenses

ARTIER comparative of arty

ARTIEST superlative of arty

ARTIFACT *n* pl. -S an object made by man

ARTIFICE *n* pl. -S a clever stratagem

ARTILY *adv* in an arty manner

ARTINESS *n* pl. -ES the quality of being arty

ARTISAN *n* pl. -S a trained or skilled workman

ARTIST *n* pl. -S one who practices one of the fine arts

ARTISTE *n* pl. -S a skilled public performer

ARTISTIC *adj* characteristic of art

ARTISTRY *n* pl. -RIES artistic quality or workmanship

ARTLESS *adj* lacking cunning or guile

ARTSY *adj* -SIER, -SIEST arty

ARTWORK *n* pl. -S illustrative or decorative work in printed matter

ARTY *adj* ARTIER, ARTIEST showily or pretentiously artistic

ARUGOLA *n* pl. -S arugula

ARUGULA *n* pl. -S a European annual herb

ARUM *n* pl. -S a flowering plant

ARUSPEX *n* pl. -PICES haruspex

ARVAL *adj* pertaining to plowed land

ARVO *n* pl. -VOS afternoon

ARYL *n* pl. -S a univalent radical

ARYTHMIA *n* pl. -S an irregularity in the rhythm of the heartbeat ARYTHMIC *adj*

AS *adv* to the same degree

ASANA *n* pl. -S a posture in yoga

ASARUM *n* pl. -S a perennial herb

ASBESTOS *n* pl. -ES a mineral ASBESTIC *adj*

ASBESTUS *n* pl. -ES asbestos

ASCARID *n* pl. -S a parasitic worm

ASCARIS *n* pl. -RIDES ascarid

ASCEND *v* -ED, -ING, -S to go or move upward

ASCENDER *n* pl. -S one that ascends

ASCENT *n* pl. -S the aet of ascending

ASCESIS *n* pl. -CESES the conduct of an ascetic

ASCETIC *n* pl. -S one who practices extreme self-denial for religious reasons

ASCI pl. of ascus

ASCIDIAN *n* pl. -S a small marine animal

ASCIDIUM *n* pl. -DIA a flask-shaped plant appendage

ASCITES *n* pl. ASCITES accumulation of serous fluid in the abdomen ASCITIC *adj*

ASCOCARP *n* pl. -S a spore-producing organ of certain fungi

ASCORBIC *adj* relieving scurvy

ASCOT *n* pl. -S a broad neck scarf

ASCRIBE v -CRIBED, -CRIBING, -CRIBES to attribute to a specified cause, source, or origin

ASCUS n pl. ASCI a spore sac in certain fungi

ASDIC n pl. -S sonar

ASEA adv at sea

ASEPSIS n pl. -SEPSES the condition of being aseptic

ASEPTIC adj free from germs

ASEXUAL adj occurring or performed without sexual action

ASH v -ED, -ING, -ES to convert into ash (the residue of a substance that has been burned)

ASHAMED adj feeling shame, guilt, or disgrace

ASHCAN n pl. -S a metal receptacle for garbage

ASHEN adj consisting of ashes

ASHFALL n pl. -S a deposit of volcanic ash

ASHIER comparative of ashy

ASHIEST superlative of ashy

ASHINESS n pl. -ES the condition of being ashy

ASHLAR v -ED, -ING, -S to build with squared stones

ASHLER v -ED, -ING, -S to ashlar

ASHLESS adj having no ashes

ASHMAN n pl. -MEN one who collects and removes ashes

ASHORE adv toward or on the shore

ASHPLANT n pl. -S a walking stick

ASHRAM n pl. -S a secluded dwelling of a Hindu sage

ASHTRAY n pl. -TRAYS a receptacle for tobacco ashes

ASHY adj ASHIER, ASHIEST covered with ashes

ASIDE n pl. -S a comment by an actor intended to be heard by the audience but not the other actors

ASININE adj obstinately stupid or silly

ASK v -ED, -ING, -S to put a question to

ASKANCE adv with a side glance

ASKANT adv askance

ASKER n pl. -S one that asks

ASKESIS n pl. ASKESES ascesis

ASKEW adv to one side

ASKING n pl. -S the act of one who asks

ASKOS n pl. ASKOI an oil jar used in ancient Greece

ASLANT adj slanting

ASLEEP adj sleeping

ASLOPE adj sloping

ASOCIAL adj avoiding the company of others

ASP n pl. -S a venomous snake

ASPARKLE adj sparkling

ASPECT n pl. -S appearance of something to the eye or mind

ASPEN n pl. -S any of several poplars

ASPER n pl. -S a Turkish money of account

ASPERATE v -ATED, -ATING, -ATES to make uneven

ASPERGES n pl. ASPERGES a Roman Catholic rite

ASPERITY n pl. -TIES acrimony

ASPERSE v -PERSED, -PERSING, -PERSES to spread false charges against

ASPERSER n pl. -S one that asperses

ASPERSOR n pl. -S asperser

ASPHALT v -ED, -ING, -S to coat with asphalt (a substance used for paving and roofing)

ASPHERIC adj varying slightly from an exactly spherical shape

ASPHODEL n pl. -S a flowering plant

ASPHYXIA n pl. -S unconsciousness caused by lack of oxygen

ASPHYXY n pl. -PHYXIES asphyxia

ASPIC n pl. -S the asp

ASPIRANT n pl. -S one that aspires

ASPIRATA n pl. -TAE a type of plosive

ASPIRATE v -RATED, -RATING, -RATES to pronounce with an initial release of breath

ASPIRE v -PIRED, -PIRING, -PIRES to have an earnest desire or ambition

ASPIRER n pl. -S an aspirant

ASPIRIN n pl. -S a pain reliever

ASPIRING present participle of aspire

ASPIS n pl. -PISES aspic

ASPISH adj resembling an asp

ASQUINT adv with a sidelong glance

ASRAMA n pl. -S ashram

ASS n pl. -ES a hoofed mammal

ASSAGAI v -GAIED, -GAIING, -GAIS to pierce with a light spear

ASSAI n pl. -S a tropical tree

ASSAIL v -ED, -ING, -S to attack

ASSAILER n pl. -S one that assails

ASSASSIN n pl. -S a murderer

ASSAULT v -ED, -ING, -S to attack

ASSAY v -ED, -ING, -S to attempt

ASSAYER n pl. -S one that assays

ASSEGAI v -GAIED, -GAIING, -GAIS to assagai

ASSEMBLE v -BLED, -BLING, -BLES to come or bring together

ASSEMBLY n pl. -BLIES the act of assembling

ASSENT v -ED, -ING, -S to express agreement

ASSENTER n pl. -S one that assents

ASSENTOR n pl. -S assenter

ASSERT v -ED, -ING, -S to state positively

ASSERTER n pl. -S one that asserts

ASSERTOR n pl. -S asserter

ASSESS v -ED, -ING, -ES to estimate the value of for taxation

ASSESSOR n pl. -S one that assesses

ASSET n pl. -S a useful quality or thing

ASSIGN v -ED, -ING, -S to set apart for a particular purpose

ASSIGNAT n pl. -S one of the notes issued as currency by the French revolutionary government

ASSIGNEE n pl. -S one to whom property or right is legally transferred

ASSIGNER n pl. -S one that assigns

ASSIGNOR n pl. -S one who legally transfers property or right

ASSIST v -ED, -ING, -S to give aid or support to

ASSISTER n pl. -S one that assists

ASSISTOR n pl. -S assister

ASSIZE n pl. -S a session of a legislative or judicial body

ASSLIKE adj resembling an ass

ASSOIL v -ED, -ING, -S to pardon

ASSONANT n pl. -S a word or syllable that resembles another in sound

ASSORT v -ED, -ING, -S to distribute into groups according to kind or class

ASSORTER n pl. -S one that assorts

ASSUAGE v -SUAGED, -SUAGING, -SUAGES to make less severe

ASSUME v -SUMED, -SUMING, -SUMES to take on

ASSUMER n pl. -S one that assumes

ASSURE v -SURED, -SURING, -SURES to insure

ASSURED n pl. -S an insured person

ASSURER n pl. -S one that assures

ASSURING present participle of assure

ASSUROR n pl. -S assurer

ASSWAGE v -SWAGED, -SWAGING, -SWAGES to assuage

ASTASIA n pl. -S inability to stand resulting from muscular incoordination

ASTATIC adj unstable

ASTATINE n pl. -S a radioactive element

ASTER n pl. -S a flowering plant

ASTERIA n pl. -S a gemstone cut to exhibit asterism

ASTERISK v -ED, -ING, -S to mark with an asterisk (a star-shaped printing mark)

ASTERISM n pl. -S a property of certain minerals of showing a starlike luminous figure

ASTERN adv at or toward the rear of a ship

ASTERNAL adj not connected to the sternum

ASTEROID n pl. -S a type of celestial body

ASTHENIA n pl. -S lack of strength

ASTHENIC n pl. -S a slender, lightly muscled person

ASTHENY n pl. -NIES asthenia

ASTHMA n pl. -S a respiratory disease

ASTIGMIA n pl. -S a visual defect

ASTILBE n pl. -S an Asian perennial

ASTIR adj moving about

ASTOMOUS adj having no stomata

ASTONISH v -ED, -ING, -ES to fill with sudden wonder or surprise

ASTONY v -TONIED, -TONYING, -TONIES to astonish

ASTOUND v -ED, -ING, -S to amaze

ASTRAGAL n pl. -S a convex molding

ASTRAL n pl. -S a type of oil lamp

ASTRALLY adv in a stellar manner

ASTRAY adv off the right course

ASTRICT v -ED, -ING, -S to restrict

ASTRIDE adv with one leg on each side

ASTRINGE v -TRINGED, -TRINGING, -TRINGES to bind or draw together

ASTUTE adj shrewd **ASTUTELY** adv

ASTYLAR adj having no columns

ASUNDER adv into pieces

ASWARM adj swarming

ASWIRL adj swirling

ASWOON adj swooning

ASYLUM n pl. -LUMS or -LA an institution for the care of the mentally ill

ASYNDETA *n/pl* omissions of certain conjunctions

AT *prep* in the position of

ATABAL *n* pl. -S a type of drum

ATACTIC *adj* showing no regularity or structure

ATAGHAN *n* pl. -S yataghan

ATALAYA *n* pl. -S a watchtower

ATAMAN *n* pl. -S a hetman

ATAMASCO *n* pl. -COS a flowering plant

ATAP *n* pl. -S the nipa palm tree

ATARAXIA *n* pl. -S peace of mind

ATARAXIC *n* pl. -S a tranquilizing drug

ATARAXY *n* pl. -RAXIES ataraxia

ATAVIC *adj* pertaining to a remote ancestor

ATAVISM *n* pl. -S the reappearance of a genetic characteristic after several generations of absence

ATAVIST *n* pl. -S an individual displaying atavism

ATAXIA *n* pl. -S loss of muscular coordination

ATAXIC *n* pl. -S one suffering from ataxia

ATAXY *n* pl. ATAXIES ataxia

ATE *n* pl. -S blind impulse or reckless ambition that drives one to ruin

ATECHNIC *adj* lacking technical knowledge

ATELIC *adj* pertaining to a type of verb form

ATELIER *n* pl. -S a workshop or studio

ATEMOYA *n* pl. -S a fruit of a hybrid tropical tree

ATHANASY *n* pl. -SIES immortality

ATHEISM *n* pl. -S the belief that there is no God

ATHEIST *n* pl. -S a believer in atheism

ATHELING *n* pl. -S an Anglo-Saxon prince or nobleman

ATHENEUM *n* pl. -S a literary institution

ATHEROMA *n* pl. -MAS or -MATA a disease of the arteries

ATHETOID *adj* affected with a type of nervous disorder

ATHIRST *adj* having a strong desire

ATHLETE *n* pl. -S one skilled in feats of physical strength and agility **ATHLETIC** *adj*

ATHODYD *n* pl. -S a type of jet engine

ATHWART *adv* from side to side

ATILT *adj* being in a tilted position

ATINGLE *adj* tingling

ATLAS *n* pl. ATLANTES or ATLASES a male figure used as a supporting column

ATLATL *n* pl. -S a device for throwing a spear or dart

ATMA *n* pl. -S atman

ATMAN *n* pl. -S the individual soul in Hinduism

ATOLL *n* pl. -S a ring-shaped coral island

ATOM *n* pl. -S the smallest unit of an element **ATOMIC, ATOMICAL** *adj*

ATOMICS *n/pl* the science dealing with atoms

ATOMIES pl. of atomy

ATOMISE *v* -ISED, -ISING, -ISES to atomize

ATOMISER *n* pl. -S atomizer

ATOMISM *n* pl. -S the theory that the universe is composed of simple, indivisible, minute particles

ATOMIST *n* pl. -S an adherent of atomism

ATOMIZE *v* -IZED, -IZING, -IZES to reduce to a fine spray

ATOMIZER *n* pl. -S a device for atomizing liquids

ATOMY *n* pl. -MIES a tiny particle

ATONAL *adj* lacking tonality **ATONALLY** *adv*

ATONE *v* ATONED, ATONING, ATONES to make amends or reparation **ATONABLE** *adj*

ATONER *n* pl. -S one that atones

ATONIC *n* pl. -S an unaccented syllable or word

ATONING present participle of atone

ATONY *n* pl. -NIES muscular weakness

ATOP *adj* being on or at the top

ATOPY *n* pl. -PIES a type of allergy **ATOPIC** *adj*

ATRAZINE *n* pl. -S an herbicide

ATREMBLE *adj* trembling

ATRESIA *n* pl. -S absence or closure of a natural bodily passage

ATRIA a pl. of atrium

ATRIAL *adj* pertaining to an atrium

ATRIP *adj* aweigh

ATRIUM *n* pl. ATRIA or ATRIUMS the main room of an ancient Roman house

ATROCITY *n* pl. -TIES a heinous act

ATROPHIA *n* pl. -S a wasting away of the body or any of its parts **ATROPHIC** *adj*

ATROPHY *v* -PHIED, -PHYING, -PHIES to waste away

ATROPIN *n* pl. -S atropine

ATROPINE *n* pl. -S a poisonous alkaloid

ATROPISM *n* pl. -S atropine poisoning

ATT *n* pl. ATT a monetary unit of Laos

ATTABOY *interj* —used to express encouragement or approval

ATTACH *v* -ED, -ING, -ES to connect as an associated part

ATTACHE *n* pl. -S a diplomatic official

ATTACHER *n* pl. -S one that attaches

ATTACK *v* -ED, -ING, -S to set upon violently

ATTACKER *n* pl. -S one that attacks

ATTAIN *v* -ED, -ING, -S to gain or achieve by mental or physical effort

ATTAINER *n* pl. -S one that attains

ATTAINT *v* -ED, -ING, -S to disgrace

ATTAR *n* pl. -S a fragrant oil

ATTEMPER *v* -ED, -ING, -S to modify the temperature of

ATTEMPT *v* -ED, -ING, -S to make an effort to do or accomplish

ATTEND *v* -ED, -ING, -S to be present at

ATTENDEE *n* pl. -S an attender

ATTENDER *n* pl. -S one that attends

ATTENT *adj* heedful

ATTEST *v* -ED, -ING, -S to affirm to be true or genuine

ATTESTER *n* pl. -S one that attests

ATTESTOR *n* pl. -S attester

ATTIC *n* pl. -S a story or room directly below the roof of a house

ATTICISM *n* pl. -S a concise and elegant expression

ATTICIST *n* pl. -S one who uses atticisms

ATTIRE *v* -TIRED, -TIRING, -TIRES to clothe

ATTITUDE *n* pl. -S a state of mind with regard to some matter

ATTORN *v* -ED, -ING, -S to acknowledge a new owner as one's landlord

ATTORNEY *n* pl. -NEYS a lawyer

ATTRACT *v* -ED, -ING, -S to cause to approach or adhere

ATTRITE *adj* attrited

ATTRITED *adj* worn down by rubbing

ATTUNE *v* -TUNED, -TUNING, -TUNES to bring into harmony

ATWAIN *adv* in two

ATWEEN *prep* between

ATWITTER *adj* twittering

ATYPIC *adj* atypical

ATYPICAL *adj* not typical

AUBADE *n* pl. -S a morning song

AUBERGE *n* pl. -S an inn

AUBRETIA *n* pl. -S aubrieta

AUBRIETA *n* pl. -S a flowering plant

AUBURN *n* pl. -S a reddish brown color

AUCTION *v* -ED, -ING, -S to sell publicly to the highest bidder

AUCUBA *n* pl. -S a shrub of the dogwood family

AUDACITY *n* pl. -TIES boldness

AUDAD *n* pl. -S aoudad

AUDIAL *adj* aural

AUDIBLE *n* pl. -S a type of play in football

AUDIBLY *adv* in a way so as to be heard

AUDIENCE *n* pl. -S a group of listeners or spectators

AUDIENT *n* pl. -S one that hears

AUDILE *n* pl. -S one whose mental imagery is chiefly auditory

AUDING *n* pl. -S the process of hearing, recognizing, and interpreting a spoken language

AUDIO *n* pl. -DIOS sound reception or transmission

AUDIT *v* -ED, -ING, -S to examine with intent to verify

AUDITION *v* -ED, -ING, -S to give a trial performance

AUDITIVE *n* pl. -S an auditory

AUDITOR *n* pl. -S one that audits

AUDITORY *n* pl. -RIES a group of listeners

AUGEND *n* pl. -S a number to which another is to be added

AUGER *n* pl. -S a tool for boring

AUGHT *n* pl. -S a zero

AUGITE *n* pl. -S a mineral **AUGITIC** *adj*

AUGMENT *v* -ED, -ING, -S to increase

AUGUR *v* -ED, -ING, -S to foretell from omens

AUGURAL *adj* pertaining to augury

AUGURER *n* pl. -S one that augurs

AUGURY *n* pl. -RIES the practice of auguring

AUGUST *adj* -GUSTER, -GUSTEST inspiring reverence or admiration **AUGUSTLY** *adv*

AUK *n pl.* -S a diving seabird

AUKLET *n pl.* -S a small auk

AULD *adj* AULDER, AULDEST old

AULIC *adj* pertaining to a royal court

AUNT *n pl.* -S the sister of one's father or mother

AUNTHOOD *n pl.* -S the state of being an aunt

AUNTIE *n pl.* -S aunt

AUNTIES *pl.* of aunty

AUNTLIKE *adj* resembling an aunt

AUNTLY *adj* -LIER, -LIEST of or suggesting an aunt

AUNTY *n pl.* AUNTIES aunt

AURA *n pl.* -RAS or -RAE an invisible emanation

AURAL *adj* pertaining to the sense of hearing **AURALLY** *adv*

AURAR *pl.* of eyrir

AURATE *adj* having ears

AURATED *adj* aurate

AUREATE *adj* golden

AUREI *pl.* of aureus

AUREOLA *n pl.* -LAS or -LAE a halo

AUREOLE *v* -OLED, -OLING, -OLES to surround with a halo

AURES *pl.* of auris

AUREUS *n pl.* -REI a gold coin of ancient Rome

AURIC *adj* pertaining to gold

AURICLE *n pl.* -S an ear or ear-shaped part **AURICLED** *adj*

AURICULA *n pl.* -LAS or -LAE an auricle

AURIFORM *adj* ear-shaped

AURIS *n pl.* AURES the ear

AURIST *n pl.* -S a specialist in diseases of the ear

AUROCHS *n pl.* -ES an extinct European ox

AURORA *n pl.* -RAS or -RAE the rising light of the morning AURORAL, AUROREAN *adj*

AUROUS *adj* pertaining to gold

AURUM *n pl.* -S gold

AUSFORM *v* -ED, -ING, -S to strengthen steel

AUSPEX *n pl.* -PICES a soothsayer of ancient Rome

AUSPICE *n pl.* -S a favorable omen

AUSTERE *adj* -TERER, -TEREST grave

AUSTRAL *n pl.* -ES or -S a former monetary unit of Argentina

AUSUBO *n pl.* -BOS a tropical tree

AUTACOID *n pl.* -S a hormone

AUTARCHY *n pl.* -CHIES absolute rule or power

AUTARKY *n pl.* -KIES national economic self-sufficiency **AUTARKIC** *adj*

AUTECISM *n pl.* -S the development of the entire life cycle of a parasitic fungus on a single host

AUTEUR *n pl.* -S the creator of a film

AUTHOR *v* -ED, -ING, -S to write

AUTISM *n pl.* -S extreme withdrawal into fantasy

AUTISTIC *n pl.* -S one who is affected with autism

AUTO *v* -ED, -ING, -S to ride in an automobile

AUTOBAHN *n pl.* -BAHNS or -BAHNEN a German superhighway

AUTOBUS *n pl.* -BUSES or -BUSSES a bus

AUTOCADE *n pl.* -S a procession of automobiles

AUTOCOID *n pl.* -S autacoid

AUTOCRAT *n pl.* -S an absolute ruler

AUTODYNE *n pl.* -S a type of electrical circuit

AUTOGAMY *n pl.* -MIES fertilization of a flower by its own pollen

AUTOGENY *n pl.* -NIES the production of living organisms from inanimate matter

AUTOGIRO *n pl.* -ROS a type of airplane

AUTOGYRO *n pl.* -ROS autogiro

AUTOLYSE *v* -LYSED, -LYSING, -LYSES to autolyze

AUTOLYZE *v* -LYZED, -LYZING, -LYZES to break down tissue by the action of self-contained enzymes

AUTOMAN *n pl.* -MEN an automobile maker

AUTOMATA *n/pl* robots

AUTOMATE *v* -MATED, -MATING, -MATES to convert to a system of automatic control

AUTOMEN *n pl.* of automan

AUTONOMY *n pl.* -MIES the state of being self-governing

AUTOPSIC *adj* pertaining to an autopsy

AUTOPSY *v* -SIED, -SYING, -SIES to examine a dead body to determine the cause of death

AUTOSOME *n pl.* -S a type of chromosome

AUTOTOMY n pl. -MIES the shedding of a damaged body part

AUTOTYPE n pl. -S a type of photographic process

AUTOTYPY n pl. -TYPIES autotype

AUTUMN n pl. -S a season of the year **AUTUMNAL** adj

AUTUNITE n pl. -S a mineral

AUXESIS n pl. AUXESES an increase in cell size without cell division

AUXETIC n pl. -S a substance that promotes auxesis

AUXIN n pl. -S a substance used to regulate plant growth **AUXINIC** adj

AVA adv at all

AVADAVAT n pl. -S a small songbird

AVAIL v -ED, -ING, -S to be of use or advantage to

AVANT adj culturally or stylistically new

AVARICE n pl. -S greed

AVAST interj — used as a command to stop

AVATAR n pl. -S the incarnation of a Hindu deity

AVAUNT interj — used as an order of dismissal

AVE n pl. -S an expression of greeting or farewell

AVELLAN adj having the four arms shaped like filberts — used of a heraldic cross

AVELLANE adj avellan

AVENGE v AVENGED, AVENGING, AVENGES to exact retribution for

AVENGER n pl. -S one that avenges

AVENS n pl. -ES a perennial herb

AVENTAIL n pl. -S ventail

AVENUE n pl. -S a wide street

AVER v AVERRED, AVERRING, AVERS to declare positively

AVERAGE v -AGED, -AGING, -AGES to calculate the arithmetic mean of

AVERMENT n pl. -S the act of averring

AVERRED past tense of aver

AVERRING present participle of aver

AVERSE adj opposed; reluctant **AVERSELY** adv

AVERSION n pl. -S a feeling of repugnance **AVERSIVE** adj

AVERT v -ED, -ING, -S to turn away

AVGAS n pl. -GASES or -GASSES gasoline for airplanes

AVIAN n pl. -S a bird

AVIANIZE v -IZED, -IZING, -IZES to make less severe by repeated culture in a chick embryo, as a virus

AVIARIST n pl. -S the keeper of an aviary

AVIARY n pl. -ARIES a large enclosure for live birds

AVIATE v -ATED, -ATING, -ATES to fly an aircraft

AVIATION n pl. -S the act of aviating

AVIATOR n pl. -S one that aviates

AVIATRIX n pl. -TRICES or -TRIXES a female aviator

AVICULAR adj pertaining to birds

AVID adj eager

AVIDIN n pl. -S a protein found in egg white

AVIDITY n pl. -TIES the state of being avid

AVIDLY adv in an avid manner

AVIDNESS n pl. -ES avidity

AVIFAUNA n pl. -NAS or -NAE the bird life of a particular region

AVIGATOR n pl. -S one that navigates aircraft

AVION n pl. -S an airplane

AVIONICS n/pl the science of electronics applied to aviation **AVIONIC** adj

AVISO n pl. -SOS advice

AVO n pl. AVOS a monetary unit of Macao

AVOCADO n pl. -DOS or -DOES the edible fruit of a tropical tree

AVOCET n pl. -S a shore bird

AVODIRE n pl. -S an African tree

AVOID v -ED, -ING, -S to keep away from

AVOIDER n pl. -S one that avoids

AVOSET n pl. -S avocet

AVOUCH v -ED, -ING, -ES to affirm

AVOUCHER n pl. -S one that avouches

AVOW v -ED, -ING, -S to declare openly **AVOWABLE** adj **AVOWABLY, AVOWEDLY** adv

AVOWAL n pl. -S an open declaration

AVOWER n pl. -S one that avows

AVULSE v AVULSED, AVULSING, AVULSES to tear off forcibly

AVULSION n pl. -S the act of avulsing

AW interj — used to express protest, disgust, or disbelief

AWA adv away

AWAIT v -ED, -ING, -S to wait for

AWAITER n pl. -S one that awaits

AWAKE v AWAKED or AWOKE, AWOKEN, AWAKING, AWAKES to wake up

AWAKEN v -ED, -ING, -S to awake

AWAKENER n pl. -S one that awakens

AWAKING present participle of awake

AWARD v -ED, -ING, -S to grant as due or merited

AWARDEE n pl. -S one that is awarded something

AWARDER n pl. -S one that awards

AWARE adj having perception or knowledge

AWASH adj covered with water

AWAY adv from a certain place

AWAYNESS n pl. -ES the state of being distant

AWE v AWED, AWING or AWEING, AWES to inspire with awe (reverential fear)

AWEARY adj weary

AWEATHER adv toward the windward side of a vessel

AWED past tense of awe

AWEE adv awhile

AWEIGH adj hanging just clear of the bottom — used of an anchor

AWELESS adj lacking awe

AWESOME adj inspiring awe

AWFUL adj -FULLER, -FULLEST extremely bad or unpleasant AWFULLY adv

AWHILE adv for a short time

AWHIRL adj whirling

AWING a present participle of awe

AWKWARD adj -WARDER, -WARDEST lacking skill, dexterity, or grace

AWL n pl. -S a pointed tool for making small holes

AWLESS adj aweless

AWLWORT n pl. -S an aquatic plant

AWMOUS n pl. AWMOUS alms

AWN n pl. -S a bristlelike appendage of certain grasses AWNED, AWNLESS, AWNY adj

AWNING n pl. -S a rooflike canvas cover AWNINGED adj

AWOKE a past tense of awake

AWOKEN a past participle of awake

AWOL n pl. -S one who is absent without leave

AWRY adv with a turn or twist to one side

AX v -ED, -ING, -ES to work on with an ax (a type of cutting tool)

AXAL adj axial

AXE v AXED, AXING, AXES to ax

AXEL n pl. -S a jump in figure skating

AXEMAN n pl. -MEN axman

AXENIC adj free from germs

AXES pl. of axis

AXIAL adj pertaining to or forming an axis AXIALLY adv

AXIALITY n pl. -TIES the state of being axial

AXIL n pl. -S the angle between the upper side of a leaf and its supporting stem

AXILE adj axial

AXILLA n pl. -LAE or -LAS the armpit

AXILLAR n pl. -S a feather on the undersurface of a bird's wing

AXILLARY n pl. -LARIES an axillar

AXING present participle of axe

AXIOLOGY n pl. -GIES the study of values and value judgments

AXIOM n pl. -S a self-evident truth

AXION n pl. -S a hypothetical subatomic particle

AXIS n pl. AXES a straight line about which a body rotates AXISED adj

AXIS n pl. AXISES an Asian deer

AXITE n pl. -S a fiber of an axon

AXLE n pl. -S a shaft upon which a wheel revolves AXLED adj

AXLETREE n pl. -S a type of axle

AXLIKE adj resembling an ax

AXMAN n pl. -MEN one who wields an ax

AXOLOTL n pl. -S a salamander of Mexico and western United States

AXON n pl. -S the central process of a neuron AXONAL adj

AXONE n pl. -S axon

AXONEMAL adj pertaining to an axoneme

AXONEME n pl. -S a part of a cilium

AXONIC adj pertaining to an axon

AXOPLASM n pl. -S the protoplasm of an axon

AXSEED n pl. -S a European herb

AY n pl. AYS aye

AYAH n pl. -S a native maid or nurse in India

AYE n pl. -S an affirmative vote

AYIN n pl. -S a Hebrew letter

AYURVEDA n pl. -S a Hindu system of medicine

AZALEA n pl. -S a flowering shrub

AZAN n pl. -S a Muslim call to prayer

AZIDE n pl. -S a type of chemical compound **AZIDO** adj

AZIMUTH n pl. -S an angle of horizontal deviation

AZINE n pl. -S a type of chemical compound

AZLON n pl. -S a textile fiber

AZO adj containing nitrogen

AZOIC adj pertaining to geologic time before the appearance of life

AZOLE n pl. -S a type of chemical compound

AZON n pl. -S a radio-controlled aerial bomb

AZONAL adj pertaining to a type of a soil group

AZONIC adj not restricted to any particular zone

AZOTE n pl. -S nitrogen **AZOTED** adj

AZOTEMIA n pl. -S an excess of nitrogenous substances in the blood **AZOTEMIC** adj

AZOTH n pl. -S mercury

AZOTIC adj pertaining to azote

AZOTISE v -TISED, -TISING, -TISES to azotize

AZOTIZE v -TIZED, -TIZING, -TIZES to treat with nitrogen

AZOTURIA n pl. -S an excess of nitrogenous substances in the urine

AZURE n pl. -S a blue color

AZURITE n pl. -S a mineral

AZYGOS n pl. -ES an azygous anatomical part

AZYGOUS adj not being one of a pair

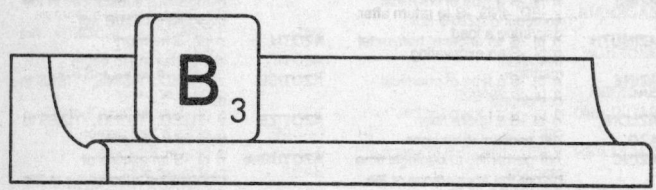

BA	*n* pl. -S the eternal soul, in Egyptian mythology
BAA	*v* -ED, -ING, -S to bleat
BAAL	*n* pl. -S or -IM a false god
BAALISM	*n* pl. -S the worship of a baal
BAAS	*n* pl. -ES master; boss
BAASKAAP	*n* pl. -S the policy of domination by white people in South Africa
BABA	*n* pl. -S a rum cake
BABASSU	*n* pl. -S a palm tree
BABBITT	*v* -ED, -ING, -S to line with babbitt (an alloy)
BABBLE	*v* -BLED, -BLING, -BLES to talk idly or excessively
BABBLER	*n* pl. -S one that babbles
BABBLING	*n* pl. -S idle talk
BABE	*n* pl. -S a baby
BABEL	*n* pl. -S confusion
BABESIA	*n* pl. -S a parasitic protozoan
BABICHE	*n* pl. -S rawhide thongs
BABIED	past tense of baby
BABIES	present 3d person sing. of baby
BABIRUSA	*n* pl. -S a wild pig
BABKA	*n* pl. -S a coffee cake
BABOO	*n* pl. -BOOS a Hindu gentleman
BABOOL	*n* pl. -S babul
BABOON	*n* pl. -S a large ape
BABU	*n* pl. -S baboo
BABUL	*n* pl. -S a North African tree
BABUSHKA	*n* pl. -S a woman's scarf
BABY	*v* -BIED, -BYING, -BIES to coddle
BABYHOOD	*n* pl. -S the state of being a baby (an infant)
BABYISH	*adj* resembling a baby
BACALAO	*n* pl. -LAOS codfish
BACCA	*n* pl. -CAE a berry
BACCARA	*n* pl. -S baccarat
BACCARAT	*n* pl. -S a card game
BACCATE	*adj* pulpy like a berry
BACCATED	*adj* baccate
BACCHANT	*n* pl. -S or -ES a carouser
BACCHIC	*adj* riotous
BACCHIUS	*n* pl. -CHII a type of metrical foot
BACH	*v* -ED, -ING, -ES to live as a bachelor
BACHELOR	*n* pl. -S an unmarried man
BACILLAR	*adj* rod-shaped
BACILLUS	*n* pl. -LI any of a class of rod-shaped bacteria
BACK	*v* -ED, -ING, -S to support
BACKACHE	*n* pl. -S a pain in the back
BACKBEAT	*n* pl. -S a type of rhythm in music
BACKBEND	*n* pl. -S an acrobatic feat
BACKBITE	*v* -BIT, -BITTEN, -BITING, -BITES to slander
BACKBONE	*n* pl. -S the spine
BACKCAST	*n* pl. -S a backward movement in casting a fishing line
BACKCHAT	*n* pl. -S repartee
BACKDATE	*v* -DATED, -DATING, -DATES to predate
BACKDOOR	*adj* secretive
BACKDROP	*v* -DROPPED or -DROPT, -DROPPING, -DROPS to provide with a scenic background
BACKER	*n* pl. -S a supporter
BACKFILL	*v* -ED, -ING, -S to refill
BACKFIRE	*v* -FIRED, -FIRING, -FIRES to have opposite results
BACKFIT	*v* -FITTED, -FITTING, -FITS to retrofit

BACKFLOW n pl. -S a flowing back toward a source

BACKHAND v -ED, -ING, -S to strike with the back of the hand

BACKHAUL v -ED, -ING, -S to return after delivering a load

BACKHOE n pl. -S an excavating machine

BACKING n pl. -S support

BACKLAND n pl. -S a region remote from cities

BACKLASH v -ED, -ING, -ES to cause a reaction

BACKLESS adj having no back

BACKLIST v -ED, -ING, -S to include in a publisher's list of older book titles

BACKLIT adj illuminated from behind

BACKLOG v -LOGGED, -LOGGING, -LOGS to accumulate

BACKMOST adj hindmost

BACKOUT n pl. -S a reversal of launching procedures

BACKPACK v -ED, -ING, -S to hike with a pack on one's back

BACKREST n pl. -S a back support

BACKROOM adj made or done in secret

BACKRUSH n pl. -ES the seaward return of water from a wave

BACKSAW n pl. -S a type of saw

BACKSEAT n pl. -S a rear seat

BACKSET n pl. -S a setback

BACKSIDE n pl. -S the hind part

BACKSLAP v -SLAPPED, -SLAPPING, -SLAPS to show much approval

BACKSLID past tense of backslide (to revert to sin)

BACKSPIN n pl. -S a backward rotation

BACKSTAY n pl. -STAYS a support for a mast

BACKSTOP v -STOPPED, -STOPPING, -STOPS to bolster

BACKUP n pl. -S a substitute

BACKWARD adv toward the back

BACKWASH v -ED, -ING, -ES to spray water backward

BACKWOOD adj uncouth

BACKWRAP n pl. -S a wraparound garment that fastens in the back

BACKYARD n pl. -S an area at the rear of a house

BACON n pl. -S a side of a pig cured and smoked

BACTERIA n pl. -S a group of microscopic organisms

BACTERIN n pl. -S a vaccine prepared from dead bacteria

BACULINE adj pertaining to a rod

BACULUM n pl. -LA or -LUMS a bone in the penis of many mammals

BAD adj BADDER, BADDEST very good

BAD adj WORSE, WORST not good in any way

BAD n pl. -S something that is bad

BADDIE n pl. -S a bad person

BADDY n pl. -DIES baddie

BADE past tense of bid

BADGE v BADGED, BADGING, BADGES to supply with an insignia

BADGER v -ED, -ING, -S to harass

BADGERLY adj bothersome

BADGING present participle of badge

BADINAGE v -NAGED, -NAGING, -NAGES to banter

BADLAND n pl. -S a barren, hilly area

BADLY adv in a bad manner

BADMAN n pl. -MEN an outlaw

BADMOUTH v -ED, -ING, -S to criticize

BADNESS n pl. -ES the state of being bad

BAFF v -ED, -ING, -S to strike under a golf ball

BAFFIES pl. of baffy

BAFFLE v -FLED, -FLING, -FLES to confuse

BAFFLER n pl. -S one that baffles

BAFFY n pl. -FIES a wooden golf club

BAG v BAGGED, BAGGING, BAGS to put into a bag (a flexible container)

BAGASS n pl. -ES bagasse

BAGASSE n pl. -S crushed sugarcane

BAGEL n pl. -S a ring-shaped roll

BAGFUL n pl. BAGFULS or BAGSFUL as much as a bag can hold

BAGGAGE n pl. -S luggage

BAGGED past tense of bag

BAGGER n pl. -S one that bags

BAGGIE n pl. -S the stomach

BAGGING n pl. -S material for making bags

BAGGY adj -GIER, -GIEST loose-fitting **BAGGILY** adv

BAGHOUSE n pl. -S a facility for removing particulates from exhaust gases

BAGMAN n pl. -MEN a traveling salesman

BAGNIO n pl. -NIOS a brothel

BAGPIPE *n* pl. -S a wind instrument
BAGPIPER *n* pl. -S one that plays bagpipes
BAGSFUL a pl. of bagful
BAGUET *n* pl. -S baguette
BAGUETTE *n* pl. -S a rectangular gem
BAGWIG *n* pl. -S a type of wig
BAGWORM *n* pl. -S the larva of certain moths
BAH *interj* — an exclamation of disgust
BAHADUR *n* pl. -S a Hindu title of respect
BAHT *n* pl. -S a monetary unit of Thailand
BAIDARKA *n* pl. -S bidarka
BAIL *v* -ED, -ING, -S to transfer property temporarily **BAILABLE** *adj*
BAILEE *n* pl. -S a person to whom property is bailed
BAILER *n* pl. -S bailor
BAILEY *n* pl. -LEYS an outer castle wall
BAILIE *n* pl. -S a Scottish magistrate
BAILIFF *n* pl. -S a court officer
BAILMENT *n* pl. -S the act of bailing
BAILOR *n* pl. -S a person who bails property to another
BAILOUT *n* pl. -S the act of parachuting from an aircraft
BAILSMAN *n* pl. -MEN one who provides security for another
BAIRN *n* pl. -S a child **BAIRNISH** *adj*
BAIRNLY *adj* -LIER, -LIEST childish
BAIT *v* -ED, -ING, -S to lure
BAITER *n* pl. -S one that baits
BAITH *adj* both
BAIZA *n* pl. -S a monetary unit of Oman
BAIZE *n* pl. -S a green, woolen fabric
BAKE *v* BAKED, BAKING, BAKES to prepare food in an oven
BAKEMEAT *n* pl. -S a pastry
BAKER *n* pl. -S one that bakes
BAKERY *n* pl. -ERIES a place where baked goods are sold
BAKESHOP *n* pl. -S a bakery
BAKING *n* pl. -S a quantity baked
BAKLAVA *n* pl. -S a Turkish pastry
BAKLAWA *n* pl. -S baklava
BAKSHISH *v* -ED, -ING, -ES to give a tip
BAL *n* pl. -S a balmoral
BALANCE *v* -ANCED, -ANCING, -ANCES to weigh
BALANCER *n* pl. -S one that balances

BALAS *n* pl. -ES a red variety of spinel
BALATA *n* pl. -S a tropical tree
BALBOA *n* pl. -S a monetary unit of Panama
BALCONY *n* pl. -NIES an elevated platform
BALD *adj* BALDER, BALDEST lacking hair
BALD *v* -ED, -ING, -S to become bald
BALDHEAD *n* pl. -S a bald person
BALDIES pl. of baldy
BALDISH *adj* somewhat bald
BALDLY *adv* in a plain and blunt manner
BALDNESS *n* pl. -ES the state of being bald
BALDPATE *n* pl. -S a baldhead
BALDRIC *n* pl. -S a shoulder belt
BALDRICK *n* pl. -S baldric
BALDY *n* pl. BALDIES a bald person
BALE *v* BALED, BALING, BALES to form into tightly compressed bundles
BALEEN *n* pl. -S whalebone
BALEFIRE *n* pl. -S a bonfire
BALEFUL *adj* menacing
BALER *n* pl. -S one that bales
BALING present participle of bale
BALISAUR *n* pl. -S a long-tailed badger
BALK *v* -ED, -ING, -S to stop short and refuse to proceed
BALKER *n* pl. -S one that balks
BALKLINE *n* pl. -S the starting line in track events
BALKY *adj* BALKIER, BALKIEST stubborn **BALKILY** *adv*
BALL *v* -ED, -ING, -S to form into a ball (a spherical object)
BALLAD *n* pl. -S a narrative poem or song **BALLADIC** *adj*
BALLADE *n* pl. -S a type of poem
BALLADRY *n* pl. -RIES ballad poetry
BALLAST *v* -ED, -ING, -S to stabilize
BALLER *n* pl. -S one that balls
BALLET *n* pl. -S a classical dance form **BALLETIC** *adj*
BALLGAME *n* pl. -S a game played with a ball
BALLHAWK *n* pl. -S a very good defensive ballplayer
BALLIES pl. of bally
BALLISTA *n* pl. -TAE an ancient weapon
BALLON *n* pl. -S lightness of movement
BALLONET *n* pl. -S a small balloon

BALLONNE *n* pl. -S a ballet jump

BALLOON *v* -ED, -ING, -S to swell out

BALLOT *v* -ED, -ING, -S to vote

BALLOTER *n* pl. -S one that ballots

BALLPARK *n* pl. -S a facility in which ballgames are played

BALLROOM *n* pl. -S a large room for dancing

BALLUTE *n* pl. -S a small inflatable parachute

BALLY *n* pl. -LIES a noisy uproar

BALLYHOO *v* -ED, -ING, -S to promote by uproar

BALLYRAG *v* -RAGGED, -RAGGING, -RAGS to bullyrag

BALM *n* pl. -S a fragrant resin **BALMLIKE** *adj*

BALMORAL *n* pl. -S a type of shoe

BALMY *adj* BALMIER, BALMIEST mild **BALMILY** *adv*

BALNEAL *adj* pertaining to baths

BALONEY *n* pl. -NEYS bologna

BALSA *n* pl. -S a tropical tree

BALSAM *v* -ED, -ING, -S to anoint with balsam (an aromatic, resinous substance)

BALSAMIC *adj* containing balsam

BALUSTER *n* pl. -S a railing support

BAM *v* BAMMED, BAMMING, BAMS to strike with a dull resounding noise

BAMBINO *n* pl. -NOS or -NI a baby

BAMBOO *n* pl. -BOOS a tropical grass

BAN *v* BANNED, BANNING, BANS to prohibit

BAN *n* pl. BANI a monetary unit of Romania

BANAL *adj* ordinary **BANALLY** *adv*

BANALITY *n* pl. -TIES something banal

BANALIZE *v* -IZED, -IZING, -IZES to make banal

BANANA *n* pl. -S an edible fruit

BANAUSIC *adj* practical

BANCO *n* pl. -COS a bet in certain gambling games

BAND *v* -ED, -ING, -S to decorate with flexible strips of material

BANDAGE *v* -DAGED, -DAGING, -DAGES to cover a wound with a strip of cloth

BANDAGER *n* pl. -S one that bandages

BANDANA *n* pl. -S bandanna

BANDANNA *n* pl. -S a large, colored handkerchief

BANDBOX *n* pl. -ES a lightweight box

BANDEAU *n* pl. -DEAUX or -DEAUS a headband

BANDER *n* pl. -S one that bands

BANDEROL *n* pl. -S a streamer

BANDIED past tense of bandy

BANDIES present 3d person sing. of bandy

BANDIT *n* pl. -DITS or -DITTI a robber

BANDITRY *n* pl. -TRIES robbery by bandits

BANDOG *n* pl. -S a watchdog

BANDORA *n* pl. -S bandore

BANDORE *n* pl. -S an ancient lute

BANDSMAN *n* pl. -MEN a member of a musical band

BANDY *v* -DIED, -DYING, -DIES to throw to and fro

BANE *v* BANED, BANING, BANES to kill with poison

BANEFUL *adj* poisonous

BANG *v* -ED, -ING, -S to hit sharply

BANGER *n* pl. -S a sausage

BANGKOK *n* pl. -S a straw hat

BANGLE *n* pl. -S a bracelet

BANGTAIL *n* pl. -S a racehorse

BANI pl. of ban

BANIAN *n* pl. -S a Hindu merchant

BANING present participle of bane

BANISH *v* -ED, -ING, -ES to expel

BANISHER *n* pl. -S one that banishes

BANISTER *n* pl. -S a handrail

BANJAX *v* -ED, -ING, -ES to damage

BANJO *n* pl. -JOS or -JOES a musical instrument

BANJOIST *n* pl. -S one who plays the banjo

BANK *v* -ED, -ING, -S to keep money in a bank (an institution dealing in money matters) **BANKABLE** *adj*

BANKBOOK *n* pl. -S a depositor's book

BANKCARD *n* pl. -S a credit card issued by a bank

BANKER *n* pl. -S one who works in a bank **BANKERLY** *adj*

BANKING *n* pl. -S the business of a bank

BANKNOTE *n* pl. -S a promissory note

BANKROLL *v* -ED, -ING, -S to supply the capital for

BANKRUPT *v* -ED, -ING, -S to impoverish

BANKSIA *n* pl. -S an Australian plant

BANKSIDE *n* pl. -S the slope of a river bank

BANNED past tense of ban

BANNER *v* -ED, -ING, -S to furnish with a flag

BANNERET n pl. -S a small flag
BANNEROL n pl. -S a banderol
BANNET n pl. -S a bonnet
BANNING present participle of ban
BANNOCK n pl. -S a type of cake
BANNS n/pl a marriage notice
BANQUET v -ED, -ING, -S to feast
BANSHEE n pl. -S a female spirit
BANSHIE n pl. -S banshee
BANTAM n pl. -S a small fowl
BANTENG n pl. -S a wild ox
BANTER v -ED, -ING, -S to exchange mildly teasing remarks
BANTERER n pl. -S one that banters
BANTLING n pl. -S a very young child
BANTY n pl. -TIES a bantam
BANYAN n pl. -S an East Indian tree
BANZAI n pl. -S a Japanese battle cry
BAOBAB n pl. -S a tropical tree
BAP n pl. -S a small bun or roll
BAPTISE v -TISED, -TISING, -TISES to baptize
BAPTISIA n pl. -S a flowering plant
BAPTISM n pl. -S a Christian ceremony
BAPTIST n pl. -S one who baptizes
BAPTIZE v -TIZED, -TIZING, -TIZES to administer baptism to
BAPTIZER n pl. -S a baptist
BAR v BARRED, BARRING, BARS to exclude
BARATHEA n pl. -S a silk fabric
BARB v -ED, -ING, -S to furnish with a barb (a sharp projection)
BARBAL adj pertaining to the beard
BARBARIC adj uncivilized
BARBASCO n pl. -COS or -COES a tropical tree
BARBATE adj bearded
BARBE n pl. -S a medieval cloth headdress
BARBECUE v -CUED, -CUING, -CUES to cook over live coals or an open fire
BARBEL n pl. -S an organ of a fish
BARBELL n pl. -S an exercise apparatus
BARBEQUE v -QUED, -QUING, -QUES barbecue
BARBER v -ED, -ING, -S to cut hair
BARBERRY n pl. -RIES a shrub
BARBET n pl. -S a tropical bird
BARBETTE n pl. -S a platform
BARBICAN n pl. -S an outer fortification
BARBICEL n pl. -S a part of a feather
BARBITAL n pl. -S a sedative
BARBLESS adj having no barbs
BARBULE n pl. -S a small barb

BARBUT n pl. -S a type of helmet
BARBWIRE n pl. -S barbed wire
BARCHAN n pl. -S a type of sand dune
BARD v -ED, -ING, -S to armor a horse
BARDE v BARDED, BARDING, BARDES to bard
BARDIC adj poetic
BARE adj BARER, BAREST naked
BARE v BARED, BARING, BARES to expose
BAREBACK adv without a saddle
BAREBOAT n pl. -S a pleasure boat rented without personnel
BAREFIT adj barefoot
BAREFOOT adj being without shoes
BAREGE n pl. -S a sheer fabric
BAREHEAD adv without a hat
BARELY adv scarcely
BARENESS n pl. -ES the state of being bare
BARER comparative of bare
BARESARK n pl. -S an ancient warrior
BAREST superlative of bare
BARF v -ED, -ING, -S to vomit
BARFLY n pl. -FLIES a drinker who frequents bars
BARGAIN v -ED, -ING, -S to discuss terms for selling or buying
BARGE v BARGED, BARGING, BARGES to move by barge (a long, large boat)
BARGEE n pl. -S a bargeman
BARGELLO n pl. -LOS a needlepoint stitch that makes a zigzag pattern
BARGEMAN n pl. -MEN the master or a crew member of a barge
BARGHEST n pl. -S a goblin
BARGING present participle of barge
BARGUEST n pl. -S barghest
BARHOP v -HOPPED, -HOPPING, -HOPS to visit a number of bars during an evening
BARIC adj pertaining to barium
BARILLA n pl. -S a chemical compound
BARING present participle of bare
BARITE n pl. -S a mineral
BARITONE n pl. -S a male singing voice
BARIUM n pl. -S a metallic element
BARK v -ED, -ING, -S to cry like a dog
BARKEEP n pl. -S a bartender
BARKER n pl. -S one that barks
BARKLESS adj having no bark; unable to bark

BARKY *adj* BARKIER, BARKIEST covered with bark (tough outer covering of a root or stem)

BARLEDUC *n pl.* -S a fruit jam

BARLESS *adj* having no restraints

BARLEY *n pl.* -LEYS a cereal grass

BARLOW *n pl.* -S a jackknife

BARM *n pl.* -S the foam on malt liquors

BARMAID *n pl.* -S a female bartender

BARMAN *n pl.* -MEN a male bartender

BARMIE *adj* barmy

BARMY *adj* BARMIER, BARMIEST full of barm; frothy

BARN *n pl.* -S a large storage building

BARNACLE *n pl.* -S a shellfish

BARNLIKE *adj* resembling a barn

BARNY *adj* BARNIER, BARNIEST resembling a barn in size, shape, or smell

BARNYARD *n pl.* -S a yard near a barn

BAROGRAM *n pl.* -S a barometric reading

BARON *n pl.* -S a lower member of nobility

BARONAGE *n pl.* -S the rank of a baron

BARONESS *n pl.* -ES the wife of a baron

BARONET *n pl.* -S the holder of a rank below that of a baron

BARONG *n pl.* -S a broad knife

BARONIAL *adj* pertaining to a baron

BARONNE *n pl.* -S a baroness

BARONY *n pl.* -ONIES the domain of a baron

BAROQUE *n pl.* -S an ornate object

BAROUCHE *n pl.* -S a type of carriage

BARQUE *n pl.* -S a sailing vessel

BARRABLE *adj* capable of being barred

BARRACK *v* -ED, -ING, -S to shout boisterously

BARRAGE *v* -RAGED, -RAGING, -RAGES to subject to a massive attack

BARRANCA *n pl.* -S a steep ravine

BARRANCO *n pl.* -COS barranca

BARRATER *n pl.* -S a barrator

BARRATOR *n pl.* -S one who commits barratry

BARRATRY *n pl.* -TRIES fraud committed by a master or crew of a ship

BARRE *v* BARRED, BARRING, BARRES to play a type of guitar chord

BARRED past tense of bar

BARREL *v* -RELED, -RELING, -RELS or -RELLED, -RELLING, -RELS to move fast

BARREN *adj* -RENER, -RENEST unproductive **BARRENLY** *adv*

BARREN *n pl.* -S a tract of barren land

BARRET *n pl.* -S a flat cap

BARRETOR *n pl.* -S barrator

BARRETRY *n pl.* -TRIES barratry

BARRETTE *n pl.* -S a hair clip

BARRIER *n pl.* -S an obstacle

BARRING present participle of bar and barre

BARRIO *n pl.* -RIOS a district

BARROOM *n pl.* -S a room where liquor is sold

BARROW *n pl.* -S a type of cart

BARSTOOL *n pl.* -S a stool in a barroom

BARTEND *v* -ED, -ING, -S to tend a barroom

BARTER *v* -ED, -ING, -S to trade

BARTERER *n pl.* -S one that barters

BARTISAN *n pl.* -S bartizan

BARTIZAN *n pl.* -S a small turret

BARWARE *n pl.* -S barroom equipment

BARYE *n pl.* -S a unit of pressure

BARYON *n pl.* -S a type of subatomic particle **BARYONIC** *adj*

BARYTA *n pl.* -S a compound of barium **BARYTIC** *adj*

BARYTE *n pl.* -S barite

BARYTONE *n pl.* -S baritone

BASAL *adj* pertaining to the foundation **BASALLY** *adv*

BASALT *n pl.* -S a volcanic rock **BASALTIC** *adj*

BASALTES *n pl.* BASALTES unglazed stoneware

BASCULE *n pl.* -S a type of seesaw

BASE *adj* BASER, BASEST morally low

BASE *v* BASED, BASING, BASES to found

BASEBALL *n pl.* -S a type of ball

BASEBORN *adj* of low birth

BASED past tense of base

BASELESS *adj* having no foundation

BASELINE *n pl.* -S a line at either end of a court in certain sports

BASELY *adv* in a base manner

BASEMAN *n pl.* -MEN a certain player in baseball

BASEMENT *n pl.* -S the part of a building below ground level

BASENESS *n pl.* -ES the state of being base

BASENJI *n* pl. -S a barkless dog

BASER comparative of base

BASES pl. of basis

BASEST superlative of base

BASH *v* -ED, -ING, -ES to smash

BASHAW *n* pl. -S a pasha

BASHER *n* pl. -S one that bashes

BASHFUL *adj* shy; timid

BASHLYK *n* pl. -S a cloth hood

BASIC *n* pl. -S a fundamental

BASICITY *n* pl. -TIES the state of being alkaline

BASIDIUM *n* pl. -IA a structure on a fungus BASIDIAL *adj*

BASIFIER *n* pl. -S one that basifies

BASIFY *v* -FIED, -FYING, -FIES to alkalize

BASIL *n* pl. -S an aromatic herb

BASILAR *adj* basal

BASILARY *adj* basilar

BASILIC *adj* pertaining to a basilica

BASILICA *n* pl. -CAS or -CAE an ancient Roman building

BASILISK *n* pl. -S a fabled serpent

BASIN *n* pl. -S a large bowl BASINAL, BASINED *adj*

BASINET *n* pl. -S a medieval helmet

BASINFUL *n* pl. -S as much as a basin can hold

BASING present participle of base

BASION *n* pl. -S a part of the skull

BASIS *n* pl. BASES the foundation of something

BASK *v* -ED, -ING, -S to lie in a pleasant warmth

BASKET *n* pl. -S a wooden container

BASKETRY *n* pl. -RIES basket weaving

BASMATI *n* pl. -S a long-grain rice

BASOPHIL *n* pl. -S a type of cell

BASQUE *n* pl. -S a bodice

BASS *n* pl. -ES an edible fish

BASSET *v* -SETED, -SETING, -SETS or -SETTED, -SETTING, -SETS to outcrop

BASSI a pl. of basso

BASSINET *n* pl. -S a basket used as a baby's crib

BASSIST *n* pl. -S a person who plays a double bass

BASSLY *adv* in a low-pitched manner

BASSNESS *n* pl. -ES the state of being low in pitch

BASSO *n* pl. -SOS or -SI a low-pitched singer

BASSOON *n* pl. -S a low-pitched instrument

BASSWOOD *n* pl. -S a linden tree

BASSY *adj* low in pitch

BAST *n* pl. -S a woody fiber

BASTARD *n* pl. -S an illegitimate child

BASTARDY *n* pl. -TARDIES the state of being a bastard

BASTE *v* BASTED, BASTING, BASTES to sew loosely together

BASTER *n* pl. -S one that bastes

BASTILE *n* pl. -S bastille

BASTILLE *n* pl. -S a prison

BASTING *n* pl. -S the thread used by a baster

BASTION *n* pl. -S a fortified place

BAT *v* BATTED, BATTING, BATS to hit a baseball

BATBOY *n* pl. -BOYS a boy who minds baseball equipment

BATCH *v* -ED, -ING, -ES to bring together

BATCHER *n* pl. -S one that batches

BATE *v* BATED, BATING, BATES to reduce the force of

BATEAU *n* pl. -TEAUX a flat-bottomed boat

BATFISH *n* pl. -ES a batlike fish

BATFOWL *v* -ED, -ING, -S to catch birds at night

BATH *n* pl. -S a washing

BATHE *v* BATHED, BATHING, BATHES to wash

BATHER *n* pl. -S one that bathes

BATHETIC *adj* trite

BATHING present participle of bathe

BATHLESS *adj* not having had a bath

BATHMAT *n* pl. -S a mat used in a bathroom

BATHOS *n* pl. -ES triteness

BATHROBE *n* pl. -S a housecoat

BATHROOM *n* pl. -S a room in which to bathe

BATHTUB *n* pl. -S a tub in which to bathe

BATHYAL *adj* pertaining to deep water

BATIK *n* pl. -S a dyeing process

BATING present participle of bate

BATISTE *n* pl. -S a sheer fabric

BATLIKE *adj* resembling a bat (a flying mammal)

BATMAN *n* pl. -MEN an orderly

BATON *n* pl. -S a short rod

BATSMAN *n* pl. -MEN one who bats

BATT *n* pl. -S a sheet of cotton

BATTALIA *n* pl. -S a military unit

BATTEAU *n* pl. -TEAUX bateau

BATTED past tense of bat

BATTEN _v_ -ED, -ING, -S to fasten with strips of wood

BATTENER _n pl._ -S one that battens

BATTER _v_ -ED, -ING, -S to beat repeatedly

BATTERIE _n pl._ -S a ballet movement

BATTERY _n pl._ -TERIES a device for generating an electric current

BATTIER comparative of batty

BATTIEST superlative of batty

BATTIK _n pl._ -S batik

BATTING _n pl._ -S a batt

BATTLE _v_ -TLED, -TLING, -TLES to fight

BATTLER _n pl._ -S one that battles

BATTU _adj_ pertaining to a ballet movement

BATTUE _n pl._ -S a type of hunt

BATTY _adj_ -TIER, -TIEST crazy

BATWING _adj_ shaped like a bat's wing

BAUBEE _n pl._ -S bawbee

BAUBLE _n pl._ -S a cheap trinket

BAUD _n pl._ -S a unit of data transmission speed

BAUDEKIN _n pl._ -S a brocaded fabric

BAUDRONS _n pl._ -ES a cat

BAUHINIA _n pl._ -S a small tropical tree

BAULK _v_ -ED, -ING, -S to balk

BAULKY _adj_ BAULKIER, BAULKIEST balky

BAUSOND _adj_ having white marks

BAUXITE _n pl._ -S an ore of aluminum **BAUXITIC** _adj_

BAWBEE _n pl._ -S a Scottish coin

BAWCOCK _n pl._ -S a fine fellow

BAWD _n pl._ -S a madam

BAWDIER comparative of bawdy

BAWDIES pl. of bawdy

BAWDIEST superlative of bawdy

BAWDILY _adv_ in a bawdy manner

BAWDRIC _n pl._ -S baldric

BAWDRY _n pl._ -RIES obscenity

BAWDY _adj_ BAWDIER, BAWDIEST obscene

BAWDY _n pl._ BAWDIES obscene language

BAWL _v_ -ED, -ING, -S to cry loudly

BAWLER _n pl._ -S one that bawls

BAWSUNT _adj_ bausond

BAWTIE _n pl._ -S a dog

BAWTY _n pl._ -TIES bawtie

BAY _v_ -ED, -ING, -S to howl

BAYADEER _n pl._ -S bayadere

BAYADERE _n pl._ -S a dancing girl

BAYAMO _n pl._ -MOS a strong wind

BAYARD _n pl._ -S a horse

BAYBERRY _n pl._ -RIES a berry tree

BAYMAN _n pl._ -MEN a person who fishes on a bay

BAYONET _v_ -NETED, -NETING, -NETS or -NETTED, -NETTING, -NETS to stab with a dagger-like weapon

BAYOU _n pl._ -S a marshy body of water

BAYWOOD _n pl._ -S a coarse mahogany

BAZAAR _n pl._ -S a marketplace

BAZAR _n pl._ -S bazaar

BAZOO _n pl._ -ZOOS the mouth

BAZOOKA _n pl._ -S a small rocket launcher

BDELLIUM _n pl._ -S a gum resin

BE _v_ present sing. 1st person AM, 2d ARE or ART, 3d IS, past sing. 1st and 3d persons WAS, 2d WERE or WAST or WERT, past participle BEEN, present participle BEING to have actuality

BEACH _v_ -ED, -ING, -ES to drive ashore

BEACHBOY _n pl._ -BOYS a male beach attendant

BEACHY _adj_ BEACHIER, BEACHIEST sandy or pebbly

BEACON _v_ -ED, -ING, -S to warn or guide

BEAD _v_ -ED, -ING, -S to adorn with beads (round pieces of glass)

BEADIER comparative of beady

BEADIEST superlative of beady

BEADILY _adv_ in a beady manner

BEADING _n pl._ -S beaded material

BEADLE _n pl._ -S a parish official

BEADLIKE _adj_ beady

BEADMAN _n pl._ -MEN beadsman

BEADROLL _n pl._ -S a list of names

BEADSMAN _n pl._ -MEN one who prays for another

BEADWORK _n pl._ -S beading

BEADY _adj_ BEADIER, BEADIEST resembling beads

BEAGLE _n pl._ -S a small hound

BEAK _n pl._ -S a bird's bill **BEAKED, BEAKLESS, BEAKLIKE** _adj_

BEAKER _n pl._ -S a large cup

BEAKY _adj_ BEAKIER, BEAKIEST resembling a beak

BEAM _v_ -ED, -ING, -S to emit in beams (rays of light)

BEAMIER comparative of beamy

BEAMIEST superlative of beamy

BEAMILY	*adv* in a beamy manner	**BEBEERU**	*n* pl. -S a tropical tree
BEAMISH	*adj* cheerful	**BEBLOOD**	*v* -ED, -ING, -S to cover with
BEAMLESS	*adj* having no beam		blood
BEAMLIKE	*adj* resembling a beam	**BEBOP**	*n* pl. -S a type of jazz
BEAMY	*adj* BEAMIER, BEAMIEST beaming	**BEBOPPER**	*n* pl. -S one that likes bebop
BEAN	*v* -ED, -ING, -S to hit on the head	**BECALM**	*v* -ED, -ING, -S to make calm
		BECAME	past tense of become
BEANBAG	*n* pl. -S a small cloth bag	**BECAP**	*v* -CAPPED, -CAPPING,
BEANBALL	*n* pl. -S a baseball thrown at the head		-CAPS to put a cap on
		BECARPET	*v* -ED, -ING, -S to cover with a
BEANERY	*n* pl. -ERIES a cheap restaurant		carpet
		BECAUSE	*conj* for the reason that
BEANIE	*n* pl. -S a small cap	**BECHALK**	*v* -ED, -ING, -S to cover with
BEANLIKE	*adj* resembling a bean		chalk
BEANO	*n* pl. BEANOS a form of bingo	**BECHAMEL**	*n* pl. -S a white sauce
BEANPOLE	*n* pl. -S a thin pole	**BECHANCE**	*v* -CHANCED, -CHANCING,
BEAR	*v* BORE, BORNE or BORN, BEARING, BEARS to endure **BEARABLE** *adj* **BEARABLY** *adv*		-CHANCES to befall
		BECHARM	*v* -ED, -ING, -S to hold under a spell
		BECK	*v* -ED, -ING, -S to beckon
BEARCAT	*n* pl. -S a small mammal	**BECKET**	*n* pl. -S a securing rope
BEARD	*v* -ED, -ING, -S to oppose boldly	**BECKON**	*v* -ED, -ING, -S to signal by sign or gesture
BEARER	*n* pl. -S one that bears	**BECKONER**	*n* pl. -S one that beckons
BEARHUG	*n* pl. -S a rough tight embrace	**BECLAMOR**	*v* -ED, -ING, -S to clamor loudly
BEARING	*n* pl. -S demeanor	**BECLASP**	*v* -ED, -ING, -S to embrace
BEARISH	*adj* resembling a bear (a large mammal)	**BECLOAK**	*v* -ED, -ING, -S to place a cloak on
BEARLIKE	*adj* bearish	**BECLOG**	*v* -CLOGGED, -CLOGGING,
BEARSKIN	*n* pl. -S the skin of a bear		-CLOGS to clog thoroughly
BEARWOOD	*n* pl. -S a small tree of the buckthorn family	**BECLOTHE**	*v* -CLOTHED, -CLOTHING, -CLOTHES to clothe
BEAST	*n* pl. -S an animal	**BECLOUD**	*v* -ED, -ING, -S to make cloudy
BEASTIE	*n* pl. -S a tiny animal		
BEASTLY	*adj* -LIER, -LIEST resembling a beast	**BECLOWN**	*v* -ED, -ING, -S to cause to appear ridiculous
BEAT	*v* BEAT, BEATEN, BEATING, BEATS to strike repeatedly **BEATABLE** *adj*	**BECOME**	*v* -CAME, -COMING, -COMES to come to be
		BECOMING	*n* pl. -S a process of change
BEATER	*n* pl. -S one that beats	**BECOWARD**	*v* -ED, -ING, -S to accuse of cowardice
BEATIFIC	*adj* blissful		
BEATIFY	*v* -FIED, -FYING, -FIES to make happy	**BECRAWL**	*v* -ED, -ING, -S to crawl over
		BECRIME	*v* -CRIMED, -CRIMING,
BEATING	*n* pl. -S a defeat		-CRIMES to make guilty of a
BEATLESS	*adj* having no rhythm		crime
BEATNIK	*n* pl. -S a nonconformist	**BECROWD**	*v* -ED, -ING, -S to crowd closely
BEAU	*n* pl. BEAUX or BEAUS a boyfriend **BEAUISH** *adj*	**BECRUST**	*v* -ED, -ING, -S to cover with a crust
BEAUCOUP	*adj* many or much		
BEAUT	*n* pl. -S something beautiful	**BECUDGEL**	*v* -GELLED, -GELLING, -GELS or -GELED, -GELING,
BEAUTIFY	*v* -FIED, -FYING, -FIES to make beautiful		-GELS to cudgel thoroughly
		BECURSE	*v* -CURSED or -CURST,
BEAUTY	*n* pl. -TIES one that is lovely		-CURSING, -CURSES to curse
BEAUX	a pl. of beau		severely
BEAVER	*v* -ED, -ING, -S to work hard		

BED v BEDDED, BEDDING, BEDS to provide with a bed (a piece of furniture used for sleeping)

BEDABBLE v -BLED, -BLING, -BLES to soil

BEDAMN v -ED, -ING, -S to swear at

BEDARKEN v -ED, -ING, -S to darken

BEDAUB v -ED, -ING, -S to besmear

BEDAZZLE v -ZLED, -ZLING, -ZLES to confuse

BEDBUG n pl. -S a bloodsucking insect

BEDCHAIR n pl. -S a chair near a bed

BEDCOVER n pl. -S a cover for a bed

BEDDABLE adj suitable for taking to bed

BEDDED past tense of bed

BEDDER n pl. -S one that makes up beds

BEDDING n pl. -S material for making up a bed

BEDEAFEN v -ED, -ING, -S to deafen

BEDECK v -ED, -ING, -S to clothe with finery

BEDEL n pl. -S an English university officer

BEDELL n pl. -S bedel

BEDEMAN n pl. -MEN beadsman

BEDESMAN n pl. -MEN beadsman

BEDEVIL v -ILED, -ILING, -ILS or -ILLED, -ILLING, -ILLS to harass

BEDEW v -ED, -ING, -S to wet with dew

BEDFAST adj confined to bed

BEDFRAME n pl. -S the frame of a bed

BEDGOWN n pl. -S a dressing gown

BEDIAPER v -ED, -ING, -S to ornament with a kind of design

BEDIGHT v -ED, -ING, -S to bedeck

BEDIM v -DIMMED, -DIMMING, -DIMS to make dim

BEDIMPLE v -PLED, -PLING, -PLES to dimple

BEDIRTY v -DIRTIED, -DIRTYING, -DIRTIES to make dirty

BEDIZEN v -ED, -ING, -S to dress gaudily

BEDLAM n pl. -S confusion

BEDLAMP n pl. -S a lamp near a bed

BEDLESS adj having no bed

BEDLIKE adj resembling a bed

BEDMAKER n pl. -S one that makes beds

BEDMATE n pl. -S a bed companion

BEDOTTED adj covered with dots

BEDOUIN n pl. -S a nomadic Arab

BEDPAN n pl. -S a toilet pan

BEDPLATE n pl. -S a frame support

BEDPOST n pl. -S a post of a bed

BEDQUILT n pl. -S a quilt for a bed

BEDRAIL n pl. -S a board at bedside

BEDRAPE v -DRAPED, -DRAPING, -DRAPES to drape

BEDRENCH v -ED, -ING, -ES to drench thoroughly

BEDRID adj bedfast

BEDRIVEL v -ELLED, -ELLING, -ELS or -ELED, -ELING, -ELS to cover with saliva

BEDROCK n pl. -S the rock under soil

BEDROLL n pl. -S a portable roll of bedding

BEDROOM n pl. -S a room for sleeping

BEDRUG v -DRUGGED, -DRUGGING, -DRUGS to make sleepy

BEDSHEET n pl. -S a sheet for a bed

BEDSIDE n pl. -S the side of a bed

BEDSIT n pl. -S a one-room apartment

BEDSONIA n pl. -S a virus

BEDSORE n pl. -S a type of sore

BEDSTAND n pl. -S a table next to a bed

BEDSTEAD n pl. -S a support for a bed

BEDSTRAW n pl. -S a woody herb

BEDTICK n pl. -S the cloth case of a mattress

BEDTIME n pl. -S a time for going to bed

BEDU n BEDU a bedouin

BEDUIN n pl. -S bedouin

BEDUMB v -ED, -ING, -S to render speechless

BEDUNCE v -DUNCED, -DUNCING, -DUNCES to make a dunce of

BEDWARD adv toward bed

BEDWARDS adv bedward

BEDWARF v -ED, -ING, -S to cause to appear small by comparison

BEE n pl. -S a winged insect

BEEBEE n pl. -S a pellet

BEEBREAD n pl. -S a pollen mixture

BEECH n pl. -ES a type of tree

BEECHEN adj

BEECHNUT n pl. -S the nut of a beech

BEECHY adj BEECHIER, BEECHIEST abounding in beeches

BEEF n pl. BEEFS or BEEVES a steer or cow fattened for food

BEEF v -ED, -ING, -S to add bulk to

BEEFALO n pl. -LOS or -LOES the offspring of an American buffalo and domestic cattle

BEEFCAKE n pl. -S pictures of male physiques

BEEFIER comparative of beefy

BEEFIEST superlative of beefy

BEEFILY   *adv* in a beefy manner

BEEFLESS   *adj* being without beef

BEEFWOOD   *n pl.* -S a hardwood tree

BEEFY   *adj* BEEFIER, BEEFIEST brawny

BEEHIVE   *n pl.* -S a hive for bees

BEELIKE   *adj* resembling a bee

BEELINE   *v* -LINED, -LINING, -LINES to go in a straight line

BEEN   past participle of be

BEEP   *v* -ED, -ING, -S to honk a horn

BEEPER   *n pl.* -S a signaling device

BEER   *n pl.* -S an alcoholic beverage

BEERY   *adj* BEERIER, BEERIEST affected by beer

BEESWAX   *n pl.* -ES a type of wax

BEESWING   *n pl.* -S a crust on old wines

BEET   *n pl.* -S a garden plant

BEETLE   *v* -TLED, -TLING, -TLES to jut out

BEETLER   *n pl.* -S one that operates a cloth-finishing machine

BEETROOT   *n pl.* -S the root of the beet

BEEVES   a *pl.* of beef

BEEYARD   *n pl.* -S an apiary

BEEZER   *n pl.* -S the nose

BEFALL   *v* -FELL, -FALLEN, -FALLING, -FALLS to happen to

BEFINGER   *v* -ED, -ING, -S to touch all over

BEFIT   *v* -FITTED, -FITTING, -FITS to be suitable to

BEFLAG   *v* -FLAGGED, -FLAGGING, -FLAGS to deck with flags

BEFLEA   *v* -ED, -ING, -S to infest with fleas

BEFLECK   *v* -ED, -ING, -S to fleck

BEFLOWER   *v* -ED, -ING, -S to cover with flowers

BEFOG   *v* -FOGGED, -FOGGING, -FOGS to envelop in fog

BEFOOL   *v* -ED, -ING, -S to deceive

BEFORE   *adv* previously

BEFOUL   *v* -ED, -ING, -S to foul

BEFOULER   *n pl.* -S one that befouls

BEFRET   *v* -FRETTED, -FRETTING, -FRETS to gnaw

BEFRIEND   *v* -ED, -ING, -S to act as a friend to

BEFRINGE   *v* -FRINGED, -FRINGING, -FRINGES to border with a fringe

BEFUDDLE   *v* -DLED, -DLING, -DLES to confuse

BEG   *v* BEGGED, BEGGING, BEGS to plead

BEGALL   *v* -ED, -ING, -S to make sore by rubbing

BEGAN   past tense of begin

BEGAZE   *v* -GAZED, -GAZING, -GAZES to gaze at

BEGET   *v* -GOT or -GAT, -GOTTEN, -GETTING, -GETS to cause to exist

BEGETTER   *n pl.* -S one that begets

BEGGAR   *v* -ED, -ING, -S to impoverish

BEGGARLY   *adj* very poor

BEGGARY   *n pl.* -GARIES extreme poverty

BEGGED   past tense of beg

BEGGING   present participle of beg

BEGIN   *v* -GAN, -GUN, -GINNING, -GINS to start

BEGINNER   *n pl.* -S one that begins

BEGIRD   *v* -GIRT or -GIRDED, -GIRDING, -GIRDS to surround

BEGIRDLE   *v* -DLED, -DLING, -DLES to surround

BEGLAD   *v* -GLADDED, -GLADDING, -GLADS to gladden

BEGLAMOR   *v* -ED, -ING, -S to dazzle with glamor

BEGLOOM   *v* -ED, -ING, -S to make gloomy

BEGONE   *interj* — used as an order of dismissal

BEGONIA   *n pl.* -S a tropical herb

BEGORAH   *interj* begorra

BEGORRA   *interj* — used as a mild oath

BEGORRAH   *interj* begorra

BEGOT   a past tense of beget

BEGOTTEN   past participle of beget

BEGRIM   *v* -GRIMMED, -GRIMMING, -GRIMS to begrime

BEGRIME   *v* -GRIMED, -GRIMING, -GRIMES to dirty

BEGROAN   *v* -ED, -ING, -S to groan at

BEGRUDGE   *v* -GRUDGED, -GRUDGING, -GRUDGES to concede reluctantly

BEGUILE   *v* -GUILED, -GUILING, -GUILES to deceive

BEGUILER   *n pl.* -S one that beguiles

BEGUINE   *n pl.* -S a lively dance

BEGULF   *v* -ED, -ING, -S to engulf

BEGUM   *n pl.* -S a Muslim lady of high rank

BEGUN   past participle of begin

BEHALF   *n pl.* -HALVES interest, support, or benefit

BEHAVE v -HAVED, -HAVING, -HAVES to act properly

BEHAVER n pl. -S one that behaves

BEHAVIOR n pl. -S demeanor

BEHEAD v -ED, -ING, -S to cut off the head of

BEHELD past tense of behold

BEHEMOTH n pl. -S a large beast

BEHEST n pl. -S a command

BEHIND n pl. -S the buttocks

BEHOLD v -HELD, -HOLDING, -HOLDS to view

BEHOLDEN adj indebted

BEHOLDER n pl. -S one that beholds

BEHOOF n pl. -HOOVES use, advantage, or benefit

BEHOOVE v -HOOVED, -HOOVING, -HOOVES to be proper for

BEHOVE v -HOVED, -HOVING, -HOVES to behoove

BEHOWL v -ED, -ING, -S to howl at

BEIGE n pl. -S a tan color

BEIGNET n pl. -S a type of fritter or doughnut

BEIGY adj of the color beige

BEING n pl. -S something that exists

BEJABERS interj bejesus

BEJEEZUS interj bejesus

BEJESUS interj — used as a mild oath

BEJEWEL v -ELED, -ELING, -ELS or -ELLED, -ELLING, -ELS to adorn with jewels

BEJUMBLE v -BLED, -BLING, -BLES to jumble

BEKISS v -ED, -ING, -ES to cover with kisses

BEKNIGHT v -ED, -ING, -S to raise to knighthood

BEKNOT v -KNOTTED, -KNOTTING, -KNOTS to tie in knots

BEL n pl. -S a unit of power

BELABOR v -ED, -ING, -S to discuss for an absurd amount of time

BELABOUR v -ED, -ING, -S to belabor

BELACED adj adorned with lace

BELADY v -DIED, -DYING, -DIES to apply the title of lady to

BELATED adj late or too late

BELAUD v -ED, -ING, -S to praise

BELAY v -ED, -ING, -S to fasten a rope

BELCH v -ED, -ING, -ES to expel gas through the mouth

BELCHER n pl. -S one that belches

BELDAM n pl. -S an old woman

BELDAME n pl. -S beldam

BELEAP v -LEAPT or -LEAPED, -LEAPING, -LEAPS to leap upon

BELFRY n pl. -FRIES a bell tower BELFRIED adj

BELGA n pl. -S a former Belgian monetary unit

BELIE v -LIED, -LYING, -LIES to misrepresent

BELIEF n pl. -S acceptance of the truth or actuality of something

BELIER n pl. -S one that belies

BELIEVE v -LIEVED, -LIEVING, -LIEVES to accept as true or real

BELIEVER n pl. -S one that believes

BELIKE adv perhaps

BELIQUOR v -ED, -ING, -S to soak with liquor

BELITTLE v -TLED, -TLING, -TLES to disparage

BELIVE adv in due time

BELL v -ED, -ING, -S to provide with a bell (a ringing device)

BELLBIRD n pl. -S a tropical bird

BELLBOY n pl. -BOYS a hotel's errand boy

BELLE n pl. -S an attractive woman

BELLEEK n pl. -S a very thin translucent porcelain

BELLHOP n pl. -S a bellboy

BELLIED past tense of belly

BELLIES present 3d person sing. of belly

BELLMAN n pl. -MEN a town crier

BELLOW v -ED, -ING, -S to shout in a deep voice

BELLOWER n pl. -S one that bellows

BELLPULL n pl. -S a cord pulled to ring a bell

BELLWORT n pl. -S a flowering plant

BELLY v -LIED, -LYING, -LIES to swell out

BELLYFUL n pl. -S an excessive amount

BELONG v -ED, -ING, -S to be a member of

BELOVED n pl. -S one who is loved

BELOW n pl. -S something that is beneath

BELT v -ED, -ING, -S to fasten with a belt (a strap or band worn around the waist)

BELTER n pl. -S one that belts

BELTING n pl. -S material for belts

BELTLESS adj having no belt

BELTLINE n pl. -S the waistline

BELTWAY n pl. -WAYS a highway around an urban area

BELUGA n pl. -S a white sturgeon

BELYING present participle of belie

BEMA n pl. -MATA or -MAS a platform in a synagogue

BEMADAM v -ED, -ING, -S to call by the title of madam

BEMADDEN v -ED, -ING, -S to madden

BEMATA a pl. of bema

BEMEAN v -ED, -ING, -S to debase

BEMINGLE v -GLED, -GLING, -GLES to mix together

BEMIRE v -MIRED, -MIRING, -MIRES to soil with mud

BEMIST v -ED, -ING, -S to envelop in a mist

BEMIX v -MIXED or -MIXT, -MIXING, -MIXES to mix thoroughly

BEMOAN v -ED, -ING, -S to lament

BEMOCK v -ED, -ING, -S to mock

BEMUDDLE v -DLED, -DLING, -DLES to confuse completely

BEMURMUR v -ED, -ING, -S to murmur at

BEMUSE v -MUSED, -MUSING, -MUSES to confuse

BEMUZZLE v -ZLED, -ZLING, -ZLES to muzzle

BEN n pl. -S an inner room

BENAME v -NAMED, -NEMPT or -NEMPTED, -NAMING, -NAMES to name

BENCH v -ED, -ING, -ES to take a player out of a game

BENCHER n pl. -S a magistrate

BEND v BENT or BENDED, BENDING, BENDS to curve BENDABLE adj

BENDAY v -ED, -ING, -S to reproduce using a certain process

BENDEE n pl. -S bendy

BENDER n pl. -S one that bends

BENDWAYS adv bendwise

BENDWISE adv diagonally

BENDY n pl. -DYS okra

BENE n pl. -S benne

BENEATH prep under

BENEDICK n pl. -S benedict

BENEDICT n pl. -S a newly married man

BENEFIC adj kindly

BENEFICE v -FICED, -FICING, -FICES to endow with land

BENEFIT v -FITED, -FITING, -FITS or -FITTED, -FITTING, -FITS to be helpful or useful to

BENEMPT a past participle of bename

BENEMPTED a past participle of bename

BENIGN adj kind BENIGNLY adv

BENISON n pl. -S a blessing

BENJAMIN n pl. -S benzoin

BENNE n pl. -S the sesame plant

BENNET n pl. -S a perennial herb

BENNI n pl. -S benne

BENNY n pl. -NIES an amphetamine tablet

BENOMYL n pl. -S a chemical compound

BENT n pl. -S an inclination

BENTHAL adj benthic

BENTHIC adj pertaining to oceanic depths

BENTHOS n pl. -ES benthic sea life

BENTWOOD n pl. -S wood bent for use in furniture

BENUMB v -ED, -ING, -S to make numb

BENZAL adj pertaining to a certain chemical group

BENZENE n pl. -S a volatile liquid

BENZIDIN n pl. -S a hydrocarbon

BENZIN n pl. -S benzine

BENZINE n pl. -S a volatile liquid

BENZOATE n pl. -S a chemical salt

BENZOIN n pl. -S a gum resin BENZOIC adj

BENZOL n pl. -S a benzene

BENZOLE n pl. -S benzol

BENZOYL n pl. -S a univalent chemical radical

BENZYL n pl. -S a univalent chemical radical BENZYLIC adj

BEPAINT v -ED, -ING, -S to tinge

BEPIMPLE v -PLED, -PLING, -PLES to cover with pimples

BEQUEATH v -ED, -ING, -S to grant by testament

BEQUEST n pl. -S a legacy

BERAKE v -RAKED, -RAKING, -RAKES to rake all over

BERASCAL v -ED, -ING, -S to accuse of being a rascal

BERATE v -RATED, -RATING, -RATES to scold severely

BERBERIN n pl. -S a medicinal alkaloid

BERBERIS n pl. -ES a barberry

BERCEUSE n pl. -S a lullaby

BERDACHE n pl. -S an American Indian male transvestite

BEREAVE v -REAVED or -REFT, -REAVING, -REAVES to deprive

BEREAVER n pl. -S one that bereaves

BERET n pl. -S a soft, flat cap

BERETTA n pl. -S biretta

BERG *n pl.* -S an iceberg

BERGAMOT *n pl.* -S a citrus tree

BERGERE *n pl.* -S an upholstered armchair

BERHYME *v* -RHYMED, -RHYMING, -RHYMES to compose in rhyme

BERIBERI *n pl.* -S a thiamine deficiency disease

BERIME *v* -RIMED, -RIMING, -RIMES to berhyme

BERINGED *adj* adorned with rings

BERLIN *n pl.* -S a type of carriage

BERLINE *n pl.* -S a limousine

BERM *n pl.* -S a ledge

BERME *n pl.* -S berm

BERMUDAS *n/pl* knee-length walking shorts

BERNICLE *n pl.* -S a wild goose

BEROBED *adj* wearing a robe

BEROUGED *adj* obviously or thickly rouged

BERRETTA *n pl.* -S biretta

BERRY *v* -RIED, -RYING, -RIES to produce berries (fleshy fruits)

BERSEEM *n pl.* -S a clover

BERSERK *n pl.* -S a fierce warrior

BERTH *v* -ED, -ING, -S to provide with a mooring

BERTHA *n pl.* -S a wide collar

BERYL *n pl.* -S a green mineral **BERYLINE** *adj*

BESCORCH *v* -ED, -ING, -ES to scorch

BESCOUR *v* -ED, -ING, -S to scour thoroughly

BESCREEN *v* -ED, -ING, -S to screen

BESEECH *v* -SOUGHT or -SEECHED, -SEECHING, -SEECHES to implore

BESEEM *v* -ED, -ING, -S to be suitable

BESET *v* -SET, -SETTING, -SETS to assail

BESETTER *n pl.* -S one that besets

BESHADOW *v* -ED, -ING, -S to cast a shadow on

BESHAME *v* -SHAMED, -SHAMING, -SHAMES to put to shame

BESHIVER *v* -ED, -ING, -S to break into small pieces

BESHOUT *v* -ED, -ING, -S to shout at

BESHREW *v* -ED, -ING, -S to curse

BESHROUD *v* -ED, -ING, -S to cover

BESIDE *prep* next to

BESIDES *adv* in addition

BESIEGE *v* -SIEGED, -SIEGING, -SIEGES to surround

BESIEGER *n pl.* -S one that besieges

BESLAVED *adj* filled with slaves

BESLIME *v* -SLIMED, -SLIMING, -SLIMES to cover with slime

BESMEAR *v* -ED, -ING, -S to smear over

BESMILE *v* -SMILED, -SMILING, -SMILES to smile on

BESMIRCH *v* -ED, -ING, -ES to dirty

BESMOKE *v* -SMOKED, -SMOKING, -SMOKES to soil with smoke

BESMOOTH *v* -ED, -ING, -S to smooth

BESMUDGE *v* -SMUDGED, -SMUDGING, -SMUDGES to smudge

BESMUT *v* -SMUTTED, -SMUTTING, -SMUTS to blacken with smut

BESNOW *v* -ED, -ING, -S to cover with snow

BESOM *n pl.* -S a broom

BESOOTHE *v* -SOOTHED, -SOOTHING -SOOTHES to soothe

BESOT *v* -SOTTED, -SOTTING, -SOTS to stupefy

BESOUGHT a past tense of beseech

BESPEAK *v* -SPOKE or -SPAKE, -SPOKEN, -SPEAKING, -SPEAKS to claim in advance

BESPOUSE *v* -SPOUSED, -SPOUSING, -SPOUSES to marry

BESPREAD *v* -SPREAD, -SPREADING, -SPREADS to spread over

BESPRENT *adj* sprinkled over

BEST *v* -ED, -ING, -S to outdo

BESTEAD *v* -ED, -ING, -S to help

BESTIAL *adj* pertaining to beasts

BESTIARY *n pl.* -ARIES a collection of animal fables

BESTIR *v* -STIRRED, -STIRRING, -STIRS to rouse

BESTOW *v* -ED, -ING, -S to present as a gift

BESTOWAL *n pl.* -S a gift

BESTREW *v* -STREWED, -STREWN, -STREWING, -STREWS to scatter

BESTRIDE *v* -STRODE or -STRID, -STRIDDEN, -STRIDING, -STRIDES to straddle

BESTROW *v* -STROWED, -STROWN, -STROWING, -STROWS to bestrew

BESTUD *v* -STUDDED, -STUDDING, -STUDS to dot

BESWARM *v* -ED, -ING, -S to swarm all over

BET *v* BET or BETTED, BETTING, BETS to wager

BETA *n pl.* -S a Greek letter

BETAINE   n pl. -S an alkaloid

BETAKE   v -TOOK, -TAKEN, -TAKING, -TAKES to cause to go

BETATRON   n pl. -S an electron accelerator

BETATTER   v -ED, -ING, -S to tatter

BETAXED   adj burdened with taxes

BETEL   n pl. -S a climbing plant

BETELNUT   n pl. -S a seed chewed as a stimulant

BETH   n pl. -S a Hebrew letter

BETHANK   v -ED, -ING, -S to thank

BETHEL   n pl. -S a holy place

BETHESDA   n pl. -S a chapel

BETHINK   v -THOUGHT, -THINKING, -THINKS to consider

BETHORN   v -ED, -ING, -S to fill with thorns

BETHUMP   v -ED, -ING, -S to thump soundly

BETIDE   v -TIDED, -TIDING, -TIDES to befall

BETIME   adv betimes

BETIMES   adv soon

BETISE   n pl. -S stupidity

BETOKEN   v -ED, -ING, -S to indicate

BETON   n pl. -S a type of concrete

BETONY   n pl. -NIES a European herb

BETOOK   past tense of betake

BETRAY   v -ED, -ING, -S to aid an enemy of

BETRAYAL   n pl. -S the act of betraying

BETRAYER   n pl. -S one that betrays

BETROTH   v -ED, -ING, -S to engage to marry

BETTA   n pl. -S a freshwater fish

BETTED   a past tense of bet

BETTER   v -ED, -ING, -S to improve

BETTING   present participle of bet

BETTOR   n pl. -S one that bets

BETWEEN   prep in the space that separates

BETWIXT   prep between

BEUNCLED   adj having many uncles

BEVATRON   n pl. -S a proton accelerator

BEVEL   v -ELED, -ELING, -ELS or -ELLED, -ELLING, -ELS to cut at an angle

BEVELER   n pl. -S one that bevels

BEVELLER   n pl. -S beveler

BEVELLING   a present participle of bevel

BEVERAGE   n pl. -S a liquid for drinking

BEVIES   pl. of bevy

BEVOMIT   v -ED, -ING, -S to vomit all over

BEVOR   n pl. -S a piece of armor for the lower face

BEVY   n pl. BEVIES a group

BEWAIL   v -ED, -ING, -S to lament

BEWAILER   n pl. -S one that bewails

BEWARE   v -WARED, -WARING, -WARES to be careful

BEWEARY   v -WEARIED, -WEARYING, -WEARIES to make weary

BEWEEP   v -WEPT, -WEEPING, -WEEPS to lament

BEWIG   v -WIGGED, -WIGGING, -WIGS to adorn with a wig

BEWILDER   v -ED, -ING, -S to confuse

BEWINGED   adj having wings

BEWITCH   v -ED, -ING, -ES to affect by witchcraft or magic

BEWORM   v -ED, -ING, -S to infest with worms

BEWORRY   v -RIED, -RYING, -RIES to worry

BEWRAP   v -WRAPPED or -WRAPT, -WRAPPING, -WRAPS to wrap completely

BEWRAY   v -ED, -ING, -S to divulge

BEWRAYER   n pl. -S one that bewrays

BEY   n pl. BEYS a Turkish ruler

BEYLIC   n pl. -S the domain of a bey

BEYLIK   n pl. -S beylic

BEYOND   n pl. -S something that lies farther ahead

BEZANT   n pl. -S a coin of ancient Rome

BEZAZZ   n pl. -ES pizazz

BEZEL   n pl. -S a slanted surface

BEZIL   n pl. -S bezel

BEZIQUE   n pl. -S a card game

BEZOAR   n pl. -S a gastric mass

BEZZANT   n pl. -S bezant

BHAKTA   n pl. -S one who practices bhakti

BHAKTI   n pl. -S a selfless devotion to a deity in Hinduism

BHANG   n pl. -S the hemp plant

BHARAL   n pl. -S a goatlike Asian mammal

BHEESTIE   n pl. -S bheesty

BHEESTY   n pl. -TIES a water carrier

BHISTIE   n pl. -S bheesty

BHOOT   n pl. -S bhut

BHUT   n pl. -S a small whirlwind

BI   n pl. -S a bisexual

BIACETYL   n pl. -S a chemical flavor enhancer

BIALI   n pl. -S bialy

BIALY   n pl. -ALYS an onion roll

BIANNUAL *adj* occurring twice a year

BIAS *v* -ASED, -ASING, -ASES or -ASSED, -ASSING, -ASSES to prejudice **BIASEDLY** *adv*

BIASNESS *n pl.* -ES the state of being slanted

BIATHLON *n pl.* -S an athletic contest

BIAXAL *adj* biaxial

BIAXIAL *adj* having two axes

BIB *v* BIBBED, BIBBING, BIBS to tipple

BIBASIC *adj* dibasic

BIBB *n pl.* -S a mast support

BIBBED past tense of bib

BIBBER *n pl.* -S a tippler

BIBBERY *n pl.* -BERIES the act of bibbing

BIBBING present participle of bib

BIBCOCK *n pl.* -S a type of faucet

BIBELOT *n pl.* -S a trinket

BIBLE *n pl.* -S an authoritative publication **BIBLICAL** *adj*

BIBLESS *adj* having no bib (a cloth covering)

BIBLIKE *adj* resembling a bib

BIBLIST *n pl.* -S one who takes the words of the Bible literally

BIBULOUS *adj* given to drinking

BICARB *n pl.* -S sodium bicarbonate

BICAUDAL *adj* having two tails

BICE *n pl.* -S a blue or green pigment

BICEPS *n pl.* -ES an arm muscle

BICHROME *adj* two-colored

BICKER *v* -ED, -ING, -S to argue

BICKERER *n pl.* -S one that bickers

BICOLOR *n pl.* -S something having two colors

BICOLOUR *n pl.* -S bicolor

BICONVEX *adj* convex on both sides

BICORN *adj* having two horns

BICORNE *n pl.* -S a type of hat

BICRON *n pl.* -S one billionth of a meter

BICUSPID *n pl.* -S a tooth

BICYCLE *v* -CLED, -CLING, -CLES to ride a bicycle (a two-wheeled vehicle)

BICYCLER *n pl.* -S one that bicycles

BICYCLIC *adj* having two cycles

BICYCLING present participle of bicycle

BID *v* BADE, BIDDEN, BIDDING, BIDS to make a bid (an offer of a price)

BIDARKA *n pl.* -S an Eskimo canoe

BIDARKEE *n pl.* -S bidarka

BIDDABLE *adj* obedient **BIDDABLY** *adv*

BIDDEN past participle of bid

BIDDER *n pl.* -S one that bids

BIDDING *n pl.* -S a command

BIDDY *n pl.* -DIES a hen

BIDE *v* BIDED or BODE, BIDING, BIDES to wait

BIDENTAL *adj* having two teeth

BIDER *n pl.* -S one that bides

BIDET *n pl.* -S a low washing basin

BIDING present participle of bide

BIELD *v* -ED, -ING, -S to shelter

BIENNALE *n pl.* -S a biennial show

BIENNIAL *n pl.* -S an event that occurs every two years

BIENNIUM *n pl.* -NIA or -NIUMS a period of two years

BIER *n pl.* -S a coffin stand

BIFACE *n pl.* -S a stone tool having a cutting edge

BIFACIAL *adj* having two faces

BIFF *v* -ED, -ING, -S to hit

BIFFIN *n pl.* -S a cooking apple

BIFFY *n pl.* -FIES a toilet

BIFID *adj* divided into two parts **BIFIDLY** *adv*

BIFIDITY *n pl.* -TIES the state of being bifid

BIFILAR *adj* having two threads

BIFLEX *adj* bent in two places

BIFOCAL *n pl.* -S a type of lens

BIFOLD *adj* twofold

BIFORATE *adj* having two perforations

BIFORKED *adj* divided into two branches

BIFORM *adj* having two forms

BIFORMED *adj* biform

BIG *adj* BIGGER, BIGGEST of considerable size

BIG *n pl.* -S one of great importance

BIGAMIES pl. of bigamy

BIGAMIST *n pl.* -S one who commits bigamy

BIGAMOUS *adj* guilty of bigamy

BIGAMY *n pl.* -MIES the act of marrying someone while married to another

BIGARADE *n pl.* -S a citrus tree

BIGAROON *n pl.* -S a type of cherry

BIGEMINY *n pl.* -NIES the state of having a double pulse

BIGEYE *n pl.* -S a marine fish

BIGFOOT *n pl.* -FEET or -FOOTS a large hairy humanlike creature

BIGGER comparative of big

BIGGEST superlative of big

BIGGETY *adj* biggity

BIGGIE n pl. -S one that is big

BIGGIN n pl. -S a house

BIGGING n pl. -S biggin

BIGGISH adj somewhat big

BIGGITY adj conceited

BIGHEAD n pl. -S a disease of animals

BIGHORN n pl. -S a wild sheep

BIGHT v -ED, -ING, -S to fasten with a loop of rope

BIGLY adv in a big manner

BIGMOUTH n pl. -S a talkative person

BIGNESS n pl. -ES the state of being big

BIGNONIA n pl. -S a climbing plant

BIGOT n pl. -S a prejudiced person

BIGOTED adj intolerant

BIGOTRY n pl. -RIES prejudice

BIGWIG n pl. -S an important person

BIHOURLY adj occurring every two hours

BIJOU n pl. -JOUX or -JOUS a jewel

BIJUGATE adj two-paired

BIJUGOUS adj bijugate

BIKE v BIKED, BIKING, BIKES to bicycle

BIKER n pl. -S one that bikes

BIKEWAY n pl. -WAYS a route for bikes

BIKIE n pl. -S biker

BIKING present participle of bike

BIKINI n pl. -S a type of bathing suit **BIKINIED** adj

BILABIAL n pl. -S a sound articulated with both lips

BILANDER n pl. -S a small ship

BILAYER n pl. -S a film with two molecular layers

BILBERRY n pl. -RIES an edible berry

BILBO n pl. -BOS or -BOES a finely tempered sword

BILBOA n pl. -S bilbo

BILE n pl. -S a fluid secreted by the liver

BILGE v BILGED, BILGING, BILGES to spring a leak

BILGY adj BILGIER, BILGIEST smelling like seepage

BILIARY adj pertaining to bile

BILINEAR adj pertaining to two lines

BILIOUS adj pertaining to bile

BILK v -ED, -ING, -S to cheat

BILKER n pl. -S one that bilks

BILL v -ED, -ING, -S to present a statement of costs to **BILLABLE** adj

BILLBUG n pl. -S a weevil

BILLER n pl. -S one that bills

BILLET v -ED, -ING, -S to lodge soldiers

BILLETER n pl. -S one that billets

BILLFISH n pl. -ES a fish with long, slender jaws

BILLFOLD n pl. -S a wallet

BILLHEAD n pl. -S a letterhead

BILLHOOK n pl. -S a cutting tool

BILLIARD n pl. -S a carom shot in billiards (a table game)

BILLIE n pl. -S a comrade

BILLIES pl. of billy

BILLING n pl. -S the relative position in which a performer is listed

BILLION n pl. -S a number

BILLON n pl. -S an alloy of silver and copper

BILLOW v -ED, -ING, -S to swell

BILLOWY adj -LOWIER, -LOWIEST swelling; surging

BILLY n pl. -LIES a short club

BILLYCAN n pl. -S a pot for heating water

BILOBATE adj having two lobes

BILOBED adj bilobate

BILSTED n pl. -S a hardwood tree

BILTONG n pl. -S dried and cured meat

BIMA n pl. -S bema

BIMAH n pl. -S bema

BIMANOUS adj two-handed

BIMANUAL adj done with two hands

BIMBO n pl. -BOS or -BOES a disreputable person

BIMENSAL adj occurring every two months

BIMESTER n pl. -S a two-month period

BIMETAL n pl. -S something composed of two metals

BIMETHYL n pl. -S ethane

BIMODAL adj having two statistical modes

BIMORPH n pl. -S a device consisting of two crystals cemented together

BIN v BINNED, BINNING, BINS to store in a large receptacle

BINAL adj twofold

BINARY n pl. -RIES a combination of two things

BINATE adj growing in pairs **BINATELY** adv

BINAURAL adj hearing with both ears

BIND v BOUND, BINDING, BINDS to tie or secure **BINDABLE** adj

BINDER n pl. -S one that binds

BINDERY n pl. -ERIES a place where books are bound

BINDI n pl. -S a dot worn on the forehead by women in India

BINDING n pl. -S the cover and fastenings of a book

BINDLE n pl. -S a bundle

BINDWEED n pl. -S a twining plant

BINE n pl. -S a twining plant stem

BINGE v BINGED, BINGEING or BINGING, BINGES to indulge in something without restraint

BINGER n pl. -S one that binges

BINGO n pl. -GOS a game of chance

BINIT n pl. -S a unit of computer information

BINNACLE n pl. -S a compass stand

BINNED past tense of bin

BINNING present participle of bin

BINOCLE n pl. -S a binocular

BINOCS n/pl binoculars

BINOMIAL n pl. -S an algebraic expression

BINT n pl. -S a woman

BIO n pl. BIOS a biography

BIOASSAY v -ED, -ING, -S to test a drug

BIOCHIP n pl. -S a hypothetical part of a computer that uses proteins to store or process data

BIOCIDE n pl. -S a substance destructive to living organisms BIOCIDAL adj

BIOCLEAN adj free of harmful organisms

BIOCYCLE n pl. -S a life-supporting region

BIOETHIC adj pertaining to ethical questions arising from advances in biology

BIOGAS n pl. -GASES or -GASSES fuel gas produced by organic waste

BIOGEN n pl. -S a hypothetical protein molecule

BIOGENIC adj produced by living organisms

BIOGENY n pl. -NIES the development of life from preexisting life

BIOHERM n pl. -S a mass of marine fossils

BIOLOGIC n pl. -S a drug obtained from an organic source

BIOLOGY n pl. -GIES the science of life

BIOLYSIS n pl. -YSES death BIOLYTIC adj

BIOMASS n pl. -ES an amount of living matter

BIOME n pl. -S an ecological community

BIOMETRY n pl. -TRIES the statistical study of biological data

BIONICS n/pl a science joining biology and electronics BIONIC adj

BIONOMY n pl. -MIES ecology BIONOMIC adj

BIONT n pl. -S a living organism BIONTIC adj

BIOPIC n pl. -S a biographical movie

BIOPLASM n pl. -S living matter

BIOPSIC adj pertaining to the examination of living tissue

BIOPSY v -SIED -SYING, -SIES to examine living tissue

BIOPTIC adj biopsic

BIOSCOPE n pl. -S an early movie projector

BIOSCOPY n pl. -PIES a type of medical examination

BIOTA n pl. -S the flora and fauna of a region

BIOTECH n pl. -S applied biological science

BIOTIC adj pertaining to life

BIOTICAL adj biotic

BIOTICS n/pl a life science

BIOTIN n pl. -S a B vitamin

BIOTITE n pl. -S a form of mica BIOTITIC adj

BIOTOPE n pl. -S a stable habitat

BIOTOXIN n pl. -S poison made by a plant or animal

BIOTRON n pl. -S a climate control chamber

BIOTYPE n pl. -S a group of genetically similar organisms BIOTYPIC adj

BIOVULAR adj derived from two ova

BIPACK n pl. -S a pair of films

BIPAROUS adj producing offspring in pairs

BIPARTED adj having two parts

BIPARTY adj of two parties

BIPED n pl. -S a two-footed animal BIPEDAL adj

BIPHASIC adj having two phases

BIPHENYL n pl. -S a hydrocarbon

BIPLANE n pl. -S a type of airplane

BIPOD n pl. -S a two-legged support

BIPOLAR adj having two poles

BIRACIAL adj including members of two races

BIRADIAL adj having dual symmetry

BIRAMOSE adj biramous

BIRAMOUS adj divided into two branches

BIRCH v -ED, -ING, -ES to whip

BIRCHEN adj made of birch wood

BIRD v -ED, -ING, -S to hunt birds (winged vertebrates)

BIRDBATH n pl. -S a bath for birds

BIRDCAGE n pl. -S a cage for birds

BIRDCALL n pl. -S the call of a bird

BIRDER n pl. -S a bird hunter

BIRDFARM n pl. -S an aircraft carrier

BIRDIE v BIRDIED, BIRDIEING, BIRDIES to shoot in one stroke under par in golf

BIRDING n pl. -S bird-watching

BIRDLIKE adj resembling a bird

BIRDLIME v -LIMED, -LIMING, -LIMES to trap small birds

BIRDMAN n pl. -MEN one who keeps birds

BIRDSEED n pl. -S a mixture of seeds used for feeding birds

BIRDSEYE n pl. -S a flowering plant

BIRDSHOT n pl. -S small shot for shooting birds

BIRDSONG n pl. -S the song of a bird

BIREME n pl. -S an ancient galley

BIRETTA n pl. -S a cap worn by clergymen

BIRK n pl. -S a birch tree

BIRKIE n pl. -S a lively person

BIRL v -ED, -ING, -S to rotate a floating log

BIRLE v BIRLED, BIRLING, BIRLES to carouse

BIRLER n pl. -S one that birls

BIRLING n pl. -S a lumberjack's game

BIRR v -ED, -ING, -S to make a whirring noise

BIRR n pl. BIRROTCH a monetary unit of Ethiopia

BIRRETTA n pl. -S biretta

BIRSE n pl. -S a bristle

BIRTH v -ED, -ING, -S to originate

BIRTHDAY n pl. -DAYS an anniversary of a birth

BIS adv twice

BISCUIT n pl. -S a small cake of shortened bread

BISE n pl. -S a cold wind

BISECT v -ED, -ING, -S to cut into two parts

BISECTOR n pl. -S something that bisects

BISEXUAL n pl. -S one who is attracted to both sexes

BISHOP v -ED, -ING, -S to appoint as a bishop (the head of a diocese)

BISK n pl. -S bisque

BISMUTH n pl. -S a metallic element

BISNAGA n pl. -S a type of cactus

BISON n pl. -S an ox-like animal

BISQUE n pl. -S a thick soup

BISTATE adj pertaining to two states

BISTER n pl. -S a brown pigment BISTERED adj

BISTORT n pl. -S a perennial herb with roots used as astringents

BISTOURY n pl. -RIES a surgical knife

BISTRE n pl. -S bister BISTRED adj

BISTRO n pl. -TROS a small tavern BISTROIC adj

BIT v BITTED, BITTING, BITS to restrain

BITABLE adj capable of being bitten

BITCH v -ED, -ING, -ES to complain

BITCHERY n pl. -ERIES bitchy behavior

BITCHY adj BITCHIER, BITCHIEST malicious BITCHILY adv

BITE v BIT, BITTEN, BITING, BITES to seize with the teeth BITEABLE adj

BITER n pl. -S one that bites

BITEWING n pl. -S a dental X-ray film

BITING present participle of bite

BITINGLY adv sarcastically

BITSTOCK n pl. -S a brace on a drill

BITSY adj tiny

BITT v -ED, -ING, -S to secure a cable

BITTED past tense of bit

BITTEN a past participle of bite

BITTER adj -TERER, -TEREST having a disagreeable taste BITTERLY adv

BITTER v -ED, -ING, -S to make bitter

BITTERN n pl. -S a wading bird

BITTIER comparative of bitty

BITTIEST superlative of bitty

BITTING n pl. -S an indentation in a key

BITTOCK n pl. -S a small amount

BITTY adj -TIER, -TIEST fragmented

BITUMEN n pl. -S an asphalt

BIUNIQUE adj being a type of correspondence between two sets

BIVALENT n pl. -S a pair of chromosomes

BIVALVE n pl. -S a bivalved mollusk

BIVALVED adj having a two-valved shell

BIVINYL n pl. -S a flammable gas used in making synthetic rubber

BIVOUAC v -OUACKED, -OUACKING, -OUACKS or -OUACS to make a camp

BIWEEKLY n pl. -LIES a publication issued every two weeks

BIYEARLY adj occurring every two years

BIZ	n pl. BIZZES business	**BLARE**	v BLARED, BLARING, BLARES to sound loudly
BIZARRE	n pl. -S a strangely striped flower	**BLARNEY**	v -NEYED, -NEYING, -NEYS to beguile with flattery
BIZE	n pl. -S bise		
BIZNAGA	n pl. -S bisnaga	**BLASE**	adj indifferent
BIZONE	n pl. -S two combined zones BIZONAL adj	**BLAST**	v -ED, -ING, -S to use an explosive
BLAB	v BLABBED, BLABBING, BLABS to talk idly	**BLASTEMA**	n pl. -MAS or -MATA a region of embryonic cells
BLABBER	v -ED, -ING, -S to blab	**BLASTER**	n pl. -S one that blasts
BLABBY	adj talkative	**BLASTIE**	n pl. -S a dwarf
BLACK	adj BLACKER, BLACKEST being of the darkest color	**BLASTIER**	comparative of blasty
		BLASTIEST	superlative of blasty
BLACK	v -ED, -ING, -S to make black	**BLASTING**	n pl. -S the act of one that blasts
BLACKBOY	n pl. -BOYS an Australian plant	**BLASTOFF**	n pl. -S the launching of a rocket
BLACKCAP	n pl. -S a small European bird		
BLACKEN	v -ED, -ING, -S to make black	**BLASTOMA**	n pl. -MAS or -MATA a type of tumor
BLACKFIN	n pl. -S a food fish		
BLACKFLY	n pl. -FLIES a biting fly	**BLASTULA**	n pl. -LAS or -LAE an early embryo
BLACKGUM	n pl. -S a tupelo		
BLACKING	n pl. -S black shoe polish	**BLASTY**	adj BLASTIER, BLASTIEST gusty
BLACKISH	adj somewhat black		
BLACKLEG	n pl. -S a cattle disease	**BLAT**	v BLATTED, BLATTING, BLATS to bleat
BLACKLY	adv in a black manner		
BLACKOUT	n pl. -S a power failure	**BLATANCY**	n pl. -CIES something blatant
BLACKTOP	v -TOPPED, -TOPPING, -TOPS to pave with asphalt	**BLATANT**	adj obvious
		BLATE	adj timid
BLADDER	n pl. -S a saclike receptacle BLADDERY adj	**BLATHER**	v -ED, -ING, -S to talk foolishly
BLADE	n pl. -S a cutting edge BLADED adj	**BLATTED**	past tense of blat
		BLATTER	v -ED, -ING, -S to chatter
BLAE	adj bluish-black	**BLATTING**	present participle of blat
BLAH	n pl. -S nonsense	**BLAUBOK**	n pl. -S an extinct antelope
BLAIN	n pl. -S a blister	**BLAW**	v BLAWED, BLAWN, BLAWING, BLAWS to blow
BLAM	n pl. -S the sound of a gunshot		
		BLAZE	v BLAZED, BLAZING, BLAZES to burn brightly
BLAMABLE	adj being at fault BLAMABLY adv		
		BLAZER	n pl. -S a lightweight jacket
BLAME	v BLAMED, BLAMING, BLAMES to find fault with	**BLAZON**	v -ED, -ING, -S to proclaim
		BLAZONER	n pl. -S one that blazons
BLAMEFUL	adj blamable	**BLAZONRY**	n pl. -RIES a great display
BLAMER	n pl. -S one that blames	**BLEACH**	v -ED, -ING, -ES to whiten
BLAMING	present participle of blame	**BLEACHER**	n pl. -S one that bleaches
BLANCH	v -ED, -ING, -ES to whiten	**BLEAK**	adj BLEAKER, BLEAKEST dreary
BLANCHER	n pl. -S a whitener		
BLAND	adj BLANDER, BLANDEST soothing BLANDLY adv	**BLEAK**	n pl. -S a freshwater fish
		BLEAKISH	adj somewhat bleak
BLANDISH	v -ED, -ING, -ES to coax by flattery	**BLEAKLY**	adv in a bleak manner
		BLEAR	v -ED, -ING, -S to dim
BLANK	adj BLANKER, BLANKEST empty	**BLEARY**	adj BLEARIER, BLEARIEST dimmed BLEARILY adv
BLANK	v -ED, -ING, -S to delete	**BLEAT**	v -ED, -ING, -S to utter the cry of a sheep
BLANKET	v -ED, -ING, -S to cover uniformly		
		BLEATER	n pl. -S one that bleats
BLANKLY	adv in a blank manner	**BLEB**	n pl. -S a blister BLEBBY adj

BLEED	v BLED, BLEEDING, BLEEDS to lose blood	**BLINTZ**	n pl. -ES blintze
BLEEDER	n pl. -S one that bleeds	**BLINTZE**	n pl. -S a thin pancake
BLEEDING	n pl. -S the act of losing blood	**BLIP**	v BLIPPED, BLIPPING, BLIPS to remove sound from a recording
BLEEP	v -ED, -ING, -S to blip		
BLELLUM	n pl. -S a babbler	**BLISS**	v -ED, -ING, -ES to experience or produce ecstasy
BLEMISH	v -ED, -ING, -ES to mar		
BLENCH	v -ED, -ING, -ES to flinch	**BLISSFUL**	adj very happy
BLENCHER	n pl. -S one that blenches	**BLISTER**	v -ED, -ING, -S to cause blisters (skin swellings)
BLEND	v BLENDED or BLENT, BLENDING, BLENDS to mix smoothly and inseparably together		
		BLISTERY	adj having blisters
		BLITE	n pl. -S an annual herb
BLENDE	n pl. -S a shiny mineral	**BLITHE**	adj BLITHER, BLITHEST merry BLITHELY adv
BLENDER	n pl. -S one that blends		
BLENNY	n pl. -NIES a marine fish	**BLITHER**	v -ED, -ING, -S to blather
BLENT	a past tense of blend	**BLITZ**	v -ED, -ING, -ES to subject to a sudden attack
BLESBOK	n pl. -S a large antelope		
BLESBUCK	n pl. -S blesbok	**BLIZZARD**	n pl. -S a heavy snowstorm
BLESS	v BLESSED or BLEST, BLESSING, BLESSES to sanctify	**BLOAT**	v -ED, -ING, -S to swell
		BLOATER	n pl. -S a smoked herring
		BLOB	v BLOBBED, BLOBBING, BLOBS to splotch
BLESSED	adj -EDER, -EDEST holy		
BLESSER	n pl. -S one that blesses	**BLOC**	n pl. -S a coalition
BLESSING	n pl. -S a prayer	**BLOCK**	v -ED, -ING, -S to obstruct
BLEST	a past tense of bless	**BLOCKADE**	v -ADED, -ADING, -ADES to block
BLET	n pl. -S a decay of fruit		
BLETHER	v -ED, -ING, -S to blather	**BLOCKAGE**	n pl. -S the act of blocking
BLEW	past tense of blow	**BLOCKER**	n pl. -S one that blocks
BLIGHT	v -ED, -ING, -S to cause decay	**BLOCKISH**	adj blocky
		BLOCKY	adj BLOCKIER, BLOCKIEST short and stout
BLIGHTER	n pl. -S one that blights		
BLIGHTY	n pl. BLIGHTIES a wound causing one to be sent home to England	**BLOKE**	n pl. -S a fellow
		BLOND	adj BLONDER, BLONDEST light-colored
BLIMEY	interj — used as an expression of surprise		
		BLOND	n pl. -S a blond person
		BLONDE	n pl. -S a blond
BLIMP	n pl. -S a nonrigid aircraft BLIMPISH adj	**BLONDISH**	adj somewhat blond
		BLOOD	v -ED, -ING, -S to stain with blood (the fluid circulated by the heart)
BLIMY	interj blimey		
BLIN	n pl. BLINI or BLINIS a blintze		
BLIND	adj BLINDER, BLINDEST sightless	**BLOODFIN**	n pl. -S a freshwater fish
		BLOODIED	past tense of bloody
BLIND	v -ED, -ING, -S to make sightless	**BLOODIER**	comparative of bloody
		BLOODIES	present 3d person sing. of bloody
BLINDAGE	n pl. -S a protective screen		
BLINDER	n pl. -S an obstruction to sight	**BLOODIEST**	superlative of bloody
BLINDLY	adv in a blind manner	**BLOODILY**	adv in a bloody manner
BLINI	a pl. of blin	**BLOODING**	n pl. -S a fox hunting ceremony
BLINIS	a pl. of blin		
BLINK	v -ED, -ING, -S to open and shut the eyes	**BLOODRED**	adj of the color of blood
		BLOODY	adj BLOODIER, BLOODIEST stained with blood
BLINKARD	n pl. -S one who habitually blinks		
		BLOODY	v BLOODIED, BLOODYING, BLOODIES to make bloody
BLINKER	v -ED, -ING, -S to put blinders on		
		BLOOEY	adj being out of order
		BLOOIE	adj blooey

BLOOM v -ED, -ING, -S to bear flowers

BLOOMER n pl. -S a blooming plant

BLOOMERY n pl. -ERIES a furnace for smelting iron

BLOOMY adj BLOOMIER, BLOOMIEST covered with flowers

BLOOP v -ED, -ING, -S to hit a short fly ball

BLOOPER n pl. -S a public blunder

BLOSSOM v -ED, -ING, -S to bloom

BLOSSOMY adj having blossoms

BLOT v BLOTTED, BLOTTING, BLOTS to spot or stain

BLOTCH v -ED, -ING, -ES to mark with large spots

BLOTCHY adj BLOTCHIER, BLOTCHIEST blotched

BLOTLESS adj spotless

BLOTTED past tense of blot

BLOTTER n pl. -S a piece of ink-absorbing paper

BLOTTIER comparative of blotty

BLOTTIEST superlative of blotty

BLOTTING present participle of blot

BLOTTO adj drunk

BLOTTY adj -TIER, -TIEST spotty

BLOUSE v BLOUSED, BLOUSING, BLOUSES to hang loosely

BLOUSON n pl. -S a woman's garment

BLOUSY adj BLOUSIER, BLOUSIEST blowsy BLOUSILY adv

BLOVIATE v -ATED, -ATING, -ATES to speak pompously

BLOW v BLEW, BLOWN, BLOWING, BLOWS to drive or impel by a current of air

BLOW v BLEW, BLOWED, BLOWING, BLOWS to damn

BLOWBACK n pl. -S an escape of gases

BLOWBALL n pl. -S a fluffy seed ball

BLOWBY n pl. -BYS leakage of exhaust fumes

BLOWDOWN n pl. -S a tree blown down by the wind

BLOWER n pl. -S one that blows

BLOWFISH n pl. -ES a marine fish

BLOWFLY n pl. -FLIES a type of fly

BLOWGUN n pl. -S a tube through which darts may be blown

BLOWHARD n pl. -S a braggart

BLOWHOLE n pl. -S an air or gas vent

BLOWIER comparative of blowy

BLOWIEST superlative of blowy

BLOWN past participle of blow

BLOWOFF n pl. -S the expelling of gas

BLOWOUT n pl. -S a sudden rupture

BLOWPIPE n pl. -S a blowgun

BLOWSED adj blowsy

BLOWSY adj -SIER, -SIEST slovenly BLOWSILY adv

BLOWTUBE n pl. -S a blowgun

BLOWUP n pl. -S an explosion

BLOWY adj BLOWIER, BLOWIEST windy

BLOWZED adj blowzy

BLOWZY adj -ZIER, -ZIEST blowsy BLOWZILY adv

BLUB v BLUBBED, BLUBBING, BLUBS to blubber

BLUBBER v -ED, -ING, -S to weep noisily

BLUBBERY adj fat; swollen

BLUCHER n pl. -S a half boot

BLUDGEON v -ED, -ING, -S to hit with a club

BLUDGER n pl. -S a loafer or shirker

BLUE adj BLUER, BLUEST having the color of the clear sky

BLUE v BLUED, BLUEING or BLUING, BLUES to make blue

BLUEBALL n pl. -S a medicinal herb

BLUEBELL n pl. -S a flowering plant

BLUEBILL n pl. -S the scaup duck

BLUEBIRD n pl. -S a songbird

BLUEBOOK n pl. -S an examination booklet

BLUECAP n pl. -S a flowering plant

BLUECOAT n pl. -S a police officer

BLUED past tense of blue

BLUEFIN n pl. -S a large tuna

BLUEFISH n pl. -ES a marine fish

BLUEGILL n pl. -S an edible sunfish

BLUEGUM n pl. -S a timber tree

BLUEHEAD n pl. -S a marine fish

BLUEING n pl. -S bluing

BLUEISH adj bluish

BLUEJACK n pl. -S an oak tree

BLUEJAY n pl. -JAYS a corvine bird

BLUELINE n pl. -S a line that divides a hockey rink

BLUELY adv in a blue manner

BLUENESS n pl. -ES the state of being blue

BLUENOSE n pl. -S a puritanical person

BLUER comparative of blue

BLUESIER comparative of bluesy

BLUESIEST superlative of bluesy

BLUESMAN n pl. -MEN one who plays the blues

BLUEST superlative of blue

BLUESTEM n pl. -S a prairie grass

BLUESY *adj* BLUESIER, BLUESIEST resembling the blues (a musical form)

BLUET *n* pl. -S a meadow flower

BLUETICK *n* pl. -S a hunting dog

BLUEWEED *n* pl. -S a bristly weed

BLUEWOOD *n* pl. -S a shrub

BLUEY *n* pl. BLUEYS a bag of clothing carried in travel

BLUFF *v* -ED, -ING, -S to mislead

BLUFF *adj* BLUFFER, BLUFFEST having a broad front **BLUFFLY** *adv*

BLUFFER *n* pl. -S one that bluffs

BLUING *n* pl. -S a fabric coloring

BLUISH *adj* somewhat blue

BLUME *v* BLUMED, BLUMING, BLUMES to blossom

BLUNDER *v* -ED, -ING, -S to make a mistake

BLUNGE *v* BLUNGED, BLUNGING, BLUNGES to mix clay with water

BLUNGER *n* pl. -S one that blunges

BLUNT *adj* BLUNTER, BLUNTEST not sharp or pointed **BLUNTLY** *adv*

BLUNT *v* -ED, -ING, -S to make blunt

BLUR *v* BLURRED, BLURRING, BLURS to make unclear

BLURB *v* -ED, -ING, -S to praise in a publicity notice

BLURRY *adj* -RIER, -RIEST unclear **BLURRILY** *adv*

BLURT *v* -ED, -ING, -S to speak abruptly

BLURTER *n* pl. -S one that blurts

BLUSH *v* -ED, -ING, -ES to become red

BLUSHER *n* pl. -S one that blushes

BLUSHFUL *adj* of a red color

BLUSTER *v* -ED, -ING, -S to blow violently

BLUSTERY *adj* windy

BLYPE *n* pl. -S a shred

BO *n* pl. BOS a pal

BOA *n* pl. -S a large snake

BOAR *n* pl. -S a male pig

BOARD *v* -ED, -ING, -S to take meals for a fixed price

BOARDER *n* pl. -S one that boards

BOARDING *n* pl. -S a surface of wooden boards

BOARDMAN *n* pl. -MEN a board member

BOARFISH *n* pl. -ES a marine fish

BOARISH *adj* swinish; coarse

BOART *n* pl. -S bort

BOAST *v* -ED, -ING, -S to brag

BOASTER *n* pl. -S one that boasts

BOASTFUL *adj* given to boasting

BOAT *v* -ED, -ING, -S to travel by boat (watercraft) **BOATABLE** *adj*

BOATBILL *n* pl. -S a wading bird

BOATEL *n* pl. -S a waterside hotel

BOATER *n* pl. -S one that boats

BOATFUL *n* pl. -S as much as a boat can hold

BOATHOOK *n* pl. -S a pole with a metal hook for use aboard a boat

BOATING *n* pl. -S the sport of traveling by boat

BOATLIKE *adj* resembling a boat

BOATLOAD *n* pl. -S the amount that a boat holds

BOATMAN *n* pl. -MEN one who works on boats

BOATSMAN *n* pl. -MEN boatman

BOATYARD *n* pl. -S a marina

BOB *v* BOBBED, BOBBING, BOBS to move up and down

BOBBER *n* pl. -S one that bobs

BOBBERY *n* pl. -BERIES a disturbance

BOBBIES pl. of bobby

BOBBIN *n* pl. -S a thread holder

BOBBINET *n* pl. -S a machine-made net

BOBBING present participle of bob

BOBBLE *v* -BLED, -BLING, -BLES to fumble

BOBBY *n* pl. -BIES a police officer

BOBCAT *n* pl. -S a lynx

BOBECHE *n* pl. -S a glass collar on a candle holder

BOBOLINK *n* pl. -S a songbird

BOBSLED *v* -SLEDDED, -SLEDDING, -SLEDS to ride on a bobsled (a racing sled)

BOBSTAY *n* pl. -STAYS a steadying rope

BOBTAIL *v* -ED, -ING, -S to cut short

BOBWHITE *n* pl. -S a game bird

BOCACCIO *n* pl. -CIOS a rockfish

BOCCE *n* pl. -S boccie

BOCCI *n* pl. -S boccie

BOCCIA *n* pl. -S boccie

BOCCIE *n* pl. -S an Italian bowling game

BOCK *n* pl. -S a dark beer

BOD *n* pl. -S a body

BODE *v* BODED, BODING, BODES to be an omen of

BODEGA *n* pl. -S a grocery store

BODEMENT *n* pl. -S an omen

BODHRAN *n* pl. -S an Irish drum

BODICE *n* pl. -S a corset

BODIED past tense of body

BODIES present 3d person sing. of body

BODILESS *adj* lacking material form

BODILY *adj* of the body

BODING *n* pl. -S an omen

BODINGLY *adv* ominously

BODKIN *n* pl. -S a sharp instrument

BODY *v* BODIED, BODYING, BODIES to give form to

BODYSUIT *n* pl. -S a one-piece garment for the torso

BODYSURF *v* -ED, -ING, -S to ride a wave without a surfboard

BODYWORK *n* pl. -S a vehicle body

BOEHMITE *n* pl. -S a mineral

BOFF *n* pl. -S a hearty laugh

BOFFIN *n* pl. -S a scientific expert

BOFFO *n* pl. -FOS a boff

BOFFOLA *n* pl. -S a boff

BOG *v* BOGGED, BOGGING, BOGS to impede

BOGAN *n* pl. -S a backwater or tributary

BOGBEAN *n* pl. -S a marsh plant

BOGEY *v* -GEYED, -GEYING, -GEYS to shoot in one stroke over par in golf

BOGEYMAN *n* pl. -MEN a terrifying creature

BOGGED past tense of bog

BOGGIER comparative of boggy

BOGGIEST superlative of boggy

BOGGING present participle of bog

BOGGISH *adj* boggy

BOGGLE *v* -GLED, -GLING, -GLES to hesitate

BOGGLER *n* pl. -S one that causes another to boggle

BOGGY *adj* -GIER, -GIEST marshy

BOGIE *n* pl. -S bogy

BOGIES pl. of bogy

BOGLE *n* pl. -S a bogy

BOGUS *adj* not genuine; fake

BOGWOOD *n* pl. -S preserved tree wood

BOGY *n* pl. -GIES a goblin

BOGYISM *n* pl. -S behavior characteristic of a bogy

BOGYMAN *n* pl. -MEN bogeyman

BOHEA *n* pl. -S a black tea

BOHEMIA *n* pl. -S a community of bohemians

BOHEMIAN *n* pl. -S an unconventional person

BOHUNK *n* pl. -S an unskilled laborer

BOIL *v* -ED, -ING, -S to vaporize liquid **BOILABLE** *adj*

BOILER *n* pl. -S a vessel for boiling

BOILOFF *n* pl. -S the vaporization of a liquid

BOING *interj* — used to express the sound of reverberation or vibration

BOISERIE *n* pl. -S wood paneling on a wall

BOITE *n* pl. -S a nightclub

BOLA *n* pl. -S a throwing weapon

BOLAR *adj* pertaining to bole

BOLAS *n* pl. -ES bola

BOLD *adj* BOLDER, BOLDEST daring **BOLDLY** *adv*

BOLD *n* pl. -S a thick type

BOLDFACE *v* -FACED, -FACING, -FACES to print in thick type

BOLDNESS *n* pl. -ES the quality of being bold

BOLE *n* pl. -S a fine clay

BOLERO *n* pl. -ROS a Spanish dance

BOLETE *n* pl. -S boletus

BOLETUS *n* pl. -TUSES or -TI a fungus

BOLIDE *n* pl. -S an exploding meteor

BOLIVAR *n* pl. -S or -ES a monetary unit of Venezuela

BOLIVIA *n* pl. -S a soft fabric

BOLL *v* -ED, -ING, -S to form pods

BOLLARD *n* pl. -S a thick post on a ship or wharf

BOLLIX *v* -ED, -ING, -ES to bungle

BOLLOX *v* -ED, -ING, -ES to bollix

BOLLWORM *n* pl. -S the larva of a certain moth

BOLO *n* pl. -LOS a machete

BOLOGNA *n* pl. -S a seasoned sausage

BOLONEY *n* pl. -NEYS bologna

BOLSHIE *n* pl. -S a Bolshevik

BOLSHY *n* pl. -SHIES bolshie

BOLSON *n* pl. -S a flat arid valley

BOLSTER *v* -ED, -ING, -S to support

BOLT *v* -ED, -ING, -S to sift

BOLTER *n* pl. -S a sifting machine

BOLTHEAD *n* pl. -S a matrass

BOLTHOLE *n* pl. -S a place or way of escape

BOLTONIA *n* pl. -S a perennial herb

BOLTROPE *n* pl. -S a rope sewn to a sail

BOLUS *n* pl. -ES a large pill

BOMB *v* -ED, -ING, -S to attack with bombs (explosive projectiles)

BOMBARD *v* -ED, -ING, -S to bomb

BOMBAST *n* pl. -S pompous language

BOMBAX *adj* pertaining to a family of tropical trees

BOMBÉ *n pl.* -S a frozen dessert

BOMBER *n pl.* -S one that bombs

BOMBESIN *n pl.* -S a combination of amino acids

BOMBING *n pl.* -S an attack with bombs

BOMBLOAD *n pl.* -S the quantity of bombs being carried

BOMBYCID *n pl.* -S a moth

BOMBYX *n pl.* -ES a silkworm

BONACI *n pl.* -S an edible fish

BONANZA *n pl.* -S a rich mine

BONBON *n pl.* -S a sugared candy

BOND *v* -ED, -ING, -S to join together **BONDABLE** *adj*

BONDAGE *n pl.* -S slavery

BONDER *n pl.* -S one that bonds

BONDING *n pl.* -S the formation of a close personal relationship

BONDMAID *n pl.* -S a female slave

BONDMAN *n pl.* -MEN a male slave

BONDSMAN *n pl.* -MEN bondman

BONDUC *n pl.* -S a prickly seed

BONE *v* BONED, BONING, BONES to debone

BONEFISH *n pl.* -ES a slender marine fish

BONEHEAD *n pl.* -S a stupid person

BONELESS *adj* having no bones (hard connective tissue)

BONEMEAL *n pl.* -S fertilizer or feed made from crushed bone

BONER *n pl.* -S a blunder

BONESET *n pl.* -S a perennial herb

BONEY *adj* BONIER, BONIEST bony

BONEYARD *n pl.* -S a junkyard

BONFIRE *n pl.* -S an open fire

BONG *v* -ED, -ING, -S to make a deep, ringing sound

BONGO *n pl.* -GOS or -GOES a small drum

BONGOIST *n pl.* -S a bongo player

BONHOMIE *n pl.* -S friendliness

BONIER comparative of bony or boney

BONIEST superlative of bony or boney

BONIFACE *n pl.* -S an innkeeper

BONINESS *n pl.* -ES the state of being bony

BONING present participle of bone

BONITA *n pl.* -S bonito

BONITO *n pl.* -TOS or -TOES a marine food fish

BONK *v* -ED, -ING, -S to hit on the head with a hollow blow

BONKERS *adj* crazy

BONNE *n pl.* -S a housemaid

BONNET *v* -ED, -ING, -S to provide with a bonnet (a type of hat)

BONNIE *adj* bonny

BONNOCK *n pl.* -S bannock

BONNY *adj* -NIER, -NIEST pretty **BONNILY** *adv*

BONSAI *n pl.* BONSAI a potted shrub that has been dwarfed

BONSPELL *n pl.* -S bonspiel

BONSPIEL *n pl.* -S a curling match or tournament

BONTEBOK *n pl.* -S an antelope

BONUS *n pl.* -ES an additional payment

BONY *adj* BONIER, BONIEST full of bones

BONZE *n pl.* -S a Buddhist monk

BONZER *adj* very good

BOO *v* -ED, -ING, -S to cry "boo"

BOOB *v* -ED, -ING, -S to make a foolish mistake

BOOBISH *adj* doltish

BOOBOO *n pl.* -BOOS a mistake

BOOBY *n pl.* -BIES a dolt

BOODLE *v* -DLED, -DLING, -DLES to take bribes

BOODLER *n pl.* -S one that boodles

BOOGER *n pl.* -S a bogeyman

BOOGEY *v* -GEYED, -GEYING, -GEYS boogie

BOOGIE *v* -GIED, -GYING, -GIES to dance to rock music

BOOGY *v* -GIED, -GYING, -GIES boogie

BOOGYMAN *n pl.* -MEN bogeyman

BOOHOO *v* -ED, -ING, -S to weep noisily

BOOK *v* -ED, -ING, -S to engage services **BOOKABLE** *adj*

BOOKCASE *n pl.* -S a case which holds books (literary volumes)

BOOKEND *n pl.* -S a support for a row of books

BOOKER *n pl.* -S one that books

BOOKFUL *n pl.* -S as much as a book can hold

BOOKIE *n pl.* -S a bet taker

BOOKING *n pl.* -S an engagement

BOOKISH *adj* pertaining to books

BOOKLET *n pl.* -S a small book

BOOKLICE *n/pl* wingless insects that damage books

BOOKLORE *n pl.* -S book learning

BOOKMAN *n pl.* -MEN a scholar

BOOKMARK *n pl.* -S a marker for finding a place in a book

BOOKRACK n pl. -S a support for an open book

BOOKREST n pl. -S a bookrack

BOOKSHOP n pl. -S a store where books are sold

BOOKWORM n pl. -S an avid book reader

BOOM v -ED, -ING, -S to make a deep, resonant sound

BOOMBOX n pl. -ES a portable radio and tape or compact disc player

BOOMER n pl. -S one that booms

BOOMIER comparative of boomy

BOOMIEST superlative of boomy

BOOMKIN n pl. -S a bumkin

BOOMLET n pl. -S a small increase in prosperity

BOOMTOWN n pl. -S a prospering town

BOOMY adj BOOMIER, BOOMIEST prospering

BOON n pl. -S a timely benefit

BOONDOCK adj pertaining to a backwoods area

BOONIES n/pl a backwoods area

BOOR n pl. -S a rude person

BOORISH adj rude

BOOST v -ED, -ING, -S to support

BOOSTER n pl. -S one that boosts

BOOT v -ED, -ING, -S to load a program into a computer **BOOTABLE** adj

BOOTEE n pl. -S a baby's sock

BOOTERY n pl. -ERIES a shoe store

BOOTH n pl. -S a small enclosure

BOOTIE n pl. -S bootee

BOOTIES pl. of booty

BOOTJACK n pl. -S a device for pulling off boots

BOOTLACE n pl. -S a shoelace

BOOTLEG v -LEGGED, -LEGGING, -LEGS to smuggle

BOOTLESS adj useless

BOOTLICK v -ED, -ING, -S to flatter servilely

BOOTY n pl. -TIES a rich gain or prize

BOOZE v BOOZED, BOOZING, BOOZES to drink liquor excessively

BOOZER n pl. -S one that boozes

BOOZY adj BOOZIER, BOOZIEST drunken **BOOZILY** adv

BOP v BOPPED, BOPPING, BOPS to hit or strike

BOPEEP n pl. -S a game of peekaboo

BOPPER n pl. -S a bebopper

BORA n pl. -S a cold wind

BORACES a pl. of borax

BORACIC adj boric

BORACITE n pl. -S a mineral

BORAGE n pl. -S a medicinal herb

BORAL n pl. -S a mixture of boron carbide and aluminum

BORANE n pl. -S a chemical compound

BORATE v -RATED, -RATING, -RATES to mix with borax or boric acid

BORAX n pl. -RAXES or -RACES a white crystalline compound

BORDEAUX n pl. BORDEAUX a red or white wine

BORDEL n pl. -S a brothel

BORDELLO n pl. -LOS a brothel

BORDER v -ED, -ING, -S to put a border (an edge) on

BORDERER n pl. -S one that borders

BORDURE n pl. -S a border around a shield

BORE v BORED, BORING, BORES to pierce with a rotary tool

BOREAL adj pertaining to the north

BORECOLE n pl. -S kale

BORED past tense of bore

BOREDOM n pl. -S tedium

BOREEN n pl. -S a lane in Ireland

BOREHOLE n pl. -S a hole bored in the earth

BORER n pl. -S one that bores

BORESOME adj tedious

BORIC adj pertaining to boron

BORIDE n pl. -S a boron compound

BORING n pl. -S an inner cavity

BORINGLY adv tediously

BORN adj having particular qualities from birth

BORNE a past participle of bear

BORNEOL n pl. -S an alcohol

BORNITE n pl. -S an ore of copper

BORON n pl. -S a nonmetallic element **BORONIC** adj

BOROUGH n pl. -S an incorporated town

BORROW v -ED, -ING, -S to take on loan

BORROWER n pl. -S one that borrows

BORSCH n pl. -ES borscht

BORSCHT n pl. -S a beet soup

BORSHT n pl. -S borscht

BORSTAL n pl. -S a reformatory

BORT n pl. -S a low-quality diamond **BORTY** adj

BORTZ n pl. -ES bort

BORZOI n pl. -S a Russian hound

BOSCAGE n pl. -S a thicket

BOSCHBOK n pl. -S bushbuck

BOSH n pl. -ES nonsense

BOSHBOK *n pl.* -S bushbuck
BOSHVARK *n pl.* -S a wild hog
BOSK *n pl.* -S a small wooded area
BOSKAGE *n pl.* -S boscage
BOSKER *adj* fine; very good
BOSKET *n pl.* -S a thicket
BOSKY *adj* BOSKIER, BOSKIEST wooded; bushy
BOSOM *v* -ED, -ING, -S to embrace
BOSOMY *adj* swelling outward
BOSON *n pl.* -S a subatomic particle
BOSQUE *n pl.* -S bosk
BOSQUET *n pl.* -S bosket
BOSS *v* -ED, -ING, -ES to supervise
BOSSDOM *n pl.* -S the domain of a political boss
BOSSIER comparative of bossy
BOSSIES pl. of bossy
BOSSISM *n pl.* -S control by political bosses
BOSSY *adj* BOSSIER, BOSSIEST domineering **BOSSILY** *adv*
BOSSY *n pl.* BOSSIES a cow
BOSTON *n pl.* -S a card game
BOSUN *n pl.* -S a boatswain
BOT *n pl.* -S the larva of a botfly
BOTA *n pl.* -S a leather bottle
BOTANIC *adj* pertaining to botany
BOTANICA *n pl.* -S a shop that sells herbs and magic charms
BOTANIES pl. of botany
BOTANISE *v* -NISED, -NISING, -NISES to botanize
BOTANIST *n pl.* -S one skilled in botany
BOTANIZE *v* -NIZED, -NIZING, -NIZES to study plants
BOTANY *n pl.* -NIES the science of plants
BOTCH *v* -ED, -ING, -ES to bungle
BOTCHER *n pl.* -S one that botches
BOTCHERY *n pl.* -ERIES something botched
BOTCHY *adj* BOTCHIER, BOTCHIEST badly done **BOTCHILY** *adv*
BOTEL *n pl.* -S a boatel
BOTFLY *n pl.* -FLIES a type of fly
BOTH *adj* being the two
BOTHER *v* -ED, -ING, -S to annoy
BOTHRIUM *n pl.* -RIA or -RIUMS a groove on a tapeworm
BOTHY *n pl.* BOTHIES a hut in Scotland
BOTONEE *adj* having arms ending in a trefoil — used of a heraldic cross
BOTONNEE *adj* botonee

BOTRYOID *adj* resembling a cluster of grapes
BOTRYOSE *adj* botryoid
BOTRYTIS *n pl.* -TISES a plant disease
BOTT *n pl.* -S bot
BOTTLE *v* -TLED, -TLING, -TLES to put into a bottle (a rigid container)
BOTTLER *n pl.* -S one that bottles
BOTTLING *n pl.* -S a bottled beverage
BOTTOM *v* -ED, -ING, -S to comprehend
BOTTOMER *n pl.* -S one that bottoms
BOTTOMRY *n pl.* -RIES a maritime contract
BOTULIN *n pl.* -S a nerve poison
BOTULISM *n pl.* -S botulin poisoning
BOUBOU *n pl.* -S a long flowing garment
BOUCHEE *n pl.* -S a small patty shell
BOUCLE *n pl.* -S a knitted fabric
BOUDOIR *n pl.* -S a woman's bedroom
BOUFFANT *n pl.* -S a woman's hairdo
BOUFFE *n pl.* -S a comic opera
BOUGH *n pl.* -S a tree branch **BOUGHED** *adj*
BOUGHPOT *n pl.* -S a large vase
BOUGHT past tense of buy
BOUGHTEN *adj* purchased
BOUGIE *n pl.* -S a wax candle
BOUILLON *n pl.* -S a clear broth
BOULDER *n pl.* -S a large rock **BOULDERY** *adj*
BOULE *n pl.* -S buhl
BOULLE *n pl.* -S buhl
BOUNCE *v* BOUNCED, BOUNCING, BOUNCES to spring back
BOUNCER *n pl.* -S one that bounces
BOUNCY *adj* BOUNCIER, BOUNCIEST tending to bounce **BOUNCILY** *adv*
BOUND *v* -ED, -ING, -S to leap
BOUNDARY *n pl.* -ARIES a dividing line
BOUNDEN *adj* obliged
BOUNDER *n pl.* -S one that bounds
BOUNTY *n pl.* -TIES a reward **BOUNTIED** *adj*
BOUQUET *n pl.* -S a bunch of flowers
BOURBON *n pl.* -S a whiskey
BOURDON *n pl.* -S a part of a bagpipe
BOURG *n pl.* -S a medieval town
BOURGEON *v* -ED, -ING, -S to burgeon
BOURN *n pl.* -S a stream
BOURNE *n pl.* -S bourn
BOURREE *n pl.* -S an old French dance
BOURRIDE *n pl.* -S a fish stew
BOURSE *n pl.* -S a stock exchange

BOURTREE *n* pl. -S a European tree

BOUSE *v* BOUSED, BOUSING, BOUSES to haul by means of a tackle

BOUSOUKI *n* pl. -KIA or -KIS bouzouki

BOUSY *adj* boozy

BOUT *n* pl. -S a contest

BOUTIQUE *n* pl. -S a small shop

BOUTON *n* pl. -S an enlarged end of a nerve fiber

BOUVIER *n* pl. -S a large dog

BOUZOUKI *n* pl. -KIA or -KIS a stringed musical instrument

BOVID *n* pl. -S a bovine

BOVINE *n* pl. -S an ox-like animal

BOVINELY *adv* stolidly

BOVINITY *n* pl. -TIES the state of being a bovine

BOW *v* -ED, -ING, -S to bend forward

BOWEL *v* -ELED, -ELING, -ELS or -ELLED, -ELLING, -ELS to disbowel

BOWER *v* -ED, -ING, -S to embower

BOWERY *n* pl. -ERIES a colonial Dutch farm

BOWFIN *n* pl. -S a freshwater fish

BOWFRONT *adj* having a curved front

BOWHEAD *n* pl. -S an arctic whale

BOWING *n* pl. -S the technique of managing the bow of a stringed instrument

BOWINGLY *adv* in a bowing manner

BOWKNOT *n* pl. -S a type of knot

BOWL *v* -ED, -ING, -S to play at bowling

BOWLDER *n* pl. -S boulder

BOWLEG *n* pl. -S an outwardly curved leg

BOWLER *n* pl. -S one that bowls

BOWLESS *adj* being without an archery bow

BOWLFUL *n* pl. -S as much as a bowl can hold

BOWLIKE *adj* curved

BOWLINE *n* pl. -S a type of knot

BOWLING *n* pl. -S a game in which balls are rolled at objects

BOWLLIKE *adj* concave

BOWMAN *n* pl. -MEN an archer

BOWPOT *n* pl. -S boughpot

BOWSE *v* BOWSED, BOWSING, BOWSES to bouse

BOWSHOT *n* pl. -S the distance an arrow is shot

BOWSPRIT *n* pl. -S a ship's spar

BOWWOW *v* -ED, -ING, -S to bark like a dog

BOWYER *n* pl. -S a maker of archery bows

BOX *v* -ED, -ING, -ES to put in a box (a rectangular container)

BOXBERRY *n* pl. -RIES an evergreen plant

BOXBOARD *n* pl. -S stiff paperboard

BOXCAR *n* pl. -S a roofed freight car

BOXER *n* pl. -S one that packs boxes

BOXFISH *n* pl. -ES a marine fish

BOXFUL *n* pl. -S as much as a box can hold

BOXHAUL *v* -ED, -ING, -S to veer a ship around

BOXIER comparative of boxy

BOXIEST superlative of boxy

BOXINESS *n* pl. -ES the state of being boxy

BOXING *n* pl. -S a casing

BOXLIKE *adj* resembling a box

BOXTHORN *n* pl. -S a thorny shrub

BOXWOOD *n* pl. -S an evergreen shrub

BOXY *adj* BOXIER, BOXIEST resembling a box

BOY *n* pl. BOYS a male child

BOYAR *n* pl. -S a former Russian aristocrat

BOYARD *n* pl. -S boyar

BOYARISM *n* pl. -S the rule of boyars

BOYCHICK *n* pl. -S boychik

BOYCHIK *n* pl. -S a young man

BOYCOTT *v* -ED, -ING, -S to refuse to buy

BOYHOOD *n* pl. -S the state of being a boy

BOYISH *adj* resembling a boy **BOYISHLY** *adv*

BOYLA *n* pl. -S a witch doctor

BOYO *n* pl. BOYOS a boy

BOZO *n* pl. -ZOS a fellow

BRA *n* pl. -S a brassiere

BRABBLE *v* -BLED, -BLING, -BLES to quarrel noisily

BRABBLER *n* pl. -S one that brabbles

BRACE *v* BRACED, BRACING, BRACES to support

BRACELET *n* pl. -S a wrist ornament

BRACER *n* pl. -S one that braces

BRACERO *n* pl. -ROS a Mexican laborer

BRACH *n* pl. -ES or -S a hound bitch

BRACHET *n* pl. -S a brach

BRACHIAL *n* pl. -S a part of the arm

BRACHIUM *n* pl. -IA the upper part of arm

BRACING *n* pl. -S a brace or reinforcement

BRACIOLA *n pl.* -S a thin slice of meat
BRACIOLE *n pl.* -S braciola
BRACKEN *n pl.* -S a large fern
BRACKET *v* -ED, -ING, -S to classify
BRACKISH *adj* salty
BRACONID *n pl.* -S any of a family of flies
BRACT *n pl.* -S a leaflike plant part BRACTEAL, BRACTED *adj*
BRACTLET *n pl.* -S a small bract
BRAD *v* BRADDED, BRADDING, BRADS to fasten with thin nails
BRADAWL *n pl.* -S a type of awl
BRADOON *n pl.* -S a bridoon
BRAE *n pl.* -S a hillside
BRAG *adj* BRAGGER, BRAGGEST first-rate
BRAG *v* BRAGGED, BRAGGING, BRAGS to speak vainly of one's deeds
BRAGGART *n pl.* -S one who brags
BRAGGER *n pl.* -S a braggart
BRAGGEST superlative of brag
BRAGGING present participle of brag
BRAGGY *adj* -GIER, -GIEST tending to brag
BRAHMA *n pl.* -S a large domestic fowl
BRAID *v* -ED, -ING, -S to weave together
BRAIDER *n pl.* -S one that braids
BRAIDING *n pl.* -S something made of braided material
BRAIL *v* -ED, -ING, -S to haul in a sail
BRAILLE *v* BRAILLED, BRAILLING, BRAILLES to write in braille (raised writing for the blind)
BRAIN *v* -ED, -ING, -S to hit on the head
BRAINIER comparative of brainy
BRAINIEST superlative of brainy
BRAINILY *adv* in a brainy manner
BRAINISH *adj* impetuous
BRAINPAN *n pl.* -S the skull
BRAINY *adj* BRAINIER, BRAINIEST smart
BRAISE *v* BRAISED, BRAISING, BRAISES to cook in fat
BRAIZE *n pl.* -S a marine fish
BRAKE *v* BRAKED, BRAKING, BRAKES to slow down or stop
BRAKEAGE *n pl.* -S the act of braking
BRAKEMAN *n pl.* -MEN a trainman
BRAKING present participle of brake
BRAKY *adj* BRAKIER, BRAKIEST abounding in shrubs or ferns

BRALESS *adj* wearing no bra
BRAMBLE *v* -BLED, -BLING, -BLES to gather berries
BRAMBLY *adj* -BLIER, -BLIEST prickly
BRAN *v* BRANNED, BRANNING, BRANS to soak in water mixed with bran (the outer coat of cereals)
BRANCH *v* -ED, -ING, -ES to form branches (offshoots)
BRANCHIA *n pl.* -CHIAE a respiratory organ of aquatic animals
BRANCHY *adj* BRANCHIER, BRANCHIEST having many branches
BRAND *v* -ED, -ING, -S to mark with a hot iron
BRANDER *n pl.* -S one that brands
BRANDISH *v* -ED, -ING, -ES to wave menacingly
BRANDY *v* -DIED, -DYING, -DIES to mix with brandy (a liquor)
BRANK *n pl.* -S a device used to restrain the tongue
BRANNED past tense of bran
BRANNER *n pl.* -S one that brans
BRANNING present participle of bran
BRANNY *adj* -NIER, -NIEST containing bran
BRANT *n pl.* -S a wild goose
BRANTAIL *n pl.* -S a singing bird
BRASH *adj* BRASHER, BRASHEST rash; hasty BRASHLY *adv*
BRASH *n pl.* -ES a mass of fragments
BRASHY *adj* BRASHIER, BRASHIEST brash
BRASIER *n pl.* -S brazier
BRASIL *n pl.* -S brazil
BRASILIN *n pl.* -S brazilin
BRASS *v* -ED, -ING, -ES to coat with brass (an alloy of copper and zinc)
BRASSAGE *n pl.* -S a fee for coining money
BRASSARD *n pl.* -S an insignia
BRASSART *n pl.* -S a brassard
BRASSICA *n pl.* -S a tall herb
BRASSIE *n pl.* -S a golf club
BRASSISH *adj* resembling brass
BRASSY *adj* BRASSIER, BRASSIEST resembling brass BRASSILY *adv*
BRAT *n pl.* -S a spoiled child BRATTISH *adj*
BRATTICE *v* -TICED, -TICING, -TICES to partition

BRATTLE v -TLED, -TLING, -TLES to clatter

BRATTY adj -TIER, -TIEST resembling a brat

BRAUNITE n pl. -S a mineral

BRAVA n pl. -S a shout of approval

BRAVADO n pl. -DOS or -DOES false bravery

BRAVE adj- BRAVER, BRAVEST showing courage **BRAVELY** adv

BRAVE v BRAVED, BRAVING, BRAVES to face with courage

BRAVER n pl. -S one that braves

BRAVERY n pl. -ERIES courage

BRAVEST superlative of brave

BRAVI a pl. of bravo

BRAVING present participle of brave

BRAVO n pl. -VOS or -VOES or -VI a hired killer

BRAVO v -ED, -ING, -ES to applaud by shouting "bravo"

BRAVURA n pl. -RAS or -RE fine musical technique

BRAW adj BRAWER, BRAWEST splendid

BRAWL v -ED, -ING, -S to fight

BRAWLER n pl. -S a fighter

BRAWLIE adv splendidly

BRAWLY adj BRAWLIER, BRAWLIEST inclined to brawl

BRAWN n pl. -S muscular strength

BRAWNY adj BRAWNIER, BRAWNIEST muscular **BRAWNILY** adv

BRAWS n/pl fine clothes

BRAXY n pl. BRAXIES a fever of sheep

BRAY v BRAYED, BRAYING, BRAYS to utter a harsh cry

BRAYER n pl. -S a roller used to spread ink

BRAZA n pl. -S a Spanish unit of length

BRAZE v BRAZED, BRAZING, BRAZES to solder together

BRAZEN v -ED, -ING, -S to face boldly

BRAZENLY adv boldly

BRAZER n pl. -S one that brazes

BRAZIER n pl. -S one who works in brass

BRAZIL n pl. -S a dyewood

BRAZILIN n pl. -S a chemical compound

BRAZING present participle of braze

BREACH v -ED, -ING, -ES to break through

BREACHER n pl. -S one that breaches

BREAD v -ED, -ING, -S to cover with crumbs of bread (a baked foodstuff made from flour)

BREADBOX n pl. -ES a container for bread

BREADNUT n pl. -S a tropical fruit

BREADTH n pl. -S width

BREADY adj resembling or characteristic of bread

BREAK v BROKE, BROKEN, BREAKING, BREAKS to reduce to fragments

BREAKAGE n pl. -S the act of breaking

BREAKER n pl. -S one that breaks

BREAKING n pl. -S the change of a pure vowel to a diphthong

BREAKOUT n pl. -S an escape

BREAKUP n pl. -S the act of breaking up

BREAM v -ED, -ING, -S to clean a ship's bottom

BREAST v -ED, -ING, -S to confront boldly

BREATH n pl. -S air inhaled and exhaled

BREATHE v BREATHED, BREATHING, BREATHES to inhale and exhale air

BREATHER n pl. -S one that breathes

BREATHY adj BREATHIER, BREATHIEST marked by loud breathing

BRECCIA n pl. -S a type of rock **BRECCIAL** adj

BRECHAM n pl. -S a collar for a horse

BRECHAN n pl. -S a brecham

BRED past tense of breed

BREDE n pl. -S a braid

BREE n pl. -S broth

BREECH v -ED, -ING, -ES to clothe with breeches (trousers)

BREED v BRED, BREEDING, BREEDS to cause to give birth

BREEDER n pl. -S one that breeds

BREEDING n pl. -S upbringing

BREEKS n/pl breeches

BREEZE v BREEZED, BREEZING, BREEZES to move swiftly

BREEZY adj BREEZIER, BREEZIEST windy **BREEZILY** adv

BREGMA n pl. -MATA a junction point of the skull **BREGMATE** adj

BREN n pl. -S a submachine gun

BRENT n pl. -S brant

BRETHREN a pl. of brother

BREVE n pl. -S a symbol used to indicate a short vowel

BREVET v -VETED, -VETING, -VETS or -VETTED, -VETTING, -VETS to confer an honorary rank upon

BREVETCY n pl. -CIES an honorary rank

BREVIARY n pl. -RIES a prayer book

BREVIER n pl. -S a size of type

BREVITY n pl. -TIES shortness of duration

BREW v -ED, -ING, -S to make beer or the like

BREWAGE n pl. -S a brewed beverage

BREWER n pl. -S one that brews

BREWERY n pl. -ERIES a place for brewing

BREWING n pl. -S a quantity brewed at one time

BREWIS n pl. BREWISES broth

BRIAR n pl. -S brier **BRIARY** adj

BRIARD n pl. -S a large dog

BRIBE v BRIBED, BRIBING, BRIBES to practice bribery **BRIBABLE** adj

BRIBEE n pl. -S one that is bribed

BRIBER n pl. -S one that bribes

BRIBERY n pl. -ERIES an act of influencing corruptly

BRIBING present participle of bribe

BRICK v -ED, -ING, -S to build with bricks (blocks of clay)

BRICKBAT n pl. -S a piece of brick

BRICKLE n pl. -S a brittle candy

BRICKY adj BRICKIER, BRICKIEST made of bricks

BRICOLE n pl. -S a cushion shot in billiards

BRIDAL n pl. -S a wedding

BRIDALLY adv in a manner befitting a bride

BRIDE n pl. -S a woman just married or about to be married

BRIDGE v BRIDGED, BRIDGING, BRIDGES to connect

BRIDGING n pl. -S a bracing

BRIDLE v -DLED, -DLING, -DLES to control with a restraint

BRIDLER n pl. -S one that bridles

BRIDOON n pl. -S a device used to control a horse

BRIE n pl. -S bree

BRIEF adj BRIEFER, BRIEFEST short

BRIEF v -ED, -ING, -S to summarize

BRIEFER n pl. -S one that briefs

BRIEFING n pl. -S a short lecture

BRIEFLY adv in a brief manner

BRIER n pl. -S a thorny shrub **BRIERY** adj

BRIG n pl. -S a two-masted ship

BRIGADE v -GADED, -GADING, -GADES to group together

BRIGAND n pl. -S a bandit

BRIGHT adj BRIGHTER, BRIGHTEST emitting much light **BRIGHTLY** adv

BRIGHT n pl. -S a light-hued tobacco

BRIGHTEN v -ED, -ING, -S to make bright

BRILL n pl. -S an edible flatfish

BRIM v BRIMMED, BRIMMING, BRIMS to fill to the top

BRIMFUL adj ready to overflow

BRIMFULL adj brimful

BRIMLESS adj having no brim (an upper edge)

BRIMMED past tense of brim

BRIMMER n pl. -S a brimming cup or glass

BRIMMING present participle of brim

BRIN n pl. -S a rib of a fan

BRINDED adj brindled

BRINDLE n pl. -S a brindled color

BRINDLED adj streaked

BRINE v BRINED, BRINING, BRINES to treat with brine (salted water)

BRINER n pl. -S one that brines

BRING v BROUGHT, BRINGING, BRINGS to take with oneself to a place

BRINGER n pl. -S one that brings

BRINIER comparative of briny

BRINIES pl. of briny

BRINIEST superlative of briny

BRINING present participle of brine

BRINISH adj resembling brine

BRINK n pl. -S an extreme edge

BRINY n pl. BRINIES the sea

BRINY adj BRINIER, BRINIEST salty

BRIO n pl. BRIOS liveliness

BRIOCHE n pl. -S a rich roll

BRIONY n pl. -NIES bryony

BRIQUET v -QUETTED, -QUETTING, -QUETS to mold into small bricks

BRIS n pl. BRISSES a Jewish circumcision rite

BRISANCE n pl. -S the shattering effect of an explosive **BRISANT** adj

BRISK adj BRISKER, BRISKEST lively

BRISK v -ED, -ING, -S to make brisk

BRISKET *n* pl. -S the breast of an animal

BRISKLY *adv* in a brisk manner

BRISLING *n* pl. -S a small herring

BRISSES pl. of bris

BRISTLE *v* -TLED, -TLING, -TLES to rise stiffly

BRISTLY *adj* -TLIER, -TLIEST stiffly erect

BRISTOL *n* pl. -S a smooth cardboard

BRIT *n* pl. -S a young herring

BRITCHES *n/pl* breeches; trousers

BRITSKA *n* pl. -S an open carriage

BRITT *n* pl. -S brit

BRITTLE *adj* -TLER, -TLEST likely to break

BRITTLE *v* -TLED, -TLING, -TLES to become brittle

BRITTLY *adv* in a brittle manner

BRITZKA *n* pl. -S britska

BRITZSKA *n* pl. -S britska

BRO *n* pl. BROS a brother

BROACH *v* -ED, -ING, -ES to pierce so as to withdraw a liquid

BROACHER *n* pl. -S one that broaches

BROAD *adj* BROADER, BROADEST wide

BROAD *n* pl. -S an expansion of a river

BROADAX *n* pl. -ES a broad-edged ax

BROADAXE *n* pl. -S broadax

BROADEN *v* -ED, -ING, -S to make broad

BROADISH *adj* somewhat broad

BROADLY *adv* in a broad manner

BROCADE *v* -CADED, -CADING, -CADES to weave with a raised design

BROCATEL *n* pl. -S a heavy fabric

BROCCOLI *n* pl. -S a vegetable related to the cabbage

BROCHE *adj* brocaded

BROCHURE *n* pl. -S a pamphlet

BROCK *n* pl. -S a badger

BROCKAGE *n* pl. -S an imperfectly minted coin

BROCKET *n* pl. -S a small, red deer

BROCOLI *n* pl. -S broccoli

BROGAN *n* pl. -S a heavy shoe

BROGUE *n* pl. -S an Irish accent

BROGUERY *n* pl. -ERIES the use of an Irish accent

BROGUISH *adj* resembling a brogue

BROIDER *v* -ED, -ING, -S to adorn with needlework

BROIDERY *n* pl. -DERIES the act of broidering

BROIL *v* -ED, -ING, -S to cook by direct heat

BROILER *n* pl. -S a device for broiling

BROKAGE *n* pl. -S the business of a broker

BROKE past tense of break

BROKEN *adj* shattered **BROKENLY** *adv*

BROKER *v* -ED, -ING, -S to act as a broker (an agent who buys and sells stocks)

BROKING *n* pl. -S the business of a broker

BROLLY *n* pl. -LIES an umbrella

BROMAL *n* pl. -S a medicinal liquid

BROMATE *v* -MATED, -MATING, -MATES to combine with bromine

BROME *n* pl. -S a tall grass

BROMELIN *n* pl. -S an enzyme

BROMIC *adj* containing bromine

BROMID *n* pl. -S bromide

BROMIDE *n* pl. -S a bromine compound

BROMIDIC *adj* commonplace; trite

BROMIN *n* pl. -S bromine

BROMINE *n* pl. -S a volatile liquid element

BROMISM *n* pl. -S a diseased condition of the skin

BROMIZE *v* -MIZED, -MIZING, -MIZES to treat with bromine or a bromide

BROMO *n* pl. -MOS a medicinal compound

BRONC *n* pl. -S bronco

BRONCHI pl. of bronchus

BRONCHIA *n/pl* the main air passages of the lungs

BRONCHO *n* pl. -CHOS bronco

BRONCHUS *n* pl. -CHI a tracheal branch

BRONCO *n* pl. -COS a wild horse

BRONZE *v* BRONZED, BRONZING, BRONZES to make brown

BRONZER *n* pl. -S one that bronzes

BRONZING *n* pl. -S a brownish coloring

BRONZY *adj* BRONZIER, BRONZIEST of a brownish color

BROO *n* pl. BROOS a bree

BROOCH *n* pl. -ES a decorative pin

BROOD *v* -ED, -ING, -S to worry

BROODER *n* pl. -S one that broods

BROODY *adj* BROODIER, BROODIEST tending to brood **BROODILY** *adv*

BROOK *v* -ED, -ING, -S to tolerate

BROOKIE *n* pl. -S a brook trout

BROOKITE *n* pl. -S a mineral

BROOKLET n pl. -S a small brook or creek

BROOM v -ED, -ING, -S to sweep

BROOMY adj BROOMIER, BROOMIEST abounding in broom (a type of shrub)

BROS pl. of bro

BROSE n pl. -S a porridge

BROSY adj smeared with brose

BROTH n pl. -S a thin clear soup

BROTHEL n pl. -S a house of prostitution

BROTHER n pl. -S or BRETHREN a male sibling

BROTHER v -ED, -ING, -S to treat like a brother

BROTHY adj resembling broth

BROUGHAM n pl. -S a type of carriage

BROUGHT past tense of bring

BROUHAHA n pl. -S an uproar

BROW n pl. -S the forehead **BROWED** adj

BROWBAND n pl. -S a band designed to cross the forehead

BROWBEAT v -BEAT, -BEATEN, -BEATING, -BEATS to intimidate

BROWLESS adj lacking eyebrows

BROWN adj BROWNER, BROWNEST of a dark color

BROWN v -ED, -ING, -S to make brown

BROWNIE n pl. -S a small sprite

BROWNIER comparative of browny

BROWNIEST superlative of browny

BROWNISH adj somewhat brown

BROWNOUT n pl. -S a power reduction

BROWNY adj BROWNIER, BROWNIEST somewhat brown

BROWSE v BROWSED, BROWSING, BROWSES to look at casually

BROWSER n pl. -S one that browses

BRR interj brrr

BRRR interj — used to indicate that one feels cold

BRUCELLA n pl. -LAE or -LAS any of a genus of harmful bacteria

BRUCIN n pl. -S brucine

BRUCINE n pl. -S a poisonous alkaloid

BRUGH n pl. -S a borough

BRUIN n pl. -S a bear

BRUISE v BRUISED, BRUISING, BRUISES to injure without breaking the surface of the skin

BRUISER n pl. -S a big, husky man

BRUIT v -ED, -ING, -S to spread news of

BRUITER n pl. -S one that bruits

BRULOT n pl. -S a biting fly

BRULYIE n pl. -S a noisy quarrel

BRULZIE n pl. -S brulyie

BRUMAL adj wintry

BRUMBY n pl. -BIES a wild horse

BRUME n pl. -S fog **BRUMOUS** adj

BRUNCH v -ED, -ING, -ES to eat a late morning meal

BRUNET n pl. -S a dark-haired male

BRUNETTE n pl. -S a dark-haired female

BRUNIZEM n pl. -S a prairie soil

BRUNT n pl. -S the main impact

BRUSH v -ED, -ING, -ES to touch lightly

BRUSHER n pl. -S one that brushes

BRUSHIER comparative of brushy

BRUSHIEST superlative of brushy

BRUSHOFF n pl. -S an abrupt dismissal

BRUSHUP n pl. -S a quick review

BRUSHY adj BRUSHIER, BRUSHIEST shaggy; rough

BRUSK adj BRUSKER, BRUSKEST brusque

BRUSQUE adj BRUSQUER, BRUSQUEST abrupt in manner

BRUT adj very dry

BRUTAL adj cruel; savage **BRUTALLY** adv

BRUTE v BRUTED, BRUTING, BRUTES to shape a diamond by rubbing it with another diamond

BRUTELY adv in a brutal manner

BRUTIFY v -FIED, -FYING, -FIES to make brutal

BRUTING present participle of brute

BRUTISH adj brutal

BRUTISM n pl. -S the state of being brutal

BRUXISM n pl. -S a nervous grinding of the teeth

BRYOLOGY n pl. -GIES the study of mosses

BRYONY n pl. -NIES a climbing plant

BRYOZOAN n pl. -S a type of small aquatic animal

BUB n pl. -S young fellow

BUBAL n pl. -S a large antelope

BUBALE n pl. -S bubal

BUBALINE adj pertaining to the bubal

BUBALIS n pl. -LISES bubal

BUBBLE	v -BLED, -BLING, -BLES to form bubbles (bodies of gas contained within a liquid)
BUBBLER	n pl. -S a drinking fountain
BUBBLY	n pl. -BLIES champagne
BUBBLY	adj -BLIER, -BLIEST full of bubbles
BUBINGA	n pl. -S an African tree
BUBO	n pl. -BOES a swelling of a lymph gland **BUBOED** adj
BUBONIC	adj pertaining to a bubo
BUCCAL	adj pertaining to the cheek **BUCCALLY** adv
BUCK	v -ED, -ING, -S to leap forward and upward suddenly
BUCKAROO	n pl. -ROOS a cowboy
BUCKAYRO	n pl. -ROS buckaroo
BUCKBEAN	n pl. -S a marsh plant
BUCKEEN	n pl. -S a poor man who acts as if wealthy
BUCKER	n pl. -S a bucking horse
BUCKEROO	n pl. -ROOS buckaroo
BUCKET	v -ED, -ING, -S to hurry
BUCKEYE	n pl. -S a nut-bearing tree
BUCKISH	adj foppish
BUCKLE	v -LED, -LING, -LES to bend under pressure
BUCKLER	v -ED, -ING, -S to shield
BUCKO	n pl. BUCKOES a bully
BUCKRAM	v -ED, -ING, -S to stiffen
BUCKSAW	n pl. -S a wood-cutting saw
BUCKSHEE	n pl. -S something extra obtained free
BUCKSHOT	n pl. -S a large lead shot
BUCKSKIN	n pl. -S the skin of a male deer
BUCKTAIL	n pl. -S a fishing lure
BUCOLIC	n pl. -S a pastoral poem
BUD	v BUDDED, BUDDING, BUDS to put forth buds (undeveloped plant parts)
BUDDER	n pl. -S one that buds
BUDDIED	past tense of buddy
BUDDIES	present 3d person sing. of buddy
BUDDING	n pl. -S a type of asexual reproduction
BUDDLE	n pl. -S an apparatus on which crushed ore is washed
BUDDLEIA	n pl. -S a tropical shrub
BUDDY	v -DIED, -DYING, -DIES to become close friends
BUDGE	v BUDGED, BUDGING, BUDGES to move slightly
BUDGER	n pl. -S one that budges

BUDGET	v -ED, -ING, -S to estimate expenditures
BUDGETER	n pl. -S one that budgets
BUDGIE	n pl. -S a small parrot
BUDGING	present participle of budge
BUDLESS	adj being without buds
BUDLIKE	adj resembling a bud
BUDWORM	n pl. -S a caterpillar that eats buds
BUFF	v -ED, -ING, -S to polish **BUFFABLE** adj
BUFFALO	n pl. -LOES or -LOS an ox-like animal
BUFFALO	v -ED, -ING, -ES to intimidate
BUFFER	v -ED, -ING, -S to cushion
BUFFET	v -ED, -ING, -S to hit sharply
BUFFETER	n pl. -S one that buffets
BUFFI	a pl. of buffo
BUFFIER	comparative of buffy
BUFFIEST	superlative of buffy
BUFFO	n pl. -FI or -FOS an operatic clown
BUFFOON	n pl. -S a clown
BUFFY	adj BUFFIER, BUFFIEST of a yellowish-brown color
BUG	v BUGGED, BUGGING, BUGS to annoy
BUGABOO	n pl. -BOOS a bugbear
BUGBANE	n pl. -S a perennial herb
BUGBEAR	n pl. -S an object or source of dread
BUGEYE	n pl. -S a small boat
BUGGED	past tense of bug
BUGGER	v -ED, -ING, -S to damn
BUGGERY	n pl. -GERIES sodomy
BUGGING	present participle of bug
BUGGY	n pl. -GIES a light carriage
BUGGY	adj -GIER, -GIEST infested with bugs
BUGHOUSE	n pl. -S an insane asylum
BUGLE	v -GLED, -GLING, -GLES to play a bugle (a brass wind instrument)
BUGLER	n pl. -S one that plays a bugle
BUGLOSS	n pl. -ES a coarse plant
BUGSEED	n pl. -S an annual herb
BUGSHA	n pl. -S buqsha
BUHL	n pl. -S a style of furniture decoration
BUHLWORK	n pl. -S buhl
BUHR	n pl. -S a heavy stone
BUILD	v BUILT or BUILDED, BUILDING, BUILDS to construct
BUILDER	n pl. -S one that builds
BUILDING	n pl. -S something that is built

BUILDUP n pl. -S an accumulation

BUILT a past tense of build

BUIRDLY adj burly

BULB n pl. -S an underground bud
BULBAR, BULBED adj

BULBEL n pl. -S bulbil

BULBIL n pl. -S a small bulb

BULBLET n pl. -S a small bulb

BULBOUS adj bulb-shaped; bulging

BULBUL n pl. -S a songbird

BULGE v BULGED, BULGING,
BULGES to swell out

BULGER n pl. -S a golf club

BULGUR n pl. -S crushed wheat

BULGY adj BULGIER, BULGIEST
bulging

BULIMIA n pl. -S insatiable appetite
BULIMIAC adj

BULIMIC n pl. -S one who is affected
with bulimia

BULK v -ED, -ING, -S to gather into
a mass

BULKAGE n pl. -S a peristaltic stimulant

BULKHEAD n pl. -S an upright partition in
a ship

BULKY adj BULKIER, BULKIEST
massive BULKILY adv

BULL v -ED, -ING, -S to push ahead

BULLA n pl. -LAE a large blister

BULLACE n pl. -S a purple plum

BULLATE adj having a blistered
appearance

BULLBAT n pl. -S a nocturnal bird

BULLDOG v -DOGGED, -DOGGING,
-DOGS to throw a steer

BULLDOZE v -DOZED, -DOZING,
-DOZES to bully

BULLET v -ED, -ING, -S to zip along

BULLETIN v -ED, -ING, -S to issue a
news item

BULLFROG n pl. -S a large frog

BULLHEAD n pl. -S a freshwater catfish

BULLHORN n pl. -S an electric megaphone

BULLIED past tense of bully

BULLIER comparative of bully

BULLIES present 3d person sing. of
bully

BULLIEST superlative of bully

BULLION n pl. -S uncoined gold or silver

BULLISH adj stubborn

BULLNECK n pl. -S a thick neck

BULLNOSE n pl. -S a disease of swine

BULLOCK n pl. -S a castrated bull
BULLOCKY adj

BULLOUS adj resembling bullae

BULLPEN n pl. -S an enclosure for bulls

BULLPOUT n pl. -S a bullhead

BULLRING n pl. -S a bullfight arena

BULLRUSH n pl. -ES bulrush

BULLSHOT n pl. -S a drink made of vodka
and bouillon

BULLWEED n pl. -S knapweed

BULLWHIP v -WHIPPED, -WHIPPING,
-WHIPS to strike with a long
whip

BULLY v -LIED, -LYING, -LIES to
treat abusively

BULLY adj -LIER, -LIEST wonderful

BULLYBOY n pl. -BOYS a ruffian

BULLYRAG v -RAGGED, -RAGGING,
-RAGS to bully

BULRUSH n pl. -ES a tall marsh plant

BULWARK v -ED, -ING, -S to fortify with a
defensive wall

BUM v BUMMED, BUMMING,
BUMS to live idly

BUM adj BUMMER, BUMMEST of
little value; worthless

BUMBLE v -BLED, -BLING, -BLES to
bungle

BUMBLER n pl. -S one that bumbles

BUMBLING n pl. -S an instance of
clumsiness

BUMBOAT n pl. -S a boat used to peddle
wares to larger ships

BUMF n pl. -S paperwork

BUMKIN n pl. -S a ship's spar

BUMMED past tense of bum

BUMMER n pl. -S one that bums

BUMMEST superlative of bum

BUMMING present participle of bum

BUMP v -ED, -ING, -S to knock
against

BUMPER v -ED, -ING, -S to fill to the
brim

BUMPH n pl. -S bumf

BUMPKIN n pl. -S an awkward rustic

BUMPY adj BUMPIER, BUMPIEST of
uneven surface BUMPILY adv

BUN n pl. -S a small bread roll

BUNCH v -ED, -ING, -ES to group
together

BUNCHY adj BUNCHIER, BUNCHIEST
clustered BUNCHILY adv

BUNCO v -ED, -ING, -S to swindle

BUNCOMBE n pl. -S nonsense

BUND n pl. -S a political association

BUNDIST n pl. -S a member of a bund

BUNDLE v -DLED, -DLING, -DLES to
fasten a group of objects
together

BUNDLER n pl. -S one that bundles

BUNDLING *n* pl. -S a former courtship custom

BUNDT *n* pl. -S a type of cake pan

BUNG *v* -ED, -ING, -S to plug with a cork or stopper

BUNGALOW *n* pl. -S a small cottage

BUNGEE *n* pl. -S an elasticized cord

BUNGHOLE *n* pl. -S a hole in a keg or barrel

BUNGLE *v* -GLED, -GLING, -GLES to work, make, or do clumsily

BUNGLER *n* pl. -S one that bungles

BUNGLING *n* pl. -S unskillful handling

BUNION *n* pl. -S a painful swelling of the foot

BUNK *v* -ED, -ING, -S to go to bed

BUNKER *v* -ED, -ING, -S to store in a large bin

BUNKMATE *n* pl. -S a person with whom sleeping quarters are shared

BUNKO *v* -ED, -ING, -S to bunco

BUNKUM *n* pl. -S nonsense

BUNN *n* pl. -S a bun

BUNNY *n* pl. -NIES a rabbit

BUNRAKU *n* pl. -S a Japanese puppet show

BUNT *v* -ED, -ING, -S to butt

BUNTER *n* pl. -S one that bunts

BUNTING *n* pl. -S a fabric used for flags

BUNTLINE *n* pl. -S a rope used to haul up a sail

BUNYA *n* pl. -S an evergreen tree

BUOY *v* -ED, -ING, -S to mark with a buoy (a warning float)

BUOYAGE *n* pl. -S a group of buoys

BUOYANCE *n* pl. -S buoyancy

BUOYANCY *n* pl. -CIES the tendency to float

BUOYANT *adj* having buoyancy

BUPPIE *n* pl. -S a black professional person working in a city

BUQSHA *n* pl. -S a monetary unit of Yemen

BUR *v* BURRED, BURRING, BURS to burr

BURA *n* pl. -S buran

BURAN *n* pl. -S a violent windstorm

BURBLE *v* -BLED, -BLING, -BLES to speak quickly and excitedly

BURBLER *n* pl. -S one that burbles

BURBLY *adj* -BLIER, -BLIEST burbling

BURBOT *n* pl. -S a freshwater fish

BURBS *n/pl* the suburbs

BURD *n* pl. -S a maiden

BURDEN *v* -ED, -ING, -S to load heavily

BURDENER *n* pl. -S one that burdens

BURDIE *n* pl. -S burd

BURDOCK *n* pl. -S a coarse weed

BUREAU *n* pl. -REAUS or -REAUX a chest of drawers

BURET *n* pl. -S burette

BURETTE *n* pl. -S a measuring tube

BURG *n* pl. -S a city or town

BURGAGE *n* pl. -S a feudal tenure

BURGEE *n* pl. -S a small flag

BURGEON *v* -ED, -ING, -S to develop rapidly

BURGER *n* pl. -S a hamburger

BURGESS *n* pl. -ES a citizen of an English borough

BURGH *n* pl. -S a Scottish borough

BURGHAL *adj*

BURGHER *n* pl. -S a citizen of a borough

BURGLAR *n* pl. -S one who commits burglary

BURGLARY *n* pl. -GLARIES a felonious theft

BURGLE *v* -GLED, -GLING, -GLES to commit burglary

BURGONET *n* pl. -S an open helmet

BURGOO *n* pl. -GOOS a thick oatmeal

BURGOUT *n* pl. -S burgoo

BURGRAVE *n* pl. -S a German nobleman

BURGUNDY *n* pl. -DIES a red wine

BURIAL *n* pl. -S the act of burying

BURIED past tense of bury

BURIER *n* pl. -S one that buries

BURIES present 3d person sing. of bury

BURIN *n* pl. -S an engraving tool

BURKE *v* BURKED, BURKING, BURKES to murder by suffocation

BURKER *n* pl. -S one that burkes

BURKITE *n* pl. -S a burker

BURL *v* -ED, -ING, -S to finish cloth by removing lumps

BURLAP *n* pl. -S a coarse fabric

BURLER *n* pl. -S one that burls

BURLESK *n* pl. -S a type of stage show

BURLEY *n* pl. -LEYS a light tobacco

BURLY *adj* -LIER, -LIEST heavy and muscular **BURLILY** *adv*

BURN *v* BURNED or BURNT, BURNING, BURNS to destroy by fire

BURNABLE *n* pl. -S something that can be burned

BURNER *n* pl. -S one that burns

BURNET *n* pl. -S a perennial herb

BURNIE *n* pl. -S a brooklet

BURNING *n* pl. -S the firing of ceramic materials

BURNISH v -ED, -ING, -ES to polish
BURNOOSE n pl. -S a hooded cloak
BURNOUS n pl. -ES burnoose
BURNOUT n pl. -S a destructive fire
BURNT a past tense of burn
BURP v -ED, -ING, -S to belch
BURR v -ED, -ING, -S to remove a rough edge from
BURRED past tense of bur
BURRER n pl. -S one that burrs
BURRIER comparative of burry
BURRIEST superlative of burry
BURRING present participle of bur
BURRITO n pl. -TOS a tortilla rolled around a filling
BURRO n pl. -ROS a small donkey
BURROW v -ED, -ING, -S to dig a hole or tunnel in the ground
BURROWER n pl. -S one that burrows
BURRY adj -RIER, -RIEST prickly
BURSA n pl. -SAS or -SAE a bodily pouch **BURSAL** adj
BURSAR n pl. -S a college treasurer
BURSARY n pl. -RIES a college treasury
BURSATE adj pertaining to a bursa
BURSE n pl. -S a small bag or pouch
BURSEED n pl. -S a coarse weed
BURSERA adj designating a family of shrubs and trees
BURSITIS n pl. -TISES inflammation of a bursa
BURST v BURST or BURSTED, BURSTING, BURSTS to break open suddenly or violently
BURSTER n pl. -S one that bursts
BURSTONE n pl. -S a heavy stone
BURTHEN v -ED, -ING, -S to burden
BURTON n pl. -S a hoisting tackle
BURWEED n pl. -S a coarse weed
BURY v BURIED, BURYING, BURIES to put in the ground and cover with earth
BUS v BUSED, BUSING, BUSES or BUSSED, BUSSING, BUSSES to transport by bus (a large motor vehicle)
BUSBAR n pl. -S a type of electrical conductor
BUSBOY n pl. -BOYS a waiter's assistant
BUSBY n pl. -BIES a tall fur hat
BUSH v -ED, -ING, -ES to cover with bushes (shrubs)
BUSHBUCK n pl. -S a small antelope

BUSHEL v -ELED, -ELING, -ELS or -ELLED, -ELLING, -ELS to mend clothing
BUSHELER n pl. -S one that bushels
BUSHER n pl. -S a minor league baseball player
BUSHFIRE n pl. -S a fire in a wooded area
BUSHGOAT n pl. -S a bushbuck
BUSHIDO n pl. -DOS the code of the samurai
BUSHIER comparative of bushy
BUSHIEST superlative of bushy
BUSHILY adv in a bushy manner
BUSHING n pl. -S a lining for a hole
BUSHLAND n pl. -S unsettled forest land
BUSHLESS adj having no bushes
BUSHLIKE adj resembling a bush
BUSHMAN n pl. -MEN a woodsman
BUSHPIG n pl. -S a wild African pig
BUSHTIT n pl. -S a titmouse
BUSHWA n pl. -S nonsense
BUSHWAH n pl. -S bushwa
BUSHY adj BUSHIER, BUSHIEST covered with bushes
BUSIED past tense of busy
BUSIER comparative of busy
BUSIES present 3d person sing. of busy
BUSIEST superlative of busy
BUSILY adv in a busy manner
BUSINESS n pl. -ES an occupation, profession, or trade
BUSING n pl. -S the act of transporting by bus
BUSK v -ED, -ING, -S to prepare
BUSKER n pl. -S a roaming entertainer
BUSKIN n pl. -S a high shoe **BUSKINED** adj
BUSLOAD n pl. -S a load that fills a bus
BUSMAN n pl. -MEN a bus operator
BUSS v -ED, -ING, -ES to kiss
BUSSED a past tense of bus
BUSSES a present 3d person sing. of bus
BUSSING n pl. -S busing
BUST v -ED, -ING, -S to burst
BUSTARD n pl. -S a game bird
BUSTER n pl. -S one that breaks up something
BUSTIC n pl. -S a tropical tree
BUSTIER n pl. -S a woman's undergarment
BUSTLE v -TLED, -TLING, -TLES to move energetically

BUSTLINE n pl. -S the distance around the bust (the upper torso of a woman)

BUSTY adj BUSTIER, BUSTIEST full-bosomed

BUSULFAN n pl. -S a medicine

BUSY adj BUSIER, BUSIEST occupied

BUSY v BUSIED, BUSYING, BUSIES to make busy

BUSYBODY n pl. -BODIES a nosy person

BUSYNESS n pl. -ES the state of being busy

BUSYWORK n pl. -S active but valueless work

BUT n pl. -S a flatfish

BUTANE n pl. -S a flammable gas

BUTANOL n pl. -S a flammable alcohol

BUTANONE n pl. -S a flammable ketone

BUTCH n pl. -ES a lesbian with a masculine appearance or manner

BUTCHER v -ED, -ING, -S to slaughter

BUTCHERY n pl. -ERIES wanton or cruel killing

BUTE n pl. BUTE a pain-relieving drug

BUTENE n pl. -S butylene

BUTEO n pl. -TEOS a hawk

BUTLE v -LED, -LING, -LES to serve as a butler

BUTLER n pl. -S a male servant

BUTLERY n pl. -LERIES a storage room

BUTLES present 3d person sing. of butle

BUTLING present participle of butle

BUTT v -ED, -ING, -S to hit with the head

BUTTALS n/pl boundary lines

BUTTE n pl. -S an isolated hill

BUTTER v -ED, -ING, -S to spread with butter (a milk product)

BUTTERY adj -TERIER, -TERIEST containing butter

BUTTERY n pl. -TERIES a wine cellar

BUTTIES pl. of butty

BUTTOCK n pl. -S either of the two rounded parts of the rump

BUTTON v -ED, -ING, -S to fasten with a button (a small disk)

BUTTONER n pl. -S one that buttons

BUTTONY adj resembling a button

BUTTRESS v -ED, -ING, -ES to prop up

BUTTY n pl. -TIES a fellow workman

BUTUT n pl. -S a monetary unit of Gambia

BUTYL n pl. -S a hydrocarbon radical

BUTYLATE v -ATED, -ATING, -ATES to add a butyl to

BUTYLENE n pl. -S a gaseous hydrocarbon

BUTYRAL n pl. -S a chemical compound

BUTYRATE n pl. -S a chemical salt

BUTYRIC adj derived from butter

BUTYRIN n pl. -S a chemical compound

BUTYROUS adj resembling butter

BUTYRYL n pl. -S a radical of butyric acid

BUXOM adj -OMER, -OMEST healthily plump BUXOMLY adv

BUY v BOUGHT, BUYING, BUYS to purchase BUYABLE adj

BUYBACK n pl. -S the repurchase by a corporation of its own stock

BUYER n pl. -S one that buys

BUYOUT n pl. -S the purchase of a business

BUZUKI n pl. -KIA or -KIS bouzouki

BUZZ v -ED, -ING, -ES to make a vibrating sound

BUZZARD n pl. -S a large bird of prey

BUZZER n pl. -S a signaling device

BUZZWIG n pl. -S a large, thick wig

BUZZWORD n pl. -S a word used to impress someone

BWANA n pl. -S master; boss

BY n pl. BYS a pass in certain card games

BYE n pl. -S a side issue

BYELAW n pl. -S bylaw

BYGONE n pl. -S a past occurrence

BYLAW n pl. -S a secondary law

BYLINE v -LINED, -LINING, -LINES to write under a byline (a line giving the author's name)

BYLINER n pl. -S one that writes under a byline

BYNAME n pl. -S a secondary name

BYPASS v -ED, -ING, -ES to avoid by going around

BYPAST adj past; gone by

BYPATH n pl. -S an indirect road

BYPLAY n pl. -PLAYS secondary action

BYRE n pl. -S a cowshed

BYRL v -ED, -ING, -S to birle

BYRNIE n pl. -S an armored shirt

BYROAD n pl. -S a side road

BYSSUS n pl. BYSSUSES or BYSSI a fine linen

BYSTREET n pl. -S a side street

BYTALK   n pl. -S small talk
BYTE   n pl. -S a group of adjacent binary digits
BYWAY   n pl. -WAYS a side road

BYWORD   n pl. -S a well-known saying
BYWORK   n pl. -S work done during leisure time
BYZANT   n pl. -S bezant

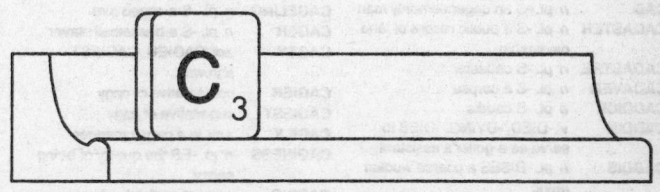

CAB   v CABBED, CABBING, CABS to take or drive a taxicab

CABAL   v -BALLED, -BALLING, -BALS to conspire

CABALA   n pl. -S an occult or secret doctrine

CABALISM   n pl. -S adherence to a cabala

CABALIST   n pl. -S one who practices cabalism

CABALLED   past tense of cabal

CABALLING   present participle of cabal

CABANA   n pl. -S a small cabin

CABARET   n pl. -S a music hall

CABBAGE   v -BAGED, -BAGING, -BAGES to steal

CABBALA   n pl. -S cabala

CABBALAH   n pl. -S cabala

CABBED   past tense of cab

CABBIE   n pl. -S cabby

CABBING   present participle of cab

CABBY   n pl. -BIES a driver of a cab

CABER   n pl. -S a heavy pole thrown as a trial of strength

CABERNET   n pl. -S a dry red wine

CABESTRO   n pl. -TROS a lasso

CABEZON   n pl. -S a large, edible fish

CABEZONE   n pl. -S cabezon

CABILDO   n pl. -DOS a town council

CABIN   v -ED, -ING, -S to live in a cabin (a roughly built house)

CABINET   n pl. -S a piece of furniture with shelves and drawers

CABLE   v -BLED, -BLING, -BLES to fasten with a cable (a heavy rope)

CABLET   n pl. -S a small cable

CABLEWAY   n pl. -WAYS a suspended cable

CABLING   present participle of cable

CABMAN   n pl. -MEN a driver of a cab

CABOB   n pl. -S kabob

CABOCHED   adj full-faced — used of an animal's head in heraldry

CABOCHON   n pl. -S a precious stone

CABOMBA   n pl. -S an aquatic plant

CABOODLE   n pl. -S a collection

CABOOSE   n pl. -S the last car of a freight train

CABOSHED   adj caboched

CABOTAGE   n pl. -S coastal trade

CABRESTA   n pl. -S cabestro

CABRESTO   n pl. -TOS cabestro

CABRETTA   n pl. -S a soft leather

CABRILLA   n pl. -S a sea bass

CABRIOLE   n pl. -S a curved furniture leg

CABSTAND   n pl. -S a place where cabs await hire

CACA   n pl. -S excrement

CACAO   n pl. -CAOS a tropical tree

CACHALOT   n pl. -S a large whale

CACHE   v CACHED, CACHING, CACHES to store in a hiding place

CACHEPOT   n pl. -S an ornamental container for a flowerpot

CACHET   v -ED, -ING, -S to print a design on an envelope

CACHEXIA   n pl. -S general ill health CACHEXIC adj

CACHEXY   n pl. -CHEXIES cachexia

CACHING   present participle of cache

CACHOU   n pl. -S catechu

CACHUCHA   n pl. -S a Spanish dance

CACIQUE   n pl. -S a tropical oriole

CACKLE   v -LED, -LING, -LES to make the sound of a hen

CACKLER   n pl. -S one that cackles

CACODYL   n pl. -S a poisonous liquid

CACOMIXL n pl. -S a raccoon-like mammal

CACTUS n pl. -TI or -TUSES a plant native to arid regions **CACTOID** adj

CAD n pl. -S an ungentlemanly man

CADASTER n pl. -S a public record of land ownership

CADASTRE n pl. -S cadaster

CADAVER n pl. -S a corpse

CADDICE n pl. -S caddis

CADDIE v -DIED, -DYING, -DIES to serve as a golfer's assistant

CADDIS n pl. -DISES a coarse woolen fabric

CADDISH adj resembling a cad

CADDY v -DIED, -DYING, -DIES to caddie

CADE n pl. -S a European shrub

CADELLE n pl. -S a small, black beetle

CADENCE v -DENCED, -DENCING, -DENCES to make rhythmic

CADENCY n pl. -CIES a rhythm

CADENT adj having rhythm

CADENZA n pl. -S an elaborate musical passage

CADET n pl. -S a student at a military school

CADGE v CADGED, CADGING, CADGES to get by begging

CADGER n pl. -S one that cadges

CADGY adj cheerful

CADI n pl. -S a Muslim judge

CADMIUM n pl. -S a metallic element **CADMIC** adj

CADRE n pl. -S a nucleus of trained personnel

CADUCEUS n pl. -CEI a heraldic wand or staff **CADUCEAN** adj

CADUCITY n pl. -TIES senility

CADUCOUS adj transitory; perishable

CAECUM n pl. -CA cecum **CAECAL** adj **CAECALLY** adv

CAEOMA n pl. -S a spore-forming organ of a fungus

CAESAR n pl. -S an emperor

CAESIUM n pl. -S cesium

CAESTUS n pl. -ES cestus

CAESURA n pl. -RAS or -RAE a pause in a line of verse **CAESURAL**, **CAESURIC** adj

CAFE n pl. -S a small restaurant

CAFF n pl. -S a cafe

CAFFEIN n pl. -S caffeine

CAFFEINE n pl. -S a bitter alkaloid used as a stimulant

CAFTAN n pl. -S a full-length tunic

CAGE v CAGED, CAGING, CAGES to confine

CAGEFUL n pl. -S the number held in a cage (an enclosure)

CAGELING n pl. -S a caged bird

CAGER n pl. -S a basketball player

CAGEY adj CAGIER, CAGIEST shrewd

CAGIER comparative of cagy

CAGIEST superlative of cagy

CAGILY adv in a cagey manner

CAGINESS n pl. -ES the quality of being cagey

CAGING present participle of cage

CAGY adj CAGIER, CAGIEST cagey

CAHIER n pl. -S a notebook

CAHOOT n pl. -S partnership

CAHOW n pl. -S a sea bird

CAID n pl. -S a Muslim leader

CAIMAN n pl. -S a tropical reptile

CAIN n pl. -S kain

CAIQUE n pl. -S a long, narrow rowboat

CAIRD n pl. -S a gypsy

CAIRN n pl. -S a mound of stones set up as a memorial **CAIRNED**, **CAIRNY** adj

CAISSON n pl. -S a watertight chamber

CAITIFF n pl. -S a despicable person

CAJAPUT n pl. -S cajeput

CAJEPUT n pl. -S an Australian tree

CAJOLE v -JOLED, -JOLING, -JOLES to persuade by flattery

CAJOLER n pl. -S one that cajoles

CAJOLERY n pl. -ERIES persuasion by flattery

CAJOLING present participle of cajole

CAJON n pl. -ES a steep-sided canyon

CAJUPUT n pl. -S cajeput

CAKE v CAKED, CAKING, CAKES to form into a hardened mass

CAKEWALK v -ED, -ING, -S to step stylishly

CAKEY adj CAKIER, CAKIEST tending to form lumps

CAKY adj CAKIER, CAKIEST cakey

CALABASH n pl. -ES a gourd

CALADIUM n pl. -S a tropical plant

CALAMAR n pl. -S calamary

CALAMARI n pl. -S squid used as food

CALAMARY n pl. -MARIES a squid

CALAMI pl. of calamus

CALAMINE *v* -MINED, -MINING, -MINES to apply an ointment for skin ailments

CALAMINT *n pl.* -S a perennial herb

CALAMITE *n pl.* -S an extinct treelike plant

CALAMITY *n pl.* -TIES a grievous misfortune

CALAMUS *n pl.* -MI a marsh plant

CALANDO *adj* gradually diminishing

CALASH *n pl.* -ES a light carriage

CALATHOS *n pl.* -THI a fruit basket

CALATHUS *n pl.* -THI calathos

CALCANEA *n/pl* calcanei

CALCANEI *n/pl* bones of the heel

CALCAR *n pl.* -CARIA an anatomical projection

CALCAR *n pl.* -S a type of oven

CALCEATE *adj* wearing shoes

CALCES a pl. of calx

CALCIC *adj* pertaining to lime or calcium

CALCIFIC *adj* containing salts of calcium

CALCIFY *v* -FIED, -FYING, -FIES to harden

CALCINE *v* -CINED, -CINING, -CINES to reduce to a calx by heat

CALCITE *n pl.* -S a mineral **CALCITIC** *adj*

CALCIUM *n pl.* -S a metallic element

CALCSPAR *n pl.* -S a calcite

CALCTUFA *n pl.* -S a mineral deposit

CALCTUFF *n pl.* -S a calctufa

CALCULUS *n pl.* -LI or -LUSES a branch of mathematics

CALDARIA *n/pl* rooms for taking hot baths

CALDERA *n pl.* -S a large crater

CALDRON *n pl.* -S a large kettle or boiler

CALECHE *n pl.* -S calash

CALENDAL *adj* pertaining to calends

CALENDAR *v* -ED, -ING, -S to schedule

CALENDER *v* -ED, -ING, -S to smooth by pressing between rollers

CALENDS *n pl.* CALENDS the first day of the Roman month

CALESA *n pl.* -S a calash

CALF *n pl.* CALVES or CALFS a young cow or bull **CALFLIKE** *adj*

CALFSKIN *n pl.* -S the skin of a calf

CALIBER *n pl.* -S the diameter of a gun barrel

CALIBRE *n pl.* -S caliber **CALIBRED** *adj*

CALICES pl. of calix

CALICHE *n pl.* -S a mineral deposit

CALICLE *n pl.* -S a cup-shaped, anatomical structure

CALICO *n pl.* -COES or -COS a cotton fabric

CALIF *n pl.* -S caliph

CALIFATE *n pl.* -S the domain of a calif

CALIPASH *n pl.* -ES an edible part of a turtle

CALIPEE *n pl.* -S an edible part of a turtle

CALIPER *v* -ED, -ING, -S to use a type of measuring device

CALIPH *n pl.* -S a Muslim leader **CALIPHAL** *adj*

CALISAYA *n pl.* -S the medicinal bark of the cinchona

CALIX *n pl.* -LICES a cup

CALK *v* -ED, -ING, -S to caulk

CALKER *n pl.* -S one that calks

CALKIN *n pl.* -S a gripping projection on a horseshoe

CALL *v* -ED, -ING, -S to summon **CALLABLE** *adj*

CALLA *n pl.* -S a tropical plant

CALLALOO *n pl.* -LOOS a crabmeat soup

CALLAN *n pl.* -S callant

CALLANT *n pl.* -S a lad

CALLBACK *n pl.* -S a recall of a defective product

CALLBOY *n pl.* -BOYS a bellboy

CALLER *n pl.* -S one that calls

CALLET *n pl.* -S a prostitute

CALLING *n pl.* -S a vocation or profession

CALLIOPE *n pl.* -S a keyboard musical instrument

CALLIPEE *n pl.* -S calipee

CALLIPER *v* -ED, -ING, -S to caliper

CALLOSE *n pl.* -S a part of a plant cell wall

CALLOUS *v* -ED, -ING, -ES to make or become hard

CALLOW *adj* -LOWER, -LOWEST immature

CALLUS *v* -ED, -ING, -ES to form a hard growth

CALM *adj* CALMER, CALMEST free from agitation **CALMLY** *adv*

CALM *v* -ED, -ING, -S to make calm

CALMNESS *n pl.* -ES the state of being calm

CALO *n pl.* CALO a Spanish argot used by Chicano youths

CALOMEL *n pl.* -S a chemical compound used as a purgative

CALORIC *n pl.* -S heat

CALORIE n pl. -S a unit of heat

CALORIZE v -RIZED, -RIZING, -RIZES to coat steel with aluminum

CALORY n pl. -RIES calorie

CALOTTE n pl. -S a skullcap

CALOTYPE n pl. -S a kind of photograph

CALOYER n pl. -S a monk of the Eastern Church

CALPAC n pl. -S a sheepskin hat

CALPACK n pl. -S calpac

CALQUE v CALQUED, CALQUING, CALQUES to model a word's meaning upon that of an analogous word in another language

CALTHROP n pl. -S caltrop

CALTRAP n pl. -S caltrop

CALTROP n pl. -S a spiny plant

CALUMET n pl. -S a ceremonial pipe

CALUMNY n pl. -NIES a false and malicious accusation

CALUTRON n pl. -S a device used for separating isotopes

CALVADOS n pl. -ES a dry apple brandy

CALVARIA n pl. -S the dome of the skull

CALVARY n pl. -RIES a representation of the Crucifixion

CALVE v CALVED, CALVING, CALVES to give birth to a calf

CALVES a pl. of calf

CALX n pl. -ES or CALCES a mineral residue

CALYCATE adj calycine

CALYCEAL adj calycine

CALYCES a pl. of calyx

CALYCINE adj pertaining to a calyx

CALYCLE n pl. -S an outer calyx

CALYCULI n/pl small, cup-shaped structures

CALYPSO n pl. -SOS or -SOES an improvised song

CALYPTER n pl. -S calyptra

CALYPTRA n pl. -S a hood-shaped organ of flowers

CALYX n pl. -LYXES or -LYCES the outer protective covering of a flower

CALZONE n pl. -S a turnover with a savory filling

CAM n pl. -S a rotating or sliding piece of machinery

CAMAIL n pl. -S a piece of armor for the neck **CAMAILED** adj

CAMAS n pl. -ES camass

CAMASS n pl. -ES a perennial herb

CAMBER v -ED, -ING, -S to arch slightly

CAMBIA a pl. of cambium

CAMBIAL adj pertaining to cambium

CAMBISM n pl. -S the theory and practice of exchange in commerce

CAMBIST n pl. -S a dealer in bills of exchange

CAMBIUM n pl. -BIUMS or -BIA a layer of plant tissue

CAMBOGIA n pl. -S a gum resin

CAMBRIC n pl. -S a fine linen

CAME n pl. -S a leaden window rod

CAMEL n pl. -S a large, humped mammal

CAMELEER n pl. -S a camel driver

CAMELIA n pl. -S camellia

CAMELLIA n pl. -S a tropical shrub

CAMEO v -ED, -ING, -S to portray in sharp, delicate relief

CAMERA n pl. -ERAS or -ERAE a judge's chamber **CAMERAL** adj

CAMION n pl. -S a military truck

CAMISA n pl. -S a shirt or chemise

CAMISADE n pl. -S camisado

CAMISADO n pl. -DOS or -DOES an attack made at night

CAMISE n pl. -S a loose shirt or gown

CAMISIA n pl. -S camise

CAMISOLE n pl. -S a brief negligee

CAMLET n pl. -S a durable fabric

CAMOMILE n pl. -S a medicinal herb

CAMORRA n pl. -S an unscrupulous secret society

CAMP v -ED, -ING, -S to live in the open

CAMPAGNA n pl. -PAGNE a flat, open plain

CAMPAIGN v -ED, -ING, -S to conduct a series of operations to reach a specific goal

CAMPER n pl. -S one that camps

CAMPFIRE n pl. -S an outdoor fire

CAMPHENE n pl. -S camphine

CAMPHINE n pl. -S an explosive liquid

CAMPHIRE n pl. -S a flowering plant

CAMPHOL n pl. -S borneol

CAMPHOR n pl. -S a volatile compound

CAMPI pl. of campo

CAMPIER comparative of campy

CAMPIEST superlative of campy

CAMPILY adv in a campy manner

CAMPING n pl. -S the act of living outdoors

CAMPION n pl. -S an herb

CAMPO *n pl.* -PI an open space in a town

CAMPO *n pl.* -POS a level, grassy plain

CAMPONG *n pl.* -S kampong

CAMPOREE *n pl.* -S a gathering of Boy Scouts

CAMPSITE *n pl.* -S an area suitable for camping

CAMPUS *v* -ED, -ING, -ES to restrict a student to the school grounds

CAMPY *adj* CAMPIER, CAMPIEST comically exaggerated

CAMSHAFT *n pl.* -S a shaft fitted with cams

CAN *v* CANNED, CANNING, CANS to put in a can (a cylindrical container)

CAN *v* present sing. 2d person CAN or CANST, past sing. 2d person COULD, COULDEST, or COULDST — used as an auxiliary to express ability

CANAILLE *n pl.* -S the common people

CANAKIN *n pl.* -S cannikin

CANAL *v* -NALLED, -NALLING, -NALS or -NALED, -NALING, -NALS to dig an artificial waterway through

CANALISE *v* -ISED, -ISING, -ISES to canalize

CANALIZE *v* -IZED, -IZING, -IZES to canal

CANALLED a past tense of canal

CANALLER *n pl.* -S a freight boat

CANALLING a present participle of canal

CANAPE *n pl.* -S a food served before a meal

CANARD *n pl.* -S a false story

CANARY *n pl.* -NARIES a songbird

CANASTA *n pl.* -S a card game

CANCAN *n pl.* -S a dance marked by high kicking

CANCEL *v* -CELED, -CELING, -CELS or -CELLED, -CELLING, -CELS to annul

CANCELER *n pl.* -S one that cancels

CANCER *n pl.* -S a malignant growth

CANCHA *n pl.* -S a jai alai court

CANCROID *n pl.* -S a skin cancer

CANDELA *n pl.* -S a unit of luminous intensity

CANDENT *adj* glowing

CANDID *adj* -DIDER, -DIDEST frank and sincere

CANDID *n pl.* -S an unposed photograph

CANDIDA *n pl.* -S a parasitic fungus

CANDIDLY *adv* in a candid manner

CANDIED past tense of candy

CANDIES present 3d person sing. of candy

CANDLE *v* -DLED, -DLING, -DLES to examine eggs in front of a light

CANDLER *n pl.* -S one that candles

CANDOR *n pl.* -S frankness; sincerity

CANDOUR *n pl.* -S candor

CANDY *v* -DIED, -DYING, -DIES to coat with sugar

CANE *v* CANED, CANING, CANES to weave or furnish with cane (hollow woody stems)

CANELLA *n pl.* -S a medicinal tree bark

CANEPHOR *n pl.* -S a Greek maiden bearing a basket on her head

CANER *n pl.* -S one that canes

CANEWARE *n pl.* -S a yellowish stoneware

CANFIELD *n pl.* -S a card game

CANFUL *n pl.* CANFULS or CANSFUL as much as a can holds

CANGUE *n pl.* -S an ancient Chinese punishing device

CANID *n pl.* -S a dog

CANIKIN *n pl.* -S cannikin

CANINE *n pl.* -S a dog

CANING present participle of cane

CANINITY *n pl.* -TIES the state of being a canine

CANISTER *n pl.* -S a small, metal box

CANITIES *n pl.* CANITIES the turning gray of the hair

CANKER *v* -ED, -ING, -S to affect with ulcerous sores

CANNA *n pl.* -S a tropical plant

CANNABIC *adj* pertaining to cannabis

CANNABIN *n pl.* -S a resin extracted from cannabis

CANNABIS *n pl.* -BISES hemp

CANNED past tense of can

CANNEL *n pl.* -S an oily, compact coal

CANNELON *n pl.* -S a stuffed roll

CANNER *n pl.* -S one that cans food

CANNERY *n pl.* -NERIES a place where food is canned

CANNIBAL *n pl.* -S one who eats his own kind

CANNIE *adj* -NIER, -NIEST canny

CANNIER comparative of canny

CANNIEST superlative of canny

CANNIKIN *n pl.* -S a small can or cup

CANNILY *adv* in a canny manner

CANNING n pl. -S the business of preserving food in airtight containers

CANNOLI n/pl a tube of pastry

CANNON v -ED, -ING, -S to fire a cannon (a heavy firearm)

CANNONRY n pl. -RIES artillery

CANNOT the negative form of can

CANNULA n pl. -LAS or -LAE a tube inserted into a bodily cavity **CANNULAR** adj

CANNY adj -NIER, -NIEST prudent

CANOE v -NOED, -NOEING, -NOES to paddle a canoe (a light, slender boat)

CANOEIST n pl. -S one who canoes

CANOLA n pl. CANOLA an oil from the seeds of a kind of herb

CANON n pl. -S a law decreed by a church council **CANONIC** adj

CANONESS n pl. -ES a woman who lives according to a canon

CANONISE v -ISED, -ISING, -ISES to canonize

CANONIST n pl. -S a specialist in canon law

CANONIZE v -IZED, -IZING, -IZES to declare to be a saint

CANONRY n pl. -RIES a clerical office

CANOODLE v -DLED, -DLING, -DLES to caress

CANOPY v -PIED, -PYING, -PIES to cover from above

CANOROUS adj melodic

CANSFUL a pl. of canful

CANSO n pl. -SOS a love song

CANST a present 2d person sing. of can

CANT v -ED, -ING, -S to tilt or slant

CANTALA n pl. -S a tropical plant

CANTATA n pl. -S a vocal composition

CANTDOG n pl. -S a device used to move logs

CANTEEN n pl. -S a small container for carrying water

CANTER v -ED, -ING, -S to ride a horse at a moderate pace

CANTHUS n pl. -THI a corner of the eye **CANTHAL** adj

CANTIC adj slanted

CANTICLE n pl. -S a hymn

CANTINA n pl. -S a saloon

CANTLE n pl. -S the rear part of a saddle

CANTO n pl. -TOS a division of a long poem

CANTON v -ED, -ING, -S to divide into cantons (districts)

CANTONAL adj pertaining to a canton

CANTOR n pl. -S a religious singer

CANTRAIP n pl. -S cantrip

CANTRAP n pl. -S cantrip

CANTRIP n pl. -S a magic spell

CANTUS n pl. CANTUS a style of church music

CANTY adj cheerful

CANULA n pl. -LAS or -LAE cannula

CANULATE v -LATED, -LATING, -LATES to insert a canula into

CANVAS v -ED, -ING, -ES to canvass

CANVASER n pl. -S one that canvases

CANVASS v -ED, -ING, -ES to examine thoroughly

CANYON n pl. -S a deep valley with steep sides

CANZONA n pl. -S canzone

CANZONE n pl. -NI or -NES a form of lyric poetry

CANZONET n pl. -S a short song

CAP v CAPPED, CAPPING, GAPS to provide with a cap (a type of head covering)

CAPABLE adj -BLER, -BLEST having ability **CAPABLY** adv

CAPACITY n pl. -TIES the ability to receive or contain

CAPE n pl. -S a sleeveless garment **CAPED** adj

CAPELAN n pl. -S capelin

CAPELET n pl. -S a small cape

CAPELIN n pl. -S a small, edible fish

CAPER v -ED, -ING, -S to frolic

CAPERER n pl. -S one that capers

CAPESKIN n pl. -S a soft leather

CAPEWORK n pl. -S a bullfighting technique

CAPFUL n pl. -S as much as a cap can hold

CAPH n pl. -S kaph

CAPIAS n pl. -ES a judicial writ

CAPITA pl. of caput

CAPITAL n pl. -S the upper part of a column

CAPITATE adj head-shaped

CAPITOL n pl. -S a building occupied by a state legislature

CAPITULA n/pl flower clusters

CAPLESS adj being without a cap

CAPLET n pl. -S a coated tablet

CAPLIN n pl. -S capelin

CAPMAKER n pl. -S one that makes caps

CAPO	n pl. -POS a pitch-raising device for fretted instruments
CAPON	n pl. -S a gelded rooster
CAPONATA	n pl. -S a relish made with eggplant
CAPONIER	n pl. -S a type of defense
CAPONIZE	v -IZED, -IZING, -IZES to geld a rooster
CAPORAL	n pl. -S a coarse tobacco
CAPOTE	n pl. -S a hooded cloak or overcoat
CAPOUCH	n pl. -ES capuche
CAPPED	past tense of cap
CAPPER	n pl. -S a capmaker
CAPPING	n pl. -S a wax covering in a honeycomb
CAPRIC	adj pertaining to a goat
CAPRICCI	n/pl caprices
CAPRICE	n pl. -S a whim
CAPRIFIG	n pl. -S a European tree
CAPRINE	adj capric
CAPRIOLE	v -OLED, -OLING, -OLES to leap
CAPRIS	n/pl pants for women
CAPROCK	n pl. -S an overlying rock layer
CAPSICIN	n pl. -S a liquid used as a flavoring
CAPSICUM	n pl. -S a tropical herb
CAPSID	n pl. -S the outer shell of a virus particle **CAPSIDAL** adj
CAPSIZE	v -SIZED, -SIZING, -SIZES to overturn
CAPSOMER	n pl. -S a protein forming the capsid
CAPSTAN	n pl. -S a machine used to hoist weights
CAPSTONE	n pl. -S the top stone of a structure
CAPSULAR	adj enclosed and compact
CAPSULE	v -SULED, -SULING, -SULES to condense into a brief form
CAPTAIN	v -ED, -ING, -S to lead or command
CAPTAN	n pl. -S a fungicide
CAPTION	v -ED, -ING, -S to provide with a title
CAPTIOUS	adj tending to find fault
CAPTIVE	n pl. -S a prisoner
CAPTOR	n pl. -S one who takes or holds a captive
CAPTURE	v -TURED, -TURING, -TURES to take by force or cunning
CAPTURER	n pl. -S one that captures
CAPUCHE	n pl. -S a hood or cowl **CAPUCHED** adj
CAPUCHIN	n pl. -S a long-tailed monkey

CAPUT	n pl. CAPITA a head or head-like part
CAPYBARA	n pl. -S a large rodent
CAR	n pl. -S an automobile
CARABAO	n pl. -BAOS a water buffalo
CARABID	n pl. -S a predatory beetle
CARABIN	n pl. -S carbine
CARABINE	n pl. -S carbine
CARACAL	n pl. -S an African lynx
CARACARA	n pl. -S a large hawk
CARACK	n pl. -S carrack
CARACOL	v -COLLED, -COLLING, -COLS to caracole
CARACOLE	v -COLED, -COLING, -COLES to perform a half turn on a horse
CARACUL	n pl. -S karakul
CARAFE	n pl. -S a glass bottle
CARAGANA	n pl. -S an Asian shrub
CARAGEEN	n pl. -S an edible seaweed
CARAMBA	interj — used to express surprise or dismay
CARAMEL	n pl. -S a chewy candy
CARANGID	n pl. -S a marine fish
CARAPACE	n pl. -S a hard, protective outer covering
CARAPAX	n pl. -ES carapace
CARASSOW	n pl. -S curassow
CARAT	n pl. -S a unit of weight for gems
CARATE	n pl. -S a tropical skin disease
CARAVAN	v -VANED, -VANING, -VANS or -VANNED, -VANNING, -VANS to travel in a group
CARAVEL	n pl. -S a small sailing ship
CARAWAY	n pl. -WAYS an herb used in cooking
CARB	n pl. -S a carburetor
CARBAMIC	adj pertaining to a type of acid
CARBAMYL	n pl. -S a chemical radical
CARBARN	n pl. -S a garage for buses
CARBARYL	n pl. -S an insecticide
CARBIDE	n pl. -S a carbon compound
CARBINE	n pl. -S a light rifle
CARBINOL	n pl. -S an alcohol
CARBO	n pl. -S a carbohydrate
CARBOLIC	n pl. -S an acidic compound
CARBON	n pl. -S a nonmetallic element **CARBONIC** adj
CARBONYL	n pl. -S a chemical compound
CARBORA	n pl. -S a wood-boring worm
CARBOXYL	n pl. -S a univalent acid radical
CARBOY	n pl. -BOYS a large bottle **CARBOYED** adj

CARBURET v -RETED, -RETING, -RETS or -RETTED, -RETTING, -RETS to combine chemically with carbon

CARCAJOU n pl. -S a carnivorous mammal

CARCANET n pl. -S a jeweled necklace

CARCASE n pl. -S a carcass

CARCASS n pl. -ES the body of a dead animal

CARCEL n pl. -S a unit of illumination

CARD v -ED, -ING, -S to provide with a card (a stiff piece of paper)

CARDAMOM n pl. -S a tropical herb

CARDAMON n pl. -S cardamom

CARDAMUM n pl. -S cardamom

CARDCASE n pl. -S a case for holding cards

CARDER n pl. -S one that does carding

CARDIA n pl. -DIAS or -DIAE an opening of the esophagus

CARDIAC n pl. -S a person with a heart disorder

CARDIGAN n pl. -S a type of sweater

CARDINAL n pl. -S a bright red bird

CARDING n pl. -S the process of combing and cleaning cotton fibers; cleaned and combed fibers

CARDIOID n pl. -S a heart-shaped curve

CARDITIS n pl. -TISES inflammation of the heart **CARDITIC** adj

CARDOON n pl. -S a perennial plant

CARE v CARED, CARING, CARES to be concerned or interested

CAREEN v -ED, -ING, -S to lurch while moving

CAREENER n pl. -S one that careens

CAREER v -ED, -ING, -S to go at full speed

CAREERER n pl. -S one that careers

CAREFREE adj being without worry or anxiety

CAREFUL adj -FULLER, -FULLEST cautious

CARELESS adj inattentive; negligent

CARER n pl. -S one that cares

CARESS v -ED, -ING, -ES to touch lovingly

CARESSER n pl. -S one that caresses

CARET n pl. -S a proofreaders' symbol

CARETAKE v -TOOK, -TAKEN, -TAKING, -TAKES to take care of someone else's house or land

CAREWORN adj haggard

CAREX n pl. CARICES a marsh plant

CARFARE n pl. -S payment for a bus or car ride

CARFUL n pl. -S as much as a car can hold

CARGO n pl. -GOS or -GOES conveyed merchandise

CARHOP n pl. -S a waitress at a drive-in restaurant

CARIBE n pl. -S the piranha

CARIBOU n pl. -S a large deer

CARICES pl. of carex

CARIES n pl. CARIES tooth decay **CARIED** adj

CARILLON v -LONNED, -LONNING, -LONS to play a set of bells

CARINA n pl. -NAS or -NAE a carinate anatomical part **CARINAL** adj

CARINATE adj shaped like the keel of a ship

CARING present participle of care

CARIOCA n pl. -S a South American dance

CARIOLE n pl. -S a small, open carriage

CARIOUS adj decayed

CARITAS n pl. -ES love for all people

CARK v -ED, -ING, -S to worry

CARL n pl. -S a peasant

CARLE n pl. -S a carl

CARLESS adj being without a car

CARLIN n pl. -S an old woman

CARLINE n pl. -S carling

CARLING n pl. -S a beam supporting a ship's deck

CARLISH adj resembling a carl

CARLOAD n pl. -S as much as a car can hold

CARMAKER n pl. -S an automobile manufacturer

CARMAN n pl. -MEN a streetcar driver

CARMINE n pl. -S a vivid red color

CARN n pl. -S cairn

CARNAGE n pl. -S great and bloody slaughter

CARNAL adj pertaining to bodily appetites **CARNALLY** adv

CARNAUBA n pl. -S a palm tree

CARNET n pl. -S an official permit

CARNEY n pl. -NEYS carny

CARNIE n pl. -S carny

CARNIES pl. of carny

CARNIFY v -FIED, -FYING, -FIES to form into flesh

CARNIVAL n pl. -S a traveling amusement show

CARNY n pl. -NIES a carnival

CAROACH n pl. -ES caroche

CAROB n pl. -S an evergreen tree
CAROCH n pl. -ES caroche
CAROCHE n pl. -S a stately carriage
CAROL v -OLED, -OLING, -OLS or -OLLED, -OLLING, -OLS to sing joyously
CAROLER n pl. -S one that carols
CAROLI a pl. of carolus
CAROLLED a past tense of carol
CAROLLER n pl. -S caroler
CAROLLING a present participle of carol
CAROLUS n pl. -LUSES or -LI an old English coin
CAROM v -ED, -ING, -S to collide with and rebound
CAROTENE n pl. -S a plant pigment
CAROTID n pl. -S an artery in the neck
CAROTIN n pl. -S carotene
CAROUSAL n pl. -S a boisterous drinking party
CAROUSE v -ROUSED, -ROUSING, -ROUSES to engage in a carousal
CAROUSEL n pl. -S an amusement park ride
CAROUSER n pl. -S one that carouses
CAROUSING present participle of carouse
CARP v -ED, -ING, -S to find fault unreasonably
CARPAL n pl. -S carpale
CARPALE n pl. -LIA a bone of the wrist
CARPEL n pl. -S a simple pistil
CARPER n pl. -S one that carps
CARPET v -ED, -ING, -S to cover a floor with a heavy fabric
CARPI pl. of carpus
CARPING n pl. -S the act of one who carps
CARPOOL v -ED, -ING, -S to take turns driving a group of commuters
CARPORT n pl. -S a shelter for a car
CARPUS n pl. -PI the wrist
CARR n pl. -S a marsh
CARRACK n pl. -S a type of merchant ship
CARREL n pl. -S a desk in a library stack for solitary study
CARRELL n pl. -S carrel
CARRIAGE n pl. -S a wheeled, horse-drawn vehicle
CARRIED past tense of carry
CARRIER n pl. -S one that carries
CARRIES present 3d person sing. of carry
CARRIOLE n pl. -S cariole

CARRION n pl. -S dead and putrefying flesh
CARRITCH n pl. -ES a religious handbook
CARROCH n pl. -ES caroche
CARROM v -ED, -ING, -S to carom
CARROT n pl. -S an edible orange root
CARROTIN n pl. -S carotene
CARROTY adj -ROTIER, -ROTIEST resembling a carrot in color
CARRY v -RIED, -RYING, -RIES to convey from one place to another
CARRYALL n pl. -S a light covered carriage
CARRYON n pl. -S a small piece of luggage
CARRYOUT n pl. -S a take-out order of food
CARSE n pl. -S low, fertile land along a river
CARSICK adj nauseated from riding in a car
CART v -ED, -ING, -S to convey in a cart (a two-wheeled vehicle) **CARTABLE** adj
CARTAGE n pl. -S the act of carting
CARTE n pl. -S a menu
CARTEL n pl. -S a business organization
CARTER n pl. -S one that carts
CARTLOAD n pl. -S as much as a cart can hold
CARTON v -ED, -ING, -S to pack in a cardboard box
CARTOON v -ED, -ING, -S to sketch a cartoon (a humorous representation) of
CARTOONY adj resembling a cartoon
CARTOP adj able to fit on top of a car
CARTOUCH n pl. -ES a scroll-like tablet
CARUNCLE n pl. -S a fleshy outgrowth
CARVE v CARVED, CARVING, CARVES to form by cutting
CARVEL n pl. -S caravel
CARVEN adj carved
CARVER n pl. -S one that carves
CARVING n pl. -S a carved figure or design
CARWASH n pl. -ES an establishment equipped to wash automobiles
CARYATIC adj resembling a caryatid
CARYATID n pl. -S or -ES a sculptured female figure used as a column
CARYOTIN n pl. -S karyotin
CASA n pl. -S a dwelling

CASABA n pl. -S a variety of melon
CASAVA n pl. -S cassava
CASBAH n pl. -S the old section of a North African city
CASCABEL n pl. -S the rear part of a cannon
CASCABLE n pl. -S cascabel
CASCADE v -CADED, -CADING, -CADES to fall like a waterfall
CASCARA n pl. -S a medicinal tree bark
CASE v CASED, CASING, CASES to put in a case (a container or receptacle)
CASEASE n pl. -S an enzyme
CASEATE v -ATED, -ATING, -ATES to become cheesy
CASEBOOK n pl. -S a law textbook
CASED past tense of case
CASEFY v -FIED, -FYING, -FIES to caseate
CASEIN n pl. -S a milk protein CASEIC adj
CASELOAD n pl. -S the number of cases being handled
CASEMATE n pl. -S a bombproof shelter
CASEMENT n pl. -S a type of window
CASEOSE n pl. -S a proteose
CASEOUS adj cheesy
CASERN n pl. -S a barracks for soldiers
CASERNE n pl. -S a casern
CASETTE n pl. -S cassette
CASEWORK n pl. -S a form of social work
CASEWORM n pl. -S an insect larva
CASH v -ED, -ING, -ES to convert into cash (ready money) CASHABLE adj
CASHAW n pl. -S cushaw
CASHBOOK n pl. -S a book of monetary records
CASHBOX n pl. -ES a container for money
CASHEW n pl. -S a nut-bearing tree
CASHIER v -ED, -ING, -S to dismiss in disgrace
CASHLESS adj having no cash
CASHMERE n pl. -S a fine wool
CASHOO n pl. -SHOOS catechu
CASIMERE n pl. -S a woolen fabric
CASIMIRE n pl. -S casimere
CASING n pl. -S a protective outer covering
CASINO n pl. -NOS or -NI a gambling room
CASITA n pl. -S a small house
CASK v -ED, -ING, -S to store in a cask (a strong barrel)

CASKET v -ED, -ING, -S to place in a casket (a burial case)
CASKY adj resembling a cask
CASQUE n pl. -S a helmet CASQUED adj
CASSABA n pl. -S casaba
CASSATA n pl. -S an Italian ice cream
CASSAVA n pl. -S a tropical plant
CASSETTE n pl. -S a small case containing audiotape or videotape
CASSIA n pl. -S a variety of cinnamon
CASSINO n pl. -NOS a card game
CASSIS n pl. -SISES a European bush
CASSOCK n pl. -S a long garment worn by clergymen
CAST v CAST, CASTING, CASTS to throw with force CASTABLE adj
CASTANET n pl. -S a rhythm instrument
CASTAWAY n pl. -WAYS an outcast
CASTE n pl. -S a system of distinct social classes
CASTEISM n pl. -S the use of a caste system
CASTER n pl. -S a small, swiveling wheel
CASTING n pl. -S something made in a mold
CASTLE v -TLED, -TLING, -TLES to make a certain move in chess
CASTOFF n pl. -S a discarded person or thing
CASTOR n pl. -S caster
CASTRATE v -TRATED, -TRATING, -TRATES to remove the testes of
CASTRATO n pl. -TI a singer castrated in boyhood
CASUAL n pl. -S one who works occasionally
CASUALLY adv informally
CASUALTY n pl. -TIES a victim of war or disaster
CASUIST n pl. -S one who resolves ethical problems
CASUS n pl. CASUS a legal occurrence or event
CAT v CATTED, CATTING, CATS to hoist an anchor to the cathead
CATACOMB n pl. -S an underground cemetery
CATALASE n pl. -S an enzyme
CATALO n pl. -LOS or -LOES a hybrid between a buffalo and a cow

CATALOG v -ED, -ING, -S to classify information descriptively

CATALPA n pl. -S a tree

CATALYST n pl. -S a substance that accelerates a chemical reaction

CATALYZE v -LYZED, -LYZING, -LYZES to act as a catalyst

CATAMITE n pl. -S a boy used in sodomy

CATAPULT v -ED, -ING, -S to hurl through the air

CATARACT n pl. -S a tremendous waterfall

CATARRH n pl. -S inflammation of a mucous membrane

CATAWBA n pl. -S a variety of fox grape

CATBIRD n pl. -S a songbird

CATBOAT n pl. -S a small sailboat

CATBRIER n pl. -S a thorny vine

CATCALL v -ED, -ING, -S to deride by making shrill sounds

CATCH v CAUGHT, CATCHING, CATCHES to capture after pursuit

CATCHALL n pl. -S a container for odds and ends

CATCHER n pl. -S one that catches

CATCHFLY n pl. -FLIES an insect-catching plant

CATCHUP n pl. -S ketchup

CATCHY adj CATCHIER, CATCHIEST pleasing and easily remembered

CATCLAW n pl. -S a flowering shrub

CATE n pl. -S a choice food

CATECHIN n pl. -S a chemical used in dyeing

CATECHOL n pl. -S a chemical used in photography

CATECHU n pl. -S a resin used in tanning

CATEGORY n pl. -RIES a division in any system of classification

CATENA n pl. -NAS or -NAE a closely linked series

CATENARY n pl. -NARIES a mathematical curve

CATENATE v -NATED, -NATING, -NATES to link together

CATENOID n pl. -S a geometric surface

CATER v -ED, -ING, -S to provide food and service for

CATERAN n pl. -S a brigand

CATERER n pl. -S one that caters

CATERESS n pl. -ES a woman who caters

CATFACE n pl. -S a deformity of fruit

CATFALL n pl. -S an anchor line

CATFIGHT n pl. -S a fight between two women

CATFISH n pl. -ES a scaleless, large-headed fish

CATGUT n pl. -S a strong cord

CATHEAD n pl. -S a beam projecting from a ship's bow

CATHECT v -ED, -ING, -S to invest with psychic energy

CATHEDRA n pl. -DRAS or -DRAE a bishop's throne

CATHETER n pl. -S a medical instrument

CATHEXIS n pl. -THEXES the concentration of psychic energy on a person or idea

CATHODE n pl. -S a negatively charged electrode CATHODAL, CATHODIC adj

CATHOLIC n pl. -S a member of the early Christian church

CATHOUSE n pl. -S a brothel

CATION n pl. -S a positively charged ion CATIONIC adj

CATKIN n pl. -S a flower cluster

CATLIKE adj resembling a cat; stealthy; silent

CATLIN n pl. -S catling

CATLING n pl. -S a surgical knife

CATMINT n pl. -S catnip

CATNAP v -NAPPED, -NAPPING, -NAPS to doze

CATNAPER n pl. -S one that steals cats

CATNIP n pl. -S an aromatic herb

CATSPAW n pl. -S a light wind

CATSUP n pl. -S ketchup

CATTAIL n pl. -S a marsh plant

CATTALO n pl. -LOS or -LOES catalo

CATTED past tense of cat

CATTERY n pl. -TERIES an establishment for breeding cats

CATTIE n pl. -S an Asian unit of weight

CATTIER comparative of catty

CATTIEST superlative of catty

CATTILY adv in a catty manner

CATTING present participle of cat

CATTISH adj catty

CATTLE n/pl domesticated bovines

CATTLEYA n pl. -S a tropical orchid

CATTY adj -TIER, -TIEST catlike; spiteful

CATWALK n pl. -S a narrow walkway

CAUCUS v -CUSED, -CUSING, -CUSES or -CUSSED, -CUSSING, -CUSSES to hold a political meeting

CAUDAD adv toward the tail

CAUDAL *adj* taillike **CAUDALLY** *adv*

CAUDATE *n pl.* -S a basal ganglion of the brain

CAUDATED *adj* having a tail

CAUDEX *n pl.* -DICES or -DEXES the woody base of some plants

CAUDILLO *n pl.* -DILLOS a military dictator

CAUDLE *n pl.* -S a warm beverage

CAUGHT past tense of catch

CAUL *n pl.* -S a fetal membrane

CAULD *n pl.* -S cold

CAULDRON *n pl.* -S caldron

CAULES pl. of caulis

CAULICLE *n pl.* -S a small stem

CAULINE *adj* pertaining to a stem

CAULIS *n pl.* -LES a plant stem

CAULK *v* -ED, -ING, -S to make the seams of a ship watertight

CAULKER *n pl.* -S one that caulks

CAULKING *n pl.* -S the material used to caulk

CAUSABLE *adj* capable of being caused

CAUSAL *n pl.* -S a word expressing cause or reason

CAUSALLY *adv* by way of causing

CAUSE *v* CAUSED, CAUSING, CAUSES to bring about

CAUSER *n pl.* -S one that causes

CAUSERIE *n pl.* -S an informal talk

CAUSEWAY *v* -ED, -ING, -S to build a causeway (a raised roadway) over

CAUSEY *n pl.* -SEYS a paved road

CAUSING present participle of cause

CAUSTIC *n pl.* -S a corrosive substance

CAUTERY *n pl.* -TERIES something used to destroy tissue

CAUTION *v* -ED, -ING, -S to warn

CAUTIOUS *adj* exercising prudence to avoid danger

CAVALERO *n pl.* -ROS a horseman

CAVALIER *v* -ED, -ING, -S to behave haughtily

CAVALLA *n pl.* -S a large food fish

CAVALLY *n pl.* -LIES cavalla

CAVALRY *n pl.* -RIES a mobile army unit

CAVATINA *n pl.* -NAS or -NE a simple song or an instrumental

CAVE *v* CAVED, CAVING, CAVES to hollow out

CAVEAT *v* -ED, -ING, -S to enter a type of legal notice

CAVEATOR *n pl.* -S one that files a caveat

CAVED past tense of cave

CAVEFISH *n pl.* -ES a sightless fish

CAVELIKE *adj* resembling a cave (an underground chamber)

CAVEMAN *n pl.* -MEN a cave dweller

CAVER *n pl.* -S one that caves

CAVERN *v* -ED, -ING, -S to hollow out

CAVETTO *n pl.* -TOS or -TI a concave molding

CAVIAR *n pl.* -S the roe of sturgeon

CAVIARE *n pl.* -S caviar

CAVICORN *adj* having hollow horns

CAVIE *n pl.* -S a hencoop

CAVIES pl. of cavy

CAVIL *v* -ILED, -ILING, -ILS or -ILLED, -ILLING, -ILS to carp

CAVILER *n pl.* -S one that cavils

CAVILLER *n pl.* -S caviler

CAVILLING a present participle of cavil

CAVING *n pl.* -S the sport of exploring caves

CAVITARY *adj* pertaining to the formation of cavities in tissue

CAVITATE *v* -TATED, -TATING, -TATES to form cavities

CAVITY *n pl.* -TIES an unfilled space within a mass **CAVITIED** *adj*

CAVORT *v* -ED, -ING, -S to frolic

CAVORTER *n pl.* -S one that cavorts

CAVY *n pl.* -VIES a short-tailed rodent

CAW *v* -ED, -ING, -S to utter the sound of a crow

CAY *n pl.* CAYS a small low island

CAYENNE *n pl.* -S a hot seasoning **CAYENNED** *adj*

CAYMAN *n pl.* -S caiman

CAYUSE *n pl.* -S an Indian pony

CAZIQUE *n pl.* -S a cacique

CEASE *v* CEASED, CEASING, CEASES to stop

CEBID *n pl.* -S ceboid

CEBOID *n pl.* -S one of a family of monkeys

CECUM *n pl.* CECA a bodily cavity with one opening **CECAL** *adj* **CECALLY** *adv*

CEDAR *n pl.* -S an evergreen tree **CEDARN** *adj*

CEDE *v* CEDED, CEDING, CEDES to yield

CEDER *n pl.* -S one that cedes

CEDI *n pl.* -S a monetary unit of Ghana

CEDILLA *n pl.* -S a pronunciation mark

CEDING present participle of cede

CEDULA *n pl.* -S a Philippine tax

CEE *n pl.* -S the letter C

CEIBA n pl. -S a tropical tree

CEIL v -ED, -ING, -S to furnish with a ceiling

CEILER n pl. -S one that ceils

CEILING n pl. -S the overhead lining of a room

CEINTURE n pl. -S a belt for the waist

CEL n pl. -S a sheet of celluloid used in animation

CELADON n pl. -S a pale green color

CELEB n pl. -S a celebrity; a famous person

CELERIAC n pl. -S a variety of celery

CELERITY n pl. -TIES swiftness

CELERY n pl. -ERIES a plant with edible stalks

CELESTA n pl. -S a keyboard instrument

CELESTE n pl. -S celesta

CELIAC n pl. -S one that has a chronic nutritional disturbance

CELIBACY n pl. -CIES abstention from sexual intercourse

CELIBATE n pl. -S one who lives a life of celibacy

CELL v -ED, -ING, -S to store in a honeycomb

CELLA n pl. -LAE the interior of an ancient temple

CELLAR v -ED, -ING, -S to store in an underground room

CELLARER n pl. -S the steward of a monastery

CELLARET n pl. -S a cabinet for wine bottles

CELLIST n pl. -S one who plays the cello

CELLMATE n pl. -S one of two or more prisoners sharing a cell

CELLO n pl. -LOS or -LI a stringed musical instrument

CELLULAR adj pertaining to a cell (a basic unit of life)

CELLULE n pl. -S a small cell

CELOM n pl. -LOMS or -LOMATA coelom

CELOSIA n pl. -S a flowering plant

CELT n pl. -S a primitive ax

CEMBALO n pl. -LI or -LOS a harpsichord

CEMENT v -ED, -ING, -S to bind firmly

CEMENTER n pl. -S one that cements

CEMENTUM n pl. -TA the hard tissue covering the roots of the teeth

CEMETERY n pl. -TERIES a burial ground

CENACLE n pl. -S a small dining room

CENOBITE n pl. -S a member of a religious order

CENOTAPH n pl. -S an empty tomb

CENOTE n pl. -S a sinkhole in limestone

CENSE v CENSED, CENSING, CENSES to perfume with incense

CENSER n pl. -S a vessel for burning incense

CENSOR v -ED, -ING, -S to delete an objectionable word or passage

CENSUAL adj pertaining to the act of censusing

CENSURE v -SURED, -SURING, -SURES to criticize severely

CENSURER n pl. -S one that censures

CENSUS v -ED, -ING, -ES to take an official count of

CENT n pl. -S the 100th part of a dollar

CENTAL n pl. -S a unit of weight

CENTARE n pl. -S a measure of land area

CENTAUR n pl. -S a mythological creature

CENTAURY n pl. -RIES a medicinal herb

CENTAVO n pl. -VOS a coin of various Spanish-American nations

CENTER v -ED, -ING, -S to place at the center (the midpoint)

CENTESIS n pl. -TESES a surgical puncture

CENTIARE n pl. -S centare

CENTILE n pl. -S a value of a statistical variable

CENTIME n pl. -S the 100th part of a franc

CENTIMO n pl. -MOS any of various small coins

CENTNER n pl. -S a unit of weight

CENTO n pl. -TONES or -TOS a literary work made up of parts from other works

CENTRA a pl. of centrum

CENTRAL n pl. -S a telephone exchange

CENTRAL adj -TRALER, -TRALEST situated at, in, or near the center

CENTRE v -TRED, -TRING, -TRES to center

CENTRIC adj situated at the center

CENTRING n pl. -S a temporary framework for an arch

CENTRISM n pl. -S moderate political philosophy

CENTRIST n pl. -S an advocate of centrism

CENTROID n pl. -S the center of mass of an object

CENTRUM n pl. -TRUMS or -TRA the body of a vertebra

CENTUM n pl. -S one hundred

CENTUPLE v -PLED, -PLING, -PLES to increase a hundredfold

CENTURY n pl. -RIES a period of 100 years

CEORL n pl. -S a freeman of low birth CEORLISH adj

CEP n pl. -S cepe

CEPE n pl. -S a large mushroom

CEPHALAD adv toward the head

CEPHALIC adj pertaining to the head

CEPHALIN n pl. -S a bodily chemical

CEPHEID n pl. -S a giant star

CERAMAL n pl. -S a heat-resistant alloy

CERAMIC n pl. -S an item made of baked clay

CERAMIST n pl. -S one who makes ceramics

CERASTES n pl. CERASTES a venomous snake

CERATE n pl. -S a medicated ointment

CERATED adj covered with wax

CERATIN n pl. -S keratin

CERATOID adj hornlike

CERCARIA n pl. -IAE or -IAS a parasitic worm

CERCIS n pl. -CISES a shrub

CERCUS n pl. CERCI a sensory appendage of an insect

CERE v CERED, CERING, CERES to wrap in a waxy cloth

CEREAL n pl. -S a food made from grain

CEREBRAL n pl. -S a kind of consonant

CEREBRUM n pl. -BRUMS or -BRA a part of the brain CEREBRIC adj

CERED past tense of cere

CEREMENT n pl. -S a waxy cloth

CEREMONY n pl. -NIES a formal observance

CEREUS n pl. -ES a tall cactus

CERIA n pl. -S a chemical compound

CERIC adj containing cerium

CERING present participle of cere

CERIPH n pl. -S serif

CERISE n pl. -S a red color

CERITE n pl. -S a mineral

CERIUM n pl. -S a metallic element

CERMET n pl. -S ceramal

CERNUOUS adj drooping or nodding

CERO n pl. CEROS a large food fish

CEROTIC adj pertaining to beeswax

CEROTYPE n pl. -S a process of engraving using wax

CEROUS adj pertaining to cerium

CERTAIN adj -TAINER, -TAINEST absolutely confident

CERTES adv in truth

CERTIFY v -FIED, -FYING, -FIES to confirm

CERULEAN n pl. -S a blue color

CERUMEN n pl. -S a waxy secretion of the ear

CERUSE n pl. -S a lead compound

CERUSITE n pl. -S a lead ore

CERVELAS n pl. -ES cervelat

CERVELAT n pl. -S a smoked sausage

CERVICAL adj pertaining to the cervix

CERVID n pl. -S of the deer family

CERVINE adj pertaining to deer

CERVIX n pl. -VICES or -VIXES the neck

CESAREAN n pl. -S a method of child delivery

CESARIAN n pl. -S cesarean

CESIUM n pl. -S a metallic element

CESS v -ED, -ING, -ES to tax or assess

CESSION n pl. -S the act of ceding

CESSPIT n pl. -S a cesspool

CESSPOOL n pl. -S a covered well or pit for sewage

CESTA n pl. -S a basket used in jai alai

CESTI pl. of cestus

CESTODE n pl. -S a tapeworm

CESTOID n pl. -S cestode

CESTOS n pl. -TOI cestus

CESTUS n pl. -TI a belt or girdle

CESTUS n pl. -ES a hand covering for ancient Roman boxers

CESURA n pl. -RAS or -RAE caesura

CETACEAN n pl. -S an aquatic mammal

CETANE n pl. -S a diesel fuel

CETE n pl. -S a group of badgers

CETOLOGY n pl. -GIES the study of whales

CEVICHE n pl. -S seviche

CHABLIS n pl. CHABLIS a dry white wine

CHABOUK n pl. -S a type of whip

CHABUK n pl. -S chabouk

CHACMA n pl. -S a large baboon

CHACONNE n pl. -S an ancient dance

CHAD n pl. -S a scrap of paper CHADLESS adj

CHADAR n pl. -DARS or -DRI chador

CHADARIM a pl. of cheder

CHADOR *n pl.* -DORS or -DRI a large shawl

CHAETA *n pl.* -TAE a bristle or seta CHAETAL *adj*

CHAFE *v* CHAFED, CHAFING, CHAFES to warm by rubbing

CHAFER *n pl.* -S a large beetle

CHAFF *v* -ED, -ING, -S to poke fun at

CHAFFER *v* -ED, -ING, -S to bargain or haggle

CHAFFY *adj* CHAFFIER, CHAFFIEST worthless

CHAFING present participle of chafe

CHAGRIN *v* -GRINED, -GRINING, -GRINS or -GRINNED, -GRINNING, -GRINS to humiliate

CHAIN *v* -ED, -ING, -S to bind with a chain (a series of connected rings)

CHAINE *n pl.* -S a series of ballet turns

CHAINMAN *n pl.* -MEN a surveyor's assistant who uses a measuring chain

CHAINSAW *v* -SAWED, -SAWING, -SAWS to cut with a chain saw

CHAIR *v* -ED, -ING, -S to install in office

CHAIRMAN *n pl.* -MEN the presiding officer of a meeting

CHAIRMAN *v* -MANED, -MANING, -MANS or -MANNED, -MANNING, -MANS to act as chairman of

CHAISE *n pl.* -S a light carriage

CHAKRA *n pl.* -S a body center in yoga

CHALAH *n pl.* -LAHS, -LOTH or -LOT challah

CHALAZA *n pl.* -ZAS or -ZAE a band of tissue in an egg CHALAZAL *adj*

CHALAZIA *n/pl* tumors of the eyelid

CHALCID *n pl.* -S a tiny fly

CHALDRON *n pl.* -S a unit of dry measure

CHALEH *n pl.* -S challah

CHALET *n pl.* -S a Swiss cottage

CHALICE *n pl.* -S a drinking cup CHALICED *adj*

CHALK *v* -ED, -ING, -S to mark with chalk (a soft limestone)

CHALKY *adj* CHALKIER, CHALKIEST resembling chalk

CHALLA *n pl.* -S challah

CHALLAH *n pl.* -LAHS, -LOTH, or -LOT a kind of bread

CHALLIE *n pl.* -S challis

CHALLIES *pl.* of chally

CHALLIS *n pl.* -LISES a light fabric

CHALLOT a *pl.* of challah

CHALLOTH a *pl.* of challah

CHALLY *n pl.* -LIES challis

CHALONE *n pl.* -S a hormone

CHALOT a *pl.* of chalah

CHALOTH a *pl.* of chalah

CHALUTZ *n pl.* -LUTZIM halutz

CHAM *n pl.* -S a khan

CHAMADE *n pl.* -S a signal made with a drum

CHAMBER *v* -ED, -ING, -S to put in a chamber (a room)

CHAMBRAY *n pl.* -BRAYS a fine fabric

CHAMFER *v* -ED, -ING, -S to groove

CHAMFRON *n pl.* -S armor for a horse's head

CHAMISE *n pl.* -S chamiso

CHAMISO *n pl.* -SOS a flowering shrub

CHAMMY *v* -MIED, -MYING, -MIES to chamois

CHAMOIS *n pl.* -OIX a soft leather

CHAMOIS *v* -ED, -ING, -ES to prepare leather like chamois

CHAMP *v* -ED, -ING, -S to chew noisily

CHAMPAC *n pl.* -S champak

CHAMPAK *n pl.* -S an East Indian tree

CHAMPER *n pl.* -S one that champs

CHAMPION *v* -ED, -ING, -S to defend or support

CHAMPY *adj* broken up by the trampling of beasts

CHANCE *v* CHANCED, CHANCING, CHANCES to risk

CHANCEL *n pl.* -S an area around a church altar

CHANCERY *n pl.* -CERIES a court of public record

CHANCIER comparative of chancy

CHANCIEST superlative of chancy

CHANCILY *adv* in a chancy manner

CHANCING present participle of chance

CHANCRE *n pl.* -S a hard-based sore

CHANCY *adj* CHANCIER, CHANCIEST risky

CHANDLER *n pl.* -S a dealer in provisions

CHANFRON *n pl.* -S chamfron

CHANG *n pl.* -S a cattle

CHANGE *v* CHANGED, CHANGING, CHANGES to make different

CHANGER *n pl.* -S one that changes

CHANNEL *v* -NELED, -NELING, -NELS or -NELLED, -NELLING, -NELS to direct along some desired course

CHANSON *n pl.* -S a song

CHANT v -ED, -ING, -S to sing

CHANTAGE n pl. -S blackmail

CHANTER n pl. -S one that chants

CHANTEY n pl. -TEYS a sailor's song

CHANTIES pl. of chanty

CHANTOR n pl. -S chanter

CHANTRY n pl. -TRIES an endowment given to a church

CHANTY n pl. -TIES chantey

CHAO n pl. CHAO a monetary unit of Vietnam

CHAOS n pl. -ES a state of total disorder; a confused mass CHAOTIC adj

CHAP v CHAPPED or CHAPT, CHAPPING, CHAPS to split, crack, or redden

CHAPATI n pl. -S an unleavened bread of India

CHAPATTI n pl. -S chapati

CHAPBOOK n pl. -S a small book of popular tales

CHAPE n pl. -S a part of a scabbard

CHAPEAU n pl. -PEAUX or -PEAUS a hat

CHAPEL n pl. -S a place of worship

CHAPERON v -ED, -ING, -S to accompany

CHAPITER n pl. -S the capital of a column

CHAPLAIN n pl. -S a clergyman attached to a chapel

CHAPLET n pl. -S a wreath for the head

CHAPMAN n pl. -MEN a peddler

CHAPPATI n pl. -S chapati

CHAPPED a past tense of chap

CHAPPING present participle of chap

CHAPT a past tense of chap

CHAPTER v -ED, -ING, -S to divide a book into chapters (main sections)

CHAQUETA n pl. -S a jacket worn by cowboys

CHAR v CHARRED, CHARRING, CHARS to burn slightly

CHARACID n pl. -S characin

CHARACIN n pl. -S a tropical fish

CHARADE n pl. -S a pantomimed word

CHARAS n pl. -ES hashish

CHARCOAL v -ED, -ING, -S to blacken with charcoal (a dark, porous carbon)

CHARD n pl. -S a variety of beet

CHARE v CHARED, CHARING, CHARES to do small jobs

CHARGE v CHARGED, CHARGING, CHARGES to accuse formally

CHARGER n pl. -S one that charges

CHARIER comparative of chary

CHARIEST superlative of chary

CHARILY adv in a chary manner

CHARING present participle of chare

CHARIOT v -ED, -ING, -S to ride in a chariot (a type of cart)

CHARISM n pl. -S charisma

CHARISMA n pl. -MATA a special magnetic appeal

CHARITY n pl. -TIES something given to the needy

CHARK v -ED, -ING, -S to char

CHARKA n pl. -S charkha

CHARKHA n pl. -S a spinning wheel

CHARLADY n pl. -DIES a cleaning woman

CHARLEY n pl. -LEYS charlie

CHARLIE n pl. -LIES a fool

CHARLOCK n pl. -S a troublesome weed

CHARM v -ED, -ING, -S to attract irresistibly

CHARMER n pl. -S one that charms

CHARMING adj -INGER, -INGEST pleasing

CHARNEL n pl. -S a room where corpses are placed

CHARPAI n pl. -S charpoy

CHARPOY n pl. -POYS a bed used in India

CHARQUI n pl. -S a type of meat CHARQUID adj

CHARR n pl. -S a small-scaled trout

CHARRED past tense of char

CHARRIER comparative of charry

CHARRIEST superlative of charry

CHARRING present participle of char

CHARRO n pl. -ROS a cowboy

CHARRY adj -RIER, -RIEST resembling charcoal

CHART v -ED, -ING, -S to map out

CHARTER v -ED, -ING, -S to lease or hire

CHARTIST n pl. -S a stock market specialist

CHARY adj CHARIER, CHARIEST cautious

CHASE v CHASED, CHASING, CHASES to pursue

CHASER n pl. -S one that chases

CHASING n pl. -S a design engraved on metal

CHASM n pl. -S a deep cleft in the earth CHASMAL, CHASMED, CHASMIC, CHASMY adj

CHASSE v CHASSED, CHASSEING, CHASSES to perform a dance movement

CHASSEUR n pl. -S a cavalry soldier

CHASSIS n pl. CHASSIS the frame of a car

CHASTE adj CHASTER, CHASTEST morally pure CHASTELY adv

CHASTEN v -ED, -ING, -S to chastise

CHASTISE v -TISED, -TISING, -TISES to discipline by punishment

CHASTITY n pl. -TIES moral purity

CHASUBLE n pl. -S a sleeveless vestment

CHAT v CHATTED, CHATTING, CHATS to converse informally

CHATCHKA n pl. -S a knickknack

CHATCHKE n pl. -S chatchka

CHATEAU n pl. -TEAUX or -TEAUS a large country house

CHATTED past tense of chat

CHATTEL n pl. -S a slave

CHATTER v -ED, -ING, -S to talk rapidly and trivially CHATTERY adj

CHATTING present participle of chat

CHATTY adj -TIER, -TIEST talkative CHATTILY adv

CHAUFER n pl. -S chauffer

CHAUFFER n pl. -S a small furnace

CHAUNT v -ED, -ING, -S to chant

CHAUNTER n pl. -S one that chaunts

CHAUSSES n/pl medieval armor

CHAW v -ED, -ING, -S to chew

CHAWER n pl. -S one that chaws

CHAY n pl. CHAYS the root of an East Indian herb

CHAYOTE n pl. -S a tropical vine

CHAZAN n pl. -ZANS or -ZANIM a cantor

CHAZZAN n pl. -ZANS or -ZANIM chazan

CHAZZEN n pl. -ZENS or -ZENIM chazan

CHEAP adj CHEAPER, CHEAPEST inexpensive

CHEAP n pl. -S a market

CHEAPEN v -ED, -ING, -S to make cheap

CHEAPIE n pl. -S one that is cheap

CHEAPISH adj somewhat cheap

CHEAPLY adv in a cheap manner

CHEAPO n pl. CHEAPOS a cheapie

CHEAT v -ED, -ING, -S to defraud

CHEATER n pl. -S one that cheats

CHEBEC n pl. -S a small bird

CHECHAKO n pl. -KOS a newcomer

CHECK v -ED, -ING, -S to inspect

CHECKER v -ED, -ING, -S to mark with squares

CHECKOFF n pl. -S a method of collecting union dues

CHECKOUT n pl. -S a test of a machine

CHECKROW v -ED, -ING, -S to plant in rows dividing land into squares

CHECKUP n pl. -S an examination

CHEDDAR n pl. -S a type of cheese

CHEDDITE n pl. -S chedite

CHEDER n pl. CHADARIM or CHEDERS heder

CHEDITE n pl. -S an explosive

CHEEK v -ED, -ING, -S to speak impudently to

CHEEKFUL n pl. -S the amount held in one's cheek

CHEEKY adj CHEEKIER, CHEEKIEST impudent CHEEKILY adv

CHEEP v -ED, -ING, -S to chirp

CHEEPER n pl. -S one that cheeps

CHEER v -ED, -ING, -S to applaud with shouts of approval

CHEERER n pl. -S one that cheers

CHEERFUL adj -FULLER, -FULLEST full of spirits

CHEERIER comparative of cheery

CHEERIEST superlative of cheery

CHEERILY adv in a cheery manner

CHEERIO n pl. -IOS a greeting

CHEERLED past tense of cheerlead

CHEERLY adv cheerily

CHEERO n pl. CHEEROS cheerio

CHEERY adj CHEERIER, CHEERIEST cheerful

CHEESE v CHEESED, CHEESING, CHEESES to stop

CHEESY adj CHEESIER, CHEESIEST resembling cheese (a food made from milk curds) CHEESILY adv

CHEETAH n pl. -S a swift-running wildcat

CHEF v CHEFFED, CHEFFING, CHEFS to work as a chef (a chief cook)

CHEFDOM n pl. -S the status or function of a chef

CHEGOE n pl. -S chigoe

CHELA n pl. -LAE a pincerlike claw

CHELA n pl. -S a pupil of a guru

CHELATE v -LATED, -LATING, -LATES to combine a metal ion with a compound

CHELATOR n pl. -S one that chelates

CHELIPED n pl. -S a claw-bearing leg

CHELOID n pl. -S keloid

CHEMIC n pl. -S a chemist

CHEMICAL n pl. -S a substance obtained by a process of chemistry

CHEMISE n pl. -S a loose dress

CHEMISM n pl. -S chemical attraction

CHEMIST n pl. -S one versed in chemistry

CHEMURGY n pl. -GIES a branch of applied chemistry

CHENILLE n pl. -S a soft fabric

CHENOPOD n pl. -S a flowering plant

CHEQUE n pl. -S a written order directing a bank to pay money

CHEQUER v -ED, -ING, -S to checker

CHERISH v -ED, -ING, -ES to hold dear

CHEROOT n pl. -S a square-cut cigar

CHERRY n pl. -RIES a fruit

CHERT n pl. -S a compact rock

CHERTY adj CHERTIER, CHERTIEST resembling chert

CHERUB n pl. -UBS or -UBIM or -UBIMS an angel **CHERUBIC** adj

CHERVIL n pl. -S an aromatic herb

CHESS n pl. -ES a weed

CHESSMAN n pl. -MEN one of the pieces used in chess (a board game for two players)

CHEST n pl. -S a part of the body **CHESTED** adj

CHESTFUL n pl. -S as much as a chest or box can hold

CHESTNUT n pl. -S an edible nut

CHESTY adj CHESTIER, CHESTIEST proud

CHETAH n pl. -S cheetah

CHETH n pl. -S heth

CHETRUM n pl. -S a monetary unit of Bhutan

CHEVALET n pl. -S a part of a stringed instrument

CHEVERON n pl. -S chevron

CHEVIED past tense of chevy

CHEVIES present 3d person sing. of chevy

CHEVIOT n pl. -S a coarse fabric

CHEVRE n pl. -S a cheese made from goat's milk

CHEVRON n pl. -S a V-shaped pattern

CHEVY v CHEVIED, CHEVYING, CHEVIES to chase about

CHEW v -ED, -ING, -S to crush or grind with the teeth **CHEWABLE** adj

CHEWER n pl. -S one that chews

CHEWINK n pl. -S a common finch

CHEWY adj CHEWIER, CHEWIEST not easily chewed

CHEZ prep at the home of

CHI n pl. -S a Greek letter

CHIA n pl. -S a Mexican herb

CHIAO n pl. CHIAO a monetary unit of China

CHIASM n pl. -S chiasrma

CHIASMA n pl. -MATA or -MAS an anatomical junction **CHIASMAL, CHIASMIC** adj

CHIASMUS n pl. -MI a reversal of word order between parallel phrases **CHIASTIC** adj

CHIAUS n pl. -ES a Turkish messenger

CHIBOUK n pl. -S a tobacco pipe

CHIC n pl. -S elegance

CHIC adj CHICER, CHICEST smartly stylish

CHICANE v -CANED, -CANING, -CANES to trick

CHICANER n pl. -S one that chicanes

CHICANO n pl. -NOS an American of Mexican descent

CHICCORY n pl. -RIES chicory

CHICHI n pl. -S elaborate ornamentation

CHICK n pl. -S a young bird

CHICKEE n pl. -S a stilt house of the Seminole Indians

CHICKEN v -ED, -ING, -S to lose one's nerve

CHICKORY n pl. -RIES chicory

CHICKPEA n pl. -S an Asian herb

CHICLE n pl. -S a tree gum

CHICLY adv in an elegant manner

CHICNESS n pl. -ES elegance

CHICO n pl. -COS a prickly shrub

CHICORY n pl. -RIES a perennial herb

CHIDE v CHIDED or CHID, CHIDDEN, CHIDING, CHIDES to scold

CHIDER n pl. -S one that chides

CHIEF adj CHIEFER, CHIEFEST highest in authority

CHIEF n pl. -S the person highest in authority

CHIEFDOM n pl. -S the domain of a chief

CHIEFLY adv above all

CHIEL n pl. -S chield

CHIELD n pl. -S a young man

CHIFFON n pl. -S a sheer fabric

CHIGETAI n pl. -S a wild ass

CHIGGER n pl. -S a parasitic mite

CHIGNON n pl. -S a woman's hairdo

CHIGOE n pl. -S a tropical flea

CHILD n pl. CHILDREN a young person

CHILDBED n pl. -S the state of a woman giving birth

CHILDE n pl. -S a youth of noble birth

CHILDING *adj* pregnant
CHILDISH *adj* resembling a child
CHILDLY *adj* -LIER, -LIEST resembling a child
CHILDREN pl. of child
CHILE *n* pl. -S chili
CHILI *n* pl. -ES a hot pepper
CHILIAD *n* pl. -S a group of one thousand
CHILIASM *n* pl. -S a religious doctrine
CHILIAST *n* pl. -S a supporter of chiliasm
CHILIDOG *n* pl. -S a hot dog topped with chili
CHILL *v* -ED, -ING, -S to make cold
CHILL *adj* CHILLER, CHILLEST cool
CHILLER *n* pl. -S one that chills
CHILLI *n* pl. -ES chili
CHILLUM *n* pl. -S a part of a water pipe
CHILLY *adj* CHILLIER, CHILLIEST cool CHILLILY *adv*
CHILOPOD *n* pl. -S a multi-legged insect
CHIMAERA *n* pl. -S a marine fish
CHIMAR *n* pl. -S chimere
CHIMB *n* pl. -S the rim of a cask
CHIMBLEY *n* pl. -BLEYS chimley
CHIMBLY *n* pl. -BLIES chimley
CHIME *v* CHIMED, CHIMING, CHIMES to ring harmoniously
CHIMER *n* pl. -S one that chimes
CHIMERA *n* pl. -S an imaginary monster
CHIMERE *n* pl. -S a bishop's robe
CHIMERIC *adj* imaginary; unreal
CHIMING present participle of chime
CHIMLA *n* pl. -S chimley
CHIMLEY *n* pl. -LEYS a chimney
CHIMNEY *n* pl. -NEYS a flue
CHIMP *n* pl. -S a chimpanzee
CHIN *v* CHINNED, CHINNING, CHINS to hold with the chin (the lower part of the face)
CHINA *n* pl. -S fine porcelain ware
CHINBONE *n* pl. -S the lower jaw
CHINCH *n* pl. -ES a bedbug
CHINCHY *adj* CHINCHIER, CHINCHIEST stingy
CHINE *v* CHINED, CHINING, CHINES to cut through the backbone of
CHINK *v* -ED, -ING, -S to fill cracks or fissures in
CHINKY *adj* CHINKIER, CHINKIEST full of cracks
CHINLESS *adj* lacking a chin
CHINNED past tense of chin
CHINNING present participle of chin
CHINO *n* pl. -NOS a strong fabric

CHINONE *n* pl. -S quinone
CHINOOK *n* pl. -S a warm wind
CHINTS *n* pl. -ES chintz
CHINTZ *n* pl. -ES a cotton fabric
CHINTZY *adj* CHINTZIER, CHINTZIEST gaudy; cheap
CHIP *v* CHIPPED, CHIPPING, CHIPS to break a small piece from
CHIPMUCK *n* pl. -S a chipmunk
CHIPMUNK *n* pl. -S a small rodent
CHIPPED past tense of chip
CHIPPER *v* -ED, -ING, -S to chirp
CHIPPIE *n* pl. -S chippy
CHIPPING present participle of chip
CHIPPY *n* pl. -PIES a prostitute
CHIPPY *adj* -PIER, -PIEST belligerent
CHIRAL *adj* pertaining to an asymmetrical molecule
CHIRK *v* -ED, -ING, -S to make a shrill noise
CHIRK *adj* CHIRKER, CHIRKEST cheerful
CHIRM *v* -ED, -ING, -S to chirp
CHIRO *n* pl. -ROS a marine fish
CHIRP *v* -ED, -ING, -S to utter a short, shrill sound
CHIRPER *n* pl. -S one that chirps
CHIRPY *adj* CHIRPIER, CHIRPIEST cheerful CHIRPILY *adv*
CHIRR *v* -ED, -ING, -S to make a harsh, vibrant sound
CHIRRE *v* CHIRRED, CHIRRING, CHIRRES to chirr
CHIRRUP *v* -ED, -ING, -S to chirp repeatedly CHIRRUPY *adj*
CHISEL *v* -ELED, -ELING, -ELS or -ELLED, -ELLING, -ELS to use a chisel (a cutting tool)
CHISELER *n* pl. -S one that chisels
CHIT *n* pl. -S a short letter
CHITAL *n* pl. CHITAL an Asian deer
CHITCHAT *v* -CHATTED, -CHATTING, -CHATS to indulge in small talk
CHITIN *n* pl. -S the main component of insect shells
CHITLIN *n* pl. -S chitling
CHITLING *n* pl. -S a part of the small intestine of swine
CHITON *n* pl. -S a tunic worn in ancient Greece
CHITOSAN *n* pl. -S a compound derived from chitin
CHITTER *v* -ED, -ING, -S to twitter
CHITTY *n* pl. -TIES a chit

CHIVALRY *n* pl. -RIES knightly behavior and skill

CHIVAREE *v* -REED, -REEING, -REES to perform a mock serenade

CHIVARI *v* -RIED, -RIING, -RIES to chivaree

CHIVE *n* pl. -S an herb used as a seasoning

CHIVVY *v* -VIED, -VYING, -VIES to chevy

CHIVY *v* CHIVIED, CHIVYING, CHIVIES to chevy

CHLAMYS *n* pl. -MYSES or -MYDES a garment worn in ancient Greece

CHLOASMA *n* pl. -MATA a skin discoloration

CHLORAL *n* pl. -S a chemical compound

CHLORATE *n* pl. -S a chemical salt

CHLORDAN *n* pl. -S a toxic compound of chlorine

CHLORIC *adj* pertaining to chlorine

CHLORID *n* pl. -S chloride

CHLORIDE *n* pl. -S a chlorine compound

CHLORIN *n* pl. -S chlorine

CHLORINE *n* pl. -S a gaseous element

CHLORITE *n* pl. -S a mineral group

CHLOROUS *adj* pertaining to chlorine

CHOANA *n* pl. -NAE a funnel-shaped opening

CHOCK *v* -ED, -ING, -S to secure with a wedge of wood or metal

CHOCKFUL *adj* full to the limit

CHOICE *n* pl. -S one that is chosen

CHOICE *adj* CHOICER, CHOICEST of fine quality **CHOICELY** *adv*

CHOIR *v* -ED, -ING, -S to sing in unison

CHOIRBOY *n* pl. -BOYS a boy who sings in a choir (a body of church singers)

CHOKE *v* CHOKED, CHOKING, CHOKES to impede the breathing of

CHOKER *n* pl. -S one that chokes

CHOKEY *adj* CHOKIER, CHOKIEST choky

CHOKING present participle of choke

CHOKY *adj* CHOKIER, CHOKIEST tending to cause choking

CHOLATE *n* pl. -S a chemical salt

CHOLENT *n* pl. -S a traditional Jewish stew

CHOLER *n* pl. -S anger

CHOLERA *n* pl. -S an acute disease

CHOLERIC *adj* bad-tempered

CHOLINE *n* pl. -S a B vitamin

CHOLLA *n* pl. -S a treelike cactus

CHOLO *n* pl. -LOS a pachuco

CHOMP *v* -ED, -ING, -S to champ

CHOMPER *n* pl. -S one that chomps

CHON *n* pl. CHON a monetary unit of South Korea

CHOOK *n* pl. -S a chicken

CHOOSE *v* CHOSE, CHOSEN, CHOOSING, CHOOSES to take by preference

CHOOSER *n* pl. -S one that chooses

CHOOSEY *adj* CHOOSIER, CHOOSIEST choosy

CHOOSING present participle of choose

CHOOSY *adj* CHOOSIER, CHOOSIEST hard to please

CHOP *v* CHOPPED, CHOPPING, CHOPS to sever with a sharp tool

CHOPIN *n* pl. -S chopine

CHOPINE *n* pl. -S a type of shoe

CHOPPED past tense of chop

CHOPPER *v* -ED, -ING, -S to travel by helicopter

CHOPPING present participle of chop

CHOPPY *adj* CHOPPIER, CHOPPIEST full of short, rough waves **CHOPPILY** *adv*

CHORAGUS *n* pl. -GI or -GUSES the leader of a chorus or choir **CHORAGIC** *adj*

CHORAL *n* pl. -S chorale

CHORALE *n* pl. -S a hymn that is sung in unison

CHORALLY *adv* harmoniously

CHORD *v* -ED, -ING, -S to play a chord (a combination of three or more musical tones)

CHORDAL *adj* pertaining to a chord

CHORDATE *n* pl. -S any of a large phylum of animals

CHORE *v* CHORED, CHORING, CHORES to do small jobs

CHOREA *n* pl. -S a nervous disorder **CHOREAL, CHOREIC** *adj*

CHOREGUS *n* pl. -GI or -GUSES choragus

CHOREMAN *n* pl. -MEN a menial worker

CHOREOID *adj* resembling chorea

CHORIAL *adj* pertaining to the chorion

CHORIAMB *n* pl. -S a type of metrical foot

CHORIC *adj* pertaining to a chorus

CHORINE *n* pl. -S a chorus girl

CHORING present participle of chore

CHORIOID *n* pl. -S choroid

CHORION *n* pl. -S an embryonic membrane

CHORIZO *n* pl. -ZOS a highly seasoned sausage

CHOROID *n* pl. -S a membrane of the eye

CHORTLE *v* -TLED, -TLING, -TLES to chuckle with glee

CHORTLER *n* pl. -S one that chortles

CHORUS *v* -RUSED, -RUSING, -RUSES or -RUSSED, -RUSSING, -RUSSES to sing in unison

CHOSE *n* pl. -S an item of personal property

CHOSEN past participle of choose

CHOTT *n* pl. -S a saline lake

CHOUGH *n* pl. -S a crow-like bird

CHOUSE *v* CHOUSED, CHOUSING, CHOUSES to swindle

CHOUSER *n* pl. -S one that chouses

CHOUSH *n* pl. -ES chiaus

CHOUSING present participle of chouse

CHOW *v* -ED, -ING, -S to eat

CHOWCHOW *n* pl. -S a relish of mixed pickles in mustard

CHOWDER *v* -ED, -ING, -S to make a thick soup of

CHOWSE *v* CHOWSED, CHOWSING, CHOWSES to chouse

CHOWTIME *n* pl. -S mealtime

CHRESARD *n* pl. -S the available water of the soil

CHRISM *n* pl. -S a consecrated oil **CHRISMAL** *adj*

CHRISMON *n* pl. -MA or -MONS a Christian monogram

CHRISOM *n* pl. -S chrism

CHRISTEN *v* -ED, -ING, -S to baptise

CHRISTIE *n* pl. -S christy

CHRISTY *n* pl. -TIES a skiing turn

CHROMA *n* pl. -S the purity of a color

CHROMATE *n* pl. -S a chemical salt

CHROME *v* CHROMED, CHROMING, CHROMES to plate with chromium

CHROMIC *adj* pertaining to chromium

CHROMIDE *n* pl. -S a tropical fish

CHROMING *n* pl. -S a chromium ore

CHROMITE *n* pl. -S a chromium ore

CHROMIUM *n* pl. -S a metallic element

CHROMIZE *v* -MIZED, -MIZING, -MIZES to chrome

CHROMO *n* pl. -MOS a type of color picture

CHROMOUS *adj* pertaining to chromium

CHROMYL *n* pl. -S a bivalent radical

CHRONAXY *n* pl. -AXIES the time required to excite a nerve cell electrically

CHRONIC *n* pl. -S one that suffers from a long-lasting disease

CHRONON *n* pl. -S a hypothetical unit of time

CHTHONIC *adj* pertaining to the gods of the underworld

CHUB *n* pl. -S a freshwater fish

CHUBASCO *n* pl. -COS a violent thunderstorm

CHUBBY *adj* -BIER, -BIEST plump **CHUBBILY** *adv*

CHUCK *v* -ED, -ING, -S to throw

CHUCKIES pl. of chucky

CHUCKLE *v* -LED, -LING, -LES to laugh quietly

CHUCKLER *n* pl. -S one that chuckles

CHUCKY *n* pl. CHUCKIES a little chick

CHUDDAH *n* pl. -S chuddar

CHUDDAR *n* pl. -S a large, square shawl

CHUDDER *n* pl. -S chuddar

CHUFA *n* pl. -S a European sedge

CHUFF *adj* CHUFFER, CHUFFEST gruff

CHUFF *v* -ED, -ING, -S to chug

CHUFFY *adj* -FIER, -FIEST plump

CHUG *v* CHUGGED, CHUGGING, CHUGS to move with a dull explosive sound

CHUGALUG *v* -LUGGED, -LUGGING, -LUGS to drink without pause

CHUGGER *n* pl. -S one that chugs

CHUKAR *n* pl. -S a game bird

CHUKKA *n* pl. -S a type of boot

CHUKKAR *n* pl. -S a chukker

CHUKKER *n* pl. -S a period of play in polo

CHUM *v* CHUMMED, CHUMMING, CHUMS to be close friends with someone

CHUMMY *adj* -MIER, -MIEST friendly **CHUMMILY** *adv*

CHUMP *v* -ED, -ING, -S to munch

CHUMSHIP *n* pl. -S friendship

CHUNK *v* -ED, -ING, -S to make a dull explosive sound

CHUNKY *adj* CHUNKIER, CHUNKIEST stocky **CHUNKILY** *adv*

CHUNTER *v* -ED, -ING, -S to mutter

CHURCH *v* -ED, -ING, -ES to bring to church (a building for Christian worship)

CHURCHLY *adj* -LIER, -LIEST pertaining to a church

CHURCHY adj CHURCHIER, CHURCHIEST churchly

CHURL n pl. -S a rude person CHURLISH adj

CHURN v -ED, -ING, -S to stir briskly in order to make butter

CHURNER n pl. -S one that churns

CHURNING n pl. -S the butter churned at one time

CHURR v -ED, -ING, -S to make a vibrant sound

CHUTE v CHUTED, CHUTING, CHUTES to convey by chute (a vertical passage)

CHUTIST n pl. -S a parachutist

CHUTNEE n pl. -S chutney

CHUTNEY n pl. -NEYS a sweet and sour sauce

CHUTZPA n pl. -S chutzpah

CHUTZPAH n pl. -S supreme self-confidence

CHYLE n pl. -S a digestive fluid CHYLOUS adj

CHYME n pl. -S semi-digested food

CHYMIC n pl. -S chemic

CHYMIST n pl. -S chemist

CHYMOSIN n pl. -S rennin

CHYMOUS adj pertaining to chyme

CIAO interj — used as an expression of greeting and farewell

CIBOL n pl. -S a variety of onion

CIBORIUM n pl. -RIA a vessel for holding holy bread

CIBOULE n pl. -S cibol

CICADA n pl. -DAS or -DAE a winged insect

CICALA n pl. -LAS or -LE cicada

CICATRIX n pl. -TRICES or -TRIXES scar tissue

CICELY n pl. -LIES a fragrant herb

CICERO n pl. -ROS a unit of measure in printing

CICERONE n pl. -NES or -NI a tour guide

CICHLID n pl. -LIDS or -LIDAE a tropical fish

CICISBEO n pl. -BEI or -BEOS a lover of a married woman

CICOREE n pl. -S a perennial herb

CIDER n pl. -S the juice pressed from apples

CIGAR n pl. -S a roll of tobacco leaf for smoking

CIGARET n pl. -S a narrow roll of finely cut tobacco for smoking

CILANTRO n pl. -TROS an herb used in cooking

CILIA pl. of cilium

CILIARY adj pertaining to cilia

CILIATE n pl. -S one of a class of ciliated protozoans

CILIATED adj having cilia

CILICE n pl. -S a coarse cloth

CILIUM n pl. CILIA a short, hairlike projection

CIMBALOM n pl. -S a Hungarian dulcimer

CIMEX n pl. -MICES a bedbug

CINCH v -ED, -ING, -ES to girth

CINCHONA n pl. -S a Peruvian tree

CINCTURE v -TURED, -TURING, -TURES to gird or encircle

CINDER v -ED, -ING, -S to reduce to cinders (ashes)

CINDERY adj containing cinders

CINE n pl. -S a motion picture

CINEAST n pl. -S a devotee of motion pictures

CINEASTE n pl. -S cineast

CINEMA n pl. -S a motion-picture theater

CINEOL n pl. -S a liquid used as an antiseptic

CINEOLE n pl. -S cineol

CINERARY adj used for cremated ashes

CINERIN n pl. -S a compound used in insecticides

CINGULUM n pl. -LA an anatomical band or girdle

CINNABAR n pl. -S the principal ore of mercury

CINNAMON n pl. -S a spice obtained from tree bark CINNAMIC adj

CINNAMYL n pl. -S a chemical used to make soap

CINQUAIN n pl. -S a stanza of five lines

CINQUE n pl. -S the number five

CION n pl. -S a cutting from a plant or tree

CIOPPINO n pl. -NOS a spicy fish stew

CIPHER v -ED, -ING, -S to solve problems in arithmetic

CIPHONY n pl. -NIES the electronic scrambling of voice transmissions

CIPOLIN n pl. -S a type of marble

CIRCA prep about; around

CIRCLE v -CLED, -CLING, -CLES to move or revolve around

CIRCLER n pl. -S one that circles

CIRCLET n pl. -S a small ring or ring-shaped object

CIRCLING present participle of circle

CIRCUIT *v* -ED, -ING, -S to move around

CIRCUITY *n pl.* -ITIES lack of straightforwardness

CIRCULAR *n pl.* -S a leaflet intended for wide distribution

CIRCUS *n pl.* -ES a public entertainment CIRCUSY *adj*

CIRE *n pl.* -S a highly glazed finish for fabrics

CIRQUE *n pl.* -S a deep, steep-walled basin on a mountain

CIRRATE *adj* having cirri

CIRRI *pl.* of cirrus

CIRRIPED *n pl.* -S any of an order of crustaceans

CIRROSE *adj* cirrous

CIRROUS *adj* having cirri

CIRRUS *n pl.* -RI a tendril or similar part

CIRSOID *adj* varicose

CIS *adj* having certain atoms on the same side of the molecule

CISCO *n pl.* -COS or -COES a freshwater fish

CISLUNAR *adj* situated between the earth and the moon

CISSOID *n pl.* -S a type of geometric curve

CISSY *n pl.* -SIES sissy

CIST *n pl.* -S a prehistoric stone coffin

CISTERN *n pl.* -S a water tank

CISTERNA *n pl.* -NAE a fluid-containing sac

CISTRON *n pl.* -S a segment of DNA

CISTUS *n pl.* -ES a flowering shrub

CITABLE *adj* citeable

CITADEL *n pl.* -S a fortress or stronghold

CITATION *n pl.* -S the act of citing CITATORY *adj*

CITATOR *n pl.* -S one that cites

CITE *v* CITED, CITING, CITES to quote as an authority or example

CITEABLE *adj* suitable for citation

CITER *n pl.* -S one that cites

CITHARA *n pl.* -S an ancient stringed instrument

CITHER *n pl.* -S cittern

CITHERN *n pl.* -S cittern

CITHREN *n pl.* -S cittern

CITIED *adj* having cities

CITIES *pl.* of city

CITIFY *v* -FIED, -FYING, -FIES to urbanize

CITING present participle of cite

CITIZEN *n pl.* -S a resident of a city or town

CITOLA *n pl.* -S a cittern

CITOLE *n pl.* -S citola

CITRAL *n pl.* -S a lemon flavoring

CITRATE *n pl.* -S a salt of citric acid CITRATED *adj*

CITREOUS *adj* having a lemonlike color

CITRIC *adj* derived from citrus fruits

CITRIN *n pl.* -S a citric vitamin

CITRINE *n pl.* -S a variety of quartz

CITRININ *n pl.* -S an antibiotic

CITRON *n pl.* -S a lemonlike fruit

CITROUS *adj* pertaining to a citrus tree

CITRUS *n pl.* -ES any of a genus of tropical, fruit-bearing trees CITRUSY *adj*

CITTERN *n pl.* -S a pear-shaped guitar

CITY *n pl.* CITIES a large town

CITYFIED *adj* having the customs and manners of city people

CITYWARD *adv* toward the city

CITYWIDE *adj* including all parts of a city

CIVET *n pl.* -S a catlike mammal

CIVIC *adj* pertaining to a city

CIVICISM *n pl.* -S a system of government based upon individual rights

CIVICS *n/pl* the science of civic affairs

CIVIE *n pl.* -S civvy

CIVIL *adj* pertaining to citizens

CIVILIAN *n pl.* -S a nonmilitary person

CIVILISE *v* -LISED, -LISING, -LISES to civilize

CIVILITY *n pl.* -TIES courtesy; politeness

CIVILIZE *v* -LIZED, -LIZING, -LIZES to bring out of savagery

CIVILLY *adv* politely

CIVISM *n pl.* -S good citizenship

CIVVY *n pl.* -VIES a civilian

CLABBER *v* -ED, -ING, -S to curdle

CLACH *n pl.* -S clachan

CLACHAN *n pl.* -S a hamlet

CLACK *v* -ED, -ING, -S to make an abrupt, dry sound

CLACKER *n pl.* -S one that clacks

CLAD *v* CLAD, CLADDING, CLADS to coat one metal over another

CLADDING *n pl.* -S something that overlays

CLADE *n pl.* -S a group of biological taxa

CLADIST n pl. -S a taxonomist who uses clades in classifying life-forms

CLADODE n pl. -S a leaflike part of a stem

CLAG v CLAGGED, CLAGGING, CLAGS to clog

CLAIM v -ED, -ING, -S to demand as one's due

CLAIMANT n pl. -S one that asserts a right or title

CLAIMER n pl. -S one that claims

CLAM v CLAMMED, CLAMMING, CLAMS to dig for clams (bivalve mollusks)

CLAMANT adj noisy

CLAMBAKE n pl. -S a beach picnic

CLAMBER v -ED, -ING, -S to climb awkwardly

CLAMMED past tense of clam

CLAMMER n pl. -S one that clams

CLAMMING present participle of clam

CLAMMY adj CLAMMIER, CLAMMIEST cold and damp **CLAMMILY** adv

CLAMOR v -ED, -ING, -S to make loud outcries

CLAMORER n pl. -S one that clamors

CLAMOUR v -ED, -ING, -S to clamor

CLAMP v -ED, -ING, -S to fasten with a clamp (a securing device)

CLAMPER n pl. -S a device worn on shoes to prevent slipping on ice

CLAMWORM n pl. -S a marine worm

CLAN n pl. -S a united group of families

CLANG v -ED, -ING, -S to ring loudly

CLANGER n pl. -S a blunder

CLANGOR v -ED, -ING, -S to clang repeatedly

CLANGOUR v -ED, -ING, -S to clangor

CLANK v -ED, -ING, -S to make a sharp, metallic sound

CLANNISH adj characteristic of a clan

CLANSMAN n pl. -MEN a member of a clan

CLAP v CLAPPED or CLAPT, CLAPPING, CLAPS to strike one palm against the other

CLAPPER n pl. -S one that claps

CLAPTRAP n pl. -S pretentious language

CLAQUE n pl. -S a group of hired applauders

CLAQUER n pl. -S claqueur

CLAQUEUR n pl. -S a member of a claque

CLARENCE n pl. -S a closed carriage

CLARET n pl. -S a dry red wine

CLARIES pl. of clary

CLARIFY v -FIED, -FYING, -FIES to make clear

CLARINET n pl. -S a woodwind instrument

CLARION v -ED, -ING, -S to proclaim by blowing a medieval trumpet

CLARITY n pl. -TIES the state of being clear

CLARKIA n pl. -S an annual herb

CLARO n pl. -ROS or -ROES a mild cigar

CLARY n pl. CLARIES an aromatic herb

CLASH v -ED, -ING, -ES to conflict or disagree

CLASHER n pl. -S one that clashes

CLASP v CLASPED or CLASPT, CLASPING, CLASPS to embrace tightly

CLASPER n pl. -S one that clasps

CLASS v -ED, -ING, -ES to classify

CLASSER n pl. -S one that classes

CLASSES pl. of classis

CLASSIC n pl. -S a work of enduring excellence

CLASSICO adj made from grapes grown in a certain part of Italy

CLASSIER comparative of classy

CLASSIEST superlative of classy

CLASSIFY v -FIED, -FYING, -FIES to arrange according to characteristics

CLASSILY adv in a classy manner

CLASSIS n pl. CLASSES a governing body in certain churches

CLASSISM n pl. -S discrimination based on social class

CLASSIST n pl. -S an advocate of classism

CLASSY adj CLASSIER, CLASSIEST stylish; elegant

CLAST n pl. -S a fragment of rock

CLASTIC n pl. -S a rock made up of other rocks

CLATTER v -ED, -ING, -S to move with a rattling noise

CLATTERY adj having a rattling noise

CLAUCHT a past tense of cleek

CLAUGHT v -ED, -ING, -S to clutch

CLAUSE n pl. -S a distinct part of a composition **CLAUSAL** adj

CLAUSTRA n/pl basal ganglia in the brain

CLAVATE adj shaped like a club

CLAVE *n pl.* -S one of a pair of percussion sticks

CLAVER *v* -ED, -ING, -S to gossip

CLAVI *pl.* of clavus

CLAVICLE *n pl.* -S a bone of the shoulder

CLAVIER *n pl.* -S a keyboard instrument

CLAVUS *n pl.* -VI a horny thickening of the skin

CLAW *v* -ED, -ING, -S to scratch with claws (sharp, curved toenails)

CLAWER *n pl.* -S one that claws

CLAWLESS *adj* having no claws

CLAWLIKE *adj* resembling a claw

CLAXON *n pl.* -S klaxon

CLAY *v* -ED, -ING, -S to treat with clay (a fine-grained, earthy material)

CLAYBANK *n pl.* -S a yellow-brown color

CLAYEY *adj* CLAYIER, CLAYIEST resembling clay

CLAYISH *adj* resembling or containing clay

CLAYLIKE *adj* resembling clay

CLAYMORE *n pl.* -S a type of sword

CLAYPAN *n pl.* -S a shallow natural depression

CLAYWARE *n pl.* -S pottery

CLEAN *adj* CLEANER, CLEANEST free from dirt or stain

CLEAN *v* -ED, -ING, -S to rid of dirt or stain

CLEANER *n pl.* -S one that cleans

CLEANLY *adj* -LIER, -LIEST habitually clean

CLEANSE *v* CLEANSED, CLEANSING, CLEANSES to clean

CLEANSER *n pl.* -S one that cleanses

CLEANUP *n pl.* -S an act of cleaning

CLEAR *adj* CLEARER, CLEAREST clean and pure

CLEAR *v* -ED, -ING, -S to remove obstructions

CLEARER *n pl.* -S one that clears

CLEARING *n pl.* -S an open space

CLEARLY *adv* in a clear manner

CLEAT *v* -ED, -ING, -S to strengthen with a strip of wood or iron

CLEAVAGE *n pl.* -S the act of cleaving

CLEAVE *v* CLEAVED, CLEFT, CLOVE or CLAVE, CLOVEN, CLEAVING, CLEAVES to split or divide

CLEAVER *n pl.* -S a heavy knife

CLEEK *v* CLAUGHT or CLEEKED, CLEEKING, CLEEKS to clutch

CLEF *n pl.* -S a musical symbol

CLEFT *v* -ED, -ING, -S to insert a scion into the stock of a plant

CLEIDOIC *adj* enclosed in a shell

CLEMATIS *n pl.* -TISES a flowering vine

CLEMENCY *n pl.* -CIES mercy

CLEMENT *adj* merciful

CLENCH *v* -ED, -ING, -ES to grasp firmly

CLENCHER *n pl.* -S one that clenches

CLEOME *n pl.* -S a tropical plant

CLEPE *v* CLEPED or CLEPT, CLEPING, CLEPES to call by name

CLERGY *n pl.* -GIES the body of persons ordained for religious service

CLERIC *n pl.* -S a member of the clergy

CLERICAL *n pl.* -S a cleric

CLERID *n pl.* -S a predatory beetle

CLERIHEW *n pl.* -S a humorous poem

CLERISY *n pl.* -SIES the well-educated class

CLERK *v* -ED, -ING, -S to serve as a clerk (an office worker)

CLERKDOM *n pl.* -S the status or function of a clerk

CLERKISH *adj* resembling or suitable to a clerk

CLERKLY *adj* -LIER, -LIEST pertaining to a clerk

CLEVEITE *n pl.* -S a radioactive mineral

CLEVER *adj* -ERER, -EREST mentally keen **CLEVERLY** *adv*

CLEVIS *n pl.* -ISES a metal fastening device

CLEW *v* -ED, -ING, -S to roll into a ball

CLICHE *n pl.* -S a trite expression **CLICHED** *adj*

CLICK *v* -ED, -ING, -S to make a short, sharp sound

CLICKER *n pl.* -S one that clicks

CLIENT *n pl.* -S a customer **CLIENTAL** *adj*

CLIFF *n pl.* -S a high, steep face of rock

CLIFFY *adj* CLIFFIER, CLIFFIEST abounding in cliffs

CLIFT *n pl.* -S cliff

CLIMATE *n pl.* -S the weather conditions characteristic of an area **CLIMATAL, CLIMATIC** *adj*

CLIMAX *v* -ED, -ING, -ES to reach a high or dramatic point

CLIMB	v CLIMBED or CLOMB, CLIMBING, CLIMBS to ascend
CLIMBER	n pl. -S one that climbs
CLIME	n pl. -S climate
CLINAL	adj pertaining to a cline
CLINALLY	adv in a clinal manner
CLINCH	v -ED, -ING, -ES to settle a matter decisively
CLINCHER	n pl. -S a decisive fact or remark
CLINE	n pl. -S a series of changes within a species
CLING	v CLUNG, CLINGING, CLINGS to adhere closely
CLING	v -ED, -ING, -S to make a high-pitched ringing sound
CLINGER	n pl. -S one that clings
CLINGY	adj CLINGIER, CLINGIEST adhesive
CLINIC	n pl. -S a medical facility CLINICAL adj
CLINK	v -ED, -ING, -S to make a soft, sharp, ringing sound
CLINKER	v -ED, -ING, -S to form fused residue in burning
CLIP	v CLIPPED or CLIPT, CLIPPING, CLIPS to trim by cutting
CLIPPER	n pl. -S one that clips
CLIPPING	n pl. -S something that is clipped out or off
CLIPT	a past participle of clip
CLIQUE	v CLIQUED, CLIQUING, CLIQUES to form a clique (an exclusive group of persons)
CLIQUEY	adj CLIQUIER, CLIQUIEST inclined to form cliques
CLIQUISH	adj cliquey
CLIQUY	adj CLIQUIER, CLIQUIEST cliquey
CLITELLA	n/pl regions in the body walls of certain annelids
CLITIC	n pl. -S a word pronounced as part of a neighboring word
CLITORIS	n pl. -RISES or -RIDES a sex organ CLITORAL, CLITORIC adj
CLIVERS	n pl. CLIVERS an annual herb
CLIVIA	n pl. -S a flowering plant
CLOACA	n pl. -ACAE or -ACAS a sewer CLOACAL adj
CLOAK	v -ED, -ING, -S to conceal
CLOBBER	v -ED, -ING, -S to trounce
CLOCHARD	n pl. -S a vagrant
CLOCHE	n pl. -S a bell-shaped hat
CLOCK	v -ED, -ING, -S to time with a stopwatch
CLOCKER	n pl. -S one that clocks
CLOD	n pl. -S a dolt CLODDISH adj
CLODDY	adj -DIER, -DIEST lumpy
CLODPATE	n pl. -S a stupid person
CLODPOLE	n pl. -S clodpate
CLODPOLL	n pl. -S clodpate
CLOG	v CLOGGED, CLOGGING, CLOGS to block up or obstruct
CLOGGER	n pl. -S one that clogs
CLOGGY	adj -GIER, -GIEST clogging or able to clog
CLOISTER	v -ED, -ING, -S to seclude
CLOMB	a past tense of climb
CLOMP	v -ED, -ING, -S to walk heavily and clumsily
CLON	n pl. -S a group of asexually derived organisms CLONAL adj CLONALLY adv
CLONE	v CLONED, CLONING, CLONES to reproduce by asexual means
CLONER	n pl. -S one that clones
CLONIC	adj pertaining to clonus
CLONING	n pl. -S a technique for reproducing by asexual means
CLONISM	n pl. -S the condition of having clonus
CLONK	v -ED, -ING, -S to make a dull thumping sound
CLONUS	n pl. -ES a form of muscular spasm
CLOOT	n pl. -S a cloven hoof
CLOP	v CLOPPED, CLOPPING, CLOPS to make the sound of a hoof striking pavement
CLOQUE	n pl. -S a fabric with an embossed design
CLOSE	adj CLOSER, CLOSEST near CLOSELY adv
CLOSE	v CLOSED, CLOSING, CLOSES to block against entry or passage CLOSABLE adj
CLOSEOUT	n pl. -S a clearance sale
CLOSER	n pl. -S one that closes
CLOSEST	superlative of close
CLOSET	v -ED, -ING, -S to enclose in a private room
CLOSING	n pl. -S a concluding part
CLOSURE	v -SURED, -SURING, -SURES to cloture
CLOT	v CLOTTED, CLOTTING, CLOTS to form into a clot (a thick mass)
CLOTH	n pl. -S fabric

CLOTHE v CLOTHED or CLAD, CLOTHING, CLOTHES to provide with clothing

CLOTHIER n pl. -S one who makes or sells clothing

CLOTHING n pl. -S wearing apparel

CLOTTED past tense of clot

CLOTTING present participle of clot

CLOTTY adj tending to clot

CLOTURE v -TURED, -TURING, -TURES to end a debate by calling for a vote

CLOUD v -ED, -ING, -S to cover with clouds (masses of visible vapor)

CLOUDLET n pl. -S a small cloud

CLOUDY adj CLOUDIER, CLOUDIEST overcast with clouds CLOUDILY adv

CLOUGH n pl. -S a ravine

CLOUR v -ED, -ING, -S to knock or bump

CLOUT v -ED, -ING, -S to hit with the hand

CLOUTER n pl. -S one that clouts

CLOVE n pl. -S a spice

CLOVEN adj split; divided

CLOVER n pl. -S a plant

CLOWDER n pl. -S a group of cats

CLOWN v -ED, -ING, -S to act like a clown (a humorous performer)

CLOWNERY n pl. -ERIES clownish behavior

CLOWNISH adj resembling or befitting a clown

CLOY v -ED, -ING, -S to gratify beyond desire

CLOZE n pl. -S a test of reading comprehension

CLUB v CLUBBED, CLUBBING, CLUBS to form a club (an organized group of persons)

CLUBABLE adj sociable

CLUBBER n pl. -S a member of a club

CLUBBING present participle of club

CLUBBISH adj clubby

CLUBBY adj -BIER, -BIEST characteristic of a club

CLUBFOOT n pl. -FEET a deformed foot

CLUBHAND n pl. -S a deformed hand

CLUBHAUL v -ED, -ING, -S to put a vessel about

CLUBMAN n pl. -MEN a male member of a club

CLUBROOM n pl. -S a room for a club's meetings

CLUBROOT n pl. -S a plant disease

CLUCK v -ED, -ING, -S to make the sound of a hen

CLUE v CLUED, CLUEING or CLUING, CLUES to give guiding information

CLUELESS adj hopelessly confused or ignorant

CLUMBER n pl. -S a stocky spaniel

CLUMP v -ED, -ING, -S to form into a thick mass

CLUMPISH adj resembling a clump (a thick mass)

CLUMPY adj CLUMPIER, CLUMPIEST lumpy

CLUMSY adj -SIER, -SIEST awkward CLUMSILY adv

CLUNG past tense of cling

CLUNK v -ED, -ING, -S to thump

CLUNKER n pl. -S a jalopy

CLUNKY adj CLUNKIER, CLUNKIEST clumsy in style

CLUPEID n pl. -S a fish of the herring family

CLUPEOID n pl. -S a clupeid

CLUSTER v -ED, -ING, -S to form into a cluster (a group of similar objects)

CLUSTERY adj pertaining to a cluster

CLUTCH v -ED, -ING, -ES to grasp and hold tightly

CLUTCHY adj tending to clutch

CLUTTER v -ED, -ING, -S to pile in a disorderly state

CLUTTERY adj characterized by disorder

CLYPEUS n pl. CLYPEI a shield-like structure CLYPEAL, CLYPEATE adj

CLYSTER n pl. -S an enema

COACH v -ED, -ING, -ES to tutor or train

COACHER n pl. -S one that coaches

COACHMAN n pl. -MEN one who drives a coach or carriage

COACT v -ED, -ING, -S to act together

COACTION n pl. -S joint action

COACTIVE adj mutually active

COACTOR n pl. -S a fellow actor in a production

COADMIRE v -MIRED, -MIRING, -MIRES to admire together

COADMIT v -MITTED, -MITTING, -MITS to admit several things equally

COAEVAL n pl. -S coeval

COAGENCY n pl. -CIES a joint agency

COAGENT n pl. -S a person, force, or other agent working together with another

COAGULUM n pl. -LA or -LUMS a clot

COAL v -ED, -ING, -S to supply with coal (a carbon fuel)

COALA n pl. -S koala

COALBIN n pl. -S a bin for storing coal

COALBOX n pl. -ES a box for storing coal

COALER n pl. -S one that supplies coal

COALESCE v -ALESCED, -ALESCING, -ALESCES to blend

COALFISH n pl. -ES a blackish fish

COALHOLE n pl. -S a compartment for storing coal

COALIER comparative of coaly

COALIEST superlative of coaly

COALIFY v -FIED, -FYING, -FIES to convert into coal

COALLESS adj lacking coal

COALPIT n pl. -S a pit from which coal is obtained

COALSACK n pl. -S a dark region of the Milky Way

COALSHED n pl. -S a shed for storing coal

COALY adj COALIER, COALIEST containing coal

COALYARD n pl. -S a yard for storing coal

COAMING n pl. -S a raised border

COANCHOR v -ED, -ING, -S to present televised news reports jointly

COANNEX v -ED, -ING, -ES to annex jointly

COAPPEAR v -ED, -ING, -S to appear together or at the same time

COAPT v -ED, -ING, -S to fit together and make fast

COARSE adj COARSER, COARSEST rough COARSELY adv

COARSEN v -ED, -ING, -S to make coarse

COASSIST v -ED, -ING, -S to assist jointly

COASSUME v -SUMED, -SUMING, -SUMES to assume together

COAST v -ED, -ING, -S to slide down a hill

COASTAL adj pertaining to or located near a seashore

COASTER n pl. -S a sled

COASTING n pl. -S coastal trade

COAT v -ED, -ING, -S to cover with a coat (an outer garment)

COATEE n pl. -S a small coat

COATER n pl. -S one that coats

COATI n pl. -S a tropical mammal

COATING n pl. -S a covering layer

COATLESS adj lacking a coat

COATRACK n pl. -S a rack or stand for coats

COATROOM n pl. -S a room for storing coats

COATTAIL n pl. -S the back lower portion of a coat

COATTEND v -ED, -ING, -S to attend together

COATTEST v -ED, -ING, -S to attest jointly

COAUTHOR v -ED, -ING, -S to write together

COAX v -ED, -ING, -ES to cajole

COAXAL adj coaxial

COAXER n pl. -S one that coaxes

COAXIAL adj having a common axis

COB n pl. -S a corncob

COBALT n pl. -S a metallic element COBALTIC adj

COBB n pl. -S a sea gull

COBBER n pl. -S a comrade

COBBIER comparative of cobby

COBBIEST superlative of cobby

COBBLE v -BLED, -BLING, -BLES to mend

COBBLER n pl. -S a mender of shoes

COBBY adj -BIER, -BIEST stocky

COBIA n pl. -S a large game fish

COBLE n pl. -S a small fishing boat

COBNUT n pl. -S an edible nut

COBRA n pl. -S a venomous snake

COBWEB v -WEBBED, -WEBBING, -WEBS to cover with cobwebs (spider webs)

COBWEBBY adj -BIER, -BIEST covered with cobwebs

COCA n pl. -S a South American shrub

COCAIN n pl. -S cocaine

COCAINE n pl. -S a narcotic alkaloid

COCCAL adj pertaining to a coccus

COCCI pl. of coccus

COCCIC adj coccal

COCCID n pl. -S an insect

COCCIDIA n/pl parasitic protozoans

COCCOID n pl. -S a spherical cell or body

COCCUS n pl. COCCI a spherical bacterium COCCOUS adj

COCCYX n pl. -CYGES or -CYXES a bone of the spine

COCHAIR v -ED, -ING, -S to serve jointly as chairman of a

COCHIN n pl. -S a large domestic chicken

COCHLEA n pl. -CHLEAE or -CHLEAS a part of the ear COCHLEAR adj

COCINERA n pl. -S a cook

COCK v -ED, -ING, -S to tilt to one side

COCKADE n pl. -S an ornament worn on a hat COCKADED adj

COCKAPOO n pl. -POOS a hybrid between a cocker spaniel and a poodle

COCKATOO n pl. -TOOS a parrot

COCKBILL v -ED, -ING, -S to raise the yardarm on a ship

COCKBOAT n pl. -S a small boat

COCKCROW n pl. -S daybreak

COCKER v -ED, -ING, -S to pamper

COCKEREL n pl. -S a young rooster

COCKEYE n pl. -S a squinting eye COCKEYED adj

COCKIER comparative of cocky

COCKIEST superlative of cocky

COCKILY adv in a cocky manner

COCKISH adj cocky

COCKLE v -LED, -LING, -LES to wrinkle or pucker

COCKLIKE adj resembling a rooster

COCKLOFT n pl. -S a small attic

COCKNEY n pl. -NEYS a resident of the East End of London

COCKPIT n pl. -S a pilot's compartment in certain airplanes

COCKSHUT n pl. -S the close of day

COCKSHY n pl. -SHIES a target in a throwing contest

COCKSPUR n pl. -S a thorny plant

COCKSURE adj certain

COCKTAIL v -ED, -ING, -S to drink alcoholic beverages

COCKUP n pl. -S a turned-up part of something

COCKY adj COCKIER, COCKIEST arrogantly self-confident

COCO n pl. -COS a tall palm tree

COCOA n pl. -S chocolate

COCOANUT n pl. -S coconut

COCOBOLA n pl. -S cocobolo

COCOBOLO n pl. -LOS a tropical tree

COCOMAT n pl. -S a matting made from coir

COCONUT n pl. -S the fruit of the coco

COCOON v -ED, -ING, -S to wrap or envelop tightly

COCOTTE n pl. -S a prostitute

COCOYAM n pl. -S a tropical tuber

COCREATE v -ATED, -ATING, -ATES to create together

COD v CODDED, CODDING, CODS to fool

CODA n pl. -S a passage at the end of a musical composition

CODABLE adj capable of being coded

CODDED past tense of cod

CODDER n pl. -S a cod fisherman

CODDING present participle of cod

CODDLE v -DLED, -DLING, -DLES to pamper

CODDLER n pl. -S one that coddles

CODE v CODED, CODING, CODES to convert into symbols

CODEBOOK n pl. -S a book listing words and their coded equivalents

CODEBTOR n pl. -S one that shares a debt

CODEC n pl. -S an integrated circuit

CODED past tense of code

CODEIA n pl. -S codeine

CODEIN n pl. -S codeine

CODEINA n pl. -S codeine

CODEINE n pl. -S a narcotic alkaloid

CODELESS adj being without a set of laws

CODEN n pl. -S a coding classification

CODER n pl. -S one that codes

CODERIVE v -RIVED, -RIVING, -RIVES to derive jointly

CODESIGN v -ED, -ING, -S to design jointly

CODEX n pl. -DICES an ancient manuscript

CODFISH n pl. -ES a food fish

CODGER n pl. -S an old man

CODICES pl. of codex

CODICIL n pl. -S a supplement to a will

CODIFIER n pl. -S one that codifies

CODIFY v -FIED, -FYING, -FIES to arrange or systematize

CODING present participle of code

CODIRECT v -ED, -ING, -S to direct jointly

CODLIN n pl. -S codling

CODLING n pl. -S an unripe apple

CODON n pl. -S a triplet of nucleotides (basic components of DNA)

CODPIECE n pl. -S a cover for the crotch in men's breeches

CODRIVE v -DROVE, -DRIVEN, -DRIVING, -DRIVES to work as a codriver

CODRIVER n pl. -S one who takes turns driving a vehicle

COED n pl. -S a female student

COEDIT v -ED, -ING, -S to edit with another person

COEDITOR n pl. -S one that coedits

COEFFECT *n pl.* -S an accompanying effect

COELIAC *adj* celiac

COELOM *n pl.* -LOMS or -LOMATA a body cavity in some animals **COELOMIC** *adj*

COELOME *n pl.* -S coelom

COEMBODY *v* -BODIED, -BODYING, -BODIES to embody jointly

COEMPLOY *v* -ED, -ING, -S to employ together

COEMPT *v* -ED, -ING, -S to buy up the entire supply of a product

COENACT *v* -ED, -ING, -S to enact jointly or at the same time

COENAMOR *v* -ED, -ING, -S to inflame with mutual love

COENDURE *v* -DURED, -DURING, -DURES to endure together

COENURE *n pl.* -S coenurus

COENURUS *n pl.* -RI a tapeworm larva

COENZYME *n pl.* -S a substance necessary for the functioning of certain enzymes

COEQUAL *n pl.* -S one who is equal with another

COEQUATE *v* -QUATED, -QUATING, -QUATES to equate with something else

COERCE *v* -ERCED, -ERCING, -ERCES to compel by force or threat

COERCER *n pl.* -S one that coerces

COERCION *n pl.* -S the act of coercing

COERCIVE *adj* serving to coerce

COERECT *v* -ED, -ING, -S to erect together

COESITE *n pl.* -S a type of silica

COEVAL *n pl.* -S one of the same era or period as another

COEVALLY *adv* contemporarily

COEVOLVE *v* -VOLVED, -VOLVING, -VOLVES to evolve together

COEXERT *v* -ED, -ING, -S to exert jointly

COEXIST *v* -ED, -ING, -S to exist together

COEXTEND *v* -ED, -ING, -S to extend through the same space or time as another

COFACTOR *n pl.* -S a coenzyme

COFF *v* COFT, COFFING, COFFS to buy

COFFEE *n pl.* -S an aromatic, mildly stimulating beverage

COFFER *v* -ED, -ING, -S to put in a strongbox

COFFIN *v* -ED, -ING, -S to put in a coffin (a burial case)

COFFLE *v* -FLED, -FLING, -FLES to chain slaves together

COFFRET *n pl.* -S a small strongbox

COFOUND *v* -ED, -ING, -S to found jointly

COFT past tense of coff

COG *v* COGGED, COGGING, COGS to cheat at dice

COGENCY *n pl.* -CIES the state of being cogent

COGENT *adj* convincing **COGENTLY** *adv*

COGGED past tense of cog

COGGING present participle of cog

COGITATE *v* -TATED, -TATING, -TATES to ponder

COGITO *n pl.* -TOS a philosophical principle

COGNAC *n pl.* -S a brandy

COGNATE *n pl.* -S one that is related to another

COGNISE *v* -NISED, -NISING, -NISES to cognize

COGNIZE *v* -NIZED, -NIZING, -NIZES to become aware of in one's mind

COGNIZER *n pl.* -S one that cognizes

COGNOMEN *n pl.* -MENS or -MINA a family name

COGNOVIT *n pl.* -S a written admission of liability

COGON *n pl.* -S a tall tropical grass

COGWAY *n pl.* -WAYS a railway operating on steep slopes

COGWHEEL *n pl.* -S a toothed wheel

COHABIT *v* -ED, -ING, -S to live together as man and wife while unmarried

COHEAD *v* -ED, -ING, -S to head jointly

COHEIR *n pl.* -S a joint heir

COHERE *v* -HERED, -HERING, -HERES to stick together

COHERENT *adj* sticking together

COHERER *n pl.* -S a device used to detect radio waves

COHERING present participle of cohere

COHESION *n pl.* -S the act or state of cohering **COHESIVE** *adj*

COHO *n pl.* -HOS a small salmon

COHOBATE *v* -BATED, -BATING, -BATES to distill again

COHOG *n pl.* -S a quahog

COHOLDER *n pl.* -S an athlete who holds a record with another

COHORT *n pl.* -S a companion or associate

COHOSH n pl. -ES a medicinal plant

COHOST v -ED, -ING, -S to host jointly

COHUNE n pl. -S a palm tree

COIF v -ED, -ING, -S to style the hair

COIFFE v COIFFED, COIFFING, COIFFES to coif

COIFFEUR n pl. -S a male hairdresser

COIFFURE v -FURED, -FURING, -FURES to coif

COIGN v -ED, -ING, -S to quoin

COIGNE v COIGNED, COIGNING, COIGNES to quoin

COIL v -ED, -ING, -S to wind in even rings

COILER n pl. -S one that coils

COIN v -ED, -ING, -S to make coins (metal currency) COINABLE adj

COINAGE n pl. -S the act of making coins

COINCIDE v -CIDED, -CIDING, -CIDES to be in the same place

COINER n pl. -S one that coins

COINFER v -FERRED, -FERRING, -FERS to infer jointly

COINHERE v -HERED, -HERING, -HERES to inhere jointly

COINMATE n pl. -S a fellow inmate

COINSURE v -SURED, -SURING, -SURES to insure with another

COINTER v -TERRED, -TERRING, -TERS to bury together

COINVENT v -ED, -ING, -S to invent together

COIR n pl. -S a fiber obtained from coconut husks

COISTREL n pl. -S a knave

COISTRIL n pl. -S coistrel

COITION n pl. -S coitus

COITUS n pl. -ES sexual intercourse COITAL adj COITALLY adv

COJOIN v -ED, -ING, -S to join with

COKE v COKED, COKING, COKES to change into a carbon fuel

COKEHEAD n pl. -S a cocaine addict

COL n pl. -S a depression between two mountains

COLA n pl. -S a carbonated beverage

COLANDER n pl. -S a kitchen utensil for draining off liquids

COLD adj COLDER, COLDEST having little or no warmth

COLD n pl. -S the relative lack of heat; a chill

COLDCOCK v -ED, -ING, -S to knock unconscious

COLDISH adj somewhat cold

COLDLY adv in a cold manner

COLDNESS n pl. -ES the state of being cold

COLE n pl. -S a plant of the cabbage family

COLEAD v -LED, -LEADING, -LEADS to lead jointly

COLEADER n pl. -S one that coleads

COLESEED n pl. -S colza

COLESLAW n pl. -S a salad made of shredded raw cabbage

COLESSEE n pl. -S a joint lessee

COLESSOR n pl. -S a joint lessor

COLEUS n pl. -ES a tropical plant

COLEWORT n pl. -S cole

COLIC n pl. -S acute abdominal pain

COLICIN n pl. -S an antibacterial substance

COLICINE n pl. -S colicin

COLICKY adj pertaining to or associated with colic

COLIES pl. of coly

COLIFORM n pl. -S a bacillus of the colon

COLIN n pl. -S the bobwhite

COLINEAR adj lying in the same straight line

COLISEUM n pl. -S a large structure for public entertainment

COLISTIN n pl. -S an antibiotic

COLITIS n pl. -TISES inflammation of the colon COLITIC adj

COLLAGE v -LAGED, -LAGING, -LAGES to arrange materials in a collage (a kind of artistic composition)

COLLAGEN n pl. -S a protein

COLLAPSE v -LAPSED, -LAPSING, -LAPSES to crumble suddenly

COLLAR v -ED, -ING, -S to provide with a collar (something worn around the neck)

COLLARD n pl. -S a variety of kale

COLLARET n pl. -S a small collar

COLLATE v -LATED, -LATING, -LATES to compare critically

COLLATOR n pl. -S one that collates

COLLECT v -ED, -ING, -S to bring together in a group

COLLEEN n pl. -S an Irish girl

COLLEGE n pl. -S a school of higher learning

COLLEGER n pl. -S a student supported by funds from his college

COLLEGIA *n/pl* soviet executive councils

COLLET *v* -ED, -ING, -S to set a gem in a rim or ring

COLLIDE *v* -LIDED, -LIDING, -LIDES to come together with violent impact

COLLIDER *n* pl. -S a type of particle accelerator

COLLIE *n* pl. -S a large dog

COLLIED past tense of colly

COLLIER *n* pl. -S a coal miner

COLLIERY *n* pl. -LIERIES a coal mine

COLLIES present 3d person sing. of colly

COLLINS *n* pl. -ES an alcoholic beverage

COLLOGUE *v* -LOGUED, -LOGUING, -LOGUES to conspire

COLLOID *n* pl. -S a type of chemical suspension

COLLOP *n* pl. -S a small portion of meat

COLLOQUY *n* pl. -QUIES a conversation

COLLUDE *v* -LUDED, -LUDING, -LUDES to conspire

COLLUDER *n* pl. -S one that colludes

COLLUVIA *n/pl* rock debris

COLLY *v* -LIED, -LYING, -LIES to blacken with coal dust

COLLYRIA *n/pl* medicinal lotions

COLOBOMA *n* pl. -MATA a lesion of the eye

COLOBUS *n* pl. -BI a long-tailed monkey

COLOCATE *v* -CATED, -CATING, -CATES to place two or more housing units in close proximity

COLOG *n* pl. -S the logarithm of the reciprocal of a number

COLOGNE *n* pl. -S a scented liquid COLOGNED *adj*

COLON *n* pl. -S a section of the large intestine

COLON *n* pl. -ES a monetary unit of Costa Rica

COLONE *n* pl. -S colon

COLONEL *n* pl. -S a military officer

COLONI pl. of colonus

COLONIAL *n* pl. -S a citizen of a colony

COLONIC *n* pl. -S irrigation of the colon

COLONIES pl. of colony

COLONISE *v* -NISED, -NISING, -NISES to colonize

COLONIST *n* pl. -S one who settles a colony

COLONIZE *v* -NIZED, -NIZING, -NIZES to establish a colony

COLONUS *n* pl. -NI a freeborn serf

COLONY *n* pl. -NIES a group of emigrants living in a new land

COLOPHON *n* pl. -S an inscription placed at the end of a book

COLOR *v* -ED, -ING, -S to give color (a visual attribute of objects) to

COLORADO *adj* of medium strength and color — used of cigars

COLORANT *n* pl. -S a pigment or dye

COLORED *adj* having color

COLORER *n* pl. -S one that colors

COLORFUL *adj* full of color

COLORING *n* pl. -S appearance in regard to color

COLORISM *n* pl. -S coloring

COLORIST *n* pl. -S a person skilled in the use of color

COLORIZE *v* -IZED, -IZING, -IZES to give color to a black-and-white film

COLORMAN *n* pl. -MEN a sportscaster who provides commentary during a game

COLOSSAL *adj* gigantic

COLOSSUS *n* pl. -LOSSI or -LOSSUSES a gigantic statue

COLOTOMY *n* pl. -MIES a surgical incision of the colon

COLOUR *v* -ED, -ING, -S to color

COLOURER *n* pl. -S colorer

COLPITIS *n* pl. -TISES a vaginal inflammation

COLT *n* pl. -S a young male horse COLTISH *adj*

COLTER *n* pl. -S a blade on a plow

COLUBRID *n* pl. -S any of a large family of snakes

OOLUGO *n* pl. -GOS a small mammal

COLUMBIC *adj* pertaining to niobium

COLUMEL *n* pl. -S a small column-like anatomical part

COLUMN *n* pl. -S a vertical cylindrical support COLUMNAL, COLUMNAR, COLUMNED *adj*

COLURE *n* pl. -S an astronomical circle

COLY *n* pl. COLIES an African bird

COLZA *n* pl. -S a plant of the cabbage family

COMA *n* pl. -S a condition of prolonged unconsciousness

COMA *n* pl. -MAE a tuft of silky hairs

COMAKE *v* -MADE, -MAKING, -MAKES to serve as comaker for another's loan

COMAKER *n* pl. -S one who assumes financial responsibility for another's default

COMAL	*adj* comose	**COMFORT**	*v* -ED, -ING, -S to soothe in time of grief
COMANAGE	*v* -AGED, -AGING, -AGES to manage jointly	**COMFREY**	*n pl.* -FREYS a coarse herb
COMATE	*n pl.* -S a companion	**COMFY**	*adj* -FIER, -FIEST comfortable
COMATIC	*adj* having blurred vision as a result of coma	**COMIC**	*n pl.* -S a comedian
COMATIK	*n pl.* -S komatik	**COMICAL**	*adj* funny
COMATOSE	*adj* affected with coma	**COMING**	*n pl.* -S arrival
COMATULA	*n pl.* -LAE a marine animal	**COMINGLE**	*v* -GLED, -GLING, -GLES to blend thoroughly
COMB	*v* -ED, -ING, -S to arrange or clean with a comb (a toothed instrument)	**COMITIA**	*n pl.* COMITIA a public assembly in ancient Rome COMITIAL *adj*
COMBAT	*v* -BATED, -BATING, -BATS or -BATTED, -BATTING, -BATS to fight against	**COMITY**	*n pl.* -TIES civility
		COMIX	*n/pl* comic books or strips
COMBATER	*n pl.* -S one that combats	**COMMA**	*n pl.* -MAS or -MATA a fragment of a few words or feet in ancient prosody
COMBE	*n pl.* -S a narrow valley		
COMBER	*n pl.* -S one that combs	**COMMAND**	*v* -ED, -ING, -S to direct with authority
COMBINE	*v* -BINED, -BINING, -BINES to blend		
		COMMANDO	*n pl.* -DOES or -DOS a military unit
COMBINER	*n pl.* -S one that combines		
COMBINGS	*n/pl* hair removed by a comb	**COMMATA**	a pl. of comma
COMBINING	present participle of combine	**COMMENCE**	*v* -MENCED, -MENCING, -MENCES to begin
COMBLIKE	*adj* resembling a comb		
COMBO	*n pl.* -BOS a small jazz band	**COMMEND**	*v* -ED, -ING, -S to praise
COMBUST	*v* -ED, -ING, -S to burn	**COMMENT**	*v* -ED, -ING, -S to remark
COME	*v* CAME, COMING, COMES or COMETH to move toward something or someone	**COMMERCE**	*v* -MERCED, -MERCING, -MERCES to commune
		COMMIE	*n pl.* -S a Communist
COMEBACK	*n pl.* -S a return to former prosperity	**COMMIES**	pl. of commy
		COMMIT	*v* -MITTED, -MITTING, -MITS to do, perform, or perpetrate
COMEDIAN	*n pl.* -S a humorous entertainer		
		COMMIX	*v* -MIXED or -MIXT, -MIXING, -MIXES to mix together
COMEDIC	*adj* pertaining to comedy		
COMEDIES	pl. of comedy		
COMEDO	*n pl.* -DOS or -DONES a skin blemish	**COMMODE**	*n pl.* -S a cabinet
		COMMON	*adj* -MONER, -MONEST ordinary
COMEDOWN	*n pl.* -S a drop in status		
COMEDY	*n pl.* -DIES a humorous play, movie, or other work	**COMMON**	*n pl.* -S a tract of publicly used land
		COMMONER	*n pl.* -S one of the common people
COMELY	*adj* -LIER, -LIEST pleasing to look at COMELILY *adv*		
		COMMONLY	*adv* in a common manner
COMEMBER	*n pl.* -S one that shares membership	**COMMOVE**	*v* -MOVED, -MOVING, -MOVES to move violently
		COMMUNAL	*adj* belonging to a community; public
COMER	*n pl.* -S one showing great promise		
COMET	*n pl.* -S a celestial body COMETARY *adj*	**COMMUNE**	*v* -MUNED, -MUNING, -MUNES to converse intimately
		COMMUTE	*v* -MUTED, -MUTING, -MUTES to exchange
COMETH	a present 3d person sing. of come		
COMETHER	*n pl.* -S an affair or matter	**COMMUTER**	*n pl.* -S one that commutes
COMETIC	*adj* pertaining to a comet	**COMMY**	*n pl.* -MIES commie
COMFIER	comparative of comfy	**COMOSE**	*adj* bearing a tuft of silky hairs
COMFIEST	superlative of comfy	**COMOUS**	*adj* comose
COMFIT	*n pl.* -S a candy		

COMP *v* -ED, -ING, -S to play a jazz accompaniment

COMPACT *adj* -PACTER, -PACTEST closely and firmly united

COMPACT *v* -ED, -ING, -S to pack closely together

COMPADRE *n pl.* -S a close friend

COMPANY *v* -NIED, -NYING, -NIES to associate with

COMPARE *v* -PARED, -PARING, -PARES to represent as similar

COMPARER *n pl.* -S one that compares

COMPART *v* -ED, -ING, -S to divide into parts

COMPASS *v* -ED, -ING, -ES to go around

COMPEER *v* -ED, -ING, -S to equal or match

COMPEL *v* -PELLED, -PELLING, -PELS to urge forcefully

COMPEND *n pl.* -S a brief summary

COMPERE *v* -PERED, -PERING, -PERES to act as master of ceremonies

COMPETE *v* -PETED, -PETING, -PETES to vie

COMPILE *v* -PILED, -PILING, -PILES to collect into a volume

COMPILER *n pl.* -S one that compiles

COMPLAIN *v* -ED, -ING, -S to express discontent

COMPLEAT *adj* highly skilled

COMPLECT *v* -ED, -ING, -S to weave together

COMPLETE *adj* -PLETER, -PLETEST having all necessary parts

COMPLETE *v* -PLETED, -PLETING, -PLETES to bring to an end

COMPLEX *adj* -PLEXER, -PLEXEST complicated

COMPLEX *v* -ED, -ING, -ES to make complex

COMPLICE *n pl.* -S an associate

COMPLIED past tense of comply

COMPLIER *n pl.* -S one that complies

COMPLIES present 3d person sing. of comply

COMPLIN *n pl.* -S compline

COMPLINE *n pl.* -S the last liturgical prayer of the day

COMPLOT *v* -PLOTTED, -PLOTTING, -PLOTS to conspire

COMPLY *v* -PLIED, -PLYING, -PLIES to obey

COMPO *n pl.* -POS a mixed substance

COMPONE *adj* compony

COMPONY *adj* composed of squares of alternating colors

COMPORT *v* -ED, -ING, -S to conduct oneself in a certain way

COMPOSE *v* -POSED, -POSING, -POSES to form the substance of

COMPOSER *n pl.* -S one that writes music

COMPOST *v* -ED, -ING, -S to fertilize

COMPOTE *n pl.* -S fruit stewed in syrup

COMPOUND *v* -ED, -ING, -S to add to

COMPRESS *v* -ED, -ING, -ES to compact

COMPRISE *v* -PRISED, -PRISING, -PRISES to include or contain

COMPRIZE *v* -PRIZED, -PRIZING, -PRIZES to comprise

COMPT *v* -ED, -ING, -S to count

COMPUTE *v* -PUTED, -PUTING, -PUTES to calculate

COMPUTER *n pl.* -S a machine that computes automatically

COMRADE *n pl.* -S a close friend

COMTE *n pl.* -S a French nobleman

CON *v* CONNED, CONNING, CONS to study carefully

CONATION *n pl.* -S the inclination to act purposefully **CONATIVE** *adj*

CONATUS *n pl.* CONATUS an effort

CONCAVE *v* -CAVED, -CAVING, -CAVES to make concave (curving inward)

CONCEAL *v* -ED, -ING, -S to keep from sight or discovery

CONCEDE *v* -CEDED, -CEDING, -CEDES to acknowledge as true

CONCEDER *n pl.* -S one that concedes

CONCEIT *v* -ED, -ING, -S to imagine

CONCEIVE *v* -CEIVED, -CEIVING, -CEIVES to understand

CONCENT *n pl.* -S harmony

CONCEPT *n pl.* -S a general idea

CONCERN *v* -ED, -ING, -S to be of interest to

CONCERT *v* -ED, -ING, -S to plan

CONCERTO *n pl.* -TOS or -TI a musical composition

CONCH *n pl.* -S or -ES a marine mollusk

CONCHA *n pl.* -CHAE an anatomical shell-like structure **CONCHAL** *adj*

CONCHIE *n pl.* -S conchy

CONCHOID *n pl.* -S a type of geometric curve

CONCHY *n pl.* -CHIES a conscientious objector

CONCISE *adj* -CISER, -CISEST succinct

CONCLAVE *n* pl. -S a secret meeting

CONCLUDE *v* -CLUDED, -CLUDING, -CLUDES to finish

CONCOCT *v* -ED, -ING, -S to prepare by combining ingredients

CONCORD *n* pl. -S a state of agreement

CONCRETE *v* -CRETED, -CRETING, -CRETES to solidify

CONCUR *v* -CURRED, -CURRING, -CURS to agree

CONCUSS *v* -ED, -ING, -ES to injure the brain by a violent blow

CONDEMN *v* -ED, -ING, -S to criticize severely

CONDENSE *v* -DENSED, -DENSING, -DENSES to compress

CONDIGN *adj* deserved; appropriate

CONDO *n* pl. -DOS or -DOES an individually owned unit in a multiunit structure

CONDOLE *v* -DOLED, -DOLING, -DOLES to mourn

CONDOLER *n* pl. -S one that condoles

CONDOM *n* pl. -S a prophylactic

CONDONE *v* -DONED, -DONING, -DONES to forgive or overlook

CONDONER *n* pl. -S one that condones

CONDOR *n* pl. -S or -ES a coin of Chile

CONDUCE *v* -DUCED, -DUCING, -DUCES to contribute to a result

CONDUCER *n* pl. -S one that conduces

CONDUCT *v* -ED, -ING, -S to lead or guide

CONDUIT *n* pl. -S a channel or pipe for conveying fluids

CONDYLE *n* pl. -S a protuberance on a bone CONDYLAR *adj*

CONE *v* CONED, CONING, CONES to shape like a cone (a geometric solid)

CONELRAD *n* pl. -S a system of defense in the event of air attack

CONENOSE *n* pl. -S a bloodsucking insect

CONEPATE *n* pl. -S a skunk

CONEPATL *n* pl. -S conepate

CONEY *n* pl. -NEYS cony

CONFAB *v* -FABBED, -FABBING, -FABS to chat

CONFECT *v* -ED, -ING, -S to prepare from various ingredients

CONFER *v* -FERRED, -FERRING, -FERS to bestow

CONFEREE *n* pl. -S one upon whom something is conferred

CONFERVA *n* pl. -VAE or -VAS a freshwater alga

CONFESS *v* -ED, -ING, -ES to acknowledge or disclose

CONFETTO *n* pl. -TI a bonbon

CONFIDE *v* -FIDED, -FIDING, -FIDES to reveal in trust or confidence

CONFIDER *n* pl. -S one that confides

CONFINE *v* -FINED, -FINING, -FINES to shut within an enclosure

CONFINER *n* pl. -S one that confines

CONFIRM *v* -ED, -ING, -S to assure the validity of

CONFIT *n* pl. -S meat cooked and preserved in its own fat

CONFLATE *v* -FLATED, -FLATING, -FLATES to blend

CONFLICT *v* -ED, -ING, -S to come into opposition

CONFLUX *n* pl. -ES a flowing together of streams

CONFOCAL *adj* having the same focus or foci

CONFORM *v* -ED, -ING, -S to become the same or similar

CONFOUND *v* -ED, -ING, -S to confuse

CONFRERE *n* pl. -S a colleague

CONFRONT *v* -ED, -ING, -S to face defiantly

CONFUSE *v* -FUSED, -FUSING, -FUSES to mix up mentally

CONFUTE *v* -FUTED, -FUTING, -FUTES to disprove

CONFUTER *n* pl. -S one that confutes

CONGA *v* -ED, -ING, -S to perform a conga (Latin American dance)

CONGE *n* pl. -S permission to depart

CONGEAL *v* -ED, -ING, -S to change from a fluid to a solid

CONGEE *v* -GEED, -GEEING, -GEES to bow politely

CONGENER *n* pl. -S one of the same kind or class

CONGER *n* pl. -S a marine eel

CONGEST *v* -ED, -ING, -S to fill to excess

CONGIUS *n* pl. -GII an ancient unit of measure

CONGLOBE *v* -GLOBED, -GLOBING, -GLOBES to become a globule

CONGO *n* pl. -GOS congou

CONGO *n* pl. -GOES an eellike amphibian

CONGOU *n* pl. -S a Chinese tea

CONGRATS *n/pl* congratulations

CONGRESS v -ED, -ING, -ES to assemble together
CONI pl. of conus
CONIC n pl. -S a geometric curve
CONICAL adj shaped like a cone
CONICITY n pl. -TIES the state of being conical
CONIDIUM n pl. -NIDIA a fungus spore CONIDIAL, CONIDIAN adj
CONIES pl. of cony
CONIFER n pl. -S an evergreen tree
CONIINE n pl. -S a poisonous alkaloid
CONIN n pl. -S coniine
CONINE n pl. -S coniine
CONING present participle of cone
CONIOSIS n pl. -OSES an infection caused by the inhalation of dust
CONIUM n pl. -S a poisonous herb
CONJOIN v -ED, -ING, -S to join together CONJOINT adj
CONJUGAL adj pertaining to marriage
CONJUNCT n pl. -S one that is joined with another
CONJURE v -JURED, -JURING, -JURES to summon a spirit
CONJURER n pl. -S a sorcerer
CONJUROR n pl. -S conjurer
CONK v -ED, -ING, -S to hit on the head
CONKER n pl. -S a chestnut used in a British game
CONKY adj full of a tree fungus
CONN v -ED, -ING, -S to direct the steering of a ship
CONNATE adj innate
CONNECT v -ED, -ING, -S to join together
CONNED past tense of con
CONNER n pl. -S one that cons
CONNING present participle of con
CONNIVE v -NIVED, -NIVING, -NIVES to feign ignorance of wrongdoing
CONNIVER n pl. -S one that connives
CONNOTE v -NOTED, -NOTING, -NOTES to imply another meaning besides the literal one
CONODONT n pl. -S a fossil
CONOID n pl. -S a geometric solid CONOIDAL adj
CONQUER v -ED, -ING, -S to overcome by force
CONQUEST n pl. -S the act of conquering
CONQUIAN n pl. -S a card game
CONSENT v -ED, -ING, -S to permit or approve

CONSERVE v -SERVED, -SERVING, -SERVES to protect from loss or depletion
CONSIDER v -ED, -ING, -S to think about
CONSIGN v -ED, -ING, -S to give over to another's care
CONSIST v -ED, -ING, -S to be made up or composed
CONSOL n pl. -S a government bond
CONSOLE v -SOLED, -SOLING, -SOLES to comfort
CONSOLER n pl. -S one that consoles
CONSOMME n pl. -S a clear soup
CONSORT v -ED, -ING, -S to keep company
CONSPIRE v -SPIRED, -SPIRING, -SPIRES to plan secretly with another
CONSTANT n pl. -S something that does not vary
CONSTRUE v -STRUED, -STRUING, -STRUES to interpret
CONSUL n pl. -S an official serving abroad CONSULAR adj
CONSULT v -ED, -ING, -S to ask an opinion of
CONSUME v -SUMED, -SUMING, -SUMES to use up
CONSUMER n pl. -S one that consumes
CONTACT v -ED, -ING, -S to communicate with
CONTAGIA n/pl causative agents of infectious diseases
CONTAIN v -ED, -ING, -S to hold within
CONTE n pl. -S a short story
CONTEMN v -ED, -ING, -S to scorn
CONTEMPT n pl. -S the feeling of one who views something as mean, vile, or worthless
CONTEND v -ED, -ING, -S to vie
CONTENT v -ED, -ING, -S to satisfy
CONTEST v -ED, -ING, -S to compete for
CONTEXT n pl. -S the part of a discourse in which a particular word or phrase appears
CONTINUA n/pl mathematical sets
CONTINUE v -UED, -UING, -UES to go on with
CONTINUO n pl. -UOS a type of instrumental part
CONTO n pl. -TOS a Portuguese money of account
CONTORT v -ED, -ING, -S to twist out of shape
CONTOUR v -ED, -ING, -S to make the outline of

CONTRA n pl. -S a Nicaraguan revolutionary

CONTRACT v -ED, -ING, -S to decrease in size or volume

CONTRAIL n pl. -S a visible trail of water vapor from an aircraft

CONTRARY n pl. -TRARIES an opposite

CONTRAST v -ED, -ING, -S to place in opposition to set off differences

CONTRITE adj deeply sorry for one's sins

CONTRIVE v -TRIVED, -TRIVING, -TRIVES to devise

CONTROL v -TROLLED, -TROLLING, -TROLS to exercise authority over

CONTUSE v -TUSED, -TUSING, -TUSES to bruise

CONUS n pl. CONI an anatomical part in mammals

CONVECT v -ED, -ING, -S to transfer heat by a process of circulation

CONVENE v -VENED, -VENING, -VENES to assemble

CONVENER n pl. -S one that convenes

CONVENOR n pl. -S convener

CONVENT v -ED, -ING, -S to convene

CONVERGE v -VERGED, -VERGING, -VERGES to come together

CONVERSE v -VERSED, -VERSING, -VERSES to speak together

CONVERT v -ED, -ING, -S to change into another form

CONVEX n pl. -ES a surface or body that is convex (curving outward)

CONVEXLY adv in a convex manner

CONVEY v -ED, -ING, -S to transport

CONVEYER n pl. -S one that conveys

CONVEYOR n pl. -S conveyer

CONVICT v -ED, -ING, -S to prove guilty

CONVINCE v -VINCED, -VINCING, -VINCES to cause to believe something

CONVOKE v -VOKED, -VOKING, -VOKES to cause to assemble

CONVOKER n pl. -S one that convokes

CONVOLVE v -VOLVED, -VOLVING, -VOLVES to roll together

CONVOY v -ED, -ING, -S to escort

CONVULSE v -VULSED, -VULSING, -VULSES to shake violently

CONY n pl. CONIES a rabbit

COO v COOED, COOING, COOS to make the sound of a dove

COOCH n pl. -ES a sinuous dance

COOCOO adj crazy

COOEE v COOEED, COOEEING, COOEES to cry out shrilly

COOER n pl. -S one that coos

COOEY v -EYED, -EYING, -EYS to cooee

COOF n pl. -S a dolt

COOINGLY adv in the manner of cooing doves; affectionately

COOK v -ED, -ING, -S to prepare food by heating **COOKABLE** adj

COOKBOOK n pl. -S a book of recipes

COOKER n pl. -S one that cooks

COOKERY n pl. -ERIES the art of cooking

COOKEY n pl. -EYS cookie

COOKIE n pl. -S a small, flat cake

COOKING n pl. -S the act of one that cooks

COOKLESS adj having no person that cooks

COOKOUT n pl. -S a meal eaten and prepared outdoors

COOKSHOP n pl. -S a shop that sells cooked food

COOKTOP n pl. -S a counter-top cooking apparatus

COOKWARE n pl. -S utensils used in cooking

COOKY n pl. COOKIES cookie

COOL adj COOLER, COOLEST moderately cold

COOL v -ED, -ING, -S to make less warm

COOLANT n pl. -S a fluid used to cool engines

COOLDOWN n pl. -S a gradual return of physiological functions to normal levels after strenuous exercise

COOLER n pl. -S something that cools

COOLIE n pl. -S an Oriental laborer

COOLIES pl. of cooly

COOLISH adj somewhat cool

COOLLY adv in a cool manner

COOLNESS n pl. -ES the state of being cool

COOLTH n pl. -S coolness

COOLY n pl. COOLIES coolie

COOMB n pl. -S combe

COOMBE n pl. -S combe

COON n pl. -S a raccoon

COONCAN n pl. -S conquian

COONSKIN n pl. -S the pelt of a raccoon

COONTIE n pl. -S a tropical plant

COOP v -ED, -ING, -S to confine

COOPER v -ED, -ING, -S to make or mend barrels

COOPERY n pl. -ERIES the trade of coopering

COOPT v -ED, -ING, -S to elect or appoint

COOPTION n pl. -S the act of coopting

COOT n pl. -S an aquatic bird

COOTER n pl. -S a turtle

COOTIE n pl. -S a body louse

COP v COPPED, COPPING, COPS to steal

COPAIBA n pl. -S a resin

COPAL n pl. -S a resin

COPALM n pl. -S a hardwood tree

COPARENT n pl. -S a fellow parent

COPASTOR n pl. -S one that shares the duties of a pastor

COPATRON n pl. -S a fellow patron

COPE v COPED, COPING, COPES to contend or strive

COPECK n pl. -S kopeck

COPEMATE n pl. -S an antagonist

COPEN n pl. -S a blue color

COPEPOD n pl. -S a minute crustacean

COPER n pl. -S a horse dealer

COPIED past tense of copy

COPIER n pl. -S one that copies

COPIES present 3d person sing. of copy

COPIHUE n pl. -S a climbing vine

COPILOT n pl. -S an assistant pilot

COPING n pl. -S the top part of a wall

COPIOUS adj abundant

COPLANAR adj lying in the same plane

COPLOT v -PLOTTED, -PLOTTING, -PLOTS to plot together

COPPED past tense of cop

COPPER v -ED, -ING, -S to cover with copper (a metallic element)

COPPERAH n pl. -S copra

COPPERAS n pl. -ES a compound used in making inks

COPPERY adj resembling copper

COPPICE v -PICED, -PICING, -PICES to cause to grow in the form of a coppice (a thicket)

COPPING present participle of cop

COPPRA n pl. -S copra

COPRA n pl. -S dried coconut meat

COPRAH n pl. -S copra

COPREMIA n pl. -S a form of blood poisoning COPREMIC adj

COPRINCE n pl. -S one of two princes ruling jointly

COPSE n pl. -S a coppice

COPTER n pl. -S a helicopter

COPULA n pl. -LAS or -LAE something that links COPULAR adj

COPULATE v -LATED, -LATING, -LATES to engage in coitus

COPURIFY v -FIED, -FYING, -FIES to become purified with another substance

COPY v COPIED, COPYING, COPIES to imitate

COPYBOOK n pl. -S a book used in teaching penmanship

COPYBOY n pl. -BOYS an office boy

COPYCAT v -CATTED, -CATTING, -CATS to imitate

COPYDESK n pl. -S an editor's desk in a newspaper office

COPYEDIT v -ED, -ING, -S to prepare copy for the printer

COPYHOLD n pl. -S a type of ownership of land

COPYIST n pl. -S an imitator

COPYREAD v -READ, -READING, -READS to copyedit

COQUET v -QUETTED, -QUETTING, -QUETS to flirt

COQUETRY n pl. -TRIES flirtatious behavior

COQUETTE v -QUETTED, -QUETTING, -QUETTES to coquet

COQUILLE n pl. -S a cooking utensil

COQUINA n pl. -S a small marine clam

COQUITO n pl. -TOS a palm tree

COR interj — used to express surprise, admiration, or irritation

CORACLE n pl. -S a small boat

CORACOID n pl. -S a bone of the shoulder girdle

CORAL n pl. -S a mass of marine animal skeletons

CORANTO n pl. -TOS or -TOES courante

CORBAN n pl. -S an offering to God

CORBEIL n pl. -S a sculptured fruit basket

CORBEL v -BELED, -BELING, -BELS or -BELLED, -BELLING, -BELS to provide a wall with a bracket

CORBIE n pl. -S a raven or crow

CORBINA n pl. -S a food and game fish

CORBY n pl. CORBIES corbie

CORD v -ED, -ING, -S to fasten with a cord (a thin rope)

CORDAGE n pl. -S the amount of wood in an area

CORDATE adj heart-shaped

CORDELLE v -DELLED, -DELLING, -DELLES to tow a boat with a cordelle (a towrope)

CORDER n pl. -S one that cords

CORDIAL n pl. -S a liqueur

CORDING n pl. -S the ribbed surface of cloth

CORDITE n pl. -S an explosive powder

CORDLESS adj having no cord

CORDLIKE adj resembling a cord

CORDOBA n pl. -S a monetary unit of Nicaragua

CORDON v -ED, -ING, -S to form a barrier around

CORDOVAN n pl. -S a fine leather

CORDUROY v -ED, -ING, -S to build a type of road

CORDWAIN n pl. -S cordovan

CORDWOOD n pl. -S wood used for fuel

CORE v CORED, CORING, CORES to remove the core (the central part) of

COREDEEM v -ED, -ING, -S to redeem jointly

COREIGN n pl. -S a joint reign

CORELATE v -LATED, -LATING, -LATES to place into mutual or reciprocal relation

CORELESS adj having no core

COREMIUM n pl. -MIA an organ of certain fungi

CORER n pl. -S a utensil for coring apples

CORF n pl. CORVES a wagon used in a mine

CORGI n pl. -S a short-legged dog

CORING present participle of core

CORIUM n pl. -RIA a skin layer

CORK v -ED, -ING, -S to stop up

CORKAGE n pl. -S a charge for wine in a restaurant

CORKER n pl. -S one that corks

CORKIER comparative of corky

CORKIEST superlative of corky

CORKLIKE adj resembling cork (a porous tree bark)

CORKWOOD n pl. -S a small tree

CORKY adj CORKIER, CORKIEST corklike

CORM n pl. -S a stem of certain plants CORMLIKE, CORMOID, CORMOUS adj

CORMEL n pl. -S a small corm

CORN v -ED, -ING, -S to preserve with salt

CORNBALL n pl. -S a hick

CORNCAKE n pl. -S a cake made of cornmeal

CORNCOB n pl. -S the woody core of an ear of corn

CORNCRIB n pl. -S a building in which corn is stored

CORNEA n pl. -S a part of the eye CORNEAL adj

CORNEL n pl. -S a hardwood tree or shrub

CORNEOUS adj of a hornlike texture

CORNER v -ED, -ING, -S to gain control of

CORNET n pl. -S a trumpetlike instrument

CORNETCY n -CIES a rank in the British cavalry

CORNFED adj fed on corn

CORNHUSK n pl. -S the husk covering an ear of corn

CORNICE v -NICED, -NICING, -NICES to decorate with a molding

CORNICHE n pl. -S a road built along a cliff

CORNICLE n pl. -S a part of an aphid

CORNIER comparative of corny

CORNIEST superlative of corny

CORNILY adv in a corny manner

CORNMEAL n pl. -S meal made from corn

CORNPONE n pl. -S bread made with cornmeal

CORNROW v -ED, -ING, -S to braid hair tightly in rows close to the scalp

CORNU n pl. -NUA a hornlike bone formation CORNUAL adj

CORNUS n pl. -ES a cornel

CORNUTE adj horn-shaped

CORNUTED adj cornute

CORNUTO n pl. -TOS the husband of an unfaithful wife

CORNY adj CORNIER, CORNIEST trite

CORODY n pl. -DIES an allowance of food or clothes

COROLLA n pl. -S a protective covering of a flower

CORONA n pl. -NAS or -NAE a luminous circle around a celestial body

CORONACH n pl. -S a dirge

CORONAL n pl. -S a wreath worn on the head

CORONARY n pl. -NARIES an artery supplying blood to the heart

CORONATE v -NATED, -NATING, -NATES to crown

CORONEL *n pl.* -S coronal

CORONER *n pl.* -S an officer who investigates questionable deaths

CORONET *n pl.* -S a small crown

CORONOID *adj* crown-shaped

COROTATE *v* -TATED, -TATING, -TATES to rotate together

CORPORA pl. of corpus

CORPORAL *n pl.* -S a military rank

CORPS *n pl.* CORPS a military unit

CORPSE *n pl.* -S a dead body

CORPSMAN *n pl.* -MEN an enlisted man trained in first aid

CORPUS *n pl.* -PORA a human or animal body

CORRADE *v* -RADED, -RADING, -RADES to erode

CORRAL *v* -RALLED, -RALLING, -RALS to place livestock in a corral (an enclosure)

CORRECT *v* -ED, -ING, -S to make free from error

CORRECT *adj* -RECTER, -RECTEST free from error

CORRIDA *n pl.* -S a bullfight

CORRIDOR *n pl.* -S a narrow hallway

CORRIE *n pl.* -S a cirque

CORRIVAL *n pl.* -S a rival or opponent

CORRODE *v* -RODED, -RODING, -RODES to eat away gradually

CORRODY *n pl.* -DIES corody

CORRUPT *adj* -RUPTER, -RUPTEST dishonest and venal

CORRUPT *v* -ED, -ING, -S to subvert the honesty or integrity of

CORSAC *n pl.* -S an Asian fox

CORSAGE *n pl.* -S a small bouquet of flowers

CORSAIR *n pl.* -S a pirate

CORSE *n pl.* -S a corpse

CORSELET *n pl.* -S a piece of body armor

CORSET *v* -ED, -ING, -S to fit with a corset (a supporting undergarment)

CORSETRY *n pl.* -RIES the work of making corsets

CORSLET *n pl.* -S corselet

CORTEGE *n pl.* -S a retinue

CORTEX *n pl.* -TICES or -TEXES the outer layer of an organ CORTICAL *adj*

CORTIN *n pl.* -S a hormone

CORTISOL *n pl.* -S a hormone

CORULER *n pl.* -S one that rules jointly

CORUNDUM *n pl.* -S a hard mineral

CORVEE *n pl.* -S an obligation to perform feudal service

CORVES pl. of corf

CORVET *n pl.* -S corvette

CORVETTE *n pl.* -S a small, swift warship

CORVINA *n pl.* -S corbina

CORVINE *adj* pertaining or belonging to the crow family of birds

CORY *n pl.* CORY a former monetary unit of Guinea

CORYBANT *n pl.* -BANTS or -BANTES a reveler

CORYMB *n pl.* -S a flower cluster CORYMBED *adj*

CORYPHEE *n pl.* -S a ballet dancer

CORYZA *n pl.* -S a head cold CORYZAL *adj*

COS *n pl.* -ES a variety of lettuce

COSCRIPT *v* -ED, -ING, -S to collaborate in preparing a script for

COSEC *n pl.* -S cosecant

COSECANT *n pl.* -S a trigonometric function of an angle

COSET *n pl.* -S a mathematical subset

COSEY *n pl.* -SEYS a cozy

COSH *v* -ED, -ING, -ES to bludgeon

COSHER *v* -ED, -ING, -S to coddle

COSIE *n pl.* -S a cozy

COSIED past tense of cosy

COSIER comparative of cosy

COSIES present 3d person sing. of cosy

COSIEST superlative of cosy

COSIGN *v* -ED, -ING, -S to sign jointly

COSIGNER *n pl.* -S one that cosigns

COSILY *adv* in a cosy manner

COSINE *n pl.* -S a trigonometric function of an angle

COSINESS *n pl.* -ES coziness

COSMETIC *n pl.* -S a beauty preparation

COSMIC *adj* pertaining to the cosmos

COSMICAL *adj* cosmic

COSMISM *n pl.* -S a philosophical theory

COSMIST *n pl.* -S a supporter of cosmism

COSMOS *n pl.* -ES the universe regarded as an orderly system

COSS *n pl.* COSS kos

COSSACK *n pl.* -S a Russian cavalryman

COSSET *v* -ED, -ING, -S to fondle

COST *v* COST or COSTED, COSTING, COSTS to estimate a price for production of

COSTA *n pl.* -TAE a rib COSTAL *adj*

COSTAR *v* -STARRED, -STARRING, -STARS to star with another actor

COSTARD *n pl.* -S a large cooking apple

COSTATE *adj* having a rib or ribs

COSTER *n pl.* -S a hawker of fruit or vegetables

COSTIVE *adj* constipated

COSTLESS *adj* free of charge

COSTLY *adj* -LIER, -LIEST expensive

COSTMARY *n pl.* -MARIES an herb used in salads

COSTREL *n pl.* -S a flask

COSTUME *v* -TUMED, -TUMING, -TUMES to supply with a costume (a style of dress)

COSTUMER *n pl.* -S one that costumes

COSTUMEY *adj* of or pertaining to a costume

COSTUMING present participle of costume

COSY *v* COSIED, COSYING, COSIES cozy

COSY *adj* COSIER, COSIEST cozy

COT *n pl.* -S a light, narrow bed

COTAN *n pl.* -S a trigonometric function of an angle

COTE *v* COTED, COTING, COTES to pass by

COTEAU *n pl.* -TEAUX the higher ground of a region

COTENANT *n pl.* -S one who is a tenant with another in the same place

COTERIE *n pl.* -S a clique

COTHURN *n pl.* -S a buskin worn by ancient Roman actors

COTHURNI *n/pl* cothurns

COTIDAL *adj* indicating coincidence of the tides

COTILLON *n pl.* -S a ballroom dance

COTING present participle of cote

COTQUEAN *n pl.* -S a vulgar woman

COTTA *n pl.* -TAE or -TAS a short surplice

COTTAGE *n pl.* -S a small house COTTAGEY *adj*

COTTAGER *n pl.* -S one that lives in a cottage

COTTAR *n pl.* -S a tenant farmer

COTTER *n pl.* -S a pin or wedge used for fastening parts together COTTERED *adj*

COTTIER *n pl.* -S cottar

COTTON *v* -ED, -ING, -S to take a liking

COTTONY *adj* resembling cotton (a soft, fibrous material)

COTYLOID *adj* cup-shaped

COTYPE *n pl.* -S a taxonomic type

COUCH *v* -ED, -ING, -ES to put into words

COUCHANT *adj* lying down

COUCHER *n pl.* -S one that couches

COUCHING *n pl.* -S a form of embroidery

COUDE *adj* pertaining to a type of telescope

COUGAR *n pl.* -S a mountain lion

COUGH *v* -ED, -ING, -S to expel air from the lungs noisily

COUGHER *n pl.* -S one that coughs

COULD past tense of can

COULDEST a past 2d person sing. of can

COULDST a past 2d person sing. of can

COULEE *n pl.* -S a small ravine

COULIS *n pl.* -LISES a thick sauce of pureed vegetable or fruit

COULISSE *n pl.* -S a side scene of a theatre stage

COULOIR *n pl.* -S a deep gorge or gully

COULOMB *n pl.* -S an electrical measure

COULTER *n pl.* -S a colter

COUMARIN *n pl.* -S a chemical compound COUMARIC *adj*

COUMAROU *n pl.* -S the seed of a tropical tree

COUNCIL *n pl.* -S a group of persons appointed for a certain function

COUNSEL *v* -SELED, -SELING, -SELS or -SELLED, -SELLING, -SELS to advise

COUNT *v* -ED, -ING, -S to list or mention the units of one by one to ascertain the total

COUNTER *v* -ED, -ING, -S to oppose

COUNTESS *n pl.* -ES a noblewoman

COUNTIAN *n pl.* -S a resident of a county

COUNTRY *n pl.* -TRIES the territory of a nation

COUNTY *n pl.* -TIES an administrative division of a state

COUP *v* -ED, -ING, -S to overturn

COUPE *n pl.* -S an automobile with two doors

COUPLE *v* -PLED, -PLING, -PLES to unite in pairs

COUPLER *n pl.* -S one that couples

COUPLET *n pl.* -S a pair of successive lines of verse

COUPLING *n pl.* -S a joining device

COUPON *n pl.* -S a certificate entitling the holder to certain benefits

COURAGE *n pl.* -S the quality that enables one to face danger fearlessly; spirit

COURANT n pl. -S courante
COURANTE n pl. -S an old, lively dance
COURANTO n pl. -TOS or -TOES courante
COURIER n pl. -S a messenger
COURLAN n pl. -S a wading bird
COURSE v COURSED, COURSING, COURSES to cause hounds to chase game
COURSER n pl. -S one that courses
COURSING n pl. -S the pursuit of game by hounds
COURT v -ED, -ING, -S to woo
COURTER n pl. -S one that courts
COURTESY v -SIED, -SYING, -SIES to curtsy
COURTIER n pl. -S one who attends a royal court
COURTLY adj -LIER, -LIEST stately
COUSCOUS n pl. -ES a North African cereal
COUSIN n pl. -S a child of one's aunt or uncle COUSINLY adj
COUSINRY n pl. -RIES cousins collectively
COUTEAU n pl. -TEAUX a knife
COUTER n pl. -S a piece of armor for the elbow
COUTH adj COUTHER, COUTHEST sophisticated
COUTH n pl. -S refinement
COUTHIE adj COUTHIER, COUTHIEST friendly
COUTURE n pl. -S the business of dressmaking
COUVADE n pl. -S a primitive birth ritual
COVALENT adj sharing electron pairs
COVE v COVED, COVING, COVES to curve over or inward
COVEN n pl. -S a group of witches
COVENANT v -ED, -ING, -S to enter into a binding agreement
COVER v -ED, -ING, -S to place something over or upon
COVERAGE n pl. -S the extent to which something is covered
COVERALL n pl. -S a one-piece work garment
COVERER n pl. -S one that covers
COVERING n pl. -S something that covers
COVERLET n pl. -S a bed covering
COVERLID n pl. -S a coverlet
COVERT n pl. -S a hiding place
COVERTLY adv secretly
COVERUP n pl. -S something used to conceal improper activity

COVET v -ED, -ING, -S to desire greatly
COVETER n pl. -S one that covets
COVETOUS adj excessively desirous
COVEY n pl. -EYS a flock of birds
COVIN n pl. -S a conspiracy to defraud
COVING n pl. -S a concave molding
COW n pl. -S or KINE a farm animal
COW v -ED, -ING, -S to intimidate
COWAGE n pl. -S a tropical vine
COWARD n pl. -S one who lacks courage
COWARDLY adj lacking courage
COWBANE n pl. -S a poisonous plant
COWBELL n pl. -S a bell around a cow's neck
COWBERRY n pl. -RIES a pasture shrub
COWBIND n pl. -S a species of bryony
COWBIRD n pl. -S a blackbird
COWBOY n pl. -BOYS a ranch worker
COWEDLY adv in a cowed manner
COWER v -ED, -ING, -S to cringe
COWFISH n pl. -ES an aquatic mammal
COWFLAP n pl. -S cowflop
COWFLOP n pl. -S a cowpat
COWGIRL n pl. -S a female ranch worker
COWHAGE n pl. -S cowage
COWHAND n pl. -S a cowboy
COWHERB n pl. -S an annual herb
COWHERD n pl. -S one who tends cattle
COWHIDE v -HIDED, -HIDING, -HIDES to flog with a leather whip
COWIER comparative of cowy
COWIEST superlative of cowy
COWINNER n pl. -S one of two or more winners
COWL v -ED, -ING, -S to cover with a hood
COWLICK n pl. -S a lock of unruly hair
COWLING n pl. -S a covering for an aircraft engine
COWMAN n pl. -MEN one who owns cattle
COWORKER n pl. -S a fellow worker
COWPAT n pl. -S a dropping of cow dung
COWPEA n pl. -S a black-eyed pea
COWPIE n pl. -S a cowpat
COWPLOP n pl. -S a cowpat
COWPOKE n pl. -S a cowboy
COWPOX n pl. -ES a cattle disease
COWRIE n pl. -S cowry
COWRITE v -WROTE, -WRITTEN, -WRITING, -WRITES to collaborate in writing

COWRY *n pl.* -RIES a glossy seashell
COWSHED *n pl.* -S a shelter for cows
COWSKIN *n pl.* -S the hide of a cow
COWSLIP *n pl.* -S a flowering plant
COWY *adj* COWIER, COWIEST suggestive of a cow
COX *v* -ED, -ING, -ES to coxswain
COXA *n pl.* COXAE the hip or hip joint COXAL *adj*
COXALGIA *n pl.* -S pain in the hip COXALGIC *adj*
COXALGY *n pl.* -GIES coxalgia
COXCOMB *n pl.* -S a conceited dandy
COXITIS *n pl.* COXITIDES inflammation of the hip joint
COXSWAIN *v* -ED, -ING, -S to steer a racing rowboat
COY *adj* COYER, COYEST shy
COY *v* -ED, -ING, -S to caress
COYDOG *n pl.* -S a hybrid between a coyote and a wild dog
COYISH *adj* somewhat coy
COYLY *adv* in a coy manner
COYNESS *n pl.* -ES the state of being coy
COYOTE *n pl.* -S a small wolf
COYPOU *n pl.* -S a coypu
COYPU *n pl.* -S an aquatic rodent
COZ *n pl.* COZES or COZZES a cousin
COZEN *v* -ED, -ING, -S to deceive
COZENAGE *n pl.* -S the practice of cozening
COZENER *n pl.* -S one that cozens
COZEY *n pl.* -ZEYS a cover for a teapot
COZIE *n pl.* -S a cozey
COZIED past tense of cozy
COZIER comparative of cozy
COZIES present 3d person sing. of cozy
COZIEST superlative of cozy
COZINESS *n pl.* -ES the state of being cozy
COZY *v* COZIED, COZYING, COZIES to attempt to get on friendly terms
COZY *adj* COZIER, COZIEST snug and comfortable COZILY *adv*
COZZES *a pl.* of coz
CRAAL *v* -ED, -ING, -S to kraal
CRAB *v* CRABBED, CRABBING, CRABS to complain
CRABBER *n pl.* -S one that crabs
CRABBY *adj* -BIER, -BIEST grumpy CRABBILY *adv*

CRABMEAT *n pl.* -S the edible part of a crab
CRABWISE *adv* sideways
CRACK *v* -ED, -ING, -S to break without dividing into parts
CRACKER *n pl.* -S a thin, crisp biscuit
CRACKING *n pl.* -S a chemical process
CRACKLE *v* -LED, -LING, -LES to make a succession of snapping sounds
CRACKLY *adj* -LIER, -LIEST brittle
CRACKNEL *n pl.* -S a hard, crisp biscuit
CRACKPOT *n pl.* -S an eccentric person
CRACKUP *n pl.* -S a collision
CRACKY *interj* — used to express surprise
CRADLE *v* -DLED, -DLING, -DLES to nurture during infancy
CRADLER *n pl.* -S one that cradles
CRAFT *v* -ED, -ING, -S to make by hand
CRAFTY *adj* CRAFTIER, CRAFTIEST skilful in deceiving CRAFTILY *adv*
CRAG *n pl.* -S a large jagged rock CRAGGED *adj*
CRAGGY *adj* -GIER, -GIEST full of crags CRAGGILY *adv*
CRAGSMAN *n pl.* -MEN one who climbs crags
CRAKE *n pl.* -S a small, harsh-voiced bird
CRAM *v* CRAMMED, CRAMMING, CRAMS to fill or pack tightly
CRAMBE *n pl.* -S an annual herb
CRAMBO *n pl.* -BOS or -BOES a word game
CRAMMED past tense of cram
CRAMMER *n pl.* -S one that crams
CRAMMING present participle of cram
CRAMOISY *n pl.* -SIES crimson cloth
CRAMP *v* -ED, -ING, -S to restrain or confine
CRAMPIT *n pl.* -S a piece of equipment used in curling
CRAMPON *n pl.* -S a device for raising heavy objects
CRAMPOON *n pl.* -S crampon
CRANCH *v* -ED, -ING, -ES to craunch
CRANE *v* CRANED, CRANING, CRANES to stretch out one's neck
CRANIA *a pl.* of cranium
CRANIAL *adj* pertaining to the skull
CRANIATE *n pl.* -S one that has a skull
CRANING present participle of crane

CRANIUM *n pl.* -NIUMS or -NIA the skull

CRANK *v* -ED, -ING, -S to start manually

CRANK *adj* CRANKER, CRANKEST lively

CRANKIER comparative of cranky

CRANKIEST superlative of cranky

CRANKILY *adv* in a cranky manner

CRANKISH *adj* eccentric

CRANKLE *v* -KLED, -KLING, -KLES to crinkle

CRANKLY *adv* in a crank manner

CRANKOUS *adj* cranky

CRANKPIN *n pl.* -S the handle of a crank

CRANKY *adj* CRANKIER, CRANKIEST grumpy

CRANNIED *adj* having crannies

CRANNIES pl. of cranny

CRANNOG *n pl.* -S an artificial island

CRANNOGE *n pl.* -S crannog

CRANNY *n pl.* -NIES a crevice CRANNIED *adj*

CRAP *v* CRAPPED, CRAPPING, CRAPS to throw a 2, 3, or 12 in a dice game

CRAPE *v* CRAPED, CRAPING, CRAPES to crepe

CRAPPIE *n pl.* -S an edible fish

CRAPPING present participle of crap

CRAPPY *adj* -PIER, -PIEST markedly inferior in quality

CRASES pl. of crasis

CRASH *v* -ED, -ING, -ES to collide noisily

CRASHER *n pl.* -S one that crashes

CRASIS *n pl.* CRASES a vowel contraction

CRASS *adj* CRASSER, CRASSEST grossly vulgar or stupid CRASSLY *adv*

CRATCH *n pl.* -ES a manger

CRATE *v* CRATED, CRATING, CRATES to put in a packing box

CRATER *v* -ED, -ING, -S to form cavities in a surface

CRATON *n pl.* -S a part of the earth's crust CRATONIC *adj*

CRAUNCH *v* -ED, -ING, -ES to crunch

CRAVAT *n pl.* -S a necktie

CRAVE *v* CRAVED, CRAVING, CRAVES to desire greatly

CRAVEN *v* -ED, -ING, -S to make cowardly

CRAVENLY *adv* in a cowardly manner

CRAVER *n pl.* -S one that craves

CRAVING *n pl.* -S a great desire

CRAW *n pl.* -S the stomach of an animal

CRAWDAD *n pl.* -S a crayfish

CRAWFISH *v* -ED, -ING, -ES to back out or retreat

CRAWL *v* -ED, -ING, -S to move with the body on or near the ground

CRAWLER *n pl.* -S one that crawls

CRAWLWAY *n pl.* -WAYS a small, low tunnel

CRAWLY *adj* CRAWLIER, CRAWLIEST creepy

CRAYFISH *n pl.* -ES a crustacean

CRAYON *v* -ED, -ING, -S to use a drawing implement

CRAZE *v* CRAZED, CRAZING, CRAZES to make insane

CRAZY *adj* -ZIER, -ZIEST insane CRAZILY *adv*

CRAZY *n pl.* -ZIES a crazy person

CREAK *v* -ED, -ING, -S to squeak

CREAKY *adj* CREAKIER, CREAKIEST creaking CREAKILY *adv*

CREAM *v* -ED, -ING, -S to form cream (a part of milk)

CREAMER *n pl.* -S a cream pitcher

CREAMERY *n pl.* -ERIES a dairy

CREAMY *adj* CREAMIER, CREAMIEST rich in cream CREAMILY *adv*

CREASE *v* CREASED, CREASING, CREASES to make a fold or wrinkle in

CREASER *n pl.* -S one that creases

CREASY *adj* CREASIER, CREASIEST having folds or wrinkles

CREATE *v* -ATED, -ATING, -ATES to cause to exist

CREATIN *n pl.* -S creatine

CREATINE *n pl.* -S a chemical compound

CREATION *n pl.* -S something created

CREATIVE *adj* having the ability to create

CREATOR *n pl.* -S one that creates

CREATURE *n pl.* -S a living being

CRECHE *n pl.* -S a day nursery

CREDAL *adj* pertaining to a creed

CREDENCE *n pl.* -S belief

CREDENDA *n/pl* articles of faith

CREDENT *adj* believing

CREDENZA *n pl.* -S a piece of furniture

CREDIBLE *adj* believable CREDIBLY *adv*

CREDIT *v* -ED, -ING, -S to accept as true

CREDITOR *n pl.* -S one to whom money is owed

CREDO *n pl.* -DOS a creed

CREED n pl. -S a statement of belief CREEDAL adj

CREEK n pl. -S a watercourse smaller than a river

CREEL v -ED, -ING, -S to put fish in a creel (a fish basket)

CREEP v CREPT, CREEPING, CREEPS to crawl

CREEPAGE n pl. -S gradual movement

CREEPER n pl. -S one that creeps

CREEPIE n pl. -S a low stool

CREEPY adj CREEPIER, CREEPIEST repugnant CREEPILY adv

CREESE n pl. -S kris

CREESH v -ED, -ING, -ES to grease

CREMAINS n/pl the ashes of a cremated body

CREMATE v -MATED, -MATING, -MATES to reduce to ashes by burning

CREMATOR n pl. -S one that cremates

CREME n pl. -S cream

CRENATE adj having an edge with rounded projections

CRENATED adj crenate

CRENEL v -ELED, -ELING, -ELS or -ELLED, -ELLING, -ELS to provide with crenelles

CRENELLE n pl. -S a rounded projection

CREODONT n pl. -S an extinct carnivore

CREOLE n pl. -S a type of mixed language

CREOLISE v -ISED, -ISING, -ISES to creolize

CREOLIZE v -IZED, -IZING, -IZES to cause a language to become a creole

CREOSOL n pl. -S a chemical compound

CREOSOTE v -SOTED, -SOTING, -SOTES to treat with a wood preservative

CREPE v CREPED, CREPING, CREPES to frizz the hair

CREPEY adj CREPIER, CREPIEST crinkly

CREPON n pl. -S a crinkled fabric

CREPT past tense of creep

CREPY adj CREPIER, CREPIEST crepey

CRESCENT n pl. -S the figure of the moon in its first or last quarter

CRESCIVE adj increasing

CRESOL n pl. -S a chemical disinfectant

CRESS n pl. -ES a plant used in salads

CRESSET n pl. -S a metal cup for burning oil

CREST v -ED, -ING, -S to reach a crest (a peak)

CRESTAL adj pertaining to a crest (a peak)

CRESTING n pl. -S a decorative coping

CRESYL n pl. -S tolyl

CRESYLIC adj pertaining to cresol

CRETIC n pl. -S a type of metrical foot

CRETIN n pl. -S an idiot

CRETONNE n pl. -S a heavy fabric

CREVALLE n pl. -S a food and game fish

CREVASSE v -VASSED, -VASSING, -VASSES to fissure

CREVICE n pl. -S a cleft CREVICED adj

CREW v -ED, -ING, -S to serve aboard a ship

CREWEL n pl. -S a woolen yarn

CREWLESS adj without any crewmen

CREWMAN n pl. -MEN one who serves on a ship

CREWMATE n pl. -S a fellow crewman

CREWNECK n pl. -S a sweater with a collarless neckline

CRIB v CRIBBED, CRIBBING, CRIBS to confine closely

CRIBBAGE n pl. -S a card game

CRIBBER n pl. -S one that cribs

CRIBBING n pl. -S a supporting framework

CRIBBLED adj covered with dots

CRIBROUS adj pierced with small holes

CRIBWORK n pl. -S a framework of logs

CRICETID n pl. -S a small rodent

CRICK v -ED, -ING, -S to cause a spasm of the neck

CRICKET v -ED, -ING, -S to play cricket (a ball game)

CRICKEY interj — used as a mild oath

CRICOID n pl. -S a cartilage of the larynx

CRIED past tense of cry

CRIER n pl. -S one that cries

CRIES present 3d person sing. of cry

CRIKEY interj — used as a mild oath

CRIME n pl. -S a violation of the law

CRIMINAL n pl. -S one who has committed a crime

CRIMMER n pl. -S krimmer

CRIMP v -ED, -ING, -S to pleat

CRIMPER n pl. -S one who crimps

CRIMPLE v -PLED, -PLING, -PLES to wrinkle

CRIMPY adj CRIMPIER, CRIMPIEST wavy

CRIMSON v -ED, -ING, -S to make crimson (a red color)

CRINGE v CRINGED, CRINGING, CRINGES to shrink in fear

CRINGER n pl. -S one that cringes

CRINGLE n pl. -S a small loop of rope

CRINITE n pl. -S a fossil crinoid

CRINKLE v -KLED, -KLING, -KLES to wrinkle

CRINKLY adj -KLIER, -KLIEST crinkled

CRINOID n pl. -S a marine animal

CRINUM n pl. -S a tropical herb

CRIOLLO n pl. -LLOS a person of Spanish ancestry

CRIPE interj — used as a mild oath

CRIPES interj — used as a mild oath

CRIPPLE v -PLED, -PLING, -PLES to disable or impair

CRIPPLER n pl. -S one that cripples

CRIS n pl. -ES kris

CRISIS n pl. CRISES a crucial turning point CRISIC adj

CRISP adj CRISPER, CRISPEST brittle

CRISP v -ED, -ING, -S to make crisp

CRISPATE adj curled

CRISPEN v -ED, -ING, -S to make crisp

CRISPER n pl. -S one that crisps

CRISPLY adv in a crisp manner

CRISPY adj CRISPIER, CRISPIEST crisp CRISPILY adv

CRISSUM n pl. CRISSA a region of feathers on a bird CRISSAL adj

CRISTA n pl. -TAE a part of a cell

CRISTATE adj having a projection on the head

CRITERIA n/pl standards of judgment

CRITIC n pl. -S one who judges the merits of something CRITICAL adj

CRITIQUE v -TIQUED, -TIQUING, -TIQUES to judge as a critic

CRITTER n pl. -S a creature

CRITTUR n pl. -S critter

CROAK v -ED, -ING, -S to utter a low, hoarse sound

CROAKER n pl. -S one that croaks

CROAKY adj CROAKIER, CROAKIEST low and hoarse CROAKILY adv

CROC n pl. -S a crocodile

CROCEIN n pl. -S a red dye

CROCEINE n pl. -S crocein

CROCHET v -ED, -ING, -S to do a type of needlework

CROCI a pl. of crocus

CROCINE adj pertaining to the crocus

CROCK v -ED, -ING, -S to stain or soil

CROCKERY n pl. -ERIES pottery

CROCKET n pl. -S an architectural ornament

CROCOITE n pl. -S a mineral

CROCUS n pl. -CUSES or -CI a flowering plant

CROFT n pl. -S a small tenant farm

CROFTER n pl. -S a tenant farmer

CROJIK n pl. -S a triangular sail

CROMLECH n pl. -S a dolmen

CRONE n pl. -S a withered old woman

CRONY n pl. CRONIES a close friend

CRONYISM n pl. -S a kind of political favoritism

CROOK v -ED, -ING, -S to bend

CROOKED adj -EDER, -EDEST dishonest

CROOKERY n pl. -ERIES crooked activity

CROON v -ED, -ING, -S to sing softly

CROONER n pl. -S one that croons

CROP v CROPPED, CROPPING, CROPS to cut off short

CROPLAND n pl. -S farmland

CROPLESS adj being without crops (agricultural produce)

CROPPED past tense of crop

CROPPER n pl. -S one that crops

CROPPIE n pl. -S crappie

CROPPING present participle of crop

CROQUET v -ED, -ING, -S to drive a ball away in a certain game

CROQUIS n pl. CROQUIS a sketch

CRORE n pl. -S a monetary unit of India

CROSIER n pl. -S a bishop's staff

CROSS v -ED, -ING, -ES to intersect

CROSS adj CROSSER, CROSSEST ill-tempered

CROSSARM n pl. -S a horizontal bar

CROSSBAR v -BARRED, -BARRING, -BARS to fasten with crossarms

CROSSBOW n pl. -S a kind of weapon

CROSSCUT v -CUT, -CUTTING, -CUTS to cut across

CROSSE n pl. -S a lacrosse stick

CROSSER n pl. -S one that crosses

CROSSING n pl. -S an intersection

CROSSLET n pl. -S a heraldic symbol

CROSSLY adv in a cross manner

CROSSTIE n pl. -S a transverse beam

CROSSWAY n pl. -WAYS a road that crosses another road

CROTCH n pl. -ES an angle formed by two diverging parts **CROTCHED** adj

CROTCHET n pl. -S a small hook

CROTON n pl. -S a tropical plant

CROUCH v -ED, -ING, -ES to stoop

CROUP n pl. -S a disease of the throat

CROUPE n pl. -S the rump of certain animals

CROUPIER n pl. -S an attendant in a casino

CROUPOUS adj pertaining to croup

CROUPY adj CROUPIER, CROUPIEST affected with croup **CROUPILY** adv

CROUSE adj lively **CROUSELY** adv

CROUTON n pl. -S a small cube of toasted bread

CROW v -ED, -ING, -S to boast

CROWBAR v -BARRED, -BARRING, -BARS to use a steel bar as a lever

CROWD v -ED, -ING, -S to press into an insufficient space

CROWDER n pl. -S one that crowds

CROWDIE n pl. -S a crowdy

CROWDY n pl. -DIES porridge

CROWER n pl. -S one that crows

CROWFOOT n pl. -FOOTS or -FEET a flowering plant

CROWN v -ED, -ING, -S to supply with a crown (a royal headpiece)

CROWNER n pl. -S a coroner

CROWNET n pl. -S a coronet

CROWSTEP n pl. -S a step on top of a wall

CROZE n pl. -S a tool used in barrel-making

CROZER n pl. -S a croze

CROZIER n pl. -S crosier

CRUCES a pl. of crux

CRUCIAL adj of supreme importance

CRUCIAN n pl. -S a European fish

CRUCIATE adj cross-shaped

CRUCIBLE n pl. -S a heat-resistant vessel

CRUCIFER n pl. -S one who carries a cross

CRUCIFIX n pl. -ES a cross bearing an image of Christ

CRUCIFY v -FIED, -FYING, -FIES to put to death on a cross

CRUCK n pl. -S a curved roof timber

CRUD v CRUDDED, CRUDDING, CRUDS to curd

CRUDDY adj -DIER, -DIEST filthy; contemptible

CRUDE adj CRUDER, CRUDEST unrefined **CRUDELY** adv

CRUDE n pl. -S unrefined petroleum

CRUDITES n/pl pieces of raw vegetables served with a dip

CRUDITY n pl. -TIES the state of being crude

CRUEL adj CRUELER, CRUELEST or CRUELLER, CRUELLEST indifferent to the pain of others **CRUELLY** adv

CRUELTY n pl. -TIES a cruel act

CRUET n pl. -S a glass bottle

CRUISE v CRUISED, CRUISING, CRUISES to sail about touching at several ports

CRUISER n pl. -S a boat that cruises

CRUISING n pl. -S the act of driving around in search of fun

CRULLER n pl. -S a small sweet cake

CRUMB v -ED, -ING, -S to break into crumbs (small pieces)

CRUMBER n pl. -S one that crumbs

CRUMBIER comparative of crumby

CRUMBIEST superlative of crumby

CRUMBLE v -BLED, -BLING, -BLES to break into small pieces

CRUMBLY adj -BLIER, -BLIEST easily crumbled

CRUMBUM n pl. -S a despicable person

CRUMBY adj CRUMBIER, CRUMBIEST full of crumbs

CRUMHORN n pl. -S a double-reed woodwind instrument

CRUMMIE n pl. -S a cow with crooked horns

CRUMMY adj -MIER, -MIEST of little or no value

CRUMP v -ED, -ING, -S to crunch

CRUMPET n pl. -S a small cake cooked on a griddle

CRUMPLE v -PLED, -PLING, -PLES to wrinkle

CRUMPLY adj -PLIER, -PLIEST easily wrinkled

CRUNCH v -ED, -ING, -ES to chew with a crackling sound

CRUNCHER n pl. -S one that crunches

CRUNCHY adj CRUNCHIER, CRUNCHIEST crisp

CRUNODE n pl. -S a point at which a curve crosses itself **CRUNODAL** adj

CRUOR n pl. -S clotted blood

CRUPPER n pl. -S the rump of a horse

CRURAL *adj* pertaining to the thigh or leg

CRUS *n pl.* CRURA a part of the leg

CRUSADE *v* -SADED, -SADING, -SADES to engage in a holy war

CRUSADER *n pl.* -S one that crusades

CRUSADO *n pl.* -DOES or -DOS an old Portuguese coin

CRUSE *n pl.* -S a small bottle

CRUSET *n pl.* -S a melting pot

CRUSH *v* -ED, -ING, -ES to press or squeeze out of shape

CRUSHER *n pl.* -S one that crushes

CRUSILY *adj* covered with crosslets

CRUST *v* -ED, -ING, -S to form a crust (a hardened outer surface)

CRUSTAL *adj* pertaining to the earth's crust

CRUSTOSE *adj* forming a thin, brittle crust

CRUSTY *adj* CRUSTIER, CRUSTIEST surly CRUSTILY *adv*

CRUTCH *v* -ED, -ING, -ES to prop up or support

CRUX *n pl.* CRUXES or CRUCES a basic or decisive point

CRUZADO *n pl.* -DOES or -DOS crusado

CRUZEIRO *n pl.* -ROS a monetary unit of Brazil

CRWTH *n pl.* -S an ancient stringed musical instrument

CRY *v* CRIED, CRYING, CRIES to weep CRYINGLY *adv*

CRYBABY *n pl.* -BIES a person who cries easily

CRYOGEN *n pl.* -S a substance for producing low temperatures

CRYOGENY *n pl.* -NIES a branch of physics

CRYOLITE *n pl.* -S a mineral

CRYONICS *n/pl* the practice of freezing dead bodies for future revival CRYONIC *adj*

CRYOSTAT *n pl.* -S a refrigerating device

CRYOTRON *n pl.* -S an electronic device

CRYPT *n pl.* -S a burial vault CRYPTAL *adj*

CRYPTIC *adj* mysterious

CRYPTO *n pl.* -TOS one who belongs secretly to a group

CRYSTAL *n pl.* -S a transparent mineral

CTENIDIA *n/pl* comblike anatomical structures

CTENOID *adj* comblike

CUB *n pl.* -S the young of certain animals

CUBAGE *n pl.* -S cubature

CUBATURE *n pl.* -S cubical content

CUBBISH *adj* resembling a cub

CUBBY *n pl.* -BIES a small, enclosed space

CUBE *v* CUBED, CUBING, CUBES to form into a cube (a regular solid)

CUBEB *n pl.* -S a woody vine

CUBER *n pl.* -S one that cubes

CUBIC *n pl.* -S a mathematical equation or expression

CUBICAL *adj* shaped like a cube

CUBICITY *n pl.* -TIES the state of being cubical

CUBICLE *n pl.* -S a small chamber

CUBICLY *adv* in the form of a cube

CUBICULA *n/pl* burial chambers

CUBIFORM *adj* shaped like a cube

CUBING present participle of cube

CUBISM *n pl.* -S a style of art CUBISTIC *adj*

CUBIST *n pl.* -S an adherent of cubism

CUBIT *n pl.* -S an ancient measure of length CUBITAL *adj*

CUBOID *n pl.* -S a bone of the foot CUBOIDAL *adj*

CUCKOLD *v* -ED, -ING, -S to make a cuckold (a cornuto) of

CUCKOO *v* -ED, -ING, -S to repeat monotonously

CUCUMBER *n pl.* -S a garden vegetable

CUCURBIT *n pl.* -S a gourd

CUD *n pl.* -S a portion of food to be chewed again

CUDBEAR *n pl.* -S a red dye

CUDDIE *n pl.* -S cuddy

CUDDIES pl. of cuddy

CUDDLE *v* -DLED, -DLING, -DLES to hug tenderly

CUDDLER *n pl.* -S one that cuddles

CUDDLY *adj* -DLIER, -DLIEST fit for cuddling

CUDDY *n pl.* -DIES a donkey

CUDGEL *v* -ELED, -ELING, -ELS or -ELLED, -ELLING, -ELS to beat with a heavy club

CUDGELER *n pl.* -S one that cudgels

CUDWEED *n pl.* -S a perennial herb

CUE *v* CUED, CUING or CUEING, CUES to give a signal to an actor

CUESTA *n pl.* -S a type of land elevation

CUFF *v* -ED, -ING, -S to furnish with a cuff (a part of a sleeve)

CUFFLESS *adj* having no cuff

CUIF	n pl. -S coof
CUING	a present participle of cue
CUIRASS	v -ED, -ING, -ES to cover with a type of armor
CUISH	n pl. -ES cuisse
CUISINE	n pl. -S a style of cooking
CUISSE	n pl. -S a piece of armor for the thigh
CUITTLE	v -TLED, -TLING, -TLES to coax
CUKE	n pl. -S a cucumber
CULCH	n pl. -ES an oyster bed
CULET	n pl. -S a piece of armor for the lower back
CULEX	n pl. CULICES a mosquito
CULICID	n pl. -S a culicine
CULICINE	n pl. -S a mosquito
CULINARY	adj pertaining to cookery
CULL	v -ED, -ING, -S to select from others
CULLAY	n pl. -LAYS quillai
CULLER	n pl. -S one that culls
CULLET	n pl. -S broken glass gathered for remelting
CULLIED	past tense of cully
CULLIES	present 3d person sing. of cully
CULLION	n pl. -S a vile fellow
CULLIS	n pl. -LISES a gutter in a roof
CULLY	v -LIED, -LYING, -LIES to trick
CULM	v -ED, -ING, -S to form a hollow stem
CULOTTE	n pl. -S a divided skirt
CULPA	n pl. -PAE negligence for which one is liable
CULPABLE	adj deserving blame or censure CULPABLY adv
CULPRIT	n pl. -S one that is guilty
CULT	n pl. -S a religious society
CULTCH	n pl. -ES culch
CULTI	a pl. of cultus
CULTIC	adj pertaining to a cult
CULTIGEN	n pl. -S a cultivar
CULTISH	adj pertaining to a cult
CULTISM	n pl. -S devotion to a cult
CULTIST	n pl. -S a member of a cult
CULTIVAR	n pl. -S a variety of plant originating under cultivation
CULTLIKE	adj resembling a cult
CULTRATE	adj sharp-edged and pointed
CULTURAL	adj produced by breeding
CULTURE	v -TURED, -TURING, -TURES to make fit for raising crops
CULTUS	n pl. -TUSES or -TI a cult
CULVER	n pl. -S a pigeon
CULVERIN	n pl. -S a medieval musket

CULVERT	n pl. -S a conduit
CUM	prep together with
CUMARIN	n pl. -S coumarin
CUMBER	v -ED, -ING, -S to hinder
CUMBERER	n pl. -S one that cumbers
CUMBROUS	adj unwieldy
CUMIN	n pl. -S a plant used in cooking
CUMMER	n pl. -S a godmother
CUMMIN	n pl. -S cumin
CUMQUAT	n pl. -S kumquat
CUMSHAW	n pl. -S a gift
CUMULATE	v -LATED, -LATING, -LATES to heap
CUMULUS	n pl. -LI a type of cloud CUMULOUS adj
CUNDUM	n pl. -S condom
CUNEAL	adj cuneate
CUNEATE	adj wedge-shaped; triangular
CUNEATED	adj cuneate
CUNEATIC	adj cuneate
CUNIFORM	n pl. -S wedge-shaped writing characters
CUNNER	n pl. -S a marine fish
CUNNING	adj -NINGER, -NINGEST crafty
CUNNING	n pl. -S skill in deception
CUP	v CUPPED, CUPPING, CUPS to place in a cup (a small, open container)
CUPBOARD	n pl. -S a cabinet
CUPCAKE	n pl. -S a small cake
CUPEL	v -PELED, -PELING, -PELS or -PELLED, -PELLING, -PELS to refine gold or silver in a cuplike vessel
CUPELER	n pl. -S cupeller
CUPELLER	n pl. -S one that cupels
CUPFUL	n pl. CUPFULS or CUPSFUL as much as a cup can hold
CUPID	n pl. -S a naked, winged representation of the Roman god of love
CUPIDITY	n pl. -TIES greed; lust
CUPLIKE	adj resembling a cup
CUPOLA	v -ED, -ING, -S to shape like a dome
CUPPA	n pl. -S a cup of tea
CUPPED	past tense of cup
CUPPER	n pl. -S one that performs cupping
CUPPING	n pl. -S an archaic medical process
CUPPY	adj -PIER, -PIEST cuplike
CUPREOUS	adj containing copper
CUPRIC	adj containing copper

CUPRITE *n pl.* -S an ore of copper
CUPROUS *adj* containing copper
CUPRUM *n pl.* -S copper
CUPSFUL a *pl.* of cupful
CUPULA *n pl.* -LAE a cup-shaped anatomical structure
CUPULAR *adj* cupulate
CUPULATE *adj* cup-shaped
CUPULE *n pl.* -S a cup-shaped anatomical structure
CUR *n pl.* -S a mongrel dog
CURABLE *adj* capable of being cured **CURABLY** *adv*
CURACAO *n pl.* -S a type of liqueur
CURACOA *n pl.* -S curacao
CURACY *n pl.* -CIES the office of a curate
CURAGH *n pl.* -S currach
CURARA *n pl.* -S curare
CURARE *n pl.* -S an arrow poison
CURARI *n pl.* -S curare
CURARINE *n pl.* -S a poisonous alkaloid
CURARIZE *v* -RIZED, -RIZING, -RIZES to poison with curare
CURASSOW *n pl.* -S a turkey-like bird
CURATE *v* -RATED, -RATING, -RATES to act as curator of
CURATIVE *n pl.* -S something that cures
CURATOR *n pl.* -S a museum manager
CURB *v* -ED, -ING, -S to restrain **CURBABLE** *adj*
CURBER *n pl.* -S one that curbs
CURBING *n pl.* -S a concrete border along a street
CURBSIDE *n pl.* -S the side of a pavement bordered by a curbing
CURCH *n pl.* -ES a kerchief
CURCULIO *n pl.* -LIOS a weevil
CURCUMA *n pl.* -S a tropical plant
CURD *v* -ED, -ING, -S to curdle
CURDIER comparative of curdy
CURDIEST superlative of curdy
CURDLE *v* -DLED, -DLING, -DLES to congeal
CURDLER *n pl.* -S one that curdles
CURDY *adj* CURDIER, CURDIEST curdled
CURE *v* CURED, CURING, CURES to restore to health
CURELESS *adj* not curable
CURER *n pl.* -S one that cures
CURET *n pl.* -S a surgical instrument
CURETTE *v* -RETTED, -RETTING, -RETTES to treat with a curet

CURF *n pl.* -S an incision made by a cutting tool
CURFEW *n pl.* -S a regulation concerning the hours which one may keep
CURIA *n pl.* -RIAE a court of justice **CURIAL** *adj*
CURIE *n pl.* -S a unit of radioactivity
CURING present participle of cure
CURIO *n pl.* -RIOS an unusual art object
CURIOSA *n/pl* pornographic books
CURIOUS *adj* -OUSER, -OUSEST eager for information
CURITE *n pl.* -S a radioactive mineral
CURIUM *n pl.* -S a radioactive element
CURL *v* -ED, -ING, -S to form into ringlets
CURLER *n pl.* -S one that curls
CURLEW *n pl.* -S a shore bird
CURLICUE *v* -CUED, -CUING, -CUES to decorate with curlicues (fancy spiral figures)
CURLING *n pl.* -S a game played on ice
CURLY *adj* CURLIER, CURLIEST tending to curl **CURLILY** *adv*
CURLYCUE *n pl.* -S curlicue
CURN *n pl.* -S grain
CURR *v* -ED, -ING, -S to purr
CURRACH *n pl.* -S a coracle
CURRAGH *n pl.* -S currach
CURRAN *n pl.* -S curn
CURRANT *n pl.* -S an edible berry
CURRENCY *n pl.* -CIES money
CURRENT *n pl.* -S a continuous flow
CURRICLE *n pl.* -S a light carriage
CURRIE *v* -RIED, -RYING, -RIES to prepare food a certain way
CURRIED past tense of curry
CURRIER *n pl.* -S one that curries leather
CURRIERY *n pl.* -ERIES the shop of a currier
CURRISH *adj* resembling a cur
CURRY *v* -RIED, -RYING, -RIES to prepare leather for use or sale
CURRYING present participle of currie
CURSE *v* CURSED or CURST, CURSING, CURSES to wish evil upon
CURSED *adj* CURSEDER, CURSEDEST wicked **CURSEDLY** *adv*
CURSER *n pl.* -S one that curses
CURSING present participle of curse
CURSIVE *n pl.* -S a style of print

CURSOR n pl. -S a light indicator on a computer display

CURSORY adj hasty and superficial

CURST a past tense of curse

CURT adj CURTER, CURTEST abrupt

CURTAIL v -ED, -ING, -S to cut short

CURTAIN v -ED, -ING, -S to provide with a hanging piece of fabric

CURTAL n pl. -S an animal with a clipped tail

CURTALAX n pl. -ES a cutlass

CURTATE adj shortened

CURTESY n pl. -SIES a type of legal tenure

CURTLY adv in a curt manner

CURTNESS n pl. -ES the quality of being curt

CURTSEY v -ED, -ING, -S to curtsy

CURTSY v -SIED, -SYING, -SIES to bow politely

CURULE adj of the highest rank

CURVE v CURVED, CURVING, CURVES to deviate from straightness **CURVEDLY** adv

CURVET v -VETED, -VETING, -VETS or -VETTED, -VETTING, -VETS to prance

CURVEY adj CURVIER, CURVIEST curvy

CURVING present participle of curve

CURVY adj CURVIER, CURVIEST curved

CUSCUS n pl. -ES an arboreal mammal

CUSEC n pl. -S a volumetric unit of flow of liquids

CUSHAT n pl. -S a pigeon

CUSHAW n pl. -S a variety of squash

CUSHIER comparative of cushy

CUSHIEST superlative of cushy

CUSHILY adv in a cushy manner

CUSHION v -ED, -ING, -S to pad with soft material

CUSHIONY adj soft

CUSHY adj CUSHIER, CUSHIEST easy

CUSK n pl. -S a marine food fish

CUSP n pl. -S a pointed end **CUSPATE, CUSPATED, CUSPED** adj

CUSPID n pl. -S a pointed tooth

CUSPIDAL adj having a cusp

CUSPIDOR n pl. -S a spittoon

CUSPIS n pl. -PIDES a cusp

CUSS v -ED, -ING, -ES to curse

CUSSEDLY adv in a cranky manner

CUSSER n pl. -S one that cusses

CUSSO n pl. -SOS an Ethiopian tree

CUSSWORD n pl. -S a profane or obscene word

CUSTARD n pl. -S a thick, soft dessert **CUSTARDY** adj

CUSTODES pl. of custos

CUSTODY n pl. -DIES guardianship

CUSTOM n pl. -S a habitual practice

CUSTOMER n pl. -S one who buys something

CUSTOS n pl. -TODES a guardian or keeper

CUSTUMAL n pl. -S a written record of laws and customs

CUT v CUT, CUTTING, CUTS to divide into parts with a sharp-edged instrument

CUTAWAY n pl. -AWAYS a type of coat

CUTBACK n pl. -S a reduction

CUTBANK n pl. -S a steep stream bank

CUTCH n pl. -ES catechu

CUTCHERY n pl. -CHERIES a judicial office in India

CUTDOWN n pl. -S a reduction

CUTE adj CUTER, CUTEST pleasingly attractive **CUTELY** adv

CUTENESS n pl. -ES the quality of being cute

CUTES a pl. of cutis

CUTESIE adj -SIER, -SIEST cutesy

CUTEST superlative of cute

CUTESY adj -SIER, -SIEST self-consciously cute

CUTEY n pl. -TEYS cutie

CUTGRASS n pl. -ES a swamp grass

CUTICLE n pl. -S the epidermis

CUTICULA n pl. -LAE the outer hard covering of an insect

CUTIE n pl. -S a cute person

CUTIN n pl. -S a waxy substance found on plants

CUTINISE v -ISED, -ISING, -ISES to cutinize

CUTINIZE v -IZED, -IZING, -IZES to become coated with cutin

CUTIS n pl. -TES or -TISES the corium

CUTLAS n pl. -ES cutlass

CUTLASS n pl. -ES a short sword

CUTLER n pl. -S one who sells and repairs cutting tools

CUTLERY n pl. -LERIES the occupation of a cutler

CUTLET n pl. -S a slice of meat

CUTLINE n pl. -S a caption

CUTOFF n pl. -S the point at which something terminates

CUTOUT n pl. -S something cut out

CUTOVER n pl. -S land cleared of trees

CUTPURSE n pl. -S a pickpocket

CUTTABLE adj capable of being cut

CUTTAGE n pl. -S a means of plant propagation

CUTTER n pl. -S one that cuts

CUTTIES pl. of cutty

CUTTING n pl. -S a section cut from a plant

CUTTLE v -TLED, -TLING, -TLES to fold cloth in a particular fashion

CUTTY n pl. -TIES a thickset girl

CUTUP n pl. -S a mischievous person

CUTWATER n pl. -S the front part of a ship's prow

CUTWORK n pl. -S a type of embroidery

CUTWORM n pl. -S a caterpillar

CUVETTE n pl. -S a small tube or vessel

CWM n pl. -S a cirque

CYAN n pl. -S a blue color

CYANAMID n pl. -S a chemical compound

CYANATE n pl. -S a chemical salt

CYANIC adj blue or bluish

CYANID n pl. -S a compound of cyanogen

CYANIDE v -NIDED, -NIDING, -NIDES to treat an ore with cyanid

CYANIN n pl. -S cyanine

CYANINE n pl. -S a blue dye

CYANITE n pl. -S a mineral **CYANITIC** adj

CYANO adj pertaining to cyanogen

CYANOGEN n pl. -S a reactive compound of carbon and nitrogen

CYANOSIS n pl. -NOSES bluish discoloration of the skin **CYANOSED, CYANOTIC** adj

CYBORG n pl. -S a human linked to a mechanical device for life support

CYCAD n pl. -S a tropical plant

CYCAS n pl. -ES a tropical plant

CYCASIN n pl. -S a sugar derivative

CYCLAMEN n pl. -S a flowering plant

CYCLASE n pl. -S an enzyme

CYCLE v -CLED, -CLING, -CLES to ride a bicycle

CYCLECAR n pl. -S a type of motor vehicle

CYCLER n pl. -S a cyclist

CYCLERY n pl. -RIES a bicycle shop

CYCLIC adj moving in complete circles **CYCLICLY** adv

CYCLICAL n pl. -S a stock whose earnings fluctuate widely with variations in the economy

CYCLING n pl. -S the act of riding a bicycle

CYCLIST n pl. -S one who rides a bicycle

CYCLITOL n pl. -S a chemical compound

CYCLIZE v -CLIZED, -CLIZING, -CLIZES to form one or more rings in a chemical compound

CYCLO n pl. -CLOS a three-wheeled motor vehicle

CYCLOID n pl. -S a geometric curve

CYCLONE n pl. -S a rotating system of winds **CYCLONAL, CYCLONIC** adj

CYCLOPS n pl. CYCLOPS a freshwater animal

CYCLOSIS n pl. -CLOSES the circulation of protoplasm within a cell

CYDER n pl. -S cider

CYESIS n pl. CYESES pregnancy

CYGNET n pl. -S a young swan

CYLINDER v -ED, -ING, -S to furnish with a cylinder (a chamber in an engine)

CYLIX n pl. CYLICES kylix

CYMA n pl. -MAS or -MAE a curved molding

CYMAR n pl. -S simar

CYMATIUM n pl. -TIA a cyma

CYMBAL n pl. -S a percussion instrument

CYMBALER n pl. -S one that plays the cymbals

CYMBALOM n pl. -S cimbalom

CYMBIDIA n/pl tropical orchids

CYMBLING n pl. -S cymling

CYME n pl. -S a flower cluster

CYMENE n pl. -S a hydrocarbon

CYMLIN n pl. -S cymling

CYMLING n pl. -S a variety of squash

CYMOGENE n pl. -S a volatile compound

CYMOID adj resembling a cyma

CYMOL n pl. -S cymene

CYMOSE adj resembling a cyme **CYMOSELY** adv

CYMOUS adj cymose

CYNIC n pl. -S a cynical person

CYNICAL adj distrusting the motives of others

CYNICISM n pl. -S cynical quality

CYNOSURE n pl. -S a center of attraction

CYPHER v -ED, -ING, -S to cipher

CYPRES n pl. -ES a legal doctrine

CYPRESS *n* pl. -ES a thin fabric

CYPRIAN *n* pl. -S a prostitute

CYPRINID *n* pl. -S a small freshwater fish

CYPRUS *n* pl. -ES cypress

CYPSELA *n* pl. -LAE an achene in certain plants

CYST *n* pl. -S a sac

CYSTEIN *n* pl. -S cysteine

CYSTEINE *n* pl. -S an amino acid

CYSTIC *adj* pertaining to a cyst

CYSTINE *n* pl. -S an amino acid

CYSTITIS *n* pl. -TITIDES inflammation of the urinary bladder

CYSTOID *n* pl. -S a cyst-like structure

CYTASTER *n* pl. -S a structure formed in a cell during mitosis

CYTIDINE *n* pl. -S a compound containing cytosine

CYTOGENY *n* pl. -NIES the formation of cells

CYTOKINE *n* pl. -S a kind of substance secreted by cells of the immune system

CYTOLOGY *n* pl. -GIES a study of cells

CYTON *n* pl. -S the body of a nerve cell

CYTOSINE *n* pl. -S a component of DNA and RNA

CYTOSOL *n* pl. -S the fluid portion of cell material

CZAR *n* pl. -S an emperor or king

CZARDAS *n* pl. CZARDAS a Hungarian dance

CZARDOM *n* pl. -S the domain of a czar

CZAREVNA *n* pl. -S the daughter of a czar

CZARINA *n* pl. -S the wife of a czar

CZARISM *n* pl. -S autocratic government

CZARIST *n* pl. -S a supporter of czarism

CZARITZA *n* pl. -S a czarina

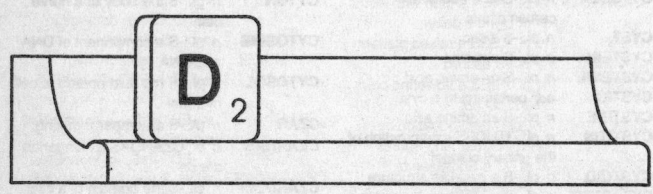

DAB v DABBED, DABBING, DABS to touch lightly

DABBER n pl. -S one that dabs

DABBLE v -BLED, -BLING, -BLES to involve oneself in a superficial interest

DABBLER n pl. -S one that dabbles

DABBLING n pl. -S a superficial interest

DABCHICK n pl. -S a small grebe

DABSTER n pl. -S a dabbler

DACE n pl. -S a freshwater fish

DACHA n pl. -S a Russian cottage

DACKER v -ED, -ING, -S to waver

DACOIT n pl. -S a bandit in India

DACOITY n pl. -COITIES robbery by dacoits

DACTYL n pl. -S a type of metrical foot

DACTYLIC n pl. -S a verse consisting of dactyls

DACTYLUS n pl. -LI a leg joint of certain insects

DAD n pl. -S father

DADA n pl. -S an artistic and literary movement

DADAISM n pl. -S the dada movement

DADAIST n pl. -S a follower of dadaism

DADDLE v -DLED, -DLING, -DLES to diddle

DADDY n pl. -DIES father

DADO v -ED, -ING, -ES or -S to set into a groove

DAEDAL adj skillful

DAEMON n pl. -S demon DAEMONIC adj

DAFF v -ED, -ING, -S to thrust aside

DAFFODIL n pl. -S a flowering plant

DAFFY adj -FIER, -FIEST silly DAFFILY adv

DAFT adj DAFTER, DAFTEST insane DAFTLY adv

DAFTNESS n pl. -ES the quality of being daft

DAG n pl. -S a hanging end or shred

DAGGA n pl. -S marijuana

DAGGER v -ED, -ING, -S to stab with a small knife

DAGGLE v -GLED, -GLING, -GLES to drag in mud

DAGLOCK n pl. -S a dirty or tangled lock of wool

DAGOBA n pl. -S a Buddhist shrine

DAGWOOD n pl. -S a large sandwich

DAH n pl. -S a dash in Morse code

DAHABEAH n pl. -S a large passenger boat

DAHABIAH n pl. -S dahabeah

DAHABIEH n pl. -S dahabeah

DAHABIYA n pl. -S dahabeah

DAHL n pl. -S dal

DAHLIA n pl. -S a flowering plant

DAHOON n pl. -S an evergreen tree

DAIKER v -ED, -ING, -S to dacker

DAIKON n pl. -S a Japanese radish

DAILY n pl. -LIES a newspaper published every weekday

DAIMEN adj occasional

DAIMIO n pl. -MIOS a former Japanese nobleman

DAIMON n pl. -S or -ES an attendant spirit DAIMONIC adj

DAIMYO n pl. -MYOS daimio

DAINTY n pl. -TIES something delicious

DAINTY adj -TIER, -TIEST delicately pretty DAINTILY adv

DAIQUIRI n pl. -S a cocktail

DAIRY *n pl.* DAIRIES an establishment dealing in milk products

DAIRYING *n pl.* -S the business of a dairy

DAIRYMAN *n pl.* -MEN a man who works in or owns a dairy

DAIS *n pl.* -ISES a raised platform

DAISHIKI *n pl.* -S dashiki

DAISY *n pl.* -SIES a flowering plant DAISIED *adj*

DAK *n pl.* -S transportation by relays of men and horses

DAKERHEN *n pl.* -S a European bird

DAKOIT *n pl.* -S dacoit

DAKOITY *n pl.* -TIES dacoity

DAL *n pl.* -S a dish of lentils and spices in India

DALAPON *n pl.* -S an herbicide used on unwanted grasses

DALASI *n pl.* DALASI or DALASIS a unit of Gambian currency

DALE *n pl.* -S a valley

DALEDH *n pl.* -S daleth

DALESMAN *n pl.* -MEN one living in a dale

DALETH *n pl.* -S a Hebrew letter

DALLES *n/pl* rapids

DALLIER *n pl.* -S one that dallies

DALLY *v* -LIED, -LYING, -LIES to waste time

DALMATIC *n pl.* -S a wide-sleeved vestment

DALTON *n pl.* -S a unit of atomic mass

DALTONIC *adj* pertaining to a form of color blindness

DAM *v* DAMMED, DAMMING, DAMS to build a barrier to obstruct the flow of water

DAMAGE *v* -AGED, -AGING, -AGES to injure

DAMAGER *n pl.* -S one that damages

DAMAN *n pl.* -S a small mammal

DAMAR *n pl.* -S dammar

DAMASK *v* -ED, -ING, -S to weave with elaborate design

DAME *n pl.* -S a matron

DAMEWORT *n pl.* -S a flowering plant

DAMMAR *n pl.* -S a hard resin

DAMMED past tense of dam

DAMMER *n pl.* -S dammar

DAMMING present participle of dam

DAMN *v* -ED, -ING, -S to curse

DAMNABLE *adj* detestable DAMNABLY *adv*

DAMNDEST *n pl.* -S utmost

DAMNED *adj* DAMNEDER, DAMNEDEST or DAMNDEST damnable

DAMNER *n pl.* -S one that damns

DAMNIFY *v* -FIED, -FYING, -FIES to cause loss or damage to

DAMOSEL *n pl.* -S damsel

DAMOZEL *n pl.* -S damsel

DAMP *adj* DAMPER, DAMPEST moist

DAMP *v* -ED, -ING, -S to lessen in intensity

DAMPEN *v* -ED, -ING, -S to moisten

DAMPENER *n pl.* -S one that dampens

DAMPER *n pl.* -S one that damps

DAMPING *n pl.* -S the ability of a device to prevent instability

DAMPISH *adj* somewhat damp

DAMPLY *adv* in a damp manner

DAMPNESS *n pl.* -ES the state of being damp

DAMSEL *n pl.* -S a maiden

DAMSON *n pl.* -S a small purple plum

DANCE *v* DANCED, DANCING, DANCES to move rhythmically to music

DANCER *n pl.* -S one that dances

DANDER *v* -ED, -ING, -S to stroll

DANDIER comparative of dandy

DANDIES pl. of dandy

DANDIEST superlative of dandy

DANDIFY *v* -FIED, -FYING, -FIES to cause to resemble a dandy

DANDILY *adv* in a dandy manner

DANDLE *v* -DLED, -DLING, -DLES to fondle

DANDLER *n pl.* -S one that dandles

DANDRIFF *n pl.* -S dandruff

DANDRUFF *n pl.* -S a scurf that forms on the scalp

DANDY *adj* -DIER, -DIEST fine

DANDY *n pl.* -DIES a man who is overly concerned about his appearance

DANDYISH *adj* suggestive of a dandy

DANDYISM *n pl.* -S the style or conduct of a dandy

DANEGELD *n pl.* -S an annual tax in medieval England

DANEWEED *n pl.* -S a danewort

DANEWORT *n pl.* -S a flowering plant

DANG *v* -ED, -ING, -S to damn

DANGER *v* -ED, -ING, -S to endanger

DANGLE *v* -GLED, -GLING, -GLES to hang loosely

DANGLER *n pl.* -S one that dangles

DANIO n pl. -NIOS an aquarium fish

DANISH n pl. DANISH a pastry of raised dough

DANK adj DANKER, DANKEST unpleasantly damp **DANKLY** adv

DANKNESS n pl. -ES the state of being dank

DANSEUR n pl. -S a male ballet dancer

DANSEUSE n pl. -S a female ballet dancer

DAP v DAPPED, DAPPING, DAPS to dip lightly or quickly into water

DAPHNE n pl. -S a flowering shrub

DAPHNIA n pl. -S a minute crustacean

DAPPED past tense of dap

DAPPER adj -PERER, -PEREST looking neat and trim **DAPPERLY** adv

DAPPING present participle of dap

DAPPLE v -PLED, -PLING, -PLES to mark with spots

DAPSONE n pl. -S a medicinal substance

DARB n pl. -S something considered extraordinary

DARBIES n/pl handcuffs

DARE v DARED or DURST, DARING, DARES to have the necessary courage

DAREFUL adj brave

DARER n pl. -S one that dares

DARESAY v to venture to say — DARESAY is the only form of this verb; it is not conjugated

DARIC n pl. -S an ancient Persian coin

DARING n pl. -S bravery

DARINGLY adv in a brave manner

DARIOLE n pl. -S a type of pastry filled with cream, custard, or jelly

DARK adj DARKER, DARKEST having little or no light

DARK v -ED, -ING, -S to darken

DARKEN v -ED, -ING, -S to make dark

DARKENER n pl. -S one that darkens

DARKISH adj somewhat dark

DARKLE v -KLED, -KLING, -KLES to become dark

DARKLY adv -LIER, -LIEST in a dark manner

DARKNESS n pl. -ES the state of being dark

DARKROOM n pl. -S a room in which film is processed

DARKSOME adj dark

DARLING n pl. -S a much-loved person

DARN v -ED, -ING, -S to mend with interlacing stitches

DARNDEST n pl. -S damndest

DARNED adj DARNEDER, DARNEDEST or DARNDEST damned

DARNEL n pl. -S an annual grass

DARNER n pl. -S one that darns

DARNING n pl. -S things to be darned

DARSHAN n pl. -S a Hindu blessing

DART v -ED, -ING, -S to move suddenly or swiftly

DARTER n pl. -S one that darts

DARTLE v -TLED, -TLING, -TLES to dart repeatedly

DASH v -ED, -ING, -ES to strike violently

DASHEEN n pl. -S a tropical plant

DASHER n pl. -S one that dashes

DASHI n pl. -S a fish broth

DASHIER comparative of dashy

DASHIEST superlative of dashy

DASHIKI n pl. -S an African tunic

DASHPOT n pl. -S a shock absorber

DASHY adj DASHIER, DASHIEST stylish

DASSIE n pl. -S a hyrax

DASTARD n pl. -S a base coward

DASYURE n pl. -S a flesh-eating mammal

DATA a pl. of datum

DATABANK n pl. -S a database

DATABASE n pl. -S a collection of data in a computer

DATABLE adj capable of being dated

DATARY n pl. -RIES a cardinal in the Roman Catholic Church

DATCHA n pl. -S a dacha

DATE v DATED, DATING, DATES to determine or record the date of **DATEABLE** adj

DATEDLY adv in an old-fashioned manner

DATELESS adj having no date

DATELINE v -LINED, -LINING, -LINES to provide a news story with its date and place of origin

DATER n pl. -S one that dates

DATING present participle of date

DATIVE n pl. -S a grammatical case **DATIVAL** adj **DATIVELY** adv

DATO n pl. -TOS datto

DATTO n pl. -TOS a Philippine tribal chief

DATUM n pl. -TA or -TUMS something used as a basis for calculating

DATURA *n* pl. -S a flowering plant
DATURIC *adj*

DAUB *v* -ED, -ING, -S to smear

DAUBE *n* pl. -S a braised meat stew

DAUBER *n* pl. -S one that daubs

DAUBERY *n* pl. -ERIES a bad or inexpert painting

DAUBRY *n* pl. -RIES daubery

DAUBY *adj* DAUBIER, DAUBIEST smeary

DAUGHTER *n* pl. -S a female child

DAUNDER *v* -ED, -ING, -S to dander

DAUNT *v* -ED, -ING, -S to intimidate

DAUNTER *n* pl. -S one that daunts

DAUPHIN *n* pl. -S the eldest son of a French king

DAUPHINE *n* pl. -S the wife of a dauphin

DAUT *v* -ED, -ING, -S to fondle

DAUTIE *n* pl. -S a small pet

DAVEN *v* -ED, -ING, -S to utter Jewish prayers

DAVIT *n* pl. -S a hoisting device on a ship

DAVY *n* pl. -VIES a safety lamp

DAW *v* DAWED, DAWEN, DAWING, DAWS to dawn

DAWDLE *v* -DLED, -DLING, -DLES to waste time

DAWDLER *n* pl. -S one that dawdles

DAWEN past participle of daw

DAWK *n* pl. -S dak

DAWN *v* -ED, -ING, -S to begin to grow light in the morning

DAWNLIKE *adj* suggestive of daybreak

DAWT *v* -ED, -ING, -S to daut

DAWTIE *n* pl. -S dautie

DAY *n* pl. DAYS the time between sunrise and sunset

DAYBED *n* pl. -S a couch that can be converted into a bed

DAYBOOK *n* pl. -S a diary

DAYBREAK *n* pl. -S the first appearance of light in the morning

DAYDREAM *v* -DREAMED or -DREAMT, -DREAMING, -DREAMS to fantasize

DAYFLY *n* pl. -FLIES a mayfly

DAYGLOW *n* pl. -S airglow seen during the day

DAYLIGHT *v* -LIGHTED or -LIT, -LIGHTING, -LIGHTS to illuminate with the light of day

DAYLILY *n* pl. -LILIES a flowering plant

DAYLONG *adj* lasting all day

DAYMARE *n* pl. -S a nightmarish fantasy experienced while awake

DAYROOM *n* pl. -S a room for reading and recreation

DAYSIDE *n* pl. -S the sun side of a planet or the moon

DAYSMAN *n* pl. -MEN an arbiter

DAYSTAR *n* pl. -S a planet visible in the east just before sunrise

DAYTIME *n* pl. -S day

DAYWORK *n* pl. -S work done on a daily basis

DAZE *v* DAZED, DAZING, DAZES to stun DAZEDLY *adv*

DAZZLE *v* -ZLED, -ZLING, -ZLES to blind by bright light

DAZZLER *n* pl. -S one that dazzles

DE *prep* of; from — used in names

DEACON *v* -ED, -ING, -S to read a hymn aloud

DEACONRY *n* pl. -RIES a clerical office

DEAD *adj* DEADER, DEADEST deprived of life

DEAD *n* pl. -S the period of greatest intensity

DEADBEAT *n* pl. -S a loafer

DEADBOLT *n* pl. -S a lock for a door

DEADEN *v* -ED, -ING, -S to diminish the sensitivity or vigor of

DEADENER *n* pl. -S one that deadens

DEADEYE *n* pl. -S an expert marksman

DEADFALL *n* pl. -S a type of animal trap

DEADHEAD *v* -ED, -ING, -S to travel without freight

DEADLIER comparative of deadly

DEADLIEST superlative of deadly

DEADLIFT *v* -ED, -ING, -S to execute a type of lift in weight lifting

DEADLINE *n* pl. -S a time limit

DEADLOCK *v* -ED, -ING, -S to come to a standstill

DEADLY *adj* -LIER, -LIEST fatal

DEADNESS *n* pl. -ES the state of being dead

DEADPAN *v* -PANNED, -PANNING, -PANS to act without emotion

DEADWOOD *n* pl. -S a reinforcement in a ship's keel

DEAERATE *v* -ATED, -ATING, -ATES to remove air or gas from

DEAF *adj* DEAFER, DEAFEST lacking the sense of hearing

DEAFEN *v* -ED, -ING, -S to make deaf

DEAFISH *adj* somewhat deaf

DEAFLY *adv* in a deaf manner

DEAFNESS *n* pl. -ES the state of being deaf

DEAIR v -ED, -ING, -S to remove air from

DEAL v DEALT, DEALING, DEALS to trade or do business

DEALATE n pl. -S an insect divested of its wings DEALATED adj

DEALER n pl. -S one that deals

DEALFISH n pl. -ES a marine fish

DEALING n pl. -S a business transaction

DEALT past tense of deal

DEAN v -ED, -ING, -S to serve as dean (the head of a faculty)

DEANERY n pl. -ERIES the office of a dean

DEANSHIP n pl. -S deanery

DEAR adj DEARER, DEAREST greatly loved

DEAR n pl. -S a loved one

DEARIE n pl. -S deary

DEARIES pl. of deary

DEARLY adv in a dear manner

DEARNESS n pl. -ES the state of being dear

DEARTH n pl. -S scarcity

DEARY n pl. DEARIES darling

DEASH v -ED, -ING, -ES to remove ash from

DEASIL adv clockwise

DEATH n pl. -S the end of life

DEATHBED n pl. -S the bed on which a person dies

DEATHCUP n pl. -S a poisonous mushroom

DEATHFUL adj fatal

DEATHLY adj fatal

DEATHY adj deathly

DEAVE v DEAVED, DEAVING, DEAVES to deafen

DEB n pl. -S a debutante

DEBACLE n pl. -S a sudden collapse

DEBAR v -BARRED, -BARRING, -BARS to exclude

DEBARK v -ED, -ING, -S to unload from a ship

DEBASE v -BASED, -BASING, -BASES to lower in character, quality, or value

DEBASER n pl. -S one that debases

DEBATE v -BATED, -BATING, -BATES to argue about

DEBATER n pl. -S one that debates

DEBAUCH v -ED, -ING, -ES to corrupt

DEBEAK v -ED, -ING, -S to remove the tip of the upper beak of

DEBILITY n pl. -TIES weakness

DEBIT v -ED, -ING, -S to charge with a debt

DEBONAIR adj suave

DEBONE v -BONED, -BONING, -BONES to remove the bones from

DEBONER n pl. -S a bone remover

DEBOUCH v -ED, -ING, -ES to march into the open

DEBOUCHE n pl. -S an opening for the passage of troops

DEBRIDE v -BRIDED, -BRIDING, -BRIDES to remove dead tissue surgically

DEBRIEF v -ED, -ING, -S to question after a mission

DEBRIS n pl. DEBRIS fragments or scattered remains

DEBRUISE v -BRUISED, -BRUISING, -BRUISES to cross a coat of arms

DEBT n pl. -S something that is owed DEBTLESS adj

DEBTOR n pl. -S one who owes something to another

DEBUG v -BUGGED, -BUGGING, -BUGS to remove bugs from

DEBUGGER n pl. -S one that debugs

DEBUNK v -ED, -ING, -S to expose the sham or falseness of

DEBUNKER n pl. -S one that debunks

DEBUT v -ED, -ING, -S to make one's first public appearance

DEBUTANT n pl. -S one who is debuting

DEBYE n pl. -S a unit of measure for electric dipole moments

DECADE n pl. -S a period of ten years DECADAL adj

DECADENT n pl. -S one in a state of mental or moral decay

DECAF n pl. -S decaffeinated coffee

DECAGON n pl. -S a ten-sided polygon

DECAGRAM n pl. -S dekagram

DECAL n pl. -S a picture or design made to be transferred to specially prepared paper

DECALOG n pl. -S the Ten Commandments

DECAMP v -ED, -ING, -S to depart from a camping ground

DECANAL adj pertaining to a dean

DECANE n pl. -S a hydrocarbon

DECANT v -ED, -ING, -S to pour from one container into another

DECANTER n pl. -S a decorative bottle

DECAPOD n pl. -S a ten-legged crustacean

DECARE n pl. -S dekare

DECAY v -ED, -ING, -S to decompose

DECAYER n pl. -S one that decays

DECEASE v -CEASED, -CEASING, -CEASES to die

DECEDENT n pl. -S a deceased person

DECEIT n pl. -S the act of deceiving

DECEIVE v -CEIVED, -CEIVING, -CEIVES to mislead by falsehood

DECEIVER n pl. -S one that deceives

DECEMVIR n pl. -VIRS or -VIRI one of a body of ten Roman magistrates

DECENARY n pl. -RIES a tithing

DECENCY n pl. -CIES the state of being decent

DECENNIA n/pl decades

DECENT adj -CENTER, -CENTEST conforming to recognized standards of propriety
DECENTLY adv

DECENTER v -ED, -ING, -S to put out of center

DECENTRE v -TRED, -TRING, -TRES to decenter

DECERN v -ED, -ING, -S to decree by judicial sentence

DECIARE n pl. -S a metric unit of area

DECIBEL n pl. -S a unit of sound intensity

DECIDE v -CIDED, -CIDING, -CIDES to make a choice or judgment

DECIDER n pl. -S one that decides

DECIDUA n pl. -UAS or -UAE a mucous membrane of the uterus
DECIDUAL adj

DECIGRAM n pl. -S one tenth of a gram

DECILE n pl. -S a statistical interval

DECIMAL n pl. -S a fraction whose denominator is some power of ten

DECIMATE v -MATED, -MATING, -MATES to destroy a large part of

DECIPHER v -ED, -ING, -S to determine the meaning of

DECISION v -ED, -ING, -S to win a victory over a boxing opponent on points

DECISIVE adj conclusive

DECK v -ED, -ING, -S to adorn

DECKEL n pl. -S deckle

DECKER n pl. -S something having a specified number of levels, floors, or layers

DECKHAND n pl. -S a seaman who performs manual duties

DECKING n pl. -S material for a ship's deck

DECKLE n pl. -S a frame used in making paper by hand

DECLAIM v -ED, -ING, -S to speak formally

DECLARE v -CLARED, -CLARING, -CLARES to state publicly

DECLARER n pl. -S one that declares

DECLASS v -ED, -ING, -ES to lower in status

DECLASSE adj lowered in status

DECLINE v -CLINED, -CLINING, -CLINES to refuse

DECLINER n pl. -S one that declines

DECO n pl. DECOS a decorative style

DECOCT v -ED, -ING, -S to extract the flavor of by boiling

DECODE v -CODED, -CODING, -CODES to convert a coded message into plain language

DECODER n pl. -S one that decodes

DECOLOR v -ED, -ING, -S to deprive of color

DECOLOUR v -ED, -ING, -S to decolor

DECOR n pl. -S room decoration

DECORATE v -RATED, -RATING, -RATES to adorn

DECOROUS adj proper

DECORUM n pl. -S proper behavior

DECOUPLE v -PLED, -PLING, -PLES to disconnect

DECOY v -ED, -ING, -S to lure into a trap

DECOYER n pl. -S one that decoys

DECREASE v -CREASED, -CREASING, -CREASES to diminish

DECREE v -CREED, -CREEING, -CREES to order or establish by law or edict

DECREER n pl. -S one that decrees

DECREPIT adj worn out by long use

DECRETAL n pl. -S a papal edict

DECRIAL n pl. -S the act of decrying

DECRIED past tense of decry

DECRIER n pl. -S one that decries

DECROWN v -ED, -ING, -S to deprive of a crown; depose

DECRY v -CRIED, -CRYING, -CRIES to denounce

DECRYPT v -ED, -ING, -S to decode

DECUMAN adj extremely large

DECUPLE v -PLED, -PLING, -PLES to increase tenfold

DECURIES pl. of decury

DECURION n pl. -S a commander of a decury

DECURVE v -CURVED, -CURVING, -CURVES to curve downward

DECURY n pl. -RIES a group of ten soldiers in ancient Rome

DEDAL adj daedal

DEDANS n pl. DEDANS a gallery for tennis spectators

DEDICATE v -CATED, -CATING, -CATES to set apart for some special use

DEDUCE v -DUCED, -DUCING, -DUCES to infer

DEDUCT v -ED, -ING, -S to subtract

DEE n pl. -S the letter D

DEED v -ED, -ING, -S to transfer by deed (a legal document)

DEEDLESS adj being without deeds

DEEDY adj DEEDIER, DEEDIEST industrious

DEEJAY n pl. -JAYS a disc jockey

DEEM v -ED, -ING, -S to hold as an opinion

DEEMSTER n pl. -S a judicial officer of the Isle of Man

DEEP adj DEEPER, DEEPEST extending far down from a surface

DEEP n pl. -S a place or thing of great depth

DEEPEN v -ED, -ING, -S to make deep

DEEPENER n pl. -S one that deepens

DEEPLY adv at or to a great depth

DEEPNESS n pl. -ES the quality of being deep

DEER n pl. -S a ruminant mammal DEERLIKE adj

DEERFLY n pl. -FLIES a bloodsucking fly

DEERSKIN n pl. -S the skin of a deer

DEERWEED n pl. -S a bushlike herb

DEERYARD n pl. -S an area where deer herd in winter

DEET n pl. -S an insect repellent

DEEWAN n pl. -S dewan

DEFACE v -FACED, -FACING, -FACES to mar the appearance of

DEFACER n pl. -S one that defaces

DEFAME v -FAMED, -FAMING, -FAMES to attack the good name of

DEFAMER n pl. -S one that defames

DEFANG v -ED, -ING, -S to make harmless

DEFAT v -FATTED, -FATTING, -FATS to remove fat from

DEFAULT v -ED, -ING, -S to fail to do something required

DEFEAT v -ED, -ING, -S to win victory over

DEFEATER n pl. -S one that defeats

DEFECATE v -CATED, -CATING, -CATES to discharge feces

DEFECT v -ED, -ING, -S to desert an allegiance

DEFECTOR n pl. -S one that defects

DEFENCE n pl. -S something that defends

DEFEND v -ED, -ING, -S to protect

DEFENDER n pl. -S one that defends

DEFENSE v -FENSED, -FENSING, -FENSES to guard against a specific attack

DEFER v -FERRED, -FERRING, -FERS to postpone

DEFERENT n pl. -S an imaginary circle around the earth

DEFERRAL n pl. -S the act of deferring

DEFERRED past tense of defer

DEFERRER n pl. -S one that defers

DEFERRING present participle of defer

DEFI n pl. -S a challenge

DEFIANCE n pl. -S bold opposition

DEFIANT adj showing defiance

DEFICIT n pl. -S a shortage

DEFIED past tense of defy

DEFIER n pl. -S one that defies

DEFIES present 3d person sing. of defy

DEFILADE v -LADED, -LADING, -LADES to shield from enemy fire

DEFILE v -FILED, -FILING, -FILES to make dirty

DEFILER n pl. -S one that defiles

DEFINE v -FINED, -FINING, -FINES to state the meaning of

DEFINER n pl. -S one that defines

DEFINITE adj known for certain

DEFLATE v -FLATED, -FLATING, -FLATES to release the air or gas from

DEFLATER n pl. -S one that deflates

DEFLATOR n pl. -S one that deflates

DEFLEA v -ED, -ING, -S to rid of fleas

DEFLECT v -ED, -ING, -S to turn aside

DEFLEXED adj bent downward

DEFLOWER v -ED, -ING, -S to deprive of flowers

DEFOAM v -ED, -ING, -S to remove foam from

DEFOAMER n pl. -S one that defoams

DEFOCUS v -CUSED, -CUSING, -CUSES or -CUSSED, -CUSSING, -CUSSES to cause to go out of focus

DEFOG v -FOGGED, -FOGGING, -FOGS to remove fog from

DEFOGGER n pl. -S one that defogs

DEFORCE v -FORCED, -FORCING, -FORCES to withhold by force

DEFOREST v -ED, -ING, -S to clear of forests

DEFORM v -ED, -ING, -S to spoil the form of

DEFORMER n pl. -S one that deforms

DEFRAUD v -ED, -ING, -S to swindle

DEFRAY v -ED, -ING, -S to pay

DEFRAYAL n pl. -S the act of defraying

DEFRAYER n pl. -S one that defrays

DEFROCK v -ED, -ING, -S to unfrock

DEFROST v -ED, -ING, -S to remove frost from

DEFT adj DEFTER, DEFTEST skillful DEFTLY adv

DEFTNESS n pl. -ES the quality of being deft

DEFUNCT adj deceased

DEFUND v -ED, -ING, -S to withdraw funding from

DEFUSE v -FUSED, -FUSING, -FUSES to remove the fuse from

DEFUZE v -FUZED, -FUZING, -FUZES to defuse

DEFY v -FIED, -FYING, -FIES to resist openly and boldly

DEGAGE adj free and relaxed in manner

DEGAME n pl. -S a tropical tree

DEGAMI n pl. -S degame

DEGAS v -GASSED, -GASSING, -GASSES or -GASES to remove gas from

DEGASSER n pl. -S one that degasses

DEGAUSS v -ED, -ING, -ES to demagnetize

DEGERM v -ED, -ING, -S to remove germs from

DEGLAZE v -GLAZED, -GLAZING, -GLAZES to remove the glaze from

DEGRADE v -GRADED, -GRADING, -GRADES to debase

DEGRADER n pl. -S one that degrades

DEGREASE v -GREASED, -GREASING, -GREASES to remove the grease from

DEGREE n pl. -S one of a series of stages DEGREED adj

DEGUM v -GUMMED, -GUMMING, -GUMS to free from gum

DEGUST v -ED, -ING, -S to taste with pleasure

DEHISCE v -HISCED, -HISCING, -HISCES to split open

DEHORN v -ED, -ING, -S to deprive of horns

DEHORNER n pl. -S one that dehorns

DEHORT v -ED, -ING, -S to try to dissuade

DEICE v -ICED, -ICING, -ICES to free from ice

DEICER n pl. -S one that deices

DEICIDE n pl. -S the killing of a god DEICIDAL adj

DEICING present participle of deice

DEICTIC adj proving directly

DEIFIC adj godlike

DEIFICAL adj deific

DEIFIED past tense of deify

DEIFIER n pl. -S one that deifies

DEIFORM adj having the form of a god

DEIFY v -FIED, -FYING, -FIES to make a god of

DEIGN v -ED, -ING, -S to lower oneself to do something

DEIL n pl. -S the devil

DEIONIZE v -IZED, -IZING, -IZES to remove ions from

DEISM n pl. -S a religious philosophy

DEIST n pl. -S an adherent of deism DEISTIC adj

DEITY n pl. -TIES a god or goddess

DEIXIS n pl. DEIXISES the specifying function of some words

DEJECT v -ED, -ING, -S to depress or discourage

DEJECTA n/pl excrements

DEJEUNER n pl. -S a late breakfast

DEKAGRAM n pl. -S a measure equal to ten grams

DEKARE n pl. -S a measure equal to ten ares

DEKE v DEKED, DEKING, DEKES to feint in hockey

DEKKO n pl. -KOS a look

DEL n pl. -S an operator in differential calculus

DELAINE n pl. -S a wool fabric

DELATE v -LATED, -LATING, -LATES to accuse

DELATION n pl. -S the act of delating

DELATOR n pl. -S one that delates

DELAY v -ED, -ING, -S to postpone

DELAYER n pl. -S one that delays

DELE v DELED, DELEING, DELES to delete

DELEAD v -ED, -ING, -S to remove lead from

DELEAVE v -LEAVED, -LEAVING, -LEAVES to separate the copies of

DELEGACY n pl. -CIES the act of delegating

DELEGATE v -GATED, -GATING, -GATES to appoint as one's representative

DELETE v -LETED, -LETING, -LETES to remove written or printed matter

DELETION n pl. -S the act of deleting

DELF n pl. -S delft

DELFT n pl. -S an earthenware

DELI n pl. DELIS a delicatessen

DELICACY n pl. -CIES a choice food

DELICATE n pl. -S a delicacy

DELICT n pl. -S an offense against civil law

DELIGHT v -ED, -ING, -S to give great pleasure to

DELIME v -LIMED, -LIMING, -LIMES to free from lime

DELIMIT v -ED, -ING, -S to mark the boundaries of

DELIRIUM n pl. -IUMS or -IA wild excitement

DELIST v -ED, -ING, -S to remove from a list

DELIVER v -ED, -ING, -S to take to the intended recipient

DELIVERY n pl. -ERIES the act of delivering

DELL n pl. -S a small, wooded valley

DELLY n pl. DELLIES deli

DELOUSE v -LOUSED, -LOUSING, -LOUSES to remove lice from

DELOUSER n pl. -S one that gets rid of lice

DELPHIC adj ambiguous

DELTA n pl. -S an alluvial deposit at the mouth of a river DELTAIC, DELTIC adj

DELTOID n pl. -S a shoulder muscle

DELUDE v -LUDED, -LUDING, -LUDES to mislead the mind or judgment of

DELUDER n pl. -S one that deludes

DELUGE v -UGED, -UGING, -UGES to flood

DELUSION n pl. -S the act of deluding

DELUSIVE adj tending to delude

DELUSORY adj delusive

DELUSTER v -ED, -ING, -S to lessen the sheen of

DELUXE adj of special elegance or luxury

DELVE v DELVED, DELVING, DELVES to search in depth

DELVER n pl. -S one that delves

DEMAGOG v -ED, -ING, -S to behave like a demagog (a leader who appeals to emotions and prejudices)

DEMAGOGY n pl. -GOGIES the rule of a demagog

DEMAND v -ED, -ING, -S to ask for with authority

DEMANDER n pl. -S one that demands

DEMARCHE n pl. -S a procedure

DEMARK v -ED, -ING, -S to delimit

DEMAST v -ED, -ING, -S to strip masts from

DEME n pl. -S a Greek district

DEMEAN v -ED, -ING, -S to conduct oneself in a particular manner

DEMEANOR n pl. -S the manner in which one conducts oneself

DEMENT v -ED, -ING, -S to make insane

DEMENTIA n pl. -S mental illness

DEMERARA n pl. -S a coarse light-brown sugar

DEMERGE v -MERGED, -MERGING, -MERGES to remove a division from a corporation

DEMERGER v -ED, -ING, -S to demerge

DEMERIT v -ED, -ING, -S to lower in rank or status

DEMERSAL adj found at the bottom of the sea

DEMESNE n pl. -S the legal possession of land as one's own

DEMETON n pl. -S an insecticide

DEMIES pl. of demy

DEMIGOD n pl. -S a lesser god

DEMIJOHN n pl. -S a narrow-necked jug

DEMILUNE n pl. -S a half-moon

DEMIREP n pl. -S a prostitute

DEMISE v -MISED, -MISING, -MISES to bequeath

DEMIT v -MITTED, -MITTING, -MITS to resign

DEMIURGE *n* pl. -S a magistrate of ancient Greece

DEMIVOLT *n* pl. -S a half turn made by a horse

DEMO *n* pl. DEMOS a demonstration

DEMOB *v* -MOBBED, -MOBBING, -MOBS to discharge from military service

DEMOCRAT *n* pl. -S one who believes in political and social equality

DEMODE *adj* demoded

DEMODED *adj* out-of-date

DEMOLISH *v* -ED, -ING, -ES to destroy

DEMON *n* pl. -S an evil spirit

DEMONESS *n* pl. -ES a female demon

DEMONIAC *n* pl. -S one regarded as possessed by a demon

DEMONIAN *adj* demonic

DEMONIC *adj* characteristic of a demon

DEMONISE *v* -ISED, -ISING, -ISES to demonize

DEMONISM *n* pl. -S belief in demons

DEMONIST *n* pl. -S one who believes in demons

DEMONIZE *v* -IZED, -IZING, -IZES to make a demon of

DEMOS *n* pl. -ES the people of an ancient Greek state

DEMOTE *v* -MOTED, -MOTING, -MOTES to lower in rank or grade

DEMOTIC *adj* pertaining to a simplified form of ancient Egyptian writing

DEMOTICS *n/pl* the study of people in society

DEMOTING present participle of demote

DEMOTION *n* pl. -S the act of demoting

DEMOTIST *n* pl. -S a student of demotic writings

DEMOUNT *v* -ED, -ING, -S to remove from a mounting

DEMPSTER *n* pl. -S a deemster

DEMUR *v* -MURRED, -MURRING, -MURS to object

DEMURE *adj* -MURER, -MUREST shy and modest DEMURELY *adv*

DEMURRAL *n* pl. -S the act of demurring

DEMURRED past tense of demur

DEMURRER *n* pl. -S one that demurs

DEMURRING present participle of demur

DEMY *n* pl. -MIES a size of paper

DEN *v* DENNED, DENNING, DENS to live in a lair

DENARIUS *n* pl. DENARII a coin of ancient Rome

DENARY *adj* containing ten

DENATURE *v* -TURED, -TURING, -TURES to deprive of natural qualities

DENAZIFY *v* -FIED, -FYING, -FIES to rid of Nazism

DENDRITE *n* pl. -S a branched part of a nerve cell

DENDROID *adj* shaped like a tree

DENDRON *n* pl. -S a dendrite

DENE *n* pl. -S a valley

DENGUE *n* pl. -S a tropical disease

DENIABLE *adj* capable of being denied DENIABLY *adv*

DENIAL *n* pl. -S the act of denying

DENIED past tense of deny

DENIER *n* pl. -S one that denies

DENIES present 3d person sing. of deny

DENIM *n* pl. -S a durable fabric

DENIZEN *v* -ED, -ING, -S to make a citizen of

DENNED past tense of den

DENNING present participle of den

DENOTE *v* -NOTED, -NOTING, -NOTES to indicate DENOTIVE *adj*

DENOUNCE *v* -NOUNCED, -NOUNCING, -NOUNCES to condemn openly

DENSE *adj* DENSER, DENSEST compact DENSELY *adv*

DENSIFY *v* -FIED, -FYING, -FIES to make denser

DENSITY *n* pl. -TIES the state of being dense

DENT *v* -ED, -ING, -S to make a depression in

DENTAL *n* pl. -S a dentally produced sound

DENTALIA *n/pl* mollusks with long, tapering shells

DENTALLY *adv* with the tip of the tongue against the upper front teeth

DENTATE *adj* having teeth

DENTATED *adj* dentate

DENTICLE *n* pl. -S a small tooth

DENTIL *n* pl. -S a small rectangular block DENTILED *adj*

DENTIN *n* pl. -S the hard substance forming the body of a tooth DENTINAL *adj*

DENTINE *n* pl. -S dentin

DENTIST *n* pl. -S one who treats the teeth

DENTOID *adj* resembling a tooth

DENTURE n pl. -S a set of teeth
DENTURAL adj

DENUDATE v -DATED, -DATING, -DATES to denude

DENUDE v -NUDED, -NUDING, -NUDES to strip of all covering

DENUDER n pl. -S one that denudes

DENY v -NIED, -NYING, -NIES to declare to be untrue

DEODAND n pl. -S property forfeited to the crown under a former English law

DEODAR n pl. -S an East Indian cedar

DEODARA n pl. -S deodar

DEONTIC adj pertaining to moral obligation

DEORBIT v -ED, -ING, -S to come out of an orbit

DEOXY adj having less oxygen than the compound from which it is derived

DEPAINT v -ED, -ING, -S to depict

DEPART v -ED, -ING, -S to go away

DEPARTEE n pl. -S one that departs

DEPEND v -ED, -ING, -S to rely

DEPERM v -ED, -ING, -S to demagnetize

DEPICT v -ED, -ING, -S to portray

DEPICTER n pl. -S one that depicts

DEPICTOR n pl. -S depicter

DEPILATE v -LATED, -LATING, -LATES to remove hair from

DEPLANE v -PLANED, -PLANING, -PLANES to get off an airplane

DEPLETE v -PLETED, -PLETING, -PLETES to lessen or exhaust the supply of

DEPLORE v -PLORED, -PLORING, -PLORES to regret strongly

DEPLORER n pl. -S one that deplores

DEPLOY v -ED, -ING, -S to position troops for battle

DEPLUME v -PLUMED, -PLUMING, -PLUMES to deprive of feathers

DEPOLISH v -ED, -ING, -ES to remove the gloss or polish of

DEPONE v -PONED, -PONING, -PONES to testify under oath

DEPONENT n pl. -S one that depones

DEPORT v -ED, -ING, -S to expel from a country

DEPORTEE n pl. -S one who is deported

DEPOSAL n pl. -S the act of deposing

DEPOSE v -POSED, -POSING, -POSES to remove from office

DEPOSER n pl. -S one that deposes

DEPOSIT v -ED, -ING, -S to place

DEPOT n pl. -S a railroad or bus station

DEPRAVE v -PRAVED, -PRAVING, -PRAVES to corrupt in morals

DEPRAVER n pl. -S one that depraves

DEPRESS v -ED, -ING, -ES to make sad

DEPRIVAL n pl. -S the act of depriving

DEPRIVE v -PRIVED, -PRIVING, -PRIVES to take something away from

DEPRIVER n pl. -S one that deprives

DEPSIDE n pl. -S an aromatic compound

DEPTH n pl. -S deepness

DEPURATE v -RATED, -RATING, -RATES to free from impurities

DEPUTE v -PUTED, -PUTING, -PUTES to delegate

DEPUTIZE v -TIZED, -TIZING, -TIZES to appoint as a deputy

DEPUTY n pl. -TIES one appointed to act for another

DERAIGN v -ED, -ING, -S to dispute a claim

DERAIL v -ED, -ING, -S to run off the rails of a track

DERANGE v -RANGED, -RANGING, -RANGES to disorder

DERAT v -RATTED, -RATTING, -RATS to rid of rats

DERATE v -RATED, -RATING, -RATES to lower the rated capability of

DERAY n pl. -RAYS disorderly revelry

DERBY n pl. -BIES a type of hat

DERE adj dire

DERELICT n pl. -S something abandoned

DERIDE v -RIDED, -RIDING, -RIDES to ridicule

DERIDER n pl. -S one that derides

DERINGER n pl. -S a short-barreled pistol

DERISION n pl. -S the act of deriding

DERISIVE adj expressing derision

DERISORY adj derisive

DERIVATE n pl. -S something derived

DERIVE v -RIVED, -RIVING, -RIVES to obtain or receive from a source

DERIVER n pl. -S one that derives

DERM n pl. -S derma

DERMA n pl. -S a layer of the skin
DERMAL adj

DERMIS n pl. -MISES derma DERMIC adj

DERMOID n pl. -S a cystic tumor

DERNIER adj last

DEROGATE v -GATED, -GATING, -GATES to detract

DERRICK n pl. -S a hoisting apparatus

DERRIERE n pl. -S the buttocks

DERRIS n pl. -RISES a climbing plant

DERRY n pl. -RIES a meaningless word used in the chorus of old songs

DERVISH n pl. -ES a member of a Muslim religious order

DESALT v -ED, -ING, -S to remove the salt from

DESALTER n pl. -S one that desalts

DESAND v -ED, -ING, -S to remove sand from

DESCANT v -ED, -ING, -S to sing a counterpoint to a melody

DESCEND v -ED, -ING, -S to come or go down

DESCENT n pl. -S the act of descending

DESCRIBE v -SCRIBED, -SCRIBING, -SCRIBES to give a verbal account of

DESCRIER n pl. -S one that descries

DESCRY v -SCRIED, -SCRYING, -SCRIES to discern

DESELECT v -ED, -ING, -S to dismiss from a training program

DESERT v -ED, -ING, -S to abandon

DESERTER n pl. -S one that deserts

DESERTIC adj arid and barren

DESERVE v -SERVED, -SERVING, -SERVES to be entitled to or worthy of

DESERVER n pl. -S one that deserves

DESEX v -ED, -ING, -ES to castrate or spay

DESIGN v -ED, -ING, -S to conceive and plan out

DESIGNEE n pl. -S one who is designated

DESIGNER n pl. -S one that designs

DESILVER v -ED, -ING, -S to remove the silver from

DESINENT adj terminating

DESIRE v -SIRED, -SIRING, -SIRES to wish for

DESIRER n pl. -S one that desires

DESIROUS adj desiring

DESIST v -ED, -ING, -S to cease doing something

DESK n pl. -S a writing table

DESKMAN n pl. -MEN one who works at a desk

DESKTOP n pl. -S the top of a desk

DESMAN n pl. -S an aquatic mammal

DESMID n pl. -S a freshwater alga

DESMOID n pl. -S a very hard tumor

DESOLATE v -LATED, -LATING, -LATES to lay waste

DESORB v -ED, -ING, -S to remove by the reverse of absorption

DESOXY adj deoxy

DESPAIR v -ED, -ING, -S to lose all hope

DESPATCH v -ED, -ING, -ES to dispatch

DESPISE v -SPISED, -SPISING, -SPISES to loathe

DESPISER n pl. -S one that despises

DESPITE v -SPITED, -SPITING, -SPITES to treat with contempt

DESPOIL v -ED, -ING, -S to plunder

DESPOND v -ED, -ING, -S to lose spirit or hope

DESPOT n pl. -S a tyrant **DESPOTIC** adj

DESSERT n pl. -S something served as the last course of a meal

DESTAIN v -ED, -ING, -S to remove stain from

DESTINE v -TINED, -TINING, -TINES to determine beforehand

DESTINY n pl. -NIES the fate or fortune to which one is destined

DESTRIER n pl. -S a war horse

DESTROY v -ED, -ING, -S to damage beyond repair or renewal

DESTRUCT v -ED, -ING, -S to destroy

DESUGAR v -ED, -ING, -S to remove sugar from

DESULFUR v -ED, -ING, -S to free from sulfur

DETACH v -ED, -ING, -ES to unfasten and separate

DETACHER n pl. -S one that detaches

DETAIL v -ED, -ING, -S to report with complete particulars

DETAILER n pl. -S one that details

DETAIN v -ED, -ING, -S to hold in custody

DETAINEE n pl. -S one who is detained

DETAINER n pl. -S the unlawful withholding of another's property

DETASSEL v -SELED, -SELING, -SELS or -SELLED, -SELLING, -SELS to remove tassels from

DETECT v -ED, -ING, -S to discover or perceive

DETECTER n pl. -S detector

DETECTOR n pl. -S one that detects

DETENT n pl. -S a locking or unlocking mechanism

DETENTE *n* pl. -S an easing of international tension

DETER *v* -TERRED, -TERRING, -TERS to stop from proceeding

DETERGE *v* -TERGED, -TERGING, -TERGES to cleanse

DETERGER *n* pl. -S one that deterges

DETERRED past tense of deter

DETERRER *n* pl. -S one that deters

DETERRING present participle of deter

DETEST *v* -ED, -ING, -S to dislike intensely

DETESTER *n* pl. -S one that detests

DETHRONE *v* -THRONED, -THRONING, -THRONES to remove from a throne

DETICK *v* -ED, -ING, -S to remove ticks from

DETICKER *n* pl. -S one that deticks

DETINUE *n* pl. -S an action to recover property wrongfully detained

DETONATE *v* -NATED, -NATING, -NATES to cause to explode

DETOUR *v* -ED, -ING, -S to take an indirect route

DETOX *v* -ED, -ING, -ES to detoxify

DETOXIFY *v* -FIED, -FYING, -FIES to remove a toxin from

DETRACT *v* -ED, -ING, -S to take away

DETRAIN *v* -ED, -ING, -S to get off a railroad train

DETRITUS *n* pl. DETRITUS particles of rock **DETRITAL** *adj*

DETRUDE *v* -TRUDED, -TRUDING, -TRUDES to thrust out

DEUCE *v* DEUCED, DEUCING, DEUCES to bring a tennis score to a tie

DEUCEDLY *adv* extremely

DEUTERIC *adj* pertaining to heavy hydrogen

DEUTERON *n* pl. -S an atomic particle

DEUTZIA *n* pl. -S an ornamental shrub

DEW *n* pl. -S deva

DEVA *n* pl. -S a Hindu god

DEVALUE *v* -UED, -UING, -UES to lessen the worth of

DEVEIN *v* -ED, -ING, -S to remove the dorsal vein from

DEVEL *v* -ED, -ING, -S to strike forcibly

DEVELOP *v* -ED, -ING, -S to bring to a more advanced or effective state

DEVELOPE *v* -OPED, -OPING, -OPES to develop

DEVERBAL *adj* derived from a verb

DEVEST *v* -ED, -ING, -S to divest

DEVIANCE *n* pl. -S the behavior of a deviant

DEVIANCY *n* pl. -CIES deviance

DEVIANT *n* pl. -S one that deviates from a norm

DEVIATE *v* -ATED, -ATING, -ATES to turn aside from a course or norm

DEVIATOR *n* pl. -S one that deviates

DEVICE *n* pl. -S something devised or constructed for a specific purpose

DEVIL *v* -ILED, -ILING, -ILS or -ILLED, -ILLING, -ILS to prepare food with pungent seasoning

DEVILISH *adj* fiendish

DEVILKIN *n* pl. -S a small demon

DEVILLED a past tense of devil

DEVILLING a present participle of devil

DEVILRY *n* pl. -RIES deviltry

DEVILTRY *n* pl. -TRIES mischief

DEVIOUS *adj* indirect

DEVISAL *n* pl. -S the act of devising

DEVISE *v* -VISED, -VISING, -VISES to form in the mind

DEVISEE *n* pl. -S one to whom a will is made

DEVISER *n* pl. -S one that devises

DEVISING present participle of devise

DEVISOR *n* pl. -S one who makes a will

DEVOICE *v* -VOICED, -VOICING, -VOICES to unvoice

DEVOID *adj* completely lacking

DEVOIR *n* pl. -S an act of civility or respect

DEVOLVE *v* -VOLVED, -VOLVING, -VOLVES to transfer from one person to another

DEVON *n* pl. -S one of a breed of small, hardy cattle

DEVOTE *v* -VOTED, -VOTING, -VOTES to give oneself wholly to

DEVOTEE *n* pl. -S an ardent follower or supporter

DEVOTION *n* pl. -S the act of devoting

DEVOUR *v* -ED, -ING, -S to eat up voraciously

DEVOURER *n* pl. -S one that devours

DEVOUT *adj* -VOUTER, -VOUTEST pious **DEVOUTLY** *adv*

DEW *v* -ED, -ING, -S to wet with dew (condensed moisture)

DEWAN *n* pl. -S an official in India

DEWAR	n pl. -S a double-walled flask
DEWATER	v -ED, -ING, -S to remove water from
DEWAX	v -ED, -ING, -ES to remove wax from
DEWBERRY	n pl. -RIES an edible berry
DEWCLAW	n pl. -S a vestigial toe
DEWDROP	n pl. -S a drop of dew
DEWFALL	n pl. -S the formation of dew
DEWIER	comparative of dewy
DEWIEST	superlative of dewy
DEWILY	adv in a dewy manner
DEWINESS	n pl. -ES the state of being dewy
DEWLAP	n pl. -S a fold of loose skin under the neck
DEWLESS	adj having no dew
DEWOOL	v -ED, -ING, -S to remove the wool from
DEWORM	v -ED, -ING, -S to rid of worms
DEWORMER	n pl. -S one that deworms
DEWY	adj DEWIER, DEWIEST moist with dew
DEX	n pl. -ES a sulfate used as a central nervous system stimulant
DEXIE	n pl. -S a tablet of dex
DEXIES	pl. of dexy
DEXTER	adj situated on the right
DEXTRAL	adj pertaining to the right
DEXTRAN	n pl. -S a substance used as a blood plasma substitute
DEXTRIN	n pl. -S a substance used as an adhesive
DEXTRINE	n pl. -S dextrin
DEXTRO	adj turning to the right
DEXTROSE	n pl. -S a form of glucose
DEXTROUS	adj adroit
DEXY	n pl. DEXIES dexie
DEY	n pl. DEYS a former North African ruler
DEZINC	v -ZINCKED, -ZINCKING, -ZINCS or -ZINCED, -ZINCING, -ZINCS to remove zinc from
DHAK	n pl. -S an Asian tree
DHAL	n pl. -S dal
DHARMA	n pl. -S conformity to Hindu law DHARMIC adj
DHARNA	n pl. -S a form of protest in India
DHOBI	n pl. -S a person who does laundry in India
DHOLE	n pl. -S a wild dog of India
DHOOLY	n pl. -LIES dooly

DHOORA	n pl. -S durra
DHOOTI	n pl. -S dhoti
DHOOTIE	n pl. -S dhoti
DHOTI	n pl. -S a loincloth worn by Hindu men
DHOURRA	n pl. -S durra
DHOW	n pl. -S an Arabian sailing vessel
DHURNA	n pl. -S dharna
DHURRIE	n pl. -S a cotton rug made in India
DHUTI	n pl. -S dhoti
DIABASE	n pl. -S an igneous rock DIABASIC adj
DIABETES	n pl. DIABETES a metabolic disorder
DIABETIC	n pl. -S one who has diabetes
DIABLERY	n pl. -RIES sorcery
DIABOLIC	adj devilish
DIABOLO	n pl. -LOS a game requiring manual dexterity
DIACETYL	n pl. -S biacetyl
DIACID	n pl. -S a type of acid DIACIDIC adj
DIACONAL	adj pertaining to a deacon
DIADEM	v -ED, -ING, -S to adorn with a crown
DIAGNOSE	v -NOSED, -NOSING, -NOSES to recognize a disease by its signs and symptoms
DIAGONAL	n pl. -S an oblique line
DIAGRAM	v -GRAMED, -GRAMING, -GRAMS or -GRAMMED, -GRAMMING, -GRAMS to illustrate by a diagram (a graphic design)
DIAGRAPH	n pl. -S a drawing device
DIAL	v DIALED, DIALING, DIALS or DIALLED, DIALLING, DIALS to manipulate a calibrated disk
DIALECT	n pl. -S a regional variety of a language
DIALER	n pl. -S one that dials
DIALING	n pl. -S the measurement of time by sundials
DIALIST	n pl. -S a dialer
DIALLAGE	n pl. -S a mineral
DIALLED	a past tense of dial
DIALLEL	adj pertaining to a genetic crossing
DIALLER	n pl. -S dialer
DIALLING	n pl. -S dialing
DIALLIST	n pl. -S dialist
DIALOG	v -ED, -ING, -S to dialogue
DIALOGER	n pl. -S one that dialogs

DIALOGIC *adj* conversational

DIALOGUE *v* -LOGUED, -LOGUING, -LOGUES to carry on a conversation

DIALYSE *v* -LYSED, -LYSING, -LYSES to dialyze

DIALYSER *n pl.* -S dialyzer

DIALYSIS *n pl.* -YSES the separation of substances in a solution by diffusion through a membrane

DIALYTIC *adj* pertaining to dialysis

DIALYZE *v* -LYZED, -LYZING, -LYZES to subject to dialysis

DIALYZER *n pl.* -S an apparatus used for dialysis

DIAMANTE *n pl.* -S a sparkling decoration

DIAMETER *n pl.* -S a straight line passing through the center of a circle and ending at the periphery

DIAMIDE *n pl.* -S a chemical compound

DIAMIN *n pl.* -S diamine

DIAMINE *n pl.* -S a chemical compound

DIAMOND *v* -ED, -ING, -S to adorn with diamonds (precious gems)

DIANTHUS *n pl.* -ES an ornamental herb

DIAPASON *n pl.* -S a burst of harmonious sound

DIAPAUSE *v* -PAUSED, -PAUSING, -PAUSES to undergo dormancy

DIAPER *v* -ED, -ING, -S to put a diaper (a baby's breechcloth) on

DIAPHONE *n pl.* -S a low-pitched foghorn

DIAPHONY *n pl.* -NIES organum

DIAPIR *n pl.* -S a bend in a layer of rock **DIAPIRIC** *adj*

DIAPSID *adj* pertaining to a type of reptile

DIARCHY *n pl.* -CHIES a government with two rulers **DIARCHIC** *adj*

DIARIES pl. of diary

DIARIST *n pl.* -S one who keeps a diary

DIARRHEA *n pl.* -S an intestinal disorder

DIARY *n pl.* -RIES a personal journal

DIASPORA *n pl.* -S migration

DIASPORE *n pl.* -S a mineral

DIASTASE *n pl.* -S an enzyme

DIASTEM *n pl.* -S an interruption in the deposition of sediment

DIASTEMA *n pl.* -MATA a space between teeth

DIASTER *n pl.* -S a stage in mitosis **DIASTRAL** *adj*

DIASTOLE *n pl.* -S the normal rhythmical dilation of the heart

DIATOM *n pl.* -S any of a class of algae

DIATOMIC *adj* composed of two atoms

DIATONIC *adj* pertaining to a type of musical scale

DIATRIBE *n pl.* -S a bitter and abusive criticism

DIATRON *n pl.* -S a circuitry design that uses diodes

DIAZEPAM *n pl.* -S a tranquilizer

DIAZIN *n pl.* -S diazine

DIAZINE *n pl.* -S a chemical compound

DIAZINON *n pl.* -S an insecticide

DIAZO *adj* containing a certain chemical group

DIAZOLE *n pl.* -S a chemical compound

DIB *v* DIBBED, DIBBING, DIBS to fish by letting the bait bob lightly on the water

DIBASIC *adj* having two replaceable hydrogen atoms

DIBBER *n pl.* -S a planting implement

DIBBING present participle of dib

DIBBLE *v* -BLED, -BLING, -BLES to dib

DIBBLER *n pl.* -S one that dibbles

DIBBUK *n pl.* -BUKS or -BUKIM dybbuk

DICAST *n pl.* -S a judge of ancient Athens **DICASTIC** *adj*

DICE *v* DICED, DICING, DICES to cut into small cubes

DICENTRA *n pl.* -S a perennial herb

DICER *n pl.* -S a device that dices food

DICEY *adj* DICIER, DICIEST dangerous

DICHASIA *n/pl* flower clusters

DICHOTIC *adj* affecting the two ears differently

DICHROIC *adj* having two colors

DICIER comparative of dicey

DICIEST superlative of dicey

DICING present participle of dice

DICK *n pl.* -S a detective

DICKENS *n pl.* -ES devil

DICKER *v* -ED, -ING, -S to bargain

DICKEY *n pl.* -EYS a blouse front

DICKIE *n pl.* -S dickey

DICKY *n pl.* DICKIES dickey

DICKY *adj* DICKIER, DICKIEST poor in condition

DICLINY *n pl.* -NIES the state of having stamens and pistils in separate flowers

DICOT *n pl.* -S a plant with two seed leaves

DICOTYL *n pl.* -S dicot

DICROTAL *adj* dicrotic

DICROTIC *adj* having a double pulse beat

DICTA a pl. of dictum

DICTATE *v* -TATED, -TATING, -TATES to read aloud for recording

DICTATOR *n* pl. -S one that dictates

DICTIER comparative of dicty

DICTIEST superlative of dicty

DICTION *n* pl. -S choice and use of words in speech or writing

DICTUM *n* pl. -TA or -TUMS an authoritative statement

DICTY *adj* -TIER, -TIEST snobbish

DICYCLIC *adj* having two maxima of population each year

DICYCLY *n* pl. -CLIES the state of being dicyclic

DID a past tense of do

DIDACT *n* pl. -S a didactic person

DIDACTIC *adj* instructive

DIDACTYL *adj* having two digits at the end of each limb

DIDAPPER *n* pl. -S a dabchick

DIDDLE *v* -DLED, -DLING, -DLES to swindle

DIDDLER *n* pl. -S one that diddles

DIDDLEY *n* pl. -DLEYS diddly

DIDDLY *n* pl. -DLIES the least amount

DIDIE *n* pl. -S didy

DIDIES pl. of didy

DIDO *n* pl. -DOS or -DOES a mischievous act

DIDST a past tense of do

DIDY *n* pl. -DIES a diaper

DIDYMIUM *n* pl. -S a mixture of rare-earth elements

DIDYMOUS *adj* occurring in pairs

DIDYNAMY *n* pl. -MIES the state of having four stamens in pairs of unequal length

DIE *v* DIED, DYING, DIES to cease living

DIE *v* DIED, DIEING, DIES to cut with a die (a device for shaping material)

DIEBACK *n* pl. -S a gradual dying of plant shoots

DIECIOUS *adj* dioicous

DIED past tense of die

DIEHARD *n* pl. -S a stubborn person

DIEL *adj* involving a full day

DIELDRIN *n* pl. -S an insecticide

DIEMAKER *n* pl. -S one that makes dies

DIENE *n* pl. -S a chemical compound

DIERESIS *n* pl. DIERESES the separation of two vowels into two syllables **DIERETIC** *adj*

DIESEL *v* -ED, -ING, -S to continue running after the ignition is turned off

DIESIS *n* pl. DIESES a reference mark in printing

DIESTER *n* pl. -S a type of chemical compound

DIESTOCK *n* pl. -S a frame for holding dies

DIESTRUM *n* pl. -S diestrus

DIESTRUS *n* pl. -ES a period of sexual inactivity

DIET *v* -ED, -ING, -S to regulate one's daily sustenance

DIETARY *n* pl. -ETARIES a system of dieting

DIETER *n* pl. -S one that diets

DIETETIC *adj* pertaining to diet

DIETHER *n* pl. -S a chemical compound

DIFFER *v* -ED, -ING, -S to be unlike

DIFFRACT *v* -ED, -ING, -S to separate into parts

DIFFUSE *v* -FUSED, -FUSING, -FUSES to spread widely or thinly

DIFFUSER *n* pl. -S one that diffuses

DIFFUSOR *n* pl. -S diffuser

DIG *v* DUG or DIGGED, DIGGING, DIGS to break up, turn over, or remove earth

DIGAMIES pl. of digamy

DIGAMIST *n* pl. -S one who practices digamy

DIGAMMA *n* pl. -S a Greek letter

DIGAMY *n* pl. -MIES a second legal marriage **DIGAMOUS** *adj*

DIGEST *v* -ED, -ING, -S to render food usable for the body

DIGESTER *n* pl. -S an apparatus in which substances are softened or decomposed

DIGESTOR *n* pl. -S digester

DIGGED a past tense of dig

DIGGER *n* pl. -S one that digs

DIGGING present participle of dig

DIGGINGS *n/pl* an excavation site

DIGHT *v* -ED, -ING, -S to adorn

DIGIT *n* pl. -S a finger or toe

DIGITAL *n* pl. -S a piano key

DIGITATE *adj* having digits

DIGITIZE *v* -TIZED, -TIZING, -TIZES to put data into digital notation

DIGLOT *n* pl. -S a bilingual book or edition

DIGNIFY v -FIED, -FYING, -FIES to add dignity to

DIGNITY n pl. -TIES stateliness and nobility of manner

DIGOXIN n pl. -S a drug to improve heart function

DIGRAPH n pl. -S a pair of letters representing a single speech sound

DIGRESS v -ED, -ING, -ES to stray from the main topic

DIHEDRAL n pl. -S a dihedron

DIHEDRON n pl. -S a figure formed by two intersecting planes

DIHYBRID n pl. -S an offspring of parents differing in two pairs of genes

DIHYDRIC adj containing two hydroxyl radicals

DIKDIK n pl. -S a small antelope

DIKE v DIKED, DIKING, DIKES to furnish with an embankment

DIKER n pl. -S one that dikes

DIKTAT n pl. -S a harsh settlement imposed on a defeated nation

DILATANT n pl. -S a dilator

DILATATE adj dilated

DILATE v -LATED, -LATING, -LATES to make wider or larger

DILATER n pl. -S a dilator

DILATION n pl. -S the act of dilating

DILATIVE adj tending to dilate

DILATOR n pl. -S one that dilates

DILATORY adj tending to delay

DILDO n pl. -DOS an object used as a penis substitute

DILDOE n pl. -S a dildo

DILEMMA n pl. -S a perplexing situation
DILEMMIC adj

DILIGENT adj persevering

DILL n pl. -S an annual herb

DILLED adj flavored with dill

DILLY n pl. DILLIES something remarkable

DILUENT n pl. -S a diluting substance

DILUTE v -LUTED, -LUTING, -LUTES to thin or reduce the concentration of

DILUTER n pl. -S one that dilutes

DILUTION n pl. -S the act of diluting

DILUTIVE adj tending to dilute

DILUTOR n pl. -S a diluter

DILUVIA a pl. of diluvium

DILUVIAL adj pertaining to a flood

DILUVIAN adj diluvial

DILUVION n pl. -S diluvium

DILUVIUM n pl. -VIA or -VIUMS coarse rock material deposited by glaciers

DIM adj DIMMER, DIMMEST obscure

DIM v DIMMED, DIMMING, DIMS to make dim

DIME n pl. -S a coin of the United States

DIMER n pl. -S a molecule composed of two identical molecules

DIMERIC adj dimerous

DIMERISM n pl. -S the state of being dimerous

DIMERIZE v -IZED, -IZING, -IZES to form a dimer

DIMEROUS adj composed of two parts

DIMETER n pl. -S a verse of two metrical feet

DIMETHYL n pl. -S ethane

DIMETRIC adj pertaining to a type of crystal system

DIMINISH v -ED, -ING, -ES to lessen

DIMITY n pl. -TIES a cotton fabric

DIMLY adv in a dim manner

DIMMABLE adj capable of being dimmed

DIMMED past tense of dim

DIMMER n pl. -S a device for varying the intensity of illumination

DIMMEST superlative of dim

DIMMING present participle of dim

DIMNESS n pl. -ES the state of being dim

DIMORPH n pl. -S either of two distinct forms

DIMOUT n pl. -S a condition of partial darkness

DIMPLE v -PLED, -PLING, -PLES to mark with indentations

DIMPLY adj -PLIER, -PLIEST dimpled

DIMWIT n pl. -S a dunce

DIN v DINNED, DINNING, DINS to make a loud noise

DINAR n pl. -S an ancient gold coin of Muslim areas

DINDLE v -DLED, -DLING, -DLES to tingle

DINE v DINED, DINING, DINES to eat dinner

DINER n pl. -S one that dines

DINERIC adj pertaining to the interface between two immiscible liquids

DINERO n pl. -ROS a former silver coin of Peru

DINETTE n pl. -S a small dining room

DING v -ED, -ING, -S to ring

DINGBAT n pl. -S a typographical ornament

DINGDONG v -ED, -ING, -S to make a ringing sound

DINGE n pl. -S the condition of being dingy

DINGER n pl. -S a home run

DINGEY n pl. -GEYS dinghy

DINGHY n pl. -GHIES a small boat

DINGIER comparative of dingy

DINGIES pl. of dingy

DINGIEST superlative of dingy

DINGILY adv in a dingy manner

DINGLE n pl. -S a dell

DINGO n pl. -GOES a wild dog of Australia

DINGUS n pl. -ES a doodad

DINGY n pl. -GIES dinghy

DINGY adj -GIER, -GIEST grimy

DINING present participle of dine

DINITRO adj containing two nitro groups

DINK v -ED, -ING, -S to adorn

DINKEY n pl. -KEYS a small locomotive

DINKIER comparative of dinky

DINKIES pl. of dinky

DINKIEST superlative of dinky

DINKLY adv neatly

DINKUM n pl. -S the truth

DINKY n pl. -KIES dinkey

DINKY adj -KIER, -KIEST small

DINNED past tense of din

DINNER n pl. -S the main meal of the day

DINNING present participle of din

DINOSAUR n pl. -S one of a group of extinct reptiles

DINT v -ED, -ING, -S to dent

DIOBOL n pl. -S a coin of ancient Greece

DIOBOLON n pl. -S diobol

DIOCESAN n pl. -S a bishop

DIOCESE n pl. -S an ecclesiastical district

DIODE n pl. -S a type of electron tube

DIOECISM n pl. -S the state of being dioicous

DIOECY n pl. DIOECIES dioecism

DIOICOUS adj unisexual

DIOL n pl. -S a chemical compound

DIOLEFIN n pl. -S a hydrocarbon

DIOPSIDE n pl. -S a mineral

DIOPTASE n pl. -S a mineral

DIOPTER n pl. -S a measure of refractive power **DIOPTRAL** adj

DIOPTRE n pl. -S diopter

DIOPTRIC adj aiding the vision by refraction

DIORAMA n pl. -S a three-dimensional exhibit **DIORAMIC** adj

DIORITE n pl. -S an igneous rock **DIORITIC** adj

DIOXAN n pl. -S dioxane

DIOXANE n pl. -S a flammable liquid

DIOXID n pl. -S dioxide

DIOXIDE n pl. -S a type of oxide

DIOXIN n pl. -S a toxic solid hydrocarbon

DIP v DIPPED or DIPT, DIPPING, DIPS to plunge into a liquid

DIPHASE adj having two phases

DIPHASIC adj diphase

DIPHENYL n pl. -S biphenyl

DIPLEGIA n pl. -S paralysis of the same part on both sides of the body

DIPLEX adj pertaining to the simultaneous transmission or reception of two radio signals

DIPLEXER n pl. -S a coupling device

DIPLOE n pl. -S a bony tissue of the cranium **DIPLOIC** adj

DIPLOID n pl. -S a cell having the basic chromosome number doubled

DIPLOIDY n pl. -DIES the condition of being a diploid

DIPLOMA n pl. -MAS or -MATA a certificate of an academic degree

DIPLOMA v -ED, -ING, -S to furnish with a diploma

DIPLOMAT n pl. -S a governmental official

DIPLONT n pl. -S an organism having a particular chromosomal structure

DIPLOPIA n pl. -S double vision **DIPLOPIC** adj

DIPLOPOD n pl. -S a multi-legged insect

DIPLOSIS n pl. -LOSES a method of chromosome formation

DIPNET v -NETTED, -NETTING, -NETS to scoop fish with a type of net

DIPNOAN n pl. -S a lungfish

DIPODY n pl. -DIES a dimeter **DIPODIC** adj

DIPOLE n pl. -S a pair of equal and opposite electric charges **DIPOLAR** adj

DIPPABLE adj capable of being dipped

DIPPED a past tense of dip

DIPPER n pl. -S one that dips

DIPPING	present participle of dip	**DISALLOW**	v -ED, -ING, -S to refuse to allow
DIPPY	adj -PIER, -PIEST foolish		
DIPSAS	n pl. DIPSADES a fabled serpent	**DISANNUL**	v -NULLED, -NULLING, -NULS to annul
DIPSO	n pl. -SOS a person who craves alcoholic liquors	**DISARM**	v -ED, -ING, -S to deprive of weapons
DIPSTICK	n pl. -S a measuring rod	**DISARMER**	n pl. -S one that disarms
DIPT	a past tense of dip	**DISARRAY**	v -ED, -ING, -S to disorder
DIPTERA	pl. of dipteron	**DISASTER**	n pl. -S a calamity
DIPTERAL	adj having two rows or columns	**DISAVOW**	v -ED, -ING, -S to disclaim responsibility for
DIPTERAN	n pl. -S a two-winged fly	**DISBAND**	v -ED, -ING, -S to break up
DIPTERON	n pl. -TERA dipteran	**DISBAR**	v -BARRED, -BARRING, -BARS to expel from the legal profession
DIPTYCA	n pl. -S diptych		
DIPTYCH	n pl. -S an ancient writing tablet	**DISBOSOM**	v -ED, -ING, -S to confess
DIQUAT	n pl. -S an herbicide	**DISBOUND**	adj not having a binding
DIRDUM	n pl. -S blame	**DISBOWEL**	v -ELED, -ELING, -ELS or -ELLED, -ELLING, -ELS to remove the intestines of
DIRE	adj DIRER, DIREST disastrous		
DIRECT	v -ED, -ING, -S to control or conduct the affairs of	**DISBUD**	v -BUDDED, -BUDDING, -BUDS to remove buds from
DIRECT	adj -RECTER, -RECTEST straightforward DIRECTLY adv	**DISBURSE**	v -BURSED, -BURSING, -BURSES to pay out
DIRECTOR	n pl. -S one that directs	**DISC**	v -ED, -ING, -S to disk
DIREFUL	adj dreadful	**DISCANT**	v -ED, -ING, -S to descant
DIRELY	adv in a dire manner	**DISCARD**	v -ED, -ING, -S to throw away
DIRENESS	n pl. -ES the state of being dire	**DISCASE**	v -CASED, -CASING, -CASES to remove the case of
DIRER	comparative of dire	**DISCEPT**	v -ED, -ING, -S to debate
DIREST	superlative of dire	**DISCERN**	v -ED, -ING, -S to perceive
DIRGE	n pl. -S a funeral song DIRGEFUL adj	**DISCI**	a pl. of discus
		DISCIPLE	v -PLED, -PLING, -PLES to cause to become a follower
DIRHAM	n pl. -S a monetary unit of Morocco	**DISCLAIM**	v -ED, -ING, -S to renounce any claim to or connection with
DIRIMENT	adj nullifying		
DIRK	v -ED, -ING, -S to stab with a small knife	**DISCLIKE**	adj disklike
		DISCLOSE	v -CLOSED, -CLOSING, -CLOSES to reveal
DIRL	v -ED, -ING, -S to tremble		
DIRNDL	n pl. -S a woman's dress	**DISCO**	v -ED, -ING, -S to dance at a discotheque
DIRT	n pl. -S earth or soil		
DIRTBAG	n pl. -S a dirty or contemptible person	**DISCOID**	n pl. -S a disk
		DISCOLOR	v -ED, -ING, -S to alter the color of
DIRTY	adj DIRTIER, DIRTIEST unclean DIRTILY adv		
		DISCORD	v -ED, -ING, -S to disagree
DIRTY	v DIRTIED, DIRTYING, DIRTIES to make dirty	**DISCOUNT**	v -ED, -ING, -S to reduce the price of
DIS	v DISSED, DISSING, DISSES to insult or criticize	**DISCOVER**	v -ED, -ING, -S to gain sight or knowledge of
DISABLE	v -ABLED, -ABLING, -ABLES to render incapable or unable	**DISCREET**	adj -CREETER, -CREETEST tactful
DISABUSE	v -ABUSED, -ABUSING, -ABUSES to free from false or mistaken ideas	**DISCRETE**	adj separate
		DISCROWN	v -ED, -ING, -S to deprive of crown
DISAGREE	v -AGREED, -AGREEING, -AGREES to differ in opinion	**DISCUS**	n pl. -CUSES or -CI a disk hurled in athletic competition

DISCUSS v -ED, -ING, -ES to talk over or write about

DISDAIN v -ED, -ING, -S to scorn

DISEASE v -EASED, -EASING, -EASES to make unhealthy

DISENDOW v -ED, -ING, -S to deprive of endowment

DISEUSE n pl. -S a female entertainer

DISFAVOR v -ED, -ING, -S to regard with disapproval

DISFROCK v -ED, -ING, -S to unfrock

DISGORGE v -GORGED, -GORGING, -GORGES to vomit

DISGRACE v -GRACED, -GRACING, -GRACES to bring shame or discredit upon

DISGUISE v -GUISED, -GUISING, -GUISES to alter the appearance of

DISGUST v -ED, -ING, -S to cause nausea or loathing in

DISH v -ED, -ING, -ES to put into a dish (a concave vessel)

DISHELM v -ED, -ING, -S to deprive of a helmet

DISHERIT v -ED, -ING, -S to deprive of an inheritance

DISHEVEL v -ELED, -ELING, -ELS or -ELLED, -ELLING, -ELS to make messy

DISHFUL n pl. -S as much as a dish can hold

DISHIER comparative of dishy

DISHIEST superlative of dishy

DISHLIKE adj resembling a dish

DISHONOR v -ED, -ING, -S to deprive of honor

DISHPAN n pl. -S a pan for washing dishes

DISHRAG n pl. -S a cloth for washing dishes

DISHWARE n pl. -S tableware used in serving food

DISHY adj DISHIER, DISHIEST attractive

DISINTER v -TERRED, -TERRING, -TERS to exhume

DISJECT v -ED, -ING, -S to disperse

DISJOIN v -ED, -ING, -S to separate

DISJOINT v -ED, -ING, -S to put out of order

DISJUNCT n pl. -S an alternative in a logical disjunction

DISK v -ED, -ING, -S to break up land with a type of farm implement

DISKETTE n pl. -S a floppy disk for a computer

DISKLIKE adj resembling a disk (a flat, circular plate)

DISLIKE v -LIKED, -LIKING, -LIKES to regard with aversion

DISLIKER n pl. -S one that dislikes

DISLIMN v -ED, -ING, -S to make dim

DISLODGE v -LODGED, -LODGING, -LODGES to remove from a firm position

DISLOYAL adj not loyal

DISMAL n pl. -S a track of swampy land

DISMAL adj -MALER, -MALEST cheerless and depressing **DISMALLY** adv

DISMAST v -ED, -ING, -S to remove the mast of

DISMAY v -ED, -ING, -S to deprive of courage or resolution

DISME n pl. -S a former coin of the United States

DISMISS v -ED, -ING, -ES to permit or cause to leave

DISMOUNT v -ED, -ING, -S to get down from an elevated position

DISOBEY v -ED, -ING, -S to fail to obey

DISOMIC adj having a number of chromosomes duplicated

DISORDER v -ED, -ING, -S to put out of order

DISOWN v -ED, -ING, -S to deny the ownership of

DISPART v -ED, -ING, -S to separate

DISPATCH v -ED, -ING, -ES to send off with speed

DISPEL v -PELLED, -PELLING, -PELS to drive off in various directions

DISPEND v -ED, -ING, -S to squander

DISPENSE v -PENSED, -PENSING, -PENSES to distribute

DISPERSE v -PERSED, -PERSING, -PERSES to scatter

DISPIRIT v -ED, -ING, -S to lower in spirit

DISPLACE v -PLACED, -PLACING, -PLACES to remove from the usual or proper place

DISPLANT v -ED, -ING, -S to dislodge

DISPLAY v -ED, -ING, -S to make evident or obvious

DISPLODE v -PLODED, -PLODING, -PLODES to explode

DISPLUME v -PLUMED, -PLUMING, -PLUMES to deplume

DISPORT v -ED, -ING, -S to amuse oneself

DISPOSAL n pl. -S the act of disposing

DISPOSE v -POSED, -POSING, -POSES to put in place

DISPOSER n pl. -S one that disposes

DISPREAD v -SPREAD, -SPREADING, -SPREADS to spread out

DISPRIZE v -PRIZED, -PRIZING, -PRIZES to disdain

DISPROOF n pl. -S the act of disproving

DISPROVE v -PROVED, -PROVEN, -PROVING, -PROVES to refute

DISPUTE v -PUTED, -PUTING, -PUTES to argue about

DISPUTER n pl. -S one that disputes

DISQUIET v -ED, -ING, -S to deprive of quiet, rest, or peace

DISRATE v -RATED, -RATING, -RATES to lower in rating or rank

DISROBE v -ROBED, -ROBING, -ROBES to undress

DISROBER n pl. -S one that disrobes

DISROOT v -ED, -ING, -S to uproot

DISRUPT v -ED, -ING, -S to throw into confusion

DISS v -ED, -ING, -ES to dis

DISSAVE v -SAVED, -SAVING, -SAVES to use savings for current expenses

DISSEAT v -ED, -ING, -S to unseat

DISSECT v -ED, -ING, -S to cut apart for scientific examination

DISSED past tense of dis

DISSEISE v -SEISED, -SEISING, -SEISES to deprive

DISSEIZE v -SEIZED, -SEIZING, -SEIZES to disseise

DISSENT v -ED, -ING, -S to disagree

DISSERT v -ED, -ING, -S to discuss in a learned or formal manner

DISSERVE v -SERVED, -SERVING, -SERVES to treat badly

DISSEVER v -ED, -ING, -S to sever

DISSES present 3d person sing. of dis

DISSING present participle of dis

DISSOLVE v -SOLVED, -SOLVING, -SOLVES to make into a solution

DISSUADE v -SUADED, -SUADING, -SUADES to persuade not to do something

DISTAFF n pl. -TAFFS or -TAVES a type of staff

DISTAIN v -ED, -ING, -S to stain

DISTAL adj located far from the point of origin **DISTALLY** adv

DISTANCE v -TANCED, -TANCING, -TANCES to leave behind

DISTANT adj far off or apart

DISTASTE v -TASTED, -TASTING, -TASTES to dislike

DISTAVES a pl. of distaff

DISTEND v -ED, -ING, -S to swell

DISTENT adj distended

DISTICH n pl. -S a couplet

DISTIL v -TILLED, -TILLING, -TILS to distill

DISTILL v -ED, -ING, -S to extract by vaporization and condensation

DISTINCT adj -TINCTER, -TINCTEST clearly different

DISTOME n pl. -S a parasitic flatworm

DISTORT v -ED, -ING, -S to twist or bend out of shape

DISTRACT v -ED, -ING, -S to divert the attention of

DISTRAIN v -ED, -ING, -S to seize and hold property as security

DISTRAIT adj absentminded

DISTRESS v -ED, -ING, -ES to cause anxiety or suffering to

DISTRICT v -ED, -ING, -S to divide into localities

DISTRUST v -ED, -ING, -S to have no trust in

DISTURB v -ED, -ING, -S to interrupt the quiet, rest, or peace of

DISULFID n pl. -S a chemical compound

DISUNION n pl. -S the state of being disunited

DISUNITE v -UNITED, -UNITING, -UNITES to separate

DISUNITY n pl. -TIES lack of unity

DISUSE v -USED, -USING, -USES to stop using

DISVALUE v -UED, -UING, -UES to treat as of little value

DISYOKE v -YOKED, -YOKING, -YOKES to free from a yoke

DIT n pl. -S a dot in Morse code

DITA n pl. -S a Philippine tree

DITCH v -ED, -ING, -ES to dig a long, narrow excavation in the ground

DITCHER n pl. -S one that ditches

DITE n pl. -S a small amount

DITHEISM n pl. -S belief in two coequal gods

DITHEIST n pl. -S an adherent of ditheism

DITHER v -ED, -ING, -S to act nervously or indecisively

DITHERER n pl. -S one that dithers

DITHERY adj nervously excited

DITHIOL adj containing two chemical groups both of which include sulfur and hydrogen

DITSY adj -SIER, -SIEST silly, eccentric

DITTANY n pl. -NIES a perennial herb

DITTO v -ED, -ING, -S to repeat

DITTY n pl. -TIES a short, simple song

DITZ n pl. -ES a ditsy person

DITZY adj -ZIER, -ZIEST ditsy

DIURESIS n pl. DIURESES excessive discharge of urine

DIURETIC n pl. -S a drug which increases urinary discharge

DIURNAL n pl. -S a diary

DIURON n pl. -S an herbicide

DIVA n pl. -S a distinguished female operatic singer

DIVAGATE v -GATED, -GATING, -GATES to wander

DIVALENT adj having a valence of two

DIVAN n pl. -S a sofa or couch

DIVE v DIVED or DOVE, DIVING, DIVES to plunge headfirst into water

DIVEBOMB v -ED, -ING, -S to drop bombs on a target from a diving airplane

DIVER n pl. -S one that dives

DIVERGE v -VERGED, -VERGING, -VERGES to move in different directions from a common point

DIVERSE adj different

DIVERT v -ED, -ING, -S to turn aside

DIVERTER n pl. -S one that diverts

DIVEST v -ED, -ING, -S to strip or deprive of anything

DIVIDE v -VIDED, -VIDING, -VIDES to separate into parts, areas, or groups

DIVIDEND n pl. -S a quantity to be divided

DIVIDER n pl. -S one that divides

DIVIDING present participle of divide

DIVIDUAL adj capable of being divided

DIVINE v -VINED, -VINING, -VINES to foretell by occult means

DIVINE adj -VINER, -VINEST pertaining to or characteristic of a god DIVINELY adv

DIVINER n pl. -S one that divines

DIVING present participle of dive

DIVINING present participle of divine

DIVINISE v -NISED, -NISING, -NISES to divinize

DIVINITY n pl. -TIES the state of being divine

DIVINIZE v -NIZED, -NIZING, -NIZES to make divine

DIVISION n pl. -S the act of dividing

DIVISIVE adj causing disunity or dissension

DIVISOR n pl. -S a number by which a dividend is divided

DIVORCE v -VORCED, -VORCING, -VORCES to terminate the marriage contract between

DIVORCEE n pl. -S a divorced woman

DIVORCER n pl. -S one that divorces

DIVORCING present participle of divorce

DIVOT n pl. -S a piece of turf

DIVULGE v -VULGED, -VULGING, -VULGES to reveal

DIVULGER n pl. -S one that divulges

DIVVY v -VIED, -VYING, -VIES to divide

DIWAN n pl. -S dewan

DIXIT n pl. -S a statement

DIZEN v -ED, -ING, -S to dress in fine clothes

DIZYGOUS adj developed from two fertilized ova

DIZZY adj -ZIER, -ZIEST having a sensation of whirling DIZZILY adv

DIZZY v -ZIED, -ZYING, -ZIES to make dizzy

DJEBEL n pl. -S jebel

DJELLABA n pl. -S a long hooded garment

DJIN n pl. -S jinni

DJINN n pl. -S jinni

DJINNI n pl. DJINN jinni

DJINNY n pl. DJINN jinni

DO v DID or DIDST, DONE, DOING, present sing. 2d person DO, DOEST or DOST, 3d person DOES, DOETH or DOTH to begin and carry through to completion

DO n pl. DOS the first tone of the diatonic musical scale

DOABLE adj able to be done

DOAT v -ED, -ING, -S to dote

DOBBER n pl. -S a float for a fishing line

DOBBIN n pl. -S a farm horse

DOBBY	n pl. -BIES a fool	
DOBIE	n pl. -S adobe	
DOBIES	pl. of doby	
DOBLA	n pl. -S a former gold coin of Spain	
DOBLON	n pl. -S or -ES a former gold coin of Spain and Spanish America	
DOBRA	n pl. -S a former gold coin of Portugal	
DOBSON	n pl. -S an aquatic insect larva	
DOBY	n pl. -BIES dobie	
DOC	n pl. -S doctor	
DOCENT	n pl. -S a college or university lecturer	
DOCETIC	adj pertaining to a religious doctrine	
DOCILE	adj easily trained DOCILELY adv	
DOCILITY	n pl. -TIES the quality of being docile	
DOCK	v -ED, -ING, -S to bring into a dock (a wharf)	
DOCKAGE	n pl. -S a charge for the use of a dock	
DOCKER	n pl. -S a dock worker	
DOCKET	v -ED, -ING, -S to supply with an identifying statement	
DOCKHAND	n pl. -S a docker	
DOCKLAND	n pl. -S the part of a port occupied by docks	
DOCKSIDE	n pl. -S the area adjacent to a dock	
DOCKYARD	n pl. -S a shipyard	
DOCTOR	v -ED, -ING, -S to treat medically	
DOCTORAL	adj pertaining to a doctor	
DOCTRINE	n pl. -S a belief or set of beliefs taught or advocated	
DOCUMENT	v -ED, -ING, -S to support by conclusive information or evidence	
DODDER	v -ED, -ING, -S to totter	
DODDERER	n pl. -S one that dodders	
DODDERY	adj feeble	
DODGE	v DODGED, DODGING, DODGES to evade	
DODGEM	n pl. -S an amusement park ride	
DODGER	n pl. -S one that dodges	
DODGERY	n pl. -ERIES evasion	
DODGING	present participle of dodge	
DODGY	adj DODGIER, DODGIEST evasive	
DODO	n pl. -DOES or -DOS an extinct flightless bird	

DODOISM	n pl. -S a stupid remark	
DOE	n pl. -S a female deer	
DOER	n pl. -S one that does something	
DOES	a present 3d person sing. of do	
DOESKIN	n pl. -S the skin of a doe	
DOEST	a present 2d person sing. of do	
DOETH	a present 3d person sing. of do	
DOFF	v -ED, -ING, -S to take off	
DOFFER	n pl. -S one that doffs	
DOG	v DOGGED, DOGGING, DOGS to follow after like a dog (a domesticated, carnivorous mammal)	
DOGBANE	n pl. -S a perennial herb	
DOGBERRY	n pl. -RIES a wild berry	
DOGCART	n pl. -S a one-horse carriage	
DOGDOM	n pl. -S the world of dogs	
DOGE	n pl. -S the chief magistrate in the former republics of Venice and Genoa	
DOGEAR	v -ED, -ING, -S to turn down a corner of a page	
DOGEDOM	n pl. -S the domain of a doge	
DOGESHIP	n pl. -S the office of a doge	
DOGEY	n pl. -GEYS dogie	
DOGFACE	n pl. -S a soldier in the U.S. Army	
DOGFIGHT	v -FOUGHT, -FIGHTING, -FIGHTS to engage in an aerial battle	
DOGFISH	n pl. -ES a small shark	
DOGGED	past tense of dog	
DOGGEDLY	adv stubbornly	
DOGGER	n pl. -S a fishing vessel	
DOGGEREL	n pl. -S trivial, awkwardly written verse	
DOGGERY	n pl. -GERIES surly behavior	
DOGGIE	n pl. -S doggy	
DOGGIER	comparative of doggy	
DOGGIES	pl. of doggy	
DOGGIEST	superlative of doggy	
DOGGING	present participle of dog	
DOGGISH	adj doglike	
DOGGO	adv in hiding	
DOGGONE	v -GONED, -GONING, -GONES to damn	
DOGGONE	adj -GONER, -GONEST damned	
DOGGONED	adj -GONEDER, -GONEDEST damned	
DOGGONING	present participle of doggone	
DOGGREL	n pl. -S doggerel	
DOGGY	n pl. -GIES a small dog	
DOGGY	adj -GIER, -GIEST resembling or suggestive of a dog	

DOGHOUSE n pl. -S a shelter for a dog

DOGIE n pl. -S a stray calf

DOGIES pl. of dogy

DOGLEG v -LEGGED, -LEGGING, -LEGS to move in an angle

DOGLIKE adj resembling a dog

DOGMA n pl. -MAS or -MATA a principle or belief put forth as authoritative **DOGMATIC** adj

DOGNAP v -NAPED, -NAPING, -NAPS or -NAPPED, -NAPPING, -NAPS to steal a dog

DOGNAPER n pl. -S one that dognaps

DOGSBODY n pl. -BODIES a menial worker

DOGSLED v -SLEDDED, -SLEDDING, -SLEDS to move on a sled drawn by dogs

DOGTOOTH n pl. -TEETH a cuspid

DOGTROT v -TROTTED, -TROTTING, -TROTS to move at a steady trot

DOGVANE n pl. -S a small vane

DOGWATCH n pl. -ES a short period of watch duty on a ship

DOGWOOD n pl. -S a tree

DOGY n pl. -GIES dogie

DOILED adj dazed

DOILY n pl. -LIES a small napkin

DOING n pl. -S an action

DOIT n pl. -S a former Dutch coin

DOITED adj old and feeble

DOJO n pl. -JOS a school that teaches judo or karate

DOL n pl. -S a unit of pain intensity

DOLCE n pl. -CI a soft-toned organ stop

DOLDRUMS n/pl a state of inactivity or stagnation

DOLE v DOLED, DOLING, DOLES to distribute in small portions

DOLEFUL adj -FULLER, -FULLEST mournful

DOLERITE n pl. -S a variety of basalt

DOLESOME adj doleful

DOLING present participle of dole

DOLL v -ED, -ING, -S to dress stylishly

DOLLAR n pl. -S a monetary unit of the United States

DOLLIED past tense of dolly

DOLLIES present 3d person sing. of dolly

DOLLISH adj pretty

DOLLOP v -ED, -ING, -S to dispense in small amounts

DOLLY v -LIED, -LYING, -LIES to move on a wheeled platform

DOLMA n pl. -MAS or -MADES a stuffed grape leaf

DOLMAN n pl. -S a Turkish robe

DOLMEN n pl. -S a prehistoric monument

DOLOMITE n pl. -S a mineral

DOLOR n pl. -S grief

DOLOROSO adj having a mournful musical quality

DOLOROUS adj mournful

DOLOUR n pl. -S dolor

DOLPHIN n pl. -S a marine mammal

DOLT n pl. -S a stupid person **DOLTISH** adj

DOM n pl. -S a title given to certain monks

DOMAIN n pl. -S an area of control

DOMAL adj domical

DOME v DOMED, DOMING, DOMES to cover with a dome (a rounded roof)

DOMELIKE adj resembling a dome

DOMESDAY n pl. -DAYS doomsday

DOMESTIC n pl. -S a household servant

DOMIC adj domical

DOMICAL adj shaped like a dome

DOMICIL v -ED, -ING, -S to domicile

DOMICILE v -CILED, -CILING, -CILES to establish in a residence

DOMINANT n pl. -S a controlling genetic character

DOMINATE v -NATED, -NATING, -NATES to control

DOMINE n pl. -S master

DOMINEER v -ED, -ING, -S to tyrannize

DOMING present participle of dome

DOMINICK n pl. -S one of an American breed of chickens

DOMINIE n pl. -S a clergyman

DOMINION n pl. -S supreme authority

DOMINIUM n pl. -S the right of ownership and control of property

DOMINO n pl. -NOES or -NOS a small mask

DON v DONNED, DONNING, DONS to put on

DONA n pl. -S a Spanish lady

DONATE v -NATED, -NATING, -NATES to contribute

DONATION n pl. -S something donated

DONATIVE n pl. -S a donation

DONATOR n pl. -S a donor

DONE past participle of do

DONEE n pl. -S a recipient of a gift

DONENESS n pl. -ES the state of being cooked enough

DONG n pl. -S a deep sound like that of a large bell

DONGA n pl. -S a gully in a veldt

DONGOLA n pl. -S a type of leather

DONJON n pl. -S the main tower of a castle

DONKEY n pl. -KEYS the domestic ass

DONNA n pl. DONNAS or DONNE an Italian lady

DONNED past tense of don

DONNEE n pl. -S the set of assumptions upon which a story proceeds

DONNERD adj donnered

DONNERED adj dazed

DONNERT adj donnered

DONNIKER n pl. -S a bathroom or privy

DONNING present participle of don

DONNISH adj scholarly

DONOR n pl. -S one that donates

DONSIE adj unlucky

DONSY adj donsie

DONUT n pl. -S doughnut

DONZEL n pl. -S a young squire

DOODAD n pl. -S an article whose name is unknown or forgotten

DOODLE v -DLED, -DLING, -DLES to draw or scribble aimlessly

DOODLER n pl. -S one that doodles

DOOFUS n pl. -ES a stupid or foolish person

DOOLEE n pl. -S a stretcher for the sick or wounded

DOOLIE n pl. -S doolee

DOOLY n pl. -LIES doolee

DOOM v -ED, -ING, -S to destine to an unhappy fate

DOOMFUL adj ominous

DOOMSDAY n pl. -DAYS judgment day

DOOMSTER n pl. -S a judge

DOOMY adj doomful DOOMILY adv

DOOR n pl. -S a movable barrier at an entranceway

DOORBELL n pl. -S a bell at a door

DOORJAMB n pl. -S a vertical piece at the side of a doorway

DOORKNOB n pl. -S a handle for opening a door

DOORLESS adj having no door

DOORMAN n pl. -MEN the door attendant of a building

DOORMAT n pl. -S a mat placed in front of a door

DOORNAIL n pl. -S a large-headed nail

DOORPOST n pl. -S a doorjamb

DOORSILL n pl. -S the sill of a door

DOORSTEP n pl. -S a step leading to a door

DOORSTOP n pl. -S an object used for holding a door open

DOORWAY n pl. -WAYS the entranceway to a room or building

DOORYARD n pl. -S a yard in front of a house

DOOZER n pl. -S an extraordinary one of its kind

DOOZIE n pl. -S doozy

DOOZY n pl. -ZIES doozer

DOPA n pl. -S a drug to treat Parkinson's disease

DOPAMINE n pl. -S a form of dopa used to stimulate the heart

DOPANT n pl. -S an impurity added to a pure substance

DOPE v DOPED, DOPING, DOPES to give a narcotic to

DOPEHEAD n pl. -S a drug addict

DOPER n pl. -S one that dopes

DOPESTER n pl. -S one who predicts the outcomes of contests

DOPEY adj DOPIER, DOPIEST lethargic; stupid

DOPIER comparative of dopy

DOPIEST superlative of dopy

DOPINESS n pl. -ES the state of being dopey

DOPING present participle of dope

DOPY adj DOPIER, DOPIEST dopey

DOR n pl. -S a black European beetle

DORADO n pl. -DOS a marine fish

DORBUG n pl. -S a dor

DORE adj gilded

DORHAWK n pl. -S a nocturnal bird

DORIES pl. of dory

DORK n pl. -S a stupid or foolish person

DORKY adj DORKIER, DORKIEST stupid, foolish

DORM n pl. -S a dormitory

DORMANCY n pl. -CIES the state of being dormant

DORMANT adj lying asleep

DORMER n pl. -S a type of window

DORMICE pl. of dormouse

DORMIE adj being ahead by as many holes in golf as remain to be played

DORMIENT adj dormant

DORMIN n pl. -S a plant hormone

DORMOUSE n pl. -MICE a small rodent

DORMY	*adj* dormie
DORNECK	*n pl.* -S domick
DORNICK	*n pl.* -S a heavy linen fabric
DORNOCK	*n pl.* -S dornick
DORP	*n pl.* -S a village
DORPER	*n pl.* -S one of a breed of mutton-producing sheep
DORR	*n pl.* -S dor
DORSA	*pl.* of dorsum
DORSAD	*adv* dorsally
DORSAL	*n pl.* -S a dorsally located anatomical part
DORSALLY	*adv* toward the back
DORSEL	*n pl.* -S a dossal
DORSER	*n pl.* -S a dosser
DORSUM	*n pl.* -SA the back
DORTY	*adj* sullen
DORY	*n pl.* -RIES a flat-bottomed boat
DOSAGE	*n pl.* -S the amount of medicine to be given
DOSE	*v* DOSED, DOSING, DOSES to give a specified quantity of medicine to
DOSER	*n pl.* -S one that doses
DOSS	*v* -ED, -ING, -ES to sleep in any convenient place
DOSSAL	*n pl.* -S an ornamental cloth hung behind an altar
DOSSEL	*n pl.* -S dossal
DOSSER	*n pl.* -S a basket carried on the back
DOSSERET	*n pl.* -S a block resting on the capital of a column
DOSSIER	*n pl.* -S a file of papers on a single subject
DOSSIL	*n pl.* -S a cloth roll for wiping ink
DOST	a present 2d person sing. of do
DOT	*v* DOTTED, DOTTING, DOTS to cover with dots (tiny round marks)
DOTAGE	*n pl.* -S a state of senility
DOTAL	*adj* pertaining to a dowry
DOTARD	*n pl.* -S a senile person DOTARDLY *adj*
DOTATION	*n pl.* -S an endowment
DOTE	*v* DOTED, DOTING, DOTES to show excessive affection
DOTER	*n pl.* -S one that dotes
DOTH	a present 3d person sing. of do
DOTIER	comparative of doty
DOTIEST	superlative of doty
DOTING	present participle of dote
DOTINGLY	*adv* in an excessively affectionate manner
DOTTED	past tense of dot
DOTTEL	*n pl.* -S dottle
DOTTER	*n pl.* -S one that dots
DOTTEREL	*n pl.* -S a shore bird
DOTTIER	comparative of dotty
DOTTIEST	superlative of dotty
DOTTILY	*adv* in a dotty manner
DOTTING	present participle of dot
DOTTLE	*n pl.* -S a mass of half-burnt pipe tobacco
DOTTREL	*n pl.* -S dotterel
DOTTY	*adj* -TIER, -TIEST crazy
DOTY	*adj* DOTIER, DOTIEST stained by decay
DOUBLE	*v* -BLED, -BLING, -BLES to make twice as great
DOUBLER	*n pl.* -S one that doubles
DOUBLET	*n pl.* -S a close-fitting jacket
DOUBLING	present participle of double
DOUBLOON	*n pl.* -S a former Spanish gold coin
DOUBLURE	*n pl.* -S the lining of a book cover
DOUBLY	*adv* to twice the degree
DOUBT	*v* -ED, -ING, -S to be uncertain about
DOUBTER	*n pl.* -S one that doubts
DOUBTFUL	*adj* uncertain
DOUCE	*adj* sedate DOUCELY *adv*
DOUCEUR	*n pl.* -S a gratuity
DOUCHE	*v* DOUCHED, DOUCHING, DOUCHES to cleanse with a jet of water
DOUGH	*n pl.* -S a flour mixture
DOUGHBOY	*n pl.* -BOYS an infantryman
DOUGHIER	comparative of doughy
DOUGHIEST	superlative of doughy
DOUGHNUT	*n pl.* -S a ring-shaped cake
DOUGHT	a past tense of dow
DOUGHTY	*adj* -TIER, -TIEST courageous
DOUGHY	*adj* DOUGHIER, DOUGHIEST resembling dough
DOUM	*n pl.* -S an African palm tree
DOUMA	*n pl.* -S duma
DOUPIONI	*n pl.* -S a silk yarn
DOUR	*adj* DOURER, DOUREST sullen
DOURA	*n pl.* -S durra
DOURAH	*n pl.* -S durra
DOURINE	*n pl.* -S a disease of horses
DOURLY	*adv* in a dour manner
DOURNESS	*n pl.* -ES the state of being dour
DOUSE	*v* DOUSED, DOUSING, DOUSES to plunge into water
DOUSER	*n pl.* -S one that douses

DOUX *adj* very sweet — used of champagne

DOUZEPER *n pl.* -S one of twelve legendary knights

DOVE *n pl.* -S a bird of the pigeon family

DOVECOT *n pl.* -S dovecote

DOVECOTE *n pl.* -S a roost for domesticated pigeons

DOVEKEY *n pl.* -KEYS dovekie

DOVEKIE *n pl.* -S a seabird

DOVELIKE *adj* resembling or suggestive of a dove

DOVEN *v* -ED, -ING, -S to daven

DOVETAIL *v* -ED, -ING, -S to fit together closely

DOVISH *adj* not warlike

DOW *v* DOWED or DOUGHT, DOWING, DOWS to prosper

DOWABLE *adj* entitled to an endowment

DOWAGER *n pl.* -S a dignified elderly woman

DOWDY *adj* DOWDIER, DOWDIEST lacking in stylishness or neatness DOWDILY *adv* DOWDYISH *adj*

DOWDY *n pl.* DOWDIES a dowdy woman

DOWEL *v* -ELED, -ELING, -ELS or -ELLED, -ELLING, -ELS to fasten with wooden pins

DOWER *v* -ED, -ING, -S to provide with a dowry

DOWERY *n pl.* -ERIES dowry

DOWIE *adj* dreary

DOWN *v* -ED, -ING, -S to cause to fall

DOWNBEAT *n pl.* -S the first beat of a musical measure

DOWNCAST *n pl.* -S an overthrow or ruin

DOWNCOME *n pl.* -S downfall

DOWNER *n pl.* -S a depressant drug

DOWNFALL *n pl.* -S a sudden fall

DOWNHAUL *n pl.* -S a rope for hauling down sails

DOWNHILL *n pl.* -S a downward slope

DOWNIER comparative of downy

DOWNIEST superlative of downy

DOWNLAND *n pl.* -S a rolling treeless upland

DOWNLINK *n pl.* -S a communications channel from a spacecraft

DOWNLOAD *v* -ED, -ING, -S to transfer data from a large computer to a smaller one

DOWNPIPE *n pl.* -S a pipe for draining water from a roof

DOWNPLAY *v* -ED, -ING, -S to de-emphasize

DOWNPOUR *n pl.* -S a heavy rain

DOWNSIDE *n pl.* -S a negative aspect

DOWNSIZE *v* -SIZED, -SIZING, -SIZES to produce in a smaller size

DOWNTICK *n pl.* -S a stock market transaction

DOWNTIME *n pl.* -S the time when a machine or factory is inactive

DOWNTOWN *n pl.* -S the business district of a city

DOWNTROD *adj* oppressed

DOWNTURN *n pl.* -S a downward turn

DOWNWARD *adv* from a higher to a lower place

DOWNWASH *n pl.* -ES a downward deflection of air

DOWNWIND *adv* in the direction that the wind blows

DOWNY *adj* DOWNIER, DOWNIEST soft

DOWRY *n pl.* -RIES the money or property a wife brings to her husband at marriage

DOWSABEL *n pl.* -S a sweetheart

DOWSE *v* DOWSED, DOWSING, DOWSES to search for underground water with a divining rod

DOWSER *n pl.* -S one that dowses

DOXIE *n pl.* -S doxy

DOXOLOGY *n pl.* -GIES a hymn or verse of praise to God

DOXY *n pl.* DOXIES a doctrine

DOYEN *n pl.* -S the senior member of a group

DOYENNE *n pl.* -S a female doyen

DOYLEY *n pl.* -LEYS doily

DOYLY *n pl.* -LIES doily

DOZE *v* DOZED, DOZING, DOZES to sleep lightly

DOZEN *v* -ED, -ING, -S to stun

DOZENTH *n pl.* -S twelfth

DOZER *n pl.* -S one that dozes

DOZIER comparative of dozy

DOZIEST superlative of dozy

DOZILY *adv* in a dozy manner

DOZINESS *n pl.* -ES the state of being dozy

DOZING present participle of doze

DOZY *adj* DOZIER, DOZIEST drowsy

DRAB *adj* DRABBER, DRABBEST cheerless

DRAB   v DRABBED, DRABBING, DRABS to consort with prostitutes

DRABBET   n pl. -S a coarse linen fabric

DRABBLE   v -BLED, -BLING, -BLES to draggle

DRABLY   adv in a drab manner

DRABNESS   n pl. -ES the quality of being drab

DRACAENA   n pl. -S a tropical plant

DRACHM   n pl. -S a unit of weight

DRACHMA   n pl. -MAS, -MAE or -MAI a monetary unit of Greece

DRACONIC   adj pertaining to a dragon

DRAFF   n pl. -S the damp remains of malt after brewing

DRAFFISH   adj draffy

DRAFFY   adj DRAFFIER, DRAFFIEST worthless

DRAFT   v -ED, -ING, -S to conscript for military service

DRAFTEE   n pl. -S one that is drafted

DRAFTER   n pl. -S one that drafts

DRAFTING   n pl. -S mechanical drawing

DRAFTY   adj DRAFTIER, DRAFTIEST having or exposed to currents of air DRAFTILY adv

DRAG   v DRAGGED, DRAGGING, DRAGS to pull along the ground

DRAGEE   n pl. -S a sugarcoated candy

DRAGGER   n pl. -S one that drags

DRAGGIER   comparative of draggy

DRAGGIEST   superlative of draggy

DRAGGING   present participle of drag

DRAGGLE   v -GLED, -GLING, -GLES to make wet and dirty

DRAGGY   adj -GIER, -GIEST sluggish

DRAGLINE   n pl. -S a line used for dragging

DRAGNET   n pl. -S a net for trawling

DRAGOMAN   n pl. -MANS or -MEN an interpreter in Near Eastern countries

DRAGON   n pl. -S a mythical, serpentlike monster

DRAGONET   n pl. -S a marine fish

DRAGOON   v -ED, -ING, -S to harass by the use of troops

DRAGROPE   n pl. -S a rope used for dragging

DRAGSTER   n pl. -S a vehicle used in drag racing

DRAIL   n pl. -S a heavy fishhook

DRAIN   v -ED, -ING, -S to draw off a liquid

DRAINAGE   n pl. -S the act of draining

DRAINER   n pl. -S one that drains

DRAKE   n pl. -S a male duck

DRAM   v DRAMMED, DRAMMING, DRAMS to tipple

DRAMA   n pl. -S a composition written for theatrical performance

DRAMATIC   adj pertaining to drama

DRAMEDY   n pl. -DIES a sitcom having dramatic scenes

DRAMMED   past tense of dram

DRAMMING   present participle of dram

DRAMMOCK   n pl. -S raw oatmeal mixed with cold water

DRAMSHOP   n pl. -S a barroom

DRANK   past tense of drink

DRAPE   v DRAPED, DRAPING, DRAPES to arrange in graceful folds DRAPABLE adj

DRAPER   n pl. -S a dealer in cloth

DRAPERY   n pl. -ERIES cloth arranged in graceful folds

DRAPEY   adj characterized by graceful folds

DRAPING   present participle of drape

DRASTIC   adj extremely severe

DRAT   v DRATTED, DRATTING, DRATS to damn

DRAUGHT   v -ED, -ING, -S to draft

DRAUGHTY   adj DRAUGHTIER, DRAUGHTIEST drafty

DRAVE   a past tense of drive

DRAW   v DREW, DRAWN, DRAWING, DRAWS to move by pulling DRAWABLE adj

DRAWBACK   n pl. -S a hindrance

DRAWBAR   n pl. -S a railroad coupler

DRAWBORE   n pl. -S a hole for joining a mortise and tenon

DRAWDOWN   n pl. -S a lowering of a water level

DRAWEE   n pl. -S the person on whom a bill of exchange is drawn

DRAWER   n pl. -S one that draws

DRAWING   n pl. -S a portrayal in lines of a form or figure

DRAWL   v -ED, -ING, -S to speak slowly with vowels greatly prolonged

DRAWLER   n pl. -S one that drawls

DRAWLY   adj DRAWLIER, DRAWLIEST marked by drawling

DRAWN   past participle of draw

DRAWTUBE   n pl. -S a tube that slides within another tube

DRAY v -ED, -ING, -S to transport by dray (a low, strong cart)

DRAYAGE n pl. -S transportation by dray

DRAYMAN n pl. -MEN one who drives a dray

DREAD v -ED, -ING, -S to fear greatly

DREADFUL n pl. -S a publication containing sensational material

DREAM v DREAMED or DREAMT, DREAMING, DREAMS to have a dream (a series of images occurring during sleep)

DREAMER n pl. -S one that dreams

DREAMFUL adj dreamy

DREAMT a past tense of dream

DREAMY adj DREAMIER, DREAMIEST full of dreams **DREAMILY** adv

DREAR n pl. -S the state of being dreary

DREARY adj DREARIER, DREARIEST dismal **DREARILY** adv

DREARY n pl. DREARIES a dismal person

DRECK n pl. -S rubbish **DRECKY** adj

DREDGE v DREDGED, DREDGING, DREDGES to clear with a dredge (a machine for scooping mud)

DREDGER n pl. -S one that dredges

DREDGING n pl. -S matter that is dredged up

DREE v DREED, DREEING, DREES to suffer

DREG n pl. -S the sediment of liquors **DREGGISH** adj

DREGGY adj -GIER, -GIEST full of dregs

DREICH adj dreary

DREIDEL n pl. -S a spinning toy

DREIDL n pl. -S dreidel

DREIGH adj dreich

DREK n pl. -S dreck

DRENCH v -ED, -ING, -ES to wet thoroughly

DRENCHER n pl. -S one that drenches

DRESS v DRESSED or DREST, DRESSING, DRESSES to put clothes on

DRESSAGE n pl. -S the training of a horse in obedience and deportment

DRESSER n pl. -S one that dresses

DRESSING n pl. -S material applied to cover a wound

DRESSY adj DRESSIER, DRESSIEST stylish **DRESSILY** adv

DREST a past tense of dress

DREW past tense of draw

DRIB v DRIBBED, DRIBBING, DRIBS to drip

DRIBBLE v -BLED, -BLING, -BLES to drivel

DRIBBLER n pl. -S one that dribbles

DRIBBLET n pl. -S driblet

DRIBBLING present participle of dribble

DRIBBLY adj tending to dribble

DRIBLET n pl. -S a small drop of liquid

DRIED past tense of dry

DRIEGH adj dreary

DRIER n pl. -S one that dries

DRIES present 3d person sing. of dry

DRIEST a superlative of dry

DRIFT v -ED, -ING, -S to move along in a current

DRIFTAGE n pl. -S the act of drifting

DRIFTER n pl. -S one that drifts

DRIFTPIN n pl. -S a metal rod for securing timbers

DRIFTY adj DRIFTIER, DRIFTIEST full of drifts (masses of wind-driven snow)

DRILL v -ED, -ING, -S to bore a hole in

DRILLER n pl. -S one that drills

DRILLING n pl. -S a heavy twilled cotton fabric

DRILY adv dryly

DRINK v DRANK, DRUNK, DRINKING, DRINKS to swallow liquid

DRINKER n pl. -S one that drinks

DRIP v DRIPPED or DRIPT, DRIPPING, DRIPS to fall in drops

DRIPLESS adj designed not to drip

DRIPPER n pl. -S something from which a liquid drips

DRIPPING n pl. -S juice drawn from meat during cooking

DRIPPY adj -PIER, -PIEST very wet

DRIPT a past tense of drip

DRIVE v DROVE or DRAVE, DRIVEN, DRIVING, DRIVES to urge or propel forward **DRIVABLE** adj

DRIVEL v -ELED, -ELING, -ELS or -ELLED, -ELLING, -ELS to let saliva flow from the mouth

DRIVELER n pl. -S one that drivels

DRIVEN past participle of drive

DRIVER n pl. -S one that drives

DRIVEWAY n pl. -WAYS a private road providing access to a building

DRIVING n pl. -S management of a motor vehicle

DRIZZLE v -ZLED, -ZLING, -ZLES to rain lightly

DRIZZLY adj -ZLIER, -ZLIEST characterized by light rain

DROGUE n pl. -S a sea anchor

DROIT n pl. -S a legal right

DROLL adj DROLLER, DROLLEST comical

DROLL v -ED, -ING, -S to jest

DROLLERY n pl. -ERIES something droll

DROLLY adv in a droll manner

DROMON n pl. -S dromond

DROMOND n pl. -S a large fast-sailing medieval galley

DRONE v DRONED, DRONING, DRONES to make a continuous low sound

DRONER n pl. -S one that drones

DRONGO n pl. -GOS a tropical bird

DRONING present participle of drone

DRONISH adj habitually lazy

DROOL v -ED, -ING, -S to drivel

DROOP v -ED, -ING, -S to hang downward

DROOPY adj DROOPIER, DROOPIEST drooping DROOPILY adv

DROP v DROPPED or DROPT, DROPPING, DROPS to fall in drops (globules)

DROPHEAD n pl. -S a convertible car

DROPKICK n pl. -S a type of kick in football

DROPLET n pl. -S a tiny drop

DROPOUT n pl. -S one who quits school prematurely

DROPPED a past tense of drop

DROPPER n pl. -S a tube for dispensing liquid in drops

DROPPING n pl. -S something that has been dropped

DROPSHOT n pl. -S a type of shot in tennis

DROPSY n pl. -SIES an excessive accumulation of serous fluid DROPSIED adj

DROPT a past tense of drop

DROPWORT n pl. -S a perennial herb

DROSERA n pl. -S a sundew

DROSHKY n pl. -KIES an open carriage

DROSKY n pl. -KIES droshky

DROSS n pl. -ES waste matter

DROSSY adj DROSSIER, DROSSIEST worthless

DROUGHT n pl. -S a dry period

DROUGHTY adj DROUGHTIER, DROUGHTIEST dry

DROUK v -ED, -ING, -S to drench

DROUTH n pl. -S drought

DROUTHY adj DROUTHIER, DROUTHIEST droughty

DROVE v DROVED, DROVING, DROVES to drive cattle or sheep

DROVER n pl. -S a driver of cattle or sheep

DROWN v -ED, -ING, -S to suffocate in water

DROWND v -ED, -ING, -S to drown

DROWNER n pl. -S one that drowns

DROWSE v DROWSED, DROWSING, DROWSES to doze

DROWSY adj DROWSIER, DROWSIEST sleepy DROWSILY adv

DRUB v DRUBBED, DRUBBING, DRUBS to beat severely

DRUBBER n pl. -S one that drubs

DRUBBING n pl. -S a severe beating

DRUDGE v DRUDGED, DRUDGING, DRUDGES to do hard, menial, or tedious work

DRUDGER n pl. -S one that drudges

DRUDGERY n pl. -ERIES hard, menial, or tedious work

DRUDGING present participle of drudge

DRUG v DRUGGED, DRUGGING, DRUGS to affect with a drug (a medicinal substance)

DRUGGET n pl. -S a coarse woolen fabric

DRUGGIE n pl. -S a drug addict

DRUGGIST n pl. -S a pharmacist

DRUGGY adj -GIER, -GIEST affected by drugs

DRUID n pl. -S one of an ancient Celtic order of priests DRUIDIC adj

DRUIDESS n pl. -ES a female druid

DRUIDISM n pl. -S the religious system of the druids

DRUM v DRUMMED, DRUMMING, DRUMS to beat a drum (a percussion instrument)

DRUMBEAT n pl. -S the sound of a drum

DRUMBLE v -BLED, -BLING, -BLES to move slowly

DRUMFIRE n pl. -S heavy, continuous gunfire

DRUMFISH n pl. -ES a fish that makes a drumming sound

DRUMHEAD *n* pl. -S the material stretched over the end of a drum

DRUMLIER comparative of drumly

DRUMLIEST superlative of drumly

DRUMLIKE *adj* resembling the head of a drum

DRUMLIN *n* pl. -S a long hill of glacial drift

DRUMLY *adj* -LIER, -LIEST dark and gloomy

DRUMMED past tense of drum

DRUMMER *n* pl. -S one that drums

DRUMMING present participle of drum

DRUMROLL *n* pl. -S a roll played on a drum

DRUNK *adj* DRUNKER, DRUNKEST intoxicated

DRUNK *n* pl. -S a drunken person

DRUNKARD *n* pl. -S one who is habitually drunk

DRUNKEN *adj* drunk

DRUPE *n* pl. -S a fleshy fruit

DRUPELET *n* pl. -S a small drupe

DRUSE *n* pl. -S a crust of small crystals lining a rock cavity

DRUTHERS *n/pl* one's preference

DRY *adj* DRIER, DRIEST or DRYER, DRYEST having no moisture

DRY *v* DRIED, DRYING, DRIES to make dry **DRYABLE** *adj*

DRY *n* pl. DRYS a prohibitionist

DRYAD *n* pl. -S or -ES a nymph of the woods **DRYADIC** *adj*

DRYER *n* pl. -S drier

DRYISH *adj* somewhat dry

DRYLAND *adj* relating to an arid region

DRYLOT *n* pl. -S an enclosure for livestock

DRYLY *adv* in a dry manner

DRYNESS *n* pl. -ES the state of being dry

DRYPOINT *n* pl. -S a method of engraving

DRYSTONE *adj* constructed of stone without mortar

DRYWALL *n* pl. -S board used instead of plaster in walls

DUAD *n* pl. -S a pair

DUAL *n* pl. -S a linguistic form

DUALISM *n* pl. -S a philosophical theory

DUALIST *n* pl. -S an adherent of dualism

DUALITY *n* pl. -TIES the state of being twofold

DUALIZE *v* -IZED, -IZING, -IZES to make twofold

DUALLY *adv* in two ways

DUB *v* DUBBED, DUBBING, DUBS to confer knighthood on

DUBBER *n* pl. -S one that dubs

DUBBIN *n* pl. -S material for softening and waterproofing leather

DUBBING *n* pl. -S dubbin

DUBIETY *n* pl. -ETIES the state of being dubious

DUBIOUS *adj* doubtful

DUBONNET *n* pl. -S a red color

DUCAL *adj* pertaining to a duke (a high-ranking nobleman) **DUCALLY** *adv*

DUCAT *n* pl. -S any of several gold coins formerly used in Europe

DUCE *n* pl. DUCES or DUCI a leader

DUCHESS *n* pl. -ES the wife or widow of a duke

DUCHY *n* pl. DUCHIES the domain of a duke

DUCI a pl. of duce

DUCK *v* -ED, -ING, -S to lower quickly

DUCKBILL *n* pl. -S a platypus

DUCKER *n* pl. -S one that ducks

DUCKIE *adj* ducky

DUCKIER comparative of ducky

DUCKIES pl. of ducky

DUCKIEST superlative of ducky

DUCKLING *n* pl. -S a young duck

DUCKPIN *n* pl. -S a type of bowling pin

DUCKTAIL *n* pl. -S a style of haircut

DUCKWALK *v* -ED, -ING, -S to walk in a squatting position

DUCKWEED *n* pl. -S an aquatic plant

DUCKY *adj* DUCKIER, DUCKIEST excellent

DUCKY *n* pl. DUCKIES a darling

DUCT *v* -ED, -ING, -S to convey through a duct (a tubular passage)

DUCTAL *adj* made up of ducts

DUCTILE *adj* easily molded or shaped

DUCTING *n* pl. -S a system of ducts

DUCTLESS *adj* being without a duct

DUCTULE *n* pl. -S a small duct

DUCTWORK *n* pl. -S a system of ducts

DUD *n* pl. -S a bomb that fails to explode

DUDDIE *adj* ragged

DUDDY *adj* duddie

DUDE *v* DUDED, DUDING, DUDES to dress up in flashy clothes

DUDEEN *n* pl. -S a short tobacco pipe

DUDGEON n pl. -S a feeling of resentment

DUDING present participle of dude

DUDISH adj resembling a dude (a dandy)

DUDISHLY adv in the manner of a dude

DUE n pl. -S something that is owed

DUECENTO n pl. -TOS the thirteenth century

DUEL v DUELED, DUELING, DUELS or DUELLED, DUELLING, DUELS to fight formally

DUELER n pl. -S one that duels

DUELIST n pl. -S a dueler

DUELLED a past tense of duel

DUELLER n pl. -S a dueler

DUELLI a pl. of duello

DUELLING a present participle of duel

DUELLIST n pl. -S duelist

DUELLO n pl. -LOS or -LI the art of dueling; a duel

DUENDE n pl. -S charisma

DUENESS n pl. -ES the state of being owed

DUENNA n pl. -S a governess

DUET v DUETTED, DUETTING, DUETS to perform a duet (a musical composition for two)

DUETTIST n pl. -S a participant in a duet

DUFF n pl. -S a thick pudding

DUFFEL n pl. -S a coarse woolen fabric

DUFFER n pl. -S a clumsy person

DUFFLE n pl. -S duffel

DUG n pl. -S the teat or udder of a female mammal

DUGONG n pl. -S an aquatic mammal

DUGOUT n pl. -S a canoe made by hollowing out a log

DUI a pl. of duo

DUIKER n pl. -S a small antelope

DUIT n pl. -S doit

DUKE v DUKED, DUKING, DUKES to fight

DUKEDOM n pl. -S a duchy

DULCET n pl. -S a soft-toned organ stop

DULCETLY adv melodiously

DULCIANA n pl. -S a soft-toned organ stop

DULCIFY v -FIED, -FYING, -FIES to sweeten

DULCIMER n pl. -S a stringed instrument

DULCINEA n pl. -S a sweetheart

DULIA n pl. -S veneration of saints

DULL adj DULLER, DULLEST mentally slow

DULL v -ED, -ING, -S to make less sharp

DULLARD n pl. -S a dolt

DULLISH adj somewhat dull

DULLNESS n pl. -ES the state of being dull

DULLY adv in a dull manner

DULNESS n pl. -ES dullness

DULSE n pl. -S an edible seaweed

DULY adv rightfully

DUMA n pl. -S a Russian council

DUMB adj DUMBER, DUMBEST incapable of speech

DUMB v -ED, -ING, -S to make silent

DUMBBELL n pl. -S a weight lifted for muscular exercise

DUMBCANE n pl. -S a tropical plant

DUMBHEAD n pl. -S a stupid person

DUMBLY adv in a dumb manner

DUMBNESS n pl. -ES the state of being dumb

DUMDUM n pl. -S a type of bullet

DUMFOUND v -ED, -ING, -S to astonish

DUMKA n pl. -KY a Slavic folk ballad

DUMMKOPF n pl. -S a dolt

DUMMY v -MIED, -MYING, -MIES to make a representation of

DUMP v -ED, -ING, -S to let fall heavily

DUMPCART n pl. -S a type of cart

DUMPER n pl. -S one that dumps

DUMPIER comparative of dumpy

DUMPIEST superlative of dumpy

DUMPILY adv in a dumpy manner

DUMPING n pl. -S the selling of large quantities of goods at below the market price

DUMPISH adj sad

DUMPLING n pl. -S a ball of dough cooked with stew or soup

DUMPY adj DUMPIER, DUMPIEST short and thick

DUN v DUNNED, DUNNING, DUNS to make demands upon for payment of a debt

DUN adj DUNNER, DUNNEST of a dull brown color

DUNAM n pl. -S a unit of land measure in Israel

DUNCE n pl. -S a stupid person DUNCICAL, DUNCISH adj

DUNCH n pl. -ES a push

DUNE *n* pl. -S a hill of sand **DUNELIKE** *adj*

DUNELAND *n* pl. -S an area having many dunes

DUNG *v* -ED, -ING, -S to fertilize with manure

DUNGAREE *n* pl. -S a coarse cotton fabric

DUNGEON *v* -ED, -ING, -S to confine in a dungeon (an underground prison)

DUNGHILL *n* pl. -S a heap of manure

DUNGY *adj* DUNGIER, DUNGIEST filthy

DUNITE *n* pl. -S an igneous rock **DUNITIC** *adj*

DUNK *v* -ED, -ING, -S to dip into liquid

DUNKER *n* pl. -S one that dunks

DUNLIN *n* pl. -S a wading bird

DUNNAGE *n* pl. -S packing material used to protect cargo

DUNNED past tense of dun

DUNNER comparative of dun

DUNNESS *n* pl. -ES the state of being dun

DUNNEST superlative of dun

DUNNING present participle of dun

DUNNITE *n* pl. -S an explosive

DUNT *v* -ED, -ING, -S to strike with a heavy blow

DUO *n* pl. DUOS or DUI an instrumental duet

DUODENUM *n* pl. -DENA or -DENUMS the first portion of the small intestine **DUODENAL** *adj*

DUOLOG *n* pl. -S duologue

DUOLOGUE *n* pl. -S a conversation between two persons

DUOMO *n* pl. -MOS or -MI a cathedral

DUOPOLY *n* pl. -LIES the market condition existing when there are two sellers only

DUOPSONY *n* pl. -NIES the market condition existing when there are two buyers only

DUOTONE *n* pl. -S an illustration in two tones

DUP *v* DUPPED, DUPPING, DUPS to open

DUPE *v* DUPED, DUPING, DUPES to deceive **DUPABLE** *adj*

DUPER *n* pl. -S one that dupes

DUPERY *n* pl. -ERIES the act of duping

DUPING present participle of dupe

DUPLE *adj* having two parts or elements

DUPLEX *v* -ED, -ING, -ES to make duple

DUPLEXER *n* pl. -S an electronic switching device

DUPPED past tense of dup

DUPPING present participle of dup

DURA *n* pl. -S durra

DURABLE *adj* able to withstand wear or decay **DURABLY** *adv*

DURABLES *n/pl* durable goods

DURAL *adj* of the dura mater (a brain membrane)

DURAMEN *n* pl. -S the central wood of a tree

DURANCE *n* pl. -S restraint by or as if by physical force

DURATION *n* pl. -S continuance in time

DURATIVE *n* pl. -S a type of verb

DURBAR *n* pl. -S the court of a native ruler in India

DURE *v* DURED, DURING, DURES to endure

DURESS *n* pl. -ES compulsion by threat

DURIAN *n* pl. -S an East Indian tree

DURING *prep* throughout the duration of

DURION *n* pl. -S durian

DURMAST *n* pl. -S a European oak

DURN *v* -ED, -ING, -S to damn

DURNED *adj* DURNEDER, DURNEDEST or DURNDEST damned

DURO *n* pl. -ROS a Spanish silver dollar

DUROC *n* pl. -S a large red hog

DURR *n* pl. -S durra

DURRA *n* pl. -S a cereal grain

DURRIE *n* pl. -S dhurrie

DURST a past tense of dare

DURUM *n* pl. -S a kind of wheat

DUSK *v* -ED, -ING, -S to become dark

DUSKISH *adj* dusky

DUSKY *adj* DUSKIER, DUSKIEST somewhat dark **DUSKILY** *adv*

DUST *v* -ED, -ING, -S to make free of dust (minute particles of matter)

DUSTBIN *n* pl. -S a trash can

DUSTER *n* pl. -S one that dusts

DUSTHEAP *n* pl. -S a pile of trash

DUSTIER comparative of dusty

DUSTIEST superlative of dusty

DUSTILY *adv* in a dusty manner

DUSTLESS *adj* being without dust

DUSTLIKE *adj* resembling dust

DUSTMAN *n pl.* -MEN a trashman

DUSTOFF *n pl.* -S a military helicopter for evacuating the wounded

DUSTPAN *n pl.* -S a pan for holding swept dust

DUSTRAG *n pl.* -S a rag used for dusting

DUSTUP *n pl.* -S an argument

DUSTY *adj* DUSTIER, DUSTIEST full of dust

DUTCH *adv* with each person paying for himself

DUTCHMAN *n pl.* -MEN something used to hide structural defects

DUTEOUS *adj* dutiful

DUTIABLE *adj* subject to import tax

DUTIFUL *adj* obedient

DUTY *n pl.* -TIES a moral or legal obligation

DUUMVIR *n pl.* -VIRS or -VIRI a magistrate of ancient Rome

DUVET *n pl.* -S a down-filled bed covering

DUVETINE *n pl.* -S duvetyn

DUVETYN *n pl.* -S a smooth lustrous velvety fabric

DUVETYNE *n pl.* -S duvetyn

DUXELLES *n pl.* DUXELLES a garnish or sauce with minced mushrooms

DWARF *adj* DWARFER, DWARFEST extremely small

DWARF *n pl.* -DWARFS or DWARVES an extremely small person

DWARF *v* -ED, -ING, -S to cause to appear small

DWARFISH *adj* resembling a dwarf

DWARFISM *n pl.* -S a condition of stunted growth

DWARVES a pl. of dwarf

DWEEB *n pl.* -S an unattractive or inept person

DWELL *v* DWELT or DWELLED, DWELLING, DWELLS to reside

DWELLER *n pl.* -S one that dwells

DWELLING *n pl.* -S a place of residence

DWELT a past tense of dwell

DWINDLE *v* -DLED, -DLING, -DLES to decrease steadily

DWINE *v* DWINED, DWINING, DWINES to pine or waste away

DYABLE *adj* dyeable

DYAD *n pl.* -S a pair of units

DYADIC *n pl.* -S a sum of mathematical dyads

DYARCHY *n pl.* -CHIES diarchy
DYARCHIC *adj*

DYBBUK *n pl.* -BUKS or -BUKIM a wandering soul in Jewish folklore

DYE *v* DYED, DYEING, DYES to treat with a dye (a coloring matter)

DYEABLE *adj* capable of being dyed

DYEING *n pl.* -S something colored with a dye

DYER *n pl.* -S one that dyes

DYESTUFF *n pl.* -S a dye

DYEWEED *n pl.* -S a shrub that yields a yellow dye

DYEWOOD *n pl.* -S a wood from which a dye is extracted

DYING *n pl.* -S a passing out of existence

DYKE *v* DYKED, DYKING, DYKES to dike

DYNAMIC *n pl.* -S a physical force

DYNAMISM *n pl.* -S a theory that explains the universe in terms of force or energy

DYNAMIST *n pl.* -S an adherent of dynamism

DYNAMITE *v* -MITED, -MITING, -MITES to blow up with a powerful explosive

DYNAMO *n pl.* -MOS a forceful energetic person

DYNAST *n pl.* -S a ruler

DYNASTY *n pl.* -TIES a succession of rulers from the same line of descent **DYNASTIC** *adj*

DYNATRON *n pl.* -S a type of electron tube

DYNE *n pl.* -S a unit of force

DYNEIN *n pl.* DYNEIN an enzyme involved in cell movement

DYNEL *n pl.* -S a synthetic fiber

DYNODE *n pl.* -S a type of electrode

DYSGENIC *adj* causing the deterioration of hereditary qualities

DYSLEXIA *n pl.* -S impairment of the ability to read

DYSLEXIC *n pl.* -S one who is affected with dyslexia

DYSPEPSY *n pl.* -SIES indigestion

DYSPNEA *n* pl. -S labored breathing **DYSPNEAL, DYSPNEIC** *adj*

DYSPNOEA *n* pl. -S dyspnea **DYSPNOIC** *adj*

DYSTAXIA *n* pl. -S a form of muscular tremor

DYSTOCIA *n* pl. -S difficult labor and delivery in childbirth

DYSTONIA *n* pl. -S a condition of disordered tonicity of muscle tissue **DYSTONIC** *adj*

DYSTOPIA *n* pl. -S a wretched place

DYSURIA *n* pl. -S painful urination **DYSURIC** *adj*

DYVOUR *n* pl. -S one who is bankrupt

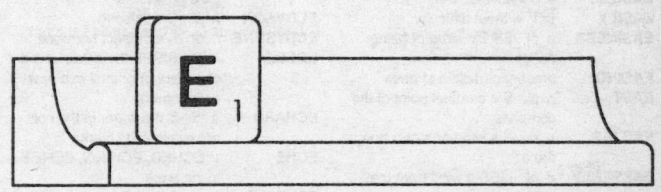

E₁

EACH	adj being one of two or more distinct individuals
EAGER	adj -GERER, -GEREST impatiently longing EAGERLY adv
EAGER	n pl. -S eagre
EAGLE	n pl. -S a large bird of prey
EAGLET	n pl. -S a young eagle
EAGRE	n pl. -S a tidal flood
EANLING	n pl. -S yeanling
EAR	v -ED, -ING, -S to form the fruiting head of a cereal
EARACHE	n pl. -S a pain in the ear (an organ of hearing)
EARDROP	n pl. -S an earring
EARDRUM	n pl. -S the tympanic membrane
EARED	adj having ears
EARFLAP	n pl. -S a part of a cap designed to cover the ears
EARFUL	n pl. -S a flow of information
EARING	n pl. -S a line on a ship
EARL	n pl. -S a British nobleman
EARLAP	n pl. -S an earflap
EARLDOM	n pl. -S the rank of an earl
EARLESS	adj lacking ears
EARLIER	comparative of early
EARLIEST	superlative of early
EARLOBE	n pl. -S a part of the ear
EARLOCK	n pl. -S a curl of hair by the ear
EARLSHIP	n pl. -S earldom
EARLY	adv -LIER, -LIEST near the beginning of a period of time or a series of events
EARMARK	v -ED, -ING, -S to designate for a specific use
EARMUFF	n pl. -S one of a pair of ear coverings
EARN	v -ED, -ING, -S to gain or deserve for one's labor or service
EARNER	n pl. -S one that earns
EARNEST	n pl. -S a down payment
EARNINGS	n/pl something earned
EARPHONE	n pl. -S a listening device worn over the ear
EARPIECE	n pl. -S an earphone
EARPLUG	n pl. -S a plug for the ear
EARRING	n pl. -S an ornament for the earlobe
EARSHOT	n pl. -S the range within which sound can be heard
EARSTONE	n pl. -S an otolith
EARTH	v -ED, -ING, -S to cover with earth (soil)
EARTHEN	adj made of earth
EARTHIER	comparative of earthy
EARTHIEST	superlative of earthy
EARTHILY	adv in an earthy manner
EARTHLY	adj -LIER, -LIEST worldly
EARTHMAN	n pl. -MEN a person from the planet earth
EARTHNUT	n pl. -S a European herb
EARTHPEA	n pl. -S a twining plant
EARTHSET	n pl. -S the setting of the earth as seen from the moon
EARTHY	adj EARTHIER, EARTHIEST composed of, resembling, or suggestive of earth
EARWAX	n pl. -ES cerumen
EARWIG	v -WIGGED, -WIGGING, -WIGS to insinuate against in secret
EARWORM	n pl. -S a bollworm
EASE	v EASED, EASING, EASES to give rest or relief to
EASEFUL	adj restful

EASEL n pl. -S a three-legged frame

EASEMENT n pl. -S relief

EASIER comparative of easy

EASIES pl. of easy

EASIEST superlative of easy

EASILY adv without difficulty

EASINESS n pl. -ES the state of being easy

EASING present participle of ease

EAST n pl. -S a cardinal point of the compass

EASTER n pl. -S a wind or storm from the east

EASTERLY n pl. -LIES a wind from the east

EASTERN adj being to, toward, or in the east

EASTING n pl. -S a movement toward the east

EASTWARD n pl. -S a direction toward the east

EASY adj EASIER, EASIEST not difficult

EASY n pl. EASIES a communications code word for the letter E

EAT v ATE or ET, EATEN, EATING, EATS to consume food

EATABLE n pl. -S an edible

EATER n pl. -S one that eats

EATERY n pl. -ERIES a lunchroom

EATH adj easy

EATING n pl. -S the act of consuming food

EAU n pl. EAUX water

EAVE n pl. -S the lower projecting edge of a roof EAVED adj

EBB v -ED, -ING, -S to recede

EBBET n pl. -S a common green newt

EBON n pl. -S ebony

EBONIES pl. of ebony

EBONISE v -ISED, -ISING, -ISES to ebonize

EBONITE n pl. -S a hard rubber

EBONIZE v -IZED, -IZING, -IZES to stain black in imitation of ebony

EBONY n pl. -NIES a hard, heavy wood

ECARTE n pl. -S a card game

ECAUDATE adj having no tail

ECBOLIC n pl. -S a type of drug

ECCLESIA n pl. -SIAE an assembly in ancient Greece

ECCRINE adj producing secretions externally

ECDYSIS n pl. -DYSES the shedding of an outer layer of skin ECDYSIAL adj

ECDYSON n pl. -S ecdysone

ECDYSONE n pl. -S an insect hormone

ECESIS n pl. -SISES the establishment of a plant or animal in a new environment

ECHARD n pl. -S the water in the soil not available to plants

ECHE v ECHED, ECHING, ECHES to increase

ECHELLE n pl. -S a device for spreading light into its component colors

ECHELON v -ED, -ING, -S to group in a particular formation

ECHIDNA n pl. -NAS or -NAE a spiny anteater

ECHINATE adj spiny

ECHING present participle of eche

ECHINOID n pl. -S a spiny marine animal

ECHINUS n pl. -NI echinoid

ECHO v -ED, -ING, -ES to produce an echo

ECHO n pl. ECHOES or ECHOS a repetition of sound by reflection of sound waves

ECHOER n pl. -S one that echoes

ECHOEY adj full of echoes

ECHOGRAM n pl. -S a record produced by a device that uses ultrasonic waves

ECHOIC adj resembling an echo

ECHOISM n pl. -S the formation of words in imitation of sounds

ECHOLESS adj producing no echo

ECLAIR n pl. -S a type of pastry

ECLAT n pl. -S brilliance

ECLECTIC n pl. -S one who draws his beliefs from various sources

ECLIPSE v ECLIPSED, ECLIPSING, ECLIPSES to obscure

ECLIPSIS n pl. ECLIPSES or ECLIPSISES an ellipsis

ECLIPTIC n pl. -S an astronomical plane

ECLOGITE n pl. -S a type of rock

ECLOGUE n pl. -S a pastoral poem

ECLOSION n pl. -S the emergence of an insect larva from an egg

ECOCIDE n pl. -S the destruction of the natural environment ECOCIDAL adj

ECOFREAK n pl. -S a zealous environmentalist

ECOLOGY *n pl.* -GIES an environmental science ECOLOGIC *adj*

ECONOBOX *n pl.* -ES a small economical car

ECONOMIC *adj* pertaining to financial matters

ECONOMY *n pl.* -MIES thrift

ECOTONE *n pl.* -S a type of ecological zone ECOTONAL *adj*

ECOTYPE *n pl.* -S a subspecies adapted to specific environmental conditions ECOTYPIC *adj*

ECRASEUR *n pl.* -S a surgical instrument

ECRU *n pl.* -S a yellowish brown color

ECSTASY *n pl.* -SIES a state of exaltation

ECSTATIC *n pl.* -S one that is subject to ecstasies

ECTASIS *n pl.* -TASES the lengthening of a usually short syllable ECTATIC *adj*

ECTHYMA *n pl.* -MATA a virus disease

ECTODERM *n pl.* -S the outermost germ layer of an embryo

ECTOMERE *n pl.* -S a cell that develops into ectoderm

ECTOPIA *n pl.* -S congenital displacement of parts or organs ECTOPIC *adj*

ECTOSARC *n pl.* -S the outermost layer of protoplasm of certain protozoans

ECTOZOAN *n pl.* -S ectozoon

ECTOZOON *n pl.* -ZOA a parasite on the body of an animal

ECTYPE *n pl.* -S a copy ECTYPAL *adj*

ECU *n pl.* -S an old French coin

ECUMENIC *adj* universal

ECZEMA *n pl.* -S a skin disease

ED *n pl.* ED education

EDACIOUS *adj* voracious

EDACITY *n pl.* -TIES gluttony

EDAPHIC *adj* pertaining to the soil

EDDO *n pl.* -DOES a tropical plant

EDDY *v* -DIED, -DYING, -DIES to move against the main current

EDEMA *n pl.* -MAS or -MATA an excessive accumulation of serous fluid

EDENIC *adj* pertaining to a paradise

EDENTATE *n pl.* -S a toothless mammal

EDGE *v* EDGED, EDGING, EDGES to provide with an edge (a bounding or dividing line)

EDGELESS *adj* lacking an edge

EDGER *n pl.* -S a tool used to trim a lawn's edge

EDGEWAYS *adv* edgewise

EDGEWISE *adv* sideways

EDGIER comparative of edgy

EDGIEST superlative of edgy

EDGILY *adv* in an edgy manner

EDGINESS *n pl.* -ES the state of being edgy

EDGING *n pl.* -S something that forms or serves as an edge

EDGY *adj* EDGIER, EDGIEST tense, nervous, or irritable

EDH *n pl.* -S an Old English letter

EDIBLE *n pl.* -S something fit to be eaten

EDICT *n pl.* -S an authoritative order having the force of law EDICTAL *adj*

EDIFICE *n pl.* -S a building

EDIFIER *n pl.* -S one that edifies

EDIFY *v* -FIED, -FYING, -FIES to enlighten

EDILE *n pl.* -S aedile

EDIT *v* -ED, -ING, -S to correct and prepare for publication EDITABLE *adj*

EDITION *n pl.* -S a particular series of printed material

EDITOR *n pl.* -S one that edits

EDITRESS *n pl.* -ES a female editor

EDUCABLE *n pl.* -S a mildly retarded person

EDUCATE *v* -CATED, -CATING, -CATES to teach

EDUCATOR *n pl.* -S one that educates

EDUCE *v* EDUCED, EDUCING, EDUCES to draw forth or bring out EDUCIBLE *adj*

EDUCT *n pl.* -S something educed

EDUCTION *n pl.* -S the act of educing EDUCTIVE *adj*

EDUCTOR *n pl.* -S one that educes

EEL *n pl.* -S a snakelike fish

EELGRASS *n pl.* -ES an aquatic plant

EELIER comparative of eely

EELIEST superlative of eely

EELLIKE *adj* resembling an eel

EELPOUT *n pl.* -S a marine fish

EELWORM *n pl.* -S a small roundworm

EELY *adj* EELIER, EELIEST resembling an eel

EERIE *adj* -RIER, -RIEST weird EERILY *adv*

EERINESS *n pl.* -ES the state of being eerie

EERY	adj -RIER, -RIEST eerie	**EGGNOG**	n pl. -S a beverage
EF	n pl. -S the letter F	**EGGPLANT**	n pl. -S a perennial herb yielding edible fruit
EFF	n pl. -S ef		
EFFABLE	adj capable of being uttered or expressed	**EGGSHELL**	n pl. -S the hard exterior of a bird's egg
EFFACE	v -FACED, -FACING, -FACES to rub or wipe out	**EGGY**	adj containing eggs
		EGIS	n pl. EGISES aegis
EFFACER	n pl. -S one that effaces	**EGLATERE**	n pl. -S a wild rose
EFFECT	v -ED, -ING, -S to bring about	**EGLOMISE**	adj made of glass with a painted picture on the back
EFFECTER	n pl. -S effector		
EFFECTOR	n pl. -S a bodily organ that responds to a nerve impulse	**EGO**	n pl. EGOS the conscious self
		EGOISM	n pl. -S extreme devotion to self-interest
EFFENDI	n pl. -S a Turkish title of respect		
		EGOIST	n pl. -S one who practices egoism EGOISTIC adj
EFFERENT	n pl. -S an organ or part conveying nervous impulses to an effector		
		EGOLESS	adj not characterized by egoism
EFFETE	adj exhausted of vigor or energy EFFETELY adv		
		EGOMANIA	n pl. -S extreme egotism
EFFICACY	n pl. -CIES effectiveness	**EGOTISM**	n pl. -S self-conceit
EFFIGIAL	adj resembling an effigy	**EGOTIST**	n pl. -S a conceited person
EFFIGY	n pl. -GIES a likeness or representation	**EGRESS**	v -ED, -ING, -ES to go out
		EGRET	n pl. -S a wading bird
EFFLUENT	n pl. -S an outflow	**EGYPTIAN**	n pl. -S a typeface with squared serifs
EFFLUVIA	n/pl byproducts in the form of waste		
		EH	interj — used to express doubt or surprise
EFFLUX	n pl. -ES an outflow		
EFFORT	n pl. -S a deliberate exertion	**EIDE**	pl. of eidos
EFFULGE	v -FULGED, -FULGING, -FULGES to shine forth	**EIDER**	n pl. -S a large sea duck
		EIDETIC	adj pertaining to vivid recall
		EIDOLIC	adj pertaining to an eidolon
EFFUSE	v -FUSED, -FUSING, -FUSES to pour forth	**EIDOLON**	n pl. -LONS or -LA a phantom
		EIDOS	n pl. EIDE an essence
EFFUSION	n pl. -S an outpouring of emotion	**EIGHT**	n pl. -S a number
		EIGHTEEN	n pl. -S a number
EFFUSIVE	adj pouring forth	**EIGHTH**	n pl. -S one of eight equal parts
EFT	n pl. -S a newt		
EFTSOON	adv soon afterward	**EIGHTHLY**	adv in the eighth place
EFTSOONS	adv eftsoon	**EIGHTVO**	n pl. -VOS octavo
EGAD	interj — used as a mild oath	**EIGHTY**	n pl. EIGHTIES a number
EGADS	interj egad	**EIKON**	n pl. -S or -ES icon
EGAL	adj equal	**EINKORN**	n pl. -S a variety of wheat
EGALITE	n pl. -S equality	**EINSTEIN**	n pl. -S a very intelligent person
EGER	n pl. -S eagre		
EGEST	v -ED, -ING, -S to discharge from the body	**EIRENIC**	adj irenic
		EISWEIN	n pl. -S a sweet German wine
EGESTA	n/pl egested matter	**EITHER**	adj being one or the other
EGESTION	n pl. -S the act of egesting EGESTIVE adj	**EJECT**	v -ED, -ING, -S to throw out forcibly
EGG	v -ED, -ING, -S to incite or urge	**EJECTA**	n/pl ejected material
		EJECTION	n pl. -S the act of ejecting
EGGAR	n pl. -S egger	**EJECTIVE**	n pl. -S a sound produced with air compressed above the closed glottis
EGGCUP	n pl. -S a cup from which an egg is eaten		
		EJECTOR	n pl. -S one that ejects
EGGER	n pl. S a kind of moth	**EKE**	v EKED, EKING, EKES to supplement with great effort
EGGHEAD	n pl. -S an intellectual		
EGGLESS	adj lacking eggs		

EKISTICS *n/pl* a science dealing with human habitats **EKISTIC** *adj*

EKPWELE *n* pl. -S a former monetary unit of Equatorial Guinea

EKTEXINE *n* pl. -S an outer layer of the exine

EKUELE *n* pl. EKUELE ekpwele

EL *n* pl. -S an elevated railroad or train

ELAIN *n* pl. -S olein

ELAN *n* pl. -S enthusiasm

ELAND *n* pl. -S a large antelope

ELAPHINE *adj* pertaining to a genus of deer

ELAPID *n* pl. -S a venomous snake

ELAPINE *adj* pertaining to a family of snakes

ELAPSE *v* ELAPSED, ELAPSING, ELAPSES to pass away

ELASTASE *n* pl. -S an enzyme

ELASTIC *n* pl. -S a stretchable material

ELASTIN *n* pl. -S a bodily protein

ELATE *v* ELATED, ELATING, ELATES to raise the spirits of **ELATEDLY** *adv*

ELATER *n* pl. -S a click beetle

ELATERID *n* pl. -S an elater

ELATERIN *n* pl. -S a chemical compound

ELATING present participle of elate

ELATION *n* pl. -S a feeling of great joy

ELATIVE *n* pl. -S an adjectival form in some languages

ELBOW *v* -ED, -ING, -S to jostle

ELD *n* pl. -S old age

ELDER *n* pl. -S an older person

ELDERLY *n* pl. -LIES a rather old person

ELDEST *adj* oldest

ELDRESS *n* pl. -ES a female elder (a church officer)

ELDRICH *adj* eldritch

ELDRITCH *adj* weird

ELECT *v* -ED, -ING, -S to select by vote for an office

ELECTEE *n* pl. -S a person who has been elected

ELECTION *n* pl. -S the act of electing

ELECTIVE *n* pl. -S an optional course of study

ELECTOR *n* pl. -S one that elects

ELECTRET *n* pl. -S a type of nonconductor

ELECTRIC *n* pl. -S something run by electricity

ELECTRO *v* -ED, -ING, -S to make a metallic copy of a page of type for printing

ELECTRON *n* pl. -S an elementary particle

ELECTRUM *n* pl. -S an alloy of gold and silver

ELEGANCE *n* pl. -S tasteful opulence

ELEGANCY *n* pl. -CIES elegance

ELEGANT *adj* tastefully opulent

ELEGIAC *n* pl. -S a type of verse

ELEGIES pl. of elegy

ELEGISE *v* -GISED, -GISING, -GISES to elegize

ELEGIST *n* pl. -S one that writes elegies

ELEGIT *n* pl. -S a type of judicial writ

ELEGIZE *v* -GIZED, -GIZING, -GIZES to write an elegy

ELEGY *n* pl. -GIES a mournful poem for one who is dead

ELEMENT *n* pl. -S a substance that cannot be separated into simpler substances by chemical means

ELEMI *n* pl. -S a fragrant resin

ELENCHUS *n* pl. -CHI a logical refutation **ELENCHIC, ELENCTIC** *adj*

ELEPHANT *n* pl. -S a large mammal

ELEVATE *v* -VATED, -VATING, -VATES to raise

ELEVATED *n* pl. -S a railway that operates on a raised structure

ELEVATOR *n* pl. -S one that elevates

ELEVEN *n* pl. -S a number

ELEVENTH *n* pl. -S one of eleven equal parts

ELEVON *n* pl. -S a type of airplane control surface

ELF *n* pl. ELVES a small, often mischievous fairy **ELFLIKE** *adj*

ELFIN *n* pl. -S an elf

ELFISH *adj* resembling an elf **ELFISHLY** *adv*

ELFLOCK *n* pl. -S a lock of tangled hair

ELHI *adj* pertaining to school grades 1 through 12

ELICIT *v* -ED, -ING, -S to educe

ELICITOR *n* pl. -S one that elicits

ELIDE *v* ELIDED, ELIDING, ELIDES to omit **ELIDIBLE** *adj*

ELIGIBLE *n* pl. -S one that is qualified to be chosen

ELIGIBLY *adv* in a qualified manner

ELINT *n* pl. -S the gathering of intelligence by electronic devices

ELISION *n* pl. -S the act of eliding

ELITE *n* pl. -S a socially superior group

ELITISM	n pl. -S belief in rule by an elite	**ELYTRON**	n pl. -TRA a hardened forewing of certain insects ELYTROID, ELYTROUS adj
ELITIST	n pl. -S an adherent of elitism		
ELIXIR	n pl. -S a medicinal beverage	**ELYTRUM**	n pl. -TRA elytron
ELK	n pl. -S a large deer	**EM**	n pl. -S the letter M
ELKHOUND	n pl. -S a hunting dog	**EMACIATE**	v -ATED, -ATING, -ATES to make thin
ELL	n pl. -S the letter L		
ELLIPSE	n pl. -S a type of plane curve	**EMANATE**	v -NATED, -NATING, -NATES to send forth
ELLIPSIS	n pl. -LIPSES an omission of a word or words in a sentence		
		EMANATOR	n pl. -S one that emanates
ELLIPTIC	adj having the shape of an ellipse	**EMBALM**	v -ED, -ING, -S to treat so as to protect from decay
ELM	n pl. -S a deciduous tree	**EMBALMER**	n pl. -S one that embalms
ELMY	adj -MIER, -MIEST abounding in elms	**EMBANK**	v -ED, -ING, -S to confine or protect with a raised structure
ELODEA	n pl. -S an aquatic herb	**EMBAR**	v -BARRED, -BARRING, -BARS to imprison
ELOIGN	v -ED, -ING, -S to remove to a distant place		
		EMBARGO	v -ED, -ING, -ES to restrain trade by a governmental order
ELOIGNER	n pl. -S one that eloigns		
ELOIN	v -ED, -ING, -S to eloign	**EMBARK**	v -ED, -ING, -S to make a start
ELOINER	n pl. -S one that eloins		
ELONGATE	v -GATED, -GATING, -GATES to lengthen	**EMBARRED**	past tense of embar
		EMBARRING	present participle of embar
ELOPE	v ELOPED, ELOPING, ELOPES to run off secretly to be married	**EMBASSY**	n pl. -SIES the headquarters of an ambassador
		EMBATTLE	v -TLED, -TLING, -TLES to prepare for battle
ELOPER	n pl. -S one that elopes		
ELOQUENT	adj fluent and convincing in speech	**EMBAY**	v -ED, -ING, -S to enclose in a bay
ELSE	adv in a different place, time, or way	**EMBED**	v -BEDDED, -BEDDING, -BEDS to fix firmly into a surrounding mass
ELUANT	n pl. -S a solvent		
ELUATE	n pl. -S the material obtained by eluting	**EMBER**	n pl. -S a glowing fragment from a fire
		EMBEZZLE	v -ZLED, -ZLING, -ZLES to appropriate fraudulently to one's own use
ELUDE	v ELUDED, ELUDING, ELUDES to evade		
ELUDER	n pl. -S one that eludes		
ELUENT	n pl. -S eluant	**EMBITTER**	v -ED, -ING, -S to make bitter
ELUSION	n pl. -S the act of eluding	**EMBLAZE**	v -BLAZED, -BLAZING, -BLAZES to set on fire
ELUSIVE	adj tending to elude		
ELUSORY	adj elusive	**EMBLAZER**	n pl. -S one that emblazes
ELUTE	v ELUTED, ELUTING, ELUTES to remove by means of a solvent	**EMBLAZON**	v -ED, -ING, -S to decorate with brilliant colors
		EMBLEM	v -ED, -ING, -S to represent with an emblem (a graphical symbol)
ELUTION	n pl. -S the act of eluting		
ELUVIA	a pl. of eluvium		
ELUVIAL	adj pertaining to an eluvium	**EMBODIER**	n pl. -S one that embodies
ELUVIATE	v -ATED, -ATING, -ATES to undergo a transfer of materials in the soil	**EMBODY**	v -BODIED, -BODYING, -BODIES to provide with a body
ELUVIUM	n pl. -VIA or -VIUMS a soil deposit	**EMBOLDEN**	v -ED, -ING, -S to instill with courage
ELVER	n pl. -S a young eel		
ELVES	pl. of elf	**EMBOLI**	pl. of embolus
ELVISH	adj elfish ELVISHLY adv	**EMBOLIES**	pl. of emboly
ELYSIAN	adj delightful		

EMBOLISM *n pl.* -S the obstruction of a blood vessel by an embolus **EMBOLIC** *adj*

EMBOLUS *n pl.* -LI an abnormal particle circulating in the blood

EMBOLY *n pl.* -LIES a phase of embryonic growth

EMBORDER *v* -ED, -ING, -S to provide with a border

EMBOSK *v* -ED, -ING, -S to conceal with foliage

EMBOSOM *v* -ED, -ING, -S to embrace

EMBOSS *v* -ED, -ING, -ES to decorate with raised designs

EMBOSSER *n pl.* -S one that embosses

EMBOW *v* -ED, -ING, -S to arch

EMBOWEL *v* -ELED, -ELING, -ELS or -ELLED, -ELLING, -ELS to disbowel

EMBOWER *v* -ED, -ING, -S to surround with foliage

EMBRACE *v* -BRACED, -BRACING, -BRACES to hug

EMBRACER *n pl.* -S one that embraces

EMBROIL *v* -ED, -ING, -S to involve in conflict

EMBROWN *v* -ED, -ING, -S to make brown

EMBRUE *v* -BRUED, -BRUING, -BRUES to imbrue

EMBRUTE *v* -BRUTED, -BRUTING, -BRUTES to imbrute

EMBRYO *n pl.* -BRYOS an organism in its early stages of development

EMBRYOID *n pl.* -S a mass of tissue that resembles an embryo

EMBRYON *n pl.* -S an embryo

EMCEE *v* -CEED, -CEEING, -CEES to serve as master of ceremonies

EME *n pl.* -S an uncle

EMEER *n pl.* -S emir

EMEERATE *n pl.* -S emirate

EMEND *v* -ED, -ING, -S to correct

EMENDATE *v* -DATED, -DATING, -DATES to emend

EMENDER *n pl.* -S one that emends

EMERALD *n pl.* -S a green gem

EMERGE *v* EMERGED, EMERGING, EMERGES to come out into view

EMERGENT *n pl.* -S a type of aquatic plant

EMERIES pl. of emery

EMERITA *n pl.* -TAE a retired woman who retains an honorary title

EMERITUS *n pl.* -TI a retired person who retains an honorary title

EMEROD *n pl.* -S a tumor

EMEROID *n pl.* -S emerod

EMERSED *adj* standing out of water

EMERSION *n pl.* -S the act of emerging

EMERY *n pl.* -ERIES a granular corundum

EMESIS *n pl.* EMESES the act of vomiting

EMETIC *n pl.* -S a substance which induces vomiting

EMETIN *n pl.* -S emetine

EMETINE *n pl.* -S an alkaloid

EMEU *n pl.* -S an emu

EMEUTE *n pl.* -S a riot

EMF *n pl.* -S a difference in electric potential

EMIC *adj* relating to a type of linguistic analysis

EMIGRANT *n pl.* -S one that emigrates

EMIGRATE *v* -GRATED, -GRATING, -GRATES to leave one country or region to settle in another

EMIGRE *n pl.* -S an emigrant

EMINENCE *n pl.* -S high station or rank

EMINENCY *n pl.* -CIES eminence

EMINENT *adj* of high station or rank

EMIR *n pl.* -S an Arab chieftain or prince

EMIRATE *n pl.* -S the rank of an emir

EMISSARY *n pl.* -SARIES a person sent on a mission

EMISSION *n pl.* -S the act of emitting **EMISSIVE** *adj*

EMIT *v* EMITTED, EMITTING, EMITS to send forth

EMITTER *n pl.* -S one that emits

EMMER *n pl.* -S a type of wheat

EMMET *n pl.* -S an ant

EMODIN *n pl.* -S a chemical compound

EMOTE *v* EMOTED, EMOTING, EMOTES to express emotion in an exaggerated manner

EMOTER *n pl.* -S one that emotes

EMOTION *n pl.* -S an affective state of consciousness

EMOTIVE *adj* pertaining to emotion

EMPALE *v* -PALED, -PALING, -PALES to impale

EMPALER *n pl.* -S one that empales

EMPANADA *n pl.* -S a pastry turnover

EMPANEL *v* -ELED, -ELING, -ELS or -ELLED, -ELLING, -ELS to impanel

EMPATHY *n pl.* -THIES imaginative identification with another's thoughts and feelings **EMPATHIC** *adj*

EMPEROR *n pl.* -S the ruler of an empire

EMPERY *n pl.* -PERIES absolute dominion

EMPHASIS *n pl.* -PHASES special significance imparted to something

EMPHATIC *adj* strongly expressive

EMPIRE *n pl.* -S a major political unit

EMPIRIC *n pl.* -S one who relies on practical experience

EMPLACE *v* -PLACED, -PLACING, -PLACES to position

EMPLANE *v* -PLANED, -PLANING, -PLANES to enplane

EMPLOY *v* -ED -ING, -S to hire

EMPLOYE *n pl.* -S employee

EMPLOYEE *n pl.* -S a person who is employed

EMPLOYER *n pl.* -S one that employs

EMPOISON *v* -ED, -ING, -S to embitter

EMPORIUM *n pl.* -RIUMS or -RIA a trading or market center

EMPOWER *v* -ED, -ING, -S to give legal power to

EMPRESS *n pl.* -ES a female ruler of an empire

EMPRISE *n pl.* -S an adventurous undertaking

EMPRIZE *n pl.* -S emprise

EMPTIED past tense of empty

EMPTIER *n pl.* -S one that empties

EMPTIES present 3d person sing. of empty

EMPTIEST superlative of empty

EMPTILY *adv* in an empty manner

EMPTINGS *n/pl* emptins

EMPTINS *n/pl* a liquid leavening

EMPTY *adj* -TIER, -TIEST containing nothing

EMPTY *v* -TIED, -TYING, -TIES to remove the contents of

EMPURPLE *v* -PLED, -PLING, -PLES to tinge with purple

EMPYEMA *n pl.* -EMATA or -EMAS a collection of pus in a body cavity **EMPYEMIC** *adj*

EMPYREAL *adj* pertaining to the sky

EMPYREAN *n pl.* -S the highest heaven

EMU *n pl.* -S a large, flightless bird

EMULATE *v* -LATED, -LATING, -LATES to try to equal or surpass

EMULATOR *n pl.* -S one that emulates

EMULOUS *adj* eager to equal or surpass another

EMULSIFY *v* -FIED, -FYING, -FIES to make into an emulsion

EMULSION *n pl.* -S a type of liquid mixture **EMULSIVE** *adj*

EMULSOID *n pl.* -S a liquid dispersed in another liquid

EMYD *n pl.* -S a freshwater tortoise

EMYDE *n pl.* -S emyd

EN *n pl.* -S the letter N

ENABLE *v* -BLED, -BLING, -BLES to make possible

ENABLER *n pl.* -S one that enables

ENACT *v* -ED, -ING, -S to make into a law

ENACTIVE *adj* having the power to enact

ENACTOR *n pl.* -S one that enacts

ENACTORY *adj* pertaining to the enactment of law

ENAMEL *v* -ELED, -ELING, -ELS or -ELLED, -ELLING, -ELS to cover with a hard, glossy surface

ENAMELER *n pl.* -S one that enamels

ENAMINE *n pl.* -S a type of amine

ENAMOR *v* -ED, -ING, -S to inspire with love

ENAMOUR *v* -ED, -ING, -S to enamor

ENATE *n pl.* -S a relative on the mother's side **ENATIC** *adj*

ENATION *n pl.* -S an outgrowth from the surface of an organ

ENCAENIA *n/pl* annual university ceremonies

ENCAGE *v* -CAGED, -CAGING, -CAGES to confine in a cage

ENCAMP *v* -ED, -ING, -S to set up a camp

ENCASE *v* -CASED, -CASING, -CASES to enclose in a case

ENCASH *v* -ED, -ING, -ES to cash

ENCEINTE *n pl.* -S an encircling fortification

ENCHAIN *v* -ED, -ING, -S to bind with chains

ENCHANT *v* -ED, -ING, -S to delight

ENCHASE *v* -CHASED, -CHASING, -CHASES to place in an ornamental setting

ENCHASER *n pl.* -S one that enchases

ENCHORIC *adj* belonging to a particular country

ENCINA *n pl.* -S an evergreen oak **ENCINAL** *adj*

ENCIPHER v -ED, -ING, -S to write in characters of hidden meaning

ENCIRCLE v -CLED, -CLING, -CLES to form a circle around

ENCLASP v -ED, -ING, -S to embrace

ENCLAVE n pl. -S a territorial unit enclosed within foreign territory

ENCLITIC n pl. -S a word pronounced as part of the preceding word

ENCLOSE v -CLOSED, -CLOSING, -CLOSES to close in on all sides

ENCLOSER n pl. -S one that encloses

ENCODE v -CODED, -CODING, -CODES to put into code

ENCODER n pl. -S one that encodes

ENCOMIUM n pl. -MIUMS or -MIA a eulogy

ENCORE v -CORED, -CORING, -CORES to call for the reappearance of a performer

ENCROACH v -ED, -ING, -ES to advance beyond the proper limits

ENCRUST v -ED, -ING, -S to cover with a crust

ENCRYPT v -ED, -ING, -S to encipher

ENCUMBER v -ED, -ING, -S to hinder in action or movement

ENCYCLIC n pl. -S a letter addressed by the pope to the bishops of the world

ENCYST v -ED, -ING, -S to enclose in a cyst

END v -ED, -ING, -S to terminate

ENDAMAGE v -AGED, -AGING, -AGES to damage

ENDAMEBA n pl. -BAS or -BAE a parasitic ameba

ENDANGER v -ED, -ING, -S to imperil

ENDARCH adj formed from the center outward

ENDARCHY n pl. -CHIES the condition of being endarch

ENDBRAIN n pl. -S a part of the brain

ENDEAR v -ED, -ING, -S to make dear or beloved

ENDEAVOR v -ED, -ING, -S to make an effort

ENDEMIAL adj peculiar to a country or people

ENDEMIC n pl. -S an endemial disease

ENDEMISM n pl. -S the state of being endemial

ENDER n pl. -S one that ends something

ENDERMIC adj acting by absorption through the skin

ENDEXINE n pl. -S an inner layer of the exine

ENDGAME n pl. -S the last stage of a chess game

ENDING n pl. -S a termination

ENDITE v -DITED, -DITING, -DITES to indite

ENDIVE n pl. -S an herb cultivated as a salad plant

ENDLEAF n pl. -LEAVES an endpaper

ENDLESS adj enduring forever

ENDLONG adv lengthwise

ENDMOST adj farthest

ENDNOTE n pl. -S a note placed at the end of the text

ENDOCARP n pl. -S the inner layer of a pericarp

ENDOCAST n pl. -S a cast of the cranial cavity

ENDODERM n pl. -S the innermost germ layer of an embryo

ENDOGAMY n pl. -MIES marriage within a particular group

ENDOGEN n pl. -S a type of plant

ENDOGENY n pl. -NIES growth from within

ENDOPOD n pl. -S a branch of a crustacean limb

ENDORSE v -DORSED, -DORSING, -DORSES to sign the back of a negotiable document

ENDORSEE n pl. -S one to whom a document is transferred by endorsement

ENDORSER n pl. -S one that endorses

ENDORSING present participle of endorse

ENDORSOR n pl. -S endorser

ENDOSARC n pl. -S a portion of a cell

ENDOSMOS n pl. -ES a form of osmosis

ENDOSOME n pl. -S a cellular particle

ENDOSTEA n/pl bone membranes

ENDOW v -ED, -ING, -S to provide with something

ENDOWER n pl. -S one that endows

ENDOZOIC adj involving passage through an animal

ENDPAPER n pl. -S a sheet of paper used in bookbinding

ENDPLATE n pl. -S a type of nerve terminal

ENDPOINT n pl. -S either of two points that mark the end of a line segment

ENDRIN n pl. -S an insecticide

ENDUE v -DUED, -DUING, -DUES to provide with some quality or gift

ENDURE v -DURED, -DURING, -DURES to last

ENDURO n pl. -DUROS a long race

ENDWAYS adv endwise

ENDWISE adv lengthwise

ENEMA n pl. -MAS or -MATA a liquid injected into the rectum

ENEMY n pl. -MIES one that is antagonistic toward another

ENERGID n pl. -S a nucleus and the body of cytoplasm with which it interacts

ENERGIES pl. of energy

ENERGISE v -GISED, -GISING, -GISES to energize

ENERGIZE v -GIZED, -GIZING, -GIZES to give energy to

ENERGY n -GIES the capacity for vigorous activity

ENERVATE v -VATED, -VATING, -VATES to deprive of strength or vitality

ENFACE v -FACED, -FACING, -FACES to write on the front of

ENFEEBLE v -BLED, -BLING, -BLES to make feeble

ENFEOFF v -ED, -ING, -S to invest with a feudal estate

ENFETTER v -ED, -ING, -S to enchain

ENFEVER v -ED, -ING, -S to fever

ENFILADE v -LADED, -LADING, -LADES to direct heavy gunfire along the length of

ENFLAME v -FLAMED, -FLAMING, -FLAMES to inflame

ENFOLD v -ED, -ING, -S to envelop

ENFOLDER n pl. -S one that enfolds

ENFORCE v -FORCED, -FORCING, -FORCES to compel obedience to

ENFORCER n pl. -S one that enforces

ENFRAME v -FRAMED, -FRAMING, -FRAMES to frame

ENG n pl. -S a phonetic symbol

ENGAGE v -GAGED, -GAGING, -GAGES to employ

ENGAGER n pl. -S one that engages

ENGENDER v -ED, -ING, -S to bring into existence

ENGILD v -ED, -ING, -S to brighten

ENGINE v -GINED, -GINING, -GINES to equip with machinery

ENGINEER v -ED, -ING, -S to carry through or manage by contrivance

ENGINERY n pl. -RIES machinery

ENGINING present participle of engine

ENGINOUS adj ingenious

ENGIRD v -GIRT or -GIRDED, -GIRDING, -GIRDS to gird

ENGIRDLE v -DLED, -DLING, -DLES to engird

ENGLISH v -ED, -ING, -ES to cause a billiard ball to spin around its vertical axis

ENGLUT v -GLUTTED, -GLUTTING, -GLUTS to gulp down

ENGORGE v -GORGED, -GORGING, -GORGES to fill with blood

ENGRAFT v -ED, -ING, -S to graft for propagation

ENGRAIL v -ED, -ING, -S to ornament the edge of with curved indentations

ENGRAIN v -ED, -ING, -S to ingrain

ENGRAM n pl. -S the durable mark caused by a stimulus upon protoplasm

ENGRAMME n pl. -S engram

ENGRAVE v -GRAVED, -GRAVING, -GRAVES to form by incision

ENGRAVER n pl. -S one that engraves

ENGROSS v -ED, -ING, -ES to occupy completely

ENGULF v -ED, -ING, -S to surround completely

ENHALO v -ED, -ING, -ES or -S to surround with a halo

ENHANCE v -HANCED, -HANCING, -HANCES to raise to a higher degree

ENHANCER n pl. -S one that enhances

ENIGMA n pl. -MAS or -MATA something that is hard to understand or explain

ENISLE v -ISLED, -ISLING, -ISLES to isolate

ENJAMBED adj marked by the continuation of a sentence from one line of a poem to the next

ENJOIN v -ED, -ING, -S to command

ENJOINER n pl. -S one that enjoins

ENJOY v -ED, -ING, -S to receive pleasure from

ENJOYER n pl. -S one that enjoys

ENKINDLE v -DLED, -DLING, -DLES to set on fire

ENLACE v -LACED, -LACING, -LACES to bind with laces

ENLARGE v -LARGED, -LARGING, -LARGES to make or become larger

ENLARGER n pl. -S a device used to enlarge photographs

ENLIST v -ED, -ING, -S to engage for military service

ENLISTEE n pl. -S one that is enlisted

ENLISTER n pl. -S one that enlists

ENLIVEN v -ED, -ING, -S to make lively

ENMESH v -ED, -ING, -ES to ensnare or entangle in a net

ENMITY n pl. -TIES hostility

ENNEAD n pl. -S a group of nine
ENNEADIC adj

ENNEAGON n pl. -S a nonagon

ENNOBLE v -BLED, -BLING, -BLES to make noble

ENNOBLER n pl. -S one that ennobles

ENNUI n pl. -S a feeling of weariness and discontent

ENNUYE adj oppressed with ennui

ENNUYEE adj ennuye

ENOKI n pl. -S a small mushroom

ENOL n pl. -S a chemical compound
ENOLIC adj

ENOLASE n pl. -S an enzyme

ENOLOGY n pl. -GIES oenology

ENORM adj enormous

ENORMITY n pl. -TIES a grave offense against decency

ENORMOUS adj huge

ENOSIS n pl. -SISES union

ENOUGH n pl. -S a sufficient supply

ENOUNCE v ENOUNCED, ENOUNCING, ENOUNCES to announce

ENOW n pl. -S enough

ENPLANE v -PLANED, -PLANING, -PLANES to board an airplane

ENQUIRE v -QUIRED, -QUIRING, -QUIRES to inquire

ENQUIRY n pl. -RIES inquiry

ENRAGE v -RAGED, -RAGING, -RAGES to make very angry

ENRAPT adj rapt

ENRAVISH v -ED, -ING, -ES to delight greatly

ENRICH v -ED, -ING, -ES to add desirable elements to

ENRICHER n pl. -S one that enriches

ENROBE v -ROBED, -ROBING, -ROBES to dress

ENROBER n pl. -S one that enrobes

ENROL v -ROLLED, -ROLLING, -ROLS to enroll

ENROLL v -ED, -ING, -S to enter the name of on a list

ENROLLEE n pl. -S one that is enrolled

ENROLLER n pl. -S one that enrolls

ENROLLING present participle of enrol

ENROOT v -ED, -ING, -S to implant

ENS n pl. ENTIA an entity

ENSAMPLE n pl. -S an example

ENSCONCE v -SCONCED, -SCONCING, -SCONCES to settle securely or comfortably

ENSCROLL v -ED, -ING, -S to write on a scroll

ENSEMBLE n pl. -S a group of complementary parts

ENSERF v -ED, -ING, -S to make a serf of

ENSHEATH v -ED, -ING, -S to enclose in a sheath

ENSHRINE v -SHRINED, -SHRINING, -SHRINES to place in a shrine

ENSHROUD v -ED, -ING, -S to conceal

ENSIFORM adj sword-shaped

ENSIGN n pl. -S a navy officer

ENSIGNCY n pl. -CIES the rank of an ensign

ENSILAGE v -LAGED, -LAGING, -LAGES to ensile

ENSILE v -SILED, -SILING, -SILES to store in a silo

ENSKY v -SKIED or -SKYED, -SKYING, -SKIES to raise to the skies

ENSLAVE v -SLAVED, -SLAVING, -SLAVES to make a slave of

ENSLAVER n pl. -S one that enslaves

ENSNARE v -SNARED, -SNARING, -SNARES to trap

ENSNARER n pl. -S one that ensnares

ENSNARL v -ED, -ING, -S to tangle

ENSORCEL v -ED, -ING, -S to bewitch

ENSOUL v -ED, -ING, -S to endow with a soul

ENSPHERE v -SPHERED, -SPHERING, -SPHERES to enclose in a sphere

ENSUE v -SUED, -SUING, -SUES to occur afterward or as a result

ENSURE v -SURED, -SURING, -SURES to make certain

ENSURER n pl. -S one that ensures

ENSWATHE v -SWATHED, -SWATHING, -SWATHES to swathe

ENTAIL v -ED, -ING, -S to restrict the inheritance of to a specified line of heirs

ENTAILER n pl. -S one that entails

ENTAMEBA n pl. -BAE or -BAS endameba

ENTANGLE v -TANGLED, -TANGLING, -TANGLES to tangle

ENTASIA *n pl.* -S spasmodic contraction of a muscle

ENTASIS *n pl.* -TASES a slight convexity in a column **ENTASTIC** *adj*

ENTELLUS *n pl.* -ES a hanuman

ENTENTE *n pl.* -S an agreement between nations

ENTER *v* -ED, -ING, -S to come or go into

ENTERA a *pl.* of enteron

ENTERAL *adj* enteric

ENTERER *n pl.* -S one that enters

ENTERIC *adj* pertaining to the enteron

ENTERON *n pl.* -TERONS or -TERA the alimentary canal

ENTHALPY *n pl.* -PIES a thermodynamic measure of heat

ENTHETIC *adj* introduced from outside

ENTHRAL *v* -THRALLED, -THRALLING, -THRALS to enthrall

ENTHRALL *v* -ED, -ING, -S to charm

ENTHRONE *v* -THRONED, -THRONING, -THRONES to place on a throne

ENTHUSE *v* -THUSED, -THUSING, -THUSES to show enthusiasm

ENTIA *pl.* of ens

ENTICE *v* -TICED, -TICING, -TICES to allure

ENTICER *n pl.* -S one that entices

ENTIRE *n pl.* -S the whole of something

ENTIRELY *adv* completely

ENTIRETY *n pl.* -TIES completeness

ENTITLE *v* -TLED, -TLING, -TLES to give a title to

ENTITY *n pl.* -TIES something that has a real existence

ENTODERM *n pl.* -S endoderm

ENTOIL *v* -ED, -ING, -S to entrap

ENTOMB *v* -ED, -ING, -S to place in a tomb

ENTOPIC *adj* situated in the normal place

ENTOZOA a *pl.* of entozoan and *pl.* of entozoon

ENTOZOAL *adj* entozoic

ENTOZOAN *n pl.* -ZOANS or -ZOA an entozoic parasite

ENTOZOIC *adj* living within an animal

ENTOZOON *n pl.* -ZOA entozoan

ENTRAILS *n/pl* the internal organs

ENTRAIN *v* -ED, -ING, -S to board a train

ENTRANCE *v* -TRANCED, -TRANCING, -TRANCES to fill with delight or wonder

ENTRANT *n pl.* -S one that enters

ENTRAP *v* -TRAPPED, -TRAPPING, -TRAPS to trap

ENTREAT *v* -ED, -ING, -S to ask for earnestly

ENTREATY *n pl.* -TREATIES an earnest request

ENTREE *n pl.* -S the principal dish of a meal

ENTRENCH *v* -ED, -ING, -ES to establish firmly

ENTREPOT *n pl.* -S a warehouse

ENTRESOL *n pl.* -S a mezzanine

ENTRIES *pl.* of entry

ENTROPY *n pl.* -PIES a thermodynamic measure of disorder **ENTROPIC** *adj*

ENTRUST *v* -ED, -ING, -S to give over for safekeeping

ENTRY *n pl.* -TRIES a place of entrance

ENTRYWAY *n pl.* -WAYS a passage serving as an entrance

ENTWINE *v* -TWINED, -TWINING, -TWINES to twine around

ENTWIST *v* -ED, -ING, -S to twist together

ENURE *v* -URED, -URING, -URES to inure

ENURESIS *n pl.* -SISES involuntary urination

ENURETIC *n pl.* -S one who is affected with enuresis

ENVELOP *v* -ED, -ING, -S to cover completely

ENVELOPE *n pl.* -S a paper container

ENVENOM *v* -ED, -ING, -S to put venom into

ENVIABLE *adj* desirable **ENVIABLY** *adv*

ENVIED past tense of envy

ENVIER *n pl.* -S one that envies

ENVIES present 3d person sing. of envy

ENVIOUS *adj* resentful and desirous of another's possessions or qualities

ENVIRON *v* -ED, -ING, -S to encircle

ENVISAGE *v* -AGED, -AGING, -AGES to form a mental image of

ENVISION *v* -ED, -ING, -S to envisage

ENVOI *n pl.* -S the closing of a poem or prose work

ENVOY *n pl.* -VOYS a representative

ENVY *v* -VIED, -VYING, -VIES to be envious of

ENWHEEL *v* -ED, -ING, -S to encircle

ENWIND *v* -WOUND, -WINDING, -WINDS to wind around

ENWOMB *v* -ED, -ING, -S to enclose as if in a womb

ENWRAP *v* -WRAPPED, -WRAPPING, -WRAPS to envelop

ENZOOTIC *n pl.* -S a type of animal disease

ENZYM *n pl.* -S enzyme

ENZYME *n pl.* -S a complex protein **ENZYMIC** *adj*

EOBIONT *n pl.* -S a type of basic organism

EOHIPPUS *n pl.* -ES an extinct horse

EOLIAN *adj* pertaining to the wind

EOLIPILE *n pl.* -S a type of engine

EOLITH *n pl.* -S a prehistoric stone tool **EOLITHIC** *adj*

EOLOPILE *n pl.* -S eolipile

EON *n pl.* -S an indefinitely long period of time

EONIAN *adj* everlasting

EONISM *n pl.* -S adoption of the dress and mannerisms of the opposite sex

EOSIN *n pl.* -S a red dye **EOSINIC** *adj*

EOSINE *n pl.* -S eosin

EPACT *n pl.* -S the difference between the lengths of the solar and lunar years

EPARCH *n pl.* -S the head of an eparchy

EPARCHY *n pl.* -CHIES a district of modern Greece

EPAULET *n pl.* -S a shoulder ornament

EPAZOTE *n pl.* -S an herb of the goosefoot family

EPEE *n pl.* -S a type of sword

EPEEIST *n pl.* -S one who fences with an epee

EPEIRIC *adj* pertaining to vertical movement of the earth's crust

EPENDYMA *n pl.* -S a membrane lining certain body cavities

EPERGNE *n pl.* -S an ornamental dish

EPHA *n pl.* -S ephah

EPHAH *n pl.* -S a Hebrew unit of dry measure

EPHEBE *n pl.* -S ephebus **EPHEBIC** *adj*

EPHEBOS *n pl.* -BOI ephebus

EPHEBUS *n pl.* -BI a young man of ancient Greece

EPHEDRA *n pl.* -S a desert shrub

EPHEDRIN *n pl.* -S an alkaloid used to treat allergies

EPHEMERA *n pl.* -ERAS or -ERAE something of very short life or duration

EPHOD *n pl.* -S an ancient Hebrew vestment

EPHOR *n pl.* -ORS or -ORI a magistrate of ancient Greece **EPHORAL** *adj*

EPHORATE *n pl.* -S the office of ephor

EPIBLAST *n pl.* -S the ectoderm

EPIBOLY *n pl.* -LIES the growth of one part around another **EPIBOLIC** *adj*

EPIC *n pl.* -S a long narrative poem **EPICAL** *adj* **EPICALLY** *adv*

EPICALYX *n pl.* -LYXES or -LYCES a set of bracts close to and resembling a calyx

EPICARP *n pl.* -S the outer layer of a pericarp

EPICEDIA *n/pl* funeral songs

EPICENE *n pl.* -S one having both male and female characteristics

EPICLIKE *adj* resembling an epic

EPICOTYL *n pl.* -S a part of a plant embryo

EPICURE *n pl.* -S a gourmet

EPICYCLE *n pl.* -S a circle that rolls on the circumference of another circle

EPIDEMIC *n pl.* -S a rapid spread of a disease

EPIDERM *n pl.* -S the outer layer of skin

EPIDOTE *n pl.* -S a mineral **EPIDOTIC** *adj*

EPIDURAL *adj* situated on the membrane that encloses the brain

EPIFAUNA *n pl.* -FAUNAE or -FAUNAS fauna living on a hard sea floor

EPIFOCAL *adj* pertaining to the point of origin of an earthquake

EPIGEAL *adj* epigeous

EPIGEAN *adj* epigeous

EPIGEIC *adj* epigeous

EPIGENE *adj* occurring near the surface of the earth

EPIGENIC *adj* pertaining to change in the mineral character of a rock

EPIGEOUS *adj* growing on or close to the ground

EPIGON *n pl.* -S epigone

EPIGONE *n* pl. -S an inferior imitator EPIGONIC *adj*

EPIGONUS *n* pl. -NI epigone

EPIGRAM *n* pl. -S a brief, witty remark

EPIGRAPH *n* pl. -S an engraved inscription

EPIGYNY *n* pl. -NIES the state of having floral organs near the top of the ovary

EPILEPSY *n* pl. -SIES a disorder of the nervous system

EPILOG *n* pl. -S a concluding section

EPILOGUE *v* -LOGUED, -LOGUING, -LOGUES to provide with a concluding section

EPIMER *n* pl. -S a type of sugar compound EPIMERIC *adj*

EPIMERE *n* pl. -S a part of an embryo

EPIMYSIA *n/pl* muscle sheaths

EPINAOS *n* pl. -NAOI a rear vestibule

EPINASTY *n* pl. -TIES a downward bending of plant parts

EPIPHANY *n* pl. -NIES an appearance of a deity

EPIPHYTE *n* pl. -S a plant growing upon another plant

EPISCIA *n* pl. -S a tropical herb

EPISCOPE *n* pl. -S a type of projector

EPISODE *n* pl. -S an incident in the course of a continuous experience EPISODIC *adj*

EPISOME *n* pl. -S a genetic determinant EPISOMAL *adj*

EPISTASY *n* pl. -SIES a suppression of genetic effect

EPISTLE *n* pl. -S a long or formal letter

EPISTLER *n* pl. -S one that writes epistles

EPISTOME *n* pl. -S a structure covering the mouth of various invertebrates

EPISTYLE *n* pl. -S a part of a classical building

EPITAPH *n* pl. -S an inscription on a tomb

EPITASIS *n* pl. -ASES the main part of a classical drama

EPITAXY *n* pl. -TAXIES a type of crystalline growth EPITAXIC *adj*

EPITHET *n* pl. -S a term used to characterize a person or thing

EPITOME *n* pl. -S a typical or ideal example EPITOMIC *adj*

EPITOPE *n* pl. -S a region on the surface of an antigen

EPIZOA pl. of epizoon

EPIZOIC *adj* living on the body of an animal

EPIZOISM *n* pl. -S the state of being epizoic

EPIZOITE *n* pl. -S an epizoic organism

EPIZOON *n* pl. -ZOA an epizoic parasite

EPIZOOTY *n* pl. -TIES a type of animal disease

EPOCH *n* pl. -S a particular period of time EPOCHAL *adj*

EPODE *n* pl. -S a type of poem

EPONYM *n* pl. -S the person for whom something is named EPONYMIC *adj*

EPONYMY *n* pl. -MIES the derivation of an eponymic name

EPOPEE *n* pl. -S an epic poem

EPOPOEIA *n* pl. -S epopee

EPOS *n* pl. -ES an epic poem

EPOXIDE *n* pl. -S an epoxy compound

EPOXY *v* EPOXIED or EPOXYED, EPOXYING, EPOXIES to glue with epoxy (a type of resin)

EPSILON *n* pl. -S a Greek letter

EQUABLE *adj* not changing or varying greatly EQUABLY *adv*

EQUAL *adj* having the same capability, quantity, or effect as another

EQUAL *v* EQUALED, EQUALING, EQUALS or EQUALLED, EQUALLING, EQUALS to be equal to

EQUALISE *v* -ISED, -ISING, -ISES to equalize

EQUALITY *n* pl. -TIES the state of being equal

EQUALIZE *v* -IZED, -IZING, -IZES to make equal

EQUALLED a past tense of equal

EQUALLING a past participle of equal

EQUALLY *adv* in an equal manner

EQUATE *v* EQUATED, EQUATING, EQUATES to make equal

EQUATION *n* pl. -S the act of equating

EQUATOR *n* pl. -S a great circle of spherical celestial bodies

EQUERRY *n* pl. -RIES an officer in charge of the care of horses

EQUID *n* pl. -S an animal of the horse family

EQUINE *n* pl. -S a horse

EQUINELY *adv* in a horselike manner

EQUINITY *n* pl. -TIES the state of being like a horse

EQUINOX	n pl. -ES a point on the celestial sphere
EQUIP	v EQUIPPED, EQUIPPING, EQUIPS to provide with whatever is needed
EQUIPAGE	n pl. -S a carriage
EQUIPPER	n pl. -S one that equips
EQUIPPING	present participle of equip
EQUISETA	n/pl rushlike plants
EQUITANT	adj overlapping
EQUITES	n/pl a privileged military class of ancient Rome
EQUITY	n pl. -TIES fairness or impartiality
EQUIVOKE	n pl. -S a play on words
ER	interj — used to express hesitation
ERA	n pl. -S an epoch
ERADIATE	v -ATED, -ATING, -ATES to radiate
ERASE	v ERASED, ERASING, ERASES to rub or scrape out ERASABLE adj
ERASER	n pl. -S one that erases
ERASION	n pl. -S an erasure
ERASURE	n pl. -S the act of erasing
ERBIUM	n pl. -S a metallic element
ERE	prep previous to; before
ERECT	v -ED, -ING, -S to build
ERECTER	n pl. -S erector
ERECTILE	adj capable of being raised upright
ERECTION	n pl. -S the act of erecting
ERECTIVE	adj tending to erect
ERECTLY	adv in an upright manner
ERECTOR	n pl. -S one that erects
ERELONG	adv soon
EREMITE	n pl. -S a hermit EREMITIC adj
EREMURUS	n pl. -URI a perennial herb
ERENOW	adv before this time
EREPSIN	n pl. -S a mixture of enzymes in the small intestine
ERETHISM	n pl. -S abnormal irritability ERETHIC adj
EREWHILE	adv some time ago
ERG	n pl. -S a unit of work or energy
ERGASTIC	adj constituting the nonliving by-products of protoplasmic activity
ERGATE	n pl. -S a worker ant
ERGATIVE	adj pertaining to a type of language
ERGO	conj therefore
ERGODIC	adj pertaining to the probability that any state will recur
ERGOT	n pl. -S a fungus ERGOTIC adj
ERGOTISM	n pl. -S poisoning produced by eating ergot-infected grain
ERICA	n pl. -S a shrub of the heath family
ERICOID	adj resembling heath
ERIGERON	n pl. -S an herb
ERINGO	n pl. -GOES or -GOS eryngo
ERISTIC	n pl. -S an expert in debate
ERLKING	n pl. -S an evil spirit of Germanic folklore
ERMINE	n pl. -S the fur of certain weasels ERMINED adj
ERN	n pl. -S erne
ERNE	n pl. -S a sea eagle
ERODE	v ERODED, ERODING, ERODES to wear away by constant friction
ERODENT	adj erosive
ERODIBLE	adj erosible
ERODING	present participle of erode
EROGENIC	adj arousing sexual desire
EROS	n pl. -ES sexual desire
EROSE	adj uneven EROSELY adv
EROSIBLE	adj capable of being eroded
EROSION	n pl. -S the act of eroding
EROSIVE	adj causing erosion
EROTIC	n pl. -S an amatory poem EROTICAL adj
EROTICA	n/pl literature or art dealing with sexual love
EROTISM	n pl. -S sexual excitement
EROTIZE	v -TIZED, -TIZING, -TIZES to give a sexual meaning to
ERR	v -ED, -ING, -S to make a mistake
ERRANCY	n pl. -CIES an instance of erring
ERRAND	n pl. -S a short trip made for a particular purpose
ERRANT	n pl. -S a wanderer
ERRANTLY	adv in a wandering manner
ERRANTRY	n pl. -RIES the state of wandering
ERRATA	n pl. -S a list of printing errors
ERRATIC	n pl. -S an eccentric person
ERRATUM	n pl. -TA a printing error
ERRHINE	n pl. -S a substance that promotes nasal discharge
ERRINGLY	adv in a mistaken manner
ERROR	n pl. -S a mistake
ERS	n pl. -ES ervil
ERSATZ	n pl. -ES a substitute

ERST *adv* formerly

ERUCT *v* -ED, -ING, -S to belch

ERUCTATE *v* -TATED, -TATING, -TATES to eruct

ERUDITE *adj* scholarly

ERUGO *n pl.* -GOS aerugo

ERUMPENT *adj* bursting forth

ERUPT *v* -ED, -ING, -S to burst forth

ERUPTION *n pl.* -S the act of erupting

ERUPTIVE *n pl.* -S a type of rock

ERVIL *n pl.* -S a European vetch

ERYNGO *n pl.* -GOES or -GOS a medicinal herb

ERYTHEMA *n pl.* -S a redness of the skin

ERYTHRON *n pl.* -S a bodily organ consisting of the red blood cells

ES *n pl.* ESES ess

ESCALADE *v* -LADED, -LADING, -LADES to enter by means of ladders

ESCALATE *v* -LATED, -LATING, -LATES to increase

ESCALLOP *v* -ED, -ING, -S to scallop

ESCALOP *v* -ED, -ING, -S to escallop

ESCAPADE *n pl.* -S a reckless adventure

ESCAPE *v* -CAPED, -CAPING, -CAPES to get away

ESCAPEE *n pl.* -S one that has escaped

ESCAPER *n pl.* -S one that escapes

ESCAPING present participle of escape

ESCAPISM *n pl.* -S the avoidance of reality by diversion of the mind

ESCAPIST *n pl.* -S one given to escapism

ESCAR *n pl.* -S escar

ESCARGOT *n pl.* -S an edible snail

ESCAROLE *n pl.* -S a variety of endive

ESCARP *v* -ED, -ING, -S to cause to slope steeply

ESCHALOT *n pl.* -S a shallot

ESCHAR *n pl.* -S a hard, dry scab

ESCHEAT *v* -ED, -ING, -S to confiscate

ESCHEW *v* -ED, -ING, -S to avoid

ESCHEWAL *n pl.* -S the act of eschewing

ESCOLAR *n pl.* -S a food fish

ESCORT *v* -ED, -ING, -S to accompany

ESCOT *v* -ED, -ING, -S to provide support for

ESCROW *v* -ED, -ING, -S to place in the custody of a third party

ESCUAGE *n pl.* -S scutage

ESCUDO *n pl.* -DOS a monetary unit of Portugal

ESCULENT *n pl.* -S something that is edible

ESERINE *n pl.* -S a toxic alkaloid

ESKAR *n pl.* -S esker

ESKER *n pl.* -S a narrow ridge of gravel and sand

ESOPHAGI *n/pl* tubes connecting the mouth to the stomach

ESOTERIC *adj* designed for a select few

ESPALIER *v* -ED, -ING, -S to furnish with a trellis

ESPANOL *n pl.* -ES a native of Spain

ESPARTO *n pl.* -TOS a perennial grass

ESPECIAL *adj* special

ESPIAL *n pl.* -S the act of espying

ESPIED past tense of espy

ESPIEGLE *adj* playful

ESPIES present 3d person sing. of espy

ESPOUSAL *n pl.* -S a marriage ceremony

ESPOUSE *v* -POUSED, -POUSING, -POUSES to marry

ESPOUSER *n pl.* -S one that espouses

ESPRESSO *n pl.* -SOS a strong coffee

ESPRIT *n pl.* -S spirit

ESPY *v* -PIED, -PYING, -PIES to catch sight of

ESQUIRE *v* -QUIRED, -QUIRING, -QUIRES to escort

ESS *n pl.* -ES the letter S

ESSAY *v* -ED, -ING, -S to try

ESSAYER *n pl.* -S one that essays

ESSAYIST *n pl.* -S a writer of essays (prose compositions)

ESSENCE *n pl.* -S a fundamental nature or quality

ESSOIN *n pl.* -S an excuse

ESSONITE *n pl.* -S a variety of garnet

ESTANCIA *n pl.* -S a cattle ranch

ESTATE *v* -TATED, -TATING, -TATES to provide with landed property

ESTEEM *v* -ED, -ING, -S to have a high opinion of

ESTER *n pl.* -S a type of chemical compound

ESTERASE *n pl.* -S a type of enzyme

ESTERIFY *v* -FIED, -FYING, -FIES to convert into an ester

ESTHESIA *n pl.* -S the ability to receive sensation

ESTHESIS *n pl.* -THESISES or -THESES esthesia

ESTHETE *n pl.* -S an esthetic person

ESTHETIC *adj* keenly appreciative of the beautiful

ESTIMATE *v* -MATED, -MATING, -MATES to make an approximate judgment of

ESTIVAL *adj* pertaining to summer

ESTIVATE v -VATED, -VATING, -VATES to spend the summer

ESTOP v -TOPPED, -TOPPING, -TOPS to impede by estoppel

ESTOPPEL n pl. -S a legal restraint preventing a person from contradicting his own previous statement

ESTOVERS n/pl necessities allowed by law

ESTRAGON n pl. -S tarragon

ESTRAL adj estrous

ESTRANGE v -TRANGED, -TRANGING, -TRANGES to alienate

ESTRAY v -ED, -ING, -S to stray

ESTREAT v -ED, -ING, -S to copy from court records for use in prosecution

ESTRIN n pl. -S estrone

ESTRIOL n pl. -S an estrogen

ESTROGEN n pl. -S a female sex hormone promoting or producing estrus

ESTRONE n pl. -S an estrogen

ESTROUS adj pertaining to estrus

ESTRUAL adj estrous

ESTRUM n pl. -S estrus

ESTRUS n pl. -ES the period of heat in female mammals

ESTUARY n pl. -ARIES an inlet of the sea at a river's lower end

ESURIENT adj greedy

ET a past tense of eat

ETA n pl. -S a Greek letter

ETAGERE n pl. -S an ornamental stand

ETALON n pl. -S an optical instrument

ETAMIN n pl. -S etamine

ETAMINE n pl. -S a loosely woven fabric

ETAPE n pl. -S a warehouse

ETATISM n pl. -S state socialism ETATIST adj

ETCETERA n pl. -S a number of additional items

ETCH v -ED, -ING, -ES to engrave with acid

ETCHANT n pl. -S a substance used in etching

ETCHER n pl. -S one that etches

ETCHING n pl. -S an etched design

ETERNAL n pl. -S something lasting forever

ETERNE adj everlasting

ETERNISE v -NISED, -NISING, -NISES to eternize

ETERNITY n pl. -TIES infinite time

ETERNIZE v -NIZED, -NIZING, -NIZES to make everlasting

ETESIAN n pl. -S an annually recurring wind

ETH n pl. -S edh

ETHANE n pl. -S a gaseous hydrocarbon

ETHANOL n pl. -S an alcohol

ETHENE n pl. -S ethylene

ETHEPHON n pl. -S a synthetic plant growth regulator

ETHER n pl. -S a volatile liquid used as an anesthetic ETHERIC adj

ETHEREAL adj airy

ETHERIFY v -FIED, -FYING, -FIES to convert into ether

ETHERISH adj resembling ether

ETHERIZE v -IZED, -IZING, -IZES to treat with ether

ETHIC n pl. -S a body of moral principles

ETHICAL n pl. -S a drug sold by prescription only

ETHICIAN n pl. -S an ethicist

ETHICIST n pl. -S a specialist in ethics

ETHICIZE v -CIZED, -CIZING, -CIZES to make ethical

ETHINYL n pl. -S ethynyl

ETHION n pl. -S a pesticide

ETHMOID n pl. -S a bone of the nasal cavity

ETHNARCH n pl. -S the ruler of a people or province

ETHNIC n pl. -S a member of a particular ethnos ETHNICAL adj

ETHNOS n pl. -ES a group of people who share a common and distinctive culture

ETHOLOGY n pl. -GIES the study of animal behavior

ETHOS n pl. -ES the fundamental character of a culture

ETHOXY n pl. -OXIES ethoxyl

ETHOXYL n pl. -S a univalent chemical radical

ETHYL n pl. -S a univalent chemical radical

ETHYLATE v -ATED, -ATING, -ATES to introduce the ethyl group into

ETHYLENE n pl. -S a flammable gas

ETHYLIC adj pertaining to ethyl

ETHYNE n pl. -S a flammable gas

ETHYNYL n pl. -S a univalent chemical radical

ETIC adj relating to a type of linguistic analysis

ETIOLATE v -LATED, -LATING, -LATES to whiten

ETIOLOGY n pl. -GIES the study of the causes of diseases

ETNA n pl. -S a container for heating liquids

ETOILE n pl. -S a star

ETOUFFEE n pl. -S a Cajun stew

ETUDE n pl. -S a piece of music for the practice of a point of technique

ETUI n pl. -S a case for holding small articles

ETWEE n pl. -S etui

ETYMON n pl. -MA or -MONS the earliest known form of a word

EUCAINE n pl. -S an anesthetic

EUCALYPT n pl. -S an evergreen tree

EUCHARIS n pl. -RISES a flowering plant

EUCHRE v -CHRED, -CHRING, -CHRES to prevent from winning three tricks in euchre (a card game)

EUCLASE n pl. -S a mineral

EUCRITE n pl. -S a type of meteorite **EUCRITIC** adj

EUDAEMON n pl. -S eudemon

EUDEMON n pl. -S a good spirit

EUGENIA n pl. -S a tropical evergreen tree

EUGENICS n/pl the science of hereditary improvement **EUGENIC** adj

EUGENIST n pl. -S a student of eugenics

EUGENOL n pl. -S an aromatic liquid

EUGLENA n pl. -S a freshwater protozoan

EULACHAN n pl. -S eulachon

EULACHON n pl. -S a marine food fish

EULOGIA n pl. -GIAE holy bread

EULOGIA n pl. -S a blessing

EULOGIES pl. of eulogy

EULOGISE v -GISED, -GISING, -GISES to eulogize

EULOGIST n pl. -S one that eulogizes

EULOGIUM n pl. -GIA or -GIUMS a eulogy

EULOGIZE v -GIZED, -GIZING, -GIZES to praise highly

EULOGY n pl. -GIES a formal expression of high praise

EUNUCH n pl. -S a castrated man

EUONYMUS n pl. -ES any of a genus of shrubs or small trees

EUPATRID n pl. -RIDS or -RIDAE an aristocrat of ancient Athens

EUPEPSIA n pl. -S good digestion **EUPEPTIC** adj

EUPEPSY n pl. -SIES eupepsia

EUPHENIC adj dealing with biological improvement

EUPHONY n pl. -NIES pleasant sound **EUPHONIC** adj

EUPHORIA n pl. -S a feeling of well-being **EUPHORIC** adj

EUPHOTIC adj pertaining to the upper layer of a body of water

EUPHRASY n pl. -SIES an annual herb

EUPHROE n pl. -S a device used to adjust a shipboard awning

EUPHUISM n pl. -S an artificially elegant style of speech or writing

EUPHUIST n pl. -S one given to euphuism

EUPLOID n pl. -S a cell having three or more identical genomes

EUPLOIDY n pl. -DIES the state of being a euploid

EUPNEA n pl. -S normal breathing **EUPNEIC** adj

EUPNOEA n pl. -S eupnea **EUPNOEIC** adj

EUREKA interj — used to express triumph upon discovering something

EURIPUS n pl. -PI a swift sea channel

EURO n pl. EUROS a large kangaroo

EUROKY n pl. -KIES the ability of an organism to live under variable conditions **EUROKOUS** adj

EUROPIUM n pl. -S a metallic element

EURYBATH n pl. -S an organism that can live in a wide range of water depths

EURYOKY n pl. -KIES euroky

EURYTHMY n pl. -MIES harmony of movement or structure

EUSTACY n pl. -CIES a worldwide change in sea level **EUSTATIC** adj

EUSTELE n pl. -S a plant part

EUTAXY n pl. -TAXIES good order

EUTECTIC n pl. -S an alloy that has the lowest possible melting point

EUTROPHY n pl. -PHIES healthful nutrition

EUXENITE n pl. -S a mineral

EVACUANT n pl. -S a cathartic medicine

EVACUATE v -ATED, -ATING, -ATES to remove from a dangerous area

EVACUEE n pl. -S one that is evacuated

EVADE v EVADED, EVADING, EVADES to escape or avoid by cleverness or deceit **EVADABLE, EVADIBLE** adj

EVADER n pl. -S one that evades

EVALUATE	v -ATED, -ATING, -ATES to determine the value of
EVANESCE	v -NESCED, -NESCING, -NESCES to fade away
EVANGEL	n pl. -S a preacher of the gospel
EVANISH	v -ED, -ING, -ES to vanish
EVASION	n pl. -S the act of evading
EVASIVE	adj tending to evade
EVE	n pl. -S evening
EVECTION	n pl. -S irregularity in the moon's motion
EVEN	adj EVENER, EVENEST flat and smooth
EVEN	v -ED, -ING, -S to make even
EVENER	n pl. -S one that evens
EVENFALL	n pl. -S twilight
EVENING	n pl. -S the latter part of the day and early part of the night
EVENLY	adv in an even manner
EVENNESS	n pl. -ES the state of being even
EVENSONG	n pl. -S an evening prayer service
EVENT	n pl. -S something that occurs
EVENTFUL	adj momentous
EVENTIDE	n pl. -S evening
EVENTUAL	adj occurring at a later time
EVER	adv at all times
EVERMORE	adv forever
EVERSION	n pl -S the act of everting
EVERT	v -ED, -ING, -S to turn outward or inside out
EVERTOR	n pl. -S a muscle that turns a part outward
EVERY	adj each without exception
EVERYDAY	adj ordinary
EVERYMAN	n pl. -MEN the typical or ordinary man
EVERYONE	pron every person
EVERYWAY	adv in every way
EVICT	v -ED, -ING, -S to expel by legal process
EVICTEE	n pl. -S one that is evicted
EVICTION	n pl. -S the act of evicting
EVICTOR	n pl. -S one that evicts
EVIDENCE	v -DENCED, -DENCING, -DENCES to indicate clearly
EVIDENT	adj clear to the vision or understanding
EVIL	adj EVILER, EVILEST or EVILLER, EVILLEST morally bad
EVIL	n pl. -S something that is evil
EVILDOER	n pl. -S one that does evil
EVILLER	a comparative of evil

EVILLEST	a superlative of evil
EVILLY	adv in an evil manner
EVILNESS	n pl. -ES the quality of being evil
EVINCE	v EVINCED, EVINCING, EVINCES to show clearly
	EVINCIVE adj
EVITE	v EVITED, EVITING, EVITES to avoid **EVITABLE** adj
EVOCABLE	adj capable of being evoked
EVOCATOR	n pl. -S one that evokes
EVOKE	v EVOKED, EVOKING, EVOKES to call forth
EVOKER	n pl. -S an evocator
EVOLUTE	n pl. -S a type of geometric curve
EVOLVE	v EVOLVED, EVOLVING, EVOLVES to develop
EVOLVER	n pl. -S one that evolves
EVONYMUS	n pl. -ES euonymus
EVULSION	n pl. -S the act of pulling out
EVZONE	n pl. -S a Greek soldier
EWE	n pl. -S a female sheep
EWER	n pl. -S a large pitcher
EX	n pl. -ES the letter X
EXACT	adj -ACTER, -ACTEST precise
EXACT	v -ED, -ING, -S to force the payment or yielding of
EXACTA	n pl. -S a type of horse racing bet
EXACTER	n pl. -S one that exacts
EXACTION	n pl. -S the act of exacting
EXACTLY	adv in an exact manner
EXACTOR	n pl. -S exacter
EXALT	v -ED, -ING, -S to raise
EXALTER	n pl. -S one that exalts
EXAM	n pl. -S an examination
EXAMEN	n pl. -S a critical study
EXAMINE	v -INED, -INING, -INES to inspect
EXAMINEE	n pl. -S one that is taking an examination
EXAMINER	n pl. -S one that examines
EXAMINING	present participle of examine
EXAMPLE	v -PLED, -PLING, -PLES to show by representation
EXANTHEM	n pl. -S a skin eruption
EXARCH	n pl. -S the ruler of a province in the Byzantine Empire **EXARCHAL** adj
EXARCHY	n pl. -CHIES the domain of an exarch
EXCAVATE	v -VATED, -VATING, -VATES to dig out
EXCEED	v -ED, -ING, -S to go beyond

EXCEEDER n pl. -S one that exceeds

EXCEL v -CELLED, -CELLING, -CELS to surpass others

EXCEPT v -ED, -ING, -S to leave out

EXCERPT v -ED, -ING, -S to pick out a passage from for quoting

EXCESS v -ED, -ING, -ES to eliminate the position of

EXCHANGE v -CHANGED, -CHANGING, -CHANGES to give and receive reciprocally

EXCIDE v -CIDED, -CIDING, -CIDES to excise

EXCIMER n pl. -S a dimer that exists in an excited state

EXCIPLE n pl. -S a rim around the hymenium of various lichens

EXCISE v -CISED, -CISING, -CISES to remove by cutting out

EXCISION n pl. -S the act of excising

EXCITANT n pl. -S a stimulant

EXCITE v -CITED, -CITING, -CITES to arouse the emotions of

EXCITER n pl. -S one that excites

EXCITON n pl. -S a phenomenon occurring in an excited crystal

EXCITOR n pl. -S exciter

EXCLAIM v -ED, -ING, -S to cry out suddenly

EXCLAVE n pl. -S a portion of a country which is isolated in foreign territory

EXCLUDE v -CLUDED, -CLUDING, -CLUDES to shut out

EXCLUDER n pl. -S one that excludes

EXCRETA n/pl excreted matter **EXCRETAL** adj

EXCRETE v -CRETED, -CRETING, -CRETES to separate and eliminate from an organic body

EXCRETER n pl. -S one that excretes

EXCURSUS n pl. -ES a long appended exposition of a topic

EXCUSE v -CUSED, -CUSING, -CUSES to apologize for

EXCUSER n pl. -S one that excuses

EXEC n pl. -S an executive officer

EXECRATE v -CRATED, -CRATING, -CRATES to curse

EXECUTE v -CUTED, -CUTING, -CUTES to carry out

EXECUTER n pl. -S executor

EXECUTOR n pl. -S one that executes

EXEDRA n pl. -DRAE a curved outdoor bench

EXEGESIS n pl. -GESES critical explanation or analysis **EXEGETIC** adj

EXEGETE n pl. -S one skilled in exegesis

EXEMPLAR n pl. -S one that is worthy of being copied

EXEMPLUM n pl. -PLA an example

EXEMPT v -ED, -ING, -S to free from an obligation required of others

EXEQUY n pl. -QUIES a funeral procession **EXEQUIAL** adj

EXERCISE v -CISED, -CISING, -CISES to make use of

EXERGUE n pl. -S a space on a coin **EXERGUAL** adj

EXERT v -ED, -ING, -S to put into action

EXERTION n pl. -S the act of exerting

EXERTIVE adj tending to exert

EXEUNT v they leave the stage — used as a stage direction

EXHALANT n pl. -S something that exhales

EXHALE v -HALED, -HALING, -HALES to expel air or vapor

EXHALENT n pl. -S exhalant

EXHAUST v -ED, -ING, -S to use up

EXHIBIT v -ED, -ING, -S to present for public viewing

EXHORT v -ED, -ING, -S to advise urgently

EXHORTER n pl. -S one that exhorts

EXHUME v -HUMED, -HUMING, -HUMES to dig out of the earth

EXHUMER n pl. -S one that exhumes

EXIGENCE n pl. -S exigency

EXIGENCY n pl. -CIES urgency

EXIGENT adj urgent

EXIGIBLE adj liable to be demanded

EXIGUITY n pl. -ITIES the state of being exiguous

EXIGUOUS adj meager

EXILE v -ILED, -ILING, -ILES to banish from one's own country

EXILIAN adj exilic

EXILIC adj pertaining to exile (banishment from one's own country)

EXILING present participle of exile

EXIMIOUS adj excellent

EXINE n pl. -S the outer layer of certain spores

EXIST v -ED, -ING, -S to be

EXISTENT n pl. -S something that exists

EXIT v -ED, -ING, -S to go out

EXITLESS adj lacking a way out

EXOCARP n pl. -S the epicarp

EXOCRINE n pl. -S an external secretion

EXODERM n pl. -S the ectoderm

EXODOS n pl. -DOI a concluding dramatic scene

EXODUS n pl. -ES a movement away

EXOERGIC adj releasing energy

EXOGAMY n pl. -MIES marriage outside of a particular group **EXOGAMIC** adj

EXOGEN n pl. -S a type of plant

EXON n pl. -S a sequence in the genetic code **EXONIC** adj

EXONUMIA n/pl numismatic items other than coins or paper money

EXORABLE adj persuadable

EXORCISE v -CISED, -CISING, -CISES to free of an evil spirit

EXORCISM n pl. -S the act of exorcising

EXORCIST n pl. -S one who practices exorcism

EXORCIZE v -CIZED, -CIZING, -CIZES to exorcise

EXORDIUM n pl. -DIUMS or -DIA a beginning **EXORDIAL** adj

EXOSMOSE n pl. -S a form of osmosis **EXOSMIC** adj

EXOSPORE n pl. -S the outer coat of a spore

EXOTERIC adj suitable for the public

EXOTIC n pl. -S something from another part of the world

EXOTICA n/pl things excitingly different or unusual

EXOTISM n pl. -S an exotic

EXOTOXIN n pl. -S an excreted toxin **EXOTOXIC** adj

EXPAND v -ED, -ING, -S to increase in size or volume

EXPANDER n pl. -S one that expands

EXPANDOR n pl. -S a type of transducer

EXPANSE n pl. -S a wide, continuous area

EXPAT n pl. -S an expatriate person

EXPECT v -ED, -ING, -S to anticipate

EXPEDITE v -DITED, -DITING, -DITES to speed up the progress of

EXPEL v -PELLED, -PELLING, -PELS to force out

EXPELLEE n pl. -S a deportee

EXPELLER n pl. -S one that expels

EXPELLING present participle of expel

EXPEND v -ED, -ING, -S to use up

EXPENDER n pl. -S one that expends

EXPENSE v -PENSED, -PENSING, -PENSES to charge with costs

EXPERT v -ED, -ING, -S to serve as an authority

EXPERTLY adv skillfully

EXPIABLE adj capable of being expiated

EXPIATE v -ATED, -ATING, -ATES to atone for

EXPIATOR n pl. -S one that expiates

EXPIRE v -PIRED, -PIRING, -PIRES to come to an end

EXPIRER n pl. -S one that expires

EXPIRY n pl. -RIES a termination

EXPLAIN v -ED, -ING, -S to make plain or understandable

EXPLANT v -ED, -ING, -S to remove from the natural site of growth and place in a medium

EXPLICIT n pl. -S a statement formerly used at the close of a book

EXPLODE v -PLODED, -PLODING, -PLODES to blow up

EXPLODER n pl. -S one that explodes

EXPLOIT v -ED, -ING, -S to take advantage of

EXPLORE v -PLORED, -PLORING, -PLORES to travel through for the purpose of discovery

EXPLORER n pl. -S one that explores

EXPO n pl. -POS a public exhibition

EXPONENT n pl. -S one who expounds

EXPORT v -ED, -ING, -S to send to other countries for commercial purposes

EXPORTER n pl. -S one that exports

EXPOSAL n pl. -S an exposure

EXPOSE v -POSED, -POSING, -POSES to lay open to view

EXPOSER n pl. -S one that exposes

EXPOSIT v -ED, -ING, -S to expound

EXPOSURE n pl. -S the act of exposing

EXPOUND v -ED, -ING, -S to explain in detail

EXPRESS v -ED, -ING, -ES to set forth in words

EXPRESSO n pl. -SOS espresso

EXPULSE v -PULSED, -PULSING, -PULSES to expel

EXPUNGE v -PUNGED, -PUNGING, -PUNGES to delete

EXPUNGER n pl. -S one that expunges

EXSCIND v -ED, -ING, -S to cut out

EXSECANT n pl. -S a trigonometric function of an angle

EXSECT v -ED, -ING, -S to cut out

EXSERT v -ED, -ING, -S to thrust out

EXTANT adj still in existence

EXTEND v -ED, -ING, -S to stretch out to full length

EXTENDER n pl. -S a substance added to another substance

EXTENSOR n pl. -S a muscle that extends a limb

EXTENT n pl. -S the range over which something extends

EXTERIOR n pl. -S a part or surface that is outside

EXTERN n pl. -S a nonresident of an institution

EXTERNAL n pl. -S an exterior

EXTERNE n pl. -S extern

EXTINCT v -ED, -ING, -S to extinguish

EXTOL v -TOLLED, -TOLLING, -TOLS to praise highly

EXTOLL v -ED, -ING, -S to extol

EXTOLLER n pl. -S one that extols

EXTOLLING present participle of extol

EXTORT v -ED, -ING, -S to obtain from a person by violence or intimidation

EXTORTER n pl. -S one that extorts

EXTRA n pl. -S something additional

EXTRACT v -ED, -ING, -S to pull or draw out

EXTRADOS n pl. -ES the outer curve of an arch

EXTREMA pl. of extremum

EXTREME adj -TREMER, -TREMEST existing in a very high degree

EXTREME n pl. -S the highest degree

EXTREMUM n pl. -MA a maximum or a minimum of a mathematical function

EXTRORSE adj facing outward

EXTRUDE v -TRUDED, -TRUDING, -TRUDES to force, thrust, or push out

EXTRUDER n pl. -S one that extrudes

EXTUBATE v -BATED, -BATING, -BATES to remove a tube from

EXUDATE n pl. -S an exuded substance

EXUDE v -UDED, -UDING, -UDES to ooze forth

EXULT v -ED, -ING, -S to rejoice greatly

EXULTANT adj exulting

EXURB n pl. -S a residential area lying beyond the suburbs of a city EXURBAN adj

EXURBIA n pl. -S an exurb

EXUVIATE v -ATED, -ATING, -ATES to molt

EXUVIUM n pl. -VIAE or -VIA the molted covering of an animal EXUVIAL adj

EYAS n pl. -ES a young hawk

EYE v EYED, EYING or EYEING, EYES to watch closely EYEABLE adj

EYE n pl. EYES, EYEN or EYNE the organ of sight

EYEBALL v -ED, -ING, -S to eye

EYEBAR n pl. -S a metal bar with a loop at one or both ends

EYEBEAM n pl. -S a glance

EYEBOLT n pl. -S a type of bolt or screw

EYEBROW n pl. -S the ridge over the eye

EYECUP n pl. -S a cup used for applying lotions to the eyes

EYED past tense of eye

EYEDNESS n pl. -ES preference for the use of one eye over the other

EYEDROPS n/pl a medicated solution for the eyes applied in drops

EYEFUL n pl. -S a complete view

EYEGLASS n pl. -ES a lens used to aid vision

EYEHOLE n pl. -S a small opening

EYEHOOK n pl. -S a type of hook

EYELASH n pl. -ES a hair growing on the edge of an eyelid

EYELESS adj lacking eyes

EYELET v -LETTED, -LETTING, -LETS to make a small hole in

EYELID n pl. -S the lid of skin that can be closed over an eyeball

EYELIKE adj resembling an eye

EYELINER n pl. -S makeup for the eyes

EYEN a pl. of eye

EYEPIECE n pl. -S the lens or lens group nearest the eye in an optical instrument

EYEPOINT n pl. -S the point at which an eye is placed in using an optical instrument

EYER n pl. -S one that eyes

EYESHADE n pl. -S a visor for shading the eyes

EYESHOT n pl. -S the range of vision

EYESIGHT n pl. -S the ability to see

EYESOME adj pleasant to look at

EYESORE n pl. -S something offensive to the sight

EYESPOT n pl. -S a simple visual organ of lower animals

EYESTALK n pl. -S a stalklike structure with an eye at its tip

EYESTONE *n* pl. -S a disk used to remove foreign matter from the eye

EYETOOTH *n* pl. -TEETH a cuspid

EYEWASH *n* pl. -ES an eye lotion

EYEWATER *n* pl. -S an eyewash

EYEWEAR *n* pl. EYEWEAR a device worn on or over the eyes

EYEWINK *n* pl. -S a wink of the eye

EYING a present participle of eye

EYNE a pl. of eye

EYRA *n* pl. -S a wild cat of tropical America

EYRE *n* pl. -S a journey

EYRIE *n* pl. -S aerie

EYRIR *n* pl. AURAR a monetary unit of Iceland

EYRY *n* pl. -RIES aerie

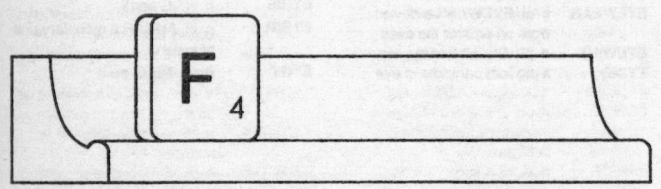

FA *n* pl. -S the fourth tone of the diatonic musical scale

FABLE *v* -BLED, -BLING, -BLES to compose or tell fictitious tales

FABLER *n* pl. -S one that fables

FABLIAU *n* pl. -AUX a short metrical tale popular in medieval France

FABLING present participle of fable

FABRIC *n* pl. -S a woven, felted, or knitted material

FABULAR *adj* legendary

FABULIST *n* pl. -S a liar

FABULOUS *adj* almost unbelievable

FACADE *n* pl. -S the front of a building

FACE *v* FACED, FACING, FACES to oppose or meet defiantly FACEABLE *adj*

FACEDOWN *adv* with the front part down

FACELESS *adj* lacking personal distinction or identity

FACER *n* pl. -S one that faces

FACET *v* -ETED, -ETING, -ETS or -ETTED, -ETTING, -ETS to cut small plane surfaces on

FACETE *adj* witty FACETELY *adv*

FACETIAE *n/pl* witty sayings or writings

FACETTED a past tense of facet

FACETTING a present participle of facet

FACEUP *adv* with the front part up

FACIA *n* pl. -S fascia

FACIAL *n* pl. -S a treatment for the face

FACIALLY *adv* with respect to the face

FACIEND *n* pl. -S a number to be multiplied by another

FACIES *n* pl. FACIES general appearance

FACILE *adj* easily achieved or performed FACILELY *adv*

FACILITY *n* pl. -TIES the quality of being facile

FACING *n* pl. -S a lining at the edge of a garment

FACT *n* pl. -S something known with certainty FACTFUL *adj*

FACTION *n* pl. -S a clique within a larger group

FACTIOUS *adj* promoting dissension

FACTOID *n* pl. -S a brief news item

FACTOR *v* -ED, -ING, -S to express as a product of two or more quantities

FACTORY *n* pl. -RIES a building or group of buildings in which goods are manufactured

FACTOTUM *n* pl. -S a person employed to do many kinds of work

FACTUAL *adj* pertaining to facts

FACTURE *n* pl. -S the act of making something

FACULA *n* pl. -LAE an unusually bright spot on the sun's surface FACULAR *adj*

FACULTY *n* pl. -TIES an inherent power or ability

FAD *n* pl. -S a practice or interest that enjoys brief popularity

FADABLE *adj* capable of fading

FADDIER comparative of faddy

FADDIEST superlative of faddy

FADDISH *adj* inclined to take up fads

FADDISM *n* pl. -S inclination to take up fads

FADDIST *n* pl. -S a faddish person

FADDY *adj* -DIER, -DIEST faddish

FADE *v* FADED, FADING, FADES to lose color or brightness FADEDLY *adv*

FADEAWAY n pl. -AWAYS a type of pitch in baseball

FADELESS adj not fading

FADER n pl. -S one that fades

FADGE v FADGED, FADGING, FADGES to succeed

FADING n pl. -S an Irish dance

FADO n pl. -DOS a Portuguese folk song

FAECES n/pl feces FAECAL adj

FAENA n pl. -S a series of passes made by a matador in a bullfight

FAERIE n pl. -S a fairy

FAERY n pl. -ERIES faerie

FAG v FAGGED, FAGGING, FAGS to make weary by hard work

FAGGOT v -ED, -ING, -S to fagot

FAGIN n pl. -S a person who instructs others in crime

FAGOT v -ED, -ING, -S to bind together into a bundle

FAGOTER n pl. -S one that fagots

FAGOTING n pl. -S a type of embroidery

FAHLBAND n pl. -S a band or stratum of rock impregnated with metallic sulfides

FAIENCE n pl. -S a variety of glazed pottery

FAIL v -ED, -ING, -S to be unsuccessful in an attempt

FAILING n pl. -S a minor fault or weakness

FAILLE n pl. -S a woven fabric

FAILURE n pl. -S the act of failing

FAIN adj FAINER, FAINEST glad

FAINEANT n pl. -S a lazy person

FAINT v -ED, -ING, -S to lose consciousness

FAINT adj FAINTER, FAINTEST lacking strength or vigor

FAINTER n pl. -S one that faints

FAINTISH adj somewhat faint

FAINTLY adv in a faint manner

FAIR adj FAIRER, FAIREST free from bias, dishonesty, or injustice

FAIR v -ED, -ING, -S to make smooth

FAIRIES pl. of fairy

FAIRING n pl. -S a structure on an aircraft serving to reduce drag

FAIRISH adj moderately good

FAIRLEAD n pl. -S a device used to hold a ship's rigging in place

FAIRLY adv in a fair manner

FAIRNESS n pl. -ES the quality of being fair

FAIRWAY n pl. -WAYS the mowed part of a golf course between tee and green

FAIRY n pl. FAIRIES an imaginary supernatural being

FAIRYISM n pl. -S the quality of being like a fairy

FAITH v -ED, -ING, -S to believe or trust

FAITHFUL n pl. -S a loyal follower or member

FAITOUR n pl. -S an impostor

FAJITA n pl. -S marinated and grilled beef, chicken, or shrimp served with a flour tortilla

FAKE v FAKED, FAKING, FAKES to contrive and present as genuine

FAKEER n pl. -S fakir

FAKER n pl. -S one that fakes

FAKERY n pl. -ERIES the practice of faking

FAKEY adj not genuine; phony

FAKING present participle of fake

FAKIR n pl. -S a Hindu ascetic

FALAFEL n pl. FALAFEL ground spiced vegetables formed into patties

FALBALA n pl. -S a trimming for a woman's garment

FALCATE adj curved and tapering to a point

FALCATED adj falcate

FALCES pl. of falx

FALCHION n pl. -S a broad-bladed sword

FALCON n pl. -S a bird of prey

FALCONER n pl. -S one that hunts with hawks

FALCONET n pl. -S a small falcon

FALCONRY n pl. -RIES the sport of hunting with falcons

FALDERAL n pl. -S nonsense

FALDEROL n pl. -S falderal

FALL v FELL, FALLEN, FALLING, FALLS to descend under the force of gravity

FALLACY n pl. -CIES a false idea

FALLAL n pl. -S a showy article of dress

FALLAWAY n pl. -AWAYS a shot in basketball

FALLBACK n pl. -S an act of retreating

FALLEN past participle of fall

FALLER n pl. -S one that falls

FALLFISH n pl. -ES a freshwater fish

FALLIBLE *adj* capable of erring **FALLIBLY** *adv*

FALLOFF *n pl.* -S a decline in quantity or quality

FALLOUT *n pl.* -S radioactive debris resulting from a nuclear explosion

FALLOW *v* -ED, -ING, -S to plow and leave unseeded

FALSE *adj* FALSER, FALSEST contrary to truth or fact **FALSELY** *adv*

FALSETTO *n pl.* -TOS an artificially high voice

FALSIE *n pl.* -S a pad worn within a brassiere

FALSIFY *v* -FIED, -FYING, -FIES to represent falsely

FALSITY *n pl.* -TIES something false

FALTBOAT *n pl.* -S a collapsible boat resembling a kayak

FALTER *v* -ED, -ING, -S to hesitate

FALTERER *n pl.* -S one that falters

FALX *n pl.* FALCES a sickle-shaped structure

FAME *v* FAMED, FAMING, FAMES to make famous

FAMELESS *adj* not famous

FAMILIAL *adj* pertaining to a family

FAMILIAR *n pl.* -S a close friend or associate

FAMILISM *n pl.* -S a social structure in which the family takes precedence over the individual

FAMILY *n pl.* -LIES a group of persons related by blood or marriage

FAMINE *n pl.* -S a widespread scarcity of food

FAMING present participle of fame

FAMISH *v* -ED, -ING, -ES to suffer extreme hunger

FAMOUS *adj* well-known **FAMOUSLY** *adv*

FAMULUS *n pl.* -LI a servant or attendant

FAN *v* FANNED, FANNING, FANS to cool or refresh with a fan (a device for putting air into motion)

FANATIC *n pl.* -S a zealot

FANCIED past tense of fancy

FANCIER *n pl.* -S one that has a special liking for something

FANCIES present 3d person sing. of fancy

FANCIFUL *adj* unrealistic

FANCIFY *v* -FIED, -FYING, -FIES to make fancy

FANCY *adj* -CIER, -CIEST ornamental **FANCILY** *adv*

FANCY *v* -CIED, -CYING, -CIES to take a liking to

FANDANGO *n pl.* -GOS a lively Spanish dance

FANDOM *n pl.* -S an aggregate of enthusiastic devotees

FANE *n pl.* -S a temple

FANEGA *n pl.* -S a Spanish unit of dry measure

FANEGADA *n pl.* -S a Spanish unit of area

FANFARE *n pl.* -S a short, lively musical flourish

FANFARON *n pl.* -S a braggart

FANFOLD *v* -ED, -ING, -S to fold paper like a fan

FANG *n pl.* -S a long, pointed tooth **FANGED, FANGLESS, FANGLIKE** *adj*

FANGA *n pl.* -S fanega

FANION *n pl.* -S a small flag

FANJET *n pl.* -S a type of jet engine

FANLIGHT *n pl.* -S a type of window

FANLIKE *adj* resembling a fan

FANNED past tense of fan

FANNER *n pl.* -S one that fans

FANNING present participle of fan

FANNY *n pl.* -NIES the buttocks

FANO *n pl.* FANOS a fanon

FANON *n pl.* -S a cape worn by the pope

FANTAIL *n pl.* -S a fan-shaped tail or end

FANTASIA *n pl.* -S a free-form musical composition

FANTASIE *n pl.* -S a fantasia

FANTASIED past tense of fantasy

FANTASIES present 3d person sing. of fantasy

FANTASM *n pl.* -S phantasm

FANTAST *n pl.* -S an impractical person

FANTASY *v* -SIED, -SYING, -SIES to imagine

FANTOD *n pl.* -S an emotional outburst

FANTOM *n pl.* -S phantom

FANUM *n pl.* -S fanon

FANWISE *adj* spread out like an open fan

FANWORT *n pl.* -S an aquatic plant

FANZINE *n pl.* -S a magazine written by and for enthusiastic devotees

FAQIR *n pl.* -S fakir

FAQUIR *n pl.* -S fakir

FAR	*adv* FARTHER, FARTHEST or FURTHER, FURTHEST at or to a great distance
FARAD	*n pl.* -S a unit of electrical capacitance
FARADAIC	*adj* faradic
FARADAY	*n pl.* -DAYS a unit of electricity
FARADIC	*adj* pertaining to a type of electric current
FARADISE	*v* -DISED, -DISING, -DISES to feradize
FARADISM	*n pl.* -S the use of faradic current for therapeutic purposes
FARADIZE	*v* -DIZED, -DIZING, -DIZES to treat by faradism
FARAWAY	*adj* distant
FARCE	*v* FARCED, FARCING, FARCES to fill out with witty material
FARCER	*n pl.* -S farceur
FARCEUR	*n pl.* -S a joker
FARCI	*adj* stuffed with finely chopped meat
FARCICAL	*adj* absurd
FARCIE	*adj* farci
FARCING	present participle of farce
FARCY	*n pl.* -CIES a disease of horses
FARD	*v* -ED, -ING, -S to apply cosmetics to
FARDEL	*n pl.* -S a bundle
FARE	*v* FARED, FARING, FARES to get along
FARER	*n pl.* -S a traveler
FAREWELL	*v* -ED, -ING, -S to say goodby
FARFAL	*n pl.* -S farfel
FARFEL	*n pl.* -S noodles in the form of small pellets or granules
FARINA	*n pl.* -S a fine meal made from cereal grain
FARING	present participle of fare
FARINHA	*n pl.* -S a meal made from the root of the cassava
FARINOSE	*adj* resembling farina
FARL	*n pl.* -S a thin oatmeal cake
FARLE	*n pl.* -S a farl
FARM	*v* -ED, -ING, -S to manage and cultivate as a farm (a tract of land devoted to agriculture) FARMABLE *adj*
FARMER	*n pl.* -S one that farms
FARMHAND	*n pl.* -S a farm laborer
FARMING	*n pl.* -S the business of operating a farm
FARMLAND	*n pl.* -S cultivated land
FARMWIFE	*n pl.* -WIVES a farmer's wife
FARMWORK	*n pl.* -S labor done on a farm
FARMYARD	*n pl.* -S an area surrounded by farm buildings
FARNESOL	*n pl.* -S an alcohol used in perfumes
FARNESS	*n pl.* -ES the state of being far off or apart
FARO	*n pl.* FAROS a card game
FAROUCHE	*adj* sullenly shy
FARRAGO	*n pl.* -GOES a confused mixture
FARRIER	*n pl.* -S one that shoes horses
FARRIERY	*n pl.* -ERIES the trade of a farrier
FARROW	*v* -ED, -ING, -S to give birth to a litter of pigs
FARSIDE	*n pl.* -S the farther side
FARTHER	a comparative of far
FARTHEST	a superlative of far
FARTHING	*n pl.* -S a former British coin
FASCES	*n pl.* FASCES an ancient Roman symbol of power
FASCIA	*n pl.* -CIAE or -CIAS a broad and distinct band of color FASCIAL, FASCIATE *adj*
FASCICLE	*n pl.* -S a small bundle
FASCINE	*n pl.* -S a bundle of sticks used in building fortifications
FASCISM	*n pl.* -S an oppressive political system
FASCIST	*n pl.* -S an advocate of fascism
FASH	*v* -ED, -ING, -ES to annoy
FASHION	*v* -ED, -ING, -S to give a particular shape or form to
FASHIOUS	*adj* annoying
FAST	*adj* FASTER, FASTEST moving or able to move quickly
FAST	*v* -ED, -ING, -S to abstain from eating
FASTBACK	*n pl.* -S a type of automobile roof
FASTBALL	*n pl.* -S a type of pitch in baseball
FASTEN	*v* -ED, -ING, -S to secure
FASTENER	*n pl.* -S one that fastens
FASTING	*n pl.* -S abstention from eating
FASTNESS	*n pl.* -ES the quality of being fast
FASTUOUS	*adj* arrogant
FAT	*adj* FATTER, FATTEST having an abundance of flesh
FAT	*v* FATTED, FATTING, FATS to make fat

FATAL	adj causing or capable of causing death	**FAUCET**	n pl. -S a device for controlling the flow of liquid from a pipe
FATALISM	n pl. -S the doctrine that all events are predetermined	**FAUCIAL**	adj pertaining to the fauces
FATALIST	n pl. -S a believer in fatalism	**FAUGH**	interj — used to express disgust
FATALITY	n pl. -TIES a death resulting from an unexpected occurrence	**FAULD**	n pl. -S a piece of armor below the breastplate
FATALLY	adv in a fatal manner	**FAULT**	v -ED, -ING, -S to criticize
FATBACK	n pl. -S a marine fish	**FAULTY**	adj FAULTIER, FAULTIEST imperfect **FAULTILY** adv
FATBIRD	n pl. -S a wading bird	**FAUN**	n pl. -S a woodland deity of Roman mythology **FAUNLIKE** adj
FATE	v FATED, FATING, FATES to destine		
FATEFUL	adj decisively important	**FAUNA**	n pl. -NAS or -NAE the animal life of a particular region **FAUNAL** adj **FAUNALLY** adv
FATHEAD	n pl. -S a dolt		
FATHER	v -ED, -ING, -S to cause to exist		
FATHERLY	adj paternal	**FAUTEUIL**	n pl. -S an armchair
FATHOM	v -ED, -ING, -S to understand	**FAUVE**	n pl. -S a fauvist
FATIDIC	adj pertaining to prophecy	**FAUVISM**	n pl. -S a movement in painting
FATIGUE	v -TIGUED, -TIGUING, -TIGUES to weary	**FAUVIST**	n pl. -S an advocate of fauvism
FATING	present participle of fate	**FAUX**	adj not genuine; fake
FATLESS	adj having no fat	**FAVA**	n pl. -S the edible seed of a climbing vine
FATLIKE	adj resembling fat		
FATLING	n pl. -S a young animal fattened for slaughter	**FAVE**	n pl. -S a favorite
		FAVELA	n pl. -S a slum area
FATLY	adv in the manner of one that is fat	**FAVELLA**	n pl. -S favela
		FAVISM	n pl. -S an acute anemia
FATNESS	n pl. -ES the state of being fat	**FAVONIAN**	adj pertaining to the west wind
FATSTOCK	n pl. -S livestock that is fat and ready for market	**FAVOR**	v -ED, -ING, -S to regard with approval
FATTED	past tense of fat	**FAVORER**	n pl. -S one that favors
FATTEN	v -ED, -ING, -S to make fat	**FAVORITE**	n pl. -S a person or thing preferred above all others
FATTENER	n pl. -S one that fattens		
FATTER	comparative of fat	**FAVOUR**	v -ED, -ING, -S to favor
FATTEST	superlative of fat	**FAVOURER**	n pl. -S favorer
FATTIER	comparative of fatty	**FAVUS**	n pl. -ES a skin disease
FATTIES	pl. of fatty	**FAWN**	v -ED, -ING, -S to seek notice or favor by servile demeanor
FATTIEST	superlative of fatty		
FATTILY	adv in a fatty manner	**FAWNER**	n pl. -S one that fawns
FATTING	present participle of fat	**FAWNLIKE**	adj resembling a young deer
FATTISH	adj somewhat fat	**FAWNY**	adj FAWNIER, FAWNIEST of a yellowish-brown color
FATTY	adj -TIER, -TIEST greasy; oily		
FATUITY	n pl. -ITIES something foolish or stupid	**FAX**	v -ED, -ING, -ES to transmit and reproduce by electronic means
FATUOUS	adj smugly stupid	**FAY**	v -ED, -ING, -S to join closely
FATWA	n pl. -S an Islamic legal decree	**FAYALITE**	n pl. -S a mineral
		FAZE	v FAZED, FAZING, FAZES to disturb the composure of
FATWOOD	n pl. -S wood used for kindling		
FAUBOURG	n pl. -S a suburb	**FAZENDA**	n pl. -S a Brazilian plantation
FAUCAL	n pl. -S a sound produced in the fauces	**FEAL**	adj loyal
		FEALTY	n pl. -TIES loyalty
FAUCES	n/pl the passage from the mouth to the pharynx	**FEAR**	v -ED, -ING, -S to be afraid of
		FEARER	n pl. -S one that fears

FEARFUL	adj -FULLER, -FULLEST afraid
FEARLESS	adj unafraid
FEARSOME	adj frightening
FEASANCE	n pl. -S the performance of a condition, obligation, or duty
FEASE	v FEASED, FEASING, FEASES to faze
FEASIBLE	adj capable of being done FEASIBLY adv
FEAST	v -ED, -ING, -S to eat sumptuously
FEASTER	n pl. -S one that feasts
FEASTFUL	adj festive
FEAT	n pl. -S a notable act or achievement
FEAT	adj FEATER, FEATEST skillful
FEATHER	v -ED, -ING, -S to cover with feathers (horny structures that form the principal covering of birds)
FEATHERY	adj -ERIER, -ERIEST resembling feathers
FEATLY	adj -LIER, -LIEST graceful
FEATURE	v -TURED, -TURING, -TURES to give special prominence to
FEAZE	v FEAZED, FEAZING, FEAZES to faze
FEBRIFIC	adj feverish
FEBRILE	adj feverish
FECAL	adj pertaining to feces
FECES	n/pl bodily waste discharged through the anus
FECIAL	n pl. -S fetial
FECK	n pl. -S value
FECKLESS	adj worthless
FECKLY	adv almost
FECULA	n pl. -LAE fecal matter
FECULENT	adj foul with impurities
FECUND	adj fruitful
FED	n pl. -S a federal agent
FEDAYEE	n pl. -YEEN an Arab commando
FEDERACY	n pl. -CIES an alliance
FEDERAL	n pl. -S a supporter of a type of central government
FEDERATE	v -ATED, -ATING, -ATES to unite in an alliance
FEDORA	n pl. -S a type of hat
FEE	v FEED, FEEING, FEES to pay a fee (a fixed charge) to
FEEBLE	adj -BLER, -BLEST weak FEEBLY adv
FEEBLISH	adj somewhat feeble
FEED	v FED, FEEDING, FEEDS to give food to FEEDABLE adj
FEEDBACK	n pl. -S the return of a portion of the output to the input
FEEDBAG	n pl. -S a bag for feeding horses
FEEDBOX	n pl. -ES a box for animal feed
FEEDER	n pl. -S one that feeds
FEEDHOLE	n pl. -S one of a series of holes in paper tape
FEEDLOT	n pl. -S a plot of land on which livestock is fattened
FEEL	v FELT, FEELING, FEELS to perceive through the sense of touch
FEELER	n pl. -S a tactile organ
FEELESS	adj requiring no fee
FEELING	n pl. -S the function or power of perceiving by touch
FEET	pl. of foot FEETLESS adj
FEEZE	v FEEZED, FEEZING, FEEZES to faze
FEH	n pl. -S peh
FEIGN	v -ED, -ING, -S to pretend
FEIGNER	n pl. -S one that feigns
FEIJOA	n pl. -S a green edible fruit
FEINT	v -ED, -ING, -S to make a deceptive movement
FEIRIE	adj nimble
FEIST	n pl. -S a small dog of mixed breed
FEISTY	adj FEISTIER, FEISTIEST full of nervous energy
FELAFEL	n pl. FELAFEL falafel
FELDSHER	n pl. -S a medical worker in Russia
FELDSPAR	n pl. -S a mineral
FELICITY	n pl. -TIES happiness
FELID	n pl. -S a feline
FELINE	n pl. -S an animal of the cat family
FELINELY	adv in a catlike manner
FELINITY	n pl. -TIES the quality of being catlike
FELL	v -ED, -ING, -S to cause to fall
FELL	adj FELLER, FELLEST cruel
FELLA	n pl. -S a man or boy
FELLABLE	adj capable of being felled
FELLAH	n pl. -LAHS, -LAHIN, or -LAHEEN a peasant or laborer in Arab countries
FELLATE	v -LATED, -LATING, -LATES to perform fellatio
FELLATIO	n pl. -TIOS oral stimulation of the penis
FELLATOR	n pl. -S one that fellates

FELLER n pl. -S one that fells

FELLIES pl. of felly

FELLNESS n pl. -ES extreme cruelty

FELLOE n pl. -S the rim of a wheel

FELLOW v -ED, -ING, -S to produce an equal to

FELLOWLY adj friendly

FELLY n pl. -LIES a felloe

FELON n pl. -S a person who has committed a felony

FELONRY n pl. -RIES the whole class of felons

FELONY n pl. -NIES a grave crime

FELSITE n pl. -S an igneous rock FELSITIC adj

FELSPAR n pl. -S feldspar

FELSTONE n pl. -S felsite

FELT v -ED, -ING, -S to mat together

FELTING n pl. -S felted material

FELTLIKE adj like a cloth made from wool

FELUCCA n pl. -S a swift sailing vessel

FELWORT n pl. -S a flowering plant

FEM n pl. -S a passive homosexual

FEMALE n pl. -S an individual that bears young or produces ova

FEME n pl. -S a wife

FEMINACY n pl. -CIES the state of being a female

FEMINIE n/pl women collectively

FEMININE n pl. -S a word or form having feminine gender

FEMINISE v -NISED, -NISING, -NISES to feminize

FEMINISM n pl. -S a doctrine advocating rights for women equal to those of men

FEMINIST n pl. -S a supporter of feminism

FEMINITY n pl. -TIES the quality of being womanly

FEMINIZE v -NIZED, -NIZING, -NIZES to make womanly

FEMME n pl. -S a woman

FEMORAL adj pertaining to the femur

FEMUR n pl. -MURS or -MORA a bone of the leg

FEN n pl. -S a marsh

FENAGLE v -GLED, -GLING, -GLES to finagle

FENCE v FENCED, FENCING, FENCES to practice the art of fencing

FENCER n pl. -S one that fences

FENCEROW n pl. -S the land occupied by a fence

FENCIBLE n pl. -S a soldier enlisted for home service only

FENCING n pl. -S the art of using a sword in attack and defense

FEND v -ED, -ING, -S to ward off

FENDER n pl. -S a metal guard over the wheel of a motor vehicle FENDERED adj

FENESTRA n pl. -TRAE a small anatomical opening

FENLAND n pl. -S marshy ground

FENNEC n pl. -S an African fox

FENNEL n pl. -S a perennial herb

FENNY adj marshy

FENTHION n pl. -S an insecticide

FENURON n pl. -S an herbicide

FEOD n pl. -S a fief

FEODARY n pl. -RIES a vassal

FEOFF v -ED, -ING, -S to grant a fief to

FEOFFEE n pl. -S one to whom a fief is granted

FEOFFER n pl. -S one that grants a fief to another

FEOFFOR n pl. -S feoffer

FER prep for

FERACITY n pl. -TIES the state of being fruitful

FERAL adj wild

FERBAM n pl. -S a fungicide

FERE n pl. -S a companion

FERETORY n pl. -RIES a receptacle in which sacred relics are kept

FERIA n pl. -RIAS or -RIAE a weekday of a church calendar on which no feast is celebrated FERIAL adj

FERINE adj feral

FERITY n pl. -TIES wildness

FERLIE n pl. -S a strange sight

FERLY n pl. -LIES ferlie

FERMATA n pl. -TAS or -TE the sustaining of a musical note, chord, or rest beyond its written time value

FERMENT v -ED, -ING, -S to undergo a type of chemical reaction

FERMI n pl. -S a unit of length

FERMION n pl. -S a type of atomic particle

FERMIUM n pl. -S a radioactive element

FERN n pl. -S a flowerless vascular plant FERNLESS, FERNLIKE adj

FERNERY *n pl.* -ERIES a place in which ferns are grown

FERNY *adj* FERNIER, FERNIEST abounding in ferns

FEROCITY *n pl.* -TIES fierceness

FERRATE *n pl.* -S a chemical salt

FERREL *v* -RELED, -RELING, -RELS or -RELLED, -RELLING, -RELS ferrule

FERREOUS *adj* containing iron

FERRET *v* -ED, -ING, -S to search out by careful investigation

FERRETER *n pl.* -S one that ferrets

FERRETY *adj* suggestive of a ferret (a polecat)

FERRIAGE *n pl.* -S transportation by ferry

FERRIC *adj* pertaining to iron

FERRIED past tense of ferry

FERRIES present 3d person sing. of ferry

FERRITE *n pl.* -S a magnetic substance FERRITIC *adj*

FERRITIN *n pl.* -S a protein that contains iron

FERROUS *adj* pertaining to iron

FERRULE *v* -RULED, -RULING, -RULES to furnish with a metal ring or cap to prevent splitting

FERRUM *n pl.* -S iron

FERRY *v* -RIED, -RYING, -RIES to transport by ferry (a type of boat)

FERRYMAN *n pl.* -MEN one who operates a ferry

FERTILE *adj* capable of reproducing

FERULA *n pl.* -LAE or -LAS a flat piece of wood

FERULE *v* -ULED, -ULING, -ULES to ferrule

FERVENCY *n pl.* -CIES fervor

FERVENT *adj* marked by fervor

FERVID *adj* fervent FERVIDLY *adv*

FERVOR *n pl.* -S great warmth or intensity

FERVOUR *n pl.* -S fervor

FESCUE *n pl.* -S a perennial grass

FESS *v* -ED, -ING, -ES to confess

FESSE *n pl.* -S a horizontal band across the middle of a heraldic shield

FESSWISE *adv* horizontally

FESTAL *adj* festive FESTALLY *adv*

FESTER *v* -ED, -ING, -S to generate pus

FESTIVAL *n pl.* -S a day or time of celebration

FESTIVE *adj* of or befitting a festival

FESTOON *v* -ED, -ING, -S to hang decorative chains or strips on

FET *v* FETTED, FETTING, FETS to fetch

FETA *n pl.* -S a Greek cheese

FETAL *adj* pertaining to a fetus

FETATION *n pl.* -S the development of a fetus

FETCH *v* -ED, -ING, -ES to go after and bring back

FETCHER *n pl.* -S one that fetches

FETE *v* FETED, FETING, FETES to honor with a celebration

FETERITA *n pl.* -S a cereal grass

FETIAL *n pl.* -S a priest of ancient Rome

FETIALIS *n pl.* -LES fetial

FETICH *n pl.* -ES fetish

FETICIDE *n pl.* -S the killing of a fetus

FETID *adj* having an offensive odor FETIDLY *adv*

FETING present participle of fete

FETISH *n pl.* -ES an object believed to have magical power

FETLOCK *n pl.* -S a joint of a horse's leg

FETOLOGY *n pl.* -GIES the branch of medicine dealing with the fetus

FETOR *n pl.* -S an offensive odor

FETTED past tense of fet

FETTER *v* -ED, -ING, -S to shackle

FETTERER *n pl.* -S one that fetters

FETTING present participle of fet

FETTLE *v* -TLED, -TLING, -TLES to cover the hearth of with fettling

FETTLING *n pl.* -S loose material thrown on the hearth of a furnace to protect it

FETUS *n pl.* -ES the unborn organism carried within the womb in the later stages of its development

FEU *v* -ED, -ING, -S to grant land to under Scottish feudal law

FEUAR *n pl.* -S one granted land under Scottish feudal law

FEUD *v* -ED, -ING, -S to engage in a feud (a bitter, continuous hostility)

FEUDAL *adj* pertaining to a political and economic system of medieval Europe FEUDALLY *adv*

FEUDARY *n pl.* -RIES a vassal

FEUDIST *n pl.* -S one that feuds

FEVER *v* -ED, -ING, -S to affect with fever (abnormal elevation of the body temperature)

FEVERFEW *n pl.* -S a perennial herb

FEVERISH	adj having a fever	**FICHU**	n pl. -S a woman's scarf
FEVEROUS	adj feverish	**FICIN**	n pl. -S an enzyme
FEW	adj FEWER, FEWEST amounting to or consisting of a small number	**FICKLE**	adj -LER, -LEST not constant or loyal FICKLY adv
		FICO	n pl. -COES something of little worth
FEWNESS	n pl. -ES the state of being few		
		FICTILE	adj moldable
FEWTRILS	n/pl things of little value	**FICTION**	n pl. -S a literary work whose content is produced by the imagination
FEY	adj FEYER, FEYEST crazy FEYLY adv		
		FICTIVE	adj imaginary
FEYNESS	n pl. -ES the state of being fey	**FICUS**	n pl. -ES a tropical tree
FEZ	n pl. FEZZES or FEZES a brimless cap worn by men in the Near East FEZZED adj	**FID**	n pl. -S a square bar used as a support for a topmast
		FIDDLE	v -DLED, -DLING, -DLES to play a violin
FIACRE	n pl. -S a small carriage		
FIANCE	n pl. -S a man engaged to be married	**FIDDLER**	n pl. -S one that fiddles
		FIDDLY	adj intricately difficult to handle
FIANCEE	n pl. -S a woman engaged to be married	**FIDEISM**	n pl. -S reliance on faith rather than reason
FIAR	n pl. -S the holder of a type of absolute ownership of land under Scottish law	**FIDEIST**	n pl. -S a believer in fideism
		FIDELITY	n pl. -TIES loyalty
		FIDGE	v FIDGED, FIDGING, FIDGES to fidget
FIASCO	n pl. -COES or -CHI a wine bottle		
		FIDGET	v -ED, -ING, -S to move nervously or restlessly
FIASCO	n pl. -COES or -COS a complete failure		
		FIDGETER	n pl. -S one that fidgets
FIAT	n pl. -S an authoritative order	**FIDGETY**	adj nervously restless
FIB	v FIBBED, FIBBING, FIBS to tell a trivial lie	**FIDGING**	present participle of fidge
		FIDO	n pl. -DOS a defective coin
FIBBER	n pl. -S one that fibs	**FIDUCIAL**	adj based on faith or trust
FIBER	n pl. -S a thread or threadlike object or structure FIBERED adj	**FIE**	interj — used to express disapproval
		FIEF	n pl. -S a feudal estate
FIBERIZE	v -IZED, -IZING, -IZES to break into fibers	**FIEFDOM**	n pl. -S a fief
		FIELD	v -ED, -ING, -S to play as a fielder
FIBRANNE	n pl. -S a fabric made of spun-rayon yarn		
		FIELDER	n pl. -S one that catches or picks up a ball in play
FIBRE	n pl. -S fiber		
FIBRIL	n pl. -S a small fiber	**FIEND**	n pl. -S a demon
FIBRILLA	n pl. -LAE a fibril	**FIENDISH**	adj extremely wicked or cruel
FIBRIN	n pl. -S an insoluble protein	**FIERCE**	adj FIERCER, FIERCEST violently hostile or aggressive FIERCELY adv
FIBROID	n pl. -S a fibroma		
FIBROIN	n pl. -S an insoluble protein		
FIBROMA	n pl. -MAS or -MATA a benign tumor composed of fibrous tissue	**FIERY**	adj -ERIER, -ERIEST intensely hot FIERILY adv
		FIESTA	n pl. -S a festival
FIBROSIS	n pl. -BROSES the development of excess fibrous tissue in a bodily organ FIBROTIC adj	**FIFE**	v FIFED, FIFING, FIFES to play a fife (a high-pitched flute)
		FIFER	n pl. -S one that plays a fife
		FIFTEEN	n pl. -S a number
FIBROUS	adj containing, consisting of, or resembling fibers	**FIFTH**	n pl. -S one of five equal parts
		FIFTHLY	adv in the fifth place
FIBULA	n pl. -LAE or -LAS a bone of the leg FIBULAR adj	**FIFTIETH**	n pl. -S one of fifty equal parts
		FIFTY	n pl. -TIES a number
FICE	n pl. -S a feist	**FIFTYISH**	adj being about fifty years old
FICHE	n pl. -S a sheet of microfilm		

FIG 199 **FIMBLE**

FIG *v* FIGGED, FIGGING, FIGS to adorn

FIGEATER *n pl.* -S a large beetle

FIGHT *v* FOUGHT, FIGHTING, FIGHTS to attempt to defeat an adversary

FIGHTER *n pl.* -S one that fights

FIGHTING *n pl.* -S the act of one that fights

FIGMENT *n pl.* -S a product of mental invention

FIGULINE *n pl.* -S a piece of pottery

FIGURAL *adj* consisting of human or animal form

FIGURANT *n pl.* -S a ballet dancer who dances only in groups

FIGURATE *adj* having a definite shape

FIGURE *v* -URED, -URING, -URES to compute

FIGURER *n pl.* -S one that figures

FIGURINE *n pl.* -S a small statue

FIGURING present participle of figure

FIGWORT *n pl.* -S a flowering plant

FIL *n pl.* -S a coin of Iraq and Jordan

FILA pl. of filum

FILAGREE *v* -GREED, -GREEING, -GREES to filigree

FILAMENT *n pl.* -S a very thin thread or threadlike structure

FILAR *adj* pertaining to a thread

FILAREE *n pl.* -S a European weed

FILARIA *n pl.* -IAE a parasitic worm FILARIAL, FILARIAN *adj*

FILARIID *n pl.* -S filaria

FILATURE *n pl.* -S the reeling of silk from cocoons

FILBERT *n pl.* -S the edible nut of a European shrub

FILCH *v* -ED, -ING, -ES to steal

FILCHER *n pl.* -S one that filches

FILE *v* FILED, FILING, FILES to arrange in order for future reference FILEABLE *adj*

FILEFISH *n pl.* -ES a marine fish

FILEMOT *adj* of a brownish yellow color

FILER *n pl.* -S one that files

FILET *v* -ED, -ING, -S to fillet

FILIAL *adj* pertaining to a son or daughter FILIALLY *adv*

FILIATE *v* -ATED, -ATING, -ATES to bring into close association

FILIBEG *n pl.* -S a pleated skirt worn by Scottish Highlanders

FILICIDE *n pl.* -S the killing of one's child

FILIFORM *adj* shaped like a filament

FILIGREE *v* -GREED, -GREEING, -GREES to adorn with intricate ornamental work

FILING *n pl.* -S a particle removed by a file

FILISTER *n pl.* -S a groove on a window frame

FILL *v* -ED, -ING, -S to put as much as can be held into

FILLE *n pl.* -S a girl

FILLER *n pl.* -S one that fills

FILLET *v* -ED, -ING, -S to cut boneless slices from

FILLIES pl. of filly

FILLING *n pl.* -S that which is used to fill something

FILLIP *v* -ED, -ING, -S to strike sharply

FILLO *n pl.* -LOS phyllo

FILLY *n pl.* -LIES a young female horse

FILM *v* -ED, -ING, -S to make a motion picture FILMABLE *adj*

FILMCARD *n pl.* -S a fiche

FILMDOM *n pl.* -S the motion-picture industry

FILMER *n pl.* -S one that films

FILMGOER *n pl.* -S one that goes to see motion pictures

FILMIC *adj* pertaining to motion pictures

FILMIER comparative of filmy

FILMIEST superlative of filmy

FILMILY *adv* in a filmy manner

FILMLAND *n pl.* -S filmdom

FILMSET *v* -SET, -SETTING, -SETS to photoset

FILMY *adj* FILMIER, FILMIEST resembling or covered with film; hazy

FILO *n pl.* -LOS phyllo

FILOSE *adj* resembling a thread

FILTER *v* -ED, -ING, -S to pass through a filter (a device for removing suspended matter)

FILTERER *n pl.* -S one that filters

FILTH *n pl.* -S foul or dirty matter

FILTHY *adj* FILTHIER, FILTHIEST offensively dirty FILTHILY *adv*

FILTRATE *v* -TRATED, -TRATING, -TRATES to filter

FILUM *n pl.* -LA a threadlike anatomical structure

FIMBLE *n pl.* -S the male hemp plant

FIMBRIA n pl. -BRIAE a fringe or fringe-like structure **FIMBRIAL** adj

FIN v FINNED, FINNING, FINS to equip with fins (external paddle-like structures)

FINABLE adj subject to the payment of a fine

FINAGLE v -GLED, -GLING, -GLES to obtain by trickery

FINAGLER n pl. -S one that finagles

FINAL n pl. -S the last examination of an academic course

FINALE n pl. -S a close or termination of something

FINALIS n pl. -LES a type of tone in medieval music

FINALISE v -ISED, -ISING, -ISES finalize

FINALISM n pl. -S the doctrine that all events are determined by ultimate purposes

FINALIST n pl. -S a contestant who reaches the last part of a competition

FINALITY n pl. -TIES the state of being conclusive

FINALIZE v -IZED, -IZING, -IZES to put into finished form

FINALLY adv at the end

FINANCE v -NANCED, -NANCING, -NANCES to supply the money for

FINBACK n pl. -S the rorqual

FINCH n pl. -ES a small bird

FIND v FOUND, FINDING, FINDS to come upon after a search **FINDABLE** adj

FINDER n pl. -S one that finds

FINDING n pl. -S something that is found

FINE adj FINER, FINEST excellent

FINE v FINED, FINING, FINES to subject to a fine (a monetary penalty)

FINEABLE adj finable

FINELY adv in a fine manner

FINENESS n pl. -ES the quality of being fine

FINER comparative of fine

FINERY n pl. -ERIES elaborate adornment

FINESPUN adj developed with extreme care

FINESSE v -NESSED, -NESSING, -NESSES to bring about by adroit maneuvering

FINEST superlative of fine

FINFISH n pl. -ES a true fish

FINFOOT n pl. -S an aquatic bird

FINGER v -ED, -ING, -S to touch with the fingers (the terminating members of the hand)

FINGERER n pl. -S one that fingers

FINIAL n pl. -S a crowning ornament **FINIALED** adj

FINICAL adj finicky

FINICKIN adj finicky

FINICKY adj -ICKIER, -ICKIEST difficult to please

FINIKIN adj finicky

FINIKING adj finicky

FINING n pl. -S the clarifying of wines

FINIS n pl. -NISES the end

FINISH v -ED, -ING, -ES to bring to an end

FINISHER n pl. -S one that finishes

FINITE n pl. -S something that is finite (having definite limits)

FINITELY adv to a finite extent

FINITUDE n pl. -S the state of being finite

FINK v -ED, -ING, -S to inform to the police

FINLESS adj having no fins

FINLIKE adj resembling a fin

FINMARK n pl. -S a monetary unit of Finland

FINNED past tense of fin

FINNICKY adj -NICKIER, -NICKIEST finicky

FINNIER comparative of finny

FINNIEST superlative of finny

FINNING present participle of fin

FINNMARK n pl. -S finmark

FINNY adj -NIER, -NIEST having or characterized by fins

FINO n pl. -NOS a very dry sherry

FINOCHIO n pl. -CHIOS a perennial herb

FIORD n pl. -S fjord

FIPPLE n pl. -S a plug of wood at the mouth of certain wind instruments

FIQUE n pl. -S a tropical plant

FIR n pl. -S an evergreen tree

FIRE v FIRED, FIRING, FIRES to project by discharging from a gun **FIREABLE** adj

FIREARM n pl. -S a weapon from which a shot is discharged by gunpowder

FIREBACK n pl. -S a cast-iron plate along the back of a fireplace

FIREBALL n pl. -S a luminous meteor

FIREBASE *n* pl. -S a military base from which fire is directed against the enemy

FIREBIRD *n* pl. -S a brightly colored bird

FIREBOAT *n* pl. -S a boat equipped with fire-fighting apparatus

FIREBOMB *v* -ED, -ING, -S to attack with incendiary bombs

FIREBOX *n* pl. -ES a chamber in which fuel is burned

FIREBRAT *n* pl. -S a small, wingless insect

FIREBUG *n* pl. -S an arsonist

FIRECLAY *n* pl. -CLAYS a heat-resistant clay

FIRED past tense of fire

FIREDAMP *n* pl. -S a combustible gas

FIREDOG *n* pl. -S an andiron

FIREFANG *v* -ED, -ING, -S to decompose by oxidation

FIREFLY *n* pl. -FLIES a luminous insect

FIREHALL *n* pl. -S a fire station

FIRELESS *adj* having no fire

FIRELIT *adj* lighted by firelight

FIRELOCK *n* pl. -S a type of gun

FIREMAN *n* pl. -MEN a man employed to extinguish fires

FIREPAN *n* pl. -S an open pan for holding live coals

FIREPINK *n* pl. -S a flowering plant

FIREPLUG *n* pl. -S a hydrant

FIREPOT *n* pl. -S a clay pot filled with burning items

FIRER *n* pl. -S one that fires

FIREROOM *n* pl. -S a room containing a ship's boilers

FIRESIDE *n* pl. -S the area immediately surrounding a fireplace

FIRETRAP *n* pl. -S a building that is likely to catch on fire

FIREWEED *n* pl. -S a perennial herb

FIREWOOD *n* pl. -S wood used as fuel

FIREWORK *n* pl. -S a device for producing a striking display of light or a loud noise

FIREWORM *n* pl. -S a glowworm

FIRING *n* pl. -S the process of maturing ceramic products by heat

FIRKIN *n* pl. -S a British unit of capacity

FIRM *adj* FIRMER, FIRMEST unyielding to pressure

FIRM *v* -ED, -ING, -S to make firm

FIRMAN *n* pl. -S an edict issued by a Middle Eastern sovereign

FIRMER *n* pl. -S a woodworking tool

FIRMLY *adv* in a firm manner

FIRMNESS *n* pl. -ES the state of being firm

FIRMWARE *n* pl. -S computer programs permanently stored on a microchip

FIRN *n* pl. -S a neve

FIRRY *adj* abounding in firs

FIRST *n* pl. -S something that precedes all others

FIRSTLY *adv* before all others

FIRTH *n* pl. -S an inlet of the sea

FISC *n* pl. -S a state or royal treasury

FISCAL *n* pl. -S a public prosecutor

FISCALLY *adv* with regard to financial matters

FISH *v* -ED, -ING, -ES to catch or try to catch fish (cold-blooded aquatic vertebrates)

FISHABLE *adj* suitable for fishing

FISHBOLT *n* pl. -S a type of bolt

FISHBONE *n* pl. -S a bone of a fish

FISHBOWL *n* pl. -S a bowl in which live fish are kept

FISHER *n* pl. -S one that fishes

FISHERY *n* pl. -ERIES a place for catching fish

FISHEYE *n* pl. -S a suspicious stare

FISHGIG *n* pl. -S a pronged implement for spearing fish

FISHHOOK *n* pl. -S a barbed hook for catching fish

FISHIER comparative of fishy

FISHIEST superlative of fishy

FISHILY *adv* in a fishy manner

FISHING *n* pl. -S the occupation or pastime of catching fish

FISHLESS *adj* having no fish

FISHLIKE *adj* resembling a fish

FISHLINE *n* pl. -S a line used in fishing

FISHMEAL *n* pl. -S ground dried fish

FISHNET *n* pl. -S a net for catching fish

FISHPOLE *n* pl. -S a fishing rod

FISHPOND *n* pl. -S a pond abounding in edible fish

FISHTAIL *v* -ED, -ING, -S to have the rear end of a moving vehicle slide from side to side

FISHWAY *n* pl. -WAYS a device for enabling fish to pass around a dam

FISHWIFE *n* pl. -WIVES a woman who sells fish

FISHWORM *n* pl. -S a worm used as bait

FISHY *adj* FISHIER, FISHIEST of or resembling fish

FISSATE *adj* deeply split

FISSILE *adj* capable of being split

FISSION *v* -ED, -ING, -S to split into parts

FISSIPED *n pl.* -S a mammal that has separated toes

FISSURE *v* -SURED, -SURING, -SURES to split

FIST *v* -ED, -ING, -S to strike with the fist (the hand closed tightly)

FISTFUL *n pl.* -S a handful

FISTIC *adj* pertaining to pugilism

FISTNOTE *n pl.* -S a part of a text to which attention is drawn by an index mark

FISTULA *n pl.* -LAE or -LAS a duct formed by the imperfect closing of a wound **FISTULAR** *adj*

FIT *adj* FITTER, FITTEST healthy

FIT *v* FITTED, FITTING, FITS to bring to a required form and size

FITCH *n pl.* -ES a polecat

FITCHEE *adj* fitchy

FITCHET *n pl.* -S a fitch

FITCHEW *n pl.* -S a fitch

FITCHY *adj* having the arms ending in a point — used of a heraldic cross

FITFUL *adj* recurring irregularly **FITFULLY** *adv*

FITLY *adv* in a fit manner

FITMENT *n pl.* -S equipment

FITNESS *n pl.* -ES the state of being fit

FITTABLE *adj* capable of being fitted

FITTED past tense of fit

FITTER *n pl.* -S one that fits

FITTEST superlative of fit

FITTING *n pl.* -S a small often standardized accessory part

FIVE *n pl.* -S a number

FIVEFOLD *adj* five times as great

FIVEPINS *n/pl* a bowling game

FIVER *n pl.* -S a five-dollar bill

FIX *v* FIXED or FIXT, FIXING, FIXES to repair **FIXABLE** *adj*

FIXATE *v* -ATED, -ATING, -ATES to make stable or stationary

FIXATIF *n pl.* -S fixative

FIXATION *n pl.* -S the act of fixating

FIXATIVE *n pl.* -S a substance for preserving paintings or drawings

FIXEDLY *adv* firmly

FIXER *n pl.* -S one that fixes

FIXINGS *n/pl* accompaniments to the main dish of a meal

FIXIT *adj* involved with fixing things

FIXITY *n pl.* -TIES stability

FIXT a past tense of fix

FIXTURE *n pl.* -S a permanent part or appendage of a house

FIXURE *n pl.* -S firmness

FIZ *n pl.* FIZZES a hissing or sputtering sound

FIZGIG *n pl.* -S fishgig

FIZZ *v* -ED, -ING, -ES to make a hissing or sputtering sound

FIZZER *n pl.* -S one that fizzes

FIZZES pl. of fiz

FIZZLE *v* -ZLED, -ZLING, -ZLES to fizz

FIZZY *adj* FIZZIER, FIZZIEST fizzing

FJELD *n pl.* -S a high, barren plateau

FJORD *n pl.* -S a narrow inlet of the sea between steep cliffs

FLAB *n pl.* -S flabby body tissue

FLABBY *adj* -BIER, -BIEST flaccid **FLABBILY** *adv*

FLABELLA *n/pl* fan-shaped anatomical structures

FLACCID *adj* lacking firmness

FLACK *v* -ED, -ING, -S to work as a press agent

FLACKERY *n pl.* -ERIES publicity

FLACON *n pl.* -S a small stoppered bottle

FLAG *v* FLAGGED, FLAGGING, FLAGS to mark with a flag (a piece of cloth used as a symbol)

FLAGELLA *n/pl* long, slender plant shoots

FLAGGER *n pl.* -S one that flags

FLAGGING *n pl.* -S a type of pavement

FLAGGY *adj* -GIER, -GIEST drooping

FLAGLESS *adj* having no flag

FLAGMAN *n pl.* -MEN one who carries a flag

FLAGON *n pl.* -S a large bulging bottle

FLAGPOLE *n pl.* -S a pole on which a flag is displayed

FLAGRANT *adj* extremely or deliberately conspicuous

FLAGSHIP *n pl.* -S a ship bearing the flag of a fleet

FLAIL *v* -ED, -ING, -S to swing freely

FLAIR *n pl.* -S a natural aptitude

FLAK *n pl.* FLAK antiaircraft fire

FLAKE v FLAKED, FLAKING, FLAKES to peel off in flakes (flat, thin pieces)

FLAKER n pl. -S one that flakes

FLAKEY adj FLAKIER, FLAKIEST flaky

FLAKY adj FLAKIER, FLAKIEST resembling flakes **FLAKILY** adv

FLAM v FLAMMED, FLAMMING, FLAMS to deceive

FLAMBE v -BEED, -BEING, -BES to douse with a liqueur and ignite

FLAMBEAU n pl. -BEAUX or -BEAUS a flaming torch

FLAMBEE adj flaming

FLAME v FLAMED, FLAMING, FLAMES to burn brightly

FLAMEN n pl. -MENS or -MINES a priest of ancient Rome

FLAMENCO n pl. -COS a strongly rhythmic style of dancing

FLAMEOUT n pl. -S a failure of a jet engine in flight

FLAMER n pl. -S one that flames

FLAMIER comparative of flamy

FLAMIEST superlative of flamy

FLAMINES a pl. of flamen

FLAMING present participle of flame

FLAMINGO n pl. -GOS or -GOES a wading bird

FLAMMED past tense of flam

FLAMMING present participle of flam

FLAMY adj FLAMIER, FLAMIEST flaming

FLAN n pl. -S or -ES a type of custard

FLANCARD n pl. -S a piece of armor

FLANERIE n pl. -S idleness

FLANEUR n pl. -S an idler

FLANGE v FLANGED, FLANGING, FLANGES to provide with a protecting rim

FLANGER n pl. -S one that flanges

FLANK v -ED, -ING, -S to be located at the side of

FLANKEN n/pl beef cut from the sides that is boiled with vegetables

FLANKER n pl. -S one that flanks

FLANNEL v -NELED, -NELING, -NELS or -NELLED, -NELLING, -NELS to cover with flannel (a soft fabric)

FLAP v FLAPPED, FLAPPING, FLAPS to wave up and down

FLAPJACK n pl. -S a pancake

FLAPLESS adj having no flap (a flat appendage)

FLAPPED past tense of flap

FLAPPER n pl. -S one that flaps

FLAPPING present participle of flap

FLAPPY adj -PIER, -PIEST flapping

FLARE v FLARED, FLARING, FLARES to burn with a bright, wavering light

FLASH v -ED, -ING, -ES to send forth a sudden burst of light

FLASHER n pl. -S one that flashes

FLASHGUN n pl. -S a photographic apparatus

FLASHING n pl. -S sheet metal used in waterproofing a roof

FLASHY adj FLASHIER, FLASHIEST gaudy **FLASHILY** adv

FLASK n pl. -S a narrow-necked container

FLASKET n pl. -S a small flask

FLAT adj FLATTER, FLATTEST having a smooth or even surface

FLAT v FLATTED, FLATTING, FLATS to flatten

FLATBED n pl. -S a type of truck or trailer

FLATBOAT n pl. -S a flat-bottomed boat

FLATCAP n pl. -S a type of hat

FLATCAR n pl. -S a railroad car without sides or roof

FLATFISH n pl. -ES any of an order of marine fishes

FLATFOOT n pl. -FEET a foot condition

FLATFOOT v -ED, -ING, -S to walk with a dragging gait

FLATHEAD n pl. -S a marine food fish

FLATIRON n pl. -S a device for pressing clothes

FLATLAND n pl. -S land lacking significant variation in elevation

FLATLET n pl. -S a type of apartment

FLATLING adv with a flat side or edge

FLATLONG adv flatling

FLATLY adv in a flat manner

FLATMATE n pl. -S one with whom an apartment is shared

FLATNESS n pl. -ES the state of being flat

FLATTED past tense of flat

FLATTEN v -ED, -ING, -S to make or become flat

FLATTER v -ED, -ING, -S to praise excessively

FLATTERY n pl. -TERIES the act of flattering

FLATTEST superlative of flat

FLATTING present participle of flat

FLATTISH adj somewhat flat

FLATTOP n pl. -S an aircraft carrier

FLATUS n pl. -ES intestinal gas

FLATWARE n pl. -S tableware that is fairly flat

FLATWASH n pl. -ES flatwork

FLATWAYS adv flatwise

FLATWISE adv with the flat side in a particular position

FLATWORK n pl. -S laundry that can be ironed mechanically

FLATWORM n pl. -S a flat-bodied worm

FLAUNT v -ED, -ING, -S to exhibit in a gaudy manner

FLAUNTER n pl. -S one that flaunts

FLAUNTY adj FLAUNTIER, FLAUNTIEST gaudy

FLAUTIST n pl. -S flutist

FLAVANOL n pl. -S flavonol

FLAVIN n pl. -S a yellow pigment

FLAVINE n pl. -S flavin

FLAVONE n pl. -S a chemical compound

FLAVONOL n pl. -S a derivative of flavone

FLAVOR v -ED, -ING, -S to give flavor (distinctive taste) to

FLAVORER n pl. -S one that flavors

FLAVORY adj full of flavor

FLAVOUR v -ED, -ING, -S to flavor

FLAVOURY adj flavory

FLAW v -ED, -ING, -S to produce a flaw (an imperfection) in

FLAWLESS adj having no flaw

FLAWY adj FLAWIER, FLAWIEST full of flaws

FLAX n pl. -ES an annual herb

FLAXEN adj of a pale yellow color

FLAXSEED n pl. -S the seed of flax

FLAXY adj FLAXIER, FLAXIEST flaxen

FLAY v -ED, -ING, -S to strip off the skin of

FLAYER n pl. -S one that flays

FLEA n pl. -S a parasitic insect

FLEABAG n pl. -S an inferior hotel

FLEABANE n pl. -S a flowering plant

FLEABITE n pl. -S the bite of a flea

FLEAM n pl. -S a surgical instrument

FLEAPIT n pl. -S a run-down movie theater

FLEAWORT n pl. -S a European herb

FLECHE n pl. -S a steeple

FLECK v -ED, -ING, -S to mark with flecks (tiny streaks or spots)

FLECKY adj flecked

FLECTION n pl. -S the act of bending

FLED past tense of flee

FLEDGE v FLEDGED, FLEDGING, FLEDGES to furnish with feathers

FLEDGY adj FLEDGIER, FLEDGIEST covered with feathers

FLEE v FLED, FLEEING, FLEES to run away

FLEECE v FLEECED, FLEECING, FLEECES to remove the coat of wool from

FLEECER n pl. -S one that fleeces

FLEECH v -ED, -ING, -ES to coax

FLEECING present participle of fleece

FLEECY adj FLEECIER, FLEECIEST woolly FLEECILY adv

FLEER v -ED, -ING, -S to deride

FLEET adj FLEETER, FLEETEST swift FLEETLY adv

FLEET v -ED, -ING, -S to move swiftly

FLEISHIG adj made of meat or meat products

FLEMISH v -ED, -ING, -ES to coil rope in a certain manner

FLENCH v -ED, -ING, -ES to flense

FLENSE v FLENSED, FLENSING, FLENSES to strip the blubber or skin from

FLENSER n pl. -S one that flenses

FLESH v -ED, -ING, -ES to plunge into the flesh (soft body tissue)

FLESHER n pl. -S one that removes flesh from animal hides

FLESHIER comparative of fleshy

FLESHIEST superlative of fleshy

FLESHING n pl. -S the distribution of the lean and fat on an animal

FLESHLY adj -LIER, -LIEST pertaining to the body

FLESHPOT n pl. -S a pot for cooking meat

FLESHY adj FLESHIER, FLESHIEST having much flesh

FLETCH v -ED, -ING, -ES to fledge

FLETCHER n pl. -S one that makes arrows

FLEURY adj having the arms terminating in three leaves — used of a heraldic cross

FLEW n pl. -S a fishing net

FLEX v -ED, -ING, -ES to bend

FLEXAGON n pl. -S a folded paper construction

FLEXIBLE adj capable of being bent FLEXIBLY adv

FLEXILE *adj* flexible

FLEXION *n* pl. -S flection

FLEXOR *n* pl. -S a muscle that serves to bend a bodily part

FLEXTIME *n* pl. -S a system that allows flexible working hours

FLEXUOSE *adj* flexuous

FLEXUOUS *adj* winding

FLEXURE *n* pl. -S the act of bending **FLEXURAL** *adj*

FLEY *v* -ED, -ING, -S to frighten

FLIC *n* pl. -S a Parisian policeman

FLICHTER *v* -ED, -ING, -S to flicker

FLICK *v* -ED, -ING, -S to strike with a quick, light blow

FLICKER *v* -ED, -ING, -S to move waveringly

FLICKERY *adj* flickering

FLIED a past tense of fly

FLIER *n* pl. -S one that flies

FLIES present 3d person sing. of fly

FLIEST superlative of fly

FLIGHT *v* -ED, -ING, -S to fly in a flock

FLIGHTY *adj* FLIGHTIER, FLIGHTIEST fickle

FLIMFLAM *v* -FLAMMED, -FLAMMING, -FLAMS to swindle

FLIMSY *adj* -SIER, -SIEST lacking solidity or strength **FLIMSILY** *adv*

FLIMSY *n* pl. -SIES a thin paper

FLINCH *v* -ED, -ING, -ES to shrink back involuntarily

FLINCHER *n* pl. -S one that flinches

FLINDER *n* pl. -S a small fragment

FLING *v* FLUNG, FLINGING, FLINGS to throw with force

FLINGER *n* pl. -S one that flings

FLINKITE *n* pl. -S a mineral

FLINT *v* -ED, -ING, -S to provide with flint (a spark-producing rock)

FLINTY *adj* FLINTIER, FLINTIEST resembling flint **FLINTILY** *adv*

FLIP *v* FLIPPED, FLIPPING, FLIPS to throw with a brisk motion

FLIP *adj* FLIPPER, FLIPPEST flippant

FLIPPANT *adj* impudent

FLIPPED past tense of flip

FLIPPER *n* pl. -S a broad, flat limb adapted for swimming

FLIPPEST superlative of flip

FLIPPING present participle of flip

FLIPPY *adj* flaring at the bottom

FLIRT *v* -ED, -ING, -S to behave amorously without serious intent

FLIRTER *n* pl. -S one that flirts

FLIRTY *adj* FLIRTIER, FLIRTIEST given to flirting

FLIT *v* FLITTED, FLITTING, FLITS to move lightly and swiftly

FLITCH *v* -ED, -ING, -ES to cut into strips

FLITE *v* FLITED, FLITING, FLITES to quarrel

FLITTED past tense of flit

FLITTER *v* -ED, -ING, -S to flutter

FLITTING present participle of flit

FLIVVER *n* pl. -S an old, battered car

FLOAT *v* -ED, -ING, -S to rest or remain on the surface of a liquid

FLOATAGE *n* pl. -S flotage

FLOATEL *n* pl. -S a houseboat used as a hotel

FLOATER *n* pl. -S one that floats

FLOATY *adj* FLOATIER, FLOATIEST tending to float

FLOC *v* FLOCCED, FLOCCING, FLOCS to aggregate into floccules

FLOCCI pl. of floccus

FLOCCOSE *adj* having woolly tufts

FLOCCULE *n* pl. -S a tuft-like mass

FLOCCULI *n/pl* small, loosely aggregated masses

FLOCCUS *n* pl. FLOCCI a floccule

FLOCK *v* -ED, -ING, -S to gather or move in a crowd

FLOCKING *n* pl. -S a velvety design in short fibers on cloth or paper

FLOCKY *adj* FLOCKIER, FLOCKIEST woolly

FLOE *n* pl. -S a large mass of floating ice

FLOG *v* FLOGGED, FLOGGING, FLOGS to beat with a whip or rod

FLOGGER *n* pl. -S one that flogs

FLOGGING *n* pl. -S a whipping

FLOKATI *n* pl. -S a Greek handwoven rug

FLONG *n* pl. -S a sheet of a certain type of paper

FLOOD *v* -ED, -ING, -S to inundate

FLOODER *n* pl. -S one that floods

FLOODLIT *adj* illuminated by floodlights

FLOODWAY *n* pl. -WAYS an overflow channel

FLOOEY _adj_ awry

FLOOIE _adj_ flooey

FLOOR _v_ -ED, -ING, -S to provide with a floor (the level base of a room)

FLOORAGE _n pl._ -S floor space

FLOORER _n pl._ -S one that floors

FLOORING _n pl._ -S a floor

FLOOSIE _n pl._ -S floozy

FLOOSY _n pl._ -SIES floozy

FLOOZIE _n pl._ -S floozy

FLOOZY _n pl._ -ZIES a prostitute

FLOP _v_ FLOPPED, FLOPPING, FLOPS to fall heavily and noisily

FLOPOVER _n pl._ -S a defect in television reception

FLOPPER _n pl._ -S one that flops

FLOPPING present participle of flop

FLOPPY _n pl._ -PIES a type of computer disk

FLOPPY _adj_ -PIER, -PIEST soft and flexible FLOPPILY _adv_

FLORA _n pl._ -RAS or -RAE the plant life of a particular region

FLORAL _n pl._ -S a design featuring flowers

FLORALLY _adv_ in a manner resembling flowers

FLORENCE _n pl._ -S florin

FLORET _n pl._ -S a small flower

FLORID _adj_ ruddy FLORIDLY _adv_

FLORIGEN _n pl._ -S a plant hormone

FLORIN _n pl._ -S a former gold coin of Europe

FLORIST _n pl._ -S a grower or seller of flowers

FLORUIT _n pl._ -S a period of flourishing

FLOSS _v_ -ED, -ING, -ES to clean between the teeth with a strong thread

FLOSSIE _n pl._ -S a floozy

FLOSSY _adj_ FLOSSIER, FLOSSIEST resembling floss (a soft, light fiber) FLOSSILY _adv_

FLOTA _n pl._ -S a fleet of Spanish ships

FLOTAGE _n pl._ -S the act of floating

FLOTILLA _n pl._ -S a fleet of ships

FLOTSAM _n pl._ -S floating wreckage of a ship or its cargo

FLOUNCE _v_ FLOUNCED, FLOUNCING, FLOUNCES to move with exaggerated motions

FLOUNCY _adj_ FLOUNCIER, FLOUNCIEST flouncing

FLOUNDER _v_ -ED, -ING, -S to struggle clumsily

FLOUR _v_ -ED, -ING, -S to cover with flour (a finely ground meal of grain)

FLOURISH _v_ -ED, -ING, -ES to thrive

FLOURY _adj_ resembling flour

FLOUT _v_ -ED, -ING, -S to treat with contempt

FLOUTER _n pl._ -S one that flouts

FLOW _v_ -ED, -ING, -S to move steadily and smoothly along

FLOWAGE _n pl._ -S the act of flowing

FLOWER _v_ -ED, -ING, -S to put forth flowers (reproductive structures of seed-bearing plants)

FLOWERER _n pl._ -S a plant that flowers at a certain time

FLOWERET _n pl._ -S a floret

FLOWERY _adj_ -ERIER, -ERIEST abounding in flowers

FLOWN a past participle of fly

FLU _n pl._ -S a virus disease

FLUB _v_ FLUBBED, FLUBBING, FLUBS to bungle

FLUBBER _n pl._ -S one that flubs

FLUBDUB _n pl._ -S pretentious nonsense

FLUE _n pl._ -S an enclosed passageway for directing a current FLUED _adj_

FLUENCY _n pl._ -CIES the quality of being fluent

FLUENT _adj_ spoken or written with effortless ease FLUENTLY _adv_

FLUERICS _n/pl_ fluidics FLUERIC _adj_

FLUFF _v_ -ED, -ING, -S to make fluffy

FLUFFY _adj_ FLUFFIER, FLUFFIEST light and soft FLUFFILY _adv_

FLUID _n pl._ -S a substance that tends to flow FLUIDAL _adj_

FLUIDICS _n/pl_ a branch of mechanical engineering FLUIDIC _adj_

FLUIDISE _v_ -ISED, -ISING, -ISES to fluidize

FLUIDITY _n pl._ -TIES the quality of being able to flow

FLUIDIZE _v_ -IZED, -IZING, -IZES to cause to flow like a fluid

FLUIDLY _adv_ with fluidity

FLUIDRAM _n pl._ -S a unit of liquid capacity

FLUKE _v_ FLUKED, FLUKING, FLUKES to obtain by chance

FLUKEY _adj_ FLUKIER, FLUKIEST fluky

FLUKY *adj* FLUKIER, FLUKIEST happening by or depending on chance

FLUME *v* FLUMED, FLUMING, FLUMES to convey by means of an artificial water channel

FLUMMERY *n pl.* -MERIES a sweet dessert

FLUMMOX *v* -ED, -ING, -ES to confuse

FLUMP *v* -ED, -ING, -S to fall heavily

FLUNG past tense of fling

FLUNK *v* -ED, -ING, -S to fail an examination or course

FLUNKER *n pl.* -S one that flunks

FLUNKEY *n pl.* -KEYS flunky

FLUNKY *n pl.* -KIES a servile follower

FLUOR *n pl.* -S fluorite FLUORIC *adj*

FLUORENE *n pl.* -S a chemical compound

FLUORID *n pl.* -S fluoride

FLUORIDE *n pl.* -S a compound of fluorine

FLUORIN *n pl.* -S fluorine

FLUORINE *n pl.* -S a gaseous element

FLUORITE *n pl.* -S a mineral

FLURRY *v* -RIED, -RYING, -RIES to confuse

FLUSH *adj* FLUSHER, FLUSHEST ruddy

FLUSH *v* -ED, -ING, -ES to blush

FLUSHER *n pl.* -S one that flushes

FLUSTER *v* -ED, -ING, -S to put into a state of nervous confusion

FLUTE *v* FLUTED, FLUTING, FLUTES to play on a flute (a woodwind instrument)

FLUTER *n pl.* -S a flutist

FLUTEY *adj* FLUTIER, FLUTIEST fluty

FLUTIER comparative of fluty

FLUTIEST superlative of fluty

FLUTING *n pl.* -S a series of parallel grooves

FLUTIST *n pl.* -S one who plays the flute

FLUTTER *v* -ED, -ING, -S to wave rapidly and irregularly

FLUTTERY *adj* marked by fluttering

FLUTY *adj* FLUTIER, FLUTIEST resembling a flute in sound

FLUVIAL *adj* pertaining to a river

FLUX *v* -ED, -ING, -ES to melt

FLUXGATE *n pl.* -S a device to measure a magnetic field

FLUXION *n pl.* -S the act of flowing

FLUYT *n pl.* -S a type of ship

FLY *v* FLEW, FLOWN, FLYING, FLIES to move through the air

FLY *v* FLIED, FLYING, FLIES to hit a ball high into the air in baseball

FLY *adj* FLIER, FLIEST clever

FLYABLE *adj* suitable for flying

FLYAWAY *n pl.* -AWAYS one that is elusive

FLYBELT *n pl.* -S an area infested with tsetse flies

FLYBLOW *v* -BLEW, -BLOWN, -BLOWING, -BLOWS to taint

FLYBOAT *n pl.* -S a small, fast boat

FLYBOY *n pl.* -BOYS a pilot in an air force

FLYBY *n pl.* -BYS a flight of aircraft close to a specified place

FLYER *n pl.* -S flier

FLYING *n pl.* -S the operation of an aircraft

FLYLEAF *n pl.* -LEAVES a blank leaf at the beginning or end of a book

FLYLESS *adj* free of flies (winged insects)

FLYMAN *n pl.* -MEN a stage worker in a theater

FLYOFF *n pl.* -S a competitive testing of model aircraft

FLYOVER *n pl.* -S a flight of aircraft over a specific location

FLYPAPER *n pl.* -S paper designed to catch or kill flies

FLYPAST *n pl.* -S a flyby

FLYSCH *n pl.* -ES a sandstone deposit

FLYSPECK *v* -ED, -ING, -S to mark with minute spots

FLYTE *v* FLYTED, FLYTING, FLYTES to flite

FLYTIER *n pl.* -S a maker of fishing flies

FLYTING *n pl.* -S a dispute in verse form

FLYTRAP *n pl.* -S a trap for catching flies

FLYWAY *n pl.* -WAYS an established air route of migratory birds

FLYWHEEL *n pl.* -S a heavy disk used in machinery

FOAL *v* -ED, -ING, -S to give birth to a horse

FOAM *v* -ED, -ING, -S to form foam (a light, bubbly, gas and liquid mass) FOAMABLE *adj*

FOAMER *n pl.* -S one that foams

FOAMIER comparative of foamy

FOAMIEST superlative of foamy

FOAMILY *adv* in a foamy manner

FOAMLESS *adj* being without foam

FOAMLIKE *adj* resembling foam

FOAMY *adj* FOAMIER, FOAMIEST covered with foam

FOB *v* FOBBED, FOBBING, FOBS to deceive

FOCACCIA *n pl.* -S a flat Italian bread

FOCAL *adj* pertaining to a focus

FOCALISE *v* -ISED, -ISING, -ISES to focalize

FOCALIZE *v* -IZED, -IZING, -IZES to focus

FOCALLY *adv* with regard to focus

FOCUS *n pl.* -CUSES or -CI a point at which rays converge or from which they diverge

FOCUS *v* -CUSED, -CUSING, -CUSES or -CUSSED, -CUSSING, -CUSSES to bring to a focus

FOCUSER *n pl.* -S one that focuses

FODDER *v* -ED, -ING, -S to feed with coarse food

FODGEL *adj* plump

FOE *n pl.* -S an enemy

FOEHN *n pl.* -S a warm, dry wind

FOEMAN *n pl.* -MEN an enemy in war

FOETAL *adj* fetal

FOETID *adj* fetid

FOETOR *n pl.* -S fetor

FOETUS *n pl.* -ES fetus

FOG *v* FOGGED, FOGGING, FOGS to cover with fog (condensed water vapor near the earth's surface)

FOGBOUND *adj* surrounded by fog

FOGBOW *n pl.* -S a nebulous arc of light sometimes seen in a fog

FOGDOG *n pl.* -S a fogbow

FOGEY *n pl.* -GEYS fogy

FOGFRUIT *n pl.* -S a flowering plant

FOGGAGE *n pl.* -S a second growth of grass

FOGGED past tense of fog

FOGGER *n pl.* -S one that fogs

FOGGING present participle of fog

FOGGY *adj* -GIER, -GIEST filled with fog FOGGILY *adv*

FOGHORN *n pl.* -S a horn sounded in a fog to give warning

FOGIE *n pl.* -S fogy

FOGLESS *adj* having no fog

FOGY *n pl.* -GIES an old-fashioned person FOGYISH *adj*

FOGYISM *n pl.* -S old-fashioned behavior

FOH *interj* faugh

FOHN *n pl.* -S foehn

FOIBLE *n pl.* -S a minor weakness

FOIL *v* -ED, -ING, -S to prevent the success of FOILABLE *adj*

FOILSMAN *n pl.* -MEN a fencer

FOIN *v* -ED, -ING, -S to thrust with a pointed weapon

FOISON *n pl.* -S strength

FOIST *v* -ED, -ING, -S to force upon slyly

FOLACIN *n pl.* -S a B vitamin

FOLATE *n pl.* -S folacin

FOLD *v* -ED, -ING, -S to lay one part over another part of FOLDABLE *adj*

FOLDAWAY *adj* designed to fold out of the way

FOLDBOAT *n pl.* -S a faltboat

FOLDER *n pl.* -S one that folds

FOLDEROL *n pl.* -S falderal

FOLDOUT *n pl.* -S a gatefold

FOLIA a pl. of folium

FOLIAGE *n pl.* -S the growth of leaves of a plant FOLIAGED *adj*

FOLIAR *adj* pertaining to a leaf

FOLIATE *v* -ATED, -ATING, -ATES to hammer into thin plates

FOLIO *v* -ED, -ING, -S to number the pages of

FOLIOSE *adj* having leaves

FOLIOUS *adj* foliose

FOLIUM *n pl.* -LIA or -LIUMS a thin layer

FOLK *n pl.* -S a people or tribe

FOLKIE *n pl.* -S a performer of folk music

FOLKISH *adj* characteristic of the common people

FOLKLIFE *n pl.* -LIVES the traditions, skills, and products of a people

FOLKLIKE *adj* folkish

FOLKLORE *n pl.* -S the lore of a people

FOLKMOOT *n pl.* -S a general assembly of the people in early England

FOLKMOT *n pl.* -S folkmoot

FOLKMOTE *n pl.* -S folkmoot

FOLKSY *adj* FOLKSIER, FOLKSIEST friendly FOLKSILY *adv*

FOLKTALE *n pl.* -S a tale forming part of the oral tradition of a people

FOLKWAY *n pl.* -WAYS a traditional custom of a people

FOLKY *n pl.* FOLKIES folkie

FOLLES pl. of follis

FOLLICLE *n pl.* -S a small bodily cavity

FOLLIES pl. of folly

FOLLIS *n pl.* -LES a coin of ancient Rome

FOLLOW v -ED, -ING, -S to come or go after

FOLLOWER n pl. -S one that follows

FOLLY n pl. -LIES a foolish idea or action

FOMENT v -ED, -ING, -S to promote the development of

FOMENTER n pl. -S one that foments

FOMITE n pl. -S an inanimate object that serves to transmit infectious organisms

FON n pl. -S foehn

FOND adj FONDER, FONDEST having an affection

FOND v -ED, -ING, -S to display affection

FONDANT n pl. -S a soft, creamy candy

FONDLE v -DLED, -DLING, -DLES to caress

FONDLER n pl. -S one that fondles

FONDLING n pl. -S one that is fondled

FONDLY adv in a fond manner

FONDNESS n pl. -ES affection

FONDU n pl. -S fondue

FONDUE n pl. -S a dish of melted cheese

FONT n pl. -S a receptacle for the water used in baptism FONTAL adj

FONTANEL n pl. -S a space in the fetal and infantile skull

FONTINA n pl. -S an Italian cheese

FOOD n pl. -S a substance taken into the body to maintain life and growth FOODLESS adj

FOODIE n pl. -S an enthusiast of foods and their preparation

FOODWAYS n/pl the eating habits of a people

FOOFARAW n pl. -S excessive ornamentation

FOOL v -ED, -ING, -S to deceive

FOOLERY n pl. -ERIES foolish behavior or speech

FOOLFISH n pl. -ES a marine fish

FOOLISH adj -ISHER, -ISHEST lacking good sense or judgment

FOOLSCAP n pl. -S a paper size

FOOT n pl. FEET the terminal part of the leg on which the body stands and moves

FOOT v -ED, -ING, -S to walk

FOOTAGE n pl. -S a length or quantity expressed in feet

FOOTBALL n pl. -S a type of ball

FOOTBATH n pl. -S a bath for the feet

FOOTBOY n pl. -BOYS a serving boy

FOOTER n pl. -S one that walks

FOOTFALL n pl. -S the sound of a footstep

FOOTGEAR n pl. -S footwear

FOOTHILL n pl. -S a low hill at the foot of higher hills

FOOTHOLD n pl. -S a secure support for the feet

FOOTIE n pl. -S footsie

FOOTIER comparative of footy

FOOTIEST superlative of footy

FOOTING n pl. -S a foothold

FOOTLE v -TLED, -TLING, -TLES to waste time

FOOTLER n pl. -S one that footles

FOOTLESS adj having no feet

FOOTLIKE adj resembling a foot

FOOTLING present participle of footle

FOOTMAN n pl. -MEN a male servant

FOOTMARK n pl. -S a mark left by the foot on a surface

FOOTNOTE v -NOTED, -NOTING, -NOTES to furnish with explanatory notes

FOOTPACE n pl. -S a walking pace

FOOTPAD n pl. -S one who robs a pedestrian

FOOTPATH n pl. -S a path for pedestrians

FOOTRACE n pl. -S a race run on foot

FOOTREST n pl. -S a support for the feet

FOOTROPE n pl. -S a rope used in sailing

FOOTSIE n pl. -S a flirting game played with the feet

FOOTSLOG v -SLOGGED, -SLOGGING, -SLOGS to march through mud

FOOTSORE adj having sore or tired feet

FOOTSTEP n pl. -S a step with the foot

FOOTSY n pl. -SIES footsie

FOOTWALL n pl. -S the layer of rock beneath a vein of ore

FOOTWAY n pl. -WAYS a footpath

FOOTWEAR n pl. FOOTWEAR wearing apparel for the feet

FOOTWORK n pl. -S the use of the feet

FOOTWORN adj footsore

FOOTY adj -TIER, -TIEST paltry

FOOZLE v -ZLED, -ZLING, -ZLES to bungle

FOOZLER n pl. -S one that foozles

FOP v FOPPED, FOPPING, FOPS to deceive

FOPPERY n pl. -PERIES foppish behavior

FOPPISH adj characteristic of a dandy

FOR prep directed or sent to

FORA a pl. of forum

FORAGE v -AGED, -AGING, -AGES to search about

FORAGER n pl. -S one that forages

FORAM n pl. -S a marine rhizopod

FORAMEN n pl. -MINA or -MENS a small anatomical opening

FORAY v -ED, -ING, -S to raid

FORAYER n pl. -S one that forays

FORB n pl. -S an herb other than grass

FORBAD a past tense of forbid

FORBADE a past tense of forbid

FORBEAR v -BORE, -BORNE, -BEARING, -BEARS to refrain from

FORBID v -BADE or -BAD, -BIDDEN, -BIDDING, -BIDS to command not to do something

FORBIDAL n pl. -S the act of forbidding

FORBODE v -BODED, -BODING, -BODES to forebode

FORBORE past tense of forbear

FORBORNE past participle of forbear

FORBY prep close by

FORBYE prep forby

FORCE v FORCED, FORCING, FORCES to overcome resistance by the exertion of strength **FORCEDLY** adv

FORCEFUL adj strong

FORCEPS n pl. -CIPES an instrument for seizing and holding objects

FORCER n pl. -S one that forces

FORCIBLE adj effected by force **FORCIBLY**

FORCING present participle of force

FORCIPES pl. of forceps

FORD v -ED, -ING, -S to cross by wading **FORDABLE** adj

FORDLESS adj unable to be forded

FORDO v -DID, -DONE, -DOING, -DOES to destroy

FORE n pl. -S the front part of something

FOREARM v -ED, -ING, -S to arm in advance

FOREBAY n pl. -BAYS a reservoir from which water is taken to run equipment

FOREBEAR n pl. -S an ancestor

FOREBODE v -BODED, -BODING, -BODES to indicate in advance

FOREBODY n pl. -BODIES the forward part of a ship

FOREBOOM n pl. -S the boom of a ship's foremast

FOREBY prep forby

FOREBYE prep forby

FORECAST v -ED, -ING, -S to estimate or calculate in advance

FOREDATE v -DATED, -DATING, -DATES to antedate

FOREDECK n pl. -S the forward part of a ship's deck

FOREDO v -DID, -DONE, -DOING, -DOES to fordo

FOREDOOM v -ED, -ING, -S to doom in advance

FOREFACE n pl. -S the front part of the head of a quadruped

FOREFEEL v -FELT, -FEELING, -FEELS to have a premonition of

FOREFEND v -ED, -ING, -S to forfend

FOREFOOT n pl. -FEET one of the front feet of an animal

FOREGO v -WENT, -GONE, -GOING, -GOES to go before

FOREGOER n pl. -S one that foregoes

FOREGUT n pl. -S the front part of the embryonic alimentary canal

FOREHAND n pl. -S a type of tennis stroke

FOREHEAD n pl. -S the part of the face above the eyes

FOREHOOF n pl. -HOOFS or -HOOVES the hoof of a forefoot

FOREIGN adj situated outside a place or country

FOREKNOW v -KNEW, -KNOWN, -KNOWING, -KNOWS to know in advance

FORELADY n pl. -DIES a woman who supervises workers

FORELAND n pl. -S a projecting mass of land

FORELEG n pl. -S one of the front legs of an animal

FORELIMB n pl. -S a foreleg

FORELOCK v -ED, -ING, -S to fasten with a linchpin

FOREMAN n pl. -MEN a man who supervises workers

FOREMAST n pl. -S the forward mast of a ship

FOREMILK n pl. -S the milk secreted immediately after childbirth

FOREMOST adj first in position

FORENAME n pl. -S a first name

FORENOON n pl. -S the period of daylight before noon

FORENSIC n pl. -S an argumentative exercise

FOREPART n pl. -S the front part

FOREPAST adj already in the past

FOREPAW n pl. -S the paw of a foreleg

FOREPEAK n pl. -S the forward part of a ship's hold

FOREPLAY n pl. -PLAYS erotic stimulation preceding sexual intercourse

FORERANK n pl. -S the first rank

FORERUN v -RAN, -RUNNING, -RUNS to run in advance of

FORESAID adj previously said

FORESAIL n pl. -S the lowest sail on a foremast

FORESEE v -SAW, -SEEN, -SEEING, -SEES to see in advance

FORESEER n pl. -S one that foresees

FORESHOW v -SHOWED, -SHOWN, -SHOWING, -SHOWS to show in advance

FORESIDE n pl. -S the front side

FORESKIN n pl. -S the prepuce

FOREST v -ED, -ING, -S to convert into a forest (a densely wooded area)

FORESTAL adj of or pertaining to a forest

FORESTAY n pl. -STAYS a wire or rope used to support a foremast

FORESTER n pl. -S one skilled in forestry

FORESTRY n pl. -RIES the science of planting and managing forests

FORETELL v -TOLD, -TELLING, -TELLS to tell of or about in advance

FORETIME n pl. -S the past

FORETOP n pl. -S a forelock

FOREVER n pl. -S an indefinite length of time

FOREWARN v -ED, -ING, -S to warn in advance

FOREWENT past tense of forego

FOREWING n pl. -S an anterior wing of an insect

FOREWORD n pl. -S an introductory statement

FOREWORN adj forworn

FOREYARD n pl. -S the lowest yard on a foremast

FORFEIT v -ED, -ING, -S to lose as a penalty

FORFEND v -ED, -ING, -S to protect

FORGAT a past tense of forget

FORGAVE past tense of forgive

FORGE v FORGED, FORGING, FORGES to fashion or reproduce for fraudulent purposes

FORGER n pl. -S one that forges

FORGERY n pl. -ERIES the act of forging

FORGET v -GOT or -GAT, -GOTTEN, -GETTING, -GETS to fail to remember

FORGING n pl. -S a forgery

FORGIVE v -GAVE, -GIVEN, -GIVING, -GIVES to pardon

FORGIVER n pl. -S one that forgives

FORGO v -WENT, -GONE, -GOING, -GOES to refrain from

FORGOER n pl. -S one that forgoes

FORGOT a past tense of forget

FORGOTTEN past participle of forget

FORINT n pl. -S a monetary unit of Hungary

FORJUDGE v -JUDGED, -JUDGING, -JUDGES to deprive by judgment of a court

FORK v -ED, -ING, -S to work with a fork (a pronged implement) **FORKEDLY** adv

FORKBALL n pl. -S a breaking pitch in baseball

FORKER n pl. -S one that forks

FORKFUL n pl. FORKFULS or FORKSFUL as much as a fork will hold

FORKIER comparative of forky

FORKIEST superlative of forky

FORKLESS adj having no fork

FORKLIFT v -ED, -ING, -S to raise or transport by means of a forklift (a machine with projecting prongs)

FORKLIKE adj resembling a fork

FORKSFUL a pl. of forkful

FORKY adj FORKIER, FORKIEST resembling a fork

FORLORN adj -LORNER, -LORNEST dreary

FORM v -ED, -ING, -S to produce **FORMABLE** adj

FORMAL n pl. -S a social event that requires evening dress

FORMALIN n pl. -S an aqueous solution of formaldehyde

FORMALLY adv in a prescribed or customary manner

FORMANT n pl. -S a characteristic component of the quality of a speech sound

FORMAT v -MATTED, -MATTING, -MATS to produce in a specified style

FORMATE n pl. -S a chemical salt

FORME n pl. -S an assemblage of printing type secured in a metal frame

FORMEE adj having the arms narrow at the center and expanding toward the ends — used of a heraldic cross

FORMER n pl. -S one that forms

FORMERLY adv previously

FORMFUL adj exhibiting good form

FORMIC adj pertaining to ants

FORMLESS adj lacking structure

FORMOL n pl. -S formalin

FORMULA n pl. -LAS or -LAE an exact method for doing something

FORMWORK n pl. -S a set of forms to hold concrete until it sets

FORMYL n pl. -S a univalent chemical radical

FORNIX n pl. -NICES an arched anatomical structure FORNICAL adj

FORRADER adv further ahead

FORRIT adv toward the front

FORSAKE v -SOOK, -SAKEN, -SAKING, -SAKES to quit or leave entirely

FORSAKER n pl. -S one that forsakes

FORSOOTH adv in truth

FORSPENT adj worn out

FORSWEAR v -SWORE, -SWORN, -SWEARING, -SWEARS to deny under oath

FORT n pl. -S a fortified enclosure or structure

FORTE n pl. -S a strong point

FORTES pl. of fortis

FORTH adv onward in time, place, or order

FORTIES pl. of forty

FORTIETH n pl. -S one of forty equal parts

FORTIFY v -FIED, -FYING, -FIES to strengthen against attack

FORTIS n pl. -TES a consonant pronounced with relatively strong release of breath

FORTRESS v -ED, -ING, -ES to fortify

FORTUITY n pl. -ITIES an accidental occurrence

FORTUNE v -TUNED, -TUNING, -TUNES to endow with wealth

FORTY n pl. -TIES a number

FORTYISH adj being about forty years old

FORUM n pl. -RUMS or -RA a public meeting place

FORWARD adj -WARDER, -WARDEST being at or near a point in advance

FORWARD v -ED, -ING, -S to help onward

FORWENT past tense of forgo

FORWHY adv for what reason

FORWORN adj worn out

FORZANDO n pl. -DOS sforzato

FOSS n pl. -ES fosse

FOSSA n pl. -SAE an anatomical depression FOSSATE adj

FOSSA n pl. -S a catlike mammal

FOSSE n pl. -S a ditch

FOSSETTE n pl. -S a small fossa

FOSSICK v -ED, -ING, -S to search for gold

FOSSIL n pl. -S the remains of an animal or plant preserved in the earth's crust

FOSTER v -ED, -ING, -S to promote the growth of

FOSTERER n pl. -S one that fosters

FOU adj drunk

FOUETTE n pl. -S a movement in ballet

FOUGHT past tense of fight

FOUGHTEN adj exhausted especially from fighting

FOUL adj FOULER, FOULEST offensive to the senses

FOUL v -ED, -ING, -S to make foul

FOULARD n pl. -S a soft fabric

FOULING n pl. -S a deposit or crust

FOULLY adv in a foul manner

FOULNESS n pl. -ES the state of being foul

FOUND v -ED, -ING, -S to establish

FOUNDER v -ED, -ING, -S to become disabled

FOUNDRY n pl. -RIES an establishment in which metal is cast

FOUNT n pl. -S a fountain

FOUNTAIN v -ED, -ING, -S to flow like a fountain (a spring of water)

FOUR n pl. -S a number

FOURCHEE adj having the end of each arm forked — used of a heraldic cross

FOURFOLD adj four times as great

FOURGON n pl. -S a wagon for baggage

FOURPLEX n pl. -ES quadplex

FOURSOME n pl. -S a group of four

FOURTEEN   n pl. -S a number
FOURTH   n pl. -S one of four equal parts
FOURTHLY   adv in the fourth place
FOVEA   n pl. -VEAE or -VEAS a shallow anatomical depression   **FOVEAL, FOVEATE, FOVEOLATED** adj
FOVEOLA   n pl. -LAE or -LAS a small fovea **FOVEOLAR** adj
FOVEOLE   n pl. -S a foveola
FOVEOLET   n pl. -S a foveola
FOWL   v -ED, -ING, -S to hunt birds
FOWLER   n pl. -S one that fowls
FOWLING   n pl. -S the hunting of birds
FOWLPOX   n pl. -ES a virus disease of poultry
FOX   v -ED, -ING, -ES to outwit
FOXFIRE   n pl. -S a glow produced by certain fungi on decaying wood
FOXFISH   n pl. -ES a large shark
FOXGLOVE   n pl. -S a flowering plant
FOXHOLE   n pl. -S a small pit used for cover in a battle area
FOXHOUND   n pl. -S a hunting dog
FOXHUNT   v -ED, -ING, -S to hunt with hounds for a fox
FOXIER   comparative of foxy
FOXIEST   superlative of foxy
FOXILY   adv in a foxy manner
FOXINESS   n pl. -ES the state of being foxy
FOXING   n pl. -S a piece of material used to cover the upper portion of a shoe
FOXLIKE   adj resembling a fox (a carnivorous mammal)
FOXSKIN   n pl. -S the skin of a fox
FOXTAIL   n pl. -S the tail of a fox
FOXTROT   v -TROTTED, -TROTTING, -TROTS to dance the fox trot (a dance for couples)
FOXY   adj FOXIER, FOXIEST crafty
FOY   n pl. FOYS a farewell feast or gift
FOYER   n pl. -S an entrance room or hall
FOZINESS   n pl. -ES the state of being fozy
FOZY   adj -ZIER, -ZIEST too ripe
FRABJOUS   adj splendid
FRACAS   n pl. -ES a brawl
FRACTAL   n pl. -S a complex geometric curve
FRACTED   adj broken
FRACTI   pl. of fractus

FRACTION   v -ED, -ING, -S to divide into portions
FRACTUR   n pl. -S fraktur
FRACTURE   v -TURED, -TURING, -TURES to break
FRACTUS   n pl. -TI a ragged cloud
FRAE   prep from
FRAENUM   n pl. -NA or -NUMS frenum
FRAG   v FRAGGED, FRAGGING, FRAGS to injure with a type of grenade
FRAGGING   n pl. -S the act of one that frags
FRAGILE   adj easily broken or damaged
FRAGMENT   v -ED, -ING, -S to break into pieces
FRAGRANT   adj having a pleasant odor
FRAIL   adj FRAILER, FRAILEST fragile **FRAILLY** adv
FRAIL   n pl. -S a basket for holding dried fruits
FRAILTY   n pl. -TIES a weakness of character
FRAISE   n pl. -S a barrier of pointed stakes
FRAKTUR   n pl. -S a style of type
FRAME   v FRAMED, FRAMING, FRAMES to construct by putting together the various parts **FRAMABLE** adj
FRAMER   n pl. -S one that frames
FRAMING   n pl. -S framework
FRANC   n pl. -S a monetary unit of France
FRANCIUM   n pl. -S a radioactive element
FRANK   adj FRANKER, FRANKEST honest and unreserved in speech
FRANK   v -ED, -ING, -S to mark (a piece of mail) for free delivery
FRANKER   n pl. -S one that franks
FRANKLIN   n pl. -S a medieval English landowner
FRANKLY   adv in a frank manner
FRANTIC   adj wildly excited
FRAP   v FRAPPED, FRAPPING, FRAPS to bind firmly
FRAPPE   n pl. -S a partly frozen drink
FRASS   n pl. -ES debris made by insects
FRAT   n pl. -S a college fraternity
FRATER   n pl. -S a comrade
FRAUD   n pl. -S trickery
FRAUGHT   v -ED, -ING, -S to load down
FRAULEIN   n pl. -S a German governess

FRAY	v -ED, -ING, -S to wear off by rubbing		**FREEZE**	v FROZE, FROZEN, FREEZING, FREEZES to become hardened into a solid body by loss of heat
FRAYING	n pl. -S something worn off by rubbing			
FRAZIL	n pl. -S tiny ice crystals formed in supercooled waters		**FREEZER**	n pl. -S an apparatus for freezing food
FRAZZLE	v -ZLED, -ZLING, -ZLES to fray		**FREIGHT**	v -ED, -ING, -S to load with goods for transportation
FREAK	v -ED, -ING, -S to streak with color		**FREMD**	adj strange
FREAKIER	comparative of freaky		**FREMITUS**	n pl. -ES a palpable vibration
FREAKIEST	superlative of freaky		**FRENA**	a pl. of frenum
FREAKILY	adv in a freaky manner		**FRENCH**	v -ED, -ING, -ES to cut into thin strips before cooking
FREAKISH	adj unusual		**FRENETIC**	n pl. -S a frantic person
FREAKOUT	n pl. -S an event marked by wild excitement		**FRENULUM**	n pl. -LA or -LUMS a frenum
FREAKY	adj FREAKIER, FREAKIEST freakish		**FRENUM**	n pl. -NA or -NUMS a connecting fold of membrane
FRECKLE	v -LED, -LING, -LES to mark with freckles (small, brownish spots)		**FRENZILY**	adv in a frantic manner
			FRENZY	v -ZIED, -ZYING, -ZIES to make frantic
FRECKLY	adj -LIER, -LIEST marked with freckles		**FREQUENT**	adj -QUENTER, -QUENTEST occurring again and again
FREE	adj FREER, FREEST not subject to restriction or control		**FREQUENT**	v -ED, -ING, -S to be in or at often
FREE	v FREED, FREEING, FREES to make free		**FRERE**	n pl. -S brother
			FRESCO	v -ED, -ING, -ES or -S to paint on a surface of plaster
FREEBASE	v -BASED, -BASING, -BASES to use a form of cocaine that is inhaled		**FRESCOER**	n pl. -S one that frescoes
			FRESH	adj FRESHER, FRESHEST new
FREEBEE	n pl. -S freebie			
FREEBIE	n pl. -S something given or received without charge		**FRESH**	v -ED, -ING, -ES to freshen
			FRESHEN	v -ED, -ING, -S to make or become fresh
FREEBOOT	v -ED, -ING, -S to plunder			
FREEBORN	adj born free		**FRESHET**	n pl. -S a sudden overflow of a stream
FREED	past tense of free			
FREEDMAN	n pl. -MEN a man who has been freed from slavery		**FRESHLY**	adv in a fresh manner
			FRESHMAN	n pl. -MEN a first-year student
FREEDOM	n pl. -S the state of being free		**FRESNEL**	n pl. -S a unit of frequency
FREEFORM	adj having a free flowing design or shape		**FRET**	v FRETTED, FRETTING, FRETS to worry
FREEHAND	adj drawn by hand without mechanical aids		**FRETFUL**	adj inclined to fret
			FRETLESS	adj having no fretwork
FREEHOLD	n pl. -S a form of tenure of real property		**FRETSAW**	n pl. -S a narrow-bladed saw
			FRETSOME	adj fretful
FREELOAD	v -ED, -ING, -S to live at the expense of others		**FRETTED**	past tense of fret
			FRETTER	n pl. -S one that frets
FREELY	adv in a free manner		**FRETTING**	present participle of fret
FREEMAN	n pl. -MEN one who is free		**FRETTY**	adj -TIER, -TIEST fretful
FREENESS	n pl. -ES freedom		**FRETWORK**	n pl. -S ornamental work consisting of interlacing parts
FREER	n pl. -S one that frees			
FREESIA	n pl. -S an African herb		**FRIABLE**	adj easily crumbled
FREEST	superlative of free		**FRIAR**	n pl. -S a member of a religious order FRIARLY adj
FREEWAY	n pl. -WAYS an express highway			
FREEWILL	adj voluntary		**FRIARY**	n pl. -ARIES a monastery of friars

FRIBBLE v -BLED, -BLING, -BLES to act foolishly

FRIBBLER n pl. -S one that fribbles

FRICANDO n pl. -DOES a roasted loin of veal

FRICTION n pl. -S the rubbing of one body against another

FRIDGE n pl. -S a refrigerator

FRIED past tense of fry

FRIEND v -ED, -ING, -S to enter into a warm association with

FRIENDLY adj -LIER, -LIEST inclined to approve, help, or support

FRIENDLY n pl. -LIES one who is friendly

FRIER n pl. -S fryer

FRIES present 3d person sing. of fry

FRIEZE n pl. -S a coarse woolen fabric

FRIGATE n pl. -S a sailing vessel

FRIGHT v -ED, -ING, -S to frighten

FRIGHTEN v -ED, -ING, -S to make afraid

FRIGID adj very cold FRIGIDLY adv

FRIJOL n pl. -ES a bean used as food

FRIJOLE n pl. -S frijol

FRILL v -ED, -ING, -S to provide with a frill (an ornamental ruffled edge)

FRILLER n pl. -S one that frills

FRILLING n pl. -S an arrangement of frills

FRILLY adj FRILLIER, FRILLIEST having frills

FRINGE v FRINGED, FRINGING, FRINGES to provide with a fringe (an ornamental border)

FRINGY adj FRINGIER, FRINGIEST resembling a fringe

FRIPPERY n pl. -PERIES excessive ornamentation

FRISE n pl. -S frieze

FRISETTE n pl. -S frizette

FRISEUR n pl. -S a hairdresser

FRISK v -ED, -ING, -S to move or leap about playfully

FRISKER n pl. -S one that frisks

FRISKET n pl. -S a frame used to protect paper in a printing press

FRISKY adj FRISKIER, FRISKIEST lively and playful FRISKILY adv

FRISSON n pl. -S a shudder

FRIT v FRITTED, FRITTING, FRITS to fuse into a vitreous substance

FRITH n pl. -S firth

FRITT v -ED, -ING, -S to frit

FRITTATA n pl. -S an unfolded omelet with chopped vegetables or meat

FRITTED past tense of frit

FRITTER v -ED, -ING, -S to squander little by little

FRITTING present participle of frit

FRITZ n pl. -ES a nonfunctioning state

FRIVOL v -OLED, -OLING, -OLS or -OLLED, -OLLING, -OLS to behave playfully

FRIVOLER n pl. -S one that frivols

FRIZ v -ED, -ING, -ES to frizz

FRIZER n pl. -S frizzer

FRIZETTE n pl. -S a frizzed fringe of hair

FRIZZ v -ED, -ING, -ES to form into small, tight curls

FRIZZER n pl. -S one that frizzes

FRIZZIER comparative of frizzy

FRIZZIEST superlative of frizzy

FRIZZILY adv in a frizzy manner

FRIZZLE v -ZLED, -ZLING, -ZLES to frizz

FRIZZLER n pl. -S one that frizzles

FRIZZLY adj -ZLIER, -ZLIEST frizzy

FRIZZY adj FRIZZIER, FRIZZIEST tightly curled

FRO adv away

FROCK v -ED, -ING, -S to clothe in a long, loose outer garment

FROE n pl. -S a cleaving tool

FROG v FROGGED, FROGGING, FROGS to hunt frogs (web-footed, tailless amphibians)

FROGEYE n pl. -S a plant disease FROGEYED adj

FROGFISH n pl. -ES a marine fish

FROGGED past tense of frog

FROGGING present participle of frog

FROGGY adj -GIER, -GIEST abounding in frogs

FROGLIKE adj resembling a frog

FROGMAN n pl. -MEN a person equipped for extended periods of underwater swimming

FROLIC v -ICKED, -ICKING, -ICS to play and run about merrily FROLICKY adj

FROM prep starting at

FROMAGE n pl. -S cheese

FROMENTY n pl. -TIES frumenty

FROND n pl. -S a type of leaf FRONDED, FRONDOSE adj

FRONDEUR n pl. -S a rebel

FRONS *n* pl. FRONTES the upper anterior portion of an insect's head

FRONT *v* -ED, -ING, -S to provide with a front (a forward part)

FRONT *adj* FRONTER articulated at the front of the oral passage

FRONTAGE *n* pl. -S the front of a building or lot

FRONTAL *n* pl. -S a bone of the skull

FRONTES pl. of frons

FRONTIER *n* pl. -S a border between two countries

FRONTLET *n* pl. -S a decorative band worn across the forehead

FRONTON *n* pl. -S a jai alai arena

FRORE *adj* frozen

FROSH *n* pl. FROSH a freshman

FROST *v* -ED, -ING, -S to cover with frost (a deposit of minute ice crystals)

FROSTBIT *adj* injured by extreme cold

FROSTED *n* pl. -S a type of milk shake

FROSTING *n* pl. -S icing

FROSTY *adj* FROSTIER, FROSTIEST covered with frost **FROSTILY** *adv*

FROTH *v* -ED, -ING, -S to foam

FROTHY *adj* FROTHIER, FROTHIEST foamy **FROTHILY** *adv*

FROTTAGE *n* pl. -S masturbation by rubbing against another person

FROTTEUR *n* pl. -S one who practices frottage

FROUFROU *n* pl. -S a rustling sound

FROUNCE *v* FROUNCED, FROUNCING, FROUNCES to pleat

FROUZY *adj* -ZIER, -ZIEST frowzy

FROW *n* pl. -S froe

FROWARD *adj* disobedient

FROWN *v* -ED, -ING, -S to contract the brow in displeasure

FROWNER *n* pl. -S one that frowns

FROWST *v* -ED, -ING, -S to lounge in a stuffy room

FROWSTY *adj* -TIER, -TIEST musty

FROWSY *adj* -SIER, -SIEST frowzy

FROWZY *adj* -ZIER, -ZIEST unkempt **FROWZILY** *adv*

FROZE past tense of freeze

FROZEN *adj* very cold **FROZENLY** *adv*

FRUCTIFY *v* -FIED, -FYING, -FIES to bear fruit

FRUCTOSE *n* pl. -S a sugar found in various fruits

FRUG *v* FRUGGED, FRUGGING, FRUGS to perform a type of vigorous dance

FRUGAL *adj* thrifty **FRUGALLY** *adv*

FRUIT *v* -ED, -ING, -S to bear fruit (usually edible reproductive bodies of a seed plant)

FRUITAGE *n* pl. -S the process of bearing fruit

FRUITER *n* pl. -S one that grows or sells fruit

FRUITFUL *adj* -FULLER, -FULLEST producing abundantly

FRUITIER comparative of fruity

FRUITIEST superlative of fruity

FRUITION *n* pl. -S the accomplishment of something desired

FRUITLET *n* pl. -S a small fruit

FRUITY *adj* FRUITIER, FRUITIEST suggestive of fruit **FRUITILY** *adv*

FRUMENTY *n* pl. -TIES a dish of wheat boiled in milk and sweetened with sugar

FRUMP *n* pl. -S a dowdy woman **FRUMPISH** *adj*

FRUMPY *adj* FRUMPIER, FRUMPIEST dowdy **FRUMPILY** *adv*

FRUSTULE *n* pl. -S the shell of a diatom

FRUSTUM *n* pl. -TA or -TUMS a part of a conical solid

FRY *v* FRIED, FRYING, FRIES to cook over direct heat in hot fat or oil

FRYER *n* pl. -S one that fries

FRYPAN *n* pl. -S a pan for frying food

FUB *v* FUBBED, FUBBING, FUBS to fob

FUBSY *adj* FUBSIER, FUBSIEST chubby and somewhat squat

FUCHSIA *n* pl. -S a flowering shrub

FUCHSIN *n* pl. -S a red dye

FUCHSINE *n* pl. -S fuchsin

FUCI a pl. of fucus

FUCOID *n* pl. -S a brown seaweed **FUCOIDAL** *adj*

FUCOSE *n* pl. -S a type of sugar

FUCOUS *adj* of or pertaining to fucoids

FUCUS *n* pl. -CI or -CUSES any of a genus of brown algae

FUD *n* pl. -S an old-fashioned person

FUDDLE *v* -DLED, -DLING, -DLES to confuse

FUDGE *v* FUDGED, FUDGING, FUDGES to falsify

FUEHRER n pl. -S fuhrer

FUEL v -ELED, -ELING, -ELS or -ELLED, -ELLING, -ELS to provide with fuel (material used to produce energy)

FUELER n pl. -S one that fuels

FUELLER n pl. -S fueler

FUELLING a present participle of fuel

FUELWOOD n pl. -S firewood

FUG v FUGGED, FUGGING, FUGS to make stuffy and odorous

FUGACITY n pl. -TIES lack of enduring qualities

FUGAL adj being in the style of a fugue **FUGALLY** adv

FUGATO n pl. -TOS a fugal composition

FUGGED past tense of fug

FUGGING present participle of fug

FUGGY adj -GIER, -GIEST stuffy and odorous **FUGGILY** adv

FUGIO n pl. -GIOS a former coin of the United States

FUGITIVE n pl. -S one who flees

FUGLE v -GLED, -GLING, -GLES to lead

FUGLEMAN n pl. -MEN a leader

FUGU n pl. -S a toxin-containing fish

FUGUE v FUGUED, FUGUING, FUGUES to compose a fugue (a type of musical composition)

FUGUIST n pl. -S one who composes fugues

FUHRER n pl. -S a leader

FUJI n pl. -S a silk fabric

FULCRUM n pl. -CRUMS or -CRA a support for a lever

FULFIL v -FILLED, -FILLING, -FILS to fulfill

FULFILL v -ED, -ING, -S to bring about the accomplishment of

FULGENT adj shining brightly

FULGID adj fulgent

FULHAM n pl. -S a loaded die

FULL adj FULLER, FULLEST filled completely

FULL v -ED, -ING, -S to shrink and thicken, as cloth

FULLAM n pl. -S fulham

FULLBACK n pl. -S an offensive back in football

FULLER v -ED, -ING, -S to groove with a type of hammer

FULLERY n pl. -ERIES a place for fulling cloth

FULLFACE n pl. -S a heavy-faced type

FULLNESS n pl. -ES the state of being full

FULLY adv in a full manner

FULMAR n pl. -S an arctic seabird

FULMINE v -MINED, -MINING, -MINES to explode loudly

FULMINIC adj highly explosive

FULNESS n pl. -ES fullness

FULSOME adj repulsive

FULVOUS adj of a brownish yellow color

FUMARASE n pl. -S an enzyme

FUMARATE n pl. -S a chemical salt

FUMARIC adj pertaining to a certain acid

FUMAROLE n pl. -S a hole from which volcanic vapors issue

FUMATORY n pl. -RIES a fumigation chamber

FUMBLE v -BLED, -BLING, -BLES to handle clumsily

FUMBLER n pl. -S one that fumbles

FUME v FUMED, FUMING, FUMES to give off fumes (gaseous exhalations)

FUMELESS adj having no fumes

FUMELIKE adj resembling fumes

FUMER n pl. -S one that fumes

FUMET n pl. -S the odor of meat while cooking

FUMETTE n pl. -S fumet

FUMIER comparative of fumy

FUMIEST superlative of fumy

FUMIGANT n pl. -S a substance used in fumigating

FUMIGATE v -GATED, -GATING, -GATES to subject to fumes in order to destroy pests

FUMING present participle of fume

FUMINGLY adv angrily

FUMITORY n pl. -RIES a climbing plant

FUMULUS n pl. -LI a thin cloud

FUMY adj FUMIER, FUMIEST producing or full of fumes

FUN v FUNNED, FUNNING, FUNS to act playfully

FUN adj FUNNER, FUNNEST providing enjoyment

FUNCTION v -ED, -ING, -S to be in action

FUNCTOR n pl. -S one that functions

FUND v -ED, -ING, -S to provide money for

FUNDUS n pl. -DI the inner basal surface of a bodily organ **FUNDIC** adj

FUNERAL n pl. -S a ceremony held for a dead person

FUNERARY adj pertaining to a funeral

FUNEREAL adj funerary

FUNEST *adj* portending death or evil
FUNFAIR *n* pl. -S an amusement park
FUNGAL *n* pl. -S a fungus
FUNGI a pl. of fungus
FUNGIBLE *n* pl. -S something that may be exchanged for an equivalent unit of the same class
FUNGIC *adj* fungous
FUNGO *n* pl. -GOES a fly ball hit to a fielder for practice in baseball
FUNGOID *n* pl. -S a growth resembling a fungus
FUNGOUS *adj* pertaining to a fungus
FUNGUS *n* pl. -GI or -GUSES any of a major group of lower plants
FUNICLE *n* pl. -S a cordlike anatomical structure
FUNICULI *n/pl* funicles
FUNK *v* -ED, -ING, -S to shrink back in fear
FUNKER *n* pl. -S one that funks
FUNKIA *n* pl. -S a flowering plant
FUNKY *adj* FUNKIER, FUNKIEST having an offensive odor
FUNNED past tense of fun
FUNNEL *v* -NELED, -NELING, -NELS or -NELLED, -NELLING, -NELS to pass through a funnel (a cone-shaped utensil)
FUNNER comparative of fun
FUNNEST superlative of fun
FUNNING present participle of fun
FUNNY *adj* -NIER, -NIEST causing laughter or amusement
FUNNILY *adv*
FUNNY *n* pl. -NIES a comic strip
FUNNYMAN *n* pl. -MEN a comedian
FUR *v* FURRED, FURRING, FURS to cover with fur (a dressed animal pelt)
FURAN *n* pl. -S a flammable liquid
FURANE *n* pl. -S furan
FURANOSE *n* pl. -S a type of sugar
FURBELOW *v* -ED, -ING, -S to decorate with ruffles
FURBISH *v* -ED, -ING, -ES to polish
FURCATE *v* -CATED, -CATING, -CATES to divide into branches
FURCRAEA *n* pl. -S a tropical plant
FURCULA *n* pl. -LAE a forked bone
FURCULAR *adj*
FURCULUM *n* pl. -LA a furcula
FURFUR *n* pl. -ES dandruff
FURFURAL *n* pl. -S a chemical compound
FURFURAN *n* pl. -S furan

FURIBUND *adj* furious
FURIES pl. of fury
FURIOSO *adv* with great force — used as a musical direction
FURIOUS *adj* extremely angry
FURL *v* -ED, -ING, -S to roll up
FURLABLE *adj*
FURLER *n* pl. -S one that furls
FURLESS *adj* having no fur
FURLONG *n* pl. -S a unit of distance
FURLOUGH *v* -ED, -ING, -S to grant a leave of absence to
FURMENTY *n* pl. -TIES frumenty
FURMETY *n* pl. -TIES frumenty
FURMITY *n* pl. -TIES frumenty
FURNACE *v* -NACED, -NACING, -NACES to subject to hea.
FURNISH *v* -ED, -ING, -ES to equip
FUROR *n* pl. -S an uproar
FURORE *n* pl. -S furor
FURRED past tense of fur
FURRIER *n* pl. -S one that deals in furs
FURRIERY *n* pl. -ERIES the business of a furrier
FURRIEST superlative of furry
FURRILY *adv* in a furry manner
FURRINER *n* pl. -S a foreigner
FURRING *n* pl. -S a trimming or lining of fur
FURROW *v* -ED, -ING, -S to make furrows (narrow depressions) in
FURROWER *n* pl. -S one that furrows
FURROWY *adj* marked by furrows
FURRY *adj* -RIER, -RIEST covered with fur
FURTHER *v* -ED, -ING, -S to help forward
FURTHEST a superlative of far
FURTIVE *adj* stealthy
FURUNCLE *n* pl. -S a painful swelling on the skin
FURY *n* pl. -RIES violent anger
FURZE *n* pl. -S a spiny shrub
FURZY *adj* FURZIER, FURZIEST abounding in furze
FUSAIN *n* pl. -S a fine charcoal used in drawing
FUSCOUS *adj* of a dusky color
FUSE *v* FUSED, FUSING, FUSES to equip with a fuse (a detonating device)
FUSEE *n* pl. -S a large-headed friction match
FUSEL *n* pl. -S an oily liquid

FUSELAGE *n* pl. -S the body of an airplane

FUSELESS *adj* lacking a fuse

FUSIBLE *adj* capable of being melted **FUSIBLY** *adv*

FUSIFORM *adj* tapering toward each end

FUSIL *n* pl. -S a type of musket

FUSILE *adj* formed by melting

FUSILEER *n* pl. -S fusilier

FUSILIER *n* pl. -S a soldier armed with a fusil

FUSILLI *n* pl. -S spiral-shaped pasta

FUSING present participle of fuse

FUSION *n* pl. -S the act of melting together

FUSS *v* -ED, -ING, -ES to be overly concerned with small details

FUSSER *n* pl. -S one that fusses

FUSSPOT *n* pl. -S a fusser

FUSSY *adj* FUSSIER, FUSSIEST overly concerned with small details **FUSSILY** *adv*

FUSTIAN *n* pl. -S a cotton fabric

FUSTIC *n* pl. -S a tropical tree

FUSTY *adj* -TIER, -TIEST musty **FUSTILY** *adv*

FUTHARC *n* pl. -S futhark

FUTHARK *n* pl. -S an ancient alphabet

FUTHORC *n* pl. -S futhark

FUTHORK *n* pl. -S futhark

FUTILE *adj* having no useful result **FUTILELY** *adv*

FUTILITY *n* pl. -TIES the quality of being futile

FUTON *n* pl. -S a cotton filled mattress for use as a bed

FUTTOCK *n* pl. -S a curved timber in the frame of a wooden ship

FUTURE *n* pl. -S the time yet to come **FUTURAL** *adj*

FUTURISM *n* pl. -S an artistic and literary movement

FUTURIST *n* pl. -S an advocate of futurism

FUTURITY *n* pl. -TIES the future

FUTZ *v* -ED, -ING, -ES to spend time aimlessly

FUZE *v* FUZED, FUZING, FUZES to fuse

FUZEE *n* pl. -S fusee

FUZIL *n* pl. -S fusil

FUZING present participle of fuze

FUZZ *v* -ED, -ING, -ES to become fuzzy

FUZZY *adj* FUZZIER, FUZZIEST blurry **FUZZILY** *adv*

FYCE *n* pl. -S feist

FYKE *n* pl. -S a bag-shaped fishnet

FYLFOT *n* pl. -S a swastika

FYTTE *n* pl. -S a division of a poem or song

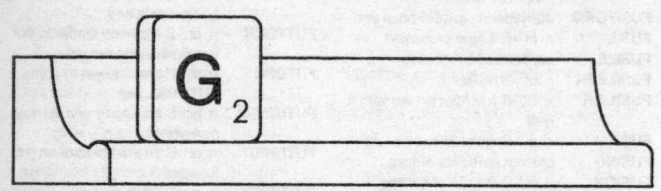

GAB v GABBED, GABBING, GABS to chatter

GABBARD n pl. -S a barge

GABBART n pl. -S gabbard

GABBED past tense of gab

GABBER n pl. -S one that gabs

GABBIER comparative of gabby

GABBIEST superlative of gabby

GABBING present participle of gab

GABBLE v -BLED, -BLING, -BLES to jabber

GABBLER n pl. -S one that gabbles

GABBRO n pl. -BROS a type of rock GABBROIC, GABBROID adj

GABBY adj -BIER, -BIEST talkative

GABELLE n pl. -S a tax on salt GABELLED adj

GABFEST n pl. -S an informal gathering for general talk

GABIES pl. of gaby

GABION n pl. -S a type of basket

GABLE v -BLED, -BLING, -BLES to form a triangular section of a wall

GABOON n pl. -S a spittoon

GABY n pl. -BIES a dolt

GAD v GADDED, GADDING, GADS to roam about restlessly

GADABOUT n pl. -S one that gads about

GADARENE adj headlong

GADDED past tense of gad

GADDER n pl. -S one that gads about

GADDI n pl. -S a hassock

GADDING present participle of gad

GADFLY n pl. -FLIES a biting fly

GADGET n pl. -S a mechanical device GADGETY adj

GADGETRY n pl. -RIES the devising or constructing of gadgets

GADI n pl. -S gaddi

GADID n pl. -S gadoid

GADOID n pl. -S a type of fish

GADROON v -ED, -ING, -S to decorate with bands of fluted or reeded molding

GADWALL n pl. -S a wild duck

GADZOOKS interj — used as a mild oath

GAE v GAED, GANE or GAEN, GAEING or GAUN, GAES to go

GAFF v -ED, -ING, -S to catch a fish with a sharp hook

GAFFE n pl. -S a social blunder

GAFFER n pl. -S an old man

GAG v GAGGED, GAGGING, GAGS to stop up the mouth

GAGA adj crazy

GAGAKU n pl. -S ancient court music of Japan

GAGE v GAGED, GAGING, GAGES to pledge as security

GAGER n pl. -S gauger

GAGGED past tense of gag

GAGGER n pl. -S one that gags

GAGGING present participle of gag

GAGGLE v -GLED, -GLING, -GLES to cackle

GAGING present participle of gage

GAGMAN n pl. -MEN one who writes jokes

GAGSTER n pl. -S a gagman

GAHNITE n pl. -S a mineral

GAIETY n pl. -ETIES festive activity

GAIJIN n pl. GAIJIN a foreigner in Japan

GAILY adv in a gay manner

GAIN v -ED, -ING, -S to acquire GAINABLE adj

GAINER n pl. -S one that gains

GAINFUL adj profitable

GAINLESS adj profitless

GAINLY adj -LIER, -LIEST graceful

GAINSAY v -SAID, -SAYING, -SAYS to deny

GAINST prep against

GAIT v -ED, -ING, -S to train a horse to move in a particular way

GAITER n pl. -S a covering for the lower leg

GAL n pl. -S a girl

GALA n pl. -S a celebration

GALABIA n pl. -S djellaba

GALABIEH n pl. -S djellaba

GALABIYA n pl. -S djellaba

GALACTIC adj pertaining to a galaxy

GALAGO n pl. -GOS a small primate

GALAH n pl. -S a cockatoo

GALANGAL n pl. -S a medicinal plant

GALATEA n pl. -S a strong cotton fabric

GALAVANT v -ED, -ING, -S to gad about

GALAX n pl. -ES an evergreen herb

GALAXY n pl. -AXIES a large system of celestial bodies

GALBANUM n pl. -S a gum resin

GALE n pl. -S a strong wind

GALEA n pl. -LEAE or -LEAS a helmet-shaped anatomical part **GALEATE, GALEATED** adj

GALENA n pl. -S the principal ore of lead **GALENIC** adj

GALENITE n pl. -S galena

GALERE n pl. -S a group of people having a common quality

GALILEE n pl. -S a type of porch

GALIOT n pl. -S a galliot

GALIPOT n pl. -S a type of turpentine

GALIVANT v -ED, -ING, -S to gad about

GALL v -ED, -ING, -S to vex or irritate

GALLANT v -ED, -ING, -S to court a woman

GALLATE n pl. -S a chemical salt

GALLEASS n pl. -ES a large war galley

GALLEIN n pl. -S a green dye

GALLEON n pl. -S a large sailing vessel

GALLERIA n pl. -S a roofed promenade or court

GALLERY v -LERIED, -LERYING, -LERIES to provide with a long covered area

GALLET v -ED, -ING, -S to fill in mortar joints with stone chips

GALLETA n pl. -S a perennial grass

GALLEY n pl. -LEYS a long, low medieval ship

GALLFLY n pl. -FLIES a small insect

GALLIARD n pl. -S a lively dance

GALLIASS n pl. -ES galleass

GALLIC adj containing gallium

GALLICAN adj pertaining to a French religious movement

GALLIED past tense of gally

GALLIES present 3d person sing. of gally

GALLIOT n pl. -S a small galley

GALLIPOT n pl. -S a small earthen jar

GALLIUM n pl. -S a metallic element

GALLNUT n pl. -S an abnormal swelling of plant tissue

GALLON n pl. -S a unit of liquid measure

GALLOON n pl. -S an ornamental braid

GALLOOT n pl. -S galoot

GALLOP v -ED, -ING, -S to ride a horse at full speed

GALLOPER n pl. -S one that gallops

GALLOUS adj containing gallium

GALLOWS n pl. -ES a structure used for hanging a condemned person

GALLUS n pl. -ES a suspender for trousers **GALLUSED** adj

GALLY v -LIED, -LYING, -LIES to frighten

GALOOT n pl. -S an awkward or uncouth person

GALOP v -ED, -ING, -S to dance a galop (a lively round dance)

GALOPADE n pl. -S a lively round dance

GALORE n pl. -S an abundance

GALOSH n pl. -ES an overshoe **GALOSHED** adj

GALOSHE n pl. -S galosh

GALUMPH v -ED, -ING, -S to move clumsily

GALVANIC adj pertaining to a direct electric current

GALYAC n pl. -S galyak

GALYAK n pl. -S a fur made from lambskin

GAM v GAMMED, GAMMING, GAMS to visit socially

GAMA n pl. -S a pasture grass

GAMASHES n/pl boots worn by horseback riders

GAMAY n pl. -MAYS a red grape

GAMB n pl. -S a leg

GAMBA n pl. -S a bass viol

GAMBADE n pl. -S a gambado

GAMBADO *n* pl. -DOES or -DOS a leap made by a horse

GAMBE *n* pl. -S gamb

GAMBESON *n* pl. -S a medieval coat

GAMBIA *n* pl. -S gambier

GAMBIER *n* pl. -S an extract obtained from an Asian vine

GAMBIR *n* pl. -S gambier

GAMBIT *n* pl. -S a type of chess opening

GAMBLE *v* -BLED, -BLING, -BLES to play a game of chance for money or valuables

GAMBLER *n* pl. -S one that gambles

GAMBOGE *n* pl. -S a gum resin

GAMBOL *v* -BOLED, -BOLING, -BOLS or -BOLLED, -BOLLING, -BOLS to leap about playfully

GAMBREL *n* pl. -S a part of a horse's leg

GAMBUSIA *n* pl. -S a small fish

GAME *adj* GAMER, GAMEST plucky

GAME *v* GAMED, GAMING, GAMES to gamble

GAMECOCK *n* pl. -S a rooster trained for fighting

GAMELAN *n* pl. -S a type of orchestra

GAMELIKE *adj* similar to a game (a contest governed by a set of rules)

GAMELY *adv* in a game manner

GAMENESS *n* pl. -ES the quality of being game

GAMER *n* pl. -S an avid game player

GAMESMAN *n* pl. -MEN one who plays games

GAMESOME *adj* playful

GAMEST superlative of game

GAMESTER *n* pl. -S a gambler

GAMETE *n* pl. -S a mature reproductive cell **GAMETIC** *adj*

GAMEY *adj* GAMIER, GAMIEST gamy

GAMIC *adj* requiring fertilization

GAMIER comparative of gamy

GAMIEST superlative of gamy

GAMILY *adv* in a game manner

GAMIN *n* pl. -S an urchin

GAMINE *n* pl. -S a tomboy

GAMINESS *n* pl. -ES the quality of being gamy

GAMING *n* pl. -S the practice of gambling

GAMMA *n* pl. -S a Greek letter

GAMMADIA *n/pl* Greek ornamental designs

GAMMED past tense of gam

GAMMER *n* pl. -S an old woman

GAMMIER comparative of gammy

GAMMIEST superlative of gammy

GAMMING present participle of gam

GAMMON *v* -ED, -ING, -S to mislead by deceptive talk

GAMMONER *n* pl. -S one that gammons

GAMMY *adj* -MIER, -MIEST lame

GAMODEME *n* pl. -S a somewhat isolated breeding community of organisms

GAMP *n* pl. -S a large umbrella

GAMUT *n* pl. -S an entire range

GAMY *adj* GAMIER, GAMIEST plucky

GAN past tense of gin

GANACHE *n* pl. -S creamy chocolate mixture

GANDER *v* -ED, -ING, -S to wander

GANE a past participle of gae

GANEF *n* pl. -S a thief

GANEV *n* pl. -S ganef

GANG *v* -ED, -ING, -S to form into a gang (a group)

GANGER *n* pl. -S a foreman of a gang of laborers

GANGLAND *n* pl. -S the criminal underworld

GANGLIA a pl. of ganglion

GANGLIAL *adj* gangliar

GANGLIAR *adj* pertaining to a ganglion

GANGLIER comparative of gangly

GANGLIEST superlative of gangly

GANGLING *adj* awkwardly tall and lanky

GANGLION *n* pl. -GLIA or -GLIONS a group of nerve cells

GANGLY *adj* -GLIER, -GLIEST gangling

GANGPLOW *n* pl. -S an agricultural implement

GANGREL *n* pl. -S a vagabond

GANGRENE *v* -GRENED, -GRENING, -GRENES to suffer the loss of tissue in part of the body

GANGSTER *n* pl. -S a member of a criminal gang

GANGUE *n* pl. -S the worthless rock in which valuable minerals are found

GANGWAY *n* pl. -WAYS a passageway

GANISTER *n* pl. -S a type of rock

GANJA *n* pl. -S cannabis used for smoking

GANJAH *n* pl. -S ganja

GANNET *n* pl. -S a large seabird

GANOF *n* pl. -S ganef

GANOID *n* pl. -S a type of fish

GANTLET *v* -ED, -ING, -S to overlap railroad tracks

GANTLINE *n pl.* -S a rope on a ship

GANTLOPE *n pl.* -S a former military punishment

GANTRY *n pl.* -TRIES a structure for supporting railroad signals

GANYMEDE *n pl.* -S a youth who serves liquors

GAOL *v* -ED, -ING, -S to jail

GAOLER *n pl.* -S jailer

GAP *v* GAPPED, GAPPING, GAPS to make an opening in

GAPE *v* GAPED, GAPING, GAPES to stare with open mouth

GAPER *n pl.* -S one that gapes

GAPESEED *n pl.* -S something that causes wonder

GAPEWORM *n pl.* -S a worm that causes a disease of young birds

GAPING present participle of gape

GAPINGLY *adv* in a gaping manner

GAPOSIS *n pl.* -SISES a gap in a row of buttons or snaps

GAPPED past tense of gap

GAPPING present participle of gap

GAPPY *adj* -PIER, -PIEST having openings

GAPY *adj* infested with gapeworms

GAR *v* GARRED, GARRING, GARS to cause or compel

GARAGE *v* -RAGED, -RAGING, -RAGES to put in a garage (a car shelter)

GARB *v* -ED, -ING, -S to clothe

GARBAGE *n pl.* -S food waste

GARBANZO *n pl.* -ZOS a chickpea

GARBLE *v* -BLED, -BLING, -BLES to distort the meaning of

GARBLER *n pl.* -S one that garbles

GARBLESS *adj* being without clothing

GARBOARD *n pl.* -S a plank on a ship's bottom

GARBOIL *n pl.* -S turmoil

GARCON *n pl.* -S a waiter

GARDANT *adj* turned directly toward the observer — used of a heraldic animal

GARDEN *v* -ED, -ING, -S to cultivate a plot of ground

GARDENER *n pl.* -S one that gardens

GARDENIA *n pl.* -S a tropical shrub or tree

GARDYLOO *interj* — used as a warning cry

GARFISH *n pl.* -ES a freshwater fish

GARGANEY *n pl.* -NEYS a small duck

GARGET *n pl.* -S mastitis of domestic animals GARGETY *adj*

GARGLE *v* -GLED, -GLING, -GLES to rinse the mouth or throat

GARGLER *n pl.* -S one that gargles

GARGOYLE *n pl.* -S an ornamental figure

GARIGUE *n pl.* -S a low scrubland

GARISH *adj* gaudy GARISHLY *adv*

GARLAND *v* -ED, -ING, -S to deck with wreaths of flowers

GARLIC *n pl.* -S an herb used in cooking GARLICKY *adj*

GARMENT *v* -ED, -ING, -S to clothe

GARNER *v* -ED, -ING, -S to gather and store

GARNET *n pl.* -S a mineral

GARNI *adj* garnished

GARNISH *v* -ED, -ING, -ES to decorate

GAROTE *v* -ROTED, -ROTING, -ROTES to garrote

GAROTTE *v* -ROTTED, -ROTTING, -ROTTES to garrote

GAROTTER *n pl.* -S one that garottes

GARPIKE *n pl.* -S a garfish

GARRED past tense of gar

GARRET *n pl.* -S an attic

GARRING present participle of gar

GARRISON *v* -ED, -ING, -S to assign to a military post

GARRON *n pl.* -S a small, sturdy horse

GARROTE *v* -ROTED, -ROTING, -ROTES to execute by strangling

GARROTER *n pl.* -S one that garrotes

GARROTTE *v* -ROTTED, -ROTTING, -ROTTES to garrote

GARTER *v* -ED, -ING, -S to fasten with an elastic band

GARTH *n pl.* -S a yard or garden

GARVEY *n pl.* -VEYS a small scow

GAS *v* GASSED, GASSING, GASES or GASSES to supply with gas (a substance capable of indefinite expansion)

GASALIER *n pl.* -S a gaselier

GASBAG *n pl.* -S a bag for holding gas

GASCON *n pl.* -S a boaster

GASELIER *n pl.* -S a gaslight chandelier

GASEOUS *adj* pertaining to gas

GASH *v* -ED, -ING, -ES to make a long deep cut in

GASH *adj* GASHER, GASHEST knowing

GASHOUSE *n pl.* -S a gasworks

GASIFIED past tense of gasify

GASIFIER *n pl.* -S one that gasifies

GASIFORM *adj* having the form of gas

GASIFY v -IFIED, -IFYING, -IFIES to convert into gas

GASKET n pl. -S packing for making something fluid-tight

GASKIN n pl. -S a part of a horse's leg

GASKING n pl. -S a gasket

GASLESS adj having no gas

GASLIGHT n pl. -S light made by burning gas

GASLIT adj illuminated by gaslight

GASMAN n pl. -MEN an employee of a gas company

GASOGENE n pl. -S gazogene

GASOHOL n pl. -S a fuel mixture of gasoline and ethyl alcohol

GASOLENE n pl. -S gasoline

GASOLIER n pl. -S gaselier

GASOLINE n pl. -S a liquid fuel

GASP v -ED, -ING, -S to breathe convulsively

GASPER n pl. -S a cigarette

GASSED past tense of gas

GASSER n pl. -S one that gasses

GASSES a present 3d person sing. of gas

GASSING n pl. -S a poisoning by noxious gas

GASSY adj -SIER, -SIEST containing gas **GASSILY** adv

GAST v -ED, -ING, -S to scare

GASTER n pl. -S the enlarged part of the abdomen in some insects

GASTIGHT adj not allowing gas to escape or enter

GASTNESS n pl. -ES fright

GASTRAEA n pl. -S a type of metazoan

GASTRAL adj pertaining to the stomach

GASTREA n pl. -S gastraea

GASTRIC adj pertaining to the stomach

GASTRIN n pl. -S a hormone

GASTRULA n pl. -LAS or -LAE a metazoan embryo

GASWORKS n pl. GASWORKS a factory where gas is produced

GAT n pl. -S a pistol

GATE v GATED, GATING, GATES to supply with a gate (a movable barrier)

GATEAU n pl. -TEAUX a rich layer cake

GATEFOLD n pl. -S a folded insert in a book or magazine

GATELESS adj lacking a gate

GATELIKE adj resembling a gate

GATEMAN n pl. -MEN a person in charge of a gate

GATEPOST n pl. -S a post from which a gate is hung

GATEWAY n pl. -WAYS a passage that may be closed by a gate

GATHER v -ED, -ING, -S to bring together into one place or group

GATHERER n pl. -S one that gathers

GATING present participle of gate

GATOR n pl. -S an alligator

GAUCHE adj GAUCHER, GAUCHEST lacking social grace **GAUCHELY** adv

GAUCHO n pl. -CHOS a cowboy of the South American pampas

GAUD n pl. -S a showy ornament

GAUDERY n pl. -ERIES finery

GAUDY adj GAUDIER, GAUDIEST tastelessly showy **GAUDILY** adv

GAUDY n pl. -DIES a festival

GAUFFER v -ED, -ING, -S to goffer

GAUGE v GAUGED, GAUGING, GAUGES to measure precisely

GAUGER n pl. -S one that gauges

GAULT n pl. -S a heavy, thick clay soil

GAUM v -ED, -ING, -S to smear

GAUN present participle of gae

GAUNT adj GAUNTER, GAUNTEST emaciated **GAUNTLY** adv

GAUNTLET v -ED, -ING, -S to gantlet

GAUNTRY n pl. -TRIES gantry

GAUR n pl. -S a wild ox

GAUSS n pl. -ES a unit of magnetic induction

GAUZE n pl. -S a transparent fabric

GAUZY adj GAUZIER, GAUZIEST resembling gauze **GAUZILY** adv

GAVAGE n pl. -S introduction of material into the stomach by a tube

GAVE past tense of give

GAVEL v -ELED, -ELING, -ELS or -ELLED, -ELLING, -ELS to signal for attention or order by use of a gavel (a small mallet)

GAVELOCK n pl. -S a crowbar

GAVIAL n pl. -S a large reptile

GAVOT n pl. -S a French dance

GAVOTTE v -VOTTED, -VOTTING, -VOTTES to dance a gavot

GAWK v -ED, -ING, -S to stare stupidly

GAWKER n pl. -S one that gawks

GAWKIER comparative of gawky

GAWKIES pl. of gawky

GAWKISH *adj* gawky
GAWKY *adj* GAWKIER, GAWKIEST awkward GAWKILY *adv*
GAWKY *n pl.* GAWKIES an awkward person
GAWP *v* -ED, -ING, -S to stare stupidly
GAWPER *n pl.* -S one that gawps
GAWSIE *adj* well-fed and healthy looking
GAWSY *adj* gawsie
GAY *adj* GAYER, GAYEST merry
GAY *n pl.* GAYS a homosexual
GAYAL *n pl.* -S a domesticated ox
GAYETY *n pl.* -ETIES gaiety
GAYLY *adv* in a gay manner
GAYNESS *n pl.* -ES gaiety
GAYWINGS *n pl.* GAYWINGS a perennial herb
GAZABO *n pl.* -BOS or -BOES a fellow
GAZANIA *n pl.* -S a South African herb
GAZAR *n pl.* -S silky sheer fabric
GAZE *v* GAZED, GAZING, GAZES to look intently
GAZEBO *n pl.* -BOS or -BOES a roofed structure open on the sides
GAZELLE *n pl.* -S a small antelope
GAZER *n pl.* -S one that gazes
GAZETTE *v* -ZETTED, -ZETTING, -ZETTES to announce in an official journal
GAZING present participle of gaze
GAZOGENE *n pl.* -S an apparatus for carbonating liquids
GAZPACHO *n pl.* -CHOS a cold, spicy soup
GAZUMP *v* -ED, -ING, -S to cheat by raising the price originally agreed upon
GAZUMPER *n pl.* -S one that gazumps
GEAR *v* -ED, -ING, -S to provide with gears (toothed machine parts)
GEARBOX *n pl.* -ES an automotive transmission
GEARCASE *n pl.* -S a casing for gears
GEARING *n pl.* -S a system of gears
GEARLESS *adj* being without gears
GECK *v* -ED, -ING, -S to mock
GECKO *n pl.* GECKOS or GECKOES a small lizard
GED *n pl.* -S a food fish
GEE *v* GEED, GEEING, GEES to turn to the right
GEEGAW *n pl.* -S gewgaw
GEEK *n pl.* -S a carnival performer

GEEKY *adj* GEEKIER, GEEKIEST socially awkward or unappealing
GEEPOUND *n pl.* -S a unit of mass
GEESE *pl.* of goose
GEEST *n pl.* -S old alluvial matter
GEEZ *interj* jeez
GEEZER *n pl.* -S an eccentric man
GEISHA *n pl.* -S a Japanese girl trained to entertain
GEL *v* GELLED, GELLING, GELS to become like jelly GELABLE *adj*
GELADA *n pl.* -S a baboon
GELANT *n pl.* -S gellant
GELATE *v* -ATED, -ATING, -ATES to gel
GELATI *a pl.* of gelato
GELATIN *n pl.* -S a glutinous substance
GELATINE *n pl.* -S gelatin
GELATING present participle of gelate
GELATION *n pl.* -S the process of gelling
GELATO *n pl.* -TI or -TOS Italian ice cream
GELD *v* -ED, -ING, -S to castrate
GELDER *n pl.* -S one that gelds
GELDING *n pl.* -S a castrated animal
GELEE *n pl.* -S a cosmetic gel
GELID *adj* icy GELIDLY *adv*
GELIDITY *n pl.* -TIES iciness
GELLANT *n pl.* -S a substance used to produce gelling
GELLED past tense of gel
GELLING present participle of gel
GELSEMIA *n/pl* medicinal plant roots
GELT *n pl.* -S money
GEM *v* GEMMED, GEMMING, GEMS to adorn with gems (precious stones)
GEMINAL *adj* of or pertaining to two substituents on the same atom
GEMINATE *v* -NATED, -NATING, -NATES to arrange in pairs
GEMLIKE *adj* resembling a gem
GEMMA *n pl.* -MAE an asexual reproductive structure
GEMMATE *v* -MATED, -MATING, -MATES to produce gemmae
GEMMED past tense of gem
GEMMIER comparative of gemmy
GEMMIEST superlative of gemmy
GEMMILY *adv* in a manner suggesting a gem
GEMMING present participle of gem
GEMMULE *n pl.* -S a small gemma

GEMMY *adj* -MIER, -MIEST resembling a gem

GEMOLOGY *n pl.* -GIES the science of gems

GEMOT *n pl.* -S a public meeting in Anglo-Saxon England

GEMOTE *n pl.* -S gemot

GEMSBOK *n pl.* -S a large antelope

GEMSBUCK *n pl.* -S gemsbok

GEMSTONE *n pl.* -S a precious stone

GEN *n pl.* -S information obtained from study

GENDARME *n pl.* -S a policeman

GENDER *v* -ED, -ING, -S to engender

GENE *n pl.* -S a hereditary unit

GENERA a *pl.* of genus

GENERAL *n pl.* -S a military officer

GENERATE *v* -ATED, -ATING, -ATES to bring into existence

GENERIC *n pl.* -S a type of drug

GENEROUS *adj* willing to give

GENESIS *n pl.* GENESES an origin

GENET *n pl.* -S a carnivorous mammal

GENETIC *adj* pertaining to genetics

GENETICS *n/pl* the science of heredity

GENETTE *n pl.* -S genet

GENEVA *n pl.* -S a liquor

GENIAL *adj* cheerful GENIALLY *adv*

GENIC *adj* pertaining to genes

GENIE *n pl.* -S jinni

GENII a *pl.* of genius

GENIP *n pl.* -S a tropical tree

GENIPAP *n pl.* -S a tropical tree

GENITAL *adj* pertaining to reproduction

GENITALS *n/pl* the sexual organs

GENITIVE *n pl.* -S a grammatical case

GENITOR *n pl.* -S a male parent

GENITURE *n pl.* -S birth

GENIUS *n pl.* GENIUSES or GENII an exceptional natural aptitude

GENOA *n pl.* -S a triangular sail

GENOCIDE *n pl.* -S the deliberate extermination of a national or racial group

GENOISE *n pl.* -S a rich spongecake

GENOM *n pl.* -S genome

GENOME *n pl.* -S a haploid set of chromosomes **GENOMIC** *adj*

GENOTYPE *n pl.* -S the genetic constitution of an organism

GENRE *n pl.* -S a type or kind

GENRO *n pl.* -ROS a group of elder statesmen in Japan

GENS *n pl.* GENTES a type of clan

GENSENG *n pl.* -S ginseng

GENT *n pl.* -S a gentleman

GENTEEL *adj* -TEELER, -TEELEST well-bred or refined

GENTES *pl.* of gens

GENTIAN *n pl.* -S a flowering plant

GENTIL *adj* kind

GENTILE *n pl.* -S a non-Jewish person

GENTLE *adj* -TLER, -TLEST mild

GENTLY *adv*

GENTLE *v* -TLED, -TLING, -TLES to tame

GENTOO *n pl.* -TOOS a gray-backed penguin

GENTRICE *n pl.* -S good breeding

GENTRIFY *v* -FIED, -FYING, -FIES to renew a decayed urban area so as to attract middle-class residents

GENTRY *n pl.* -TRIES people of high social class

GENU *n pl.* GENUA the knee

GENUINE *adj* authentic

GENUS *n pl.* GENERA or GENUSES a kind, sort, or class

GEODE *n pl.* -S a type of rock

GEODESIC *n pl.* -S a geometric line

GEODESY *n pl.* -SIES geographical surveying

GEODETIC *adj* pertaining to geodesy

GEODIC *adj* of or pertaining to a geode

GEODUCK *n pl.* -S a large, edible clam

GEOGNOSY *n pl.* -SIES a branch of geology

GEOID *n pl.* -S a hypothetical surface of the earth **GEOIDAL** *adj*

GEOLOGER *n pl.* -S a specialist in geology

GEOLOGY *n pl.* -GIES the science that deals with the origin and structure of the earth **GEOLOGIC** *adj*

GEOMANCY *n pl.* -CIES a method of foretelling the future by geographical features

GEOMETER *n pl.* -S a specialist in geometry

GEOMETRY *n pl.* -TRIES a branch of mathematics

GEOPHAGY *n pl.* -GIES the practice of eating earthy substances

GEOPHONE *n pl.* -S a device that detects vibrations in the earth

GEOPHYTE *n pl.* -S a plant having underground buds

GEOPONIC *adj* pertaining to farming

GEOPROBE *n pl.* -S a spacecraft for exploring space near the earth

GEORGIC *n pl.* -S a poem about farming

GEOTAXIS _n_ pl. -TAXES the movement of an organism in response to gravity

GERAH _n_ pl. -S a Hebrew unit of weight

GERANIAL _n_ pl. -S citral

GERANIOL _n_ pl. -S an alcohol used in perfumes

GERANIUM _n_ pl. -S a flowering plant

GERARDIA _n_ pl. -S an herb

GERBERA _n_ pl. -S an herb

GERBIL _n_ pl. -S a burrowing rodent

GERBILLE _n_ pl. -S gerbil

GERENT _n_ pl. -S a ruler or manager

GERENUK _n_ pl. -S a long-necked antelope

GERM _n_ pl. -S a microorganism that causes disease

GERMAN _n_ pl. -S an elaborate dance

GERMANE _adj_ relevant

GERMANIC _adj_ containing germanium (a metallic element)

GERMEN _n_ pl. -MENS or -MINA something that serves as an origin

GERMFREE _adj_ free from germs

GERMIER comparative of germy

GERMIEST superlative of germy

GERMINA a pl. of germen

GERMINAL _adj_ being in the earliest stage of development

GERMY _adj_ GERMIER, GERMIEST full of germs

GERONTIC _adj_ pertaining to old age

GERUND _n_ pl. -S a verbal noun

GESNERIA _adj_ designating a type of flowering plant

GESSO _n_ pl. -SOES a plaster mixture

GESSOED _adj_ having gesso as a coating or constituent part

GEST _n_ pl. -S a feat

GESTALT _n_ pl. -STALTS or -STALTEN a unified whole

GESTAPO _n_ pl. -POS a secret-police organization

GESTATE _v_ -TATED, -TATING, -TATES to carry in the uterus during pregnancy

GESTE _n_ pl. -S gest

GESTIC _adj_ pertaining to bodily motion

GESTICAL _adj_ gestic

GESTURAL _adj_ pertaining to or consisting of gestures (expressive bodily motions)

GESTURE _v_ -TURED, -TURING, -TURES to express by bodily motion

GESTURER _n_ pl. -S one that gestures

GET _v_ GOT, GOTTEN, GETTING, GETS to obtain or acquire GETABLE, GETTABLE _adj_

GET _n_ pl. GITTIN a divorce by Jewish law

GETA _n_ pl. -S a Japanese wooden clog

GETAWAY _n_ pl. -AWAYS an escape

GETTER _v_ -ED, -ING, -S to purify with a chemically active substance

GETTING present participle of get

GETUP _n_ pl. -S a costume

GEUM _n_ pl. -S a perennial herb

GEWGAW _n_ pl. -S a showy trinket

GEY _adv_ very

GEYSER _n_ pl. -S a spring that ejects jets of hot water and steam

GHARIAL _n_ pl. -S a large reptile

GHARRI _n_ pl. -S gharry

GHARRY _n_ pl. -RIES a carriage used in India

GHAST _adj_ ghastly

GHASTFUL _adj_ frightful

GHASTLY _adj_ -LIER, -LIEST terrifying

GHAT _n_ pl. -S a passage leading down to a river

GHAUT _n_ pl. -S ghat

GHAZI _n_ pl. -S or -ES a Muslim war hero

GHEE _n_ pl. -S a kind of liquid butter made in India

GHERAO _v_ -ED, -ING, -ES to coerce by physical means

GHERKIN _n_ pl. -S a small cucumber

GHETTO _v_ -ED, -ING, -S or -ES to isolate in a slum

GHI _n_ pl. -S ghee

GHIBLI _n_ pl. -S a hot desert wind

GHILLIE _n_ pl. -S a type of shoe

GHOST _v_ -ED, -ING, -S to haunt

GHOSTING _n_ pl. -S a false image on a television screen

GHOSTLY _adj_ -LIER, -LIEST spectral

GHOSTY _adj_ GHOSTIER, GHOSTIEST ghostly

GHOUL _n_ pl. -S a demon GHOULISH _adj_

GHOULIE _n_ pl. -S a ghoul

GHYLL _n_ pl. -S a ravine

GIANT _n_ pl. -S a person or thing of great size

GIANTESS _n_ pl. -ES a female giant

GIANTISM _n_ pl. -S the condition of being a giant

GIAOUR _n_ pl. -S a non-Muslim

GIB v GIBBED, GIBBING, GIBS to fasten with a wedge of wood or metal

GIBBER v -ED, -ING, -S to jabber

GIBBET v -BETED, -BETING, -BETS or -BETTED, -BETTING, -BETS to execute by hanging

GIBBING present participle of gib

GIBBON n pl. -S an arboreal ape

GIBBOSE adj gibbous

GIBBOUS adj irregularly rounded

GIBBSITE n pl. -S a mineral

GIBE v GIBED, GIBING, GIBES to jeer GIBINGLY adv

GIBER n pl. -S one that gibes

GIBLET n pl. -S an edible part of a fowl

GIBSON n pl. -S a martini served with a tiny onion

GID n pl. -S a disease of sheep

GIDDAP interj — used as a command to a horse to go faster

GIDDY adj -DIER, -DIEST dizzy GIDDILY adv

GIDDY v -DIED, -DYING, -DIES to make giddy

GIDDYAP interj giddap

GIDDYUP interj giddap

GIE v GIED, GIEN, GIEING, GIES to give

GIFT v -ED, -ING, -S to present with a gift (something given without charge)

GIFTEDLY adv in a talented manner

GIFTLESS adj being without a gift

GIFTWARE n pl. -S wares suitable for gifts

GIG v GIGGED, GIGGING, GIGS to catch fish with a pronged spear

GIGA n pl. GIGHE a gigue

GIGABIT n pl. -S a unit of information

GIGABYTE n pl. -S 1,073,741,824 bytes

GIGANTIC adj huge

GIGAS adj pertaining to variations in plant development

GIGATON n pl. -S a unit of weight

GIGAWATT n pl. -S a unit of power

GIGGED past tense of gig

GIGGING present participle of gig

GIGGLE v -GLED, -GLING, -GLES to laugh in a silly manner

GIGGLER n pl. -S one that giggles

GIGGLY adj -GLIER, -GLIEST tending to giggle

GIGHE pl. of giga

GIGLET n pl. -S a playful girl

GIGLOT n pl. -S giglet

GIGOLO n pl. -LOS a man supported financially by a woman

GIGOT n pl. -S a leg of lamb

GIGUE n pl. -S a lively dance

GILBERT n pl. -S a unit of magnetomotive force

GILD v GILDED or GILT, GILDING, GILDS to cover with a thin layer of gold

GILDER n pl. -S one that gilds

GILDHALL n pl. -S a town hall

GILDING n pl. -S the application of gilt

GILL v -ED, -ING, -S to catch fish with a type of net

GILLER n pl. -S one that gills

GILLIE n pl. -S ghillie

GILLNET v -NETTED, -NETTING, -NETS to gill

GILLY v -LIED, -LYING, -LIES to transport on a type of wagon

GILT n pl. -S the gold with which something is gilded

GILTHEAD n pl. -S a marine fish

GIMBAL v -BALED, -BALING, -BALS or -BALLED, -BALLING, -BALS to support on a set of rings

GIMCRACK n pl. -S a gewgaw

GIMEL n pl. -S a Hebrew letter

GIMLET v -ED, -ING, -S to pierce with a boring tool

GIMMAL n pl. -S a pair of interlocked rings

GIMME n pl. -S something easily won

GIMMICK v -ED, -ING, -S to provide with a gimmick (a novel or tricky feature)

GIMMICKY adj having or being like a gimmick

GIMMIE n pl. -MIES an easy golf putt conceded to an opponent

GIMP v -ED, -ING, -S to limp

GIMPIER comparative of gimpy

GIMPIEST superlative of gimpy

GIMPY adj GIMPIER, GIMPIEST limping

GIN v GINNED, GINNING, GINS to remove seeds from cotton

GIN v GAN, GUNNEN, GINNING, GINS to begin

GINGAL n pl. -S jingal

GINGALL n pl. -S jingal

GINGELEY n pl. -LEYS gingelly

GINGELI n pl. -S gingelly

GINGELIES pl. of gingely

GINGELLI n pl. -S gingelly

GINGELLY *n pl.* -LIES the sesame seed or its oil

GINGELY *n pl.* -LIES gingelly

GINGER *v* -ED, -ING, -S to flavor with ginger (a pungent spice)

GINGERLY *adv* in a careful manner

GINGERY *adj* having the characteristics of ginger

GINGHAM *n pl.* -S a cotton fabric

GINGILI *n pl.* -LIS gingelly

GINGILLI *n pl.* -S gingelly

GINGIVA *n pl.* -VAE the fleshy tissue that surrounds the teeth GINGIVAL *adj*

GINGKO *n pl.* -KOES ginkgo

GINK *n pl.* -S a fellow

GINKGO *n pl.* -GOES or -GOS an ornamental tree

GINNED past tense of gin

GINNER *n pl.* -S one that gins cotton

GINNING *n pl.* -S cotton as it comes from a gin

GINNY *adj* GINNIER, GINNIEST affected with gin (a strong liquor)

GINSENG *n pl.* -S a perennial herb

GIP *v* GIPPED, GIPPING, GIPS to gyp

GIPON *n pl.* -S jupon

GIPPER *n pl.* -S one that gips

GIPPING present participle of gip

GIPSY *v* -SIED, -SYING, -SIES to gypsy

GIRAFFE *n pl.* -S a long-necked mammal

GIRASOL *n pl.* -S a variety of opal

GIRASOLE *n pl.* -S girasol

GIRD *v* GIRDED or GIRT, GIRDING, GIRDS to surround

GIRDER *n pl.* -S a horizontal support

GIRDLE *v* -DLED, -DLING, -DLES to encircle with a belt

GIRDLER *n pl.* -S one that girdles

GIRL *n pl.* -S a female child

GIRLHOOD *n pl.* -S the state of being a girl

GIRLIE *adj* featuring scantily clothed women

GIRLISH *adj* of, pertaining to, or having the characteristics of a girl

GIRLY *adj* girlie

GIRN *v* -ED, -ING, -S to snarl

GIRO *n pl.* -ROS an autogiro

GIRON *n pl.* -S gyron

GIROSOL *n pl.* -S girasol

GIRSH *n pl.* -ES qursh

GIRT *v* -ED, -ING, -S to gird

GIRTH *v* -ED, -ING, -S to encircle

GISARME *n pl.* -S a medieval weapon

GISMO *n pl.* -MOS a gadget

GIST *n pl.* -S the main point of a matter

GIT *n pl.* -S a foolish person

GITANO *n pl.* -NOS a Spanish gypsy

GITTERN *n pl.* -S a medieval guitar

GITTIN *pl.* of get

GIVE *v* GAVE, GIVEN, GIVING, GIVES to transfer freely to another's possession GIVEABLE *adj*

GIVEAWAY *n pl.* -AWAYS something given away free of charge

GIVEBACK *n pl.* -S a worker's benefit given back to management

GIVEN *n pl.* -S something assigned as a basis for a calculation

GIVER *n pl.* -S one that gives

GIVING present participle of give

GIZMO *n pl.* -MOS gismo

GIZZARD *n pl.* -S a digestive organ

GJETOST *n pl.* -S a hard brown cheese

GLABELLA *n pl.* -BELLAE the smooth area between the eyebrows

GLABRATE *adj* glabrous

GLABROUS *adj* smooth

GLACE *v* -CEED, -CEING, -CES to cover with icing

GLACIAL *adj* of or pertaining to glaciers

GLACIATE *v* -ATED, -ATING, -ATES to cover with glaciers

GLACIER *n pl.* -S a huge mass of ice

GLACIS *n pl.* -CISES a slope

GLAD *adj* GLADDER, GLADDEST feeling pleasure

GLAD *v* GLADDED, GLADDING, GLADS to gladden

GLADDEN *v* -ED, -ING, -S to make glad

GLADDER comparative of glad

GLADDEST superlative of glad

GLADDING present participle of glad

GLADE *n pl.* -S an open space in a forest

GLADIATE *adj* shaped like a sword

GLADIER comparative of glady

GLADIEST superlative of glady

GLADIOLA *n pl.* -S a flowering plant

GLADIOLI *n/pl* segments of the sternum

GLADLY *adv* -LIER, -LIEST in a glad manner

GLADNESS *n pl.* -ES the state of being glad

GLADSOME *adj* -SOMER, -SOMEST glad

GLADY	*adj* GLADIER, GLADIEST having glades
GLAIKET	*adj* glaikit
GLAIKIT	*adj* foolish
GLAIR	*v* -ED, -ING, -S to coat with egg white
GLAIRE	*v* GLAIRED, GLAIRING, GLAIRES to glair
GLAIRY	*adj* GLAIRIER, GLAIRIEST resembling egg white
GLAIVE	*n pl.* -S a sword GLAIVED *adj*
GLAMOR	*n pl.* -S alluring attractiveness
GLAMOUR	*v* -ED, -ING, -S to bewitch
GLANCE	*v* GLANCED, GLANCING, GLANCES to look quickly
GLANCER	*n pl.* -S one that glances
GLAND	*n pl.* -S a secreting organ
GLANDERS	*n/pl* a disease of horses
GLANDULE	*n pl.* -S a small gland
GLANS	*n pl.* GLANDES the tip of the penis or clitoris
GLARE	*v* GLARED, GLARING, GLARES to shine with a harshly brilliant light
GLARY	*adj* GLARIER, GLARIEST glaring
GLASNOST	*n pl.* -S a Soviet policy of open political discussion
GLASS	*v* -ED, -ING, -ES to encase in glass (a transparent substance)
GLASSFUL	*n pl.* -FULS as much as a drinking glass will hold
GLASSIE	*n pl.* -S a type of playing marble
GLASSIER	comparative of glassy
GLASSIEST	superlative of glassy
GLASSILY	*adv* in a glassy manner
GLASSINE	*n pl.* -S a type of paper
GLASSMAN	*n pl.* -MEN a glazier
GLASSY	*adj* GLASSIER, GLASSIEST resembling glass
GLAUCOMA	*n pl.* -S a disease of the eye
GLAUCOUS	*adj* bluish green
GLAZE	*v* GLAZED, GLAZING, GLAZES to fit windows with glass panes
GLAZER	*n pl.* -S a glazier
GLAZIER	*n pl.* -S one that glazes
GLAZIERY	*n pl.* -ZIERIES the work of a glazier
GLAZING	*n pl.* -S glaziery
GLAZY	*adj* GLAZIER, GLAZIEST covered with a smooth, glossy coating

GLEAM	*v* -ED, -ING, -S to shine with a soft radiance
GLEAMER	*n pl.* -S one that gleams
GLEAMY	*adj* GLEAMIER, GLEAMIEST gleaming
GLEAN	*v* -ED, -ING, -S to gather little by little
GLEANER	*n pl.* -S one that gleans
GLEANING	*n pl.* -S something that is gleaned
GLEBA	*n pl.* -BAE a spore-bearing mass of some fungi
GLEBE	*n pl.* -S the soil or earth
GLED	*n pl.* -S a glede
GLEDE	*n pl.* -S a bird of prey
GLEE	*n pl.* -S an unaccompanied song
GLEED	*n pl.* -S a glowing coal
GLEEFUL	*adj* merry
GLEEK	*v* -ED, -ING, -S to gibe
GLEEMAN	*n pl.* -MEN a minstrel
GLEESOME	*adj* gleeful
GLEET	*v* -ED, -ING, -S to discharge mucus from the urethra
GLEETY	*adj* GLEETIER, GLEETIEST resembling mucus
GLEG	*adj* alert GLEGLY *adv*
GLEGNESS	*n pl.* -ES alertness
GLEN	*n pl.* -S a small valley GLENLIKE *adj*
GLENOID	*adj* having the shallow or slightly cupped form of a bone socket
GLEY	*n pl.* GLEYS a clay soil layer GLEYED *adj*
GLEYING	*n pl.* -S development of gley
GLIA	*n pl.* -S supporting tissue that binds nerve tissue
GLIADIN	*n pl.* -S a simple protein
GLIADINE	*n pl.* -S gliadin
GLIAL	*adj* pertaining to the supporting tissue of the central nervous system
GLIB	*adj* GLIBBER, GLIBBEST fluent GLIBLY *adv*
GLIBNESS	*n pl.* -ES the quality of being glib
GLIDE	*v* GLIDED, GLIDING, GLIDES to move effortlessly
GLIDER	*n pl.* -S a type of aircraft
GLIFF	*n pl.* -S a brief moment
GLIM	*n pl.* -S a light or lamp
GLIME	*v* GLIMED, GLIMING, GLIMES to glance slyly
GLIMMER	*v* -ED, -ING, -S to shine faintly or unsteadily

GLIMPSE v GLIMPSED, GLIMPSING, GLIMPSES to see for an instant

GLIMPSER n pl. -S one that glimpses

GLINT v -ED, -ING, -S to glitter

GLIOMA n pl. -MAS or -MATA a type of tumor

GLISSADE v -SADED, -SADING, -SADES to perform a gliding dance step

GLISTEN v -ED, -ING, -S to shine by reflection

GLISTER v -ED, -ING, -S to glisten

GLITCH n pl. -ES a malfunction

GLITCHY adj characterized by glitches

GLITTER v -ED, -ING, -S to sparkle

GLITTERY adj glittering

GLITZ n pl. -ES gaudy showiness

GLITZY adj GLITZIER, GLITZIEST showy

GLOAM n pl. -S twilight

GLOAMING n pl. -S twilight

GLOAT v -ED, -ING, -S to regard with great or excessive satisfaction

GLOATER n pl. -S one that gloats

GLOB n pl. -S a rounded mass

GLOBAL adj spherical GLOBALLY adv

GLOBATE adj spherical

GLOBATED adj spherical

GLOBBY adj -BIER, -BIEST full of globs

GLOBE v GLOBED, GLOBING, GLOBES to form into a perfectly round body

GLOBIN n pl. -S a simple protein

GLOBOID n pl. -S a spheroid

GLOBOSE adj spherical

GLOBOUS adj spherical

GLOBULAR adj spherical

GLOBULE n pl. -S a small spherical mass

GLOBULIN n pl. -S a simple protein

GLOCHID n pl. -S a barbed hair on some plants

GLOGG n pl. -S an alcoholic beverage

GLOM v GLOMMED, GLOMMING, GLOMS to steal

GLOMUS n pl. -MERA a type of vascular tuft

GLONOIN n pl. -S nitroglycerin

GLOOM v -ED, -ING, -S to become dark

GLOOMFUL adj gloomy

GLOOMING n pl. -S glooming

GLOOMY adj GLOOMIER, GLOOMIEST dismally dark GLOOMILY adv

GLOP v GLOPPED, GLOPPING, GLOPS to cover with glop (a messy mass or mixture)

GLOPPY adj being or resembling glop

GLORIA n pl. -S a halo

GLORIED past tense of glory

GLORIES present 3d person sing. of glory

GLORIFY v -FIED, -FYING, -FIES to bestow honor or praise on

GLORIOLE n pl. -S a halo

GLORIOUS adj magnificent

GLORY v -RIED, -RYING, -RIES to rejoice proudly

GLOSS v -ED, -ING, -ES to make lustrous

GLOSSA n pl. -SAE or -SAS the tongue GLOSSAL adj

GLOSSARY n pl. -RIES a list of terms and their definitions

GLOSSEME n pl. -S the smallest linguistic unit that signals a meaning

GLOSSER n pl. -S one that glosses

GLOSSIER comparative of glossy

GLOSSIES pl. of glossy

GLOSSINA n pl. -S a tsetse fly

GLOSSY adj GLOSSIER, GLOSSIEST lustrous GLOSSILY adv

GLOSSY n pl. GLOSSIES a type of photograph

GLOST n pl. -S pottery that has been coated with a glassy surface

GLOTTIS n pl. -TISES or -TIDES the opening between the vocal cords GLOTTAL, GLOTTIC adj

GLOUT v -ED, -ING, -S to scowl

GLOVE v GLOVED, GLOVING, GLOVES to furnish with gloves (hand coverings)

GLOVER n pl. -S a maker or seller of gloves

GLOW v -ED, -ING, -S to emit light and heat

GLOWER v -ED, -ING, -S to scowl

GLOWFLY n pl. -FLIES a firefly

GLOWWORM n pl. -S a luminous insect

GLOXINIA n pl. -S a tropical plant

GLOZE v GLOZED, GLOZING, GLOZES to explain away

GLUCAGON n pl. -S a hormone

GLUCAN n pl. -S a polymer of glucose

GLUCINUM n pl. -S a metallic element GLUCINIC adj

GLUCOSE n pl. -S a sugar GLUCOSIC adj

GLUE *v* GLUED, GLUING or GLUEING, GLUES to fasten with glue (an adhesive substance)

GLUELIKE *adj* resembling glue

GLUEPOT *n pl.* -S a pot for melting glue

GLUER *n pl.* -S one that glues

GLUEY *adj* GLUIER, GLUIEST resembling glue GLUILY *adv*

GLUG *v* GLUGGED, GLUGGING, GLUGS to make a gurgling sound

GLUING present participle of glue

GLUM *adj* GLUMMER, GLUMMEST being in low spirits GLUMLY *adv*

GLUME *n pl.* -S a bract on grassy plants

GLUMNESS *n pl.* -ES the state of being glum

GLUMPY *adj* GLUMPIER, GLUMPIEST glum GLUMPILY *adv*

GLUNCH *v* -ED, -ING, -ES to frown

GLUON *n pl.* -S a hypothetical massless particle binding quarks together

GLUT *v* GLUTTED, GLUTTING, GLUTS to feed or fill to excess

GLUTEAL *adj* of or pertaining to the buttock muscles

GLUTEI *pl.* of gluteus

GLUTELIN *n pl.* -S a plant protein

GLUTEN *n pl.* -S a tough elastic plant protein substance

GLUTEUS *n pl.* -TEI a buttock muscle

GLUTTED past tense of glut

GLUTTING present participle of glut

GLUTTON *n pl.* -S a person who eats to excess

GLUTTONY *n pl.* -TONIES excessive eating

GLYCAN *n pl.* -S a carbohydrate

GLYCERIN *n pl.* -S a glycerol GLYCERIC *adj*

GLYCEROL *n pl.* -S a syrupy alcohol

GLYCERYL *n pl.* -S a radical derived from glycerol

GLYCIN *n pl.* -S a compound used in photography

GLYCINE *n pl.* -S an amino acid

GLYCOGEN *n pl.* -S a carbohydrate

GLYCOL *n pl.* -S an alcohol GLYCOLIC *adj*

GLYCONIC *n pl.* -S a type of verse line

GLYCOSYL *n pl.* -S a radical derived from glucose

GLYCYL *n pl.* -S a radical derived from glycine

GLYPH *n pl.* -S an ornamental groove GLYPHIC *adj*

GLYPTIC *n pl.* -S the art or process of engraving on gems

GNAR *v* GNARRED, GNARRING, GNARS to snarl

GNARL *v* -ED, -ING, -S to twist into a state of deformity

GNARLY *adj* GNARLIER, GNARLIEST gnarled

GNARR *v* -ED, -ING, -S to gnar

GNARRED past tense of gnarr

GNARRING present participle of gnar

GNASH *v* -ED, -ING, -ES to grind the teeth together

GNAT *n pl.* -S a small winged insect

GNATHAL *adj* gnathic

GNATHIC *adj* of or pertaining to the jaw

GNATHION *n pl.* -S the tip of the chin

GNATHITE *n pl.* -S a jawlike appendage of an insect

GNATLIKE *adj* resembling a gnat

GNATTY *adj* -TIER, -TIEST infested with gnats

GNAW *v* GNAWED, GNAWN, GNAWING, GNAWS to wear away by persistent biting GNAWABLE *adj*

GNAWER *n pl.* -S one that gnaws

GNAWING *n pl.* -S a persistent dull pain

GNAWN a past participle of gnaw

GNEISS *n pl.* -ES a type of rock GNEISSIC *adj*

GNOCCHI *n/pl* dumplings made of pasta

GNOME *n pl.* -S a dwarf

GNOMIC *adj* resembling or containing aphorisms

GNOMICAL *adj* gnomic

GNOMISH *adj* resembling a gnome

GNOMIST *n pl.* -S a writer of aphorisms

GNOMON *n pl.* -S a part of a sundial GNOMONIC *adj*

GNOSIS *n pl.* GNOSES mystical knowledge

GNOSTIC *adj* possessing knowledge

GNU *n pl.* -S a large antelope

GO *v* WENT, GONE, GOING, GOES to move along

GOA *n pl.* -S an Asian gazelle

GOAD *v* -ED, -ING, -S to drive animals with a goad (a pointed stick)

GOADLIKE *adj* resembling a goad

GOAL v -ED, -ING, -S to score a goal (a point-scoring play in some games)

GOALIE n pl. -S a player who defends against goals

GOALLESS adj having no goal

GOALPOST n pl. -S a post that marks a boundary of the scoring area in some games

GOALWARD adv toward a goal (a point-scoring area)

GOANNA n pl. -S a large monitor lizard

GOAT n pl. -S a horned mammal

GOATEE n pl. -S a small pointed beard GOATEED adj

GOATFISH n pl. -ES a tropical fish

GOATHERD n pl. -S one who tends goats

GOATISH adj resembling a goat

GOATLIKE adj goatish

GOATSKIN n pl. -S the hide of a goat

GOB v GOBBED, GOBBING, GOBS to fill a mine pit with waste material

GOBAN n pl. -S gobang

GOBANG n pl. -S a Japanese game

GOBBED past tense of gob

GOBBET n pl. -S a piece of raw meat

GOBBING present participle of gob

GOBBLE v -BLED, -BLING, -BLES to eat hastily

GOBBLER n pl. -S a male turkey

GOBIES pl. of goby

GOBIOID n pl. -S a fish of the goby family

GOBLET n pl. -S a drinking vessel

GOBLIN n pl. -S an evil or mischievous creature

GOBO n pl. -BOS or -BOES a device used to shield a microphone from extraneous sounds

GOBONEE adj gobony

GOBONY adj compony

GOBY n pl. GOBIES a small fish

GOD v GODDED, GODDING, GODS to treat as a god (a supernatural being)

GODCHILD n pl. -CHILDREN one whom a person sponsors at baptism

GODDAM v -DAMMED, -DAMMING, -DAMS goddamn

GODDAMN v -ED, -ING, -S to damn

GODDED past tense of god

GODDESS n pl. -ES a female god

GODDING present participle of god

GODET n pl. -S insert of cloth in a seam

GODHEAD n pl. -S godhood

GODHOOD n pl. -S the state of being a god

GODLESS adj worshiping no god

GODLIER comparative of godly

GODLIEST superlative of godly

GODLIKE adj divine

GODLING n pl. -S a lesser god

GODLY adj -LIER, -LIEST pious GODLILY adv

GODOWN n pl. -S an oriental warehouse

GODROON n pl. -S gadroon

GODSEND n pl. -S an unexpected boon

GODSHIP n pl. -S the rank of a god

GODSON n pl. -S a male godchild

GODWIT n pl. -S a wading bird

GOER n pl. -S one that goes

GOETHITE n pl. -S an ore of iron

GOFER n pl. -S an employee who runs errands

GOFFER v -ED, -ING, -S to press ridges or pleats into

GOGGLE v -GLED, -GLING, -GLES to stare with wide eyes

GOGGLER n pl. -S one that goggles

GOGGLY adj -GLIER, -GLIEST wide-eyed

GOGLET n pl. -S a long-necked jar

GOGO n pl. -GOS a discotheque

GOING n pl. -S an advance toward an objective

GOITER n pl. -S an enlargement of the thyroid gland GOITROUS adj

GOITRE n pl. -S goiter

GOLCONDA n pl. -S a source of great wealth

GOLD n pl. -S a precious metallic element

GOLD adj GOLDER, GOLDEST golden

GOLDARN n pl. -S an expression of anger

GOLDBUG n pl. -S a gold beetle

GOLDEN adj -ENER, -ENEST of the color of gold GOLDENLY adv

GOLDEYE n pl. -S a freshwater fish

GOLDFISH n pl. -ES a freshwater fish

GOLDURN n pl. -S goldarn

GOLEM n pl. -S a legendary creature

GOLF v -ED, -ING, -S to play golf (a type of ball game)

GOLFER n pl. -S one that golfs

GOLFING n pl. -S the game of golf

GOLGOTHA n pl. -S a place of burial

GOLIARD n pl. -S a wandering student

GOLLIWOG n pl. -S a grotesque doll

GOLLY *interj* — used as a mild oath

GOLLYWOG *n* pl. -S golliwog

GOLOSH *n* pl. -ES galosh

GOLOSHE *n* pl. -S galosh

GOMBO *n* pl. -BOS gumbo

GOMBROON *n* pl. -S a kind of Persian pottery

GOMERAL *n* pl. -S a fool

GOMEREL *n* pl. -S gomeral

GOMERIL *n* pl. -S gomeral

GOMUTI *n* pl. -S a palm tree

GONAD *n* pl. -S a sex gland GONADAL, GONADIAL, GONADIC *adj*

GONDOLA *n* pl. -S a long, narrow boat

GONE *adj* departed

GONEF *n* pl. -S ganef

GONENESS *n* pl. -ES a state of exhaustion

GONER *n* pl. -S one who is in a hopeless situation

GONFALON *n* pl. -S a banner

GONFANON *n* pl. -S gonfalon

GONG *v* -ED, -ING, -S to make the sound of a gong (a disk-shaped percussion instrument)

GONGLIKE *adj* resembling a gong

GONIA pl. of gonion and of gonium

GONIDIUM *n* pl. -IA an asexual reproductive cell GONIDIAL, GONIDIC *adj*

GONIF *n* pl. -S ganef

GONIFF *n* pl. -S ganef

GONION *n* pl. -NIA a part of the lower jaw

GONIUM *n* pl. -NIA an immature reproductive cell

GONOCYTE *n* pl. -S a cell that produces gametes

GONOF *n* pl. -S ganef

GONOPH *n* pl. -S ganef

GONOPORE *n* pl. -S a genital pore

GONZO *adj* bizarre

GOO *n* pl. GOOS a sticky or viscid substance

GOOBER *n* pl. -S a peanut

GOOD *adj* BETTER, BEST having positive or desirable qualities

GOOD *n* pl. -S something that is good

GOODBY *n* pl. -BYS goodbye

GOODBYE *n* pl. -S a concluding remark or gesture at parting

GOODIE *n* pl. -S goody

GOODIES pl. of goody

GOODISH *adj* somewhat good

GOODLY *adj* -LIER, -LIEST of pleasing appearance

GOODMAN *n* pl. -MEN the master of a household

GOODNESS *n* pl. -ES the state of being good

GOODWIFE *n* pl. -WIVES the mistress of a household

GOODWILL *n* pl. -S an attitude of friendliness

GOODY *n* pl. GOODIES a desirable food

GOOEY *adj* GOOIER, GOOIEST sticky or viscid

GOOF *v* -ED, -ING, -S to blunder

GOOFBALL *n* pl. -S a sleeping pill

GOOFY *adj* GOOFIER, GOOFIEST silly GOOFILY *adv*

GOOGLY *n* pl. -GLIES a type of bowled ball in cricket

GOOGOL *n* pl. -S an enormous number

GOOIER comparative of gooey

GOOIEST superlative of gooey

GOOK *n* pl. -S goo GOOKY *adj*

GOOMBAH *n* pl. -S an older man who is a friend

GOOMBAY *n* pl. -BAYS calypso music of the Bahamas

GOON *n* pl. -S a hired thug

GOONEY *n* pl. -NEYS an albatross

GOONIE *n* pl. -S gooney

GOONY *n* pl. -NIES gooney

GOOP *n* pl. -S goo, gunk

GOOPY *adj* GOOPIER, GOOPIEST sticky, gooey

GOORAL *n* pl. -S goral

GOOSE *n* pl. GEESE a swimming bird

GOOSE *v* GOOSED, GOOSING, GOOSES to poke between the buttocks

GOOSEY *adj* GOOSIER, GOOSIEST goosy

GOOSY *adj* GOOSIER, GOOSIEST resembling a goose

GOPHER *n* pl. -S a burrowing rodent

GOR *interj* — used as a mild oath

GORAL *n* pl. -S a goat antelope

GORBELLY *n* pl. -LIES a potbelly

GORBLIMY *interj* blimey

GORCOCK *n* pl. -S the male red grouse

GORE *v* GORED, GORING, GORES to pierce with a horn or tusk

GORGE *v* GORGED, GORGING, GORGES to stuff with food GORGEDLY *adv*

GORGEOUS *adj* beautiful

GORGER *n* pl. -S one that gorges

GORGERIN *n* pl. -S a part of a column

GORGET n pl. -S a piece of armor for the throat **GORGETED** adj

GORGING present participle of gorge

GORGON n pl. -S an ugly woman

GORHEN n pl. -S the female red grouse

GORIER comparative of gory

GORIEST superlative of gory

GORILLA n pl. -S a large ape

GORILY adv in a gory manner

GORINESS n pl. -ES the state of being gory

GORING present participle of gore

GORMAND n pl. -S gourmand

GORMLESS adj stupid

GORP n pl. -S a snack for quick energy

GORSE n pl. -S furze

GORSY adj GORSIER, GORSIEST abounding in gorse

GORY adj GORIER, GORIEST bloody

GOSH interj — used as an exclamation of surprise

GOSHAWK n pl. -S a large hawk

GOSLING n pl. -S a young goose

GOSPEL n pl. -S the message concerning Christ, the kingdom of God, and salvation

GOSPELER n pl. -S one that teaches the gospel

GOSPORT n pl. -S a communication device in an airplane

GOSSAMER n pl. -S a fine film of cobwebs

GOSSAN n pl. -S a type of decomposed rock

GOSSIP v -SIPED, -SIPING, -SIPS or -SIPPED, -SIPPING, -SIPS to talk idly about the affairs of others

GOSSIPER n pl. -S one that gossips

GOSSIPRY n pl. -RIES the practice of gossiping

GOSSIPY adj inclined to gossip

GOSSOON n pl. -S a boy

GOSSYPOL n pl. -S a toxic pigment

GOT past tense of get

GOTHIC n pl. -S a style of printing

GOTHITE n pl. -S goethite

GOTTEN past participle of get

GOUACHE n pl. -S a method of painting

GOUGE v GOUGED, GOUGING, GOUGES to cut or scoop out

GOUGER n pl. -S one that gouges

GOULASH n pl. -ES a beef stew

GOURAMI n pl. -S or -ES a food fish

GOURD n pl. -S a hard-shelled fruit

GOURDE n pl. -S a monetary unit of Haiti

GOURMAND n pl. -S one who loves to eat

GOURMET n pl. -S a connoisseur of fine food and drink

GOUT n pl. -S a metabolic disease

GOUTY adj GOUTIER, GOUTIEST affected with gout **GOUTILY** adv

GOVERN v -ED, -ING, -S to rule or direct

GOVERNOR n pl. -S one that governs

GOWAN n pl. -S a daisy **GOWANED**, **GOWANY** adj

GOWD n pl. -S gold

GOWK n pl. -S a fool

GOWN v -ED, -ING, -S to dress in a gown (a long, loose outer garment)

GOWNSMAN n pl. -MEN a professional or academic person

GOX n pl. -ES gaseous oxygen

GRAAL n pl. -S grail

GRAB v GRABBED, GRABBING, GRABS to grasp suddenly

GRABBER n pl. -S one that grabs

GRABBIER comparative of grabby

GRABBIEST superlative of grabby

GRABBING present participle of grab

GRABBLE v -BLED, -BLING, -BLES to grope

GRABBLER n pl. -S one that grabbles

GRABBY adj -BIER, -BIEST tending to grab

GRABEN n pl. -S a depression of the earth's crust

GRACE v GRACED, GRACING, GRACES to give beauty to

GRACEFUL adj -FULLER, -FULLEST having beauty of form or movement

GRACILE adj gracefully slender

GRACILIS n pl. -LES a thigh muscle

GRACING present participle of grace

GRACIOSO n pl. -SOS a clown in Spanish comedy

GRACIOUS adj marked by kindness and courtesy

GRACKLE n pl. -S a blackbird

GRAD n pl. -S a graduate

GRADATE v -DATED, -DATING, -DATES to change by degrees

GRADE v GRADED, GRADING, GRADES to arrange in steps or degrees **GRADABLE** adj

GRADER n pl. -S one that grades

GRADIENT *n pl.* -S a rate of inclination

GRADIN *n pl.* -S gradine

GRADINE *n pl.* -S one of a series of steps

GRADING present participle of grade

GRADUAL *n pl.* -S a hymn sung in alternate parts

GRADUAND *n pl.* -S one who is about to graduate

GRADUATE *v* -ATED, -ATING, -ATES to receive an academic degree or diploma

GRADUS *n pl.* -ES a dictionary of prosody

GRAECIZE *v* -CIZED, -CIZING, -CIZES to grecize

GRAFFITO *n pl.* -TI an inscription or drawing made on a rock or wall

GRAFT *v* -ED, -ING, -S to unite with a growing plant by insertion

GRAFTAGE *n pl.* -S the process of grafting

GRAFTER *n pl.* -S one that grafts

GRAHAM *n pl.* -S whole-wheat flour

GRAIL *n pl.* -S the object of a long quest

GRAIN *v* -ED, -ING, -S to form into small particles

GRAINER *n pl.* -S one that grains

GRAINY *adj* GRAINIER, GRAINIEST granular

GRAM *pl.* -S a unit of mass and weight

GRAMA *n pl.* -S a pasture grass

GRAMARY *n pl.* -RIES gramarye

GRAMARYE *n pl.* -S occult learning; magic

GRAMERCY *n pl.* -CIES an expression of gratitude

GRAMMAR *n pl.* -S the study of the formal features of a language

GRAMME *n pl.* -S gram

GRAMP *n pl.* -S grandfather

GRAMPUS *n pl.* -ES a marine mammal

GRAN *n pl.* -S a grandmother

GRANA *pl.* of granum

GRANARY *n pl.* -RIES a storehouse for grain

GRAND *adj* GRANDER, GRANDEST large and impressive

GRAND *n pl.* -S a type of piano

GRANDAD *n pl.* -S granddad

GRANDAM *n pl.* -S a grandmother

GRANDAME *n pl.* -S grandam

GRANDDAD *n pl.* -S a grandfather

GRANDDAM *n pl.* -S the female parent of an animal with offspring

GRANDEE *n pl.* -S man of high social position

GRANDEUR *n pl.* -S the state of being grand

GRANDKID *n pl.* -S the child of one's son or daughter

GRANDLY *adv* in a grand manner

GRANDMA *n pl.* -S a grandmother

GRANDPA *n pl.* -S a grandfather

GRANDSIR *n pl.* -S a grandfather

GRANDSON *n pl.* -S a son of one's son or daughter

GRANGE *n pl.* -S a farm

GRANGER *n pl.* -S a farmer

GRANITA *n pl.* -S an iced dessert

GRANITE *n pl.* -S a type of rock **GRANITIC** *adj*

GRANNIE *n pl.* -S granny

GRANNY *n pl.* -NIES a grandmother

GRANOLA *n pl.* -S a breakfast cereal

GRANT *v* -ED, -ING, -S to bestow upon

GRANTEE *n pl.* -S one to whom something is granted

GRANTER *n pl.* -S one that grants

GRANTOR *n pl.* -S granter

GRANULAR *adj* composed of granules

GRANULE *n pl.* -S a small particle

GRANUM *n pl.* GRANA a part of a plant chloroplast

GRAPE *n pl.* -S an edible berry

GRAPERY *n pl.* -ERIES a vinery

GRAPEY *adj* GRAPIER, GRAPIEST grapy

GRAPH *v* -ED, -ING, -S to represent by means of a diagram

GRAPHEME *n pl.* -S a unit of a writing system

GRAPHIC *n pl.* -S a product of the art of representation

GRAPHITE *n pl.* -S a variety of carbon

GRAPIER comparative of grapy

GRAPIEST superlative of grapy

GRAPLIN *n pl.* -S a grapnel

GRAPLINE *n pl.* -S graplin

GRAPNEL *n pl.* -S a type of anchor

GRAPPA *n pl.* -S an Italian brandy

GRAPPLE *v* -PLED, -PLING, -PLES to struggle or contend

GRAPPLER *n pl.* -S one that grapples

GRAPY *adj* GRAPIER, GRAPIEST resembling grapes

GRASP *v* -ED, -ING, -S to seize firmly with the hand

GRASPER *n pl.* -S one that grasps

GRASS   v -ED, -ING, -ES to cover with grass (herbaceous plants)

GRASSY   adj GRASSIER, GRASSIEST of, resembling, or pertaining to grass **GRASSILY** adv

GRAT   past tense of greet (to weep)

GRATE   v GRATED, GRATING, GRATES to reduce to shreds by rubbing

GRATEFUL   adj -FULLER, -FULLEST deeply thankful

GRATER   n pl. -S one that grates

GRATIFY   v -FIED, -FYING, -FIES to satisfy

GRATIN   n pl. -S a type of food crust

GRATINE   adj covered with a crust

GRATINEE   v -NEED, -NEEING, -NEES to cook food that is covered with a crust

GRATING   n pl. -S a network of bars covering an opening

GRATIS   adj free of charge

GRATUITY   n pl. -ITIES a gift of money

GRAUPEL   n pl. -S precipitation consisting of granular snow pellets

GRAVAMEN   n pl. -MENS or -MINA the most serious part of an accusation

GRAVE   adj GRAVER, GRAVEST extremely serious

GRAVE   v GRAVED, GRAVEN, GRAVING, GRAVES to engrave

GRAVEL   v -ELED, -ELING, -ELS or -ELLED, -ELLING, -ELS to pave with gravel (a mixture of rock fragments)

GRAVELLY   adj containing gravel

GRAVELY   adv in a grave manner

GRAVEN   past participle of grave

GRAVER   n pl. -S an engraver

GRAVEST   superlative of grave

GRAVID   adj pregnant **GRAVIDLY** adv

GRAVIDA   n pl. -DAS or -DAE a pregnant woman

GRAVIES   pl. of gravy

GRAVING   present participle of grave

GRAVITAS   n pl. -ES reserved, dignified behavior

GRAVITON   n pl. -S a hypothetical particle

GRAVITY   n pl. -TIES the force of attraction toward the earth's center

GRAVLAKS   n pl. GRAVLAKS gravlax

GRAVLAX   n pl. GRAVLAX cured salmon

GRAVURE   n pl. -S a printing process

GRAVY   n pl. -VIES a sauce of the fat and juices from cooked meat

GRAY   adj GRAYER, GRAYEST of a color between white and black

GRAY   v -ED, -ING, -S to make gray

GRAYBACK   n pl. -S a gray bird

GRAYFISH   n pl. -ES a dogfish

GRAYISH   adj somewhat gray

GRAYLAG   n pl. -S a wild goose

GRAYLING   n pl. -S a food fish

GRAYLY   adv in a gray manner

GRAYMAIL   n pl. -S pressure on an official to reveal sensitive information

GRAYNESS   n pl. -ES the state of being gray

GRAYOUT   n pl. -S a temporary blurring of vision

GRAZE   v GRAZED, GRAZING, GRAZES to feed on growing grass **GRAZABLE** adj

GRAZER   n pl. -S one that grazes

GRAZIER   n pl. -S one that grazes cattle

GRAZING   n pl. -S land used for grazing

GRAZIOSO   adj graceful in style

GREASE   v GREASED, GREASING, GREASES to smear with grease (a lubricating substance)

GREASER   n pl. -S one that greases

GREASY   adj GREASIER, GREASIEST containing or resembling grease **GREASILY** adv

GREAT   adj GREATER, GREATEST large

GREAT   n pl. -S an outstanding person

GREATEN   v -ED, -ING, -S to make greater

GREATLY   adv in a great manner

GREAVE   n pl. -S a piece of armor for the leg **GREAVED** adj

GREBE   n pl. -S a diving bird

GRECIZE   v -CIZED, -CIZING, -CIZES to provide with a Greek style

GREE   v GREED, GREEING, GREES to agree

GREED   n pl. -S excessive desire for gain or wealth

GREEDY   adj GREEDIER, GREEDIEST marked by greed **GREEDILY** adv

GREEGREE   n pl. -S grigri

GREEK   n pl. GREEK something unintelligible

GREEN   adj GREENER, GREENEST of the color of growing foliage

GREEN v -ED, -ING, -S to become green

GREENBUG n pl. -S a green aphid

GREENERY n pl. -ERIES green vegetation

GREENFLY n pl. -FLIES a green aphid

GREENIE n pl. -S an amphetamine pill

GREENIER comparative of greeny

GREENIEST superlative of greeny

GREENING n pl. -S a variety of apple

GREENISH adj somewhat green

GREENLET n pl. -S a vireo

GREENLY adv in a green manner

GREENTH n pl. -S verdure

GREENWAY n pl. -WAYS piece of undeveloped land in a city

GREENY adj GREENIER, GREENIEST somewhat green

GREET v -ED, -ING, -S to address in a friendly and courteous way

GREET v GRAT, GRUTTEN, GREETING, GREETS to weep

GREETER n pl. -S one that greets

GREETING n pl. -S a salutation

GREGO n pl. -GOS a hooded coat

GREIGE n pl. -S unfinished fabric

GREISEN n pl. -S a type of rock

GREMIAL n pl. -S a lap cloth used by a bishop during a service

GREMLIN n pl. -S a mischievous gnome

GREMMIE n pl. -S an inexperienced surfer

GREMMY n pl. -MIES gremmie

GRENADE n pl. -S an explosive device

GREW past tense of grow

GREWSOME adj -SOMER, -SOMEST gruesome

GREY adj GREYER, GREYEST gray

GREY v -ED, -ING, -S to gray

GREYHEN n pl. -S the female black grouse

GREYISH adj grayish

GREYLAG n pl. -S graylag

GREYLY adv grayly

GREYNESS n pl. -ES grayness

GRIBBLE n pl. -S a marine isopod

GRID n pl. -S a grating

GRIDDER n pl. -S a football player

GRIDDLE v -DLED, -DLING, -DLES to cook on a flat pan

GRIDE v GRIDED, GRIDING, GRIDES to scrape harshly

GRIDIRON n pl. -S a grate for broiling food

GRIDLOCK v -ED, -ING, -S to bring to a standstill

GRIEF n pl. -S intense mental distress

GRIEVANT n pl. -S one that submits a complaint for arbitration

GRIEVE v GRIEVED, GRIEVING, GRIEVES to feel grief

GRIEVER n pl. -S one that grieves

GRIEVOUS adj causing grief

GRIFF n pl. -S griffe

GRIFFE n pl. -S the offspring of a black person and a mulatto

GRIFFIN n pl. -S a mythological creature

GRIFFON n pl. -S griffin

GRIFT v -ED, -ING, -S to swindle

GRIFTER n pl. -S a swindler

GRIG n pl. -S a lively person

GRIGRI n pl. -S a fetish or amulet

GRILL v -ED, -ING, -S to broil on a gridiron

GRILLADE n pl. -S a dish of grilled meat

GRILLAGE n pl. -S a framework of timber

GRILLE n pl. -S a grating

GRILLER n pl. -S one that grills

GRILSE n pl. -S a young salmon

GRIM adj GRIMMER, GRIMMEST stern and unrelenting

GRIMACE v -MACED, -MACING, -MACES to contort the facial features

GRIMACER n pl. -S one that grimaces

GRIME v GRIMED, GRIMING, GRIMES to make dirty

GRIMIER comparative of grimy

GRIMIEST superlative of grimy

GRIMILY adv in a grimy manner

GRIMING present participle of grime

GRIMLY adv in a grim manner

GRIMMER comparative of grim

GRIMMEST superlative of grim

GRIMNESS n pl. -ES the quality of being grim

GRIMY adj GRIMIER, GRIMIEST dirty

GRIN v GRINNED, GRINNING, GRINS to smile broadly

GRINCH n pl. -ES one who spoils the fun of others

GRIND v GROUND or GRINDED, GRINDING, GRINDS to wear, smooth, or sharpen by friction

GRINDER n pl. -S one that grinds

GRINDERY n pl. -ERIES a place where tools are ground

GRINNED past tense of grin

GRINNER n pl. -S one that grins

GRINNING present participle of grin

GRIOT n pl. -S a tribal entertainer in West Africa

GRIP v GRIPPED or GRIPT, GRIPPING, GRIPS to grasp

GRIPE v GRIPED, GRIPING, GRIPES to grasp

GRIPER n pl. -S one that gripes

GRIPEY adj GRIPIER, GRIPIEST gripy

GRIPIER comparative of gripy

GRIPIEST superlative of gripy

GRIPING present participle of gripe

GRIPMAN n pl. -MEN a cable car operator

GRIPPE n pl. -S a virus disease

GRIPPED a past tense of grip

GRIPPER n pl. -S one that grips

GRIPPIER comparative of grippy

GRIPPIEST superlative of grippy

GRIPPING present participle of grip

GRIPPLE adj greedy

GRIPPY adj GRIPPIER, GRIPPIEST affected with the grippe

GRIPSACK n pl. -S a valise

GRIPT a past tense of grip

GRIPY adj GRIPIER, GRIPIEST causing sharp pains in the bowels

GRISEOUS adj grayish

GRISETTE n pl. -S a young French working-class girl

GRISKIN n pl. -S the lean part of a loin of pork

GRISLY adj -LIER, -LIEST horrifying

GRISON n pl. -S a carnivorous mammal

GRIST n pl. -S grain for grinding

GRISTLE n pl. -S the tough part of meat

GRISTLY adj -TLIER, -TLIEST containing gristle

GRIT v GRITTED, GRITTING, GRITS to press the teeth together

GRITH n pl. -S sanctuary for a limited period of time

GRITTY adj -TIER, -TIEST plucky GRITTILY adv

GRIVET n pl. -S a small monkey

GRIZZLE v -ZLED, -ZLING, -ZLES to complain

GRIZZLER n pl. -S one that grizzles

GRIZZLY adj -ZLIER, -ZLIEST grayish

GRIZZLY n pl. -ZLIES a large bear

GROAN v -ED, -ING, -S to utter a low, mournful sound

GROANER n pl. -S one that groans

GROAT n pl. -S an old English coin

GROCER n pl. -S a dealer in foodstuffs and household supplies

GROCERY n pl. -CERIES a grocer's store

GROG n pl. -S a mixture of liquor and water

GROGGERY n pl. -GERIES a barroom

GROGGY adj -GIER, -GIEST dazed GROGGILY adv

GROGRAM n pl. -S a coarse silk fabric

GROGSHOP n pl. -S a groggery

GROIN v -ED, -ING, -S to build with intersecting arches

GROMMET n pl. -S a reinforcing ring of metal

GROMWELL n pl. -S an herb

GROOM v -ED, -ING, -S to clean and care for

GROOMER n pl. -S one that grooms

GROOVE v GROOVED, GROOVING, GROOVES to form a groove (a long, narrow depression)

GROOVER n pl. -S one that grooves

GROOVY adj GROOVIER, GROOVIEST marvelous

GROPE v GROPED, GROPING, GROPES to feel about with the hands

GROPER n pl. -S one that gropes

GROSBEAK n pl. -S a finch

GROSCHEN n pl. GROSCHEN an Austrian coin

GROSS adj GROSSER, GROSSEST flagrant

GROSS v -ED, -ING, -ES to earn exclusive of deductions

GROSSER n pl. -S a product yielding a large volume of business

GROSSLY adv in a gross manner

GROSZ n pl. GROSZY a Polish coin

GROSZE n pl. GROSZY grosz

GROT n pl. -S a grotto

GROTTO n pl. -TOES or -TOS a cave

GROTTY adj -TIER, -TIEST wretched

GROUCH v -ED, -ING, -ES to complain

GROUCHY adj GROUCHIER, GROUCHIEST ill-tempered

GROUND v -ED, -ING, -S to place on a foundation

GROUNDER n pl. -S a type of batted baseball

GROUP v -ED, -ING, -S to arrange in a group (an assemblage of persons or things)

GROUPER n pl. -S a food fish

GROUPIE n pl. -S a female follower of rock groups

GROUPING n pl. -S a set of objects

GROUPOID n pl. -S a type of mathematical set

GROUSE v GROUSED, GROUSING, GROUSES to complain

GROUSER n pl. -S one that grouses

GROUT v -ED, -ING, -S to fill with a thin mortar

GROUTER n pl. -S one that grouts

GROUTY adj GROUTIER, GROUTIEST surly

GROVE n pl. -S a small forested area GROVED adj

GROVEL v -ELED, -ELING, -ELS or -ELLED, -ELLING, -ELS to crawl in an abject manner

GROVELER n pl. -S one that grovels

GROW v GREW, GROWN, GROWING, GROWS to cultivate GROWABLE adj

GROWER n pl. -S one that grows

GROWL v -ED, -ING, -S to utter a deep, harsh sound

GROWLER n pl. -S one that growls

GROWLY adj GROWLIER, GROWLIEST deep and harsh in speech

GROWN adj mature

GROWNUP n pl. -S a mature person

GROWTH n pl. -S development

GROWTHY adj GROWTHIER, GROWTHIEST fast-growing

GROYNE n pl. -S a structure built to protect a shore from erosion

GRUB v GRUBBED, GRUBBING, GRUBS to dig

GRUBBER n pl. -S one that grubs

GRUBBY adj -BIER, -BIEST dirty GRUBBILY adv

GRUBWORM n pl. -S the larva of some insects

GRUDGE v GRUDGED, GRUDGING, GRUDGES to be unwilling to give or admit

GRUDGER n pl. -S one that grudges

GRUE n pl. -S a shudder of fear

GRUEL v -ELED, -ELING, -ELS or -ELLED, -ELLING, -ELS to disable by hard work

GRUELER n pl. -S one that gruels

GRUELING n pl. -S an exhausting experience

GRUELLED a past tense of gruel

GRUELLER n pl. -S grueler

GRUELLING present participle of gruel

GRUESOME adj -SOMER, -SOMEST repugnant

GRUFF adj GRUFFER, GRUFFEST low and harsh in speech

GRUFF v -ED, -ING, -S to utter in a gruff voice

GRUFFIER comparative of gruffy

GRUFFIEST superlative of gruffy

GRUFFILY adv in a gruffy manner

GRUFFISH adj somewhat gruff

GRUFFLY adv in a gruff manner

GRUFFY adj GRUFFIER, GRUFFIEST gruff

GRUGRU n pl. -S a palm tree

GRUIFORM adj designating an order of birds

GRUM adj GRUMMER, GRUMMEST morose

GRUMBLE v -BLED, -BLING, -BLES to mutter in discontent GRUMBLY adj

GRUMBLER n pl. -S one that grumbles

GRUME n pl. -S a thick, viscid substance

GRUMMER comparative of grum

GRUMMEST superlative of grum

GRUMMET n pl. -S grommet

GRUMOSE adj grumous

GRUMOUS adj consisting of clustered grains

GRUMP v -ED, -ING, -S to complain

GRUMPHIE n pl. -S a pig

GRUMPHY n pl. GRUMPHIES grumphie

GRUMPISH adj grumpy

GRUMPY adj GRUMPIER, GRUMPIEST ill-tempered GRUMPILY adv

GRUNGE n pl. -S dirt

GRUNGY adj -GIER, -GIEST dirty

GRUNION n pl. -S a small food fish

GRUNT v -ED, -ING, -S to utter a deep, guttural sound

GRUNTER n pl. -S one that grunts

GRUNTLE v -TLED, -TLING, -TLES to put in a good humor

GRUSHIE adj thriving

GRUTCH v -ED, -ING, -ES to grudge

GRUTTEN past participle of greet (to weep)

GRUYERE n pl. -S a Swiss cheese

GRYPHON n pl. -S griffin

GUACHARO n pl. -ROS or -ROES a tropical bird

GUACO n pl. -COS a tropical plant

GUAIAC n pl. -S guaiacum

GUAIACOL n pl. -S a chemical compound

GUAIACUM n pl. -S a medicinal resin

GUAIOCUM n pl. -S guaiacum

GUAN n pl. -S a large bird

GUANACO n pl. -COS a South American mammal

GUANASE n pl. -S an enzyme

GUANAY n pl. -NAYS a Peruvian cormorant

GUANIDIN n pl. -S a chemical compound

GUANIN n pl. -S guanine

GUANINE n pl. -S a chemical compound

GUANO n pl. -NOS the accumulated excrement of sea birds

GUAR n pl. -S a drought-tolerant legume

GUARANI n pl. -NIS or -NIES a monetary unit of Paraguay

GUARANTY v -TIED, -TYING, -TIES to assume responsibility for the quality of

GUARD v -ED, -ING, -S to protect

GUARDANT n pl. -S a guardian

GUARDER n pl. -S one that guards

GUARDIAN n pl. -S one that guards

GUAVA n pl. -S a tropical shrub

GUAYULE n pl. -S a shrub that is a source of rubber

GUCK n pl. -S a messy substance

GUDE n pl. -S good

GUDGEON v -ED, -ING, -S to dupe

GUENON n pl. -S a long-tailed monkey

GUERDON v -ED, -ING, -S to reward

GUERIDON n pl. -S a small stand or table

GUERILLA n pl. -S a member of a small independent band of soldiers

GUERNSEY n pl. -SEYS a woolen shirt

GUESS v -ED, -ING, -ES to form an opinion from little or no evidence

GUESSER n pl. -S one that guesses

GUEST v -ED, -ING, -S to appear as a visitor

GUFF n pl. -S foolish talk

GUFFAW v -ED, -ING, -S to laugh loudly

GUGGLE v -GLED, -GLING, -GLES to gurgle

GUGLET n pl. -S a goglet

GUID n pl. -S good

GUIDANCE n pl. -S advice

GUIDE v GUIDED, GUIDING, GUIDES to show the way to GUIDABLE adj

GUIDER n pl. -S one that guides

GUIDEWAY n pl. -WAYS a track for controlling the line of motion of something

GUIDON n ol. -S a small flag

GUILD n pl. -S an association of people of the same trade

GUILDER n pl. -S a monetary unit of the Netherlands

GUILE v GUILED, GUILING, GUILES to beguile

GUILEFUL adj cunning

GUILT n pl. -S the fact of having committed an offense

GUILTY adj GUILTIER, GUILTIEST worthy of blame for an offense GUILTILY adv

GUIMPE n pl. -S a short blouse

GUINEA n pl. -S a former British coin

GUIPURE n pl. -S a type of lace

GUIRO n pl. -ROS a percussion instrument

GUISARD n pl. -S a masker

GUISE v GUISED, GUISING, GUISES to disguise

GUITAR n pl. -S a stringed musical instrument

GUITGUIT n pl. -S a tropical American bird

GUL n pl. -S a design in oriental carpets

GULAG n pl. -S a forced-labor camp

GULAR adj of or pertaining to the throat

GULCH n pl. -ES a deep, narrow ravine

GULDEN n pl. -S a guilder

GULES n pl. GULES the color red

GULF v -ED, -ING, -S to swallow up

GULFIER comparative of gulfy

GULFIEST superlative of gulfy

GULFLIKE adj resembling a deep chasm

GULFWEED n pl. -S a brownish seaweed

GULFY adj GULFIER, GULFIEST full of whirlpools

GULL v -ED, -ING, -S to deceive

GULLABLE adj gullible GULLABLY adv

GULLET n pl. -S the throat

GULLEY n pl. -LEYS a ravine

GULLIBLE adj easily deceived GULLIBLY adv

GULLY v -LIED, -LYING, -LIES to form ravines by the action of water

GULOSITY n pl. -TIES gluttony

GULP v -ED, -ING, -S to swallow rapidly

GULPER n pl. -S one that gulps

GULPY adj GULPIER, GULPIEST marked by gulping

GUM	v GUMMED, GUMMING, GUMS to smear, seal, or clog with gum (a sticky, viscid substance)	**GUNMETAL**	n pl. -S a dark gray color
		GUNNED	past tense of gun
		GUNNEL	n pl. -S a marine fish
		GUNNEN	past participle of gin
GUMBO	n pl. -BOS the okra plant	**GUNNER**	n pl. -S one that operates a gun
GUMBOIL	n pl. -S an abscess in the gum		
GUMBOOT	n pl. -S a rubber boot	**GUNNERY**	n pl. -NERIES the use of guns
GUMBOTIL	n pl. -S a sticky clay	**GUNNING**	n pl. -S the sport of hunting with a gun
GUMDROP	n pl. -S a chewy candy		
GUMLESS	adj having no gum	**GUNNY**	n pl. -NIES a coarse fabric
GUMLIKE	adj resembling gum	**GUNNYBAG**	n pl. -S a bag made of gunny
GUMMA	n pl. -MAS or -MATA a soft tumor	**GUNPAPER**	n pl. -S a type of explosive paper
GUMMED	past tense of gum		
GUMMER	n pl. -S one that gums	**GUNPLAY**	n pl. -PLAYS the shooting of guns
GUMMIER	comparative of gummy		
GUMMIEST	superlative of gummy	**GUNPOINT**	n pl. -S the point or aim of a gun
GUMMING	present participle of gum		
GUMMITE	n pl. -S a mixture of various minerals	**GUNROOM**	n pl. -S a room on a British warship
		GUNSEL	n pl. -S a gunman
GUMMOSE	adj gummy	**GUNSHIP**	n pl. -S an armed helicopter
GUMMOSIS	n pl. -MOSES a disease of plants	**GUNSHOT**	n pl. -S a projectile fired from a gun
GUMMOUS	adj gummy	**GUNSMITH**	n pl. -S one who makes or repairs firearms
GUMMY	adj -MIER, -MIEST resembling gum		
		GUNSTOCK	n pl. -S the rear wooden part of a rifle
GUMPTION	n pl. -S shrewdness		
GUMSHOE	v -SHOED, -SHOEING, -SHOES to investigate stealthily	**GUNWALE**	n pl. -S the upper edge of a ship's side
		GUPPY	n pl. -PIES a small, tropical fish
GUMTREE	n pl. -S a tree that yields gum		
GUMWEED	n pl. -S a plant covered with a gummy substance	**GURGE**	v GURGED, GURGING, GURGES to swirl
GUMWOOD	n pl. -S the wood of a gumtree	**GURGLE**	v -GLED, -GLING, -GLES to flow unevenly
GUN	v GUNNED, GUNNING, GUNS to shoot with a gun (a portable firearm)		
		GURGLET	n pl. -S goglet
		GURNARD	n pl. -S a marine fish
GUNBOAT	n pl. -S an armed vessel	**GURNET**	n pl. -S a gurnard
GUNDOG	n pl. -S a hunting dog	**GURNEY**	n pl. -NEYS a wheeled cot
GUNFIGHT	v -FOUGHT, -FIGHTING, -FIGHTS to fight with guns	**GURRY**	n pl. -RIES fish offal
		GURSH	n pl. -ES qursh
GUNFIRE	n pl. -S the firing of guns	**GURU**	n pl. -S a Hindu spiritual teacher
GUNFLINT	n pl. -S the flint in a flintlock		
GUNFOUGHT	past tense of gunfight	**GURUSHIP**	n pl. -S the office of a guru
GUNITE	n pl. -S a mixture of cement, sand, and water	**GUSH**	v -ED, -ING, -ES to flow forth forcefully
		GUSHER	n pl. -S a gushing oil well
GUNK	n pl. -S filthy, sticky, or greasy matter **GUNKY** adj	**GUSHY**	adj GUSHIER, GUSHIEST overly sentimental **GUSHILY** adv
GUNKHOLE	v -HOLED, -HOLING, -HOLES to make a series of short boat trips		
		GUSSET	v -ED, -ING, -S to furnish with a reinforcing piece of material
GUNLESS	adj having no gun		
GUNLOCK	n pl. -S the mechanism which ignites the charge of a gun	**GUSSIE**	v -SIED, -SYING, -SIES gussy
		GUSSY	v -SIED, -SYING, -SIES to dress up in fine or showy clothes
GUNMAN	n pl. -MEN one who is armed with a gun		

GUST *v* -ED, -ING, -S to blow in gusts (sudden blasts of wind)
GUSTABLE *n pl.* -S a savory food
GUSTIER comparative of gusty
GUSTIEST superlative of gusty
GUSTILY *adv* in a gusty manner
GUSTLESS *adj* having no gusts
GUSTO *n pl.* -TOES vigorous enjoyment
GUSTY *adj* GUSTIER, GUSTIEST blowing in gusts
GUT *v* GUTTED, GUTTING, GUTS to remove the guts (intestines) of
GUTLESS *adj* lacking courage
GUTLIKE *adj* resembling guts
GUTSILY *adv* in a gutsy manner
GUTSY *adj* GUTSIER, GUTSIEST brave
GUTTA *n pl.* -TAE a drop of liquid
GUTTATE *adj* resembling a drop
GUTTATED *adj* guttate
GUTTED past tense of gut
GUTTER *v* -ED, -ING, -S to form channels for draining off water
GUTTERY *adj* marked by extreme vulgarity or indecency
GUTTIER comparative of gutty
GUTTIEST superlative of gutty
GUTTING present participle of gut
GUTTLE *v* -TLED, -TLING, -TLES to eat rapidly
GUTTLER *n pl.* -S one that guttles
GUTTURAL *n pl.* -S a throaty sound
GUTTY *adj* -TIER, -TIEST marked by courage
GUV *n pl.* -S a governor
GUY *v* -ED, -ING, -S to ridicule
GUYLINE *n pl.* -S a rope, chain, or wire used as a brace
GUYOT *n pl.* -S a flat-topped seamount
GUZZLE *v* -ZLED, -ZLING, -ZLES to drink rapidly
GUZZLER *n pl.* -S one that guzzles
GWEDUC *n pl.* -S geoduck
GWEDUCK *n pl.* -S geoduck
GYBE *v* GYBED, GYBING, GYBES to shift from side to side while sailing
GYM *n pl.* -S a room for athletic activities

GYMKHANA *n pl.* -S an athletic meet
GYMNASIA *n/pl* gyms
GYMNAST *n pl.* -S one who is skilled in physical exercises
GYNAECEA *n/pl* gynecia
GYNAECIA *n/pl* gynecia
GYNANDRY *n pl.* -DRIES the condition of having both male and female sexual organs
GYNARCHY *n pl.* -CHIES government by women
GYNECIC *adj* pertaining to women
GYNECIUM *n pl.* -CIA the pistil of a flower
GYNECOID *adj* resembling a woman
GYNIATRY *n pl.* -TRIES the treatment of women's diseases
GYNOECIA *n/pl* gynecia
GYP *v* GYPPED, GYPPING, GYPS to swindle
GYPLURE *n pl.* -S a synthetic attractant to trap gypsy moths
GYPPER *n pl.* -S one that gyps
GYPSEIAN *adj* of or pertaining to gypsies
GYPSEOUS *adj* containing gypsum
GYPSTER *n pl.* -S one that gyps
GYPSUM *n pl.* -S a mineral
GYPSY *v* -SIED, -SYING, -SIES to live like a gypsy (a wanderer)
GYPSYDOM *n pl.* -S the realm of gypsies
GYPSYISH *adj* resembling a gypsy
GYPSYISM *n pl.* -S the mode of life of gypsies
GYRAL *adj* gyratory **GYRALLY** *adv*
GYRASE *n pl.* -S an enzyme
GYRATE *v* -RATED, -RATING, -RATES to revolve or rotate
GYRATION *n pl.* -S the act of gyrating
GYRATOR *n pl.* -S one that gyrates
GYRATORY *adj* moving in a circle or spiral
GYRE *v* GYRED, GYRING, GYRES to move in a circle or spiral
GYRENE *n pl.* -S a marine
GYRI pl. of gyrus
GYRING present participle of gyre
GYRO *n pl.* -ROS a gyroscope
GYROIDAL *adj* spiral in arrangement
GYRON *n pl.* -S a heraldic design
GYROSE *adj* marked with wavy lines
GYROSTAT *n pl.* -S a type of stabilizing device
GYRUS *n pl.* -RI a ridge in the brain
GYVE *v* GYVED, GYVING, GYVES to shackle

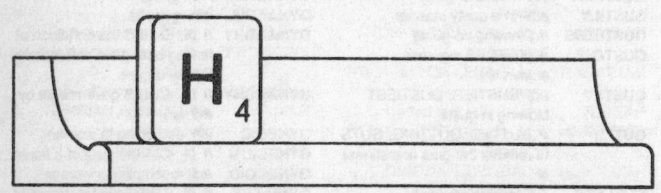

HA *n pl.* -S a sound of surprise

HAAF *n pl.* -S a deep-sea fishing ground

HAAR *n pl.* -S a fog

HABANERA *n pl.* -S a Cuban dance

HABDALAH *n pl.* -S a Jewish ceremony

HABILE *adj* skillful

HABIT *v* -ED, -ING, -S to clothe or dress

HABITAN *n pl.* -S a French settler

HABITANT *n pl.* -S an inhabitant

HABITAT *n pl.* -S the natural environment of an organism

HABITUAL *adj* occurring frequently or constantly

HABITUDE *n pl.* -S a usual course of action

HABITUE *n pl.* -S a frequent customer

HABITUS *n pl.* HABITUS bodily build and constitution

HABOOB *n pl.* -S a violent sandstorm

HABU *n pl.* -S a poisonous snake

HACEK *n pl.* -S a mark placed over a letter to modify it

HACHURE *v* -CHURED, -CHURING, -CHURES to make a hatching on a map

HACIENDA *n pl.* -S an estate

HACK *v* -ED, -ING, -S to cut or chop roughly

HACKBUT *n pl.* -S a type of gun

HACKEE *n pl.* -S a chipmunk

HACKER *n pl.* -S one that hacks

HACKIE *n pl.* -S a taxicab driver

HACKLE *v* -LED, -LING, -LES to hack

HACKLER *n pl.* -S one that hackles

HACKLY *adj* -LIER, -LIEST jagged

HACKMAN *n pl.* -MEN a hackie

HACKNEY *v* -NEYED, -NEYING, -NEYS to make common

HACKSAW *n pl.* -S a type of saw

HACKWORK *n pl.* -S artistic work done according to formula

HAD a past tense of have

HADAL *adj* pertaining to deep parts of the ocean

HADARIM a pl. of heder

HADDEST a past 2d person sing. of have

HADDOCK *n pl.* -S a food fish

HADE *v* HADED, HADING, HADES to incline

HADITH *n pl.* HADITH or HADITHS a record of the sayings of Muhammed

HADJ *n pl.* -ES a pilgrimage to Mecca

HADJEE *n pl.* -S hadji

HADJI *n pl.* -S one who has made a hadj

HADRON *n pl.* -S an elementary particle **HADRONIC** *adj*

HADST a past 2d person sing. of have

HAE *v* HAED, HAEN, HAEING, HAES to have

HAEM *n pl.* -S heme

HAEMAL *adj* hemal

HAEMATAL *adj* hemal

HAEMATIC *n pl.* -S hematic

HAEMATIN *n pl.* -S hematin

HAEMIC *adj* hemic

HAEMIN *n pl.* -S hemin

HAEMOID *adj* hemoid

HAEN past participle of hae

HAERES *n pl.* -REDES heres

HAET *n pl.* -S a small amount

HAFFET *n pl.* -S the cheekbone and temple

HAFFIT n pl. -S haffet

HAFIZ n pl. HAFIS a Muslim who knows the Koran by heart

HAFNIUM n pl. -S a metallic element

HAFT v -ED, -ING, -S to supply with a handle

HAFTARA n pl. -RAS, -ROT or -ROTH haphtara

HAFTARAH n pl. -RAHS, -ROT or -ROTH haphtara

HAFTER n pl. -S one that hafts

HAFTORAH n pl. -RAHS, -ROT or -ROTH haphtara

HAG v HAGGED, HAGGING, HAGS to hack

HAGADIC adj haggadic

HAGADIST n pl. -S a haggadic scholar

HAGBERRY n pl. -RIES a small cherry

HAGBORN adj born of a witch

HAGBUSH n pl. -ES a large tree

HAGBUT n pl. -S a hackbut

HAGDON n pl. -S a seabird

HAGFISH n pl. -ES an eellike fish

HAGGADA n pl. -DAS, -DOT or -DOTH haggadah

HAGGADAH n pl. -DAHS, -DOT or -DOTH a biblical narrative **HAGGADIC** adj

HAGGARD n pl. -S an adult hawk

HAGGED past tense of hag

HAGGING present participle of hag

HAGGIS n pl. -GISES a Scottish dish

HAGGISH adj resembling a hag

HAGGLE v -GLED, -GLING, -GLES to bargain

HAGGLER n pl. -S one that haggles

HAGRIDE v -RODE, -RIDDEN, -RIDING, -RIDES to harass

HAH n pl. -S ha

HAHA n pl. -S a fence set in a ditch

HAHNIUM n pl. -S a radioactive element

HAIK n pl. HAIKS or HAIKA an outer garment worn by Arabs

HAIKU n pl. HAIKU a Japanese poem

HAIL v -ED, -ING, -S to welcome

HAILER n pl. -S one that hails

HAIR n pl. -S a threadlike growth

HAIRBALL n pl. -S a ball of hair

HAIRBAND n pl. -S a headband

HAIRCAP n pl. -S a hat

HAIRCUT n pl. -S a cutting of the hair

HAIRDO n pl. -DOS a style of wearing the hair

HAIRED adj having hair

HAIRIER comparative of hairy

HAIRIEST superlative of hairy

HAIRLESS adj having no hair

HAIRLIKE adj resembling a hair

HAIRLINE n pl. -S a very thin line

HAIRLOCK n pl. -S a lock of hair

HAIRNET n pl. -S a net worn to keep the hair in place

HAIRPIN n pl. -S a hair fastener

HAIRWORK n pl. -S the making of articles from hair

HAIRWORM n pl. -S a parasitic worm

HAIRY adj HAIRIER, HAIRIEST covered with hair

HAJ n pl. -ES hadj

HAJI n pl. -S hadji

HAJJ n pl. -ES hadj

HAJJI n pl. -S hadji

HAKE n pl. -S a marine fish

HAKEEM n pl. -S hakim

HAKIM n pl. -S a Muslim physician

HALACHA n pl. -CHAS or -CHOT halakah

HALAKAH n pl. -KAHS or -KOTH the legal part of the Talmud

HALAKHA n pl. -KHAS or -KHOT halakah

HALAKIC adj pertaining to the halakah

HALAKIST n pl. -S a halakic writer

HALAKOTH a pl. of halakah

HALALA n pl. -S a Saudi Arabian coin

HALALAH n pl. -S halala

HALATION n pl. -S a blurring of light in photographs

HALAVAH n pl. -S halvah

HALAZONE n pl. -S a disinfectant for drinking water

HALBERD n pl. -S an axlike weapon of the 15th and 16th centuries

HALBERT n pl. -S halberd

HALCYON n pl. -S a mythical bird

HALE adj HALER, HALEST healthy

HALE v HALED, HALING, HALES to compel to go

HALENESS n pl. -ES the state of being hale

HALER n pl. -LERS or -LERU a coin of the Czech Republic

HALEST superlative of hale

HALF n pl. HALVES one of two equal parts

HALFBACK n pl. -S a football player

HALFBEAK n pl. -S a marine fish

HALFLIFE n pl. -LIVES a measure of radioactive decay

HALFNESS n pl. -ES the state of being half

HALFTIME n pl. -S an intermission in a football game

HALFTONE n pl. -S a shade between light and dark

HALFWAY adj being in the middle

HALIBUT n pl. -S a flatfish

HALID n pl. -S halide

HALIDE n pl. -S a chemical compound

HALIDOM n pl. -S something holy

HALIDOME n pl. -S halidom

HALING present participle of hale

HALITE n pl. -S a mineral

HALITUS n pl. -ES an exhalation

HALL n pl. -S a large room for assembly

HALLAH n pl. -LAHS, -LOTH or -LOT challah

HALLEL n pl. -S a chant of praise

HALLIARD n pl. -S a halyard

HALLMARK v -ED, -ING, -S to mark with an official stamp

HALLO v -ED, -ING, -S or -ES to shout

HALLOA v -ED, -ING, -S to hallo

HALLOO v -ED, -ING, -S to hallo

HALLOT a pl. of haliah

HALLOTH a pl. of hallah

HALLOW v -ED, -ING, -S to make holy

HALLOWER n pl. -S one that hallows

HALLUX n pl. -LUCES the big toe

HALLWAY n pl. -WAYS a hall

HALM n pl. -S haulm

HALMA n pl. -S a board game

HALO v -ED, -ING, -ES or -S to form a halo (a ring of light)

HALOGEN n pl. -S a nonmetallic element

HALOID n pl. -S a chemical salt

HALOLIKE adj resembling a halo

HALT v -ED, -ING, -S to stop

HALTER v -ED, -ING, -S to put restraint upon

HALTERE n pl. -S a pair of wings of an insect

HALTLESS adj not hesitant

HALUTZ n pl. -LUTZIM an Israeli farmer

HALVA n pl. -S halvah

HALVAH n pl. -S a Turkish confection

HALVE v HALVED, HALVING, HALVES to divide into two equal parts

HALVERS n pl. HALVERS half shares

HALVES pl. of half

HALVING present participle of halve

HALYARD n pl. -S a line used to hoist a sail

HAM v HAMMED, HAMMING, HAMS to overact

HAMADA n pl. -S hammada

HAMAL n pl. -S a porter in eastern countries

HAMARTIA n pl. -S a defect of character

HAMATE n pl. -S a wrist bone

HAMAUL n pl. -S hamal

HAMBONE v -BONED, -BONING, -BONES to overact

HAMBURG n pl. -S a patty of ground beef

HAME n pl. -S a part of a horse collar

HAMLET n pl. -S a small town

HAMMADA n pl. -S a desert plateau of bedrock

HAMMAL n pl. -S hamal

HAMMED past tense of ham

HAMMER v -ED, -ING, -S to strike repeatedly

HAMMERER n pl. -S one that hammers

HAMMIER comparative of hammy

HAMMIEST superlative of hammy

HAMMILY adv in a hammy manner

HAMMING present participle of ham

HAMMOCK n pl. -S a hanging cot

HAMMY adj -MIER, -MIEST overly theatrical

HAMPER v -ED, -ING, -S to hinder

HAMPERER n pl. -S one that hampers

HAMSTER n pl. -S a burrowing rodent

HAMULUS n pl. -LI a small hook HAMULAR, HAMULATE, HAMULOSE, HAMULOUS adj

HAMZA n pl. -S an Arabic diacritical mark

HAMZAH n pl. -S hamza

HANAPER n pl. -S a wicker receptacle

HANCE n pl. -S a side of an arch

HAND v -ED, -ING, -S to present with the hand (the end of the forearm)

HANDBAG n pl. -S a small carrying bag

HANDBALL n pl. -S a small rubber ball

HANDBELL n pl. -S a small bell with a handle

HANDBILL n pl. -S a circular

HANDBOOK n pl. -S a manual

HANDCAR n pl. -S a hand-operated railroad car

HANDCART n pl. -S a cart pushed by hand

HANDCUFF v -ED, -ING, -S to fetter with restraining cuffs

HANDFAST v -ED, -ING, -S to grip securely

HANDFUL n pl. HANDFULS or HANDSFUL as much as the hand can hold

HANDGRIP *n pl.* -S a grip by the hand or hands

HANDGUN *n pl.* -S a small firearm

HANDHELD *n pl.* -S something held in the hand

HANDHOLD *n pl.* -S a handgrip

HANDICAP *v* -CAPPED, -CAPPING, -CAPS to hinder

HANDIER comparative of handy

HANDIEST superlative of handy

HANDILY *adv* in a handy manner

HANDLE *v* -DLED, -DLING, -DLES to touch with the hands

HANDLER *n pl.* -S one that handles

HANDLESS *adj* having no hands

HANDLIKE *adj* resembling a hand

HANDLING *n pl.* -S the manner in which something is handled

HANDLIST *n pl.* -S a reference list

HANDLOOM *n pl.* -S a manually operated loom

HANDMADE *adj* made by hand

HANDMAID *n pl.* -S a female servant

HANDOFF *n pl.* -S a play in football

HANDOUT *n pl.* -S something given out free

HANDOVER *n pl.* -S an instance of giving up control

HANDPICK *v* -ED, -ING, -S to choose carefully

HANDRAIL *n pl.* -S a railing used for support

HANDSAW *n pl.* -S a saw used manually

HANDSEL *v* -SELED, -SELING, -SELS or -SELLED, -SELLING, -SELS to give a gift to

HANDSET *n pl.* -S a type of telephone

HANDSEWN *adj* sewn by hand

HANDSFUL *a pl.* of handful

HANDSOME *adj* -SOMER, -SOMEST attractive

HANDWORK *n pl.* -S manual labor

HANDWRIT *adj* written by hand

HANDY *adj* HANDIER, HANDIEST convenient for handling

HANDYMAN *n pl.* -MEN a man who does odd jobs

HANG *v* HUNG or HANGED, HANGING, HANGS to attach from above only **HANGABLE** *adj*

HANGAR *v* -ED, -ING, -S to place in an aircraft shelter

HANGBIRD *n pl.* -S a type of bird

HANGDOG *n pl.* -S a sneaky person

HANGER *n pl.* -S one that hangs

HANGFIRE *n pl.* -S a delay in detonation

HANGING *n pl.* -S an execution by strangling with a suspended noose

HANGMAN *n pl.* -MEN an executioner

HANGNAIL *n pl.* -S an agnail

HANGNEST *n pl.* -S a hangbird

HANGOUT *n pl.* -S a place often visited

HANGOVER *n pl.* -S the physical effects following a drinking binge

HANGTAG *n pl.* -S a type of tag used commercially

HANGUL *n* the Korean alphabetic script

HANGUP *n pl.* -S an inhibition or obsession

HANIWA *n/pl* Japanese clay sculptures

HANK *v* -ED, -ING, -S to fasten a sail

HANKER *v* -ED, -ING, -S to long for

HANKERER *n pl.* -S one that hankers

HANKIE *n pl.* -S hanky

HANKY *n pl.* -KIES a handkerchief

HANSA *n pl.* -S hanse

HANSE *n pl.* -S a guild of merchants

HANSEL *v* -SELED, -SELING, -SELS or -SELLED, -SELLING, -SELS to handsel

HANSOM *n pl.* -S a light carriage

HANT *v* -ED, -ING, -S to haunt

HANTLE *n pl.* -S a large amount

HANUMAN *n pl.* -S an East Indian monkey

HAO *n pl.* HAO a monetary unit of Vietnam

HAP *v* HAPPED, HAPPING, HAPS to happen

HAPAX *n pl.* -ES a word that occurs only once

HAPHTARA *n pl.* -RAS, -ROT or -ROTH a biblical selection

HAPLESS *adj* luckless

HAPLITE *n pl.* -S aplite

HAPLOID *n pl.* -S a cell having only one set of chromosomes

HAPLOIDY *n pl.* -DIES the state of being a haploid

HAPLONT *n pl.* -S an organism having a particular chromosomal structure

HAPLOPIA *n pl.* -S normal vision

HAPLOSIS *n pl.* -LOSES the halving of the chromosome number

HAPLY *adv* by chance

HAPPED past tense of hap

HAPPEN *v* -ED, -ING, -S to occur

HAPPING present participle of hap

HAPPY	adj -PIER, -PIEST marked by joy **HAPPILY** adv
HAPTEN	n pl. -S a substance similar to an antigen **HAPTENIC** adj
HAPTENE	n pl. -S hapten
HAPTIC	adj pertaining to the sense of touch
HAPTICAL	adj haptic
HARANGUE	v -RANGUED, -RANGUING, -RANGUES to deliver a tirade to
HARASS	v -ED, -ING, -ES to bother persistently
HARASSER	n pl. -S one that harasses
HARBOR	v -ED, -ING, -S to shelter
HARBORER	n pl. -S one that harbors
HARBOUR	v -ED, -ING, -S to harbor
HARD	adj HARDER, HARDEST firm and unyielding
HARDBACK	n pl. -S a hardcover book
HARDBALL	n pl. -S baseball
HARDBOOT	n pl. -S a horseman
HARDCASE	adj tough
HARDCORE	adj unyielding
HARDEDGE	n pl. -S a geometric painting
HARDEN	v -ED, -ING, -S to make hard
HARDENER	n pl. -S one that hardens
HARDHACK	n pl. -S a woody plant
HARDHAT	n pl. -S a conservative
HARDHEAD	n pl. -S a practical person
HARDIER	comparative of hardy
HARDIES	pl. of hardy
HARDIEST	superlative of hardy
HARDILY	adv in a hardy manner
HARDLINE	adj unyielding
HARDLY	adv scarcely
HARDNESS	n pl. -ES the state of being hard
HARDNOSE	n pl. -S a stubborn person
HARDPAN	n pl. -S a layer of hard subsoil
HARDS	n/pl the coarse refuse of flax
HARDSET	adj rigid
HARDSHIP	n pl. -S a difficult, painful condition
HARDTACK	n pl. -S a hard biscuit
HARDTOP	n pl. -S a type of car
HARDWARE	n pl. -S metal goods
HARDWIRE	v -WIRED, -WIRING, -WIRES to permanently connect electronic components
HARDWOOD	n pl. -S the hard, compact wood of various trees
HARDY	adj -DIER, -DIEST very sturdy
HARDY	n pl. -DIES a blacksmith's chisel

HARE	v HARED, HARING, HARES to run
HAREBELL	n pl. -S a perennial herb
HAREEM	n pl. -S harem
HARELIKE	adj resembling a hare (a long-eared mammal)
HARELIP	n pl. -S a deformity of the upper lip
HAREM	n pl. -S the section of a Muslim household reserved for women
HARIANA	n pl. -S a breed of cattle
HARICOT	n pl. -S the seed of various string beans
HARIJAN	n pl. -S an outcaste in India
HARING	present participle of hare
HARK	v -ED, -ING, -S to listen to
HARKEN	v -ED, -ING, -S to hearken
HARKENER	n pl. -S one that harkens
HARL	n pl. -S a herl
HARLOT	n pl. -S a prostitute
HARLOTRY	n pl. -RIES prostitution
HARM	v -ED, -ING, -S to injure
HARMER	n pl. -S one that harms
HARMFUL	adj capable of harming
HARMIN	n pl. -S harmine
HARMINE	n pl. -S an alkaloid used as a stimulant
HARMLESS	adj not harmful
HARMONIC	n pl. -S an overtone
HARMONY	n pl. -NIES agreement
HARNESS	v -ED, -ING, -ES to put tackle on a draft animal
HARP	v -ED, -ING, -S to play on a harp (a type of stringed musical instrument)
HARPER	n pl. -S a harpist
HARPIES	pl. of harpy
HARPIN	n pl. -S harping
HARPING	n pl. -S a wooden plank used in shipbuilding
HARPIST	n pl. -S one that plays the harp
HARPOON	v -ED, -ING, -S to strike with a harpoon
HARPY	n pl. -PIES a shrewish person
HARRIDAN	n pl. -S a haggard woman
HARRIED	past tense of harry
HARRIER	n pl. -S a hunting dog
HARRIES	present 3d person sing. of harry
HARROW	v -ED, -ING, -S to break up and level soil
HARROWER	n pl. -S one that harrows
HARRUMPH	v -ED, -ING, -S to make a guttural sound

HARRY v -RIED, -RYING, -RIES to pillage

HARSH adj HARSHER, HARSHEST severe **HARSHLY** adv

HARSHEN v -ED, -ING, -S to make harsh

HARSLET n pl. -S haslet

HART n pl. -S a male deer

HARTAL n pl. -S a stoppage of work

HARUMPH v -ED, -ING, -S harrumph

HARUSPEX n pl. -PICES a soothsayer of ancient Rome

HARVEST v -ED, -ING, -S to gather a crop

HAS a present 3d person sing. of have

HASH v -ED, -ING, -ES to mince

HASHEESH n pl. -ES hashish

HASHHEAD n pl. -S a hashish addict

HASHISH n pl. -ES a mild narcotic

HASLET n pl. -S the edible viscera of an animal

HASP v -ED, -ING, -S to fasten with a clasp

HASSEL n pl. -S an argument

HASSLE v -SLED, -SLING, -SLES to argue

HASSOCK n pl. -S a footstool

HAST a present 2d person sing. of have

HASTATE adj triangular

HASTE v HASTED, HASTING, HASTES to hasten

HASTEFUL adj hasty

HASTEN v -ED, -ING, -S to hurry

HASTENER n pl. -S one that hastens

HASTING present participle of haste

HASTY adj HASTIER, HASTIEST speedy **HASTILY** adv

HAT v HATTED, HATTING, HATS to provide with a hat (a covering for the head)

HATABLE adj hateable

HATBAND n pl. -S a band worn on a hat

HATBOX n pl. -ES a box for a hat

HATCH v -ED, -ING, -ES to bring forth young from an egg

HATCHECK adj pertaining to the checking of hats

HATCHEL v -ELED, -ELING, -ELS or -ELLED, -ELLING, -ELS to separate flax fibers with a comb

HATCHER n pl. -S one that hatches

HATCHERY n pl. -ERIES a place for hatching eggs

HATCHET n pl. -S a small ax

HATCHING n pl. -S a series of lines used to show shading

HATCHWAY n pl. -WAYS an opening in the deck of a ship

HATE v HATED, HATING, HATES to despise

HATEABLE adj meriting hatred

HATEFUL adj detestable

HATER n pl. -S one that hates

HATFUL n pl. HATSFUL or HATFULS as much as a hat can hold

HATH a present 3d person sing. of have

HATING present participle of hate

HATLESS adj lacking a hat

HATLIKE adj resembling a hat

HATMAKER n pl. -S one that makes hats

HATPIN n pl. -S a pin for securing a hat

HATRACK n pl. -S a rack for hats

HATRED n pl. -S intense dislike or aversion

HATSFUL a pl. of hatful

HATTED past tense of hat

HATTER n pl. -S a hatmaker

HATTERIA n pl. -S a reptile

HATTING present participle of hat

HAUBERK n pl. -S a coat of armor

HAUGH n pl. -S a low-lying meadow

HAUGHTY adj -TIER, -TIEST arrogant

HAUL v -ED, -ING, -S to pull with force

HAULAGE n pl. -S the act of hauling

HAULER n pl. -S one that hauls

HAULIER n pl. -S hauler

HAULM n pl. -S a plant stem

HAULMY adj HAULMIER, HAULMIEST having haulms

HAULYARD n pl. -S halyard

HAUNCH n pl. -ES the hindquarter **HAUNCHED** adj

HAUNT v -ED, -ING, -S to visit frequently

HAUNTER n pl. -S one that haunts

HAUSEN n pl. -S a Russian sturgeon

HAUSFRAU n pl. -FRAUS or -FRAUEN a housewife

HAUT adj haute

HAUTBOIS n pl. HAUTBOIS hautboy

HAUTBOY n pl. -BOYS an oboe

HAUTE adj high-class

HAUTEUR n pl. -S haughty manner or spirit

HAVARTI n pl. -S a Danish cheese

HAVDALAH n pl. -S habdalah

HAVE v past 2d person sing. HAD, HADDEST or HADST, present participle HAVING, present 2d person sing. HAVE or HAST, 3d person sing. HAS or HATH to be in possession of

HAVE n pl. -S a wealthy person

HAVELOCK n pl. -S a covering for a cap

HAVEN v -ED, -ING, -S to shelter

HAVER v -ED, -ING, -S to hem and haw

HAVEREL n pl. -S a fool

HAVING present participle of have

HAVIOR n pl. -S behavior

HAVIOUR n pl. -S havior

HAVOC v -OCKED, -OCKING, -OCS to destroy

HAVOCKER n pl. -S one that havocs

HAW v -ED, -ING, -S to turn left

HAWFINCH n pl. -ES a Eurasian finch

HAWK v -ED, -ING, -S to peddle

HAWKBILL n pl. -S a sea turtle

HAWKER n pl. -S one that hawks

HAWKEY n pl. -EYS a hawkie

HAWKEYED adj having keen sight

HAWKIE n pl. -S a white-faced cow

HAWKING n pl. -S falconry

HAWKISH adj warlike

HAWKLIKE adj resembling a hawk (a bird of prey)

HAWKMOTH n pl. -S a large moth

HAWKNOSE n pl. -S a large, curved nose

HAWKSHAW n pl. -S a detective

HAWKWEED n pl. -S a weedlike herb

HAWSE n pl. -S a part of a ship's bow

HAWSER n pl. -S a mooring rope

HAWTHORN n pl. -S a thorny shrub

HAY v -ED, -ING, -S to convert into hay (grass, cut and dried for fodder)

HAYCOCK n pl. -S a pile of hay

HAYER n pl. -S one that hays

HAYFIELD n pl. -S a field where grasses for hay are grown

HAYFORK n pl. -S a tool for pitching hay

HAYING n pl. -S the season for harvesting hay

HAYLAGE n pl. -S a type of hay

HAYLOFT n pl. -S a loft for hay storage

HAYMAKER n pl. -S one that makes hay

HAYMOW n pl. -S a hayloft

HAYRACK n pl. -S a frame used in hauling hay

HAYRICK n pl. -S a haystack

HAYRIDE n pl. -S a wagon ride

HAYSEED n pl. -S a bumpkin

HAYSTACK n pl. -S a pile of hay

HAYWARD n pl. -S an officer who tends cattle

HAYWIRE n pl. -S wire used in baling hay

HAZAN n pl. -ZANIM or -ZANS a cantor

HAZARD v -ED, -ING, -S to venture

HAZE v HAZED, HAZING, HAZES to subject to a humiliating initiation

HAZEL n pl. -S a shrub

HAZELHEN n pl. -S a European grouse

HAZELLY adj yellowish brown

HAZELNUT n pl. -S an edible nut

HAZER n pl. -S one that hazes

HAZIER comparative of hazy

HAZIEST superlative of hazy

HAZILY adv in a hazy manner

HAZINESS n pl. -ES the state of being hazy

HAZING n pl. -S an attempt to embarrass or ridicule

HAZY adj HAZIER, HAZIEST unclear

HAZZAN n pl. HAZZANIM or HAZZANS hazan

HE n pl. -S a male person

HEAD v -ED, -ING, -S to be chief of

HEADACHE n pl. -S a pain inside the head

HEADACHY adj -ACHIER, -ACHIEST having a headache

HEADBAND n pl. -S a band worn on the head

HEADER n pl. -S a grain harvester

HEADFISH n pl. -ES a marine fish

HEADGATE n pl. -S a gate to control the flow of water

HEADGEAR n pl. -S a covering for the head

HEADHUNT v -ED, -ING, -S to seek out, decapitate, and preserve the heads of enemies

HEADIER comparative of heady

HEADIEST superlative of heady

HEADILY adv in a heady manner

HEADING n pl. -S a title

HEADLAMP n pl. -S a light on the front of a car

HEADLAND n pl. -S a cliff

HEADLESS adj lacking a head

HEADLINE v -LINED, -LINING, -LINES to provide with a title

HEADLOCK n pl. -S a wrestling hold

HEADLONG adj rash; impetuous

HEADMAN n pl. -MEN a foreman

HEADMOST adj foremost

HEADNOTE n pl. -S a prefixed note

HEADPIN n pl. -S a bowling pin

HEADRACE n pl. -S a water channel

HEADREST n pl. -S a support for the head

HEADROOM n pl. -S clear vertical space

HEADSAIL n pl. -S a type fo sail

HEADSET n pl. -S a pair of earphones

HEADSHIP n pl. -S the position of a leader

HEADSMAN n pl. -MEN an executioner

HEADSTAY n pl. -STAYS a support for a ship's foremast

HEADWAY n pl. -WAYS forward movement

HEADWIND n pl. -S an oncoming wind

HEADWORD n pl. -S a word put at the beginning

HEADWORK n pl. -S mental work

HEADY adj HEADIER, HEADIEST intoxicating

HEAL v -ED, -ING, -S to make sound or whole HEALABLE adj

HEALER n pl. -S one that heals

HEALTH n pl. -S the physical condition of an organism

HEALTHY adj HEALTHIER, HEALTHIEST having good health

HEAP v -ED, -ING, -S to pile up

HEAR v HEARD, HEARING, HEARS to perceive by the ear HEARABLE adj

HEARER n pl. -S one that hears

HEARING n pl. -S a preliminary examination

HEARKEN v -ED, -ING, -S to listen to

HEARSAY n pl. -SAYS secondhand information

HEARSE v HEARSED, HEARSING, HEARSES to transport in a hearse (a vehicle for conveying corpses)

HEART v -ED, -ING, -S to hearten

HEARTEN v -ED, -ING, -S to give courage to

HEARTH n pl. -S the floor of a fireplace

HEARTY adj HEARTIER, HEARTIEST very friendly HEARTILY adv

HEARTY n pl. HEARTIES a comrade

HEAT v HEATED or HET, HEATING, HEATS to make hot HEATABLE adj

HEATEDLY adv in an inflamed or excited manner

HEATER n pl. -S an apparatus for heating

HEATH n pl. -S an evergreen shrub

HEATHEN n pl. -S an uncivilized person

HEATHER n pl. -S an evergreen shrub HEATHERY adj

HEATHY adj HEATHIER, HEATHIEST abounding in heath

HEATLESS adj having no warmth

HEAUME n pl. -S a medieval helmet

HEAVE v HEAVED or HOVE, HEAVING, HEAVES to lift forcefully

HEAVEN n pl. -S the sky

HEAVENLY adj -LIER, -LIEST full of beauty and peace

HEAVER n pl. -S one that heaves

HEAVIER comparative of heavy

HEAVIES pl. of heavy

HEAVING present participle of heave

HEAVY adj HEAVIER, HEAVIEST having much weight HEAVILY adv

HEAVY n pl. HEAVIES a villain

HEAVYSET adj solidly built; stocky

HEBDOMAD n pl. -S the number seven

HEBETATE v -TATED, -TATING, -TATES to make dull

HEBETIC adj pertaining to puberty

HEBETUDE n pl. -S mental dullness

HEBRAIZE v -IZED, -IZING, -IZES to make Hebrew

HECATOMB n pl. -S a great sacrifice or slaughter

HECK n pl. -S hell

HECKLE v -LED, -LING, -LES to harass a speaker

HECKLER n pl. -S one that heckles

HECTARE n pl. -S a unit of area

HECTIC adj filled with turmoil HECTICLY adv

HECTICAL adj hectic

HECTOR v -ED, -ING, -S to bully

HEDDLE n pl. -S a part of a loom

HEDER n pl. HEDERS or HADARIM a Jewish school

HEDGE v HEDGED, HEDGING, HEDGES to surround with a hedge (a dense row of shrubs)

HEDGEHOG n pl. -S a small mammal

HEDGEHOP v -HOPPED, -HOPPING, -HOPS to fly near the ground

HEDGEPIG n pl. -S a hedgehog

HEDGER n pl. -S one that hedges

HEDGEROW n pl. -S a row of bushes

HEDGING present participle of hedge

HEDGY *adj* HEDGIER, HEDGIEST abounding in hedges

HEDONIC *adj* pertaining to pleasure

HEDONICS *n/pl* a branch of psychology

HEDONISM *n* pl. -S the pursuit of pleasure

HEDONIST *n* pl. -S a follower of hedonism

HEED *v* -ED, -ING, -S to pay attention to

HEEDER *n* pl. -S one that heeds

HEEDFUL *adj* paying close attention

HEEDLESS *adj* paying little or no attention

HEEHAW *v* -ED, -ING, -S to guffaw

HEEL *v* -ED, -ING, -S to supply with a heel (the raised part of a shoe)

HEELBALL *n* pl. -S a composition used for polishing

HEELER *n* pl. -S one that puts heels on shoes

HEELING *n* pl. -S the act of inclining laterally

HEELLESS *adj* lacking heels

HEELPOST *n* pl. -S a post fitted to the end of something

HEELTAP *n* pl. -S material put on the heel of a shoe

HEEZE *v* HEEZED, HEEZING, HEEZES to hoist

HEFT *v* -ED, -ING, -S to lift up

HEFTER *n* pl. -S one that hefts

HEFTY *adj* HEFTIER, HEFTIEST heavy HEFTILY *adv*

HEGARI *n* pl. -S a grain

HEGEMONY *n* pl. -NIES great authority

HEGIRA *n* pl. -S an exodus

HEGUMEN *n* pl. -S the head of a monastery

HEGUMENE *n* pl. -S the head of a nunnery

HEGUMENY *n* pl. -NIES the office of a hegumen

HEH *n* pl. -S a Hebrew letter

HEIFER *n* pl. -S a young cow

HEIGH *interj* — used to attract attention

HEIGHT *n* pl. -S the highest point

HEIGHTEN *v* -ED, -ING, -S to raise

HEIGHTH *n* pl. -S height

HEIL *v* -ED, -ING, -S to salute

HEIMISH *adj* homelike

HEINIE *n* pl. -S the buttocks

HEINOUS *adj* very wicked

HEIR *v* -ED, -ING, -S to inherit

HEIRDOM *n* pl. -S heirship

HEIRESS *n* pl. -ES a female inheritor

HEIRLESS *adj* having no inheritors

HEIRLOOM *n* pl. -S an inherited possession

HEIRSHIP *n* pl. -S the right to inheritance

HEISHI *n/pl* tiny beads made from shells

HEIST *v* -ED, -ING, -S to steal

HEISTER *n* pl. -S one that heists

HEJIRA *n* pl. -S hegira

HEKTARE *n* pl. -S hectare

HELD past tense of hold

HELIAC *adj* heliacal

HELIACAL *adj* pertaining to the sun

HELIAST *n* pl. -S an Athenian judge

HELICAL *adj* shaped like a helix

HELICES a pl. of helix

HELICITY *n* pl. -TIES a component of a particle's spin

HELICOID *n* pl. -S a type of geometrical surface

HELICON *n* pl. -S a large bass tuba

HELICOPT *v* -ED, -ING, -S to travel by helicopter

HELILIFT *v* -ED, -ING, -S to transport by helicopter

HELIO *n* pl. -LIOS a signaling mirror

HELIPAD *n* pl. -S a heliport

HELIPORT *n* pl. -S an airport for helicopters

HELISTOP *n* pl. -S a heliport

HELIUM *n* pl. -S a gaseous element

HELIX *n* pl. -LIXES or -LICES something spiral in form

HELL *v* -ED, -ING, -S to behave raucously

HELLBENT *adj* stubbornly determined

HELLBOX *n* pl. -ES a printer's receptacle

HELLCAT *n* pl. -S a shrewish person

HELLER *n* pl. -S a hellion

HELLERI *n* pl. -ES a tropical fish

HELLERY *n* pl. -LERIES rough play

HELLFIRE *n* pl. -S the torment of hell

HELLHOLE *n* pl. -S a horrible place

HELLION *n* pl. -S a troublesome person

HELLISH *adj* horrible

HELLKITE *n* pl. -S a cruel person

HELLO *v* -ED, -ING, -ES or -S to greet

HELLUVA *adj* disagreeable

HELM *v* -ED, -ING, -S to steer a ship

HELMET *v* -ED, -ING, -S to supply with a helmet (a protective covering for the head)

HELMINTH *n* pl. -S a worm

HELMLESS *adj* lacking a helm (a steering system)

HELMSMAN *n* pl. -MEN one that steers a ship

HELO *n pl.* HELOS a helicopter

HELOT *n pl.* -S a slave or serf

HELOTAGE *n pl.* -S helotism

HELOTISM *n pl.* -S slavery or serfdom

HELOTRY *n pl.* -RIES helotism

HELP *v* HELPED or HOLP, HELPED or HOLPEN, HELPING, HELPS to give assistance to HELPABLE *adj*

HELPER *n pl.* -S one that helps

HELPFUL *adj* being of service or assistance

HELPING *n pl.* -S a portion of food

HELPLESS *adj* defenseless

HELPMATE *n pl.* -S a helpful companion

HELPMEET *n pl.* -S a helpmate

HELVE *v* HELVED, HELVING, HELVES to provide with a handle

HEM *v* HEMMED, HEMMING, HEMS to provide with an edge

HEMAGOG *n pl.* -S an agent that promotes blood flow

HEMAL *adj* pertaining to the blood

HEMATAL *adj* hemal

HEMATEIN *n pl.* -S a chemical compound

HEMATIC *n pl.* -S a medicine for a blood disease

HEMATIN *n pl.* -S heme

HEMATINE *n pl.* -S hematin

HEMATITE *n pl.* -S an ore of iron

HEMATOID *adj* resembling blood

HEMATOMA *n pl.* -MAS or -MATA a swelling filled with blood

HEME *n pl.* -S a component of hemoglobin

HEMIC *adj* hemal

HEMIN *n pl.* -S a chloride of heme

HEMIOLA *n pl.* -S a rhythmic alteration in music

HEMIOLIA *n pl.* -S hemiola

HEMIPTER *n pl.* -S an insect

HEMLINE *n pl.* -S the bottom edge of a garment

HEMLOCK *n pl.* -S a poisonous herb

HEMMED past tense of hem

HEMMER *n pl.* -S one that hems

HEMMING present participle of hem

HEMOCOEL *n pl.* -S a body cavity

HEMOCYTE *n pl.* -S a blood cell

HEMOID *adj* hemal

HEMOLYZE *v* -LYZED, -LYZING, -LYZES to break down red blood cells

HEMOSTAT *n pl.* -S an instrument for reducing bleeding

HEMP *n pl.* -S a tall herb

HEMPEN *adj* made of hemp

HEMPIE *adj* HEMPIER, HEMPIEST hempy

HEMPIER comparative of hempy

HEMPIEST superlative of hempy

HEMPLIKE *adj* resembling hemp

HEMPSEED *n pl.* -S the seed of hemp

HEMPWEED *n pl.* -S a climbing plant

HEMPY *adj* HEMPIER, HEMPIEST mischievous

HEN *n pl.* -S a female chicken

HENBANE *n pl.* -S a poisonous herb

HENBIT *n pl.* -S a perennial herb

HENCE *adv* consequently

HENCHMAN *n pl.* -MEN an unscrupulous supporter

HENCOOP *n pl.* -S a cage for hens

HENEQUEN *n pl.* -S a fiber used to make ropes

HENEQUIN *n pl.* -S henequen

HENHOUSE *n pl.* -S a shelter for poultry

HENIQUEN *n pl.* -S henequen

HENLIKE *adj* resembling a hen

HENNA *v* -ED, -ING, -S to dye with a reddish coloring

HENNERY *n pl.* -NERIES a poultry farm

HENPECK *v* -ED, -ING, -S to dominate by nagging

HENRY *n pl.* -RIES or -RYS a unit of inductance

HENT *v* -ED, -ING, -S to grasp

HEP *adj* hip

HEPARIN *n pl.* -S a biochemical

HEPATIC *n pl.* -S a drug acting on the liver

HEPATICA *n pl.* -CAS or -CAE a perennial herb

HEPATIZE *v* -TIZED, -TIZING, -TIZES to convert tissue into a firm mass

HEPATOMA *n pl.* -MAS or -MATA a tumor of the liver

HEPCAT *n pl.* -S a jazz enthusiast

HEPTAD *n pl.* -S a group of seven

HEPTAGON *n pl.* -S a seven-sided polygon

HEPTANE *n pl.* -S a hydrocarbon used as a solvent

HEPTARCH *n pl.* -S one of a group of seven rulers

HEPTOSE *n pl.* -S a chemical compound

HER *pron* the objective or possessive case of the pronoun she

HERALD *v* -ED, -ING, -S to proclaim

HERALDIC *adj* pertaining to heraldry

HERALDRY *n pl.* -RIES the art or science of armorial bearings

HERB *n pl.* -S a flowering plant with a nonwoody stem

HERBAGE *n pl.* -S nonwoody plant life

HERBAL *n pl.* -S a book about herbs and plants

HERBARIA *n/pl* collections of dried plants

HERBED *adj* flavored with herbs

HERBIER comparative of herby

HERBIEST superlative of herby

HERBLESS *adj* lacking herbs

HERBLIKE *adj* resembling an herb

HERBY *adj* HERBIER, HERBIEST abounding in herbs

HERCULES *n pl.* -LESES any man of great size and strength

HERD *v* -ED, -ING, -S to bring together in a herd (a group of animals)

HERDER *n pl.* -S one who tends a herd

HERDIC *n pl.* -S a type of carriage

HERDLIKE *adj* resembling a herd

HERDMAN *n pl.* -MEN herdsman

HERDSMAN *n pl.* -MEN a herder

HERE *n pl.* -S this place

HEREAT *adv* at this time

HEREAWAY *adv* in this vicinity

HEREBY *adv* by this means

HEREDES *pl.* of heres

HEREDITY *n pl.* -TIES the genetic transmission of chracterics

HEREIN *adv* in this

HEREINTO *adv* into this place

HEREOF *adv* of this

HEREON *adv* on this

HERES *n pl.* HEREDES an heir

HERESY *n pl.* -SIES a belief contrary to a church doctrine

HERETIC *n pl.* -S one that upholds heresy

HERETO *adv* to this matter

HERETRIX *n pl.* -TRIXES or -TRICES heritrix

HEREUNTO *adv* hereto

HEREUPON *adv* immediately following this

HEREWITH *adv* along with this

HERIOT *n pl.* -S a feudal tribute or payment

HERITAGE *n pl.* -S something that is inherited

HERITOR *n pl.* -S one that inherits

HERITRIX *n pl.* -TRIXES or -TRICES a female heritor

HERL *n pl.* -S a feathered fishing lure

HERM *n pl.* -S a type of statue

HERMA *n pl.* -MAE or -MAI a herm HERMAEAN *adj*

HERMETIC *adj* airtight

HERMIT *n pl.* -S a recluse HERMITIC *adj*

HERMITRY *n pl.* -RIES the state of being a hermit

HERN *n pl.* -S a heron

HERNIA *n pl.* -NIAS or -NIAE the protrusion of an organ through its surrounding wall HERNIAL *adj*

HERNIATE *v* -ATED, -ATING, -ATES to protrude through an abnormal bodily opening

HERO *n pl.* -ROES or -ROS a hoagie

HEROIC *n pl.* -S an epic verse

HEROICAL *adj* courageous; noble

HEROIN *n pl.* -S an addictive narcotic

HEROINE *n pl.* -S a brave woman

HEROISM *n pl.* -S heroic behavior

HEROIZE *v* -IZED, -IZING, -IZES to make heroic

HERON *n pl.* -S a wading bird

HERONRY *n pl.* -RIES a place where herons breed

HERPES *n pl.* HERPES a skin infection HERPETIC *adj*

HERRING *n pl.* -S a food fish

HERRY *v* -RIED, -RYING, -RIES to harry

HERS *pron* the possessive case of the pronoun she

HERSELF *pron* a form of the 3d person sing. feminine pronoun

HERSTORY *n pl.* -RIES history with a feminist viewpoint

HERTZ *n pl.* -ES a unit of frequency

HESITANT *adj* tending to hesitate

HESITATE *v* -TATED, -TATING, -TATES to hold back in uncertainty

HESSIAN *n pl.* -S a coarse cloth

HESSITE *n pl.* -S a mineral

HEST *n pl.* -S a command

HET *n pl.* -S heth

HETAERA *n pl.* -RAE or -RAS a concubine HETAERIC *adj*

HETAIRA *n pl.* -RAI or -RAS hetaera

HETERO *n pl.* -EROS a heterosexual

HETH *n pl.* -S a Hebrew letter

HETMAN *n pl.* -S a cossack leader

HEUCH *n pl.* -S heugh

HEUGH *n pl.* -S a steep cliff

HEW *v* HEWED, HEWN, HEWING, HEWS to cut with an ax HEWABLE *adj*

HEWER n pl. -S one that hews

HEX v -ED, -ING, -ES to cast an evil spell upon

HEXAD n pl. -S a group of six **HEXADIC** adj

HEXADE n pl. -S hexad

HEXAGON n pl. -S a polygon having six sides

HEXAGRAM n pl. -S a six-pointed star

HEXAMINE n pl. -S a chemical compound

HEXANE n pl. -S a volatile liquid

HEXAPLA n pl. -S an edition in which six texts are set in parallel columns **HEXAPLAR** adj

HEXAPOD n pl. -S a six-legged insect

HEXAPODY n pl. -DIES a line of verse with six feet

HEXARCHY n pl. -CHIES a group of six separate states

HEXER n pl. -S one that hexes

HEXEREI n pl. -S witchcraft

HEXONE n pl. -S a hydrocarbon solvent

HEXOSAN n pl. -S a carbohydrate

HEXOSE n pl. -S a simple sugar

HEXYL n pl. -S a hydrocarbon radical

HEY interj — used to attract attention

HEYDAY n pl. -DAYS the period of one's greatest success

HEYDEY n pl. -DEYS heyday

HI interj — used as a greeting

HIATUS n pl. -ES a gap or missing section **HIATAL** adj

HIBACHI n pl. -S a cooking device

HIBERNAL adj pertaining to winter

HIBISCUS n pl. -ES a tropical plant

HIC interj — used to represent a hiccup

HICCOUGH v -ED, -ING, -S to hiccup

HICCUP v -CUPED, -CUPING, -CUPS or -CUPPED, -CUPPING, -CUPS to make a peculiar-sounding, spasmodic inhalation

HICK n pl. -S a rural person **HICKISH** adj

HICKEY n pl. HICKEYS or HICKIES a gadget

HICKORY n pl. -RIES a hardwood tree

HID a past tense of hide

HIDABLE adj able to be hidden

HIDALGO n pl. -GOS a minor Spanish nobleman

HIDDEN adj concealed; obscure **HIDDENLY** adv

HIDE v HID, HIDDEN, HIDING, HIDES to conceal

HIDE v HIDED, HIDING, HIDES to flog

HIDEAWAY n pl. -AWAYS a hideout

HIDELESS adj lacking a skin

HIDEOUS adj very ugly

HIDEOUT n pl. -S a place of refuge

HIDER n pl. -S one that hides

HIDING n pl. -S a beating

HIDROSIS n pl. -DROSES abnormal perspiration

HIDROTIC n pl. -S a drug that induces perspiration

HIE v HIED, HIEING or HYING, HIES to hurry

HIEMAL adj pertaining to winter

HIERARCH n pl. -S a religious leader

HIERATIC adj pertaining to priests

HIGGLE v -GLED, -GLING, -GLES to haggle

HIGGLER n pl. -S one that higgles

HIGH adj HIGHER, HIGHEST reaching far upward

HIGH n pl. -S a high level

HIGHBALL v -ED, -ING, -S to go at full speed

HIGHBORN adj of noble birth

HIGHBOY n pl. -BOYS a tall chest of drawers

HIGHBRED adj highborn

HIGHBROW n pl. -S a person who has superior tastes

HIGHBUSH adj forming a tall bush

HIGHJACK v -ED, -ING, -S to hijack

HIGHLAND n pl. -S an elevated region

HIGHLIFE n pl. -S the lifestyle of fashionable society

HIGHLY adv to a high degree

HIGHNESS n pl. -ES the state of being high

HIGHROAD n pl. -S a highway

HIGHSPOT n pl. -S an event of major importance

HIGHT v -ED, -ING, -S to command

HIGHTAIL v -ED, -ING, -S to retreat rapidly

HIGHTH n pl. -S height

HIGHWAY n pl. -WAYS a main road

HIJACK v -ED, -ING, -S to seize a vehicle while in transit

HIJACKER n pl. -S one that hijacks

HIJINKS n/pl mischievous fun

HIKE v HIKED, HIKING, HIKES to walk a long distance

HIKER n pl. -S one that hikes

HILA pl. of hilum

HILAR *adj* pertaining to a hilum

HILARITY *n* pl. -TIES noisy merriment

HILDING *n* pl. -S a vile person

HILI pl. of hilus

HILL *v* -ED, -ING, -S to form into a hill (a rounded elevation)

HILLER *n* pl. -S one that hills

HILLIER comparative of hilly

HILLIEST superlative of hilly

HILLO *v* -ED, -ING, -S or -ES to hallo

HILLOA *v* -ED, -ING, -S to hallo

HILLOCK *n* pl. -S a small hill **HILLOCKY** *adj*

HILLSIDE *n* pl. -S the side of a hill

HILLTOP *n* pl. -S the top of a hill

HILLY *adj* HILLIER, HILLIEST abounding in hills

HILT *v* -ED, -ING, -S to provide with a hilt (a handle for a weapon)

HILTLESS *adj* having no hilt

HILUM *n* pl. HILA a small opening in a bodily organ

HILUS *n* pl. HILI hilum

HIM *pron* the objective case of the pronoun he

HIMATION *n* pl. -MATIA or -MATIONS a loose outer garment

HIMSELF *pron* a form of the 3d person sing. masculine pronoun

HIN *n* pl. -S a Hebrew unit of liquid measure

HIND *n* pl. -S a female red deer

HINDER *v* -ED, -ING, -S to impede

HINDERER *n* pl. -S one that hinders

HINDGUT *n* pl. -S the rear part of the alimentary canal

HINDMOST *adj* farthest to the rear

HINGE *v* HINGED, HINGING, HINGES to attach a jointed device

HINGER *n* pl. -S one that hinges

HINNY *v* -NIED, -NYING, -NIES to whinny

HINT *v* -ED, -ING, -S to suggest indirectly

HINTER *n* pl. -S one that hints

HIP *v* HIPPED, HIPPING, HIPS to build a type of roof

HIP *adj* HIPPER, HIPPEST aware of the most current styles and trends

HIPBONE *n* pl. -S a pelvic bone

HIPLESS *adj* lacking a hip (the pelvic joint)

HIPLIKE *adj* suggestive of a hip

HIPLINE *n* pl. -S the distance around the hips

HIPNESS *n* pl. -ES the state of being hip

HIPPARCH *n* pl. -S a cavalry commander in ancient Greece

HIPPED past tense of hip

HIPPER comparative of hip

HIPPEST superlative of hip

HIPPIE *n* pl. -S a nonconformist

HIPPIER comparative of hippy

HIPPIEST superlative of hippy

HIPPING present participle of hip

HIPPISH *adj* depressed; sad

HIPPO *n* pl. -POS a hippopotamus

HIPPY *adj* -PIER, -PIEST having big hips

HIPSHOT *adj* lame; awkward

HIPSTER *n* pl. -S one that is hip

HIRABLE *adj* available for hire

HIRAGANA *n* pl. -S a Japanese cursive script

HIRCINE *adj* pertaining to a goat

HIRE *v* HIRED, HIRING, HIRES to engage the services of for payment **HIREABLE** *adj*

HIRELING *n* pl. -S one that works for money only

HIRER *n* pl. -S one that hires

HIRING present participle of hire

HIRPLE *v* -PLED, -PLING, -PLES to limp

HIRSEL *v* -SELED, -SELING, -SELS or -SELLED, -SELLING, -SELS to herd sheep

HIRSLE *v* -SLED, -SLING, -SLES to slide along

HIRSUTE *adj* hairy

HIRUDIN *n* pl. -S an anticoagulant

HIS *pron* the possessive form of the pronoun he

HISN *pron* his

HISPID *adj* covered with stiff hairs

HISS *v* -ED, -ING, -ES to make a sibilant sound

HISSELF *pron* himself

HISSER *n* pl. -S one that hisses

HISSING *n* pl. -S an object of scorn

HISSY *n* pl. HISSIES a tantrum

HIST *v* -ED, -ING, -S to hoist

HISTAMIN *n* pl. -S an amine released in allergic reactions

HISTIDIN *n* pl. -S an amino acid

HISTOGEN *n* pl. -S interior plant tissue

HISTOID *adj* pertaining to connective tissue

HISTONE *n* pl. -S a simple protein

HISTORIC *adj* important in history

HISTORY *n pl.* -RIES a chronological record of past events

HIT *v* HIT, HITTING, HITS to strike forcibly

HITCH *v* -ED, -ING, -ES to fasten with a knot or hook

HITCHER *n pl.* -S one that hitches

HITHER *adv* toward this place

HITHERTO *adv* up to now

HITLESS *adj* being without a hit

HITTER *n pl.* -S one that hits

HITTING present participle of hit

HIVE *v* HIVED, HIVING, HIVES to cause to enter a hive (a bee's nest)

HIVELESS *adj* lacking a hive

HIZZONER *n pl.* -S — used as a title for a mayor

HM *interj* hmm

HMM *interj* — used to express thoughtful consideration

HO *interj* — used to express surprise

HOACTZIN *n pl.* -S or -ES hoatzin

HOAGIE *n pl.* -S a long sandwich

HOAGY *n pl.* -GIES hoagie

HOAR *n pl.* -S a white coating

HOARD *v* -ED, -ING, -S to gather and store away

HOARDER *n pl.* -S one that hoards

HOARDING *n pl.* -S something hoarded

HOARIER comparative of hoary

HOARIEST superlative of hoary

HOARILY *adv* in a hoary manner

HOARSE *adj* HOARSER, HOARSEST low and rough in sound
HOARSELY *adv*

HOARSEN *v* -ED, -ING, -S to make hoarse

HOARY *adj* HOARIER, HOARIEST white with age

HOATZIN *n pl.* -S or -ES a tropical bird

HOAX *v* -ED, -ING, -ES to deceive

HOAXER *n pl.* -S one that hoaxes

HOB *v* HOBBED, HOBBING, HOBS to furnish with hobnails

HOBBIES pl. of hobby

HOBBIT *n pl.* -S a fictitious creature that lives underground

HOBBLE *v* -BLED, -BLING, -BLES to limp

HOBBLER *n pl.* -S one that hobbles

HOBBY *n pl.* -BIES a recreational pastime

HOBBYIST *n pl.* -S one that pursues a hobby

HOBLIKE *adj* suggestive of an elf

HOBNAIL *v* -ED, -ING, -S to put hobnails (short nails with a broad head) on a shoe sole

HOBNOB *v* -NOBBED, -NOBBING, -NOBS to associate in a friendly way

HOBO *v* -ED, -ING, -S or -ES to live like a hobo (a vagrant or tramp)

HOBOISM *n pl.* -S the state of being a hobo

HOCK *v* -ED, -ING, -S to pawn

HOCKER *n pl.* -S one that hocks

HOCKEY *n pl.* -EYS a game played on ice

HOCKSHOP *n pl.* -S a pawnshop

HOCUS *v* -CUSED, -CUSING, -CUSES or -CUSSED, -CUSSING, -CUSSES to deceive or cheat

HOD *n pl.* -S a portable trough

HODAD *n pl.* -S a nonsurfer

HODADDY *n pl.* -DIES hodad

HODDEN *n pl.* -S a coarse cloth

HODDIN *n pl.* -S hodden

HOE *v* HOED, HOEING, HOES to use a hoe (a gardening tool)

HOECAKE *n pl.* -S a cornmeal cake

HOEDOWN *n pl.* -S a square dance

HOELIKE *adj* resembling a hoe

HOER *n pl.* -S one that hoes

HOG *v* HOGGED, HOGGING, HOGS to take more than one's share

HOGAN *n pl.* -S a Navaho Indian dwelling

HOGBACK *n pl.* -S a sharp ridge

HOGFISH *n pl.* -ES a tropical fish

HOGG *n pl.* -S a young sheep

HOGGED past tense of hog

HOGGER *n pl.* -S one that hogs

HOGGET *n pl.* -S a young unshorn sheep

HOGGING present participle of hog

HOGGISH *adj* coarsely selfish

HOGLIKE *adj* hoggish

HOGMANAY *n pl.* -NAYS a Scottish celebration

HOGMANE *n pl.* -S hogmanay

HOGMENAY *n pl.* -NAYS hogmanay

HOGNOSE *n pl.* -S a nonvenomous snake

HOGNUT *n pl.* -S a hickory nut

HOGSHEAD *n pl.* -S a large cask

HOGTIE v -TIED, -TIEING or -TYING, -TIES to tie together the legs of

HOGWASH n pl. -ES meaningless talk

HOGWEED n pl. -S a coarse plant

HOICK v -ED, -ING, -S to change directions abruptly

HOIDEN v -ED, -ING, -S to hoyden

HOISE v HOISED, HOISING, HOISES to hoist

HOIST v -ED, -ING, -S to haul up by some mechanical means

HOISTER n pl. -S one that hoists

HOKE v HOKED, HOKING, HOKES to give false value to

HOKEY adj HOKIER, HOKIEST false; contrived HOKILY adv

HOKINESS n pl. -ES the state of being hokey

HOKKU n pl. HOKKU haiku

HOKUM n pl. -S nonsense

HOKYPOKY n pl. -KIES trickery

HOLARD n pl. -S the total quantity of water in the soil

HOLD v HELD, HOLDEN, HOLDING, HOLDS to maintain possession of HOLDABLE adj

HOLDALL n pl. -S a carrying case

HOLDBACK n pl. -S a restraining device

HOLDEN a past participle of hold

HOLDER n pl. -S one that holds

HOLDFAST n pl. -S a fastening device

HOLDING n pl. -S something held

HOLDOUT n pl. -S one who delays signing a contract

HOLDOVER n pl. -S something left over

HOLDUP n pl. -S a delay

HOLE v HOLED, HOLING, HOLES to make a hole (a cavity in a solid)

HOLELESS adj lacking a hole

HOLEY adj full of holes

HOLIBUT n pl. -S halibut

HOLIDAY v -ED, -ING, -S to take a vacation

HOLIER comparative of holy

HOLIES pl. of holy

HOLIEST superlative of holy

HOLILY adv in a holy manner

HOLINESS n pl. -ES the state of being holy

HOLING present participle of hole

HOLISM n pl. -S a philosophical theory

HOLIST n pl. -S one who adheres to the theory of holism HOLISTIC adj

HOLK v -ED, -ING, -S to howk

HOLLA v -ED, -ING, -S to hallo

HOLLAND n pl. -S a cotton fabric

HOLLER v -ED, -ING, -S to yell

HOLLIES pl. of holly

HOLLO v -ED, -ING, -S or -ES to hallo

HOLLOA v -ED, -ING, -S to hallo

HOLLOO v -ED, -ING, -S to hallo

HOLLOW adj -LOWER, -LOWEST not solid HOLLOWLY adv

HOLLOW v -ED, -ING, -S to make hollow

HOLLY n pl. -LIES a tree

HOLM n pl. -S an island in a river

HOLMIUM n pl. -S a metallic element HOLMIC adj

HOLOGAMY n pl. -MIES the state of having gametes of the same size and form as other cells

HOLOGRAM n pl. -S a three-dimensional photograph

HOLOGYNY n pl. -NIES a trait transmitted solely in the female line

HOLOTYPE n pl. -S an animal or plant specimen

HOLOZOIC adj eating solid foods

HOLP a past tense of help

HOLPEN a past participle of help

HOLS n/pl a vacation

HOLSTEIN n pl. -S a breed of cattle

HOLSTER n pl. -S a case for a pistol

HOLT n pl. -S a grove

HOLY adj -LIER, -LIEST having a divine nature or origin

HOLY n pl. -LIES a holy place

HOLYDAY n pl. -DAYS a religious holiday

HOLYTIDE n pl. -S a time of religious observance

HOMAGE v -AGED, -AGING, -AGES to pay tribute to

HOMAGER n pl. -S a feudal vassal

HOMBRE n pl. -S a fellow

HOMBURG n pl. -S a felt hat

HOME v HOMED, HOMING, HOMES to return to one's home (place of residence)

HOMEBODY n pl. -BODIES one who likes to stay at home

HOMEBOY n pl. -BOYS a boy or man from one's neighborhood

HOMEBRED n pl. -S a native athlete

HOMED past tense of home

HOMELAND n pl. -S one's native land

HOMELESS adj lacking a home

HOMELIKE adj suggestive of a home

HOMELY adj -LIER, -LIEST unattractive

HOMEMADE *adj* made at home

HOMEOBOX *n pl.* -ES a short DNA sequence

HOMEOTIC *adj* being a gene producing a shift in development

HOMEPORT *v* -ED, -ING, -S to assign a ship to a port

HOMER *v* -ED, -ING, -S to hit a home run

HOMEROOM *n pl.* -S the classroom where pupils report before classes begin

HOMESICK *adj* longing for home

HOMESITE *n pl.* -S a location for a house

HOMESPUN *n pl.* -S a loosely woven fabric

HOMESTAY *n pl.* -STAYS a period during which a visitor in a foreign country lives with a local family

HOMETOWN *n pl.* -S the town of one's birth or residence

HOMEWARD *adv* toward home

HOMEWORK *n pl.* -S work done at home

HOMEY *adj* HOMIER, HOMIEST homelike

HOMICIDE *n pl.* -S the killing of one person by another

HOMIER comparative of homy

HOMIEST superlative of homy

HOMILIST *n pl.* -S one that delivers a homily

HOMILY *n pl.* -LIES a sermon

HOMINES a pl. of homo

HOMINESS *n pl.* -ES the quality of being homey

HOMING present participle of home

HOMINIAN *n pl.* -S a hominid

HOMINID *n pl.* -S a manlike creature

HOMINIES pl. of hominy

HOMININE *adj* characteristic of man

HOMINIZE *v* -NIZED, -NIZING, -NIZES to alter the environment to conform with evolving man

HOMINOID *n pl.* -S a manlike animal

HOMINY *n pl.* -NIES hulled, dried corn

HOMMOCK *n pl.* -S a ridge in an ice field

HOMMOS *n pl.* -ES hummus

HOMO *n pl.* HOMINES or HOMOS a member of the genus that includes modern man

HOMOGAMY *n pl.* -MIES the bearing of sexually similar flowers

HOMOGENY *n pl.* -NIES correspondence in form or structure

HOMOGONY *n pl.* -NIES the condition of having flowers with uniform stamens and pistils

HOMOLOG *n pl.* -S something that exhibits homology

HOMOLOGY *n pl.* -GIES similarity in structure

HOMONYM *n pl.* -S a namesake

HOMONYMY *n pl.* -MIES the condition of having the same name

HOMOSEX *n pl.* -ES homosexuality

HOMY *adj* HOMIER, HOMIEST homey

HON *n pl.* -S a honeybun

HONAN *n pl.* -S a fine silk

HONCHO *v* -ED, -ING, -S to take charge of

HONDA *n pl.* -S a part of a lariat

HONDLE *v* -DLED, -DLING, -DLES to haggle

HONE *v* HONED, HONING, HONES to sharpen

HONER *n pl.* -S one that hones

HONEST *adj* -ESTER, -ESTEST truthful **HONESTLY** *adv*

HONESTY *n pl.* -TIES the quality of being honest

HONEWORT *n pl.* -S a perennial herb

HONEY *v* HONEYED or HONIED, HONEYING, HONEYS to sweeten with honey (a sweet, viscid fluid)

HONEYBEE *n pl.* -S a type of bee

HONEYBUN *n pl.* -S a sweetheart

HONEYDEW *n pl.* -S a sweet fluid

HONEYFUL *adj* containing much honey

HONG *n pl.* -S a Chinese factory

HONIED a past tense of honey

HONING present participle of hone

HONK *v* -ED, -ING, -S to emit a cry like that of a goose

HONKER *n pl.* -S one that honks

HONOR *v* -ED, -ING, -S to treat with respect

HONORAND *n pl.* -S an honoree

HONORARY *n pl.* -ARIES an honor society

HONOREE *n pl.* -S one that receives an honor

HONORER *n pl.* -S one that honors

HONOUR *v* -ED, -ING, -S to honor

HONOURER *n pl.* -S honorer

HOOCH *n pl.* -ES cheap whiskey

HOOD *v* -ED, -ING, -S to furnish with a hood (a covering for the head)

HOODIE *n pl.* -S a gray crow of Europe

HOODLESS *adj* lacking a hood

HOODLIKE *adj* resembling a hood

HOODLUM *n pl.* -S a thug

HOODOO v -ED, -ING, -S to bring bad luck to

HOODWINK v -ED, -ING, -S to trick

HOODY adj HOODIER, HOODIEST resembling a hoodlum

HOOEY n pl. -EYS nonsense

HOOF v -ED, -ING, -S to dance

HOOF n pl. HOOVES or HOOFS the hard covering on the feet of certain animals

HOOFBEAT n pl. -S the sound of hooves striking the ground

HOOFER n pl. -S a professional dancer

HOOFLESS adj lacking hooves

HOOFLIKE adj resembling a hoof

HOOK v -ED, -ING, -S to catch with a hook (a bent piece of metal)

HOOKA n pl. -S hookah

HOOKAH n pl. -S a water pipe

HOOKER n pl. -S a prostitute

HOOKEY n pl. -EYS hooky

HOOKIER comparative of hooky

HOOKIES pl. of hooky

HOOKIEST superlative of hooky

HOOKLESS adj lacking a hook

HOOKLET n pl. -S a small hook

HOOKLIKE adj resembling a hook

HOOKNOSE n pl. -S an aquiline nose

HOOKUP n pl. -S an electrical assemblage

HOOKWORM n pl. -S a parasitic worm

HOOKY n pl. HOOKIES truancy

HOOKY adj HOOKIER, HOOKIEST full of hooks

HOOLIE adj easy; slow

HOOLIGAN n pl. -S a hoodlum

HOOLY adj hoolie

HOOP v -ED, -ING, -S to fasten with a hoop (a circular band of metal)

HOOPER n pl. -S one that hoops

HOOPLA n pl. -S commotion

HOOPLESS adj lacking a hoop

HOOPLIKE adj suggestive of a hoop

HOOPOE n pl. -S a European bird

HOOPOO n pl. -POOS hoopoe

HOOPSTER n pl. -S a basketball player

HOORAH v -ED, -ING, -S to hurrah

HOORAY v -ED, -ING, -S to hurrah

HOOSEGOW n pl. -S a jail

HOOSGOW n pl. -S hoosegow

HOOT v -ED, -ING, -S to cry like an owl

HOOTCH n pl. -ES hooch

HOOTER n pl. -S one that hoots

HOOTY adj HOOTIER, HOOTIEST sounding like the cry of an owl

HOOVED adj having hooves

HOOVES a pl. of hoof

HOP v HOPPED, HOPPING, HOPS to move by quick leaps

HOPE v HOPED, HOPING, HOPES to have a desire or expectation

HOPEFUL n pl. -S one that aspires

HOPELESS adj despairing

HOPER n pl. -S one that hopes

HOPHEAD n pl. -S a drug addict

HOPING present participle of hope

HOPLITE n pl. -S a foot soldier of ancient Greece HOPLITIC adj

HOPPED past tense of hop

HOPPER n pl. -S one that hops

HOPPING n pl. -S a going from one place to another of the same kind

HOPPLE v -PLED, -PLING, -PLES to hobble

HOPPY adj -PIER, -PIEST having the taste of hops (catkins of a particular vine)

HOPSACK n pl. -S a coarse fabric

HOPTOAD n pl. -S a toad

HORA n pl. -S an Israeli dance

HORAH n pl. -S hora

HORAL adj hourly

HORARY adj hourly

HORDE v HORDED, HORDING, HORDES to gather in a large group

HORDEIN n pl. -S a simple protein

HORIZON n pl. -S the line where the sky seems to meet the earth

HORMONE n pl. -S a secretion of the endocrine organs HORMONAL, HORMONIC adj

HORN v -ED, -ING, -S to form a horn (a hard, bonelike projection)

HORNBEAM n pl. -S a small tree

HORNBILL n pl. -S a large-billed bird

HORNBOOK n pl. -S a primer

HORNET n pl. -S a stinging insect

HORNFELS n pl. HORNFELS a silicate rock

HORNIER comparative of horny

HORNIEST superlative of horny

HORNILY adv in a horny manner

HORNIST n pl. -S a French horn player

HORNITO n pl. -TOS a mound of volcanic matter

HORNLESS adj lacking a horn

HORNLIKE adj resembling a horn

HORNPIPE n pl. -S a musical instrument

HORNPOUT n pl. -S a catfish
HORNTAIL n pl. -S a wasplike insect
HORNWORM n pl. -S the larva of a hawkmoth
HORNWORT n pl. -S an aquatic herb
HORNY adj HORNIER, HORNIEST hornlike in hardness
HOROLOGE n pl. -S a timepiece
HOROLOGY n pl. -GIES the science of measuring time
HORRENT adj bristling; standing erect
HORRIBLE n pl. -S something that causes horror
HORRIBLY adv dreadfully
HORRID adj repulsive HORRIDLY adv
HORRIFIC adj causing horror
HORRIFY v -FIED, -FYING, -FIES to cause to feel horror
HORROR n pl. -S a feeling of intense fear or repugnance
HORSE v HORSED, HORSING, HORSES to provide with a horse (a large, hoofed mammal)
HORSECAR n pl. -S a streetcar drawn by a horse
HORSEFLY n pl. -FLIES a large fly
HORSEMAN n pl. -MEN one who rides a horse
HORSEPOX n pl. -ES a skin disease of horses
HORSEY adj HORSIER, HORSIEST horsy
HORSIER comparative of horsy
HORSIEST superlative of horsy
HORSILY adv in a horsy manner
HORSING present participle of horse
HORST n pl. -S a portion of the earth's crust
HORSTE n pl. -S horst
HORSY adj HORSIER, HORSIEST resembling a horse
HOSANNA v -ED, -ING, -S to praise
HOSANNAH interj — used to express praise to God
HOSE v HOSED, HOSING, HOSES to spray with water
HOSE n pl. HOSEN stockings or socks
HOSEL n pl. -S a part of a golf club
HOSEPIPE n pl. -S a flexible tube for conveying fluids
HOSIER n pl. -S one that makes hose
HOSIERY n pl. -SIERIES hose
HOSING present participle of hose
HOSPICE n pl. -S a shelter

HOSPITAL n pl. -S a medical institution
HOSPITIA n/pl places of shelter
HOSPODAR n pl. -S a governor of a region under Turkish rule
HOST v -ED, -ING, -S to entertain socially
HOSTA n pl. -S a plantain lily
HOSTAGE n pl. -S a person held as security
HOSTEL v -TELED, -TELING, -TELS or -TELLED, -TELLING, -TELS to stay at inns overnight while traveling
HOSTELER n pl. -S an innkeeper
HOSTELRY n pl. -RIES an inn
HOSTESS v -ED, -ING, -ES to act as a hostess (a woman who entertains socially)
HOSTILE n pl. -S an unfriendly person
HOSTLER n pl. -S a person who tends horses or mules
HOSTLY adj pertaining to one who hosts
HOT adj HOTTER, HOTTEST having a high temperature
HOT v HOTTED, HOTTING, HOTS to heat
HOTBED n pl. -S a bed of rich soil
HOTBLOOD n pl. -S a thoroughbred horse
HOTBOX n pl. -ES an overheated bearing of a railroad car
HOTCAKE n pl. -S a pancake
HOTCH v -ED, -ING, -ES to wiggle
HOTCHPOT n pl. -S the combining of properties in order to divide them equally among heirs
HOTDOG v -DOGGED, -DOGGING, -DOGS to show off
HOTEL n pl. -S a public lodging
HOTELDOM n pl. -S hotels and hotel workers
HOTELIER n pl. -S a hotel manager
HOTELMAN n pl. -MEN a hotelier
HOTFOOT v -FOOTED, -FOOTING, -FOOTS to hurry
HOTHEAD n pl. -S a quick-tempered person
HOTHOUSE n pl. -S a heated greenhouse
HOTLINE n pl. -S a direct communications system for immediate contact
HOTLY adv in a hot manner
HOTNESS n pl. -ES the state of being hot
HOTPRESS v -ED, -ING, -ES to subject to heat and pressure
HOTROD n pl. -S a car modified for high speeds

HOTSHOT *n* pl. -S a showily skillful person

HOTSPUR *n* pl. -S a hothead

HOTTED past tense of hot

HOTTER comparative of hot

HOTTEST superlative of hot

HOTTING present participle of hot

HOTTISH *adj* somewhat hot

HOUDAH *n* pl. -S howdah

HOUND *v* -ED, -ING, -S to pursue relentlessly

HOUNDER *n* pl. -S one that hounds

HOUR *n* pl. -S a period of sixty minutes

HOURI *n* pl. -S a beautiful maiden in Muslim belief

HOURLY *adj* occurring every hour

HOUSE *v* HOUSED, HOUSING, HOUSES to lodge in a house (a building in which people live)

HOUSEBOY *n* pl. -BOYS a male servant

HOUSEFLY *n* pl. -FLIES a common fly

HOUSEFUL *n* pl. -S as much as a house will hold

HOUSEL *v* -SELED, -SELING, -SELS or -SELLED, -SELLING, -SELS to administer the Eucharist to

HOUSEMAN *n* pl. -MEN a male servant

HOUSER *n* pl. -S one who organizes housing projects

HOUSESIT *v* -SAT, -SITTING, -SITS to occupy a dwelling while the tenants are away

HOUSETOP *n* pl. -S the roof of a house

HOUSING *n* pl. -S any dwelling place

HOVE a past tense of heave

HOVEL *v* -ELED, -ELING, -ELS or -ELLED, -ELLING, -ELS to live in a small, miserable dwelling

HOVER *v* -ED, -ING, -S to hang suspended in the air

HOVERER *n* pl. -S something that hovers

HOW *n* pl. -S a method of doing something

HOWBEIT *adv* nevertheless

HOWDAH *n* pl. -S a seat on an elephant or camel for riders

HOWDIE *n* pl. -S a midwife

HOWDY *v* -DIED, -DYING, -DIES to greet with the words "how do you do"

HOWE *n* pl. -S a valley

HOWEVER *adv* nevertheless

HOWF *n* pl. -S a place frequently visited

HOWFF *n* pl. -S howf

HOWITZER *n* pl. -S a short cannon

HOWK *v* -ED, -ING, -S to dig

HOWL *v* -ED, -ING, -S to cry like a dog

HOWLER *n* pl. -S one that howls

HOWLET *n* pl. -S an owl

HOY *n* pl. HOYS a heavy barge or scow

HOYA *n* pl. -S a flowering plant

HOYDEN *v* -ED, -ING, -S to act like a tomboy

HOYLE *n* pl. -S a rule book

HUARACHE *n* pl. -S a flat-heeled sandal

HUARACHO *n* pl. -CHOS huarache

HUB *n* pl. -S the center of a wheel

HUBBLY *adj* having an uneven surface

HUBBUB *n* pl. -S an uproar

HUBBY *n* pl. -BIES a husband

HUBCAP *n* pl. -S a covering for the hub of a wheel

HUBRIS *n* pl. -BRISES arrogance

HUCK *n* pl. -S a durable fabric

HUCKLE *n* pl. -S the hip

HUCKSTER *v* -ED, -ING, -S to peddle

HUDDLE *v* -DLED, -DLING, -DLES to crowd together

HUDDLER *n* pl. -S one that huddles

HUE *n* pl. -S color HUED, HUELESS *adj*

HUFF *v* -ED, -ING, -S to breathe heavily

HUFFISH *adj* sulky

HUFFY *adj* HUFFIER, HUFFIEST easily offended HUFFILY *adv*

HUG *v* HUGGED, HUGGING, HUGS to clasp tightly in the arms

HUGE *adj* HUGER, HUGEST very large HUGELY *adv*

HUGENESS *n* pl. -ES the quality of being huge

HUGEOUS *adj* huge

HUGER comparative of huge

HUGEST superlative of huge

HUGGABLE *adj* cuddlesome

HUGGED past tense of hug

HUGGER *n* pl. -S one that hugs

HUGGING present participle of hug

HUH *interj* — used to express surprise

HUIC *interj* — used to encourage hunting hounds

HUIPIL *n* pl. -S or -ES an embroidered blouse or dress of Mexico

HUISACHE *n* pl. -S a flowering plant

HULA n pl. -S a Hawaiian dance

HULK v -ED, -ING, -S to appear impressively large

HULKY adj HULKIER, HULKIEST massive

HULL v -ED, -ING, -S to remove the shell from a seed

HULLER n pl. -S one that hulls

HULLO v -ED, -ING, -S or -ES to hallo

HULLOA v -ED, -ING, -S to hallo

HUM v HUMMED, HUMMING, HUMS to sing without opening the lips or saying words

HUMAN n pl. -S a person

HUMANE adj -MANER, -MANEST compassionate **HUMANELY** adv

HUMANISE v -ISED, -ISING, -ISES to humanize

HUMANISM n pl. -S the quality of being human

HUMANIST n pl. -S one who studies human nature

HUMANITY n pl. -TIES the human race

HUMANIZE v -IZED, -IZING, -IZES to make human

HUMANLY adv in a human manner

HUMANOID n pl. -S something having human form

HUMATE n pl. -S a chemical salt

HUMBLE adj -BLER, -BLEST modest

HUMBLE v -BLED, -BLING, -BLES to reduce the pride of

HUMBLER n pl. -S one that humbles

HUMBLEST superlative of humble

HUMBLING present participle of humble

HUMBLY adv in a humble manner

HUMBUG v -BUGGED, -BUGGING, -BUGS to deceive

HUMDRUM n pl. -S a dull, boring person

HUMERAL n pl. -S a bone of the shoulder

HUMERUS n pl. -MERI the large bone of the upper arm

HUMIC adj derived from humus

HUMID adj having much humidity

HUMIDIFY v -FIED, -FYING, -FIES to make humid

HUMIDITY n pl. -TIES moisture of the air

HUMIDLY adv in a humid manner

HUMIDOR n pl. -S a cigar case

HUMIFIED adj converted into humus

HUMILITY n pl. -TIES the quality of being humble

HUMMABLE adj capable of being hummed

HUMMED past tense of hum

HUMMER n pl. -S one that hums

HUMMING present participle of hum

HUMMOCK v -ED, -ING, -S to form into hummocks (small rounded hills)

HUMMOCKY adj abounding in hummocks

HUMMUS n pl. -ES a paste of pureed chickpeas and tahini

HUMOR v -ED, -ING, -S to indulge

HUMORAL adj pertaining to bodily fluids

HUMORFUL adj humorous

HUMORIST n pl. -S a humorous writer or entertainer

HUMOROUS adj funny; witty

HUMOUR v -ED, -ING, -S to humor

HUMP v -ED, -ING, -S to arch into a hump (a rounded protuberance)

HUMPBACK n pl. -S a humped back

HUMPH v -ED, -ING, -S to utter a grunt

HUMPLESS adj lacking a hump

HUMPY adj HUMPIER, HUMPIEST full of humps

HUMUS n pl. -ES decomposed organic matter

HUMVEE n pl. -S a type of motor vehicle

HUN n pl. -S a barbarous, destructive person

HUNCH v -ED, -ING, -ES to arch forward

HUNDRED n pl. -S a number

HUNG a past tense of hang

HUNGER v -ED, -ING, -S to crave

HUNGOVER adj suffering from a hangover

HUNGRY adj -GRIER, -GRIEST wanting food **HUNGRILY** adv

HUNH interj — used to ask for a repetition of an utterance

HUNK n pl. -S a large piece

HUNKER v -ED, -ING, -S to squat

HUNKY adj HUNKIER, HUNKIEST muscular and attractive

HUNNISH adj resembling a hun

HUNT v -ED, -ING, -S to pursue for food or sport **HUNTABLE** adj **HUNTEDLY** adv

HUNTER n pl. -S one that hunts

HUNTING n pl. -S an instance of searching

HUNTRESS n pl. -ES a female hunter

HUNTSMAN n pl. -MEN a hunter

HUP interj — used to mark a marching cadence

HURDIES n/pl the buttocks

HURDLE v -DLED, -DLING, -DLES to jump over

HURDLER n pl. -S one that hurdles

HURDS *n/pl* hards

HURL *v* -ED, -ING, -S to throw with great force

HURLER *n* pl. -S one that hurls

HURLEY *n* pl. -LEYS hurling

HURLING *n* pl. -S an Irish game

HURLY *n* pl. -LIES commotion

HURRAH *v* -ED, -ING, -S to cheer

HURRAY *v* -ED, -ING, -S to hurrah

HURRIER *n* pl. -S one that hurries

HURRY *v* -RIED, -RYING, -RIES to move swiftly

HURST *n* pl. -S a small hill

HURT *v* HURT, HURTING, HURTS to injure

HURTER *n* pl. -S one that hurts

HURTFUL *adj* causing injury

HURTLE *v* -TLED, -TLING, -TLES to rush violently

HURTLESS *adj* harmless

HUSBAND *v* -ED, -ING, -S to spend wisely

HUSH *v* -ED, -ING, -ES to quiet HUSHEDLY *adv*

HUSHABY *v* go to sleep — used imperatively to soothe a child

HUSHFUL *adj* quiet

HUSK *v* -ED, -ING, -S to remove the husk (the outer covering) from

HUSKER *n* pl. -S one that husks

HUSKIER comparative of husky

HUSKIES pl. of husky

HUSKIEST superlative of husky

HUSKILY *adv* in a husky manner

HUSKING *n* pl. -S a gathering of families to husk corn

HUSKLIKE *adj* resembling a husk

HUSKY *adj* -KIER, -KIEST hoarse

HUSKY *n* pl. -KIES an Eskimo dog

HUSSAR *n* pl. -S a cavalry soldier

HUSSY *n* pl. -SIES a lewd woman

HUSTINGS *n* pl. HUSTINGS a British court

HUSTLE *v* -TLED, -TLING, -TLES to hurry

HUSTLER *n* pl. -S one that hustles

HUSWIFE *n* pl. -WIFES or -WIVES a sewing kit

HUT *v* HUTTED, HUTTING, HUTS to live in a hut (a simple shelter)

HUTCH *v* -ED, -ING, -ES to store away

HUTLIKE *adj* resembling a hut

HUTMENT *n* pl. -S a group of huts

HUTTED past tense of hut

HUTTING present participle of hut

HUTZPA *n* pl. -S chutzpah

HUTZPAH *n* pl. -S chutzpah

HUZZA *v* -ED, -ING, -S to cheer

HUZZAH *v* -ED, -ING, -S to huzza

HWAN *n* pl. HWAN a monetary unit of South Korea

HYACINTH *n* pl. -S a flowering plant

HYAENA *n* pl. -S hyena HYAENIC *adj*

HYALIN *n* pl. -S hyaline

HYALINE *n* pl. -S a transparent substance

HYALITE *n* pl. -S a colorless opal

HYALOGEN *n* pl. -S a substance found in animal cells

HYALOID *n* pl. -S a membrane of the eye

HYBRID *n* pl. -S the offspring of genetically dissimilar parents

HYBRIS *n* pl. -BRISES hubris

HYDATID *n* pl. -S a cyst caused by a tapeworm

HYDRA *n* pl. -DRAS or -DRAE a freshwater polyp

HYDRACID *n* pl. -S an acid

HYDRAGOG *n* pl. -S a purgative causing watery discharges

HYDRANT *n* pl. -S an outlet from a water main

HYDRANTH *n* pl. -S the oral opening of a hydra

HYDRASE *n* pl. -S an enzyme

HYDRATE *v* -DRATED, -DRATING, -DRATES to combine with water

HYDRATOR *n* pl. -S one that hydrates

HYDRIA *n* pl. -DRIAE a water jar

HYDRIC *adj* pertaining to moisture

HYDRID *n* pl. -S hydride

HYDRIDE *n* pl. -S a chemical compound

HYDRO *n* pl. -DROS electricity produced by waterpower

HYDROGEL *n* pl. -S a colloid

HYDROGEN *n* pl. -S a gaseous element

HYDROID *n* pl. -S a polyp

HYDROMEL *n* pl. -S a mixture of honey and water

HYDRONIC *adj* pertaining to heating and cooling by water

HYDROPIC *adj* affected with hydropsy

HYDROPS *n* pl. -ES hydropsy

HYDROPSY *n* pl. -SIES dropsy

HYDROSKI *n* pl. -S a plate attached to a seaplane to facilitate takeoffs and landings

HYDROSOL n pl. -S an aqueous solution of a colloid

HYDROUS adj containing water

HYDROXY adj containing hydroxyl

HYDROXYL n pl. -S the radical or group containing oxygen and hydrogen

HYENA n pl. -S a wolflike mammal HYENIC, HYENINE, HYENOID adj

HYETAL adj pertaining to rain

HYGEIST n pl. -S an expert in hygiene

HYGIEIST n pl. -S hygeist

HYGIENE n pl. -S the science of health HYGIENIC adj

HYING present participle of hie

HYLA n pl. -S a tree frog

HYLOZOIC adj pertaining to the doctrine that life and matter are inseparable

HYMEN n pl. -S a vaginal membrane HYMENAL adj

HYMENEAL n pl. -S a wedding song or poem

HYMENIUM n pl. -NIA or -NIUMS a layer in certain fungi HYMENIAL adj

HYMN v -ED, -ING, -S to sing a hymn (a song of praise to God)

HYMNAL n pl. -S a book of hymns

HYMNARY n pl. -RIES a hymnal

HYMNBOOK n pl. -S a hymnal

HYMNIST n pl. -S one who composes hymns

HYMNLESS adj lacking a hymn

HYMNLIKE adj resembling a hymn

HYMNODY n pl. -DIES the singing of hymns

HYOID n pl. -S a bone of the tongue HYOIDAL, HYOIDEAN adj

HYOSCINE n pl. -S a sedative

HYP n pl. -S hypochondria

HYPE v HYPED, HYPING, HYPES to promote extravagantly

HYPER adj very excitable

HYPERGOL n pl. -S a rocket fuel

HYPERON n pl. -S an atomic particle

HYPEROPE n pl. -S a farsighted person

HYPHA n pl. -PHAE a threadlike element of a fungus HYPHAL adj

HYPHEMIA n pl. -S deficiency of blood

HYPHEN v -ED, -ING, -S to connect words or syllables with a hyphen (a mark of punctuation)

HYPING present participle of hype

HYPNIC adj pertaining to sleep

HYPNOID adj pertaining to hypnosis or sleep

HYPNOSIS n pl. -NOSES an artificially induced state resembling sleep

HYPNOTIC n pl. -S a sleep-inducing drug

HYPO v -ED, -ING, -S to inject with a hypodermic needle

HYPOACID adj having a lower than normal degree of acidity

HYPODERM n pl. -S a skin layer

HYPOGEA pl. of hypogeum

HYPOGEAL adj underground

HYPOGEAN adj hypogeal

HYPOGENE adj formed underground

HYPOGEUM n pl. -GEA an underground chamber

HYPOGYNY n pl. -NIES the condition of having flowers with organs situated below the ovary

HYPONEA n pl. -S hyponoia

HYPONOIA n pl. -S dulled mental activity

HYPOPNEA n pl. -S abnormally shallow breathing

HYPOPYON n pl. -S an accumulation of pus in the eye

HYPOTHEC n pl. -S a type of mortgage

HYPOXIA n pl. -S a deficiency of oxygen in body tissue HYPOXIC adj

HYRACOID n pl. -S a hyrax

HYRAX n pl. -RAXES or -RACES a small, harelike mammal

HYSON n pl. -S a Chinese tea

HYSSOP n pl. -S a medicinal herb

HYSTERIA n pl. -S uncontrollable excitement or fear

HYSTERIC n pl. -S one who is subject to fits of hysteria

HYTE adj insane

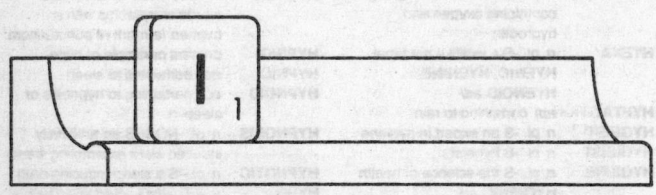

IAMB	n pl. -S a type of metrical foot	**ICHOR**	n pl. -S a watery discharge from a wound ICHOROUS adj
IAMBIC	n pl. -S an iamb		
IAMBUS	n pl. -BUSES or -BI an iamb	**ICHTHYIC**	adj pertaining to fishes
IATRIC	adj pertaining to medicine	**ICICLE**	n pl. -S a hanging spike of ice
IATRICAL	adj iatric		ICICLED adj
IBEX	n pl. IBEXES or IBICES a wild goat	**ICIER**	comparative of icy
		ICIEST	superlative of icy
IBIDEM	adv in the same place	**ICILY**	adv in an icy manner
IBIS	n pl. IBISES a wading bird	**ICINESS**	n pl. -ES the state of being icy
IBOGAINE	n pl. -S an alkaloid used as an antidepressant	**ICING**	n pl. -S a sweet mixture for covering cakes
ICE	v ICED, ICING, ICES to cover with ice (frozen water)	**ICK**	interj — used to express disgust
ICEBERG	n pl. -S a large floating body of ice	**ICKER**	n pl. -S a head of grain
ICEBLINK	n pl. -S a glare over an ice field	**ICKINESS**	n pl. -ES the state of being icky
ICEBOAT	n pl. -S a vehicle that sails on ice	**ICKY**	adj ICKIER, ICKIEST repulsive ICKILY adv
ICEBOUND	adj surrounded by ice	**ICON**	n pl. -S or -ES a representation ICONIC, ICONICAL adj
ICEBOX	n pl. -ES a cabinet for cooling food		
ICECAP	n pl. -S a covering of ice and snow	**ICTERIC**	n pl. -S a remedy for icterus
		ICTERUS	n pl. -ES a diseased condition of the liver
ICED	past tense of ice		
ICEFALL	n pl. -S a kind of frozen waterfall	**ICTUS**	n pl. -ES a recurring stress or beat in a poetical form ICTIC adj
ICEHOUSE	n pl. -S a building for storing ice	**ICY**	adj ICIER, ICIEST covered with ice
ICEKHANA	n pl. -S an automotive event held on a frozen lake	**ID**	n pl. -S a part of the psyche
ICELESS	adj having no ice	**IDEA**	n pl. -S a conception existing in the mind IDEALESS adj
ICELIKE	adj resembling ice		
ICEMAN	n pl. -MEN a man who supplies ice	**IDEAL**	n pl. -S a standard of perfection
ICH	n pl. ICHS a disease of certain fishes	**IDEALISE**	v -ISED, -ISING, -ISES to idealize
ICHNITE	n pl. -S a fossil footprint	**IDEALISM**	n pl. -S the pursuit of noble goals

IDEALIST *n* pl. -S an adherent of idealism

IDEALITY *n* pl. -TIES the state of being perfect; something idealized

IDEALIZE *v* -IZED, -IZING, -IZES to regard as perfect

IDEALLY *adv* perfectly

IDEALOGY *n* pl. -GIES ideology

IDEATE *v* -ATED, -ATING, -ATES to form an idea

IDEATION *n* pl. -S the act of ideating

IDEATIVE *adj* pertaining to ideation

IDEM *adj* the same

IDENTIC *adj* identical

IDENTIFY *v* -FIED, -FYING, -FIES to establish the identity of

IDENTITY *n* pl. -TIES the essential character of a person or thing

IDEOGRAM *n* pl. -S a type of written symbol

IDEOLOGY *n* pl. -GIES a systematic body of ideas

IDES *n* pl. IDES a certain day in the ancient Roman calendar

IDIOCY *n* pl. -CIES the condition of being an idiot

IDIOLECT *n* pl. -S one's speech pattern

IDIOM *n* pl. -S an expression peculiar to a language

IDIOT *n* pl. -S a mentally deficient person IDIOTIC *adj*

IDIOTISM *n* pl. -S idiocy

IDLE *adj* IDLER, IDLEST inactive

IDLE *v* IDLED, IDLING, IDLES to pass time idly

IDLENESS *n* pl. -ES the state of being idle

IDLER *n* pl. -S one that idles

IDLESSE *n* pl. -S idleness

IDLEST superlative of idle

IDLING present participle of idle

IDLY *adv* in an idle manner

IDOCRASE *n* pl. -S a mineral

IDOL *n* pl. -S an object of worship

IDOLATER *n* pl. -S one that worships idols

IDOLATOR *n* pl. -S idolater

IDOLATRY *n* pl. -TRIES the worship of idols

IDOLISE *v* -ISED, -ISING, -ISES to idolize

IDOLISER *n* pl. -S one that idolises

IDOLISM *n* pl. -S idolatry

IDOLIZE *v* -IZED, -IZING, -IZES to worship

IDOLIZER *n* pl. -S one that idolizes

IDONEITY *n* pl. -TIES the state of being idoneous

IDONEOUS *adj* suitable

IDYL *n* pl. -S a poem or prose work depicting scenes of rural simplicity

IDYLIST *n* pl. -S a writer of idyls

IDYLL *n* pl. -S idyl IDYLLIC *adj*

IDYLLIST *n* pl. -S idylist

IF *n* pl. -S a possibility

IFF *conj* if and only if

IFFINESS *n* pl. -ES the state of being iffy

IFFY *adj* IFFIER, IFFIEST full of uncertainty

IGLOO *n* pl. -LOOS an Eskimo dwelling

IGLU *n* pl. -S igloo

IGNATIA *n* pl. -S a medicinal seed

IGNEOUS *adj* pertaining to fire

IGNIFY *v* -FIED, -FYING, -FIES to burn

IGNITE *v* -NITED, -NITING, -NITES to set on fire

IGNITER *n* pl. -S one that ignites

IGNITION *n* pl. -S the act of igniting

IGNITOR *n* pl. -S a igniter

IGNITRON *n* pl. -S a type of rectifier tube

IGNOBLE *adj* of low character IGNOBLY *adv*

IGNOMINY *n* pl. -NIES disgrace or dishonor

IGNORANT *adj* having no knowledge

IGNORE *v* -NORED, -NORING, -NORES to refuse to notice

IGNORER *n* pl. -S one that ignores

IGUANA *n* pl. -S a tropical lizard

IGUANIAN *n* pl. -S a lizard related to the iguana

IHRAM *n* pl. -S the garb worn by Muslim pilgrims

IKAT *n* pl. -S a fabric of tie-dyed yams

IKEBANA *n* pl. -S the Japanese art of flower arranging

IKON *n* pl. -S icon

ILEA pl. of ileum

ILEAC *adj* pertaining to the ileum

ILEAL *adj* ileac

ILEITIS *n* pl. ILEITIDES inflammation of the ileum

ILEUM *n* pl. ILEA a part of the small intestine

ILEUS *n* pl. -ES intestinal obstruction

ILEX *n* pl. -ES a holly

ILIA pl. of ilium

ILIAC *adj* pertaining to the ilium

ILIAD n pl. -S a long poem

ILIAL adj iliac

ILIUM n pl. ILIA a bone of the pelvis

ILK n pl. -S a class or kind

ILKA adj each

ILL n pl. -S an evil

ILLATION n pl. -S the act of inferring

ILLATIVE n pl. -S a word or phrase introducing an inference

ILLEGAL n pl. -S a person who enters a country without authorization

ILLICIT adj not permitted

ILLINIUM n pl. -S a radioactive element

ILLIQUID adj not readily convertible into cash

ILLITE n pl. -S a group of minerals
ILLITIC adj

ILLNESS n pl. -ES sickness

ILLOGIC n pl. -S absence of logic

ILLUME v -LUMED, -LUMING, -LUMES to illuminate

ILLUMINE v -MINED, -MINING, -MINES to illuminate

ILLUSION n pl. -S a false perception

ILLUSIVE adj illusory

ILLUSORY adj based on illusion

ILLUVIUM n pl. -VIA or -VIUMS a type of material accumulated in soil
ILLUVIAL adj

ILLY adv badly

ILMENITE n pl. -S a mineral

IMAGE v -AGED, -AGING, -AGES to imagine

IMAGER n pl. -S one that images

IMAGERY n pl. -ERIES mental pictures

IMAGINAL adj pertaining to an imago

IMAGINE v -INED, -INING, -INES to form a mental picture of

IMAGINER n pl. -S one that imagines

IMAGING n pl. -S the action of producing a visible representation

IMAGINING present participle of imagine

IMAGISM n pl. -S a movement in poetry

IMAGIST n pl. -S an adherent of imagism

IMAGO n pl. -GOES or -GOS an adult insect

IMAM n pl. -S a Muslim priest

IMAMATE n pl. -S the office of an imam

IMARET n pl. -S a Turkish inn

IMAUM n pl. -S imam

IMBALM v -ED, -ING, -S to embalm

IMBALMER n pl. -S embalmer

IMBARK v -ED, -ING, -S to embark

IMBECILE n pl. -S a mentally deficient person

IMBED v -BEDDED, -BEDDING, -BEDS to embed

IMBIBE v -BIBED, -BIBING, -BIBES to drink

IMBIBER n pl. -S one that imbibes

IMBITTER v -ED, -ING, -S to embitter

IMBLAZE v -BLAZED, -BLAZING, -BLAZES to emblaze

IMBODY v -BODIED, -BODYING, -BODIES to embody

IMBOLDEN v -ED, -ING, -S to embolden

IMBOSOM v -ED, -ING, -S to embosom

IMBOWER v -ED, -ING, -S to embower

IMBROWN v -ED, -ING, -S to embrown

IMBRUE v -BRUED, -BRUING, -BRUES to stain

IMBRUTE v -BRUTED, -BRUTING, -BRUTES to make brutal

IMBUE v -BUED, -BUING, -BUES to make thoroughly wet

IMID n pl. -S imide

IMIDE n pl. -S a chemical compound
IMIDIC adj

IMIDO adj containing an imide

IMINE n pl. -S a chemical compound

IMINO adj containing an imine

IMITABLE adj capable of being imitated

IMITATE v -TATED, -TATING, -TATES to behave in the same way as

IMITATOR n pl. -S one that imitates

IMMANE adj great in size

IMMANENT adj existing within

IMMATURE n pl. -S an individual that is not fully grown or developed

IMMENSE adj -MENSER, -MENSEST great in size

IMMERGE v -MERGED, -MERGING, -MERGES to immerse

IMMERSE v -MERSED, -MERSING, -MERSES to plunge into a liquid

IMMESH v -ED, -ING, -ES to enmesh

IMMIES pl. of immy

IMMINENT adj ready to take place

IMMINGLE v -GLED, -GLING, -GLES to blend

IMMIX v -ED, -ING, -ES to mix in

IMMOBILE adj incapable of being moved

IMMODEST adj not modest

IMMOLATE v -LATED, -LATING, -LATES to kill as a sacrifice

IMMORAL adj contrary to established morality

IMMORTAL n pl. -S one who is not subject to death

IMMOTILE adj lacking mobility

IMMUNE *n* pl. -S one who is protected from a disease

IMMUNISE *v* -NISED, -NISING, -NISES to immunize

IMMUNITY *n* pl. -TIES the state of being protected from a disease

IMMUNIZE *v* -NIZED, -NIZING, -NIZES to protect from a disease

IMMURE *v* -MURED, -MURING, -MURES to imprison

IMMY *n* pl. -MIES a type of playing marble

IMP *v* -ED, -ING, -S to graft feathers onto a bird's wing

IMPACT *v* -ED, -ING, -S to pack firmly together

IMPACTER *n* pl. -S one that impacts

IMPACTOR *n* pl. -S impacter

IMPAINT *v* -ED, -ING, -S to paint or depict

IMPAIR *v* -ED, -ING, -S to make worse

IMPAIRER *n* pl. -S one that impairs

IMPALA *n* pl. -S an African antelope

IMPALE *v* -PALED, -PALING, -PALES to pierce with a pointed object

IMPALER *n* pl. -S one that impales

IMPANEL *v* -ELED, -ELING, -ELS or -ELLED, -ELLING, -ELS to enter on a list for jury duty

IMPARITY *n* pl. -TIES lack of equality

IMPARK *v* -ED, -ING, -S to confine in a park

IMPART *v* -ED, -ING, -S to make known

IMPARTER *n* pl. -S one that imparts

IMPASSE *n* pl. -S a road or passage having no exit

IMPASTE *v* -PASTED, -PASTING, -PASTES to make into a paste

IMPASTO *n* pl. -TOS a painting technique

IMPAVID *adj* brave

IMPAWN *v* -ED, -ING, -S to pawn

IMPEACH *v* -ED, -ING, -ES to charge with misconduct in office

IMPEARL *v* -ED, -ING, -S to make pearly

IMPEDE *v* -PEDED, -PEDING, -PEDES to obstruct the progress of

IMPEDER *n* pl. -S one that impedes

IMPEL *v* -PELLED, -PELLING, -PELS to force into action

IMPELLER *n* pl. -S one that impels

IMPELLOR *n* pl. -S impeller

IMPEND *v* -ED, -ING, -S to be imminent

IMPERIA a pl. of imperium

IMPERIAL *n* pl. -S an emperor or empress

IMPERIL *v* -ILED, -ILING, -ILS or -ILLED, -ILLING, -ILS to place in jeopardy

IMPERIUM *n* pl. -RIUMS or -RIA absolute power

IMPETIGO *n* pl. -GOS a skin disease

IMPETUS *n* pl. -ES an impelling force

IMPHEE *n* pl. -S an African grass

IMPI *n* pl. -S a body of warriors

IMPIETY *n* pl. -TIES lack of piety

IMPING *n* pl. -S the process of grafting

IMPINGE *v* -PINGED, -PINGING, -PINGES to collide

IMPINGER *n* pl. -S one that impinges

IMPIOUS *adj* not pious

IMPISH *adj* mischievous IMPISHLY *adv*

IMPLANT *v* -ED, -ING, -S to set securely

IMPLEAD *v* -ED, -ING, -S to sue in a court of law

IMPLEDGE *v* -PLEDGED, -PLEDGING, -PLEDGES to pawn

IMPLICIT *adj* implied

IMPLIED past tense of imply

IMPLIES present 3d person sing. of imply

IMPLODE *v* -PLODED, -PLODING, -PLODES to collapse inward

IMPLORE *v* -PLORED, -PLORING, -PLORES to beg for urgently

IMPLORER *n* pl. -S one that implores

IMPLY *v* -PLIED, -PLYING, -PLIES to indicate or suggest indirectly

IMPOLICY *n* pl. -CIES an unwise course of action

IMPOLITE *adj* not polite

IMPONE *v* -PONED, -PONING, -PONES to wager

IMPOROUS *adj* extremely dense

IMPORT *v* -ED, -ING, -S to bring into a country from abroad

IMPORTER *n* pl. -S one that imports

IMPOSE *v* -POSED, -POSING, -POSES to establish as compulsory

IMPOSER *n* pl. -S one that imposes

IMPOST *v* -ED, -ING, -S to determine customs duties

IMPOSTER *n* pl. -S impostor

IMPOSTOR *n* pl. -S one that poses as another for deceptive purposes

IMPOTENT *n* pl. -S one that is powerless

IMPOUND v -ED, -ING, -S to seize and retain in legal custody

IMPOWER v -ED, -ING, -S to empower

IMPREGN v -ED, -ING, -S to make pregnant

IMPRESA n pl. -S a type of emblem

IMPRESE n pl. -S impresa

IMPRESS v -ED, -ING, -ES to affect strongly

IMPREST n pl. -S a loan or advance of money

IMPRIMIS adv in the first place

IMPRINT v -ED, -ING, -S to produce a mark by pressure

IMPRISON v -ED, -ING, -S to confine

IMPROPER adj not proper

IMPROV n pl. -S improvisation

IMPROVE v -PROVED, -PROVING, -PROVES to make better

IMPROVER n pl. -S one that improves

IMPUDENT adj offensively bold or disrespectful

IMPUGN v -ED, -ING, -S to make insinuations against

IMPUGNER n pl. -S one that impugns

IMPULSE v -PULSED, -PULSING, -PULSES to give impetus to

IMPUNITY n pl. -TIES exemption from penalty

IMPURE adj not pure **IMPURELY** adv

IMPURITY n pl. -TIES something that is impure

IMPUTE v -PUTED, -PUTING, -PUTES to credit to a person or a cause

IMPUTER n pl. -S one that imputes

IN v INNED, INNING, INS to harvest

INACTION n pl. -S lack of action

INACTIVE adj not active

INANE adj INANER, INANEST nonsensical **INANELY** adv

INANE n pl. -S empty space

INANITY n pl. -TIES something that is inane

INAPT adj not apt **INAPTLY** adv

INARABLE adj not arable

INARCH v -ED, -ING, -ES to graft with in a certain way

INARM v -ED, -ING, -S to encircle with the arms

INBEING n pl. -S the state of being inherent

INBOARD n pl. -S a type of boat motor

INBORN adj existing in one from birth

INBOUND v -ED, -ING, -S to put a basketball in play from out of bounds

INBOUNDS adj being within certain boundaries

INBRED n pl. -S a product of inbreeding

INBREED v -BRED, -BREEDING, -BREEDS to breed closely related stock

INBUILT adj forming an integral part of a structure

INBURST n pl. -S the act of bursting inward

INBY adv inward

INBYE adv inby

INCAGE v -CAGED, -CAGING, -CAGES to encage

INCANT v -ED, -ING, -S to utter ritually

INCASE v -CASED, -CASING, -CASES to encase

INCENSE v -CENSED, -CENSING, -CENSES to make angry

INCENTER n pl. -S the point where the three lines bisecting the angles of a triangle meet

INCEPT v -ED, -ING, -S to take in

INCEPTOR n pl. -S one that incepts

INCEST n pl. -S sexual intercourse between closely related persons

INCH v -ED, -ING, -ES to move very slowly

INCHMEAL adv little by little

INCHOATE adj being in an early stage

INCHWORM n pl. -S a type of worm

INCIDENT n pl. -S an event

INCIPIT n pl. -S the opening words of a text

INCISAL adj being the cutting edge of a tooth

INCISE v -CISED, -CISING, -CISES to cut into

INCISION n pl. -S the act of incising

INCISIVE adj penetrating

INCISOR n pl. -S a cutting tooth

INCISORY adj adapted for cutting

INCISURE n pl. -S a notch or cleft of a body part

INCITANT n pl. -S something that incites

INCITE v -CITED, -CITING, -CITES to arouse to action

INCITER n pl. -S one that incites

INCIVIL adj discourteous

INCLASP v -ED, -ING, -S to enclasp

INCLINE v -CLINED, -CLINING, -CLINES to slant

INCLINER n pl. -S one that inclines

INCLIP v -CLIPPED, -CLIPPING, -CLIPS to clasp

INCLOSE v -CLOSED, -CLOSING, -CLOSES to enclose

INCLOSER n pl. -S one that incloses

INCLUDE v -CLUDED, -CLUDING, -CLUDES to have as a part

INCOG n pl. -S a disguised person

INCOME n pl. -S a sum of money earned regularly

INCOMER n pl. -S one that comes in

INCOMING n pl. -S an arrival

INCONNU n pl. -S a large food fish

INCONY adj pretty

INCORPSE v -CORPSED, -CORPSING, -CORPSES to become combined with

INCREASE v -CREASED, -CREASING, -CREASES to make or become greater

INCREATE adj not created

INCROSS v -ED, -ING, -ES to inbreed

INCRUST v -ED, -ING, -S to encrust

INCUBATE v -BATED, -BATING, -BATES to warm eggs for hatching

INCUBUS n pl. -BI or -BUSES a demon

INCUDAL adj pertaining to the incus

INCUDATE adj incudal

INCUDES pl. of incus

INCULT adj uncultivated

INCUMBER v -ED, -ING, -S to encumber

INCUR v -CURRED, -CURRING, -CURS to bring upon oneself

INCURVE v -CURVED, -CURVING, -CURVES to curve inward

INCUS n pl. INCUDES a bone in the middle ear

INCUSE v -CUSED, -CUSING, -CUSES to mark by stamping

INDABA n pl. -S a meeting of South African tribes

INDAGATE v -GATED, -GATING, -GATES to investigate

INDAMIN n pl. -S indamine

INDAMINE n pl. -S a chemical compound

INDEBTED adj beholden

INDECENT adj -CENTER, -CENTEST not decent

INDEED adv in truth

INDENE n pl. -S a hydrocarbon

INDENT v -ED, -ING, -S to cut or tear irregularly

INDENTER n pl. -S one that indents

INDENTOR n pl. -S indenter

INDEVOUT adj not devout

INDEX n pl. INDEXES or INDICES a type of reference guide at the end of a book

INDEX v -ED, -ING, -ES to provide with an index

INDEXER n pl. -S one that indexes

INDEXING n pl. -S the linking of wages and prices to cost-of-living levels

INDICAN n pl. -S a chemical compound

INDICANT n pl. -S something that indicates

INDICATE v -CATED, -CATING, -CATES to point out

INDICES a pl. of index

INDICIA n pl. -S a distinctive mark

INDICIUM n pl. -S an indicia

INDICT v -ED, -ING, -S to charge with a crime

INDICTEE n pl. -S one that is indicted

INDICTER n pl. -S one that indicts

INDICTOR n pl. -S indicter

INDIE n pl. -S a person who is independent

INDIGEN n pl. -S indigene

INDIGENE n pl. -S a native

INDIGENT n pl. -S a needy person

INDIGN adj disgraceful **INDIGNLY** adv

INDIGO n pl. -GOS or -GOES a blue dye

INDIGOID n pl. -S a blue dye

INDIRECT adj not direct

INDITE v -DITED, -DITING, -DITES to write or compose

INDITER n pl. -S one that indites

INDIUM n pl. -S a metallic element

INDOCILE adj not docile

INDOL n pl. -S indole

INDOLE n pl. -S a chemical compound

INDOLENT adj lazy

INDOOR adj pertaining to the interior of a building

INDOORS adv in or into a house

INDORSE v -DORSED, -DORSING, -DORSES to endorse

INDORSEE n pl. -S endorsee

INDORSER n pl. -S endorser

INDORSING present participle of indorse

INDORSOR n pl. -S endorsor

INDOW v -ED, -ING, -S to endow

INDOXYL n pl. -S a chemical compound

INDRAFT n pl. -S an inward flow or current

INDRAWN adj drawn in

INDRI *n pl.* -S a short-tailed lemur

INDUCE *v* -DUCED, -DUCING, -DUCES to influence into doing something

INDUCER *n pl.* -S one that induces

INDUCT *v* -ED, -ING, -S to bring into military service

INDUCTEE *n pl.* -S one that is inducted

INDUCTOR *n pl.* -S one that inducts

INDUE *v* -DUED, -DUING, -DUES to endue

INDULGE *v* -DULGED, -DULGING, -DULGES to yield to the desire of

INDULGER *n pl.* -S one that indulges

INDULIN *n pl.* -S induline

INDULINE *n pl.* -S a blue dye

INDULT *n pl.* -S a privilege granted by the pope

INDURATE *v* -RATED, -RATING, -RATES to make hard

INDUSIUM *n pl.* -SIA an enclosing membrane **INDUSIAL** *adj*

INDUSTRY *n pl.* -TRIES a group of productive enterprises

INDWELL *v* -DWELT, -DWELLING, -DWELLS to live within

INEARTH *v* -ED, -ING, -S to bury

INEDIBLE *adj* not fit to be eaten

INEDITA *n/pl* unpublished literary works

INEDITED *adj* not published

INEPT *adj* not suitable **INEPTLY** *adv*

INEQUITY *n pl.* -TIES unfairness

INERRANT *adj* free from error

INERT *n pl.* -S something that lacks active properties

INERTIA *n pl.* -TIAS or -TIAE the tendency of a body to resist acceleration **INERTIAL** *adj*

INERTLY *adv* inactively

INEXACT *adj* not exact

INEXPERT *n pl.* -S a novice

INFALL *n pl.* -S movement under the influence of gravity toward a celestial object

INFAMOUS *adj* having a vile reputation

INFAMY *n pl.* -MIES the state of being infamous

INFANCY *n pl.* -CIES the state of being an infant

INFANT *n pl.* -S a child in the earliest stages of life

INFANTA *n pl.* -S a daughter of a Spanish or Portuguese monarch

INFANTE *n pl.* -S a younger son of a Spanish or Portuguese monarch

INFANTRY *n pl.* -TRIES a branch of the army composed of foot soldiers

INFARCT *n pl.* -S an area of dead or dying tissue

INFARE *n pl.* -S a reception for newlyweds

INFAUNA *n pl.* -NAS or -NAE fauna living on a soft sea floor **INFAUNAL** *adj*

INFECT *v* -ED, -ING, -S to contaminate with disease-producing germs

INFECTER *n pl.* -S one that infects

INFECTOR *n pl.* -S infecter

INFECUND *adj* barren

INFEOFF *v* -ED, -ING, -S to enfeoff

INFER *v* -FERRED, -FERRING, -FERS to reach or derive by reasoning

INFERIOR *n pl.* -S one of lesser rank

INFERNAL *adj* pertaining to hell

INFERNO *n pl.* -NOS a place that resembles or suggests hell

INFERRED past tense of infer

INFERRER *n pl.* -S one that infers

INFERRING present participle of infer

INFEST *v* -ED, -ING, -S to overrun in large numbers

INFESTER *n pl.* -S one that infests

INFIDEL *n pl.* -S one who has no religious faith

INFIELD *n pl.* -S a part of a baseball field

INFIGHT *v* -FOUGHT, -FIGHTING, -FIGHTS to contend with others within the same group

INFINITE *n pl.* -S something that has no limits

INFINITY *n pl.* -TIES the state of having no limits

INFIRM *v* -ED, -ING, -S to weaken or destroy the validity of

INFIRMLY *adv* in a feeble manner

INFIX *v* -ED, -ING, -ES to implant

INFIXION *n pl.* -S the act of infixing

INFLAME *v* -FLAMED, -FLAMING, -FLAMES to set on fire

INFLAMER *n pl.* -S one that inflames

INFLATE *v* -FLATED, -FLATING, -FLATES to cause to expand by filling with gas or air

INFLATER *n pl.* -S one that inflates

INFLATOR *n pl.* -S inflater

INFLECT	v -ED, -ING, -S to bend
INFLEXED	adj bent inward
INFLICT	v -ED, -ING, -S to cause to be endured; impose
INFLIGHT	adj done during an air voyage
INFLOW	n pl. -S the act of flowing in
INFLUENT	n pl. -S a tributary
INFLUX	n pl. -ES a flowing in
INFO	n pl. -FOS information
INFOLD	v -ED, -ING, -S to fold inward
INFOLDER	n pl. -S one that infolds
INFORM	v -ED, -ING, -S to supply with information
INFORMAL	adj marked by the absence of formality or ceremony
INFORMER	n pl. -S one that informs
INFOUGHT	past tense of infight
INFRA	adv below
INFRACT	v -ED, -ING, -S to break a legal rule
INFRARED	n pl. -S a part of the invisible spectrum
INFRINGE	v -FRINGED, -FRINGING, -FRINGES to violate an oath or a law
INFRUGAL	adj not frugal
INFUSE	v -FUSED, -FUSING, -FUSES to permeate with something
INFUSER	n pl. -S one that infuses
INFUSION	n pl. -S the act of infusing
INFUSIVE	adj capable of infusing
INGATE	n pl. -S a channel by which molten metal enters a mold
INGATHER	v -ED, -ING, -S to gather in
INGENUE	n pl. -S a naive young woman
INGEST	v -ED, -ING, -S to take into the body
INGESTA	n/pl ingested material
INGLE	n pl. -S a fire
INGOING	adj entering
INGOT	v -ED, -ING, -S to shape into a convenient form for storage
INGRAFT	v -ED, -ING, -S to engraft
INGRAIN	v -ED, -ING, -S to impress firmly on the mind
INGRATE	n pl. -S an ungrateful person
INGRESS	n pl. -ES the act of entering
INGROUP	n pl. -S a group united by common interests
INGROWN	adj grown into the flesh
INGROWTH	n pl. -S growth inward
INGUINAL	adj pertaining to the groin
INGULF	v -ED, -ING, -S to engulf
INHABIT	v -ED, -ING, -S to live in
INHALANT	n pl. -S something that is inhaled

INHALE	v -HALED, -HALING, -HALES to take into the lungs
INHALER	n pl. -S one that inhales
INHAUL	n pl. -S a line for bringing in a sail
INHAULER	n pl. -S an inhaul
INHERE	v -HERED, -HERING, -HERES to be inherent
INHERENT	adj existing in something as an essential characteristic
INHERIT	v -ED, -ING, -S to receive by legal succession
INHESION	n pl. -S the state of inhering
INHIBIN	n pl. -S a human hormone
INHIBIT	v -ED, -ING, -S to restrain or hold back
INHUMAN	adj lacking desirable human qualities
INHUMANE	adj not humane
INHUME	v -HUMED, -HUMING, -HUMES to bury
INHUMER	n pl. -S one that inhumes
INIMICAL	adj unfriendly
INION	n pl. INIA a part of the skull
INIQUITY	n pl. -TIES a gross injustice
INITIAL	v -TIALED, -TIALING, -TIALS or -TIALLED, -TIALLING, -TIALS to mark with the first letters of one's name
INITIATE	v -ATED, -ATING, -ATES to originate
INJECT	v -ED, -ING, -S to force a fluid into
INJECTOR	n pl. -S one that injects
INJURE	v -JURED, -JURING, -JURES to do or cause injury to
INJURER	n pl. -S one that injures
INJURY	n pl. -RIES harm inflicted or suffered
INK	v -ED, -ING, -S to mark with ink (a colored fluid used for writing)
INKBERRY	n pl. -RIES a small shrub
INKBLOT	n pl. -S a blotted pattern of spilled ink
INKER	n pl. -S one that inks
INKHORN	n pl. -S a small container for ink
INKIER	comparative of inky
INKIEST	superlative of inky
INKINESS	n pl. -ES the state of being inky
INKJET	adj being a high-speed printing process using jets of ink

INKLE	n pl. -S a tape used for trimming	**INOSITOL**	n pl. -S an alcohol found in plant and animal tissue
INKLESS	adj being without ink	**INPHASE**	adj having matching electrical phases
INKLIKE	adj resembling ink		
INKLING	n pl. -S a slight suggestion	**INPOUR**	v -ED, -ING, -S to pour in
INKPOT	n pl. -S an inkwell	**INPUT**	v -PUTTED, -PUTTING, -PUTS to enter data into a computer
INKSTAND	n pl. -S an inkwell		
INKSTONE	n pl. -S a stone on which dry ink and water are mixed	**INQUEST**	n pl. -S a legal inquiry
		INQUIET	v -ED, -ING, -S to disturb
INKWELL	n pl. -S a small container for ink	**INQUIRE**	v -QUIRED, -QUIRING, -QUIRES to ask about
INKWOOD	n pl. -S an evergreen tree	**INQUIRER**	n pl. -S one that inquires
INKY	adj INKIER, INKIEST resembling ink	**INQUIRY**	n pl. -RIES a question
		INRO	n pl. INRO a Japanese ornamental container
INLACE	v -LACED, -LACING, -LACES to enlace	**INROAD**	n pl. -S a hostile invasion
INLAID	past tense of inlay	**INRUSH**	n pl. -ES a rushing in
INLAND	n pl. -S the interior of a region	**INSANE**	adj -SANER, -SANEST mentally unsound INSANELY adv
INLANDER	n pl. -S one living in the interior of a region		
INLAY	v -LAID, -LAYING, -LAYS to set into a surface	**INSANITY**	n pl. -TIES the state of being insane; something utterly foolish
INLAYER	n pl. -S one that inlays	**INSCAPE**	n pl. -S the inner essential quality of something
INLET	v -LET, -LETTING, -LETS to insert		
INLIER	n pl. -S a type of rock formation	**INSCRIBE**	v -SCRIBED, -SCRIBING, -SCRIBES to write or engrave as a lasting record
INLY	adv inwardly		
INMATE	n pl. -S one who is confined to an institution	**INSCROLL**	v -ED, -ING, -S to enscroll
		INSCULP	v -ED, -ING, -S to engrave
INMESH	v -ED, -ING, -ES to enmesh	**INSEAM**	n pl. -S an inner seam
INMOST	adj farthest within	**INSECT**	n pl. -S any of a class of small invertebrate animals
INN	v -ED, -ING, -S to put up at an inn (a public lodging house)		
		INSECTAN	adj pertaining to insects
INNARDS	n/pl the internal organs	**INSECURE**	adj unsafe
INNATE	adj inborn INNATELY adv	**INSERT**	v -ED, -ING, -S to put in
INNED	past tense of in	**INSERTER**	n pl. -S one that inserts
INNER	n pl. -S something that is within	**INSET**	v -SETTED, -SETTING, -SETS to insert
INNERLY	adv inwardly		
INNERVE	v -NERVED, -NERVING, -NERVES to stimulate	**INSETTER**	n pl. -S one that inserts
		INSHEATH	v -ED, -ING, -S to ensheath
INNING	n pl. -S a division of a baseball game	**INSHORE**	adj near the shore
		INSHRINE	v -SHRINED, -SHRINING, -SHRINES to enshrine
INNLESS	adj having no inns		
INNOCENT	adj -CENTER, -CENTEST free from guilt or sin	**INSIDE**	n pl. -S something that lies within
INNOCENT	n pl. -S an innocent person	**INSIDER**	n pl. -S an accepted member of a clique
INNOVATE	v -VATED, -VATING, -VATES to introduce something new	**INSIGHT**	n pl. -S a perception of the inner nature of things
INNUENDO	v -ED, -ING, -S or -ES to make a derogatory implication	**INSIGNE**	n pl. INSIGNIA an insignia
		INSIGNIA	n pl. -S an emblem of authority or honor
INOCULUM	n pl. -LA or -LUMS the material used in an inoculation		
INOSITE	n pl. -S inositol	**INSIPID**	adj dull and uninteresting

INSIST	v -ED, -ING, -S to be resolute on some matter		**INSULANT**	n pl. -S an insulating material
INSISTER	n pl. -S one that insists		**INSULAR**	n pl. -S an islander
INSNARE	v -SNARED, -SNARING, -SNARES to ensnare		**INSULATE**	v -LATED, -LATING, -LATES to separate with nonconducting material
INSNARER	n pl. -S ensnarer		**INSULIN**	n pl. -S a hormone
INSOFAR	adv to such an extent		**INSULT**	v -ED, -ING, -S to treat offensively
INSOLATE	v -LATED, -LATING, -LATES to expose to sunlight		**INSULTER**	n pl. -S one that insults
INSOLE	n pl. -S the inner sole of a boot or shoe		**INSURANT**	n pl. -S one who is insured
INSOLENT	n pl. -S an extremely rude person		**INSURE**	v -SURED, -SURING, -SURES to guarantee against loss
INSOMNIA	n pl. -S chronic inability to sleep		**INSURED**	n pl. -S one who is insured
INSOMUCH	adv to such a degree		**INSURER**	n pl. -S one that insures
INSOUL	v -ED, -ING, -S to ensoul		**INSURING**	present participle of insure
INSPAN	v -SPANNED, -SPANNING, -SPANS to harness or yoke to a vehicle		**INSWATHE**	v -SWATHED, -SWATHING, -SWATHES to enswathe
INSPECT	v -ED, -ING, -S to look carefully at or over		**INSWEPT**	adj narrowed in front
INSPHERE	v -SPHERED, -SPHERING, -SPHERES to ensphere		**INTACT**	adj not damaged in any way
INSPIRE	v -SPIRED, -SPIRING, -SPIRES to animate the mind or emotions of		**INTAGLIO**	n pl. -GLIOS or -GLI an incised or sunken design
			INTAGLIO	v -ED, -ING, -S to engrave in intaglio
INSPIRER	n pl. -S one that inspires		**INTAKE**	n pl. -S the act of taking in
INSPIRIT	v -ED, -ING, -S to fill with spirit or life		**INTARSIA**	n pl. -S a decorative technique
INSTABLE	adj unstable		**INTEGER**	n pl. -S a whole number
INSTAL	v -STALLED, -STALLING, -STALS to install		**INTEGRAL**	n pl. -S a total unit
INSTALL	v -ED, -ING, -S to place in position for use		**INTEND**	v -ED, -ING, -S to have as a specific aim or purpose
INSTANCE	v -STANCED, -STANCING, -STANCES to cite as an example		**INTENDED**	n pl. -S one's spouse to-be
			INTENDER	n pl. -S one that intends
INSTANCY	n pl. -CIES urgency		**INTENSE**	adj -TENSER, -TENSEST existing in an extreme degree
INSTANT	n pl. -S a very short time		
INSTAR	v -STARRED, -STARRING, -STARS to adorn with stars		**INTENT**	n pl. -S a purpose
			INTENTLY	adv in an unwavering manner
INSTATE	v -STATED, -STATING, -STATES to place in office		**INTER**	v -TERRED, -TERRING, -TERS to bury
INSTEAD	adv as a substitute or equivalent		**INTERACT**	v -ED, -ING, -S to act on each other
INSTEP	n pl. -S a part of the foot		**INTERAGE**	adj including persons of various ages
INSTIL	v -STILLED, -STILLING, -STILS to instill		**INTERBED**	v -BEDDED, -BEDDING, -BEDS to insert between other layers
INSTILL	v -ED, -ING, -S to infuse slowly		**INTERCOM**	n pl. -S a type of communication system
INSTINCT	n pl. -S an inborn behavioral pattern		**INTERCUT**	v -CUT, -CUTTING, -CUTS to alternate camera shots
INSTROKE	n pl. -S an inward stroke		**INTEREST**	v -ED, -ING, -S to engage the attention of
INSTRUCT	v -ED, -ING, -S to supply with knowledge		**INTERIM**	n pl. -S an interval
			INTERIOR	n pl. -S the inside
			INTERLAP	v -LAPPED, -LAPPING, -LAPS to lap one over another

INTERLAY *v* -LAID, -LAYING, -LAYS to place between

INTERMIT *v* -MITTED, -MITTING, -MITS to stop temporarily

INTERMIX *v* -ED, -ING, -ES to mix together

INTERN *v* -ED, -ING, -S to confine during a war

INTERNAL *n pl.* -S an inner attribute

INTERNE *n pl.* -S a recent medical school graduate on a hospital staff

INTERNEE *n pl.* -S one who has been interned

INTERRED past tense of inter

INTERREX *n pl.* -REGES a type of sovereign

INTERRING present participle of inter

INTERROW *adj* existing between rows

INTERSEX *n pl.* -ES a person having characteristics of both sexes

INTERTIE *n pl.* -S a type of electrical connection

INTERVAL *n pl.* -S a space of time between periods or events

INTERWAR *adj* happening between wars

INTHRAL *v* -THRALLED, -THRALLING, -THRALS to enthrall

INTHRALL *v* -ED, -ING, -S to enthrall

INTHRONE *v* -THRONED, -THRONING, -THRONES to enthrone

INTI *n pl.* -S a monetary unit of Peru

INTIMA *n pl.* -MAE or -MAS the innermost layer of an organ **INTIMAL** *adj*

INTIMACY *n pl.* -CIES the state of being closely associated

INTIMATE *v* -MATED, -MATING, -MATES to make known indirectly

INTIME *adj* cozy

INTIMIST *n pl.* -S a writer or artist who deals with deep personal experiences

INTINE *n pl.* -S the inner wall of a spore

INTITLE *v* -TLED, -TLING, -TLES to entitle

INTITULE *v* -ULED, -ULING, -ULES to entitle

INTO *prep* to the inside of

INTOMB *v* -ED, -ING, -S to entomb

INTONATE *v* -NATED, -NATING, -NATES to intone

INTONE *v* -TONED, -TONING, -TONES to speak in a singing voice

INTONER *n pl.* -S one that intones

INTORT *v* -ED, -ING, -S to twist inward

INTOWN *adj* located in the center of a city

INTRADAY *adj* occurring within a single day

INTRADOS *n pl.* -ES the inner curve of an arch

INTRANT *n pl.* -S an entrant

INTREAT *v* -ED, -ING, -S to entreat

INTRENCH *v* -ED, -ING, -ES to entrench

INTREPID *adj* fearless

INTRIGUE *v* -TRIGUED, -TRIGUING, -TRIGUES to arouse the curiosity of

INTRO *n pl.* -TROS an introduction

INTROFY *v* -FIED, -FYING, -FIES to increase the wetting properties of

INTROIT *n pl.* -S music sung at the beginning of a worship service

INTROMIT *v* -MITTED, -MITTING, -MITS to put in

INTRON *n pl.* -S an intervening sequence in the genetic code

INTRORSE *adj* facing inward

INTRUDE *v* -TRUDED, -TRUDING, -TRUDES to thrust or force oneself in

INTRUDER *n pl.* -S one that intrudes

INTRUST *v* -ED, -ING, -S to entrust

INTUBATE *v* -BATED, -BATING, -BATES to insert a tube into

INTUIT *v* -ED, -ING, -S to know without conscious reasoning

INTURN *n pl.* -S a turning inward **INTURNED** *adj*

INTWINE *v* -TWINED, -TWINING, -TWINES to entwine

INTWIST *v* -ED, -ING, -S to entwist

INULASE *n pl.* -S an enzyme

INULIN *n pl.* -S a chemical compound

INUNDANT *adj* inundating

INUNDATE *v* -DATED, -DATING, -DATES to overwhelm with water

INURBANE *adj* not urbane

INURE *v* -URED, -URING, -URES to accustom to accept something undesirable

INURN *v* -ED, -ING, -S to put in an urn

INUTILE *adj* useless

INVADE	v -VADED, -VADING, -VADES to enter for conquest or plunder
INVADER	n pl. -S one that invades
INVALID	v -ED, -ING, -S to disable physically
INVAR	n pl. -S an iron-nickel alloy
INVASION	n pl. -S the act of invading **INVASIVE** adj
INVECTED	adj edged by convex curves
INVEIGH	v -ED, -ING, -S to protest angrily
INVEIGLE	v -GLED, -GLING, -GLES to induce by guile or flattery
INVENT	v -ED, -ING, -S to devise originally
INVENTER	n pl. -S inventor
INVENTOR	n pl. -S one that invents
INVERITY	n pl. -TIES lack of truth
INVERSE	n pl. -S something that is opposite
INVERT	v -ED, -ING, -S to turn upside down
INVERTER	n pl. -S one that inverts
INVERTOR	n pl. -S a type of electrical device
INVEST	v -ED, -ING, -S to commit something of value for future profit
INVESTOR	n pl. -S one that invests
INVIABLE	adj not viable **INVIABLY** adv
INVIRILE	adj not virile
INVISCID	adj not viscid
INVITAL	adj not vital
INVITE	v -VITED, -VITING, -VITES to request the presence of
INVITEE	n pl. -S one that is invited
INVITER	n pl. -S one that invites
INVITING	present participle of invite
INVOCATE	v -CATED, -CATING, -CATES to invoke
INVOICE	v -VOICED, -VOICING, -VOICES to bill
INVOKE	v -VOKED, -VOKING, -VOKES to appeal to for aid
INVOKER	n pl. -S one that invokes
INVOLUTE	v -LUTED, -LUTING, -LUTES to roll or curl up
INVOLVE	v -VOLVED, -VOLVING, -VOLVES to contain or include as a part
INVOLVER	n pl. -S one that involves
INWALL	v -ED, -ING, -S to surround with a wall
INWARD	adv toward the inside
INWARDLY	adv on the inside
INWARDS	adv inward
INWEAVE	v -WOVE or -WEAVED, -WOVEN, -WEAVING, -WEAVES to weave together
INWIND	v -WOUND, -WINDING, -WINDS to enwind
INWRAP	v -WRAPPED, -WRAPPING, -WRAPS to enwrap
IODATE	v -DATED, -DATING, -DATES to iodize
IODATION	n pl. -S the act of iodating
IODIC	adj pertaining to iodine
IODID	n pl. -S iodide
IODIDE	n pl. -S a compound of iodine
IODIN	n pl. -S iodine
IODINATE	v -ATED, -ATING, -ATES to iodize
IODINE	n pl. -S a nonmetallic element
IODISE	v -DISED, -DISING, -DISES iodize
IODISM	n pl. -S iodine poisoning
IODIZE	v -DIZED, -DIZING, -DIZES to treat with iodine
IODIZER	n pl. -S one that iodizes
IODOFORM	n pl. -S an iodine compound
IODOPHOR	n pl. -S an iodine compound
IODOPSIN	n pl. -S a pigment in the retina
IODOUS	adj pertaining to iodine
IOLITE	n pl. -S a mineral
ION	n pl. -S an electrically charged atom
IONIC	n pl. -S a style of type
IONICITY	n pl. -TIES the state of existing as or like an ion
IONISE	v -ISED, -ISING, -ISES to ionize
IONIUM	n pl. -S an isotope of thorium
IONIZE	v -IZED, -IZING, -IZES to convert into ions
IONIZER	n pl. -S one that ionizes
IONOGEN	n pl. -S a compound capable of forming ions
IONOMER	n pl. -S a type of plastic
IONONE	n pl. -S a chemical compound
IOTA	n pl. -S a Greek letter
IOTACISM	n pl. -S excessive use of the letter iota
IPECAC	n pl. -S a medicinal plant
IPOMOEA	n pl. -S a flowering plant
IRACUND	adj easily angered
IRADE	n pl. -S a decree of a Muslim ruler
IRATE	adj IRATER, IRATEST angry **IRATELY** adv
IRE	v IRED, IRING, IRES to anger
IREFUL	adj angry **IREFULLY** adv

IRELESS *adj* not angry
IRENIC *adj* peaceful in purpose
IRENICAL *adj* irenic
IRENICS *n/pl* a branch of theology
IRID *n* pl. -S a plant of the iris family
IRIDES a pl. of iris
IRIDIC *adj* pertaining to iridium
IRIDIUM *n* pl. -S a metallic element
IRING present participle of ire
IRIS *n* pl. IRISES or IRIDES a part of the eye
IRIS *v* -ED, -ING, -ES to give the form of a rainbow to
IRITIS *n* pl. -TISES inflammation of the iris IRITIC *adj*
IRK *v* -ED, -ING, -S to annoy or weary
IRKSOME *adj* tending to irk
IROKO *n* pl. -KOS a large African tree
IRON *v* -ED, -ING, -S to furnish with iron (a metallic element)
IRONBARK *n* pl. -S a timber tree
IRONCLAD *n* pl. -S an armored warship
IRONE *n* pl. -S an aromatic oil
IRONER *n* pl. -S a machine for pressing clothes
IRONIC *adj* pertaining to irony
IRONICAL *adj* ironic
IRONIES pl. of irony
IRONING *n* pl. -S clothes pressed or to be pressed
IRONIST *n* pl. -S one who uses irony
IRONIZE *v* -NIZED, -NIZING, -NIZES to mix with nutritional iron
IRONLIKE *adj* resembling iron
IRONNESS *n* pl. -ES the state of being iron
IRONSIDE *n* pl. -S a man of great strength
IRONWARE *n* pl. -S articles made of iron
IRONWEED *n* pl. -S a shrub
IRONWOOD *n* pl. -S a hardwood tree
IRONWORK *n* pl. -S objects made of iron
IRONY *n* pl. -NIES the use of words to express the opposite of what is literally said
IRREAL *adj* not real
IRRIGATE *v* -GATED, -GATING, -GATES to supply with water by artificial means
IRRITANT *n* pl. -S something that irritates
IRRITATE *v* -TATED, -TATING, -TATES to excite to impatience or anger

IRRUPT *v* -ED, -ING, -S to rush in forcibly
IS present 3d person sing. of be
ISAGOGE *n* pl. -S a type of introduction to a branch of study
ISAGOGIC *n* pl. -S a branch of theology
ISARITHM *n* pl. -S an isopleth
ISATIN *n* pl. -S a chemical compound ISATINIC *adj*
ISATINE *n* pl. -S isatin
ISBA *n* pl. -S a Russian log hut
ISCHEMIA *n* pl. -S a type of anemia ISCHEMIC *adj*
ISCHIUM *n* pl. -CHIA a pelvic bone ISCHIAL *adj*
ISLAND *v* -ED, -ING, -S to make into an island (a land area entirely surrounded by water)
ISLANDER *n* pl. -S one that lives on an island
ISLE *v* ISLED, ISLING, ISLES to place on an isle (a small island)
ISLELESS *adj* lacking an isle
ISLET *n* pl. -S a small island
ISLING present participle of isle
ISM *n* pl. -S a distinctive theory or doctrine
ISOBAR *n* pl. -S a type of atom ISOBARIC *adj*
ISOBARE *n* pl. -S isobar
ISOBATH *n* pl. -S a line on a map connecting points of equal water depth
ISOCHEIM *n* pl. -S a type of isotherm
ISOCHIME *n* pl. -S isocheim
ISOCHOR *n* pl. -S isochore
ISOCHORE *n* pl. -S a curve used to show a relationship between pressure and temperature
ISOCHRON *n* pl. -S a line on a chart connecting points representing the same time
ISOCLINE *n* pl. -S a type of rock formation
ISOCRACY *n* pl. -CIES a form of government
ISODOSE *adj* pertaining to zones that receive equal doses of radiation
ISOGAMY *n* pl. -MIES the fusion of two similar gametes
ISOGENIC *adj* genetically similar
ISOGENY *n* pl. -NIES the state of being of similar origin

ISOGLOSS n pl. -ES a line on a map between linguistically varied areas

ISOGON n pl. -S a polygon having equal angles

ISOGONAL n pl. -S isogone

ISOGONE n pl. -S a line on a map used to show characteristics of the earth's magnetic field

ISOGONIC n pl. -S isogone

ISOGONY n pl. -NIES an equivalent relative growth of parts

ISOGRAFT v -ED, -ING, -S to transplant from one individual to another of the same species

ISOGRAM n pl. -S a line on a map connecting points of equal value

ISOGRAPH n pl. -S a line on a map indicating areas that are linguistically similar

ISOGRIV n pl. -S a line drawn on a map such that all points have equal grid variation

ISOHEL n pl. -S a line on a map connecting points receiving equal sunshine

ISOHYET n pl. -S a line on a map connecting points having equal rainfall

ISOLABLE adj capable of being isolated

ISOLATE v -LATED, -LATING, -LATES to set apart from others

ISOLATOR n pl. -S one that isolates

ISOLEAD n pl. -S a line on a ballistic graph

ISOLINE n pl. -S an isogram

ISOLOG n pl. -S isologue

ISOLOGUE n pl. -S a type of chemical compound

ISOMER n pl. -S a type of chemical compound **ISOMERIC** adj

ISOMETRY n pl. -TRIES equality of measure

ISOMORPH n pl. -S something similar to something else in form

ISONOMY n pl. -MIES equality of civil rights **ISONOMIC** adj

ISOPACH n pl. -S an isogram connecting points of equal thickness

ISOPHOTE n pl. -S a curve on a chart joining points of equal light intensity

ISOPLETH n pl. -S a type of isogram

ISOPOD n pl. -S a kind of crustacean

ISOPODAN n pl. -S an isopod

ISOPRENE n pl. -S a volatile liquid

ISOSPIN n pl. -S a type of quantum number

ISOSPORY n pl. -RIES the condition of producing sexual or asexual spores of but one kind

ISOSTASY n pl. -SIES the state of balance in the earth's crust

ISOTACH n pl. -S a line on a map connecting points of equal wind velocity

ISOTHERE n pl. -S a type of isotherm

ISOTHERM n pl. -S a line on a map connecting points of equal mean temperature

ISOTONE n pl. -S a type of atom

ISOTONIC adj of equal tension

ISOTOPE n pl. -S a form of an element **ISOTOPIC** adj

ISOTOPY n pl. -PIES the state of being an isotope

ISOTROPY n pl. -PIES the state of being identical in all directions

ISOTYPE n pl. -S a type of diagram **ISOTYPIC** adj

ISOZYME n pl. -S a type of enzyme **ISOZYMIC** adj

ISSEI n pl. -S a Japanese immigrant to the United States

ISSUABLE adj authorized for issuing **ISSUABLY** adv

ISSUANCE n pl. -S the act of issuing

ISSUANT adj coming forth

ISSUE v -SUED, -SUING, -SUES to come forth

ISSUER n pl. -S one that issues

ISTHMI a pl. of isthmus

ISTHMIAN n pl. -S a native of an isthmus

ISTHMIC adj pertaining to an isthmus

ISTHMOID adj isthmic

ISTHMUS n pl. -MUSES or -MI a strip of land connecting two larger land masses

ISTLE n pl. -S a strong fiber

IT pron the 3d person sing. neuter pronoun

ITALIC n pl. -S a style of print

ITCH v -ED, -ING, -ES to have an uneasy or tingling skin sensation

ITCHING n pl. -S an uneasy or tingling skin sensation

ITCHY adj ITCHIER, ITCHIEST causing an itching sensation **ITCHILY** adv

ITEM v -ED, -ING, -S to itemize

ITEMISE	v -ISED, -ISING, -ISES itemize
ITEMIZE	v -IZED, -IZING, -IZES to set down the particulars of
ITEMIZER	n pl. -S one that itemizes
ITERANCE	n pl. -S repetition
ITERANT	adj repeating
ITERATE	v -ATED, -ATING, -ATES to repeat
ITERUM	adv again; once more
ITHER	adj other
ITS	pron the possessive form of the pronoun it
ITSELF	pron a reflexive form of the pronoun it

IVIED	adj covered with ivy
IVORY	n pl. -RIES a hard white substance found in elephant tusks
IVY	n pl. IVIES a climbing vine
IVYLIKE adj	
IWIS	adv certainly
IXIA	n pl. -S a flowering plant
IXODID	n pl. -S a bloodsucking insect
IXORA	n pl. -S a flowering plant
IXTLE	n pl. -S istle
IZAR	n pl. -S an outer garment worn by Muslim women
IZZARD	n pl. -S the letter Z

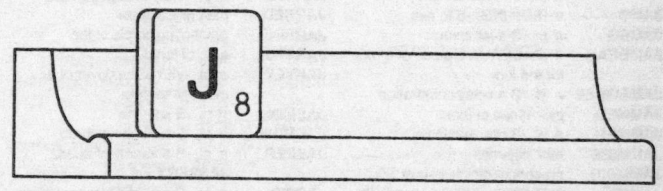

JAB	v JABBED, JABBING, JABS to poke sharply	**JADE**	v JADED, JADING, JADES to weary JADEDLY adv
JABBER	v -ED, -ING, -S to talk rapidly	**JADEITE**	n pl. -S a mineral JADITIC adj
JABBERER	n pl. -S one that jabbers	**JADISH**	adj worn-out JADISHLY adv
JABBING	present participle of jab	**JAEGER**	n pl. -S a hunter
JABIRU	n pl. -S a wading bird	**JAG**	v JAGGED, JAGGING, JAGS to cut unevenly
JABOT	n pl. -S a decoration on a shirt		
JACAL	n pl. -ES or -S a hut	**JAGER**	n pl. -S jaeger
JACAMAR	n pl. -S a tropical bird	**JAGG**	v -ED, -ING, -S to jag
JACANA	n pl. -S a wading bird	**JAGGARY**	n pl. -RIES jaggery
JACINTH	n pl. -S a variety of zircon	**JAGGED**	adj -GEDER, -GEDEST having a sharply uneven edge or surface JAGGEDLY adv
JACINTHE	n pl. -S an orange color		
JACK	v -ED, -ING, -S to raise with a type of lever		
		JAGGER	n pl. -S one that jags
JACKAL	n pl. -S a doglike mammal	**JAGGERY**	n pl. -GERIES a coarse, dark sugar
JACKAROO	n pl. -ROOS jackeroo		
JACKASS	n pl. -ES a male donkey	**JAGGHERY**	n pl. -GHERIES jaggery
JACKBOOT	n pl. -S a heavy boot	**JAGGING**	present participle of jag
JACKDAW	n pl. -S a crowlike bird	**JAGGY**	adj -GIER, -GIEST jagged
JACKER	n pl. -S one that jacks	**JAGLESS**	adj smooth and even
JACKEROO	n pl. -ROOS an inexperienced ranch hand	**JAGRA**	n pl. -S jaggery
		JAGUAR	n pl. -S a large feline animal
JACKET	v -ED, -ING, -S to provide with a jacket (a short coat)	**JAIL**	v -ED, -ING, -S to put in jail (a place of confinement)
JACKFISH	n pl. -ES a food fish		
JACKIES	pl. of jacky	**JAILBAIT**	n pl. JAILBAIT a girl under the age of consent with whom sexual intercourse constitutes statutory rape
JACKLEG	n pl. -S an unskilled worker		
JACKPOT	n pl. -S a top prize or reward		
JACKROLL	v -ED, -ING, -S to rob a drunken or sleeping person		
		JAILBIRD	n pl. -S a prisoner
JACKSTAY	n pl. -STAYS a rope on a ship	**JAILER**	n pl. -S a keeper of a jail
JACKY	n pl. JACKIES a sailor	**JAILOR**	n pl. -S jailer
JACOBIN	n pl. -S a pigeon	**JAKE**	adj all right; fine
JACOBUS	n pl. -ES an old English coin	**JAKES**	n/pl an outhouse
JACONET	n pl. -S a cotton cloth	**JALAP**	n pl. -S a Mexican plant JALAPIC adj
JACQUARD	n pl. -S a fabric of intricate weave		
		JALAPENO	n pl. -NOS a hot pepper
JACULATE	v -LATED, -LATING, -LATES to throw	**JALAPIN**	n pl. -S a medicinal substance contained in jalap
		JALOP	n pl. -S jalap

JALOPPY	n pl. -PIES jalopy
JALOPY	n pl. -LOPIES a decrepit car
JALOUSIE	n pl. -S a type of window
JAM	v JAMMED, JAMMING, JAMS to force together tightly
JAMB	v -ED, -ING, -S to jam
JAMBE	n pl. -S a jambeau
JAMBEAU	n pl. -BEAUX a piece of armor for the leg
JAMBOREE	n pl. -S a noisy celebration
JAMMED	past tense of jam
JAMMER	n pl. -S one that jams
JAMMIES	n/pl pajamas
JAMMING	present participle of jam
JAMMY	adj -MIER, -MIEST sticky with jam (boiled fruit and sugar)
JANE	n pl. -S a girl or woman
JANGLE	v -GLED, -GLING, -GLES to make a harsh, metallic sound
JANGLER	n pl. -S one that jangles
JANGLY	adj -GLIER, -GLIEST jangling
JANIFORM	adj hypocritical
JANISARY	n pl. -SARIES janizary
JANITOR	n pl. -S a maintenance man
JANIZARY	n pl. -ZARIES a Turkish soldier
JANTY	adj jaunty
JAPAN	v -PANNED, -PANNING, -PANS to coat with a glossy, black lacquer
JAPANIZE	v -NIZED, -NIZING, -NIZES to make Japanese
JAPANNER	n pl. -S one that japans
JAPANNING	present participle of japan
JAPE	v JAPED, JAPING, JAPES to mock
JAPER	n pl. -S one that japes
JAPERY	n pl. -ERIES mockery
JAPING	present participle of jape
JAPINGLY	adv in a japing manner
JAPONICA	n pl. -S an Asian shrub
JAR	v JARRED, JARRING, JARS to cause to shake
JARFUL	n pl. JARFULS or JARSFUL the quantity held by a jar (a cylindrical container)
JARGON	v -ED, -ING, -S to speak or write an obscure and often pretentious kind of language
JARGONEL	n pl. -S a variety of pear
JARGOON	n pl. -S a variety of zircon
JARHEAD	n pl. -S a marine soldier
JARINA	n pl. -S the hard seed of a palm tree
JARL	n pl. -S a Scandinavian nobleman
JARLDOM	n pl. -S the domain of a jarl
JAROSITE	n pl. -S a mineral
JAROVIZE	v -VIZED, -VIZING, -VIZES to hasten the flowering of a plant
JARRAH	n pl. -S an evergreen tree
JARRED	past tense of jar
JARRING	present participle of jar
JARSFUL	a pl. of jarful
JARVEY	n pl. -VEYS the driver of a carriage for hire
JASMIN	n pl. -S jasmine
JASMINE	n pl. -S a climbing shrub
JASPER	n pl. -S a variety of quartz
JASPERY	adj
JASSID	n pl. -S any of a family of plant pests
JATO	n pl. -TOS a takeoff aided by jet propulsion
JAUK	v -ED, -ING, -S to dawdle
JAUNCE	v JAUNCED, JAUNCING, JAUNCES to prance
JAUNDICE	v -DICED, -DICING, -DICES to prejudice unfavorably
JAUNT	v -ED, -ING, -S to make a pleasure trip
JAUNTY	adj -TIER, -TIEST having a lively and self-confident manner JAUNTILY adv
JAUP	v -ED, -ING, -S to splash
JAVA	n pl. -S coffee
JAVELIN	v -ED, -ING, -S to pierce with a javelin (a light spear)
JAVELINA	n pl. -S a peccary
JAW	v -ED, -ING, -S to jabber
JAWAN	n pl. -S a soldier of India
JAWBONE	v -BONED, -BONING, -BONES to attempt to convince
JAWBONER	n pl. -S one that jawbones
JAWLIKE	adj resembling the jaw (the framework of the mouth)
JAWLINE	n pl. -S the outline of the lower jaw
JAY	n pl. JAYS a corvine bird
JAYBIRD	n pl. -S a jay
JAYGEE	n pl. -S a military officer
JAYVEE	n pl. -S a junior varsity player
JAYWALK	v -ED, -ING, -S to cross a street recklessly
JAZZ	v -ED, -ING, -ES to enliven
JAZZER	n pl. -S one that jazzes
JAZZLIKE	adj resembling a type of music
JAZZMAN	n pl. -MEN a type of musician
JAZZY	adj JAZZIER, JAZZIEST lively JAZZILY adv

JEALOUS *adj* resentful of another's advantages

JEALOUSY *n pl.* -SIES a jealous feeling

JEAN *n pl.* -S a durable cotton fabric

JEBEL *n pl.* -S a mountain

JEE *v* JEED, JEEING, JEES to gee

JEEP *v* -ED, -ING, -S to travel by a small type of motor vehicle

JEEPERS *interj* — used as a mild oath

JEEPNEY *n pl.* -NEYS a Philippine jitney

JEER *v* -ED, -ING, -S to mock

JEERER *n pl.* -S one that jeers

JEEZ *interj* — used as a mild oath

JEFE *n pl.* -S a chief

JEHAD *n pl.* -S jihad

JEHU *n pl.* -S a fast driver

JEJUNA *pl.* of jejunum

JEJUNAL *adj* pertaining to the jejunum

JEJUNE *adj* uninteresting; childish JEJUNELY *adv*

JEJUNITY *n pl.* -TIES something that is jejune

JEJUNUM *n pl.* -NA a part of the small intestine

JELL *v* -ED, -ING, -S to congeal

JELLABA *n pl.* -S djellaba

JELLIFY *v* -FIED, -FYING, -FIES to jelly

JELLY *v* -LIED, -LYING, -LIES to make into a jelly (a soft, semisolid substance)

JELUTONG *n pl.* -S a tropical tree

JEMADAR *n pl.* -S an officer in the army of India

JEMIDAR *n pl.* -S jemadar

JEMMY *v* -MIED, -MYING, -MIES to jimmy

JENNET *n pl.* -S a small horse

JENNY *n pl.* -NIES a female donkey

JEON *n pl.* JEON a monetary unit of South Korea

JEOPARD *v* -ED, -ING, -S to imperil

JEOPARDY *n pl.* -DIES risk of loss or injury

JERBOA *n pl.* -S a small rodent

JEREED *n pl.* -S a wooden javelin

JEREMIAD *n pl.* -S a tale of woe

JERID *n pl.* -S jereed

JERK *v* -ED, -ING, -S to move with a sharp, sudden motion

JERKER *n pl.* -S one that jerks

JERKIES *pl.* of jerky

JERKIN *n pl.* -S a sleeveless jacket

JERKY *adj* JERKIER, JERKIEST characterized by jerking movements JERKILY *adv*

JERKY *n pl.* -KIES dried meat

JEROBOAM *n pl.* -S a wine bottle

JERREED *n pl.* -S jereed

JERRICAN *n pl.* -S jerrycan

JERRID *n pl.* -S jereed

JERRY *n pl.* -RIES a German soldier

JERRYCAN *n pl.* -S a fuel container

JERSEY *n pl.* -SEYS a close-fitting knitted shirt JERSEYED *adj*

JESS *v* -ED, -ING, -ES to fasten straps around the legs of a hawk

JESSANT *adj* shooting forth

JESSE *v* JESSED, JESSING, JESSES to jess

JEST *v* -ED, -ING, -S to joke

JESTER *n pl.* -S one that jests

JESTFUL *adj* tending to jest

JESTING *n pl.* -S the act of one who jests

JET *v* JETTED, JETTING, JETS to spurt forth in a stream

JETBEAD *n pl.* -S an ornamental shrub

JETE *n pl.* -S a ballet leap

JETLIKE *adj* resembling a jet airplane

JETLINER *n pl.* -S a type of aircraft

JETON *n pl.* -S jetton

JETPORT *n pl.* -S a type of airport

JETSAM *n pl.* -S goods cast overboard

JETSOM *n pl.* -S jetsam

JETTED past tense of jet

JETTIED past tense of jetty

JETTIER comparative of jetty

JETTIES present 3d person sing. of jetty

JETTIEST superlative of jetty

JETTING present participle of jet

JETTISON *v* -ED, -ING, -S to cast overboard

JETTON *n pl.* -S a piece used in counting

JETTY *v* -TIED, -TYING, -TIES to jut

JETTY *adj* -TIER, -TIEST having the color jet black

JEU *n pl.* JEUX a game

JEWEL *v* -ELED, -ELING, -ELS or -ELLED, -ELLING, -ELS to adorn or equip with jewels (precious stones)

JEWELER *n pl.* -S a dealer or maker of jewelry

JEWELLER *n pl.* -S jeweler

JEWELLING a present participle of jewel

JEWELRY *n pl.* -RIES an article or articles for personal adornment

JEWFISH *n pl.* -ES a large marine fish

JEZAIL *n pl.* -S a type of firearm

JEZEBEL *n pl.* -S a scheming, wicked woman

JIAO *n pl.* JIAO chiao

JIB *v* JIBBED, JIBBING, JIBS to refuse to proceed further

JIBB *v* -ED, -ING, -S to shift from side to side while sailing

JIBBER *n pl.* -S a horse that jibs

JIBBING present participle of jib

JIBBOOM *n pl.* -S a ship's spar

JIBE *v* JIBED, JIBING, JIBES to gibe JIBINGLY *adv*

JIBER *n pl.* -S one that jibes

JICAMA *n pl.* -S a tropical plant with edible roots

JIFF *n pl.* -S jiffy

JIFFY *n pl.* -FIES a short time

JIG *v* JIGGED, JIGGING, JIGS to bob

JIGGER *v* -ED, -ING, -S to jerk up and down

JIGGERED *adj* damned

JIGGING present participle of jig

JIGGLE *v* -GLED, -GLING, -GLES to shake lightly

JIGGLY *adj* -GLIER, -GLIEST unsteady

JIGSAW *v* -SAWED, -SAWN, -SAWING, -SAWS to cut with a type of saw

JIHAD *n pl.* -S a Muslim holy war

JILL *n pl.* -S a unit of liquid measure

JILLION *n pl.* -S a very large number

JILT *v* -ED, -ING, -S to reject a lover

JILTER *n pl.* -S one that jilts

JIMINY *interj* — used to express surprise

JIMJAMS *n/pl* violent delirium

JIMMINY *interj* jiminy

JIMMY *v* -MIED, -MYING, -MIES to pry open with a crowbar

JIMP *adj* JIMPER, JIMPEST natty JIMPLY *adv*

JIMPY *adj* jimp

JIN *n pl.* -S jinn

JINGAL *n pl.* -S a heavy musket

JINGALL *n pl.* -S a jingal

JINGKO *n pl.* -KOES ginkgo

JINGLE *v* -GLED, -GLING, -GLES to make a tinkling sound

JINGLER *n pl.* -S one that jingles

JINGLY *adj* -GLIER, -GLIEST jingling

JINGO *n pl.* -GOES a zealous patriot JINGOISH *adj*

JINGOISM *n pl.* -S the spirit or policy of jingoes

JINGOIST *n pl.* -S a jingo

JINK *v* -ED, -ING, -S to move quickly out of the way

JINKER *n pl.* -S one that jinks

JINN *n pl.* -S a supernatural being in Muslim mythology

JINNEE *n pl.* JINN jinn

JINNI *n pl.* JINN jinn

JINX *v* -ED, -ING, -ES to bring bad luck to

JIPIJAPA *n pl.* -S a tropical plant

JITNEY *n pl.* -NEYS a small bus

JITTER *v* -ED, -ING, -S to fidget

JITTERY *adj* -TERIER, -TERIEST extremely nervous

JIUJITSU *n pl.* -S jujitsu

JIUJUTSU *n pl.* -S jujitsu

JIVE *v* JIVED, JIVING, JIVES to play jazz or swing music

JIVEASS *adj* insincere, phony

JIVER *n pl.* -S one that jives

JIVEY *adj* JIVIER, JIVIEST jazzy, lively

JNANA *n pl.* -S knowledge acquired through meditation

JO *n pl.* JOES a sweetheart

JOANNES *n pl.* JOANNES johannes

JOB *v* JOBBED, JOBBING, JOBS to work by the piece

JOBBER *n pl.* -S a pieceworker

JOBBERY *n pl.* -BERIES corruption in public office

JOBBING present participle of job

JOBLESS *adj* having no job

JOBNAME *n pl.* -S a computer code for a job instruction

JOCK *n pl.* -S an athletic supporter

JOCKETTE *n pl.* -S a woman who rides horses in races

JOCKEY *v* -EYED, -EYING, -EYS to maneuver for an advantage

JOCKO *n pl.* JOCKOS a monkey

JOCOSE *adj* humorous JOCOSELY *adv*

JOCOSITY *n pl.* -TIES the state of being jocose

JOCULAR *adj* given to joking

JOCUND *adj* cheerful JOCUNDLY *adv*

JODHPUR *n pl.* -S a type of boot

JOE *n pl.* -S a fellow

JOEY n pl. -EYS a young kangaroo

JOG v JOGGED, JOGGING, JOGS to run at a slow, steady pace

JOGGER n pl. -S one that jogs

JOGGING n pl. -S the practice of running at a slow, steady pace

JOGGLE v -GLED, -GLING, -GLES to shake slightly

JOGGLER n pl. -S one that joggles

JOHANNES n pl. JOHANNES a Portuguese coin

JOHN n pl. -S a toilet

JOHNBOAT n pl. -S a narrow square-ended boat

JOHNNY n pl. -NIES a sleeveless hospital gown

JOIN v -ED, -ING, -S to unite JOINABLE adj

JOINDER n pl. -S a joining of parties in a lawsuit

JOINER n pl. -S a carpenter

JOINERY n pl. -ERIES the trade of a joiner

JOINING n pl. -S a juncture

JOINT v -ED, -ING, -S to fit together by means of a junction

JOINTER n pl. -S one that joints

JOINTLY adv together

JOINTURE v -TURED, -TURING, -TURES to set aside property as an inheritance

JOIST v -ED, -ING, -S to support with horizontal beams

JOJOBA n pl. -S a small tree

JOKE v JOKED, JOKING, JOKES to say something amusing

JOKER n pl. -S one that jokes

JOKESTER n pl. -S a practical joker

JOKEY adj JOKIER, JOKIEST amusing JOKILY adv

JOKIER comparative of jokey

JOKIEST superlative of jokey

JOKINESS n pl. -ES the state of being jokey

JOKING present participle of joke

JOKINGLY adv in a joking manner

JOKY adj JOKIER, JOKIEST jokey

JOLE n pl. -S jowl

JOLLIED past tense of jolly

JOLLIER comparative of jolly

JOLLIES present 3d person sing. of jolly

JOLLIEST superlative of jolly

JOLLIFY v -FIED, -FYING, -FIES to make jolly

JOLLITY n pl. -TIES mirth

JOLLY adj -LIER, -LIEST cheerful JOLLILY adv

JOLLY v -LIED, -LYING, -LIES to put in a good humor for one's own purposes

JOLT v -ED, -ING, -S to jar or shake roughly

JOLTER n pl. -S one that jolts

JOLTY adj JOLTIER, JOLTIEST marked by a jolting motion JOLTILY adv

JONES n pl. JONESES a drug addiction

JONGLEUR n pl. -S a minstrel

JONQUIL n pl. -S a perennial herb

JORAM n pl. -S a jorum

JORDAN n pl. -S a type of container

JORUM n pl. -S a large drinking bowl

JOSEPH n pl. -S a woman's long cloak

JOSH v -ED, -ING, -ES to tease

JOSHER n pl. -S one that joshes

JOSS n pl. -ES a Chinese idol

JOSTLE v -TLED, -TLING, -TLES to bump or push roughly

JOSTLER n pl. -S one that jostles

JOT v JOTTED, JOTTING, JOTS to write down quickly

JOTA n pl. -S a Spanish dance

JOTTER n pl. -S one that jots

JOTTING n pl. -S a brief note

JOTTY adj written down quickly

JOUAL n pl. -S a dialect of Canadian French

JOUK v -ED, -ING, -S to dodge

JOULE n pl. -S a unit of energy

JOUNCE v JOUNCED, JOUNCING, JOUNCES to move roughly up and down

JOUNCY adj JOUNCIER, JOUNCIEST marked by a jouncing motion

JOURNAL n pl. -S a record of daily events

JOURNEY v -ED, -ING, -S to travel

JOUST v -ED, -ING, -S to engage in personal combat

JOUSTER n pl. -S one that jousts

JOVIAL adj good-humored JOVIALLY adv

JOVIALTY n pl. -TIES the quality or state of being jovial

JOW v -ED, -ING, -S to toll

JOWAR n pl. -S a durra grown in India

JOWL n pl. -S the fleshy part under the lower jaw JOWLED adj

JOWLY adj JOWLIER, JOWLIEST having prominent jowls

JOY	v -ED, -ING, -S to rejoice
JOYANCE	n pl. -S gladness
JOYFUL	adj -FULLER, -FULLEST happy **JOYFULLY** adv
JOYLESS	adj being without gladness
JOYOUS	adj joyful **JOYOUSLY** adv
JOYPOP	v -POPPED, -POPPING, -POPS to use habit-forming drugs occasionally
JOYRIDE	v -RODE, -RIDDEN, -RIDING, -RIDES to take an automobile ride for pleasure
JOYRIDER	n pl. -S one that joyrides
JOYSTICK	n pl. -S the control stick in an airplane
JUBA	n pl. -S a lively dance
JUBBAH	n pl. -S a loose outer garment
JUBE	n pl. -S a platform in a church
JUBHAH	n pl. -S jubbah
JUBILANT	adj exultant
JUBILATE	v -LATED, -LATING, -LATES to exult
JUBILE	n pl. -S jubilee
JUBILEE	n pl. -S a celebration
JUDAS	n pl. -ES a peephole
JUDDER	v -ED, -ING, -S to vibrate
JUDGE	v JUDGED, JUDGING, JUDGES to decide on critically
JUDGER	n pl. -S one that judges
JUDGMENT	n pl. -S an authoritative opinion
JUDICIAL	adj pertaining to courts of law
JUDO	n pl. -DOS a form of jujitsu
JUDOIST	n pl. -S one skilled in judo
JUDOKA	n pl. -S a judoist
JUG	v JUGGED, JUGGING, JUGS to put into a jug (a large, deep container with a narrow mouth and a handle)
JUGA	a pl. of jugum
JUGAL	adj pertaining to the cheek or cheekbone
JUGATE	adj occurring in pairs
JUGFUL	n pl. JUGFULS or JUGSFUL as much as a jug will hold
JUGGED	past tense of jug
JUGGING	present participle of jug
JUGGLE	v -GLED, -GLING, -GLES to perform feats of manual dexterity
JUGGLER	n pl. -S one that juggles
JUGGLERY	n pl. -GLERIES the art of a juggler
JUGGLING	n pl. -S jugglery
JUGHEAD	n pl. -S a dolt
JUGSFUL	a pl. of jugful

JUGULA	pl. of jugulum
JUGULAR	n pl. -S a vein of the neck
JUGULATE	v -LATED, -LATING, -LATES to suppress a disease by extreme measures
JUGULUM	n pl. -LA a part of a bird's neck
JUGUM	n pl. -GA or -GUMS a pair of the opposite leaflets of a pinnate leaf
JUICE	v JUICED, JUICING, JUICES to extract the juice (the liquid part of a fruit or vegetable) from
JUICER	n pl. -S a juice extractor
JUICY	adj JUICIER, JUICIEST full of juice **JUICILY** adv
JUJITSU	n pl. -S a Japanese art of self-defense
JUJU	n pl. -S an object regarded as having magical power
JUJUBE	n pl. -S a fruit-flavored candy
JUJUISM	n pl. -S the system of beliefs connected with jujus
JUJUIST	n pl. -S a follower of jujuism
JUJUTSU	n pl. -S jujitsu
JUKE	v JUKED, JUKING, JUKES to fake out of position
JUKEBOX	n pl. -ES a coin-operated phonograph
JULEP	n pl. -S a sweet drink
JULIENNE	v -ENNED, -ENNING, -ENNES to cut food into long thin strips
JUMBAL	n pl. -S a ring-shaped cookie
JUMBLE	v -BLED, -BLING, -BLES to mix in a disordered manner
JUMBLER	n pl. -S one that jumbles
JUMBO	n pl. -BOS a very large specimen of its kind
JUMBUCK	n pl. -S a sheep
JUMP	v -ED, -ING, -S to spring off the ground
JUMPER	n pl. -S one that jumps
JUMPOFF	n pl. -S a starting point
JUMPSUIT	n pl. -S a one-piece garment
JUMPY	adj JUMPIER, JUMPIEST nervous **JUMPILY** adv
JUN	n pl. JUN a coin of North Korea
JUNCO	n pl. -COS or -COES a small finch
JUNCTION	n pl. -S a place where things join
JUNCTURE	n pl. -S the act of joining

JUNGLE *n* pl. -S land covered with dense tropical vegetation JUNGLED *adj*

JUNGLY *adj* -GLIER, -GLIEST resembling a jungle

JUNIOR *n* pl. -S a person who is younger than another

JUNIPER *n* pl. -S an evergreen tree

JUNK *v* -ED, -ING, -S to discard as trash

JUNKER *n* pl. -S something ready for junking

JUNKET *v* -ED, -ING, -S to banquet

JUNKETER *n* pl. -S one that junkets

JUNKIE *n* pl. -S a drug addict

JUNKMAN *n* pl. -MEN one who buys and sells junk

JUNKY *adj* JUNKIER, JUNKIEST worthless

JUNKYARD *n* pl. -S a place where junk is stored

JUNTA *n* pl. -S a political or governmental council

JUNTO *n* pl. -TOS a political faction

JUPE *n* pl. -S a woman's jacket

JUPON *n* pl. -S a tunic

JURA pl. of jus

JURAL *adj* pertaining to law JURALLY *adv*

JURANT *n* pl. -S one that takes an oath

JURAT *n* pl. -S a statement on an affidavit

JURATORY *adj* pertaining to an oath

JUREL *n* pl. -S a food fish

JURIDIC *adj* pertaining to the law

JURIST *n* pl. -S one versed in the law JURISTIC *adj*

JUROR *n* pl. -S a member of a jury

JURY *v* -RIED, -RYING, -RIES to select material for exhibition

JURYMAN *n* pl. -MEN a juror

JUS *n* pl. JURA a legal right

JUSSIVE *n* pl. -S a word used to express command

JUST *v* -ED, -ING, -S to joust

JUST *adj* JUSTER, JUSTEST acting in conformity with what is morally good

JUSTER *n* pl. -S jouster

JUSTICE *n* pl. -S a judge

JUSTIFY *v* -FIED, -FYING, -FIES to show to be just, right, or valid

JUSTLE *v* -TLED, -TLING, -TLES to jostle

JUSTLY *adv* in a just manner

JUSTNESS *n* pl. -ES the quality of being just

JUT *v* JUTTED, JUTTING, JUTS to protrude

JUTE *n* pl. -S a strong, coarse fiber

JUTTY *v* -TIED, -TYING, -TIES to jut

JUVENAL *n* pl. -S a young bird's plumage

JUVENILE *n* pl. -S a young person

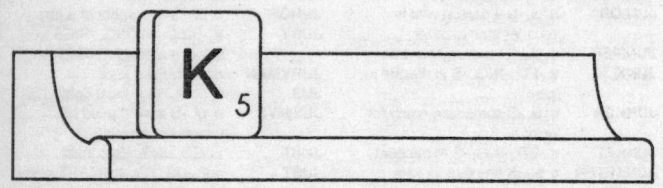

KA   *n* pl. -S the spiritual self of a human being in Egyptian religion

KAAS   *n* pl. KAAS kas

KAB   *n* pl. -S an ancient Hebrew unit of measure

KABAB   *n* pl. -S kabob

KABAKA   *n* pl. -S a Ugandan emperor

KABALA   *n* pl. -S cabala

KABAR   *n* pl. -S a caber

KABAYA   *n* pl. -S a cotton jacket

KABBALA   *n* pl. -S cabala

KABBALAH   *n* pl. -S cabala

KABELJOU   *n* pl. -S a large food fish

KABIKI   *n* pl. -S a tropical tree

KABOB   *n* pl. -S cubes of meat cooked on a skewer

KABUKI   *n* pl. -S a form of Japanese theater

KACHINA   *n* pl. -S an ancestral spirit

KADDISH   *n* pl. -DISHIM a Jewish prayer

KADI   *n* pl. -S cadi

KAE   *n* pl. -S a bird resembling a crow

KAF   *n* pl. -S kaph

KAFFIR   *n* pl. -S kafir

KAFFIYEH   *n* pl. -S a large, square kerchief

KAFIR   *n* pl. -S a cereal grass

KAFTAN   *n* pl. -S caftan

KAGU   *n* pl. -S a flightless bird

KAHUNA   *n* pl. -S a medicine man

KAIAK   *n* pl. -S kayak

KAIF   *n* pl. -S kef

KAIL   *n* pl. -S kale

KAILYARD   *n* pl. -S kaleyard

KAIN   *n* pl. -S a tax paid in produce or livestock

KAINIT   *n* pl. -S kainite

KAINITE   *n* pl. -S a mineral salt

KAISER   *n* pl. -S an emperor

KAISERIN   *n* pl. -S a kaiser's wife

KAJEPUT   *n* pl. -S cajuput

KAKA   *n* pl. -S a parrot

KAKAPO   *n* pl. -POS a flightless parrot

KAKEMONO   *n* pl. -NOS a Japanese scroll

KAKI   *n* pl. -S a Japanese tree

KAKIEMON   *n* pl. -S a Japanese porcelain

KALAM   *n* pl. -S a type of Muslim theology

KALE   *n* pl. -S a variety of cabbage

KALENDS   *n* pl. KALENDS calends

KALEWIFE   *n* pl. -WIVES a female vegetable vendor

KALEYARD   *n* pl. -S a kitchen garden

KALIAN   *n* pl. -S a hookah

KALIF   *n* pl. -S caliph

KALIFATE   *n* pl. -S califate

KALIMBA   *n* pl. -S an African musical instrument

KALIPH   *n* pl. -S caliph

KALIUM   *n* pl. -S potassium

KALLIDIN   *n* pl. -S a hormone

KALMIA   *n* pl. -S an evergreen shrub

KALONG   *n* pl. -S a fruit-eating bat

KALPA   *n* pl. -S a period of time in Hindu religion

KALPAK   *n* pl. -S calpac

KALYPTRA   *n* pl. -S a thin veil

KAMAAINA   *n* pl. -S a longtime resident of Hawaii

KAMACITE   *n* pl. -S an alloy of nickel and iron

KAMALA   *n* pl. -S an Asian tree

KAME   *n* pl. -S a mound of detrital material

KAMI   *n* pl. KAMI a sacred power or force

KAMIK *n* pl. -S a type of boot
KAMIKAZE *n* pl. -S a plane to be flown in a suicide crash on a target
KAMPONG *n* pl. -S a small village
KAMSEEN *n* pl. -S khamsin
KAMSIN *n* pl. -S khamsin
KANA *n* pl. -S the Japanese syllabic script
KANBAN *n* pl. -S a manufacturing strategy wherein parts are delivered only as needed
KANE *n* pl. -S kain
KANGAROO *n* pl. -ROOS an Australian mammal
KANJI *n* pl. -S a system of Japanese writing
KANTAR *n* pl. -S a unit of weight
KANTELE *n* pl. -S a type of harp
KAOLIANG *n* pl. -S an Asian sorghum
KAOLIN *n* pl. -S a fine white clay KAOLINIC *adj*
KAOLINE *n* pl. -S kaolin
KAON *n* pl. -S a type of meson
KAPA *n* pl. -S a coarse cloth
KAPH *n* pl. -S a Hebrew letter
KAPOK *n* pl. -S a mass of silky fibers
KAPPA *n* pl. -S a Greek letter
KAPUT *adj* ruined
KAPUTT *adj* kaput
KARAKUL *n* pl. -S an Asian sheep
KARAOKE *n* pl. -S a musical device to which a user sings along
KARAT *n* pl. -S a unit of quality for gold
KARATE *n* pl. -S a Japanese art of self-defense
KARMA *n* pl. -S the force generated by a person's actions KARMIC *adj*
KARN *n* pl. -S cairn
KAROO *n* pl. -ROOS karroo
KAROSS *n* pl. -ES an African garment
KARROO *n* pl. -ROOS a dry plateau
KARST *n* pl. -S a limestone region KARSTIC *adj*
KART *n* pl. -S a small motor vehicle
KARTING *n* pl. -S the sport of racing karts
KARYOTIN *n* pl. -S the nuclear material of a cell
KAS *n* pl. KAS a large cupboard
KASBAH *n* pl. -S casbah
KASHA *n* pl. -S a cooked cereal
KASHER *v* -ED, -ING, -S to kosher
KASHMIR *n* pl. -S cashmere
KASHRUT *n* pl. -S kashruth

KASHRUTH *n* pl. -S the Jewish dietary laws
KAT *n* pl. -S an evergreen shrub
KATA *n* pl. -S an exercise of set movements
KATAKANA *n* pl. -S a Japanese syllabic symbol
KATCHINA *n* pl. -S kachina
KATCINA *n* pl. -S kachina
KATHODE *n* pl. -S cathode KATHODAL, KATHODIC *adj*
KATION *n* pl. -S cation
KATYDID *n* pl. -S a grasshopper
KAURI *n* pl. -S a timber tree
KAURY *n* pl. -RIES kauri
KAVA *n* pl. -S a tropical shrub
KAVAKAVA *n* pl. -S kava
KAVASS *n* pl. -ES a Turkish policeman
KAY *n* pl. KAYS the letter K
KAYAK *v* -ED, -ING, -S to travel in a kayak (an Eskimo canoe)
KAYAKER *n* pl. -S one that rides in a kayak
KAYAKING *n* pl. -S the act or skill of managing a kayak
KAYLES *n/pl* a British game
KAYO *v* -ED, -ING, -S or -ES to knock out
KAZACHOK *n* pl. -ZACHKI a Russian folk dance
KAZATSKI *n* pl. -ES kazachok
KAZATSKY *n* pl. -SKIES kazachok
KAZOO *n* pl. -ZOOS a toy musical instrument
KBAR *n* pl. -S a kilobar
KEA *n* pl. -S a parrot
KEBAB *n* pl. -S a kabob
KEBAR *n* pl. -S a caber
KEBBIE *n* pl. -S a rough walking stick
KEBBOCK *n* pl. -S kebbuck
KEBBUCK *n* pl. -S a whole cheese
KEBLAH *n* pl. -S a kiblah
KEBOB *n* pl. -S a kabob
KECK *v* -ED, -ING, -S to retch
KECKLE *v* -LED, -LING, -LES to wind with rope to prevent chafing
KEDDAH *n* pl. -S an enclosure for elephants
KEDGE *v* KEDGED, KEDGING, KEDGES to move a vessel with the use of an anchor
KEDGEREE *n* pl. -S a food in India
KEEF *n* pl. -S kef
KEEK *v* -ED, -ING, -S to peep
KEEL *v* -ED, -ING, -S to capsize

KEELAGE *n* pl. -S the amount paid to keep a boat in a harbor

KEELBOAT *n* pl. -S a freight boat

KEELHALE *v* -HALED, -HALING, -HALES to keelhaul

KEELHAUL *v* -ED, -ING, -S to rebuke severely

KEELLESS *adj* having no keel (the main structural part of a ship)

KEELSON *n* pl. -S a beam in a ship

KEEN *adj* KEENER, KEENEST enthusiastic

KEEN *v* -ED, -ING, -S to wail loudly over the dead

KEENER *n* pl. -S one that keens

KEENLY *adv* in a keen manner

KEENNESS *n* pl. -ES sharpness

KEEP *v* KEPT, KEEPING, KEEPS to continue to possess **KEEPABLE** *adj*

KEEPER *n* pl. -S one that keeps

KEEPING *n* pl. -S custody

KEEPSAKE *n* pl. -S a memento

KEESHOND *n* pl. -HONDS or -HONDEN a small, heavy-coated dog

KEESTER *n* pl. -S a keister

KEET *n* pl. -S a young guinea fowl

KEEVE *n* pl. -S a tub or vat

KEF *n* pl. -S hemp smoked to produce euphoria

KEFFIYEH *n* pl. -S kaffiyeh

KEFIR *n* pl. -S a fermented beverage made from cow's milk

KEG *n* pl. -S a small barrel

KEGELER *n* pl. -S kegler

KEGLER *n* pl. -S a bowler

KEGLING *n* pl. -S bowling

KEIR *n* pl. -S kier

KEISTER *n* pl. -S the buttocks

KEITLOA *n* pl. -S a rhinoceros

KELEP *n* pl. -S a stinging ant

KELIM *n* pl. -S kilim

KELLY *n* pl. -LIES a bright green color

KELOID *n* pl. -S a scar caused by excessive growth of fibrous tissue **KELOIDAL** *adj*

KELP *v* -ED, -ING, -S to burn a type of seaweed

KELPIE *n* pl. -S a water sprite

KELPY *n* pl. -PIES kelpie

KELSON *n* pl. -S keelson

KELTER *n* pl. -S kilter

KELVIN *n* pl. -S a unit of temperature

KEMP *n* pl. -S a champion

KEMPT *adj* neatly kept

KEN *v* KENNED or KENT, KENNING, KENS to know

KENAF *n* pl. -S an East Indian plant

KENCH *n* pl. -ES a bin for salting fish

KENDO *n* pl. -DOS a Japanese sport

KENNED a past tense of ken

KENNEL *v* -NELED, -NELING, -NELS or -NELLED, -NELLING, -NELS to keep in a shelter for dogs

KENNING *n* pl. -S a metaphorical compound word or phrase

KENO *n* pl. -NOS a game of chance

KENOSIS *n* pl. -SISES the incarnation of Christ **KENOTIC** *adj*

KENOTRON *n* pl. -S a type of diode

KENT a past tense of ken

KEP *v* KEPPED, KEPPEN or KIPPEN, KEPPING, KEPS to catch

KEPHALIN *n* pl. -S cephalin

KEPI *n* pl. -S a type of cap

KEPPED past tense of kep

KEPPEN a past participle of kep

KEPPING present participle of kep

KEPT past tense of keep

KERAMIC *n* pl. -S ceramic

KERATIN *n* pl. -S a fibrous protein

KERATOID *adj* horny

KERATOMA *n* pl. -MAS or -MATA a skin disease

KERATOSE *adj* of or resembling horny tissue

KERB *v* -ED, -ING, -S to provide with curbing

KERCHIEF *n* pl. -CHIEFS or -CHIEVES a cloth worn as a head covering

KERCHOO *interj* ahchoo

KERF *v* -ED, -ING, -S to make an incision with a cutting tool

KERMES *n* pl. KERMES a red dye

KERMESS *n* pl. -ES kermis

KERMESSE *n* pl. -S kermis

KERMIS *n* pl. -MISES a festival

KERN *v* -ED, -ING, -S to be formed with a projecting typeface

KERNE *n* pl. -S a medieval foot soldier

KERNEL *v* -NELED, -NELING, -NELS or -NELLED, -NELLING, -NELS to envelop as a kernel (the inner part of a nut)

KERNITE *n* pl. -S a mineral

KEROGEN *n* pl. -S a substance found in shale

KEROSENE *n* pl. -S a fuel oil

KEROSINE *n* pl. -S kerosene

KERPLUNK v -ED, -ING, -S to fall or drop with a heavy sound

KERRIA n pl. -S a Chinese shrub

KERRY n pl. -RIES one of an Irish breed of cattle

KERSEY n pl. -SEYS a coarse woolen cloth

KERYGMA n pl. -MATA the preaching of the gospel

KESTREL n pl. -S a small falcon

KETCH n pl. -ES a sailing vessel

KETCHUP n pl. -S a spicy tomato sauce

KETENE n pl. -S a toxic gas

KETO adj of or pertaining to ketone

KETOL n pl. -S a chemical compound

KETONE n pl. -S a type of chemical compound **KETONIC** adj

KETOSE n pl. -S a simple sugar

KETOSIS n pl. -TOSES a buildup of ketones in the body **KETOTIC** adj

KETTLE n pl. -S a vessel for boiling liquids

KEVEL n pl. -S a belaying cleat or peg

KEVIL n pl. -S kevel

KEX n pl. -ES a dry, hollow stalk

KEY v -ED, -ING, -S to provide with a key (a device used to turn the bolt in a lock)

KEYBOARD v -ED, -ING, -S to operate a machine by means of a keyset

KEYCARD n pl. -S a coded card for operating a device

KEYHOLE n pl. -S a hole for a key

KEYLESS adj being without a key

KEYNOTE v -NOTED, -NOTING, -NOTES to deliver the main speech at a function

KEYNOTER n pl. -S one that keynotes

KEYPAD n pl. -S a small keyboard

KEYPUNCH v -ED, -ING, -ES to perforate with a machine

KEYSET n pl. -S a system of finger levers

KEYSTER n pl. -S keister

KEYSTONE n pl. -S the central stone of an arch

KEYWAY n pl. -WAYS a slot for a key

KEYWORD n pl. -S a significant word

KHADDAR n pl. -S a cotton cloth

KHADI n pl. -S khaddar

KHAF n pl. -S kaph

KHAKI n pl. -S a durable cloth

KHALIF n pl. -S caliph

KHALIFA n pl. -S caliph

KHAMSEEN n pl. -S khamsin

KHAMSIN n pl. -S a hot, dry wind

KHAN n pl. -S an Asian ruler

KHANATE n pl. -S the domain of a khan

KHAPH n pl. -S kaph

KHAT n pl. -S kat

KHAZEN n pl. -ZENS or -ZENIM hazzan

KHEDA n pl. -S keddah

KHEDAH n pl. -S keddah

KHEDIVE n pl. -S a Turkish viceroy **KHEDIVAL** adj

KHET n pl. -S heth

KHETH n pl. -S heth

KHI n pl. -S chi

KHIRKAH n pl. -S a patchwork garment

KHOUM n pl. -S a monetary unit of Mauritania

KIANG n pl. -S a wild ass

KIAUGH n pl. -S trouble; worry

KIBBE n pl. -S a Near Eastern dish of ground lamb and bulgur

KIBBEH n pl. -S kibbe

KIBBI n pl. -S kibbe

KIBBITZ v -ED, -ING, -ES kibitz

KIBBLE v -BLED, -BLING, -BLES to grind coarsely

KIBBUTZ n pl. -BUTZIM a collective farm in Israel

KIBE n pl. -S a sore caused by exposure to cold

KIBEI n pl. -S one born in America of immigrant Japanese parents and educated in Japan

KIBITZ v -ED, -ING, -ES to meddle

KIBITZER n pl. -S one that kibitzes

KIBLA n pl. -S kiblah

KIBLAH n pl. -S the direction toward which Muslims face while praying

KIBOSH v -ED, -ING, -ES to stop

KICK v -ED, -ING, -S to strike out with the foot or feet **KICKABLE** adj

KICKBACK n pl. -S a strong reaction

KICKBALL n pl. -S baseball using an inflated ball that is kicked

KICKER n pl. -S one that kicks

KICKIER comparative of kicky

KICKIEST superlative of kicky

KICKOFF n pl. -S the kick that begins play in football

KICKSHAW n pl. -S a trifle or trinket

KICKUP n pl. -S a noisy argument

KICKY adj KICKIER, KICKIEST exciting

KID v KIDDED, KIDDING, KIDS to tease

KIDDER n pl. -S one that kids

KIDDIE n pl. -S a small child

KIDDIES pl. of kiddy

KIDDING present participle of kid

KIDDISH adj childish

KIDDO n pl. -DOS or -DOES — used as a form of familiar address

KIDDUSH n pl. -ES a Jewish prayer

KIDDY n pl. -DIES kiddie

KIDLIKE adj resembling a child

KIDNAP v -NAPED, -NAPING, -NAPS or -NAPPED, -NAPPING, -NAPS to take a person by force and often for ransom

KIDNAPEE n pl. -S one that is kidnaped

KIDNAPER n pl. -S one that kidnaps

KIDNAPPER n pl. -S kidnaper

KIDNAPPING present participle of kidnap

KIDNEY n pl. -NEYS a bodily organ

KIDSKIN n pl. -S a type of leather

KIDVID n pl. -S television programs for children

KIEF n pl. -S kef

KIELBASA n pl. -BASAS, -BASI, or -BASY a smoked sausage

KIER n pl. -S a vat for boiling and dyeing fabrics

KIESTER n pl. -S keister

KIF n pl. -S kef

KILIM n pl. -S an oriental tapestry

KILL v -ED, -ING, -S to cause to die

KILLDEE n pl. -S killdeer

KILLDEER n pl. -S a wading bird

KILLER n pl. -S one that kills

KILLICK n pl. -S a small anchor

KILLIE n pl. -S a freshwater fish

KILLING n pl. -S a sudden notable success

KILLJOY n pl. -JOYS one who spoils the fun of others

KILLOCK n pl. -S killick

KILN v -ED, -ING, -S to bake in a type of oven

KILO n pl. KILOS a kilogram or kilometer

KILOBAR n pl. -S a unit of atmospheric pressure

KILOBASE n pl. -S unit of measure of a nucleic-acid chain

KILOBAUD n pl. -S a unit of data transmission speed

KILOBIT n pl. -S a unit of computer information

KILOBYTE n pl. -S 1,024 bytes

KILOGRAM n pl. -S a unit of mass and weight

KILOMOLE n pl. -S one thousand moles

KILORAD n pl. -S a unit of nuclear radiation

KILOTON n pl. -S a unit of weight

KILOVOLT n pl. -S a unit of electromotive force

KILOWATT n pl. -S a unit of power

KILT v -ED, -ING, -S to make creases or pleats in

KILTER n pl. -S good condition

KILTIE n pl. -S one who wears a kilt (a type of skirt)

KILTING n pl. -S an arrangement of kilt pleats

KILTY n pl. KILTIES kiltie

KIMCHEE n pl. -S kimchi

KIMCHI n pl. -S a spicy Korean dish of pickled cabbage

KIMONO n pl. -NOS a loose robe KIMONOED adj

KIN n pl. -S a group of persons of common ancestry

KINA n pl. -S a monetary unit of Papua New Guinea

KINASE n pl. -S an enzyme

KIND adj KINDER, KINDEST having a gentle, giving nature

KIND n pl. -S a class of similar or related objects or individuals

KINDLE v -DLED, -DLING, -DLES to cause to burn

KINDLER n pl. -S one that kindles

KINDLESS adj lacking kindness

KINDLING n pl. -S material that is easily ignited

KINDLY adj -LIER, -LIEST kind

KINDNESS n pl. -ES the quality of being kind

KINDRED n pl. -S a natural grouping

KINE n pl. -S a type of television tube

KINEMA n pl. -S cinema

KINESIC adj pertaining to kinesics

KINESICS n/pl the study of body motion in relation to communication

KINESIS n pl. -NESES a type of movement

KINETIC adj pertaining to motion

KINETICS n/pl a branch of science dealing with motion

KINETIN n pl. -S a substance that increases plant growth

KINFOLK n/pl relatives

KINFOLKS n/pl kinfolk

KING v -ED, -ING, -S to reign as king (a male monarch)

KINGBIRD *n pl.* -S an American bird

KINGBOLT *n pl.* -S a kingpin

KINGCUP *n pl.* -S a marsh plant

KINGDOM *n pl.* -S the area ruled by a king

KINGFISH *n pl.* -ES a marine food fish

KINGHOOD *n pl.* -S the office of a king

KINGLESS *adj* having no king

KINGLET *n pl.* -S a king who rules over a small area

KINGLIKE *adj* resembling a king

KINGLY *adj* -LIER, -LIEST of or befitting a king

KINGPIN *n pl.* -S a central bolt connecting an axle to a vehicle

KINGPOST *n pl.* -S a supporting structure of a roof

KINGSHIP *n pl.* -S the power or position of a king

KINGSIDE *n pl.* -S a part of a chessboard

KINGWOOD *n pl.* -S a hardwood tree

KININ *n pl.* -S a hormone

KINK *v* -ED, -ING, -S to form a tight curl or bend in

KINKAJOU *n pl.* -S an arboreal mammal

KINKY *adj* KINKIER, KINKIEST tightly curled **KINKILY** *adv*

KINO *n pl.* -NOS a gum resin

KINSFOLK *n/pl* kinfolk

KINSHIP *n pl.* -S relationship

KINSMAN *n pl.* -MEN a male relative

KIOSK *n pl.* -S an open booth

KIP *v* KIPPED, KIPPING, KIPS to sleep

KIPPEN *a* past participle of kep

KIPPER *v* -ED, -ING, -S to cure fish by salting and smoking

KIPPERER *n pl.* -S one that kippers

KIPPING present participle of kip

KIPSKIN *n pl.* -S an animal hide that has not been tanned

KIR *n pl.* -S an alcoholic beverage

KIRIGAMI *n pl.* -S the Japanese art of folding paper

KIRK *n pl.* -S a church

KIRKMAN *n pl.* -MEN a member of a church

KIRMESS *n pl.* -ES kermis

KIRN *v* -ED, -ING, -S to churn

KIRSCH *n pl.* -ES a kind of brandy

KIRTLE *n pl.* -S a man's tunic or coat **KIRTLED** *adj*

KISHKA *n pl.* -S kishke

KISHKE *n pl.* -S a sausage

KISMAT *n pl.* -S kismet

KISMET *n pl.* -S destiny **KISMETIC** *adj*

KISS *v* -ED, -ING, -ES to touch with the lips as a sign of affection **KISSABLE** *adj* **KISSABLY** *adv*

KISSER *n pl.* -S one that kisses

KISSY *adj* inclined to kiss

KIST *n pl.* -S a chest, box, or coffin

KISTFUL *n pl.* -S as much as a kist can hold

KIT *v* KITTED, KITTING, KITS to equip

KITCHEN *n pl.* -S a room where food is cooked

KITE *v* KITED, KITING, KITES to obtain money or credit fraudulently

KITELIKE *adj* resembling a kite (a light, covered frame flown in the wind)

KITER *n pl.* -S one that kites

KITH *n pl.* -S one's friends and neighbors

KITHARA *n pl.* -S cithara

KITHE *v* KITHED, KITHING, KITHES to make known

KITING present participle of kite

KITLING *n pl.* -S a young animal

KITSCH *n pl.* -ES faddish art or literature **KITSCHY** *adj*

KITTED past tense of kit

KITTEL *n pl.* KITTEL a Jewish ceremonial robe

KITTEN *v* -ED, -ING, -S to bear kittens (young cats)

KITTIES pl. of kitty

KITTING present participle of kit

KITTLE *v* -TLED, -TLING, -TLES to tickle

KITTLE *adj* -TLER, -TLEST ticklish

KITTY *n pl.* -TIES a kitten or cat

KIVA *n pl.* -S an underground ceremonial chamber

KIWI *n pl.* -S a flightless bird

KLATCH *n pl.* -ES a social gathering

KLATSCH *n pl.* -ES klatch

KLAVERN *n pl.* -S a local branch of the Ku Klux Klan

KLAXON *n pl.* -S a low-pitched horn

KLEAGLE *n pl.* -S an official in the Ku Klux Klan

KLEPHT *n pl.* -S a Greek guerrilla **KLEPHTIC** *adj*

KLEZMER *n pl.* -MORIM a Jewish folk musician

KLISTER *n pl.* -S a wax for skis

KLONG *n pl.* -S a canal

KLOOF n pl. -S a ravine

KLUDGE n pl. -S a system composed of ill-fitting components

KLUGE n pl. -S kludge

KLUTZ n pl. -ES a clumsy person

KLUTZY adj KLUTZIER, KLUTZIEST clumsy

KLYSTRON n pl. -S a type of electron tube

KNACK v -ED, -ING, -S to strike sharply

KNACKER n pl. -S one that buys old livestock

KNACKERY n pl. -ERIES the place of business of a knacker

KNAP v KNAPPED, KNAPPING, KNAPS to strike sharply

KNAPPER n pl. -S one that knaps

KNAPSACK n pl. -S a bag carried on the back

KNAPWEED n pl. -S a meadow plant

KNAR n pl. -S a bump on a tree KNARRED, KNARRY adj

KNAUR n pl. -S knar

KNAVE n pl. -S a dishonest person KNAVISH adj

KNAVERY n pl. -ERIES trickery

KNAWEL n pl. -S a Eurasian plant

KNEAD v -ED, -ING, -S to work into a uniform mixture with the hands

KNEADER n pl. -S one that kneads

KNEE v KNEED, KNEEING, KNEES to strike with the knee (a joint of the leg)

KNEECAP v -CAPPED, -CAPPING, -CAPS to maim by shooting in the kneecap (a bone at the front of the knee)

KNEEHOLE n pl. -S a space for the knees

KNEEL v KNELT or KNEELED, KNEELING, KNEELS to rest on the knees

KNEELER n pl. -S one that kneels

KNEEPAD n pl. -S a covering for a knee

KNEEPAN n pl. -S the kneecap

KNEESOCK n pl. -S a sock reaching up to the knee

KNELL v -ED, -ING, -S to sound a bell

KNELT a past tense of kneel

KNESSET n pl. -S the Israeli parliament

KNEW past tense of know

KNICKERS n/pl loose-fitting pants gathered at the knee

KNIFE n pl. KNIVES a sharp-edged instrument used for cutting

KNIFE v KNIFED, KNIFING, KNIFES to cut with a knife

KNIFER n pl. -S one that knifes

KNIGHT v -ED, -ING, -S to make a knight (a medieval gentleman-soldier) of

KNIGHTLY adj of or befitting a knight

KNISH n pl. -ES dough stuffed with filling and fried

KNIT v KNITTED, KNITTING, KNITS to make a fabric by joining loops of yarn

KNITTER n pl. -S one that knits

KNITTING n pl. -S work done by a knitter

KNITWEAR n pl. KNITWEAR knitted clothing

KNIVES pl. of knife

KNOB n pl. -S a rounded protuberance KNOBBED, KNOBLIKE adj

KNOBBLY adj -BLIER, -BLIEST having very small knobs

KNOBBY adj -BIER, -BIEST full of knobs

KNOCK v -ED, -ING, -S to strike sharply

KNOCKER n pl. -S one that knocks

KNOCKOFF n pl. -S a copy that sells for less than the original

KNOCKOUT n pl. -S a blow that induces unconsciousness

KNOLL v -ED, -ING, -S to knell

KNOLLER n pl. -S one that knolls

KNOLLY adj hilly

KNOP n pl. -S a knob KNOPPED adj

KNOSP n pl. -S a knob

KNOT v KNOTTED, KNOTTING, KNOTS to tie in a knot (a closed loop)

KNOTHOLE n pl. -S a hole in a plank

KNOTLESS adj having no knots

KNOTLIKE adj resembling a knot

KNOTTED past tense of knot

KNOTTER n pl. -S one that knots

KNOTTING n pl. -S a fringe made of knotted threads

KNOTTY adj -TIER, -TIEST full of knots KNOTTILY adv

KNOTWEED n pl. -S a common weed

KNOUT v -ED, -ING, -S to flog with a leather whip

KNOW v KNEW, KNOWN, KNOWING, KNOWS to have a true understanding of KNOWABLE adj

KNOWER n pl. -S one that knows

KNOWING adj -INGER, -INGEST astute

KNOWING n pl. -S knowledge

KNOWN n pl. -S a mathematical quantity whose value is given

KNUBBY adj -BIER, -BIEST nubby

KNUCKLE v -LED, -LING, -LES to hit with the knuckles (the joints of the fingers)

KNUCKLER n pl. -S a type of baseball pitch

KNUCKLY adj -LIER, -LIEST having prominent knuckles

KNUR n pl. -S a bump on a tree

KNURL v -ED, -ING, -S to make grooves or ridges in

KNURLY adj KNURLIER, KNURLIEST gnarly

KOA n pl. -S a timber tree

KOALA n pl. -S an Australian mammal

KOAN n pl. -S a paradox meditated on by Buddhist monks

KOB n pl. -S a reddish brown antelope

KOBO n pl. KOBO a monetary unit of Nigeria

KOBOLD n pl. -S an elf

KOEL n pl. -S an Australian bird

KOHL n pl. -S a type of eye makeup

KOHLRABI n pl. -ES a variety of cabbage

KOI n pl. KOI a large and colorful fish

KOINE n pl. -S a type of dialect

KOKANEE n pl. -S a food fish

KOLA n pl. -S cola

KOLACKY n pl. KOLACKY a kind of pastry

KOLBASI n pl. -S kielbasa

KOLBASSI n pl. -S kielbasa

KOLHOZ n pl. -HOZY or -HOZES kolkhoz

KOLINSKI n pl. -ES kolinsky

KOLINSKY n pl. -SKIES an Asian mink

KOLKHOS n pl. -KHOSY or -KHOSES kolkhoz

KOLKHOZ n pl. -KHOZY or -KHOZES a collective farm in Russia

KOLKOZ n pl. -KOZY or -KOZES kolkhoz

KOLO n pl. -LOS a European folk dance

KOMATIK n pl. -S an Eskimo sledge

KOMONDOR n pl. -DORS, -DOROK, or -DOROCK a large, shaggy-coated dog

KONK v -ED, -ING, -S conk

KOODOO n pl. -DOOS kudu

KOOK n pl. -S an eccentric person

KOOKIE adj KOOKIER, KOOKIEST kooky

KOOKY adj KOOKIER, KOOKIEST eccentric

KOP n pl. -S a hill

KOPECK n pl. -S a Russian coin

KOPEK n pl. -S kopeck

KOPH n pl. -S a Hebrew letter

KOPJE n pl. -S a small hill

KOPPA n pl. -S a Greek letter

KOPPIE n pl. -S kopje

KOR n pl. -S a Hebrew unit of measure

KORAT n pl. -S a cat having a silver-blue coat

KORE n pl. -RAI an ancient Greek statue of a young woman

KORUNA n pl. KORUNAS, KORUNY, or KORUN a monetary unit of the Czech Republic

KOS n pl. KOS a land measure in India

KOSHER v -ED, -ING, -S to make fit to be eaten according to Jewish dietary laws

KOSS n pl. KOSS kos

KOTO n pl. -TOS a musical instrument

KOTOW v -ED, -ING, -S to kowtow

KOTOWER n pl. -S one that kotows

KOUMIS n pl. -MISES koumiss

KOUMISS n pl. -ES a beverage made from camel's milk

KOUMYS n pl. -ES koumiss

KOUMYSS n pl. -ES koumiss

KOUPREY n pl. -PREYS a short-haired ox

KOUROS n pl. -ROI an ancient Greek statue of a young man

KOUSSO n pl. -SOS cusso

KOWTOW v -ED, -ING, -S to behave in a servile manner

KOWTOWER n pl. -S one that kowtows

KRAAL v -ED, -ING, -S to pen in a type of enclosure

KRAFT n pl. -S a strong paper

KRAIT n pl. -S a venomous snake

KRAKEN n pl. -S a legendary sea monster

KRATER n pl. -S a type of vase

KRAUT n pl. -S sauerkraut

KREEP n pl. -S a basaltic lunar rock

KREMLIN n pl. -S a Russian citadel

KREPLACH n pl. KREPLACH dumplings filled with ground meat or cheese

KREUTZER n pl. -S a former monetary unit of Austria

KREUZER n pl. -S kreutzer

KRILL n pl. -S an aggregate of small marine crustaceans

KRIMMER n pl. -S a kind of fur

KRIS n pl. -ES a short sword

KRONA n pl. KRONUR a monetary unit of Iceland

KRONA n pl. KRONOR a monetary unit of Sweden

KRONE n pl. KRONER a monetary unit of Denmark

KRONE n pl. KRONEN a former monetary unit of Austria

KRONOR pl. of krona

KRONUR pl. of krona

KROON n pl. KROONS or KROONI a former monetary unit of Estonia

KRUBI n pl. -S a tropical plant

KRUBUT n pl. -S krubi

KRULLER n pl. -S cruller

KRUMHORN n pl. -S crumhorn

KRYOLITE n pl. -S cryolite

KRYOLITH n pl. -S cryolite

KRYPTON n pl. -S a gaseous element

KUCHEN n pl. KUCHEN a coffee cake

KUDO n pl. -DOS award; honor

KUDU n pl. -S a large antelope

KUDZU n pl. -S an Asian vine

KUE n pl. -S the letter Q

KUGEL n pl. -S a baked pudding of potatoes or noodles

KUKRI n pl. -S a long, curved knife of Nepal

KULAK n pl. -LAKS or -LAKI a rich Russian peasant

KULTUR n pl. -S culture; civilization

KUMISS n pl. -ES koumiss

KUMMEL n pl. -S a type of liqueur

KUMQUAT n pl. -S a citrus fruit

KUMYS n pl. -ES koumiss

KUNZITE n pl. -S a mineral

KURBASH v -ED, -ING, -ES to flog with a leather whip

KURGAN n pl. -S a mound of earth over a grave

KURTA n pl. -S a shirt worn in India

KURTOSIS n pl. -SISES the relative degree of curvature in a statistical curve

KURU n pl. -S a disease of the nervous system

KUSSO n pl. -SOS cusso

KUVASZ n pl. -VASZOK a large dog having a white coat

KVAS n pl. -ES kvass

KVASS n pl. -ES a Russian beer

KVETCH v -ED, -ING, -ES to complain

KVETCHY adj KVETCHIER, KVETCHIEST habitually complaining

KWACHA n pl. KWACHA a monetary unit of Zambia

KWANZA n pl. -S a monetary unit of Angola

KYACK n pl. -S a packsack

KYAK n pl. -S a kayak (an Eskimo canoe)

KYANISE v -ISED, -ISING, -ISES to kyanize

KYANITE n pl. -S cyanite

KYANIZE v -IZED, -IZING, -IZES to treat wood with a type of preservative

KYAR n pl. -S coir

KYAT n pl. -S a monetary unit of Myanmar

KYBOSH v -ED, -ING, -ES to kibosh

KYLIX n pl. -LIKES a drinking vessel

KYMOGRAM n pl. -S a record of fluid pressure

KYPHOSIS n pl. -PHOSES abnormal curvature of the spine KYPHOTIC adj

KYRIE n pl. -S a religious petition for mercy

KYTE n pl. -S the stomach

KYTHE v KYTHED, KYTHING, KYTHES to kithe

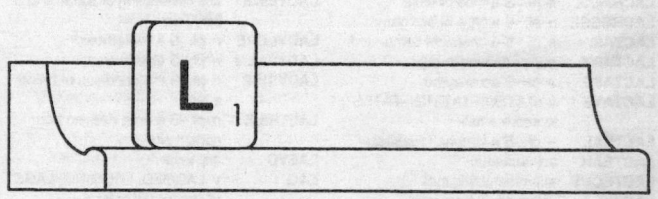

LA *n pl.* -S the sixth tone of the diatonic musical scale

LAAGER *v* -ED, -ING, -S to form a defensive encampment

LAARI *n pl.* LAARI a monetary unit of the Maldives

LAB *n pl.* -S a laboratory

LABARUM *n pl.* -RA or -RUMS an ecclesiastical banner

LABDANUM *n pl.* -S a fragrant resin

LABEL *v* -BELED, -BELING, -BELS or -BELLED, -BELLING, -BELS to describe or designate

LABELER *n pl.* -S one that labels

LABELLA *pl.* of labellum

LABELLED a past tense of label

LABELLER *n pl.* -S labeler

LABELLING a present participle of label

LABELLUM *n pl.* -LA the lower petal of an orchid

LABIA *pl.* of labium

LABIAL *n pl.* -S a labially produced sound

LABIALLY *adv* by means of the lips

LABIATE *n pl.* -S a labiated plant

LABIATED *adj* having corollas that are divided into two liplike parts

LABILE *adj* likely to change

LABILITY *n pl.* -TIES the state of being labile

LABIUM *n pl.* -BIA a fold of the vulva

LABOR *v* -ED, -ING, -S to work

LABORER *n pl.* -S one that labors

LABORITE *n pl.* -S a supporter of labor interests

LABOUR *v* -ED, -ING, -S to labor

LABOURER *n pl.* -S laborer

LABRA *a pl.* of labrum

LABRADOR *n pl.* -S a hunting dog

LABRET *n pl.* -S an ornament worn in a perforation of the lip

LABROID *n pl.* -S a marine fish

LABRUM *n pl.* -BRA or -BRUMS a lip or liplike structure

LABRUSCA *adj* designating a fox grape

LABURNUM *n pl.* -S an ornamental tree

LAC *n pl.* -S a resinous substance secreted by certain insects

LACE *v* LACED, LACING, LACES to fasten by means of a lace (a cord for drawing together two edges)

LACELESS *adj* lacking lace

LACELIKE *adj* resembling lace

LACER *n pl.* -S one that laces

LACERATE *v* -ATED, -ATING, -ATES to tear roughly

LACERTID *n pl.* -S a type of lizard

LACEWING *n pl.* -S a winged insect

LACEWOOD *n pl.* -S an Australian tree

LACEWORK *n pl.* -S a delicate openwork fabric

LACEY *adj* LACIER, LACIEST lacy

LACHES *n pl.* LACHES undue delay in asserting a legal right

LACIER comparative of lacy

LACIEST superlative of lacy

LACILY *adv* in a lacy manner

LACINESS *n pl.* -ES the quality of being lacy

LACING *n pl.* -S a contrasting marginal band of color

LACK *v* -ED, -ING, -S to be without

LACKADAY *interj* — used to express regret

LACKER *v* -ED, -ING, -S to lacquer

LACKEY *v* -ED, -ING, -S to act in a servile manner

LACONIC *adj* using a minimum of words

LACONISM *n pl.* -S brevity of expression

LACQUER *v* -ED, -ING, -S to coat with a glossy substance

LACQUEY *v* -ED, -ING, -S to lackey

LACRIMAL *n pl.* -S a type of vase

LACROSSE *n pl.* -S a type of ball game

LACTAM *n pl.* -S a chemical compound

LACTARY *adj* pertaining to milk

LACTASE *n pl.* -S an enzyme

LACTATE *v* -TATED, -TATING, -TATES to secrete milk

LACTEAL *n pl.* -S a lymphatic vessel

LACTEAN *adj* lacteous

LACTEOUS *adj* resembling milk

LACTIC *adj* derived from milk

LACTONE *n pl.* -S any of a group of esters **LACTONIC** *adj*

LACTOSE *n pl.* -S a lactic sugar

LACUNA *n pl.* -NAE or -NAS an empty space or missing part **LACUNAL, LACUNARY, LACUNATE** *adj*

LACUNAR *n pl.* -NARS or -NARIA a ceiling with recessed panels

LACUNE *n pl.* -S lacuna

LACUNOSE *adj* marked by shallow depressions

LACY *adj* **LACIER, LACIEST** resembling lacework

LAD *n pl.* -S a boy or youth

LADANUM *n pl.* -S labdanum

LADDER *v* -ED, -ING, -S to cause a run in a stocking

LADDIE *n pl.* -S a lad

LADE *v* **LADED, LADEN, LADING, LADES** to load with a cargo

LADEN *v* -ED, -ING, -S to lade

LADER *n pl.* -S one that lades

LADIES pl. of lady

LADING *n pl.* -S cargo; freight

LADINO *n pl.* -NOS a fast-growing clover

LADLE *v* -DLED, -DLING, -DLES to lift out with a ladle (a type of spoon)

LADLEFUL *n pl.* -S as much as a ladle will hold

LADLER *n pl.* -S one that ladles

LADLING present participle of ladle

LADRON *n pl.* -S ladrone

LADRONE *n pl.* -S a thief

LADY *n pl.* -DIES a woman of refinement and gentle manners

LADYBIRD *n pl.* -S a ladybug

LADYBUG *n pl.* -S a small beetle

LADYFISH *n pl.* -ES a bonefish

LADYHOOD *n pl.* -S the state of being a lady

LADYISH *adj* somewhat ladylike

LADYKIN *n pl.* -S a small lady

LADYLIKE *adj* resembling or suitable to a lady

LADYLOVE *n pl.* -S a sweetheart

LADYPALM *n pl.* -S a palm tree

LADYSHIP *n pl.* -S the condition of being a lady

LAETRILE *n pl.* -S a drug derived from apricot pits

LAEVO *adj* levo

LAG *v* **LAGGED, LAGGING, LAGS** to stay or fall behind

LAGAN *n pl.* -S goods thrown into the sea with a buoy attached to enable recovery

LAGEND *n pl.* -S lagan

LAGER *v* -ED, -ING, -S to laager

LAGGARD *n pl.* -S one that lags

LAGGED past tense of lag

LAGGER *n pl.* -S a laggard

LAGGING *n pl.* -S an insulating material

LAGNAPPE *n pl.* -S a small gift given to a customer with his purchase

LAGOON *n pl.* -S a shallow body of water **LAGOONAL** *adj*

LAGUNA *n pl.* -S lagoon

LAGUNE *n pl.* -S lagoon

LAHAR *n pl.* -S a flowing mass of volcanic debris

LAIC *n pl.* -S a layman **LAICAL** *adj* **LAICALLY** *adv*

LAICH *n pl.* -S laigh

LAICISE *v* -ICISED, -ICISING, -ICISES to laicize

LAICISM *n pl.* -S a political system free from clerical control

LAICIZE *v* -ICIZED, -ICIZING, -ICIZES to free from clerical control

LAID a past tense of lay

LAIGH *n pl.* -S a lowland

LAIN past participle of lie

LAIR *v* -ED, -ING, -S to live in a lair (a wild animal's resting or dwelling place)

LAIRD *n pl.* -S the owner of a landed estate **LAIRDLY** *adj*

LAITANCE *n pl.* -S a milky deposit on the surface of fresh concrete

LAITH *adj* loath **LAITHLY** *adv*

LAITY *n pl.* -ITIES the nonclerical membership of a religious faith

LAKE *n pl.* -S a sizable inland body of water **LAKELIKE** *adj*

LAKED *adj* subjected to the process of laking

LAKEPORT *n pl.* -S a city located on the shore of a lake

LAKER *n pl.* -S a lake fish

LAKESIDE *n pl.* -S the land along the edge of a lake

LAKH *n pl.* -S the sum of one hundred thousand

LAKING *n pl.* -S the reddening of blood plasma by the release of hemoglobin from the red corpuscles

LAKY *adj* LAKIER, LAKIEST of the color of blood

LALL *v* -ED, -ING, -S to articulate the letter r as l

LALLAN *n pl.* -S a lowland

LALLAND *n pl.* -S a lowland

LALLYGAG *v* -GAGGED, -GAGGING, -GAGS to dawdle

LAM *v* LAMMED, LAMMING, LAMS to flee hastily

LAMA *n pl.* -S a Buddhist monk

LAMASERY *n pl.* -SERIES a monastery of lamas

LAMB *v* -ED, -ING, -S to give birth to a lamb (a young sheep)

LAMBAST *v* -ED, -ING, -S to lambaste

LAMBASTE *v* -BASTED, -BASTING, -BASTES to beat severely

LAMBDA *n pl.* -S a Greek letter **LAMBDOID** *adj*

LAMBENCY *n pl.* -CIES the quality or an instance of being lambent

LAMBENT *adj* flickering lightly and gently over a surface

LAMBER *n pl.* -S a ewe that is lambing

LAMBERT *n pl.* -S a unit of brightness

LAMBIE *n pl.* -S a lambkin

LAMBIER comparative of lamby

LAMBIEST superlative of lamby

LAMBKILL *n pl.* -S an evergreen shrub

LAMBKIN *n pl.* -S a small lamb

LAMBLIKE *adj* resembling a lamb

LAMBSKIN *n pl.* -S the skin of a lamb

LAMBY *adj* LAMBIER, LAMBIEST resembling a lamb

LAME *adj* LAMER, LAMEST physically disabled

LAME *v* LAMED, LAMING, LAMES to make lame

LAMED *n pl.* -S a Hebrew letter

LAMEDH *n pl.* -S lamed

LAMELLA *n pl.* -LAE or -LAS a thin plate, scale, or membrane **LAMELLAR** *adj*

LAMELY *adv* in a lame manner

LAMENESS *n pl.* -ES the state of being lame

LAMENT *v* -ED, -ING, -S to express sorrow or regret for

LAMENTER *n pl.* -S one that laments

LAMER comparative of lame

LAMEST superlative of lame

LAMIA *n pl.* -MIAS or -MIAE a female demon

LAMINA *n pl.* -NAE or -NAS a thin plate, scale, or layer **LAMINAL, LAMINAR, LAMINARY** *adj*

LAMINATE *v* -NATED, -NATING, -NATES to compress into a thin plate

LAMING present participle of lame

LAMINOSE *adj* composed of laminae

LAMINOUS *adj* laminose

LAMISTER *n pl.* -S lamster

LAMMED past tense of lam

LAMMING present participle of lam

LAMP *v* -ED, -ING, -S to look at

LAMPAD *n pl.* -S a candlestick

LAMPAS *n pl.* -ES inflammation of the roof of a horse's mouth

LAMPERS *n pl.* -ES lampas

LAMPION *n pl.* -S a type of light-generating device

LAMPOON *v* -ED, -ING, -S to ridicule in a satirical composition

LAMPPOST *n pl.* -S a post supporting a streetlight

LAMPREY *n pl.* -PREYS an eellike fish

LAMPYRID *n pl.* -S any of a family of beetles

LAMSTER *n pl.* -S a fugitive

LANAI *n pl.* -S a veranda

LANATE *adj* covered with wool

LANATED *adj* lanate

LANCE *v* LANCED, LANCING, LANCES to pierce with a lance (a spearlike weapon)

LANCELET *n pl.* -S a small marine organism

LANCER *n pl.* -S a cavalryman armed with a lance

LANCET *n pl.* -S a narrow, pointed arch **LANCETED** *adj*

LANCIERS *n pl.* LANCIERS a French dance

LANCING present participle of lance

LAND *v* -ED, -ING, -S to set down upon land (solid ground)

LANDAU *n pl.* -S a type of carriage

LANDER *n pl.* -S one that lands

LANDFALL *n pl.* -S a sighting or approach to land

LANDFILL *n pl.* -S a system of waste disposal

LANDFORM *n pl.* -S a natural feature of the earth's surface

LANDGRAB *n pl.* -S a swift and often fraudulent seizure of land

LANDING *n pl.* -S a place for discharging or taking on passengers or cargo

LANDLADY *n pl.* -DIES a female landlord

LANDLER *n pl.* -S a slow Austrian dance

LANDLESS *adj* owning no land

LANDLINE *n pl.* -S a line of communication on land

LANDLORD *n pl.* -S one who owns and rents out real estate

LANDMAN *n pl.* -MEN one who lives and works on land

LANDMARK *n pl.* -S an object that marks a boundary line

LANDMASS *n pl.* -ES a large area of land

LANDMEN pl. of landman

LANDSIDE *n pl.* -S a part of a plow

LANDSKIP *n pl.* -S landscape

LANDSLEIT pl. of landsman

LANDSLID past tense of landslide (to win an election by an overwhelming majority)

LANDSLIP *n pl.* -S the fall of a mass of earth

LANDSMAN *n pl.* LANDSLEIT a fellow Jew coming from one's own section of Eastern Europe

LANDSMAN *n pl.* -MEN landman

LANDWARD *adv* toward the land

LANE *n pl.* -S a narrow passageway

LANELY *adj* lonely

LANEWAY *n pl.* -WAYS a lane

LANG *adj* long

LANGLAUF *n pl.* -S a cross-country ski run

LANGLEY *n pl.* -LEYS a unit of illumination

LANGRAGE *n pl.* -S a shot formerly used in naval warfare

LANGREL *n pl.* -S langrage

LANGSHAN *n pl.* -S any of a breed of large domestic fowl

LANGSYNE *n pl.* -S time long past

LANGUAGE *n pl.* -S a body of words and systems serving as a means of communication

LANGUE *n pl.* -S a type of language

LANGUET *n pl.* -S a tonguelike part

LANGUID *adj* lacking in vigor or vitality

LANGUISH *v* -ED, -ING, -ES to lose vigor or vitality

LANGUOR *n pl.* -S the state of being languid

LANGUR *n pl.* -S an Asian monkey

LANIARD *n pl.* -S lanyard

LANIARY *n pl.* -ARIES a cuspid

LANITAL *n pl.* -S a woollike fiber

LANK *adj* LANKER, LANKEST long and slender **LANKLY** *adv*

LANKNESS *n pl.* -ES the state of being lank

LANKY *adj* LANKIER, LANKIEST ungracefully tall and thin **LANKILY** *adv*

LANNER *n pl.* -S a falcon of Europe and Asia

LANNERET *n pl.* -S a male lanner

LANOLIN *n pl.* -S a fatty substance obtained from wool

LANOLINE *n pl.* -S lanolin

LANOSE *adj* lanate

LANOSITY *n pl.* -TIES the state of being lanose

LANTANA *n pl.* -S a tropical shrub

LANTERN *n pl.* -S a protective case for a light

LANTHORN *n pl.* -S a lantern

LANUGO *n pl.* -GOS fine, soft hair

LANYARD *n pl.* -S a fastening rope on a ship

LAP *v* LAPPED, LAPPING, LAPS to fold over or around something

LAPBOARD *n pl.* -S a flat board used as a table or desk

LAPDOG *n pl.* -S a small dog

LAPEL *n pl.* -S an extension of the collar of a garment **LAPELED, LAPELLED** *adj*

LAPFUL *n pl.* -S as much as the lap can hold

LAPIDARY *n pl.* -DARIES one who works with precious stones

LAPIDATE *v* -DATED, -DATING, -DATES to hurl stones at

LAPIDES pl. of lapis

LAPIDIFY *v* -FIED, -FYING, -FIES to turn to stone

LAPIDIST *n pl.* -S a lapidary

LAPILLUS *n pl.* -LI a small fragment of lava

LAPIN *n pl.* -S a rabbit

LAPIS *n pl.* LAPIDES a stone

LAPIS *n pl.* -PISES a mineral

LAPPED past tense of lap

LAPPER *v* -ED, -ING, -S to lopper

LAPPET *n pl.* -S a decorative flap on a garment **LAPPETED** *adj*

LAPPING present participle of lap

LAPSE *v* LAPSED, LAPSING, LAPSES to fall from a previous standard **LAPSABLE, LAPSIBLE** *adj*

LAPSER *n pl.* -S one that lapses

LAPSUS *n pl.* LAPSUS a mistake

LAPTOP *n pl.* -S a small computer for use on one's lap

LAPWING *n pl.* -S a shore bird

LAR *n pl.* -ES or -S a tutelary god or spirit of an ancient Roman household

LARBOARD *n pl.* -S the left-hand side of a ship

LARCENER *n pl.* -S one that commits larceny

LARCENY *n pl.* -NIES the felonious taking and removal of another's personal goods

LARCH *n pl.* -ES a coniferous tree

LARD *v* -ED, -ING, -S to coat with lard (the melted fat of hogs)

LARDER *n pl.* -S a place where food is stored

LARDIER comparative of lardy

LARDIEST superlative of lardy

LARDLIKE *adj* resembling lard

LARDON *n pl.* -S a thin slice of bacon or pork

LARDOON *n pl.* -S lardon

LARDY *adj* LARDIER, LARDIEST resembling lard

LAREE *n pl.* -S lari

LARES a pl. of lar

LARGANDO *adj* becoming gradually slower — used as a musical direction

LARGE *adj* LARGER, LARGEST of considerable size or quantity **LARGELY** *adv*

LARGE *n pl.* -S generosity

LARGESS *n pl.* -ES generosity

LARGESSE *n pl.* -S largess

LARGEST superlative of large

LARGISH *adj* somewhat large

LARGO *n pl.* -GOS a slow musical movement

LARI *n pl.* -S a monetary unit of Maldives

LARIAT *v* -ED, -ING, -S to lasso

LARINE *adj* resembling a gull

LARK *v* -ED, -ING, -S to behave playfully

LARKER *n pl.* -S one that larks

LARKIER comparative of larky

LARKIEST superlative of larky

LARKISH *adj* playful

LARKSOME *adj* playful

LARKSPUR *n pl.* -S a flowering plant

LARKY *adj* LARKIER, LARKIEST playful

LARRIGAN *n pl.* -S a type of moccasin

LARRIKIN *n pl.* -S a rowdy

LARRUP *v* -ED, -ING, -S to beat or thrash

LARRUPER *n pl.* -S one that larrups

LARUM *n pl.* -S an alarm

LARVA *n pl.* -VAE or -VAS the immature form of various insects and animals when newly hatched **LARVAL** *adj*

LARYNX *n pl.* LARYNGES or LARYNXES an organ of the respiratory tract **LARYNGAL** *adj*

LASAGNA *n pl.* -S an Italian baked dish

LASAGNE *n pl.* -S lasagna

LASCAR *n pl.* -S an East Indian sailor

LASE *v* LASED, LASING, LASES to function as a laser

LASER *n pl.* -S a device that amplifies light waves

LASH *v* -ED, -ING, -ES to strike with a whip

LASHER *n pl.* -S one that lashes

LASHING *n pl.* -S a flogging

LASHINS *n/pl* an abundance

LASHKAR *n pl.* -S lascar

LASING present participle of lase

LASS *n pl.* -ES a young woman

LASSIE *n pl.* -S a lass

LASSO *v* -ED, -ING, -S or -ES to catch with a lasso (a long rope with a running noose)

LASSOER *n pl.* -S one that lassos

LAST *v* -ED, -ING, -S to continue in existence

LASTER *n pl.* -S one that lasts

LASTING *n pl.* -S a durable fabric

LASTLY *adv* in conclusion

LAT *n pl.* LATS or LATI a former monetary unit of Latvia

LATAKIA n pl. -S a variety of Turkish tobacco

LATCH v -ED, -ING, -ES to close with a type of fastening device

LATCHET n pl. -S a thong used to fasten a shoe

LATCHKEY n pl. -KEYS a key for opening a latched door

LATE adj LATER, LATEST coming or occurring after the expected time

LATED adj belated

LATEEN n pl. -S a sailing vessel

LATEENER n pl. -S a lateen

LATELY adv not long ago

LATEN v -ED, -ING, -S to become late

LATENCY n pl. -CIES the state of being present but not manifest

LATENESS n pl. -ES the state of being late

LATENT n pl. -S a barely visible fingerprint that can be developed for study

LATENTLY adv dormantly

LATER comparative of late

LATERAD adv toward the side

LATERAL v -ED, -ING, -S to throw a sideward pass in football

LATERITE n pl. -S a type of soil

LATERIZE v -IZED, -IZING, -IZES to convert to laterite

LATEST n pl. -S the most recent development

LATEWOOD n pl. -S a part of an annual ring of wood

LATEX n pl. LATICES or LATEXES a milky liquid of certain plants

LATH v -ED, -ING, -S to cover with laths (thin strips of wood)

LATHE v LATHED, LATHING, LATHES to cut or shape on a type of machine

LATHER v -ED, -ING, -S to cover with lather (a light foam)

LATHERER n pl. -S one that lathers

LATHERY adj covered with lather

LATHI n pl. -S a heavy stick of bamboo and iron in India

LATHIER comparative of lathy

LATHIEST superlative of lathy

LATHING n pl. -S work made of or using laths

LATHWORK n pl. -S lathing

LATHY adj LATHIER, LATHIEST long and slender

LATI a pl. of lat

LATICES a pl. of latex

LATIGO n pl. -GOS or -GOES a strap used to fasten a saddle

LATINITY n pl. -TIES a manner of writing or speaking Latin

LATINIZE v -IZED, -IZING, -IZES to translate into Latin

LATINO n pl. -NOS a Latin American

LATISH adj somewhat late

LATITUDE n pl. -S freedom from narrow restrictions

LATKE n pl. -S a potato pancake

LATOSOL n pl. -S a tropical soil

LATRIA n pl. -S the supreme worship given to God only, in Roman Catholicism

LATRINE n pl. -S a type of toilet

LATTEN n pl. -S a brass-like alloy

LATTER adj being the second mentioned of two

LATTERLY adv lately

LATTICE v -TICED, -TICING, -TICES to form a structure consisting of interlaced strips of material

LATTIN n pl. -S latten

LAUAN n pl. -S a Philippine timber

LAUD v -ED, -ING, -S to praise

LAUDABLE adj worthy of praise **LAUDABLY** adv

LAUDANUM n pl. -S a type of opium preparation

LAUDATOR n pl. -S a lauder

LAUDER n pl. -S one that lauds

LAUGH v -ED, -ING, -S to express emotion, typically mirth, by a series of inarticulate sounds

LAUGHER n pl. -S one that laughs

LAUGHING n pl. -S laughter

LAUGHTER n pl. -S the act or sound of one that laughs

LAUNCE n pl. -S a marine fish

LAUNCH v -ED, -ING, -ES to set in motion

LAUNCHER n pl. -S a launching device

LAUNDER v -ED, -ING, -S to wash clothes

LAUNDRY n pl. -DRIES a collection of clothes to be washed

LAURA n pl. -RAS or -RAE a type of monastery

LAUREATE v -ATED, -ATING, -ATES to laurel

LAUREL v -RELED, -RELING, -RELS or -RELLED, -RELLING, -RELS to crown with a wreath of evergreen leaves

LAUWINE n pl. -S an avalanche

LAV n pl. -S a lavatory

LAVA n pl. -S molten rock that issues from a volcano

LAVABO n pl. -BOES or -BOS a ceremonial washing in certain Christian churches

LAVAGE n pl. -S a washing

LAVALAVA n pl. -S a Polynesian garment

LAVALIER n pl. -S a pendant worn on a chain around the neck

LAVALIKE adj resembling lava

LAVATION n pl. -S the acting of washing

LAVATORY n pl. -RIES a room equipped with washing and toilet facilities

LAVE v LAVED, LAVING, LAVES to wash

LAVEER v -ED, -ING, -S to sail against the wind

LAVENDER v -ED, -ING, -S to sprinkle with a type of perfume

LAVER n pl. -S a vessel used for ancient Hebrew ceremonial washings

LAVEROCK n pl. -S a songbird

LAVING present participle of lave

LAVISH adj -ISHER, -ISHEST expending or giving in great amounts LAVISHLY adv

LAVISH v -ED, -ING, -ES to expend or give in great amounts

LAVISHER n pl. -S one that lavishes

LAVROCK n pl. -S laverock

LAW v -ED, -ING, -S to take a complaint to court for settlement

LAWBOOK n pl. -S a book containing or dealing with laws

LAWFUL adj allowed by law (the body of rules governing the affairs of a community) LAWFULLY adv

LAWGIVER n pl. -S one who institutes a legal system

LAWINE n pl. -S lauwine

LAWING n pl. -S a bill for food or drink in a tavern

LAWLESS adj having no system of laws

LAWLIKE adj being like the law

LAWMAKER n pl. -S a legislator

LAWMAN n pl. -MEN a law-enforcement officer

LAWN n pl. -S an area of grass-covered land LAWNY adj

LAWSUIT n pl. -S a legal action

LAWYER v -ED, -ING, -S to work as a member of the legal profession

LAWYERLY adj befitting a member of the legal profession

LAX adj LAXER, LAXEST not strict or stringent

LAXATION n pl. -S the act of relaxing

LAXATIVE n pl. -S a drug that stimulates evacuation of the bowels

LAXITY n pl. -ITIES the state of being lax

LAXLY adv in a lax manner

LAXNESS n pl. -ES laxity

LAY v LAID or LAYED, LAYING, LAYS to deposit as a wager

LAYABOUT n pl. -S a lazy person

LAYAWAY n pl. -AWAYS an item that has been reserved with a down payment

LAYER v -ED, -ING, -S to form a layer (a single thickness, coating, or covering)

LAYERAGE n pl. -S a method of plant propagation

LAYERING n pl. -S layerage

LAYETTE n pl. -S an outfit of clothing and equipment for a newborn child

LAYMAN n pl. -MEN a member of the laity

LAYOFF n pl. -S the suspension or dismissal of employees

LAYOUT n pl. -S an arrangement or plan

LAYOVER n pl. -S a stopover

LAYUP n pl. -S a shot in basketball

LAYWOMAN n pl. -WOMEN a female member of the laity

LAZAR n pl. -S a beggar afflicted with a loathsome disease

LAZARET n pl. -S a hospital treating contagious diseases

LAZE v LAZED, LAZING, LAZES to pass time lazily

LAZIED past tense of lazy

LAZIER comparative of lazy

LAZIES present 3d person sing. of lazy

LAZIEST superlative of lazy

LAZILY adv in a lazy manner

LAZINESS n pl. -ES the state of being lazy

LAZING present participle of laze

LAZULI n pl. -S a mineral

LAZULITE *n pl.* -S a mineral

LAZURITE *n pl.* -S a mineral

LAZY *adj* LAZIER, LAZIEST disinclined toward work or exertion

LAZY *v* LAZIED, LAZYING, LAZIES to move or lie lazily

LAZYISH *adj* somewhat lazy

LEA *n pl.* -S a meadow

LEACH *v* -ED, -ING, -ES to subject to the filtering action of a liquid

LEACHATE *n pl.* -S a solution obtained by leaching

LEACHER *n pl.* -S one that leaches

LEACHY *adj* LEACHIER, LEACHIEST porous

LEAD *v* LED, LEADING, LEADS to show the way to by going in advance

LEAD *v* -ED, -ING, -S to cover with lead (a heavy metallic element)

LEADEN *adj* oppressively heavy **LEADENLY** *adv*

LEADER *n pl.* -S one that leads or guides

LEADIER comparative of leady

LEADIEST superlative of leady

LEADING *n pl.* -S a covering or border of lead

LEADLESS *adj* having no lead

LEADMAN *n pl.* -MEN a worker in charge of other workers

LEADOFF *n pl.* -S an opening play or move

LEADSMAN *n pl.* -MEN a seaman who measures the depth of water

LEADWORK *n pl.* -S something made of lead

LEADWORT *n pl.* -S a tropical plant

LEADY *adj* LEADIER, LEADIEST resembling lead

LEAF *n pl.* LEAVES a usually green, flattened organ of vascular plants

LEAF *v* -ED, -ING, -S to turn pages rapidly

LEAFAGE *n pl.* -S foliage

LEAFIER comparative of leafy

LEAFIEST superlative of leafy

LEAFLESS *adj* having no leaves

LEAFLET *v* -LETED, -LETING, -LETS or -LETTED, -LETTING, -LETS to distribute printed sheets of paper

LEAFLIKE *adj* resembling a leaf

LEAFWORM *n pl.* -S a moth larva that feeds on leaves

LEAFY *adj* LEAFIER, LEAFIEST covered with leaves

LEAGUE *v* LEAGUED, LEAGUING, LEAGUES to come together for a common purpose

LEAGUER *v* -ED, -ING, -S to besiege

LEAK *v* -ED, -ING, -S to permit the escape of something through a breach or flaw

LEAKAGE *n pl.* -S the act or an instance of leaking

LEAKER *n pl.* -S one that leaks

LEAKLESS *adj* designed not to leak

LEAKY *adj* LEAKIER, LEAKIEST tending to leak **LEAKILY** *adv*

LEAL *adj* loyal **LEALLY** *adv*

LEALTY *n pl.* -TIES loyalty

LEAN *v* LEANED or LEANT, LEANING, LEANS to deviate from a vertical position

LEAN *adj* LEANER, LEANEST having little fat **LEANLY** *adv*

LEANER *n pl.* -S one that leans

LEANING *n pl.* -S a tendency

LEANNESS *n pl.* -ES the state of being lean

LEANT a past tense of lean

LEAP *v* LEAPED or LEAPT or LEPT, LEAPING, LEAPS to spring off the ground

LEAPER *n pl.* -S one that leaps

LEAPFROG *v* -FROGGED, -FROGGING, -FROGS to jump over with the legs wide apart

LEAPT a past tense of leap

LEAR *n pl.* -S learning

LEARIER comparative of leary

LEARIEST superlative of leary

LEARN *v* LEARNED or LEARNT, LEARNING, LEARNS to gain knowledge by experience, instruction, or study

LEARNER *n pl.* -S one that learns

LEARNING *n pl.* -S acquired knowledge

LEARNT a past tense of learn

LEARY *adj* LEARIER, LEARIEST leery

LEASE *v* LEASED, LEASING, LEASES to grant temporary use of in exchange for rent **LEASABLE** *adj*

LEASER *n pl.* -S one that leases

LEASH *v* -ED, -ING, -ES to restrain an animal with a line or thong

LEASING n pl. -S a falsehood

LEAST n pl. -S something that is smallest in size or degree

LEATHER v -ED, -ING, -S to cover with leather (the dressed or tanned hide of an animal)

LEATHERN adj made of leather

LEATHERY adj resembling leather

LEAVE v LEFT, LEAVING, LEAVES to go away from

LEAVED adj having a leaf or leaves

LEAVEN v -ED, -ING, -S to produce fermentation in

LEAVER n pl. -S one that leaves

LEAVES pl. of leaf

LEAVING n pl. -S a leftover

LEAVY adj LEAVIER, LEAVIEST leafy

LEBEN n pl. -S a type of liquid food

LECH v -ED, -ING, -ES to engage in lechery

LECHAYIM n pl. -S lehayim

LECHER v -ED, -ING, -S to engage in lechery

LECHERY n pl. -ERIES excessive sexual indulgence

LECHWE n pl. -S an African antelope

LECITHIN n pl. -S any of a group of fatty substances found in plant and animal tissues

LECTERN n pl. -S a reading desk

LECTIN n pl. -S a protein that binds to a sugar molecule

LECTION n pl. -S a portion of sacred writing read in a church service

LECTOR n pl. -S a reader of the lessons in a church service

LECTURE v -TURED, -TURING, -TURES to expound on a specific subject

LECTURER n pl. -S one that lectures

LECYTHIS adj designating a family of tropical shrubs

LECYTHUS n pl. -THI lekythos

LED past tense of lead

LEDGE n pl. -S a narrow, shelflike projection

LEDGER n pl. -S an account book of final entry

LEDGY adj LEDGIER, LEDGIEST abounding in ledges

LEE n pl. -S shelter from the wind

LEEBOARD n pl. -S a board attached to a sailing vessel to prevent leeway

LEECH v -ED, -ING, -ES to cling to and feed upon or drain

LEEK n pl. -S an herb used in cookery

LEER v -ED, -ING, -S to look with a sideways glance

LEERY adj LEERIER, LEERIEST suspicious LEERILY adv

LEET n pl. -S a former English court for petty offenses

LEEWARD n pl. -S the direction toward which the wind is blowing

LEEWAY n pl. -WAYS the lateral drift of a ship

LEFT adj LEFTER, LEFTEST pertaining to the side of the body to the north when one faces east

LEFT n pl. -S the left side or hand

LEFTIES pl. of lefty

LEFTISH adj inclined to be a leftist

LEFTISM n pl. -S a liberal political philosophy

LEFTIST n pl. -S an advocate of leftism

LEFTOVER n pl. -S an unused or unconsumed portion

LEFTWARD adv toward the left

LEFTWING adj favoring leftism

LEFTY n pl. LEFTIES a left-handed person

LEG v LEGGED, LEGGING, LEGS to move with the legs (appendages that serve as a means of support and locomotion)

LEGACY n pl. -CIES something bequeathed

LEGAL n pl. -S an authorized investment that may be made by investors such as savings banks

LEGALESE n pl. -S the specialized language of lawyers

LEGALISE v -ISED, -ISING, -ISES to legalize

LEGALISM n pl. -S strict conformity to the law

LEGALIST n pl. -S an adherent of legalism

LEGALITY n pl. -TIES the condition of being lawful

LEGALIZE v -IZED, -IZING, -IZES to make lawful

LEGALLY adv in a lawful manner

LEGATE v -GATED, -GATING, -GATES to bequeath

LEGATEE n pl. -S the inheritor of a legacy

LEGATINE *adj* pertaining to an official envoy

LEGATING present participle of legate

LEGATION *n pl.* -S the sending of an official envoy

LEGATO *n pl.* -TOS a smooth and flowing musical style

LEGATOR *n pl.* -S one that legates

LEGEND *n pl.* -S an unverified story from earlier times

LEGENDRY *n pl.* -RIES a collection of legends

LEGER *n pl.* -S fishing bait made to lie on the bottom

LEGERITY *n pl.* -TIES quickness of the mind or body

LEGES pl. of lex

LEGGED past tense of leg

LEGGIER comparative of leggy

LEGGIERO *adv* in a light or graceful manner — used as a musical direction

LEGGIEST superlative of leggy

LEGGIN *n pl.* -S legging

LEGGING *n pl.* -S a covering for the leg

LEGGY *adj* -GIER, -GIEST having long legs

LEGHORN *n pl.* -S a smooth, plaited straw

LEGIBLE *adj* capable of being read **LEGIBLY** *adv*

LEGION *n pl.* -S a large military force

LEGIST *n pl.* -S one learned or skilled in the law

LEGIT *n pl.* -S legitimate drama

LEGLESS *adj* having no legs

LEGLIKE *adj* resembling a leg

LEGMAN *n pl.* -MEN a newspaperman assigned to gather information

LEGONG *n pl.* -S a Balinese dance

LEGROOM *n pl.* -S space in which to extend the legs

LEGUME *n pl.* -S a type of plant

LEGUMIN *n pl.* -S a plant protein

LEGWORK *n pl.* -S work that involves extensive walking

LEHAYIM *n pl.* -S a traditional Jewish toast

LEHR *n pl.* -S a type of oven

LEHUA *n pl.* -S a tropical tree

LEI *n pl.* -S a wreath of flowers

LEISTER *v* -ED, -ING, -S to spear with a three-pronged fishing implement

LEISURE *n pl.* -S freedom from the demands of work or duty **LEISURED** *adj*

LEK *n pl.* LEKS or LEKE or LEKU a monetary unit of Albania

LEKVAR *n pl.* -S a prune butter

LEKYTHOS *n pl.* -THOI an oil jar used in ancient Greece

LEKYTHUS *n pl.* -THI lekythos

LEMAN *n pl.* -S a lover

LEMMA *n pl.* -MAS or -MATA a type of proposition in logic

LEMMING *n pl.* -S a mouselike rodent

LEMNISCI *n/pl* bands of nerve fibers

LEMON *n pl.* -S a citrus fruit **LEMONISH, LEMONY** *adj*

LEMONADE *n pl.* -S a beverage

LEMPIRA *n pl.* -S a monetary unit of Honduras

LEMUR *n pl.* -S an arboreal mammal related to the monkeys

LEMURES *n/pl* the ghosts of the dead in ancient Roman religion

LEMURINE *adj* pertaining to a lemur

LEMUROID *n pl.* -S a lemur

LEND *v* LENT, LENDING, LENDS to give the temporary use of **LENDABLE** *adj*

LENDER *n pl.* -S one that lends

LENES pl. of lenis

LENGTH *n pl.* -S the longer or longest dimension of an object

LENGTHEN *v* -ED, -ING, -S to make or become longer

LENGTHY *adj* LENGTHIER, LENGTHIEST very long

LENIENCE *n pl.* -S leniency

LENIENCY *n pl.* -CIES the quality of being lenient

LENIENT *adj* gently tolerant

LENIS *n pl.* LENES a speech sound pronounced with little or no aspiration

LENITION *n pl.* -S a change in articulation

LENITIVE *n pl.* -S a soothing medicine

LENITY *n pl.* -TIES leniency

LENO *n pl.* -NOS a style of weaving

LENS *n pl.* -ES a piece of transparent material used in changing the convergence of light rays **LENSLESS** *adj*

LENS *v* -ED, -ING, -ES to make a film of

LENSE *n pl.* -S lens

LENSMAN *n pl.* -MEN a photographer

LENT	past tense of lend	**LETHAL**	n pl. -S a death-causing genetic defect
LENTANDO	adv becoming slower — used as a musical direction	**LETHALLY**	adv in a deadly manner
LENTEN	adj meager	**LETHARGY**	n pl. -GIES drowsiness; sluggishness
LENTIC	adj pertaining to still water	**LETHE**	n pl. -S forgetfulness
LENTICEL	n pl. -S a mass of cells on a plant stem	**LETHEAN** adj	
LENTIGO	n pl. -TIGINES a freckle	**LETTED**	past tense of let
LENTIL	n pl. -S a Eurasian annual plant	**LETTER**	v -ED, -ING, -S to mark with letters (written symbols representing speech sounds)
LENTISK	n pl. -S an evergreen tree	**LETTERER**	n pl. -S one that letters
LENTO	n pl. -TOS a slow musical movement	**LETTING**	present participle of let
LENTOID	adj lens-shaped	**LETTUCE**	n pl. -S an herb cultivated as a salad plant
LEONE	n pl. -S a monetary unit of Sierra Leone	**LETUP**	n pl. -S a lessening or relaxation
LEONINE	adj pertaining to a lion	**LEU**	n pl. LEI a monetary unit of Romania
LEOPARD	n pl. -S a large, carnivorous feline mammal	**LEUCEMIA**	n pl. -S leukemia **LEUCEMIC** adj
LEOTARD	n pl. -S a close-fitting garment	**LEUCIN**	n pl. -S leucine
LEPER	n pl. -S one affected with leprosy	**LEUCINE**	n pl. -S an amino acid
LEPIDOTE	n pl. -S a flowering shrub	**LEUCITE**	n pl. -S a mineral **LEUCITIC** adj
LEPORID	n pl. -RIDS or -RIDAE a gnawing mammal	**LEUCOMA**	n pl. -S leukoma
LEPORINE	adj resembling a rabbit or hare	**LEUD**	n pl. -S or -ES a feudal vassal
LEPROSE	adj leprous	**LEUKEMIA**	n pl. -S a disease of the blood-forming organs
LEPROSY	n pl. -SIES a chronic disease characterized by skin lesions and deformities	**LEUKEMIC**	n pl. -S one affected with leukemia
LEPROTIC	adj leprous	**LEUKOMA**	n pl. -S an opacity of the cornea
LEPROUS	adj affected with leprosy		
LEPT	a past tense of leap	**LEUKON**	n pl. -S a bodily organ consisting of the white blood cells
LEPTON	n pl. -TA a monetary unit of Greece		
LEPTON	n pl. -S a subatomic particle **LEPTONIC** adj	**LEUKOSIS**	n pl. -KOSES leukemia **LEUKOTIC** adj
LESBIAN	n pl. -S a female homosexual	**LEV**	n pl. LEVA a monetary unit of Bulgaria
LESION	n pl. -S an abnormal change in the structure of an organ or tissue **LESIONED** adj	**LEVANT**	v -ED, -ING, -S to avoid a debt
LESS	adj LESSER, LEAST not as great in quantity or degree	**LEVANTER**	n pl. -S an easterly Mediterranean wind
LESSEE	n pl. -S one to whom a lease is granted	**LEVATOR**	n pl. -ES or -S a muscle that raises an organ or part
LESSEN	v -ED, -ING, -S to make or become less	**LEVEE**	v LEVEED, LEVEEING, LEVEES to provide with an embankment
LESSER	adj not as large or important		
LESSON	v -ED, -ING, -S to instruct	**LEVEL**	v -ELED, -ELING, -ELS or -ELLED, -ELLING, -ELS to make even
LESSOR	n pl. -S one that grants a lease		
LEST	conj for fear that	**LEVELER**	n pl. -S one that levels
LET	v LETTED, LETTING, LETS to hinder	**LEVELLER**	n pl. -S leveler
LETCH	v -ED, -ING, -ES lech	**LEVELLING**	a present participle of level
LETDOWN	n pl. -S a decrease	**LEVELLY**	adv in an even manner

LEVER v -ED, -ING, -S to move with a lever (a rigid body used to lift weight)

LEVERAGE v -AGED, -AGING, -AGES to provide with a type of economic advantage

LEVERET n pl. -S a young hare

LEVIABLE adj liable to be levied

LEVIED past tense of levy

LEVIER n pl. -S one that levies

LEVIES present 3d person sing. of levy

LEVIGATE v -GATED, -GATING, -GATES to reduce to a fine powder

LEVIN n pl. -S lightning

LEVIRATE n pl. -S the custom of marrying the widow of one's brother

LEVITATE v -TATED, -TATING, -TATES to rise and float in the air

LEVITY n pl. -TIES conduct characterized by a lack of seriousness

LEVO adj turning toward the left

LEVODOPA n pl. -S a form of dopa

LEVOGYRE adj turning toward the left

LEVULIN n pl. -S a chemical compound

LEVULOSE n pl. -S a very sweet sugar

LEVY v LEVIED, LEVYING, LEVIES to impose or collect by legal authority

LEWD adj LEWDER, LEWDEST obscene **LEWDLY** adv

LEWDNESS n pl. -ES the state of being lewd

LEWIS n pl. -ISES a hoisting device

LEWISITE n pl. -S a vesicant liquid

LEWISSON n pl. -S lewis

LEX n pl. LEGES law

LEXEME n pl. -S a linguistic unit **LEXEMIC** adj

LEXICAL adj pertaining to the words of a language

LEXICON n pl. -CA or -CONS a dictionary

LEXIS n pl. LEXES the vocabulary of a language, a group, or a subject field

LEY n pl. LEYS lea

LI n pl. -S a Chinese unit of distance

LIABLE adj subject or susceptible to something possible or likely

LIAISE v LIAISED, LIAISING, LIAISES to establish liaison

LIAISON n pl. -S a means for maintaining communication

LIANA n pl. -S a tropical vine

LIANE n pl. -S liana

LIANG n pl. -S a Chinese unit of weight

LIANOID adj pertaining to a liana

LIAR n pl. -S one that speaks falsely

LIARD n pl. -S a former silver coin of France

LIB n pl. -S liberation

LIBATION n pl. -S a ceremonial pouring of a liquid

LIBECCIO n pl. -CIOS a southwest wind

LIBEL v -BELED, -BELING, -BELS or -BELLED, -BELLING, -BELS to make or publish a defamatory statement about

LIBELANT n pl. -S a plaintiff in a type of lawsuit

LIBELEE n pl. -S a defendant in a type of lawsuit

LIBELER n pl. -S one that libels

LIBELIST n pl. -S a libeler

LIBELLED a past tense of libel

LIBELLEE n pl. -S libelee

LIBELLER n pl. -S libeler

LIBELLING a present participle of libel

LIBELOUS adj defamatory

LIBER n pl. LIBRI or LIBERS a book of public records

LIBERAL n pl. -S a person favorable to progress or reform

LIBERATE v -ATED, -ATING, -ATES to set free

LIBERTY n pl. -TIES the state of being free

LIBIDO n pl. -DOS the energy derived from instinctual biological drives

LIBLAB n pl. -S a person supporting a coalition of liberal and labor groups

LIBRA n pl. -BRAE an ancient Roman unit of weight

LIBRA n pl. -S a former gold coin of Peru

LIBRARY n pl. -BRARIES a place where literary materials are kept for reading and reference

LIBRATE v -BRATED, -BRATING, -BRATES to move from side to side

LIBRETTO n pl. -TOS or -TI the text of an opera

LIBRI a pl. of liber

LICE pl. of louse

LICENCE v -CENCED, -CENCING, -CENCES to license

LICENCEE n pl. -S licensee

LICENCER n pl. -S licenser

LICENSE v -CENSED, -CENSING, -CENSES to issue or grant authoritative permission to

LICENSEE n pl. -S one that is licensed

LICENSER n pl. -S one that licenses

LICENSOR n pl. -S licenser

LICENTE a pl. of sente

LICH n pl. -ES a corpse

LICHEE n pl. -S litchi

LICHEN v -ED, -ING, -S to cover with lichens (flowerless plants)

LICHENIN n pl. -S a chemical compound

LICHI n pl. -S litchi

LICHT v -ED, -ING, -S to light

LICHTLY adv lightly

LICIT adj lawful LICITLY adv

LICK v -ED, -ING, -S to pass the tongue over the surface of

LICKER n pl. -S one that licks

LICKING n pl. -S a thrashing or beating

LICKSPIT n pl. -S a fawning person

LICORICE n pl. -S a perennial herb

LICTOR n pl. -S a magistrate's attendant in ancient Rome

LID v LIDDED, LIDDING, LIDS to provide with a lid (a movable cover)

LIDAR n pl. -S an electronic locating device

LIDLESS adj having no lid

LIDO n pl. -DOS a fashionable beach resort

LIE v LIED, LYING, LIES to speak falsely

LIE v LAY, LAIN, LYING, LIES to be in or get into a horizontal position

LIED n pl. LIEDER a German song

LIEF adj LIEFER, LIEFEST willing LIEFLY adv

LIEGE n pl. -S a feudal lord

LIEGEMAN n pl. -MEN a feudal vassal

LIEN n pl. -S a legal right to hold or sell a debtor's property

LIENABLE adj capable of being subjected to a lien

LIENAL adj pertaining to the spleen

LIENTERY n pl. -TERIES a form of diarrhea

LIER n pl. -S one that lies or reclines

LIERNE n pl. -S a connecting part in Gothic vaulting

LIEU n pl. -S place; stead

LIEVE adv LIEVER, LIEVEST gladly

LIFE n pl. LIVES the quality that distinguishes animals and plants from inanimate matter

LIFEBOAT n pl. -S a small rescue boat

LIFEFUL adj full of life

LIFELESS adj having no life

LIFELIKE adj resembling a living thing

LIFELINE n pl. -S a rope used to aid a person in distress

LIFELONG adj lasting for a lifetime

LIFER n pl. -S a prisoner serving a life sentence

LIFETIME n pl. -S the period of living existence

LIFEWAY n pl. -WAYS a way of living

LIFEWORK n pl. -S the major work of one's lifetime

LIFT v -ED, -ING, -S to move to a higher position LIFTABLE adj

LIFTER n pl. -S one that lifts

LIFTGATE n pl. -S a rear panel on a station wagon that opens upward

LIFTMAN n pl. -MEN an elevator operator

LIFTOFF n pl. -S the vertical takeoff of a rocket

LIGAMENT n pl. -S a band of firm, fibrous tissue

LIGAN n pl. -S lagan

LIGAND n pl. -S a type of ion or molecule

LIGASE n pl. -S an enzyme

LIGATE v -GATED, -GATING, -GATES to bind

LIGATION n pl. -S the act of ligating LIGATIVE adj

LIGATURE v -TURED, -TURING, -TURES to ligate

LIGER n pl. -S the offspring of a male lion and a female tiger

LIGHT adj LIGHTER, LIGHTEST having little weight

LIGHT v LIGHTED or LIT, LIGHTING, LIGHTS to illuminate

LIGHTEN v -ED, -ING, -S to reduce the weight of

LIGHTER v -ED, -ING, -S to convey in a type of barge

LIGHTFUL adj brightly illuminated

LIGHTING n pl. -S illumination

LIGHTISH adj somewhat light

LIGHTLY *adv* to a moderate degree

LIGNEOUS *adj* of or resembling wood

LIGNIFY *v* -FIED, -FYING, -FIES to convert into wood

LIGNIN *n pl.* -S an essential part of woody tissue

LIGNITE *n pl.* -S a type of coal **LIGNITIC** *adj*

LIGROIN *n pl.* -S a flammable liquid

LIGROINE *n pl.* -S ligroin

LIGULA *n pl.* -LAE or -LAS a strap-shaped organ or part **LIGULAR, LIGULATE, LIGULOID** *adj*

LIGULE *n pl.* -S a strap-shaped plant part

LIGURE *n pl.* -S a precious stone

LIKABLE *adj* pleasant

LIKE *v* LIKED, LIKING, LIKES to find pleasant

LIKE *adj* LIKER, LIKEST possessing the same or almost the same characteristics

LIKEABLE *adj* likable

LIKED past tense of like

LIKELY *adj* -LIER, -LIEST probable

LIKEN *v* -ED, -ING, -S to represent as similar

LIKENESS *n pl.* -ES a pictorial representation

LIKER *n pl.* -S one that likes

LIKEST superlative of like

LIKEWISE *adv* in a similar manner

LIKING *n pl.* -S a feeling of attraction or affection

LIKUTA *n pl.* MAKUTA a monetary unit of Zaire

LILAC *n pl.* -S a flowering shrub

LILIED *adj* covered with lilies

LILIES *pl.* of lily

LILLIPUT *n pl.* -S a very small person

LILT *v* -ED, -ING, -S to sing or speak rhythmically

LILY *n pl.* LILIES a flowering plant **LILYLIKE** *adj*

LIMA *n pl.* -S the edible seed of a tropical American plant

LIMACINE *adj* resembling a type of mollusk

LIMACON *n pl.* -S a type of geometric curve

LIMAN *n pl.* -S a lagoon

LIMB *v* -ED, -ING, -S to cut off the arms or legs of

LIMBA *n pl.* -S an African tree

LIMBATE *adj* having an edge of a different color

LIMBECK *n pl.* -S alembic

LIMBER *adj* -BERER, -BEREST flexible **LIMBERLY** *adv*

LIMBER *v* -ED, -ING, -S to make flexible

LIMBI a *pl.* of limbus

LIMBIC *adj* pertaining to a system of the brain

LIMBIER comparative of limby

LIMBIEST superlative of limby

LIMBLESS *adj* having no arms or legs

LIMBO *n pl.* -BOS a condition of oblivion or neglect

LIMBUS *n pl.* -BUSES or -BI a distinctive border

LIMBY *adj* LIMBIER, LIMBIEST having many large branches

LIME *v* LIMED, LIMING, LIMES to treat with lime (a calcium compound)

LIMEADE *n pl.* -S a beverage

LIMEKILN *n pl.* -S a furnace in which shells are burned to produce lime

LIMELESS *adj* having no lime

LIMEN *n pl.* -MENS or -MINA a sensory threshold

LIMERICK *n pl.* -S a humorous verse

LIMES *n pl.* LIMITES a fortified boundary

LIMEY *n pl.* -EYS a British sailor

LIMIER comparative of limy

LIMIEST superlative of limy

LIMINA a *pl.* of limen

LIMINAL *adj* pertaining to the limen

LIMINESS *n pl.* -ES the state of being limy

LIMING present participle of lime

LIMIT *v* -ED, -ING, -S to restrict

LIMITARY *adj* limiting

LIMITED *n pl.* -S a train or bus making few stops

LIMITER *n pl.* -S one that limits

LIMITES *pl.* of limes

LIMMER *n pl.* -S a scoundrel

LIMN *v* -ED, -ING, -S to depict by painting or drawing

LIMNER *n pl.* -S one that limns

LIMNETIC *adj* pertaining to the open water of a lake or pond

LIMNIC *adj* limnetic

LIMO *n pl.* LIMOS a limousine

LIMONENE *n pl.* -S a chemical compound

LIMONITE *n pl.* -S a major ore of iron

LIMP *v* -ED, -ING, -S to walk lamely

LIMP *adj* LIMPER, LIMPEST lacking rigidity

LIMPA *n pl.* -S rye bread made with molasses

LIMPER *n pl.* -S one that limps

LIMPET *n pl.* -S a type of mollusk

LIMPID *adj* transparent **LIMPIDLY** *adv*

LIMPKIN *n pl.* -S a wading bird

LIMPLY *adv* in a limp manner

LIMPNESS *n pl.* -ES the state of being limp

LIMPSEY *adj* -SIER, -SIEST limpsy

LIMPSY *adj* -SIER, -SIEST lacking strength or vigor

LIMULOID *n pl.* -S a horseshoe crab

LIMULUS *n pl.* -LI a horseshoe crab

LIMY *adj* LIMIER, LIMIEST resembling or containing lime

LIN *n pl.* -S linn

LINABLE *adj* lineable

LINAC *n pl.* -S a device for imparting high velocities to charged particles

LINAGE *n pl.* -S the number of lines of printed material

LINALOL *n pl.* -S linalool

LINALOOL *n pl.* -S a fragrant alcohol

LINCHPIN *n pl.* -S a locking pin inserted in the end of a shaft

LINDANE *n pl.* -S an insecticide

LINDEN *n pl.* -S a tall forest tree

LINDY *n pl.* -DIES a lively dance

LINE *v* LINED, LINING, LINES to mark with lines (slender, continuous marks)

LINEABLE *adj* lying in a straight line

LINEAGE *n pl.* -S direct descent from an ancestor

LINEAL *adj* being directly descended from an ancestor **LINEALLY** *adv*

LINEAR *adj* of or resembling a straight line **LINEARLY** *adv*

LINEATE *adj* marked with lines

LINEATED *adj* lineate

LINEBRED *adj* produced by interbreeding within a particular line of descent

LINECUT *n pl.* -S a type of printing plate

LINED past tense of line

LINELESS *adj* having no lines

LINELIKE *adj* resembling a line

LINEMAN *n pl.* -MEN one who installs or repairs telephone wires

LINEN *n pl.* -S a fabric woven from the fibers of flax **LINENY** *adj*

LINER *n pl.* -S a commercial ship or airplane

LINESMAN *n pl.* -MEN a football official

LINEUP *n pl.* -S a row of persons

LINEY *adj* LINIER, LINIEST liny

LING *n pl.* -S a heath plant

LINGA *n pl.* -S lingam

LINGAM *n pl.* -S a Hindu phallic symbol

LINGCOD *n pl.* -S a marine food fish

LINGER *v* -ED, -ING, -S to delay leaving

LINGERER *n pl.* -S one that lingers

LINGERIE *n pl.* -S women's underwear

LINGIER comparative of lingy

LINGIEST superlative of lingy

LINGO *n pl.* -GOES strange or incomprehensible language

LINGUA *n pl.* -GUAE the tongue or a tonguelike part

LINGUAL *n pl.* -S a sound articulated with the tongue

LINGUINE *n pl.* -S linguini

LINGUINI *n pl.* -S a type of pasta

LINGUIST *n pl.* -S a person skilled in several languages

LINGY *adj* LINGIER, LINGIEST covered with heaths

LINIER comparative of liney and liny

LINIEST superlative of liney and liny

LINIMENT *n pl.* -S a medicinal liquid

LININ *n pl.* -S a substance in the nucleus of a cell

LINING *n pl.* -S an inner layer

LINK *v* -ED, -ING, -S to connect **LINKABLE** *adj*

LINKAGE *n pl.* -S the act of linking

LINKBOY *n pl.* -BOYS a man or boy hired to carry a torch to light the way along dark streets

LINKER *n pl.* -S one that links

LINKMAN *n pl.* -MEN a linkboy

LINKSMAN *n pl.* -MEN a golfer

LINKUP *n pl.* -S something that serves as a linking device

LINKWORK *n pl.* -S something composed of interlocking rings

LINKY *adj* full of interlocking rings

LINN *n pl.* -S a waterfall

LINNET *n pl.* -S a European songbird

LINO *n pl.* -NOS linoleum

LINOCUT *n pl.* -S a print made from a design cut into linoleum

LINOLEUM *n pl.* -S a durable material used as a floor covering

LINSANG n pl. -S a carnivorous mammal

LINSEED n pl. -S flaxseed

LINSEY n pl. -SEYS a coarse fabric

LINSTOCK n pl. -S a stick having one end divided to hold a match

LINT n pl. -S an accumulation of bits of fiber

LINTEL n pl. -S a horizontal supporting beam

LINTER n pl. -S a machine for removing fibers from cotton seeds

LINTIER comparative of linty

LINTIEST superlative of linty

LINTLESS adj free from lint

LINTOL n pl. -S lintel

LINTY adj LINTIER, LINTIEST covered with lint

LINUM n pl. -S a plant of the flax family

LINURON n pl. -S a herbicide

LINY adj LINIER, LINIEST resembling a line

LION n pl. -S a large, carnivorous feline mammal

LIONESS n pl. -ES a female lion

LIONFISH n pl. -ES a tropical fish

LIONISE v -ISED, -ISING, -ISES to lionize

LIONISER n pl. -S one that lionises

LIONIZE v -IZED, -IZING, -IZES to treat or regard as a celebrity

LIONIZER n pl. -S one that lionizes

LIONLIKE adj resembling a lion

LIP v LIPPED, LIPPING, LIPS to touch with the lips (the folds of flesh around the mouth)

LIPASE n pl. -S an enzyme

LIPID n pl. -S any of a class of fatty substances LIPIDIC adj

LIPIDE n pl. -S lipid

LIPIN n pl. -S a lipid

LIPLESS adj having no lips

LIPLIKE adj resembling a lip

LIPOCYTE n pl. -S a fat-producing cell

LIPOID n pl. -S a lipid LIPOIDAL adj

LIPOMA n pl. -MAS or -MATA a tumor of fatty tissue

LIPOSOME n pl. -S a microscopic globule composed of lipids

LIPPED past tense of lip

LIPPEN v -ED, -ING, -S to trust

LIPPER v -ED, -ING, -S to ripple

LIPPING n pl. -S a liplike outgrowth of bone

LIPPY adj -PIER, -PIEST impudent

LIPSTICK n pl. -S a cosmetic used to color the lips

LIQUATE v -QUATED, -QUATING, -QUATES to purify metal by heating

LIQUEFY v -FIED, -FYING, -FIES to make or become liquid

LIQUEUR n pl. -S a sweetened alcoholic beverage

LIQUID n pl. -S a substance that flows freely

LIQUIDLY adv in a free-flowing manner

LIQUIFY v -FIED, -FYING, -FIES to liquefy

LIQUOR v -ED, -ING, -S to intoxicate with liquor (an alcoholic beverage)

LIRA n pl. LIRI a monetary unit of Malta

LIRA n pl. LIRE or LIRAS a monetary unit of Italy

LIRA n pl. LIROTH or LIROT a former monetary unit of Israel

LIRIPIPE n pl. -S a long scarf

LISENTE a pl. of sente

LISLE n pl. -S a fine, tightly twisted cotton thread

LISP v -ED, -ING, -S to pronounce the letters s and z imperfectly

LISPER n pl. -S one that lisps

LISSOM adj lissome LISSOMLY adv

LISSOME adj lithe

LIST v -ED, -ING, -S to write down in a particular order LISTABLE adj

LISTEE n pl. -S one that is on a list

LISTEL n pl. -S a narrow molding

LISTEN v -ED, -ING, -S to make conscious use of the sense of hearing

LISTENER n pl. -S one that listens

LISTER n pl. -S a type of plow

LISTING n pl. -S something that is listed

LISTLESS adj languid

LIT n pl. -S the litas

LITANY n pl. -NIES a ceremonial form of prayer

LITAS n pl. LITAI or LITU a former monetary unit of Lithuania

LITCHI n pl. -S the edible fruit of a Chinese tree

LITE adj lower in calories or having less of some ingredient

LITER n pl. -S a unit of capacity

LITERACY n pl. -CIES the ability to read and write

LITERAL n pl. -S a small error in printing or writing

LITERARY adj of, pertaining to, or having the characteristics of books and writings

LITERATE n pl. -S one who can read and write

LITERATI n/pl scholars collectively

LITHARGE n pl. -S a monoxide of lead

LITHE adj LITHER, LITHEST bending easily LITHELY adv

LITHEMIA n pl. -S an excess of uric acid in the blood LITHEMIC adj

LITHIA n pl. -S an oxide of lithium

LITHIC adj pertaining to lithium

LITHIFY v -FIED, -FYING, -FIES to petrify

LITHIUM n pl. -S a metallic element

LITHO v -ED, -ING, -S to make prints by lithography

LITHOID adj resembling stone

LITHOSOL n pl. -S a type of soil

LITIGANT n pl. -S one who is engaged in a lawsuit

LITIGATE v -GATED, -GATING, -GATES to subject to legal proceedings

LITMUS n pl. -ES a blue coloring matter

LITORAL adj pertaining to a coastal region

LITOTES n pl. LITOTES a figure of speech in which an assertion is made by the negation of its opposite LITOTIC adj

LITRE n pl. -S liter

LITTEN adj lighted

LITTER v -ED, -ING, -S to scatter rubbish about

LITTERER n pl. -S one that litters

LITTERY adj covered with rubbish

LITTLE adj -TLER, -TLEST small

LITTLE n pl. -S a small amount

LITTLISH adj somewhat little

LITTORAL n pl. -S a coastal region

LITU a pl. of litas

LITURGY n pl. -GIES a prescribed system of public worship LITURGIC adj

LIVABLE adj suitable for living in

LIVE v LIVED, LIVING, LIVES to function as an animal or plant

LIVE adj LIVER, LIVEST having life

LIVEABLE adj livable

LIVELONG adj long in passing

LIVELY adj -LIER, -LIEST full of energy LIVELILY adv

LIVEN v -ED, -ING, -S to make lively

LIVENER n pl. -S one that livens

LIVENESS n pl. -ES the state of being live

LIVER n pl. -S a secreting organ

LIVERIED adj wearing a livery

LIVERISH adj having a liver disorder

LIVERY n pl. -ERIES a uniform worn by servants

LIVES pl. of life

LIVEST superlative of live

LIVETRAP v -TRAPPED, -TRAPPING, -TRAPS to capture in a type of animal trap

LIVID adj having the skin abnormally discolored LIVIDLY adv

LIVIDITY n pl. -TIES the state of being livid

LIVIER n pl. -S livyer

LIVING n pl. -S a means of subsistence

LIVINGLY adv realistically

LIVRE n pl. -S a former monetary unit of France

LIVYER n pl. -S a permanent resident of Newfoundland

LIXIVIUM n pl. -IA or -IUMS a solution obtained by leaching LIXIVIAL adj

LIZARD n pl. -S any of a suborder of reptiles

LLAMA n pl. -S a ruminant mammal

LLANO n pl. -NOS an open, grassy plain

LO interj — used to attract attention or to express surprise

LOACH n pl. -ES a freshwater fish

LOAD v -ED, -ING, -S to place in or on a means of conveyance

LOADER n pl. -S one that loads

LOADING n pl. -S a burden

LOADSTAR n pl. -S lodestar

LOAF n pl. LOAVES a shaped mass of bread

LOAF v -ED, -ING, -S to pass time idly

LOAFER n pl. -S one that loafs

LOAM v -ED, -ING, -S to cover with loam (a type of soil)

LOAMLESS adj having no loam

LOAMY adj LOAMIER, LOAMIEST resembling loam

LOAN v -ED, -ING, -S to lend LOANABLE adj

LOANER n pl. -S one that loans

LOANING n pl. -S a lane

LOANWORD n pl. -S a word taken from another language

LOATH adj unwilling

LOATHE v LOATHED, LOATHING, LOATHES to detest greatly

LOATHER n pl. -S one that loathes

LOATHFUL adj repulsive

LOATHING n pl. -S extreme dislike

LOATHLY adj repulsive

LOAVES pl. of loaf

LOB v LOBBED, LOBBING, LOBS to throw or hit in a high arc

LOBAR adj pertaining to a lobe

LOBATE adj having lobes **LOBATELY** adv

LOBATED adj lobate

LOBATION n pl. -S the formation of lobes

LOBBED past tense of lob

LOBBER n pl. -S one that lobs

LOBBING present participle of lob

LOBBY v -BIED, -BYING, -BIES to attempt to influence legislators

LOBBYER n pl. -S a lobbyist

LOBBYGOW n pl. -S an errand boy

LOBBYISM n pl. -S the practice of lobbying

LOBBYIST n pl. -S one who lobbies

LOBE n pl. -S a rounded, projecting anatomical part **LOBED** adj

LOBEFIN n pl. -S a bony fish

LOBELIA n pl. -S a flowering plant

LOBELINE n pl. -S a poisonous alkaloid

LOBLOLLY n pl. -LIES a pine tree

LOBO n pl. -BOS the timber wolf

LOBOTOMY n pl. -MIES a type of surgical operation

LOBSTER v -ED, -ING, -S to fish for lobsters (marine crustaceans)

LOBSTICK n pl. -S a tree with its lower branches trimmed

LOBULE n pl. -S a small lobe **LOBULAR, LOBULATE, LOBULOSE** adj

LOBWORM n pl. -S a lugworm

LOCA a pl. of locus

LOCAL n pl. -S a train or bus making all stops

LOCALE n pl. -S a locality

LOCALISE v -ISED, -ISING, -ISES to localize

LOCALISM n pl. -S a custom or mannerism peculiar to a locality

LOCALIST n pl. -S one who is strongly concerned with the matters of a locality

LOCALITE n pl. -S a resident of a locality

LOCALITY n pl. -TIES an area or neighborhood

LOCALIZE v -IZED, -IZING, -IZES to confine to a particular area

LOCALLY adv in a particular area

LOCATE v -CATED, -CATING, -CATES to determine the position of

LOCATER n pl. -S one that locates

LOCATION n pl. -S the place where something is at a given moment

LOCATIVE n pl. -S a type of grammatical case

LOCATOR n pl. -S locater

LOCH n pl. -S a lake

LOCHAN n pl. -S a small lake

LOCHIA n pl. LOCHIA a vaginal discharge following childbirth **LOCHIAL** adj

LOCI a pl. of locus

LOCK v -ED, -ING, -S to secure by means of a mechanical fastening device **LOCKABLE** adj

LOCKAGE n pl. -S a toll on a ship passing through a canal

LOCKBOX n pl. -ES a box that locks

LOCKDOWN n pl. -S the confinement of prisoners to their cells

LOCKER n pl. -S an enclosure that may be locked

LOCKET n pl. -S a small ornamental case

LOCKJAW n pl. -S a form of tetanus

LOCKNUT n pl. -S a nut which keeps another from loosening

LOCKOUT n pl. -S a closing of a business to coerce employees to agree to terms

LOCKRAM n pl. -S a coarse, linen fabric

LOCKSTEP n pl. -S a mode of marching in close file

LOCKUP n pl. -S a jail

LOCO n pl. -COS or -COES locoweed

LOCO v -ED, -ING, -S to poison with locoweed

LOCOFOCO n pl. -COS a type of friction match

LOCOISM n pl. -S a disease of livestock

LOCOMOTE v -MOTED, -MOTING, -MOTES to move about

LOCOWEED *n* pl. **-S** a plant that causes poisoning when eaten by livestock

LOCULAR *adj* having or divided into loculi

LOCULATE *adj* locular

LOCULE *n* pl. **-S** loculus **LOCULED** *adj*

LOCULUS *n* pl. **-LI** a small, cell-like chamber

LOCUM *n* pl. **-S** a temporary substitute

LOCUS *n* pl. **LOCI** or **LOCA** a place

LOCUST *n* pl. **-S** a migratory grasshopper

LOCUSTA *n* pl. **-TAE** a spikelet **LOCUSTAL** *adj*

LOCUTION *n* pl. **-S** a particular form of expression

LOCUTORY *n* pl. **-RIES** a room in a monastery

LODE *n* pl. **-S** a deposit of ore

LODEN *n* pl. **-S** a thick, woolen fabric

LODESTAR *n* pl. **-S** a star used as a point of reference

LODGE *v* **LODGED, LODGING, LODGES** to furnish with temporary quarters

LODGER *n* pl. **-S** one that resides in rented quarters

LODGING *n* pl. **-S** a temporary place to live

LODGMENT *n* pl. **-S** a lodging

LODICULE *n* pl. **-S** a scale at the base of the ovary of a grass

LOESS *n* pl. **-ES** a soil deposit **LOESSAL, LOESSIAL** *adj*

LOFT *v* **-ED, -ING, -S** to store in a loft (an upper room)

LOFTER *n* pl. **-S** a type of golf club

LOFTIER comparative of lofty

LOFTIEST superlative of lofty

LOFTILY *adv* in a lofty manner

LOFTLESS *adj* having no loft

LOFTLIKE *adj* resembling a loft

LOFTY *adj* **LOFTIER, LOFTIEST** extending high in the air

LOG *v* **LOGGED, LOGGING, LOGS** to cut down trees for timber

LOGAN *n* pl. **-S** a stone balanced to permit easy movement

LOGANIA *adj* designating a family of flowering plants

LOGBOOK *n* pl. **-S** a record book of a ship or aircraft

LOGE *n* pl. **-S** a small compartment

LOGGATS *n/pl* loggets

LOGGED past tense of log

LOGGER *n* pl. **-S** one that logs

LOGGETS *n/pl* an old English throwing game

LOGGIA *n* pl. **-GIAS** or **-GIE** an open gallery

LOGGING *n* pl. **-S** the business of cutting down trees for timber

LOGGY *adj* **-GIER, -GIEST** logy

LOGIA a pl. of logion

LOGIC *n* pl. **-S** the science of reasoning

LOGICAL *adj* pertaining to logic

LOGICIAN *n* pl. **-S** one who is skilled in logic

LOGICISE *v* **-CISED, -CISING, -CISES** to logicize

LOGICIZE *v* **-CIZED, -CIZING, -CIZES** to reason

LOGIER comparative of logy

LOGIEST superlative of logy

LOGILY *adv* in a logy manner

LOGINESS *n* pl. **-ES** the state of being logy

LOGION *n* pl. **-GIA** or **-GIONS** a saying attributed to Jesus

LOGISTIC *n* pl. **-S** symbolic logic

LOGJAM *n* pl. **-S** a tangled mass of logs

LOGO *n* pl. **LOGOS** an identifying symbol

LOGOGRAM *n* pl. **-S** a symbol used to represent an entire word

LOGOMACH *n* pl. **-S** one given to arguing about words

LOGOS *n* pl. **LOGOI** the rational principle that governs the universe in ancient Greek philosophy

LOGOTYPE *n* pl. **-S** a piece of type bearing a syllable, word, or words

LOGOTYPY *n* pl. **-TYPIES** the use of logotypes

LOGROLL *v* **-ED, -ING, -S** to obtain passage of by exchanging political favors

LOGWAY *n* pl. **-WAYS** a ramp used in logging

LOGWOOD *n* pl. **-S** a tropical tree

LOGY *adj* **-GIER, -GIEST** sluggish

LOIN *n* pl. **-S** a part of the side and back between the ribs and the hipbone

LOITER *v* **-ED, -ING, -S** to stand idly about

LOITERER *n* pl. **-S** one that loiters

LOLL	v -ED, -ING, -S to lounge		LONGSPUR	n pl. -S a long-clawed finch
LOLLER	n pl. -S one that lolls		LONGTIME	adj of long duration
LOLLIES	pl. of lolly		LONGUEUR	n pl. -S a dull and tedious section
LOLLIPOP	n pl. -S a piece of candy on the end of a stick		LONGWAYS	adv longwise
LOLLOP	v -ED, -ING, -S to loll		LONGWISE	adv lengthwise
LOLLY	n pl. -LIES a lollipop		LOO	v -ED, -ING, -S to subject to a forfeit at loo (a card game)
LOLLYGAG	v -GAGGED, -GAGGING, -GAGS to lallygag		LOOBY	n pl. -BIES a large, awkward person
LOLLYPOP	n pl. -S lollipop		
LOMEIN	n pl. -S a Chinese dish of noodles, meat, and vegetables		LOOEY	n pl. -EYS looie
LOMENT	n pl. -S a type of plant pod		LOOF	n pl. -S the palm of the hand
LOMENTUM	n pl. -TA or -TUMS loment		LOOFA	n pl. -S loofah
LONE	adj having no companions		LOOFAH	n pl. -S a tropical vine
LONELY	adj -LIER, -LIEST sad from lack of companionship LONELILY adv		LOOIE	n pl. -S a lieutenant of the armed forces
			LOOK	v -ED, -ING, -S to use one's eyes in seeing
LONENESS	n pl. -ES the state of being lone		LOOKDOWN	n pl. -S a marine fish
LONER	n pl. -S one that avoids others		LOOKER	n pl. -S one that looks
LONESOME	n pl. -S self		LOOKOUT	n pl. -S one engaged in keeping watch
LONG	adj LONGER, LONGEST extending for a considerable distance		LOOKUP	n pl. -S the process of looking something up
LONG	v -ED, -ING, -S to desire strongly		LOOM	v -ED, -ING, -S to appear in an enlarged and indistinct form
LONGAN	n pl. -S the edible fruit of a Chinese tree		LOON	n pl. -S a diving waterfowl
LONGBOAT	n pl. -S the largest boat carried by a sailing vessel		LOONEY	adj -NIER, -NIEST loony
			LOONEY	n pl. -EYS loony
LONGBOW	n pl. -S a type of archery bow		LOONY	adj -NIER, -NIEST crazy
LONGE	v LONGED, LONGEING, LONGES to guide a horse by means of a long rope		LOONY	n pl. -NIES a loony person
			LOOP	v -ED, -ING, -S to form loops (circular or oval openings)
LONGER	n pl. -S one that longs		LOOPER	n pl. -S one that loops
LONGERON	n pl. -S a longitudinal support of an airplane		LOOPHOLE	v -HOLED, -HOLING, -HOLES to make small openings in
LONGHAIR	n pl. -S an intellectual		
LONGHAND	n pl. -S ordinary handwriting		LOOPY	adj LOOPIER, LOOPIEST full of loops
LONGHEAD	n pl. -S a person having a long skull		LOOSE	adj LOOSER, LOOSEST not firm, taut, or rigid LOOSELY adv
LONGHORN	n pl. -S one of a breed of long-horned cattle		
LONGIES	n/pl long underwear		LOOSE	v LOOSED, LOOSING, LOOSES to set free
LONGING	n pl. -S a strong desire		LOOSEN	v -ED, -ING, -S to make looser
LONGISH	adj somewhat long		
LONGLEAF	n pl. -LEAVES an evergreen tree		LOOSENER	n pl. -S one that loosens
			LOOSER	comparative of loose
LONGLINE	n pl. -S a type of fishing line		LOOSEST	superlative of loose
LONGLY	adv for a considerable distance		LOOSING	present participle of loose
			LOOT	v -ED, -ING, -S to plunder
LONGNESS	n pl. -ES the state of being long		LOOTER	n pl. -S one that loots
			LOP	v LOPPED, LOPPING, LOPS to cut off branches or twigs from
LONGSHIP	n pl. -S a medieval ship		
LONGSOME	adj tediously long		LOPE	v LOPED, LOPING, LOPES to run with a steady, easy gait

LOPER	n pl. -S one that lopes	**LOSING**	n pl. -S a loss
LOPPED	past tense of lop	**LOSINGLY**	adv in a manner characterized
LOPPER	v -ED, -ING, -S to curdle		by defeat
LOPPING	present participle of lop	**LOSS**	n pl. -ES the act of one that
LOPPY	adj -PIER, -PIEST hanging		loses
	limply	**LOSSY**	adj causing dissipation of
LOPSIDED	adj leaning to one side		electrical energy
LOPSTICK	n pl. -S lobstick	**LOST**	adj not to be found or
LOQUAT	n pl. -S a small yellow fruit		recovered
LORAL	adj pertaining to the space	**LOSTNESS**	n pl. -ES the state of being
	between the eye and bill of a		lost
	bird	**LOT**	v LOTTED, LOTTING, LOTS
LORAN	n pl. -S a type of navigational		to distribute proportionally
	system	**LOTA**	n pl. -S lotah
LORD	v -ED, -ING, -S to invest with	**LOTAH**	n pl. -S a small water vessel
	the power of a lord (a person		used in India
	having dominion over others)	**LOTH**	adj loath
LORDING	n pl. -S a lordling	**LOTHARIO**	n pl. -IOS a seducer of women
LORDLESS	adj having no lord	**LOTHSOME**	adj repulsive
LORDLIER	comparative of lordly	**LOTI**	n pl. MALOTI a monetary unit
LORDLIEST	superlative of lordly		of Lesotho
LORDLIKE	adj lordly	**LOTIC**	adj pertaining to moving water
LORDLING	n pl. -S an unimportant lord	**LOTION**	n pl. -S a liquid preparation for
LORDLY	adj -LIER, -LIEST of or		external application
	befitting a lord	**LOTOS**	n pl. -ES lotus
LORDOMA	n pl. -S lordosis	**LOTTE**	n pl. -S a monkfish
LORDOSIS	n pl. -DOSES a curvature of	**LOTTED**	past tense of lot
	the spinal column **LORDOTIC**	**LOTTERY**	n pl. -TERIES a type of
	adj		gambling game
LORDSHIP	n pl. -S the power of a lord	**LOTTING**	present participle of lot
LORE	n pl. -S traditional knowledge	**LOTTO**	n pl. -TOS a game of chance
	or belief	**LOTUS**	n pl. -ES an aquatic plant
LOREAL	adj loral	**LOUCHE**	adj not reputable
LORGNON	n pl. -S a pair of eyeglasses	**LOUD**	adj LOUDER, LOUDEST
	with a handle		strongly audible
LORICA	n pl. -CAE a protective	**LOUDEN**	v -ED, -ING, -S to make or
	covering or shell		become louder
LORICATE	n pl. -S an animal having a	**LOUDISH**	adj somewhat loud
	lorica	**LOUDLY**	adv -LIER, -LIEST in a loud
LORIES	pl. of lory		manner
LORIKEET	n pl. -S a small parrot	**LOUDNESS**	n pl. -ES the quality of being
LORIMER	n pl. -S a maker of implements		loud
	for harnesses and saddles	**LOUGH**	n pl. -S a lake
LORINER	n pl. -S lorimer	**LOUIE**	n pl. -S looie
LORIS	n pl. -RISES an Asian lemur	**LOUIS**	n pl. LOUIS a former gold coin
LORN	adj abandoned		of France
LORNNESS	n pl. -ES the state of being	**LOUNGE**	v LOUNGED, LOUNGING,
	lorn		LOUNGES to recline or lean in
LORRY	n pl. -RIES a type of wagon or		a relaxed, lazy manner
	truck	**LOUNGER**	n pl. -S one that lounges
LORY	n pl. -RIES a small parrot	**LOUNGY**	adj suitable for lounging
LOSE	v LOST, LOSING, LOSES to	**LOUP**	v LOUPED, LOUPEN,
	come to be without and be		LOUPING, LOUPS to leap
	unable to find **LOSABLE** adj	**LOUPE**	n pl. -S a small magnifying
LOSEL	n pl. -S a worthless person		glass
LOSER	n pl. -S one that loses	**LOUR**	v -ED, -ING, -S to lower

LOURY *adj* lowery

LOUSE *n pl.* LICE a parasitic insect

LOUSE *v* LOUSED, LOUSING, LOUSES to spoil or bungle

LOUSY *adj* LOUSIER, LOUSIEST mean or contemptible LOUSILY *adv*

LOUT *v* -ED, -ING, -S to bow in respect

LOUTISH *adj* clumsy

LOUVER *n pl.* -S a type of window LOUVERED *adj*

LOUVRE *n pl.* -S louver

LOVABLE *adj* having qualities that attract love LOVABLY *adv*

LOVAGE *n pl.* -S a perennial herb

LOVAT *n pl.* -S a chiefly green color mixture in fabrics

LOVE *v* LOVED, LOVING, LOVES to feel great affection for

LOVEABLE *adj* lovable LOVEABLY *adv*

LOVEBIRD *n pl.* -S a small parrot

LOVEBUG *n pl.* -S a small black fly that swarms along highways

LOVED past tense of love

LOVELESS *adj* feeling no love

LOVELIER comparative of lovely

LOVELIES pl. of lovely

LOVELIEST superlative of lovely

LOVELILY *adv* in a lovely manner

LOVELOCK *n pl.* -S a lock of hair hanging separately

LOVELORN *adj* not loved

LOVELY *adj* -LIER, -LIEST beautiful

LOVELY *n pl.* -LIES a beautiful woman

LOVER *n pl.* -S one that loves another LOVERLY *adj*

LOVESICK *adj* languishing with love

LOVESOME *adj* lovely

LOVEVINE *n pl.* -S a twining herb

LOVING *adj* affectionate

LOVINGLY *adv* in a loving manner

LOW *adj* LOWER, LOWEST having relatively little upward extension

LOW *v* -ED, -ING, -S to utter the sound characteristic of cattle

LOWBALL *v* -ED, -ING, -S to give a customer a deceptively low price

LOWBORN *adj* of humble birth

LOWBOY *n pl.* -BOYS a low chest of drawers

LOWBRED *adj* lowborn

LOWBROW *n pl.* -S an uncultivated person

LOWDOWN *n pl.* -S the whole truth

LOWE *v* LOWED, LOWING, LOWES to blaze

LOWER *v* -ED, -ING, -S to appear dark and threatening

LOWERY *adj* dark and threatening

LOWING *n pl.* -S the sound characteristic of cattle

LOWISH *adj* somewhat low

LOWLAND *n pl.* -S an area of land lying lower than the adjacent country

LOWLIFE *n pl.* -LIFES or -LIVES a despicable person

LOWLIFER *n pl.* -S a lowlife

LOWLIGHT *n pl.* -S an unpleasant event, detail, or part

LOWLY *adj* -LIER, -LIEST low in position or rank

LOWN *adj* peaceful

LOWNESS *n pl.* -ES the state of being low

LOWRIDER *n pl.* -S a car having a lowered suspension

LOWSE *adj* loose

LOX *v* -ED, -ING, -ES to supply with lox (liquid oxygen)

LOYAL *adj* -ALER, -ALEST faithful to one's allegiance

LOYALISM *n pl.* -S loyalty

LOYALIST *n pl.* -S one who is loyal

LOYALLY *adv* in a loyal manner

LOYALTY *n pl.* -TIES the state of being loyal

LOZENGE *n pl.* -S a small, often medicated candy

LUAU *n pl.* -S a Hawaiian feast

LUBBER *n pl.* -S a clumsy person LUBBERLY *adj*

LUBE *n pl.* -S a lubricant

LUBRIC *adj* slippery

LUBRICAL *adj* lubric

LUCARNE *n pl.* -S a type of window

LUCE *n pl.* -S a freshwater fish

LUCENCE *n pl.* -S lucency

LUCENCY *n pl.* -CIES the quality of being lucent

LUCENT *adj* giving off light LUCENTLY *adv*

LUCERN *n pl.* -S lucerne

LUCERNE *n pl.* -S alfalfa

LUCES a pl. of lux

LUCID *adj* easily understood LUCIDLY *adv*

LUCIDITY *n pl.* -TIES the quality of being lucid

LUCIFER *n pl.* -S a friction match

LUCK v -ED, -ING, -S to succeed by chance or good fortune

LUCKIE n pl. -S an old woman

LUCKLESS adj unlucky

LUCKY adj LUCKIER, LUCKIEST having good fortune LUCKILY adv

LUCRE n pl. -S monetary gain

LUCULENT adj lucid

LUDE n pl. -S a methaqualone pill

LUDIC adj aimlessly playful

LUES n pl. LUES syphilis

LUETIC n pl. -S one infected with syphilis

LUFF v -ED, -ING, -S to steer a sailing vessel nearer into the wind

LUFFA n pl. -S loofah

LUG v LUGGED, LUGGING, LUGS to carry or pull with effort

LUGE v LUGED, LUGEING, LUGES to race on a luge (a small sled)

LUGER n pl. -S one that luges

LUGGAGE n pl. -S articles containing a traveler's belongings

LUGGED past tense of lug

LUGGER n pl. -S a small sailing vessel

LUGGIE n pl. -S a small wooden dish or pail

LUGGING present participle of lug

LUGSAIL n pl. -S a type of sail

LUGWORM n pl. -S a burrowing marine worm

LUKEWARM adj moderately warm

LULL v -ED, -ING, -S to cause to sleep or rest

LULLABY v -BIED, -BYING, -BIES to lull with a soothing song

LULU n pl. -S something remarkable

LUM n pl. -S a chimney

LUMBAGO n pl. -GOS pain in the lower back

LUMBAR n pl. -S an anatomical part situated near the loins

LUMBER v -ED, -ING, -S to cut down and prepare timber for market

LUMBERER n pl. -S one that lumbers

LUMEN n pl. -MENS or -MINA the inner passage of a tubular organ LUMENAL, LUMINAL adj

LUMINARY n pl. -NARIES a body that gives light

LUMINISM n pl. -S a style of painting

LUMINIST n pl. -S a painter who uses the effects of light

LUMINOUS adj giving off light

LUMMOX n pl. -ES a clumsy person

LUMP v -ED, -ING, -S to make into lumps (shapeless masses)

LUMPEN n pl. -S an uprooted individual

LUMPER n pl. -S a laborer employed to load and unload ships

LUMPFISH n pl. -ES a marine fish

LUMPISH adj stupid

LUMPY adj LUMPIER, LUMPIEST full of lumps LUMPILY adv

LUNA n pl. -S an alchemical designation for silver

LUNACY n pl. -CIES insanity

LUNAR n pl. -S an observation of the moon taken for navigational purposes

LUNARIAN n pl. -S a supposed inhabitant of the moon

LUNATE adj crescent-shaped LUNATELY adv

LUNATED adj lunate

LUNATIC n pl. -S an insane person

LUNATION n pl. -S the interval between two successive new moons

LUNCH v -ED, -ING, -ES to eat a noonday meal

LUNCHEON n pl. -S a noonday meal

LUNCHER n pl. -S one that lunches

LUNE n pl. -S a crescent-shaped figure

LUNET n pl. -S lunette

LUNETTE n pl. -S a crescent-shaped object

LUNG n pl. -S a respiratory organ

LUNGAN n pl. -S longan

LUNGE v LUNGED, LUNGING, LUNGES to make a forceful forward movement

LUNGEE n pl. -S lungi

LUNGER n pl. -S one that lunges

LUNGFISH n pl. -ES a type of fish

LUNGFUL n pl. -S as much as the lungs can hold

LUNGI n pl. -S a loincloth worn by men in India

LUNGING present participle of lunge

LUNGWORM n pl. -S a parasitic worm

LUNGWORT n pl. -S a European herb

LUNGYI n pl. -S lungi

LUNIER comparative of luny

LUNIES pl. of luny

LUNIEST superlative of luny

LUNK n pl. -S a lunkhead

LUNKER n pl. -S a large game fish

LUNKHEAD n pl. -S a stupid person

LUNT *v* -ED, -ING, -S to emit smoke

LUNULA *n* pl. -LAE a small crescent-shaped structure **LUNULAR**, **LUNULATE** *adj*

LUNULE *n* pl. -S lunula

LUNY *adj* -NIER, -NIEST loony

LUNY *n* pl. -NIES a loony

LUPANAR *n* pl. -S a brothel

LUPIN *n* pl. -S lupine

LUPINE *n* pl. -S a flowering plant

LUPOUS *adj* pertaining to lupus

LUPULIN *n* pl. -S a medicinal powder obtained from the hop plant

LUPUS *n* pl. -ES a skin disease

LURCH *v* -ED, -ING, -ES to sway abruptly

LURCHER *n* pl. -S one that lurks or prowls

LURDAN *n* pl. -S a lazy or stupid person

LURDANE *n* pl. -S lurdan

LURE *v* LURED, LURING, LURES to attract with something desirable

LURER *n* pl. -S one that lures

LURID *adj* causing shock or horror **LURIDLY** *adv*

LURING present participle of lure

LURK *v* -ED, -ING, -S to wait in concealment

LURKER *n* pl. -S one that lurks

LUSCIOUS *adj* having a very pleasing taste or smell

LUSH *adj* LUSHER, LUSHEST abounding in vegetation **LUSHLY** *adv*

LUSH *v* -ED, -ING, -ES to drink to excess

LUSHNESS *n* pl. -ES the state of being lush

LUST *v* -ED, -ING, -S to have an intense desire

LUSTER *v* -ED, -ING, -S to make or become lustrous

LUSTFUL *adj* marked by excessive sexual desire

LUSTIER comparative of lusty

LUSTIEST superlative of lusty

LUSTILY *adv* in a lusty manner

LUSTRA *a* pl. of lustrum

LUSTRAL *adj* pertaining to a lustrum

LUSTRATE *v* -TRATED, -TRATING, -TRATES to purify ceremonially

LUSTRE *v* -TRED, -TRING, -TRES to luster

LUSTRING *n* pl. -S a glossy silk fabric

LUSTROUS *adj* reflecting light evenly and efficiently

LUSTRUM *n* pl. -TRUMS or -TRA a ceremonial purification of the population in ancient Rome

LUSTY *adj* LUSTIER, LUSTIEST full of vigor

LUSUS *n* pl. -ES an abnormality

LUTANIST *n* pl. -S one who plays the lute

LUTE *v* LUTED, LUTING, LUTES to play a lute (a stringed musical instrument)

LUTEA pl. of luteum

LUTEAL *adj* pertaining to the luteum

LUTECIUM *n* pl. -S lutetium

LUTED past tense of lute

LUTEFISK *n* pl. -S dried codfish

LUTEIN *n* pl. -S a yellow pigment

LUTENIST *n* pl. -S lutanist

LUTEOLIN *n* pl. -S a yellow pigment

LUTEOUS *adj* light to moderate greenish yellow in color

LUTETIUM *n* pl. -S a metallic element

LUTEUM *n* pl. -TEA a hormone-secreting body

LUTHERN *n* pl. -S a type of window

LUTHIER *n* pl. -S one who makes stringed instruments

LUTING *n* pl. -S a substance used as a sealant

LUTIST *n* pl. -S a lutanist

LUTZ *n* pl. -ES a jump in figure skating

LUV *n* pl. -S a sweetheart

LUX *n* pl. LUXES or LUCES a unit of illumination

LUXATE *v* -ATED, -ATING, -ATES to put out of joint

LUXATION *n* pl. -S the act of luxating

LUXE *n* pl. -S luxury

LUXURY *n* pl. -RIES free indulgence in that which affords pleasure or comfort

LWEI *n* pl. -S a monetary unit of Angola

LYARD *adj* streaked with gray

LYART *adj* lyard

LYASE *n* pl. -S an enzyme

LYCEE *n* pl. -S a French secondary school

LYCEUM *n* pl. -CEUMS or -CEA a hall for public lectures or discussions

LYCHEE *n* pl. -S litchi

LYCHNIS *n* pl. -NISES a flowering plant

LYCOPENE *n* pl. -S a red pigment

LYCOPOD *n pl.* -S an evergreen plant

LYDDITE *n pl.* -S an explosive

LYE *n pl.* -S a solution used in making soap

LYING *n pl.* -S the act of telling lies

LYINGLY *adv* falsely

LYMPH *n pl.* -S a body fluid containing white blood cells **LYMPHOID** *adj*

LYMPHOMA *n pl.* -MAS or -MATA a type of tumor

LYNCEAN *adj* of or resembling a lynx

LYNCH *v* -ED, -ING, -ES to put to death without legal sanction

LYNCHER *n pl.* -S one that lynches

LYNCHING *n pl.* -S the act of one who lynches

LYNCHPIN *n pl.* -S linchpin

LYNX *n pl.* -ES a short-tailed wildcat

LYOPHILE *adj* pertaining to a type of colloid

LYRATE *adj* having the shape of a lyre **LYRATELY** *adv*

LYRATED *adj* lyrate

LYRE *n pl.* -S an ancient harp-like instrument

LYREBIRD *n pl.* -S an Australian bird

LYRIC *n pl.* -S a lyrical poem

LYRICAL *adj* having the form of a song

LYRICISE *v* -CISED, -CISING, -CISES to lyricize

LYRICISM *n pl.* -S the quality of being lyrics

LYRICIST *n pl.* -S one who writes the words for songs

LYRICIZE *v* -CIZED, -CIZING, -CIZES to write lyrics

LYRIFORM *adj* lyrate

LYRISM *n pl.* -S lyricism

LYRIST *n pl.* -S one who plays the lyre

LYSATE *n pl.* -S a product of lysis

LYSE *v* LYSED, LYSING, LYSES to cause to undergo lysis

LYSIN *n pl.* -S a substance capable of disintegrating blood cells or bacteria

LYSINE *n pl.* -S an amino acid

LYSING present participle of lyse

LYSIS *n pl.* LYSES the disintegration of cells by lysins

LYSOGEN *n pl.* -S a type of antigen

LYSOGENY *n pl.* -NIES the state of being like a lysogen

LYSOSOME *n pl.* -S a saclike part of a cell

LYSOZYME *n pl.* -S an enzyme

LYSSA *n pl.* -S rabies

LYTIC *adj* pertaining to lysis

LYTTA *n pl.* -TAE or -TAS a fibrous band in the tongue of certain carnivorous mammals

M _3_

MA _n_ pl. -S mother

MAAR _n_ pl. -S a volcanic crater

MABE _n_ pl. -S a cultured pearl

MAC _n_ pl. -S a raincoat

MACABER _adj_ macabre

MACABRE _adj_ gruesome

MACACO _n_ pl. -COS a lemur

MACADAM _n_ pl. -S a type of pavement

MACAQUE _n_ pl. -S a short-tailed monkey

MACARONI _n_ pl. -NIS or -NIES a tubular pasta

MACAROON _n_ pl. -S a type of cookie

MACAW _n_ pl. -S a large parrot

MACCABAW _n_ pl. -S maccaboy

MACCABOY _n_ pl. -BOYS a type of snuff

MACCHIA _n_ pl. -CHIE a dense growth of small trees and shrubs

MACCOBOY _n_ pl. -BOYS maccaboy

MACE _v_ MACED, MACING, MACES to attack with a clublike weapon

MACER _n_ pl. -S an official who carries a ceremonial staff

MACERATE _v_ -ATED, -ATING, -ATES to soften by soaking in liquid

MACH _n_ pl. -S a number indicating the ratio of the speed of a body to the speed of sound

MACHE _n_ pl. -S a European herb

MACHETE _n_ pl. -S a large, heavy knife

MACHINE _v_ -CHINED, -CHINING, -CHINES to process by machine (a mechanical device)

MACHISMO _n_ pl. -MOS strong masculinity

MACHO _n_ pl. -CHOS a person who exhibits machismo

MACHREE _n_ pl. -S dear

MACHZOR _n_ pl. -ZORIM or -ZORS mahzor

MACING present participle of mace

MACK _n_ pl. -S mac

MACKEREL _n_ pl. -S a marine food fish

MACKINAW _n_ pl. -S a woolen fabric

MACKLE _v_ -LED, -LING, -LES to blur in printing

MACLE _n_ pl. -S a spot or discoloration in a mineral **MACLED** _adj_

MACON _n_ pl. -S a red or white French wine

MACRAME _n_ pl. -S a trimming of knotted thread or cord

MACRO _n_ pl. -ROS a type of computer instruction

MACRON _n_ pl. -S a symbol placed over a vowel to show that it has a long sound

MACRURAL _adj_ pertaining to macruran

MACRURAN _n_ pl. -S any of a suborder of crustaceans

MACULA _n_ pl. -LAE or -LAS a spot **MACULAR** _adj_

MACULATE _v_ -LATED, -LATING, -LATES to mark with spots

MACULE _v_ -ULED, -ULING, -ULES to mackle

MACUMBA _n_ pl. -S a religion practiced in Brazil

MAD _adj_ MADDER, MADDEST insane

MAD _v_ MADDED, MADDING, MADS to madden

MADAM _n_ pl. -S a woman who manages a brothel

MADAME _n_ pl. -S madam

MADAME _n_ pl. MESDAMES the French title of respect for a married woman

MADCAP _n_ pl. -S an impulsive person

MADDED　past tense of mad

MADDEN　v -ED, -ING, -S to make or become mad

MADDER　n pl. -S a perennial herb

MADDEST　superlative of mad

MADDING　present participle of mad

MADDISH　adj somewhat mad

MADE　past tense of make

MADEIRA　n pl. -S a white wine

MADHOUSE　n pl. -S an insane asylum

MADLY　adv in a mad manner

MADMAN　n pl. -MEN a man who is insane

MADNESS　n pl. -ES the state of being mad

MADONNA　n pl. -S a former Italian title of respect for a woman

MADRAS　n pl. -ES a cotton fabric

MADRE　n pl. -S mother

MADRIGAL　n pl. -S a short lyric poem

MADRONA　n pl. -S an evergreen tree

MADRONE　n pl. -S madrona

MADRONO　n pl. -NOS madrona

MADURO　n pl. -ROS a dark-colored, relatively strong cigar

MADWOMAN　n pl. -WOMEN a woman who is insane

MADWORT　n pl. -S a flowering plant

MADZOON　n pl. -S matzoon

MAE　n pl. -S more

MAENAD　n pl. -S or -ES a female participant in ancient Greek orgies MAENADIC adj

MAESTOSO　n pl. -SOS a stately musical passage

MAESTRO　n pl. -STROS or -STRI a master of an art

MAFFIA　n pl. -S mafia

MAFFICK　v -ED, -ING, -S to celebrate boisterously

MAFIA　n pl. -S a secret criminal organization

MAFIC　adj pertaining to minerals rich in magnesium and iron

MAFIOSO　n pl. -SI a member of the mafia

MAFTIR　n pl. -S the concluding section of a parashah

MAG　n pl. -S a magazine

MAGAZINE　n pl. -S a type of periodical publication

MAGDALEN　n pl. -S a reformed prostitute

MAGE　n pl. -S a magician

MAGENTA　n pl. -S a purplish red dye

MAGGOT　n pl. -S the legless larva of certain insects MAGGOTY adj

MAGI　pl. of magus

MAGIAN　n pl. -S a magus

MAGIC　v -ICKED, -ICKING, -ICS to affect by magic (sorcery)

MAGICAL　adj resembling magic

MAGICIAN　n pl. -S one skilled in magic

MAGICKED　past tense of magic

MAGICKING　present participle of magic

MAGILP　n pl. -S megilp

MAGISTER　n pl. -S a master or teacher

MAGLEV　adj pertaining to a railroad system using magnets to move a train above the tracks

MAGMA　n pl. -MAS or -MATA the molten matter from which igneous rock is formed MAGMATIC adj

MAGNATE　n pl. -S a powerful or influential person

MAGNESIA　n pl. -S a medicinal compound MAGNESIC adj

MAGNET　n pl. -S a body that possesses the property of attracting iron

MAGNETIC　n pl. -S a magnet

MAGNETO　n pl. -TOS a type of electric generator

MAGNETON　n pl. -S a unit of magnetic moment

MAGNIFIC　adj magnificent

MAGNIFY　v -FIED, -FYING, -FIES to increase the perceived size of

MAGNOLIA　n pl. -S a flowering shrub or tree

MAGNUM　n pl. -S a large wine bottle

MAGOT　n pl. -S a tailless ape

MAGPIE　n pl. -S a corvine bird

MAGUEY　n pl. -GUEYS a tropical plant

MAGUS　n pl. -GI a magician

MAHARAJA　n pl. -S a king or prince in India

MAHARANI　n pl. -S the wife of a maharaja

MAHATMA　n pl. -S a Hindu sage

MAHIMAHI　n pl. MAHIMAHI a food fish in Hawaii

MAHJONG　n pl. -S a game of Chinese origin

MAHJONGG　n pl. -S mahjong

MAHOE　n pl. -S a tropical tree

MAHOGANY　n pl. -NIES a tropical tree

MAHONIA　n pl. -S a flowering shrub

MAHOUT　n pl. -S the keeper and driver of an elephant

MAHUANG　n pl. -S an Asian plant

MAHZOR　n pl. -ZORIM or -ZORS a Jewish prayer book

MAID n pl. -S a maiden **MAIDISH** adj

MAIDEN n pl. -S a young unmarried woman **MAIDENLY** adj

MAIDHOOD n pl. -S the state of being a maiden

MAIEUTIC adj pertaining to a method of eliciting knowledge

MAIGRE adj containing neither flesh nor its juices

MAIHEM n pl. -S mayhem

MAIL v -ED, -ING, -S to send by a governmental postal system. **MAILABLE** adj

MAILBAG n pl. -S a bag for carrying mail (postal material)

MAILBOX n pl. -ES a box for depositing mail

MAILE n pl. -S a Pacific island vine

MAILER n pl. -S one that mails

MAILING n pl. -S a rented farm

MAILL n pl. -S a payment

MAILLESS adj having no armor

MAILLOT n pl. -S a woman's one-piece bathing suit

MAILMAN n pl. -MEN a man who carries and delivers mail

MAIM v -ED, -ING, -S to injure so as to cause lasting damage

MAIMER n pl. -S one that maims

MAIN n pl. -S the principal part

MAINLAND n pl. -S a principal land mass

MAINLINE v -LINED, -LINING, -LINES to inject a narcotic into a major vein

MAINLY adv for the most part

MAINMAST n pl. -S the principal mast of a vessel

MAINSAIL n pl. -S the principal sail of a vessel

MAINSTAY n pl. -STAYS a principal support

MAINTAIN v -ED, -ING, -S to keep in proper condition

MAINTOP n pl. -S a platform at the head of a mainmast

MAIOLICA n pl. -S majolica

MAIR n pl. -S more

MAIST n pl. -S most

MAIZE n pl. -S an American cereal grass

MAJAGUA n pl. -S a tropical tree

MAJESTIC adj having majesty

MAJESTY n pl. -TIES regal dignity

MAJOLICA n pl. -S a type of pottery

MAJOR v -ED, -ING, -S to pursue a specific principal course of study

MAJORITY n pl. -TIES the greater number or part

MAJORLY adv mainly

MAKAR n pl. -S a poet

MAKE v MADE, MAKING, MAKES to cause to exist **MAKABLE**, **MAKEABLE** adj

MAKEBATE n pl. -S one that encourages quarrels

MAKEFAST n pl. -S an object to which a boat is tied

MAKEOVER n pl. -S a changing of appearance

MAKER n pl. -S one that makes

MAKEUP n pl. -S the way in which the parts or ingredients of something are put together

MAKIMONO n pl. -NOS a Japanese ornamental scroll

MAKING n pl. -S material from which something can be developed

MAKO n pl. -KOS a large shark

MAKUTA pl. of likuta

MALACCA n pl. -S the cane of an Asian rattan palm

MALADY n pl. -DIES an illness

MALAISE n pl. -S a feeling of vague discomfort

MALAMUTE n pl. -S an Alaskan sled dog

MALANGA n pl. -S a yautia

MALAPERT n pl. -S an impudent person

MALAPROP n pl. -S a humorous misuse of a word

MALAR n pl. -S the cheekbone

MALARIA n pl. -S an infectious disease **MALARIAL, MALARIAN** adj

MALARKEY n pl. -KEYS nonsense

MALARKY n pl. -KIES malarkey

MALAROMA n pl. -S a malodor

MALATE n pl. -S a chemical salt

MALE n pl. -S an individual that begets young by fertilizing the female

MALEATE n pl. -S a chemical salt

MALEDICT v -ED, -ING, -S to curse

MALEFIC adj producing or causing evil

MALEMIUT n pl. -S malamute

MALEMUTE n pl. -S malamute

MALENESS n pl. -ES the quality of being a male

MALFED adj badly fed

MALGRE prep in spite of

MALIC adj pertaining to apples

MALICE n pl. -S a desire to injure another

MALIGN v -ED, -ING, -S to speak evil of

MALIGNER n pl. -S one that maligns

MALIGNLY adv in an evil manner

MALIHINI n pl. -S a newcomer to Hawaii

MALINE n pl. -S a delicate net used for veils

MALINGER v -ED, -ING, -S to feign illness in order to avoid duty or work

MALISON n pl. -S a curse

MALKIN n pl. -S an untidy woman

MALL v -ED, -ING, -S to maul

MALLARD n pl. -S a wild duck

MALLEE n pl. -S an evergreen tree

MALLEI pl. of malleus

MALLEOLI n/pl bony protuberances of the ankle

MALLET n pl. -S a type of hammer

MALLEUS n pl. -LEI a bone of the middle ear

MALLOW n pl. -S a flowering plant

MALM n pl. -S a soft, friable limestone

MALMSEY n pl. -SEYS a white wine

MALMY adj MALMIER, MALMIEST resembling malm

MALODOR n pl. -S an offensive odor

MALOTI pl. of loti

MALPOSED adj being in the wrong position

MALT v -ED, -ING, -S to treat or combine with malt (germinated grain)

MALTASE n pl. -S an enzyme

MALTED n pl. -S a sweet beverage

MALTHA n pl. -S a natural tar

MALTIER comparative of malty

MALTIEST superlative of malty

MALTOL n pl. -S a chemical compound

MALTOSE n pl. -S a type of sugar

MALTREAT v -ED, -ING, -S to treat badly

MALTSTER n pl. -S one that makes malt

MALTY adj MALTIER, MALTIEST resembling malt

MALVASIA n pl. -S malmsey

MAMA n pl. -S mother

MAMALIGA n pl. -S a cornmeal porridge

MAMBA n pl. -S a venomous snake

MAMBO v -ED, -ING, -ES or -S to perform a ballroom dance

MAMELUKE n pl. -S a slave in Muslim countries

MAMEY n pl. -MEYS or -MEYES a tropical tree

MAMIE n pl. -S mamey

MAMLUK n pl. -S mameluke

MAMMA n pl. -S mama

MAMMA n pl. -MAE a milk-secreting organ

MAMMAL n pl. -S any of a class of warm-blooded vertebrates

MAMMARY adj pertaining to the mammae

MAMMATE adj having mammae

MAMMATUS n pl. -TI a type of cloud

MAMMEE n pl. -S mamey

MAMMER v -ED, -ING, -S to hesitate

MAMMET n pl. -S maumet

MAMMEY n pl. -MEYS mamey

MAMMIE n pl. -S mammy

MAMMIES pl. of mammy

MAMMILLA n pl. -LAE a nipple

MAMMITIS n pl. -MITIDES mastitis

MAMMOCK v -ED, -ING, -S to shred

MAMMON n pl. -S material wealth

MAMMOTH n pl. -S an extinct elephant

MAMMY n pl. -MIES mother

MAN n pl. MEN an adult human male

MAN v MANNED, MANNING, MANS to supply with men

MANA n pl. -S a supernatural force in certain Pacific island religions

MANACLE v -CLED, -CLING, -CLES to handcuff

MANAGE v -AGED, -AGING, -AGES to control or direct

MANAGER n pl. -S one that manages

MANAKIN n pl. -S a tropical bird

MANANA n pl. -S tomorrow

MANATEE n pl. -S an aquatic mammal MANATOID adj

MANCHE n pl. -S a heraldic design

MANCHET n pl. -S a small loaf of fine white bread

MANCIPLE n pl. -S an officer authorized to purchase provisions

MANDALA n pl. -S a Hindu or Buddhist graphic symbol of the universe MANDALIC adj

MANDAMUS v -ED, -ING, -ES to command by means of writ issued by a superior court

MANDARIN n pl. -S a citrus fruit

MANDATE v -DATED, -DATING, -DATES to authorize or decree

MANDATOR n pl. -S one that mandates

MANDIBLE n pl. -S the bone of the lower jaw

MANDIOCA n pl. -S manioc

MANDOLA n pl. -S an ancient lute

MANDOLIN *n pl.* -S a stringed musical instrument

MANDRAKE *n pl.* -S a European herb

MANDREL *n pl.* -S a shaft on which a tool is mounted

MANDRIL *n pl.* -S mandrel

MANDRILL *n pl.* -S a large baboon

MANE *n pl.* -S the long hair growing on and about the neck of some animals **MANED, MANELESS** *adj*

MANEGE *n pl.* -S the art of training and riding horses

MANEUVER *v* -ED, -ING, -S to change the position of for a specific purpose

MANFUL *adj* courageous **MANFULLY** *adv*

MANGABEY *n pl.* -BEYS a long-tailed monkey

MANGABY *n pl.* -BIES mangabey

MANGANIC *adj* containing manganese (a metallic element)

MANGE *n pl.* -S a skin disease of domestic animals

MANGEL *n pl.* -S a variety of beet

MANGER *n pl.* -S a trough or box from which horses or cattle eat

MANGEY *adj* **MANGIER, MANGIEST** mangy

MANGIER comparative of mangy

MANGIEST superlative of mangy

MANGILY *adv* in a mangy manner

MANGLE *v* -GLED, -GLING, -GLES to cut, slash, or crush so as to disfigure

MANGLER *n pl.* -S one that mangles

MANGO *n pl.* -GOES or -GOS an edible tropical fruit

MANGOLD *n pl.* -S mangel

MANGONEL *n pl.* -S a medieval military device for hurling stones

MANGROVE *n pl.* -S a tropical tree or shrub

MANGY *adj* **MANGIER, MANGIEST** affected with mange

MANHOLE *n pl.* -S a hole providing entrance to an underground or enclosed structure

MANHOOD *n pl.* -S the state of being a man

MANHUNT *n pl.* -S an intensive search for a person

MANIA *n pl.* -S an excessive interest or enthusiasm

MANIAC *n pl.* -S an insane person **MANIACAL** *adj*

MANIC *n pl.* -S one that is affected with mania

MANICURE *v* -CURED, -CURING, -CURES to trim and polish the fingernails of

MANIFEST *v* -ED, -ING, -S to show clearly

MANIFOLD *v* -ED, -ING, -S to make several copies of

MANIHOT *n pl.* -S a tropical plant

MANIKIN *n pl.* -S an anatomical model of the human body

MANILA *n pl.* -S a strong paper

MANILLA *n pl.* -S manila

MANILLE *n pl.* -S the second highest trump in certain card games

MANIOC *n pl.* -S a tropical plant

MANIOCA *n pl.* -S manioc

MANIPLE *n pl.* -S a silk band worn on the left arm as a vestment

MANITO *n pl.* -TOS manitou

MANITOU *n pl.* -S an Algonquian Indian deity

MANITU *n pl.* -S manitou

MANKIND *n pl.* MANKIND the human race

MANLESS *adj* destitute of men

MANLIKE *adj* resembling men

MANLY *adj* -LIER, -LIEST having the qualities of a man **MANLILY** *adv*

MANMADE *adj* made by man

MANNA *n pl.* -S divinely supplied food

MANNAN *n pl.* -S a type of sugar

MANNED past tense of man

MANNER *n pl.* -S a way of acting **MANNERED** *adj*

MANNERLY *adj* polite

MANNIKIN *n pl.* -S manikin

MANNING present participle of man

MANNISH *adj* resembling or characteristic of a man

MANNITE *n pl.* -S mannitol **MANNITIC** *adj*

MANNITOL *n pl.* -S an alcohol

MANNOSE *n pl.* -S a type of sugar

MANO *n pl.* -NOS a stone used for grinding foods

MANOR *n pl.* -S a landed estate or territorial unit **MANORIAL** *adj*

MANPACK *adj* designed to be carried by one person

MANPOWER *n pl.* -S the number of men available for service

MANQUE *adj* frustrated in the fulfillment of one's aspirations

MANROPE n pl. -S a rope used as a handrail

MANSARD n pl. -S a type of roof

MANSE n pl. -S a clergyman's house

MANSION n pl. -S a large, impressive house

MANTA n pl. -S a cotton fabric

MANTEAU n pl. -TEAUS or -TEAUX a loose cloak

MANTEL n pl. -S a shelf above a fireplace

MANTELET n pl. -S a mobile screen used to protect soldiers

MANTES a pl. of mantis

MANTIC adj having powers of prophecy

MANTID n pl. -S mantis

MANTILLA n pl. -S a woman's scarf

MANTIS n pl. -TISES or -TES a predatory insect

MANTISSA n pl. -S the decimal part of a logarithm

MANTLE v -TLED, -TLING, -TLES to cloak

MANTLET n pl. -S mantelet

MANTLING n pl. -S an ornamental cloth

MANTRA n pl. -S a mystical formula of prayer or incantation in Hinduism **MANTRIC** adj

MANTRAP n pl. -S a trap for catching men

MANTUA n pl. -S a woman's gown

MANUAL n pl. -S a small reference book

MANUALLY adv by means of the hands

MANUARY adj involving the hands

MANUBRIA n/pl handle-shaped anatomical parts

MANUMIT v -MITTED, -MITTING, -MITS to free from slavery

MANURE v -NURED, -NURING, -NURES to fertilize with manure (animal excrement)

MANURER n pl. -S one that manures

MANURIAL adj of or pertaining to manure

MANURING present participle of manure

MANUS n pl. MANUS the end of the forelimb in vertebrates

MANWARD adv toward man

MANWARDS adv manward

MANWISE adv in a manner characteristic of man

MANY adj MORE, MOST consisting of or amounting to a large number

MANYFOLD adv by many times

MAP v MAPPED, MAPPING, MAPS to delineate on a map (a representation of a region)

MAPLE n pl. -S a hardwood tree

MAPLIKE adj resembling a map

MAPMAKER n pl. -S one that makes maps

MAPPABLE adj capable of being mapped

MAPPED past tense of map

MAPPER n pl. -S one that maps

MAPPING n pl. -S a mathematical correspondence

MAQUETTE n pl. -S a small preliminary model

MAQUI n pl. -S maquis

MAQUIS n pl. MAQUIS a thick underbrush

MAR v MARRED, MARRING, MARS to detract from the perfection or wholeness of

MARABOU n pl. -S an African stork

MARABOUT n pl. -S a marabou

MARACA n pl. -S a percussion instrument

MARANTA n pl. -S a tropical plant

MARASCA n pl. -S a wild cherry

MARASMUS n pl. -ES a wasting away of the body **MARASMIC** adj

MARATHON n pl. -S a long-distance race

MARAUD v -ED, -ING, -S to rove in search of booty

MARAUDER n pl. -S one that marauds

MARAVEDI n pl. -S a former coin of Spain

MARBLE v -BLED, -BLING, -BLES to give a mottled appearance to

MARBLER n pl. -S one that marbles

MARBLING n pl. -S an intermixture of fat and lean in meat

MARBLY adj -BLIER, -BLIEST mottled

MARC n pl. -S the residue remaining after a fruit has been pressed

MARCATO adv with strong accentuation—used as a musical direction

MARCEL v -CELLED, -CELLING, -CELS to make a deep, soft wave in the hair

MARCH v -ED, -ING, -ES to walk in a formal military manner

MARCHEN n pl. MARCHEN a folktale

MARCHER n pl. -S one that marches

MARCHESA n pl. -CHESE the wife or widow of a marchese

MARCHESE n pl. -CHESI an Italian nobleman

MARE n pl. -S a mature female horse

MARE n pl. -RIA a dark area on the surface of the moon or Mars

MAREMMA n pl. -REMME a marshy coastal region

MARENGO adj served with a sauce of mushrooms, tomatoes, oil, and wine

MARGARIC adj pearly

MARGARIN n pl. -S a butter substitute

MARGAY n pl. -GAYS a small American wildcat

MARGE n pl. -S a margin

MARGENT v -ED, -ING, -S to margin

MARGIN v -ED, -ING, -S to provide with a margin (a border)

MARGINAL adj of or pertaining to a margin

MARGRAVE n pl. -S the military governor of a medieval German border province

MARIA pl. of mare

MARIACHI n pl. -S a Mexican musical band

MARIGOLD n pl. -S a flowering plant

MARIMBA n pl. -S a percussion instrument

MARINA n pl. -S a docking area for small boats

MARINADE v -NADED, -NADING, -NADES to marinate

MARINARA n pl. -S a seasoned tomato sauce

MARINATE v -NATED, -NATING, -NATES to soak in a seasoned liquid before cooking

MARINE n pl. -S a soldier trained for service at sea and on land

MARINER n pl. -S a sailor

MARIPOSA n pl. -S a flowering plant

MARISH n pl. -ES a marsh

MARITAL adj pertaining to marriage

MARITIME adj pertaining to navigation or commerce on the sea

MARJORAM n pl. -S fragrant herb

MARK v -ED, -ING, -S to make a visible impression on

MARKDOWN n pl. -S a reduction in price

MARKEDLY adv in an evident manner

MARKER n pl. -S one that marks

MARKET v -ED, -ING, -S to offer for sale

MARKETER n pl. -S one that markets

MARKHOOR n pl. -S markhor

MARKHOR n pl. -S a wild goat

MARKING n pl. -S a pattern of marks

MARKKA n pl. -KAA or -KAS a monetary unit of Finland

MARKSMAN n pl. -MEN a person skillful at hitting a target

MARKUP n pl. -S an increase in price

MARL v -ED, -ING, -S to fertilize with marl (an earthy deposit containing lime, clay, and sand)

MARLIER comparative of marly

MARLIEST superlative of marly

MARLIN n pl. -S a marine game fish

MARLINE n pl. -S a rope used on a ship

MARLING n pl. -S marline

MARLITE n pl. -S a type of marl **MARLITIC** adj

MARLY adj MARLIER, MARLIEST abounding with marl

MARMITE n pl. -S a large soup kettle

MARMOSET n pl. -S a small monkey

MARMOT n pl. -S a burrowing rodent

MAROCAIN n pl. -S a light crinkled fabric

MAROON v -ED, -ING, -S to abandon in an isolated place

MARPLOT n pl. -S one that ruins a plan by meddling

MARQUE n pl. -S reprisal

MARQUEE n pl. -S a rooflike structure projecting over an entrance

MARQUESS n pl. -ES marquis

MARQUIS n pl. -ES a European nobleman

MARQUISE n pl. -S the wife or widow of a marquis

MARRAM n pl. -S a beach grass

MARRANO n pl. -NOS a Jew in Spain who professed Christianity to avoid persecution

MARRED past tense of mar

MARRER n pl. -S one that mars

MARRIAGE n pl. -S the legal union of a man and woman

MARRIED n pl. -S one who has entered into marriage

MARRIER n pl. -S one that marries

MARRIES present 3d person sing. of marry

MARRING present participle of mar

MARRON n pl. -S a variety of chestnut

MARROW v -ED, -ING, -S to marry

MARROWY adj pithy

MARRY v -RIED, -RYING, -RIES to enter into marriage

MARSALA n pl. -S a Sicilian wine

MARSE n pl. -S master

MARSH n pl. -ES a tract of low, wet land

MARSHAL v -ED, -ING, -S to put in proper order

MARSHALL v -ED, -ING, -S to marshal

MARSHY *adj* MARSHIER, MARSHIEST resembling a marsh

MARSUPIA *n/pl* abdominal pouches of certain mammals

MART *v* -ED, -ING, -S to market

MARTAGON *n* pl. -S a flowering plant

MARTELLO *n* pl. -LOS a circular fort

MARTEN *n* pl. -S a carnivorous mammal

MARTIAL *adj* pertaining to war

MARTIAN *n* pl. -S a supposed inhabitant of the planet Mars

MARTIN *n* pl. -S a small bird

MARTINET *n* pl. -S one who demands rigid adherence to rules

MARTINI *n* pl. -S an alcoholic beverage

MARTLET *n* pl. -S a martin

MARTYR *v* -ED, -ING, -S to put to death for adhering to a belief

MARTYRLY *adj* resembling a martyr

MARTYRY *n* pl. -TYRIES a shrine erected in honor of a martyred person

MARVEL *v* -VELED, -VELING, -VELS or -VELLED, -VELLING, -VELS to be filled with wonder or astonishment

MARVY *adj* marvelous

MARYJANE *n* pl. -S marijuana

MARZIPAN *n* pl. -S an almond candy

MASCARA *v* -ED, -ING, -S to color the eyelashes or eyebrows with a cosmetic

MASCON *n* pl. -S a concentration of dense mass beneath the moon's surface

MASCOT *n* pl. -S a person, animal, or object believed to bring good luck

MASER *n* pl. -S a device for amplifying electrical impulses

MASH *v* -ED, -ING, -ES to reduce to a pulpy mass

MASHER *n* pl. -S one that mashes

MASHIE *n* pl. -S a golf club

MASHY *n* pl. MASHIES mashie

MASJID *n* pl. -S a mosque

MASK *v* -ED, -ING, -S to cover with a mask (a covering used to disguise the face) MASKABLE *adj*

MASKEG *n* pl. -S muskeg

MASKER *n* pl. -S one that wears a mask

MASKING *n* pl. -S a piece of scenery used to conceal parts of a stage from the audience

MASKLIKE *adj* suggestive of a mask

MASON *v* -ED, -ING, -S to build with stone or brick

MASONIC *adj* pertaining to masonry

MASONRY *n* pl. -RIES a structure built of stone or brick

MASQUE *n* pl. -S a dramatic entertainment formerly popular in England

MASQUER *n* pl. -S masker

MASS *v* -ED, -ING, -ES to assemble in a mass (a body of coherent matter)

MASSA *n* pl. -S master

MASSACRE *v* -CRED, -CRING, -CRES to kill indiscriminately

MASSAGE *v* -SAGED, -SAGING, -SAGES to manipulate parts of the body for remedial or hygienic purposes

MASSAGER *n* pl. -S one that massages

MASSCULT *n* pl. -S culture as popularized by the mass media

MASSE *n* pl. -S a type of shot in billiards

MASSEDLY *adv* in a massed manner

MASSETER *n* pl. -S a muscle that raises the lower jaw

MASSEUR *n* pl. -S a man who massages

MASSEUSE *n* pl. -S a woman who massages

MASSICOT *n* pl. -S a yellow pigment

MASSIER comparative of massy

MASSIEST superlative of massy

MASSIF *n* pl. -S a principal mountain mass

MASSIVE *adj* of considerable size

MASSLESS *adj* having no mass

MASSY *adj* MASSIER, MASSIEST massive

MAST *v* -ED, -ING, -S to provide with a mast (a long pole on a ship that supports the sails and rigging)

MASTABA *n* pl. -S an ancient Egyptian tomb

MASTABAH *n* pl. -S mastaba

MASTER *v* -ED, -ING, -S to become skilled in

MASTERLY *adj* very skillful

MASTERY *n* pl. -TERIES superior knowledge or skill

MASTHEAD *v* -ED, -ING, -S to raise to the top of a mast

MASTIC *n* pl. -S an aromatic resin

MASTICHE *n* pl. -S mastic

MASTIFF n pl. -S a large, short-haired dog

MASTITIS n pl. -TITIDES inflammation of the breast **MASTITIC** adj

MASTIX n pl. -ES mastic

MASTLESS adj having no mast

MASTLIKE adj resembling a mast

MASTODON n pl. -S an extinct elephant-like mammal

MASTOID n pl. -S the rear portion of the temporal bone

MASURIUM n pl. -S a metallic element

MAT v MATTED, MATTING, MATS to pack down so as to form a dense mass

MATADOR n pl. -S the bullfighter who kills the bull in a bullfight

MATAMBALA a pl. of tambala

MATCH v -ED, -ING, -ES to set in competition or opposition

MATCHBOX n pl. -ES a small box

MATCHER n pl. -S one that matches

MATCHUP n pl. -S a setting of two players against each other

MATE v MATED, MATING, MATES to join as mates (partners in a union)

MATELESS adj having no mate

MATELOT n pl. -S a sailor

MATELOTE n pl. -S a fish stew

MATER n pl. -TERS or -TRES mother

MATERIAL n pl. -S the substance of which anything is or may be composed

MATERIEL n pl. -S the aggregate of equipment and supplies used by an organization

MATERNAL adj pertaining to a mother

MATESHIP n pl. -S the state of being a mate

MATEY n pl. -EYS a friend

MATH n pl. -S mathematics

MATILDA n pl. -S a hobo's bundle

MATIN n pl. -S a morning song, as of birds

MATINAL adj pertaining to the morning

MATINEE n pl. -S a daytime performance

MATINESS n pl. -ES friendliness

MATING n pl. -S the period during which a seasonal-breeding animal can mate

MATLESS adj having no mats (small floor coverings)

MATRASS n pl. -ES a long-necked glass vessel

MATRES a pl. of mater

MATRIX n pl. -TRICES or -TRIXES something within which something else originates or develops

MATRON n pl. -S a married woman of established social position **MATRONAL, MATRONLY** adj

MATSAH n pl. -S matzo

MATT v -ED, -ING, -S to matte

MATTE v MATTED, MATTING, MATTES to produce a dull finish on

MATTED past tense of mat, matt, and matte

MATTEDLY adv in a tangled manner

MATTER v -ED, -ING, -S to be of importance

MATTERY adj producing pus

MATTIN n pl. -S matin

MATTING n pl. -S a woven fabric used as a floor covering

MATTOCK n pl. -S a digging tool

MATTOID n pl. -S a mentally unbalanced person

MATTRASS n pl. -ES matrass

MATTRESS n pl. -ES a large pad filled with resilient material used on or as a bed

MATURATE v -RATED, -RATING, -RATES to mature

MATURE adj -TURER, -TUREST fully developed **MATURELY** adv

MATURE v -TURED, -TURING, -TURES to make or become mature

MATURITY n pl. -TIES the state of being mature

MATZA n pl. -S matzo

MATZAH n pl. -S matzo

MATZO n pl. -ZOS, -ZOT, or -ZOTH an unleavened bread

MATZOH n pl. -S matzo

MATZOON n pl. -S a food made from milk

MATZOT a pl. of matzo

MATZOTH a pl. of matzo

MAUD n pl. -S a Scottish gray and black plaid

MAUDLIN adj excessively emotional

MAUGER prep maugre

MAUGRE prep in spite of

MAUL v -ED, -ING, -S to injure by beating

MAULER n pl. -S one that mauls

MAUMET n pl. -S an idol

MAUMETRY n pl. -RIES idolatry

MAUN v must — MAUN is the only form of this verb; it cannot be conjugated

MAUND n pl. -S an Asian unit of weight

MAUNDER v -ED, -ING, -S to talk incoherently

MAUNDY n pl. -DIES the religious ceremony of washing the feet of the poor

MAUSOLEA n/pl large, stately tombs

MAUT n pl. -S malt

MAUVE n pl. -S a purple color

MAVEN n pl. -S mavin

MAVERICK n pl. -S an unbranded range animal

MAVIE n pl. -S mavis

MAVIN n pl. -S an expert

MAVIS n pl. -VISES a songbird

MAW v MAWED, MAWN, MAWING, MAWS to mow

MAWKISH adj offensively sentimental

MAX n pl. -ES maximum

MAXI n pl. -S a long skirt or coat

MAXICOAT n pl. -S a long coat

MAXILLA n pl. -LAE or -LAS the upper jaw or jawbone

MAXIM n pl. -S a brief statement of a general truth or principle

MAXIMA a pl. of maximum

MAXIMAL n pl. -S an element of a mathematical set that is followed by no other

MAXIMIN n pl. -S the maximum of a set of minima

MAXIMISE v -MISED, -MISING, -MISES to maximize

MAXIMITE n pl. -S a powerful explosive

MAXIMIZE v -MIZED, -MIZING, -MIZES to make as great as possible

MAXIMUM n pl. -MUMS or -MA the greatest possible amount, quantity, or degree

MAXIXE n pl. -S a Brazilian dance

MAXWELL n pl. -S a unit of magnetic flux

MAY v present 2d person sing. MAY, MAYEST, or MAYST, past tense MIGHT — used as an auxiliary to express permission

MAY v -ED, -ING, -S to gather flowers in the spring

MAYA n pl. -S the power to produce illusions in Hindu philosophy **MAYAN** adj

MAYAPPLE n pl. -S a perennial herb

MAYBE n pl. -S an uncertainty

MAYBUSH n pl. -ES a flowering shrub

MAYDAY n pl. -DAYS a radio distress call

MAYEST a present 2d person sing. of may

MAYFLY n pl. -FLIES a winged insect

MAYHAP adv maybe

MAYHEM n pl. -S the offense of willfully maiming a person

MAYING n pl. -S the gathering of spring flowers

MAYO n pl. -YOS mayonnaise

MAYOR n pl. -S the chief executive official of a city or borough **MAYORAL** adj

MAYORESS n pl. -ES a female mayor

MAYPOLE n pl. -S a decorated pole used in a spring celebration

MAYPOP n pl. -S a flowering vine

MAYST a present 2d person sing. of may

MAYVIN n pl. -S mavin

MAYWEED n pl. -S a malodorous weed

MAZAEDIA n/pl spore-producing organs of certain lichens

MAZARD n pl. -S the head or face

MAZE v MAZED, MAZING, MAZES to bewilder **MAZEDLY** adv

MAZELIKE adj mazy

MAZER n pl. -S a large drinking bowl

MAZIER comparative of mazy

MAZIEST superlative of mazy

MAZILY adv in a mazy manner

MAZINESS n pl. -ES the quality of being mazy

MAZING present participle of maze

MAZOURKA n pl. -S mazurka

MAZUMA n pl. -S money

MAZURKA n pl. -S a Polish dance

MAZY adj MAZIER, MAZIEST full of confusing turns and passages

MAZZARD n pl. -S a wild cherry

MBIRA n pl. -S an African musical instrument

ME pron the objective case of the pronoun I

MEAD n pl. -S an alcoholic beverage

MEADOW n pl. -S a tract of grassland **MEADOWY** adj

MEAGER adj deficient in quantity or quality **MEAGERLY** adv

MEAGRE adj meager **MEAGRELY** adv

MEAL n pl. -S the food served and eaten in one sitting

MEALIE n pl. -S an ear of corn

MEALIER comparative of mealy

MEALIEST superlative of mealy
MEALLESS adj lacking a meal
MEALTIME n pl. -S the usual time for a meal
MEALWORM n pl. -S the destructive larva of certain beetles
MEALY adj MEALIER, MEALIEST soft, dry, and friable
MEALYBUG n pl. -S a destructive insect
MEAN v MEANT, MEANING, MEANS to intend
MEAN adj MEANER, MEANEST inferior in grade, quality, or character
MEANDER v -ED, -ING, -S to wander
MEANER n pl. -S one that means
MEANIE n pl. -S a nasty person
MEANIES pl. of meany
MEANING n pl. -S something that one intends to convey by language
MEANLY adv in a mean manner
MEANNESS n pl. -ES the state of being mean
MEANT past tense of mean
MEANTIME n pl. -S the intervening time
MEANY n pl. MEANIES meanie
MEASLE n pl. -S a tapeworm larva MEASLED adj
MEASLY adj -SLIER, -SLIEST meager
MEASURE v -SURED, -SURING, -SURES to ascertain the dimensions, quantity, or capacity of
MEASURER n pl. -S one that measures
MEAT n pl. -S animal flesh used as food MEATED adj
MEATAL adj pertaining to a meatus
MEATBALL n pl. -S a small ball of chopped meat
MEATHEAD n pl. -S a dolt
MEATIER comparative of meaty
MEATIEST superlative of meaty
MEATILY adv in a meaty manner
MEATLESS adj having no meat
MEATLOAF n pl. -LOAVES a baked loaf of ground meat
MEATMAN n pl. -MEN a vendor of meat
MEATUS n pl. -ES a natural body passage
MEATY adj MEATIER, MEATIEST full of meat
MECCA n pl. -S a place visited by many people
MECHANIC n pl. -S a person who works with machines

MECONIUM n pl. -S the first fecal excretion of a newborn child
MED adj medical
MEDAKA n pl. -S a Japanese fish
MEDAL v -ALED, -ALING, -ALS or -ALLED, -ALLING, -ALS to honor with a medal (a commemorative piece of metal)
MEDALIST n pl. -S a person to whom a medal has been awarded
MEDALLIC adj of or pertaining to a medal
MEDALLING a present participle of medal
MEDDLE v -DLED, -DLING, -DLES to interest oneself in what is not one's concern
MEDDLER n pl. -S one that meddles
MEDEVAC v -VACKED, -VACKING, -VACS to evacuate the wounded from a battlefield by helicopter
MEDFLY n pl. -FLIES a Mediterranean fruit fly
MEDIA n pl. -DIAE the middle layer of a blood or lymph vessel
MEDIA n pl. -S a channel of communication
MEDIACY n pl. -CIES the act of mediating
MEDIAD adv toward the middle of a body or part
MEDIAE pl. of media
MEDIAL n pl. -S a sound, syllable, or letter in the middle of a word
MEDIALLY adv in a central manner
MEDIAN n pl. -S a central part
MEDIANLY adv medially
MEDIANT n pl. -S a type of musical tone
MEDIATE v -ATED, -ATING, -ATES to act between disputing parties in order to bring about a settlement
MEDIATOR n pl. -S one that mediates
MEDIC n pl. -S one engaged in medical work
MEDICAID n pl. -S a type of governmental health program
MEDICAL n pl. -S a physical examination
MEDICARE n pl. -S a type of governmental health program
MEDICATE v -CATED, -CATING, -CATES to treat with medicine
MEDICINE v -CINED, -CINING, -CINES to administer medicine (a substance used in the treatment of disease) to

MEDICK n pl. -S a flowering plant

MEDICO n pl. -COS a doctor or medical student

MEDIEVAL n pl. -S a person belonging to the Middle Ages

MEDII pl. of medius

MEDINA n pl. -S the native quarter of a North African city

MEDIOCRE adj neither good nor bad

MEDITATE v -TATED, -TATING, -TATES to ponder

MEDIUM n pl. -DIA or -DIUMS a surrounding environment in which something functions and thrives

MEDIUS n pl. -DII the middle finger

MEDLAR n pl. -S a Eurasian tree

MEDLEY n pl. -LEYS a mixture

MEDULLA n pl. -LAS or -LAE the central tissue in the stems of certain plants MEDULLAR adj

MEDUSA n pl. -SAE or -SAS a jellyfish MEDUSAL adj

MEDUSAN n pl. -S medusa

MEDUSOID n pl. -S medusa

MEED n pl. -S a deserved reward

MEEK adj MEEKER, MEEKEST lacking in spirit and courage MEEKLY adv

MEEKNESS n pl. -ES the quality of being meek

MEERKAT n pl. -S an African mongoose

MEET v MET, MEETING, MEETS to come into the company or presence of

MEETER n pl. -S one that meets

MEETING n pl. -S an assembly for a common purpose

MEETLY adv suitably

MEETNESS n pl. -ES suitability

MEGABAR n pl. -S a unit of pressure

MEGABIT n pl. -S a unit of computer information

MEGABUCK n pl. -S one million dollars

MEGABYTE n pl. -S 1,048,576 bytes

MEGACITY n pl. -CITIES a very large city

MEGADEAL n pl. -S a business deal involving a lot of money

MEGADOSE n pl. -S an abnormally large dose

MEGADYNE n pl. -S a unit of force

MEGAHIT n pl. -S something extremely successful

MEGALITH n pl. -S a huge stone used in prehistoric monuments

MEGALOPS n pl. -LOPSES a larval stage of most crabs

MEGAPOD n pl. -S megapode

MEGAPODE n pl. -S a large-footed bird

MEGASS n pl. -ES a bagasse

MEGASSE n pl. -S megass

MEGASTAR n pl. -S an extremely successful performer

MEGATON n pl. -S a unit of explosive force

MEGAVOLT n pl. -S a unit of electromotive force

MEGAWATT n pl. -S a unit of power

MEGILLAH n pl. -S a long, involved story

MEGILP n pl. -S a substance with which pigments are mixed in painting

MEGILPH n pl. -S megilp

MEGOHM n pl. -S a unit of electrical resistance

MEGRIM n pl. -S a migraine

MEIKLE adj large

MEINIE n pl. -S meiny

MEINY n pl. -NIES a retinue

MEIOSIS n pl. -OSES a type of cell division MEIOTIC adj

MEL n pl. -S honey

MELAMED n pl. -LAMDIM a teacher in a Jewish school

MELAMINE n pl. -S a chemical compound

MELANGE n pl. -S a mixture

MELANIAN adj pertaining to dark pigmentation

MELANIC n pl. -S one who is affected with melanism

MELANIN n pl. -S a dark pigment

MELANISM n pl. -S abnormally dark pigmentation of the skin

MELANIST n pl. -S a melanic

MELANITE n pl. -S a black variety of garnet

MELANIZE v -NIZED, -NIZING, -NIZES to make dark

MELANOID n pl. -S a dark pigment

MELANOMA n pl. -MAS or -MATA a darkly pigmented tumor

MELANOUS adj having dark skin and hair

MELD v -ED, -ING, -S to blend

MELDER n pl. -S the amount of grain ground at one time

MELEE n pl. -S a confused struggle

MELIC adj pertaining to song

MELILITE n pl. -S a mineral group

MELILOT n pl. -S a flowering plant

MELINITE n pl. -S a powerful explosive

MELISMA n pl. -MAS or -MATA melodic embellishment

MELL v -ED, -ING, -S to mix

MELLIFIC adj producing honey

MELLOW adj -LOWER, -LOWEST soft and full-flavored from ripeness **MELLOWLY** adv

MELLOW v -ED, -ING, -S to make or become mellow

MELODEON n pl. -S a musical instrument

MELODIA n pl. -S a type of organ stop

MELODIC adj pertaining to melody

MELODICA n pl. -S a harmonica with a small keyboard at one end

MELODIES pl. of melody

MELODISE v -DISED, -DISING, -DISES to melodize

MELODIST n pl. -S a composer of melodies

MELODIZE v -DIZED, -DIZING, -DIZES to compose a melody

MELODY n pl. -DIES an agreeable succession of musical sounds

MELOID n pl. -S a type of beetle

MELON n pl. -S any of various gourds

MELT v -ED, -ING, -S to change from a solid to a liquid state by heat **MELTABLE** adj

MELTAGE n pl. -S the process of melting

MELTDOWN n pl. -S the melting of the core of a nuclear reactor

MELTER n pl. -S one that melts

MELTON n pl. -S a heavy woolen fabric

MEM n pl. -S a Hebrew letter

MEMBER n pl. -S a distinct part of a whole **MEMBERED** adj

MEMBRANE n pl. -S a thin, pliable layer of tissue

MEMENTO n pl. -TOS or -TOES something that serves as a reminder of the past

MEMO n pl. MEMOS a note designating something to be remembered

MEMOIR n pl. -S a biography

MEMORIAL n pl. -S something that serves as a remembrance of a person or event

MEMORISE v -ISED, -ISING, -ISES memorize

MEMORIZE v -RIZED, -RIZING, -RIZES to commit to memory

MEMORY n pl. -RIES the mental faculty of retaining and recalling past experience

MEMSAHIB n pl. -S a European woman living in colonial India

MEN pl. of man

MENACE v -ACED, -ACING, -ACES to theaten

MENACER n pl. -S one that menaces

MENAD n pl. -S maenad

MENAGE n pl. -S a household

MENARCHE n pl. -S the first occurrence of menstruation

MENAZON n pl. -S an insecticide

MEND v -ED, -ING, -S to repair **MENDABLE** adj

MENDER n pl. -S one that mends

MENDIGO n pl. -GOS a freshwater fish

MENDING n pl. -S an accumulation of articles to be mended

MENFOLK n/pl the men of a family or community

MENFOLKS n/pl menfolk

MENHADEN n pl. -S a marine fish

MENHIR n pl. -S a prehistoric monument

MENIAL n pl. -S a domestic servant

MENIALLY adv in a servile manner

MENINX n pl. -NINGES any of the membranes enclosing the brain and spinal cord

MENISCUS n pl. -CI or -CUSES a crescent-shaped body **MENISCAL** adj

MENO adv less — used as a musical direction

MENOLOGY n pl. -GIES an ecclesiastical calendar

MENORAH n pl. -S a candleholder used in Jewish worship

MENSA n pl. -SAS or -SAE the grinding surface of a tooth

MENSAL adj pertaining to or used at the table

MENSCH n pl. MENSCHES or MENSCHEN an admirable person

MENSE v MENSED, MENSING, MENSES to do honor to

MENSEFUL adj proper

MENSTRUA n/pl solvents

MENSURAL adj pertaining to measure

MENSWEAR n pl. MENSWEAR clothing for men

MENTA pl. of mentum

MENTAL adj pertaining to the mind **MENTALLY** adv

MENTHENE n pl. -S a liquid hydrocarbon

MENTHOL n pl. -S an alcohol

MENTION v -ED, -ING, -S to refer to in a casual manner

MENTOR v -ED, -ING, -S to serve as a friend and teacher to

MENTUM n pl. -TA the chin

MENU n pl. -S a list of the dishes available in a restaurant

MEOU v -ED, -ING, -S meow

MEOW v -ED, -ING, -S to make the crying sound of a cat

MEPHITIS n pl. -TISES an offensive odor **MEPHITIC** adj

MERCAPTO adj containing a particular chemical group

MERCER n pl. -S a dealer in textiles

MERCERY n pl. -CERIES a mercer's shop

MERCHANT v -ED, -ING, -S to buy and sell goods for profit

MERCIES pl. of mercy

MERCIFUL adj full of mercy

MERCURY n pl. -RIES a metallic element **MERCURIC** adj

MERCY n pl. -CIES compassion shown to an offender or enemy

MERE n pl. -S a pond or lake

MERE adj MERER, MEREST being nothing more than **MERELY** adv

MERENGUE n pl. -S a ballroom dance

MERGE v MERGED, MERGING, MERGES to combine

MERGENCE n pl. -S the act of merging

MERGER n pl. -S the union of two or more businesses into a single enterprise

MERGING present participle of merge

MERIDIAN n pl. -S a circle around the earth passing through both poles

MERINGUE n pl. -S a topping for pastries

MERINO n pl. -NOS a fine wool

MERISIS n pl. MERISES growth

MERISTEM n pl. -S formative plant tissue

MERISTIC adj made up of segments

MERIT v -ED, -ING, -S to earn

MERK n pl. -S a former coin of Scotland

MERL n pl. -S merle

MERLE n pl. -S a blackbird

MERLIN n pl. -S a European falcon

MERLON n pl. -S the solid part of an indented parapet

MERLOT n pl. -S a dry red wine

MERMAID n pl. -S a legendary marine creature

MERMAN n pl. -MEN a legendary marine creature

MEROPIA n pl. -S partial blindness **MEROPIC** adj

MERRY adj -RIER, -RIEST cheerful **MERRILY** adv

MESA n pl. -S a land formation having a flat top and steep sides

MESALLY adv medially

MESARCH adj originating in a mesic habitat

MESCAL n pl. -S a cactus

MESDAMES pl. of madame

MESEEMS v past tense MESEEMED present 3d person sing. MESEEMETH it seems to me — MESEEMS is an impersonal verb and is used only in the 3d person sing.

MESH v -ED, -ING, -ES to entangle

MESHIER comparative of meshy

MESHIEST superlative of meshy

MESHUGA adj crazy

MESHUGAH adj meshuga

MESHUGGA adj meshuga

MESHUGGE adj meshuga

MESHWORK n pl. -S a network

MESHY adj MESHIER, MESHIEST netty

MESIAL adj situated in the middle **MESIALLY** adv

MESIAN adj mesial

MESIC adj characterized by a medium supply of moisture

MESMERIC adj pertaining to hypnotism

MESNALTY n pl. -TIES a type of feudal estate

MESNE n pl. -S a feudal lord holding land from a superior

MESOCARP n pl. -S the middle layer of a pericarp

MESODERM n pl. -S the middle germ layer of an embryo

MESOGLEA n pl. -S a gelatinous material in sponges

MESOMERE n pl. -S an embryonic segment

MESON n pl. -S a subatomic particle **MESONIC** adj

MESOPHYL n pl. -S the soft tissue of a leaf

MESOSOME n pl. -S a specialized cellular part

MESOTRON n pl. -S a meson

MESQUIT n pl. -S mesquite

MESQUITE n pl. -S a spiny tree or shrub

MESS v -ED, -ING, -ES to make dirty or untidy

MESSAGE v -SAGED, -SAGING, -SAGES to send as a message (an oral, written, or signaled communication)

MESSAN n pl. -S a lapdog

MESSIAH n pl. -S an expected liberator

MESSIER comparative of messy

MESSIEST superlative of messy

MESSIEURS pl. of monsieur

MESSILY adv in a messy manner

MESSMAN n pl. -MEN a serviceman who works in a dining facility

MESSMATE n pl. -S a person with whom one eats regularly

MESSUAGE n pl. -S a dwelling house with its adjacent buildings and land

MESSY adj MESSIER, MESSIEST dirty or untidy

MESTEE n pl. -S mustee

MESTESO n pl. -SOS or -SOES mestizo

MESTINO n pl. -NOS or -NOES mestizo

MESTIZA n pl. -S a female mestizo

MESTIZO n pl. -ZOS or -ZOES a person of mixed ancestry

MET past tense of meet

META adj pertaining to positions in a benzene ring separated by one carbon atom

METAGE n pl. -S an official measurement of weight or contents

METAL v -ALED, -ALING, -ALS or -ALLED, -ALLING, -ALS to cover with metal (any of various ductile, fusible, and lustrous substances)

METALISE v -ISED, -ISING, -ISES to metalize

METALIST n pl. -S one who works with metals

METALIZE v -IZED, -IZING, -IZES to treat with metal

METALLED a past tense of metal

METALLIC n pl. -S a fabric or yarn made of or coated with metal

METALLING a present participle of metal

METAMER n pl. -S a type of chemical compound

METAMERE n pl. -S a somite

METAPHOR n pl. -S a type of figure of speech

METATE n pl. -S a stone used for grinding grains

METAZOAN n pl. -S any of a major division of multicellular animals METAZOAL, METAZOIC adj

METAZOON n pl. -ZOA a metazoan

METE v METED, METING, METES to distribute by measure

METEOR n pl. -S a small celestial body that enters the earth's atmosphere METEORIC adj

METEPA n pl. -S a chemical compound

METER v -ED, -ING, -S to measure by mechanical means

METERAGE n pl. -S the process of metering

METH n pl. -S a stimulant drug

METHADON n pl. -S a narcotic drug

METHANE n pl. -S a flammable gas

METHANOL n pl. -S a toxic alcohol

METHINKS v past tense METHOUGHT it seems to me — METHINKS is an impersonal verb and is used only in the 3d person sing.

METHOD n pl. -S a means of procedure

METHODIC adj systematic

METHOUGHT past tense of methinks

METHOXY adj containing a certain chemical group

METHOXYL adj methoxy

METHYL n pl. -S a univalent radical METHYLIC adj

METHYLAL n pl. -S a flammable liquid

METICAL n pl. -CAIS or -CALS a monetary unit of Mozambique

METIER n pl. -S a vocation

METING present participle of mete

METIS n pl. METIS a person of mixed ancestry

METISSE n pl. -S a female metis

METONYM n pl. -S a word used in metonymy

METONYMY n pl. -MIES a type of figure of speech

METOPE n pl. -PES or -PAE a space between two triglyphs

METOPIC adj pertaining to the forehead

METOPON n pl. -S a narcotic drug

METRE v -TRED, -TRING, -TRES to meter

METRIC n pl. -S a standard of measurement

METRICAL adj pertaining to or composed in a system of arranged and measured rhythm

METRIFY v -FIED, -FYING, -FIES to compose in metrical form

METRING present participle of metre

METRIST n pl. -S one who metrifies

METRITIS n pl. -TISES inflammation of the uterus

METRO n pl. -ROS a subway

METTLE n pl. -S quality of character **METTLED** adj

METUMP n pl. -S a tumpline

MEUNIERE adj cooked in browned butter

MEW v -ED, -ING, -S to confine

MEWL v -ED, -ING, -S to whimper

MEWLER n pl. -S one that mewls

MEZCAL n pl. -S mescal

MEZE n pl. -S a Greek or Middle Eastern appetizer

MEZEREON n pl. -S a flowering shrub

MEZEREUM n pl. -S mezereon

MEZQUIT n pl. -S mesquite

MEZQUITE n pl. -S mesquite

MEZUZA n pl. -S mezuzah

MEZUZAH n pl. -ZAHS, -ZOT, or -ZOTH a Judaic scroll

MEZZO n pl. -ZOS a female voice of a full, deep quality

MHO n pl. MHOS a unit of electrical conductance

MI n pl. -S the third tone of the diatonic musical scale

MIAOU v -ED, -ING, -S to meow

MIAOW v -ED, -ING, -S to meow

MIASM n pl. -S miasma

MIASMA n pl. -MAS or -MATA a noxious vapor **MIASMAL, MIASMIC** adj

MIAUL v -ED, -ING, -S to meow

MIB n pl. -S a type of playing marble

MICA n pl. -S a mineral

MICAWBER n pl. -S a person who remains hopeful despite adversity

MICE pl. of mouse

MICELL n pl. -S micelle

MICELLA n pl. -LAE micelle

MICELLE n pl. -S a coherent strand or structure in a fiber **MICELLAR** adj

MICHE v MICHED, MICHING, MICHES to skulk

MICKEY n pl. -EYS a drugged drink

MICKLE adj -LER, -LEST large

MICKLE n pl. -S a large amount

MICRA a pl. of micron

MICRIFY v -FIED, -FYING, -FIES to make small

MICRO n pl. -CROS a very small computer

MICROBAR n pl. -S a unit of atmospheric pressure

MICROBE n pl. -S a minute life form **MICROBIC** adj

MICROBUS n pl. -BUSES or -BUSSES a small bus

MICRODOT n pl. -S a copy of printed matter reduced to the size of a dot

MICROHM n pl. -S a unit of electrical resistance

MICROLUX n pl. -LUXES or -LUCES a unit of illumination

MICROMHO n pl. -S a unit of electrical conductance

MICRON n pl. -CRONS or -CRA a unit of length

MICRURGY n pl. -GIES the use of minute tools under high magnification

MID n pl. -S the middle

MIDAIR n pl. -S a region in the middle of the air

MIDBRAIN n pl. -S the middle region of the brain

MIDCULT n pl. -S middle-class culture

MIDDAY n pl. -DAYS the middle of the day

MIDDEN n pl. -S a dunghill

MIDDIES pl. of middy

MIDDLE v -DLED, -DLING, -DLES to place in the middle (the area or point equidistant from extremes or limits)

MIDDLER n pl. -S a student in an intermediate grade

MIDDLING n pl. -S a cut of pork

MIDDY n pl. -DIES a loosely fitting blouse

MIDFIELD n pl. -S the middle portion of a playing field

MIDGE n pl. -S a small winged insect

MIDGET n pl. -S a very small person

MIDGUT n pl. -S the middle part of the embryonic digestive tract

MIDI n pl. -S a skirt or coat that extends to the middle of the calf

MIDIRON n pl. -S a golf club

MIDLAND n pl. -S the middle part of a country

MIDLEG n pl. -S the middle of the leg

MIDLIFE n pl. -LIVES middle age

MIDLINE n pl. -S a median line

MIDMONTH n pl. -S the middle of the month

MIDMOST *n pl.* -S a part exactly in the middle

MIDNIGHT *n pl.* -S the middle of the night

MIDNOON *n pl.* -S midday

MIDPOINT *n pl.* -S a point at the middle

MIDRANGE *n pl.* -S the middle of a range

MIDRASH *n pl.* -RASHIM or -RASHOTH an early Jewish interpretation of a biblical text

MIDRIB *n pl.* -S the central vein of a leaf

MIDRIFF *n pl.* -S the middle part of the body

MIDSHIP *adj* pertaining to the middle of a ship

MIDSHIPS *adv* toward the middle of a ship

MIDSIZE *adj* of intermediate size

MIDSIZED *adj* midsize

MIDSOLE *n pl.* -S a middle layer of the sole of a shoe

MIDSPACE *n pl.* -S the middle of a space

MIDST *n pl.* -S the middle

MIDSTORY *n pl.* -RIES the middle of a story

MIDTERM *n pl.* -S an examination given in the middle of an academic semester

MIDTOWN *n pl.* -S the central part of a city

MIDWATCH *n pl.* -ES a watch on a ship between midnight and 4 A.M.

MIDWAY *n pl.* -WAYS an avenue at a fair or carnival for concessions and amusements

MIDWEEK *n pl.* -S the middle of the week

MIDWIFE *v* -WIFED, -WIFING, -WIFES or -WIVED, -WIVING, -WIVES to assist a woman in childbirth

MIDYEAR *n pl.* -S the middle of the year

MIEN *n pl.* -S demeanor

MIFF *v* -ED, -ING, -S to annoy

MIFFY *adj* MIFFIER, MIFFIEST easily annoyed

MIG *n pl.* -S a type of playing marble

MIGG *n pl.* -S mig

MIGGLE *n pl.* -S a mig

MIGHT *n pl.* -S strength

MIGHTY *adj* MIGHTIER, MIGHTIEST strong MIGHTILY *adv*

MIGNON *n pl.* -S a cut of beef

MIGNONNE *adj* daintily small

MIGRAINE *n pl.* -S a severe headache

MIGRANT *n pl.* -S one that migrates

MIGRATE *v* -GRATED, -GRATING, -GRATES to move from one region to another

MIGRATOR *n pl.* -S a migrant

MIHRAB *n pl.* -S a niche in a mosque

MIJNHEER *n pl.* -S mynheer

MIKADO *n pl.* -DOS an emperor of Japan

MIKE *v* MIKED, MIKING, MIKES to amplify or record by use of a microphone

MIKRON *n pl.* -KRONS or -KRA micron

MIKVAH *n pl.* -VAHS or -VOTH a place for ritual bathing by Orthodox Jews

MIKVEH *n pl.* -S mikvah

MIL *n pl.* -S a unit of length

MILADI *n pl.* -S milady

MILADY *n pl.* -DIES an English gentlewoman

MILAGE *n pl.* -S mileage

MILCH *adj* giving milk

MILCHIG *adj* made of or derived from milk

MILD *adj* MILDER, MILDEST not harsh or rough

MILDEN *v* -ED, -ING, -S to make or become mild

MILDEW *v* -ED, -ING, -S to affect with mildew (a whitish growth produced by fungi)

MILDEWY *adj* affected with or resembling mildew

MILDLY *adj* in a mild manner

MILDNESS *n pl.* -ES the quality of being mild

MILE *n pl.* -S a unit of distance

MILEAGE *n pl.* -S total distance expressed in miles

MILEPOST *n pl.* -S a post indicating distance in miles

MILER *n pl.* -S one that runs a mile race

MILESIMO *n pl.* -MOS a former monetary unit of Chile

MILFOIL *n pl.* -S a perennial herb

MILIA *pl.* of milium

MILIARIA *n pl.* -S a skin disease

MILIARY *adj* made up of many small projections

MILIEU *n pl.* -LIEUS or -LIEUX environment

MILITANT *n pl.* -S a person who is aggressively engaged in a cause

MILITARY *n pl.* -TARIES armed forces

MILITATE v -TATED, -TATING, -TATES to have influence or effect

MILITIA n pl. -S a citizen army

MILIUM n pl. -IA a small, whitish lump in the skin

MILK v -ED, -ING, -S to draw milk (a whitish, nutritious liquid) from the udder of

MILKER n pl. -S one that milks

MILKFISH n pl. -ES a marine food fish

MILKIER comparative of milky

MILKIEST superlative of milky

MILKILY adv in a milky manner

MILKMAID n pl. -S a woman who milks cows

MILKMAN n pl. -MEN a man who sells or delivers milk

MILKSHED n pl. -S a region supplying milk to a particular community

MILKSOP n pl. -S an effeminate man

MILKWEED n pl. -S a plant that secretes a milky juice

MILKWOOD n pl. -S a tropical tree

MILKWORT n pl. -S a flowering plant

MILKY adj MILKIER, MILKIEST resembling or suggestive of milk

MILL v -ED, -ING, -S to grind by mechanical means **MILLABLE** adj

MILLAGE n pl. -S a type of monetary rate

MILLCAKE n pl. -S a residue from pressed linseed

MILLDAM n pl. -S a dam built to form a millpond

MILLE n pl. -S a thousand

MILLEPED n pl. -S milliped

MILLER n pl. -S one that mills

MILLET n pl. -S a cereal grass

MILLIARD n pl. -S a billion

MILLIARE n pl. -S a unit of area

MILLIARY n pl. -ARIES an ancient Roman milestone

MILLIBAR n pl. -S a unit of atmospheric pressure

MILLIEME n pl. -S unit of value of Egypt and Sudan

MILLIER n pl. -S a unit of weight

MILLIGAL n pl. -S a unit of acceleration

MILLILUX n pl. -LUXES or -LUCES a unit of illumination

MILLIME n pl. -S a coin of Tunisia

MILLIMHO n pl. -MHOS a unit of electrical conductance

MILLINE n pl. -S a unit of advertising space

MILLINER n pl. -S one who makes or sells women's hats

MILLING n pl. -S a corrugated edge on a coin

MILLIOHM n pl. -S a unit of electrical resistance

MILLION n pl. -S a number

MILLIPED n pl. -S a multi-legged arthropod

MILLIREM n pl. -S a quantity of ionizing radiation

MILLPOND n pl. -S a pond for supplying water to run a mill wheel (a type of waterwheel)

MILLRACE n pl. -S the current of water that drives a mill wheel

MILLRUN n pl. -S a millrace

MILLWORK n pl. -S woodwork produced by milling

MILNEB n pl. -S a fungicide

MILO n pl. -LOS a cereal grass

MILORD n pl. -S an English gentleman

MILPA n pl. -S a field that is cleared from a jungle for farming purposes

MILREIS n pl. MILREIS a former monetary unit of Portugal

MILT v -ED, -ING, -S to impregnate with milt (fish sperm)

MILTER n pl. -S a male fish at breeding time

MILTY adj MILTIER, MILTIEST full of milt

MIM adj primly demure

MIMBAR n pl. -S a pulpit in a mosque

MIME v MIMED, MIMING, MIMES to mimic

MIMEO v -ED, -ING, -S to make copies of by use of a mimeograph

MIMER n pl. -S one that mimes

MIMESIS n pl. -SISES mimicry **MIMETIC** adj

MIMETITE n pl. -S an ore of lead

MIMIC v -ICKED, -ICKING, -ICS to imitate closely

MIMICAL adj of the nature of mimicry

MIMICKER n pl. -S one that mimics

MIMICKING present participle of mimic

MIMICRY n pl. -RIES an instance of mimicking

MIMING present participle of mime

MIMOSA n pl. -S a tropical plant

MINA *n pl.* -NAS or -NAE an ancient unit of weight and value

MINABLE *adj* capable of being mined

MINACITY *n pl.* -TIES the state of being threatening

MINAE a *pl.* of mina

MINARET *n pl.* -S a slender tower attached to a mosque

MINATORY *adj* threatening

MINCE *v* MINCED, MINCING, MINCES to cut into very small pieces

MINCER *n pl.* -S one that minces

MINCY *adj* MINCIER, MINCIEST affectedly dainty

MIND *v* -ED, -ING, -S to heed

MINDER *n pl.* -S one that minds

MINDFUL *adj* heedful

MINDLESS *adj* lacking intelligence

MINDSET *n pl.* -S a fixed mental attitude

MINE *v* MINED, MINING, MINES to dig into for valuable materials

MINEABLE *adj* minable

MINER *n pl.* -S one that mines

MINERAL *n pl.* -S a naturally occurring inorganic substance having a characteristic set of physical properties

MINGIER comparative of mingy

MINGIEST superlative of mingy

MINGLE *v* -GLED, -GLING, -GLES to mix together

MINGLER *n pl.* -S one that mingles

MINGY *adj* -GIER, -GIEST mean and stingy

MINI *n pl.* -S something distinctively smaller than others of its kind

MINIBIKE *n pl.* -S a small motorcycle

MINIBUS *n pl.* -BUSES or -BUSSES a small bus

MINICAB *n pl.* -S a small taxicab

MINICAMP *n pl.* -S a short training camp for football players

MINICAR *n pl.* -S a small automobile

MINIFY *v* -FIED, -FYING, -FIES to make small or smaller

MINIKIN *n pl.* -S a small or dainty creature

MINILAB *n pl.* -S a retail outlet offering rapid on-site film development

MINIM *n pl.* -S a unit of liquid measure

MINIMA a *pl.* of minimum

MINIMAL *n pl.* -S an element of a mathematical set that precedes all others

MINIMAX *n pl.* -ES the minimum of a set of maxima

MINIMILL *n pl.* -S a small-scale steel mill

MINIMISE *v* -MISED, -MISING, -MISES to minimize

MINIMIZE *v* -MIZED, -MIZING, -MIZES to make as small as possible

MINIMUM *n pl.* -MUMS or -MA the least possible amount, quantity, or degree

MINING *n pl.* -S the process or business of working mines (excavations in the earth)

MINION *n pl.* -S a servile follower

MINIPARK *n pl.* -S a small city park

MINISH *v* -ED, -ING, -ES to diminish

MINISKI *n pl.* -S a short ski

MINISTER *v* -ED, -ING, -S to give aid or service

MINISTRY *n pl.* -TRIES the act of ministering

MINIUM *n pl.* -S a red pigment

MINIVAN *n pl.* -S a small van

MINIVER *n pl.* -S a white fur

MINK *n pl.* -S a carnivorous mammal

MINKE *n pl.* -S a small whale

MINNOW *n pl.* -S a small fish

MINNY *n pl.* -NIES minnow

MINOR *v* -ED, -ING, -S to pursue a specific subordinate course of study

MINORCA *n pl.* -S any of a breed of large domestic fowls

MINORITY *n pl.* -TIES the smaller number or part

MINSTER *n pl.* -S a large or important church

MINSTREL *n pl.* -S a medieval musician

MINT *v* -ED, -ING, -S to produce by stamping metal, as coins

MINTAGE *n pl.* -S the act of minting

MINTER *n pl.* -S one that mints

MINTY *adj* MINTIER, MINTIEST having the flavor mint (an aromatic herb)

MINUEND *n pl.* -S a number from which another is to be subtracted

MINUET *n pl.* -S a slow, stately dance

MINUS *n pl.* -ES a negative quantity

MINUTE *v* -UTED, -UTING, -UTES to make a brief note of

MINUTE *adj* -NUTER, -NUTEST very small MINUTELY *adv*

MINUTIA *n pl.* -TIAE a small detail MINUTIAL *adj*

MINUTING present participle of minute

MINX n pl. -ES a pert girl **MINXISH** adj

MINYAN n pl. -YANS or -YANIM the minimum number required to be present for the conduct of a Jewish service

MIOSIS n pl. -OSES excessive contraction of the pupil of the eye

MIOTIC n pl. -S an agent that causes miosis

MIQUELET n pl. -S a former Spanish or French soldier

MIR n pl. MIRS or MIRI a Russian peasant commune

MIRACLE n pl. -S an event ascribed to supernatural or divine origin

MIRADOR n pl. -S an architectural feature designed to afford an extensive view

MIRAGE n pl. -S a type of optical illusion

MIRE v MIRED, MIRING, MIRES to cause to stick in swampy ground

MIREX n pl. -ES an insecticide

MIRI a pl. of mir

MIRIER comparative of miry

MIRIEST superlative of miry

MIRINESS n pl. -ES the state of being miry

MIRING present participle of mire

MIRK adj MIRKER, MIRKEST murk

MIRK n pl. -S murk

MIRKY adj MIRKIER, MIRKIEST murky **MIRKILY** adv

MIRLITON n pl. -S a chayote

MIRROR v -ED, -ING, -S to reflect an image of

MIRTH n pl. -S spirited gaiety **MIRTHFUL** adj

MIRY adj MIRIER, MIRIEST swampy

MIRZA n pl. -S a Persian title of honor

MISACT v -ED, -ING, -S to act badly

MISADAPT v -ED, -ING, -S to adapt wrongly

MISADD v -ED, -ING, -S to add incorrectly

MISAGENT n pl. -S a bad agent

MISAIM v -ED, -ING, -S to aim badly

MISALIGN v -ED, -ING, -S to align improperly

MISALLY v -LIED, -LYING, -LIES to ally badly

MISALTER v -ED, -ING, -S to alter wrongly

MISANDRY n pl. -DRIES hatred of men

MISAPPLY v -PLIED, -PLYING, -PLIES to apply wrongly

MISASSAY v -ED, -ING, -S to attempt unsuccessfully

MISATE past tense of miseat

MISATONE v -ATONED, -ATONING, -ATONES to atone wrongly

MISAVER v -AVERRED, -AVERRING, -AVERS to speak erroneously

MISAWARD v -ED, -ING, -S to award wrongly

MISBEGIN v -GAN, -GUN, -GINNING, -GINS to begin wrongly

MISBEGOT adj born out of wedlock

MISBIAS v -ASED, -ASING, -ASES or -ASSED, -ASSING, -ASSES to bias wrongly

MISBILL v -ED, -ING, -S to bill wrongly

MISBIND v -BOUND, -BINDING, -BINDS to bind imperfectly

MISBRAND v -ED, -ING, -S to brand incorrectly

MISBUILD v -BUILT, -BUILDING, -BUILDS to build imperfectly

MISCALL v -ED, -ING, -S to call by a wrong name

MISCARRY v -RIED, -RYING, -RIES to be unsuccessful

MISCAST v -CAST, -CASTING, -CASTS to cast in an unsuitable role

MISCHIEF n pl. -S action that causes irritation, harm, or trouble

MISCIBLE adj capable of being mixed

MISCITE v -CITED, -CITING, -CITES to misquote

MISCLAIM v -ED, -ING, -S to claim wrongfully

MISCLASS v -ED, -ING, -ES to put in the wrong class

MISCODE v -CODED, -CODING, -CODES to code wrongly

MISCOIN v -ED, -ING, -S to coin improperly

MISCOLOR v -ED, -ING, -S to color incorrectly

MISCOOK v -ED, -ING, -S to cook badly

MISCOPY v -COPIED, -COPYING, -COPIES to copy incorrectly

MISCOUNT v -ED, -ING, -S to count incorrectly

MISCUE v -CUED, -CUING, -CUES to make a faulty stroke in billiards

MISCUT v -CUT, -CUTTING, -CUTS to cut incorrectly

MISDATE v -DATED, -DATING, -DATES to date incorrectly

MISDEAL v -DEALT, -DEALING, -DEALS to deal cards incorrectly

MISDEED n pl. -S an evil act

MISDEEM v -ED, -ING, -S to judge unfavorably

MISDIAL v -DIALED, -DIALING, -DIALS or -DIALLED, -DIALLING, -DIALS to dial wrongly

MISDO v -DID, -DONE, -DOING, -DOES to do wrongly

MISDOER n pl. -S one that misdoes

MISDOING n pl. -S an instance of doing wrong

MISDONE past participle of misdo

MISDOUBT v -ED, -ING, -S to doubt

MISDRAW v -DREW, -DRAWN, -DRAWING, -DRAWS to draw incorrectly

MISDRIVE v -DROVE, -DRIVEN, -DRIVING, -DRIVES to drive wrongly or improperly

MISE n pl. -S an agreement or settlement

MISEASE n pl. -S discomfort

MISEAT v -ATE, -EATEN, -EATING, -EATS to eat improperly

MISEDIT v -ED, -ING, -S to edit incorrectly

MISENROL v -ROLLED, -ROLLING, -ROLS to misenroll

MISENROLL v -ED, -ING, -S to enroll improperly

MISENTER v -ED, -ING, -S to enter erroneously

MISENTRY n pl. -TRIES an erroneous entry

MISER n pl. -S one who hoards money greedily

MISERERE n pl. -S a part of a church seat

MISERLY adj characteristic of a miser

MISERY n pl. -ERIES a state of great suffering

MISEVENT n pl. -S a mishap

MISFAITH n pl. -S lack of faith; disbelief

MISFIELD v -ED, -ING, -S to field badly

MISFILE v -FILED, -FILING, -FILES to file in the wrong place

MISFIRE v -FIRED, -FIRING, -FIRES to fail to fire

MISFIT v -FITTED, -FITTING, -FITS to fit badly

MISFOCUS v -CUSED, -CUSING, -CUSES or -CUSSED, -CUSSING, -CUSSES to focus badly

MISFORM v -ED, -ING, -S to misshape

MISFRAME v -FRAMED, -FRAMING, -FRAMES to frame badly

MISGAUGE v -GAUGED, -GAUGING, -GAUGES to gauge wrongly or inaccurately

MISGIVE v -GAVE, -GIVEN, -GIVING, -GIVES to make doubtful or fearful

MISGRADE v -GRADED, -GRADING, -GRADES to grade incorrectly

MISGRAFT v -ED, -ING, -S to graft wrongly

MISGROW v -GREW, -GROWN, -GROWING, -GROWS to grow abnormally

MISGUESS v -ED, -ING, -ES to guess wrongly

MISGUIDE v -GUIDED, -GUIDING, -GUIDES to guide wrongly

MISHAP n pl. -S an unfortunate accident

MISHEAR v -HEARD, -HEARING, -HEARS to hear incorrectly

MISHIT v -HIT, -HITTING, -HITS to hit poorly

MISHMASH n pl. -ES a confused mixture

MISHMOSH n pl. -ES mishmash

MISINFER v -FERRED, -FERRING, -FERS to infer wrongly

MISINTER v -TERRED, -TERRING, -TERS to inter improperly

MISJOIN v -ED, -ING, -S to join improperly

MISJUDGE v -JUDGED, -JUDGING, -JUDGES to judge wrongly

MISKAL n pl. -S an Oriental unit of weight

MISKEEP v -KEPT, -KEEPING, -KEEPS to keep wrongly

MISKICK v -ED, -ING, -S to kick badly

MISKNOW v -KNEW, -KNOWN, -KNOWING, -KNOWS to fail to understand or recognize

MISLABEL v -BELED, -BELING, -BELS or -BELLED, -BELLING, -BELS to label incorrectly or falsely

MISLABOR v -ED, -ING, -S to labor badly

MISLAIN past participle of mislie

MISLAY v -LAID, -LAYING, -LAYS to put in a forgotten place

MISLAYER n pl. -S one that mislays

MISLEAD v -LED, -LEADING, -LEADS to lead astray

MISLEARN v -LEARNED or -LEARNT, -LEARNING, -LEARNS to learn wrongly

MISLIE v -LAY, -LAIN, -LYING, -LIES to lie in a wrong position

MISLIGHT v -LIGHTED or -LIT, -LIGHTING, -LIGHTS to lead astray by its light

MISLIKE v -LIKED, -LIKING, -LIKES to dislike

MISLIKER n pl. -S one that mislikes

MISLIT a past tense of mislight

MISLIVE v -LIVED, -LIVING, -LIVES to live a bad life

MISLODGE v -LODGED, -LODGING, -LODGES to lodge in a wrong place

MISLYING present participle of mislie

MISMAKE v -MADE, -MAKING, -MAKES to make incorrectly

MISMARK v -ED, -ING, -S to mark wrongly

MISMATCH v -ED, -ING, -ES to match badly

MISMATE v -MATED, -MATING, -MATES to mate unsuitably

MISMEET v -MET, -MEETING, -MEETS to meet under unfortunate circumstances

MISMOVE v -MOVED, -MOVING, -MOVES to move wrongly

MISNAME v -NAMED, -NAMING, -NAMES to call by a wrong name

MISNOMER n pl. -S a name wrongly used

MISO n pl. -SOS a type of food paste

MISOGAMY n pl. -MIES a hatred of marriage

MISOGYNY n pl. -NIES a hatred of women

MISOLOGY n pl. -GIES a hatred of debate or reasoning

MISORDER v -ED, -ING, -S to order incorrectly

MISPAGE v -PAGED, -PAGING, -PAGES to page incorrectly

MISPAINT v -ED, -ING, -S to paint wrongly

MISPARSE v -PARSED, -PARSING, -PARSES to parse incorrectly

MISPART v -ED, -ING, -S to part badly

MISPATCH v -ED, -ING, -ES to patch badly

MISPEN v -PENNED, -PENNING, -PENS to write incorrectly

MISPLACE v -PLACED, -PLACING, -PLACES to put in a wrong place

MISPLAN v -PLANNED, -PLANNING, -PLANS to plan badly

MISPLANT v -ED, -ING, -S to plant wrongly

MISPLAY v -ED, -ING, -S to make a bad play in a game

MISPLEAD v -PLEADED or -PLED, -PLEADING, -PLEADS to plead wrongly or falsely

MISPOINT v -ED, -ING, -S to point improperly

MISPOISE v -POISED, -POISING, -POISES to poise incorrectly

MISPRICE v -PRICED, -PRICING, -PRICES to price incorrectly

MISPRINT v -ED, -ING, -S to print incorrectly

MISPRIZE v -PRIZED, -PRIZING, -PRIZES to despise

MISQUOTE v -QUOTED, -QUOTING, -QUOTES to quote incorrectly

MISRAISE v -RAISED, -RAISING, -RAISES to raise wrongly

MISRATE v -RATED, -RATING, -RATES to rate incorrectly

MISREAD v -READ, -READING, -READS to read incorrectly

MISREFER v -FERRED, -FERRING, -FERS to refer incorrectly

MISRELY v -LIED, -LYING, -LIES to rely wrongly

MISROUTE v -ROUTED, -ROUTING, -ROUTES to route incorrectly

MISRULE v -RULED, -RULING, -RULES to rule unwisely or unjustly

MISS v -ED, -ING, -ES to make contact with

MISSABLE adj able to be missed

MISSAL n pl. -S a prayer book

MISSAY v -SAID, -SAYING, -SAYS to say incorrectly

MISSEAT v -ED, -ING, -S to seat wrongly

MISSEL n pl. -S a European thrush

MISSEND v -SENT, -SENDING, -SENDS to send incorrectly

MISSENSE n pl. -S a form of genetic mutation

MISSET v -SET, -SETTING, -SETS to set incorrectly

MISSHAPE v -SHAPED, -SHAPEN, -SHAPING, -SHAPES to shape badly

MISSHOD adj improperly shod

MISSIES pl. of missy

MISSILE n pl. -S an object or weapon that is thrown or projected

MISSILRY n pl. -RIES the science of designing and operating guided missiles

MISSION v -ED, -ING, -S to send to perform a specific task

MISSIS n pl. -SISES a wife

MISSIVE n pl. -S a written communication

MISSORT v -ED, -ING, -S to sort badly or improperly

MISSOUND v -ED, -ING, -S to sound wrongly

MISSOUT n pl. -S a losing throw of dice

MISSPACE v -SPACED, -SPACING, -SPACES to space incorrectly

MISSPEAK v -SPOKE, -SPOKEN, -SPEAKING, -SPEAKS to speak incorrectly

MISSPELL v -SPELLED or -SPELT, -SPELLING, -SPELLS to spell incorrectly

MISSPEND v -SPENT, -SPENDING, -SPENDS to spend wrongly

MISSPOKE past tense of misspeak

MISSPOKEN past participle of misspeak

MISSTART v -ED, -ING, -S to start off badly

MISSTATE v -STATED, -STATING, -STATES to state wrongly

MISSTEER v -ED, -ING, -S to steer wrongly

MISSTEP n pl. -S a false step

MISSTOP v -STOPPED, -STOPPING, -STOPS to stop wrongly

MISSTYLE v -STYLED, -STYLING, -STYLES to style or call wrongly

MISSUIT v -ED, -ING, -S to suit badly

MISSUS n pl. -ES missis

MISSY n pl. MISSIES a young girl

MIST v -ED, -ING, -S to become blurry

MISTAKE v -TOOK or -TEUK, -TAKEN, -TAKING, -TAKES to interpret wrongly

MISTAKER n pl. -S one that mistakes

MISTBOW n pl. -S a fogbow

MISTEACH v -TAUGHT, -TEACHING, -TEACHES to teach wrongly or badly

MISTEND v -ED, -ING, -S to tend to improperly

MISTER n pl. -S sir

MISTERM v -ED, -ING, -S to call by a wrong name

MISTEUK a past tense of mistake

MISTHINK v -THOUGHT, -THINKING, -THINKS to thinks wrongly

MISTHROW v -THREW, -THROWN, -THROWING, -THROWS to throw errantly

MISTIER comparative of misty

MISTIEST superlative of misty

MISTILY adv in a misty manner

MISTIME v -TIMED, -TIMING, -TIMES to time wrongly

MISTITLE v -TLED, -TLING, -TLES to call by a wrong title

MISTOOK a past tense of mistake

MISTOUCH v -ED, -ING, -ES to touch improperly

MISTRACE v -TRACED, -TRACING, -TRACES to trace wrongly

MISTRAIN v -ED, -ING, -S to train improperly

MISTRAL n pl. -S a cold, dry wind

MISTREAT v -ED, -ING, -S to treat badly

MISTRESS n pl. -ES a woman in a position of authority

MISTRIAL n pl. -S a trial made invalid because of some error in procedure

MISTRUST v -ED, -ING, -S to distrust

MISTRUTH n pl. -S a lie

MISTRYST v -ED, -ING, -S to fail to keep an appointment with

MISTUNE v -TUNED, -TUNING, -TUNES to tune incorrectly

MISTUTOR v -ED, -ING, -S to instruct or bring up badly

MISTY adj MISTIER, MISTIEST blurry

MISTYPE v -TYPED, -TYPING, -TYPES to type incorrectly

MISUNION n pl. -S a bad union

MISUSAGE n pl. -S incorrect use

MISUSE v -USED, -USING, -USES to use incorrectly

MISUSER n pl. -S one that misuses

MISVALUE v -UED, -UING, -UES to value incorrectly

MISWORD v -ED, -ING, -S to word wrongly

MISWRITE v -WROTE or -WRIT, -WRITTEN, -WRITING, -WRITES to write incorrectly

MISYOKE v -YOKED, -YOKING, -YOKES to yoke improperly

MITE n pl. -S a small arachnid

MITER v -ED, -ING, -S to raise to the rank of a bishop

MITERER n pl. -S one that miters

MITHER n pl. -S mother

MITICIDE n pl. -S a substance used to kill mites

MITIER comparative of mity

MITIEST superlative of mity

MITIGATE v -GATED, -GATING, -GATES to make less severe

MITIS n pl. -TISES a type of wrought iron

MITOGEN n pl. -S a substance that induces mitosis

MITOSIS n pl. -TOSES a type of cell division **MITOTIC** adj

MITRAL adj pertaining to a valve of the heart

MITRE v -TRED, -TRING, -TRES to miter

MITSVAH n pl. -VAHS or -VOTH mitzvah

MITT n pl. -S a type of baseball glove

MITTEN n pl. -S a type of covering for the hand

MITTIMUS n pl. -ES a warrant committing a person to prison

MITY adj MITIER, MITIEST infested with mites

MITZVAH n pl. -VAHS or -VOTH a commandment of Jewish law

MIX v MIXED or MIXT, MIXING, MIXES to put together into one mass **MIXABLE, MIXIBLE** adj

MIXER n pl. -S one that mixes

MIXOLOGY n pl. -GIES the art of making mixed drinks

MIXT a past tense of mix

MIXTURE n pl. -S something produced by mixing

MIXUP n pl. -S a state of confusion

MIZEN n pl. -S mizzen

MIZZEN n pl. -S a type of sail

MIZZLE v -ZLED, -ZLING, -ZLES to rain in fine droplets

MIZZLY adj characterized by a fine rain

MM interj — used to express assent or satisfaction

MNEMONIC n pl. -S a device to assist the memory

MO n pl. MOS a moment

MOA n pl. -S an extinct flightless bird

MOAN v -ED, -ING, -S to utter a low, mournful sound

MOANER n pl. -S one that moans

MOANFUL adj moaning

MOAT v -ED, -ING, -S to surround with a moat (a water-filled trench)

MOATLIKE adj suggestive of a moat

MOB v MOBBED, MOBBING, MOBS to crowd about

MOBBER n pl. -S one that mobs

MOBBISH adj characteristic of a mob (a disorderly crowd of people)

MOBCAP n pl. -S a woman's cap

MOBILE n pl. -S a form of sculpture

MOBILISE v -LISED, -LISING, -LISES to mobilize

MOBILITY n pl. -TIES the ability to move

MOBILIZE v -LIZED, -LIZING, -LIZES to put into movement

MOBLED adj wrapped in or as if in a hood

MOBOCRAT n pl. -S a supporter of mob rule

MOBSTER n pl. -S a gangster

MOC n pl. -S a moccasin

MOCCASIN n pl. -S a type of shoe

MOCHA n pl. -S a choice, pungent coffee

MOCHILA n pl. -S a leather covering for a saddle

MOCK v -ED, -ING, -S to ridicule **MOCKABLE** adj

MOCKER n pl. -S one that mocks

MOCKERY n pl. -ERIES the act of mocking

MOCKUP n pl. -S a full-sized model

MOD n pl. -S one who wears boldly stylish clothes

MODAL adj pertaining to a mode **MODALLY** adv

MODALITY n pl. -TIES the state of being modal

MODE n pl. -S a method of doing or acting

MODEL v -ELED, -ELING, -ELS or -ELLED, -ELLING, -ELS to plan or form after a pattern

MODELER n pl. -S one that models

MODELING n pl. -S the treatment of volume in sculpture

MODELIST *n pl.* -S one who makes models

MODELLED a past tense of model

MODELLER *n pl.* -S a modeler

MODELLING a present participle of model

MODEM *n pl.* -S a device for converting signals from one form to another

MODERATE *v* -ATED, -ATING, -ATES to make less extreme

MODERATO *n pl.* -TOS a musical passage played at a medium tempo

MODERN *adj* -ERNER, -ERNEST pertaining to present or recent time **MODERNLY** *adv*

MODERN *n pl.* -S a person of modern times or views

MODERNE *adj* pretentiously modern

MODEST *adj* -ESTER, -ESTEST having a moderate regard for oneself **MODESTLY** *adv*

MODESTY *n pl.* -TIES the quality of being modest

MODI pl. of modus

MODICUM *n pl.* -CA or -CUMS a small amount

MODIFIER *n pl.* -S one that modifies

MODIFY *v* -FIED, -FYING, -FIES to change in form or character

MODIOLUS *n pl.* -LI a bony shaft of the inner ear

MODISH *adj* stylish **MODISHLY** *adv*

MODISTE *n pl.* -S a dealer in stylish women's clothing

MODULAR *adj* pertaining to a module

MODULATE *v* -LATED, -LATING, -LATES to adjust to a certain proportion

MODULE *n pl.* -S a standard of measurement

MODULO *adv* with respect to a modulus

MODULUS *n pl.* -LI a number that produces the same remainder when divided into each of two numbers

MODUS *n pl.* -DI a mode

MOFETTE *n pl.* -S a noxious emanation from a fissure in the earth

MOFFETTE *n pl.* -S mofette

MOG *v* MOGGED, MOGGING, MOGS to move away

MOGGIE *n pl.* -S moggy

MOGGY *n pl.* -GIES a cat

MOGUL *n pl.* -S an important person

MOHAIR *n pl.* -S the long, silky hair of the Angora goat

MOHEL *n pl.* -HALIM, -HELIM or -HELS a person who performs Jewish ritual circumcisions

MOHUR *n pl.* -S a former gold coin of India

MOIDORE *n pl.* -S a former gold coin of Portugal

MOIETY *n pl.* -ETIES a half

MOIL *v* -ED, -ING, -S to work hard

MOILER *n pl.* -S one that moils

MOIRA *n pl.* -RAI fate or destiny, in ancient Greek religion

MOIRE *n pl.* -S a fabric having a wavy pattern

MOIST *adj* MOISTER, MOISTEST slightly wet

MOISTEN *v* -ED, -ING, -S to make or become moist

MOISTFUL *adj* moist

MOISTLY *adv* in a moist manner

MOISTURE *n pl.* -S condensed or diffused liquid

MOJARRA *n pl.* -S a marine fish

MOJO *n pl.* -JOS or -JOES a magic charm

MOKE *n pl.* -S a donkey

MOL *n pl.* -S mole

MOLA *n pl.* -S a marine fish

MOLAL *adj* pertaining to a mole

MOLALITY *n pl.* -TIES the number of moles of solute per liter of solvent

MOLAR *n pl.* -S a grinding tooth

MOLARITY *n pl.* -TIES the number of moles of solute per liter of solution

MOLASSES *n pl.* -LASSESES a thick syrup

MOLD *v* -ED, -ING, -S to work into a particular shape **MOLDABLE** *adj*

MOLDER *v* -ED, -ING, -S to turn to dust by natural decay

MOLDIER comparative of moldy

MOLDIEST superlative of moldy

MOLDING *n pl.* -S a long, narrow strip used to decorate a surface

MOLDWARP *n pl.* -S a burrowing mammal

MOLDY *adj* MOLDIER, MOLDIEST musty

MOLE *n pl.* -S the quantity of a compound that has a weight equal to the compound's molecular weight

MOLECULE *n pl.* -S the smallest physical unit of an element

MOLEHILL n pl. -S a small mound of earth

MOLESKIN n pl. -S a cotton fabric

MOLEST v -ED, -ING, -S to disturb or annoy

MOLESTER n pl. -S one that molests

MOLIES pl. of moly

MOLINE adj having arms forked and curved at the ends — used of a heraldic cross

MOLL n pl. -S a gangster's girlfriend

MOLLAH n pl. -S mullah

MOLLIE n pl. -S a tropical fish

MOLLIES pl. of molly

MOLLIFY v -FIED, -FYING, -FIES to soothe

MOLLUSC n pl. -S mollusk

MOLLUSK n pl. -S any of a phylum of soft-bodied invertebrates

MOLLY n pl. -LIES mollie

MOLOCH n pl. -S a spiny lizard

MOLT v -ED, -ING, -S to cast off an outer covering

MOLTEN adj made liquid by heat
MOLTENLY adv

MOLTER n pl. -S one that molts

MOLTO adv very — used in musical directions

MOLY n pl. -LIES a wild garlic

MOLYBDIC adj pertaining to a certain metallic element

MOM n pl. -S mother

MOME n pl. -S a fool

MOMENT n pl. -S a brief period of time

MOMENTA a pl. of momentum

MOMENTLY adv from moment to moment

MOMENTO n pl. -TOS or -TOES memento

MOMENTUM n pl. -TA or -TUMS force of movement

MOMI a pl. of momus

MOMISM n pl. -S an excessive dependence on mothers

MOMMA n pl. -S mother

MOMMY n pl. -MIES mother

MOMSER n pl. -S a bastard

MOMUS n pl. -MUSES or -MI a carping person

MOMZER n pl. -S momser

MON n pl. MEN man

MONACHAL adj pertaining to monks

MONACID n pl. -S monoacid

MONAD n pl. -S a single-celled organism **MONADAL, MONADIC** adj

MONADES pl. of monas

MONADISM n pl. -S a philosophical doctrine

MONANDRY n pl. -DRIES the condition of having one husband at a time

MONARCH n pl. -S an absolute ruler

MONARCHY n pl. -CHIES rule by a monarch

MONARDA n pl. -S an aromatic herb

MONAS n pl. MONADES a monad

MONASTIC n pl. -S a monk

MONAURAL adj pertaining to sound transmission, recording, or reproduction involving a single transmission path

MONAXIAL adj having one axis

MONAXON n pl. -S a straight spicule in sponges

MONAZITE n pl. -S a mineral

MONDE n pl. -S the world

MONDO n pl. -DOS a rapid question and answer technique employed in Zen Buddhism

MONECIAN adj having both male and female sex organs in the same individual

MONELLIN n pl. -S a protein extracted from a West African red berry

MONERAN n pl. -S a cellular organism that does not have a distinct nucleus

MONETARY adj pertaining to money

MONETISE v -TISED, -TISING, -TISES to monetize

MONETIZE v -TIZED, -TIZING, -TIZES to coin into money

MONEY n pl. MONEYS or MONIES an official medium of exchange and measure of value

MONEYBAG n pl. -S a bag for holding money

MONEYED adj having much money

MONEYER n pl. -S one that coins money

MONEYMAN n pl. -MEN a person who invests large sums of money

MONGEESE a pl. of mongoose

MONGER v -ED, -ING, -S to peddle

MONGO n pl. -GOS mungo

MONGOE n pl. -S mungo

MONGOL n pl. -S a person affected with a form of mental deficiency

MONGOOSE n pl. -GOOSES or -GEESE a carnivorous mammal

MONGREL n pl. -S an animal or plant of mixed breed

MONGST prep amongst

MONICKER n pl. -S moniker

MONIE *adj* many

MONIED *adj* moneyed

MONIES a pl. of money

MONIKER *n pl.* -S a name

MONISH *v* -ED, -ING, -ES to warn

MONISM *n pl.* -S a philosophical theory

MONIST *n pl.* -S an adherent of monism **MONISTIC** *adj*

MONITION *n pl.* -S a warning

MONITIVE *adj* giving warning

MONITOR *v* -ED, -ING, -S to keep track of

MONITORY *n pl.* -RIES a letter of warning

MONK *n pl.* -S a man who is a member of a secluded religious order

MONKERY *n pl.* -ERIES the mode of life of monks

MONKEY *v* -ED, -ING, -S to mimic

MONKFISH *n pl.* -ES a marine fish

MONKHOOD *n pl.* -S the state of being a monk

MONKISH *adj* pertaining to monks

MONO *n pl.* MONOS an infectious disease

MONOACID *n pl.* -S a type of acid

MONOCARP *n pl.* -S a plant that yields fruit only once before dying

MONOCLE *n pl.* -S an eyeglass for one eye **MONOCLED** *adj*

MONOCOT *n pl.* -S a type of seed plant

MONOCRAT *n pl.* -S an autocrat

MONOCYTE *n pl.* -S a type of white blood cell

MONODIST *n pl.* -S one who writes monodies

MONODY *n pl.* -DIES an elegy performed by one person **MONODIC** *adj*

MONOECY *n pl.* -CIES the condition of being monecian

MONOFIL *n pl.* -S a single filament of synthetic fiber

MONOFUEL *n pl.* -S a type of rocket propellant

MONOGAMY *n pl.* -MIES marriage with one person at a time

MONOGENY *n pl.* -NIES asexual reproduction

MONOGERM *adj* being a fruit that produces a single plant

MONOGLOT *n pl.* -S a person speaking or writing only one language

MONOGRAM *v* -GRAMED, -GRAMING, -GRAMS or -GRAMMED, -GRAMMING, -GRAMS to mark with a design of one's initials

MONOGYNY *n pl.* -NIES the condition of having one wife at a time

MONOHULL *n pl.* -S a vessel with a single hull

MONOLITH *n pl.* -S a large block of stone

MONOLOG *n pl.* -S a lengthy speech by one person

MONOLOGY *n pl.* -GIES the act of uttering a monolog

MONOMER *n pl.* -S a type of chemical compound

MONOMIAL *n pl.* -S an algebraic expression consisting of a single term

MONOPODE *n pl.* -S a creature having one foot

MONOPODY *n pl.* -DIES a measure consisting of a single metrical foot

MONOPOLE *n pl.* -S a type of radio antenna

MONOPOLY *n pl.* -LIES exclusive control of a commodity or service in a particular market

MONORAIL *n pl.* -S a single rail serving as a track for a wheeled vehicle

MONOSOME *n pl.* -S an unpaired chromosome

MONOSOMY *n pl.* -MIES a condition of having one unpaired chromosome

MONOTINT *n pl.* -S a painting done in different shades of one color

MONOTONE *n pl.* -S a vocal utterance in one unvaried tone

MONOTONY *n pl.* -NIES tedious sameness

MONOTYPE *n pl.* -S the only representative of its group

MONOXIDE *n pl.* -S a type of oxide

MONS *n pl.* MONTES a protuberance of the body

MONSIEUR *n pl.* MESSIEURS a French title of courtesy for a man

MONSOON *n pl.* -S a seasonal wind

MONSTER *n pl.* -S a strange or terrifying creature

MONSTERA *n pl.* -S a tropical American plant

MONTAGE *v* -TAGED, -TAGING, -TAGES to combine into a composite picture

MONTANE n pl. -S the lower vegetation belt of a mountain

MONTE n pl. -S a card game

MONTEITH n pl. -S a large punch bowl

MONTERO n pl. -ROS a type of cap

MONTES pl. of mons

MONTH n pl. -S a period of approximately 30 days

MONTHLY n pl. -LIES a publication issued once a month

MONUMENT n pl. -S a structure built as a memorial

MONURON n pl. -S an herbicide

MONY adj many

MOO v -ED, -ING, -S to make the deep, moaning sound of a cow

MOOCH v -ED, -ING, -ES to obtain without paying

MOOCHER n pl. -S one that mooches

MOOD n pl. -S a person's emotional state at a particular moment

MOODY adj MOODIER, MOODIEST given to changing moods MOODILY adv

MOOL n pl. -S soft soil

MOOLA n pl. -S moolah

MOOLAH n pl. -S money

MOOLEY n pl. -EYS muley

MOON v -ED, -ING, -S to spend time idly

MOONBEAM n pl. -S a ray of light from the moon (the earth's natural satellite)

MOONBOW n pl. -S a rainbow formed by light from the moon

MOONCALF n pl. -CALVES a foolish person

MOONDUST n pl. -S dust on the moon

MOONEYE n pl. -S a freshwater fish

MOONFISH n pl. -ES a marine fish

MOONIER comparative of moony

MOONIEST superlative of moony

MOONILY adv in a moony manner

MOONISH adj fickle

MOONLESS adj lacking the light of the moon

MOONLET n pl. -S a small satellite

MOONLIKE adj resembling the moon

MOONLIT adj lighted by the moon

MOONPORT n pl. -S a facility for launching spacecraft to the moon

MOONRISE n pl. -S the rising of the moon above the horizon

MOONSAIL n pl. -S a light, square sail

MOONSEED n pl. -S a climbing plant

MOONSET n pl. -S the setting of the moon below the horizon

MOONSHOT n pl. -S the launching of a spacecraft to the moon

MOONWALK n pl. -S an instance of walking on the moon

MOONWARD adv toward the moon

MOONWORT n pl. -S a flowering plant

MOONY adj MOONIER, MOONIEST resembling the moon

MOOR v -ED, -ING, -S to secure a vessel by means of cables

MOORAGE n pl. -S the act of mooring

MOORCOCK n pl. -S the male moorfowl

MOORFOWL n pl. -S a game bird

MOORHEN n pl. -S the female moorfowl

MOORIER comparative of moory

MOORIEST superlative of moory

MOORING n pl. -S a place where a vessel may be moored

MOORISH adj marshy

MOORLAND n pl. -S a tract of marshy land

MOORWORT n pl. -S a marsh plant

MOORY adj MOORIER, MOORIEST marshy

MOOSE n pl. MOOSE a ruminant mammal

MOOT v -ED, -ING, -S to bring up for discussion

MOOTER n pl. -S one that moots

MOP v MOPPED, MOPPING, MOPS to wipe with a mop (an implement for cleaning floors)

MOPBOARD n pl. -S a board at the base of a wall

MOPE v MOPED, MOPING, MOPES to act in a dejected or gloomy manner

MOPED n pl. -S a type of motorbike

MOPER n pl. -S one that mopes

MOPERY n pl. -PERIES an act of dawdling

MOPEY adj MOPIER, MOPIEST dejected

MOPIER comparative of mopy

MOPIEST superlative of mopy

MOPING present participle of mope

MOPINGLY adv in a moping manner

MOPISH adj given to moping MOPISHLY adv

MOPOKE n pl. -S an Australian bird

MOPPED past tense of mop

MOPPER n pl. -S one that mops

MOPPET n pl. -S a child

MOPPING present participle of mop

MOPY *adj* MOPIER, MOPIEST mopey

MOQUETTE *n pl.* -S a woolen fabric

MOR *n pl.* -S a forest humus

MORA *n pl.* -RAE or -RAS a unit of metrical time in prosody

MORAINE *n pl.* -S an accumulation of debris deposited by a glacier MORAINAL, MORAINIC *adj*

MORAL *adj* pertaining to principles of right and wrong MORALLY *adv*

MORALE *n pl.* -S the state of the spirits of an individual or group

MORALISE *v* -ISED, -ISING, -ISES to moralize

MORALISM *n pl.* -S the practice of moralizing

MORALIST *n pl.* -S a teacher of morality

MORALITY *n pl.* -TIES conformity to the rules of right conduct

MORALIZE *v* -IZED, -IZING, -IZES to explain in a moral sense

MORALS *n/pl* rules of conduct with respect to right and wrong

MORASS *n pl.* -ES a marsh MORASSY *adj*

MORATORY *adj* authorizing delay of payment

MORAY *n pl.* -RAYS a tropical eel

MORBID *adj* gruesome MORBIDLY *adv*

MORBIFIC *adj* causing disease

MORBILLI *n/pl* a virus disease

MORCEAU *n pl.* -CEAUX a short literary or musical composition

MORDANCY *n pl.* -CIES a sarcastic quality

MORDANT *v* -ED, -ING, -S to treat with a caustic substance

MORDENT *n pl.* -S a melodic embellishment

MORE *n pl.* -S a greater amount

MOREEN *n pl.* -S a heavy fabric

MOREL *n pl.* -S an edible mushroom

MORELLE *n pl.* -S a flowering plant

MORELLO *n pl.* -LOS a variety of sour cherry

MOREOVER *adv* in addition

MORESQUE *n pl.* -S an ancient decorative style

MORGAN *n pl.* -S a unit of distance between genes

MORGEN *n pl.* -S a Dutch unit of land area

MORGUE *n pl.* -S a place where dead bodies are kept for identification

MORIBUND *adj* being about to die

MORION *n pl.* -S a type of helmet

MORN *n pl.* -S morning

MORNING *n pl.* -S the early part of the day

MOROCCO *n pl.* -COS a soft leather

MORON *n pl.* -S a mentally deficient person MORONIC *adj*

MORONISM *n pl.* -S the condition of being a moron

MORONITY *n pl.* -TIES moronism

MOROSE *adj* sullen MOROSELY *adv*

MOROSITY *n pl.* -TIES the state of being morose

MORPH *n pl.* -S a type of phoneme

MORPHEME *n pl.* -S a linguistic unit

MORPHIA *n pl.* -S morphine

MORPHIC *adj* pertaining to form

MORPHIN *n pl.* -S morphine

MORPHINE *n pl.* -S a narcotic alkaloid

MORPHO *n pl.* -PHOS a tropical butterfly

MORRION *n pl.* -S morion

MORRIS *n pl.* -RISES an English folk dance

MORRO *n pl.* -ROS a rounded elevation

MORROW *n pl.* -S the next day

MORSE *adj* designating a code used in telegraphy

MORSEL *v* -SELED, -SELING, -SELS or -SELLED, -SELLING, -SELS to divide into small pieces

MORT *n pl.* -S a note sounded on a hunting horn to announce the killing of an animal

MORTAL *n pl.* -S a human being

MORTALLY *adv* fatally

MORTAR *v* -ED, -ING, -S to secure with mortar (a type of cement)

MORTARY *adj* containing or resembling mortar

MORTGAGE *v* -GAGED, -GAGING, -GAGES to pledge to a creditor as security

MORTICE *v* -TICED, -TICING, -TICES to mortise

MORTIFY *v* -FIED, -FYING, -FIES to humiliate

MORTISE *v* -TISED, -TISING, -TISES to join or fasten securely

MORTISER *n pl.* -S one that mortises

MORTMAIN *n pl.* -S perpetual ownership of land

MORTUARY *n pl.* -ARIES a place where dead bodies are kept until burial

MORULA n pl. -LAE or -LAS an embryonic mass of cells **MORULAR** adj

MOSAIC v -ICKED, -ICKING, -ICS to form into a mosaic (a type of inlaid surface decoration)

MOSASAUR n pl. -S an extinct lizard

MOSCHATE adj musky

MOSEY v -ED, -ING, -S to saunter

MOSHAV n pl. -SHAVIM a cooperative settlement of small farms in Israel

MOSK n pl. -S mosque

MOSQUE n pl. -S a Muslim house of worship

MOSQUITO n pl. -TOES or -TOS a winged insect

MOSS v -ED, -ING, -ES to cover with moss (a growth of small, leafy-stemmed plants)

MOSSBACK n pl. -S a large, old fish

MOSSER n pl. -S one that gathers or works with moss

MOSSIER comparative of mossy

MOSSIEST superlative of mossy

MOSSLIKE adj resembling moss

MOSSO adv rapidly — used as a musical direction

MOSSY adj MOSSIER, MOSSIEST covered with moss

MOST n pl. -S the greatest amount

MOSTE past tense of mote

MOSTEST n pl. -S most

MOSTLY adv mainly

MOT n pl. -S a witty saying

MOTE v past tense MOSTE may

MOTE n pl. -S a small particle

MOTEL n pl. -S a roadside hotel

MOTET n pl. -S a type of choral composition

MOTEY adj full of motes

MOTH n pl. -S a winged insect

MOTHBALL v -ED, -ING, -S to put into storage

MOTHER v -ED, -ING, -S to give birth to

MOTHERLY adj maternal

MOTHERY adj slimy

MOTHLIKE adj resembling a moth

MOTHY adj MOTHIER, MOTHIEST full of moths

MOTIF n pl. -S a recurring thematic element in an artistic work **MOTIFIC** adj

MOTILE n pl. -S one whose mental imagery consists chiefly of inner feelings of action

MOTILITY n pl. -TIES the ability to move

MOTION v -ED, -ING, -S to signal by a bodily movement

MOTIONAL adj pertaining to movement

MOTIONER n pl. -S one that motions

MOTIVATE v -VATED, -VATING, -VATES to provide with an incentive

MOTIVE v -TIVED, -TIVING, -TIVES to motivate

MOTIVIC adj pertaining to a musical motif

MOTIVITY n pl. -TIES the ability to move

MOTLEY adj -LEYER, -LEYEST or -LIER, -LIEST composed of diverse elements

MOTLEY n pl. -LEYS a garment of various colors

MOTMOT n pl. -S a tropical bird

MOTOR v -ED, -ING, -S to travel by automobile

MOTORBUS n pl. -BUSES or -BUSSES a bus

MOTORCAR n pl. -S an automobile

MOTORDOM n pl. -S the motor vehicle industry

MOTORIC adj pertaining to muscular movement

MOTORING n pl. -S the recreation of traveling by automobile

MOTORISE v -ISED, -ISING, -ISES to motorize

MOTORIST n pl. -S one who travels by automobile

MOTORIZE v -IZED, -IZING, -IZES to equip with motor vehicles

MOTORMAN n pl. -MEN one who operates an electric streetcar or subway train

MOTORWAY n pl. -WAYS a type of highway

MOTT n pl. -S a motte

MOTTE n pl. -S a small growth of trees on a prairie

MOTTLE v -TLED, -TLING, -TLES to mark with spots or streaks of different colors

MOTTLER n pl. -S one that mottles

MOTTO n pl. -TOES or -TOS a short expression of a guiding principle

MOUCH v -ED, -ING, -ES to mooch

MOUCHOIR n pl. -S a small handkerchief

MOUE n pl. -S a pouting grimace

MOUFFLON n pl. -S mouflon

MOUFLON n pl. -S a wild sheep

MOUILLE *adj* pronounced with the front of the tongue against the palate

MOUJIK *n pl.* -S muzhik

MOULAGE *n pl.* -S the making of a cast or mold of a mark for use in a criminal investigation

MOULD *v* -ED, -ING, -S to mold

MOULDER *v* -ED, -ING, -S to molder

MOULDING *n pl.* -S molding

MOULDY *adj* MOULDIER, MOULDIEST moldy

MOULIN *n pl.* -S a vertical cavity in a glacier

MOULT *v* -ED, -ING, -S to molt

MOULTER *n pl.* -S molter

MOUND *v* -ED, -ING, -S to pile

MOUNT *v* -ED, -ING, -S to get up on

MOUNTAIN *n pl.* -S a large, natural elevation of the earth's surface

MOUNTER *n pl.* -S one that mounts

MOUNTING *n pl.* -S something that provides a backing or appropriate setting for something else

MOURN *v* -ED, -ING, -S to feel or express grief or sorrow

MOURNER *n pl.* -S one that mourns

MOURNFUL *adj* -FULLER, -FULLEST expressing grief or sorrow

MOURNING *n pl.* -S an outward sign of grief

MOUSE *n pl.* MICE a small rodent

MOUSE *v* MOUSED, MOUSING, MOUSES to catch mice

MOUSER *n pl.* -S an animal that catches mice

MOUSEY *adj* MOUSIER, MOUSIEST mousy

MOUSIER comparative of mousy

MOUSIEST superlative of mousy

MOUSILY *adv* in a mousy manner

MOUSING *n pl.* -S a wrapping around the shank end of a hook

MOUSSAKA *n pl.* -S a Middle Eastern dish of meat and eggplant

MOUSSE *v* MOUSSED, MOUSSING, MOUSSES to style with mousse (foamy preparation used in styling hair)

MOUSY *adj* MOUSIER, MOUSIEST resembling a mouse

MOUTH *v* -ED, -ING, -S to put into the mouth

MOUTHER *n pl.* -S a speaker

MOUTHFUL *n pl.* -S as much as the mouth can hold

MOUTHY *adj* MOUTHIER, MOUTHIEST very talkative **MOUTHILY** *adv*

MOUTON *n pl.* -S sheepskin processed to resemble seal or beaver

MOVABLE *n pl.* -S something that can be moved

MOVABLY *adv* so as to be capable of being moved

MOVE *v* MOVED, MOVING, MOVES to change from one position to another

MOVEABLE *n pl.* -S movable

MOVEABLY *adv* movably

MOVED past tense of move

MOVELESS *adj* incapable of movement

MOVEMENT *n pl.* -S the act of moving

MOVER *n pl.* -S one that moves

MOVIE *n pl.* -S a motion picture

MOVIEDOM *n pl.* -S filmdom

MOVIEOLA *n pl.* -S a device for viewing and editing film

MOVING present participle of move

MOVINGLY *adv* so as to affect the emotions

MOVIOLA *n pl.* -S movieola

MOW *v* MOWED, MOWN, MOWING, MOWS to cut down standing herbage

MOWER *n pl.* -S one that mows

MOWING *n pl.* -S the act of cutting down standing herbage

MOXA *n pl.* -S a Chinese plant

MOXIE *n pl.* -S spirit or courage

MOZETTA *n pl.* -TAS or -TE mozzetta

MOZO *n pl.* -ZOS a manual laborer

MOZZETTA *n pl.* -TAS or -TE a hooded cape worn by bishops

MRIDANGA *n pl.* -S a drum of India

MU *n pl.* -S a Greek letter

MUCH *n pl.* -ES a great amount

MUCHACHO *n pl.* -CHOS a young man

MUCHLY *adv* very much

MUCHNESS *n pl.* -ES the quality of being great

MUCID *adj* musty

MUCIDITY *n pl.* -TIES the state of being mucid

MUCILAGE *n pl.* -S an adhesive substance

MUCIN *n pl.* -S a protein secreted by the mucous membranes **MUCINOID, MUCINOUS** *adj*

MUCK *v* -ED, -ING, -S to fertilize with manure

MUCKER n pl. -S a vulgar person

MUCKIER comparative of mucky

MUCKIEST superlative of mucky

MUCKILY adv in a mucky manner

MUCKLE n pl. -S a large amount

MUCKLUCK n pl. -S mukluk

MUCKRAKE v -RAKED, -RAKING, -RAKES to search for and expose corruption

MUCKWORM n pl. -S a worm found in manure

MUCKY adj MUCKIER, MUCKIEST filthy

MUCLUC n pl. -S mukluk

MUCOID n pl. -S a complex protein **MUCOIDAL** adj

MUCOR n pl. -S a type of fungus

MUCOSA n pl. -SAE or -SAS a mucous membrane **MUCOSAL** adj

MUCOSE adj mucous

MUCOSITY n pl. -TIES the state of being mucous

MUCOUS adj secreting or containing mucus

MUCRO n pl. -CRONES a sharp point at the end of certain plant and animal organs

MUCUS n pl. -ES a viscid bodily fluid

MUD v MUDDED, MUDDING, MUDS to cover with mud (soft, wet earth)

MUDCAP v -CAPPED, -CAPPING, -CAPS to cover an explosive with mud before detonating

MUDCAT n pl. -S a type of catfish

MUDDER n pl. -S a racehorse that runs well on a muddy track

MUDDIED past tense of muddy

MUDDIER comparative of muddy

MUDDIES present 3d person sing. of muddy

MUDDIEST superlative of muddy

MUDDILY adv in a muddy manner

MUDDING present participle of mud

MUDDLE v -DLED, -DLING, -DLES to mix in a disordered manner

MUDDLER n pl. -S one that muddles

MUDDLY adj disordered

MUDDY adj -DIER, -DIEST covered or filled with mud

MUDDY v -DIED, -DYING, -DIES to make or become muddy

MUDFISH n pl. -ES a fish found in mud or muddy water

MUDFLAT n pl. -S a level tract alternately covered and left bare by the tide

MUDFLOW n pl. -S a moving mass of mud

MUDGUARD n pl. -S a fender

MUDHOLE n pl. -S a hole or hollow place full of mud

MUDLARK n pl. -S a street urchin

MUDPACK n pl. -S cosmetic paste for the face

MUDPUPPY n pl. -PIES a large salamander

MUDRA n pl. -S a hand gesture in East Indian classical dancing

MUDROCK n pl. -S pelite

MUDROOM n pl. -S a room for shedding muddy clothing or footwear

MUDSILL n pl. -S the lowest supporting timber of a structure

MUDSLIDE n pl. -S a mudflow down a slope

MUDSTONE n pl. -S a type of rock

MUEDDIN n pl. -S muezzin

MUENSTER n pl. -S a mild cheese

MUESLI n pl. -S a breakfast cereal

MUEZZIN n pl. -S a Muslim crier who calls the faithful to prayer

MUFF v -ED, -ING, -S to bungle

MUFFIN n pl. -S a small, round bread

MUFFLE v -FLED, -FLING, -FLES to wrap with something to deaden sound

MUFFLER n pl. -S a device for deadening sound

MUFTI n pl. -S a judge who interprets Muslim religious law

MUG v MUGGED, MUGGING, MUGS to assault with intent to rob

MUGFUL n pl. -S as much as a mug can hold

MUGG v -ED, -ING, -S to make funny faces

MUGGAR n pl. -S mugger

MUGGED past tense of mug

MUGGEE n pl. -S one who is mugged

MUGGER n pl. -S a large Asian crocodile

MUGGIER comparative of muggy

MUGGIEST superlative of muggy

MUGGILY adv in a muggy manner

MUGGING n pl. -S a street assault or beating

MUGGINS n pl. MUGGINS a card game

MUGGUR n pl. -S mugger

MUGGY adj -GIER, -GIEST warm and humid

MUGWORT n pl. -S a flowering plant

MUGWUMP n pl. -S a political independent

MUHLY n pl. MUHLIES a perennial grass

MUJIK n pl. -S muzhik

MUKLUK n pl. -S a soft boot worn by Eskimos

MUKTUK n pl. -S whale skin used for food

MULATTO n pl. -TOES or -TOS the offspring of one white and one black parent

MULBERRY n pl. -RIES a tree bearing an edible, berrylike fruit

MULCH v -ED, -ING, -ES to provide with a protective covering for the soil

MULCT v -ED, -ING, -S to defraud

MULE v MULED, MULING, MULES to strike from dies belonging to two different issues, as a coin

MULETA n pl. -S a red cloth used by a matador

MULETEER n pl. -S one who drives mules (hoofed work animals)

MULEY n pl. -LEYS a hornless cow

MULING present participle of mule

MULISH adj stubborn MULISHLY adv

MULL v -ED, -ING, -S to ponder

MULLA n pl. -S mullah

MULLAH n pl. -S a Muslim religious leader or teacher

MULLEIN n pl. -S a Eurasian herb

MULLEN n pl. -S mullein

MULLER n pl. -S a grinding implement

MULLET n pl. -S an edible fish

MULLEY n pl. -LEYS muley

MULLIGAN n pl. -S a stew of various meats and vegetables

MULLION v -ED, -ING, -S to provide with vertical dividing strips

MULLITE n pl. -S a mineral

MULLOCK n pl. -S waste earth or rock from a mine MULLOCKY adj

MULTIAGE adj including people of various ages

MULTICAR adj owning or involving several cars

MULTIFID adj divided into many parts

MULTIJET adj having more than two jets

MULTIPED n pl. -S an animal having many feet

MULTIPLE n pl. -S the product of a quantity by an integer

MULTIPLY v -PLIED, -PLYING, -PLIES to increase in number

MULTITON adj weighing many tons

MULTIUSE adj having many uses

MULTURE n pl. -S a fee paid to a miller for grinding grain

MUM v MUMMED, MUMMING, MUMS to act in a disguise

MUMBLE v -BLED, -BLING, -BLES to speak unclearly

MUMBLER n pl. -S one that mumbles

MUMBLY adj given to mumbling

MUMM v -ED, -ING, -S to mum

MUMMED past tense of mum and mumm

MUMMER n pl. -S one that mums

MUMMERY n pl. -MERIES a performance by mummers

MUMMIED past tense of mummy

MUMMIES present 3d person sing. of mummy

MUMMIFY v -FIED, -FYING, -FIES to preserve by embalming

MUMMING present participle of mum

MUMMY v -MIED, -MYING, -MIES to mummify

MUMP v -ED, -ING, -S to beg

MUMPER n pl. -S one that mumps

MUMU n pl. -S muumuu

MUN n pl. -S man; fellow

MUNCH v -ED, -ING, -ES to chew with a crackling sound

MUNCHER n pl. -S one that munches

MUNCHIES n/pl hunger pangs

MUNCHKIN n pl. -S a small friendly person

MUNDANE adj ordinary

MUNDUNGO n pl. -GOS a foul-smelling tobacco

MUNGO n pl. -GOS a low-quality wool

MUNGOOSE n pl. -S mongoose

MUNI n pl. -S a security issued by a state or local government

MUNIMENT n pl. -S a means of defense

MUNITION v -ED, -ING, -S to furnish with war materiel

MUNNION n pl. -S a muntin

MUNSTER n pl. -S muenster

MUNTIN n pl. -S a dividing strip for window panes

MUNTING n pl. -S muntin

MUNTJAC n pl. -S a small Asian deer

MUNTJAK n pl. -S muntjac

MUON n pl. -S a subatomic particle MUONIC adj

MUONIUM n pl. -S an electron and a positive muon bound together

MURA n pl. -S a Japanese village

MURAENID n pl. -S a moray

MURAL *n pl.* -S a painting applied directly to a wall or ceiling

MURALIST *n pl.* -S a painter of murals

MURDER *v* -ED, -ING, -S to kill unlawfully with premediated malice

MURDEREE *n pl.* -S one that is murdered

MURDERER *n pl.* -S one that murders

MURE *v* MURED, MURING, MURES to immure

MUREIN *n pl.* -S a type of polymer

MUREX *n pl.* -RICES or -REXES a marine mollusk

MURIATE *n pl.* -S chloride

MURIATED *adj* pickled

MURICATE *adj* covered with short, sharp points

MURICES a pl. of murex

MURID *n pl.* -S a murine

MURINE *n pl.* -S any of a family of small rodents

MURING present participle of mure

MURK *adj* MURKER, MURKEST dark **MURKLY** *adv*

MURK *n pl.* -S darkness

MURKY *adj* MURKIER, MURKIEST dark **MURKILY** *adv*

MURMUR *v* -ED, -ING, -S to speak unclearly

MURMURER *n pl.* -S one that murmurs

MURPHY *n pl.* -PHIES a potato

MURR *n pl.* -S murre

MURRA *n pl.* -S a substance used to make fine vases and cups in ancient Rome

MURRAIN *n pl.* -S a disease of cattle

MURRE *n pl.* -S a diving bird

MURRELET *n pl.* -S a small diving bird

MURREY *n pl.* -REYS a dark purple color

MURRHA *n pl.* -S murra **MURRHINE** *adj*

MURRINE *adj* pertaining to murra

MURRY *n pl.* -RIES a moray

MURTHER *v* -ED, -ING, -S to murder

MUSCA *n pl.* -CAE any of a genus of flies

MUSCADEL *n pl.* -S muscatel

MUSCADET *n pl.* -S a dry white French wine

MUSCAT *n pl.* -S a sweet, white grape

MUSCATEL *n pl.* -S a wine made from muscat grapes

MUSCID *n pl.* -S musca

MUSCLE *v* -CLED, -CLING, -CLES to proceed by force

MUSCLY *adj* composed of muscle (tissue that produces bodily movement)

MUSCULAR *adj* pertaining to muscle

MUSE *v* MUSED, MUSING, MUSES to ponder

MUSEFUL *adj* pensive

MUSER *n pl.* -S one that muses

MUSETTE *n pl.* -S a small bagpipe

MUSEUM *n pl.* -S a place where objects of lasting interest or value are cared for and exhibited

MUSH *v* -ED, -ING, -ES to travel over snow with a dog sled

MUSHER *n pl.* -S one that mushes

MUSHROOM *v* -ED, -ING, -S to grow or spread rapidly

MUSHY *adj* MUSHIER, MUSHIEST pulpy **MUSHILY** *adv*

MUSIC *n pl.* -S vocal or instrumental sounds organized to produce a unified composition

MUSICAL *n pl.* -S a play in which dialogue is interspersed with songs and dances

MUSICALE *n pl.* -S a program of music performed at a social gathering

MUSICIAN *n pl.* -S one who performs or composes music

MUSING *n pl.* -S contemplation

MUSINGLY *adv* in a pensive manner

MUSJID *n pl.* -S a mosque

MUSK *n pl.* -S a strongly odorous substance secreted by certain animals

MUSKEG *n pl.* -S a marsh

MUSKET *n pl.* -S a type of firearm

MUSKETRY *n pl.* -RIES the technique of firing small arms

MUSKIE *n pl.* -S a freshwater fish

MUSKIER comparative of musky

MUSKIEST superlative of musky

MUSKILY *adv* in a musky manner

MUSKIT *n pl.* -S mesquite

MUSKRAT *n pl.* -S an aquatic rodent

MUSKY *adj* MUSKIER, MUSKIEST resembling musk

MUSLIN *n pl.* -S a cotton fabric

MUSPIKE *n pl.* -S a freshwater fish

MUSQUASH *n pl.* -ES the muskrat

MUSS *v* -ED, -ING, -ES to mess

MUSSEL *n pl.* -S a bivalve mollusk

MUSSY *adj* MUSSIER, MUSSIEST messy **MUSSILY** *adv*

MUST *v* -ED, -ING, -S to become musty

MUSTACHE *n* pl. -S a growth of hair on the upper lip

MUSTANG *n* pl. -S a wild horse

MUSTARD *n* pl. -S a pungent seasoning

MUSTARDY *adj* resembling mustard

MUSTEE *n* pl. -S an octoroon

MUSTER *v* -ED, -ING, -S to summon or assemble

MUSTH *n* pl. -S a state of frenzy occurring in male elephants

MUSTY *adj* MUSTIER, MUSTIEST having a stale odor **MUSTILY** *adv*

MUT *n* pl. -S mutt

MUTABLE *adj* capable of change **MUTABLY** *adv*

MUTAGEN *n* pl. -S a substance that causes biological mutation

MUTANT *n* pl. -S something that undergoes mutation

MUTASE *n* pl. -S an enzyme

MUTATE *v* -TATED, -TATING, -TATES to undergo mutation

MUTATION *n* pl. -S the act of changing **MUTATIVE** *adj*

MUTCH *n* pl. -ES a close-fitting cap

MUTCHKIN *n* pl. -S a Scottish unit of liquid measure

MUTE *adj* MUTER, MUTEST characterized by an absence of speech **MUTELY** *adv*

MUTE *v* MUTED, MUTING, MUTES to deaden the sound of **MUTEDLY** *adv*

MUTENESS *n* pl. -ES the state of being mute

MUTER comparative of mute

MUTEST superlative of mute

MUTICOUS *adj* lacking a point

MUTILATE *v* -LATED, -LATING, -LATES to deprive of a limb or other essential part

MUTINE *v* -TINED, -TINING, -TINES to mutiny

MUTINEER *v* -ED, -ING, -S to mutiny

MUTING present participle of mute

MUTINIED past tense of mutiny

MUTINIES present 3d person sing. of mutiny

MUTINING present participle of mutine

MUTINOUS *adj* disposed to mutiny

MUTINY *v* -NIED, -NYING, -NIES to revolt against constituted authority

MUTISM *n* pl. -S muteness

MUTON *n* pl. -S a unit of nucleic acid

MUTT *n* pl. -S a mongrel dog

MUTTER *v* -ED, -ING, -S to speak unclearly

MUTTERER *n* pl. -S one that mutters

MUTTON *n* pl. -S the flesh of sheep used as food **MUTTONY** *adj*

MUTUAL *adj* shared in common **MUTUALLY** *adv*

MUTUEL *n* pl. -S a system of betting on races

MUTULE *n* pl. -S an ornamental block used in classical Greek architecture **MUTULAR** *adj*

MUUMUU *n* pl. -S a long, loose dress

MUZHIK *n* pl. -S a Russian peasant

MUZJIK *n* pl. -S muzhik

MUZZIER comparative of muzzy

MUZZIEST superlative of muzzy

MUZZILY *adv* in a muzzy manner

MUZZLE *v* -ZLED, -ZLING, -ZLES to put a covering over the mouth of to prevent biting or eating

MUZZLER *n* pl. -S one that muzzles

MUZZY *adj* -ZIER, -ZIEST confused

MY *pron* the possessive form of the pronoun I

MYALGIA *n* pl. -S muscular pain **MYALGIC** *adj*

MYASIS *n* pl. MYASES myiasis

MYCELE *n* pl. -S mycelium

MYCELIUM *n* pl. -LIA the vegetative portion of a fungus **MYCELIAL, MYCELIAN, MYCELOID** *adj*

MYCETOMA *n* pl. -MAS or -MATA a fungous infection

MYCOLOGY *n* pl. -GIES the branch of botany dealing with fungi

MYCOSIS *n* pl. -COSES a disease caused by a fungus **MYCOTIC** *adj*

MYELIN *n* pl. -S a fatty substance that encases certain nerve fibers **MYELINIC** *adj*

MYELINE *n* pl. -S myelin

MYELITIS *n* pl. -LITIDES inflammation of the bone marrow

MYELOID *adj* pertaining to bone marrow

MYELOMA *n* pl. -MAS or -MATA a tumor of the bone marrow

MYIASIS *n* pl. MYIASES infestation of human tissue by fly maggots

MYLONITE *n* pl. -S a type of rock

MYNA *n* pl. -S an Asian bird

MYNAH *n* pl. -S myna

MYNHEER *n* pl. -S a Dutch title of courtesy for a man

MYOBLAST *n* pl. -S a cell capable of giving rise to muscle cells

MYOGENIC *adj* originating in muscle tissue

MYOGRAPH *n* pl. -S an instrument for recording muscular contractions

MYOID *adj* resembling muscle

MYOLOGY *n* pl. -GIES the study of muscles **MYOLOGIC** *adj*

MYOMA *n* pl. -MAS or -MATA a tumor composed of muscle tissue

MYOPATHY *n* pl. -THIES a disorder of muscle tissue

MYOPE *n* pl. -S one who is affected with myopia

MYOPIA *n* pl. -S a visual defect **MYOPIC** *adj*

MYOPY *n* pl. -PIES myopia

MYOSCOPE *n* pl. -S an instrument for observing muscular contractions

MYOSIN *n* pl. -S a protein found in muscle tissue

MYOSIS *n* pl. MYOSES miosis

MYOSITIS *n* pl. -TISES muscular pain from infection

MYOSOTE *n* pl. -S myosotis

MYOSOTIS *n* pl. -TISES a flowering plant

MYOTIC *n* pl. -S miotic

MYOTOME *n* pl. -S a portion of an embryonic somite

MYOTONIA *n* pl. -S temporary muscular rigidity **MYOTONIC** *adj*

MYRIAD *n* pl. -S a very large number

MYRIAPOD *n* pl. -S a multi-legged arthropod

MYRICA *n* pl. -S a medicinal tree bark

MYRIOPOD *n* pl. -S myriapod

MYRMIDON *n* pl. -S a loyal follower

MYRRH *n* pl. -S an aromatic gum resin **MYRRHIC** *adj*

MYRTLE *n* pl. -S an evergreen shrub

MYSELF *pron* a form of the 1st person sing. pronoun

MYSID *n* pl. -S a small crustacean

MYSOST *n* pl. -S a mild cheese

MYSTAGOG *n* pl. -S a teacher of religious mysteries

MYSTERY *n* pl. -TERIES something that is not or cannot be known, understood, or explained

MYSTIC *n* pl. -S one who professes to have had mystical experiences

MYSTICAL *adj* spiritually significant or symbolic

MYSTICLY *adv* in a mystical manner

MYSTIFY *v* -FIED, -FYING, -FIES to perplex

MYSTIQUE *n* pl. -S an aura of mystery or mystical power surrounding a particular person or thing

MYTH *n* pl. -S a type of traditional story

MYTHIC *adj* mythical

MYTHICAL *adj* based on or described in a myth

MYTHOS *n* pl. -THOI a myth

MYTHY *adj* MYTHIER, MYTHIEST resembling myth

MYXEDEMA *n* pl. -S a disease caused by decreased activity of the thyroid gland

MYXOCYTE *n* pl. -S a large cell found in mucous tissue

MYXOID *adj* containing mucus

MYXOMA *n* pl. -MAS or -MATA a tumor composed of mucous tissue

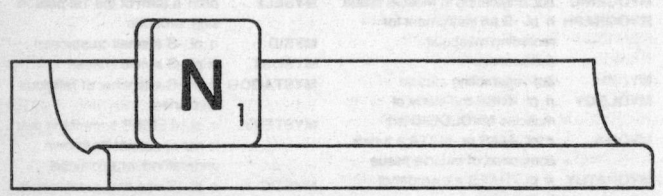

NA   *adv* no; not

NAAN   *n* pl. **-S** nan

NAB   *v* **NABBED, NABBING, NABS** to capture or arrest

NABBER   *n* pl. **-S** one that nabs

NABE   *n* pl. **-S** a neighborhood movie theater

NABIS   *n* pl. **NABIS** a group of French artists

NABOB   *n* pl. **-S** one who becomes rich and prominent **NABOBISH** *adj*

NABOBERY   *n* pl. **-ERIES** the state of being a nabob

NABOBESS   *n* pl. **-ES** a female nabob

NABOBISM   *n* pl. **-S** great wealth and luxury

NACELLE   *n* pl. **-S** a shelter on an aircraft

NACHAS   *n* pl. **NACHAS** pride in another's accomplishments

NACHES   *n* pl. **NACHES** nachas

NACHO   *n* pl. **-CHOS** a tortilla chip topped with cheese and a savory mixture and broiled

NACRE   *n* pl. **-S** the pearly internal layer of certain shells **NACRED, NACREOUS** *adj*

NADA   *n* pl. **-S** nothing

NADIR   *n* pl. **-S** a point on the celestial sphere **NADIRAL** *adj*

NAE   *adv* no; not

NAETHING   *n* pl. **-S** nothing

NAEVUS   *n* pl. **-VI** nevus **NAEVOID** *adj*

NAG   *v* **NAGGED, NAGGING, NAGS** to find fault incessantly

NAGANA   *n* pl. **-S** a disease of horses in Africa

NAGGER   *n* pl. **-S** one that nags

NAGGING   present participle of nag

NAGGY   *adj* **-GIER, -GIEST** given to nagging

NAH   *adv* no

NAIAD   *n* pl. **-S** or **-ES** a water nymph

NAIF   *n* pl. **-S** a naive person

NAIL   *v* **-ED, -ING, -S** to fasten with a nail (a slender piece of metal)

NAILER   *n* pl. **-S** one that nails

NAILFOLD   *n* pl. **-S** a fold of skin around the fingernail

NAILHEAD   *n* pl. **-S** the top of a nail

NAILSET   *n* pl. **-S** a steel rod for driving a nail into something

NAINSOOK   *n* pl. **-S** a cotton fabric

NAIRA   *n* pl. **NAIRA** a monetary unit of Nigeria

NAIVE   *adj* **NAIVER, NAIVEST** lacking sophistication **NAIVELY** *adv*

NAIVE   *n* pl. **-S** a naive person

NAIVETE   *n* pl. **-S** the quality of being naive

NAIVETY   *n* pl. **-TIES** naivete

NAKED   *adj* **-KEDER, -KEDEST** being without clothing or covering **NAKEDLY** *adv*

NALED   *n* pl. **-S** an insecticide

NALOXONE   *n* pl. **-S** a chemical compound

NAM   a past tense of nim

NAME   *v* **NAMED, NAMING, NAMES** to give a title to **NAMABLE, NAMEABLE** *adj*

NAMELESS   *adj* lacking distinction or fame

NAMELY   *adv* that is to say

NAMER   *n* pl. **-S** one that names

NAMESAKE   *n* pl. **-S** one who is named after another

NAMETAG   *n* pl. **-S** a tag bearing one's name worn for identification

NAMING	present participle of name
NAN	n pl. -S a round flat bread
NANA	n pl. -S a grandmother
NANDIN	n pl. -S an evergreen shrub
NANDINA	n pl. -S an Asian shrub
NANISM	n pl. -S abnormal smallness
NANKEEN	n pl. -S a cotton fabric
NANKIN	n pl. -S nankeen
NANNIE	n pl. -S nanny
NANNY	n pl. -NIES a children's nurse
NANOGRAM	n pl. -S a unit of mass and weight
NANOWATT	n pl. -S a unit of power
NAOS	n pl. NAOI an ancient temple
NAP	v NAPPED, NAPPING, NAPS to sleep briefly
NAPALM	v -ED, -ING, -S to assault with a type of incendiary bomb
NAPE	n pl. -S the back of the neck
NAPERY	n pl. -PERIES table linen
NAPHTHA	n pl. -S a volatile liquid
NAPHTHOL	n pl. -S a chemical compound
NAPHTHYL	n pl. -S a radical derived from naphthalene
NAPHTOL	n pl. -S naphthol
NAPIFORM	adj shaped like a turnip
NAPKIN	n pl. -S a piece of material used to wipe the hands and mouth
NAPLESS	adj threadbare
NAPOLEON	n pl. -S a type of pastry
NAPPE	n pl. -S a type of rock formation
NAPPED	past tense of nap
NAPPER	n pl. -S one that naps
NAPPIE	n pl. -S a diaper
NAPPING	present participle of nap
NAPPY	adj -PIER, -PIEST kinky
NARC	n pl. -S an undercover drug agent
NARCEIN	n pl. -S narceine
NARCEINE	n pl. -S an opium derivative
NARCISM	n pl. -S excessive love of oneself
NARCISSI	n/pl bulbous flowering plants
NARCIST	n pl. -S one given to narcism
NARCO	n pl. -COS narc
NARCOSE	adj characterized by stupor
NARCOSIS	n pl. -COSES a drug-induced stupor
NARCOTIC	n pl. -S a drug that dulls the senses
NARD	n pl. -S a fragrant ointment **NARDINE** adj
NARES	pl. of naris

NARGHILE	n pl. -S a hookah
NARGILE	n pl. -S narghile
NARGILEH	n pl. -S narghile
NARIS	n pl. NARES a nostril **NARIAL, NARIC, NARINE** adj
NARK	v -ED, -ING, -S to spy or inform
NARKY	adj irritable
NARRATE	v -RATED, -RATING, -RATES to tell a story
NARRATER	n pl. -S narrator
NARRATOR	n pl. -S one that narrates
NARROW	adj -ROWER, -ROWEST of little width **NARROWLY** adv
NARROW	v -ED, -ING, -S to make narrow
NARTHEX	n pl. -ES a vestibule in a church
NARWAL	n pl. -S narwhal
NARWHAL	n pl. -S an arctic aquatic mammal
NARWHALE	n pl. -S narwhal
NARY	adj not one
NASAL	n pl. -S a sound uttered through the nose
NASALISE	v -ISED, -ISING, -ISES to nasalize
NASALITY	n pl. -TIES the quality or an instance of being produced nasally
NASALIZE	v -IZED, -IZING, -IZES to produce sounds nasally
NASALLY	adv through the nose
NASCENCE	n pl. -S naascency
NASCENCY	n pl. -CIES birth; origin
NASCENT	adj coming into existence
NASION	n pl. -S a point in the skull **NASIAL** adj
NASTIC	adj pertaining to an automatic response of plants
NASTY	adj -TIER, -TIEST offensive to the senses **NASTILY** adv
NASTY	n pl. -TIES something that is nasty
NATAL	adj pertaining to one's birth
NATALITY	n pl. -TIES birth rate
NATANT	adj floating or swimming **NATANTLY** adv
NATATION	n pl. -S the act of swimming
NATATORY	adj pertaining to swimming
NATCH	adv naturally
NATES	n/pl the buttocks
NATHLESS	adv nevertheless

NATION n pl. -S a politically organized people who share a territory, customs, and history

NATIONAL n pl. -S a citizen of a nation

NATIVE n pl. -S an original inhabitant of an area

NATIVELY adv in an inborn manner

NATIVISM n pl. -S a policy of favoring the interests of native inhabitants

NATIVIST n pl. -S an advocate of nativism

NATIVITY n pl. -TIES the process of being born

NATRIUM n pl. -S sodium

NATRON n pl. -S a chemical compound

NATTER v -ED, -ING, -S to chatter

NATTY adj -TIER, -TIEST neatly dressed **NATTILY** adv

NATURAL n pl. -S a type of musical note

NATURE n pl. -S the essential qualities of a person or thing **NATURED** adj

NATURISM n pl. -S nudism

NATURIST n pl. -S a nudist

NAUGHT n pl. -S a zero

NAUGHTY adj -TIER, -TIEST disobedient

NAUMACHY n pl. -CHIES a mock sea battle

NAUPLIUS n pl. -PLII a form of certain crustaceans **NAUPLIAL** adj

NAUSEA n pl. -S a stomach disturbance

NAUSEANT n pl. -S an agent that induces nausea

NAUSEATE v -ATED, -ATING, -ATES to affect with nausea

NAUSEOUS adj affected with nausea

NAUTCH n pl. -ES a dancing exhibition in India

NAUTICAL adj pertaining to ships

NAUTILUS n pl. -LUSES or -LI a spiral-shelled mollusk

NAVAID n pl. -S a navigational device

NAVAL adj pertaining to ships **NAVALLY** adv

NAVAR n pl. -S a system of air navigation

NAVE n pl. -S the main part of a church

NAVEL n pl. -S a depression in the abdomen

NAVETTE n pl. -S a gem cut in a pointed oval form

NAVICERT n pl. -S a document permitting a vessel passage through a naval blockade

NAVIES pl. of navy

NAVIGATE v -GATED, -GATING, -GATES to plan and control the course of

NAVVY n pl. -VIES a manual laborer

NAVY n pl. -VIES a nation's warships

NAW adv no

NAWAB n pl. -S a nabob

NAY n pl. NAYS a negative vote

NAYSAYER n pl. -S one that denies or opposes something

NAZI n pl. -S a type of fascist

NAZIFY v -FIED, -FYING, -FIES to cause to be like a nazi

NE adj born with the name of

NEAP n pl. -S a tide of lowest range

NEAR adj NEARER, NEAREST situated within a short distance

NEAR v -ED, -ING, -S to approach

NEARBY adj near

NEARLY adv -LIER, -LIEST with close approximation

NEARNESS n pl. -ES the state of being near

NEARSIDE n pl. -S the left side

NEAT adj NEATER, NEATEST being in a state of cleanliness and order

NEAT n pl. -S a bovine

NEATEN v -ED, -ING, -S to make neat

NEATH prep beneath

NEATHERD n pl. -S a cowherd

NEATLY adv in a neat manner

NEATNESS n pl. -ES the state of being neat

NEB n pl. -S the beak of a bird

NEBBISH n pl. -ES a meek person **NEBBISHY** adj

NEBULA n pl. -LAS or -LAE a cloud-like interstellar mass **NEBULAR** adj

NEBULE adj composed of successive short curves

NEBULISE v -LISED, -LISING, -LISES to nebulize

NEBULIZE v -LIZED, -LIZING, -LIZES to reduce to a fine spray

NEBULOSE adj nebulous

NEBULOUS adj unclear

NEBULY adj nebule

NECK v -ED, -ING, -S to kiss and caress in lovemaking

NECKBAND n pl. -S a band worn around the neck (the part of the body joining the head to the trunk)

NECKER *n pl.* -S one that necks

NECKING *n pl.* -S a small molding near the top of a column

NECKLACE *n pl.* -S an ornament worn around the neck

NECKLESS *adj* having no neck

NECKLIKE *adj* resembling the neck

NECKLINE *n pl.* -S the line formed by the neck opening of a garment

NECKTIE *n pl.* -S a strip of fabric worn around the neck

NECKWEAR *n pl.* NECKWEAR something that is worn around the neck

NECROPSY *v* -SIED, -SYING, -SIES to perform an autopsy on

NECROSE *v* -CROSED, -CROSING, -CROSES to affect with necrosis

NECROSIS *n pl.* -CROSES the death of living tissue NECROTIC *adj*

NECTAR *n pl.* -S a delicious drink

NECTARY *n pl.* -TARIES a plant gland

NEE *adj* born with the name of

NEED *v* -ED, -ING, -S to have an urgent or essential use for

NEEDER *n pl.* -S one that needs

NEEDFUL *n pl.* -S something that is needed

NEEDIER comparative of needy

NEEDIEST superlative of needy

NEEDILY *adv* in a needy manner

NEEDLE *v* -DLED, -DLING, -DLES to sew with a slender, pointed instrument

NEEDLER *n pl.* -S one that needles

NEEDLESS *adj* not necessary

NEEDLING *n pl.* -S the act of one who needles

NEEDY *adj* NEEDIER, NEEDIEST in a state of poverty

NEEM *n pl.* -S an East Indian tree

NEEP *n pl.* -S a turnip

NEGATE *v* -GATED, -GATING, -GATES to nullify

NEGATER *n pl.* -S one that negates

NEGATION *n pl.* -S the act of negating

NEGATIVE *v* -TIVED, -TIVING, -TIVES to veto

NEGATON *n pl.* -S negatron

NEGATOR *n pl.* -S negater

NEGATRON *n pl.* -S an electron

NEGLECT *v* -ED, -ING, -S to fail to pay attention to

NEGLIGE *n pl.* -S negligee

NEGLIGEE *n pl.* -S a woman's dressing gown

NEGROID *n pl.* -S member of the black race

NEGRONI *n pl.* -S an alcoholic beverage

NEGUS *n pl.* -ES an alcoholic beverage

NEIF *n pl.* -S nieve

NEIGH *v* -ED, -ING, -S to utter the cry of a horse

NEIGHBOR *v* -ED, -ING, -S to live close to

NEIST *adj* next

NEITHER *adj* not one or the other

NEKTON *n pl.* -S free-swimming marine animals NEKTONIC *adj*

NELLIE *n pl.* -S an effeminate male

NELLY *n pl.* -LIES nellie

NELSON *n pl.* -S a wrestling hold

NELUMBO *n pl.* -BOS an aquatic herb

NEMA *n pl.* -S a nematode

NEMATIC *adj* pertaining to a phase of a liquid crystal

NEMATODE *n pl.* -S a kind of worm

NEMESIS *n pl.* NEMESES an unbeatable opponent

NENE *n pl.* NENE a Hawaiian goose

NEOLITH *n pl.* -S an ancient stone implement

NEOLOGY *n pl.* -GIES a new word or phrase NEOLOGIC *adj*

NEOMORPH *n pl.* -S a type of biological structure

NEOMYCIN *n pl.* -S an antibiotic drug

NEON *n pl.* -S a gaseous element NEONED *adj*

NEONATE *n pl.* -S a newborn child NEONATAL *adj*

NEOPHYTE *n pl.* -S a novice

NEOPLASM *n pl.* -S a tumor

NEOPRENE *n pl.* -S a synthetic rubber

NEOTENY *n pl.* -NIES attainment of sexual maturity in the larval stage NEOTENIC *adj*

NEOTERIC *n pl.* -S a modern author

NEOTYPE *n pl.* -S a specimen of a species

NEPENTHE *n pl.* -S a drug that induces forgetfulness

NEPHEW *n pl.* -S a son of one's brother or sister

NEPHRIC *adj* renal

NEPHRISM *n pl.* -S ill health caused by a kidney disease

NEPHRITE *n pl.* -S a mineral

NEPHRON *n pl.* -S an excretory unit of a kidney

NEPOTISM *n pl.* -S favoritism shown to a relative NEPOTIC *adj*

NEPOTIST n pl. -S one who practices nepotism

NERD n pl. -S a socially inept person NERDISH adj

NERDY adj NERDIER, NERDIEST socially inept

NEREID n pl. -S a sea nymph

NEREIS n pl. -REIDES a marine worm

NERITIC adj pertaining to shallow water

NEROL n pl. -S a fragrant alcohol

NEROLI n pl. -S a fragrant oil

NERTS interj — used to express defiance or disgust

NERTZ interj nerts

NERVATE adj having veins

NERVE v NERVED, NERVING, NERVES to give courage to

NERVIER comparative of nervy

NERVIEST superlative of nervy

NERVILY adv in a nervy manner

NERVINE n pl. -S a soothing medicine

NERVING n pl. -S a type of veterinary operation

NERVOUS adj easily excited

NERVULE n pl. -S nervure

NERVURE n pl. -S a vein on a leaf

NERVY adj NERVIER, NERVIEST impudent

NESCIENT n pl. -S one who is ignorant

NESS n pl. -ES a headland

NEST v -ED, -ING, -S to build a nest (a structure for holding bird eggs)

NESTABLE adj capable of being fitted closely within another container

NESTER n pl. -S one that nests

NESTLE v -TLED, -TLING, -TLES to lie snugly

NESTLER n pl. -S one that nestles

NESTLIKE adj resembling a nest

NESTLING n pl. -S a young bird

NESTOR n pl. -S a wise old man

NET v NETTED, NETTING, NETS to catch in a net (a type of openwork fabric)

NETHER adj situated below

NETLESS adj having no net

NETLIKE adj resembling a net

NETOP n pl. -S friend; companion

NETSUKE n pl. -S a button-like fixture on Japanese clothing

NETT v -ED, -ING, -S to net

NETTABLE adj capable of being netted

NETTED past tense of net, nett

NETTER n pl. -S one that nets

NETTIER comparative of netty

NETTIEST superlative of netty

NETTING n pl. -S a net

NETTLE v -TLED, -TLING, -TLES to make angry

NETTLER n pl. -S one that nettles

NETTLY adj -TLIER, -TLIEST prickly

NETTY adj -TIER, -TIEST resembling a net

NETWORK v -ED, -ING, -S to cover with or as if with crossing lines

NEUK n pl. -S nook

NEUM n pl. -S neume

NEUME n pl. -S a sign used in musical notation NEUMATIC, NEUMIC adj

NEURAL adj pertaining to the nervous system NEURALLY adv

NEURAXON n pl. -S a part of a neuron

NEURINE n pl. -S a ptomaine poison

NEURITIC n pl. -S one affected with neuritis

NEURITIS n pl. -RITIDES or -RITISES inflammation of a nerve

NEUROID adj resembling a nerve

NEUROMA n pl. -MAS or -MATA a type of tumor

NEURON n pl. -S the basic cellular unit of the nervous system NEURONAL, NEURONIC adj

NEURONE n pl. -S neuron

NEUROSIS n pl. -ROSES a type of emotional disturbance NEUROSAL adj

NEUROTIC n pl. -S one affected with a neurosis

NEURULA n pl. -LAE or -LAS a vertebrate embryo

NEUSTON n pl. -S an aggregate of small aquatic organisms

NEUTER v -ED, -ING, -S to castrate

NEUTRAL n pl. -S one that is impartial

NEUTRINO n pl. -NOS a subatomic particle

NEUTRON n pl. -S a subatomic particle

NEVE n pl. -S a granular snow

NEVER adv at no time

NEVUS n pl. -VI a birthmark NEVOID adj

NEW adj NEWER, NEWEST existing only a short time

NEW n pl. -S something that is new

NEWBORN n pl. -S a recently born infant

NEWCOMER n pl. -S one that has recently arrived

NEWEL n pl. -S a staircase support

NEWFOUND adj newly found

NEWIE n pl. -S something new

NEWISH adj somewhat new

NEWLY adv recently

NEWLYWED n pl. -S a person recently married

NEWMOWN adj recently mown

NEWNESS n pl. -ES the state of being new

NEWS n/pl a report of recent events

NEWSBOY n pl. -BOYS a boy who delivers or sells newspapers

NEWSCAST n pl. -S a news broadcast

NEWSHAWK n pl. -S a newspaper reporter

NEWSIE n pl. -S newsy

NEWSIER comparative of newsy

NEWSIES pl. of newsy

NEWSIEST superlative of newsy

NEWSLESS adj having no news

NEWSMAN n pl. -MEN a news reporter

NEWSPEAK n pl. -S a deliberately ambiguous language

NEWSREEL n pl. -S a short movie presenting current events

NEWSROOM n pl. -S a room where the news is gathered

NEWSY adj NEWSIER, NEWSIEST full of news

NEWSY n pl. NEWSIES a newsboy

NEWT n pl. -S a small salamander

NEWTON n pl. -S a unit of force

NEXT adj coming immediately after; adjoining

NEXTDOOR adj located in the next building or room

NEXUS n pl. -ES a connection or link

NGULTRUM n pl. -S a monetary unit of Bhutan

NGWEE n pl. NGWEE a monetary unit of Zambia

NIACIN n pl. -S a B vitamin

NIB v NIBBED, NIBBING, NIBS to provide with a penpoint

NIBBLE v -BLED, -BLING, -BLES to eat with small bites

NIBBLER n pl. -S one that nibbles

NIBLICK n pl. -S a golf club

NIBLIKE adj resembling a penpoint

NICAD n pl. -S nickel cadmium

NICE adj NICER, NICEST pleasing to the senses NICELY adv

NICENESS n pl. -ES the quality of being nice

NICETY n pl. -TIES a fine point or distinction

NICHE v NICHED, NICHING, NICHES to place in a receding space or hollow

NICK v -ED, -ING, -S to make a shallow cut in

NICKEL v -ELED, -ELING, -ELS or -ELLED, -ELLING, -ELS to plate with nickel (a metallic element)

NICKELIC adj pertaining to or containing nickel

NICKER v -ED, -ING, -S to neigh

NICKLE v -LED, -LING, -LES nickel

NICKNACK n pl. -S a trinket

NICKNAME v -NAMED, -NAMING, -NAMES to give an alternate name to

NICOL n pl. -S a type of prism

NICOTIN n pl. -S nicotine

NICOTINE n pl. -S a poisonous alkaloid in tobacco

NICTATE n -TATED, -TATING, -TATES to wink

NIDAL adj pertaining to a nidus

NIDE n NIDED, NIDING, NIDES to nest

NIDERING n pl. -S a coward

NIDGET n pl. -S an idiot

NIDI a pl. of nidus

NIDIFY v -FIED, -FYING, -FIES to nest

NIDING present participle of nide

NIDUS n pl. NIDI or NIDUSES a nest or breeding place

NIECE n pl. -S a daughter of one's brother or sister

NIELLIST n pl. -S one that niellos

NIELLO n pl. -LI or -LOS a black metallic substance

NIELLO v -ED, -ING, -S to decorate with niello

NIEVE n pl. -S the fist or hand

NIFFER v -ED, -ING, -S to barter

NIFTY adj -TIER, -TIEST stylish; pleasing NIFTILY adv

NIFTY n pl. -TIES something that is nifty

NIGGARD v -ED, -ING, -S to act stingily

NIGGLE v -GLED, -GLING, -GLES to worry over petty details

NIGGLER n pl. -S one that niggles

NIGGLING n pl. -S petty or meticulous work

NIGH adj NIGHER, NIGHEST near

NIGH v -ED, -ING, -S to approach

NIGHNESS n pl. -ES the state of being nigh

NIGHT n pl. -S the period from sunset to sunrise

NIGHTCAP n pl. -S a cap worn to bed

NIGHTIE n pl. -S a nightgown

NIGHTIES pl. of nighty

NIGHTJAR n pl. -S a nocturnal bird

NIGHTLY adv every night; at night

NIGHTY n pl. NIGHTIES nightie

NIGRIFY v -FIED, -FYING, -FIES to make black

NIGROSIN n pl. -S a type of dye

NIHIL n pl. -S nothing

NIHILISM n pl. -S a doctrine that denies traditional values

NIHILIST n pl. -S an adherent of nihilism

NIHILITY n pl. -TIES the state of being nothing

NIL n pl. -S nothing

NILGAI n pl. -S a large antelope

NILGAU n pl. -S nilgai

NILGHAI n pl. -S nilgai

NILGHAU n pl. -S nilgai

NILL v -ED, -ING, -S to be unwilling

NIM v NAM or NIMMED, NIMMING, NIMS to steal

NIMBLE adj -BLER, -BLEST agile NIMBLY adv

NIMBUS n pl. -BI or -BUSES a luminous cloud NIMBUSED adj

NIMIETY n pl. -ETIES excess NIMIOUS adj

NIMMED past tense of nim

NIMMING present participle of nim

NIMROD n pl. -S a hunter

NINE n pl. -S a number

NINEBARK n pl. -S a flowering shrub

NINEFOLD adj nine times as great

NINEPIN n pl. -S a wooden pin used in a bowling game

NINETEEN n pl. -S a number

NINETY n pl. -TIES a number

NINJA n pl. -S a feudal Japanese warrior

NINNY n pl. -NIES a fool NINNYISH adj

NINON n pl. -S a sheer fabric

NINTH n pl. -S one of nine equal parts

NINTHLY adv in the ninth place

NIOBATE n pl. -S a chemical salt

NIOBIUM n pl. -S a metallic element NIOBIC, NIOBOUS adj

NIP v NIPPED, NIPPING, NIPS to pinch

NIPA n pl. -S a palm tree

NIPPER n pl. -S one that nips

NIPPIER comparative of nippy

NIPPIEST superlative of nippy

NIPPILY adv in a nippy manner

NIPPING present participle of nip

NIPPLE n pl. -S a protuberance on the breast NIPPLED adj

NIPPY adj -PIER, -PIEST sharp or biting

NIRVANA n pl. -S a blessed state in Buddhism NIRVANIC adj

NISEI n pl. -S one born in America of immigrant Japanese parents

NISI adj not yet final

NISUS n pl. NISUS an effort

NIT n pl. -S the egg of a parasitic insect

NITE n pl. -S night

NITER n pl. -S a chemical salt

NITERIE n pl. -S a nitery

NITERY n pl. -ERIES a nightclub

NITID adj bright

NITINOL n pl. -S an alloy of nickel and titanium

NITON n pl. -S radon

NITPICK v -ED, -ING, -S to fuss over petty details

NITPICKY adj -PICKIER, -PICKIEST tending to nitpick

NITRATE v -TRATED, -TRATING, -TRATES to treat with nitric acid

NITRATOR n pl. -S one that nitrates

NITRE n pl. -S niter

NITRIC adj containing nitrogen

NITRID n pl. -S nitride

NITRIDE v -TRIDED, -TRIDING, -TRIDES to convert into a nitride (a compound of nitrogen)

NITRIFY v -FIED, -FYING, -FIES to combine with nitrogen

NITRIL n pl. -S nitrile

NITRILE n pl. -S a chemical compound

NITRITE n pl. -S a salt of nitrous acid

NITRO n pl. -TROS a nitrated product

NITROGEN n pl. -S a gaseous element

NITROLIC adj pertaining to a class of acids

NITROSO adj containing nitrosyl

NITROSYL n pl. -S a univalent radical

NITROUS adj containing nitrogen

NITTY adj -TIER, -TIEST full of nits

NITWIT *n pl.* -S a stupid person

NIVAL *adj* pertaining to snow

NIVEOUS *adj* resembling snow

NIX *v* -ED, -ING, -ES to veto

NIX *n pl.* NIXES or NIXE a water sprite

NIXIE *n pl.* -S a female water sprite

NIXY *n pl.* NIXIES an undeliverable piece of mail

NIZAM *n pl.* -S a former sovereign of India

NIZAMATE *n pl.* -S the territory of a nizam

NO *n pl.* NOS or NOES a negative reply

NOB *n pl.* -S a wealthy person

NOBBIER comparative of nobby

NOBBIEST superlative of nobby

NOBBILY *adv* in a nobby manner

NOBBLE *v* -BLED, -BLING, -BLES to disable a racehorse

NOBBLER *n pl.* -S one that nobbles

NOBBY *adj* -BIER, -BIEST elegant

NOBELIUM *n pl.* -S a radioactive element

NOBILITY *n pl.* -TIES the social class composed of nobles

NOBLE *adj* -BLER, -BLEST possessing qualities of excellence

NOBLE *n pl.* -S a person of high birth, rank, or title

NOBLEMAN *n pl.* -MEN a noble

NOBLER comparative of noble

NOBLESSE *n pl.* -S the nobility

NOBLEST superlative of noble

NOBLY *adv* in a noble manner

NOBODY *n pl.* -BODIES an unimportant person

NOCENT *adj* harmful

NOCK *v* -ED, -ING, -S to notch a bow or arrow

NOCTUID *n pl.* -S a night-flying moth **NOCTUOID** *adj*

NOCTULE *n pl.* -S a large bat

NOCTURN *n pl.* -S a religious service

NOCTURNE *n pl.* -S a musical composition

NOCUOUS *adj* harmful

NOD *v* NODDED, NODDING, NODS to briefly lower the head forward

NODAL *adj* of the nature of a node **NODALLY** *adv*

NODALITY *n pl.* -TIES the state of being nodal

NODDED past tense of nod

NODDER *n pl.* -S one that nods

NODDIES pl. of noddy

NODDING present participle of nod

NODDLE *v* -DLED, -DLING, -DLES to nod frequently

NODDY *n pl.* -DIES a fool

NODE *n pl.* -S a swollen enlargement

NODI pl. of nodus

NODICAL *adj* pertaining to an astronomical point

NODOSE *adj* having nodes

NODOSITY *n pl.* -TIES the state of being nodose

NODOUS *adj* nodose

NODULE *n pl.* -S a small node **NODULAR, NODULOSE, NODULOUS** *adj*

NODUS *n pl.* -DI a difficulty

NOEL *n pl.* -S a Christmas carol

NOES a pl. of no

NOESIS *n pl.* -SISES the process of reason

NOETIC *adj* pertaining to reason

NOG *v* NOGGED, NOGGING, NOGS to fill in a space in a wall with bricks

NOGG *n pl.* -S a strong ale

NOGGIN *n pl.* -S a small cup

NOGGING *n pl.* -S a type of masonry

NOH *n pl.* NOH the classical drama of Japan

NOHOW *adv* in no manner

NOIL *n pl.* -S a kind of short fiber **NOILY** *adj*

NOIR *n pl.* -S a bleak type of crime fiction **NOIRISH** *adj*

NOISE *v* NOISED, NOISING, NOISES to spread as a rumor or report

NOISETTE *n pl.* -S a small round piece of meat

NOISOME *adj* disgusting; harmful

NOISY *adj* NOISIER, NOISIEST making loud sounds **NOISILY** *adv*

NOLO *n pl.* -LOS a type of legal plea

NOM *n pl.* -S a name

NOMA *n pl.* -S a severe inflammation of the mouth

NOMAD *n pl.* -S a wanderer **NOMADIC** *adj*

NOMADISM *n pl.* -S the mode of life of a nomad

NOMARCH *n pl.* -S the head of a nome

NOMARCHY *n pl.* -ARCHIES a nome

NOMBLES *n/pl* numbles

NOMBRIL *n pl.* -S a point on a heraldic shield

NOME *n pl.* -S a province of modern Greece

NOMEN *n pl.* -MINA the second name of an ancient Roman

NOMINAL *n pl.* -S a word functioning as a noun

NOMINATE *v* -NATED, -NATING, -NATES to name as a candidate

NOMINEE *n pl.* -S one that is nominated

NOMISM *n pl.* -S strict adherence to moral law **NOMISTIC** *adj*

NOMOGRAM *n pl.* -S a type of graph

NOMOLOGY *n pl.* -GIES the science of law

NOMOS *n pl.* NOMOI law

NONA *n pl.* -S a virus disease

NONACID *n pl.* -S a substance that is not an acid

NONACTOR *n pl.* -S a person who is not an actor

NONADULT *n pl.* -S a person who is not an adult

NONAGE *n pl.* -S a period of immaturity

NONAGON *n pl.* -S a nine-sided polygon

NONART *n pl.* -S something that is not art

NONBANK *n pl.* -S a business that is not a bank

NONBASIC *adj* not basic

NONBEING *n pl.* -S lack of being

NONBLACK *n pl.* -S one that is not black

NONBODY *n pl.* -BODIES a person's nonphysical nature

NONBOOK *n pl.* -S a book of little literary merit

NONBRAND *adj* lacking a brand name

NONCASH *adj* other than cash

NONCE *n pl.* -S the present occasion

NONCLASS *n pl.* -ES a lack of class

NONCLING *adj* not clinging

NONCOLA *adj* being a drink that is not a cola

NONCOLOR *n pl.* -S a lack of color

NONCOM *n pl.* -S a noncommissioned officer

NONCRIME *n pl.* -S something that is not a crime

NONDAIRY *adj* having no milk products

NONDANCE *n pl.* -S an unrhythmic dance

NONDRUG *adj* not involving drugs

NONE *n pl.* -S one of seven canonical daily periods for prayer and devotion

NONEGO *n pl.* -GOS all that is not part of the ego

NONELECT *adj* not chosen

NONELITE *adj* not belonging to an elite group

NONEMPTY *adj* not empty

NONENTRY *n pl.* -TRIES the fact of not entering

NONEQUAL *n pl.* -S one that is not equal

NONESUCH *n pl.* -ES one without equal

NONET *n pl.* -S a composition for nine instruments or voices

NONEVENT *n pl.* -S an expected event that does not occur

NONFACT *n pl.* -S a statement not based on fact

NONFAN *n pl.* -S a person who is not a fan (an enthusiast)

NONFARM *adj* not pertaining to the farm

NONFAT *adj* having no fat solids

NONFATAL *adj* not fatal

NONFATTY *adj* not fatty

NONFINAL *adj* not being the last

NONFLUID *n pl.* -S a substance that is not a fluid

NONFOCAL *adj* not focal

NONFOOD *adj* pertaining to something other than food

NONFUEL *adj* not used as a fuel

NONGAME *adj* not hunted for food, sport, or fur

NONGAY *n pl.* -S a person who is not a homosexual

NONGLARE *adj* that does not glare

NONGREEN *adj* not green

NONGUEST *n pl.* -S one who is not a guest

NONGUILT *n pl.* -S the absence of guilt

NONHARDY *adj* not hardy

NONHEME *adj* not containing iron that is bound like that of heme

NONHERO *n pl.* -ROES an antihero

NONHOME *adj* not taking place in the home

NONHUMAN *adj* not human

NONIDEAL *adj* not ideal

NONIMAGE *adj* not having an image

NONIONIC *adj* not ionic

NONIRON *adj* not needing to be ironed

NONISSUE *n pl.* -S a topic that is not controversial

NONJUROR *n pl.* -S one who refuses to take a required oath

NONJURY *adj* not involving a jury

NONLABOR *adj* not pertaining to labor

NONLEAFY *adj* not having leaves

NONLEGAL *adj* not legal

NONLIFE *n pl.* -LIVES the absence of life

NONLOCAL *n pl.* -S one that is not local

NONMAJOR *n* pl. -S a student who is not majoring in a specified subject

NONMAN *n* pl. -MEN a being that is not a man

NONMEAT *adj* not containing meat

NONMETAL *n* pl. -S an element that lacks metallic properties

NONMETRO *adj* not metropolitan

NONMODAL *adj* not modal

NONMONEY *adj* not involving money

NONMORAL *adj* not pertaining to morals

NONMUSIC *n* pl. -S inferior music

NONNAVAL *adj* not naval

NONNEWS *adj* not being news

NONNOVEL *n* pl. -S a literary work that is not a novel

NONOBESE *adj* not obese

NONOHMIC *adj* not measured in ohms

NONOILY *adj* not oily

NONOWNER *n* pl. -S one who is not the owner

NONPAGAN *n* pl. -S one who is not a pagan

NONPAID *adj* not paid

NONPAPAL *adj* not papal

NONPAR *adj* being a stock that has no face value

NONPARTY *adj* not affiliated with any political party

NONPAST *n* pl. -S a verb form that lacks an inflection for a past tense

NONPEAK *adj* being a time when something is not at its highest level

NONPLAY *n* pl. -PLAYS a theatrical work that is not a play

NONPLUS *v* -PLUSED, -PLUSING, -PLUSES or -PLUSSED, -PLUSSING, -PLUSSES to baffle

NONPOINT *adj* not occurring at a definite single site

NONPOLAR *adj* not polar

NONPOOR *adj* not being poor

NONPRINT *adj* not involving printed material

NONPROS *v* -PROSSED, -PROSSING, -PROSSES to enter a judgment against a plaintiff who fails to prosecute

NONQUOTA *adj* not included in or subject to a quota

NONRATED *adj* not rated

NONRIGID *adj* not rigid

NONRIVAL *n* pl. -S an unimportant rival

NONROYAL *adj* not royal

NONRURAL *adj* not rural

NONSELF *n* pl. -SELVES foreign material in a body

NONSENSE *n* pl. -S behavior or language that is meaningless or absurd

NONSKED *n* pl. -S an airline without scheduled flying times

NONSKID *adj* designed to inhibit skidding

NONSKIER *n* pl. -S one that does not ski

NONSLIP *adj* designed to prevent slipping

NONSOLAR *adj* not solar

NONSOLID *n* pl. -S a substance that is not a solid

NONSTICK *adj* allowing of easy removal of cooked food particles

NONSTOP *adj* making no stops

NONSTORY *n* pl. -RIES an insignificant news story

NONSTYLE *n* pl. -S a style that is not identifiable

NONSUCH *n* pl. -ES nonsuch

NONSUGAR *n* pl. -S a substance that is not a sugar

NONSUIT *v* -ED, -ING, -S to dismiss the lawsuit of

NONTAX *n* pl. -ES a tax of little consequence

NONTIDAL *adj* not tidal

NONTITLE *adj* pertaining to an athletic contest in which a title is not at stake

NONTONAL *adj* lacking tonality

NONTOXIC *adj* not toxic

NONTRUMP *adj* not having a trump

NONTRUTH *n* pl. -S something that is not true

NONUNION *n* pl. -S failure of a broken bone to heal

NONUPLE *n* pl. -S a number nine times as great as another

NONURBAN *adj* not urban

NONUSE *n* pl. -S failure to use

NONUSER *n* pl. -S one that is not a user

NONUSING *adj* not using

NONVALID *adj* not valid

NONVIRAL *adj* not viral

NONVOCAL *adj* not vocal

NONVOTER *n* pl. -S one that does not vote

NONWAR *n* pl. -S a war that is not officially declared

NONWHITE *n* pl. -S a person who is not of the white race

NONWOODY *adj* not woody

NONWORD *n* pl. -S a word that has no meaning

NONWORK *adj* not involving work

NONWOVEN *n pl.* -S a fabric not made by weaving

NONYL *n pl.* -S an alkyl radical

NONZERO *adj* having a value other than zero

NOO *adv* now

NOODGE *v* NOODGED, NOODGING, NOODGES to nag

NOODLE *v* -DLED, -DLING, -DLES to play idly on a musical instrument

NOOK *n pl.* -S a corner, as in a room

NOOKLIKE *adj*

NOON *n pl.* -S midday

NOONDAY *n pl.* -DAYS noon

NOONING *n pl.* -S a meal eaten at noon

NOONTIDE *n pl.* -S noon

NOONTIME *n pl.* -S noon

NOOSE *v* NOOSED, NOOSING, NOOSES to secure with a type of loop

NOOSER *n pl.* -S one that nooses

NOPAL *n pl.* -S a cactus

NOPE *adv* no

NOR *conj* and not

NORDIC *adj* pertaining to cross-country ski racing and ski jumping

NORI *n pl.* -S dried seaweed pressed into sheets

NORIA *n pl.* -S a type of waterwheel

NORITE *n pl.* -S a granular rock

NORITIC *adj*

NORLAND *n pl.* -S a region in the north

NORM *n pl.* -S a standard regarded as typical for a specific group

NORMAL *n pl.* -S the usual or expected state or form

NORMALCY *n pl.* -CIES conformity with the norm

NORMALLY *adv* as a rule; usually

NORMANDE *adj* prepared with foods associated with Normandy

NORMED *adj* having a norm

NORMLESS *adj* having no norm

NORTH *n pl.* -S a point of the compass

NORTHER *n pl.* -S a wind or storm from the north

NORTHERN *n pl.* -S a person living in the north

NORTHING *n pl.* -S movement toward the north

NOSE *v* NOSED, NOSING, NOSES to sniff with the nose (the organ of smell)

NOSEBAG *n pl.* -S a feedbag

NOSEBAND *n pl.* -S a part of a horse's bridle

NOSED past tense of nose

NOSEDIVE *n pl.* -S a steep downward plunge

NOSEGAY *n pl.* -GAYS a bouquet

NOSELESS *adj* having no nose

NOSELIKE *adj* resembling a nose

NOSEY *adj* NOSIER, NOSIEST nosy

NOSH *v* -ED, -ING, -ES to eat snacks between meals

NOSHER *n pl.* -S one that noshes

NOSIER comparative of nosy, nosey

NOSIEST superlative of nosy, nosey

NOSILY *adv* in a nosy manner

NOSINESS *n pl.* -ES the quality of being nosy

NOSING *n pl.* -S a projecting edge

NOSOLOGY *n pl.* -GIES a classification of diseases

NOSTOC *n pl.* -S a freshwater alga

NOSTRIL *n pl.* -S an external opening of the nose

NOSTRUM *n pl.* -S a medicine of one's own invention

NOSY *adj* NOSIER, NOSIEST unduly curious

NOT *adv* in no way

NOTA *pl.* of notum

NOTABLE *n pl.* -S a person of distinction

NOTABLY *adv* in a distinguished manner

NOTAL *adj* pertaining to a notum

NOTARIAL *adj* pertaining to a notary

NOTARIZE *v* -RIZED, -RIZING, -RIZES to certify through a notary

NOTARY *n pl.* -RIES a public officer who certifies documents

NOTATE *v* -TATED, -TATING, -TATES to put into notation

NOTATION *n pl.* -S a system of symbols

NOTCH *v* -ED, -ING, -ES to make an angular cut in

NOTCHER *n pl.* -S one that notches

NOTE *v* NOTED, NOTING, NOTES to write down

NOTEBOOK *n pl.* -S a book in which to write

NOTECASE *n pl.* -S a billfold

NOTED past tense of note

NOTEDLY *adv* in a famous manner

NOTELESS *adj* undistinguished

NOTEPAD *n pl.* -S a number of sheets of paper glued together at one end

NOTER *n pl.* -S one that notes

NOTHER *adj* different

NOTHING *n* pl. -S the absence of all quantity or magnitude

NOTICE *v* -TICED, -TICING, -TICES to become aware of

NOTICER *n* pl. -S one that notices

NOTIFIER *n* pl. -S one that notifies

NOTIFY *v* -FIED, -FYING, -FIES to inform

NOTING present participle of note

NOTION *n* pl. -S a general idea **NOTIONAL** *adj*

NOTORNIS *n pl.* NOTORNIS a flightless bird

NOTTURNO *n* pl. -NI a nocturne

NOTUM *n* pl. -TA a part of the thorax of an insect

NOUGAT *n* pl. -S a chewy candy

NOUGHT *n* pl. -S naught

NOUMENON *n* pl. -MENA an object of intellectual intuition **NOUMENAL** *adj*

NOUN *n* pl. -S a word used to denote the name of something **NOUNAL, NOUNLESS** *adj* **NOUNALLY** *adv*

NOURISH *v* -ED, -ING, -ES to sustain with food

NOUS *n* pl. -ES mind, reason, or intellect

NOUVEAU *adj* newly arrived or developed

NOUVELLE *adj* pertaining to a form of French cooking

NOVA *n* pl. -VAS or -VAE a type of star **NOVALIKE** *adj*

NOVATION *n* pl. -S the substitution of a new legal obligation for an old one

NOVEL *n* pl. -S a fictional prose narrative

NOVELISE *v* -ISED, -ISING, -ISES to novelize

NOVELIST *n* pl. -S a writer of novels

NOVELIZE *v* -IZED, -IZING, -IZES to put into the form of a novel

NOVELLA *n* pl. -LAS or -LE a short novel

NOVELLY *adv* in a new or unusual manner

NOVELTY *n* pl. -TIES something new or unusual

NOVENA *n* pl. -NAS or -NAE a religious devotion lasting nine days

NOVERCAL *adj* pertaining to a stepmother

NOVICE *n* pl. -S a person new to any field or activity

NOW *n* pl. -S the present time

NOWADAYS *adv* in these times

NOWAY *adv* in no way

NOWAYS *adv* noway

NOWHERE *n* pl. -S a nonexistent place

NOWISE *adv* not at all

NOWNESS *n* pl. -ES the state of existing at the present time

NOWT *n* pl. -S naught

NOXIOUS *adj* harmful to health

NOYADE *n* pl. -S an execution by drowning

NOZZLE *n* pl. -S a projecting spout

NTH *adj* pertaining to an indefinitely large ordinal number

NU *n* pl. -S a Greek letter

NUANCE *n* pl. -S a slight variation **NUANCED** *adj*

NUB *n* pl. -S a protuberance or knob

NUBBIER comparative of nubby

NUBBIEST superlative of nubby

NUBBIN *n* pl. -S an undeveloped fruit

NUBBLE *n* pl. -S a small nub

NUBBLY *adj* -BLIER, -BLIEST having nubbles

NUBBY *adj* -BIER, -BIEST having nubs

NUBIA *n* pl. -S a woman's scarf

NUBILE *adj* suitable for marriage

NUBILITY *n* pl. -TIES the quality of being nubile

NUBILOSE *adj* nubilous

NUBILOUS *adj* cloudy

NUCELLUS *n* pl. -LI the essential part of a plant ovule **NUCELLAR** *adj*

NUCHA *n* pl. -CHAE the nape of the neck

NUCHAL *n* pl. -S an anatomical part lying in the region of the nape

NUCLEAL *adj* nuclear

NUCLEAR *adj* pertaining to a nucleus

NUCLEASE *n* pl. -S an enzyme

NUCLEATE *v* -ATED, -ATING, -ATES to form into a nucleus

NUCLEI a pl. of nucleus

NUCLEIN *n* pl. -S a protein found in nuclei

NUCLEOID *n* pl. -S the DNA-containing area of certain cells

NUCLEOLE *n* pl. -S a part of a nucleus

NUCLEOLI *n/pl* nucleoles

NUCLEON *n* pl. -S a subatomic particle

NUCLEUS *n* pl. -CLEI or -CLEUSES an essential part of a cell

NUCLIDE *n* pl. -S a species of atom **NUCLIDIC** *adj*

NUDE *adj* NUDER, NUDEST being without clothing or covering **NUDELY** *adv*

NUDE *n* pl. -S a nude figure

NUDENESS *n* pl. -ES nudity

NUDER comparative of nude

NUDEST superlative of nude

NUDGE *v* NUDGED, NUDGING, NUDGES to push gently

NUDGER *n* pl. -S one that nudges

NUDICAUL *adj* having leafless stems

NUDIE *n* pl. -S a movie featuring nude performers

NUDISM *n* pl. -S the practice of going nude

NUDIST *n* pl. -S an advocate of nudism

NUDITY *n* pl. -TIES the state of being nude

NUDNICK *n* pl. -S nudnik

NUDNIK *n* pl. -S an annoying person

NUDZH *v* -ED, -ING, -ES to noodge

NUGATORY *adj* having no power

NUGGET *n* pl. -S a mass of solid matter **NUGGETY** *adj*

NUISANCE *n* pl. -S a source of annoyance

NUKE *v* NUKED, NUKING, NUKES to attack with nuclear weapons

NULL *v* -ED, -ING, -S to reduce to nothing

NULLAH *n* pl. -S a ravine

NULLIFY *v* -FIED, -FYING, -FIES to make useless or ineffective

NULLITY *n* pl. -TIES something of no legal force

NUMB *adj* NUMBER, NUMBEST lacking sensation

NUMB *v* -ED, -ING, -S to make numb

NUMBAT *n* pl. -S a small Australian mammal

NUMBER *v* -ED, -ING, -S to count

NUMBERER *n* pl. -S one that numbers

NUMBFISH *n* pl. -ES a fish capable of emitting electric shocks

NUMBLES *n/pl* animal entrails

NUMBLY *adv* in a numb manner

NUMBNESS *n* pl. -ES the state of being numb

NUMEN *n* pl. -MINA a deity

NUMERACY *n* pl. -CIES the ability to understand basic mathematics

NUMERAL *n* pl. -S a symbol that expresses a number

NUMERARY *adj* pertaining to numbers

NUMERATE *v* -ATED, -ATING, -ATES to count

NUMERIC *n* pl. -S a numeral

NUMEROUS *adj* many

NUMINA pl. of numen

NUMINOUS *n* pl. -ES the presence or revelation of the numen

NUMMARY *adj* pertaining to coins

NUMMULAR *adj* shaped like a coin

NUMSKULL *n* pl. -S a dunce

NUN *n* pl. -S a woman belonging to a religious order

NUNATAK *n* pl. -S a mountain peak completely surrounded by glacial ice

NUNCHAKU *n* pl. -S a Japanese weapon

NUNCIO *n* pl. -CIOS an ambassador from the pope

NUNCLE *n* pl. -S an uncle

NUNLIKE *adj* resembling a nun

NUNNERY *n* pl. -NERIES a religious house for nuns

NUNNISH *adj* of, pertaining to, or characteristic of a nun

NUPTIAL *n* pl. -S a wedding

NURD *n* pl. -S nerd

NURL *v* -ED, -ING, -S to knurl

NURSE *v* NURSED, NURSING, NURSES to care for the sick or infirm

NURSER *n* pl. -S a baby's bottle

NURSERY *n* pl. -ERIES a room for young children

NURSING *n* pl. -S the profession of one who nurses

NURSLING *n* pl. -S an infant

NURTURAL *adj* pertaining to the process of nurturing

NURTURE *v* -TURED, -TURING, -TURES to nourish

NURTURER *n* pl. -S one that nurtures

NUT *v* NUTTED, NUTTING, NUTS to gather nuts (hard-shelled dry fruits)

NUTANT *adj* drooping

NUTATE *v* -TATED, -TATING, -TATES to exhibit nutation

NUTATION *n* pl. -S an oscillatory movement of the axis of a rotating body

NUTBROWN *adj* of a dark brown

NUTCASE *n* pl. -S a crazy person

NUTGALL *n* pl. -S a gallnut

NUTGRASS *n* pl. -ES a perennial herb

NUTHATCH *n* pl. -ES a small bird

NUTHOUSE *n* pl. -S an insane asylum

NUTLET *n* pl. -S a small nut

NUTLIKE *adj* resembling a nut

NUTMEAT *n* pl. -S the edible kernel of a nut

NUTMEG *n* pl. -S an aromatic seed used as a spice

NUTPICK *n* pl. -S a device for extracting the kernels from nuts

NUTRIA *n* pl. -S the coypu

NUTRIENT *n* pl. -S a nourishing substance

NUTSEDGE *n* pl. -S nutgrass

NUTSHELL *n* pl. -S the shell of a nut

NUTSY *adj* NUTSIER, NUTSIEST crazy

NUTTED past tense of nut

NUTTER *n* pl. -S one that gathers nuts

NUTTING *n* pl. -S the act of gathering nuts

NUTTY *adj* -TIER, -TIEST silly; crazy **NUTTILY** *adv*

NUTWOOD *n* pl. -S a nut-bearing tree

NUZZLE *v* -ZLED, -ZLING, -ZLES to push with the nose

NUZZLER *n* pl. -S one that nuzzles

NYALA *n* pl. -S an antelope

NYLGHAI *n* pl. -S nilgai

NYLGHAU *n* pl. -S nilgai

NYLON *n* pl. -S a synthetic material

NYMPH *n* pl. -S a female spirit **NYMPHAL, NYMPHEAN** *adj*

NYMPHA *n* pl. -PHAE a fold of the vulva

NYMPHET *n* pl. -S a young nymph

NYMPHO *n* pl. -PHOS a woman obsessed by sexual desire

NYSTATIN *n* pl. -S an antibiotic

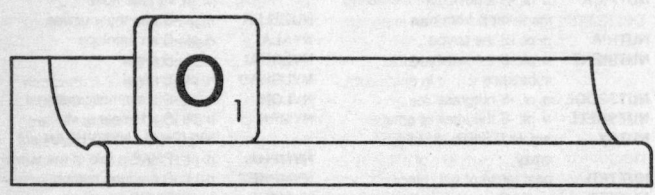

O₁

OAF n pl. OAFS or OAVES a clumsy, stupid person **OAFISH** adj **OAFISHLY** adv

OAK n pl. -S a hardwood tree or shrub **OAKEN, OAKLIKE** adj

OAKMOSS n pl. -ES a lichen that grows on oak trees

OAKUM n pl. -S loosely twisted hemp fiber

OAR v -ED, -ING, -S to propel with oars (long, broad-bladed poles)

OARFISH n pl. -ES a marine fish

OARLESS adj having no oars

OARLIKE adj resembling an oar

OARLOCK n pl. -S a device for holding an oar in place

OARSMAN n pl. -MEN a person who rows a boat

OASIS n pl. OASES a green area in a desert region

OAST n pl. -S a type of kiln

OAT n pl. -S a cereal grass

OATCAKE n pl. -S a cake made of oatmeal

OATEN adj pertaining to oats

OATER n pl. -S a cowboy movie

OATH n pl. -S a formal declaration or promise to fulfill a pledge

OATLIKE adj resembling oats

OATMEAL n pl. -S meal made from oats

OAVES a pl. of oaf

OBCONIC adj conical with the apex below

OBDURACY n pl. -CIES the quality or an instance of being obdurate

OBDURATE adj stubborn

OBE n pl. -S obeah

OBEAH n pl. -S a form of sorcery of African origin

OBEAHISM n pl. -S the use of obeah

OBEDIENT adj obeying or willing to obey

OBEISANT adj reverent; respectful

OBELI pl. of obelus

OBELIA n pl. -S a marine hydroid

OBELISE v -LISED, -LISING, -LISES to obelize

OBELISK n pl. -S a four-sided shaft of stone with a pyramidal top

OBELISM n pl. -S the act of obelizing

OBELIZE v -LIZED, -LIZING, -LIZES to mark with an obelus

OBELUS n pl. -LI a symbol used in ancient manuscripts to indicate a doubtful passage

OBESE adj very fat **OBESELY** adv

OBESITY n pl. -TIES the state or condition of being obese

OBEY v -ED, -ING, -S to follow the commands or guidance of **OBEYABLE** adj

OBEYER n pl. -S one that obeys

OBI n pl. -S obeah

OBIA n pl. -S obeah

OBIISM n pl. -S obeahism

OBIT n pl. -S an obituary

OBITUARY n pl. -ARIES a published notice of a death

OBJECT v -ED, -ING, -S to argue in opposition

OBJECTOR n pl. -S one that objects

OBJET n pl. -S an article of artistic value

OBLAST n pl. -LASTS or -LASTI an administrative division of Russia

OBLATE n pl. -S a layman residing in a monastery

OBLATELY adv elliptically

OBLATION *n pl.* -S the act of making a religious offering **OBLATORY** *adj*

OBLIGATE *v* -GATED, -GATING, -GATES to oblige

OBLIGATO *n pl.* -TI or -TOS an important musical part

OBLIGE *v* OBLIGED, OBLIGING, OBLIGES to put in one's debt by a favor or service

OBLIGEE *n pl.* -S one that is obliged

OBLIGER *n pl.* -S one that obliges

OBLIGING present participle of oblige

OBLIGOR *n pl.* -S one who places himself under a legal obligation

OBLIQUE *v* OBLIQUED, OBLIQUING, OBLIQUES to slant

OBLIVION *n pl.* -S the state of being forgotten; the act of forgetting

OBLONG *n pl.* -S something that is oblong (elongated)

OBLONGLY *adv* in an oblong manner

OBLOQUY *n pl.* -QUIES abusive language

OBOE *n pl.* -S a woodwind instrument

OBOIST *n pl.* -S one who plays the oboe

OBOL *n pl.* -S a coin of ancient Greece

OBOLE *n pl.* -S a coin of medieval France

OBOLUS *n pl.* -LI an obol

OBOVATE *adj* ovate with the narrow end at the base

OBOVOID *adj* ovoid with the narrow end at the base

OBSCENE *adj* -SCENER, -SCENEST indecent

OBSCURE *adj* -SCURER, -SCUREST dark or indistinct

OBSCURE *v* -SCURED, -SCURING, -SCURES to make obscure

OBSEQUY *n pl.* -QUIES a funeral rite

OBSERVE *v* -SERVED, -SERVING, -SERVES to look attentively

OBSERVER *n pl.* -S one that observes

OBSESS *v* -ED, -ING, -ES to dominate the thoughts of

OBSESSOR *n pl.* -S something that obsesses

OBSIDIAN *n pl.* -S a volcanic glass

OBSOLETE *v* -LETED, -LETING, -LETES to make out-of-date

OBSTACLE *n pl.* -S something that obstructs

OBSTRUCT *v* -ED, -ING, -S to get in the way of

OBTAIN *v* -ED, -ING, -S to gain possession of

OBTAINER *n pl.* -S one that obtains

OBTECT *adj* covered by a hardened secretion

OBTECTED *adj* obtect

OBTEST *v* -ED, -ING, -S to beseech

OBTRUDE *v* -TRUDED, -TRUDING, -TRUDES to thrust forward

OBTRUDER *n pl.* -S one that obtrudes

OBTUND *v* -ED, -ING, -S to deaden

OBTURATE *v* -RATED, -RATING, -RATES to close or stop up

OBTUSE *adj* -TUSER, -TUSEST dull **OBTUSELY** *adv*

OBTUSITY *n pl.* -TIES the state of being obtuse

OBVERSE *n pl.* -S the side of a coin bearing the main design

OBVERT *v* -ED, -ING, -S to turn so as to show a different surface

OBVIATE *v* -ATED, -ATING, -ATES to prevent or eliminate by effective measures **OBVIABLE** *adj*

OBVIATOR *n pl.* -S one that obviates

OBVIOUS *adj* easily perceived or understood

OBVOLUTE *adj* rolled or tuned in

OCA *n pl.* -S a South American herb

OCARINA *n pl.* -S a wind instrument

OCCASION *v* -ED, -ING, -S to cause

OCCIDENT *n pl.* -S the west

OCCIPUT *n pl.* -PITA or -PUTS the back part of the skull

OCCLUDE *v* -CLUDED, -CLUDING, -CLUDES to close or stop up

OCCLUSAL *adj* pertaining to the biting surface of a tooth

OCCULT *v* -ED, -ING, -S to conceal

OCCULTER *n pl.* -S one that occults

OCCULTLY *adv* secretly

OCCUPANT *n pl.* -S a resident

OCCUPIER *n pl.* -S one that occupies

OCCUPY *v* -PIED, -PYING, -PIES to engage the attention or energies of

OCCUR *v* -CURRED, -CURRING, -CURS to take place

OCEAN *n pl.* -S the vast body of salt water that covers most of the earth's surface **OCEANIC** *adj*

OCEANAUT *n pl.* -S an aquanaut

OCELLAR *adj* pertaining to an ocellus

OCELLATE *adj* having ocelli

OCELLUS *n pl.* -LI a minute simple eye

OCELOT *n pl.* -S an American wildcat OCELOID *adj*

OCHER *v* -ED, -ING, -S to color with ocher (a red or yellow iron ore used as a pigment)

OCHEROUS *adj* containing or resembling ocher

OCHERY *adj* ocherous

OCHONE *interj* — used to express grief

OCHRE *v* OCHRED, OCHRING, OCHRES to ocher

OCHREA *n pl.* -REAE ocrea

OCHREOUS *adj* ocherous

OCHRING present participle of ochre

OCHROID *adj* ocherous

OCHROUS *adj* ocherous

OCHRY *adj* ochery

OCKER *n pl.* -S a boorish person

OCOTILLO *n pl.* -LOS a Mexican shrub

OCREA *n pl.* -REAE a sheathing plant part

OCREATE *adj* having ocreae

OCTAD *n pl.* -S a group of eight OCTADIC *adj*

OCTAGON *n pl.* -S an eight-sided polygon

OCTAL *adj* pertaining to a number system with a base of eight

OCTAN *n pl.* -S a fever recurring every eighth day

OCTANE *n pl.* -S a liquid hydrocarbon

OCTANGLE *n pl.* -S an octagon

OCTANOL *n pl.* -S an alcohol

OCTANT *n pl.* -S an eighth of a circle OCTANTAL *adj*

OCTARCHY *n pl.* -TARCHIES a government by eight persons

OCTAVE *n pl.* -S a type of musical interval OCTAVAL *adj*

OCTAVO *n pl.* -VOS a page size

OCTET *n pl.* -S a group of eight

OCTETTE *n pl.* -S octet

OCTONARY *n pl.* -NARIES a stanza of eight lines

OCTOPOD *n pl.* -S any of an order of eight-armed mollusks

OCTOPUS *n pl.* -PUSES, -PI, or -PODES a nocturnal octopod

OCTOROON *n pl.* -S a person of one-eighth black ancestry

OCTROI *n pl.* -S a tax on certain articles brought into a city

OCTUPLE *v* -PLED, -PLING, -PLES to multiply by eight

OCTUPLET *n pl.* -S a group of eight related items

OCTUPLEX *adj* being eight times as great

OCTUPLING present participle of octuple

OCTUPLY *adv* to eight times the degree

OCTYL *n pl.* -S a univalent radical

OCULAR *n pl.* -S an eyepiece

OCULARLY *adv* by means of the eyes or sight

OCULIST *n pl.* -S a physician who treats diseases of the eye

OCULUS *n pl.* -LI a circular window

OD *n pl.* -S a hypothetical force of natural power

ODALISK *n pl.* -S a female slave in a harem

ODD *adj* ODDER, ODDEST unusual

ODD *n pl.* -S one that is odd

ODDBALL *n pl.* -S an eccentric person

ODDISH *adj* somewhat odd

ODDITY *n pl.* -TIES one that is odd

ODDLY *adv* in an odd manner

ODDMENT *n pl.* -S a remnant

ODDNESS *n pl.* -ES the state of being odd

ODE *n pl.* -S a lyric poem

ODEON *n pl.* -S odeum

ODEUM *n pl.* ODEA or ODEUMS a theater or concert hall

ODIC *adj* pertaining to an ode

ODIOUS *adj* deserving or causing hatred ODIOUSLY *adv*

ODIST *n pl.* -S one who writes odes

ODIUM *n pl.* -S hatred

ODOGRAPH *n pl.* -S an odometer

ODOMETER *n pl.* -S a device for measuring distance traveled

ODOMETRY *n pl.* -TRIES the process of using an odometer

ODONATE *n pl.* -S any of an order of predacious insects

ODONTOID *n pl.* -S a toothlike vertebral projection

ODOR *n pl.* -S the property of a substance that affects the sense of smell ODORED, ODORFUL *adj*

ODORANT *n pl.* -S an odorous substance

ODORIZE *v* -IZED, -IZING, -IZES to make odorous

ODORLESS *adj* having no odor

ODOROUS *adj* having an odor

ODOUR *n pl.* -S odor ODOURFUL *adj*

ODYL *n pl.* -S an od

ODYLE *n pl.* -S odyl

ODYSSEY n pl. -SEYS a long, wandering journey

OE n pl. -S a whirlwind off the Faeroe islands

OECOLOGY n pl. -GIES ecology

OEDEMA n pl. -MAS or -MATA edema

OEDIPAL adj pertaining to the libidinal feelings in a child toward the parent of the opposite sex

OEDIPEAN adj oedipal

OEILLADE n pl. -S an amorous look

OENOLOGY n pl. -GIES the study of wines

OENOMEL n pl. -S an ancient Greek beverage of wine and honey

OERSTED n pl. -S a unit of magnetic intensity

OESTRIN n pl. -S estrin

OESTRIOL n pl. -S estriol

OESTRONE n pl. -S estrone

OESTROUS adj estrous

OESTRUM n pl. -S estrum

OESTRUS n pl. -ES estrus

OEUVRE n pl. -S a work of art

OF prep coming from

OFF v -ED, -ING, -S to go away

OFFAL n pl. -S waste material

OFFBEAT n pl. -S an unaccented beat in a musical measure

OFFCAST n pl. -S a castoff

OFFCUT n pl. -S something that is cut off

OFFENCE n pl. -S offense

OFFEND v -ED, -ING, -S to commit an offense

OFFENDER n pl. -S one that offends

OFFENSE n pl. -S a violation of a moral or social code

OFFER v -ED, -ING, -S to present for acceptance or rejection

OFFERER n pl. -S one that offers

OFFERING n pl. -S a contribution

OFFEROR n pl. -S offerer

OFFHAND adv without preparation

OFFICE n pl. -S a position of authority

OFFICER v -ED, -ING, -S to furnish with officers (persons holding positions of authority)

OFFICIAL n pl. -S one that holds a position of authority

OFFING n pl. -S the near future

OFFISH adj aloof OFFISHLY adv

OFFKEY adj pitched higher or lower than the correct musical tone

OFFLOAD v -ED, -ING, -S to unload

OFFPRINT v -ED, -ING, -S to reprint an excerpt

OFFRAMP n pl. -S a road leading off an expressway

OFFSET v -SET, -SETTING, -SETS to compensate for

OFFSHOOT n pl. -S a lateral shoot from a main stem

OFFSHORE adv away from the shore

OFFSIDE n pl. -S an improper football play

OFFSTAGE n pl. -S a part of a stage not visible to the audience

OFFTRACK adj away from a racetrack

OFT adv OFTER, OFTEST often

OFTEN adv -ENER, -ENEST frequently

OFTTIMES adv often

OGAM n pl. -S ogham

OGDOAD n pl. -S a group of eight

OGEE n pl. -S an S-shaped molding

OGHAM n pl. -S an Old Irish alphabet OGHAMIC adj

OGHAMIST n pl. -S one who writes in ogham

OGIVE n pl. -S a pointed arch OGIVAL adj

OGLE v OGLED, OGLING, OGLES to stare at

OGLER n pl. -S one that ogles

OGRE n pl. -S a monster

OGREISH adj resembling an ogre

OGREISM n pl. -S the state of being ogreish

OGRESS n pl. -ES a female ogre

OGRISH adj ogreish OGRISHLY adv

OGRISM n pl. -S ogreism

OH v -ED, -ING, -S to exclaim in surprise, pain, or desire

OHIA n pl. -S lehua

OHM n pl. -S a unit of electrical resistance OHMIC adj

OHMAGE n pl. -S electrical resistance expressed in ohms

OHMMETER n pl. -S an instrument for measuring ohmage

OHO interj — used to express surprise or exultation

OIDIUM n pl. OIDIA a type of fungus

OIL v -ED, -ING, -S to supply with oil (a greasy liquid used for lubrication, fuel, or illumination)

OILBIRD n pl. -S a tropical bird

OILCAMP n pl. -S a living area for workers at an oil well

OILCAN n pl. -S a can for applying lubricating oil

OILCLOTH n pl. -S a waterproof fabric

OILCUP	n pl. -S a closed cup for supplying lubricant
OILER	n pl. -S one that oils
OILHOLE	n pl. -S a hole through which lubricating oil is injected
OILIER	comparative of oily
OILIEST	superlative of oily
OILILY	adv in an oily manner
OILINESS	n pl. -ES the state of being oily
OILMAN	n pl. -MEN one who owns or operates oil wells
OILPAPER	n pl. -S a water-resistant paper
OILPROOF	adj impervious to oil
OILSEED	n pl. -S a seed from which oil is pressed out
OILSKIN	n pl. -S a waterproof fabric
OILSTONE	n pl. -S a stone for sharpening tools
OILTIGHT	adj being so tight as to prevent the passage of oil
OILWAY	n pl. -WAYS a channel for the passage of oil
OILY	adj OILIER, OILIEST covered or soaked with oil
OINK	v -ED, -ING, -S to utter the natural grunt of a hog
OINOLOGY	n pl. -GIES oenology
OINOMEL	n pl. -S oenomel
OINTMENT	n pl. -S a viscous preparation applied to the skin as a medicine or cosmetic
OITICICA	n pl. -S a South American tree
OKA	n pl. -S a Turkish unit of weight
OKAPI	n pl. -S an African ruminant mammal
OKAY	v -ED, -ING, -S to approve
OKE	n pl. -S oka
OKEH	n pl. -S approval
OKEYDOKE	adj perfectly all right
OKRA	n pl. -S a tall annual herb
OLD	adj OLDER, OLDEST or ELDER, ELDEST living or existing for a relatively long time
OLD	n pl. -S an individual of a specified age
OLDEN	adj pertaining to a bygone era
OLDIE	n pl. -S a popular song of an earlier day
OLDISH	adj somewhat old
OLDNESS	n pl. -ES the state of being old
OLDSQUAW	n pl. -S a sea duck
OLDSTER	n pl. -S an old person
OLDSTYLE	n pl. -S a style of printing type
OLDWIFE	n pl. -WIVES a marine fish
OLDY	n pl. OLDIES oldie
OLE	n pl. -S a shout of approval
OLEA	pl. of oleum
OLEANDER	n pl. -S a flowering shrub
OLEASTER	n pl. -S a flowering shrub
OLEATE	n pl. -S a chemical salt
OLEFIN	n pl. -S an alkene OLEFINIC adj
OLEFINE	n pl. -S olefin
OLEIC	adj pertaining to oil
OLEIN	n pl. -S the liquid portion of a fat
OLEINE	n pl. -S olein
OLEO	n pl. OLEOS margarine
OLEUM	n pl. OLEA oil
OLEUM	n pl. -S a corrosive liquid
OLIBANUM	n pl. -S a fragrant resin
OLIGARCH	n pl. -S a ruler in a government by the few
OLIGOMER	n pl. -S a type of polymer
OLIGURIA	n pl. -S reduced excretion of urine
OLIO	n pl. OLIOS a miscellaneous collection
OLIVARY	adj shaped like an olive
OLIVE	n pl. -S the small oval fruit of a Mediterranean tree
OLIVINE	n pl. -S a mineral OLIVINIC adj
OLLA	n pl. -S a wide-mouthed pot or jar
OLOGIST	n pl. -S an expert in a particular ology
OLOGY	n pl. -GIES a branch of knowledge
OLOROSO	n pl. -SOS a dark sherry
OLYMPIAD	n pl. -S a celebration of the Olympic Games
OM	n pl. -S a mantra used in contemplation of ultimate reality
OMASUM	n pl. -SA the third stomach of a ruminant
OMBER	n pl. -S ombre
OMBRE	n pl. -S a card game
OMEGA	n pl. -S a Greek letter
OMELET	n pl. -S a dish of beaten eggs cooked and folded around a filling
OMELETTE	n pl. S omelet
OMEN	v -ED, -ING, -S to be an omen (a prophetic sign) of

OMENTUM n pl. -TA or -TUMS a fold in an abdominal membrane OMENTAL adj

OMER n pl. -S a Hebrew unit of dry measure

OMICRON n pl. -S a Greek letter

OMIKRON n pl. -S omicron

OMINOUS adj portending evil

OMISSION n pl. -S something left undone

OMISSIVE adj marked by omission

OMIT v OMITTED, OMITTING, OMITS to leave out

OMITTER n pl. -S one that omits

OMNIARCH n pl. -S an almighty ruler

OMNIBUS n pl. -ES a bus

OMNIFIC adj unlimited in creative power

OMNIFORM adj of all forms

OMNIMODE adj of all modes

OMNIVORA n/pl omnivores

OMNIVORE n pl. -S an animal that eats all kinds of food

OMOPHAGY n pl. -GIES the eating of raw flesh

OMPHALOS n pl. -LI a central point

ON n pl. -S the side of the wicket where a batsman stands in cricket

ONAGER n pl. -GERS or -GRI a wild ass of central Asia

ONANISM n pl. -S coitus deliberately interrupted to prevent insemination

ONANIST n pl. -S one who practices onanism

ONBOARD adj carried aboard a vehicle

ONCE n one single time

ONCIDIUM n pl. -S a tropical orchid

ONCOGENE n pl. -S a gene that causes a cell to become cancerous

ONCOLOGY n pl. -GIES the science of tumors

ONCOMING n pl. -S an approach

ONDOGRAM n pl. -S a graph of electric wave forms

ONE n pl. -S a number

ONEFOLD adj constituting a single, undivided whole

ONEIRIC adj pertaining to dreams

ONENESS n pl. -ES unity

ONEROUS adj burdensome or oppressive

ONERY adj -ERIER, -ERIEST ornery

ONESELF pron a person's self

ONETIME adj former

ONGOING adj continuing without interruption

ONION n pl. -S the edible bulb of a cultivated herb ONIONY adj

ONIUM adj characterized by a complex cation

ONLOOKER n pl. -S a spectator

ONLY adv with nothing or no one else

ONRUSH n pl. -ES a forward rush or flow

ONSET n pl. -S a beginning

ONSHORE adv toward the shore

ONSIDE adj not offside

ONSTAGE adj being on a part of the stage visible to the audience

ONSTREAM adv in or into production

ONTIC adj having real being or existence

ONTO prep to a position upon

ONTOGENY n pl. -NIES the development of an individual organism

ONTOLOGY n pl. -GIES the branch of philosophy that deals with being

ONUS n pl. -ES a burden or responsibility

ONWARD adv toward a point ahead or in front

ONWARDS adv onward

ONYX n pl. -ES a variety of quartz

OOCYST n pl. -S a zygote

OOCYTE n pl. -S an egg before maturation

OODLES n pl. OODLES a large amount

OODLINS n pl. OODLINS oodles

OOGAMETE n pl. -S a female gamete of certain protozoa

OOGAMOUS adj having structurally dissimilar gametes

OOGAMY n pl. -MIES the state of being oogamous

OOGENY n pl. -NIES the development of ova

OOGONIUM n pl. -NIA or -NIUMS a female sexual organ in certain algae and fungi OOGONIAL adj

OOH v -ED, -ING, -S to exclaim in amazement, joy, or surprise

OOLACHAN n pl. -S eulachon

OOLITE n pl. -S a variety of limestone OOLITIC adj

OOLITH n pl. -S oolite

OOLOGIST n pl. -S an expert in oology

OOLOGY n pl. -GIES the study of birds' eggs OOLOGIC adj

OOLONG n pl. -S a dark Chinese tea

OOMIAC n pl. -S umiak

OOMIACK n pl. -S umiak

OOMIAK n pl. -S umiak

OOMPAH v -ED, -ING, -S to play a repeated rhythmic bass accompaniment

OOMPH n pl. -S spirited vigor

OOPHYTE n pl. -S a stage of development in certain plants **OOPHYTIC** adj

OOPS interj — used to express mild apology, surprise, or dismay

OORALI n pl. -S curare

OORIE adj ourie

OOSPERM n pl. -S a fertilized egg

OOSPHERE n pl. -S an unfertilized egg within an oogonium

OOSPORE n pl. -S a fertilized egg within an oogonium **OOSPORIC** adj

OOT n pl. -S out

OOTHECA n pl. -CAE an egg case of certain insects **OOTHECAL** adj

OOTID n pl. -S one of the four sections into which a mature ovum divides

OOZE v OOZED, OOZING, OOZES to flow or leak out slowly

OOZINESS n pl. -ES the state of being oozy

OOZY adj OOZIER, OOZIEST containing or resembling soft mud or slime **OOZILY** adv

OP n pl. -S a style of abstract art

OPACIFY v -FIED, -FYING, -FIES to make opaque

OPACITY n pl. -TIES something that is opaque

OPAH n pl. -S a marine fish

OPAL n pl. -S a mineral

OPALESCE v -ESCED, -ESCING, -ESCES to emit an iridescent shimmer of colors

OPALINE n pl. -S an opaque white glass

OPAQUE adj OPAQUER, OPAQUEST impervious to light **OPAQUELY** adv

OPAQUE v OPAQUED, OPAQUING, OPAQUES to make opaque

OPE v OPED, OPING, OPES to open

OPEN adj OPENER, OPENEST affording unobstructed access, passage, or view

OPEN v -ED, -ING, -S to cause to become open **OPENABLE** adj

OPENCAST adj worked from a surface open to the air

OPENER n pl. -S one that opens

OPENING n pl. -S a vacant or unobstructed space

OPENLY adv in an open manner

OPENNESS n pl. -ES the state of being open

OPENWORK n pl. -S ornamental or structural work containing numerous openings

OPERA n pl. -S a form of musical drama

OPERABLE adj usable **OPERABLY** adv

OPERAND n pl. -S a quantity on which a mathematical operation is performed

OPERANT n pl. -S one that operates

OPERATE v -ATED, -ATING, -ATES to perform a function

OPERATIC n pl. -S the technique of staging operas

OPERATOR n pl. -S a symbol that represents a mathematical function

OPERCELE n pl. -S opercule

OPERCULA n/pl opercules

OPERCULE n pl. -S an anatomical part that serves as a lid or cover

OPERETTA n pl. -S a light musical drama with spoken dialogue

OPERON n pl. -S a type of gene cluster

OPEROSE adj involving great labor

OPHIDIAN n pl. -S a snake

OPHITE n pl. -S an igneous rock **OPHITIC** adj

OPIATE v -ATED, -ATING, -ATES to treat with opium

OPINE v OPINED, OPINING, OPINES to hold or state as an opinion

OPING present participle of ope

OPINION n pl. -S a conclusion or judgment one holds to be true

OPIOID n pl. -S a peptide that acts like opium

OPIUM n pl. -S an addictive narcotic

OPIUMISM n pl. -S opium addiction

OPOSSUM n pl. -S an arboreal mammal

OPPIDAN n pl. -S a townsman

OPPILATE v -LATED, -LATING, -LATES to obstruct **OPPILANT** adj

OPPONENT n pl. -S one that opposes another

OPPOSE v -POSED, -POSING, -POSES to be in contention or conflict with

OPPOSER n pl. -S one that opposes

OPPOSITE n pl. -S one that is radically different from another in some related way

OPPRESS v -ED, -ING, -ES to burden by abuse of power or authority

OPPUGN v -ED, -ING, -S to assail with argument

OPPUGNER n pl. -S one that oppugns

OPSIN n pl. -S a type of protein

OPSONIC adj pertaining to opsonin

OPSONIFY v -FIED, -FYING, -FIES to opsonize

OPSONIN n pl. -S an antibody of blood serum

OPSONIZE v -NIZED, -NIZING, -NIZES to form opsonins in

OPT v -ED, -ING, -S to choose

OPTATIVE n pl. -S a mood of verbs that expresses a wish or desire

OPTIC n pl. -S an eye

OPTICAL adj pertaining to sight

OPTICIAN n pl. -S one who makes or deals in optical goods

OPTICIST n pl. -S one engaged in the study of light and vision

OPTIMA a pl. of optimum

OPTIMAL adj most desirable or satisfactory

OPTIME n pl. -S an honor student in mathematics at Cambridge University

OPTIMISE v -MISED, -MISING, -MISES to optimize

OPTIMISM n pl. -S a disposition to look on the favorable side of things

OPTIMIST n pl. -S one who exhibits optimism

OPTIMIZE v -MIZED, -MIZING, -MIZES to make as perfect, useful, or effective as possible

OPTIMUM n pl. -MA or -MUMS the most favorable condition for obtaining a given result

OPTION v -ED, -ING, -S to grant an option (a right to buy or sell something at a specified price within a specified time) on

OPTIONAL n pl. -S an elective course of study

OPTIONEE n pl. -S one who holds a legal option

OPULENCE n pl. -S wealth

OPULENCY n pl. -CIES opulence

OPULENT adj wealthy

OPUNTIA n pl. -S an American cactus

OPUS n pl. OPERA or OPUSES a literary or musical work

OPUSCULA n/pl opuscules

OPUSCULE n pl. -S a minor work

OQUASSA n pl. -S a small lake trout

OR n pl. -S the heraldic color gold

ORA pl. of os

ORACH n pl. -ES a cultivated plant

ORACHE n pl. -S orach

ORACLE n pl. -S a person through whom a deity is believed to speak **ORACULAR** adj

ORAD adv toward the mouth

ORAL n pl. -S an examination requiring spoken answers

ORALISM n pl. -S the use of oral methods of teaching the deaf

ORALIST n pl. -S an advocate of oralism

ORALITY n pl. -TIES the state of being produced orally

ORALLY adv through the mouth

ORANG n pl. -S a large ape

ORANGE n pl. -S a citrus fruit

ORANGERY n pl. -RIES a place where orange trees are cultivated

ORANGEY adj -ANGIER, -ANGIEST orangy

ORANGISH adj of a somewhat orange color

ORANGY adj -ANGIER, -ANGIEST resembling or suggestive of an orange

ORATE v ORATED, ORATING, ORATES to speak formally

ORATION n pl. -S a formal speech

ORATOR n pl. -S one that orates

ORATORIO n pl. -RIOS a type of musical composition

ORATORY n pl. -RIES the art of public speaking

ORATRESS n pl. -ES oratrix

ORATRIX n pl. -TRICES a female orator

ORB v -ED, -ING, -S to form into a circle or sphere

ORBIER comparative of orby

ORBIEST superlative of orby

ORBIT v -ED, -ING, -S to move or revolve around

ORBITAL n pl. -S a subdivision of a nuclear shell

ORBITER n pl. -S one that orbits

ORBY adj ORBIER, ORBIEST resembling a circle or sphere

ORC n pl. -S a marine mammal

ORCA n pl. -S orc

ORCEIN n pl. -S a reddish brown dye

ORCHARD n pl. -S an area for the cultivation of fruit trees

ORCHID n pl. -S a flowering plant

ORCHIL n pl. -S a purple dye

ORCHIS n pl. -CHISES an orchid

ORCHITIS n pl. -TISES inflammation of the testicle ORCHITIC adj

ORCIN n pl. -S orcinol

ORCINOL n pl. -S a chemical compound

ORDAIN v -ED, -ING, -S to invest with holy authority

ORDAINER n pl. -S one that ordains

ORDEAL n pl. -S a severely difficult or painful experience

ORDER v -ED, -ING, -S to give a command or instruction to

ORDERER n pl. -S one that orders

ORDERLY n pl. -LIES a male attendant

ORDINAL n pl. -S a number designating position in a series

ORDINAND n pl. -S a person about to be ordained

ORDINARY adj -NARIER, -NARIEST of a kind to be expected in the normal order of events

ORDINARY n pl. -NARIES something that is ordinary

ORDINATE n pl. -S a particular geometric coordinate

ORDINES a pl. of ordo

ORDNANCE n pl. -S artillery; a cannon

ORDO n pl. -DINES or -DOS a calendar of religious directions

ORDURE n pl. -S manure

ORE n pl. -S a mineral or rock containing a valuable metal

OREAD n pl. -S a mountain nymph in Greek mythology

ORECTIC adj pertaining to appetites or desires

ORECTIVE adj orectic

OREGANO n pl. -NOS an aromatic herb used as a seasoning

OREIDE n pl. -S oroide

ORFRAY n pl. -FRAYS orphrey

ORGAN n pl. -S a differentiated part of an organism performing a specific function

ORGANA a pl. of organon and organum

ORGANDIE n pl. -S organdy

ORGANDY n pl. -DIES a cotton fabric

ORGANIC n pl. -S a substance of animal or vegetable origin

ORGANISE v -NISED, -NISING, -NISES to organize

ORGANISM n pl. -S any form of animal or plant life

ORGANIST n pl. -S one who plays the organ (a keyboard musical instrument)

ORGANIZE v -NIZED, -NIZING, -NIZES to form into an orderly whole

ORGANON n pl. -GANA or -GANONS a system of rules for scientific investigation

ORGANUM n pl. -GANA or -GANUMS organon

ORGANZA n pl. -S a sheer fabric

ORGASM n pl. -S the climax of sexual excitement ORGASMIC, ORGASTIC adj

ORGEAT n pl. -S an almond-flavored syrup

ORGIAC adj of the nature of an orgy

ORGIC adj orgiac

ORGONE n pl. -S a postulated energy pervading the universe

ORGULOUS adj proud

ORGY n pl. -GIES a party marked by unrestrained sexual indulgence

ORIBATID n pl. -S any of a family of eyeless mites

ORIBI n pl. -S an African antelope

ORIEL n pl. -S a type of projecting window

ORIENT v -ED, -ING, -S to adjust in relation to something else

ORIENTAL n pl. -S an inhabitant of an eastern country

ORIFICE n pl. -S a mouth or mouthlike opening

ORIGAMI n pl. -S the Japanese art of paper folding

ORIGAN n pl. -S marjoram

ORIGANUM n pl. -S an aromatic herb

ORIGIN n pl. -S a coming into being

ORIGINAL n pl. -S the first form of something

ORINASAL n pl. -S a sound pronounced through both the mouth and nose

ORIOLE n pl. -S an American songbird

ORISON n pl. -S a prayer

ORLE n pl. -S a heraldic border

ORLOP n pl. -S the lowest deck of a ship

ORMER n pl. -S an abalone

ORMOLU n pl. -S an alloy used to imitate gold

ORNAMENT	v -ED, -ING, -S to decorate	OSCULATE	v -LATED, -LATING, -LATES to kiss
ORNATE	adj elaborately or excessively ornamented ORNATELY adv		
		OSCULE	n pl. -S osculum
ORNERY	adj -NERIER, -NERIEST stubborn and mean-spirited	OSCULUM	n pl. -LA an opening in a sponge
ORNIS	n pl. ORNITHES avifauna	OSE	n pl. -S an esker
ORNITHIC	adj pertaining to birds	OSIER	n pl. -S a European tree
OROGENY	n pl. -NIES the process of mountain formation OROGENIC adj	OSMATIC	adj depending mainly on the sense of smell
		OSMICS	n/pl the study of the sense of smell
OROIDE	n pl. -S an alloy used to imitate gold	OSMIUM	n pl. -S a metallic element OSMIC, OSMIOUS adj
OROLOGY	n pl. -GIES the study of mountains	OSMOL	n pl. -S a unit of osmotic pressure OSMOLAL adj
OROMETER	n pl. -S a type of barometer	OSMOLAR	adj osmotic
OROTUND	adj full and clear in sound	OSMOLE	n pl. -S osmol
ORPHAN	v -ED, -ING, -S to deprive of both parents	OSMOSE	v -MOSED, -MOSING, -MOSES to undergo osmosis
ORPHIC	adj mystical	OSMOSIS	n pl. -MOSES a form of diffusion of a fluid through a membrane
ORPHICAL	adj orphic		
ORPHREY	n pl. -PHREYS an ornamental band or border	OSMOTIC	adj pertaining to osmosis
ORPIMENT	n pl. -S a yellow dye	OSMOUS	adj containing osmium
ORPIN	n pl. -S orpine	OSMUND	n pl. -S any of a genus of large ferns
ORPINE	n pl. -S a perennial herb		
ORRA	adj occasional	OSMUNDA	n pl. -S osmund
ORRERY	n pl. -RERIES a mechanical model of the solar system	OSNABURG	n pl. -S a cotton fabric
		OSPREY	n pl. -PREYS an American hawk
ORRICE	n pl. -S orris		
ORRIS	n pl. -RISES a flowering plant	OSSA	pl. of os
ORT	n pl. -S a scrap of food	OSSEIN	n pl. -S a protein substance in bone
ORTHICON	n pl. -S a type of television camera tube		
		OSSEOUS	adj resembling bone
ORTHO	adj pertaining to reproduction in a photograph of the full range of colors in nature	OSSIA	conj or else — used as a musical direction
		OSSICLE	n pl. -S a small bone
ORTHODOX	n pl. -ES one holding traditional beliefs	OSSIFIC	adj pertaining to the formation of bone
ORTHOEPY	n pl. -EPIES the study of correct pronunciation	OSSIFIER	n pl. -S one that ossifies
		OSSIFY	v -FIED, -FYING, -FIES to convert into bone
ORTHOSIS	n pl. -THOSES an orthotic		
ORTHOTIC	n pl. -S a brace for weak joints or muscles	OSSUARY	n pl. -ARIES a receptacle for the bones of the dead
ORTOLAN	n pl. -S a European bird	OSTEAL	adj osseous
ORYX	n pl. -ES an African antelope	OSTEITIS	n pl. -ITIDES inflammation of bone OSTEITIC adj
ORZO	n pl. -ZOS rice-shaped pasta		
OS	n pl. ORA an orifice	OSTEOID	n pl. -S uncalcified bone matrix
OS	n pl. OSSA a bone		
OS	n pl. OSAR an esker	OSTEOMA	n pl. -MAS or -MATA a tumor of bone tissue
OSCINE	n pl. -S any of a family of songbirds OSCININE adj		
		OSTEOSIS	n pl. -OSES or -OSISES the formation of bone
OSCITANT	adj yawning		
OSCULA	pl. of osculum	OSTIA	pl. of ostium
OSCULANT	adj adhering closely	OSTIARY	n pl. -ARIES a doorkeeper at a church
OSCULAR	adj pertaining to the mouth		

OSTINATO n pl. -TOS a constantly recurring musical phrase

OSTIOLE n pl. -S a small bodily opening OSTIOLAR adj

OSTIUM n pl. OSTIA an opening in a bodily organ

OSTLER n pl. -S hostler

OSTMARK n pl. -S a former East German monetary unit

OSTOMY n pl. -MIES a type of surgical operation

OSTOSIS n pl. -TOSES or -TOSISES the formation of bone

OSTRACOD n pl. -S a minute freshwater crustacean

OSTRACON n pl. -CA a fragment containing an inscription

OSTRICH n pl. -ES a large, flightless bird

OTALGIA n pl. -S pain in the ear OTALGIC adj

OTALGY n pl. -GIES otalgia

OTHER n pl. -S one that remains of two or more

OTIC adj pertaining to the ear

OTIOSE adj lazy OTIOSELY adv

OTIOSITY n pl. -TIES the state of being otiose

OTITIS n pl. OTITIDES inflammation of the ear OTITIC adj

OTOCYST n pl. -S an organ of balance in many invertebrates

OTOLITH n pl. -S a hard mass that forms in the inner ear

OTOLOGY n pl. -GIES the science of the ear

OTOSCOPE n pl. -S an instrument for examining the ear

OTOSCOPY n pl. -PIES the use of an otoscope

OTOTOXIC adj adversely affecting hearing or balance

OTTAR n pl. -S attar

OTTAVA n pl. -S an octave

OTTER n pl. -S a carnivorous mammal

OTTO n pl. -TOS attar

OTTOMAN n pl. -S a type of sofa

OUABAIN n pl. -S a cardiac stimulant

OUCH v -ED, -ING, -ES to ornament with ouches (settings for precious stones)

OUD n pl. -S a stringed instrument of northern Africa

OUGHT v -ED, -ING, -S to owe

OUGUIYA n pl. OUGUIYA a monetary unit of Mauritania

OUISTITI n pl. -S a South American monkey

OUNCE n pl. -S a unit of weight

OUPH n pl. -S ouphe

OUPHE n pl. -S an elf

OUR pron a possessive form of the pronoun we

OURANG n pl. -S orang

OURARI n pl. -S curare

OUREBI n pl. -S oribi

OURIE adj shivering with cold

OURS pron a possessive form of the pronoun we

OURSELF pron myself — used in formal or regal contexts

OUSEL n pl. -S ouzel

OUST v -ED, -ING, -S to expel or remove from a position or place

OUSTER n pl. -S the act of ousting

OUT v -ED, -ING, -S to be revealed

OUTACT v -ED, -ING, -S to surpass in acting

OUTADD v -ED, -ING, -S to surpass in adding

OUTAGE n pl. -S a failure or interruption in use or functioning

OUTARGUE v -GUED, -GUING, -GUES to get the better of by arguing

OUTASK v -ED, -ING, -S to surpass in asking

OUTATE past tense of outeat

OUTBACK n pl. -S isolated rural country

OUTBAKE v -BAKED, -BAKING, -BAKES to surpass in baking

OUTBARK v -ED, -ING, -S to surpass in barking

OUTBAWL v -ED, -ING, -S to surpass in bawling

OUTBEAM v -ED, -ING, -S to surpass in beaming

OUTBEG v -BEGGED, -BEGGING, -BEGS to surpass in begging

OUTBID v -BID, -BIDDEN, -BIDDING, -BIDS to bid higher than

OUTBITCH v -ED, -ING, -ES to surpass in bitching

OUTBLAZE v -BLAZED, -BLAZING, -BLAZES to surpass in brilliance of light

OUTBLEAT v -ED, -ING, -S to surpass in bleating

OUTBLESS v -ED, -ING, -ES to surpass in blessing

OUTBLOOM v -ED, -ING, -S to surpass in blooming

OUTBLUFF v -ED, -ING, -S to surpass in bluffing

OUTBLUSH v -ED, -ING, -ES to surpass in blushing

OUTBOARD n pl. -S a type of motor

OUTBOAST v -ED, -ING, -S to surpass in boasting

OUTBOUGHT past tense of outbuy

OUTBOUND adj outward bound

OUTBOX v -ED, -ING, -ES to surpass in boxing

OUTBRAG v -BRAGGED, -BRAGGING, -BRAGS to surpass in bragging

OUTBRAVE v -BRAVED, -BRAVING, -BRAVES to surpass in courage

OUTBRAWL v -ED, -ING, -S to surpass in brawling

OUTBREAK n pl. -S a sudden eruption

OUTBREED v -BRED, -BREEDING, -BREEDS to interbreed relatively unrelated stocks

OUTBRIBE v -BRIBED, -BRIBING, -BRIBES to surpass in bribing

OUTBUILD v -BUILT, -BUILDING, -BUILDS to surpass in building

OUTBULK v -ED, -ING, -S to surpass in bulking

OUTBULLY v -LIED, -LYING, -LIES to surpass in bullying

OUTBURN v -BURNED or -BURNT, -BURNING, -BURNS to burn longer than

OUTBURST n pl. -S a sudden and violent outpouring

OUTBUY v -BOUGHT, -BUYING, -BUYS to surpass in buying

OUTBY adv outdoors

OUTBYE adv outby

OUTCAPER v -ED, -ING, -S to surpass in capering

OUTCAST n pl. -S one that is cast out

OUTCASTE n pl. -S a Hindu who has been expelled from his caste

OUTCATCH v -CAUGHT, -CATCHING, -CATCHES to surpass in catching

OUTCAVIL v -ILED, -ILING, -ILS or -ILLED, -ILLING, -ILS to surpass in caviling

OUTCHARM v -ED, -ING, -S to surpass in charming

OUTCHEAT v -ED, -ING, -S to surpass in cheating

OUTCHIDE v -CHIDED or -CHID, -CHIDDEN, -CHIDING, -CHIDES to surpass in chiding

OUTCLASS v -ED, -ING, -ES to surpass so decisively as to appear of a higher class

OUTCLIMB v -CLIMBED or -CLOMB, -CLIMBING, -CLIMBS to surpass in climbing

OUTCOACH v -ED, -ING, -ES to surpass in coaching

OUTCOME n pl. -S a result

OUTCOOK v -ED, -ING, -S to surpass in cooking

OUTCOUNT v -ED, -ING, -S to surpass in counting

OUTCRAWL v -ED, -ING, -S to surpass in crawling

OUTCRIED past tense of outcry

OUTCRIES present 3d person sing. of outcry

OUTCROP v -CROPPED, -CROPPING, -CROPS to protrude above the soil

OUTCROSS v -ED, -ING, -ES to cross with a relatively unrelated individual

OUTCROW v -ED, -ING, -S to surpass in crowing

OUTCRY v -CRIED, -CRYING, -CRIES to cry louder than

OUTCURSE v -CURSED, -CURSING, -CURSES to surpass in cursing

OUTCURVE n pl. -S a type of pitch in baseball

OUTDANCE v -DANCED, -DANCING, -DANCES to surpass in dancing

OUTDARE v -DARED, -DARING, -DARES to surpass in daring

OUTDATE v -DATED, -DATING, -DATES to make out-of-date

OUTDO v -DID, -DONE, -DOING, -DOES to exceed in performance

OUTDODGE v -DODGED, -DODGING, -DODGES to surpass in dodging

OUTDOER n pl. -S one that outdoes

OUTDONE past participle of outdo

OUTDOOR adj pertaining to the open air

OUTDOORS adv in the open air

OUTDRAG v -DRAGGED, -DRAGGING, -DRAGS to surpass in drag racing

OUTDRANK past tense of outdrink

OUTDRAW v -DREW, -DRAWN, -DRAWING, -DRAWS to attract a larger audience than

OUTDREAM v -DREAMED or -DREAMT, -DREAMING, -DREAMS to surpass in dreaming

OUTDRESS v -ED, -ING, -ES to surpass in dressing

OUTDREW past tense of outdraw

OUTDRINK v -DRANK, -DRUNK, -DRINKING, -DRINKS to surpass in drinking

OUTDRIVE v -DROVE, -DRIVEN, -DRIVING, -DRIVES to drive a golf ball farther than

OUTDROP v -DROPPED, -DROPPING, -DROPS to surpass in dropping

OUTDRUNK past participle of outdrink

OUTDUEL v -DUELED, -DUELING, -DUELS or -DUELLED, -DUELLING, -DUELS to surpass in dueling

OUTEARN v -ED, -ING, -S to surpass in earning

OUTEAT v -ATE, -EATEN, -EATING, -EATS to surpass in eating

OUTECHO v -ED, -ING, -ES to surpass in echoing

OUTER n pl. -S a part of a target

OUTFABLE v -BLED, -BLING, -BLES to surpass in fabling

OUTFACE v -FACED, -FACING, -FACES to confront unflinchingly

OUTFALL n pl. -S the outlet of a body of water

OUTFAST v -ED, -ING, -S to surpass in fasting

OUTFAWN v -ED, -ING, -S to surpass in fawning

OUTFEAST v -ED, -ING, -S to surpass in feasting

OUTFEEL v -FELT, -FEELING, -FEELS to surpass in feeling

OUTFIELD n pl. -S a part of a baseball field

OUTFIGHT v -FOUGHT, -FIGHTING, -FIGHTS to defeat

OUTFIND v -FOUND, -FINDING, -FINDS to surpass in finding

OUTFIRE v -FIRED, -FIRING, -FIRES to surpass in firing

OUTFISH v -ED, -ING, -ES to surpass in fishing

OUTFIT v -FITTED, -FITTING, -FITS to equip

OUTFLANK v -ED, -ING, -S to gain a tactical advantage over

OUTFLOW v -ED, -ING, -S to flow out

OUTFLY v -FLEW, -FLOWN, -FLYING, -FLIES to surpass in speed of flight

OUTFOOL v -ED, -ING, -S to surpass in fooling

OUTFOOT v -ED, -ING, -S to surpass in speed

OUTFOUGHT past tense of outfight

OUTFOUND past tense of outfind

OUTFOX v -ED, -ING, -ES to outwit

OUTFROWN v -ED, -ING, -S to frown more than

OUTGAIN v -ED, -ING, -S to gain more than

OUTGAS v -GASSED, -GASSING, -GASSES to remove gas from

OUTGIVE v -GAVE, -GIVEN, -GIVING, -GIVES to give more than

OUTGLARE v -GLARED, -GLARING, -GLARES to surpass in glaring

OUTGLOW v -ED, -ING, -S to surpass in glowing

OUTGNAW v -GNAWED, -GNAWN, -GNAWING, -GNAWS to surpass in gnawing

OUTGO v -WENT, -GONE, -GOING, -GOES to go beyond

OUTGOING n pl. -S a departure

OUTGREW past tense of outgrow

OUTGRIN v -GRINNED, -GRINNING, -GRINS to surpass in grinning

OUTGROSS v -ED, -ING, -ES to surpass in gross earnings

OUTGROUP n pl. -S a group of people outside one's own group

OUTGROW v -GREW, -GROWN, -GROWING, -GROWS to grow too large for

OUTGUESS v -ED, -ING, -ES to anticipate the actions of

OUTGUIDE v -GUIDED, -GUIDING, -GUIDES to surpass in guiding

OUTGUN v -GUNNED, -GUNNING, -GUNS to surpass in firepower

OUTGUSH n pl. -ES a gushing out

OUTHAUL n pl. -S a rope for extending a sail along a spar

OUTHEAR v -HEARD, -HEARING, -HEARS to surpass in hearing

OUTHIT v -HIT, -HITTING, -HITS to get more hits than

OUTHOMER v -ED, -ING, -S to surpass in hitting home runs

OUTHOUSE n pl. -S a toilet housed in a small structure
OUTHOWL v -ED, -ING, -S to surpass in howling
OUTHUMOR v -ED, -ING, -S to surpass in humoring
OUTHUNT v -ED, -ING, -S to surpass in hunting
OUTING n pl. -S a short pleasure trip
OUTJINX v -ED, -ING, -ES to surpass in jinxing
OUTJUMP v -ED, -ING, -S to surpass in jumping
OUTJUT v -JUTTED, -JUTTING, -JUTS to stick out
OUTKEEP v -KEPT, -KEEPING, -KEEPS to surpass in keeping
OUTKICK v -ED, -ING, -S to surpass in kicking
OUTKILL v -ED, -ING, -S to surpass in killing
OUTKISS v -ED, -ING, -ES to surpass in kissing
OUTLAID past tense of outlay
OUTLAIN past participle of outlie
OUTLAND n pl. -S a foreign land
OUTLAST v -ED, -ING, -S to last longer than
OUTLAUGH v -ED, -ING, -S to surpass in laughing
OUTLAW v -ED, -ING, -S to prohibit
OUTLAWRY n pl. -RIES habitual defiance of the law
OUTLAY v -LAID, -LAYING, -LAYS to pay out
OUTLEAP v -LEAPED or -LEAPT, -LEAPING, -LEAPS to surpass in leaping
OUTLEARN v -LEARNED or -LEARNT, -LEARNING, -LEARNS to surpass in learning
OUTLET n pl. -S a passage for escape or discharge
OUTLIE v -LAY, -LAIN, -LYING, -LIES to lie beyond
OUTLIER n pl. -S an outlying area or portion
OUTLINE v -LINED, -LINING, -LINES to indicate the main features or different parts of
OUTLINER n pl. -S one that outlines
OUTLIVE v -LIVED, -LIVING, -LIVES to live longer than
OUTLIVER n pl. -S one that outlives
OUTLOOK n pl. -S a point of view

OUTLOVE v -LOVED, -LOVING, -LOVES to surpass in loving
OUTLYING present participle of outlie
OUTMAN v -MANNED, -MANNING, -MANS to surpass in manpower
OUTMARCH v -ED, -ING, -ES to surpass in marching
OUTMATCH v -ED, -ING, -ES to outdo
OUTMODE v -MODED, -MODING, -MODES to outdate
OUTMOST adj farthest out
OUTMOVE v -MOVED, -MOVING, -MOVES to move faster or farther than
OUTPACE v -PACED, -PACING, -PACES to surpass in speed
OUTPAINT v -ED, -ING, -S to surpass in painting
OUTPASS v -ED, -ING, -ES to excel in passing a football
OUTPITCH v -ED, -ING, -ES to surpass in pitching
OUTPITY v -PITIED, -PITYING, -PITIES to surpass in pitying
OUTPLAN v -PLANNED, -PLANNING, -PLANS to surpass in planning
OUTPLAY v -ED, -ING, -S to excel or defeat in a game
OUTPLOD v -PLODDED, -PLODDING, -PLODS to surpass in plodding
OUTPLOT v -PLOTTED, -PLOTTING, -PLOTS to surpass in plotting
OUTPOINT v -ED, -ING, -S to score more points than
OUTPOLL v -ED, -ING, -S to get more votes than
OUTPORT n pl. -S a port of export or departure
OUTPOST n pl. -S a body of troops stationed at a distance from the main body
OUTPOUR v -ED, -ING, -S to pour out
OUTPOWER v -ED, -ING, -S to surpass in power
OUTPRAY v -ED, -ING, -S to surpass in praying
OUTPREEN v -ED, -ING, -S to surpass in preening
OUTPRESS v -ED, -ING, -ES to surpass in pressing
OUTPRICE v -PRICED, -PRICING, -PRICES to surpass in pricing
OUTPULL v -ED, -ING, -S to attract a larger audience or following than

OUTPUNCH v -ED, -ING, -ES to surpass in punching

OUTPUSH v -ED, -ING, -ES to surpass in pushing

OUTPUT v -PUTTED, -PUTTING, -PUTS to produce

OUTQUOTE v -QUOTED, -QUOTING, -QUOTES to surpass in quoting

OUTRACE v -RACED, -RACING, -RACES to run faster or farther than

OUTRAGE v -RAGED, -RAGING, -RAGES to arouse anger or resentment in

OUTRAISE v -RAISED, -RAISING, -RAISES to surpass in raising

OUTRAN past tense of outrun

OUTRANCE n pl. -S the last extremity

OUTRANG past tense of outring

OUTRANGE v -RANGED, -RANGING, -RANGES to surpass in range

OUTRANK v -ED, -ING, -S to rank higher than

OUTRATE v -RATED, -RATING, -RATES to surpass in a rating

OUTRAVE v -RAVED, -RAVING, -RAVES to surpass in raving

OUTRE adj deviating from what is usual or proper

OUTREACH v -ED, -ING, -ES to reach beyond

OUTREAD v -READ, -READING, -READS to surpass in reading

OUTRIDE v -RODE, -RIDDEN, -RIDING, -RIDES to ride faster or better than

OUTRIDER n pl. -S a mounted attendant who rides before or beside a carriage

OUTRIGHT adj being without limit or reservation

OUTRING v -RANG, -RUNG, -RINGING, -RINGS to ring louder than

OUTRIVAL v -VALED, -VALING, -VALS or -VALLED, -VALLING, -VALS to outdo in a competition or rivalry

OUTROAR v -ED, -ING, -S to roar louder than

OUTROCK v -ED, -ING, -S to surpass in rocking

OUTRODE past tense of outride

OUTROLL v -ED, -ING, -S to roll out

OUTROOT v -ED, -ING, -S to pull up by the roots

OUTROW v -ED, -ING, -S to surpass in rowing

OUTRUN v -RAN, -RUNNING, -RUNS to run faster than

OUTRUNG past participle of outring

OUTRUSH v -ED, -ING, -ES to surpass in rushing

OUTSAIL v -ED, -ING, -S to sail faster than

OUTSANG past tense of outsing

OUTSAT past tense of outsit

OUTSAVOR v -ED, -ING, -S to surpass in a distinctive taste or smell

OUTSAW past tense of outsee

OUTSCOLD v -ED, -ING, -S to surpass in scolding

OUTSCOOP v -ED, -ING, -S to surpass in scooping

OUTSCORE v -SCORED, -SCORING, -SCORES to score more points than

OUTSCORN v -ED, -ING, -S to surpass in scorning

OUTSEE v -SAW, -SEEN, -SEEING, -SEES to see beyond

OUTSELL v -SOLD, -SELLING, -SELLS to sell more than

OUTSERT n pl. -S a folded sheet placed around a folded section of printed matter

OUTSERVE v -SERVED, -SERVING, -SERVES to surpass in serving

OUTSET n pl. -S a beginning

OUTSHAME v -SHAMED, -SHAMING, -SHAMES to surpass in shaming

OUTSHINE v -SHONE or -SHINED, -SHINING, -SHINES to shine brighter than

OUTSHOOT v -SHOT, -SHOOTING, -SHOOTS to shoot better than

OUTSHOUT v -ED, -ING, -S to shout louder than

OUTSIDE n pl. -S the outer side, surface, or part

OUTSIDER n pl. -S one that does not belong to a particular group

OUTSIGHT n pl. -S the power of perceiving external things

OUTSIN v -SINNED, -SINNING, -SINS to surpass in sinning

OUTSING v -SANG, -SUNG, -SINGING, -SINGS to surpass in singing

OUTSIT v -SAT, -SITTING, -SITS to remain sitting or in session longer than

OUTSIZE *n* pl. -S an unusual size
OUTSIZED *adj*

OUTSKATE *v* -SKATED, -SKATING, -SKATES to surpass in skating

OUTSKIRT *n* pl. -S an outlying area

OUTSLEEP *v* -SLEPT, -SLEEPING, -SLEEPS to sleep later than

OUTSLICK *v* -ED, -ING, -S to get the better of by trickery or cunning

OUTSMART *v* -ED, -ING, -S to outwit

OUTSMILE *v* -SMILED, -SMILING, -SMILES to surpass in smiling

OUTSMOKE *v* -SMOKED, -SMOKING, -SMOKES to surpass in smoking

OUTSNORE *v* -SNORED, -SNORING, -SNORES to surpass in snoring

OUTSOAR *v* -ED, -ING, -S to soar beyond

OUTSOLD past tense of outsell

OUTSOLE *n* pl. -S the outer sole of a boot or shoe

OUTSPAN *v* -SPANNED, -SPANNING, -SPANS to unharness a draft animal

OUTSPEAK *v* -SPOKE, -SPOKEN, -SPEAKING, -SPEAKS to outdo in speaking

OUTSPEED *v* -SPED or -SPEEDED, -SPEEDING, -SPEEDS to go faster than

OUTSPELL *v* -SPELLED or -SPELT, -SPELLING, -SPELLS to surpass in spelling

OUTSPEND *v* -SPENT, -SPENDING, -SPENDS to exceed the limits of in spending

OUTSPOKE past tense of outspeak

OUTSPOKEN past participle of outspeak

OUTSTAND *v* -STOOD, -STANDING, -STANDS to endure beyond

OUTSTARE *v* -STARED, -STARING, -STARES to outface

OUTSTART *v* -ED, -ING, -S to get ahead of at the start

OUTSTATE *v* -STATED, -STATING, -STATES to surpass in stating

OUTSTAY *v* -ED, -ING, -S to surpass in staying power

OUTSTEER *v* -ED, -ING, -S to surpass in steering

OUTSTOOD past tense of outstand

OUTSTRIP *v* -STRIPPED, -STRIPPING, -STRIPS to go faster or farther than

OUTSTUDY *v* -STUDIED, -STUDYING, -STUDIES to surpass in studying

OUTSTUNT *v* -ED, -ING, -S to surpass in stunting

OUTSULK *v* -ED, -ING, -S to surpass in sulking

OUTSUNG past participle of outsing

OUTSWEAR *v* -SWORE or -SWARE, -SWORN, -SWEARING, -SWEARS to surpass in swearing

OUTSWIM *v* -SWAM, -SWUM, -SWIMMING, -SWIMS to swim faster or farther than

OUTTAKE *n* pl. -S a passage outwards

OUTTALK *v* -ED, -ING, -S to surpass in talking

OUTTASK *v* -ED, -ING, -S to surpass in tasking

OUTTELL *v* -TOLD, -TELLING, -TELLS to say openly

OUTTHANK *v* -ED, -ING, -S to surpass in thanking

OUTTHINK *v* -THOUGHT, -THINKING, -THINKS to get the better of by thinking

OUTTHROB *v* -THROBBED, -THROBBING, -THROBS to surpass in throbbing

OUTTHROW *v* -THREW, -THROWN, -THROWING, -THROWS to throw farther or more accurately than

OUTTOLD past tense of outtell

OUTTOWER *v* -ED, -ING, -S to tower above

OUTTRADE *v* -TRADED, -TRADING, -TRADES to get the better of in a trade

OUTTRICK *v* -ED, -ING, -S to get the better of by trickery

OUTTROT *v* -TROTTED, -TROTTING, -TROTS to surpass in trotting

OUTTRUMP *v* -ED, -ING, -S to outplay

OUTTURN *n* pl. -S a quantity produced

OUTVALUE *v* -UED, -UING, -UES to be worth more than

OUTVAUNT *v* -ED, -ING, -S to surpass in vaunting

OUTVIE *v* -VIED, -VYING, -VIES to surpass in a competition

OUTVOICE *v* -VOICED, -VOICING, -VOICES to surpass in loudness of voice

OUTVOTE v -VOTED, -VOTING, -VOTES to defeat by a majority of votes

OUTVYING present participle of outvie

OUTWAIT v -ED, -ING, -S to exceed in patience

OUTWALK v -ED, -ING, -S to surpass in walking

OUTWAR v -WARRED, -WARRING, -WARS to surpass in warring

OUTWARD adv toward the outside

OUTWARDS adv outward

OUTWARRED past tense of outwar

OUTWARRING present participle of outwar

OUTWASH n pl. -ES detritus washed from a glacier

OUTWASTE v -WASTED, -WASTING, -WASTES to surpass in wasting

OUTWATCH v -ED, -ING, -ES to watch longer than

OUTWEAR v -WORE, -WORN, -WEARING, -WEARS to last longer than

OUTWEARY v -RIED, -RYING, -RIES to surpass in wearying

OUTWEEP v -WEPT, -WEEPING, -WEEPS to weep more than

OUTWEIGH v -ED, -ING, -S to weigh more than

OUTWENT past tense of outgo

OUTWEPT past tense of outweep

OUTWHIRL v -ED, -ING, -S to surpass in whirling

OUTWILE v -WILED, -WILING, -WILES to surpass in wiling

OUTWILL v -ED, -ING, -S to surpass in willpower

OUTWIND v -ED, -ING, -S to cause to be out of breath

OUTWISH v -ED, -ING, -ES to surpass in wishing

OUTWIT v -WITTED, -WITTING, -WITS to get the better of by superior cleverness

OUTWORE past tense of outwear

OUTWORK v -WORKED or -WROUGHT, -WORKING, -WORKS to work faster or better than

OUTWORN past participle of outwear

OUTWRITE v -WROTE or -WRIT, -WRITTEN, -WRITING, -WRITES to write better than

OUTWROUGHT a past tense of outwork

OUTYELL v -ED, -ING, -S to yell louder than

OUTYELP v -ED, -ING, -S to surpass in yelping

OUTYIELD v -ED, -ING, -S to surpass in yield

OUZEL n pl. -S a European bird

OUZO n pl. -ZOS a Greek liqueur

OVA pl. of ovum

OVAL n pl. -S an oval (egg-shaped) figure or object

OVALITY n pl. -TIES ovalness

OVALLY adv in the shape of an oval

OVALNESS n pl. -ES the state of being oval

OVARIAL adj ovarian

OVARIAN adj pertaining to an ovary

OVARIES pl. of ovary

OVARIOLE n pl. -S one of the tubes of which the ovaries of most insects are composed

OVARITIS n pl. -RITIDES inflammation of an ovary

OVARY n pl. -RIES a female reproductive gland

OVATE adj egg-shaped **OVATELY** adv

OVATION n pl. -S an expression or demonstration of popular acclaim

OVEN n pl. -S an enclosed compartment in which substances are heated **OVENLIKE** adj

OVENBIRD n pl. -S an American songbird

OVENWARE n pl. -S heat-resistant dishes for baking and serving food

OVER v -ED, -ING, -S to leap above and to the other side of

OVERABLE adj excessively able

OVERACT v -ED, -ING, -S to act with exaggeration

OVERAGE n pl. -S an amount in excess

OVERAGED adj too old to be useful

OVERALL n pl. -S a loose outer garment

OVERAPT adj excessively apt

OVERARCH v -ED, -ING, -ES to form an arch over

OVERARM adj done with the arm above the shoulder

OVERATE past tense of overeat

OVERAWE v -AWED, -AWING, -AWES to subdue by inspiring awe

OVERBAKE v -BAKED, -BAKING, -BAKES to bake too long

OVERBEAR v -BORE, -BORNE or -BORN, -BEARING, -BEARS to bring down by superior weight or force

OVERBEAT v -BEAT, -BEATEN, -BEATING, -BEATS to beat too much

OVERBED adj spanning a bed

OVERBET v -BET or -BETTED, -BETTING, -BETS to bet too much

OVERBID v -BID, -BID or -BIDDEN, -BIDDING, -BIDS to bid higher than

OVERBIG adj too big

OVERBILL v -ED, -ING, -S to bill too much

OVERBITE n pl. -S a faulty closure of the teeth

OVERBLOW v -BLEW, -BLOWN, -BLOWING, -BLOWS to give excessive importance to

OVERBOIL v -ED, -ING, -S to boil too long

OVERBOLD adj excessively bold or forward

OVERBOOK v -ED, -ING, -S to issue reservations in excess of the space available

OVERBORE past tense of overbear

OVERBORN a past participle of overbear

OVERBORNE a past participle of overbear

OVERBOUGHT past tense of overbuy

OVERBRED adj bred too finely or to excess

OVERBURN v -BURNED or -BURNT, -BURNING, -BURNS to burn too long

OVERBUSY adj too busy

OVERBUY v -BOUGHT, -BUYING, -BUYS to buy in quantities exceeding need or demand

OVERCALL v -ED, -ING, -S to overbid

OVERCAME past tense of overcome

OVERCAST v -CAST or -CASTED, -CASTING, -CASTS to become cloudy or dark

OVERCOAT n pl. -S a warm coat worn over indoor clothing

OVERCOLD adj too cold

OVERCOME v -CAME, -COMING, -COMES to get the better of

OVERCOOK v -ED, -ING, -S to cook too long

OVERCOOL v -ED, -ING, -S to make too cool

OVERCOY adj too coy

OVERCRAM v -CRAMMED, -CRAMMING, -CRAMS to stuff or cram to excess

OVERCROP v -CROPPED, -CROPPING, -CROPS to exhaust the fertility of by cultivating to excess

OVERCURE v -CURED, -CURING, -CURES to cure too long

OVERCUT v -CUT, -CUTTING, -CUTS to cut too much

OVERDARE v -DARED, -DARING, -DARES to become too daring

OVERDEAR adj too dear; too costly

OVERDECK v -ED, -ING, -S to adorn extravagantly

OVERDO v -DID, -DONE, -DOING, -DOES to do to excess

OVERDOER n pl. -S one that overdoes

OVERDOG n pl. -S one that is dominant or victorious

OVERDOSE v -DOSED, -DOSING, -DOSES to give an excessive dose to

OVERDRAW v -DREW, -DRAWN, -DRAWING, -DRAWS to draw checks on in excess of the balance

OVERDRY v -DRIED, -DRYING, -DRIES to dry too much

OVERDUB v -DUBBED, -DUBBING, -DUBS to add sound to an existing recording

OVERDUE adj not paid when due

OVERDYE v -DYED, -DYEING, -DYES to dye with too much color

OVEREASY adj too easy

OVEREAT v -ATE, -EATEN, -EATING, -EATS to eat to excess

OVEREDIT v -ED, -ING, -S to edit more than necessary

OVERFAR adj too great in distance, extent, or degree

OVERFAST adj too fast

OVERFAT adj too fat

OVERFEAR v -ED, -ING, -S to fear too much

OVERFEED v -FED, -FEEDING, -FEEDS to feed too much

OVERFILL v -ED, -ING, -S to fill to overflowing

OVERFISH v -ED, -ING, -ES to deplete the supply of fish in an area by fishing to excess

OVERFLOW v -FLOWED, -FLOWN, -FLOWING, -FLOWS to flow over the top of

OVERFLY v -FLEW, -FLOWN, -FLYING, -FLIES to fly over

OVERFOND adj too fond or affectionate

OVERFOUL adj too foul

OVERFREE adj too free

OVERFULL adj too full

OVERFUND v -ED, -ING, -S to fund more than required

OVERGILD v -GILDED or -GILT, -GILDING, -GILDS to gild over

OVERGIRD v -GIRDED or -GIRT, -GIRDING, -GIRDS to gird to excess

OVERGLAD adj too glad

OVERGOAD v -ED, -ING, -S to goad too much

OVERGROW v -GREW, -GROWN, -GROWING, -GROWS to grow over

OVERHAND v -ED, -ING, -S to sew with short, vertical stitches

OVERHANG v -HUNG, -HANGING, -HANGS to hang or project over

OVERHARD adj too hard

OVERHATE v -HATED, -HATING, -HATES to hate to excess

OVERHAUL v -ED, -ING, -S to examine carefully for needed repairs

OVERHEAD n pl. -S the general cost of running a business

OVERHEAP v -ED, -ING, -S to heap up or accumulate to excess

OVERHEAR v -HEARD, -HEARING, -HEARS to hear without the speaker's knowledge or intention

OVERHEAT v -ED, -ING, -S to heat to excess

OVERHIGH adj too high

OVERHOLD v -HELD, -HOLDING, -HOLDS to rate too highly

OVERHOLY adj too holy

OVERHOPE v -HOPED, -HOPING, -HOPES to hope exceedingly

OVERHOT adj too hot

OVERHUNG past tense of overhang

OVERHUNT v -ED, -ING, -S to deplete the supply of game in an area by hunting to excess

OVERHYPE v -HYPED, -HYPING, -HYPES to hype to excess

OVERIDLE adj too idle

OVERJOY v -ED, -ING, -S to fill with great joy

OVERJUST adj too just

OVERKEEN adj too keen

OVERKILL v -ED, -ING, -S to destroy with more nuclear force than required

OVERKIND adj too kind

OVERLADE v -LADED, -LADEN, -LADING, -LADES to load with too great a burden

OVERLAID past tense of overlay

OVERLAIN past participle of overlie

OVERLAND n pl. -S a train or stagecoach that travels over land

OVERLAP v -LAPPED, -LAPPING, -LAPS to extend over and cover a part of

OVERLATE adj too late

OVERLAX adj too lax

OVERLAY v -LAID, -LAYING, -LAYS to lay over

OVERLEAF adv on the other side of the page

OVERLEAP v -LEAPED or -LEAPT, -LEAPING, -LEAPS to leap over

OVERLEND v -LENT, -LENDING, -LENDS to lend too much

OVERLET v -LET, -LETTING, -LETS to let to excess

OVERLEWD adj too lewd

OVERLIE v -LAY, -LAIN, -LYING, -LIES to lie over

OVERLIT a past tense of overlight

OVERLIVE v -LIVED, -LIVING, -LIVES to outlive

OVERLOAD v -ED, -ING, -S to load to excess

OVERLONG adj too long

OVERLOOK v -ED, -ING, -S to fail to notice

OVERLORD v -ED, -ING, -S to rule tyrannically

OVERLOUD adj too loud

OVERLOVE v -LOVED, -LOVING, -LOVES to love to excess

OVERLUSH adj excessively lush

OVERLY adv to an excessive degree

OVERLYING present participle of overlie

OVERMAN n pl. -MEN a foreman

OVERMAN v -MANNED, -MANNING, -MANS to provide with more men than are needed

OVERMANY adj too many

OVERMEEK adj excessively meek

OVERMELT v -ED, -ING, -S to melt too much

OVERMEN pl. of overman

OVERMILD adj too mild

OVERMILK v -ED, -ING, -S to milk to excess

OVERMINE v -MINED, -MINING, -MINES to mine to excess

OVERMIX v -ED, -ING, -ES to mix too much

OVERMUCH n pl. -ES an excess

OVERNEAR adj too near

OVERNEAT adj too neat

OVERNEW adj too new

OVERNICE adj excessively nice

OVERPASS v -PASSED or -PAST, -PASSING, -PASSES to pass over

OVERPAY v -PAID, -PAYING, -PAYS to pay too much

OVERPERT adj too pert

OVERPLAN v -PLANNED, -PLANNING, -PLANS to plan to excess

OVERPLAY v -ED, -ING, -S to exaggerate

OVERPLOT v -PLOTTED, -PLOTTING, -PLOTS to devise an overly complex plot for

OVERPLUS n pl. -ES a surplus

OVERPLY v -PLIED, -PLYING, -PLIES to ply to excess; overwork

OVERPUMP v -ED, -ING, -S to pump to excess

OVERRAN past tense of overrun

OVERRANK adj too luxuriant in growth

OVERRASH adj too rash

OVERRATE v -RATED, -RATING, -RATES to rate too highly

OVERRICH adj too rich

OVERRIDE v -RODE, -RIDDEN, -RIDING, -RIDES to ride over

OVERRIFE adj too rife

OVERRIPE adj too ripe

OVERRODE past tense of override

OVERRUDE adj excessively rude

OVERRUFF v -ED, -ING, -S to trump with a higher trump card than has already been played

OVERRULE v -RULED, -RULING, -RULES to disallow the arguments of

OVERRUN v -RAN, -RUNNING, -RUNS to spread or swarm over

OVERSAD adj excessively sad

OVERSALE n pl. -S the act of overselling

OVERSALT v -ED, -ING, -S to salt to excess

OVERSAVE v -SAVED, -SAVING, -SAVES to save too much

OVERSAW past tense of oversee

OVERSEA adv overseas

OVERSEAS adv beyond or across the sea

OVERSEE v -SAW, -SEEN, -SEEING, -SEES to watch over and direct

OVERSEED v -ED, -ING, -S to seed to excess

OVERSEER n pl. -S one that oversees

OVERSELL v -SOLD, -SELLING, -SELLS to sell more of than can be delivered

OVERSET v -SET, -SETTING, -SETS to turn or tip over

OVERSEW v -SEWED, -SEWN, -SEWING, -SEWS to overhand

OVERSHOE n pl. -S a protective outer shoe

OVERSHOT n pl. -S a type of fabric weave

OVERSICK adj too sick

OVERSIDE n pl. -S the other side of a phonograph record

OVERSIZE n pl. -S an unusually large size

OVERSLIP v -SLIPPED or -SLIPT, -SLIPPING, -SLIPS to leave out

OVERSLOW adj too slow

OVERSOAK v -ED, -ING, -S to soak too much

OVERSOFT adj too soft

OVERSOLD past tense of oversell

OVERSOON adv too soon

OVERSOUL n pl. -S a supreme reality or mind in transcendentalism

OVERSPIN n pl. -S a forward spin imparted to a ball

OVERSTAY v -ED, -ING, -S to stay beyond the limits or duration of

OVERSTEP v -STEPPED, -STEPPING, -STEPS to go beyond

OVERSTIR v -STIRRED, -STIRRING, -STIRS to stir too much

OVERSUDS v -ED, -ING, -ES to form an excessive amount of suds

OVERSUP v -SUPPED, -SUPPING, -SUPS to sup to excess

OVERSURE adj too sure

OVERT adj open to view

OVERTAKE v -TOOK, -TAKEN, -TAKING, -TAKES to catch up with

OVERTALK v -ED, -ING, -S to talk to excess

OVERTAME adj too tame

OVERTART adj too tart

OVERTASK v -ED, -ING, -S to task too severely

OVERTAX v -ED, -ING, -ES to tax too heavily

OVERTHIN *adj* too thin

OVERTIME *v* -TIMED, -TIMING, -TIMES to exceed the desired timing for

OVERTIP *v* -TIPPED, -TIPPING, -TIPS to tip more than what is customary

OVERTIRE *v* -TIRED, -TIRING, -TIRES to tire excessively

OVERTLY *adj* in an overt manner

OVERTOIL *v* -ED, -ING, -S to wear out or exhaust by excessive toil

OVERTONE *n* pl. -S a higher partial tone

OVERTOOK past tense of overtake

OVERTOP *v* -TOPPED, -TOPPING, -TOPS to rise above the top of

OVERTRIM *v* -TRIMMED, -TRIMMING, -TRIMS to trim too much

OVERTURE *v* -TURED, -TURING, -TURES to propose

OVERTURN *v* -ED, -ING, -S to turn over

OVERURGE *v* -URGED, -URGING, -URGES to urge too much

OVERUSE *v* -USED, -USING, -USES to use too much

OVERVIEW *n* pl. -S a summary

OVERVOTE *v* -VOTED, -VOTING, -VOTES to defeat by a majority of votes

OVERWARM *v* -ED, -ING, -S to warm too much

OVERWARY *adj* too wary

OVERWEAK *adj* too weak

OVERWEAR *v* -WORE, -WORN, -WEARING, -WEARS to wear out

OVERWEEN *v* -ED, -ING, -S to be arrogant

OVERWET *v* -WETTED, -WETTING, -WETS to wet too much

OVERWIDE *adj* too wide

OVERWILY *adj* too wily

OVERWIND *v* -WOUND, -WINDING, -WINDS to wind too much, as a watch

OVERWISE *adj* too wise

OVERWORD *n* pl. -S a word or phrase repeated at intervals in a song

OVERWORE past tense of overwear

OVERWORK *v* -WORKED or -WROUGHT, -WORKING, -WORKS to cause to work too hard

OVERWORN past participle of overwear

OVERWOUND past tense of overwind

OVERWROUGHT a past tense of overwork

OVERZEAL *n* pl. -S excess of zeal

OVIBOS *n* pl. OVIBOS a wild ox

OVICIDE *n* pl. -S an agent that kills eggs **OVICIDAL** *adj*

OVIDUCT *n* pl. -S a tube through which ova travel from an ovary **OVIDUCAL** *adj*

OVIFORM *adj* shaped like an egg

OVINE *n* pl. -S a sheep or a closely related animal

OVIPARA *n/pl* egg-laying animals

OVIPOSIT *v* -ED, -ING, -S to lay eggs

OVISAC *n* pl. -S a sac containing an ovum or ova

OVOID *n* pl. -S an egg-shaped body **OVOIDAL** *adj*

OVOLO *n* pl. -LI or -LOS a convex molding

OVONIC *n* pl. -S an electronic device

OVULATE *v* -LATED, -LATING, -LATES to produce ova

OVULE *n* pl. -S a rudimentary seed **OVULAR, OVULARY** *adj*

OVUM *n* pl. OVA the female reproductive cell of animals

OW *interj* — used to express sudden pain

OWE *v* OWED, OWING, OWES to be under obligation to pay or repay

OWL *n* pl. -S a nocturnal bird

OWLET *n* pl. -S a young owl

OWLISH *adj* resembling an owl **OWLISHLY** *adv*

OWLLIKE *adj* owlish

OWN *v* -ED, -ING, -S to have as a belonging **OWNABLE** *adj*

OWNER *n* pl. -S one that owns

OWSE *n* pl. OWSEN ox

OX *n* pl. OXEN a hoofed mammal

OX *n* pl. -ES a clumsy person

OXALATE *v* -LATED, -LATING, -LATES to treat with an oxalate (a chemical salt)

OXALIS *n* pl. -ALISES a flowering plant **OXALIC** *adj*

OXAZEPAM *n* pl. -S a tranquilizing drug

OXAZINE *n* pl. -S a chemical compound

OXBLOOD *n* pl. -S a deep red color

OXBOW *n* pl. -S a U-shaped piece of wood in an ox yoke

OXCART *n* pl. -S an ox-drawn cart

OXEN pl. of ox

OXEYE *n* pl. -S a flowering plant

OXFORD *n* pl. -S a type of shoe

OXHEART *n* pl. -S a variety of sweet cherry

OXID *n* pl. -S oxide

OXIDABLE *adj* capable of being oxidized

OXIDANT *n* pl. -S an oxidizing agent

OXIDASE *n* pl. -S an oxidizing enzyme **OXIDASIC** *adj*

OXIDATE *v* -DATED, -DATING, -DATES to oxidize

OXIDE *n* pl. -S a binary compound of oxygen with another element or radical **OXIDIC** *adj*

OXIDISE *v* -DISED, -DISING, -DISES to oxidize

OXIDISER *n* pl. -S oxidizer

OXIDIZE *v* -DIZED, -DIZING, -DIZES to combine with oxygen

OXIDIZER *n* pl. -S an oxidant

OXIM *n* pl. -S oxime

OXIME *n* pl. -S a chemical compound

OXLIP *n* pl. -S a flowering plant

OXO *adj* containing oxygen

OXPECKER *n* pl. -S an African bird

OXTAIL *n* pl. -S the tail of an ox

OXTER *n* pl. -S the armpit

OXTONGUE *n* pl. -S a European herb

OXY *adj* containing oxygen

OXYACID *n* pl. -S an acid that contains oxygen

OXYGEN *n* pl. -S a gaseous element **OXYGENIC** *adj*

OXYMORON *n* -MORA a combination of contradictory or incongruous words

OXYPHIL *n* pl. -S oxyphile

OXYPHILE *n* pl. -S an organism that thrives in a relatively acid environment

OXYSALT *n* pl. -S a salt of an oxyacid

OXYSOME *n* pl. -S a structural unit of cellular cristae

OXYTOCIC *n* pl. -S a drug that hastens the process of childbirth

OXYTOCIN *n* pl. -S a pituitary hormone

OXYTONE *n* pl. -S a word having heavy stress on the last syllable

OY *interj* — used to express dismay or pain

OYER *n* pl. -S a type of legal writ

OYES *n* pl. OYESSES oyez

OYEZ *n* pl. OYESSES a cry used to introduce the opening of a court of law

OYSTER *v* -ED, -ING, -S to gather oysters (edible mollusks)

OYSTERER *n* pl. -S one that gathers or sells oysters

OZONATE *v* -ATED, -ATING, -ATES to treat or combine with ozone

OZONE *n* pl. -S a form of oxygen **OZONIC** *adj*

OZONIDE *n* pl. -S a compound of ozone

OZONISE *v* -ISED, -ISING, -ISES to ozonize

OZONIZE *v* -IZED, -IZING, -IZES to convert into ozone

OZONIZER *n* pl. -S a device for co oxygen into ozone

OZONOUS *adj* pertaining to ozone

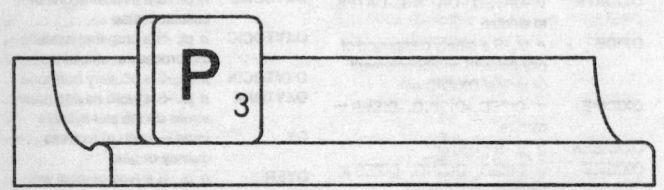

PA	*n* pl. **-S** a father	**PACKER**	*n* pl. **-S** one that packs
PABLUM	*n* pl. **-S** insipid writing or speech	**PACKET**	*v* **-ED, -ING, -S** to make into a small package
PABULUM	*n* pl. **-S** food **PABULAR** *adj*	**PACKING**	*n* pl. **-S** material used to pack
PAC	*n* pl. **-S** a shoe patterned after a moccasin	**PACKLY**	*adv* intimately
PACA	*n* pl. **-S** a large rodent	**PACKMAN**	*n* pl. **-MEN** a peddler
PACE	*v* **PACED, PACING, PACES** to walk with a regular step	**PACKNESS**	*n* pl. **-ES** intimacy
		PACKSACK	*n* pl. **-S** a carrying bag to be worn on the back
PACER	*n* pl. **-S** a horse whose gait is a pace	**PACKWAX**	*n* pl. **-ES** paxwax
PACHA	*n* pl. **-S** a pasha	**PACT**	*n* pl. **-S** an agreement
PACHADOM	*n* pl. **-S** pashadom	**PACTION**	*n* pl. **-S** a pact
PACHALIC	*n* pl. **-S** pashalik	**PAD**	*v* **PADDED, PADDING, PADS** to line or stuff with soft material
PACHINKO	*n* pl. **-KOS** a Japanese pinball game	**PADAUK**	*n* pl. **-S** a tropical tree
PACHISI	*n* pl. **-S** a board game of India	**PADDER**	*n* pl. **-S** one that pads
PACHOULI	*n* pl. **-S** an East Indian herb	**PADDIES**	pl. of paddy
PACHUCO	*n* pl. **-COS** a flashy Mexican-American youth	**PADDING**	*n* pl. **-S** cushioning material
		PADDLE	*v* **-DLED, -DLING, -DLES** to propel with a broad-bladed implement
PACIFIC	*adj* peaceful		
PACIFIED	past tense of pacify		
PACIFIER	*n* pl. **-S** one that pacifies	**PADDLER**	*n* pl. **-S** one that paddles
PACIFIES	present 3d person sing. of pacify	**PADDLING**	*n* pl. **-S** the act of one who paddles
PACIFISM	*n* pl. **-S** opposition to war or violence	**PADDOCK**	*v* **-ED, -ING, -S** to confine in an enclosure for horses
PACIFIST	*n* pl. **-S** an advocate of pacifism	**PADDY**	*n* pl. **-DIES** a rice field
PACIFY	*v* **-FIED, -FYING, -FIES** to make peaceful	**PADI**	*n* pl. **-S** paddy
		PADISHAH	*n* pl. **-S** a sovereign
		PADLE	*n* pl. **-S** a hoe
PACING	present participle of pace	**PADLOCK**	*v* **-ED, -ING, -S** to secure with a type of lock
PACK	*v* **-ED, -ING, -S** to put into a receptacle for transportation or storage **PACKABLE** *adj*	**PADNAG**	*n* pl. **-S** a horse that moves along at an easy pace
		PADOUK	*n* pl. **-S** padauk
PACKAGE	*v* **-AGED, -AGING, -AGES** to make into a package (a wrapped or boxed object)	**PADRE**	*n* pl. **PADRES** or **PADRI** a Christian clergyman
		PADRONE	*n* pl. **-NES** or **-NI** a master
PACKAGER	*n* pl. **-S** one that packages	**PADSHAH**	*n* pl. **-S** padishah

PADUASOY n pl. -SOYS a strong silk fabric

PAEAN n pl. -S a song of joy

PAEANISM n pl. -S the chanting of a paean

PAELLA n pl. -S a saffron-flavored stew

PAEON n pl. -S a metrical foot of four syllables

PAESAN n pl. -S paesano

PAESANO n pl. -NI or -NOS a fellow countryman

PAGAN n pl. -S an irreligious person

PAGANDOM n pl. -S the realm of pagans

PAGANISE v -ISED, -ISING, -ISES to paganize

PAGANISH adj resembling a pagan

PAGANISM n pl. -S an irreligious attitude

PAGANIST n pl. -S a pagan

PAGANIZE v -IZED, -IZING, -IZES to make irreligious

PAGE v PAGED, PAGING, PAGES to summon by calling out the name of

PAGEANT n pl. -S an elaborate public spectacle

PAGEBOY n pl. -BOYS a woman's hairstyle

PAGED past tense of page

PAGER n pl. -S a beeper

PAGINAL adj pertaining to the pages of a book

PAGINATE v -NATED, -NATING, -NATES to number the pages of

PAGING n pl. -S a transfer of computer pages

PAGOD n pl. -S pagoda

PAGODA n pl. -S a Far Eastern temple

PAGURIAN n pl. -S a hermit crab

PAGURID n pl. -S pagurian

PAH interj — used as an exclamation of disgust

PAHLAVI n pl. -S a former coin of Iran

PAHOEHOE n pl. -S smooth solidified lava

PAID a past tense of pay

PAIK v -ED, -ING, -S to beat or strike

PAIL n pl. -S a watertight cylindrical container

PAILFUL n pl. PAILFULS or PAILSFUL as much as a pail can hold

PAILLARD n pl. -S a slice of meat pounded thin and grilled

PAIN v -ED, -ING, -S to cause pain (suffering or distress)

PAINCH n pl. -ES paunch

PAINFUL adj -FULLER, -FULLEST causing pain

PAINLESS adj not causing pain

PAINT v -ED, -ING, -S to make a representation of with paints (coloring substances)

PAINTER n pl. -S one that paints

PAINTING n pl. -S a picture made with paints

PAINTY adj PAINTIER, PAINTIEST covered with paint

PAIR v -ED, -ING, -S to arrange in sets of two

PAIRING n pl. -S a matching of two opponents in a tournament

PAISA n pl. PAISE or PAISAS a coin of Pakistan

PAISAN n pl. -S paisano

PAISANA n pl. -S a female compatriot

PAISANO n pl. -NOS a fellow countryman

PAISE a pl. of paisa

PAISLEY n pl. -LEYS a patterned wool fabric

PAJAMA n pl. -S a garment for sleeping or lounging

PAJAMAED adj wearing pajamas

PAKEHA n pl. -S a person who is not of Maori descent

PAL v PALLED, PALLING, PALS to associate as friends

PALABRA n pl. -S a word

PALACE n pl. -S a royal residence PALACED adj

PALADIN n pl. -S a knightly champion

PALAIS n pl. PALAIS a palace

PALATAL n pl. -S a bone of the palate

PALATE n pl. -S the roof of the mouth

PALATIAL adj resembling a palace

PALATINE n pl. -S a high officer of an empire

PALAVER v -ED, -ING, -S to chatter

PALAZZO n pl. -ZI an impressive building

PALAZZOS n/pl wide-legged pants for women

PALE adj PALER, PALEST lacking intensity of color

PALE v PALED, PALING, PALES to make or become pale

PALEA n pl. -LEAE a small bract PALEAL adj

PALEFACE n pl. -S a white person

PALELY adv in a pale manner

PALENESS n pl. -ES the quality of being pale

PALEOSOL n pl. -S a layer of ancient soil

PALER comparative of pale

PALEST superlative of pale

PALESTRA n pl. -TRAS or -TRAE a school for athletics in ancient Greece

PALET n pl. -S a palea

PALETOT n pl. -S a loose overcoat

PALETTE n pl. -S a board on which an artist mixes colors

PALEWAYS adv palewise

PALEWISE adv vertically

PALFREY n pl. -FREYS a riding horse

PALIER comparative of paly

PALIEST superlative of paly

PALIKAR n pl. -S a Greek soldier

PALIMONY n pl. -NIES an allowance paid to one member of an unmarried couple who have separated

PALING n pl. -S a picket fence

PALINODE n pl. -S a formal retraction

PALISADE v -SADED, -SADING, -SADES to fortify with a heavy fence

PALISH adj somewhat pale

PALL v -ED, -ING, -S to become insipid

PALLADIA n/pl safeguards

PALLADIC adj pertaining to the metallic element palladium

PALLED past tense of pal

PALLET n pl. -S a bed or mattress of straw

PALLETTE n pl. -S a piece of armor protecting the armpit

PALLIA a pl. of pallium

PALLIAL adj pertaining to a part of the brain

PALLIATE v -ATED, -ATING, -ATES to conceal the seriousness of

PALLID adj pale PALLIDLY adv

PALLIER comparative of pally

PALLIEST superlative of pally

PALLING present participle of pal

PALLIUM n pl. -LIA or -LIUMS a cloak worn in ancient Rome

PALLOR n pl. -S paleness

PALLY adj -LIER, -LIEST marked by close friendship

PALM v -ED, -ING, -S to touch with the palm (inner surface) of the hand

PALMAR adj pertaining to the palm

PALMARY adj worthy of praise

PALMATE adj resembling an open hand

PALMATED adj palmate

PALMER n pl. -S a religious pilgrim

PALMETTE n pl. -S a type of ornament

PALMETTO n pl. -TOS or -TOES a tropical tree

PALMIER comparative of palmy

PALMIEST superlative of palmy

PALMIST n pl. -S a fortune-teller

PALMITIN n pl. -S a chemical compound

PALMLIKE adj resembling a palm tree

PALMY adj PALMIER, PALMIEST marked by prosperity

PALMYRA n pl. -S a tropical tree

PALOMINO n pl. -NOS a slender-legged horse

PALOOKA n pl. -S an inferior boxer

PALP n pl. -S a palpus

PALPABLE adj capable of being felt PALPABLY adv

PALPAL adj pertaining to a palpus

PALPATE v -PATED, -PATING, -PATES to examine by touch

PALPATOR n pl. -S one that palpates

PALPEBRA n pl. -BRAE an eyelid

PALPUS n pl. -PI a sensory organ of an arthropod

PALSHIP n pl. -S the relation existing between close friends

PALSY v -SIED, -SYING, -SIES to paralyze

PALTER v -ED, -ING, -S to talk or act insincerely

PALTERER n pl. -S one that palters

PALTRY adj -TRIER, -TRIEST petty PALTRILY adv

PALUDAL adj pertaining to a marsh

PALUDISM n pl. -S malaria

PALY adj PALIER, PALIEST somewhat pale

PAM n pl. -S the jack of clubs in certain card games

PAMPA n pl. -S a grassland of South America

PAMPEAN n pl. -S a native of the pampas

PAMPER v -ED, -ING, -S to treat with extreme or excessive indulgence

PAMPERER n pl. -S one that pampers

PAMPERO n pl. -ROS a cold, dry wind

PAMPHLET n pl. -S a printed work with a paper cover

PAN v PANNED, PANNING, PANS to criticize harshly

PANACEA n pl. -S a remedy for all diseases or ills PANACEAN adj

PANACHE *n* pl. -S an ornamental tuft of feathers

PANADA *n* pl. -S a thick sauce

PANAMA *n* pl. -S a lightweight hat

PANATELA *n* pl. -S a long, slender cigar

PANBROIL *v* -ED, -ING, -S to fry in a pan with little or no fat

PANCAKE *v* -CAKED, -CAKING, -CAKES to land an airplane in a certain manner

PANCETTA *n* pl. -S unsmoked Italian bacon

PANCHAX *n* pl. -ES a tropical fish

PANCREAS *n* pl. -ES a large gland

PANDA *n* pl. -S an herbivorous mammal

PANDANUS *n* pl. -NI or -NUSES a tropical plant

PANDECT *n* pl. -S a complete body of laws

PANDEMIC *n* pl. -S a widespread disease

PANDER *v* -ED, -ING, -S to provide gratification for others' desires

PANDERER *n* pl. -S one that panders

PANDIED past tense of pandy

PANDIES present 3d person sing. of pandy

PANDIT *n* pl. -S a wise or learned man in India

PANDOOR *n* pl. -S pandour

PANDORA *n* pl. -S bandore

PANDORE *n* pl. -S bandore

PANDOUR *n* pl. -S a marauding soldier

PANDOWDY *n* pl. -DIES an apple dessert

PANDURA *n* pl. -S bandore

PANDY *v* -DIED, -DYING, -DIES to punish by striking the hand

PANE *n* pl. -S a sheet of glass for a window PANED *adj*

PANEL *v* -ELED, -ELING, -ELS or -ELLED, -ELLING, -ELS to decorate with thin sheets of material

PANELING *n* pl. -S material with which to panel

PANELIST *n* pl. -S a member of a discussion or advisory group

PANELLED a past tense of panel

PANELLING a present participle of panel

PANETELA *n* pl. -S panatela

PANFISH *n* pl. -ES any small fish that can be fried whole

PANFRY *v* -FRIED, -FRYING, -FRIES to fry in a frying pan

PANFUL *n* pl. -S as much as a pan will hold

PANG *v* -ED, -ING, -S to cause to have spasms of pain

PANGA *n* pl. -S a large knife

PANGEN *n* pl. -S a hypothetical heredity-controlling particle of protoplasm

PANGENE *n* pl. -S pangen

PANGOLIN *n* pl. -S a toothless mammal

PANHUMAN *adj* pertaining to all humanity

PANIC *v* -ICKED, -ICKING, -ICS to be overwhelmed by fear

PANICKY *adj* -ICKIER, -ICKIEST tending to panic

PANICLE *n* pl. -S a loosely branched flower cluster PANICLED *adj*

PANICUM *n* pl. -S a grass

PANIER *n* pl. -S pannier

PANMIXIA *n* pl. -S random mating within a breeding population

PANMIXIS *n* pl. -MIXES panmixia

PANNE *n* pl. -S a lustrous velvet

PANNED past tense of pan

PANNIER *n* pl. -S a large basket

PANNIKIN *n* pl. -S a small saucepan

PANNING present participle of pan

PANOCHA *n* pl. -S a coarse Mexican sugar

PANOCHE *n* pl. -S panocha

PANOPLY *n* pl. -PLIES a suit of armor

PANOPTIC *adj* including everything visible in one view

PANORAMA *n* pl. -S a complete view

PANPIPE *n* pl. -S a musical instrument

PANSOPHY *n* pl. -PHIES universal knowledge

PANSY *n* pl. -SIES a flowering plant

PANT *v* -ED, -ING, -S to breathe quickly and with difficulty

PANTHEON *n* pl. -S a temple dedicated to all the gods

PANTHER *n* pl. -S a leopard

PANTIE *n* pl. -S a woman's or child's undergarment

PANTIES pl. of panty

PANTILE *n* pl. -S a roofing tile PANTILED *adj*

PANTO *n* pl. -TOS a pantomime

PANTOFLE *n* pl. -S a slipper

PANTOUM *n* pl. -S a verse form

PANTRY *n* pl. -TRIES a closet or room for storing kitchen utensils

PANTSUIT *n* pl. -S a type of woman's suit

PANTY *n* pl. PANTIES pantie

PANZER *n* pl. -S an armored combat vehicle

PAP *n* pl. -S a soft food for infants

PAPA *n* pl. -S a father

PAPACY *n* pl. -CIES the office of the pope

PAPAIN *n* pl. -S an enzyme

PAPAL *adj* pertaining to the pope **PAPALLY** *adv*

PAPAW *n* pl. -S a fleshy fruit

PAPAYA *n* pl. -S a melon-like fruit **PAPAYAN** *adj*

PAPER *v* -ED, -ING, -S to cover or wrap with paper (a thin sheet material made of cellulose pulp)

PAPERBOY *n* pl. -BOYS a newsboy

PAPERER *n* pl. -S one that papers

PAPERY *adj* resembling paper

PAPHIAN *n* pl. -S a prostitute

PAPILLA *n* pl. -LAE a nipple-like projection **PAPILLAR** *adj*

PAPILLON *n* pl. -S a small dog having large ears

PAPOOSE *n* pl. -S an American Indian baby

PAPPI a pl. of pappus

PAPPIER comparative of pappy

PAPPIES pl. of pappy

PAPPIEST superlative of pappy

PAPPOOSE *n* pl. -S papoose

PAPPUS *n* pl. -PI a tuft of bristles on the achene of certain plants **PAPPOSE, PAPPOUS** *adj*

PAPPY *adj* -PIER, -PIEST resembling pap

PAPPY *n* pl. -PIES a father

PAPRICA *n* pl. -S paprika

PAPRIKA *n* pl. -S a seasoning made from red peppers

PAPULA *n* pl. -LAE papule

PAPULE *n* pl. -S a pimple **PAPULAR, PAPULOSE** *adj*

PAPYRUS *n* pl. -RUSES or -RI a tall aquatic plant **PAPYRAL, PAPYRIAN, PAPYRINE** *adj*

PAR *v* PARRED, PARRING, PARS to shoot in a standard number of strokes in golf

PARA *n* pl. -S a monetary unit of Yugoslavia

PARABLE *n* pl. -S a simple story conveying a moral or religious lesson

PARABOLA *n* pl. -S a conic section

PARACHOR *n* pl. S a mathematical constant that relates molecular volume to surface tension

PARADE *v* -RADED, -RADING, -RADES to march in a public procession

PARADER *n* pl. -S one that parades

PARADIGM *n* pl. -S a pattern or example

PARADING present participle of parade

PARADISE *n* pl. -S a place of extreme beauty or delight

PARADOR *n* pl. -S a government-owned hotel in Spain

PARADOS *n* pl. -ES a protective embankment

PARADOX *n* pl. -ES a statement seemingly contradictory or absurd yet perhaps true

PARADROP *v* -DROPPED, -DROPPING, -DROPS to deliver by parachute

PARAFFIN *v* -ED, -ING, -S to coat with a waxy substance

PARAFORM *n* pl. -S a substance used as an antiseptic

PARAGOGE *n* pl. -S the addition of a sound or sounds at the end of a word

PARAGON *v* -ED, -ING, -S to compare with

PARAKEET *n* pl. -S a small parrot

PARAKITE *n* pl. -S a parachute kite for towing a person through the air by a motorboat

PARALLAX *n* pl. -ES an apparent optical displacement of an object

PARALLEL *v* -LELED, -LELING, -LELS or -LELLED, -LELLING, -LELS to be similar or analogous to

PARALYSE *v* -LYSED, -LYSING, -LYSES to paralyze

PARALYZE *v* -LYZED, -LYZING, -LYZES to render incapable of movement

PARAMENT *n* pl. -MENTS or -MENTA an ornamental vestment

PARAMO *n* pl. -MOS a plateau region of South America

PARAMOUR *n* pl. -S an illicit lover

PARANG *n* pl. -S a heavy knife

PARANOEA *n* pl. -S paranoia

PARANOIA *n* pl. -S a mental disorder

PARANOIC *n* pl. -S a paranoid

PARANOID *n* pl. -S one affected with paranoia

PARAPET *n* pl. -S a protective wall

PARAPH *n* pl. S a flourish at the end of a signature

PARAQUAT *n* pl. -S a weed killer

PARAQUET *n pl.* -S parakeet

PARASANG *n pl.* -S a Persian unit of distance

PARASHAH *n pl.* -SHOTH or -SHIOTH a passage in Jewish scripture

PARASITE *n pl.* -S an organism that lives and feeds on or in another organism

PARASOL *n pl.* -S a small, light umbrella

PARAVANE *n pl.* -S an underwater device used to cut cables

PARAWING *n pl.* -S a winglike parachute

PARAZOAN *n pl.* -S any of a major division of multicellular animals

PARBOIL *v* -ED, -ING, -S to cook partially by boiling for a short time

PARCEL *v* -CELED, -CELING, -CELS or -CELLED, -CELLING, -CELS to divide into parts or shares

PARCENER *n pl.* -S a joint heir

PARCH *v* -ED, -ING, -ES to make very dry

PARCHESI *n pl.* -S pachisi

PARCHISI *n pl.* -S pachisi

PARD *n pl.* -S a leopard

PARDAH *n pl.* -S purdah

PARDEE *interj* pardi

PARDI *interj* — used as a mild oath

PARDIE *interj* pardi

PARDINE *adj* pertaining to a leopard

PARDNER *n pl.* -S chum; friend

PARDON *v* -ED, -ING, -S to release from liability for an offense

PARDONER *n pl.* -S one that pardons

PARDY *interj* pardi

PARE *v* PARED, PARING, PARES to cut off the outer covering of

PARECISM *n pl.* -S the state of having the male and female sexual organs beside or near each other

PAREIRA *n pl.* -S a medicinal plant root

PARENT *v* -ED, -ING, -S to exercise the functions of a parent (a father or mother)

PARENTAL *adj* pertaining to a parent

PAREO *n pl.* -REOS pareu

PARER *n pl.* -S one that pares

PARERGON *n pl.* -GA a composition derived from a larger work

PARESIS *n pl.* -RESES partial loss of the ability to move

PARETIC *n pl.* -S one affected with paresis

PAREU *n pl.* -S a Polynesian garment

PAREVE *adj* parve

PARFAIT *n pl.* -S a frozen dessert

PARFLESH *n pl.* -ES a rawhide soaked in lye to remove the hair and dried

PARFOCAL *adj* having lenses with the corresponding focal points in the same plane

PARGE *v* PARGED, PARGING, PARGES to parget

PARGET *v* -GETED, -GETING, -GETS or -GETTED, -GETTING, -GETS to cover with plaster

PARGING *n pl.* -S a thin coat of mortar or plaster for sealing masonry

PARGO *n pl.* -GOS a food fish

PARHELIA *n/pl* bright circular spots appearing on a solar halo

PARHELIC *adj* pertaining to parhelia

PARIAH *n pl.* -S a social outcast

PARIAN *n pl.* -S a hard, white porcelain

PARIES *n pl.* PARIETES the wall of an organ

PARIETAL *n pl.* -S a bone of the skull

PARING *n pl.* -S something pared off

PARIS *n pl.* -ISES a European herb

PARISH *n pl.* -ES an ecclesiastical district

PARITY *n pl.* -TIES equality

PARK *v* -ED, -ING, -S to leave a vehicle in a location for a time

PARKA *n pl.* -S a hooded garment

PARKER *n pl.* -S one that parks

PARKING *n pl.* -S an area in which vehicles may be left

PARKLAND *n pl.* -S a grassland region with isolated or grouped trees

PARKLIKE *adj* resembling an outdoor recreational area

PARKWAY *n pl.* -WAYS a wide highway

PARLANCE *n pl.* -S a manner of speaking

PARLANDO *adj* sung in a manner suggestive of speech

PARLANTE *adj* parlando

PARLAY *v* -ED, -ING, -S to bet an original wager and its winnings on a subsequent event

PARLE *v* PARLED, PARLING, PARLES to parley

PARLEY *v* -LEYED, -LEYING, -LEYS to discuss terms with an enemy

PARLEYER *n pl.* -S one that parleys

PARLING present participle of parle

PARLOR *n pl.* -S a room for the entertainment of visitors

PARLOUR *n pl.* -S parlor
PARLOUS *adj* dangerous
PARODIC *adj* comically imitative
PARODIED past tense of parody
PARODIES present 3d person sing. of parody
PARODIST *n pl.* -S one who parodies
PARODOS *n pl.* -DOI an ode sung in ancient Greek drama
PARODY *v* -DIED, -DYING, -DIES to imitate a serious literary work for comic effect
PAROL *n pl.* -S an utterance
PAROLE *v* -ROLED, -ROLING, -ROLES to release from prison before completion of the imposed sentence
PAROLEE *n pl.* -S one who is paroled
PARONYM *n pl.* -S a word having the same root as another
PAROQUET *n pl.* -S a parakeet
PAROTIC *adj* situated near the ear
PAROTID *n pl.* -S a salivary gland
PAROTOID *n pl.* -S a gland of certain toads and frogs
PAROUS *adj* having produced offspring
PAROXYSM *n pl.* -S a sudden fit or attack
PARQUET *v* -ED, -ING, -S to furnish with a floor of inlaid design
PARR *n pl.* -S a young salmon
PARRAL *n pl.* -S parrel
PARRED past tense of par
PARREL *n pl.* -S a sliding loop of rope or chain used on a ship
PARRIDGE *n pl.* -S porridge
PARRIED past tense of parry
PARRIES present 3d person sing. of parry
PARRING present participle of par
PARRITCH *n pl.* -ES porridge
PARROKET *n pl.* -S parakeet
PARROT *v* -ED, -ING, -S to repeat or imitate without thought or understanding
PARROTER *n pl.* -S one that parrots
PARROTY *adj* resembling a parrot (a hook-billed tropical bird)
PARRY *v* -RIED, -RYING, -RIES to ward off a blow
PARSE *v* PARSED, PARSING, PARSES to describe and analyze grammatically
PARSABLE *adj*
PARSEC *n pl.* -S a unit of astronomical distance
PARSER *n pl.* -S one that parses

PARSING present participle of parse
PARSLEY *n pl.* -LEYS a cultivated herb
PARSLEYED, PARSLIED *adj*
PARSNIP *n pl.* -S a European herb
PARSON *n pl.* -S a clergyman
PARSONIC *adj*
PART *v* -ED, -ING, -S to divide or break into separate pieces
PARTAKE *v* -TOOK, -TAKEN, -TAKING, -TAKES to participate
PARTAKER *n pl.* -S one that partakes
PARTAN *n pl.* -S an edible crab
PARTERRE *n pl.* -S a section of a theater
PARTIAL *n pl.* -S a simple component of a complex tone
PARTIBLE *adj* divisible
PARTICLE *n pl.* -S a very small piece or part
PARTIED past tense of party
PARTIER *n pl.* -S partyer
PARTIES present 3d person sing. of party
PARTING *n pl.* -S a division or separation
PARTISAN *n pl.* -S a firm supporter of a person, party, or cause
PARTITA *n pl.* -S a set of related instrumental pieces
PARTITE *adj* divided into parts
PARTIZAN *n pl.* -S partisan
PARTLET *n pl.* -S a woman's garment
PARTLY *adv* in some measure or degree
PARTNER *v* -ED, -ING, -S to associate with in some activity of common interest
PARTON *n pl.* -S a hypothetical atomic particle
PARTOOK past tense of partake
PARTWAY *adv* to some extent
PARTY *v* -TIED, -TYING, -TIES to attend a social gathering
PARTYER *n pl.* -S one that parties
PARURA *n pl.* -S parure
PARURE *n pl.* -S a set of matched jewelry
PARVE *adj* made without milk or meat
PARVENU *n pl.* -S one who has suddenly risen above his class
PARVENUE *adj* characteristic of a parvenu
PARVIS *n pl.* -VISES an enclosed area in front of a church
PARVISE *n pl.* -S parvis
PARVO *n pl.* -VOS a contagious disease of dogs

PARVOLIN *n* pl. -S an oily liquid obtained from fish

PAS *n* pl. PAS a dance step

PASCAL *n* pl. -S a unit of pressure

PASCHAL *n* pl. -S a candle used in certain religious ceremonies

PASE *n* pl. -S a movement of a matador's cape

PASEO *n* pl. -SEOS a leisurely stroll

PASH *v* -ED, -ING, -ES to strike violently

PASHA *n* pl. -S a former Turkish high official

PASHADOM *n* pl. -S the rank of a pasha

PASHALIC *n* pl. -S pashalik

PASHALIK *n* pl. -S the territory of a pasha

PASQUIL *n* pl. -S a satire or lampoon

PASS *v* -ED, -ING, -ES to go by

PASSABLE *adj* fairly good or acceptable
PASSABLY *adv*

PASSADE *n* pl. -S a turn of a horse backward or forward on the same ground

PASSADO *n* pl. -DOS or -DOES a forward thrust in fencing

PASSAGE *v* -SAGED, -SAGING, -SAGES to make a voyage

PASSANT *adj* walking with the farther forepaw raised — used of a heraldic animal

PASSBAND *n* pl. -S a frequency band that permits transmission with maximum efficiency

PASSBOOK *n* pl. -S a bankbook

PASSE *adj* outmoded

PASSEE *adj* passe

PASSEL *n* pl. -S a large quantity or number

PASSER *n* pl. -S one that passes

PASSERBY *n* pl. PASSERSBY one who passes by

PASSIBLE *adj* capable of feeling or suffering

PASSIM *adv* here and there

PASSING *n* pl. -S a death

PASSION *n* pl. -S an intense emotion

PASSIVE *n* pl. -S a verb form

PASSKEY *n* pl. -KEYS a key that opens several different locks

PASSLESS *adj* incapable of being traveled over or through

PASSOVER *n* pl. -S the lamb eaten at the feast of a Jewish holiday

PASSPORT *n* pl. -S a document allowing travel from one country to another

PASSUS *n* pl. -ES a section of a story or poem

PASSWORD *n* pl. -S a secret word that must be spoken to gain admission

PAST *n* pl. -S time gone by

PASTA *n* pl. -S a food made of dough

PASTE *v* PASTED, PASTING, PASTES to fasten with a sticky mixture

PASTEL *n* pl. -S a soft, delicate hue

PASTER *n* pl. -S one that pastes

PASTERN *n* pl. -S a part of a horse's foot

PASTEUP *n* pl. -S a finished copy to be photographed for making a printing plate

PASTICCI *n/pl* pastiches

PASTICHE *n* pl. -S an artistic work made of fragments from various sources

PASTIE *n* pl. -S pasty

PASTIER comparative of pasty

PASTIES pl. of pasty

PASTIEST superlative of pasty

PASTIL *n* pl. -S pastille

PASTILLE *n* pl. -S a lozenge

PASTIME *n* pl. -S a recreational activity

PASTINA *n* pl. -S a type of macaroni

PASTING present participle of paste

PASTIS *n* pl. -TISES a French liqueur

PASTLESS *adj* having no past

PASTNESS *n* pl. -ES the state of being past or gone by

PASTOR *v* -ED, -ING, -S to serve as the spiritual overseer of

PASTORAL *n* pl. -S a literary or artistic work that depicts country life

PASTRAMI *n* pl. -S a highly seasoned smoked beef

PASTROMI *n* pl. -S pastrami

PASTRY *n* pl. -TRIES a sweet baked food

PASTURAL *adj* pertaining to a pasture

PASTURE *v* -TURED, -TURING, -TURES to put in a pasture (a grazing area)

PASTURER *n* pl. -S one that pastures livestock

PASTY *adj* PASTIER, PASTIEST pale and unhealthy in appearance

PASTY *n* pl. PASTIES a meat pie

PAT *v* PATTED, PATTING, PATS to touch lightly

PATACA *n* pl. -S a monetary unit of Macao

PATAGIAL *adj* pertaining to a patagium

PATAGIUM n pl. -GIA a wing membrane of a bat

PATAMAR n pl. -S a sailing vessel

PATCH v -ED, -ING, -ES to mend or cover a hole or weak spot in

PATCHER n pl. -S one that patches

PATCHY adj PATCHIER, PATCHIEST uneven in quality **PATCHILY** adv

PATE n pl. -S the top of the head **PATED** adj

PATELLA n pl. -LAE or -LAS the flat movable bone at the front of the knee **PATELLAR** adj

PATEN n pl. -S a plate

PATENCY n pl. -CIES the state of being obvious

PATENT v -ED, -ING, -S to obtain a patent (a government grant protecting the rights of an inventor) on

PATENTEE n pl. -S one that holds a patent

PATENTLY adv obviously

PATENTOR n pl. -S one that grants a patent

PATER n pl. -S a father

PATERNAL adj pertaining to a father

PATH n pl. -S a trodden way or track

PATHETIC adj arousing pity

PATHLESS adj having no path

PATHOGEN n pl. -S any disease-producing organism

PATHOS n pl. -ES a quality that arouses feelings of pity or compassion

PATHWAY n pl. -WAYS a path

PATIENCE n pl. -S the quality of being patient

PATIENT adj -TIENTER, -TIENTEST able to endure disagreeable circumstances without complaint

PATIENT n pl. -S one who is under medical treatment

PATIN n pl. -S paten

PATINA n pl. -NAE or -NAS a green film that forms on bronze

PATINATE v -NATED, -NATING, -NATES to give a patina to

PATINE v -TINED, -TINING, -TINES to cover with a patina

PATINIZE v -NIZED, -NIZING, -NIZES to patinate

PATIO n pl. -TIOS an outdoor paved area adjoining a house

PATLY adv suitably

PATNESS n pl. -ES suitability

PATOIS n pl. PATOIS a dialect

PATRIOT n pl. -S one who loves his country

PATROL v -TROLLED, -TROLLING, -TROLS to pass through an area for the purposes of observation or security

PATRON n pl. -S a regular customer **PATRONAL, PATRONLY** adj

PATROON n pl. -S a landowner granted manorial rights under old Dutch law

PATSY n pl. -SIES a person who is easily fooled

PATTAMAR n pl. -S patamar

PATTED past tense of pat

PATTEE adj paty

PATTEN n pl. -S a shoe having a thick wooden sole

PATTER v -ED, -ING, -S to talk glibly or rapidly

PATTERER n pl. -S one that patters

PATTERN v -ED, -ING, -S to make according to a prescribed design

PATTIE n pl. -S patty

PATTING present participle of pat

PATTY n pl. -TIES a small, flat cake of chopped food

PATTYPAN n pl. -S a pan in which patties are baked

PATULENT adj patulous

PATULOUS adj spreading; open

PATY adj formee

PATZER n pl. -S an inept chess player

PAUCITY n pl. -TIES smallness of number or quantity

PAUGHTY adj arrogant

PAULDRON n pl. -S a piece of armor for the shoulder

PAULIN n pl. -S a sheet of waterproof material

PAUNCH n pl. -ES the belly or abdomen **PAUNCHED** adj

PAUNCHY adj PAUNCHIER, PAUNCHIEST having a protruding belly

PAUPER v -ED, -ING, -S to reduce to poverty

PAUSAL adj pertaining to a break or rest in speaking or writing

PAUSE v PAUSED, PAUSING, PAUSES to stop temporarily

PAUSER n pl. -S one that pauses

PAVAN n pl. -S a slow, stately dance

PAVANE n pl. -S pavan

PAVE v PAVED, PAVING, PAVES to cover with material that forms a firm, level surface

PAVEED adj set close together to conceal a metal base

PAVEMENT n pl. -S a paved surface

PAVER n pl. -S one that paves

PAVID adj timid

PAVILION v -ED, -ING, -S to cover with a large tent

PAVILLON n pl. -S the bell of a wind instrument

PAVIN n pl. -S pavan

PAVING n pl. -S pavement

PAVIOR n pl. -S a paver

PAVIOUR n pl. -S a paver

PAVIS n pl. -ISES a large medieval shield

PAVISE n pl. -S pavis

PAVISER n pl. -S a soldier carrying a pavis

PAVLOVA n pl. -S a meringue dessert

PAVONINE adj resembling a peacock

PAW v -ED, -ING, -S to strike or scrape with a beating motion

PAWER n pl. -S one that paws

PAWKY adj PAWKIER, PAWKIEST sly PAWKILY adv

PAWL n pl. -S a hinged mechanical part

PAWN v -ED, -ING, -S to give as security for something borrowed PAWNABLE adj

PAWNAGE n pl. -S an act of pawning

PAWNEE n pl. -S one to whom something is pawned

PAWNER n pl. -S one that pawns something

PAWNOR n pl. -S pawner

PAWNSHOP n pl. -S a place where things are pawned

PAWPAW n pl. -S papaw

PAX n pl. -ES a ceremonial embrace given to signify Christian love and unity

PAXWAX n pl. -ES the nuchal ligament of a quadruped

PAY v PAID or PAYED, PAYING, PAYS to give money or something of value in exchange for goods or services

PAYABLE adj profitable PAYABLY adv

PAYABLES n/pl accounts payable

PAYBACK n pl. -S a return on an investment equal to the original capital outlay

PAYCHECK n pl. -S a check in payment of wages or salary

PAYDAY n pl. -DAYS the day on which wages are paid

PAYEE n pl. -S one to whom money is paid

PAYER n pl. -S one that pays

PAYGRADE n pl. -S the grade of military personnel according to a base pay scale

PAYLOAD n pl. -S the part of a cargo producing income

PAYMENT n pl. -S something that is paid

PAYNIM n pl. -S a pagan

PAYOFF n pl. -S the act of distributing gains

PAYOLA n pl. -S a secret payment for favors

PAYOR n pl. -S payer

PAYOUT n pl. -S money that is paid out

PAYROLL n pl. -S a list of employees entitled to payment

PAZAZZ n pl. -ES pizazz

PE n pl. -S a Hebrew letter

PEA n pl. -S the edible seed of an annual herb

PEACE v PEACED, PEACING, PEACES to be or become silent

PEACEFUL adj -FULLER, -FULLEST undisturbed; calm

PEACENIK n pl. -S one who demonstrates against a war

PEACH v -ED, -ING, -ES to inform against someone

PEACHER n pl. -S one that peaches

PEACHY adj PEACHIER, PEACHIEST dandy

PEACING present participle of peace

PEACOAT n pl. -S a heavy woolen jacket

PEACOCK v -ED, -ING, -S to strut vainly

PEACOCKY adj -COCKIER, -COCKIEST vain

PEAFOWL n pl. -S a large pheasant

PEAG n pl. -S wampum

PEAGE n pl. -S peag

PEAHEN n pl. -S a female peafowl

PEAK v -ED, -ING, -S to reach a maximum

PEAKIER comparative of peaky

PEAKIEST superlative of peaky

PEAKISH adj somewhat sickly

PEAKLESS *adj* having no peak (a pointed top)

PEAKLIKE *adj* resembling a peak

PEAKY *adj* PEAKIER, PEAKIEST sickly

PEAL *v* -ED, -ING, -S to ring out

PEALIKE *adj* resembling a pea

PEAN *n pl.* -S paean

PEANUT *n pl.* -S the nutlike seed or pod of an annual vine

PEAR *n pl.* -S a fleshy fruit

PEARL *v* -ED, -ING, -S to adorn with pearls (smooth, rounded masses formed in certain mollusks)

PEARLASH *n pl.* -ES an alkaline compound

PEARLER *n pl.* -S one that dives for pearls

PEARLITE *n pl.* -S a cast-iron alloy

PEARLY *adj* PEARLIER, PEARLIEST resembling a pearl

PEARMAIN *n pl.* -S a variety of apple

PEART *adj* PEARTER, PEARTEST lively **PEARTLY** *adv*

PEASANT *n pl.* -S a person of inferior social rank

PEASCOD *n pl.* -S peasecod

PEASE *n pl.* PEASEN or PEASES a pea

PEASECOD *n pl.* -S a pea pod

PEAT *n pl.* -S a substance composed of partially decayed vegetable matter

PEATY *adj* PEATIER, PEATIEST resembling or containing peat

PEAVEY *n pl.* -VEYS a lever used to move logs

PEAVY *n pl.* -VIES peavey

PEBBLE *v* -BLED, -BLING, -BLES to cover with pebbles (small, rounded stones)

PEBBLY *adj* -BLIER, -BLIEST resembling pebbles

PEC *n pl.* -S a chest muscle

PECAN *n pl.* -S a nut-bearing tree

PECCABLE *adj* liable to sin

PECCANCY *n pl.* -CIES the state of being peccant

PECCANT *adj* sinful

PECCARY *n pl.* -RIES a hoofed mammal

PECCAVI *n pl.* -S a confession of sin

PECH *v* -ED, -ING, -S to pant

PECHAN *n pl.* -S the stomach

PECK *v* -ED, -ING, -S to strike with the beak or something pointed

PECKER *n pl.* -S one that pecks

PECKISH *adj* irritable

PECKY *adj* PECKIER, PECKIEST marked by decay caused by fungi

PECORINO *n pl.* -NOS or -NI a hard cheese made from sheep's milk

PECTASE *n pl.* -S an enzyme

PECTATE *n pl.* -S a chemical salt

PECTEN *n pl.* -TENS or -TINES a comblike anatomical part

PECTIN *n pl.* -S a carbohydrate derivative **PECTIC** *adj*

PECTIZE *v* -TIZED, -TIZING, -TIZES to change into a jelly

PECTORAL *n pl.* -S something worn on the breast

PECULATE *v* -LATED, -LATING, -LATES to embezzle

PECULIAR *n pl.* -S something belonging exclusively to a person

PECULIUM *n pl.* -LIA private property

PED *n pl.* -S a natural soil aggregate

PEDAGOG *n pl.* -S a teacher

PEDAGOGY *n pl.* -GIES the work of a teacher

PEDAL *v* -ALED, -ALING, -ALS or -ALLED, -ALLING, -ALS to operate by means of foot levers

PEDALFER *n pl.* -S a type of soil

PEDALIER *n pl.* -S the pedal keyboard of an organ

PEDALLED a past tense of pedal

PEDALLING a present participle of pedal

PEDALO *n pl.* -LOS a paddleboat powered by pedals

PEDANT *n pl.* -S one who makes a display of his knowledge **PEDANTIC** *adj*

PEDANTRY *n pl.* -RIES ostentatious display of knowledge

PEDATE *adj* resembling a foot **PEDATELY** *adv*

PEDDLE *v* -DLED, -DLING, -DLES to travel about selling wares

PEDDLER *n pl.* -S one that peddles

PEDDLERY *n pl.* -RIES the trade of a peddler

PEDDLING present tense of peddle

PEDERAST *n pl.* -S a man who engages in sexual activities with boys

PEDES *pl.* of pes

PEDESTAL v -TALED, -TALING, -TALS or -TALLED, -TALLING, -TALS to provide with an architectural support or base

PEDICAB n pl. -S a passenger vehicle that is pedaled

PEDICEL n pl. -S a slender basal part of an organism

PEDICLE n pl. -S pedicel PEDICLED adj

PEDICURE v -CURED, -CURING, -CURES to administer a cosmetic treatment to the feet and toenails

PEDIFORM adj shaped like a foot

PEDIGREE n pl. -S a line of ancestors

PEDIMENT n pl. -S a triangular architectural part

PEDIPALP n pl. -S an appendage of an arachnid

PEDLAR n pl. -S peddler

PEDLARY n pl. -LARIES peddlery

PEDLER n pl. -S peddler

PEDLERY n pl. -LERIES peddlery

PEDOCAL n pl. -S a type of soil

PEDOLOGY n pl. -GIES the scientific study of the behavior and development of children

PEDRO n pl. -DROS a card game

PEDUNCLE n pl. -S a flower stalk

PEE n pl. -S the letter P

PEEBEEN n pl. -S a large hardwood evergreen tree

PEEK v -ED, -ING, -S to look furtively or quickly

PEEKABOO n pl. -BOOS a children's game

PEEL v -ED, -ING, -S to strip off an outer covering of PEELABLE adj

PEELER n pl. -S one that peels

PEELING n pl. -S a piece or strip that has been peeled off

PEEN v -ED, -ING, -S to beat with the non-flat end of a hammerhead

PEEP v -ED, -ING, -S to utter a short, shrill cry

PEEPER n pl. -S one that peeps

PEEPHOLE n pl. -S a small opening through which one may look

PEEPSHOW n pl. -S an exhibition viewed through a small opening

PEEPUL n pl. -S pipal

PEER v -ED, -ING, -S to look narrowly or searchingly

PEERAGE n pl. -S the rank of a nobleman

PEERESS n pl. -ES a noblewoman

PEERIE n pl. -S peery

PEERLESS adj having no equal

PEERY n pl. PEERIES a child's toy

PEESWEEP n pl. -S a lapwing

PEETWEET n pl. -S a wading bird

PEEVE v PEEVED, PEEVING, PEEVES to annoy

PEEVISH adj irritable

PEEWEE n pl. -S an unusually small person or thing

PEEWIT n pl. -S pewit

PEG v PEGGED, PEGGING, PEGS to fasten with a peg (a wooden pin)

PEGBOARD n pl. -S a board with holes for pegs

PEGBOX n pl. -ES a part of a stringed instrument

PEGGED past tense of peg

PEGGING present participle of peg

PEGLESS adj lacking a peg

PEGLIKE adj resembling a peg

PEH n pl. -S pe

PEIGNOIR n pl. -S a woman's gown

PEIN v -ED, -ING, -S to peen

PEISE v PEISED, PEISING, PEISES to weigh

PEKAN n pl. -S a carnivorous mammal

PEKE n pl. -S a small, long-haired dog

PEKIN n pl. -S a silk fabric

PEKOE n pl. -S a black tea

PELAGE n pl. -S the coat or covering of a mammal PELAGIAL adj

PELAGIC adj oceanic

PELE n pl. -S a medieval fortified tower

PELERINE n pl. -S a woman's cape

PELF n pl. -S money or wealth

PELICAN n pl. -S a large, web-footed bird

PELISSE n pl. -S a long outer garment

PELITE n pl. -S a rock composed of fine fragments PELITIC adj

PELLAGRA n pl. -S a niacin-deficiency disease

PELLET v -ED, -ING, -S to strike with pellets (small rounded masses)

PELLETAL adj resembling a pellet

PELLICLE n pl. -S a thin skin or film

PELLMELL n pl. -S a jumbled mass

PELLUCID adj transparent

PELMET n pl. -S a decorative cornice

PELON	*adj* hairless	**PEND**	*v* -ED, -ING, -S to remain undecided or unsettled
PELORIA	*n pl.* -S abnormal regularity of a flower form **PELORIAN**, **PELORIC** *adj*	**PENDANT**	*n pl.* -S a hanging ornament
PELORUS	*n pl.* -ES a navigational instrument	**PENDENCY**	*n pl.* -CIES a pending state
		PENDENT	*n pl.* -S pendant
PELOTA	*n pl.* -S a court game of Spanish origin	**PENDULUM**	*n pl.* -S a type of free swinging body **PENDULAR** *adj*
PELT	*v* -ED, -ING, -S to strike repeatedly with blows or missiles	**PENES**	*a pl.* of penis
		PENGO	*n pl.* -GOS a former monetary unit of Hungary
PELTAST	*n pl.* -S a soldier of ancient Greece	**PENGUIN**	*n pl.* -S a flightless, aquatic bird
PELTATE	*adj* shaped like a shield	**PENICIL**	*n pl.* -S a small tuft of hairs
PELTER	*v* -ED, -ING, -S to pelt	**PENIS**	*n pl.* -NES or -NISES the male organ of copulation **PENIAL**, **PENILE** *adj*
PELTRY	*n pl.* -RIES an animal skin		
PELVIC	*n pl.* -S a bone of the pelvis		
PELVIS	*n pl.* -VES or -VISES a part of the skeleton	**PENITENT**	*n pl.* -S a person who repents his sins
PEMBINA	*n pl.* -S a variety of cranberry	**PENKNIFE**	*n pl.* -KNIVES a small pocketknife
PEMICAN	*n pl.* -S pemmican		
PEMMICAN	*n pl.* -S a food prepared by North American Indians	**PENLIGHT**	*n pl.* -S a small flashlight
		PENLITE	*n pl.* -S penlight
PEMOLINE	*n pl.* -S a drug used as a stimulant	**PENMAN**	*n pl.* -MEN an author
		PENNA	*n pl.* -NAE any of the feathers that determine a bird's shape
PEMPHIX	*n pl.* -ES a skin disease		
PEN	*v* PENNED, PENNING, PENS to write with a pen (an instrument for writing with fluid ink)	**PENNAME**	*n pl.* -S a name used by an author instead of his real name
		PENNANT	*n pl.* -S a long, narrow flag
		PENNATE	*adj* having wings or feathers
PENAL	*adj* pertaining to punishment	**PENNATED**	*adj* pennate
PENALISE	*v* -ISED, -ISING, -ISES to penalize	**PENNE**	*n pl.* PENNE short tubular pasta
PENALITY	*n pl.* -TIES liability to punishment	**PENNED**	past tense of pen
		PENNER	*n pl.* -S one that pens
PENALIZE	*v* -IZED, -IZING, -IZES to subject to a penalty	**PENNI**	*n pl.* -NIA or -NIS a Finnish coin
PENALLY	*adv* in a penal manner	**PENNIES**	*a pl.* of penny
PENALTY	*n pl.* -TIES a punishment imposed for violation of a law, rule, or agreement	**PENNINE**	*n pl.* -S a mineral
		PENNING	present participle of pen
		PENNON	*n pl.* -S a pennant **PENNONED** *adj*
PENANCE	*v* -ANCED, -ANCING, -ANCES to impose a type of punishment upon		
		PENNY	*n pl.* PENNIES or PENCE a coin of the United Kingdom
PENANG	*n pl.* -S a cotton fabric		
PENATES	*n/pl* the Roman gods of the household	**PENOCHE**	*n pl.* -S penuche
		PENOLOGY	*n pl.* -GIES the science of the punishment of crime
PENCE	*a pl.* of penny		
PENCEL	*n pl.* -S a small flag	**PENONCEL**	*n pl.* -S a small pennon
PENCHANT	*n pl.* -S a strong liking for something	**PENPOINT**	*n pl.* -S the point of a pen
		PENSEE	*n pl.* -S a thought
PENCIL	*v* -CILED, -CILING, -CILS or -CILLED, -CILLING, -CILS to produce by using a pencil (a writing and drawing implement)	**PENSIL**	*n pl.* -S pencel
		PENSILE	*adj* hanging loosely
		PENSION	*v* -ED, -ING, -S to grant a retirement allowance to
		PENSIONE	*n pl.* -S a boarding house
PENCILER	*n pl.* -S one that pencils	**PENSIVE**	*adj* engaged in deep thought
		PENSTER	*n pl.* -S a writer

PENSTOCK *n pl.* -S a conduit for conveying water to a waterwheel

PENT *adj* confined

PENTACLE *n pl.* -S a five-pointed star

PENTAD *n pl.* -S a group of five

PENTAGON *n pl.* -S a five-sided polygon

PENTANE *n pl.* -S a volatile liquid

PENTANOL *n pl.* -S an alcohol

PENTARCH *n pl.* -S one of five joint rulers

PENTENE *n pl.* -S a liquid hydrocarbon

PENTODE *n pl.* -S a type of electron tube

PENTOMIC *adj* made up of five battle groups

PENTOSAN *n pl.* -S a complex carbohydrate

PENTOSE *n pl.* -S a sugar having five carbon atoms per molecule

PENTYL *n pl.* -S amyl

PENUCHE *n pl.* -S a fudge-like candy

PENUCHI *n pl.* -S penuche

PENUCHLE *n pl.* -S pinochle

PENUCKLE *n pl.* -S pinochle

PENULT *n pl.* -S the next to last syllable in a word

PENUMBRA *n pl.* -BRAE or -BRAS a partial shadow

PENURY *n pl.* -RIES extreme poverty

PEON *n pl.* -S or -ES an unskilled laborer

PEONAGE *n pl.* -S the condition of being a peon

PEONISM *n pl.* -S peonage

PEONY *n pl.* -NIES a flowering plant

PEOPLE *v* -PLED, -PLING, -PLES to furnish with inhabitants

PEOPLER *n pl.* -S one that peoples

PEP *v* PEPPED, PEPPING, PEPS to fill with energy

PEPERONI *n pl.* -S a highly seasoned sausage

PEPLOS *n pl.* -ES a garment worn by women in ancient Greece

PEPLUM *n pl.* -LUMS or -LA a short section attached to the waistline of a garment PEPLUMED *adj*

PEPLUS *n pl.* -ES peplos

PEPO *n pl.* -POS a fruit having a fleshy interior and a hard rind

PEPONIDA *n pl.* -S pepo

PEPONIUM *n pl.* -S pepo

PEPPED past tense of pep

PEPPER *v* -ED, -ING, -S to season with pepper (a pungent condiment)

PEPPERER *n pl.* -S one that peppers

PEPPERY *adj* resembling pepper

PEPPING present participle of pep

PEPPY *adj* -PIER, -PIEST full of energy PEPPILY *adv*

PEPSIN *n pl.* -S a digestive enzyme of the stomach

PEPSINE *n pl.* -S pepsin

PEPTIC *n pl.* -S a substance that promotes digestion

PEPTID *n pl.* -S peptide

PEPTIDE *n pl.* -S a combination of amino acids PEPTIDIC *adj*

PEPTIZE *v* -TIZED, -TIZING, -TIZES to increase the colloidal dispersion of

PEPTIZER *n pl.* -S one that peptizes

PEPTONE *n pl.* -S a protein compound PEPTONIC *adj*

PER *prep* for each

PERACID *n pl.* -S a type of acid

PERCALE *n pl.* -S a cotton fabric

PERCEIVE *v* -CEIVED, -CEIVING, -CEIVES to become aware of through the senses

PERCENT *n pl.* -S one part in a hundred

PERCEPT *n pl.* -S something perceived

PERCH *v* -ED, -ING, -ES to sit or rest on an elevated place

PERCHER *n pl.* -S one that perches

PERCOID *n pl.* -S a spiny-finned fish

PERCUSS *v* -ED, -ING, -ES to strike with force

PERDIE *interj* pardi

PERDU *n pl.* -S a soldier sent on a dangerous mission

PERDUE *n pl.* -S perdu

PERDURE *v* -DURED, -DURING, -DURES to continue to exist

PERDY *interj* pardi

PEREGRIN *n pl.* -S a swift falcon much used in falconry

PEREION *n pl.* -REIA the thorax of some crustaceans

PEREON *n pl.* -REA pereion

PEREOPOD *n pl.* -S an appendage of the pereion

PERFECT *adj* -FECTER, -FECTEST lacking fault or defect; of an extreme kind

PERFECT *v* -ED, -ING, -S to make perfect

PERFECTA *n pl.* -S a system of betting

PERFECTO *n pl.* -TOS a medium-sized cigar

PERFIDY *n pl.* -DIES deliberate breach of faith or trust

PERFORCE adv of necessity

PERFORM v -ED, -ING, -S to begin and carry through to completion

PERFUME v -FUMED, -FUMING, -FUMES to fill with a fragrant odor

PERFUMER n pl. -S one that perfumes

PERFUSE v -FUSED, -FUSING, -FUSES to spread over or through something

PERGOLA n pl. -S a shaded shelter or passageway

PERHAPS n pl. -ES something open to doubt or conjecture

PERI n pl. -S a supernatural being of Persian mythology

PERIANTH n pl. -S an outer covering of a flower

PERIAPT n pl. -S an amulet

PERIBLEM n pl. -S a region of plant tissue

PERICARP n pl. -S the wall of a ripened plant ovary or fruit

PERICOPE n pl. -PES or -PAE a selection from a book

PERIDERM n pl. -S an outer layer of plant tissue

PERIDIUM n pl. -IA the covering of the spore-bearing organ in many fungi **PERIDIAL** adj

PERIDOT n pl. -S a mineral

PERIGEE n pl. -S the point in the orbit of a celestial body which is nearest to the earth **PERIGEAL, PERIGEAN** adj

PERIGON n pl. -S an angle equal to 360 degrees

PERIGYNY n pl. -NIES the state of being situated on a cuplike organ surrounding the pistil

PERIL v -ILED, -ILING, -ILS or -ILLED, -ILLING, -ILS to imperil

PERILLA n pl. -S an Asian herb

PERILOUS adj dangerous

PERILUNE n pl. -S the point in the orbit of a celestial body which is nearest to the moon

PERINEUM n pl. -NEA a region of the body at the lower end of the trunk **PERINEAL** adj

PERIOD n pl. -S a portion of time

PERIODIC adj recurring at regular intervals

PERIODID n pl. -S an iodide

PERIOTIC adj surrounding the ear

PERIPETY n pl. -TIES a sudden change in a course of events

PERIPTER n pl. -S a structure with a row of columns around all sides

PERIQUE n pl. -S a dark tobacco

PERISARC n pl. -S a protective covering of certain hydrozoans

PERISH v -ED, -ING, -ES to die

PERIWIG n pl. -S a wig

PERJURE v -JURED, -JURING, -JURES to make a perjurer of

PERJURER n pl. -S one guilty of perjury

PERJURY n pl. -RIES the willful giving of false testimony under oath in a judicial proceeding

PERK v -ED, -ING, -S to carry oneself jauntily

PERKISH adj somewhat perky

PERKY adj PERKIER, PERKIEST jaunty **PERKILY** adv

PERLITE n pl. -S a volcanic glass **PERLITIC** adj

PERM v -ED, -ING, -S to give hair a permanent wave

PERMEANT adj that permeates

PERMEASE n pl. -S a catalyzing agent

PERMEATE v -ATED, -ATING, -ATES to spread through

PERMIT v -MITTED, -MITTING, -MITS to allow

PERMUTE v -MUTED, -MUTING, -MUTES to change the order of

PERONEAL adj pertaining to the fibula

PERORAL adj occurring through the mouth

PERORATE v -RATED, -RATING, -RATES to make a lengthy speech

PEROXID n pl. -S peroxide

PEROXIDE v -IDED, -IDING, -IDES to treat with peroxide (a bleaching agent)

PEROXY adj containing the bivalent group O_2

PERPEND v -ED, -ING, -S to ponder

PERPENT n pl. -S a large building stone

PERPLEX v -ED, -ING, -ES to make mentally uncertain

PERRON n pl. -S an outdoor stairway

PERRY n pl. -RIES a beverage of pear juice often fermented

PERSALT n pl. -S a chemical salt

PERSE n pl. -S a blue color

PERSIST v -ED, -ING, -S to continue resolutely in some activity

PERSON n pl. -S a human being

PERSONA *n pl.* -NAE a character in a literary work

PERSONA *n pl.* -S the public role that a person assumes

PERSONAL *n pl.* -S a brief, private notice in a newspaper

PERSPIRE *v* -SPIRED, -SPIRING, -SPIRES to give off moisture through the pores of the skin PERSPIRY *adj*

PERSUADE *v* -SUADED, -SUADING, -SUADES to cause to do something by means of argument, reasoning, or entreaty

PERT *adj* PERTER, PERTEST impudent PERTLY *adv*

PERTAIN *v* -ED, -ING, -S to have reference or relation

PERTNESS *n pl.* -ES the quality of being pert

PERTURB *v* -ED, -ING, -S to disturb greatly

PERUKE *n pl.* -S a wig PERUKED *adj*

PERUSAL *n pl.* -S the act of perusing

PERUSE *v* -RUSED, -RUSING, -RUSES to read

PERUSER *n pl.* -S one that peruses

PERVADE *v* -VADED, -VADING, -VADES to spread through every part of

PERVADER *n pl.* -S one that pervades

PERVERSE *adj* willfully deviating from desired or expected conduct

PERVERT *v* -ED, -ING, -S to turn away from the right course of action

PERVIOUS *adj* capable of being penetrated

PES *n pl.* PEDES a foot or footlike part

PESADE *n pl.* -S the position of a horse when rearing

PESETA *n pl.* -S a monetary unit of Spain

PESEWA *n pl.* -S a monetary unit of Ghana

PESKY *adj* -KIER, -KIEST annoying PESKILY *adv*

PESO *n pl.* -SOS a monetary unit of various Spanish-speaking countries

PESSARY *n pl.* -RIES a contraceptive device worn in the vagina

PEST *n pl.* -S an annoying person or thing

PESTER *v* -ED, -ING, -S to bother

PESTERER *n pl.* -S one that pesters

PESTHOLE *n pl.* -S a place liable to epidemic disease

PESTLE *v* -TLED, -TLING, -TLES to crush with a tool for grinding

PESTO *n pl.* -TOS a sauce of basil, garlic, and olive oil

PESTY *adj* PESTIER, PESTIEST annoying

PET *v* PETTED, PETTING, PETS to caress with the hand

PETAL *n pl.* -S a leaflike part of a corolla PETALED, PETALLED *adj*

PETALINE *adj* resembling a petal

PETALODY *n pl.* -DIES the changing of floral organs into petals

PETALOID *adj* resembling a petal

PETALOUS *adj* having petals

PETARD *n pl.* -S an explosive device

PETASOS *n pl.* -ES petasus

PETASUS *n pl.* -ES a broad-brimmed hat worn in ancient Greece

PETCOCK *n pl.* -S a small valve or faucet

PETECHIA *n pl.* -CHIAE a small hemorrhagic spot on a body surface

PETER *v* -ED, -ING, -S to diminish gradually

PETIOLAR *adj* pertaining to a petiole

PETIOLE *n pl.* -S the stalk of a leaf PETIOLED *adj*

PETIT *adj* small; minor

PETITE *n pl.* -S a clothing size for short women

PETITION *v* -ED, -ING, -S to make a formal request

PETNAP *v* -NAPPED, -NAPPING, -NAPS to steal a pet for profit

PETRALE *n pl.* -S a food fish

PETREL *n pl.* -S a small seabird

PETRIFY *v* -FIED, -FYING, -FIES to convert into stone or a stony substance

PETROL *n pl.* -S gasoline

PETROLIC *adj* derived from petroleum

PETRONEL *n pl.* -S a portable firearm

PETROSAL *adj* petrous

PETROUS *adj* resembling stone in hardness

PETSAI *n pl.* -S Chinese cabbage

PETTED past tense of pet

PETTEDLY *adv* peevishly

PETTER *n pl.* -S one that pets

PETTI *pl.* of petto

PETTIER comparative of petty

PETTIEST superlative of petty

PETTIFOG v -FOGGED, -FOGGING, -FOGS to quibble

PETTILY adv in a petty manner

PETTING n pl. -S amorous caressing and kissing

PETTISH adj peevish

PETTLE v -TLED, -TLING, -TLES to caress

PETTO n pl. -TI the breast

PETTY adj -TIER, -TIEST insignificant

PETULANT adj peevish

PETUNIA n pl. -S a tropical herb

PETUNTSE n pl. -S a mineral

PETUNTZE n pl. -S petuntse

PEW n pl. -S a bench for seating people in church

PEWEE n pl. -S a small bird

PEWIT n pl. -S the lapwing

PEWTER n pl. -S a tin alloy

PEWTERER n pl. -S one that makes articles of pewter

PEYOTE n pl. -S a cactus

PEYOTL n pl. -S peyote

PEYTRAL n pl. -S a piece of armor for the breast of a horse

PEYTREL n pl. -S peytral

PFENNIG n pl. -NIGS or -NIGE a bronze coin of Germany

PFFT interj — used to express a sudden ending

PFUI interj phooey

PHAETON n pl. -S a light carriage

PHAGE n pl. -S an organism that destroys bacteria

PHALANGE n pl. -S any bone of a finger or toe

PHALANX n pl. -ES a formation of infantry in ancient Greece

PHALLI a pl. of phallus

PHALLIC adj pertaining to a phallus

PHALLISM n pl. -S worship of the phallus as symbolic of nature's creative power

PHALLIST n pl. -S one who practices phallism

PHALLUS n pl. -LI or -LUSES the penis

PHANTASIED past tense of phantasy

PHANTASIES present 3d person sing. of phantasy

PHANTASM n pl. -S a creation of the imagination

PHANTAST n pl. -S fantast

PHANTASY v -SIED, -SYING, -SIES to fantasy

PHANTOM n pl. -S something existing in appearance only

PHARAOH n pl. -S a ruler of ancient Egypt

PHARISEE n pl. -S a hypocritically self-righteous person

PHARMACY n pl. -CIES a drugstore

PHAROS n pl. -ES a lighthouse or beacon to guide seamen

PHARYNX n pl. -YNGES or -YNXES a section of the digestive tract

PHASE v PHASED, PHASING, PHASES to plan or carry out by phases (distinct stages of development) PHASEAL, PHASIC adj

PHASEOUT n pl. -S a gradual stopping of operations

PHASIS n pl. PHASES a phase

PHASMID n pl. -S a tropical insect

PHAT adj susceptible of easy and rapid typesetting

PHATIC adj sharing feelings rather than ideas

PHEASANT n pl. -S a large, long-tailed bird

PHELLEM n pl. -S a layer of plant cells

PHELONIA n/pl liturgical vestments

PHENATE n pl. -S a salt of carbolic acid

PHENAZIN n pl. -S a chemical compound

PHENETIC adj pertaining to a type of classificatory system

PHENETOL n pl. -S a volatile liquid

PHENIX n pl. -ES phoenix

PHENOL n pl. -S a caustic compound

PHENOLIC n pl. -S a synthetic resin

PHENOM n pl. -S a person of extraordinary ability or promise

PHENOXY adj containing a radical derived from phenol

PHENYL n pl. -S a univalent chemical radical PHENYLIC adj

PHEW interj — used to express relief, fatigue, or disgust

PHI n pl. -S a Greek letter

PHIAL n pl. -S a vial

PHILABEG n pl. -S filibeg

PHILIBEG n pl. -S filibeg

PHILOMEL n pl. -S a songbird

PHILTER v -ED, -ING, -S to put under the spell of a love potion

PHILTRE v -TRED, -TRING, -TRES to philter

PHILTRUM n pl. -TRA the indentation between the upper lip and the nose

PHIMOSIS n pl. -MOSES the abnormal constriction of the opening of the prepuce **PHIMOTIC** adj

PHIZ n pl. -ES a face or facial expression

PHLEGM n pl. -S a thick mucus secreted in the air passages

PHLEGMY adj PHLEGMIER, PHLEGMIEST resembling phlegm

PHLOEM n pl. -S a complex plant tissue

PHLOX n pl. -ES a flowering plant

PHOBIA n pl. -S an obsessive or irrational fear

PHOBIC n pl. -S one affected with a phobia

PHOCINE adj pertaining to seals

PHOEBE n pl. -S a small bird

PHOEBUS n pl. -ES the sun

PHOENIX n pl. -ES a mythical bird

PHON n pl. -S a unit of loudness

PHONAL adj pertaining to speech sounds

PHONATE v -NATED, -NATING, -NATES to produce speech sounds

PHONE v PHONED, PHONING, PHONES to telephone

PHONEME n pl. -S a unit of speech **PHONEMIC** adj

PHONETIC adj pertaining to speech sounds

PHONEY v -ED, -ING, -S to phony

PHONEY adj -NIER, -NIEST phony

PHONIC adj pertaining to the nature of sound

PHONICS n/pl the science of sound

PHONIED past tense of phony

PHONIER comparative of phoney and phony

PHONIES present 3d person sing. of phony

PHONIEST superlative of phoney and phony

PHONILY adv in a phony manner

PHONING present participle of phone

PHONO n pl. -NOS a record player

PHONON n pl. -S a quantum of vibrational energy

PHONY adj -NIER, -NIEST not genuine or real

PHONY v -NIED, -NYING, -NIES to alter so as to make appear genuine

PHOOEY interj — used as an exclamation of disgust or contempt

PHORATE n pl. -S an insecticide

PHORONID n pl. -S a wormlike marine animal

PHOSGENE n pl. -S a poisonous gas

PHOSPHID n pl. -S a chemical compound

PHOSPHIN n pl. -S a poisonous gas

PHOSPHOR n pl. -S a substance that will emit light when exposed to radiation

PHOT n pl. -S a unit of illumination

PHOTIC adj pertaining to light

PHOTICS n/pl the science of light

PHOTO v -ED, -ING, -S to photograph

PHOTOG n pl. -S one who takes photographs

PHOTOMAP v -MAPPED, -MAPPING, -MAPS to map by means of aerial photography

PHOTON n pl. -S an elementary particle **PHOTONIC** adj

PHOTOPIA n pl. -S vision in bright light **PHOTOPIC** adj

PHOTOSET v -SET, -SETTING, -SETS to prepare for printing by photographic means

PHPHT interj pht

PHRASAL adj pertaining to a group of two or more associated words

PHRASE v PHRASED, PHRASING, PHRASES to express in words

PHRASING n pl. -S manner or style of verbal expression

PHRATRY n pl. -TRIES a tribal unit among primitive peoples **PHRATRAL, PHRATRIC** adj

PHREATIC adj pertaining to underground waters

PHRENIC adj pertaining to the mind

PHRENSY v -SIED, -SYING, -SIES to frenzy

PHT interj — used as an expression of mild anger or annoyance

PHTHALIC adj pertaining to a certain acid

PHTHALIN n pl. -S a chemical compound

PHTHISIC n pl. -S phthisis

PHTHISIS n pl. PHTHISES a disease of the lungs

PHUT n pl. -S a dull, abrupt sound

PHYLA pl. of phylon and phylum

PHYLAE pl. of phyle

PHYLAR adj pertaining to a phylum

PHYLAXIS n pl. -AXISES an inhibiting of infection by the body

PHYLE n pl. -LAE a political subdivision in ancient Greece **PHYLIC** adj

PHYLESIS *n* pl. -LESES or -LESISES the course of evolutionary development **PHYLETIC** *adj*

PHYLLARY *n* pl. -RIES a bract of certain plants

PHYLLITE *n* pl. -S a foliated rock

PHYLLO *n* pl. -LOS very thin pastry dough

PHYLLODE *n* pl. -S a flattened petiole that serves as a leaf

PHYLLOID *n* pl. -S a leaflike plant part

PHYLLOME *n* pl. -S a leaf of a plant

PHYLON *n* pl. -LA a genetically related group

PHYLUM *n* pl. -LA a taxonomic division

PHYSED *n* pl. -S physical education

PHYSES pl. of physis

PHYSIC *v* -ICKED, -ICKING, -ICS to treat with medicine

PHYSICAL *n* pl. -S a medical examination of the body

PHYSIQUE *n* pl. -S the form or structure of the body

PHYSIS *n* pl. PHYSES the principle of growth or change in nature

PHYTANE *n* pl. -S a chemical compound

PHYTOID *adj* resembling a plant

PHYTOL *n* pl. -S an alcohol

PHYTON *n* pl. -S a structural unit of a plant **PHYTONIC** *adj*

PI *n* pl. -S a Greek letter

PI *v* PIED, PIEING or PIING, PIES to jumble or disorder

PIA *n* pl. -S a membrane of the brain

PIACULAR *adj* atoning

PIAFFE *v* PIAFFED, PIAFFING, PIAFFES to perform a piaffer

PIAFFER *n* pl. -S a movement in horsemanship

PIAL *adj* pertaining to a pia

PIAN *n* pl. -S a tropical disease **PIANIC** *adj*

PIANISM *n* pl. -S performance on the piano

PIANIST *n* pl. -S one who plays the piano

PIANO *n* pl. -NOS a musical instrument

PIASABA *n* pl. -S piassava

PIASAVA *n* pl. -S piassava

PIASSABA *n* pl. -S piassava

PIASSAVA *n* pl. -S a coarse, stiff fiber

PIASTER *n* pl. -S a monetary unit of several Arab countries

PIASTRE *n* pl. -S piaster

PIAZZA *n* pl. -ZAS or -ZE a public square in an Italian town

PIBAL *n* pl. -S a small balloon for determining the direction and speed of the wind

PIBROCH *n* pl. -S a musical piece played on the bagpipe

PIC *n* pl. -S a photograph

PICA *n* pl. -S a craving for unnatural food

PICACHO *n* pl. -CHOS an isolated peak of a hill

PICADOR *n* pl. -ES or -S a horseman in a bullfight

PICAL *adj* resembling a pica

PICARA *n* pl. -S a female picaro

PICARO *n* pl. -ROS a vagabond

PICAROON *v* -ED, -ING, -S to act as a pirate

PICAYUNE *n* pl. -S a former Spanish-American coin

PICCOLO *n* pl. -LOS a small flute

PICE *n* pl. PICE a former coin of India and Pakistan

PICEOUS *adj* glossy-black in color

PICIFORM *adj* pertaining to an order of birds

PICK *v* -ED, -ING, -S to select

PICKADIL *n* pl. -S a type of collar

PICKAX *v* -ED, -ING, -ES to use a pickax (a tool for breaking hard surfaces)

PICKAXE *v* -AXED, -AXING, -AXES to pickax

PICKEER *v* -ED, -ING, -S to skirmish in advance of an army

PICKER *n* pl. -S one that picks

PICKEREL *n* pl. -S a freshwater fish

PICKET *v* -ED, -ING, -S to stand outside of some location, as a business, to publicize one's grievances against it

PICKETER *n* pl. -S one who pickets

PICKIER comparative of picky

PICKIEST superlative of picky

PICKING *n* pl. -S the act of one that picks

PICKLE *v* -LED, -LING, -LES to preserve or flavor in a solution of brine or vinegar

PICKLOCK *n* pl. -S a tool for opening locks

PICKOFF *n* pl. -S a play in baseball

PICKUP *n* pl. -S a small truck

PICKWICK *n* pl. -S a device for raising wicks in oil lamps

PICKY *adj* PICKIER, PICKIEST fussy

PICLORAM *n pl.* -S an herbicide

PICNIC *v* -NICKED, -NICKING, -NICS to go on a picnic (an outdoor excursion with food)

PICNICKY *adj* pertaining to a picnic

PICOGRAM *n pl.* -S one trillionth of a gram

PICOLIN *n pl.* -S picoline

PICOLINE *n pl.* -S a chemical compound

PICOMOLE *n pl.* -S one trillionth of a mole

PICOT *v* -ED, -ING, -S to edge with ornamental loops

PICOTEE *n pl.* -S a variety of carnation

PICQUET *n pl.* -S piquet

PICRATE *n pl.* -S a chemical salt PICRATED *adj*

PICRIC *adj* having a very bitter taste

PICRITE *n pl.* -S an igneous rock PICRITIC *adj*

PICTURE *v* -TURED, -TURING, -TURES to make a visual representation of

PICUL *n pl.* -S an Asian unit of weight

PIDDLE *v* -DLED, -DLING, -DLES to waste time

PIDDLER *n pl.* -S one that piddles

PIDDLY *adj* insignificant

PIDDOCK *n pl.* -S a bivalve mollusk

PIDGIN *n pl.* -S a mixed language

PIE *v* PIED, PIEING, PIES to pi

PIEBALD *n pl.* -S a spotted animal

PIECE *v* PIECED, PIECING, PIECES to join into a whole

PIECER *n pl.* -S one that pieces

PIECING *n pl.* -S material to be sewn together

PIECRUST *n pl.* -S the crust of a pie

PIED past tense of pie

PIEDFORT *n pl.* -S piefort

PIEDMONT *n pl.* -S an area lying at the foot of a mountain

PIEFORT *n pl.* -S an unusually thick coin

PIEING a present participle of pi

PIEPLANT *n pl.* -S a rhubarb

PIER *n pl.* -S a structure extending from land out over water

PIERCE *v* PIERCED, PIERCING, PIERCES to cut or pass into or through

PIERCER *n pl.* -S one that pierces

PIEROGI *n pl.* -ES a small dumpling with a filling

PIERROT *n pl.* -S a clown

PIETA *n pl.* -S a representation of the Virgin Mary mourning over the body of Christ

PIETIES pl. of piety

PIETISM *n pl.* -S piety

PIETIST *n pl.* -S a pious person

PIETY *n pl.* -TIES the quality or state of being pious

PIFFLE *v* -FLED, -FLING, -FLES to babble

PIG *v* PIGGED, PIGGING, PIGS to bear pigs (cloven-hoofed mammals)

PIGBOAT *n pl.* -S a submarine

PIGEON *n pl.* -S a short-legged bird

PIGFISH *n pl.* -ES a marine fish

PIGGED past tense of pig

PIGGERY *n pl.* -GERIES a pigpen

PIGGIE *n pl.* -S piggy

PIGGIER comparative of piggy

PIGGIES pl. of piggy

PIGGIEST superlative of piggy

PIGGIN *n pl.* -S a small wooden pail

PIGGING present participle of pig

PIGGISH *adj* greedy or dirty

PIGGY *n pl.* -GIES a small pig

PIGGY *adj* -GIER, -GIEST piggish

PIGLET *n pl.* -S a small pig

PIGLIKE *adj* resembling a pig

PIGMENT *v* -ED, -ING, -S to add a coloring matter to

PIGMY *n pl.* -MIES pygmy

PIGNOLI *n pl.* -S pignolia

PIGNOLIA *n pl.* -S the edible seed of nut pines

PIGNUS *n pl.* -NORA property held as security for a debt

PIGNUT *n pl.* -S a hickory nut

PIGOUT *n pl.* -S an instance of eating to excess

PIGPEN *n pl.* -S a place where pigs are kept

PIGSKIN *n pl.* -S the skin of a pig

PIGSNEY *n pl.* -NEYS a darling

PIGSTICK *v* -ED, -ING, -S to hunt for wild boar

PIGSTY *n pl.* -STIES a pigpen

PIGTAIL *n pl.* -S a tight braid of hair

PIGWEED *n pl.* -S a weedy plant

PIING a present participle of pi

PIKA *n pl.* -S a small mammal

PIKAKE *n pl.* -S an East Indian vine

PIKE *v* PIKED, PIKING, PIKES to pierce with a pike (a long spear)

PIKEMAN *n pl.* -MEN a soldier armed with a pike

PIKER *n pl.* -S a stingy person

PIKI *n* pl. -S thin blue cornmeal bread

PIKING present participle of pike

PILAF *n* pl. -S a dish made of seasoned rice and often meat

PILAFF *n* pl. -S pilaf

PILAR *adj* pertaining to hair

PILASTER *n* pl. -S a rectangular column

PILAU *n* pl. -S pilaf

PILAW *n* pl. -S pilaf

PILCHARD *n* pl. -S a small marine fish

PILE *v* PILED, PILING, PILES to lay one upon the other

PILEA pl. of pileum

PILEATE *adj* having a pileus

PILEATED *adj* pileate

PILED past tense of pile

PILEI pl. of pileus

PILELESS *adj* not having a raised surface of yam

PILEOUS *adj* pilose

PILEUM *n* pl. -LEA the top of a bird's head

PILEUP *n* pl. -S a collision involving several motor vehicles

PILEUS *n* pl. -LEI the umbrella-shaped portion of a mushroom

PILEWORT *n* pl. -S a medicinal plant

PILFER *v* -ED, -ING, -S to steal

PILFERER *n* pl. -S one that pilfers

PILGRIM *n* pl. -S a traveler or wanderer

PILI *n* pl. -S a Philippine tree

PILIFORM *adj* resembling a hair

PILING *n* pl. -S a structure of building supports

PILL *v* -ED, -ING, -S to dose with pills (small, rounded masses of medicine)

PILLAGE *v* -LAGED, -LAGING, -LAGES to plunder

PILLAGER *n* pl. -S one that pillages

PILLAR *v* -ED, -ING, -S to provide with vertical building supports

PILLBOX *n* pl. -ES a small box for pills

PILLION *n* pl. -S a pad or cushion for an extra rider on a horse or motorcycle

PILLORY *v* -RIED, -RYING, -RIES to expose to public ridicule or abuse

PILLOW *v* -ED, -ING, -S to rest on a pillow (a cushion for the head)

PILLOWY *adj* resembling a pillow

PILOSE *adj* covered with hair

PILOSITY *n* pl. -TIES the state of being pilose

PILOT *v* -ED, -ING, -S to control the course of

PILOTAGE *n* pl. -S the act of piloting

PILOTING *n* pl. -S a branch of navigation

PILOUS *adj* pilose

PILSENER *n* pl. -S pilsner

PILSNER *n* pl. -S a light beer

PILULE *n* pl. -S a small pill PILULAR *adj*

PILUS *n* pl. -LI a hair or hairlike structure

PILY *adj* divided into a number of wedge-shaped heraldic designs

PIMA *n* pl. -S a strong, high-grade cotton

PIMENTO *n* pl. -TOS pimiento

PIMIENTO *n* pl. -TOS a sweet pepper

PIMP *v* -ED, -ING, -S to solicit clients for a prostitute

PIMPLE *n* pl. -S an inflamed swelling of the skin PIMPLED *adj*

PIMPLY *adj* -PLIER, -PLIEST covered with pimples

PIN *v* PINNED, PINNING, PINS to fasten with a pin (a slender, pointed piece of metal)

PINA *n* pl. -S a pineapple

PINAFORE *n* pl. -S a child's apron

PINANG *n* pl. -S a palm tree

PINASTER *n* pl. -S a pine tree

PINATA *n* pl. -S a pottery jar used in a Mexican game

PINBALL *n* pl. -S an electric game

PINBONE *n* pl. -S the hipbone

PINCER *n* pl. -S one of the two pivoted parts of a grasping tool

PINCH *v* -ED, -ING, -ES to squeeze between two edges or surfaces

PINCHBUG *n* pl. -S a large beetle

PINCHECK *n* pl. -S a fabric design

PINCHER *n* pl. -S one that pinches

PINDER *n* pl. -S an official who formerly impounded stray animals

PINDLING *adj* puny or sickly

PINE *v* PINED, PINING, PINES to yearn intensely

PINEAL *n* pl. -S a gland in the brain

PINECONE *n* pl. -S a cone-shaped fruit of a pine tree

PINED past tense of pine

PINELAND *n* pl. -S land forested with pine

PINELIKE *adj* resembling a pine (an evergreen tree)

PINENE n pl. -S the main constituent of turpentine

PINERY n pl. -ERIES an area where pineapples are grown

PINESAP n pl. -S a fragrant herb

PINETUM n pl. -TA a plantation of pine trees

PINEWOOD n pl. -S the wood of a pine tree

PINEY adj PINIER, PINIEST piny

PINFISH n pl. -ES a small marine fish

PINFOLD v -ED, -ING, -S to confine in an enclosure for stray animals

PING v -ED, -ING, -S to produce a brief, high-pitched sound

PINGER n pl. -S a device for producing pulses of sound

PINGO n pl. -GOS a hill forced up by the effects of frost

PINGRASS n pl. -ES a European weed

PINGUID adj greasy

PINHEAD n pl. -S the head of a pin

PINHOLE n pl. -S a small hole made by a pin

PINIER comparative of piney and piny

PINIEST superlative of piney and piny

PINING present participle of pine

PINION v -ED, -ING, -S to remove or bind the wing feathers of to prevent flight

PINITE n pl. -S a mineral

PINITOL n pl. -S an alcohol

PINK adj PINKER, PINKEST of a pale reddish hue

PINK v -ED, -ING, -S to cut a saw-toothed edge on cloth

PINKEN v -ED, -ING, -S to become pink

PINKER n pl. -S one that pinks

PINKEY n pl. -EYS a ship with a narrow overhanging stern

PINKEYE n pl. -S an inflammation of the eye

PINKIE n pl. -S the little finger

PINKIES pl. of pinky

PINKING n pl. -S a method of cutting or decorating

PINKISH adj somewhat pink

PINKLY adv with a pink hue

PINKNESS n pl. -ES the state of being pink

PINKO n pl. PINKOS or PINKOES a person who holds somewhat radical political views

PINKROOT n pl. -S a medicinal plant root

PINKY n pl. PINKIES pinkie

PINNA n pl. -NAE or -NAS a feather, wing, or winglike part

PINNACE n pl. -S a small sailing ship

PINNACLE v -CLED, -CLING, -CLES to place on a summit

PINNAE a pl. of pinna

PINNAL adj pertaining to a pinna

PINNATE adj resembling a feather

PINNATED adj pinnate

PINNED past tense of pin

PINNER n pl. -S one that pins

PINNIES pl. of pinny

PINNING present participle of pin

PINNIPED n pl. -S a mammal with limbs modified into flippers

PINNULA n pl. -LAE pinnule PINNULAR adj

PINNULE n pl. -S a pinnate part or organ

PINNY n pl. -NIES a pinafore

PINOCHLE n pl. -S a card game

PINOCLE n pl. -S pinochle

PINOLE n pl. -S a finely ground flour

PINON n pl. -S or -ES a pine tree

PINOT n pl. -S a red or white grape

PINPOINT v -ED, -ING, -S to locate precisely

PINPRICK v -ED, -ING, -S to puncture with a pin

PINSCHER n pl. -S a large, short-haired dog

PINT n pl. -S a liquid and dry measure of capacity

PINTA n pl. -S a skin disease

PINTADA n pl. -S pintado

PINTADO n pl. -DOS or -DOES a large food fish

PINTAIL n pl. -S a river duck

PINTANO n pl. -NOS a tropical fish

PINTLE n pl. -S a pin on which something turns

PINTO n pl. -TOS or -TOES a spotted horse

PINTSIZE adj small

PINUP n pl. -S a picture that may be pinned up on a wall

PINWALE n pl. -S a type of fabric

PINWEED n pl. -S a perennial herb

PINWHEEL v -ED, -ING, -S to revolve at the end of a stick

PINWORK n pl. -S a type of embroidery

PINWORM n pl. -S a parasitic worm

PINY adj PINIER, PINIEST suggestive of or covered with pine trees

PINYIN *n* a system for transliterating Chinese ideograms into the Latin alphabet

PINYON *n* pl. -S pinon

PIOLET *n* pl. -S an ice ax

PION *n* pl. -S a subatomic particle **PIONIC** *adj*

PIONEER *v* -ED, -ING, -S to take part in the beginnings of

PIOSITY *n* pl. -TIES an excessive show of piety

PIOUS *adj* marked by religious reverence **PIOUSLY** *adv*

PIP *v* PIPPED, PIPPING, PIPS to break through the shell of an egg

PIPAGE *n* pl. -S a system of pipes

PIPAL *n* pl. -S a fig tree of India

PIPE *v* PIPED, PIPING, PIPES to convey by means of a pipe (a hollow cylinder)

PIPEAGE *n* pl. -S pipage

PIPEFISH *n* pl. -ES a slender fish

PIPEFUL *n* pl. -S a quantity sufficient to fill a tobacco pipe

PIPELESS *adj* having no pipe

PIPELIKE *adj* resembling a pipe

PIPELINE *v* -LINED, -LINING, -LINES to convey by a line of pipe

PIPER *n* pl. -S one that plays on a tubular musical instrument

PIPERINE *n* pl. -S a chemical compound

PIPESTEM *n* pl. -S the stem of a tobacco pipe

PIPET *v* -PETTED, -PETTING, -PETS to pipette

PIPETTE *v* -PETTED, -PETTING, -PETTES to measure liquid with a calibrated tube

PIPIER comparative of pipy

PIPIEST superlative of pipy

PIPINESS *n* pl. -ES the quality of being pipy

PIPING *n* pl. -S a system of pipes

PIPINGLY *adv* shrilly

PIPIT *n* pl. -S a songbird

PIPKIN *n* pl. -S a small pot

PIPPED past tense of pip

PIPPIN *n* pl. -S any of several varieties of apple

PIPPING present participle of pip

PIPY *adj* PIPIER, PIPIEST shrill

PIQUANCE *n* pl. -S piquancy

PIQUANCY *n* pl. -CIES the quality of being piquant

PIQUANT *adj* having an agreeably sharp taste

PIQUE *v* PIQUED, PIQUING, PIQUES to arouse anger or resentment in

PIQUET *n* pl. -S a card game

PIRACY *n* pl. -CIES robbery on the high seas

PIRAGUA *n* pl. -S a dugout canoe

PIRANA *n* pl. -S piranha

PIRANHA *n* pl. -S a voracious fish

PIRARUCU *n* pl. -S a large food fish

PIRATE *v* -RATED, -RATING, -RATES to commit piracy

PIRATIC *adj* pertaining to piracy

PIRAYA *n* pl. -S piranha

PIRIFORM *adj* pyriform

PIRN *n* pl. -S a spinning-wheel bobbin

PIROG *n* pl. -ROGEN, -ROGHI or -ROGI a large Russian pastry

PIROGI *n* pl. -ES pierogi

PIROGUE *n* pl. -S piragua

PIROQUE *n* pl. -S piragua

PIROZHOK *n* pl. -ROZHKI, -ROSHKI or -ROJKI a small Russian pastry

PISCARY *n* pl. -RIES a place for fishing

PISCATOR *n* pl. -S a fisherman

PISCINA *n* pl. -NAE or -NAS a basin used in certain church ceremonies **PISCINAL** *adj*

PISCINE *adj* pertaining to fish

PISCO *n* pl. -COS a Peruvian brandy

PISH *v* -ED, -ING, -ES to express contempt

PISHOGE *n* pl. -S pishogue

PISHOGUE *n* pl. -S an evil spell

PISIFORM *n* pl. -S a small bone of the wrist

PISMIRE *n* pl. -S an ant

PISO *n* pl. -SOS the Philippine peso

PISOLITE *n* pl. -S a limestone

PISSOIR *n* pl. -S a public urinal

PISTACHE *n* pl. -S a shade of green

PISTE *n* pl. -S a downhill ski trail

PISTIL *n* pl. -S the seed-bearing organ of flowering plants

PISTOL *v* -TOLED, -TOLING, -TOLS or -TOLLED, -TOLLING, -TOLS to shoot with a small firearm

PISTOLE *n* pl. S a former European gold coin

PISTON *n* pl. -S a part of an engine

PIT	v PITTED, PITTING, PITS to mark with cavities or depressions	**PIX**	n pl. -ES pyx
		PIXEL	n pl. -S a basic unit of a video image
PITA	n pl. -S a strong fiber	**PIXIE**	n pl. -S pixy PIXIEISH adj
PITAPAT	v -PATTED, -PATTING, -PATS to make a repeated tapping sound	**PIXINESS**	n pl. -ES the state of being playfully mischievous
PITCH	v -ED, -ING, -ES to throw	**PIXY**	n pl. PIXIES a playfully mischievous fairy or elf PIXYISH adj
PITCHER	n pl. -S a container for holding and pouring liquids		
PITCHIER	comparative of pitchy	**PIZAZZ**	n pl. -ES the quality of being exciting or attractive
PITCHIEST	superlative of pitchy		
PITCHILY	adv in a very dark manner	**PIZAZZY**	adj having pizazz
PITCHMAN	n pl. -MEN a salesman of small wares	**PIZZA**	n pl. -S an Italian open pie
		PIZZERIA	n pl. -S a place where pizzas are made and sold
PITCHOUT	n pl. -S a type of pitch in baseball	**PIZZLE**	n pl. -S the penis of an animal
PITCHY	adj PITCHIER, PITCHIEST tarry	**PLACABLE**	adj capable of being placated PLACABLY adv
PITEOUS	adj pitiful	**PLACARD**	v -ED, -ING, -S to publicize by means of posters
PITFALL	n pl. -S a hidden danger or difficulty		
PITH	v -ED, -ING, -S to sever the spinal cord of	**PLACATE**	v -CATED, -CATING, -CATES to soothe or mollify
PITHEAD	n pl. -S a mine entrance	**PLACATER**	n pl. -S one that placates
PITHLESS	adj lacking force	**PLACE**	v PLACED, PLACING, PLACES to set in a particular position
PITHY	adj PITHIER, PITHIEST concise PITHILY adv		
PITIABLE	adj pitiful PITIABLY adv	**PLACEBO**	n pl. -BOS or -BOES a substance containing no medication that is given for its psychological effect
PITIED	past tense of pity		
PITIER	n pl. -S one that pities		
PITIES	present 3d person sing. of pity	**PLACEMAN**	n pl. -MEN a political appointee to a public office
PITIFUL	adj -FULLER, -FULLEST arousing pity		
		PLACENTA	n pl. -TAS or -TAE a vascular organ in most mammals
PITILESS	adj having no pity		
PITMAN	n pl. -MEN a mine worker	**PLACER**	n pl. -S one that places
PITMAN	n pl. -S a connecting rod	**PLACET**	n pl. -S a vote of assent
PITON	n pl. -S a metal spike used in mountain climbing	**PLACID**	adj calm or peaceful PLACIDLY adv
PITSAW	n pl. -S a large saw for cutting logs	**PLACING**	present participle of place
		PLACK	n pl. -S a former coin of Scotland
PITTANCE	n pl. -S a small allowance of money	**PLACKET**	n pl. -S a slit in a garment
PITTED	past tense of pit	**PLACOID**	n pl. -S a fish having platelike scales
PITTING	n pl. -S an arrangement of cavities or depressions		
		PLAFOND	n pl. -S an elaborately decorated ceiling
PITY	v PITIED, PITYING, PITIES to feel pity (sorrow aroused by another's misfortune)	**PLAGAL**	adj designating a medieval musical mode
		PLAGE	n pl. -S a bright region on the sun
PIU	adv more — used as a musical direction	**PLAGIARY**	n pl. -RIES the act of passing off another's work as one's own
PIVOT	v -ED, -ING, -S to turn on a shaft or rod		
PIVOTAL	adj critically important	**PLAGUE**	v PLAGUED, PLAGUING, PLAGUES to harass or torment
PIVOTMAN	n pl. -MEN a center on a basketball team		

PLAGUER *n* pl. -S one that plagues

PLAGUEY *adj* plaguy

PLAGUING present participle of plague

PLAGUY *adj* troublesome **PLAGUILY** *adv*

PLAICE *n* pl. -S a European flatfish

PLAID *n* pl. -S a woolen scarf of a checkered pattern **PLAIDED** *adj*

PLAIN *adj* **PLAINER, PLAINEST** evident **PLAINLY** *adv*

PLAIN *v* -ED, -ING, -S to complain

PLAINT *n* pl. -S a complaint

PLAISTER *v* -ED, -ING, -S to plaster

PLAIT *v* -ED, -ING, -S to braid

PLAITER *n* pl. -S one that plaits

PLAITING *n* pl. -S something that is plaited

PLAN *v* **PLANNED, PLANNING, PLANS** to formulate a plan (a method for achieving an end)

PLANAR *adj* flat

PLANARIA *n* pl. -S an aquatic flatworm

PLANATE *adj* having a flat surface

PLANCH *n* pl. -ES a plank

PLANCHE *n* pl. -S planch

PLANCHET *n* pl. -S a flat piece of metal for stamping into a coin

PLANE *v* **PLANED, PLANING, PLANES** to make smooth or even

PLANER *n* pl. -S one that planes

PLANET *n* pl. -S a celestial body

PLANFORM *n* pl. -S the contour of an object as viewed from above

PLANGENT *adj* resounding loudly

PLANING present participle of plane

PLANISH *v* -ED, -ING, -ES to toughen and smooth by hammering lightly

PLANK *v* -ED, -ING, -S to cover with planks (long, flat pieces of lumber)

PLANKING *n* pl. -S covering made of planks

PLANKTER *n* pl. -S any organism that is an element of plankton

PLANKTON *n* pl. -S the minute animal and plant life of a body of water

PLANLESS *adj* having no plan

PLANNED past tense of plan

PLANNER *n* pl. -S one that plans

PLANNING *n* pl. -S the establishment of goals or policies

PLANOSOL *n* pl. -S a type of soil

PLANT *v* -ED, -ING, -S to place in the ground for growing

PLANTAIN *n* pl. -S a short-stemmed herb

PLANTAR *adj* pertaining to the sole of the foot

PLANTER *n* pl. -S one that plants

PLANTING *n* pl. -S an area where plants are grown

PLANTLET *n* pl. -S a small plant

PLANULA *n* pl. -LAE the free-swimming larva of certain organisms **PLANULAR** *adj*

PLAQUE *n* pl. -S an ornamental plate or disk

PLASH *v* -ED, -ING, -ES to weave together

PLASHER *n* pl. -S one that plashes

PLASHY *adj* **PLASHIER, PLASHIEST** marshy

PLASM *n* pl. -S plasma

PLASMA *n* pl. -S the liquid part of blood **PLASMIC** *adj*

PLASMID *n* pl. -S a hereditary structure of a cell

PLASMIN *n* pl. -S an enzyme

PLASMOID *n* pl. -S a type of high energy particle

PLASMON *n* pl. -S a determinant of inheritance believed to exist in cells

PLASTER *v* -ED, -ING, -S to cover with plaster (a mixture of lime, sand, and water)

PLASTERY *adj* resembling plaster

PLASTIC *n* pl. -S any of a group of synthetic or natural moldable materials

PLASTID *n* pl. -S a structure in plant cells

PLASTRON *n* pl. -S a part of the shell of a turtle **PLASTRAL** *adj*

PLASTRUM *n* pl. -S plastron

PLAT *v* **PLATTED, PLATTING, PLATS** to plait

PLATAN *n* pl. -S a large tree

PLATANE *n* pl. -S platan

PLATE *v* **PLATED, PLATING, PLATES** to coat with a thin layer of metal

PLATEAU *n* pl. -TEAUS or -TEAUX a level stretch of elevated land

PLATEAU *v* -ED, -ING, -S to reach a period or condition of stability

PLATED past tense of plate

PLATEFUL *n* pl. PLATEFULS or PLATESFUL the quantity that fills a plate (a shallow dish)

PLATELET *n* pl. -S a small, flattened body

PLATEN *n* pl. -S the roller of a typewriter

PLATER *n* pl. -S one that plates

PLATESFUL a pl. of plateful

PLATFORM *n* pl. -S a raised floor or flat surface

PLATIER comparative of platy

PLATIES a pl. of platy

PLATIEST superlative of platy

PLATINA *n* pl. -S platinum

PLATING *n* pl. -S a thin layer of metal

PLATINIC *adj* pertaining to platinum

PLATINUM *n* pl. -S a metallic element

PLATONIC *adj* purely spiritual and free from sensual desire

PLATOON *v* -ED, -ING, -S to alternate with another player at the same position

PLATTED past tense of plat

PLATTER *n* pl. -S a large, shallow dish

PLATTING present participle of plat

PLATY *adj* PLATIER, PLATIEST split into thin, flat pieces

PLATY *n* pl. PLATYS or PLATIES a small tropical fish

PLATYPUS *n* pl. -PUSES or -PI an aquatic mammal

PLAUDIT *n* pl. -S an expression of praise

PLAUSIVE *adj* expressing praise

PLAY *v* -ED, -ING, -S to engage in amusement or sport
PLAYABLE *adj*

PLAYA *n* pl. -S the bottom of a desert basin

PLAYACT *v* -ED, -ING, -S to take part in a theatrical performance

PLAYBACK *n* pl. -S the act of replaying a newly made recording

PLAYBILL *n* pl. -S a program for a theatrical performance

PLAYBOOK *n* pl. -S a book containing one or more literary works for the stage

PLAYBOY *n* pl. -BOYS a man devoted to pleasurable activities

PLAYDATE *n* pl. -S the scheduled date for showing a theatrical production

PLAYDAY *n* pl. -DAYS a holiday

PLAYDOWN *n* pl. -S a playoff

PLAYER *n* pl. -S one that plays

PLAYFUL *adj* frolicsome

PLAYGIRL *n* pl. -S a woman devoted to pleasurable activities

PLAYGOER *n* pl. -S one who attends the theater

PLAYLAND *n* pl. -S a recreational area

PLAYLESS *adj* lacking playfulness

PLAYLET *n* pl. -S a short theatrical performance

PLAYLIKE *adj* resembling a theatrical performance

PLAYLIST *n* pl. -S a list of recordings to be played on the air

PLAYMATE *n* pl. -S a companion in play

PLAYOFF *n* pl. -S a series of games played to determine a championship

PLAYPEN *n* pl. -S an enclosure in which a young child may play

PLAYROOM *n* pl. -S a recreation room

PLAYSUIT *n* pl. -S a sports outfit for women and children

PLAYTIME *n* pl. -S a time for play or amusement

PLAYWEAR *n* pl. PLAYWEAR clothing worn for leisure activities

PLAZA *n* pl. -S a public square

PLEA *n* pl. -S an entreaty

PLEACH *v* -ED, -ING, -ES to weave together

PLEAD *v* PLEADED or PLED, PLEADING, PLEADS to ask for earnestly

PLEADER *n* pl. -S one that pleads

PLEADING *n* pl. -S an allegation in a legal action

PLEASANT *adj* -ANTER, -ANTEST pleasing

PLEASE *v* PLEASED, PLEASING, PLEASES to give enjoyment or satisfaction to

PLEASER *n* pl. -S one that pleases

PLEASURE *v* -SURED, -SURING, -SURES to please

PLEAT *v* -ED, -ING, -S to fold in an even manner

PLEATER *n* pl. -S one that pleats

PLEB *n* pl. -S a commoner

PLEBE *n* pl. -S a freshman at a military or naval academy

PLEBEIAN *n* pl. -S a commoner

PLECTRON *n* pl. -TRONS or -TRA plectrum

PLECTRUM *n* pl. -TRUMS or -TRA an implement used to pluck the strings of a stringed instrument

PLED a past tense of plead

PLEDGE v PLEDGED, PLEDGING, PLEDGES to give as security for something borrowed

PLEDGEE n pl. -S one to whom something is pledged

PLEDGEOR n pl. -S pledger

PLEDGER n pl. -S one that pledges something

PLEDGET n pl. -S a pad of absorbent cotton

PLEDGING present participle of pledge

PLEDGOR n pl. -S pledger

PLEIAD n pl. -S or -ES a group of seven illustrious persons

PLENA a pl. of plenum

PLENARY adj complete in every respect

PLENCH n pl. -ES a tool serving as pliers and a wrench

PLENISH v -ED, -ING, -ES to fill up

PLENISM n pl. -S the doctrine that space is fully occupied by matter

PLENIST n pl. -S an advocate of plenism

PLENTY n pl. -TIES a sufficient or abundant amount

PLENUM n pl. -NUMS or -NA space considered as fully occupied by matter

PLEONASM n pl. -S the use of needless words

PLEOPOD n pl. -S an appendage of crustaceans

PLESSOR n pl. -S plexor

PLETHORA n pl. -S an excess

PLEURA n pl. -RAE or -RAS a membrane that envelops the lungs **PLEURAL** adj

PLEURISY n pl. -SIES inflammation of the pleura

PLEURON n pl. -RA a part of a thoracic segment of an insect

PLEUSTON n pl. -S aquatic vegetation

PLEW n pl. -S a beaver skin

PLEXAL adj pertaining to a plexus

PLEXOR n pl. -S a small, hammer-like medical instrument

PLEXUS n pl. -ES an interlacing of parts

PLIABLE adj easily bent **PLIABLY** adv

PLIANCY n pl. -CIES the quality of being pliant

PLIANT adj easily bent **PLIANTLY** adv

PLICA n pl. -CAE a fold of skin **PLICAL** adj

PLICATE adj pleated

PLICATED adj plicate

PLIE n pl. -S a movement in ballet

PLIED past tense of ply

PLIER n pl. -S one that plies

PLIES present 3d person sing. of ply

PLIGHT v -ED, -ING, -S to promise or bind by a solemn pledge

PLIGHTER n pl. -S one that plights

PLIMSOL n pl. -S plimsoll

PLIMSOLE n pl. -S plimsoll

PLIMSOLL n pl. -S a rubber-soled cloth shoe

PLINK v -ED, -ING, -S to shoot at random targets

PLINKER n pl. -S one that plinks

PLINTH n pl. -S a stone or slab upon which a column or pedestal rests

PLIOTRON n pl. -S a type of vacuum tube

PLISKIE n pl. -S a practical joke

PLISKY n pl. -KIES pliskie

PLISSE n pl. -S a puckered texture of cloth

PLOD v PLODDED, PLODDING, PLODS to walk heavily

PLODDER n pl. -S one that plods

PLOIDY n pl. -DIES the extent of repetition of the basic number of chromosomes

PLONK v -ED, -ING, -S to plunk

PLOP v PLOPPED, PLOPPING, PLOPS to drop or fall heavily

PLOSION n pl. -S a release of breath after the articulation of certain consonants

PLOSIVE n pl. -S a sound produced by plosion

PLOT v PLOTTED, PLOTTING, PLOTS to plan secretly

PLOTLESS adj planless

PLOTLINE n pl. -S the main story of a book

PLOTTAGE n pl. -S an area of land

PLOTTED past tense of plot

PLOTTER n pl. -S one that plots

PLOTTIER comparative of plotty

PLOTTIES pl. of plotty

PLOTTING present participle of plot

PLOTTY adj -TIER, -TIEST full of intrigue, as a novel

PLOTTY n pl. -TIES a hot, spiced beverage

PLOTZ v -ED, -ING, -ES to be overwhelmed by an emotion

PLOUGH v -ED, -ING, -S to plow

PLOUGHER n pl. -S one that ploughs

PLOVER n pl. -S a shore bird

PLOW v -ED, -ING, -S to turn up land with a plow (a farm implement) **PLOWABLE** adj

PLOWBACK n pl. -S a reinvestment of profits in a business

PLOWBOY n pl. -BOYS a boy who leads a plow team

PLOWER n pl. -S one that plows

PLOWHEAD n pl. -S the clevis of a plow

PLOWLAND n pl. -S land suitable for cultivation

PLOWMAN n pl. -MEN a man who plows

PLOY v -ED, -ING, -S to move from a line into column

PLUCK v -ED, -ING, -S to pull out or off

PLUCKER n pl. -S one that plucks

PLUCKY adj PLUCKIER, PLUCKIEST brave and spirited **PLUCKILY** adv

PLUG v PLUGGED, PLUGGING, PLUGS to seal or close with a plug (a piece of material used to fill a hole)

PLUGGER n pl. -S one that plugs

PLUGLESS adj having no plug

PLUGOLA n pl. -S free incidental advertising on radio or television

PLUGUGLY n pl. -LIES a hoodlum

PLUM n pl. -S a fleshy fruit

PLUMAGE n pl. -S the feathers of a bird **PLUMAGED** adj

PLUMATE adj resembling a feather

PLUMB v -ED, -ING, -S to determine the depth of

PLUMBAGO n pl. -GOS graphite

PLUMBER n pl. -S one who installs and repairs plumbing

PLUMBERY n pl. -ERIES the work of a plumber

PLUMBIC adj containing lead

PLUMBING n pl. -S the pipe system of a building

PLUMBISM n pl. -S lead poisoning

PLUMBOUS adj containing lead

PLUMBUM n pl. -S lead

PLUME v PLUMED, PLUMING, PLUMES to cover with feathers

PLUMELET n pl. -S a small feather

PLUMERIA n pl. -S a flowering shrub

PLUMIER comparative of plumy

PLUMIEST superlative of plumy

PLUMING present participle of plume

PLUMIPED n pl. -S a bird having feathered feet

PLUMLIKE adj resembling a plum

PLUMMET v -ED, -ING, -S to drop straight down

PLUMMY adj -MIER, -MIEST full of plums

PLUMOSE adj having feathers

PLUMP adj PLUMPER, PLUMPEST well-rounded and full in form

PLUMP v -ED, -ING, -S to make plump

PLUMPEN v -ED, -ING, -S to plump

PLUMPER n pl. -S a heavy fall

PLUMPISH adj somewhat plump

PLUMPLY adv in a plump way

PLUMULE n pl. -S the primary bud of a plant embryo **PLUMULAR** adj

PLUMY adj PLUMIER, PLUMIEST covered with feathers

PLUNDER v -ED, -ING, -S to rob of goods by force

PLUNGE v PLUNGED, PLUNGING, PLUNGES to throw or thrust suddenly or forcibly into something

PLUNGER n pl. -S one that plunges

PLUNK v -ED, -ING, -S to fall or drop heavily

PLUNKER n pl. -S one that plunks

PLURAL n pl. -S a word that expresses more than one

PLURALLY adv in a manner or form that expresses more than one

PLUS n pl. PLUSES or PLUSSES an additional quantity

PLUSH adj PLUSHER, PLUSHEST luxurious **PLUSHLY** adv

PLUSH n pl. -ES a fabric with a long pile

PLUSHY adj PLUSHIER, PLUSHIEST luxurious **PLUSHILY** adv

PLUSSAGE n pl. -S an amount over and above another

PLUSSES a pl. of plus

PLUTEUS n pl. -TEI the larva of a sea urchin

PLUTON n pl. -S a formation of igneous rock **PLUTONIC** adj

PLUVIAL n pl. -S a prolonged period of wet climate

PLUVIAN adj characterized by much rain

PLUVIOSE adj pluvious

PLUVIOUS adj pertaining to rain

PLY v PLIED, PLYING, PLIES to supply with or offer repeatedly PLYINGLY adv

PLYER n pl. -S plier

PLYWOOD n pl. -S a building material

PNEUMA n pl. -S the soul or spirit

POACEOUS adj pertaining to plants of the grass family

POACH v -ED, -ING, -ES to trespass for the purpose of taking game or fish

POACHER n pl. -S one that poaches

POACHY adj POACHIER, POACHIEST swampy

POCHARD n pl. -S a sea duck

POCK v -ED, -ING, -S to mark with pocks (pustules caused by an eruptive disease)

POCKET v -ED, -ING, -S to place in a pouch sewed into a garment

POCKETER n pl. -S one that pockets

POCKMARK v -ED, -ING, -S to mark with scars caused by an eruptive disease

POCKY adj POCKIER, POCKIEST covered with pocks POCKILY adv

POCO adv a little — used as a musical direction

POCOSIN n pl. -S an upland swamp

POD v PODDED, PODDING, PODS to produce seed vessels

PODAGRA n pl. -S gout in the foot PODAGRAL, PODAGRIC adj

PODESTA n pl. -S an Italian magistrate

PODGY adj PODGIER, PODGIEST pudgy PODGILY adv

PODIA a pl. of podium

PODIATRY n pl. -TRIES the study and treatment of the human foot

PODITE n pl. -S a limb segment of an arthropod PODITIC adj

PODIUM n pl. -DIUMS or -DIA a small platform

PODLIKE adj resembling a pod (a seed vessel)

PODOCARP adj designating a family of evergreen trees

PODOMERE n pl. -S a podite

PODSOL n pl. -S podzol PODSOLIC adj

PODZOL n pl. -S an infertile soil PODZOLIC adj

POECHORE n pl. -S a semiarid region

POEM n pl. -S a composition in verse

POESY n pl. -ESIES poetry

POET n pl. -S one who writes poems

POETESS n pl. -ES a female poet

POETIC adj pertaining to poetry

POETICAL adj poetic

POETICS n/pl poetic theory or practice

POETISE v -ISED, -ISING, -ISES to poetize

POETISER n pl. -S poetizer

POETIZE v -IZED, -IZING, -IZES to write poetry

POETIZER n pl. -S one that poetizes

POETLESS adj lacking a poet

POETLIKE adj resembling a poet

POETRY n pl. -RIES literary work in metrical form

POGEY n pl. -GEYS any form of government relief

POGIES pl. of pogy

POGONIA n pl. -S a small orchid

POGONIP n pl. -S a dense fog of suspended ice particles

POGROM v -ED, -ING, -S to massacre systematically

POGY n pl. -GIES a marine fish

POH interj — used to express disgust

POI n pl. -S a Hawaiian food

POIGNANT adj emotionally distressing

POILU n pl. -S a French soldier

POIND v -ED, -ING, -S to seize and sell the property of to satisfy a debt

POINT v -ED, -ING, -S to indicate direction with the finger

POINTE n pl. -S a ballet position

POINTER n pl. -S one that points

POINTMAN n pl. -MEN a certain player in hockey

POINTY adj POINTIER, POINTIEST coming to a sharp, tapering end

POISE v POISED, POISING, POISES to hold in a state of equilibrium

POISER n pl. -S one that poises

POISHA n pl. POISHA the paisa of Bangladesh

POISON v -ED, -ING, -S to administer a harmful substance to

POISONER n pl. -S one that poisons

POITREL n pl. -S peytral

POKE v POKED, POKING, POKES to push or prod

POKER n pl. -S one that pokes

POKEROOT n pl. -S pokeweed

POKEWEED n pl. -S a perennial herb

POKEY *n* pl. -KEYS poky

POKIER comparative of poky

POKIES pl. of poky

POKIEST superlative of poky

POKILY *adv* in a poky manner

POKINESS *n* pl. -ES the state of being poky

POKING present participle of poke

POKY *n* pl. POKIES a jail

POKY *adj* POKIER, POKIEST slow

POL *n* pl. -S a politician

POLAR *n* pl. -S a straight line related to a point

POLARISE *v* -ISED, -ISING, -ISES to polarize

POLARITY *n* pl. -TIES the possession of two opposite qualities

POLARIZE *v* -IZED, -IZING, -IZES to give polarity to

POLARON *n* pl. -S a type of electron

POLDER *n* pl. -S a tract of low land reclaimed from a body of water

POLE *v* POLED, POLING, POLES to propel with a pole (a long, thin piece of wood or metal)

POLEAX *v* -ED, -ING, -ES to strike with an axlike weapon

POLEAXE *v* -AXED, -AXING, -AXES to poleax

POLECAT *n* pl. -S a carnivorous mammal

POLED past tense of pole

POLEIS pl. of polis

POLELESS *adj* having no pole

POLEMIC *n* pl. -S a controversial argument

POLEMIST *n* pl. -S one who engages in polemics

POLEMIZE *v* -MIZED, -MIZING, -MIZES to engage in polemics

POLENTA *n* pl. -S a thick mush of cornmeal

POLER *n* pl. -S one that poles

POLESTAR *n* pl. -S a guiding principle

POLEWARD *adv* in the direction of either extremity of the earth's axis

POLEYN *n* pl. -S a protective piece of leather for the knee

POLICE *v* -LICED, -LICING, -LICES to make clean or orderly

POLICY *n* pl. -CIES an action or a procedure considered with reference to prudence or expediency

POLING present participle of pole

POLIO *n* pl. -LIOS an infectious virus disease

POLIS *n* pl. -LEIS an ancient Greek city-state

POLISH *v* -ED, -ING, -ES to make smooth and lustrous by rubbing

POLISHER *n* pl. -S one that polishes

POLITE *adj* -LITER, -LITEST showing consideration for others **POLITELY** *adv*

POLITIC *adj* shrewd

POLITICK *v* -ED, -ING, -S to engage in politics

POLITICO *n* pl. -COS or -COES one who politicks

POLITICS *n/pl* the art or science of government

POLITY *n* pl. -TIES a form or system of government

POLKA *v* -ED, -ING, -S to perform a lively dance

POLL *v* -ED, -ING, -S to question for the purpose of surveying public opinion

POLLACK *n* pl. -S a marine food fish

POLLARD *v* -ED, -ING, -S to cut the top branches of a tree back to the trunk

POLLEE *n* pl. -S one who is polled

POLLEN *v* -ED, -ING, -S to convey pollen (the fertilizing element in a seed plant) to

POLLER *n* pl. -S one that polls

POLLEX *n* pl. -LICES the innermost digit of the forelimb **POLLICAL** *adj*

POLLINIA *n/pl* masses of pollen grains

POLLINIC *adj* pertaining to pollen

POLLIST *n* pl. -S a poller

POLLIWOG *n* pl. -S a tadpole

POLLOCK *n* pl. -S pollack

POLLSTER *n* pl. -S a poller

POLLUTE *v* -LUTED, -LUTING, -LUTES to make unclean or impure

POLLUTER *n* pl. -S one that pollutes

POLLYWOG *n* pl. -S polliwog

POLO *n* pl. -LOS a game played on horseback

POLOIST *n* pl. -S a polo player

POLONIUM *n* pl. -S a radioactive element

POLTROON *n* pl. -S a base coward

POLY *n* pl. POLYS a type of white blood cell

POLYBRID *n* pl. -S a type of hybrid plant

POLYCOT *n* pl. -S a type of plant

POLYENE *n* pl. -S a chemical compound **POLYENIC** *adj*

POLYGALA *n pl.* -S a flowering plant

POLYGAMY *n pl.* -MIES the condition of having more than one spouse at the same time

POLYGENE *n pl.* -S a type of gene

POLYGLOT *n pl.* -S one that speaks or writes several languages

POLYGON *n pl.* -S a closed plane figure bounded by straight lines

POLYGONY *n pl.* -NIES an herb

POLYGYNY *n pl.* -NIES the condition of having more than one wife at the same time

POLYMATH *n pl.* -S a person of great and varied learning

POLYMER *n pl.* -S a complex chemical compound

POLYNYA *n pl.* -YAS or -YI an area of open water surrounded by sea ice

POLYOMA *n pl.* -S a type of virus

POLYP *n pl.* -S an invertebrate

POLYPARY *n pl.* -ARIES the common supporting structure of a polyp colony

POLYPI *a pl.* of polypus

POLYPIDE *n pl.* -S a polyp

POLYPNEA *n pl.* -S rapid breathing

POLYPOD *n pl.* -S a many-footed organism

POLYPODY *n pl.* -DIES a fern

POLYPOID *adj* resembling a polyp

POLYPORE *n pl.* -S a type of fungus

POLYPOUS *adj* pertaining to a polyp

POLYPUS *n pl.* -PI or -PUSES a growth protruding from the mucous lining of an organ

POLYSEMY *n pl.* -MIES diversity of meanings

POLYSOME *n pl.* -S a cluster of protein particles

POLYTENE *adj* having chromosomes of a certain type

POLYTENY *n pl.* -NIES the state of being polytene

POLYTYPE *n pl.* -S a crystal structure

POLYURIA *n pl.* -S excessive urination
POLYURIC *adj*

POLYZOAN *n pl.* -S a bryozoan

POLYZOIC *adj* composed of many zooids

POMACE *n pl.* -S the pulpy residue of crushed fruits

POMADE *v* -MADED, -MADING, -MADES to apply a perfumed hair dressing to

POMANDER *n pl.* -S a mixture of aromatic substances

POMATUM *n pl.* -S a perfumed hair dressing

POME *n pl.* -S a fleshy fruit with a core

POMELO *n pl.* -LOS a grapefruit

POMFRET *n pl.* -S a marine fish

POMMEE *adj* having arms with knoblike ends — used of a heraldic cross

POMMEL *v* -MELED, -MELING, -MELS or -MELLED, -MELLING, -MELS to strike with the fists

POMOLOGY *n pl.* -GIES the study of fruits

POMP *n pl.* -S stately or splendid display

POMPANO *n pl.* -NOS a marine food fish

POMPOM *n pl.* -S an antiaircraft cannon

POMPON *n pl.* -S an ornamental tuft or ball

POMPOUS *adj* marked by exaggerated self-importance

PONCE *v* PONCED, PONCING, PONCES to pimp

PONCHO *n pl.* -CHOS a type of cloak

POND *v* -ED, -ING, -S to collect into a pond (a small body of water)

PONDER *v* -ED, -ING, -S to consider something deeply and thoroughly

PONDERER *n pl.* -S one that ponders

PONDWEED *n pl.* -S an aquatic plant

PONE *n pl.* -S a corn bread

PONENT *adj* affirmative

PONG *v* -ED, -ING, -S to stink

PONGEE *n pl.* -S a type of silk

PONGID *n pl.* -S an anthropoid ape

PONIARD *v* -ED, -ING, -S to stab with a dagger

PONIED past tense of pony

PONIES present 3d person sing. of pony

PONS *n pl.* PONTES a band of nerve fibers in the brain

PONTIFEX *n pl.* -FICES an ancient Roman priest

PONTIFF *n pl.* -S a pope or bishop

PONTIFIC *adj* pertaining to a pope or bishop

PONTIFICES *pl.* of pontifex

PONTIL *n pl.* -S a punty

PONTINE *adj* pertaining to bridges

PONTON *n pl.* -S pontoon

PONTOON *n pl.* -S a flat-bottomed boat

PONY	*v* -NIED, -NYING, -NIES to prepare lessons with the aid of a literal translation
PONYTAIL	*n pl.* -S a hairstyle
POOCH	*v* -ED, -ING, -ES to bulge
POOD	*n pl.* -S a Russian unit of weight
POODLE	*n pl.* -S a heavy-coated dog
POOF	*interj* — used to indicate an instantaneous occurrence
POOH	*v* -ED, -ING, -S to express contempt for
POOL	*v* -ED, -ING, -S to combine in a common fund
POOLHALL	*n pl.* -S a poolroom
POOLROOM	*n pl.* -S an establishment for the playing of billiards
POOLSIDE	*n pl.* -S the area surrounding a swimming pool
POON	*n pl.* -S an East Indian tree
POOP	*v* -ED, -ING, -S to tire out
POOR	*adj* POORER, POOREST lacking the means of support
POORI	*n pl.* -S a light, flat wheat cake
POORISH	*adj* somewhat poor
POORLY	*adv* in a poor manner
POORNESS	*n pl.* -ES the state of being poor
POORTITH	*n pl.* -S poverty
POP	*v* POPPED, POPPING, POPS to make a sharp, explosive sound
POPCORN	*n pl.* -S a variety of corn
POPE	*n pl.* -S the head of the Roman Catholic Church POPELESS, POPELIKE *adj*
POPEDOM	*n pl.* -S the office of a pope
POPEYED	*adj* having bulging eyes
POPGUN	*n pl.* -S a toy gun
POPINJAY	*n pl.* -JAYS a vain person
POPLAR	*n pl.* -S a fast-growing tree
POPLIN	*n pl.* -S a durable fabric
POPLITIC	*adj* pertaining to the part of the leg behind the knee
POPOVER	*n pl.* -S a very light egg muffin
POPPA	*n pl.* -S papa
POPPED	past tense of pop
POPPER	*n pl.* -S one that pops
POPPET	*n pl.* -S a mechanical valve
POPPIED	*adj* covered with poppies
POPPIES	pl. of poppy
POPPING	present participle of pop
POPPLE	*v* -PLED, -PLING, -PLES to move in a bubbling or rippling manner
POPPY	*n pl.* -PIES a flowering plant
POPSIE	*n pl.* -S popsy
POPSY	*n pl.* -SIES a girlfriend
POPULACE	*n pl.* -S the common people
POPULAR	*adj* liked by many people
POPULATE	*v* -LATED, -LATING, -LATES to inhabit
POPULISM	*n pl.* -S populists' doctrines
POPULIST	*n pl.* -S a member of a party which represents the common people
POPULOUS	*adj* containing many inhabitants
PORCH	*n pl.* -ES a covered structure at the entrance to a building
PORCINE	*adj* pertaining to swine
PORCINO	*n pl.* -NI an edible mushroom
PORE	*v* PORED, PORING, PORES to gaze intently
PORGY	*n pl.* -GIES a marine food fish
PORISM	*n pl.* -S a type of mathematical proposition
PORK	*n pl.* -S the flesh of swine used as food
PORKER	*n pl.* -S a pig
PORKIER	comparative of porky
PORKIES	pl. of porky
PORKIEST	superlative of porky
PORKPIE	*n pl.* -S a man's hat
PORKWOOD	*n pl.* -S a tropical tree
PORKY	*adj* PORKIER, PORKIEST resembling pork
PORKY	*n pl.* -KIES a porcupine
PORN	*n pl.* -S pornography
PORNO	*n pl.* -NOS pornography
PORNY	*adj* PORNIER, PORNIEST pornographic
POROSE	*adj* porous
POROSITY	*n pl.* -TIES the state of being porous
POROUS	*adj* having minute openings POROUSLY *adv*
PORPHYRY	*n pl.* -RIES an igneous rock
PORPOISE	*n pl.* -S an aquatic mammal
PORRECT	*adj* extended forward
PORRIDGE	*n pl.* -S a soft food PORRIDGY *adj*
PORT	*v* -ED, -ING, -S to shift to the left side
PORTABLE	*n pl.* -S something that can be carried
PORTABLY	*adv* so as to be capable of being carried
PORTAGE	*v* -TAGED, -TAGING, -TAGES to transport from one navigable waterway to another

PORTAL *n pl.* -S a door, gate, or entrance **PORTALED** *adj*

PORTANCE *n pl.* -S demeanor

PORTAPAK *n pl.* -S a portable combined video recorder and camera

PORTEND *v* -ED, -ING, -S to serve as an omen of

PORTENT *n pl.* -S an omen

PORTER *v* -ED, -ING, -S to carry luggage for pay

PORTHOLE *n pl.* -S a small window in a ship's side

PORTICO *n pl.* -COS or -COES a type of porch

PORTIERE *n pl.* -S a curtain for a doorway

PORTION *v* -ED, -ING, -S to divide into shares for distribution

PORTLESS *adj* having no place for ships to load or unload

PORTLY *adj* -LIER, -LIEST rather heavy or fat

PORTRAIT *n pl.* -S a likeness of a person

PORTRAY *v* -ED, -ING, -S to represent pictorially

PORTRESS *n pl.* -ES a female doorkeeper

POSADA *n pl.* -S an inn

POSE *v* POSED, POSING, POSES to assume a fixed position

POSER *n pl.* -S one that poses

POSEUR *n pl.* -S an affected or insincere person

POSH *adj* POSHER, POSHEST stylish or elegant **POSHLY** *adv*

POSHNESS *n pl.* -ES the quality of being posh

POSIES *pl.* of posy

POSING present participle of pose

POSINGLY *adv* in a posing manner

POSIT *v* -ED, -ING, -S to place

POSITION *v* -ED, -ING, -S to put in a particular location

POSITIVE *adj* -TIVER, -TIVEST certain

POSITIVE *n pl.* -S a quantity greater than zero

POSITRON *n pl.* -S a subatomic particle

POSOLOGY *n pl.* -GIES a branch of medicine that deals with drug dosages

POSSE *n pl.* -S a body of men summoned to aid a peace officer

POSSESS *v* -ED, -ING, -ES to have as property

POSSET *n pl.* -S a hot, spiced drink

POSSIBLE *adj* -BLER, -BLEST capable of happening or proving true **POSSIBLY** *adv*

POSSUM *n pl.* -S opossum

POST *v* -ED, -ING, -S to affix in a public place

POSTAGE *n pl.* -S the charge for mailing an item

POSTAL *n pl.* -S a postcard

POSTALLY *adv* in a manner pertaining to the mails

POSTANAL *adj* situated behind the anus

POSTBAG *n pl.* -S a mailbag

POSTBASE *adj* following a base word

POSTBOX *n pl.* -ES a mailbox

POSTBOY *n pl.* -BOYS a boy who carries mail

POSTBURN *adj* following a burn

POSTCARD *n pl.* -S a card for use in the mail

POSTCAVA *n pl.* -VAE a vein in higher vertebrates

POSTCODE *n pl.* -S a code of numbers and letters used in a mailing address

POSTCOUP *adj* following a coup

POSTDATE *v* -DATED, -DATING, -DATES to give a date later than the actual date to

POSTDIVE *adj* following a dive

POSTDOC *n pl.* -S one engaged in postdoctoral study

POSTDRUG *adj* following the taking of a drug

POSTEEN *n pl.* -S an Afghan outer garment

POSTER *n pl.* -S a printed or written notice for posting

POSTERN *n pl.* -S a rear door or gate

POSTFACE *n pl.* -S a brief note placed at the end of a publication

POSTFIRE *adj* following a fire

POSTFIX *v* -ED, -ING, -ES to affix at the end of something

POSTFORM *v* -ED, -ING, -S to shape subsequently

POSTGAME *adj* following a game

POSTHEAT *n pl.* -S heat applied to a metal after welding

POSTHOLE *n pl.* -S a hole dug to secure a fence post

POSTICHE *n pl.* -S an imitation

POSTIN *n pl.* -S posteen

POSTING *n pl.* -S the act of transferring to a ledger

POSTIQUE *n pl.* -S postiche

POSTLUDE n pl. -S a closing musical piece

POSTMAN n pl. -MEN a mailman

POSTMARK v -ED, -ING, -S to stamp mail with an official mark

POSTORAL adj situated behind the mouth

POSTPAID adv with the postage prepaid

POSTPONE v -PONED, -PONING, -PONES to put off to a future time

POSTRACE adj following a race

POSTRIOT adj following a riot

POSTSHOW adj following a show

POSTSYNC v -ED, -ING, -S to add sound to a film after a scene has been photographed

POSTTAX adj remaining after taxes

POSTTEEN adj occurring after one's teenage years

POSTTEST n pl. -S a test given after a course of instruction

POSTURAL adj pertaining to the position of the body

POSTURE v -TURED, -TURING, -TURES to assume a particular position

POSTURER n pl. -S one that postures

POSTWAR adj occurring or existing after a war

POSY n pl. -SIES a flower or bouquet

POT v POTTED, POTTING, POTS to put in a pot (a round, fairly deep container)

POTABLE n pl. -S a liquid suitable for drinking

POTAGE n pl. -S a thick soup

POTAMIC adj pertaining to rivers

POTASH n pl. -ES a white chemical salt

POTASSIC adj pertaining to potassium (a metallic element)

POTATION n pl. -S the act of drinking

POTATO n pl. -TOES the edible tuber of a cultivated plant

POTATORY adj pertaining to drinking

POTBELLY n pl. -LIES a protruding abdominal region

POTBOIL v -ED, -ING, -S to produce a literary or artistic work of poor quality

POTBOY n pl. -BOYS a boy who serves customers in a tavern

POTEEN n pl. -S Irish whiskey that is distilled unlawfully

POTENCE n pl. -S potency

POTENCY n pl. -CIES the quality of being potent

POTENT adj powerful **POTENTLY** adv

POTFUL n pl. -S as much as a pot can hold

POTHEAD n pl. -S one who smokes marijuana

POTHEEN n pl. -S poteen

POTHER v -ED, -ING, -S to trouble

POTHERB n pl. -S any herb used as a food or seasoning

POTHOLE n pl. -S a deep hole in a road **POTHOLED** adj

POTHOOK n pl. -S a hook for lifting or hanging pots

POTHOUSE n pl. -S a tavern

POTICHE n pl. -S a type of vase

POTION n pl. -S a magical or medicinal drink

POTLACH n pl. -ES a ceremonial feast

POTLACHE n pl. -S potlach

POTLATCH v -ED, -ING, -ES to hold a ceremonial feast for

POTLIKE adj resembling a pot

POTLINE n pl. -S a row of electrolytic cells

POTLUCK n pl. -S food which is incidentally available

POTMAN n pl. -MEN a man who serves customers in a tavern

POTPIE n pl. -S a deep-dish pie containing meat and vegetables

POTSHARD n pl. -S potsherd

POTSHERD n pl. -S a fragment of broken pottery

POTSHOT v -SHOT, -SHOTTING, -SHOTS to shoot randomly at

POTSIE n pl. -S potsy

POTSTONE n pl. -S a variety of steatite

POTSY n pl. -SIES a children's game

POTTAGE n pl. -S a thick soup

POTTED past tense of pot

POTTEEN n pl. -S poteen

POTTER v -ED, -ING, -S to putter

POTTERER n pl. -S one that potters

POTTERY n pl. -TERIES ware molded from clay and hardened by heat

POTTIER comparative of potty

POTTIES pl. of potty

POTTIEST superlative of potty

POTTING present participle of pot

POTTLE n pl. -S a drinking vessel

POTTO n pl. -TOS a lemur of tropical Africa

POTTY adj -TIER, -TIEST of little importance

POTTY *n pl.* -TIES a small toilet seat

POTZER *n pl.* -S patzer

POUGH *v* -ED, -ING, -ES to put in a pouch (a small, flexible receptacle)

POUCHY *adj* POUCHIER, POUCHIEST resembling a pouch

POUF *n pl.* -S a loose roll of hair POUFED *adj*

POUFF *n pl.* -S pouf POUFFED *adj*

POUFFE *n pl.* -S pouf

POULARD *n pl.* -S a spayed hen

POULARDE *n pl.* -S poulard

POULT *n pl.* -S a young domestic fowl

POULTER *n pl.* -S one that deals in poultry

POULTICE *v* -TICED, -TICING, -TICES to apply a healing substance to

POULTRY *n pl.* -TRIES domestic fowls kept for eggs or meat

POUNCE *v* POUNCED, POUNCING, POUNCES to make a sudden assault or approach

POUNCER *n pl.* -S one that pounces

POUND *v* -ED, -ING, -S to strike heavily and repeatedly

POUNDAGE *n pl.* -S the act of impounding

POUNDAL *n pl.* -S a unit of force

POUNDER *n pl.* -S one that pounds

POUR *v* -ED, -ING, -S to cause to flow POURABLE *adj*

POURER *n pl.* -S one that pours

POUSSIE *n pl.* -S pussy

POUT *v* -ED, -ING, -S to protrude the lips in ill humor

POUTER *n pl.* -S one that pouts

POUTFUL *adj* pouty

POUTY *adj* POUTIER, POUTIEST tending to pout

POVERTY *n pl.* -TIES the state of being poor

POW *n pl.* -S an explosive sound

POWDER *v* -ED, -ING, -S to reduce to powder (matter in a finely divided state)

POWDERER *n pl.* -S one that powders

POWDERY *adj* resembling powder

POWER *v* -ED, -ING, -S to provide with means of propulsion

POWERFUL *adj* possessing great force

POWTER *n pl.* -S a domestic pigeon

POWWOW *v* -ED, -ING, -S to hold a conference

POX *v* -ED, -ING, -ES to infect with syphilis

POXVIRUS *n pl.* -ES a type of virus

POYOU *n pl.* -S an armadillo of Argentina

POZZOLAN *n pl.* -S a finely divided material used to make cement

PRAAM *n pl.* -S pram

PRACTIC *adj* practical

PRACTICE *v* -TICED, -TICING, -TICES to perform often so as to acquire skill

PRACTISE *v* -TISED, -TISING, -TISES to practice

PRAECIPE *n pl.* -S a legal writ

PRAEDIAL *adj* pertaining to land

PRAEFECT *n pl.* -S prefect

PRAELECT *v* -ED, -ING, -S to prelect

PRAETOR *n pl.* -S an ancient Roman magistrate

PRAHU *n pl.* -S prau

PRAIRIE *n pl.* -S a tract of grassland

PRAISE *v* PRAISED, PRAISING, PRAISES to express approval or admiration of

PRAISER *n pl.* -S one that praises

PRALINE *n pl.* -S a confection made of nuts cooked in sugar

PRAM *n pl.* -S a flat-bottomed boat

PRANCE *v* PRANCED, PRANCING, PRANCES to spring forward on the hind legs

PRANCER *n pl.* -S one that prances

PRANDIAL *adj* pertaining to a meal

PRANG *v* -ED, -ING, -S to cause to crash

PRANK *v* -ED, -ING, -S to adorn gaudily

PRANKISH *adj* mischievous

PRAO *n pl.* PRAOS prau

PRASE *n pl.* -S a mineral

PRAT *n pl.* -S the buttocks

PRATE *v* PRATED, PRATING, PRATES to chatter

PRATER *n pl.* -S one that prates

PRATFALL *n pl.* -S a fall on the buttocks

PRATING present participle of prate

PRATIQUE *n pl.* -S clearance given a ship by the health authority of a port

PRATTLE *v* -TLED, -TLING, -TLES to babble

PRATTLER *n pl.* -S one that prattles

PRAU *n pl.* -S a swift Malaysian sailing vessel

PRAWN *v* -ED, -ING, -S to fish for prawns (edible shellfish)

PRAWNER *n pl.* -S one that prawns

PRAXIS n pl. PRAXISES or PRAXES practical use of a branch of learning

PRAY v -ED, -ING, -S to address prayers to

PRAYER n pl. -S a devout petition to a deity

PREACH v -ED, -ING, -ES to advocate or recommend urgently

PREACHER n pl. -S one that preaches

PREACHY adj PREACHIER, PREACHIEST tending to preach

PREACT v -ED, -ING, -S to act beforehand

PREADAPT v -ED, -ING, -S to adapt beforehand

PREADMIT v -MITTED, -MITTING, -MITS to admit beforehand

PREADOPT v -ED, -ING, -S to adopt beforehand

PREADULT adj preceding adulthood

PREAGED adj previously aged

PREALLOT v -LOTTED, -LOTTING, -LOTS to allot beforehand

PREAMBLE n pl. -S an introduction

PREAMP n pl. -S an amplifier

PREANAL adj situated in front of the anus

PREARM v -ED, -ING, -S to arm beforehand

PREAUDIT n pl. -S an audit made prior to a final settlement of a transaction

PREAVER v -VERRED, -VERRING, -VERS to aver or assert beforehand

PREAXIAL adj situated in front of an axis

PREBAKE v -BAKED, -BAKING, -BAKES to bake beforehand

PREBASAL adj situated in front of a base

PREBEND n pl. -S a clergyman's stipend

PREBILL v -ED, -ING, -S to bill beforehand

PREBIND v -BOUND, -BINDING, -BINDS to bind in durable materials for library use

PREBLESS v -ED, -ING, -ES to bless beforehand

PREBOIL v -ED, -ING, -S to boil beforehand

PREBOOK v -ED, -ING, -S to book beforehand

PREBOOM adj preceding a sudden expansion of business

PREBOUND past tense of prebind

PRECAST v -CAST, -CASTING, -CASTS to cast and finish before placing into position

PRECAVA n pl. -VAE a vein in higher vertebrates **PRECAVAL** adj

PRECEDE v -CEDED, -CEDING, -CEDES to go before

PRECENT v -ED, -ING, -S to lead a church choir in singing

PRECEPT n pl. -S a rule of conduct

PRECESS v -ED, -ING, -ES to rotate with a complex motion

PRECHECK v -ED, -ING, -S to check beforehand

PRECHILL v -ED, -ING, -S to chill beforehand

PRECIEUX adj excessively refined

PRECINCT n pl. -S a subdivision of a city or town

PRECIOUS n pl. -ES a darling

PRECIPE n pl. -S praecipe

PRECIS v -ED, -ING, -ES to make a concise summary of

PRECISE adj -CISER, -CISEST sharply and clearly defined or stated

PRECITED adj previously cited

PRECLEAN v -ED, -ING, -S to clean beforehand

PRECLEAR v -ED, -ING, -S to clear beforehand

PRECLUDE v -CLUDED, -CLUDING, -CLUDES to make impossible

PRECODE v -CODED, -CODING, -CODES to code beforehand

PRECOOK v -ED, -ING, -S to cook beforehand

PRECOOL v -ED, -ING, -S to cool beforehand

PRECOUP adj preceding a coup

PRECRASH adj preceding a crash

PRECURE v -CURED, -CURING, -CURES to cure beforehand

PRECUT v -CUT, -CUTTING, -CUTS to cut beforehand

PREDATE v -DATED, -DATING, -DATES to antedate

PREDATOR n pl. -S one that plunders

PREDAWN n pl. -S the time just before dawn

PREDIAL adj praedial

PREDICT v -ED, -ING, -S to foretell

PREDIVE adj preceding a dive

PREDRILL v -ED, -ING, -S to drill beforehand

PREDUSK n pl. -S the time just before dusk

PREE v PREED, PREEING, PREES to test by tasting

PREEDIT v -ED, -ING, -S to edit beforehand

PREELECT v -ED, -ING, -S to elect or choose beforehand

PREEMIE n pl. -S an infant born prematurely

PREEMPT v -ED, -ING, -S to acquire by prior right

PREEN v -ED, -ING, -S to smooth or clean with the beak or tongue

PREENACT v -ED, -ING, -S to enact beforehand

PREENER n pl. -S one that preens

PREERECT v -ED, -ING, -S to erect beforehand

PREEXIST v -ED, -ING, -S to exist before

PREFAB v -FABBED, -FABBING, -FABS to build beforehand

PREFACE v -ACED, -ACING, -ACES to provide with an introductory statement

PREFACER n pl. -S one that prefaces

PREFADE v -FADED, -FADING, -FADES to fade beforehand

PREFECT n pl. -S an ancient Roman official

PREFER v -FERRED, -FERRING, -FERS to hold in higher regard or esteem

PREFIGHT adj preceding a fight

PREFILE v -FILED, -FILING, -FILES to file beforehand

PREFIRE v -FIRED, -FIRING, -FIRES to fire beforehand

PREFIX v -ED, -ING, -ES to add as a prefix (a form affixed to the beginning of a root word)

PREFIXAL adj pertaining to or being a prefix

PREFLAME adj preceding a flame

PREFOCUS v -CUSED, -CUSING, -CUSES or -CUSSED, -CUSSING, -CUSSES to focus beforehand

PREFORM v -ED, -ING, -S to form beforehand

PREFRANK v -ED, -ING, -S to frank beforehand

PREFREEZE v -FROZE, -FROZEN, -FREEZING, -FREEZES to freeze beforehand

PREGAME adj preceding a game

PREGGERS adj pregnant

PREGNANT adj carrying a developing fetus in the uterus

PREHEAT v -ED, -ING, -S to heat beforehand

PREHUMAN n pl. -S a prototype of man

PREJUDGE v -JUDGED, -JUDGING, -JUDGES to judge beforehand

PRELACY n pl. -CIES the office of a prelate

PRELATE n pl. -S a high-ranking clergyman PRELATIC adj

PRELECT v -ED, -ING, -S to lecture

PRELEGAL adj occurring before the commencement of studies in law

PRELIFE n pl. -LIVES a life conceived as lived before one's earthly life

PRELIM n pl. -S a minor match preceding the main event

PRELIMIT v -ED, -ING, -S to limit beforehand

PRELUDE v -LUDED, -LUDING, -LUDES to play a musical introduction

PRELUDER n pl. -S one that preludes

PRELUNCH adj preceding lunch

PREMADE adj made beforehand

PREMAN n pl. -MEN a hypothetical ancestor of man

PREMEAL adj preceding a meal

PREMED n pl. -S a student preparing for the study of medicine

PREMEDIC n pl. -S a premed

PREMEET adj preceding a meet

PREMEN pl. of preman

PREMIE n pl. -S preemie

PREMIER n pl. -S a prime minister

PREMIERE v -MIERED, -MIERING, -MIERES to present publicly for the first time

PREMISE v -MISED, -MISING, -MISES to state in advance

PREMISS n pl. -ES a proposition in logic

PREMIUM n pl. -S an additional payment

PREMIX v -MIXED, or -MIXT, -MIXING, -MIXES to mix before use

PREMOLAR n pl. -S a tooth

PREMOLD v -ED, -ING, -S to mold beforehand

PREMOLT adj preceding a molt

PREMORAL adj preceding the development of a moral code

PREMORSE adj ending abruptly, as if bitten off

PREMUNE adj resistant to a disease

PRENAME n pl. -S a forename

PRENATAL adj prior to birth

PRENOMEN *n* pl. -MENS or -MINA the first name of an ancient Roman

PRENOON *adj* preceding noon

PRENTICE *v* -TICED, -TICING, -TICES to place with an employer for instruction in a trade

PREORDER *v* -ED, -ING, -S to order beforehand

PREP *v* PREPPED, PREPPING, PREPS to attend a preparatory school

PREPACK *v* -ED, -ING, -S to package before retail distribution

PREPAID past tense of prepay

PREPARE *v* -PARED, -PARING, -PARES to put in proper condition or readiness

PREPARER *n* pl. -S one that prepares

PREPASTE *v* -PASTED, -PASTING, -PASTES to paste beforehand

PREPAY *v* -PAID, -PAYING, -PAYS to pay in advance

PREPENSE *adj* planned in advance

PREPILL *adj* preceding the development of a contraceptive pill

PREPLACE *v* -PLACED, -PLACING, -PLACES to place beforehand

PREPLAN *v* -PLANNED, -PLANNING, -PLANS to plan in advance

PREPLANT *adj* occurring before planting

PREPPED past tense of prep

PREPPIE *n* pl. -S one who preps

PREPPING present participle of prep

PREPPY *adj* -PIER, -PIEST associated with the style and behavior of preparatory school students PREPPILY *adv*

PREPREG *n* pl. -S reinforcing material already impregnated with a synthetic resin

PREPRICE *v* -PRICED, -PRICING, -PRICES to price beforehand

PREPRINT *v* -ED, -ING, -S to print in advance

PREPUCE *n* pl. -S a fold of skin covering the penis

PREPUNCH *v* -ED, -ING, -ES to punch in advance

PREPUPAL *adj* preceding the pupal stage

PREQUEL *n* pl. -S a book whose story precedes that of an earlier work

PRERACE *adj* preceding a race

PRERENAL *adj* situated in front of the kidney

PRERINSE *n* pl. -S a rinsing beforehand

PRERIOT *adj* preceding a riot

PREROCK *adj* preceding the development of rock music

PRESA *n* pl. -SE a musical symbol

PRESAGE *v* -SAGED, -SAGING, -SAGES to foretell

PRESAGER *n* pl. -S one that presages

PRESALE *adj* preceding a sale

PRESCIND *v* -ED, -ING, -S to consider separately

PRESCORE *v* -SCORED, -SCORING, -SCORES to record the sound of before filming

PRESE pl. of presa

PRESELL *v* -SOLD, -SELLING, -SELLS to promote a product not yet being sold to the public

PRESENCE *n* pl. -S close proximity

PRESENT *v* -ED, -ING, -S to bring into the presence of someone

PRESERVE *v* -SERVED, -SERVING, -SERVES to keep free from harm or danger

PRESET *v* -SET, -SETTING, -SETS to set beforehand

PRESHAPE *v* -SHAPED, -SHAPING, -SHAPES to shape beforehand

PRESHOW *v* -SHOWED, -SHOWN, -SHOWING, -SHOWS to show beforehand

PRESIDE *v* -SIDED, -SIDING, -SIDES to occupy the position of authority

PRESIDER *n* pl. -S one that presides

PRESIDIA *n/pl* Soviet executive committees

PRESIDIO *n* pl. -DIOS a Spanish fort

PRESIFT *v* -ED, -ING, -S to sift beforehand

PRESLEEP *adj* preceding sleep

PRESLICE *v* -SLICED, -SLICING, -SLICES to slice beforehand

PRESOAK *v* -ED, -ING, -S to soak beforehand

PRESOLD past tense of presell

PRESONG *adj* preceding a song

PRESORT *v* -ED, -ING, -S to sort beforehand

PRESPLIT *adj* preceding a split

PRESS *v* -ED, -ING, -ES to act upon with steady force

PRESSER *n* pl. -S one that presses

PRESSING *n* pl. -S an instance of stamping with a press

PRESSMAN *n* pl. -MEN a printing press operator

PRESSOR *n* pl. -S a substance that raises blood pressure

PRESSRUN *n* pl. -S a continuous operation of a printing press

PRESSURE *v* -SURED, -SURING, -SURES to apply force to

PREST *n* pl. -S a loan

PRESTAMP *v* -ED, -ING, -S to stamp beforehand

PRESTER *n* pl. -S a priest

PRESTIGE *n* pl. -S distinction or reputation in the eyes of people

PRESTO *n* pl. -TOS a musical passage played in rapid tempo

PRESUME *v* -SUMED, -SUMING, -SUMES to take for granted

PRESUMER *n* pl. -S one that presumes

PRETAPE *v* -TAPED, -TAPING, -TAPES to tape beforehand

PRETASTE *v* -TASTED, -TASTING, -TASTES to taste beforehand

PRETAX *adj* existing before provision for taxes

PRETEEN *n* pl. -S a child under the age of thirteen

PRETENCE *n* pl. -S pretense

PRETEND *v* -ED, -ING, -S to assume or display a false appearance of

PRETENSE *n* pl. -S the act of pretending

PRETERIT *n* pl. -S a past tense in grammar

PRETERM *adj* pertaining to premature birth

PRETEST *v* -ED, -ING, -S to give a preliminary test to

PRETEXT *v* -ED, -ING, -S to allege as an excuse

PRETOR *n* pl. -S praetor

PRETRAIN *v* -ED, -ING, -S to train beforehand

PRETREAT *v* -ED, -ING, -S to treat beforehand

PRETRIAL *n* pl. -S a proceeding that precedes a trial

PRETRIM *v* -TRIMMED, -TRIMMING, -TRIMS to trim beforehand

PRETTIED past tense of pretty

PRETTIER comparative of pretty

PRETTIES present 3d person sing. of pretty

PRETTIEST superlative of pretty

PRETTIFY *v* -FIED, -FYING, -FIES to make pretty

PRETTY *v* -TIED, -TYING, -TIES to make pretty

PRETTY *adj* -TIER, -TIEST pleasing to the eye **PRETTILY** *adv*

PRETYPE *v* -TYPED, -TYPING, -TYPES to type beforehand

PRETZEL *n* pl. -S a glazed, salted cracker

PREUNION *n* pl. -S a union beforehand

PREUNITE *v* -UNITED, -UNITING, -UNITES to unite beforehand

PREVAIL *v* -ED, -ING, -S to triumph

PREVENT *v* -ED, -ING, -S to keep from happening

PREVIEW *v* -ED, -ING, -S to view or exhibit in advance

PREVIOUS *adj* coming or occurring before in time or order

PREVISE *v* -VISED, -VISING, -VISES to foresee

PREVISOR *n* pl. -S one that previses

PREVUE *v* -VUED, -VUING, -VUES to preview

PREWAR *adj* occurring or existing before a war

PREWARM *v* -ED, -ING, -S to warm beforehand

PREWARN *v* -ED, -ING, -S to warn in advance

PREWASH *v* -ED, -ING, -ES to wash beforehand

PREWORK *adj* preceding work

PREWRAP *v* -WRAPPED, -WRAPPING, -WRAPS to wrap beforehand

PREX *n* pl. -ES prexy

PREXY *n* pl. PREXIES a president

PREY *v* -ED, -ING, -S to seize and devour animals for food

PREYER *n* pl. -S one that preys

PREZ *n* pl. -ES a president

PRIAPEAN *adj* priapic

PRIAPI a pl. of priapus

PRIAPIC *adj* phallic

PRIAPISM *n* pl. -S a persistent erection of the penis

PRIAPUS *n* pl. -PUSES or -PI a representation of the phallus

PRICE *v* PRICED, PRICING, PRICES to set a value on

PRICER *n* pl. -S one that prices

PRICEY *adj* PRICIER, PRICIEST expensive

PRICIER comparative of pricey and pricy

PRICIEST superlative of pricey and pricy

PRICING present participle of price

PRICK *v* -ED, -ING, -S to puncture slightly

PRICKER *n* pl. -S one that pricks

PRICKET n pl. -S a spike for holding a candle upright

PRICKIER comparative of pricky

PRICKIEST superlative of pricky

PRICKING n pl. -S a prickly feeling

PRICKLE v -LED, -LING, -LES to prick

PRICKLY adj -LIER, -LIEST having many sharp points

PRICKY adj PRICKIER, PRICKIEST prickly

PRICY adj PRICIER, PRICIEST pricey

PRIDE v PRIDED, PRIDING, PRIDES to feel pride (a feeling of self-esteem)

PRIDEFUL adj full of pride

PRIED past tense of pry

PRIEDIEU n pl. -DIEUS or -DIEUX a piece of furniture for kneeling on during prayer

PRIER n pl. -S one that pries

PRIES present 3d person sing. of pry

PRIEST v -ED, -ING, -S to ordain as a priest (one authorized to perform religious rites)

PRIESTLY adj -LIER, -LIEST characteristic of or befitting a priest

PRIG v PRIGGED, PRIGGING, PRIGS to steal

PRIGGERY n pl. -GERIES priggism

PRIGGISH adj marked by priggism

PRIGGISM n pl. -S prim adherence to convention

PRILL v -ED, -ING, -S to convert into pellets

PRIM adj PRIMMER, PRIMMEST formally precise or proper

PRIM v PRIMMED, PRIMMING, PRIMS to give a prim expression to

PRIMA n pl. -S primo

PRIMACY n pl. -CIES the state of being first

PRIMAGE n pl. -S an amount paid as an addition to freight charges

PRIMAL adj being at the beginning or foundation

PRIMARY n pl. -RIES a preliminary election

PRIMATAL n pl. -S a primate

PRIMATE n pl. -S any of an advanced order of mammals

PRIME v PRIMED, PRIMING, PRIMES to make ready

PRIMELY adv excellently

PRIMER n pl. -S a book that covers the basics of a subject

PRIMERO n pl. -ROS a card game

PRIMEVAL adj pertaining to the earliest ages

PRIMI a pl. of primo

PRIMINE n pl. -S the outer covering of an ovule

PRIMING n pl. -S the act of one that primes

PRIMLY adv in a prim manner

PRIMMED past tense of prim

PRIMMER comparative of prim

PRIMMEST superlative of prim

PRIMMING present participle of prim

PRIMNESS n pl. -ES the state of being prim

PRIMO n pl. -MOS or -MI the main part in a musical piece

PRIMP v -ED, -ING, -S to dress or adorn carefully

PRIMROSE n pl. -S a perennial herb

PRIMSIE adj prim

PRIMULA n pl. -S primrose

PRIMUS n pl. -ES the head bishop of Scotland

PRINCE n pl. -S a non-reigning male member of a royal family

PRINCELY adj -LIER, -LIEST of or befitting a prince

PRINCESS n pl. -ES a non-reigning female member of a royal family

PRINCIPE n pl. -PI a prince

PRINCOCK n pl. -S a coxcomb

PRINCOX n pl. -ES princock

PRINK v -ED, -ING, -S to dress or adorn in a showy manner

PRINKER n pl. -S one that prinks

PRINT v -ED, -ING, -S to produce by pressed type on a surface

PRINTER n pl. -S one that prints

PRINTERY n pl. -ERIES a place where printing is done

PRINTING n pl. -S a reproduction from a printing surface

PRINTOUT n pl. -S the printed output of a computer

PRION n pl. -S a protein particle

PRIOR n pl. -S an officer in a monastery

PRIORATE n pl. -S the office of a prior

PRIORESS n pl. -ES a nun corresponding in rank to a prior

PRIORIES pl. of priory

PRIORITY *n* pl. -TIES precedence established by importance

PRIORLY *adv* previously

PRIORY *n* pl. -RIES a religious house

PRISE *v* PRISED, PRISING, PRISES to raise or force with a lever

PRISERE *n* pl. -S a succession of vegetational stages

PRISM *n* pl. -S a solid which disperses light into a spectrum

PRISMOID *n* pl. -S a geometric solid

PRISON *v* -ED, -ING, -S to imprison

PRISONER *n* pl. -S one that is imprisoned

PRISS *v* -ED, -ING, -ES to act in a prissy manner

PRISSY *adj* -SIER, -SIEST excessively or affectedly proper **PRISSILY** *adv*

PRISSY *n* pl. -SIES one who is prissy

PRISTANE *n* pl. -S a chemical compound

PRISTINE *adj* pertaining to the earliest time or state

PRITHEE *interj* — used to express a wish or request

PRIVACY *n* pl. -CIES the state of being private

PRIVATE *adj* -VATER, -VATEST secluded from the sight, presence, or intrusion of others

PRIVATE *n* pl. -S a soldier of lower rank

PRIVET *n* pl. -S an ornamental shrub

PRIVIER comparative of privy

PRIVIES pl. of privy

PRIVITY *n* pl. -TIES private knowledge

PRIVY *adj* PRIVIER, PRIVIEST private **PRIVILY** *adv*

PRIVY *n* pl. PRIVIES an outhouse

PRIZE *v* PRIZED, PRIZING, PRIZES to value highly

PRIZER *n* pl. -S one who vies for a reward

PRO *n* pl. PROS an argument or vote in favor of something

PROA *n* pl. -S prau

PROBABLE *n* pl. -S something likely to occur or prove true

PROBABLY *adv* without much doubt

PROBAND *n* pl. -S one whose reactions or responses are studied

PROBANG *n* pl. -S a surgical rod

PROBATE *v* -BATED, -BATING, -BATES to establish the validity of

PROBE *v* PROBED, PROBING, PROBES to investigate or examine thoroughly

PROBER *n* pl. -S one that probes

PROBIT *n* pl. -S a unit of statistical probability

PROBITY *n* pl. -TIES complete and confirmed integrity

PROBLEM *n* pl. -S a perplexing question or situation

PROCAINE *n* pl. -S a compound used as a local anesthetic

PROCARP *n* pl. -S a female sexual organ in certain algae

PROCEED *v* -ED, -ING, -S to go forward or onward

PROCESS *v* -ED, -ING, -ES to treat or prepare by a special method

PROCHAIN *adj* prochein

PROCHEIN *adj* nearest in time, relation, or degree

PROCLAIM *v* -ED, -ING, -S to make known publicly or officially

PROCTOR *v* -ED, -ING, -S to supervise

PROCURAL *n* pl. -S the act of procuring

PROCURE *v* -CURED, -CURING, -CURES to obtain by effort

PROCURER *n* pl. -S one that procures

PROD *v* PRODDED, PRODDING, PRODS to jab with something pointed

PRODDER *n* pl. -S one that prods

PRODIGAL *n* pl. -S one who spends lavishly and foolishly

PRODIGY *n* pl. -GIES a child having exceptional talent or ability

PRODROME *n* pl. -DROMES or -DROMATA a sign of impending disease

PRODUCE *v* -DUCED, -DUCING, -DUCES to bring into existence

PRODUCER *n* pl. -S one that produces

PRODUCT *n* pl. -S something produced by labor or effort

PROEM *n* pl. -S an introductory statement **PROEMIAL** *adj*

PROETTE *n* pl. -S a female professional athlete

PROF *n* pl. -S a professor

PROFANE *v* -FANED, -FANING, -FANES to treat with irreverence or abuse

PROFANER *n* pl. -S one that profanes

PROFESS *v* -ED, -ING, -ES to affirm openly

PROFFER *v* -ED, -ING, -S to present for acceptance

PROFILE *v* -FILED, -FILING, -FILES to draw an outline of

PROFILER *n* pl. -S one that profiles

PROFIT v -ED, -ING, -S to gain an advantage or benefit

PROFITER n pl. -S one that profits

PROFOUND adj -FOUNDER, -FOUNDEST intellectually deep and penetrating

PROFOUND n pl. -S something that is very deep

PROFUSE adj pouring forth generously

PROG v PROGGED, PROGGING, PROGS to prowl about for food or plunder

PROGENY n pl. -NIES a descendant or offspring

PROGERIA n pl. -S premature aging

PROGGER n pl. -S one that progs

PROGGING present participle of prog

PROGNOSE v -NOSED, -NOSING, -NOSES to forecast the probable course of a disease

PROGRADE adj pertaining to the orbital motion of a body

PROGRAM v -GRAMED, -GRAMING, -GRAMS or -GRAMMED, -GRAMMING, -GRAMS to arrange in a plan of proceedings

PROGRESS v -ED, -ING, -ES to move forward or onward

PROHIBIT v -ED, -ING, -S to forbid by authority

PROJECT v -ED, -ING, -S to extend outward

PROJET n pl. -S a plan or outline

PROLABOR adj favoring organized labor

PROLAMIN n pl. -S a simple protein

PROLAN n pl. -S a sex hormone

PROLAPSE v -LAPSED, -LAPSING, -LAPSES to fall or slip out of place

PROLATE adj extended lengthwise

PROLE n pl. -S a member of the working class

PROLEG n pl. -S an abdominal leg of certain insect larvae

PROLIFIC adj producing abundantly

PROLINE n pl. -S an amino acid

PROLIX adj tediously long and wordy PROLIXLY adv

PROLOG v -ED, -ING, -S to prologue

PROLOGUE v -LOGUED, -LOGUING, -LOGUES to preface

PROLONG v -ED, -ING, -S to lengthen in duration

PROLONGE n pl. -S a rope used for pulling a gun carriage

PROM n pl. -S a formal dance

PROMINE n pl. -S a substance that promotes growth

PROMISE v -ISED, -ISING, -ISES to make a declaration of assurance

PROMISEE n pl. -S one who is promised something

PROMISER n pl. -S promisor

PROMISING present participle of promise

PROMISOR n pl. -S one that promises

PROMO n pl. -MOS a promotional presentation

PROMOTE v -MOTED, -MOTING, -MOTES to contribute to the progress of

PROMOTER n pl. -S one that promotes

PROMPT adj PROMPTER, PROMPTEST quick to act or respond

PROMPT v -ED, -ING, -S to induce to action

PROMPTER n pl. -S one that prompts

PROMPTLY adv in a prompt manner

PROMULGE v -MULGED, -MULGING, -MULGES to proclaim

PRONATE v -NATED, -NATING, -NATES to turn the palm downward or backward

PRONATOR n pl. -S or -ES a forearm or forelimb muscle

PRONE adj lying with the front or face downward PRONELY adv

PRONG v -ED, -ING, -S to pierce with a pointed projection

PRONOTUM n pl. -NOTA a hard outer plate of an insect

PRONOUN n pl. -S a word that may be used in place of a noun

PRONTO adv quickly

PROOF v -ED, -ING, -S to examine for errors

PROOFER n pl. -S one that proofs

PROP v PROPPED, PROPPING, PROPS to keep from falling

PROPANE n pl. -S a flammable gas

PROPEL v -PELLED, -PELLING, -PELS to cause to move forward or onward

PROPEND v -ED, -ING, -S to have a tendency toward

PROPENE n pl. -S a flammable gas

PROPENOL n pl. -S a flammable liquid

PROPENSE adj tending toward

PROPENYL adj pertaining to a certain chemical group

PROPER adj -ERER, -EREST suitable PROPERLY adv

PROPER n pl. -S a portion of the Mass

PROPERTY n pl. -TIES something owned

PROPHAGE n pl. -S a form of virus

PROPHASE n pl. -S the first stage in mitosis

PROPHECY n pl. -CIES a prediction

PROPHESY v -SIED, -SYING, -SIES to predict

PROPHET n pl. -S one who predicts

PROPINE v -PINED, -PINING, -PINES to offer as a gift

PROPJET n pl. -S a type of airplane

PROPMAN n pl. -MEN a man in charge of stage properties

PROPOLIS n pl. -LISES a resinous substance used as a cement by bees

PROPONE v -PONED, -PONING, -PONES to propose

PROPOSAL n pl. -S something that is proposed

PROPOSE v -POSED, -POSING, -POSES to put forward for consideration or acceptance

PROPOSER n pl. -S one that proposes

PROPOUND v -ED, -ING, -S to propose

PROPPED past tense of prop

PROPPING present participle of prop

PROPYL n pl. -S a univalent radical PROPYLIC adj

PROPYLON n pl. -LA an entrance to a temple

PRORATE v -RATED, -RATING, -RATES to divide proportionately

PROROGUE v -ROGUED, -ROGUING, -ROGUES to discontinue a session of

PROSAIC adj pertaining to prose

PROSAISM n pl. -S a prosaic style

PROSAIST n pl. -S a writer of prose

PROSE v PROSED, PROSING, PROSES to write prose (writing without metrical structure)

PROSECT v -ED, -ING, -S to dissect

PROSER n pl. -S a prosaist

PROSIER comparative of prosy

PROSIEST superlative of prosy

PROSILY adv in a prosy manner

PROSING present participle of prose

PROSIT interj— used as a drinking toast

PROSO n pl. -SOS millet

PROSODY n pl. -DIES the study of poetical forms PROSODIC adj

PROSOMA n pl. -S the front region of the body of an invertebrate PROSOMAL adj

PROSPECT v -ED, -ING, -S to explore for mineral deposits

PROSPER v -ED, -ING, -S to be successful or fortunate

PROSS n pl. -ES a prostitute

PROSSIE n pl. -S a prostitute

PROST interj prosit

PROSTATE n pl. -S a gland in male mammals

PROSTIE n pl. -S a prostitute

PROSTYLE n pl. -S a building having a row of columns across the front only

PROSY adj PROSIER, PROSIEST prosaic

PROTAMIN n pl. -S a simple protein

PROTASIS n pl. -ASES the introductory part of a classical drama PROTATIC adj

PROTEA n pl. -S an evergreen shrub

PROTEAN n pl. -S a type of protein

PROTEASE n pl. -S an enzyme

PROTECT v -ED, -ING, -S to keep from harm, attack, or injury

PROTEGE n pl. -S one whose career is promoted by an influential person

PROTEGEE n pl. -S a female protege

PROTEI pl. of proteus

PROTEID n pl. -S protein

PROTEIDE n pl. -S proteid

PROTEIN n pl. -S a nitrogenous organic compound

PROTEND v -ED, -ING, -S to extend

PROTEOSE n pl. -S a water-soluble protein

PROTEST v -ED, -ING, -S to express strong objection

PROTEUS n pl. -TEI any of a genus of aerobic bacteria

PROTEUS n pl. -ES one that readily changes his appearance or principles

PROTIST n pl. -S any of a group of unicellular organisms

PROTIUM n pl. -S an isotope of hydrogen

PROTOCOL v -COLED, -COLING, -COLS or -COLLED, -COLLING, -COLS to form a preliminary draft of an official document

PROTON n pl. -S a subatomic particle **PROTONIC** adj

PROTOPOD n pl. -S a part of a crustacean appendage

PROTOXID n pl. -S an oxide

PROTOZOA n/pl unicellular microscopic organisms

PROTRACT v -ED, -ING, -S to prolong

PROTRUDE v -TRUDED, -TRUDING, -TRUDES to extend beyond the main portion

PROTYL n pl. -S protyle

PROTYLE n pl. -S a hypothetical substance from which all the elements are supposedly derived

PROUD adj PROUDER, PROUDEST having or displaying pride **PROUDLY** adv

PROUDFUL adj prideful

PROUNION adj favoring labor unions

PROVE v PROVED, PROVEN, PROVING, PROVES to establish the truth or validity of **PROVABLE** adj **PROVABLY** adv

PROVENLY adv without doubt

PROVER n pl. -S one that proves

PROVERB v -ED, -ING, -S to make a byword of

PROVIDE v -VIDED, -VIDING, -VIDES to supply

PROVIDER n pl. -S one that provides

PROVINCE n pl. -S an administrative division of a country

PROVING present participle of prove

PROVIRUS n pl. -ES a form of virus **PROVIRAL** adj

PROVISO n pl. -SOS or -SOES a clause in a document introducing a condition or restriction

PROVOKE v -VOKED, -VOKING, -VOKES to incite to anger or resentment

PROVOKER n pl. -S one that provokes

PROVOST n pl. -S a high-ranking university official

PROW n pl. -S the forward part of a ship

PROW adj PROWER, PROWEST brave

PROWAR adj favoring war

PROWESS n pl. -ES exceptional ability

PROWL v -ED, -ING, -S to move about stealthily

PROWLER n pl. -S one that prowls

PROXEMIC adj pertaining to a branch of environmental study

PROXIES pl. of proxy

PROXIMAL adj located near the point of origin

PROXIMO adj of or occurring in the following month

PROXY n pl. PROXIES a person authorized to act for another

PRUDE n pl. -S a prudish person

PRUDENCE n pl. -S the quality of being prudent

PRUDENT adj having, showing, or exercising good judgment

PRUDERY n pl. -ERIES excessive regard for propriety, modesty, or morality

PRUDISH adj marked by prudery

PRUINOSE adj having a powdery covering

PRUNE v PRUNED, PRUNING, PRUNES to cut off branches or parts from **PRUNABLE** adj

PRUNELLA n pl. -S a strong woolen fabric

PRUNELLE n pl. -S a plum-flavored liqueur

PRUNELLO n pl. -LOS prunella

PRUNER n pl. -S one that prunes

PRUNING present participle of prune

PRUNUS n pl. -ES a flowering tree

PRURIENT adj having lustful thoughts or desires

PRURIGO n pl. -GOS a skin disease

PRURITUS n pl. -ES intense itching **PRURITIC** adj

PRUSSIC adj pertaining to a type of acid

PRUTA n pl. PRUTOT prutah

PRUTAH n pl. PRUTOTH a monetary unit of Israel

PRY v PRIED, PRYING, PRIES to inquire impertinently into private matters **PRYINGLY** adv

PRYER n pl. -S prier

PRYTHEE interj prithee

PSALM v -ED, -ING, -S to praise in psalms (sacred songs)

PSALMIC adj of or pertaining to a psalm

PSALMIST n pl. -S a writer of psalms

PSALMODY n pl. -DIES the use of psalms in worship

PSALTER n pl. -S a book of psalms

PSALTERY n pl. -TERIES an ancient stringed musical instrument

PSALTRY n pl. -TRIES psaltery

PSAMMITE n pl. -S a fine-grained rock

PSAMMON *n pl.* -S a group of microorganisms living in waterlogged sands

PSCHENT *n pl.* -S a crown worn by ancient Egyptian kings

PSEPHITE *n pl.* -S a rock composed of small pebbles

PSEUD *n pl.* -S a person pretending to be an intellectual

PSEUDO *n pl.* PSEUDOS a pseud

PSHAW *v* -ED, -ING, -S to utter an expression of disapproval

PSI *n pl.* -S a Greek letter

PSILOCIN *n pl.* -S a hallucinogenic drug

PSILOSIS *n pl.* -LOSES a tropical disease PSILOTIC *adj*

PSOAS *n pl.* PSOAI or PSOAE a muscle of the loin PSOATIC *adj*

PSOCID *n pl.* -S a minute winged insect

PSORALEA *n pl.* -S a plant of the bean family

PSORALEN *n pl.* -S a drug used to treat psoriasis

PSST *interj* — used to attract someone's attention

PSYCH *v* -ED, -ING, -S to put into the proper frame of mind

PSYCHE *n pl.* -S the mental structure of a person

PSYCHIC *n pl.* -S one sensitive to extrasensory phenomena

PSYCHO *n pl.* -CHOS a mentally unstable person

PSYLLA *n pl.* -S any of various plant lice

PSYLLID *n pl.* -S psylla

PSYLLIUM *n pl.* -S the seed of a fleawort

PSYWAR *n pl.* -S psychological warfare

PTERIN *n pl.* -S a chemical compound

PTEROPOD *n pl.* -S a type of mollusk

PTERYGIA *n/pl* fleshy growths over the cornea

PTERYLA *n pl.* -LAE a feathered area on the skin of a bird

PTISAN *n pl.* -S a tea of herbs or barley

PTOMAIN *n pl.* -S ptomaine

PTOMAINE *n pl.* -S a compound produced by the decomposition of protein

PTOSIS *n pl.* PTOSES a drooping of the upper eyelid PTOTIC *adj*

PTYALIN *n pl.* -S a salivary enzyme

PTYALISM *n pl.* -S an excessive flow of saliva

PUB *n pl.* -S a tavern

PUBERTY *n pl.* -TIES a period of sexual maturation PUBERAL, PUBERTAL *adj*

PUBIC *adj* pertaining to the pubes or pubis

PUBIS *n pl.* PUBES the forward portion of either of the hipbones

PUBLIC *n pl.* -S the community or the people as a whole

PUBLICAN *n pl.* -S one who owns or manages a pub

PUBLICLY *adv* by the public

PUBLISH *v* -ED, -ING, -ES to print and issue to the public

PUCCOON *n pl.* -S an herb that yields a red dye

PUCE *n pl.* -S a dark red color

PUCK *n pl.* -S a rubber disk used in ice hockey

PUCKA *adj* pukka

PUCKER *v* -ED, -ING, -S to gather into small wrinkles or folds

PUCKERER *n pl.* -S one that puckers

PUCKERY *adj* -ERIER, -ERIEST having a tendency to pucker

PUCKISH *adj* impish

PUD *n pl.* -S pudding

PUDDING *n pl.* -S a thick, soft dessert

PUDDLE *v* -DLED, -DLING, -DLES to strew with puddles (small pools of water)

PUDDLER *n pl.* -S one who subjects iron to puddling

PUDDLING *n pl.* -S the process of converting pig iron to wrought iron

PUDDLY *adj* -DLIER, -DLIEST full of puddles

PUDENCY *n pl.* -CIES modesty

PUDENDUM *n pl.* -DA the external genital organs of a woman PUDENDAL *adj*

PUDGY *adj* PUDGIER, PUDGIEST short and fat PUDGILY *adv*

PUDIBUND *adj* prudish

PUDIC *adj* to the pudendum

PUEBLO *n pl.* -LOS a communal dwelling of certain Indian tribes

PUERILE *adj* childish

PUFF *v* -ED, -ING, -S to blow in short gusts

PUFFBALL *n pl.* -S any of various globular fungi

PUFFER *n pl.* -S one that puffs

PUFFERY *n pl.* -ERIES excessive public praise

PUFFIN *n pl.* -S a sea bird

PUFFY *adj* -FIER, -FIEST swollen **PUFFILY** *adv*

PUG *v* PUGGED, PUGGING, PUGS to fill in with clay or mortar

PUGAREE *n pl.* -S pugree

PUGGAREE *n pl.* -S pugree

PUGGED past tense of pug

PUGGIER comparative of puggy

PUGGIEST superlative of puggy

PUGGING present participle of pug

PUGGISH *adj* somewhat stubby

PUGGREE *n pl.* -S pugree

PUGGRY *n pl.* -GRIES pugree

PUGGY *adj* -GIER, -GIEST puggish

PUGH *interj* — used to express disgust

PUGILISM *n pl.* -S the art or practice of fighting with the fists

PUGILIST *n pl.* -S one who fights with his fists

PUGMARK *n pl.* -S a footprint

PUGREE *n pl.* -S a cloth band wrapped around a hat

PUISNE *n pl.* -S one of lesser rank

PUISSANT *adj* powerful

PUJA *n pl.* -S a Hindu prayer ritual

PUJAH *n pl.* -S puja

PUKE *v* PUKED, PUKING, PUKES to vomit

PUKKA *adj* genuine

PUL *n pl.* PULS or PULI a coin of Afghanistan

PULA *n pl.* PULA a monetary unit of Botswana

PULE *v* PULED, PULING, PULES to whine

PULER *n pl.* -S one that pules

PULI *n pl.* -LIK or -LIS a long-haired sheepdog

PULICENE *adj* pertaining to fleas

PULICIDE *n pl.* -S an agent used for destroying fleas

PULIK a pl. of puli

PULING *n pl.* -S a plaintive cry

PULINGLY *adv* in a whining manner

PULL *v* -ED, -ING, -S to exert force in order to cause motion toward the force

PULLBACK *n pl.* -S a restraint or drawback

PULLER *n pl.* -S one that pulls

PULLET *n pl.* -S a young hen

PULLEY *n pl.* -LEYS a device used for lifting weight

PULLMAN *n pl.* -S a railroad sleeping car

PULLOUT *n pl.* -S a withdrawal

PULLOVER *n pl.* -S a garment that is put on by being drawn over the head

PULLUP *n pl.* -S the act of raising oneself while hanging by the hands

PULMONIC *adj* pertaining to the lungs

PULMOTOR *n pl.* -S a respiratory device

PULP *v* -ED, -ING, -S to reduce to pulp (a soft, moist mass of matter)

PULPAL *adj* pertaining to pulp **PULPALLY** *adv*

PULPER *n pl.* -S one that pulps

PULPIER comparative of pulpy

PULPIEST superlative of pulpy

PULPILY *adv* in a pulpy manner

PULPIT *n pl.* -S a platform in a church **PULPITAL** *adj*

PULPLESS *adj* having no pulp

PULPOUS *adj* pulpy

PULPWOOD *n pl.* -S soft wood used in making paper

PULPY *adj* PULPIER, PULPIEST resembling pulp

PULQUE *n pl.* -S a fermented Mexican beverage

PULSANT *adj* pulsating

PULSAR *n pl.* -S a celestial source of radio waves

PULSATE *v* -SATED, -SATING, -SATES to expand and contract rhythmically

PULSATOR *n pl.* -S something that pulsates

PULSE *v* PULSED, PULSING, PULSES to pulsate

PULSEJET *n pl.* -S a type of engine

PULSER *n pl.* -S a device that causes pulsations

PULSING present participle of pulse

PULSION *n pl.* -S propulsion

PULSOJET *n pl.* -S pulsejet

PULVILLI *n/pl* pads between the claws of an insect's foot

PULVINUS *n* pl. -NI a swelling at the base of a leaf **PULVINAR** *adj*

PUMA *n* pl. -S a cougar

PUMELO *n* pl. -LOS pomelo

PUMICE *v* -ICED, -ICING, -ICES to polish with a porous volcanic rock

PUMICER *n* pl. -S one that pumices

PUMICITE *n* pl. -S a porous volcanic rock

PUMMEL *v* -MELED, -MELING, -MELS or -MELLED, -MELLING, -MELS to pommel

PUMMELO *n* pl. -LOS a shaddock

PUMP *v* -ED, -ING, -S to cause to flow by means of a pump (a device for moving fluids)

PUMPER *n* pl. -S one that pumps

PUMPKIN *n* pl. -S a large, edible fruit

PUMPLESS *adj* lacking a pump

PUMPLIKE *adj* resembling a pump

PUN *v* PUNNED, PUNNING, PUNS to make a pun (a play on words)

PUNA *n* pl. -S a cold, arid plateau

PUNCH *v* -ED, -ING, -ES to perforate with a type of tool

PUNCHEON *n* pl. -S a vertical supporting timber

PUNCHER *n* pl. -S one that punches

PUNCHY *adj* PUNCHIER, PUNCHIEST dazed **PUNCHILY** *adv*

PUNCTATE *adj* covered with dots

PUNCTUAL *adj* being on time

PUNCTURE *v* -TURED, -TURING, -TURES to pierce with a pointed object

PUNDIT *n* pl. -S a Hindu scholar **PUNDITIC** *adj*

PUNDITRY *n* pl. -RIES the learning of pundits

PUNG *n* pl. -S a box-shaped sleigh

PUNGENCY *n* pl. -CIES the state of being pungent

PUNGENT *adj* sharply affecting the organs of taste or smell

PUNGLE *v* -GLED, -GLING, -GLES to contribute

PUNIER comparative of puny

PUNIEST superlative of puny

PUNILY *adv* in a puny manner

PUNINESS *n* pl. -ES the state of being puny

PUNISH *v* -ED, -ING, -ES to impose a penalty on in requital for wrongdoing

PUNISHER *n* pl. -S one that punishes

PUNITION *n* pl. -S the act of punishing; punishment

PUNITIVE *adj* inflicting punishment

PUNITORY *adj* punitive

PUNK *n* pl. -S dry, decayed wood used as tinder

PUNK *adj* PUNKER, PUNKEST of inferior quality

PUNKA *n* pl. -S a ceiling fan used in India

PUNKAH *n* pl. -S punka

PUNKER *n* pl. -S a punk rock musician

PUNKEY *n* pl. -KEYS punkie

PUNKIE *n* pl. -S a biting gnat

PUNKIN *n* pl. -S pumpkin

PUNKISH *adj* pertaining to a style inspired by punk rock

PUNKY *adj* PUNKIER, PUNKIEST resembling punk

PUNNED past tense of pun

PUNNER *n* pl. -S a punster

PUNNET *n* pl. -S a small basket

PUNNING present participle of pun

PUNNY *adj* -NIER, -NIEST being or involving a pun

PUNSTER *n* pl. -S one who is given to punning

PUNT *v* -ED, -ING, -S to propel through water with a pole

PUNTER *n* pl. -S one that punts

PUNTO *n* pl. -TOS a hit or thrust in fencing

PUNTY *n* pl. -TIES an iron rod used in glassmaking

PUNY *adj* PUNIER, PUNIEST of inferior size, strength, or significance

PUP *v* PUPPED, PUPPING, PUPS to give birth to puppies

PUPA *n* pl. -PAS or -PAE an intermediate stage of a metamorphic insect **PUPAL** *adj*

PUPARIUM *n* pl. -IA a pupal shell **PUPARIAL** *adj*

PUPATE *v* -PATED, -PATING, -PATES to pass through the pupal stage

PUPATION *n* pl. -S the act of pupating

PUPFISH *n* pl. -ES a small, freshwater fish

PUPIL *n* pl. -S a student under the close supervision of a teacher

PUPILAGE *n* pl. -S the state of being a pupil

PUPILAR *adj* pertaining to a part of the eye

PUPILARY *adj* pupilar

PUPPED past tense of pup

PUPPET *n* pl. -S a small figure, as of a person or animal, manipulated by the hand

PUPPETRY *n* pl. -RIES the art of making or manipulating puppets

PUPPING present participle of pup

PUPPY *n* pl. -PIES a young dog **PUPPYISH** *adj*

PUPPYDOM *n* pl. -S the world of puppies

PUR *v* PURRED, PURRING, PURS to purr

PURANA *n* pl. -S a Hindu scripture **PURANIC** *adj*

PURBLIND *adj* partially blind

PURCHASE *v* -CHASED, -CHASING, -CHASES to acquire by the payment of money

PURDA *n* pl. -S purdah

PURDAH *n* pl. -S a curtain used in India to seclude women

PURE *adj* PURER, PUREST free from anything different, inferior, or contaminating

PUREBRED *n* pl. -S an animal of unmixed stock

PUREE *v* -REED, -REEING, -REES to reduce to a thick pulp by cooking and sieving

PURELY *adv* in a pure manner

PURENESS *n* pl. -ES the quality of being pure

PURER comparative of pure

PUREST superlative of pure

PURFLE *v* -FLED, -FLING, -FLES to decorate the border of

PURFLING *n* pl. -S an ornamental border

PURGE *v* PURGED, PURGING, PURGES to purify

PURGER *n* pl. -S one that purges

PURGING *n* pl. -S the act of purifying

PURI *n* pl. -S poori

PURIFIER *n* pl. -S one that purifies

PURIFY *v* -FIED, -FYING, -FIES to free from impurities

PURIN *n* pl. -S purine

PURINE *n* pl. -S a chemical compound

PURISM *n* pl. -S strict adherence to traditional correctness

PURIST *n* pl. -S one who practices purism **PURISTIC** *adj*

PURITAN *n* pl. -S a rigorously moral or religious person

PURITY *n* pl. -TIES the quality of being pure

PURL *v* -ED, -ING, -S to knit with a particular stitch

PURLIEU *n* pl. -S an outlying or neighboring area

PURLIN *n* pl. -S a horizontal supporting timber

PURLINE *n* pl. -S purlin

PURLOIN *v* -ED, -ING, -S to steal

PURPLE *adj* -PLER, -PLEST of a color intermediate between red and blue

PURPLE *v* -PLED, -PLING, -PLES to make purple

PURPLISH *adj* somewhat purple

PURPLY *adj* purplish

PURPORT *v* -ED, -ING, -S to profess or claim

PURPOSE *v* -POSED, -POSING, -POSES to resolve to perform or accomplish

PURPURA *n* pl. -S a disease characterized by purple spots on the skin

PURPURE *n* pl. -S the heraldic color purple

PURPURIC *adj* pertaining to purpura

PURPURIN *n* pl. -S a reddish dye

PURR *v* -ED, -ING, -S to utter a low, vibrant sound

PURRED past tense of pur and purr

PURRING present participle of pur and purr

PURSE *v* PURSED, PURSING, PURSES to pucker

PURSER *n* pl. -S an officer in charge of a ship's accounts

PURSIER comparative of pursy

PURSIEST superlative of pursy

PURSILY *adv* in a pursy manner

PURSING present participle of purse

PURSLANE *n* pl. -S a common garden herb

PURSUANT *adv* in accordance

PURSUE *v* -SUED, -SUING, -SUES to follow in order to overtake or capture

PURSUER *n* pl. -S one that pursues

PURSUIT *n* pl. -S the act of pursuing

PURSY *adj* PURSIER, PURSIEST short of breath

PURULENT *adj* secreting pus

PURVEY *v* -ED, -ING, -S to supply

PURVEYOR *n* pl. -S one that purveys

PURVIEW n pl. -S the extent of operation, authority, or concern

PUS n pl. -ES a viscous fluid formed in infected tissue

PUSH v -ED, -ING, -ES to exert force in order to cause motion away from the force

PUSHBALL n pl. -S a type of ball game

PUSHCART n pl. -S a light cart pushed by hand

PUSHDOWN n pl. -S a store of computer data

PUSHER n pl. -S one that pushes

PUSHFUL adj pushy

PUSHIER comparative of pushy

PUSHIEST superlative of pushy

PUSHILY adv in a pushy manner

PUSHOVER n pl. -S an easily defeated person or team

PUSHPIN n pl. -S a large-headed pin

PUSHROD n pl. -S a rod for operating the valves in an engine

PUSHUP n pl. -S a type of exercise

PUSHY adj PUSHIER, PUSHIEST offensively aggressive

PUSLEY n pl. -LEYS pussley

PUSLIKE adj resembling pus

PUSS n pl. -ES a cat

PUSSIER comparative of pussy

PUSSIES pl. of pussy

PUSSIEST superlative of pussy

PUSSLEY n pl. -LEYS purslane

PUSSLIKE adj catlike

PUSSLY n pl. -LIES pussley

PUSSY n pl. PUSSIES a cat

PUSSY adj -SIER, -SIEST full of pus

PUSSYCAT n pl. -S a cat

PUSTULE n pl. -S a small elevation of the skin containing pus **PUSTULAR, PUSTULED** adj

PUT v PUT, PUTTING, PUTS to place in a particular position

PUTAMEN n pl. -MINA the hard covering of the kernel of certain fruits

PUTATIVE adj generally regarded as such

PUTLOG n pl. -S a horizontal supporting timber

PUTOFF n pl. -S an excuse

PUTON n pl. -S a hoax or deception

PUTOUT n pl. -S an act of causing an out in baseball

PUTREFY v -FIED, -FYING, -FIES to make or become putrid

PUTRID adj being in a decomposed, foul-smelling state **PUTRIDLY** adv

PUTSCH n pl. -ES a suddenly executed attempt to overthrow a government

PUTT v -ED, -ING, -S to hit with a light stroke in golf

PUTTEE n pl. -S a strip of cloth wound around the leg

PUTTER v -ED, -ING, -S to occupy oneself in a leisurely or ineffective manner

PUTTERER n pl. -S one that putters

PUTTI pl. of putto

PUTTIED past tense of putty

PUTTIER n pl. -S one that putties

PUTTING present participle of put

PUTTO n pl. -TI an infant boy in art

PUTTY v -TIED, -TYING, -TIES to fill with a type of cement

PUTZ v -ED, -ING, -ES to waste time

PUZZLE v -ZLED, -ZLING, -ZLES to cause uncertainty and indecision in

PUZZLER n pl. -S something that puzzles

PYA n pl. -S a copper coin of Burma

PYAEMIA n pl. -S pyemia **PYAEMIC** adj

PYCNIDIA n/pl spore-bearing organs of certain fungi

PYCNOSIS n pl. -NOSES pyknosis

PYCNOTIC adj pyknotic

PYE n pl. -S a book of ecclesiastical rules in the pre-Reformation English church

PYELITIS n pl. -TISES inflammation of the pelvis or the kidney **PYELITIC** adj

PYEMIA n pl. -S the presence of pus in the blood **PYEMIC** adj

PYGIDIUM n pl. -IA the posterior region of certain invertebrates **PYGIDIAL** adj

PYGMY n pl. -MIES a small person **PYGMAEAN, PYGMEAN, PYGMOID, PYGMYISH** adj

PYGMYISM n pl. -S a stunted or dwarfish condition

PYIC adj pertaining to pus

PYIN n pl. -S a protein compound contained in pus

PYJAMAS n pl. PYJAMAS pajamas

PYKNIC n pl. -S a person having a broad, stocky build

PYKNOSIS n pl. -NOSES a shrinking and thickening of a cell nucleus

PYKNOTIC adj exhibiting pyknosis

PYLON n pl. -S a tall structure marking an entrance or approach

PYLORUS n pl. -RI or -RUSES the opening between the stomach and the duodenum **PYLORIC** adj

PYODERMA n pl. -S a pus-causing skin disease

PYOGENIC adj producing pus

PYOID adj puslike

PYORRHEA n pl. -S a discharge of pus

PYOSIS n pl. -OSES the formation of pus

PYRALID n pl. -S a long-legged moth

PYRAMID v -ED, -ING, -S to raise or increase by adding amounts gradually

PYRAN n pl. -S a chemical compound **PYRANOID** adj

PYRANOSE n pl. -S a simple sugar

PYRE n pl. -S a pile of combustible material

PYRENE n pl. -S a putamen

PYRENOID n pl. -S a protein body of certain lower organisms

PYRETIC adj pertaining to fever

PYREXIA n pl. -S fever **PYREXIAL, PYREXIC** adj

PYRIC adj pertaining to burning

PYRIDINE n pl. -S a flammable liquid **PYRIDIC** adj

PYRIFORM adj pear-shaped

PYRITE n pl. -S a metallic sulfide **PYRITIC, PYRITOUS** adj

PYROGEN n pl. -S a substance that produces fever

PYROLA n pl. -S a perennial herb

PYROLOGY n pl. -GIES the scientific examination of materials by heat

PYROLYZE v -LYZED, -LYZING, -LYZES to affect compounds by the application of heat

PYRONE n pl. -S a chemical compound

PYRONINE n pl. -S a dye

PYROPE n pl. -S a variety of garnet

PYROSIS n pl. -SISES heartburn

PYROSTAT n pl. -S a thermostat

PYROXENE n pl. -S any of a group of minerals common in igneous rocks

PYRRHIC n pl. -S a type of metrical foot

PYRROL n pl. -S pyrrole

PYRROLE n pl. -S a chemical compound **PYRROLIC** adj

PYRUVATE n pl. -S a chemical salt

PYTHON n pl. -S a large snake **PYTHONIC** adj

PYURIA n pl. -S the presence of pus in the urine

PYX n pl. -ES a container in which the eucharistic bread is kept

PYXIDES pl. of pyxis

PYXIDIUM n pl. -IA a type of seed vessel

PYXIE n pl. -S an evergreen shrub

PYXIS n pl. PYXIDES a pyxidium

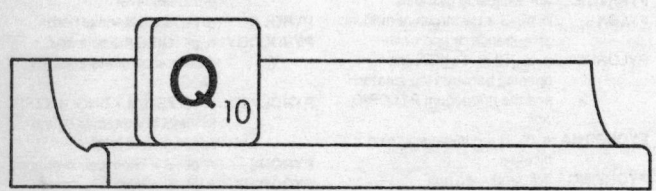

QAID	*n* pl. -S caid	
QANAT	*n* pl. -S a system of underground tunnels and wells in the Middle East	
QAT	*n* pl. -S kat	
QINDAR	*n* pl. -DARS or -DARKA qintar	
QINTAR	*n* pl. -S a monetary unit of Albania	
QIVIUT	*n* pl. -S the wool of a musk-ox	
QOPH	*n* pl. -S koph	
QUA	*adv* in the capacity of	
QUAALUDE	*n* pl. -S a sedative drug	
QUACK	*v* -ED, -ING, -S to utter the characteristic cry of a duck	
QUACKERY	*n* pl. -ERIES fraudulent practice	
QUACKISH	*adj* fraudulent	
QUACKISM	*n* pl. -S quackery	
QUAD	*v* QUADDED, QUADDING, QUADS to space out by means of quadrats	
QUADPLEX	*n* pl. -ES a building having four units	
QUADRANS	*n* pl. -RANTES an ancient Roman coin	
QUADRANT	*n* pl. -S a quarter section of a circle	
QUADRAT	*n* pl. -S a piece of type metal used for filling spaces	
QUADRATE	*v* -RATED, -RATING, -RATES to correspond or agree	
QUADRIC	*n* pl. -S a type of geometric surface	
QUADRIGA	*n* pl. -GAE a chariot drawn by four horses	
QUADROON	*n* pl. -S a person of one-quarter black ancestry	
QUAERE	*n* pl. -S a question	

QUAESTOR	*n* pl. -S an ancient Roman magistrate	
QUAFF	*v* -ED, -ING, -S to drink deeply	
QUAFFER	*n* pl. -S one that quaffs	
QUAG	*n* pl. -S a quagmire	
QUAGGA	*n* pl. -S an extinct zebralike mammal	
QUAGGY	*adj* -GIER, -GIEST marshy	
QUAGMIRE	*n* pl. -S an area of marshy ground	
QUAGMIRY	*adj* -MIRIER, -MIRIEST marshy	
QUAHAUG	*n* pl. -S quahog	
QUAHOG	*n* pl. -S an edible clam	
QUAI	*n* pl. -S a quay	
QUAICH	*n* pl. -ES or -S a small drinking vessel	
QUAIGH	*n* pl. -S quaich	
QUAIL	*v* -ED, -ING, -S to cower	
QUAINT	*adj* QUAINTER, QUAINTEST pleasingly old-fashioned or unfamiliar QUAINTLY *adv*	
QUAKE	*v* QUAKED, QUAKING, QUAKES to shake or vibrate	
QUAKER	*n* pl. -S one that quakes	
QUAKY	*adj* QUAKIER, QUAKIEST tending to quake QUAKILY *adv*	
QUALE	*n* pl. -LIA a property considered apart from things having the property	
QUALIFY	*v* -FIED, -FYING, -FIES to make suitable or capable	
QUALITY	*n* pl. -TIES a characteristic or attribute	
QUALM	*n* pl. -S a feeling of doubt or misgiving	
QUALMISH	*adj* having qualms	

QUALMY adj QUALMIER, QUALMIEST qualmish

QUAMASH n pl. -ES camass

QUANDANG n pl. -S quandong

QUANDARY n pl. -RIES a dilemma

QUANDONG n pl. -S an Australian tree

QUANGO n pl. -GOS a public administrative board

QUANT v -ED, -ING, -S to propel through water with a pole

QUANTA pl. of quantum

QUANTAL adj pertaining to a quantum

QUANTIC n pl. -S a type of mathematical function

QUANTIFY v -FIED, -FYING, -FIES to determine the quantity of

QUANTILE n pl. -S any of the values of a random variable that divides a frequency distribution

QUANTITY n pl. -TIES a specified or indefinite amount or number

QUANTIZE v -TIZED, -TIZING, -TIZES to limit the possible values of to a discrete set

QUANTONG n pl. -S quandong

QUANTUM n pl. -TA a fundamental unit of energy

QUARE adj queer

QUARK n pl. -S a hypothetical atomic particle

QUARREL v -RELED, -RELING, -RELS or -RELLED, -RELLING, -RELS to engage in an angry dispute

QUARRIER n pl. -S one that quarries

QUARRY v -RIED, -RYING, -RIES to dig stone from an excavation

QUART n pl. -S a liquid measure of capacity

QUARTAN n pl. -S a recurrent malarial fever

QUARTE n pl. -S a fencing thrust

QUARTER v -ED, -ING, -S to divide into four equal parts

QUARTERN n pl. -S one-fourth of something

QUARTET n pl. -S a group of four

QUARTIC n pl. -S a type of mathematical function

QUARTILE n pl. -S a portion of a frequency distribution

QUARTO n pl. -TOS the size of a piece of paper cut four from a sheet

QUARTZ n pl. -ES a mineral

QUASAR n pl. -S a distant celestial object emitting strong radio waves

QUASH v -ED, -ING, -ES to suppress completely

QUASHER n pl. -S one that quashes

QUASI adj similar but not exactly the same

QUASS n pl. -ES kvass

QUASSIA n pl. -S a tropical tree

QUASSIN n pl. -S a medicinal compound obtained from the wood of a quassia

QUATE adj quiet

QUATORZE n pl. -S a set of four cards of the same denomination scoring fourteen points

QUATRAIN n pl. -S a stanza of four lines

QUATRE n pl. -S the four at cards or dice

QUAVER v -ED, -ING, -S to quiver

QUAVERER n pl. -S one that quavers

QUAVERY adj quivery

QUAY n pl. QUAYS a wharf QUAYLIKE adj

QUAYAGE n pl. -S a charge for the use of a quay

QUAYSIDE n pl. -S the area adjacent to a quay

QUEAN n pl. -S a harlot

QUEASY adj -SIER, -SIEST easily nauseated QUEASILY adv

QUEAZY adj -ZIER, -ZIEST queasy

QUEEN v -ED, -ING, -S to make a queen (a female monarch) of

QUEENDOM n pl. -S the area ruled by a queen

QUEENLY adj -LIER, -LIEST of or befitting a queen

QUEER adj QUEERER, QUEEREST deviating from the expected or normal

QUEER v -ED, -ING, -S to spoil the effect or success of

QUEERISH adj somewhat queer

QUEERLY adv in a queer manner

QUELL v -ED, -ING, -S to suppress

QUELLER n pl. -S one that quells

QUENCH v -ED, -ING, -ES to put out or extinguish

QUENCHER n pl. -S one that quenches

QUENELLE n pl. -S a type of dumpling

QUERCINE adj pertaining to oaks

QUERIDA n pl. -S a female sweetheart

QUERIED past tense of query

QUERIER n pl. -S a querist

QUERIES	present 3d person sing. of query
QUERIST	n pl. -S one who queries
QUERN	n pl. -S a hand-turned grain mill
QUERY	v -RIED, -RYING, -RIES to question
QUEST	v -ED, -ING, -S to make a search
QUESTER	n pl. -S one that quests
QUESTION	v -ED, -ING, -S to put a question (an inquiry) to
QUESTOR	n pl. -S quaestor
QUETZAL	n pl. -S or -ES a tropical bird
QUEUE	v QUEUED, QUEUING or QUEUEING, QUEUES to line up
QUEUER	n pl. -S one that queues
QUEY	n pl. QUEYS a young cow
QUEZAL	n pl. -S or -ES quetzal
QUIBBLE	v -BLED, -BLING, -BLES to argue over trivialities
QUIBBLER	n pl. -S one that quibbles
QUICHE	n pl. -S a custard-filled pastry
QUICK	adj QUICKER, QUICKEST acting or capable of acting with speed
QUICK	n pl. -S a sensitive area of flesh
QUICKEN	v -ED, -ING, -S to speed up
QUICKIE	n pl. -S something done quickly
QUICKLY	adv in a quick manner
QUICKSET	n pl. -S a plant suitable for hedges
QUID	n pl. -S a portion of something to be chewed
QUIDDITY	n pl. -TIES the true nature of a thing
QUIDNUNC	n pl. -S a nosy person
QUIET	adj -ETER, -ETEST making little or no noise
QUIET	v -ED, -ING, -S to cause to be quiet
QUIETEN	v -ED, -ING, -S to quiet
QUIETER	n pl. -S one that quiets
QUIETISM	n pl. -S a form of religious mysticism
QUIETIST	n pl. -S an advocate of quietism
QUIETLY	adv in a quiet manner
QUIETUDE	n pl. -S a state of tranquillity
QUIETUS	n pl. -ES a final settlement
QUIFF	n pl. -S a forelock
QUILL	v -ED, -ING, -S to press small ridges in

QUILLAI	n pl. -S an evergreen tree
QUILLAIA	n pl. -S a quillai
QUILLAJA	n pl. -S a quillai
QUILLET	n pl. -S a trivial distinction
QUILLING	n pl. -S material that is quilled
QUILT	v -ED, -ING, -S to stitch together with padding in between
QUILTER	n pl. -S one that quilts
QUILTING	n pl. -S material that is used for making quilts
QUIN	n pl. -S a quintuplet
QUINARY	n pl. -RIES a group of five
QUINATE	adj arranged in groups of five
QUINCE	n pl. -S an apple-like fruit
QUINCUNX	n pl. -ES an arrangement of five objects
QUINELA	n pl. -S a quinella
QUINELLA	n pl. -S a type of bet in horse racing
QUINIC	adj pertaining to quinine
QUINIELA	n pl. -S a quinella
QUININ	n pl. -S quinine
QUININA	n pl. -S quinine
QUININE	n pl. -S a medicinal alkaloid
QUINNAT	n pl. -S a food fish
QUINOA	n pl. -S a weedy plant
QUINOID	n pl. -S a chemical compound
QUINOL	n pl. -S a chemical compound
QUINOLIN	n pl. -S a chemical compound
QUINONE	n pl. -S a chemical compound
QUINSY	n pl. -SIES an inflammation of the tonsils
QUINT	n pl. -S a group of five
QUINTA	n pl. -S a country estate in Portugal or Latin America
QUINTAIN	n pl. -S an object used as a target in a medieval sport
QUINTAL	n pl. -S a unit of weight
QUINTAN	n pl. -S a recurrent fever
QUINTAR	n pl. -S qintar
QUINTE	n pl. -S a position in fencing
QUINTET	n pl. -S a group of five
QUINTIC	n pl. -S a type of mathematical function
QUINTILE	n pl. -S a portion of a frequency distribution
QUINTIN	n pl. -S a fine linen
QUIP	v QUIPPED, QUIPPING, QUIPS to make witty remarks
QUIPPER	n pl. -S one that quips
QUIPPISH	adj witty
QUIPPU	n pl. -S quipu
QUIPSTER	n pl. -S one that quips
QUIPU	n pl. -S an ancient calculating device

QUIRE *v* QUIRED, QUIRING, QUIRES to arrange sheets of paper in sets of twenty-four

QUIRK *v* -ED, -ING, -S to twist

QUIRKISH *adj* quirky

QUIRKY *adj* QUIRKIER, QUIRKIEST peculiar QUIRKILY *adv*

QUIRT *v* -ED, -ING, -S to strike with a riding whip

QUISLING *n pl.* -S a traitor who aids the invaders of his country

QUIT *v* QUITTED, QUITTING, QUITS to end one's engagement in or occupation with

QUITCH *n pl.* -ES a perennial grass

QUITE *adv* to the fullest extent

QUITRENT *n pl.* -S a fixed rent due from a socage tenant

QUITTED past tense of quit

QUITTER *n pl.* -S one that quits

QUITTING present participle of quit

QUITTOR *n pl.* -S an inflammation of an animal's hoof

QUIVER *v* -ED, -ING, -S to shake with a slight but rapid motion

QUIVERER *n pl.* -S one that quivers

QUIVERY *adj* marked by quivering

QUIXOTE *n pl.* -S a quixotic person

QUIXOTIC *adj* extremely idealistic

QUIXOTRY *n pl.* -TRIES quixotic action or thought

QUIZ *v* QUIZZED, QUIZZING, QUIZZES to test the knowledge of by asking questions

QUIZZER *n pl.* -S one that quizzes

QUOD *n pl.* -S a prison

QUOHOG *n pl.* -S quahog

QUOIN *v* -ED, -ING, -S to secure with a type of wedge

QUOIT *v* -ED, -ING, -S to play a throwing game similar to ringtoss

QUOKKA *n pl.* -S a short-tailed wallaby

QUOMODO *n pl.* -DOS a means or manner

QUONDAM *adj* that once was

QUORUM *n pl.* -S a particularly chosen group

QUOTA *n pl.* -S a proportional part or share

QUOTE *v* QUOTED, QUOTING, QUOTES to repeat the words of QUOTABLE *adj* QUOTABLY *adv*

QUOTER *n pl.* -S one that quotes

QUOTH *v* said — QUOTH is the only accepted form of this verb; it cannot be conjugated

QUOTHA *interj* — used to express surprise or sarcasm

QUOTIENT *n pl.* -S the number resulting from the division of one number by another

QUOTING present participle of quote

QURSH *n pl.* -ES a monetary unit of Saudi Arabia

QURUSH *n pl.* -ES qursh

QWERTY *n pl.* -TYS a standard keyboard

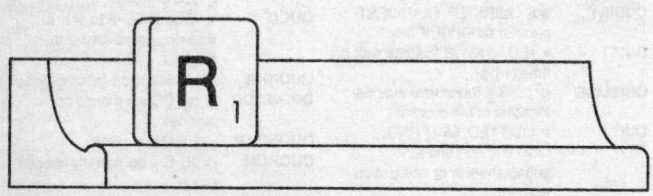

RABAT *n pl.* -S a dickey attached to a clerical collar

RABATO *n pl.* -TOS a wide, lace-edged collar

RABBET *v* -ED, -ING, -S to cut a groove in

RABBI *n pl.* -S or -ES a Jewish spiritual leader

RABBIN *n pl.* -S rabbi

RABBINIC *adj* pertaining to rabbis

RABBIT *v* -ED, -ING, -S to hunt rabbits (rodent-like mammals)

RABBITER *n pl.* -S one that rabbits

RABBITRY *n pl.* -RIES a place where rabbits are kept

RABBITY *adj* resembling a rabbit

RABBLE *v* -BLED, -BLING, -BLES to mob

RABBLER *n pl.* -S an iron bar used in puddling

RABBONI *n pl.* -S master; teacher — used as a Jewish title of respect

RABIC *adj* pertaining to rabies

RABID *adj* affected with rabies **RABIDLY** *adv*

RABIDITY *n pl.* -TIES the state of being rabid

RABIES *n pl.* RABIES an infectious virus disease **RABIETIC** *adj*

RACCOON *n pl.* -S a carnivorous mammal

RACE *v* RACED, RACING, RACES to compete in a contest of speed

RACEMATE *n pl.* -S a chemical salt

RACEME *n pl.* -S a mode of arrangement of flowers along an axis **RACEMED** *adj*

RACEMIC *adj* pertaining to a racemate

RACEMISM *n pl.* -S the state of being racemic

RACEMIZE *v* -MIZED, -MIZING, -MIZES to convert into a racemic compound

RACEMOID *adj* pertaining to a raceme

RACEMOSE *adj* having the form of a raceme

RACEMOUS *adj* racemose

RACER *n pl.* -S one that races

RACEWAY *n pl.* -WAYS a channel for conducting water

RACHET *n pl.* -S ratchet

RACHILLA *n pl.* -LAE the central stalk of a grass spikelet

RACHIS *n pl.* -CHISES or -CHIDES the spinal column **RACHIAL** *adj*

RACHITIS *n pl.* -TIDES rickets **RACHITIC** *adj*

RACIAL *adj* pertaining to an ethnic group **RACIALLY** *adv*

RACIER comparative of racy

RACIEST superlative of racy

RACILY *adv* in a racy manner

RACINESS *n pl.* -ES the quality of being racy

RACING *n pl.* -S the sport of engaging in contests of speed

RACISM *n pl.* -S a doctrine of racial superiority

RACIST *n pl.* -S an advocate of racism

RACK *v* -ED, -ING, -S to place in a type of framework

RACKER *n pl.* -S one that racks

RACKET *v* -ED, -ING, -S to make a loud noise

RACKETY *adj* -ETIER, -ETIEST noisy

RACKFUL *n pl.* -S as much as a rack can hold

RACKLE *adj* impetuous; rash
RACKWORK *n pl.* -S a type of mechanism
RACLETTE *n pl.* -S a cheese dish
RACON *n pl.* -S a type of radar transmitter
RACOON *n pl.* -S raccoon
RACQUET *n pl.* -S a lightweight implement used in various ball games
RACY *adj* RACIER, RACIEST bordering on impropriety or indecency
RAD *v* RADDED, RADDING, RADS to fear
RADAR *n pl.* -S an electronic locating device
RADDLE *v* -DLED, -DLING, -DLES to weave together
RADIABLE *adj* capable of radiating
RADIAL *n pl.* -S a part diverging from a center
RADIALE *n pl.* -LIA a bone of the carpus
RADIALLY *adv* in a diverging manner
RADIAN *n pl.* -S a unit of angular measure
RADIANCE *n pl.* -S brightness
RADIANCY *n pl.* -CIES radiance
RADIANT *n pl.* -S a point from which rays are emitted
RADIATE *v* -ATED, -ATING, -ATES to emit rays
RADIATOR *n pl.* -S a heating device
RADICAL *n pl.* -S a group of atoms that acts as a unit in chemical compounds
RADICAND *n pl.* -S a quantity in mathematics
RADICATE *v* -CATED, -CATING, -CATES to cause to take root
RADICEL *n pl.* -S a rootlet
RADICES a *pl.* of radix
RADICLE *n pl.* -S a part of a plant embryo
RADII a *pl.* of radius
RADIO *v* -ED, -ING, -S to transmit by radio (an apparatus for wireless communication)
RADIOMAN *n pl.* -MEN a radio operator or technician
RADISH *n pl.* -ES a pungent, edible root
RADIUM *n pl.* -S a radioactive element
RADIUS *n pl.* -DII or -DIUSES a straight line from the center of a circle to the circumference

RADIX *n pl.* -DICES or -DIXES the root of a plant
RADOME *n pl.* -S a domelike device used to shelter a radar antenna
RADON *n pl.* -S a radioactive element
RADULA *n pl.* -LAE or -LAS a tonguelike organ of mollusks RADULAR *adj*
RADWASTE *n pl.* -S radioactive waste
RAFF *n pl.* -S riffraff
RAFFIA *n pl.* -S a palm tree
RAFFISH *adj* tawdry
RAFFLE *v* -FLED, -FLING, -FLES to dispose of by a form of lottery
RAFFLER *n pl.* -S one that raffles
RAFT *v* -ED, -ING, -S to transport on a raft (a type of buoyant structure)
RAFTER *n pl.* -S a supporting beam
RAFTERED *adj* furnished with rafters
RAFTSMAN *n pl.* -MEN one who manages a raft
RAG *v* RAGGED, RAGGING, RAGS to scold
RAGA *n pl.* -S a Hindu musical form
RAGBAG *n pl.* -S a bag for storing scraps of cloth
RAGE *v* RAGED, RAGING, RAGES to act or speak with violent anger
RAGEE *n pl.* -S ragi
RAGGED *adj* -GEDER, -GEDEST tattered RAGGEDLY *adv*
RAGGEDY *adj* somewhat ragged
RAGGEE *n pl.* -S ragi
RAGGIES *pl.* of raggy
RAGGING present participle of rag
RAGGLE *n pl.* -S a groove cut in masonry
RAGGY *n pl.* -GIES ragi
RAGI *n pl.* -S an East Indian cereal grass
RAGING present participle of rage
RAGINGLY *adv* in a furious manner
RAGLAN *n pl.* -S a type of overcoat
RAGMAN *n pl.* -MEN one who gathers and sells scraps of cloth
RAGOUT *v* -ED, -ING, -S to make into a highly seasoned stew
RAGTAG *n pl.* -S riffraff
RAGTIME *n pl.* -S a style of American dance music
RAGTOP *n pl.* -S a convertible automobile
RAGWEED *n pl.* -S a weedy herb

RAGWORT n pl. -S a flowering plant

RAH interj — used to cheer on a team or player

RAIA n pl. -S rayah

RAID v -ED, -ING, -S to make a sudden assault on

RAIDER n pl. -S one that raids

RAIL v -ED, -ING, -S to scold in abusive or insolent language

RAILBIRD n pl. -S a racing enthusiast

RAILBUS n pl. -BUSES or -BUSSES a passenger car equipped for operation on rails

RAILCAR n pl. -S a railroad car

RAILER n pl. -S one that rails

RAILHEAD n pl. -S the end of a railroad line

RAILING n pl. -S a fence-like barrier

RAILLERY n pl. -LERIES good-natured teasing

RAILROAD v -ED, -ING, -S to transport by railroad (a type of road on which locomotives are run)

RAILWAY n pl. -WAYS a railroad

RAIMENT n pl. -S clothing

RAIN v -ED, -ING, -S to fall like rain (drops of water condensed from atmospheric vapor)

RAINBAND n pl. -S a dark band in the solar spectrum

RAINBIRD n pl. -S a type of bird

RAINBOW n pl. -S an arc of spectral colors formed in the sky

RAINCOAT n pl. -S a waterproof coat

RAINDROP n pl. -S a drop of rain

RAINFALL n pl. -S a fall of rain

RAINIER comparative of rainy

RAINIEST superlative of rainy

RAINILY adv in a rainy manner

RAINLESS adj having no rain

RAINOUT n pl. -S atomic fallout occurring in precipitation

RAINWASH v -ED, -ING, -ES to wash material downhill by rain

RAINWEAR n pl. RAINWEAR waterproof clothing

RAINY adj RAINIER, RAINIEST marked by rain

RAISE v RAISED, RAISING, RAISES to move to a higher position RAISABLE adj

RAISER n pl. -S one that raises

RAISIN n pl. -S a dried grape RAISINY adj

RAISING n pl. -S an elevation

RAISONNE adj arranged systematically

RAJ n pl. -ES dominion; sovereignty

RAJA n pl. -S rajah

RAJAH n pl. -S a king or prince in India

RAKE v RAKED, RAKING, RAKES to gather with a toothed implement

RAKEE n pl. -S raki

RAKEHELL n pl. -S a man lacking in moral restraint

RAKEOFF n pl. -S a share of profits

RAKER n pl. -S one that rakes

RAKI n pl. -S a Turkish liqueur

RAKING present participle of rake

RAKISH adj dapper RAKISHLY adv

RALE n pl. -S an abnormal respiratory sound

RALLIED past tense of rally

RALLIER n pl. -S one that rallies

RALLINE adj pertaining to a family of marsh birds

RALLY v -LIED, -LYING, -LIES to call together for a common purpose

RALLYE n pl. -S a type of automobile race

RALLYING n pl. -S the sport of driving in rallyes

RALLYIST n pl. -S a participant in a rallye

RALPH v -ED, -ING, -S to vomit

RAM v RAMMED, RAMMING, RAMS to strike with great force

RAMATE adj having branches

RAMBLE v -BLED, -BLING, -BLES to wander

RAMBLER n pl. -S one that rambles

RAMBUTAN n pl. -S the edible fruit of a Malayan tree

RAMEE n pl. -S ramie

RAMEKIN n pl. -S a cheese dish

RAMENTUM n pl. -TA a scale formed on the surface of leaves

RAMEQUIN n pl. -S ramekin

RAMET n pl. -S an independent member of a clone

RAMI pl. of ramus

RAMIE n pl. -S an Asian shrub

RAMIFORM adj shaped like a branch

RAMIFY v -FIED, -FYING, -FIES to divide into branches

RAMILIE n pl. -S ramillie

RAMILLIE n pl. -S a type of wig

RAMJET n pl. -S a type of engine

RAMMED past tense of ram

RAMMER n pl. -S one that rams

RAMMIER comparative of rammy

RAMMIEST superlative of rammy

RAMMING present participle of ram

RAMMISH *adj* resembling a ram (a male sheep)

RAMMY *adj* -MIER, -MIEST rammish

RAMOSE *adj* having many branches RAMOSELY *adv*

RAMOSITY *n* pl. -TIES the state of being ramose

RAMOUS *adj* ramose

RAMP *v* -ED, -ING, -S to rise or stand on the hind legs

RAMPAGE *v* -PAGED, -PAGING, -PAGES to move about wildly or violently

RAMPAGER *n* pl. -S one that rampages

RAMPANCY *n* pl. -CIES the state of being rampant

RAMPANT *adj* unrestrained

RAMPART *v* -ED, -ING, -S to furnish with a fortifying embankment

RAMPIKE *n* pl. -S a standing dead tree

RAMPION *n* pl. -S a European plant

RAMPOLE *n* pl. -S rampike

RAMROD *v* -RODDED, -RODDING, -RODS to supervise

RAMSHORN *n* pl. -S a snail used as an aquarium scavenger

RAMSON *n* pl. -S a broad-leaved garlic

RAMTIL *n* pl. -S a tropical plant

RAMULOSE *adj* having many small branches

RAMULOUS *adj* ramulose

RAMUS *n* pl. -MI a branch-like part of a structure

RAN past tense of run and rin

RANCE *n* pl. -S a variety of marble

RANCH *v* -ED, -ING, -ES to work on a ranch (an establishment for raising livestock)

RANCHER *n* pl. -S one that owns or works on a ranch

RANCHERO *n* pl. -ROS a rancher

RANCHMAN *n* pl. -MEN a rancher

RANCHO *n* pl. -CHOS a ranch

RANCID *adj* having an unpleasant odor or taste RANCIDLY *adv*

RANCOR *n* pl. -S bitter and vindictive enmity RANCORED *adj*

RANCOUR *n* pl. -S rancor

RAND *n* pl. -S a strip of leather at the heel of a shoe

RANDAN *n* pl. -S a boat rowed by three persons

RANDIER comparative of randy

RANDIES pl. of randy

RANDIEST superlative of randy

RANDOM *n* pl. -S a haphazard course

RANDOMLY *adv* in a haphazard manner

RANDY *adj* -DIER, -DIEST lustful

RANDY *n* pl. RANDIES a rude person

RANEE *n* pl. -S rani

RANG past tense of ring

RANGE *v* RANGED, RANGING, RANGES to place in a particular order

RANGER *n* pl. -S an officer supervising the care of a forest

RANGY *adj* RANGIER, RANGIEST tall and slender

RANI *n* pl. -S the wife of a rajah

RANID *n* pl. -S any of a large family of frogs

RANK *v* -ED, -ING, -S to determine the relative position of

RANK *adj* RANKER, RANKEST strong and disagreeable in odor or taste

RANKER *n* pl. -S an enlisted soldier

RANKING *n* pl. -S a listing of ranked individuals

RANKISH *adj* somewhat rank

RANKLE *v* -KLED, -KLING, -KLES to cause irritation or resentment in

RANKLY *adv* in a rank manner

RANKNESS *n* pl. -ES the state of being rank

RANPIKE *n* pl. -S rampike

RANSACK *v* -ED, -ING, -S to search thoroughly

RANSOM *v* -ED, -ING, -S to obtain the release of by paying a demanded price

RANSOMER *n* pl. -S one that ransoms

RANT *v* -ED, -ING, -S to speak in a loud or vehement manner

RANTER *n* pl. -S one that rants

RANULA *n* pl. -S a cyst formed under the tongue

RAP *v* RAPPED, RAPPING, RAPS to strike sharply

RAPACITY *n* pl. -TIES the quality of being ravenous

RAPE *v* RAPED, RAPING, RAPES to force to submit to sexual intercourse

RAPER *n* pl. -S a rapist

RAPESEED *n* pl. -S the seed of a European herb

RAPHE n pl. RAPHAE or RAPHES a seamlike ridge between two halves of an organ or part

RAPHIA n pl. -S raffia

RAPHIDE n pl. -S a needle-shaped crystal occurring in plant cells

RAPHIS n pl. -PHIDES raphide

RAPID adj -IDER, -IDEST moving or acting with great speed **RAPIDLY** adv

RAPID n pl. -S a fast-moving part of a river

RAPIDITY n pl. -TIES the state of being rapid

RAPIER n pl. -S a long, slender sword **RAPIERED** adj

RAPINE n pl. -S the taking of property by force

RAPING present participle of rape

RAPINI n/pl rappini

RAPIST n pl. -S one who rapes

RAPPAREE n pl. -S a plunderer

RAPPED past tense of rap

RAPPEE n pl. -S a strong snuff

RAPPEL v -PELED, -PELING, -PELS or -PELLED, -PELLING, -PELS to descend from a steep height by means of a rope

RAPPEN n pl. RAPPEN a monetary unit of Switzerland

RAPPER n pl. -S one that raps

RAPPING present participle of rap

RAPPINI n/pl immature turnip plants

RAPPORT n pl. -S a harmonious relationship

RAPT adj deeply engrossed **RAPTLY** adv

RAPTNESS n pl. -ES the state of being rapt

RAPTOR n pl. -S a bird of prey

RAPTURE v -TURED, -TURING, -TURES to fill with great joy

RARE adj RARER, RAREST occurring infrequently

RARE v RARED, RARING, RARES to be enthusiastic

RAREBIT n pl. -S a cheese dish

RAREFIER n pl. -S one that rarefies

RAREFY v -EFIED, -EFYING, -EFIES to make less dense

RARELY adv not often

RARENESS n pl. -ES the quality of being rare

RARER comparative of rare

RARERIPE n pl. -S a fruit that ripens early

RAREST superlative of rare

RARIFY v -FIED, -FYING, -FIES to rarefy

RARING adj full of enthusiasm

RARITY n pl. -TIES rareness

RAS n pl. -ES an Ethiopian prince

RASBORA n pl. -S a tropical fish

RASCAL n pl. -S an unscrupulous or dishonest person

RASCALLY adj characteristic of a rascal

RASE v RASED, RASING, RASES to raze

RASER n pl. -S one that rases

RASH adj RASHER, RASHEST acting without due caution or forethought

RASH n pl. -ES a skin eruption **RASHLIKE** adj

RASHER n pl. -S a thin slice of meat

RASHLY adv in a rash manner

RASHNESS n pl. -ES the state of being rash

RASING present participle of rase

RASORIAL adj habitually scratching the ground for food

RASP v -ED, -ING, -S to rub with something rough

RASPER n pl. -S one that rasps

RASPISH adj irritable

RASPY adj RASPIER, RASPIEST rough

RASSLE v -SLED, -SLING, -SLES to wrestle

RASTER n pl. -S the area reproducing images on the picture tube of a television set

RASURE n pl. -S erasure

RAT v RATTED, RATTING, RATS to hunt rats (long-tailed rodents)

RATABLE adj capable of being rated **RATABLY** adv

RATAFEE n pl. -S ratafia

RATAFIA n pl. -S an almond-flavored liqueur

RATAL n pl. -S an amount on which rates are assessed

RATAN n pl. -S rattan

RATANY n pl. -NIES rhatany

RATAPLAN v -PLANNED, -PLANNING, -PLANS to make a rapidly repeating sound

RATATAT n pl. -S a quick, sharp rapping sound

RATBAG n pl. -S an eccentric or disagreeable person

RATCH n pl. -ES a ratchet

RATCHET v -ED, -ING, -S to increase or decrease by small amounts

RATE v RATED, RATING, RATES to estimate the value of

RATEABLE adj ratable **RATEABLY** adv

RATEL n pl. -S a carnivorous mammal

RATER n pl. -S one that rates

RATFINK n pl. -S a contemptible person

RATFISH n pl. -ES a marine fish

RATH adj rathe

RATHE adj appearing or ripening early

RATHER adv preferably

RATHOLE n pl. -S a hole made by a rat

RATICIDE n pl. -S a substance for killing rats

RATIFIER n pl. -S one that ratifies

RATIFY v -FIED, -FYING, -FIES to approve and sanction formally

RATINE n pl. -S a heavy fabric

RATING n pl. -S relative estimate or evaluation

RATIO n pl. -TIOS a proportional relationship

RATION v -ED, -ING, -S to distribute in fixed portions

RATIONAL n pl. -S a number that can be expressed as a quotient of integers

RATITE n pl. -S a flightless bird

RATLIKE adj resembling a rat

RATLIN n pl. -S ratline

RATLINE n pl. -S one of the ropes forming the steps of a rope ladder on a ship

RATO n pl. -TOS a rocket-assisted airplane takeoff

RATOON v -ED, -ING, -S to sprout from a root planted the previous year

RATOONER n pl. -S a plant that ratoons

RATSBANE n pl. -S rat poison

RATTAIL n pl. -S a marine fish

RATTAN n pl. -S a palm tree

RATTED past tense of rat

RATTEEN n pl. -S a coarse woolen fabric

RATTEN v -ED, -ING, -S to harass

RATTENER n pl. -S one that rattens

RATTER n pl. -S an animal used for catching rats

RATTIER comparative of ratty

RATTIEST superlative of ratty

RATTING present participle of rat

RATTISH adj ratlike

RATTLE v -TLED, -TLING, -TLES to make a quick succession of short, sharp sounds

RATTLER n pl. -S one that rattles

RATTLING n pl. -S ratline

RATTLY adj tending to rattle

RATTON n pl. -S a rat

RATTOON v -ED, -ING, -S to ratoon

RATTRAP n pl. -S a trap for catching rats

RATTY adj -TIER, -TIEST infested with rats

RAUCITY n pl. -TIES the state of being raucous

RAUCOUS adj loud and unruly

RAUNCH n pl. -ES vulgarity

RAUNCHY adj -CHIER, -CHIEST slovenly

RAVAGE v -AGED, -AGING, -AGES to destroy

RAVAGER n pl. -S one that ravages

RAVE v RAVED, RAVING, RAVES to speak irrationally or incoherently

RAVEL v -ELED, -ELING, -ELS or -ELLED, -ELLING, -ELS to separate the threads of

RAVELER n pl. -S one that ravels

RAVELIN n pl. -S a type of fortification

RAVELING n pl. -S a loose thread

RAVELLED a past tense of ravel

RAVELLER n pl. -S raveler

RAVELLING n pl. -S raveling

RAVELLY adj tangled

RAVEN v -ED, -ING, -S to eat in a ravenous manner

RAVENER n pl. -S one that ravens

RAVENING n pl. -S rapacity

RAVENOUS adj extremely hungry

RAVER n pl. -S one that raves

RAVIGOTE n pl. -S a spiced vinegar sauce

RAVIN v -ED, -ING, -S to raven

RAVINE n pl. -S a narrow, steep-sided valley

RAVING n pl. -S irrational, incoherent speech

RAVINGLY adv in a delirious manner

RAVIOLI n pl. -S an Italian pasta dish made of small cases of dough with a savory filling

RAVISH v -ED, -ING, -ES to seize and carry off by force

RAVISHER n pl. -S one that ravishes

RAW adj RAWER, RAWEST uncooked

RAW n pl. -S a sore or irritated spot

RAWBONED adj having little flesh

RAWHIDE v -HIDED, -HIDING, -HIDES to beat with a type of whip

RAWIN *n* pl. -S a wind measurement made by tracking a balloon with radar

RAWISH *adj* somewhat raw

RAWLY *adv* in a raw manner

RAWNESS *n* pl. -ES the state of being raw

RAX *v* -ED, -ING, -ES to stretch out

RAY *v* -ED, -ING, -S to emit rays (narrow beams of light)

RAYA *n* pl. -S rayah

RAYAH *n* pl. -S a non-Muslim inhabitant of Turkey

RAYGRASS *n* pl. -ES ryegrass

RAYLESS *adj* having no rays

RAYLIKE *adj* resembling a narrow beam of light

RAYON *n* pl. -S a synthetic fiber

RAZE *v* RAZED, RAZING, RAZES to tear down or demolish

RAZEE *v* -ZEED, -ZEEING, -ZEES to make lower by removing the upper deck, as a ship

RAZER *n* pl. -S one that razes

RAZING present participle of raze

RAZOR *v* -ED, -ING, -S to shave or cut with a sharp-edged instrument

RAZZ *v* -ED, -ING, -ES to deride

RE *n* pl. -S the second tone of the diatonic musical scale

Following is a list of self-explanatory verbs containing the prefix RE- (again):

REABSORB *v* -ED, -ING, -S

REACCEDE *v* -CEDED, -CEDING, -CEDES

REACCENT *v* -ED, -ING, -S

REACCEPT *v* -ED, -ING, -S

REACCUSE *v* -CUSED, -CUSING, -CUSES

READAPT *v* -ED, -ING, -S

READD *v* -ED, -ING, -S

READDICT *v* -ED, -ING, -S

READJUST *v* -ED, -ING, -S

READMIT *v* -MITTED, -MITTING, -MITS

READOPT *v* -ED, -ING, -S

READORN *v* -ED, -ING, -S

REAFFIRM *v* -ED, -ING, -S

REAFFIX *v* -ED, -ING, -ES

REALIGN *v* -ED, -ING, -S

REALLOT *v* -LOTTED, -LOTTING, -LOTS

REALTER *v* -ED, -ING, -S

REANNEX *v* -ED, -ING, -ES

REANOINT *v* -ED, -ING, -S

REAPPEAR *v* -ED, -ING, -S

REAPPLY *v* -PLIED, -PLYING, -PLIES

REARGUE *v* -GUED, -GUING, -GUES

REARM *v* -ED, -ING, -S

REAROUSE *v* -AROUSED, -AROUSING, -AROUSES

REARREST *v* -ED, -ING, -S

REASCEND *v* -ED, -ING, -S

REASSAIL *v* -ED, -ING, -S

REASSERT *v* -ED, -ING, -S

REASSESS *v* -ED, -ING, -ES

REASSIGN *v* -ED, -ING, -S

REASSORT *v* -ED, -ING, -S

REASSUME *v* -SUMED, -SUMING, -SUMES

REASSURE *v* -SURED, -SURING, -SURES

REATTACH *v* -ED, -ING, -ES

REATTACK *v* -ED, -ING, -S

REATTAIN *v* -ED, -ING, -S

REAVAIL *v* -ED, -ING, -S

REAVOW *v* -ED, -ING, -S

REAWAKE *v* -AWAKED or -AWOKE, -AWOKEN, -AWAKING, -AWAKES

REAWAKEN *v* -ED, -ING, -S

REBAIT *v* -ED, -ING, -S

REBEGIN *v* -GAN, -GUN, -GINNING, -GINS

REBID *v* -BID, -BIDDEN, -BIDDING, -BIDS

REBILL *v* -ED, -ING, -S

REBIND *v* -BOUND, -BINDING, -BINDS

REBLEND *v* -ED, -ING, -S

REBLOOM *v* -ED, -ING, -S

REBOARD *v* -ED, -ING, -S

REBODY *v* -BODIED, -BODYING, -BODIES

REBOIL *v* -ED, -ING, -S

REBOOK *v* -ED, -ING, -S

REBOOT *v* -ED, -ING, -S

REBORE *v* -BORED, -BORING, -BORES

REBOTTLE *v* -TLED, -TLING, -TLES

REBOUGHT past tense of rebuy

REBOUND past tense of rebind

REBREED *v* -BRED, -BREEDING, -BREEDS

REBUILD	v -BUILT or -BUILDED, -BUILDING, -BUILDS	**REDIAL**	v -DIALED, -DIALING, -DIALS or -DIALLED, -DIALLING, -DIALS
REBURY	v -BURIED, -BURYING, -BURIES		
REBUTTON	v -ED, -ING, -S	**REDID**	past tense of redo
REBUY	v -BOUGHT, -BUYING, -BUYS	**REDIGEST**	v -ED, -ING, -S
		REDIP	v -DIPPED or -DIPT, -DIPPING, -DIPS
RECANE	v -CANED, -CANING, -CANES		
		REDIVIDE	v -VIDED, -VIDING, -VIDES
RECARRY	v -RIED, -RYING, -RIES	**REDO**	v -DID, -DONE, -DOING, -DOES
RECAST	v -CAST, -CASTING, -CASTS		
RECHANGE	v -CHANGED, -CHANGING, -CHANGES	**REDOCK**	v -ED, -ING, -S
		REDON	v -DONNED, -DONNING, -DONS
RECHARGE	v -CHARGED, -CHARGING, -CHARGES		
		REDONE	past participle of redo
RECHART	v -ED, -ING, -S	**REDRAW**	v -DREW, -DRAWN, -DRAWING, -DRAWS
RECHECK	v -ED, -ING, -S		
RECHEW	v -ED, -ING, -S	**REDREAM**	v -DREAMED or -DREAMT, -DREAMING, -DREAMS
RECHOOSE	v -CHOSE, -CHOSEN, -CHOOSING, -CHOOSES		
		REDRIED	past tense of redry
RECIRCLE	v -CLED, -CLING, -CLES	**REDRIES**	present 3d person sing. of redry
RECLAD	a past tense of reclothe		
RECLASP	v -ED, -ING, -S	**REDRILL**	v -ED, -ING, -S
RECLEAN	v -ED, -ING, -S	**REDRIVE**	v -DROVE, -DRIVEN, -DRIVING, -DRIVES
RECLOTHE	v -CLOTHED or -CLAD, -CLOTHING, -CLOTHES		
		REDRY	v -DRIED, -DRYING, -DRIES
RECOAL	v -ED, -ING, -S	**REDUB**	v -DUBBED, -DUBBING, -DUBS
RECOCK	v -ED, -ING, -S		
RECODE	v -CODED, -CODING, -CODES	**REDYE**	v -DYED, -DYEING, -DYES
		REEARN	v -ED, -ING, -S
RECODIFY	v -FIED, -FYING, -FIES	**REECHO**	v -ED, -ING, -ES
RECOIN	v -ED, -ING, -S	**REEDIT**	v -ED, -ING, -S
RECOLOR	v -ED, -ING, -S	**REEJECT**	v -ED, -ING, -S
RECOMB	v -ED, -ING, -S	**REELECT**	v -ED, -ING, -S
RECOMMIT	v -MITTED, -MITTING, -MITS	**REEMBARK**	v -ED, -ING, -S
RECOOK	v -ED, -ING, -S	**REEMBODY**	v -BODIED, -BODYING, -BODIES
RECOPY	v -COPIED, -COPYING, -COPIES		
		REEMERGE	v -EMERGED, -EMERGING, -EMERGES
RECORK	v -ED, -ING, -S		
RECOUPLE	v -PLED, -PLING, -PLES	**REEMIT**	v -EMITTED, -EMITTING, -EMITS
RECRATE	v -CRATED, -CRATING, -CRATES		
		REEMPLOY	v -ED, -ING, -S
RECROSS	v -ED, -ING, -ES	**REENACT**	v -ED, -ING, -S
RECROWN	v -ED, -ING, -S	**REENDOW**	v -ED, -ING, -S
RECUT	v -CUT, -CUTTING, -CUTS	**REENGAGE**	v -GAGED, -GAGING, -GAGES
REDAMAGE	v -AGED, -AGING, -AGES		
REDATE	v -DATED, -DATING, -DATES	**REENJOY**	v -ED, -ING, -S
REDECIDE	v -CIDED, -CIDING, -CIDES	**REENLIST**	v -ED, -ING, -S
REDEFEAT	v -ED, -ING, -S	**REENROLL**	v -ED, -ING, -S
REDEFECT	v -ED, -ING, -S	**REENTER**	v -ED, -ING, -S
REDEFINE	v -FINED, -FINING, -FINES	**REEQUIP**	v -EQUIPPED, -EQUIPPING, -EQUIPS
REDEFY	v -FIED, -FYING, -FIES		
REDEMAND	v -ED, -ING, -S	**REERECT**	v -ED, -ING, -S
REDENY	v -NIED, -NYING, -NIES	**REEVOKE**	v -EVOKED, -EVOKING, -EVOKES
REDEPLOY	v -ED, -ING, -S		
REDESIGN	v -ED, -ING, -S	**REEXPEL**	v -PELLED, -PELLING, -PELS
		REEXPORT	v -ED, -ING, -S

REEXPOSE v -POSED, -POSING, -POSES

REFALL v -FELL, -FALLEN, -FALLING, -FALLS

REFASTEN v -ED, -ING, -S

REFEED v -FED, -FEEDING, -FEEDS

REFEEL v -FELT, -FEELING, -FEELS

REFELL past tense of refall

REFENCE v -FENCED, -FENCING, -FENCES

REFIGHT v -FOUGHT, -FIGHTING, -FIGHTS

REFIGURE v -URED, -URING, -URES

REFILE v -FILED, -FILING, -FILES

REFILL v -ED, -ING, -S

REFILM v -ED, -ING, -S

REFILTER v -ED, -ING, -S

REFIND v -FOUND, -FINDING, -FINDS

REFIRE v -FIRED, -FIRING, -FIRES

REFIX v -ED, -ING, -ES

REFLEW past tense of refly

REFLIES present 3d person sing. of refly

REFLOAT v -ED, -ING, -S

REFLOOD v -ED, -ING, -S

REFLOW v -ED, -ING, -S

REFLOWER v -ED, -ING, -S

REFLY v -FLEW, -FLOWN, -FLYING, -FLIES

REFOCUS v -CUSED, -CUSING, -CUSES or -CUSSED, -CUSSING, -CUSSES

REFOLD v -ED, -ING, -S

REFORGE v -FORGED, -FORGING, -FORGES

REFORMAT v -MATTED, -MATTING, -MATS

REFOUGHT past tense of refight

REFOUND v -ED, -ING, -S

REFRAME v -FRAMED, -FRAMING, -FRAMES

REFREEZE v -FROZE, -FROZEN, -FREEZING, -FREEZES

REFRONT v -ED, -ING, -S

REFRY v -FRIED, -FRYING, -FRIES

REFUEL v -ELED, -ELING, -ELS or -ELLED, -ELLING, -ELS

REGAIN v -ED, -ING, -S

REGATHER v -ED, -ING, -S

REGAUGE v -GAUGED, -GAUGING, -GAUGES

REGAVE past tense of regive

REGEAR v -ED, -ING, -S

REGILD v -GILDED or -GILT, -GILDING, -GILDS

REGIVE v -GAVE, -GIVEN, -GIVING, -GIVES

REGLAZE v -GLAZED, -GLAZING, -GLAZES

REGLOSS v -ED, -ING, -ES

REGLOW v -ED, -ING, -S

REGLUE v -GLUED, -GLUING, -GLUES

REGRADE v -GRADED, -GRADING, -GRADES

REGRAFT v -ED, -ING, -S

REGRANT v -ED, -ING, -S

REGREEN v -ED, -ING, -S

REGREW past tense of regrow

REGRIND v -GROUND, -GRINDING, -GRINDS

REGROOM v -ED, -ING, -S

REGROOVE v -GROOVED, -GROOVING, -GROOVES

REGROUND past tense of regrind

REGROUP v -ED, -ING, -S

REGROW v -GREW, -GROWN, -GROWING, -GROWS

REHAMMER v -ED, -ING, -S

REHANDLE v -DLED, -DLING, -DLES

REHANG v -HUNG or -HANGED, -HANGING, -HANGS

REHARDEN v -ED, -ING, -S

REHASH v -ED, -ING, -ES

REHEAR v -HEARD, -HEARING, -HEARS

REHEAT v -ED, -ING, -S

REHEEL v -ED, -ING, -S

REHEM v -HEMMED, -HEMMING, -HEMS

REHINGE v -HINGED, -HINGING, -HINGES

REHIRE v -HIRED, -HIRING, -HIRES

REHUNG a past tense of rehang

REIGNITE v -NITED, -NITING, -NITES

REIMAGE v -AGED, -AGING, -AGES

REIMPORT v -ED, -ING, -S

REIMPOSE v -POSED, -POSING, -POSES

REINCITE v -CITED, -CITING, -CITES

REINCUR v -CURRED, -CURRING, -CURS

REINDEX v -ED, -ING, -ES

REINDICT v -ED, -ING, -S

REINDUCE v -DUCED, -DUCING, -DUCES

REINDUCT v -ED, -ING, -S

REINFECT v -ED, -ING, -S

REINFORM v -ED, -ING, -S

REINFUSE v -FUSED, -FUSING, -FUSES

REINJECT v -ED, -ING, -S

REINJURE v -JURED, -JURING, -JURES

REINK v -ED, -ING, -S

REINSERT v -ED, -ING, -S

REINSURE	v -SURED, -SURING, -SURES
REINTER	v -TERRED, -TERRING, -TERS
REINVADE	v -VADED, -VADING, -VADES
REINVENT	v -ED, -ING, -S
REINVEST	v -ED, -ING, -S
REINVITE	v -VITED, -VITING, -VITES
REINVOKE	v -VOKED, -VOKING, -VOKES
REISSUE	v -SUED, -SUING, -SUES
REJACKET	v -ED, -ING, -S
REJOIN	v -ED, -ING, -S
REJUDGE	v -JUDGED, -JUDGING, -JUDGES
REJUGGLE	v -GLED, -GLING, -GLES
REKEY	v -ED, -ING, -S
REKINDLE	v -DLED, -DLING, -DLES
REKNIT	v -KNITTED, -KNITTING, -KNITS
RELABEL	v -BELED, -BELING, -BELS or -BELLED, -BELLING, -BELS
RELACE	v -LACED, -LACING, -LACES
RELAUNCH	v -ED, -ING, -ES
RELAY	v -LAID, -LAYING, -LAYS
RELEARN	v -LEARNED or -LEARNT, -LEARNING, -LEARNS
RELEND	v -LENT, -LENDING, -LENDS
RELET	v -LET, -LETTING, -LETS
RELETTER	v -ED, -ING, -S
RELIGHT	v -LIGHTED or -LIT, -LIGHTING, -LIGHTS
RELINE	v -LINED, -LINING, -LINES
RELINK	v -ED, -ING, -S
RELIST	v -ED, -ING, -S
RELIT	a past tense of relight
RELOAD	v -ED, -ING, -S
RELOAN	v -ED, -ING, -S
RELOCK	v -ED, -ING, -S
RELOOK	v -ED, -ING, -S
REMAIL	v -ED, -ING, -S
REMAKE	v -MADE, -MAKING, -MAKES
REMAP	v -MAPPED, -MAPPING, -MAPS
REMARKET	v -ED, -ING, -S
REMARRY	v -RIED, -RYING, -RIES
REMASTER	v -ED, -ING, -S
REMATCH	v -ED, -ING, -ES
REMATE	v -MATED, -MATING, -MATES
REMEET	v -MET, -MEETING, -MEETS
REMELT	v -ED, -ING, -S
REMEND	v -ED, -ING, -S
REMERGE	v -MERGED, -MERGING, -MERGES
REMET	past tense of remeet
REMIX	v -MIXED or -MIXT, -MIXING, -MIXES
REMODIFY	v -FIED, -FYING, -FIES
REMOLD	v -ED, -ING, -S
REMOUNT	v -ED, -ING, -S
RENAIL	v -ED, -ING, -S
RENAME	v -NAMED, -NAMING, -NAMES
RENEST	v -ED, -ING, -S
RENOTIFY	v -FIED, -FYING, -FIES
RENUMBER	v -ED, -ING, -S
REOBJECT	v -ED, -ING, -S
REOBTAIN	v -ED, -ING, -S
REOCCUPY	v -PIED, -PYING, -PIES
REOCCUR	v -CURRED, -CURRING, -CURS
REOIL	v -ED, -ING, -S
REOPEN	v -ED, -ING, -S
REOPPOSE	v -POSED, -POSING, -POSES
REORDAIN	v -ED, -ING, -S
REORDER	v -ED, -ING, -S
REORIENT	v -ED, -ING, -S
REOUTFIT	v -FITTED, -FITTING, -FITS
REPACIFY	v -FIED, -FYING, -FIES
REPACK	v -ED, -ING, -S
REPAINT	v -ED, -ING, -S
REPANEL	v -ELED, -ELING, -ELS or -ELLED, -ELLING, -ELS
REPAPER	v -ED, -ING, -S
REPARK	v -ED, -ING, -S
REPASS	v -ED, -ING, -ES
REPATCH	v -ED, -ING, -ES
REPAVE	v -PAVED, -PAVING, -PAVES
REPEG	v -PEGGED, -PEGGING, -PEGS
REPEOPLE	v -PLED, -PLING, -PLES
REPERK	v -ED, -ING, -S
REPHRASE	v -PHRASED, -PHRASING, -PHRASES
REPIN	v -PINNED, -PINNING, -PINS
REPLAN	v -PLANNED, -PLANNING, -PLANS
REPLANT	v -ED, -ING, -S
REPLATE	v -PLATED, -PLATING, -PLATES
REPLAY	v -ED, -ING, -S
REPLEAD	v -PLEADED or -PLED, -PLEADING, -PLEADS
REPLEDGE	v -PLEDGED, -PLEDGING, -PLEDGES
REPLOT	v -PLOTTED, -PLOTTING, -PLOTS
REPLUMB	v -ED, -ING, -S

REPLUNGE v -PLUNGED, -PLUNGING, -PLUNGES

REPOLISH v -ED, -ING, -ES

REPOLL v -ED, -ING, -S

REPOT v -POTTED, -POTTING, -POTS

REPOUR v -ED, -ING, -S

REPOWER v -ED, -ING, -S

REPRICE v -PRICED, -PRICING, -PRICES

REPRINT v -ED, -ING, -S

REPROBE v -PROBED, -PROBING, -PROBES

REPUMP v -ED, -ING, -S

REPURIFY v -FIED, -FYING, -FIES

REPURSUE v -SUED, -SUING, -SUES

RERACK v -ED, -ING, -S

RERAISE v -RAISED, -RAISING, -RAISES

REREAD v -READ, -READING, -READS

RERECORD v -ED, -ING, -S

REREMIND v -ED, -ING, -S

REREPEAT v -ED, -ING, -S

REREVIEW v -ED, -ING, -S

RERIG v -RIGGED, -RIGGING, -RIGS

RERISE v -ROSE, -RISEN, -RISING, -RISES

REROLL v -ED, -ING, -S

REROOF v -ED, -ING, -S

REROSE past tense of rerise

REROUTE v -ROUTED, -ROUTING, -ROUTES

RESADDLE v -DLED, -DLING, -DLES

RESAID past tense of resay

RESAIL v -ED, -ING, -S

RESALUTE v -LUTED, -LUTING, -LUTES

RESAMPLE v -PLED, -PLING, -PLES

RESAW v -SAWED, -SAWN, -SAWING, -SAWS

RESAY v -SAID, -SAYING, -SAYS

RESCHOOL v -ED, -ING, -S

RESCORE v -SCORED, -SCORING, -SCORES

RESCREEN v -ED, -ING, -S

RESCULPT v -ED, -ING, -S

RESEAL v -ED, -ING, -S

RESEASON v -ED, -ING, -S

RESEAT v -ED, -ING, -S

RESECURE v -CURED, -CURING, -CURES

RESEE v -SAW, -SEEN, -SEEING, -SEES

RESEED v -ED, -ING, -S

RESEEK v -SOUGHT, -SEEKING, -SEEKS

RESEEN past participle of resee

RESEIZE v -SEIZED, -SEIZING, -SEIZES

RESELL v -SOLD, -SELLING, -SELLS

RESEND v -SENT, -SENDING, -SENDS

RESET v -SET, -SETTING, -SETS

RESETTLE v -TLED, -TLING, -TLES

RESEW v -SEWED, -SEWN, -SEWING, -SEWS

RESHAPE v -SHAPED, -SHAPING, -SHAPES

RESHAVE v -SHAVED, -SHAVEN, -SHAVING, -SHAVES

RESHINE v -SHONE or -SHINED, -SHINING, -SHINES

RESHIP v -SHIPPED, -SHIPPING, -SHIPS

RESHOE v -SHOD, -SHOEING, -SHOES

RESHONE a past tense of reshine

RESHOOT v -SHOT, -SHOOTING, -SHOOTS

RESHOW v -SHOWED, -SHOWN, -SHOWING, -SHOWS

RESIFT v -ED, -ING, -S

RESIGHT v -ED, -ING, -S

RESILVER v -ED, -ING, -S

RESITE v -SITED, -SITING, -SITES

RESIZE v -SIZED, -SIZING, -SIZES

RESKETCH v -ED, -ING, -ES

RESLATE v -SLATED, -SLATING, -SLATES

RESMELT v -ED, -ING, -S

RESMOOTH v -ED, -ING, -S

RESOAK v -ED, -ING, -S

RESOD v -SODDED, -SODDING, -SODS

RESOLD past tense of resell

RESOLDER v -ED, -ING, -S

RESOLE v -SOLED, -SOLING, -SOLES

RESOUGHT past tense of reseek

RESOW v -SOWED, -SOWN, -SOWING, -SOWS

RESPACE v -SPACED, -SPACING, -SPACES

RESPADE v -SPADED, -SPADING, -SPADES

RESPEAK v -SPOKE, -SPOKEN, -SPEAKING, -SPEAKS

RESPELL v -SPELLED or -SPELT, -SPELLING, SPELLS

RESPLICE v -SPLICED, -SPLICING, -SPLICES

RESPLIT	v -SPLIT, -SPLITTING, -SPLITS
RESPOKE	past tense of respeak
RESPOKEN	past participle of respeak
RESPOT	v -SPOTTED, -SPOTTING, -SPOTS
RESPRANG	a past tense of respring
RESPRAY	v -ED, -ING, -S
RESPREAD	v -SPREAD, -SPREADING, -SPREADS
RESPRING	v -SPRANG or -SPRUNG, -SPRINGING, -SPRINGS
RESPROUT	v -ED, -ING, -S
RESTACK	v -ED, -ING, -S
RESTAFF	v -ED, -ING, -S
RESTAGE	v -STAGED, -STAGING, -STAGES
RESTAMP	v -ED, -ING, -S
RESTART	v -ED, -ING, -S
RESTATE	v -STATED, -STATING, -STATES
RESTITCH	v -ED, -ING, -ES
RESTOCK	v -ED, -ING, -S
RESTOKE	v -STOKED, -STOKING, -STOKES
RESTRESS	v -ED, -ING, -ES
RESTRIKE	v -STRUCK, -STRICKEN, -STRIKING, -STRIKES
RESTRING	v -STRUNG, -STRINGING, -STRINGS
RESTRIVE	v -STROVE, -STRIVEN, -STRIVING, -STRIVES
RESTRUCK	past tense of restrike
RESTRUNG	past tense of restring
RESTUDY	v -STUDIED, -STUDYING, -STUDIES
RESTUFF	v -ED, -ING, -S
RESTYLE	v -STYLED, -STYLING, -STYLES
RESUBMIT	v -MITTED, -MITTING, -MITS
RESUMMON	v -ED, -ING, -S
RESUPPLY	v -PLIED, -PLYING, -PLIES
RESURVEY	v -ED, -ING, -S
RETACK	v -ED, -ING, -S
RETACKLE	v -LED, -LING, -LES
RETAG	v -TAGGED, -TAGGING, -TAGS
RETAILOR	v -ED, -ING, -S
RETAPE	v -TAPED, -TAPING, -TAPES
RETARGET	v -ED, -ING, -S
RETASTE	v -TASTED, -TASTING, -TASTES
RETAX	v -ED, -ING, -ES
RETEACH	v -TAUGHT, -TEACHING, -TEACHES
RETEAM	v -ED, -ING, -S

RETEAR	v -TORE, -TORN, -TEARING, -TEARS
RETELL	v -TOLD, -TELLING, -TELLS
RETEMPER	v -ED, -ING, -S
RETEST	v -ED, -ING, -S
RETHINK	v -THOUGHT, -THINKING, -THINKS
RETHREAD	v -ED, -ING, -S
RETIE	v -TIED, -TYING, -TIES
RETILE	v -TILED, -TILING, -TILES
RETIME	v -TIMED, -TIMING, -TIMES
RETINT	v -ED, -ING, -S
RETITLE	v -TLED, -TLING, -TLES
RETOLD	past tense of retell
RETORE	past tense of retear
RETORN	past participle of retear
RETRACK	v -ED, -ING, -S
RETRAIN	v -ED, -ING, -S
RETRIM	v -TRIMMED, -TRIMMING, -TRIMS
RETRY	v -TRIED, -TRYING, -TRIES
RETUNE	v -TUNED, -TUNING, -TUNES
RETWIST	v -ED, -ING, -S
RETYING	present participle of retie
RETYPE	v -TYPED, -TYPING, -TYPES
REUNIFY	v -FIED, -FYING, -FIES
REUNITE	v -UNITED, -UNITING, -UNITES
REUSE	v -USED, -USING, -USES
REUTTER	v -ED, -ING, -S
REVALUE	v -UED, -UING, -UES
REVERIFY	v -FIED, -FYING, -FIES
REVEST	v -ED, -ING, -S
REVIEW	v -ED, -ING, -S
REVISIT	v -ED, -ING, -S
REVOICE	v -VOICED, -VOICING, -VOICES
REVOTE	v -VOTED, -VOTING, -VOTES
REWAKE	v -WAKED or -WOKE, -WOKEN, -WAKING, -WAKES
REWAKEN	v -ED, -ING, -S
REWAN	a past tense of rewin
REWARM	v -ED, -ING, -S
REWASH	v -ED, -ING, -ES
REWAX	v -ED, -ING, -ES
REWEAVE	v -WOVE or -WEAVED, -WOVEN, -WEAVING, -WEAVES
REWED	v -WEDDED, -WEDDING, -WEDS
REWEIGH	v -ED, -ING, -S
REWELD	v -ED, -ING, -S
REWET	v -WETTED, -WETTING, -WETS
REWIDEN	v -ED, -ING, -S

REWIN v -WON or -WAN, -WINNING, -WINS

REWIND v -WOUND or -WINDED, -WINDING, -WINDS

REWIRE v -WIRED, -WIRING, -WIRES

REWOKE a past tense of rewake

REWOKEN past participle of rewake

REWON a past tense of rewin

REWORK v -WORKED or -WROUGHT, -WORKING, -WORKS

REWOUND a past tense of rewind

REWOVE a past tense of reweave

REWOVEN past participle of reweave

REWRAP v -WRAPPED, or -WRAPT, -WRAPPING, -WRAPS

REWRITE v -WROTE, -WRITTEN, -WRITING, -WRITES

REWROUGHT a past tense of rework

REZONE v -ZONED, -ZONING, -ZONES

REACH v -ED, -ING, -ES to stretch out or put forth

REACHER n pl. -S one that reaches

REACT v -ED, -ING, -S to respond to a stimulus

REACTANT n pl. -S one that reacts

REACTION n pl. -S the act of reacting

REACTIVE adj tending to react

REACTOR n pl. -S one that reacts

READ v READ, READING, READS to look at so as to take in the meaning of, as something written or printed READABLE adj READABLY adv

READER n pl. -S one that reads

READERLY adj typical of a reader

READIED past tense of ready

READIER comparative of ready

READIES present 3d person sing. of ready

READIEST superlative of ready

READILY adv in a ready manner

READING n pl. -S material that is read

READOUT n pl. -S a presentation of computer data

READY adj READIER, READIEST prepared

READY v READIED, READYING, READIES to make ready

REAGENT n pl. -S a substance used in a chemical reaction to ascertain the nature or composition of another

REAGIN n pl. -S a type of antibody REAGINIC adj

REAL adj REALER, REALEST having actual existence

REAL n pl. -S or -ES a former monetary unit of Spain

REAL n pl. REIS a former monetary unit of Portugal and Brazil

REALGAR n pl. -S a mineral

REALIA n/pl objects used by a teacher to illustrate everyday living

REALISE v -ISED, -ISING, -ISES to realize

REALISER n pl. -S one that realises

REALISM n pl. -S concern with fact or reality

REALIST n pl. -S one who is concerned with fact or reality

REALITY n pl. -TIES something that is real

REALIZE v -IZED, -IZING, -IZES to understand completely

REALIZER n pl. -S one that realizes

REALLY adv actually

REALM n pl. -S a kingdom

REALNESS n pl. -ES the state of being real

REALTY n pl. -TIES property in buildings and land

REAM v -ED, -ING, -S to enlarge with a reamer

REAMER n pl. -S a tool used to enlarge holes

REAP v -ED, -ING, -S to cut for harvest REAPABLE adj

REAPER n pl. -S one that reaps

REAPHOOK n pl. -S an implement used in reaping

REAR v -ED, -ING, -S to lift upright

REARER n pl. -S one that rears

REARMICE n/pl reremice

REARMOST adj coming or situated last

REARWARD n pl. -S the rearmost division of an army

REASCENT n pl. -S a new or second ascent

REASON v -ED, -ING, -S to derive inferences or conclusions from known or presumed facts

REASONER n pl. -S one that reasons

REATA n pl. -S riata

REAVE v REAVED or REFT, REAVING, REAVES to plunder

REAVER n pl. -S one that reaves

REB n pl. -S a Confederate soldier

REBAR *n pl.* -S a steel rod for use in reinforced concrete

REBATE *v* -BATED, -BATING, -BATES to deduct or return from a payment or bill

REBATER *n pl.* -S one that rebates

REBATO *n pl.* -TOS rabato

REBBE *n pl.* -S a rabbi

REBEC *n pl.* -S an ancient stringed instrument

REBECK *n pl.* -S rebec

REBEL *v* -BELLED, -BELLING, -BELS to oppose the established government of one's land

REBELDOM *n pl.* -S an area controlled by rebels

REBIRTH *n pl.* -S a new or second birth

REBOANT *adj* resounding loudly

REBOP *n pl.* -S a type of music

REBORN *adj* born again

REBOUND *v* -ED, -ING, -S to spring back

REBOZO *n pl.* -ZOS a long scarf

REBRANCH *v* -ED, -ING, -ES to form secondary branches

REBUFF *v* -ED, -ING, -S to reject or refuse curtly

REBUKE *v* -BUKED, -BUKING, -BUKES to criticize sharply

REBUKER *n pl.* -S one that rebukes

REBURIAL *n pl.* -S a second burial

REBUS *n pl.* -ES a type of puzzle

REBUT *v* -BUTTED, -BUTTING, -BUTS to refute

REBUTTAL *n pl.* -S argument or proof that rebuts

REBUTTER *n pl.* -S one that rebuts

REBUTTING present participle of rebut

REC *n pl.* -S recreation

RECALL *v* -ED, -ING, -S to call back

RECALLER *n pl.* -S one that recalls

RECAMIER *n pl.* -S a backless couch

RECANT *v* -ED, -ING, -S to make a formal retraction or disavowal of

RECANTER *n pl.* -S one that recants

RECAP *v* -CAPPED, -CAPPING, -CAPS to review by a brief summary

RECCE *n pl.* -S a recon

RECEDE *v* -CEDED, -CEDING, -CEDES to move back or away

RECEIPT *v* -ED, -ING, -S to mark as having been paid

RECEIVE *v* -CEIVED, -CEIVING, -CEIVES to come into possession of

RECEIVER *n pl.* -S one that receives

RECENCY *n pl.* -CIES the state of being recent

RECENT *adj* -CENTER, -CENTEST of or pertaining to a time not long past RECENTLY *adv*

RECEPT *n pl.* -S a type of mental image

RECEPTOR *n pl.* -S a nerve ending specialized to receive stimuli

RECESS *v* -ED, -ING, -ES to place in a receding space or hollow

RECHEAT *n pl.* -S a hunting call

RECIPE *n pl.* -S a set of instructions for making something

RECISION *n pl.* -S a cancellation

RECITAL *n pl.* -S a detailed account

RECITE *v* -CITED, -CITING, -CITES to declaim or say from memory

RECITER *n pl.* -S one that recites

RECK *v* -ED, -ING, -S to be concerned about

RECKLESS *adj* foolishly heedless of danger

RECKON *v* -ED, -ING, -S to count or compute

RECKONER *n pl.* -S one that reckons

RECLAIM *v* -ED, -ING, -S to make suitable for cultivation or habitation

RECLAME *n pl.* -S publicity

RECLINE *v* -CLINED, -CLINING, -CLINES to lean or lie back

RECLINER *n pl.* -S one that reclines

RECLUSE *n pl.* -S one who lives in solitude and seclusion

RECOIL *v* -ED, -ING, -S to draw back in fear or disgust

RECOILER *n pl.* -S one that recoils

RECON *n pl.* -S a preliminary survey

RECONVEY *v* -ED, -ING, -S to convey back to a previous position

RECORD *v* -ED, -ING, -S to set down for preservation

RECORDER *n pl.* -S one that records

RECOUNT *v* -ED, -ING, -S to relate in detail

RECOUP *v* -ED, -ING, -S to get back the equivalent of

RECOUPE *adj* divided twice

RECOURSE *n pl.* -S a turning or applying to someone or something for aid

RECOVER *v* -ED, -ING, -S to obtain again after losing

RECOVERY *n pl.* -ERIES an economic upturn

RECREANT *n pl.* -S a coward

RECREATE *v* -ATED, -ATING, -ATES to refresh mentally or physically

RECRUIT *v* -ED, -ING, -S to engage for military service

RECTA a *pl.* of rectum

RECTAL *adj* pertaining to the rectum RECTALLY *adv*

RECTI *pl.* of rectus

RECTIFY *v* -FIED, -FYING, -FIES to correct

RECTO *n pl.* -TOS a right-hand page of a book

RECTOR *n pl.* -S a clergyman in charge of a parish

RECTORY *n pl.* -RIES a rector's dwelling

RECTRIX *n pl.* -TRICES a feather of a bird's tail

RECTUM *n pl.* -TUMS or -TA the terminal portion of the large intestine

RECTUS *n pl.* -TI a straight muscle

RECUR *v* -CURRED, -CURRING, -CURS to happen again

RECURVE *v* -CURVED, -CURVING, -CURVES to curve backward or downward

RECUSAL *n pl.* -S the act of recusing

RECUSANT *n pl.* -S one who refuses to accept established authority

RECUSE *v* -CUSED, -CUSING, -CUSES to disqualify or challenge as judge in a particular case

RECYCLE *v* -CLED, -CLING, -CLES to process in order to extract useful materials

RECYCLER *n pl.* -S one that recycles

RED *adj* REDDER, REDDEST of the color of blood

RED *v* REDDED, REDDING, REDS to redd

REDACT *v* -ED, -ING, -S to prepare for publication

REDACTOR *n pl.* -S one that redacts

REDAN *n pl.* -S a type of fortification

REDARGUE *v* -GUED, -GUING, -GUES to disprove

REDBAIT *v* -ED, -ING, -S to denounce as Communist

REDBAY *n pl.* -BAYS a small tree

REDBIRD *n pl.* -S a bird with red plummage

REDBONE *n pl.* -S a hunting dog

REDBRICK *n pl.* -S a modern British university

REDBUD *n pl.* -S a small tree

REDBUG *n pl.* -S a chigger

REDCAP *n pl.* -S a porter

REDCOAT *n pl.* -S a British soldier during the American Revolution

REDD *v* -ED, -ING, -S to put in order

REDDED past tense of red and redd

REDDEN *v* -ED, -ING, -S to make or become red

REDDER *n pl.* -S one that redds

REDDEST superlative of red

REDDING present participle of red and redd

REDDISH *adj* somewhat red

REDDLE *v* -DLED, -DLING, -DLES to ruddle

REDE *v* REDED, REDING, REDES to advise

REDEAR *n pl.* -S a common sunfish

REDEEM *v* -ED, -ING, -S to buy back

REDEEMER *n pl.* -S one that redeems

REDEYE *n pl.* -S a railroad danger signal

REDFIN *n pl.* -S a freshwater fish

REDFISH *n pl.* -ES an edible rockfish

REDHEAD *n pl.* -S a person with red hair

REDHORSE *n pl.* -S a freshwater fish

REDIA *n pl.* -DIAE or -DIAS the larva of certain flatworms REDIAL *adj*

REDING present participle of rede

REDIRECT *v* -ED, -ING, -S to change the course or direction of

REDLEG *n pl.* -S a bird with red legs

REDLINE *v* -LINED, -LINING, -LINES to withhold loans or insurance from certain neighborhoods

REDLY *adv* with red color

REDNESS *n pl.* -ES the state of being red

REDO *n pl.* -DOS something that is done again

REDOLENT *adj* fragrant

REDOUBLE *v* -BLED, -BLING, -BLES to double

REDOUBT *n pl.* -S an enclosed fortification

REDOUND *v* -ED, -ING, -S to have an effect or consequence

REDOUT *n pl.* -S a condition in which blood is driven to the head

REDOWA *n pl.* -S a lively dance

REDOX *n pl.* -ES a type of chemical reaction

REDPOLL n pl. -S a small finch

REDRAFT v -ED, -ING, -S to make a revised copy of

REDRAWER n pl. -S one that redraws

REDRESS v -ED, -ING, -ES to set right

REDROOT n pl. -S a perennial herb

REDSHANK n pl. -S a shore bird

REDSHIFT n pl. -S a displacement of the spectrum of a celestial body toward the longer wavelengths

REDSHIRT v -ED, -ING, -S to keep a college athlete out of varsity play in order to extend his eligibility

REDSTART n pl. -S a small songbird

REDTAIL n pl. -S a type of hawk

REDTOP n pl. -S a type of grass

REDUCE v -DUCED, -DUCING, -DUCES to diminish

REDUCER n pl. -S one that reduces

REDUCTOR n pl. -S an apparatus for the reduction of metallic ions in solution

REDUVIID n pl. -S a bloodsucking insect

REDUX adj brought back

REDWARE n pl. -S an edible seaweed

REDWING n pl. -S a European thrush

REDWOOD n pl. -S a very tall evergreen tree

REE n pl. -S the female Eurasian sandpiper

REECHY adj REECHIER, REECHIEST foul, rancid

REED v -ED, -ING, -S to fasten with reeds (the stalks of tall grasses)

REEDBIRD n pl. -S the bobolink

REEDBUCK n pl. -S an African antelope

REEDIER comparative of reedy

REEDIEST superlative of reedy

REEDIFY v -FIED, -FYING, -FIES to rebuild

REEDILY adv with a thin, piping sound

REEDING n pl. -S a convex molding

REEDLIKE adj resembling a reed

REEDLING n pl. -S a marsh bird

REEDMAN n pl. -MEN one who plays a reed instrument

REEDY adj REEDIER, REEDIEST abounding in reeds

REEF v -ED, -ING, -S to reduce the area of a sail **REEFABLE** adj

REEFER n pl. -S one that reefs

REEFY adj REEFIER, REEFIEST abounding in ridges of rock

REEK v -ED, -ING, -S to give off a strong, unpleasant odor

REEKER n pl. -S one that reeks

REEKY adj REEKIER, REEKIEST reeking

REEL v -ED, -ING, -S to wind on a type of rotary device **REELABLE** adj

REELER n pl. -S one that reels

REENTRY n pl. -TRIES a new entry

REEST v -ED, -ING, -S to balk

REEVE v REEVED or ROVE, ROVEN, REEVING, REEVES to fasten by passing through or around something

REF v REFFED, REFFING, REFS to referee

REFACE v -FACED, -FACING, -FACES to repair the outer surface of

REFECT v -ED, -ING, -S to refresh with food and drink

REFEL v -FELLED, -FELLING, -FELS to reject

REFER v -FERRED, -FERRING, -FERS to direct to a source for help or information

REFEREE v -EED, -EEING, -EES to supervise the play in certain sports

REFERENT n pl. -S something referred to

REFERRAL n pl. -S one that is referred

REFERRED past tense of refer

REFERRER n pl. -S one that refers

REFERRING present participle of refer

REFFED past tense of ref

REFFING present participle of ref

REFINE v -FINED, -FINING, -FINES to free from impurities

REFINER n pl. -S one that refines

REFINERY n pl. -ERIES a place where crude material is refined

REFINING present participle of refine

REFINISH v -ED, -ING, -ES to give a new surface to

REFIT v -FITTED, -FITTING, -FITS to prepare for additional use

REFLATE v -FLATED, -FLATING, -FLATES to inflate again

REFLECT v -ED, -ING, -S to turn or throw back from a surface

REFLET n pl. -S special brilliance of surface

REFLEX v -ED, -ING, -ES to bend back

REFLEXLY adv in a reflexed manner

REFLUENT adj flowing back

REFLUX *v* -ED, -ING, -ES to cause to flow back

REFOREST *v* -ED, -ING, -S to replant with trees

REFORM *v* -ED, -ING, -S to change to a better state

REFORMER *n pl.* -S one that reforms

REFRACT *v* -ED, -ING, -S to deflect in a particular manner, as a ray of light

REFRAIN *v* -ED, -ING, -S to keep oneself back

REFRESH *v* -ED, -ING, -ES to restore the well-being and vigor of

REFT a past tense of reave

REFUGE *v* -UGED, -UGING, -UGES to give or take shelter

REFUGEE *n pl.* -S one who flees for safety

REFUGIUM *n pl.* -GIA a stable area during a period of continental climactic change

REFUND *v* -ED, -ING, -S to give back

REFUNDER *n pl.* -S one that refunds

REFUSAL *n pl.* -S the act of refusing

REFUSE *v* -FUSED, -FUSING, -FUSES to express oneself as unwilling to accept, do, or comply with

REFUSER *n pl.* -S one that refuses

REFUSNIK *n pl.* -S a Soviet citizen who is refused permission to emigrate

REFUTAL *n pl.* -S the act of refuting

REFUTE *v* -FUTED, -FUTING, -FUTES to prove to be false or erroneous

REFUTER *n pl.* -S one that refutes

REG *n pl.* -S a regulation

REGAINER *n pl.* -S one that regains

REGAL *adj* of or befitting a king

REGALE *v* -GALED, -GALING, -GALES to delight

REGALER *n pl.* -S one that regales

REGALIA *n/pl* the rights and privileges of a king

REGALITY *n pl.* -TIES regal authority

REGALLY *adv* in a regal manner

REGARD *v* -ED, -ING, -S to look upon with a particular feeling

REGATTA *n pl.* -S a boat race

REGELATE *v* -LATED, -LATING, -LATES to refreeze ice by reducing the pressure

REGENCY *n pl.* -CIES the office of a regent

REGENT *n pl.* -S one who rules in the place of a sovereign **REGENTAL** *adj*

REGES pl. of rex

REGGAE *n pl.* -S a form of popular Jamaican music

REGICIDE *n pl.* -S the killing of a king

REGIME *n pl.* -S a system of government

REGIMEN *n pl.* -S a systematic plan

REGIMENT *v* -ED, -ING, -S to form into military units

REGINA *n pl.* -NAE or -NAS queen **REGINAL** *adj*

REGION *n pl.* -S an administrative area or division

REGIONAL *n pl.* -S something that serves as a region

REGISTER *v* -ED, -ING, -S to record officially

REGISTRY *n pl.* -TRIES the act of registering

REGIUS *adj* holding a professorship founded by the sovereign

REGLET *n pl.* -S a flat, narrow molding

REGMA *n pl.* -MATA a type of fruit

REGNA pl. of regnum

REGNAL *adj* pertaining to a king or his reign

REGNANCY *n pl.* -CIES the state of being regnant

REGNANT *adj* reigning

REGNUM *n pl.* -NA dominion

REGOLITH *n pl.* -S a layer of loose rock

REGORGE *v* -GORGED, -GORGING, -GORGES to vomit

REGOSOL *n pl.* -S a type of soil

REGRATE *v* -GRATED, -GRATING, -GRATES to buy up in order to sell for a higher price in the same area

REGREET *v* -ED, -ING, -S to greet in return

REGRESS *v* -ED, -ING, -ES to go back

REGRET *v* -GRETTED, -GRETTING, -GRETS to look back upon with sorrow or remorse

REGROWTH *n pl.* -S a new or second growth

REGULAR *n pl.* -S an habitual customer

REGULATE *v* -LATED, -LATING, -LATES to control according to rule

REGULUS *n pl.* -LI or -LUSES a mass that forms beneath the slag in a furnace **REGULINE** *adj*

REHAB v -HABBED, -HABBING, -HABS to restore to a good condition

REHABBER n pl. -S one that rehabs

REHEARSE v -HEARSED, -HEARSING, -HEARSES to practice in preparation for a public appearance

REHEATER n pl. -S one that reheats

REHOBOAM n pl. -S a wine bottle

REHOUSE v -HOUSED, -HOUSING, -HOUSES to establish in a new housing unit

REI n pl. -S an erroneous English form for a former Portuguese coin

REIF n pl. -S robbery

REIFIER n pl. -S one that reifies

REIFY v -IFIED, -IFYING, -IFIES to regard as real or concrete

REIGN v -ED, -ING, -S to exercise sovereign power

REIN v -ED, -ING, -S to restrain

REINDEER n pl. -S a large deer

REINJURY n pl. -RIES a second injury

REINLESS adj unrestrained

REINSMAN n pl. -MEN a skilled rider of horses

REIS pl. of real

REISSUER n pl. -S one that reissues

REITBOK n pl. -S the reedbuck

REIVE v REIVED, REIVING, REIVES to plunder

REIVER n pl. -S one that reives

REJECT v -ED, -ING, -S to refuse to accept, consider, or make use of

REJECTEE n pl. -S one that is rejected

REJECTER n pl. -S one that rejects

REJECTOR n pl. -S rejecter

REJIGGER v -ED, -ING, -S to alter

REJOICE v -JOICED, -JOICING, -JOICES to feel joyful

REJOICER n pl. -S one that rejoices

RELAPSE v -LAPSED, -LAPSING, -LAPSES to fall or slip back into a former state

RELAPSER n pl. -S one that relapses

RELATE v -LATED, -LATING, -LATES to give an account of

RELATER n pl. -S one that relates

RELATION n pl. -S a significant association between two or more things

RELATIVE n pl. -S one who is connected with another by blood or marriage

RELATOR n pl. -S relater

RELAX v -ED, -ING, -ES to make less tense or rigid

RELAXANT n pl. -S a drug that relieves muscular tension

RELAXER n pl. -S one that relaxes

RELAXIN n pl. -S a female hormone

RELAY v -ED, -ING, -S to send along by using fresh sets to replace tired ones

RELEASE v -LEASED, -LEASING, -LEASES to set free

RELEASER n pl. -S one that releases

RELEGATE v -GATED, -GATING, -GATES to assign

RELENT v -ED, -ING, -S to become less severe

RELEVANT adj pertaining to the matter at hand

RELEVE n pl. -S a raising onto the toe in ballet

RELIABLE n pl. -S one that can be relied on

RELIABLY adv in a manner that can be relied on

RELIANCE n pl. -S confident or trustful dependence

RELIANT adj showing reliance

RELIC n pl. -S a surviving memorial of something past

RELICT n pl. -S an organism surviving in a changed environment

RELIED past tense of rely

RELIEF n pl. -S aid in the form of money or necessities

RELIER n pl. -S one that relies

RELIES present 3d person sing. of rely

RELIEVE v -LIEVED, -LIEVING, -LIEVES to lessen or free from pain or discomfort

RELIEVER n pl. -S one that relieves

RELIEVO n pl. -VOS the projection of figures or forms from a flat background

RELIGION n pl. -S the worship of a god or the supernatural

RELIQUE n pl. -S relic

RELISH v -ED, -ING, -ES to enjoy

RELIVE v -LIVED, -LIVING, -LIVES to experience again

RELOADER n pl. -S one that reloads

RELOCATE v -CATED, -CATING, -CATES to establish in a new place

RELUCENT *adj* reflecting light

RELUCT *v* -ED, -ING, -S to show opposition

RELUME *v* -LUMED, -LUMING, -LUMES to light again

RELUMINE *v* -MINED, -MINING, -MINES to relume

RELY *v* -LIED, -LYING, -LIES to place trust or confidence

REM *n pl.* -S a quantity of ionizing radiation

REMAIN *v* -ED, -ING, -S to continue in the same state

REMAKER *n pl.* -S one that remakes

REMAN *v* -MANNED, -MANNING, -MANS to furnish with a fresh supply of men

REMAND *v* -ED, -ING, -S to send back

REMANENT *adj* remaining

REMANNED past tense of reman

REMANNING present participle of reman

REMARK *v* -ED, -ING, -S to say or write briefly or casually

REMARKER *n pl.* -S one that remarks

REMARQUE *n pl.* -S a mark made in the margin of an engraved plate

REMEDIAL *adj* intended to correct something

REMEDY *v* -DIED, -DYING, -DIES to relieve or cure

REMEMBER *v* -ED, -ING, -S to bring to mind again

REMEX *n pl.* REMIGES a flight feather of a bird's wing **REMIGIAL** *adj*

REMIND *v* -ED, -ING, -S to cause to remember

REMINDER *n pl.* -S one that reminds

REMINT *v* -ED, -ING, -S to melt down and make into new coin

REMISE *v* -MISED, -MISING, -MISES to give up a claim to

REMISS *adj* careless **REMISSLY** *adv*

REMIT *v* -MITTED, -MITTING, -MITS to send money in payment

REMITTAL *n pl.* -S the act of remitting

REMITTER *n pl.* -S one that remits

REMITTING present participle of remit

REMITTOR *n pl.* -S remitter

REMNANT *n pl.* -S something remaining

REMODEL *v* -ELED, -ELING, -ELS or -ELLED, -ELLING, -ELS to make over

REMOLADE *n pl.* -S a piquant sauce

REMORA *n pl.* -S a type of marine fish **REMORID** *adj*

REMORSE *n pl.* -S deep anguish caused by a sense of guilt

REMOTE *adj* -MOTER, -MOTEST situated far away **REMOTELY** *adv*

REMOTE *n pl.* -S a broadcast originating outside a studio

REMOTION *n pl.* -S the act of removing

REMOVAL *n pl.* -S the act of removing

REMOVE *v* -MOVED, -MOVING, -MOVES to take or move away

REMOVER *n pl.* -S one that removes

REMUDA *n pl.* -S a herd of horses

RENAL *adj* pertaining to the kidneys

RENATURE *v* -TURED, -TURING, -TURES to restore natural qualities

REND *v* RENT or RENDED, RENDING, RENDS to tear apart forcibly

RENDER *v* -ED, -ING, -S to cause to be or become

RENDERER *n pl.* -S one that renders

RENDIBLE *adj* capable of being rent

RENDZINA *n pl.* -S a type of soil

RENEGADE *v* -GADED, -GADING, -GADES to become a traitor

RENEGADO *n pl.* -DOS or -DOES a traitor

RENEGE *v* -NEGED, -NEGING, -NEGES to fail to carry out a promise or commitment

RENEGER *n pl.* -S one that reneges

RENEW *v* -ED, -ING, -S to make new or as if new again

RENEWAL *n pl.* -S the act of renewing

RENEWER *n pl.* -S one that renews

RENIFORM *adj* kidney-shaped

RENIG *v* -NIGGED, -NIGGING, -NIGS to renege

RENIN *n pl.* -S an enzyme

RENITENT *adj* resisting physical pressure

RENMINBI *n pl.* RENMINBI currency in the People's Republic of China

RENNASE *n pl.* -S rennin

RENNET *n pl.* -S a lining membrane in the stomach of certain young animals

RENNIN *n pl.* -S an enzyme

RENOGRAM *n pl.* -S a photographic depiction of the course of renal excretion

RENOUNCE *v* -NOUNCED, -NOUNCING, -NOUNCES to disown

RENOVATE *v* -VATED, -VATING, -VATES to make like new

RENOWN v -ED, -ING, -S to make famous

RENT v -ED, -ING, -S to obtain temporary use of in return for compensation **RENTABLE** adj

RENTAL n pl. -S an amount paid or collected as rent

RENTE n pl. -S annual income under French law

RENTER n pl. -S one that rents

RENTIER n pl. -S one that receives a fixed income

RENVOI n pl. -S the expulsion by a government of an alien

REOFFER v -ED, -ING, -S to offer for public sale

REOVIRUS n pl. -ES a type of virus

REP n pl. -S a cross-ribbed fabric

REPAID past tense of repay

REPAIR v -ED, -ING, -S to restore to good condition

REPAIRER n pl. -S one that repairs

REPAND adj having a wavy margin **REPANDLY** adv

REPARTEE n pl. -S a quick, witty reply

REPAST v -ED, -ING, -S to eat or feast

REPAY v -PAID, -PAYING, -PAYS to pay back

REPEAL v -ED, -ING, -S to revoke

REPEALER n pl. -S one that repeals

REPEAT v -ED, -ING, -S to say or do again

REPEATER n pl. -S one that repeats

REPEL v -PELLED, -PELLING, -PELS to drive back

REPELLER n pl. -S one that repels

REPENT v -ED, -ING, -S to feel remorse or self-reproach for a past action

REPENTER n pl. -S one that repents

REPETEND n pl. -S a phrase or sound that is repeated

REPINE v -PINED, -PINING, -PINES to express discontent

REPINER n pl. -S one that repines

REPLACE v -PLACED, -PLACING, -PLACES to take the place of

REPLACER n pl. -S one that replaces

REPLETE adj abundantly supplied

REPLEVIN v -ED, -ING, -S to replevy

REPLEVY v -PLEVIED, -PLEVYING, -PLEVIES to regain possession of by legal action

REPLICA n pl. -S a close copy or reproduction

REPLICON n pl. -S a section of nucleic acid that replicates as a unit

REPLIER n pl. -S one that replies

REPLY v -PLIED, -PLYING, -PLIES to answer

REPO n pl. -POS something repossessed

REPORT v -ED, -ING, -S to give an account of

REPORTER n pl. -S one that reports

REPOSAL n pl. -S the act of reposing

REPOSE v -POSED, -POSING, -POSES to lie at rest

REPOSER n pl. -S one that reposes

REPOSIT v -ED, -ING, -S to put away

REPOUSSE n pl. -S a raised design hammered in metal

REPP n pl. -S rep

REPPED adj resembling rep

REPRESS v -ED, -ING, -ES to keep under control

REPRIEVE v -PRIEVED, -PRIEVING, -PRIEVES to postpone the punishment of

REPRISAL n pl. -S an act of retaliation

REPRISE v -PRISED, -PRISING, -PRISES to take back by force

REPRO n pl. -PROS a trial sheet of printed material suitable for photographic reproduction

REPROACH v -ED, -ING, -ES to find fault with

REPROOF n pl. -S criticism for a fault

REPROVAL n pl. -S reproof

REPROVE v -PROVED, -PROVING, -PROVES to rebuke

REPROVER n pl. -S one that reproves

REPTANT adj creeping or crawling

REPTILE n pl. -S any of a class of cold-blooded, air-breathing vertebrates

REPUBLIC n pl. -S a constitutional form of government

REPUGN v -ED, -ING, -S to oppose

REPULSE v -PULSED, -PULSING, -PULSES to drive back

REPULSER n pl. -S one that repulses

REPUTE v -PUTED, -PUTING, -PUTES to consider to be as specified

REQUEST v -ED, -ING, -S to express a desire for

REQUIEM n pl. -S a musical composition for the dead

REQUIN n pl. -S a voracious shark

REQUIRE v -QUIRED, -QUIRING, -QUIRES to have need of

REQUIRER n pl. -S one that requires

REQUITAL n pl. -S something given in return, compensation, or retaliation

REQUITE v -QUITED, -QUITING, -QUITES to make equivalent return for

REQUITER n pl. -S one that requites

RERAN past tense of rerun

REREDOS n pl. -ES an ornamental screen behind an altar

REREMICE n/pl bats (flying mammals)

REREWARD n pl. -S rearward

REROLLER n pl. -S one that rerolls

RERUN v -RAN, -RUNNING, -RUNS to present a repetition of a recorded performance

RES n pl. RES a particular thing or matter

RESALE n pl. -S the act of selling again

RESCALE v -SCALED, -SCALING, -SCALES to plan on a new scale

RESCIND v -ED, -ING, -S to annul

RESCRIPT n pl. -S something rewritten

RESCUE v -CUED, -CUING, -CUES to free from danger

RESCUER n pl. -S one that rescues

RESEARCH v -ED, -ING, -ES to investigate thoroughly

RESEAU n pl. -SEAUS or -SEAUX a filter screen for making color films

RESECT v -ED, -ING, -S to excise part of an organ or structure surgically

RESEDA n pl. -S a flowering plant

RESELLER n pl. -S one that resells

RESEMBLE v -BLED, -BLING, -BLES to be similar to

RESENT v -ED, -ING, -S to feel or express annoyance or ill will at

RESERVE v -SERVED, -SERVING, -SERVES to keep back for future use

RESERVER n pl. -S one that reserves

RESETTER n pl. -S one that resets

RESH n pl. -ES a Hebrew letter

RESHAPER n pl. -S one that reshapes something

RESID n pl. -S a type of fuel oil

RESIDE v -SIDED, -SIDING, -SIDES to dwell permanently or continuously

RESIDENT n pl. -S one who resides

RESIDER n pl. -S a resident

RESIDUA a pl. of residuum

RESIDUAL n pl. -S something left over

RESIDUE n pl. -S something remaining after the removal of a part

RESIDUUM n pl. -SIDUA or -SIDUUMS residue

RESIGN v -ED, -ING, -S to give up one's office or position

RESIGNER n pl. -S one that resigns

RESILE v -SILED, -SILING, -SILES to spring back

RESIN v -ED, -ING, -S to treat with resin (a viscous substance obtained from certain plants)

RESINATE v -ATED, -ATING, -ATES to resin

RESINIFY v -FIED, -FYING, -FIES to convert into resin

RESINOID n pl. -S a resinous substance

RESINOUS adj resembling resin

RESINY adj resinous

RESIST v -ED, -ING, -S to strive against

RESISTER n pl. -S one that resists

RESISTOR n pl. -S a device in an electric circuit

RESOJET n pl. -S a pulsejet

RESOLUTE adj -LUTER, -LUTEST characterized by firmness or determination

RESOLUTE n pl. -S one who is resolute

RESOLVE v -SOLVED, -SOLVING, -SOLVES to make a firm decision about

RESOLVER n pl. -S one that resolves

RESONANT n pl. -S a resounding sound

RESONATE v -NATED, -NATING, -NATES to resound

RESORB v -ED, -ING, -S to absorb again

RESORCIN n pl. -S a chemical compound

RESORT v -ED, -ING, -S to go frequently or habitually

RESORTER n pl. -S one that resorts

RESOUND v -ED, -ING, -S to make a loud, long, or echoing sound

RESOURCE n pl. -S an available supply

RESPECT v -ED, -ING, -S to have a high regard for

RESPIRE v -SPIRED, -SPIRING, -SPIRES to breathe

RESPITE v -SPITED, -SPITING, -SPITES to relieve temporarily

RESPOND v -ED, -ING, -S to say or act in return

RESPONSA n/pl written rabbinic decisions

RESPONSE *n pl.* -S a reply or reaction

REST *v* -ED, -ING, -S to refresh oneself by ceasing work or activity

RESTER *n pl.* -S one that rests

RESTFUL *adj* -FULLER, -FULLEST tranquil

RESTIVE *adj* difficult to control

RESTLESS *adj* unable or disinclined to remain at rest

RESTORAL *n pl.* -S the act of restoring

RESTORE *v* -STORED, -STORING, -STORES to bring back to a former or original condition

RESTORER *n pl.* -S one that restores

RESTRAIN *v* -ED, -ING, -S to hold back from action

RESTRICT *v* -ED, -ING, -S to keep within certain boundaries

RESTROOM *n pl.* -S a room furnished with toilets and sinks

RESULT *v* -ED, -ING, -S to occur as a consequence

RESUME *v* -SUMED, -SUMING, -SUMES to take up again after interruption

RESUMER *n pl.* -S one that resumes

RESUPINE *adj* lying on the back

RESURGE *v* -SURGED, -SURGING, -SURGES to rise again

RET *v* RETTED, RETTING, RETS to soak in order to loosen the fiber from the woody tissue

RETABLE *n pl.* -S a raised shelf above an altar

RETAIL *v* -ED, -ING, -S to sell in small quantities

RETAILER *n pl.* -S one that retails

RETAIN *v* -ED, -ING, -S to keep possession of

RETAINER *n pl.* -S one that retains

RETAKE *v* -TOOK, -TAKEN, -TAKING, -TAKES to take back

RETAKER *n pl.* -S one that retakes

RETARD *v* -ED, -ING, -S to slow the progress of

RETARDER *n pl.* -S one that retards

RETCH *v* -ED, -ING, -ES to make an effort to vomit

RETE *n pl.* -TIA an anatomical mesh or network

RETEM *n pl.* -S a desert shrub

RETENE *n pl.* -S a chemical compound

RETIA *pl.* of rete

RETIAL *adj* pertaining to a rete

RETIARII *n/pl* ancient Roman gladiators

RETIARY *adj* resembling a net

RETICENT *adj* tending to be silent

RETICLE *n pl.* -S a network of lines in the eyepiece of an optical instrument

RETICULA *n/pl* netlike structures

RETICULE *n pl.* -S a woman's handbag

RETIFORM *adj* arranged like a net

RETINA *n pl.* -NAS or -NAE a membrane of the eye

RETINAL *n pl.* -S retinene

RETINE *n pl.* -S a substance in cells that retards growth and cell division

RETINENE *n pl.* -S a pigment in the retina

RETINITE *n pl.* -S a fossil resin

RETINOID *n pl.* -S a compound analogous to vitamin A

RETINOL *n pl.* -S a liquid hydrocarbon

RETINUE *n pl.* -S a group of attendants RETINUED *adj*

RETINULA *n pl.* -LAE or -LAS a neural receptor of an arthropod's eye

RETIRANT *n pl.* -S a retiree

RETIRE *v* -TIRED, -TIRING, -TIRES to go away or withdraw

RETIREE *n pl.* -S one who has retired from his vocation

RETIRER *n pl.* -S one that retires

RETIRING *adj* shy

RETOOK past tense of retake

RETOOL *v* -ED, -ING, -S to reequip with tools

RETORT *v* -ED, -ING, -S to answer back sharply

RETORTER *n pl.* -S one that retorts

RETOUCH *v* -ED, -ING, -ES to add new details or touches to

RETRACE *v* -TRACED, -TRACING, -TRACES to go back over

RETRACT *v* -ED, -ING, -S to take back

RETRAL *adj* situated toward the back RETRALLY *adv*

RETREAD *v* -ED, -ING, -S to furnish with a new tread

RETREAT *v* -ED, -ING, -S to go back or backward

RETRENCH *v* -ED, -ING, -ES to curtail

RETRIAL *n pl.* -S a second trial

RETRIEVE *v* -TRIEVED, -TRIEVING, -TRIEVES to get back

RETRO *n pl.* -ROS a rocket on a spacecraft that produces thrust in a direction opposite to the line of flight

RETROACT *v* -ED, -ING, -S to act in return

RETROFIT v -FITTED, -FITTING, -FITS to furnish with new parts not originally available

RETRORSE adj bent backward

RETSINA n pl. -S a resin-flavored Greek wine

RETTED past tense of ret

RETTING present participle of ret

RETURN v -ED, -ING, -S to come or go back

RETURNEE n pl. -S one that has returned

RETURNER n pl. -S one that returns

RETUSE adj having a rounded apex with a shallow notch — used of leaves

REUNION n pl. -S a reuniting of persons after separation

REUNITER n pl. -S one that reunites

REUSABLE adj capable of being used again

REV v REVVED, REVVING, REVS to increase the speed of

REVAMP v -ED, -ING, -S to make over

REVAMPER n pl. -S one that revamps

REVANCHE n pl. -S a political policy designed to regain lost territory

REVEAL v -ED, -ING, -S to make known

REVEALER n pl. -S one that reveals

REVEHENT adj carrying back

REVEILLE n pl. -S a morning bugle call

REVEL v -ELED, -ELING, -ELS or -ELLED, -ELLING, -ELS to engage in revelry

REVELER n pl. -S one that revels

REVELLER n pl. -S reveler

REVELLING present participle of revel

REVELRY n pl. -RIES noisy merrymaking

REVENANT n pl. -S one that returns

REVENGE v -VENGED, -VENGING, -VENGES to inflict injury in return for

REVENGER n pl. -S one that revenges

REVENUE n pl. -S the income of a government REVENUAL, REVENUED adj

REVENUER n pl. -S a revenue officer

REVERB v -ED, -ING, -S to continue in a series of echoes

REVERE v -VERED, -VERING, -VERES to regard with great respect

REVEREND n pl. -S a clergyman

REVERENT adj deeply respectful

REVERER n pl. -S one that reveres

REVERIE n pl. -S a daydream

REVERIES pl. of revery

REVERING present participle of revere

REVERS n pl. REVERS a part of a garment turned back to show the inside

REVERSAL n pl. -S the act of reversing

REVERSE v -VERSED, -VERSING, -VERSES to turn or move in the opposite direction

REVERSER n pl. -S one that reverses

REVERSO n pl. -VERSOS verso

REVERT v -ED, -ING, -S to return to a former state

REVERTER n pl. -S one that reverts

REVERY n pl. -ERIES reverie

REVET v -VETTED, -VETTING, -VETS to face with masonry

REVIEWAL n pl. -S the act of reviewing

REVIEWER n pl. -S one that reviews

REVILE v -VILED, -VILING, -VILES to denounce with abusive language

REVILER n pl. -S one that reviles

REVISAL n pl. -S a revision

REVISE v -VISED, -VISING, -VISES to make a new or improved version of

REVISER n pl. -S one that revises

REVISION n pl. -S a revised version

REVISOR n pl. -S reviser

REVISORY adj pertaining to revision

REVIVAL n pl. -S renewed attention to or interest in something

REVIVE v -VIVED, -VIVING, -VIVES to bring back to life or consciousness

REVIVER n pl. -S one that revives

REVIVIFY v -FIED, -FYING, -FIES to give new life to

REVIVING present participle of revive

REVOKE v -VOKED, -VOKING, -VOKES to annul by taking back

REVOKER n pl. -S one that revokes

REVOLT v -ED, -ING, -S to rise up against authority

REVOLTER n pl. -S one that revolts

REVOLUTE adj rolled backward or downward

REVOLVE v -VOLVED, -VOLVING, -VOLVES to turn about an axis

REVOLVER n pl. -S a type of handgun

REVUE n pl. -S a type of musical show

REVUIST n pl. -S a writer of revues

REVULSED adj affected with revulsion

REVVED past tense of rev

REVVING	present participle of rev
REWARD	v -ED, -ING, -S to give recompense to for worthy behavior
REWARDER	n pl. -S one that rewards
REWINDER	n pl. -S one that rewinds
REWORD	v -ED, -ING, -S to state again in other words
REWRITER	n pl. -S one that rewrites
REX	n pl. REGES king
REX	n pl. -ES an animal with a single wavy layer of hair
REYNARD	n pl. -S a fox
RHABDOM	n pl. -S a rodlike structure in the retinula
RHABDOME	n pl. -S rhabdom
RHACHIS	n pl. -CHISES or -CHIDES rachis
RHAMNOSE	n pl. -S a sugar found in plants
RHAMNUS	n pl. -ES a thorny tree or shrub
RHAPHE	n pl. -PHAE or -PHES raphe
RHAPSODE	n pl. -S a reciter of epic poetry in ancient Greece
RHAPSODY	n pl. -DIES an exalted expression of feeling
RHATANY	n pl. -NIES a South American shrub
RHEA	n pl. -S a flightless bird
RHEBOK	n pl. -S a large antelope
RHEMATIC	adj pertaining to a verb
RHENIUM	n pl. -S a metallic element
RHEOBASE	n pl. -S the smallest amount of electricity required to stimulate a nerve
RHEOLOGY	n pl. -GIES the study of matter in the fluid state
RHEOPHIL	adj living in flowing water
RHEOSTAT	n pl. -S a resistor used to control electric current
RHESUS	n pl. -ES an Asian monkey
RHETOR	n pl. -S a teacher of rhetoric
RHETORIC	n pl. -S the study of effective speech and writing
RHEUM	n pl. -S a watery discharge from the eyes or nose RHEUMIC adj
RHEUMY	adj RHEUMIER, RHEUMIEST marked by rheum
RHINAL	adj pertaining to the nose
RHINITIS	n pl. RHINITIDES inflammation of the mucous membranes of the nose
RHINO	n pl. -NOS a rhinoceros
RHIZOBIA	n/pl rod-shaped bacteria

RHIZOID	n pl. -S a rootlike structure
RHIZOMA	n pl. -MATA rhizome
RHIZOME	n pl. -S a rootlike, underground stem RHIZOMIC adj
RHIZOPOD	n pl. -S any of a class of protozoans
RHIZOPUS	n pl. -PI or -PUSES any of a genus of mold fungi
RHO	n pl. RHOS a Greek letter
RHODAMIN	n pl. -S a red dye
RHODIUM	n pl. -S a metallic element RHODIC adj
RHODORA	n pl. -S a flowering shrub
RHOMB	n pl. -S a rhombus
RHOMBI	a pl. of rhombus
RHOMBIC	adj having the shape of a rhombus
RHOMBOID	n pl. -S a type of geometric figure
RHOMBUS	n pl. -BUSES or -BI a type of geometric figure
RHONCHUS	n pl. -CHI a rattling respiratory sound RHONCHAL adj
RHUBARB	n pl. -S a perennial herb
RHUMB	n pl. -S a point of the mariner's compass
RHUMBA	v -ED, -ING, -S to rumba
RHUS	n pl. -ES any of a genus of shrubs and trees
RHYME	v RHYMED, RHYMING, RHYMES to compose verse with corresponding terminal sounds
RHYMER	n pl. -S one that rhymes
RHYOLITE	n pl. -S a volcanic rock
RHYTA	pl. of rhyton
RHYTHM	n pl. -S movement or procedure with uniform recurrence of strong and weak elements
RHYTHMIC	n pl. -S the science of rhythm
RHYTON	n pl. -TONS or -TA an ancient Greek drinking horn
RIA	n pl. -S a long, narrow inlet
RIAL	n pl. -S a monetary unit of Iran
RIALTO	n pl. -TOS a marketplace
RIANT	adj cheerful RIANTLY adv
RIATA	n pl. -S a lasso
RIB	v RIBBED, RIBBING, RIBS to poke fun at
RIBALD	n pl. -S one who uses crude language
RIBALDLY	adv crudely
RIBALDRY	n pl. -RIES crude language
RIBAND	n pl. -S a ribbon

RIBBAND n pl. -S a long, narrow strip used in shipbuilding

RIBBED past tense of rib

RIBBER n pl. -S one that ribs

RIBBIER comparative of ribby

RIBBIEST superlative of ribby

RIBBING n pl. -S the act of one that ribs

RIBBON v -ED, -ING, -S to decorate with ribbons (narrow strips of fine fabric)

RIBBONY adj resembling ribbon

RIBBY adj -BIER, -BIEST marked by prominent ribs (curved bony rods in the body)

RIBES n pl. RIBES a flowering shrub

RIBGRASS n pl. -ES a weedy plant

RIBIER n pl. -S a large, black grape

RIBLESS adj having no ribs

RIBLET n pl. -S the rib end in a breast of lamb or veal

RIBLIKE adj resembling a rib

RIBOSE n pl. -S a pentose sugar

RIBOSOME n pl. -S a particle composed of protein and ribonucleic acid

RIBWORT n pl. -S ribgrass

RICE v RICED, RICING, RICES to press through a ricer

RICEBIRD n pl. -S the bobolink

RICER n pl. -S a kitchen utensil consisting of a container perforated with small holes

RICERCAR n pl. -S an instrumental composition

RICH adj RICHER, RICHEST having wealth

RICHEN v -ED, -ING, -S to make rich

RICHES n/pl wealth

RICHLY adv in a rich manner

RICHNESS n pl. -ES the state of being rich

RICHWEED n pl. -S a flowering plant

RICIN n pl. -S a poisonous protein

RICING present participle of rice

RICINUS n pl. -ES a large-leaved plant

RICK v -ED, -ING, -S to pile hay in stacks

RICKETS n/pl a disease resulting from vitamin D deficiency

RICKETY adj -ETIER, -ETIEST likely to fall or collapse

RICKEY n pl. -EYS an alcoholic beverage containing lime juice, sugar, and soda water

RICKRACK n pl. -S a flat braid used as a trimming

RICKSHA n pl. -S rickshaw

RICKSHAW n pl. -S a small, two-wheeled passenger vehicle

RICOCHET v -CHETED, -CHETING, -CHETS or -CHETTED, -CHETTING, -CHETS to rebound from a surface

RICOTTA n pl. -S an Italian cheese

RICRAC n pl. -S rickrack

RICTUS n pl. -ES the expanse of the open mouth RICTAL adj

RID v RID or RIDDED, RIDDING, RIDS to free from something objectionable

RIDABLE adj capable of being ridden

RIDDANCE n pl. -S deliverance

RIDDED a past tense of rid

RIDDEN past participle of ride

RIDDER n pl. -S one that rids

RIDDING present participle of rid

RIDDLE v -DLED, -DLING, -DLES to pierce with many holes

RIDDLER n pl. -S one that riddles

RIDE v RODE, RIDDEN, RIDING, RIDES to sit on, control, and be conveyed by an animal or machine

RIDEABLE adj ridable

RIDENT adj laughing

RIDER n pl. -S one that rides

RIDGE v RIDGED, RIDGING, RIDGES to form into ridges (long, narrow elevations)

RIDGEL n pl. -S a ridgling

RIDGIER comparative of ridgy

RIDGIEST superlative of ridgy

RIDGIL n pl. -S a ridgling

RIDGING present participle of ridge

RIDGLING n pl. -S a male animal with undescended testicles

RIDGY adj RIDGIER, RIDGIEST having ridges

RIDICULE v -CULED, -CULING, -CULES to make fun of

RIDING n pl. -S the act of one that rides

RIDLEY n pl. -LEYS a sea turtle

RIDOTTO n pl. -TOS a public musical entertainment in 18th century England

RIEL n pl. -S a monetary unit of Cambodia

RIESLING n pl. -S a white Rhine wine

RIEVER n pl. -S reaver

RIF v RIFFED, RIFFING, RIFS to dismiss from employment

RIFAMPIN n pl. -S an antibiotic

RIFE	adj RIFER, RIFEST abundant RIFELY adv	**RIGIDITY**	n pl. -TIES the state of being rigid
RIFENESS	n pl. -ES the state of being rife	**RIGIDLY**	adv in a rigid manner
RIFF	v -ED, -ING, -S to riffle	**RIGOR**	n pl. -S strictness or severity
RIFFED	past tense of rif	**RIGORISM**	n pl. -S strictness or severity
RIFFING	present participle of rif		in conduct or attitude
RIFFLE	v -FLED, -FLING, -FLES to flip through hastily	**RIGORIST**	n pl. -S one that professes rigorism
RIFFLER	n pl. -S a filing and scraping tool	**RIGOROUS**	adj characterized by rigor
		RIGOUR	n pl. -S rigor
RIFFRAFF	n pl. -S the disreputable element of society	**RIKISHA**	n pl. -S rickshaw
		RIKSHAW	n pl. -S rickshaw
RIFLE	v -FLED, -FLING, -FLES to search through and rob	**RILE**	v RILED, RILING, RILES to anger
RIFLEMAN	n pl. -MEN a soldier armed with a rifle (a type of firearm)	**RILEY**	adj angry
		RILIEVO	n pl. -VI relievo
RIFLER	n pl. -S one that rifles	**RILING**	present participle of rile
RIFLERY	n pl. -RIES the practice of shooting at targets with a rifle	**RILL**	v -ED, -ING, -S to flow like a rill (a small brook)
RIFLING	n pl. -S the system of grooves in a gun barrel	**RILLE**	n pl. -S a valley on the moon's surface
RIFT	v -ED, -ING, -S to form rifts (clefts)	**RILLET**	n pl. -S a small rill
		RIM	v RIMMED, RIMMING, RIMS
RIFTLESS	adj having no rift		to provide with a rim (an outer edge)
RIG	v RIGGED, RIGGING, RIGS to put in proper condition for use	**RIME**	v RIMED, RIMING, RIMES to rhyme
RIGADOON	n pl. -S a lively dance	**RIMER**	n pl. -S one that rimes
RIGATONI	n pl. -S a tubular pasta	**RIMESTER**	n pl. -S a rimer
RIGAUDON	n pl. -S rigadoon	**RIMFIRE**	n pl. -S a cartridge having the primer set in the rim of the shell
RIGGED	past tense of rig		
RIGGER	n pl. -S one that rigs	**RIMIER**	comparative of rimy
RIGGING	n pl. -S the system of lines, chains, and tackle used aboard a ship	**RIMIEST**	superlative of rimy
		RIMINESS	n pl. -ES the condition of being rimy
RIGHT	adj RIGHTER, RIGHTEST being in accordance with what is good, proper, or just	**RIMING**	present participle of rime
		RIMLAND	n pl. -S an outlying area
RIGHT	v -ED, -ING, -S to put in proper order or condition	**RIMLESS**	adj having no rim
		RIMMED	past tense of rim
RIGHTER	n pl. -S one that rights	**RIMMER**	n pl. -S a reamer
RIGHTFUL	adj just or proper	**RIMMING**	present participle of rim
RIGHTIES	pl. of righty	**RIMOSE**	adj marked by cracks RIMOSELY adv
RIGHTISM	n pl. -S a conservative political philosophy		
		RIMOSITY	n pl. -TIES the state of being rimose
RIGHTIST	n pl. -S an advocate of rightism	**RIMOUS**	adj rimose
RIGHTLY	adv in a right manner	**RIMPLE**	v -PLED, -PLING, -PLES to wrinkle
RIGHTO	interj — used to express cheerful consent	**RIMROCK**	n pl. -S a type of rock formation
RIGHTY	n pl. RIGHTIES a right-handed person	**RIMY**	adj RIMIER, RIMIEST frosty
RIGID	adj not flexible	**RIN**	v RAN, RINNING, RINS to run or melt
RIGIDIFY	v -FIED, -FYING, -FIES to make rigid	**RIND**	n pl. -S a thick and firm outer covering RINDED adj

RING	v -ED, -ING, -S to form a ring (a circular band) around	**RIPEN**	v -ED, -ING, -S to become ripe
RING	v RANG, RUNG, RINGING, RINGS to give forth a clear, resonant sound	**RIPENER**	n pl. -S one that ripens
		RIPENESS	n pl. -ES the state of being ripe
RINGBARK	v -ED, -ING, -S to make an encircling cut through the bark of	**RIPER**	comparative of ripe
		RIPEST	superlative of ripe
RINGBOLT	n pl. -S a type of eyebolt	**RIPIENO**	n pl. -NI or -NOS tutti
RINGBONE	n pl. -S a bony growth on a horse's foot	**RIPING**	present participle of ripe
		RIPOFF	n pl. -S an instance of stealing
RINGDOVE	n pl. -S a European pigeon	**RIPOST**	v -ED, -ING, -S to riposte
RINGENT	adj having open liplike parts	**RIPOSTE**	v -POSTED, -POSTING, -POSTES to make a return thrust in fencing
RINGER	n pl. -S one that rings		
RINGGIT	n pl. -S a monetary unit of Malaysia	**RIPPABLE**	adj capable of being ripped
		RIPPED	past tense of rip
RINGHALS	n pl. -ES a venomous snake	**RIPPER**	n pl. -S one that rips
RINGLET	n pl. -S a small ring	**RIPPING**	adj excellent
RINGLIKE	adj resembling a ring	**RIPPLE**	v -PLED, -PLING, -PLES to form ripples (small waves)
RINGNECK	n pl. -S a bird having a ring of color around the neck		
		RIPPLER	n pl. -S a toothed tool for cleaning flax fiber
RINGSIDE	n pl. -S the area just outside a boxing or wrestling ring (a square enclosure)	**RIPPLET**	n pl. -S a small ripple
		RIPPLING	present participle of ripple
RINGTAIL	n pl. -S an animal having a tail with ringlike markings	**RIPPLY**	adj -PLIER, -PLIEST marked by ripples
RINGTAW	n pl. -S a game of marbles	**RIPRAP**	v -RAPPED, -RAPPING, -RAPS to strengthen with a foundation of broken stones
RINGTOSS	n pl. -ES a game in which the object is to toss a ring onto an upright stick		
		RIPSAW	n pl. -S a type of saw
RINGWORM	n pl. -S a skin disease	**RIPSTOP**	n pl. -S a fabric woven so that small tears do not spread
RINK	n pl. -S a surface of ice for skating		
		RIPTIDE	n pl. -S a tide that opposes other tides
RINNING	present participle of rin		
RINSE	v RINSED, RINSING, RINSES to cleanse with clear water RINSABLE, RINSIBLE adj	**RISE**	v ROSE, RISEN, RISING, RISES to move upward
		RISER	n pl. -S one that rises
RINSER	n pl. -S one that rinses	**RISHI**	n pl. -S a Hindu sage
RINSING	n pl. -S the act of one that rinses	**RISIBLE**	adj inclined to laugh RISIBLY adv
RIOJA	n pl. -S a dry red Spanish wine	**RISIBLES**	n/pl a sense of the ridiculous
		RISING	n pl. -S the act of one that rises
RIOT	v -ED, -ING, -S to take part in a violent public disturbance		
		RISK	v -ED, -ING, -S to expose to a risk (a chance of injury or loss)
RIOTER	n pl. -S one that riots		
RIOTOUS	adj characterized by rioting	**RISKER**	n pl. -S one that risks
RIP	v RIPPED, RIPPING, RIPS to tear or cut apart roughly	**RISKLESS**	adj free of risk
		RISKY	adj RISKIER, RISKIEST dangerous RISKILY adv
RIPARIAN	adj pertaining to the bank of a river		
		RISOTTO	n pl. -TOS a rice dish
RIPCORD	n pl. -S a cord pulled to release a parachute	**RISQUE**	adj bordering on impropriety or indecency
RIPE	adj RIPER, RIPEST fully developed RIPELY adv	**RISSOLE**	n pl. -S a small roll filled with meat or fish
RIPE	v RIPED, RIPING, RIPES to cleanse	**RISUS**	n pl. -ES a grin or laugh

RITARD *n pl.* -S a musical passage with a gradual slackening in tempo

RITE *n pl.* -S a ceremonial act or procedure

RITTER *n pl.* -S a knight

RITUAL *n pl.* -S a system of rites

RITUALLY *adv* ceremonially

RITZ *n pl.* -ES pretentious display

RITZY *adj* RITZIER, RITZIEST elegant RITZILY *adv*

RIVAGE *n pl.* -S a coast, shore, or bank

RIVAL *v* -VALED, -VALING, -VALS or -VALLED, -VALLING, -VALS to strive to equal or surpass

RIVALRY *n pl.* -RIES competition

RIVE *v* RIVED, RIVEN, RIVING, RIVES to tear apart

RIVER *n pl.* -S a large, natural stream of water

RIVERBED *n pl.* -S the area covered or once covered by a river

RIVERINE *adj* pertaining to a river

RIVET *v* -ETED, -ETING, -ETS or -ETTED, -ETTING, -ETS to fasten with a type of metal bolt

RIVETER *n pl.* -S one that rivets

RIVIERA *n pl.* -S a coastal resort area

RIVIERE *n pl.* -S a necklace of precious stones

RIVING present participle of rive

RIVULET *n pl.* -S a small stream

RIVULOSE *adj* having narrow, winding lines

RIYAL *n pl.* -S a monetary unit of Saudi Arabia

ROACH *v* -ED, -ING, -ES to cause to arch

ROAD *n pl.* -S an open way for public passage

ROADBED *n pl.* -S the foundation for a railroad track

ROADEO *n pl.* -EOS a competition for truck drivers

ROADIE *n pl.* -S a person who works for traveling entertainers

ROADKILL *n pl.* -S an animal that has been killed on a road

ROADLESS *adj* having no roads

ROADSHOW *n pl.* -S a theatrical show on tour

ROADSIDE *n pl.* -S the area along the side of a road

ROADSTER *n pl.* -S a light, open automobile

ROADWAY *n pl.* -WAYS a road

ROADWORK *n pl.* -S outdoor running as a form of physical conditioning

ROAM *v* -ED, -ING, -S to move about without purpose or plan

ROAMER *n pl.* -S one that roams

ROAN *n pl.* -S an animal having a coat sprinkled with white or gray

ROAR *v* -ED, -ING, -S to utter a loud, deep sound

ROARER *n pl.* -S one that roars

ROARING *n pl.* -S a loud, deep sound

ROAST *v* -ED, -ING, -S to cook with dry heat

ROASTER *n pl.* -S one that roasts

ROB *v* ROBBED, ROBBING, ROBS to take property from illegally

ROBALO *n pl.* -LOS a marine food fish

ROBAND *n pl.* -S a piece of yarn used to fasten a sail

ROBBED past tense of rob

ROBBER *n pl.* -S one that robs

ROBBERY *n pl.* -BERIES the act of one who robs

ROBBIN *n pl.* -S a roband

ROBBING present participle of rob

ROBE *v* ROBED, ROBING, ROBES to cover with a robe (a long, loose outer garment)

ROBIN *n pl.* -S a songbird

ROBLE *n pl.* -S an oak tree

ROBORANT *n pl.* -S an invigorating drug

ROBOT *n pl.* -S a humanlike machine that performs various functions ROBOTIC *adj*

ROBOTICS *n/pl* a field of interest concerned with robots

ROBOTISM *n pl.* -S the state of being a robot

ROBOTIZE *v* -IZED, -IZING, -IZES to make automatic

ROBOTRY *n pl.* -RIES the science of robots

ROBUST *adj* -BUSTER, -BUSTEST strong and healthy ROBUSTLY *adv*

ROBUSTA *n pl.* -S a coffee grown in Africa

ROC *n pl.* -S a legendary bird of prey

ROCAILLE *n pl.* -S rococo

ROCHET *n pl.* -S a linen vestment

ROCK *v* -ED, -ING, -S to move back and forth

ROCKABY n pl. -BIES a song used to lull a child to sleep

ROCKABYE n pl. -S rockaby

ROCKAWAY n pl. -WAYS a light carriage

ROCKER n pl. -S a rocking chair

ROCKERY n pl. -ERIES a rock garden

ROCKET v -ED, -ING, -S to convey by means of a rocket (a device propelled by the reaction of escaping gases)

ROCKETER n pl. -S one that designs or launches rockets

ROCKETRY n pl. -RIES the science of rockets

ROCKFALL n pl. -S a mass of fallen rocks

ROCKFISH n pl. -ES a fish living around rocks

ROCKIER comparative of rocky

ROCKIEST superlative of rocky

ROCKLESS adj having no rocks

ROCKLIKE adj resembling a rock (a large mass of stone)

ROCKLING n pl. -S a marine fish

ROCKOON n pl. -S a small rocket

ROCKROSE n pl. -S a flowering plant

ROCKWEED n pl. -S a brown seaweed

ROCKWORK n pl. -S a natural mass of rocks

ROCKY adj ROCKIER, ROCKIEST unsteady

ROCOCO n pl. -COS a style of architecture and decoration

ROD v RODDED, RODDING, RODS to provide with a rod (a straight, slender piece of wood, metal, or other material)

RODE past tense of ride

RODENT n pl. -S a gnawing mammal

RODEO v -ED, -ING, -S to perform cowboy skills in a contest

RODLESS adj having no rod

RODLIKE adj resembling a rod

RODMAN n pl. -MEN a surveyor's assistant

RODSMAN n pl. -MEN rodman

ROE n pl. -S the mass of eggs within a female fish

ROEBUCK n pl. -S the male of a small Eurasian deer

ROENTGEN n pl. -S a unit of radiation dosage

ROGATION n pl. -S the proposal of a law in ancient Rome

ROGATORY adj requesting information

ROGER n pl. -S the pirate flag bearing the skull and crossbones

ROGUE v ROGUED, ROGUEING or ROGUING, ROGUES to defraud

ROGUERY n pl. -ERIES roguish conduct

ROGUISH adj dishonest

ROIL v -ED, -ING, -S to make muddy

ROILY adj ROILIER, ROILIEST muddy

ROISTER v -ED, -ING, -S to revel

ROLAMITE n pl. -S a nearly frictionless mechanical device

ROLE n pl. -S an actor's part

ROLF v -ED, -ING, -S to practice a type of massage

ROLFER n pl. -S one that rolfs

ROLL v -ED, -ING, -S to move along by repeatedly turning over

ROLLAWAY adj mounted on rollers for easy movement

ROLLBACK n pl. -S a return to a lower level of prices or wages

ROLLER n pl. -S a cylindrical device that rolls or rotates

ROLLICK v -ED, -ING, -S to frolic

ROLLICKY adj given to rollicking

ROLLING n pl. -S the act of one that rolls

ROLLMOP n pl. -S a fillet of herring

ROLLOUT n pl. -S a type of play in football

ROLLOVER n pl. -S an accident in which a vehicle overturns

ROLLTOP adj having a flexible, sliding cover

ROLLWAY n pl. -WAYS an incline for rolling logs

ROM n pl. -S a Gypsy man or boy

ROMAINE n pl. -S a variety of lettuce

ROMAN n pl. -S a metrical narrative of medieval France

ROMANCE v -MANCED, -MANCING, -MANCES to woo

ROMANCER n pl. -S one that romances

ROMANISE v -ISED, -ISING, -ISES to romanize

ROMANIZE v -IZED, -IZING, -IZES to write in the Roman alphabet

ROMANO n pl. -NOS an Italian cheese

ROMANTIC n pl. -S a fanciful person

ROMAUNT n pl. -S a long, medieval tale

ROMEO n pl. -MEOS a male lover

ROMP v -ED, -ING, -S to play boisterously

ROMPER n pl. -S one that romps

ROMPISH adj inclined to romp

RONDEAU *n pl.* -DEAUX a short poem of fixed form

RONDEL *n pl.* -S a rondeau of 14 lines

RONDELET *n pl.* -S a rondeau of 5 or 7 lines

RONDELLE *n pl.* -S rondel

RONDO *n pl.* -DOS a type of musical composition

RONDURE *n pl.* -S a circle or sphere

RONION *n pl.* -S a mangy animal or person

RONNEL *n pl.* -S an insecticide

RONTGEN *n pl.* -S roentgen

RONYON *n pl.* -S ronion

ROOD *n pl.* -S a crucifix

ROOF *v* -ED, -ING, -S to provide with a roof (the external upper covering of a building)

ROOFER *n pl.* -S one that builds or repairs roofs

ROOFING *n pl.* -S material for a roof

ROOFLESS *adj* having no roof

ROOFLIKE *adj* resembling a roof

ROOFLINE *n pl.* -S the profile of a roof

ROOFTOP *n pl.* -S a roof

ROOFTREE *n pl.* -S a horizontal timber in a roof

ROOK *v* -ED, -ING, -S to swindle

ROOKERY *n pl.* -ERIES a colony of rooks (European crows)

ROOKIE *n pl.* -S a novice

ROOKY *adj* ROOKIER, ROOKIEST abounding in rooks

ROOM *v* -ED, -ING, -S to occupy a room (a walled space within a building)

ROOMER *n pl.* -S a lodger

ROOMETTE *n pl.* -S a small room

ROOMFUL *n pl.* -S as much as a room can hold

ROOMIE *n pl.* -S a roommate

ROOMMATE *n pl.* -S one with whom a room is shared

ROOMY *adj* ROOMIER, ROOMIEST spacious ROOMILY *adv*

ROORBACH *n pl.* -S roorback

ROORBACK *n pl.* -S a false story used for political advantage

ROOSE *v* ROOSED, ROOSING, ROOSES to praise

ROOSER *n pl.* -S one that rooses

ROOST *v* -ED, -ING, -S to settle down for rest or sleep

ROOSTER *n pl.* -S a male chicken

ROOT *v* -ED, -ING, -S to put forth a root (an underground portion of a plant)

ROOTAGE *n pl.* -S a system of roots

ROOTER *n pl.* -S one that gives encouragement or support

ROOTHOLD *n pl.* -S the embedding of a plant to soil through the growing of roots

ROOTIER comparative of rooty

ROOTIEST superlative of rooty

ROOTLESS *adj* having no roots

ROOTLET *n pl.* -S a small root

ROOTLIKE *adj* resembling a root

ROOTY *adj* ROOTIER, ROOTIEST full of roots

ROPE *v* ROPED, ROPING, ROPES to bind with a rope (a thick line of twisted fibers) ROPABLE *adj*

ROPELIKE *adj* resembling a rope

ROPER *n pl.* -S one that ropes

ROPERY *n pl.* -ERIES a place where ropes are made

ROPEWALK *n pl.* -S a long path where ropes are made

ROPEWAY *n pl.* -WAYS an aerial cable used to transport freight

ROPEY *adj* ROPIER, ROPIEST ropy

ROPIER comparative of ropy

ROPIEST superlative of ropy

ROPILY *adv* in a ropy manner

ROPINESS *n pl.* -ES the quality of being ropy

ROPING present participle of rope

ROPY *adj* ROPIER, ROPIEST resembling a rope or ropes

ROQUE *n pl.* -S a form of croquet

ROQUET *v* -ED, -ING, -S to cause one's own ball to hit another in croquet

RORQUAL *n pl.* -S a large whale

ROSARIAN *n pl.* -S a cultivator of roses

ROSARIUM *n pl.* -IA or -IUMS a rose garden

ROSARY *n pl.* -RIES a series of prayers in the Roman Catholic Church

ROSCOE *n pl.* -S a pistol

ROSE *v* ROSED, ROSING, ROSES to make the color of a rose (a reddish flower)

ROSEATE *adj* rose-colored

ROSEBAY *n pl.* -BAYS an evergreen shrub

ROSEBUD *n pl.* -S the bud of a rose

ROSEBUSH n pl. -ES a shrub that bears roses

ROSED past tense of rose

ROSEFISH n pl. -ES a marine food fish

ROSELIKE adj resembling a rose

ROSELLE n pl. -S a tropical plant

ROSEMARY n pl. -MARIES an evergreen shrub

ROSEOLA n pl. -S a rose-colored skin rash ROSEOLAR adj

ROSEROOT n pl. -S a perennial herb

ROSERY n pl. -ERIES a place where roses are grown

ROSESLUG n pl. -S a larval sawfly that eats rose leaves

ROSET n pl. -S resin

ROSETTE n pl. -S an ornament resembling a rose

ROSEWOOD n pl. -S a tropical tree

ROSIER comparative of rosy

ROSIEST superlative of rosy

ROSILY adv in a rosy manner

ROSIN v -ED, -ING, -S to treat with rosin (a brittle resin)

ROSINESS n pl. -ES the state of being rosy

ROSING present participle of rose

ROSINOL n pl. -S rosin oil

ROSINOUS adj resembling rosin

ROSINY adj rosinous

ROSOLIO n pl. -LIOS a liqueur made from raisins and brandy

ROSTELLA n/pl small, beaklike structures

ROSTER n pl. -S a list of names

ROSTRA a pl. of rostrum

ROSTRAL adj pertaining to a rostrum

ROSTRATE adj having a rostrum

ROSTRUM n pl. -TRA or -TRUMS a beaklike process or part

ROSULATE adj arranged in the form of a rosette

ROSY adj ROSIER, ROSIEST rose-colored

ROT v ROTTED, ROTTING, ROTS to decompose

ROTA n pl. -S a roster

ROTARY n pl. -RIES a rotating part or device

ROTATE v -TATED, -TATING, -TATES to turn about an axis

ROTATION n pl. -S the act or an instance of rotating ROTATIVE adj

ROTATOR n pl. -S one that rotates

ROTATOR n pl. -ES a muscle serving to rotate a part of the body

ROTATORY adj pertaining to rotation

ROTCH n pl. -ES rotche

ROTCHE n pl. -S a seabird

ROTE n pl. -S mechanical routine

ROTENONE n pl. -S an insecticide

ROTGUT n pl. -S inferior liquor

ROTI n pl. -S an unleavened bread

ROTIFER n pl. -S a microscopic aquatic organism

ROTIFORM adj shaped like a wheel

ROTL n pl. ROTLS or ARTAL a unit of weight in Muslim countries

ROTO n pl. -TOS a type of printing process

ROTOR n pl. -S a rotating part of a machine

ROTOTILL v -ED, -ING, -S to till soil with a type of farming implement

ROTTE n pl. -S a medieval stringed instrument

ROTTED past tense of rot

ROTTEN adj -TENER, -TENEST being in a state of decay ROTTENLY adv

ROTTER n pl. -S a scoundrel

ROTTING present participle of rot

ROTUND adj marked by roundness ROTUNDLY adv

ROTUNDA n pl. -S a round building

ROTURIER n pl. -S a commoner

ROUBLE n pl. -S ruble

ROUCHE n pl. -S ruche

ROUE n pl. -S a lecherous man

ROUEN n pl. -S any of a breed of domestic ducks

ROUGE v ROUGED, ROUGING, ROUGES to color with a red cosmetic

ROUGH adj ROUGHER, ROUGHEST having an uneven surface

ROUGH v -ED, -ING, -S to make rough

ROUGHAGE n pl. -S coarse, bulky food

ROUGHDRY v -DRIED, -DRYING, -DRIES to dry without ironing, as washed clothes

ROUGHEN v -ED, -ING, -S to make rough

ROUGHER n pl. -S one that roughs

ROUGHHEW v -HEWED, -HEWN, -HEWING, -HEWS to shape roughly

ROUGHISH adj somewhat rough

ROUGHLEG n pl. -S a large hawk

ROUGHLY adv in a rough manner

ROUGING present participle of rouge

ROUILLE n pl. -S a peppery garlic sauce

ROULADE n pl. -S a musical embellishment

ROULEAU *n* pl. -LEAUX or -LEAUS a roll of coins wrapped in paper

ROULETTE *v* -LETTED, -LETTING, -LETTES to make tiny slits in

ROUND *adj* ROUNDER, ROUNDEST shaped like a sphere

ROUND *v* -ED, -ING, -S to make round

ROUNDEL *n* pl. -S a round figure or object

ROUNDER *n* pl. -S a tool for rounding

ROUNDISH *adj* somewhat round

ROUNDLET *n* pl. -S a small circle

ROUNDLY *adv* in a round manner

ROUNDUP *n* pl. -S the driving together of cattle scattered over a range

ROUP *v* -ED, -ING, -S to auction

ROUPET *adj* roupy

ROUPY *adj* ROUPIER, ROUPIEST hoarse ROUPILY *adv*

ROUSE *v* ROUSED, ROUSING, ROUSES to bring out of a state of sleep or inactivity

ROUSER *n* pl. -S one that rouses

ROUSSEAU *n* pl. -S fried pemmican

ROUST *v* -ED, -ING, -S to arouse and drive out

ROUSTER *n* pl. -S a wharf laborer and deckhand

ROUT *v* -ED, -ING, -S to defeat overwhelmingly

ROUTE *v* ROUTED, ROUTING, ROUTES to send on a particular course

ROUTEMAN *n* pl. -MEN one who conducts business on a customary course

ROUTER *n* pl. -S a scooping tool

ROUTEWAY *n* pl. -WAYS an established course of travel

ROUTH *n* pl. -S an abundance

ROUTINE *n* pl. -S a regular course of procedure

ROUTING present participle of route

ROUX *n* pl. ROUX a mixture of butter and flour

ROVE *v* ROVED, ROVING, ROVES to roam

ROVEN a past participle of reeve

ROVER *n* pl. -S one that roves

ROVING *n* pl. -S a roll of textile fibers

ROVINGLY *adv* in a roving manner

ROW *v* -ED, -ING, -S to propel by means of oars ROWABLE *adj*

ROWAN *n* pl. -S a Eurasian tree

ROWBOAT *n* pl. -S a small boat designed to be rowed

ROWDY *adj* -DIER, -DIEST disorderly in behavior ROWDILY *adv*

ROWDY *n* pl. -DIES a rowdy person

ROWDYISH *adj* tending to be rowdy

ROWDYISM *n* pl. -S disorderly behavior

ROWEL *v* -ELED, -ELING, -ELS or -ELLED, -ELLING, -ELS to prick with a spiked wheel in order to urge forward

ROWEN *n* pl. -S a second growth of grass

ROWER *n* pl. -S one that rows

ROWING *n* pl. -S the sport of racing in light, long, and narrow rowboats

ROWLOCK *n* pl. -S an oarlock

ROWTH *n* pl. -S routh

ROYAL *n* pl. -S a size of printing paper

ROYALISM *n* pl. -S support of a monarch or monarchy

ROYALIST *n* pl. -S a supporter of a monarch or monarchy

ROYALLY *adv* in a kingly manner

ROYALTY *n* pl. -TIES the status or power of a monarch

ROYSTER *v* -ED, -ING, -S to roister

ROZZER *n* pl. -S a policeman

RUANA *n* pl. -S a woolen poncho

RUB *v* RUBBED, RUBBING, RUBS to move along the surface of a body with pressure

RUBABOO *n* pl. -BOOS a type of soup

RUBACE *n* pl. -S rubasse

RUBAIYAT *n* pl. RUBAIYAT four-lined stanzas in Persian poetry

RUBASSE *n* pl. -S a variety of quartz

RUBATO *n* pl. -TOS a fluctuation of speed within a musical phrase

RUBBABOO *n* pl. -BOOS rubaboo

RUBBED past tense of rub

RUBBER *v* -ED, -ING, -S to stretch one's neck in looking at something

RUBBERY *adj* resembling rubber (an elastic substance)

RUBBING *n* pl. -S an image produced by rubbing

RUBBISH *n* pl. -ES worthless, unwanted matter RUBBISHY *adj*

RUBBLE *v* -BLED, -BLING, -BLES to reduce to rubble (broken pieces)

RUBBLY *adj* -BLIER, -BLIEST abounding in rubble

RUBDOWN n pl. -S a brisk rubbing of the body

RUBE n pl. -S a rustic

RUBELLA n pl. -S a virus disease

RUBEOLA n pl. -S a virus disease RUBEOLAR adj

RUBICUND adj ruddy

RUBIDIUM n pl. -S a metallic element RUBIDIC adj

RUBIED past tense of ruby

RUBIER comparative of ruby

RUBIES present 3d person sing. of ruby

RUBIEST superlative of ruby

RUBIGO n pl. -GOS red iron oxide

RUBIOUS adj ruby-colored

RUBLE n pl. -S a monetary unit of the Soviet Union

RUBOFF n pl. -S a deep impression made by close contact

RUBOUT n pl. -S an instance of obliterating something

RUBRIC n pl. -S a part of a manuscript or book that appears in red RUBRICAL adj

RUBUS n pl. RUBUS a plant of the rose family

RUBY v -BIED, -BYING, -BIES to tint with the color of a ruby (a deep-red precious stone)

RUBY adj -BIER, -BIEST of a deep-red color

RUBYLIKE adj resembling a ruby

RUCHE n pl. -S a pleated strip of fine fabric

RUCHED adj trimmed with a ruche

RUCHING n pl. -S a ruche

RUCK v -ED, -ING, -S to wrinkle or crease

RUCKLE v -LED, -LING, -LES to ruck

RUCKSACK n pl. -S a knapsack

RUCKUS n pl. -ES a noisy disturbance

RUCTION n pl. -S a ruckus

RUCTIOUS adj quarrelsome

RUDD n pl. -S a freshwater fish

RUDDER n pl. -S a vertical blade used to direct the course of a vessel

RUDDIER comparative of ruddy

RUDDIEST superlative of ruddy

RUDDILY adv in a ruddy manner

RUDDLE v -DLED, -DLING, -DLES to color with a red dye

RUDDOCK n pl. -S a European bird

RUDDY adj -DIER, -DIEST having a healthy, reddish color

RUDE adj RUDER, RUDEST discourteous or impolite RUDELY adv

RUDENESS n pl. -ES the quality of being rude

RUDERAL n pl. -S a plant growing in poor land

RUDESBY n pl. -BIES a rude person

RUDEST superlative of rude

RUDIMENT n pl. -S a basic principle or element

RUE v RUED, RUING, RUES to feel sorrow or remorse for

RUEFUL adj feeling sorrow or remorse RUEFULLY adv

RUER n pl. -S one that rues

RUFF v -ED, -ING, -S to trump

RUFFE n pl. -S a freshwater fish

RUFFIAN n pl. -S a tough, lawless person

RUFFLE v -FLED, -FLING, -FLES to destroy the smoothness of

RUFFLER n pl. -S one that ruffles

RUFFLIER comparative of ruffly

RUFFLIEST superlative of ruffly

RUFFLIKE adj resembling a ruff (a pleated collar)

RUFFLING present participle of ruffle

RUFFLY adj -FLIER, -FLIEST not smooth

RUFIYAA n pl. RUFIYAA a monetary unit of the Maldives

RUFOUS adj reddish

RUG v RUGGED, RUGGING, RUGS to tear roughly

RUGA n pl. -GAE an anatomical fold or wrinkle RUGAL, RUGATE adj

RUGBY n pl. -BIES a form of football

RUGGED adj -GEDER, -GEDEST having an uneven surface RUGGEDLY adv

RUGGER n pl. -S rugby

RUGGING present participle of rug

RUGLIKE adj resembling a rug (a thick fabric used as a floor covering)

RUGOLA n pl. -S arugula

RUGOSA n pl. -S a flowering plant

RUGOSE adj full of wrinkles RUGOSELY adv

RUGOSITY n pl. -TIES the state of being rugose

RUGOUS adj rugose

RUGULOSE adj having small wrinkles

RUIN v -ED, -ING, -S to destroy RUINABLE adj

RUINATE	v -ATED, -ATING, -ATES to ruin	**RUNABOUT**	n pl. -S a small, open auto
		RUNAGATE	n pl. -S a deserter
RUINER	n pl. -S one that ruins	**RUNAWAY**	n pl. -AWAYS one that runs away
RUING	present participle of rue		
RUINOUS	adj destructive	**RUNBACK**	n pl. -S a type of run in football
RULE	v RULED, RULING, RULES to exercise control over		
		RUNDLE	n pl. -S a rung
	RULABLE adj	**RUNDLET**	n pl. -S a small barrel
RULELESS	adj not restrained or regulated by law	**RUNDOWN**	n pl. -S a summary
		RUNE	n pl. -S a letter of an ancient
RULER	n pl. -S one that rules		alphabet **RUNELIKE** adj
RULING	n pl. -S an authoritative decision	**RUNG**	n pl. -S a crosspiece forming a step of a ladder **RUNGLESS** adj
RULY	adj RULIER, RULIEST orderly		
RUM	n pl. -S an alcoholic liquor	**RUNIC**	adj pertaining to a rune
RUM	adj RUMMER, RUMMEST odd	**RUNKLE**	v -KLED, -KLING, -KLES to wrinkle
RUMAKI	n pl. -S chicken liver wrapped together with water chestnuts in a bacon slice	**RUNLESS**	adj scoring no runs in baseball
		RUNLET	n pl. -S a small stream
		RUNNEL	n pl. -S a small stream
RUMBA	v -ED, -ING, -S to perform a ballroom dance	**RUNNER**	n pl. -S one that runs
		RUNNING	n pl. -S a race
RUMBLE	v -BLED, -BLING, -BLES to make a deep, thunderous sound	**RUNNY**	adj -NIER, -NIEST tending to drip
		RUNOFF	n pl. -S rainfall that is not absorbed by the soil
RUMBLER	n pl. -S one that rumbles		
RUMBLING	n pl. -S a deep, thunderous sound	**RUNOUT**	n pl. -S the end of a film strip
		RUNOVER	n pl. -S matter for publication that exceeds the allotted space
RUMBLY	adj tending to rumble		
RUMEN	n pl. -MINA or -MENS a part of the stomach of a ruminant **RUMINAL** adj	**RUNROUND**	n pl. -S evasive action
		RUNT	n pl. -S a small person or animal **RUNTISH** adj
RUMINANT	n pl. -S a hoofed, even-toed mammal	**RUNTY**	adj RUNTIER, RUNTIEST small
RUMINATE	v -NATED, -NATING, -NATES to chew again	**RUNWAY**	n pl. -WAYS a landing and takeoff strip for aircraft
RUMMAGE	v -MAGED, -MAGING, -MAGES to search thoroughly through	**RUPEE**	n pl. -S a monetary unit of India
		RUPIAH	n pl. -S a monetary unit of Indonesia
RUMMAGER	n pl. -S one that rummages		
RUMMER	n pl. -S a large drinking glass	**RUPTURE**	v -TURED, -TURING, -TURES to burst
RUMMEST	superlative of rum		
RUMMY	n pl. -MIES a card game	**RURAL**	adj pertaining to the country
RUMMY	adj -MIER, -MIEST odd	**RURALISE**	v -ISED, -ISING, -ISES to ruralize
RUMOR	v -ED, -ING, -S to spread by hearsay		
		RURALISM	n pl. -S the state of being rural
RUMOUR	v -ED, -ING, -S to rumor	**RURALIST**	n pl. -S one who lives in the country
RUMP	n pl. -S the lower and back part of the trunk **RUMPLESS** adj		
		RURALITE	n pl. -S a ruralist
		RURALITY	n pl. -TIES the state of being rural
RUMPLE	v -PLED, -PLING, -PLES to wrinkle		
		RURALIZE	v -IZED, -IZING, -IZES to make rural
RUMPLY	adj -PLIER, -PLIEST rumpled		
RUMPUS	n pl. -ES a noisy disturbance	**RURALLY**	adv in a rural manner
RUN	v RAN, RUNNING, RUNS to move by rapid steps	**RURBAN**	adj partially rural and urban
		RUSE	n pl. -S a deception

RUSH	v -ED, -ING, -ES to move swiftly
RUSHEE	n pl. -S a college student seeking admission to a fraternity or sorority
RUSHER	n pl. -S one that rushes
RUSHIER	comparative of rushy
RUSHIEST	superlative of rushy
RUSHING	n pl. -S yardage gained in football by running plays
RUSHLIKE	adj resembling a rush (a grasslike marsh plant)
RUSHY	adj RUSHIER, RUSHIEST abounding in rushes
RUSINE	adj pertaining to a genus of deer
RUSK	n pl. -S a sweetened biscuit
RUSSET	n pl. -S a reddish or yellowish brown color RUSSETY adj
RUSSIFY	v -FIED, -FYING, -FIES to make Russian
RUST	v -ED, -ING, -S to form rust (a reddish coating that forms on iron) RUSTABLE adj
RUSTIC	n pl. -S one who lives in the country
RUSTICAL	n pl. -S a rustic
RUSTICLY	adv in a rural manner
RUSTIER	comparative of rusty
RUSTIEST	superlative of rusty
RUSTILY	adv in a rusty manner
RUSTLE	v -TLED, -TLING, -TLES to make a succession of slight, soft sounds
RUSTLER	n pl. -S one that rustles

RUSTLESS	adj free from rust
RUSTLING	present participle of rustle
RUSTY	adj RUSTIER, RUSTIEST covered with rust
RUT	v RUTTED, RUTTING, RUTS to make ruts (grooves) in
RUTABAGA	n pl. -S a plant having a thick, edible root
RUTH	n pl. -S compassion
RUTHENIC	adj pertaining to a rare, metallic element
RUTHFUL	adj full of compassion
RUTHLESS	adj having no compassion
RUTILANT	adj having a reddish glow
RUTILE	n pl. -S a mineral
RUTIN	n pl. -S a chemical compound
RUTTED	past tense of rut
RUTTIER	comparative of rutty
RUTTIEST	superlative of rutty
RUTTILY	adv in a rutty manner
RUTTING	present participle of rut
RUTTISH	adj lustful
RUTTY	adj -TIER, -TIEST marked by ruts
RYA	n pl. -S a Scandinavian handwoven rug
RYE	n pl. -S a cereal grass
RYEGRASS	n pl. -ES a European grass
RYKE	v RYKED, RYKING, RYKES to reach
RYND	n pl. -S an iron support
RYOKAN	n pl. -S a Japanese inn
RYOT	n pl. -S a tenant farmer in India

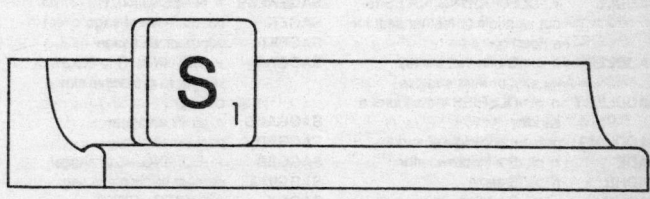

SAB *v* SABBED, SABBING, SABS to sob

SABATON *n pl.* -S a piece of armor for the foot

SABAYON *n pl.* -S a sauce of whipped egg yolks, sugar, and wine

SABBAT *n pl.* -S an assembly of demons and witches

SABBATH *n pl.* -S sabbat

SABBATIC *adj* bringing a period of rest

SABBED past tense of sab

SABBING present participle of sab

SABE *v* SABED, SABEING, SABES to savvy

SABER *v* -ED, -ING, -S to strike with a saber (a type of sword)

SABIN *n pl.* -S a unit of sound absorption

SABINE *n pl.* -S savin

SABIR *n pl.* -S a French-based pidgin language

SABLE *n pl.* -S a carnivorous mammal

SABOT *n pl.* -S a wooden shoe

SABOTAGE *v* -TAGED, -TAGING, -TAGES to destroy maliciously

SABOTEUR *n pl.* -S one who sabotages

SABRA *n pl.* -S a native Israeli

SABRE *v* -BRED, -BRING, -BRES to saber

SABULOSE *adj* sabulous

SABULOUS *adj* sandy

SAC *n pl.* -S a pouchlike structure in an animal or plant

SACATON *n pl.* -S a perennial grass

SACBUT *n pl.* -S sackbut

SACCADE *n pl.* -S a rapid, jerky movement of the eye SACCADIC *adj*

SACCATE *adj* having a sac

SACCULAR *adj* resembling a sac

SACCULE *n pl.* -S a small sac

SACCULUS *n pl.* -LI saccule

SACHEM *n pl.* -S a North American Indian chief SACHEMIC *adj*

SACHET *n pl.* -S a small bag containing perfumed powder SACHETED *adj*

SACK *v* -ED, -ING, -S to put into a sack (a large bag)

SACKBUT *n pl.* -S a medieval trombone

SACKER *n pl.* -S one that sacks

SACKFUL *n pl.* SACKFULS or SACKSFUL as much as a sack can hold

SACKING *n pl.* -S material for making sacks

SACKLIKE *adj* resembling a sack

SACKSFUL a pl. of sackful

SACLIKE *adj* resembling a sac

SACQUE *n pl.* -S a loose-fitting dress

SACRA pl. of sacrum

SACRAL *n pl.* -S a vertebra or nerve situated near the sacrum

SACRARIA *n/pl* ancient Roman shrines

SACRED *adj* dedicated to or set apart for the worship of a deity SACREDLY *adv*

SACRING *n pl.* -S the consecration of bread and wine of the Eucharist

SACRIST *n pl.* -S a person in charge of a sacristy

SACRISTY *n pl.* -TIES a room in which sacred vessels and vestments are kept

SACRUM *n pl.* -CRA or -CRUMS a bone of the pelvis

SAD — *adj* SADDER, SADDEST unhappy

SADDEN — *v* -ED, -ING, -S to make sad

SADDHU — *n pl.* -S sadhu

SADDLE — *v* -DLED, -DLING, -DLES to put a saddle (a leather seat for a rider) on

SADDLER — *n pl.* -S one that makes, repairs, or sells saddles

SADDLERY — *n pl.* -DLERIES the shop of a saddler

SADDLING — present participle of saddle

SADE — *n pl.* -S a Hebrew letter

SADHE — *n pl.* -S sade

SADHU — *n pl.* -S a Hindu holy man

SADI — *n pl.* -S sade

SADIRON — *n pl.* -S a heavy flatiron

SADISM — *n pl.* -S a tendency to take delight in inflicting pain

SADIST — *n pl.* -S one marked by sadism **SADISTIC** *adj*

SADLY — *adv* in a sad manner

SADNESS — *n pl.* -ES the state of being sad

SAE — *adv* so

SAFARI — *v* -ED, -ING, -S to go on a hunting expedition

SAFE — *adj* SAFER, SAFEST free from danger **SAFELY** *adv*

SAFE — *n pl.* -S a metal receptacle for storing valuables

SAFENESS — *n pl.* -ES the quality of being safe

SAFER — comparative of safe

SAFEST — superlative of safe

SAFETY — *v* -TIED, -TYING, -TIES to protect against failure, breakage, or accident

SAFFRON — *n pl.* -S a flowering plant

SAFRANIN — *n pl.* -S a red dye

SAFROL — *n pl.* -S safrole

SAFROLE — *n pl.* -S a poisonous liquid

SAG — *v* SAGGED, SAGGING, SAGS to bend or sink downward from weight or pressure

SAGA — *n pl.* -S a medieval Scandinavian narrative

SAGACITY — *n pl.* -TIES wisdom

SAGAMAN — *n pl.* -MEN a writer of sagas

SAGAMORE — *n pl.* -S an Algonquian Indian chief

SAGANASH — *n pl.* -ES a white man — an Algonquian Indian term

SAGBUT — *n pl.* -S sackbut

SAGE — *adj* SAGER, SAGEST wise **SAGELY** *adv*

SAGE — *n pl.* -S an aromatic herb used as seasoning

SAGENESS — *n pl.* -ES wisdom

SAGER — comparative of sage

SAGEST — superlative of sage

SAGGAR — *v* -ED, -ING, -S to bake in a saggar (a protective clay casing)

SAGGARD — *n pl.* -S a saggar

SAGGED — past tense of sag

SAGGER — *v* -ED, -ING, -S to saggar

SAGGING — present participle of sag

SAGGY — *adj* -GIER, -GIEST characterized by sagging

SAGIER — comparative of sagy

SAGIEST — superlative of sagy

SAGITTAL — *adj* resembling an arrow or arrowhead

SAGO — *n pl.* -GOS a tropical tree

SAGUARO — *n pl.* -ROS a tall cactus

SAGUM — *n pl.* -GA a cloak worn by ancient Roman soldiers

SAGY — *adj* SAGIER, SAGIEST flavored with sage

SAHIB — *n pl.* -S sir; master — used as a term of respect in colonial India

SAHIWAL — *n pl.* -S any of a breed of humped dairy cattle

SAHUARO — *n pl.* -ROS saguaro

SAICE — *n pl.* -S syce

SAID — *n pl.* -S sayyid

SAIGA — *n pl.* -S a small antelope

SAIL — *v* -ED, -ING, -S to move across the surface of water by the action of wind **SAILABLE** *adj*

SAILBOAT — *n pl.* -S a boat that sails

SAILER — *n pl.* -S a vessel that sails

SAILFISH — *n pl.* -ES a large marine fish

SAILING — *n pl.* -S the act of one that sails

SAILOR — *n pl.* -S a member of a ship's crew **SAILORLY** *adj*

SAIMIN — *n pl.* -S a Hawaiian noodle soup

SAIN — *v* -ED, -ING, -S to make the sign of the cross on

SAINFOIN — *n pl.* -S a perennial herb

SAINT — *v* -ED, -ING, -S to declare to be a saint (a person of exceptional holiness)

SAINTDOM — *n pl.* -S the condition of being a saint

SAINTLY *adj* -LIER, -LIEST of or befitting a saint

SAITH a present 3d person sing. of say

SAITHE *n pl.* SAITHE a marine food fish

SAIYID *n pl.* -S sayyid

SAJOU *n pl.* -S a capuchin

SAKE *n pl.* -S benefit, interest, or advantage

SAKER *n pl.* -S a Eurasian falcon

SAKI *n pl.* -S a Japanese liquor

SAL *n pl.* -S salt

SALAAM *v* -ED, -ING, -S to greet with a low bow

SALABLE *adj* capable of being or fit to be sold **SALABLY** *adv*

SALACITY *n pl.* -TIES lewdness

SALAD *n pl.* -S a dish of green, raw vegetables

SALADANG *n pl.* -S a wild ox

SALAL *n pl.* -S a small shrub

SALAMI *n pl.* -S a seasoned sausage

SALARIAT *n pl.* -S the class of salaried persons

SALARY *v* -RIED, -RYING, -RIES to pay a periodic, fixed compensation to

SALCHOW *n pl.* -S a figure-skating jump

SALE *n pl.* -S the act or an instance of selling

SALEABLE *adj* salable **SALEABLY** *adv*

SALEP *n pl.* -S a starchy meal ground from the roots of certain orchids

SALEROOM *n pl.* -S a room in which goods are displayed for sale

SALESMAN *n pl.* -MEN a man who sells merchandise

SALIC *adj* pertaining to a group of igneous rocks

SALICIN *n pl.* -S a chemical compound

SALICINE *n pl.* -S salicin

SALIENCE *n pl.* -S a projecting feature or detail

SALIENCY *n pl.* -CIES salience

SALIENT *n pl.* -S the part of a fortification projecting closest to the enemy

SALIFY *v* -FIED, -FYING, -FIES to combine with a salt

SALINA *n pl.* -S a pond, marsh, or lake containing salt water

SALINE *n pl.* -S a salt solution

SALINITY *n pl.* -TIES a concentration of salt

SALINIZE *v* -NIZED, -NIZING, -NIZES to treat with salt

SALIVA *n pl.* -S a fluid secreted by the glands of the mouth **SALIVARY** *adj*

SALIVATE *v* -VATED, -VATING, -VATES to secrete saliva

SALL *v* shall — SALL is the only form of this verb; it cannot be conjugated

SALLET *n pl.* -S a light medieval helmet

SALLIED past tense of sally

SALLIER *n pl.* -S one that sallies

SALLIES present 3d person sing. of sally

SALLOW *adj* -LOWER, -LOWEST of a sickly yellowish color **SALLOWLY** *adv*

SALLOW *v* -ED, -ING, -S to make sallow

SALLOWY *adj* abounding in willow trees

SALLY *v* -LIED, -LYING, -LIES to rush out suddenly

SALMI *n pl.* -S a dish of roasted game birds

SALMON *n pl.* -S a food fish

SALMONID *n pl.* -S a fish of the salmon family

SALOL *n pl.* -S a chemical compound

SALON *n pl.* -S a large room in which guests are received

SALOON *n pl.* -S a tavern

SALOOP *n pl.* -S a hot drink made from an infusion of aromatic herbs

SALP *n pl.* -S salpa

SALPA *n pl.* -PAE or -PAS a free-swimming tunicate

SALPIAN *n pl.* -S salpa

SALPID *n pl.* -S salpa

SALPINX *n pl.* -PINGES an anatomical tube

SALSA *n pl.* -S a spicy sauce of tomatoes, onions, and peppers

SALSIFY *n pl.* -FIES a European herb

SALSILLA *n pl.* -S a tropical plant

SALT *v* -ED, -ING, -S to treat with salt (a crystalline compound used as a seasoning and preservative)

SALT *adj* SALTER, SALTEST salty

SALTANT *adj* jumping or dancing

SALTBOX *n pl.* -ES a type of house

SALTBUSH *n pl.* -ES a salt-tolerant plant

SALTER *n pl.* -S one that salts

SALTERN *n pl.* -S a place where salt is produced

SALTIE *n pl.* -S a deep-sea vessel sailing the Great Lakes

SALTIER *n pl.* -S saltire

SALTIEST superlative of salty

SALTILY *adv* in a salty manner

SALTINE *n pl.* -S a salted cracker

SALTING *n pl.* -S land regularly flooded by tides

SALTIRE *n pl.* -S a heraldic design

SALTISH *adj* somewhat salty

SALTLESS *adj* having no salt

SALTLIKE *adj* resembling salt

SALTNESS *n pl.* -ES the state of being salty

SALTPAN *n pl.* -S a large pan for making salt by evaporation

SALTWORK *n pl.* -S a saltern

SALTWORT *n pl.* -S a seaside herb

SALTY *adj* SALTIER, SALTIEST tasting of or containing salt

SALUKI *n pl.* -S a tall, slender dog

SALUTARY *adj* producing a beneficial effect

SALUTE *v* -LUTED, -LUTING, -LUTES to greet with a sign of welcome or respect

SALUTER *n pl.* -S one that salutes

SALVABLE *adj* capable of being saved **SALVABLY** *adv*

SALVAGE *v* -VAGED, -VAGING, -VAGES to save from loss or destruction

SALVAGEE *n pl.* -S one in whose favor salvage has been effected

SALVAGER *n pl.* -S one that salvages

SALVAGING present participle of salvage

SALVE *v* SALVED, SALVING, SALVES to soothe

SALVER *n pl.* -S a tray or serving platter

SALVIA *n pl.* -S a flowering plant

SALVIFIC *adj* having the power to save

SALVING present participle of salve

SALVO *v* -ED, -ING, -S or -ES to discharge firearms simultaneously

SALVOR *n pl.* -S a salvager

SAMARA *n pl.* -S a dry, one-seeded fruit

SAMARIUM *n pl.* -S a metallic element

SAMBA *v* -ED, -ING, -S to perform a Brazilian dance

SAMBAR *n pl.* -S a large Asian deer

SAMBHAR *n pl.* -S sambar

SAMBHUR *n pl.* -S sambar

SAMBO *n pl.* -BOS a Latin American of mixed black and Indian ancestry

SAMBUCA *n pl.* -S an ancient stringed instrument

SAMBUKE *n pl.* -S sambuca

SAMBUR *n pl.* -S sambar

SAME *adj* resembling in every relevant respect

SAMECH *n pl.* -S samek

SAMEK *n pl.* -S a Hebrew letter

SAMEKH *n pl.* -S samek

SAMENESS *n pl.* -ES lack of change or variety

SAMIEL *n pl.* -S the simoom

SAMISEN *n pl.* -S a Japanese stringed instrument

SAMITE *n pl.* -S a silk fabric

SAMIZDAT *n pl.* -S a system in the Soviet Union for printing and distributing unauthorized literature

SAMLET *n pl.* -S a young salmon

SAMOSA *n pl.* -S a filled pastry turnover

SAMOVAR *n pl.* -S a metal urn for heating water

SAMP *n pl.* -S coarsely ground corn

SAMPAN *n pl.* -S a flat-bottomed Chinese skiff

SAMPHIRE *n pl.* -S a European herb

SAMPLE *v* -PLED, -PLING, -PLES to test a representative portion of a whole

SAMPLER *n pl.* -S one that samples

SAMPLING *n pl.* -S a small part selected for analysis

SAMSARA *n pl.* -S the cycle of birth, death, and rebirth in Buddhism

SAMSHU *n pl.* -S a Chinese liquor

SAMURAI *n pl.* -S a Japanese warrior

SANATIVE *adj* having the power to cure or heal

SANCTA a pl. of sanctum

SANCTIFY *v* -FIED, -FYING, -FIES to make holy

SANCTION *v* -ED, -ING, -S to authorize

SANCTITY *n pl.* -TIES holiness

SANCTUM *n pl.* -TUMS or -TA a sacred place

SAND *v* -ED, -ING, -S to cover with sand (a loose, granular rock material)

SANDAL *v* -DALED, -DALING, -DALS or -DALLED, -DALLING, -DALS to provide with sandals (light, open shoes)

SANDARAC *n* pl. -S an aromatic resin

SANDBAG *v* -BAGGED, -BAGGING, -BAGS to surround with bags of sand

SANDBANK *n* pl. -S a large mass of sand

SANDBAR *n* pl. -S a ridge of sand formed in a river or sea

SANDBOX *n* pl. -ES a box containing sand for children to play in

SANDBUR *n* pl. -S an annual herb

SANDBURR *n* pl. -S sandbur

SANDDAB *n* pl. -S a small flatfish

SANDER *n* pl. -S one that sands

SANDFISH *n* pl. -ES a marine fish

SANDFLY *n* pl. -FLIES a biting fly

SANDHI *n* pl. -S a process of phonetic modification

SANDHOG *n* pl. -S a worker who digs or works in sand

SANDIER comparative of sandy

SANDIEST superlative of sandy

SANDLIKE *adj* resembling sand

SANDLING *n* pl. -S a marine fish

SANDLOT *n* pl. -S a vacant lot

SANDMAN *n* pl. -MEN a mythical person who makes children sleepy by sprinkling sand in their eyes

SANDPEEP *n* pl. -S a wading bird

SANDPILE *n* pl. -S a pile of sand

SANDPIT *n* pl. -S a pit dug in sandy soil

SANDSHOE *n* pl. -S a lightweight sneaker

SANDSOAP *n* pl. -S a type of soap

SANDSPUR *n* pl. -S a sandbur

SANDWICH *v* -ED, -ING, -ES to place between two layers or objects

SANDWORM *n* pl. -S a sand-dwelling worm

SANDWORT *n* pl. -S a flowering plant

SANDY *adj* SANDIER, SANDIEST containing or covered with sand

SANE *adj* SANER, SANEST mentally sound SANELY *adv*

SANE *v* SANED, SANING, SANES to sain

SANENESS *n* pl. -ES sanity

SANER comparative of sane

SANEST superlative of sane

SANG past tense of sing

SANGA *n* pl. -S sangar

SANGAR *n* pl. -S a temporary fortification for two or three men

SANGAREE *n* pl. -S an alcoholic beverage

SANGER *n* pl. -S sangar

SANGH *n* pl. -S an association promoting unity between the different groups in Hinduism

SANGRIA *n* pl. -S an alcoholic beverage

SANGUINE *n* pl. -S a red color

SANICLE *n* pl. -S a medicinal herb

SANIES *n* pl. SANIES a fluid discharged from wounds SANIOUS *adj*

SANING present participle of sane

SANITARY *n* pl. -TARIES a public urinal

SANITATE *v* -TATED, -TATING, -TATES to sanitize

SANITIES pl. of sanity

SANITISE *v* -TISED, -TISING, -TISES to sanitize

SANITIZE *v* -TIZED, -TIZING, -TIZES to guard against infection or disease by cleaning or sterilizing

SANITY *n* pl. -TIES the state of being sane

SANJAK *n* pl. -S an administrative district of Turkey

SANK past tense of sink

SANNOP *n* pl. -S sannup

SANNUP *n* pl. -S a married male American Indian

SANNYASI *n* pl. -S a Hindu monk

SANS *prep* without

SANSAR *n* pl. -S sarsar

SANSEI *n* pl. -S a grandchild of Japanese immigrants to the United States

SANSERIF *n* pl. -S a typeface without serifs

SANTALIC *adj* pertaining to sandalwood

SANTALOL *n* pl. -S sandalwood oil

SANTIMS *n* pl. -TIMI a former coin of Latvia

SANTIR *n* pl. -S a Persian dulcimer

SANTO *n* pl. -TOS a wooden image of a saint

SANTOL *n* pl. -S a tropical tree

SANTONIN *n* pl. -S a chemical compound

SANTOUR *n* pl. -S santir

SANTUR *n* pl. -S santir

SAP *v* SAPPED, SAPPING, SAPS to deplete or weaken gradually

SAPAJOU *n* pl. -S a capuchin

SAPHEAD *n* pl. -S a foolish, stupid, or gullible person

SAPHENA *n* pl. -NAE a vein of the leg

SAPID *adj* pleasant to the taste

SAPIDITY *n* pl. -TIES the state of being sapid

SAPIENCE *n pl.* -S wisdom

SAPIENCY *n pl.* -CIES sapience

SAPIENS *adj* pertaining to recent man

SAPIENT *adj* wise

SAPLESS *adj* lacking vitality

SAPLING *n pl.* -S a young tree

SAPONIFY *v* -FIED, -FYING, -FIES to convert into soap

SAPONIN *n pl.* -S a soapy substance obtained from plants

SAPONINE *n pl.* -S saponin

SAPONITE *n pl.* -S a mineral found in veins and cavities of rocks

SAPOR *n pl.* -S flavor **SAPOROUS** *adj*

SAPOTA *n pl.* -S an evergreen tree

SAPOTE *n pl.* -S a tropical American tree

SAPOUR *n pl.* -S sapor

SAPPED past tense of sap

SAPPER *n pl.* -S a military engineer

SAPPHIC *n pl.* -S a type of verse form

SAPPHIRE *n pl.* -S a blue gem

SAPPHISM *n pl.* -S lesbianism

SAPPHIST *n pl.* -S a lesbian

SAPPING present participle of sap

SAPPY *adj* -PIER, -PIEST silly **SAPPILY** *adv*

SAPREMIA *n pl.* -S a form of blood poisoning **SAPREMIC** *adj*

SAPROBE *n pl.* -S an organism that derives its nourishment from decaying organic matter **SAPROBIC** *adj*

SAPROPEL *n pl.* -S mud consisting chiefly of decaying organic matter

SAPSAGO *n pl.* -GOS a hard green cheese

SAPWOOD *n pl.* -S the newly formed outer wood of a tree

SARABAND *n pl.* -S a stately Spanish dance

SARAN *n pl.* -S a thermoplastic resin

SARAPE *n pl.* -S serape

SARCASM *n pl.* -S a sharply mocking or contemptuous remark

SARCENET *n pl.* -S a silk fabric

SARCOID *n pl.* -S a disease of horses

SARCOMA *n pl.* -MAS or -MATA a type of tumor

SARCOUS *adj* composed of flesh or muscle

SARD *n pl.* -S a variety of quartz

SARDANA *n pl.* -S a Spanish folk dance

SARDAR *n pl.* -S sirdar

SARDINE *n pl.* -S a small food fish

SARDIUS *n pl.* -ES sard

SARDONIC *adj* mocking

SARDONYX *n pl.* -ES a variety of quartz

SAREE *n pl.* -S sari

SARGASSO *n pl.* -GASSOS a brownish seaweed

SARGE *n pl.* -S sergeant

SARI *n pl.* -S an outer garment worn by Hindu women

SARIN *n pl.* -S a toxic gas

SARK *n pl.* -S a shirt

SARKY *adj* SARKIER, SARKIEST sarcastic

SARMENT *n pl.* -S a type of plant stem

SARMENTA *n/pl* sarments

SAROD *n pl.* -S a lute of northern India

SARODE *n pl.* -S sarod

SARODIST *n pl.* -S one who plays the sarod

SARONG *n pl.* -S an outer garment worn in the Pacific islands

SAROS *n pl.* -ES the eclipse cycle of the sun and moon

SARSAR *n pl.* -S a cold, whistling wind

SARSEN *n pl.* -S a large sandstone block

SARSENET *n pl.* -S sarcenet

SARTOR *n pl.* -S a tailor

SARTORII *n/pl* narrow thigh muscles

SASH *v* -ED, -ING, -ES to furnish with a frame in which glass is set

SASHAY *v* -ED, -ING, -S to flounce

SASHIMI *n pl.* -S a Japanese dish of sliced raw fish

SASIN *n pl.* -S an antelope of India

SASS *v* -ED, -ING, -ES to talk impudently to

SASSABY *n pl.* -BIES an African antelope

SASSIER comparative of sassy

SASSIES pl. of sassy

SASSIEST superlative of sassy

SASSILY *adv* in a sassy manner

SASSWOOD *n pl.* -S an African tree

SASSY *n pl.* -SIES sasswood

SASSY *adj* SASSIER, SASSIEST impudent

SASTRUGA *n pl.* -GI a ridge of snow formed by the wind in polar regions

SAT past tense of sit

SATANG *n pl.* -S a monetary unit of Thailand

SATANIC *adj* extremely evil

SATANISM *n pl.* -S worship of the powers of evil

SATANIST n pl. -S one who practices satanism

SATARA n pl. -S a woolen fabric

SATAY n pl. -TAYS marinated meat that is skewered and broiled and dipped in peanut sauce

SATCHEL n pl. -S a small carrying bag

SATE v SATED, SATING, SATES to satiate

SATEEN n pl. -S a cotton fabric

SATEM adj pertaining to a group of Indo-European languages

SATI n pl. -S suttee

SATIABLE adj capable of being satiated SATIABLY adv

SATIATE v -ATED, -ATING, -ATES to satisfy to or beyond capacity

SATIETY n pl. -ETIES the state of being satiated

SATIN n pl. -S a smooth fabric

SATINET n pl. -S a thin satin

SATING present participle of sate

SATINPOD n pl. -S a flowering plant

SATINY adj resembling satin

SATIRE n pl. -S the use of derisive wit to attack folly or wickedness SATIRIC adj

SATIRISE v -RISED, -RISING, -RISES to satirize

SATIRIST n pl. -S one who satirizes

SATIRIZE v -RIZED, -RIZING, -RIZES to subject to satire

SATISFY v -FIED, -FYING, -FIES to provide fully with what is desired, expected, or needed

SATORI n pl. -S the illumination of spirit sought by Zen Buddhists

SATRAP n pl. -S a governor of a province in ancient Persia

SATRAPY n pl. -PIES the territory of a satrap

SATSUMA n pl. -S a variety of orange

SATURANT n pl. -S a substance used to saturate

SATURATE v -RATED, -RATING, -RATES to fill completely with something that permeates

SATYR n pl. -S a woodland deity of Greek mythology SATYRIC adj

SATYRID n pl. -S a brownish butterfly

SAU n pl. SAU xu

SAUCE v SAUCED, SAUCING, SAUCES to season with sauce (a flavorful liquid dressing)

SAUCEBOX n pl. -ES a saucy person

SAUCEPAN n pl. -S a cooking utensil

SAUCER n pl. -S a small, shallow dish

SAUCH n pl. -S saugh

SAUCING present participle of sauce

SAUCY adj SAUCIER, SAUCIEST impudent SAUCILY adv

SAUGER n pl. -S a freshwater fish

SAUGH n pl. -S a willow tree SAUGHY adj

SAUL n pl. -S soul

SAULT n pl. -S a waterfall

SAUNA n pl. -S a Finnish steam bath

SAUNTER v -ED, -ING, -S to walk in a leisurely manner

SAUREL n pl. -S a marine fish

SAURIAN n pl. -S any of a suborder of reptiles

SAUROPOD n pl. -S any of a suborder of large dinosaurs

SAURY n pl. -RIES a marine fish

SAUSAGE n pl. -S finely chopped and seasoned meat stuffed into a casing

SAUTE v -TEED or -TED, -TEING, -TES to fry in a small amount of fat

SAUTERNE n pl. -S a sweet white wine

SAUTOIR n pl. -S a saltire

SAUTOIRE n pl. -S sautoir

SAVABLE adj capable of being saved

SAVAGE adj -AGER, -AGEST fierce SAVAGELY adv

SAVAGE v -AGED, -AGING, -AGES to attack or treat brutally

SAVAGERY n pl. -RIES the quality of being savage

SAVAGEST superlative of savage

SAVAGING present participle of savage

SAVAGISM n pl. -S savagery

SAVANNA n pl. -S a flat, treeless grassland

SAVANNAH n pl. -S savanna

SAVANT n pl. -S a man of profound learning

SAVARIN n pl. -S a yeast cake baked in a ring mold

SAVATE n pl. -S a pugilistic sport

SAVE v SAVED, SAVING, SAVES to rescue from danger, injury, or loss SAVEABLE adj

SAVELOY n pl. -LOYS a highly seasoned sausage

SAVER n pl. -S one that saves

SAVIN n pl. -S an evergreen shrub

SAVINE n pl. -S savin

SAVING n pl. -S the act or an instance of saving

SAVINGLY adv in a thrifty manner

SAVIOR n pl. -S one that saves

SAVIOUR n pl. -S savior

SAVOR v -ED, -ING, -S to taste or smell with pleasure

SAVORER n pl. -S one that savors

SAVORIER comparative of savory

SAVORIES pl. of savory

SAVOROUS adj savory

SAVORY adj -VORIER, -VORIEST pleasant to the taste or smell SAVORILY adv

SAVORY n pl. -VORIES a savory dish served before or after a meal

SAVOUR v -ED, -ING, -S to savor

SAVOURER n pl. -S savorer

SAVOURY adj -VOURIER, -VOURIEST savory

SAVOURY n pl. -VOURIES a savory

SAVOY n pl. -VOYS a variety of cabbage

SAVVY v -VIED, -VYING, -VIES to understand

SAVVY adj -VIER, -VIEST shrewd

SAW v SAWED, SAWN, SAWING, SAWS to cut or divide with a saw (a type of cutting tool)

SAWBILL n pl. -S a tropical bird

SAWBONES n pl. -BONESES a surgeon

SAWBUCK n pl. -S a sawhorse

SAWDUST n pl. -S small particles of wood produced in sawing

SAWER n pl. -S one that saws

SAWFISH n pl. -ES a marine fish

SAWFLY n pl. -FLIES a winged insect

SAWHORSE n pl. -S a rack used to support a piece of wood being sawed

SAWLIKE adj resembling a saw

SAWLOG n pl. -S a log large enough to saw into boards

SAWMILL n pl. -S a place where logs are sawed

SAWN a past participle of saw

SAWNEY n pl. -NEYS a foolish person

SAWTOOTH n pl. -TEETH a cutting edge on a saw

SAWYER n pl. -S one that saws wood for a living

SAX n pl. -ES a saxophone

SAXATILE adj living or growing among rocks

SAXHORN n pl. -S a brass wind instrument

SAXONY n pl. -NIES a woolen fabric

SAXTUBA n pl. -S a bass saxhorn

SAY v SAID, SAYING, present sing. 2d person SAY, SAYEST, or SAYST, 3d person SAYS or SAITH to utter SAYABLE adj

SAYER n pl. -S one that says

SAYID n pl. -S sayyid

SAYING n pl. -S a maxim

SAYONARA n pl. -S goodby

SAYST a present 2d person sing. of say

SAYYID n pl. -S lord; sir — used as a title of respect for a Muslim dignitary

SCAB v SCABBED, SCABBING, SCABS to become covered with a scab (a crust that forms over a healing wound)

SCABBARD v -ED, -ING, -S to put into a sheath, as a sword

SCABBLE v -BLED, -BLING, -BLES to shape roughly

SCABBY adj -BIER, -BIEST covered with scabs SCABBILY adv

SCABIES n pl. SCABIES a skin disease

SCABIOSA n pl. -S scabious

SCABIOUS n pl. -ES a flowering plant

SCABLAND n pl. -S rocky land with little soil cover

SCABLIKE adj resembling a scab

SCABROUS adj roughened with small projections

SCAD n pl. -S a marine fish

SCAFFOLD v -ED, -ING, -S to provide with a scaffold (a temporary platform for workmen)

SCAG n pl. -S heroin

SCALABLE adj capable of being scaled SCALABLY adv

SCALADE n pl. -S an act of scaling the walls of a fortification

SCALADO n pl. -DOS scalade

SCALAGE n pl. -S a percentage deduction to compensate for shrinkage

SCALAR n pl. -S a mathematical quantity possessing only magnitude

SCALARE n pl. -S a tropical fish

SCALAWAG n pl. -S a rascal

SCALD v -ED, -ING, -S to burn with hot liquid or steam

SCALDIC adj skaldic

SCALE v SCALED, SCALING, SCALES to climb up or over

SCALENE *adj* designating a triangle having no two sides equal

SCALENUS *n pl.* -NI a muscle of the neck

SCALEPAN *n pl.* -S a pan on a weighing scale

SCALER *n pl.* -S one that scales

SCALEUP *n pl.* -S an increase based on a fixed ratio

SCALIER comparative of scaly

SCALIEST superlative of scaly

SCALING present participle of scale

SCALL *n pl.* -S a scaly eruption of the skin

SCALLION *n pl.* -S an onion-like plant

SCALLOP *v* -ED, -ING, -S to bake in a sauce topped with bread crumbs

SCALP *v* -ED, -ING, -S to remove an upper part from

SCALPEL *n pl.* -S a small surgical knife

SCALPER *n pl.* -S one that scalps

SCALY *adj* SCALIER, SCALIEST peeling off in flakes

SCAM *v* SCAMMED, SCAMMING, SCAMS to cheat or swindle

SCAMMONY *n pl.* -NIES a climbing plant

SCAMP *v* -ED, -ING, -S to perform in a hasty or careless manner

SCAMPER *v* -ED, -ING, -S to run playfully about

SCAMPI *n pl.* SCAMPI or SCAMPIES large shrimp used in Italian cooking

SCAMPISH *adj* rascally

SCAN *v* SCANNED, SCANNING, SCANS to examine closely

SCANDAL *v* -DALED, -DALING, -DALS or -DALLED, -DALLING, -DALS to defame

SCANDENT *adj* climbing, as a plant

SCANDIA *n pl.* -S an oxide of scandium

SCANDIUM *n pl.* -S a metallic element **SCANDIC** *adj*

SCANNED past tense of scan

SCANNER *n pl.* -S one that scans

SCANNING *n pl.* -S close examination

SCANSION *n pl.* -S the analysis of verse into metrical feet and rhythm patterns

SCANT *adj* SCANTER, SCANTEST meager

SCANT *v* -ED, -ING, -S to provide with a meager portion

SCANTIER comparative of scanty

SCANTIES *n/pl* brief panties for women

SCANTLY *adv* in a scant manner

SCANTY *adj* SCANTIER, SCANTIEST meager **SCANTILY** *adv*

SCAPE *v* SCAPED, SCAPING, SCAPES to escape

SCAPHOID *n pl.* -S a bone of the wrist

SCAPOSE *adj* bearing a leafless stalk

SCAPULA *n pl.* -LAE or -LAS a bone of the shoulder

SCAPULAR *n pl.* -S a sleeveless outer garment worn by monks

SCAR *v* SCARRED, SCARRING, SCARS to form a scar (a mark left by the healing of injured tissue)

SCARAB *n pl.* -S a large, black beetle

SCARCE *adj* SCARCER, SCARCEST infrequently seen or found

SCARCELY *adv* by a narrow margin

SCARCITY *n pl.* -TIES the quality of being scarce

SCARE *v* SCARED, SCARING, SCARES to frighten

SCARER *n pl.* -S one that scares

SCAREY *adj* SCARIER, SCARIEST scary

SCARF *n pl.* SCARFS or SCARVES a piece of cloth worn for warmth or protection

SCARF *v* -ED, -ING, -S to cover with a scarf

SCARFPIN *n pl.* -S a tiepin

SCARIER comparative of scarey and scary

SCARIEST superlative of scarey and scary

SCARIFY *v* -FIED, -FYING, -FIES to make superficial cuts in

SCARILY *adv* in a scary manner

SCARING present participle of scare

SCARIOSE *adj* scarious

SCARIOUS *adj* thin, dry, and membranous

SCARLESS *adj* having no scars

SCARLET *n pl.* -S a red color

SCARP *v* -ED, -ING, -S to cut or make into a steep slope

SCARPER *v* -ED, -ING, -S to flee

SCARPH *v* -ED, -ING, -S to unite by means of a type of joint

SCARRED past tense of scar

SCARRING present participle of scar

SCARRY *adj* -RIER, -RIEST marked with scars

SCART *v* -ED, -ING, -S to scratch

SCARVES a *pl.* of scarf

SCARY *adj* SCARIER, SCARIEST frightening

SCAT v SCATTED, SCATTING, SCATS to leave hastily

SCATBACK n pl. -S a type of player in football

SCATHE v SCATHED, SCATHING, SCATHES to criticize severely

SCATT n pl. -S a tax

SCATTED past tense of scat

SCATTER v -ED, -ING, -S to go or send in various directions

SCATTING present participle of scat

SCATTY adj -TIER, -TIEST crazy

SCAUP n pl. -S a sea duck

SCAUPER n pl. -S an engraving tool

SCAUR n pl. -S a protruding, isolated rock

SCAVENGE v -ENGED, -ENGING, -ENGES to search through rubbish for usable items

SCENA n pl. -S an elaborate composition for a single voice

SCENARIO n pl. -IOS a summary of the plot of a dramatic work

SCEND v -ED, -ING, -S to rise upward, as a ship on a wave

SCENE n pl. -S the place where some action or event occurs

SCENERY n pl. -ERIES a picturesque landscape or view

SCENIC adj pertaining to scenery

SCENICAL adj scenic

SCENT v -ED, -ING, -S to fill with an odor

SCEPTER v -ED, -ING, -S to invest with royal authority

SCEPTIC n pl. -S skeptic

SCEPTRAL adj pertaining to royal authority

SCEPTRE v -TRED, -TRING, -TRES to scepter

SCHAPPE n pl. -S a silk fabric

SCHAV n pl. -S a chilled soup

SCHEDULE v -ULED, -ULING, -ULES to assign to a certain date or time

SCHEMA n pl. -MATA or -MAS a generalized diagram or plan

SCHEME v SCHEMED, SCHEMING, SCHEMES to plan or plot

SCHEMER n pl. -S one that schemes

SCHERZO n pl. -ZOS or -ZI a lively musical movement

SCHILLER n pl. -S a brownish luster occurring on certain minerals

SCHISM n pl. -S a division into opposing parties

SCHIST n pl. -S a rock that readily splits into parallel layers

SCHIZIER comparative of schizy

SCHIZIEST superlative of schizy

SCHIZO n pl. SCHIZOS a schizoid

SCHIZOID n pl. -S a person affected with a type of psychotic disorder

SCHIZONT n pl. -S an organism that reproduces by a form of asexual reproduction

SCHIZY adj SCHIZIER, SCHIZIEST affected with schizophrenia

SCHIZZY adj SCHIZZIER, SCHIZZIEST schizy

SCHLEP v SCHLEPPED, SCHLEPPING, SCHLEPS to lug or drag

SCHLEPP v -ED, -ING, -S to schlep

SCHLIERE n pl. -REN a small streak in an igneous rock

SCHLOCK n pl. -S inferior merchandise

SCHLOCKY adj of inferior quality

SCHLUMP v -ED, -ING, -S to go about lazily or sloppily dressed

SCHMALTZ n pl. -ES excessive sentimentality

SCHMALZ n pl. -ES schmaltz

SCHMALZY adj SCHMALZIER, SCHMALZIEST characterized by schmalz

SCHMEAR n pl. -S an aggregate of related things

SCHMEER v -ED, -ING, -S to bribe

SCHMELZE n pl. -S a type of decorative glass

SCHMO n pl. SCHMOES or SCHMOS a stupid person

SCHMOE n pl. -S schmo

SCHMOOS v -ED, -ING, -ES to schmooze

SCHMOOSE v SCHMOOSED, SCHMOOSING, SCHMOOSES to schmooze

SCHMOOZE v SCHMOOZED, SCHMOOZING, SCHMOOZES to gossip

SCHMUCK n pl. -S a foolish or clumsy person

SCHNAPPS n pl. SCHNAPPS a strong liquor

SCHNAPS n pl. SCHNAPS schnapps

SCHNECKE n pl. -KEN a sweet roll

SCHNOOK n pl. -S an easily deceived person

SCHNOZ n pl. SCHNOZZES the nose

SCHNOZZ n pl. -ES schnoz

SCHOLAR n pl. -S a learned person

SCHOLIUM *n* pl. -LIA or -LIUMS an explanatory marginal note

SCHOOL *v* -ED, -ING, -S to educate in an institution of learning

SCHOONER *n* pl. -S a sailing vessel

SCHORL *n* pl. -S a mineral

SCHRIK *n* pl. -S sudden fright

SCHROD *n* pl. -S scrod

SCHTICK *n* pl. -S shtick

SCHTIK *n* pl. -S shtick

SCHUIT *n* pl. -S a Dutch sailing vessel

SCHUL *n* pl. SCHULN shul

SCHUSS *v* -ED, -ING, -ES to make a fast, straight run in skiing

SCHUSSER *n* pl. -S one that schusses

SCHWA *n* pl. -S a type of vowel sound

SCIAENID *n* pl. -S a carnivorous fish

SCIATIC *n* pl. -S a nerve, vein, or artery situated near the hip

SCIATICA *n* pl. -S a painful disorder of the hip and adjoining areas

SCIENCE *n* pl. -S a department of systematized knowledge

SCILICET *adv* namely

SCILLA *n* pl. -S a flowering plant

SCIMETAR *n* pl. -S scimitar

SCIMITAR *n* pl. -S a curved Oriental sword

SCIMITER *n* pl. -S scimitar

SCINCOID *n* pl. -S one of a family of smooth, short-limbed lizards

SCIOLISM *n* pl. -S superficial knowledge

SCIOLIST *n* pl. -S one whose knowledge is superficial

SCION *n* pl. -S a child or descendant

SCIROCCO *n* pl. -COS sirocco

SCIRRHUS *n* pl. -RHI or -RHUSES a hard tumor

SCISSILE *adj* capable of being cut or split easily

SCISSION *n* pl. -S the act of cutting or splitting

SCISSOR *v* -ED, -ING, -S to cut with a two-bladed cutting implement

SCISSURE *n* pl. -S a lengthwise cut

SCIURID *n* pl. -S a sciurine

SCIURINE *n* pl. -S a rodent of the squirrel family

SCIUROID *adj* resembling a squirrel

SCLAFF *v* -ED, -ING, -S to strike the ground with the club before hitting the ball in golf

SCLAFFER *n* pl. -S one that sclaffs

SCLERA *n* pl. -RAS or -RAE the white, fibrous outer coat of the eyeball **SCLERAL** *adj*

SCLEREID *n* pl. -S a type of plant cell

SCLERITE *n* pl. -S one of the hard plates forming the outer covering of an arthropod

SCLEROID *adj* sclerous

SCLEROMA *n* pl. -MATA a hardened patch of cellular tissue

SCLEROSE *v* -ROSED, -ROSING, -ROSES to become hard, as tissue

SCLEROUS *adj* hardened

SCOFF *v* -ED, -ING, -S to express rude doubt or derision

SCOFFER *n* pl. -S one that scoffs

SCOFFLAW *n* pl. -S an habitual law violator

SCOLD *v* -ED, -ING, -S to rebuke harshly

SCOLDER *n* pl. -S one that scolds

SCOLDING *n* pl. -S a harsh reproof

SCOLEX *n* pl. -LECES or -LICES the knoblike head of a tapeworm

SCOLIOMA *n* pl. -S abnormal curvature of the spine

SCOLLOP *v* -ED, -ING, -S to scallop

SCONCE *v* SCONCED, SCONCING, SCONCES to fine

SCONE *n* pl. -S a flat, round cake

SCOOP *v* -ED, -ING, -S to take up with a scoop (a spoonlike utensil)

SCOOPER *n* pl. -S one that scoops

SCOOPFUL *n* pl. SCOOPFULS or SCOOPSFUL as much as a scoop will hold

SCOOT *v* -ED, -ING, -S to go quickly

SCOOTER *n* pl. -S a two-wheeled vehicle

SCOP *n* pl. -S an Old English poet

SCOPE *v* SCOPED, SCOPING, SCOPES to look at in order to evaluate

SCOPULA *n* pl. -LAE or -LAS a dense tuft of hairs

SCORCH *v* -ED, -ING, -ES to burn slightly so as to alter the color or taste

SCORCHER *n* pl. -S one that scorches

SCORE *v* SCORED, SCORING, SCORES to make a point in a game or contest

SCOREPAD *n* pl. -S a pad on which scored points are recorded

SCORER *n* pl. -S one that scores

SCORIA *n* pl. -RIAE the refuse of a smelted metal or ore

SCORIFY *v* -FIED, -FYING, -FIES to reduce to scoria

SCORING	present participle of score
SCORN	v -ED, -ING, -S to treat or regard with contempt
SCORNER	n pl. -S one that scorns
SCORNFUL	adj feeling or expressing contempt
SCORPION	n pl. -S a stinging arachnid
SCOT	n pl. -S a tax
SCOTCH	v -ED, -ING, -ES to put a definite end to
SCOTER	n pl. -S a sea duck
SCOTIA	n pl. -S a concave molding
SCOTOMA	n pl. -MAS or -MATA a blind spot in the field of vision
SCOTOPIA	n pl. -S vision in dim light SCOTOPIC adj
SCOTTIE	n pl. -S a short-legged terrier
SCOUR	v -ED, -ING, -S to cleanse or polish by hard rubbing
SCOURER	n pl. -S one that scours
SCOURGE	v SCOURGED, SCOURGING, SCOURGES to punish severely
SCOURGER	n pl. -S one that scourges
SCOURING	n pl. -S material removed by scouring
SCOUSE	n pl. -S a type of meat stew
SCOUT	v -ED, -ING, -S to observe for the purpose of obtaining information
SCOUTER	n pl. -S one that scouts
SCOUTH	n pl. -S plenty
SCOUTHER	v -ED, -ING, -S to scorch
SCOUTING	n pl. -S the act of one that scouts
SCOW	v -ED, -ING, -S to transport by scow (a flat-bottomed boat)
SCOWDER	v -ED, -ING, -S to scouther
SCOWL	v -ED, -ING, -S to frown angrily
SCOWLER	n pl. -S one that scowls
SCRABBLE	v -BLED, -BLING, -BLES to claw or grope about frantically
SCRABBLY	adj -BLIER, -BLIEST raspy
SCRAG	v SCRAGGED, SCRAGGING, SCRAGS to wring the neck of
SCRAGGLY	adj -GLIER, -GLIEST uneven
SCRAGGY	adj -GIER, -GIEST scrawny
SCRAICH	v -ED, -ING, -S to utter a shrill cry
SCRAIGH	v -ED, -ING, -S to scraich
SCRAM	v SCRAMMED, SCRAMMING, SCRAMS to leave quickly
SCRAMBLE	v -BLED, -BLING, -BLES to move or climb hurriedly

SCRAMJET	n pl. -S a type of aircraft engine
SCRANNEL	n pl. -S a thin person
SCRAP	v SCRAPPED, SCRAPPING, SCRAPS to discard
SCRAPE	v SCRAPED, SCRAPING, SCRAPES to rub so as to remove an outer layer
SCRAPER	n pl. -S one that scrapes
SCRAPIE	n pl. -S a disease of sheep
SCRAPING	n pl. -S something scraped off
SCRAPPED	past tense of scrap
SCRAPPER	n pl. -S a fighter
SCRAPPIER	comparative of scrappy
SCRAPPIEST	superlative of scrappy
SCRAPPING	present participle of scrap
SCRAPPLE	n pl. -S a seasoned mixture of ground meat and cornmeal
SCRAPPY	adj -PIER, -PIEST marked by fighting spirit
SCRATCH	v -ED, -ING, -ES to make a thin, shallow cut or mark on
SCRATCHY	adj SCRATCHIER, SCRATCHIEST made by scratching
SCRAWL	v -ED, -ING, -S to write hastily or illegibly
SCRAWLER	n pl. -S one that scrawls
SCRAWLY	adj SCRAWLIER, SCRAWLIEST written hastily or illegibly
SCRAWNY	adj -NIER, -NIEST extremely thin
SCREAK	v -ED, -ING, -S to screech
SCREAKY	adj screechy
SCREAM	v -ED, -ING, -S to utter a prolonged, piercing cry
SCREAMER	n pl. -S one that screams
SCREE	n pl. -S a mass of rocks at the foot of a slope
SCREECH	v -ED, -ING, -ES to utter a harsh, shrill cry
SCREECHY	adj SCREECHIER, SCREECHIEST screaching
SCREED	v -ED, -ING, -S to shred
SCREEN	v -ED, -ING, -S to provide with a screen (a device designed to divide, conceal, or protect)
SCREENER	n pl. -S one that screens
SCREW	v -ED, -ING, -S to attach with a screw (a type of metal fastener)
SCREWER	n pl. -S one that screws
SCREWUP	n pl. -S an instance of bungling

SCREWY adj SCREWIER, SCREWIEST crazy

SCRIBAL adj pertaining to a public clerk or secretary

SCRIBBLE v -BLED, -BLING, -BLES to write hastily or carelessly

SCRIBE v SCRIBED, SCRIBING, SCRIBES to mark with a scriber

SCRIBER n pl. -S a pointed instrument used for marking off material to be cut

SCRIED past tense of scry

SCRIES present 3d person sing. of scry

SCRIEVE v SCRIEVED, SCRIEVING, SCRIEVES to move along swiftly and smoothly

SCRIM n pl. -S a cotton fabric

SCRIMP v -ED, -ING, -S to be very or overly thrifty

SCRIMPER n pl. -S one that scrimps

SCRIMPIT adj meager

SCRIMPY adj SCRIMPIER, SCRIMPIEST meager

SCRIP n pl. -S a small piece of paper

SCRIPT v -ED, -ING, -S to prepare a written text for, as a play or motion picture

SCRIPTER n pl. -S one that scripts

SCRIVE v SCRIVED, SCRIVING, SCRIVES to engrave

SCROD n pl. -S a young cod

SCROFULA n pl. -S a disease of the lymph glands

SCROGGY adj -GIER, -GIEST of stunted growth

SCROLL v -ED, -ING, -S to move text across a display screen

SCROOCH v -ED, -ING, -ES to crouch

SCROOGE n pl. -S a miserly person

SCROOP v -ED, -ING, -S to make a harsh, grating sound

SCROOTCH v -ED, -ING, -ES to scrooch

SCROTUM n pl. -TA or -TUMS the pouch of skin that contains the testes **SCROTAL** adj

SCROUGE v SCROUGED, SCROUGING, SCROUGES to crowd

SCROUNGE v SCROUNGED, SCROUNGING, SCROUNGES to gather by foraging

SCROUNGY adj SCROUNGIER, SCROUNGIEST dirty

SCRUB v SCRUBBED, SCRUBBING, SCRUBS to rub hard in order to clean

SCRUBBER n pl. -S one that scrubs

SCRUBBY adj -BIER, -BIEST inferior in size or quality

SCRUFF n pl. -S the back of the neck

SCRUFFY adj -FIER, -FIEST shabby

SCRUM v SCRUMMED, SCRUMMING, SCRUMS to engage in a scrummage (a formation around the ball in rugby)

SCRUNCH v -ED, -ING, -ES to crush

SCRUPLE v -PLED, -PLING, -PLES to hesitate because of ethical considerations

SCRUTINY n pl. -NIES a close examination

SCRY v SCRIED, SCRYING, SCRIES to engage in crystal gazing

SCUBA n pl. -S an underwater breathing device

SCUD v SCUDDED, SCUDDING, SCUDS to run or move swiftly

SCUDO n pl. -DI a former Italian coin

SCUFF v -ED, -ING, -S to walk without lifting the feet

SCUFFLE v -FLED, -FLING, -FLES to struggle in a rough, confused manner

SCUFFLER n pl. -S one that scuffles

SCULK v -ED, -ING, -S to skulk

SCULKER n pl. -S skulker

SCULL v -ED, -ING, -S to propel with a type of oar

SCULLER n pl. -S one that sculls

SCULLERY n pl. -LERIES a room in which kitchen utensils are cleaned and stored

SCULLION n pl. -S a kitchen servant who does menial work

SCULP v -ED, -ING, -S to sculpt

SCULPIN n pl. -S a freshwater fish

SCULPT v -ED, -ING, -S to form an image or representation of from solid material

SCULPTOR n pl. -S one that sculpts

SCUM v SCUMMED, SCUMMING, SCUMS to remove the scum (impure or extraneous matter) from

SCUMBAG n pl. -S a dirtbag

SCUMBLE v -BLED, -BLING, -BLES to soften the outlines or colors of by rubbing lightly

SCUMLIKE adj resembling scum

SCUMMED past tense of scum

SCUMMER n pl. -S one that scums

SCUMMING present participle of scum

SCUMMY adj -MIER, -MIEST covered with scum

SCUNNER v -ED, -ING, -S to feel loathing or disgust

SCUP n pl. -S a marine food fish

SCUPPAUG n pl. -S scup

SCUPPER v -ED, -ING, -S to ambush

SCURF n pl. -S scaly or shredded dry skin

SCURFY adj SCURFIER, SCURFIEST covered with scurf

SCURRIED past tense of scurry

SCURRIES present 3d person sing. of scurry

SCURRIL adj scurrile

SCURRILE adj expressed in coarse and abusive language

SCURRY v -RIED, -RYING, -RIES to move hurriedly

SCURVY adj -VIER, -VIEST base or contemptible **SCURVILY** adv

SCURVY n pl. -VIES a disease resulting from vitamin C deficiency

SCUT n pl. -S a short tail, as of a rabbit

SCUTA pl. of scutum

SCUTAGE n pl. -S a tax exacted by a feudal lord in lieu of military service

SCUTATE adj shaped like a shield

SCUTCH v -ED, -ING, -ES to separate the woody fiber from by beating

SCUTCHER n pl. -S one that scutches

SCUTE n pl. -S a horny plate or scale

SCUTELLA n/pl small, scutate organs or parts

SCUTTER v -ED, -ING, -S to scurry

SCUTTLE v -TLED, -TLING, -TLES to scurry

SCUTUM n pl. -TA scute

SCUZZY adj -ZIER, -ZIEST dirty or shabby

SCYPHATE adj shaped like a cup

SCYPHUS n pl. -PHI a Greek cup with two handles

SCYTHE v SCYTHED, SCYTHING, SCYTHES to cut with a scythe (a single-bladed cutting implement)

SEA n pl. -S the ocean

SEABAG n pl. -S a bag used by a sailor

SEABEACH n pl. -ES a beach lying along the sea

SEABED n pl. -S a seafloor

SEABIRD n pl. -S a bird frequenting the ocean or seacoast

SEABOARD n pl. -S the seacoast

SEABOOT n pl. -S a waterproof boot

SEABORNE adj carried on or over the sea

SEACOAST n pl. -S land bordering on the sea

SEACOCK n pl. -S a valve in a ship's hull

SEACRAFT n pl. -S skill in sea navigation

SEADOG n pl. -S a fogbow

SEADROME n pl. -S an airport in the sea

SEAFARER n pl. -S a sailor

SEAFLOOR n pl. -S the bottom of a sea

SEAFOOD n pl. -S edible fish or shellfish from the sea

SEAFOWL n pl. -S a seabird

SEAFRONT n pl. -S an area along the edge of the sea

SEAGIRT adj surrounded by the sea

SEAGOING adj designed for use on the sea

SEAGULL n pl. -S a gull frequenting the sea

SEAL v -ED, -ING, -S to close or make secure against access, leakage, or passage **SEALABLE** adj

SEALANT n pl. -S a sealing agent

SEALER n pl. -S one that seals

SEALERY n pl. -ERIES the occupation of hunting seals

SEALLIKE adj resembling a seal (an aquatic mammal)

SEALSKIN n pl. -S the skin of a seal

SEAM v -ED, -ING, -S to join with a seam (a line formed by sewing two pieces of fabric together)

SEAMAN n pl. -MEN a sailor **SEAMANLY** adj

SEAMARK n pl. -S a landmark serving as a navigational guide to mariners

SEAMER n pl. -S one that seams

SEAMIER comparative of seamy

SEAMIEST superlative of seamy

SEAMLESS adj having no seam

SEAMLIKE adj resembling a seam

SEAMOUNT n pl. -S an undersea mountain

SEAMSTER n pl. -S a person whose occupation is sewing

SEAMY adj SEAMIER, SEAMIEST unpleasant

SEANCE n pl. -S a meeting of persons seeking spiritualistic messages

SEAPIECE n pl. -S a seascape

SEAPLANE n pl. -S an airplane designed to take off from or land on the water

SEAPORT n pl. -S a harbor or town accessible to seagoing ships

SEAQUAKE n pl. -S an undersea earthquake

SEAR adj SEARER, SEAREST sere

SEAR v -ED, -ING, -S to burn the surface of

SEARCH v -ED, -ING, -ES to look through or over carefully in order to find something

SEARCHER n pl. -S one that searches

SEAROBIN n pl. -S a marine fish

SEASCAPE n pl. -S a picture of the sea

SEASCOUT n pl. -S a boy scout trained in water activities

SEASHELL n pl. -S the shell of a marine mollusk

SEASHORE n pl. -S land bordering on the sea

SEASICK adj affected with nausea caused by the motion of a vessel at sea

SEASIDE n pl. -S the seashore

SEASON v -ED, -ING, -S to heighten or improve the flavor of by adding savory ingredients

SEASONAL adj occurring at a certain time of the year

SEASONER n pl. -S one that seasons

SEAT v -ED, -ING, -S to place on a seat (something on which one sits)

SEATER n pl. -S one that seats

SEATING n pl. -S material for covering seats

SEATLESS adj having no seat

SEATMATE n pl. -S one with whom one shares a seat

SEATRAIN n pl. -S a ship equipped to carry railroad cars

SEATWORK n pl. -S work done at one's seat

SEAWALL n pl. -S a wall to protect a shoreline from erosion

SEAWAN n pl. -S wampum

SEAWANT n pl. -S seawan

SEAWARD n pl. -S the direction toward the open sea

SEAWARE n pl. -S seaweed used as fertilizer

SEAWATER n pl. -S water from the sea

SEAWAY n pl. -WAYS the headway made by a ship

SEAWEED n pl. -S a plant growing in the sea

SEBACIC adj derived from a certain acid

SEBASIC adj sebacic

SEBUM n pl. -S a fatty matter secreted by certain glands of the skin

SEC n pl. -S secant

SECALOSE n pl. -S a complex carbohydrate

SECANT n pl. -S a trigonometric function of an angle

SECANTLY adv in an intersecting manner

SECATEUR n pl. -S a pruning tool

SECCO n pl. -COS the art of painting on dry plaster

SECEDE v -CEDED, -CEDING, -CEDES to withdraw formally from an alliance or association

SECEDER n pl. -S one that secedes

SECERN v -ED, -ING, -S to discern as separate

SECLUDE v -CLUDED, -CLUDING, -CLUDES to remove or set apart from others

SECOND v -ED, -ING, -S to give support or encouragement to

SECONDE n pl. -S a position in fencing

SECONDER n pl. -S one that seconds

SECONDLY adv in the next place after the first

SECONDO n pl. -DI the lower part in a piano duet

SECPAR n pl. -S a parsec

SECRECY n pl. -CIES the condition of being secret

SECRET adj -CRETER, -CRETEST kept from knowledge or view

SECRET n pl. -S something kept from the knowledge of others

SECRETE v -CRETED, -CRETING, -CRETES to generate and separate out from cells or bodily fluids

SECRETIN n pl. -S a hormone

SECRETLY adv in a secret manner

SECRETOR n pl. -S one that secretes

SECT *n pl.* -S a group of people united by common beliefs or interests

SECTARY *n pl.* -RIES a member of a sect

SECTILE *adj* capable of being cut smoothly

SECTION *v* -ED, -ING, -S to divide into sections (distinct parts)

SECTOR *v* -ED, -ING, -S to divide into sectors (sections)

SECTORAL *adj* of or pertaining to a sector

SECULAR *n pl.* -S a layman

SECUND *adj* having the parts or organs arranged on one side only **SECUNDLY** *adv*

SECUNDUM *adv* according to

SECURE *adj* -CURER, -CUREST free from danger **SECURELY** *adv*

SECURE *v* -CURED, -CURING, -CURES to make firm or tight

SECURER *n pl.* -S one that secures

SECUREST superlative of secure

SECURING present participle of secure

SECURITY *n pl.* -TIES the state of being secure

SEDAN *n pl.* -S a type of automobile

SEDARIM a pl. of seder

SEDATE *adj* -DATER, -DATEST calm **SEDATELY** *adv*

SEDATE *v* -DATED, -DATING, -DATES to administer a sedative to

SEDATION *n pl.* -S the reduction of stress or excitement by the use of sedatives

SEDATIVE *n pl.* -S a drug that induces a calm state

SEDER *n pl.* -DARIM or -DERS a Jewish ceremonial dinner

SEDERUNT *n pl.* -S a prolonged sitting

SEDGE *n pl.* -S a marsh plant

SEDGY *adj* SEDGIER, SEDGIEST abounding in sedge

SEDILE *n pl.* -LIA one of the seats in a church for the use of the officiating clergy

SEDILIUM *n pl.* -LIA sedile

SEDIMENT *v* -ED, -ING, -S to settle to the bottom of a liquid

SEDITION *n pl.* -S incitement of rebellion against a government

SEDUCE *v* -DUCED, -DUCING, -DUCES to lead astray **SEDUCIVE** *adj*

SEDUCER *n pl.* -S one that seduces

SEDULITY *n pl.* -TIES the state of being sedulous

SEDULOUS *adj* diligent

SEDUM *n pl.* -S a flowering plant

SEE *v* SAW, SEEN, SEEING, SEES to perceive with the eyes **SEEABLE** *adj*

SEECATCH *n pl.* -CATCHIE an adult male fur seal

SEED *v* -ED, -ING, -S to plant seeds (propagative plant structures) in

SEEDBED *n pl.* -S land prepared for seeding

SEEDCAKE *n pl.* -S a sweet cake containing aromatic seeds

SEEDCASE *n pl.* -S a pericarp

SEEDER *n pl.* -S one that seeds

SEEDIER comparative of seedy

SEEDIEST superlative of seedy

SEEDILY *adv* in a seedy manner

SEEDLESS *adj* having no seeds

SEEDLIKE *adj* resembling a seed

SEEDLING *n pl.* -S a young plant

SEEDMAN *n pl.* -MEN seedsman

SEEDPOD *n pl.* -S a type of seed vessel

SEEDSMAN *n pl.* -MEN a dealer in seeds

SEEDTIME *n pl.* -S the season for sowing seeds

SEEDY *adj* SEEDIER, SEEDIEST containing seeds; inferior in condition or quality

SEEING *n pl.* -S the act of one that sees

SEEK *v* SOUGHT, SEEKING, SEEKS to go in search of

SEEKER *n pl.* -S one that seeks

SEEL *v* -ED, -ING, -S to stitch closed the eyes of, as a falcon during training

SEELY *adj* frail

SEEM *v* -ED, -ING, -S to give the impression of being

SEEMER *n pl.* -S one that seems

SEEMING *n pl.* -S outward appearance

SEEMLY *adj* -LIER, -LIEST of pleasing appearance

SEEN past participle of see

SEEP *v* -ED, -ING, -S to pass slowly through small openings

SEEPAGE *n pl.* -S the quantity of fluid that has seeped

SEEPY *adj* SEEPIER, SEEPIEST soaked or oozing with water

SEER *n pl.* -S a prophet

SEERESS *n pl.* -ES a female seer

SEESAW   v -ED, -ING, -S to move up and down or back and forth

SEETHE   v SEETHED, SEETHING, SEETHES to surge or foam as if boiling

SEG   n pl. -S one who advocates racial segregation

SEGETAL   adj growing in fields of grain

SEGGAR   n pl. -S a saggar

SEGMENT   v -ED, -ING, -S to divide into sections

SEGNO   n pl. -GNI or -GNOS a musical sign

SEGO   n pl. -GOS a perennial herb

SEGUE   v -GUED, -GUEING, -GUES to proceed without pause from one musical theme to another

SEI   n pl. -S a rorqual

SEICENTO   n pl. -TOS the seventeenth century

SEICHE   n pl. -S an oscillation of the surface of a lake or landlocked sea

SEIDEL   n pl. -S a large beer glass

SEIF   n pl. -S a long, narrow sand dune

SEIGNEUR   n pl. -S seignior

SEIGNIOR   n pl. -S a feudal lord

SEIGNORY   n pl. -GNORIES the power of a seignior

SEINE   v SEINED, SEINING, SEINES to catch fish with a large, vertically hanging net

SEINER   n pl. -S one that seines

SEISE   v SEISED, SEISING, SEISES to seize **SEISABLE** adj

SEISER   n pl. -S seizer

SEISIN   n pl. -S seizin

SEISING   n pl. -S seizing

SEISM   n pl. -S an earthquake **SEISMAL, SEISMIC** adj

SEISMISM   n pl. -S the natural activity involved in earthquakes

SEISOR   n pl. -S seizor

SEISURE   n pl. -S seizure

SEIZE   v SEIZED, SEIZING, SEIZES to take hold of suddenly and forcibly **SEIZABLE** adj

SEIZER   n pl. -S one that seizes

SEIZIN   n pl. -S legal possession of land

SEIZING   n pl. -S the act of one that seizes

SEIZOR   n pl. -S one that takes seizin

SEIZURE   n pl. -S the act of seizing

SEJANT   adj represented in a sitting position — used of a heraldic animal

SEJEANT   adj sejant

SEL   n pl. -S self

SELADANG   n pl. -S saladang

SELAH   n pl. -S a word of unknown meaning often marking the end of a verse in the Psalms

SELAMLIK   n pl. -S the portion of a Turkish house reserved for men

SELCOUTH   adj unusual

SELDOM   adj infrequent **SELDOMLY** adv

SELECT   v -ED, -ING, -S to choose

SELECTEE   n pl. -S one that is selected

SELECTLY   adv by selection

SELECTOR   n pl. -S one that selects

SELENATE   n pl. -S a chemical salt

SELENIC   adj pertaining to selenium

SELENIDE   n pl. -S a compound of selenium

SELENITE   n pl. -S a variety of gypsum

SELENIUM   n pl. -S a nonmetallic element **SELENOUS** adj

SELF   n pl. SELVES the total, essential, or particular being of one person

SELF   v -ED, -ING, -S to inbreed

SELFDOM   n pl. -S selfhood

SELFHEAL   n pl. -S a perennial herb

SELFHOOD   n pl. -S the state of being an individual person

SELFISH   adj concerned chiefly or only with oneself

SELFLESS   adj unselfish

SELFNESS   n pl. -ES selfhood

SELFSAME   adj identical

SELFWARD   adv toward oneself

SELL   v SOLD, SELLING, SELLS to give up to another for money or other valuable consideration **SELLABLE** adj

SELLE   n pl. -S a saddle

SELLER   n pl. -S one that sells

SELLOUT   n pl. -S a performance for which all seats have been sold

SELSYN   n pl. -S a type of remote-control device

SELTZER   n pl. -S carbonated mineral water

SELVA   n pl. -S a tropical rain forest

SELVAGE   n pl. -S the edge of a woven fabric finished to prevent raveling **SELVAGED** adj

SELVEDGE n pl. -S selvage

SELVES pl. of self

SEMANTIC adj pertaining to meaning

SEMATIC adj serving as a warning

SEME n pl. -S a type of ornamental pattern

SEMEME n pl. -S the meaning of a morpheme SEMEMIC adj

SEMEN n pl. -MINA or -MENS a fluid produced in the male reproductive organs

SEMESTER n pl. -S a period constituting half of an academic year

SEMI n pl. -S a freight trailer

SEMIARID adj characterized by light rainfall

SEMIBALD adj partly bald

SEMICOMA n pl. -S a coma from which a person can be aroused

SEMIDEAF adj partly deaf

SEMIDOME n pl. -S a half dome

SEMIDRY adj moderately dry

SEMIFIT adj conforming somewhat to the lines of the body

SEMIGALA adj somewhat gala

SEMIHARD adj moderately hard

SEMIHIGH adj moderately high

SEMIHOBO n pl. -BOS or -BOES a person having some of the characteristics of a hobo

SEMILOG n pl. -S having one scale logarithmic and the other arithmetic

SEMIMAT adj having a slight luster

SEMIMATT adj semimat

SEMIMUTE adj having partially lost the faculty of speech

SEMINA a pl. of semen

SEMINAL adj pertaining to semen

SEMINAR n pl. -S an advanced study group at a college or university

SEMINARY n pl. -NARIES a school for the training of priests, ministers, or rabbis

SEMINUDE adj partly nude

SEMIOSIS n pl. -OSES a process in which something functions as a sign to an organism

SEMIOTIC n pl. -S a general theory of signs and symbolism

SEMIPRO n pl. -PROS one who is engaged in some field or sport for pay on a part-time basis

SEMIRAW adj somewhat raw

SEMIS n pl. -MISES a coin of ancient Rome

SEMISOFT adj moderately soft

SEMITIST n pl. -S one who favors Jewish interests

SEMITONE n pl. -S a type of musical tone

SEMIWILD adj somewhat wild

SEMOLINA n pl. -S a granular product of wheat used for pasta

SEMPLE adj of humble birth

SEMPLICE adj simple — used as a musical direction

SEMPRE adv in the same manner throughout — used as a musical direction

SEN n pl. SEN a monetary unit of Japan

SENARIUS n pl. -NARII a Greek or Latin verse consisting of six metrical feet

SENARY adj pertaining to the number six

SENATE n pl. -S an assembly having high deliberative and legislative functions

SENATOR n pl. -S a member of a senate

SEND v SENT, SENDING, SENDS to cause to go SENDABLE adj

SEND v -ED, -ING, -S to scend

SENDAL n pl. -S a silk fabric

SENDER n pl. -S one that sends

SENDOFF n pl. -S a farewell celebration

SENDUP n pl. -S a parody

SENE n pl. SENE a monetary unit of Western Samoa

SENECA n pl. -S a senega

SENECIO n pl. -CIOS a flowering plant

SENEGA n pl. -S a medicinal plant root

SENGI n pl. SENGI a monetary unit of Zaire

SENHOR n pl. -S or -ES a Portuguese or Brazilian gentleman

SENHORA n pl. -S a married Portuguese or Brazilian woman

SENILE n pl. -S one who exhibits senility

SENILELY adv in a senile manner

SENILITY n pl. -TIES mental and physical infirmity due to old age

SENIOR n pl. -S a person who is older than another

SENITI n pl. SENITI a monetary unit of Tonga

SENNA n pl. -S a medicinal plant

SENNET n pl. -S a call sounded on a trumpet signaling the entrance or exit of actors

SENNIGHT n pl. -S a week

SENNIT n pl. -S braided straw used in making hats

SENOPIA n pl. -S an improvement of near vision

SENOR n pl. -S or -ES a Spanish gentleman

SENORA n pl. -S a married Spanish woman

SENORITA n pl. -S an unmarried Spanish girl or woman

SENRYU n pl. SENRYU a Japanese poem

SENSA pl. of sensum

SENSATE v -SATED, -SATING, -SATES to sense

SENSE v SENSED, SENSING, SENSES to perceive by the senses (any of certain agencies through which an individual receives impressions of the external world)

SENSEFUL adj sensible

SENSIBLE adj -BLER, -BLEST having or showing good judgment SENSIBLY adv

SENSIBLE n pl. -S something that can be sensed

SENSILLA n pl. -LAE a simple sense organ

SENSING present participle of sense

SENSOR n pl. -S a device that receives and responds to a stimulus

SENSORIA n/pl the parts of the brain concerned with the reception and interpretation of sensory stimuli

SENSORY adj pertaining to the senses or sensation

SENSUAL adj pertaining to the physical senses

SENSUM n pl. -SA an object of perception or sensation

SENSUOUS adj pertaining to or derived from the senses

SENT past tense of send (to cause to go)

SENTE n pl. LICENTE or LISENTE a monetary unit of Lesotho

SENTENCE v -TENCED, -TENCING, -TENCES to declare judicially the extent of punishment to be imposed

SENTI n pl. SENTI a former monetary unit of Tanzania

SENTIENT n pl. -S a person or thing capable of sensation

SENTIMO n pl. -MOS a monetary unit of the Philippines

SENTINEL v -NELED, -NELING, -NELS or -NELLED, -NELLING, -NELS to stand guard

SENTRY n pl. -TRIES one who stands guard

SEPAL n pl. -S one of the individual leaves of a calyx SEPALED, SEPALINE, SEPALLED, SEPALOID, SEPALOUS adj

SEPARATE v -RATED, -RATING, -RATES to set or keep apart

SEPIA n pl. -S a brown pigment SEPIC adj

SEPOY n pl. -POYS a native of India serving in the British army

SEPPUKU n pl. -S a Japanese form of suicide

SEPSIS n pl. SEPSES bacterial invasion of the body

SEPT n pl. -S a clan

SEPTA pl. of septum

SEPTAL adj pertaining to a septum

SEPTARIA n/pl limestone nodules

SEPTATE adj having a septum

SEPTET n pl. -S a group of seven

SEPTETTE n pl. -S septet

SEPTIC n pl. -S an agent producing sepsis SEPTICAL adj

SEPTIME n pl. -S a position in fencing

SEPTUM n pl. -TA or -TUMS a dividing membrane or partition

SEPTUPLE v -PLED, -PLING, -PLES to make seven times as great

SEQUEL n pl. -S something that follows and serves as a continuation

SEQUELA n pl. -QUELAE an abnormal condition resulting from a preceding disease

SEQUENCE v -QUENCED, -QUENCING, -QUENCES to arrange in consecutive order

SEQUENCY n pl. -CIES the following of one thing after another

SEQUENT n pl. -S something that follows

SEQUIN n pl. -S a shiny ornamental disk SEQUINED adj

SEQUITUR n pl. -S the conclusion of an inference

SEQUOIA n pl. -S a large evergreen tree

SER n pl. -S a unit of weight of India

SERA a pl. of serum

SERAC *n pl.* -S a large mass of ice broken off of a glacier

SERAGLIO *n pl.* -GLIOS a harem

SERAI *n pl.* -S a Turkish palace

SERAIL *n pl.* -S a seraglio

SERAL *adj* pertaining to a series of ecological changes

SERAPE *n pl.* -S a colorful woolen shawl

SERAPH *n pl.* -APHS, -APHIM, or -APHIN a winged celestial being **SERAPHIC** *adj*

SERAPHIM *n pl.* -S seraph

SERDAB *n pl.* -S a chamber within an ancient Egyptian tomb

SERE *adj* SERER, SEREST withered; dry

SERE *v* SERED, SERING, SERES to sear

SEREIN *n pl.* -S a fine rain falling from an apparently clear sky

SERENADE *v* -NADED, -NADING, -NADES to perform an honorific evening song for

SERENATA *n pl.* -TAS or -TE a dramatic cantata

SERENE *adj* SERENER, SERENEST calm; tranquil **SERENELY** *adv*

SERENE *n pl.* -S a serene condition or expanse

SERENITY *n pl.* -TIES the state of being serene

SERER comparative of sere

SEREST superlative of sere

SERF *n pl.* -S a feudal slave

SERFAGE *n pl.* -S serfdom

SERFDOM *n pl.* -S the state of being a serf

SERFHOOD *n pl.* -S serfdom

SERFISH *adj* characteristic of a serf

SERFLIKE *adj* serfish

SERGE *n pl.* -S a twilled fabric

SERGEANT *n pl.* -S a noncommissioned military officer

SERGING *n pl.* -S a process of finishing the raw edges of a fabric

SERIAL *n pl.* -S a literary or dramatic work presented in successive installments

SERIALLY *adv* in the manner or form of a serial

SERIATE *v* -ATED, -ATING, -ATES to put into a series

SERIATIM *adv* serially

SERICIN *n pl.* -S a kind of protein

SERIEMA *n pl.* -S a Brazilian bird

SERIES *n pl.* SERIES an arrangement of one after another

SERIF *n pl.* -S a fine line used to finish off the main stroke of a letter **SERIFED, SERIFFED** *adj*

SERIN *n pl.* -S a European finch

SERINE *n pl.* -S an amino acid

SERING present participle of sere

SERINGA *n pl.* -S a Brazilian tree

SERIOUS *adj* thoughtful or subdued in appearance or manner

SERJEANT *n pl.* -S sergeant

SERMON *n pl.* -S a religious discourse **SERMONIC** *adj*

SEROLOGY *n pl.* -GIES the science of serums

SEROSA *n pl.* -SAS or -SAE a thin membrane lining certain bodily cavities **SEROSAL** *adj*

SEROSITY *n pl.* -TIES the quality or state of being serous

SEROTINE *n pl.* -S a European bat

SEROTYPE *n pl.* -S a group of closely related organisms distinguished by a common set of antigens

SEROUS *adj* of or resembling serum

SEROW *n pl.* -S an Asian antelope

SERPENT *n pl.* -S a snake

SERPIGO *n pl.* -GOES or -GINES a spreading skin eruption

SERRANID *n pl.* -S a marine fish

SERRANO *n pl.* -NOS a small hot pepper

SERRATE *v* -RATED, -RATING, -RATES to furnish with toothlike projections

SERRY *v* -RIED, -RYING, -RIES to crowd together

SERUM *n pl.* -RUMS or -RA the watery portion of whole blood **SERUMAL** *adj*

SERVABLE *adj* capable of serving or being served

SERVAL *n pl.* -S an African wildcat

SERVANT *n pl.* -S one that serves others

SERVE *v* SERVED, SERVING, SERVES to work for

SERVER *n pl.* -S one that serves another

SERVICE *v* -VICED, -VICING, -VICES to repair

SERVICER *n pl.* -S one that services

SERVILE *adj* slavishly submissive

SERVING *n pl.* -S a portion of food

SERVITOR *n pl.* -S a male servant

SERVO n pl. -VOS an automatic device used to control another mechanism

SESAME n pl. -S an East Indian plant

SESAMOID n pl. -S a nodular mass of bone or cartilage
adj permanently attached

SESSILE adj permanently attached

SESSION n pl. -S a meeting of a legislative or judicial body for the transaction of business

SESSPOOL n pl. -S cesspool

SESTERCE n pl. -S a coin of ancient Rome

SESTET n pl. -S a stanza of six lines

SESTINA n pl. -S a type of verse form

SESTINE n pl. -S sestina

SET v SET, SETTING, SETS to put in a particular position

SETA n pl. -TAE a coarse, stiff hair
SETAL adj

SETBACK n pl. -S a defeat

SETENANT n pl. -S a postage stamp that differs in design from others in the same sheet

SETIFORM adj having the form of a seta

SETLINE n pl. -S a strong fishing line

SETOFF n pl. -S something that offsets something else

SETON n pl. -S a type of surgical thread

SETOSE adj covered with setae

SETOUS adj setose

SETOUT n pl. -S a display

SETSCREW n pl. -S a type of screw

SETT n pl. -S the burrow of a badger

SETTEE n pl. -S a long seat with a high back

SETTER n pl. -S one that sets

SETTING n pl. -S the scenery used in a dramatic production

SETTLE v -TLED, -TLING, -TLES to place in a desired state or order

SETTLER n pl. -S one that settles

SETTLING n pl. -S sediment

SETTLOR n pl. -S one that makes a legal settlement

SETULOSE adj covered with seta

SETULOUS adj setulose

SETUP n pl. -S the way something is arranged

SEVEN n pl. -S a number

SEVENTH n pl. -S one of seven equal parts

SEVENTY n pl. -TIES a number

SEVER v -ED, -ING, -S to divide or cut into parts

SEVERAL n pl. -S a few persons or things

SEVERE adj -VERER, -VEREST unsparing in the treatment of others **SEVERELY** adv

SEVERITY n pl. -TIES the quality or state of being severe

SEVICHE n pl. -S a dish of raw fish

SEW v SEWED, SEWN, SEWING, SEWS to mend or fasten with a needle and thread
SEWABLE adj

SEWAGE n pl. -S the waste matter carried off by sewers

SEWAN n pl. -S seawan

SEWAR n pl. -S a medieval servant

SEWER v -ED, -ING, -S to clean or maintain sewers (underground conduits for waste)

SEWERAGE n pl. -S sewage

SEWING n pl. -S material that has been or is to be sewed

SEWN a past participle of sew

SEX v -ED, -ING, -ES to determine the sex (the property by which organisms are classified according to reproductive functions) of

SEXIER comparative of sexy

SEXIEST superlative of sexy

SEXILY adv in a sexy manner

SEXINESS n pl. -ES the quality or state of being sexy

SEXISM n pl. -S prejudice or discrimination against women

SEXIST n pl. -S one that practices sexism

SEXLESS adj lacking sexual characteristics

SEXOLOGY n pl. -GIES the study of human sexual behavior

SEXPOT n pl. -S a sexually attractive woman

SEXT n pl. -S one of seven canonical daily periods for prayer and devotion

SEXTAIN n pl. -S a stanza of six lines

SEXTAN n pl. -S a recurrent malarial fever

SEXTANT n pl. -S an instrument for measuring angular distances

SEXTARII n/pl ancient Roman units of liquid measure

SEXTET n pl. -S a group of six

SEXTETTE n pl. -S sextet

SEXTILE n pl. -S the position of two celestial bodies when they are sixty degrees apart

SEXTO n pl. -TOS sixmo

SEXTON n pl. -S a maintenance worker of a church

SEXTUPLE v -PLED, -PLING, -PLES to make six times as great

SEXTUPLY adv to six times as much or as many

SEXUAL adj pertaining to sex **SEXUALLY** adv

SEXY adj SEXIER, SEXIEST arousing sexual desire

SFERICS n/pl an electronic detector of storms

SFORZATO n pl. -TOS the playing of a tone or chord with sudden force

SFUMATO n pl. -TOS a technique used in painting

SH interj — used to urge silence

SHA interj — used to urge silence

SHABBY adj -BIER, -BIEST ragged **SHABBILY** adv

SHACK n pl. -S a shanty

SHACKLE v -LED, -LING, -LES to confine with metal fastenings placed around the wrists or ankles

SHACKLER n pl. -S one that shackles

SHACKO n pl. -KOS or -KOES shako

SHAD n pl. -S a food fish

SHADBLOW n pl. -S a shadbush

SHADBUSH n pl. -ES a flowering tree or shrub

SHADCHAN n pl. -CHANIM or -CHANS a Jewish marriage broker

SHADDOCK n pl. -S a citrus fruit

SHADE v SHADED, SHADING, SHADES to screen from light or heat

SHADER n pl. -S one that shades

SHADFLY n pl. -FLIES a winged insect

SHADIER comparative of shady

SHADIEST superlative of shady

SHADILY adv in a shady manner

SHADING n pl. -S protection against light or heat

SHADOOF n pl. -S a device used in Egypt for raising water for irrigation

SHADOW v -ED, -ING, -S to make dark or gloomy

SHADOWER n pl. -S one that shadows

SHADOWY adj -OWIER, -OWIEST dark

SHADRACH n pl. -S a mass of unfused material in the hearth of a blast furnace

SHADUF n pl. -S shadoof

SHADY adj SHADIER, SHADIEST shaded

SHAFT v -ED, -ING, -S to push or propel with a pole

SHAFTING n pl. -S a system of rods for transmitting motion or power

SHAG v SHAGGED, SHAGGING, SHAGS to make shaggy

SHAGBARK n pl. -S a hardwood tree

SHAGGY adj -GIER, -GIEST covered with long, coarse hair **SHAGGILY** adv

SHAGREEN n pl. -S the rough skin of certain sharks

SHAH n pl. -S an Iranian ruler

SHAHDOM n pl. -S the territory ruled by a shah

SHAIRD n pl. -S shard

SHAIRN n pl. -S sharn

SHAITAN n pl. -S an evil spirit

SHAKE v SHOOK, SHAKEN, SHAKING, SHAKES to move to and fro with short, rapid movements **SHAKABLE** adj

SHAKEOUT n pl. -S a minor economic recession

SHAKER n pl. -S one that shakes

SHAKEUP n pl. -S a total reorganization

SHAKIER comparative of shaky

SHAKIEST superlative of shaky

SHAKILY adv in a shaky manner

SHAKING present participle of shake

SHAKO n pl. -KOS or -KOES a type of military hat

SHAKY adj SHAKIER, SHAKIEST shaking

SHALE n pl. -S a fissile rock

SHALED adj having a shell or husk

SHALEY adj SHALIER, SHALIEST shaly

SHALIER comparative of shaly

SHALIEST superlative of shaly

SHALL v present sing. 2d person SHALL or SHALT, past sing. 2d person SHOULD, SHOULDST, or SHOULDEST — used as an auxiliary to express futurity, inevitability, or command

SHALLOON n pl. -S a woolen fabric

SHALLOP n pl. -S a small, open boat

SHALLOT   *n* pl. -S a plant resembling an onion

SHALLOW   *adj* -LOWER, -LOWEST having little depth

SHALLOW   *v* -ED, -ING, -S to make shallow

SHALOM   *n* pl. -S a word used as a Jewish greeting or farewell

SHALT   a present 2d person sing. of shall

SHALY   *adj* SHALIER, SHALIEST resembling shale

SHAM   *v* SHAMMED, SHAMMING, SHAMS to feign

SHAMABLE   *adj* capable of being shamed

SHAMAN   *n* pl. -S a medicine man among certain North American Indians SHAMANIC *adj*

SHAMAS   *n* pl. -MOSIM shammes

SHAMBLE   *v* -BLED, -BLING, -BLES to walk awkwardly

SHAME   *v* SHAMED, SHAMING, SHAMES to cause to feel a painful sense of guilt or degradation

SHAMEFUL   *adj* disgraceful

SHAMES   *n* pl. -MOSIM shammes

SHAMING   present participle of shame

SHAMMAS   *n* pl. -MASIM shammes

SHAMMASH   *n* pl. -MASHIM shammes

SHAMMED   past tense of sham

SHAMMER   *n* pl. -S one that shams

SHAMMES   *n* pl. -MOSIM a minor official of a synagogue

SHAMMIED   past tense of shammy

SHAMMIES   present 3d person sing. of shammy

SHAMMING   present participle of sham

SHAMMOS   *n* pl. -MOSIM shammes

SHAMMOSIM   pl. of shammes

SHAMMY   *v* -MIED, -MYING, -MIES to chamois

SHAMOIS   *n* pl. SHAMOIS chamois

SHAMOS   *n* pl. -MOSIM shammes

SHAMOSIM   pl. of shames

SHAMOY   *v* -ED, -ING, -S to chamois

SHAMPOO   *v* -ED, -ING, -S to cleanse with a special preparation

SHAMROCK   *n* pl. -S a three-leaved plant

SHAMUS   *n* pl. -ES a private detective

SHANDY   *n* pl. -DIES an alcoholic drink

SHANGHAI   *v* -ED, -ING, -S to kidnap for service aboard a ship

SHANK   *v* -ED, -ING, -S to hit sharply to the right, as a golf ball

SHANNY   *n* pl. -NIES a marine fish

SHANTEY   *n* pl. -TEYS chantey

SHANTI   *n* pl. -S peace

SHANTIES   pl. of shanty

SHANTIH   *n* pl. -S shanti

SHANTUNG   *n* pl. -S a silk fabric

SHANTY   *n* pl. -TIES a small, crudely built dwelling

SHAPE   *v* SHAPED, SHAPEN, SHAPING, SHAPES to give shape (outward form) to SHAPABLE *adj*

SHAPELY   *adj* -LIER, -LIEST having a pleasing shape

SHAPER   *n* pl. -S one that shapes

SHAPEUP   *n* pl. -S a system of hiring a work crew

SHAPING   present participle of shape

SHARD   *n* pl. -S a fragment of broken pottery

SHARE   *v* SHARED, SHARING, SHARES to have, get, or use in common with another or others SHARABLE *adj*

SHARER   *n* pl. -S one that shares

SHARIF   *n* pl. -S sherif

SHARING   present participle of share

SHARK   *v* -ED, -ING, -S to live by trickery

SHARKER   *n* pl. -S one that sharks

SHARN   *n* pl. -S cow dung SHARNY *adj*

SHARP   *adj* SHARPER, SHARPEST suitable for or capable of cutting or piercing

SHARP   *v* -ED, -ING, -S to raise in pitch, as a musical tone

SHARPEN   *v* -ED, -ING, -S to make sharp

SHARPER   *n* pl. -S a swindler

SHARPIE   *n* pl. -S a very alert person

SHARPLY   *adv* in a sharp manner

SHARPY   *n* pl. SHARPIES sharpie

SHASHLIK   *n* pl. -S kabob

SHASLIK   *n* pl. -S shashlik

SHATTER   *v* -ED, -ING, -S to break into pieces

SHAUGH   *n* pl. -S a thicket

SHAUL   *v* -ED, -ING, -S to shoal

SHAVE   *v* SHAVED, SHAVEN, SHAVING, SHAVES to sever the hair close to the roots SHAVABLE *adj*

SHAVER   *n* pl. -S one that shaves

SHAVIE   *n* pl. -S a trick or prank

SHAVING   *n* pl. -S something shaved off

SHAW   *v* SHAWED, SHAWN, SHAWING, SHAWS to show

SHAWL *v* -ED, -ING, -S to wrap in a shawl (a piece of cloth worn as a covering)

SHAWM *n pl.* -S an early woodwind instrument

SHAWN past participle of shaw

SHAY *n pl.* SHAYS a chaise

SHE *n pl.* -S a female person

SHEA *n pl.* -S an African tree

SHEAF *v* -ED, -ING, -S to sheave

SHEAL *n pl.* -S shealing

SHEALING *n pl.* -S a shepherd's hut

SHEAR *v* SHEARED or SHORE, SHORN, SHEARING, SHEARS to cut the hair or wool from

SHEARER *n pl.* -S one that shears

SHEARING *n pl.* -S an instance of cutting hair or wool

SHEATH *v* -ED, -ING, -S to sheathe

SHEATHE *v* SHEATHED, SHEATHING, SHEATHES to put into a protective case

SHEATHER *n pl.* -S one that sheathes

SHEAVE *v* SHEAVED, SHEAVING, SHEAVES to gather into a bundle

SHEBANG *n pl.* -S a situation, organization, or matter

SHEBEAN *n pl.* -S shebeen

SHEBEEN *n pl.* -S a place where liquor is sold illegally

SHED *v* SHEDDED, SHEDDING, SHEDS to house in a shed (a small, low structure)

SHEDABLE *adj* capable of being cast off

SHEDDER *n pl.* -S one that casts off something

SHEDDING present participle of shed

SHEDLIKE *adj* resembling a shed

SHEEN *v* -ED, -ING, -S to shine

SHEENFUL *adj* shining

SHEENY *adj* SHEENIER, SHEENIEST shining

SHEEP *n pl.* SHEEP a ruminant mammal

SHEEPCOT *n pl.* -S an enclosure for sheep

SHEEPDOG *n pl.* -S a dog trained to guard and herd sheep

SHEEPISH *adj* embarrassed

SHEEPMAN *n pl.* -MEN a person who raises sheep

SHEER *v* -ED, -ING, -S to swerve

SHEER *adj* SHEERER, SHEEREST of very thin texture **SHEERLY** *adv*

SHEET *v* -ED, -ING, -S to cover with a sheet (a thin, rectangular piece of material)

SHEETER *n pl.* -S one that sheets

SHEETFED *adj* pertaining to a type of printing press

SHEETING *n pl.* -S material in the form of sheets

SHEEVE *n pl.* -S a grooved pulley wheel

SHEIK *n pl.* -S an Arab chief

SHEIKDOM *n pl.* -S the area ruled by a sheik

SHEIKH *n pl.* -S sheik

SHEILA *n pl.* -S a young woman

SHEITAN *n pl.* -S shaitan

SHEKEL *n pl.* -S an ancient unit of weight and money

SHELDUCK *n pl.* -S a European duck

SHELF *n pl.* SHELVES a flat rigid structure used to support articles

SHELFFUL *n pl.* -S as much as a shelf can hold

SHELL *v* -ED, -ING, -S to divest of a shell (a hard outer covering)

SHELLAC *v* -LACKED, -LACKING, -LACS to cover with a thin varnish

SHELLACK *v* -ED, -ING, -S to shellac

SHELLER *n pl.* -S one that shells

SHELLY *adj* SHELLIER, SHELLIEST abounding in seashells

SHELTA *n pl.* -S an esoteric jargon of Gaelic

SHELTER *v* -ED, -ING, -S to provide cover or protection for

SHELTIE *n pl.* -S a small, shaggy pony

SHELTY *n pl.* -TIES sheltie

SHELVE *v* SHELVED, SHELVING, SHELVES to place on a shelf

SHELVER *n pl.* -S one that shelves

SHELVES *pl.* of shelf

SHELVING *n pl.* -S material for shelves

SHELVY *adj* SHELVIER, SHELVIEST inclining gradually

SHEND *v* SHENT, SHENDING, SHENDS to disgrace

SHEOL *n pl.* -S hell

SHEPHERD *v* -ED, -ING, -S to watch over carefully

SHEQEL *n pl.* SHEQALIM shekel

SHERBERT *n pl.* -S sherbet

SHERBET *n* pl. -S a frozen fruit-flavored mixture

SHERD *n* pl. -S shard

SHEREEF *n* pl. -S sherif

SHERIF *n* pl. -S an Arab ruler

SHERIFF *n* pl. -S a law-enforcement officer of a county

SHERLOCK *n* pl. -S a detective

SHEROOT *n* pl. -S cheroot

SHERPA *n* pl. -S a soft fabric for linings

SHERRIS *n* pl. -RISES sherry

SHERRY *n* pl. -RIES a type of wine

SHETLAND *n* pl. -S a wool yarn

SHEUCH *n* pl. -S sheugh

SHEUGH *n* pl. -S a ditch

SHEW *v* SHEWED, SHEWN, SHEWING, SHEWS to show

SHEWER *n* pl. -S one that shews

SHH *interj* sh

SHIATSU *n* pl. -S a massage using finger pressure

SHIATZU *n* pl. -S shiatsu

SHIBAH *n* pl. -S shiva

SHICKER *n* pl. -S a drunkard

SHIED past tense of shy

SHIEL *n* pl. -S shieling

SHIELD *v* -ED, -ING, -S to provide with a protective cover or shelter

SHIELDER *n* pl. -S one that shields

SHIELING *n* pl. -S shealing

SHIER *n* pl. -S a horse having a tendency to shy

SHIES present 3d person sing. of shy

SHIEST a superlative of shy

SHIFT *v* -ED, -ING, -S to move from one position to another

SHIFTER *n* pl. -S one that shifts

SHIFTY *adj* SHIFTIER, SHIFTIEST tricky SHIFTILY *adv*

SHIGELLA *n* pl. -LAE or -LAS any of a genus of aerobic bacteria

SHIITAKE *n* pl. -S a dark Oriental mushroom

SHIKAR *v* -KARRED, -KARRING, -KARS to hunt

SHIKAREE *n* pl. -S a big game hunter

SHIKARI *n* pl. -S shikaree

SHIKARRED past tense of shikar

SHIKARRING present participle of shikar

SHIKKER *n* pl. -S shicker

SHILINGI *n* pl. SHILINGI a monetary unit of Tanzania

SHILL *v* -ED, -ING, -S to act as a decoy

SHILLALA *n* pl. -S a short, thick club

SHILLING *n* pl. -S a former monetary unit of Great Britain

SHILPIT *adj* sickly

SHILY *adv* in a shy manner

SHIM *v* SHIMMED, SHIMMING, SHIMS to fill out or level by inserting a thin wedge

SHIMMER *v* -ED, -ING, -S to glimmer

SHIMMERY *adj* shimmering

SHIMMING present participle of shim

SHIMMY *v* -MIED, -MYING, -MIES to vibrate or wobble

SHIN *v* SHINNED, SHINNING, SHINS to climb by gripping and pulling alternately with the hands and legs

SHINBONE *n* pl. -S the tibia

SHINDIG *n* pl. -S an elaborate dance or party

SHINDY *n* pl. -DYS or -DIES a shindig

SHINE *v* SHONE or SHINED, SHINING, SHINES to emit light

SHINER *n* pl. -S one that shines

SHINGLE *v* -GLED, -GLING, -GLES to cover with shingles (thin, oblong pieces of building material)

SHINGLER *n* pl. -S one that shingles

SHINGLY *adj* covered with small, loose stones

SHINIER comparative of shiny

SHINIEST superlative of shiny

SHINILY *adv* in a shiny manner

SHINING *adj* emitting or reflecting light

SHINLEAF *n* pl. -LEAFS or -LEAVES a perennial herb

SHINNED past of shin

SHINNERY *n* pl. -NERIES a dense growth of small trees

SHINNEY *v* -ED, -ING, -S to play a form of hockey

SHINNING present participle of shin

SHINNY *v* -NIED, -NYING, -NIES to shin

SHINY *adj* SHINIER, SHINIEST filled with light

SHIP *v* SHIPPED, SHIPPING, SHIPS to transport by ship (a vessel suitable for navigation in deep water)

SHIPLAP *n* pl. -S an overlapping joint used in carpentry

SHIPLOAD *n* pl. -S as much as a ship can carry

SHIPMAN *n* pl. -MEN a sailor

SHIPMATE *n* pl. -S a fellow sailor

SHIPMENT n pl. -S something that is shipped

SHIPPED past tense of ship

SHIPPEN n pl. -S a cowshed

SHIPPER n pl. -S one that ships

SHIPPING n pl. -S the business of one that ships

SHIPPON n pl. -S shippen

SHIPSIDE n pl. -S the area alongside a ship

SHIPWAY n pl. -WAYS a canal deep enough to serve ships

SHIPWORM n pl. -S a wormlike mollusk

SHIPYARD n pl. -S a place where ships are built or repaired

SHIRE n pl. -S a territorial division of Great Britain

SHIRK v -ED, -ING, -S to avoid work or duty

SHIRKER n pl. -S one that shirks

SHIRR v -ED, -ING, -S to draw into three or more parallel rows, as cloth

SHIRRING n pl. -S a shirred arrangement of cloth

SHIRT n pl. -S a garment for the upper part of the body

SHIRTING n pl. -S fabric used for making shirts

SHIRTY adj SHIRTIER, SHIRTIEST angry

SHIST n pl. -S schist

SHITAKE n pl. -S shiitake

SHITTAH n pl. -S a hardwood tree

SHITTIM n pl. -S the wood of the shittah

SHIV n pl. -S a knife

SHIVA n pl. -S a period of mourning

SHIVAH n pl. -S shiva

SHIVAREE v -REED, -REEING, -REES to chivaree

SHIVE n pl. -S a thin fragment

SHIVER v -ED, -ING, -S to tremble with fear or cold

SHIVERER n pl. -S one that shivers

SHIVERY adj shivering

SHLEMIEL n pl. -S an unlucky bungler

SHLEP v SHLEPPED, SHLEPPING, SHLEPS to schlep

SHLEPP v -ED, -ING, -S to schlep

SHLOCK n pl. -S schlock

SHLUMP v -ED, -ING, -S to schlump

SHLUMPY adj slovenly

SHMALTZ n pl. -ES schmaltz

SHMALTZY adj SHMALTZIER, SHMALTZIEST schmalzy

SHMEAR n pl. -S schmear

SHMO n pl. SHMOES schmo

SHMOOZE v SHMOOZED, SHMOOZING, SHMOOZES to schmooze

SHMUCK n pl. -S schmuck

SHNAPS n pl. SHNAPS schnapps

SHNOOK n pl. -S schnook

SHOAL adj SHOALER, SHOALEST shallow

SHOAL v -ED, -ING, -S to become shallow

SHOALY adj SHOALIER, SHOALIEST full of shallow areas

SHOAT n pl. -S a young hog

SHOCK v -ED, -ING, -S to strike with great surprise, horror, or disgust

SHOCKER n pl. -S one that shocks

SHOD a past tense of shoe

SHODDEN a past participle of shoe

SHODDY adj -DIER, -DIEST of inferior quality SHODDILY adv

SHODDY n pl. -DIES a low-quality wool

SHOE n pl. SHOES or SHOON a covering for the foot

SHOE v SHOD or SHOED, SHODDEN, SHOEING, SHOES to provide with shoes

SHOEBILL n pl. -S a wading bird

SHOEHORN v -ED, -ING, -S to force into a small space

SHOELACE n pl. -S a lace for fastening a shoe

SHOELESS adj having no shoe

SHOEPAC n pl. -S a waterproof boot

SHOEPACK n pl. -S shoepac

SHOER n pl. -S one that shoes horses

SHOETREE n pl. -S a device shaped like a foot that is inserted into a shoe to preserve its shape

SHOFAR n pl. SHOFARS or SHOFROTH a ram's-horn trumpet blown in certain Jewish rituals

SHOG v SHOGGED, SHOGGING, SHOGS to move along

SHOGUN n pl. -S a former military leader of Japan SHOGUNAL adj

SHOJI n pl. -S a paper screen used as a partition or door in a Japanese house

SHOLOM n pl. -S shalom

SHONE a past tense of shine

SHOO v -ED, -ING, -S to drive away

SHOOFLY n pl. -FLIES a child's rocker

SHOOK n pl. -S a set of parts for assembling a barrel or packing

SHOOL v -ED, -ING, -S to shovel

SHOON a pl. of shoe

SHOOT v SHOT, SHOOTING, SHOOTS to hit, wound, or kill with a missile discharged from a weapon

SHOOTER n pl. -S one that shoots

SHOOTING n pl. -S the act of one that shoots

SHOOTOUT n pl. -S a battle fought with handguns or rifles

SHOP v SHOPPED, SHOPPING, SHOPS to examine goods with intent to buy

SHOPBOY n pl. -BOYS a salesclerk

SHOPGIRL n pl. -S a salesgirl

SHOPHAR n pl. -PHARS or -PHROTH shofar

SHOPLIFT v -ED, -ING, -S to steal goods from a store

SHOPMAN n pl. -MEN one who owns or operates a small store

SHOPPE n pl. -S a small store

SHOPPED past tense of shop

SHOPPER n pl. -S one that shops

SHOPPING n pl. -S the act of one that shops

SHOPTALK n pl. -S conversation concerning one's business or occupation

SHOPWORN adj worn out from being on display in a store

SHORAN n pl. -S a type of navigational system

SHORE v SHORED, SHORING, SHORES to prop with a supporting timber

SHORING n pl. -S a system of supporting timbers

SHORL n pl. -S schorl

SHORN a past participle of shear

SHORT adj SHORTER, SHORTEST having little length

SHORT v -ED, -ING, -S to cause a type of electrical malfunction in

SHORTAGE n pl. -S an insufficient supply or amount

SHORTCUT v -CUT, -CUTTING, -CUTS to take a shorter or quicker way

SHORTEN v -ED, -ING, -S to make or become shorter

SHORTIA n pl. -S a perennial herb

SHORTIE n pl. -S shorty

SHORTIES pl. of shorty

SHORTISH adj somewhat short

SHORTLY adv in a short time

SHORTY n pl. SHORTIES one that is short

SHOT v SHOTTED, SHOTTING, SHOTS to load with shot (small lead or steel pellets)

SHOTE n pl. -S shoat

SHOTGUN v -GUNNED, -GUNNING, -GUNS to shoot with a type of gun

SHOTT n pl. -S chott

SHOTTED past tense of shot

SHOTTEN adj having spawned — used of a fish

SHOTTING present participle of shot

SHOULD past tense of shall

SHOULDER v -ED, -ING, -S to assume the burden or responsibility of

SHOULDEST a 2d person sing. past tense of shall

SHOULDST a 2d person sing. past tense of shall

SHOUT v -ED, -ING, -S to utter loudly

SHOUTER n pl. -S one that shouts

SHOVE v SHOVED, SHOVING, SHOVES to push roughly

SHOVEL v -ELED, -ELING, -ELS or -ELLED, -ELLING, -ELS to take up with a shovel (a digging implement)

SHOVELER n pl. -S one that shovels

SHOVER n pl. -S one that shoves

SHOVING present participle of shove

SHOW v SHOWED, SHOWN, SHOWING, SHOWS to cause or permit to be seen **SHOWABLE** adj

SHOWBIZ n pl. -BIZZES show business

SHOWBOAT v -ED, -ING, -S to show off

SHOWCASE v -CASED, -CASING, -CASES to exhibit

SHOWDOWN n pl. -S an event that forces the conclusion of an issue

SHOWER v -ED, -ING, -S to bathe in a spray of water

SHOWERER n pl. -S one that showers

SHOWERY adj abounding with brief periods of rain

SHOWGIRL n pl. -S a chorus girl

SHOWIER comparative of showy

SHOWIEST superlative of showy

SHOWILY adv in a showy manner

SHOWING n pl. -S an exhibition or display

SHOWMAN n pl. -MEN a theatrical producer

SHOWN past participle of show

SHOWOFF n pl. -S one given to pretentious display

SHOWRING n pl. -S a ring where animals are displayed

SHOWROOM n pl. -S a room used for the display of merchandise

SHOWY adj SHOWIER, SHOWIEST making a great or brilliant display

SHOYU n pl. -S soy sauce

SHRANK past tense of shrink

SHRAPNEL n pl. SHRAPNEL fragments from an exploding bomb, mine, or shell

SHRED v SHREDDED, SHREDDING, SHREDS to tear into small strips

SHREDDER n pl. -S one that shreds

SHREW v -ED, -ING, -S to curse

SHREWD adj SHREWDER, SHREWDEST having keen insight SHREWDLY adv

SHREWDIE n pl. -S a shrewd person

SHREWISH adj ill-tempered

SHRI n pl. -S sri

SHRIEK v -ED, -ING, -S to utter a shrill cry

SHRIEKER n pl. -S one that shrieks

SHRIEKY adj SHRIEKIER, SHRIEKIEST shrill

SHRIEVAL adj pertaining to a sheriff

SHRIEVE v SHRIEVED, SHRIEVING, SHRIEVES to shrive

SHRIFT n pl. -S the act of shriving

SHRIKE n pl. -S a predatory bird

SHRILL adj SHRILLER, SHRILLEST having a high-pitched and piercing quality SHRILLY adv

SHRILL v -ED, -ING, -S to utter a shrill sound

SHRIMP v -ED, -ING, -S to catch shrimps (small marine decapods)

SHRIMPER n pl. -S a shrimp fisher

SHRIMPY adj SHRIMPIER, SHRIMPIEST abounding in shrimp

SHRINE v SHRINED, SHRINING, SHRINES to place in a shrine (a receptacle for sacred relics)

SHRINK v SHRANK, SHRUNK or SHRUNKEN, SHRINKING, SHRINKS to contract or draw back

SHRINKER n pl. -S one that shrinks

SHRIVE v SHROVE or SHRIVED, SHRIVEN, SHRIVING, SHRIVES to hear the confession of and grant absolution to

SHRIVEL v -ELED, -ELING, -ELS or -ELLED, -ELLING, -ELS to contract into wrinkles

SHRIVER n pl. -S one that shrives

SHRIVING present participle of shrive

SHROFF v -ED, -ING, -S to test the genuineness of, as a coin

SHROUD v -ED, -ING, -S to wrap in burial clothing

SHROVE a past tense of shrive

SHRUB n pl. -S a low, woody plant

SHRUBBY adj -BIER, -BIEST covered with shrubs

SHRUG v SHRUGGED, SHRUGGING, SHRUGS to raise and contract the shoulders

SHRUNK a past tense of shrink

SHRUNKEN a past participle of shrink

SHTETEL n pl. SHTETLACH or SHTETELS a Jewish village

SHTETL n pl. SHTETLACH or SHTETLS shtetel

SHTICK n pl. -S an entertainment routine

SHTIK n pl. -S shtick

SHUCK v -ED, -ING, -S to remove the husk or shell from

SHUCKER n pl. -S one that shucks

SHUCKING n pl. -S the act of one that shucks

SHUDDER v -ED, -ING, -S to tremble

SHUDDERY adj shuddering

SHUFFLE v -FLED, -FLING, -FLES to walk without lifting the feet

SHUFFLER n pl. -S one that shuffles

SHUL n pl. SHULN or SHULS a synagogue

SHUN v SHUNNED, SHUNNING, SHUNS to avoid

SHUNNER n pl. -S one that shuns

SHUNPIKE v -PIKED, -PIKING, -PIKES to travel on side roads to avoid expressways

SHUNT v -ED, -ING, -S to turn aside

SHUNTER n pl. -S one that shunts

SHUSH v -ED, -ING, -ES to silence

SHUT   *v* SHUT, SHUTTING, SHUTS to close

SHUTDOWN   *n* pl. -S a temporary closing of an industrial plant

SHUTE   *v* SHUTED, SHUTING, SHUTES to chute

SHUTEYE   *n* pl. -S sleep

SHUTOFF   *n* pl. -S a device that shuts something off

SHUTOUT   *n* pl. -S a game in which one team fails to score

SHUTTER   *v* -ED, -ING, -S to provide with shutters (hinged window covers)

SHUTTING   present participle of shut

SHUTTLE   *v* -TLED, -TLING, -TLES to move or travel back and forth

SHWANPAN   *n* pl. -S swanpan

SHY   *adj* SHIER, SHIEST or SHYER, SHYEST timid

SHY   *v* SHIED, SHYING, SHIES to move suddenly back or aside, as in fear

SHYER   *n* pl. -S shier

SHYLOCK   *v* -ED, -ING, -S to lend money at high interest rates

SHYLY   *adv* in a shy manner

SHYNESS   *n* pl. -ES the state of being shy

SHYSTER   *n* pl. -S an unscrupulous lawyer or politician

SI   *n* pl. -S ti

SIAL   *n* pl. -S a type of rock formation SIALIC *adj*

SIALID   *n* pl. -S an alderfly

SIALIDAN   *n* pl. -S sialid

SIALOID   *adj* resembling saliva

SIAMANG   *n* pl. -S a large, black gibbon

SIAMESE   *n* pl. -S a water pipe with a connection for two hoses

SIB   *n* pl. -S a sibling

SIBB   *n* pl. -S sib

SIBILANT   *n* pl. -S a speech sound produced by the fricative passage of breath through a narrow orifice

SIBILATE   *v* -LATED, -LATING, -LATES to hiss

SIBLING   *n* pl. -S one having the same parents as another

SIBYL   *n* pl. -S a female prophet SIBYLIC, SIBYLLIC *adj*

SIC   *v* SICCED, SICCING, SICS to urge to attack

SICCAN   *adj* such

SICE   *n* pl. -S syce

SICK   *adj* SICKER, SICKEST affected with disease or ill health

SICK   *v* -ED, -ING, -S to sic

SICKBAY   *n* pl. -BAYS a ship's hospital

SICKBED   *n* pl. -S a sick person's bed

SICKEE   *n* pl. -S sickie

SICKEN   *v* -ED, -ING, -S to make sick

SICKENER   *n* pl. -S one that sickens

SICKERLY   *adv* securely

SICKIE   *n* pl. -S an emotionally sick person

SICKISH   *adj* somewhat sick

SICKLE   *v* -LED, -LING, -LES to cut with an agricultural implement having a single blade

SICKLY   *adj* -LIER, -LIEST appearing as if sick SICKLILY *adv*

SICKLY   *v* -LIED, -LYING, -LIES to make sickly

SICKNESS   *n* pl. -ES the state of being sick

SICKO   *n* pl. SICKOS sickie

SICKOUT   *n* pl. -S an organized absence of workers claiming to be sick

SICKROOM   *n* pl. -S a room occupied by a sick person

SIDDUR   *n* pl. -DURIM or -DURS a Jewish prayer book

SIDE   *v* SIDED, SIDING, SIDES to agree with or support

SIDEARM   *adj* thrown with a sideways sweep of the arm

SIDEBAND   *n* pl. -S a band of radio frequencies

SIDEBAR   *n* pl. -S a short news story accompanying a major story

SIDECAR   *n* pl. -S a passenger car attached to a motorcycle

SIDED   past tense of side

SIDEHILL   *n* pl. -S a hillside

SIDEKICK   *n* pl. -S a close friend

SIDELINE   *v* -LINED, -LINING, -LINES to put out of action

SIDELING   *adj* sloping

SIDELONG   *adj* directed to one side

SIDEMAN   *n* pl. -MEN a member of a jazz band

SIDEREAL   *adj* pertaining to the stars

SIDERITE   *n* pl. -S a mineral

SIDESHOW   *n* pl. -S a small show offered in addition to a main attraction

SIDESLIP   *v* -SLIPPED, -SLIPPING, -SLIPS to slip to one side

SIDESPIN   *n* pl. -S a type of spin imparted to a ball

SIDESTEP *v* -STEPPED, -STEPPING, -STEPS to step to one side

SIDEWALK *n pl.* -S a paved walk for pedestrians

SIDEWALL *n pl.* -S a side surface of a tire

SIDEWARD *adv* toward one side

SIDEWAY *adv* sideways

SIDEWAYS *adv* toward or from one side

SIDEWISE *adv* sideways

SIDING *n pl.* -S material used for surfacing a frame building

SIDLE *v* -DLED, -DLING, -DLES to move sideways

SIDLER *n pl.* -S one that sidles

SIEGE *v* SIEGED, SIEGING, SIEGES to attempt to capture or gain

SIEMENS *n pl.* SIEMENS a unit of electrical conductance

SIENITE *n pl.* -S syenite

SIENNA *n pl.* -S a brown pigment

SIEROZEM *n pl.* -S a type of soil

SIERRA *n pl.* -S a mountain range SIERRAN *adj*

SIESTA *n pl.* -S an afternoon nap or rest

SIEUR *n pl.* -S an old French title of respect for a man

SIEVE *v* SIEVED, SIEVING, SIEVES to pass through a sieve (a utensil for separating the coarse parts from the fine parts of loose matter)

SIFAKA *n pl.* -S a lemur of Madagascar

SIFFLEUR *n pl.* -S an animal that makes a whistling noise

SIFT *v* -ED, -ING, -S to sieve

SIFTER *n pl.* -S one that sifts

SIFTING *n pl.* -S the work of a sifter

SIGANID *n pl.* -S any of a family of fishes

SIGH *v* -ED, -ING, -S to let out a sigh (a deep, audible breath)

SIGHER *n pl.* -S one that sighs

SIGHLESS *adj* uttering no sigh

SIGHLIKE *adj* resembling a sigh

SIGHT *v* -ED, -ING, -S to observe or notice

SIGHTER *n pl.* -S one that sights

SIGHTING *n pl.* -S an observation

SIGHTLY *adj* -LIER, -LIEST pleasing to look at

SIGHTSEE *v* -SAW, -SEEN, -SEEING, -SEES to visit and view places of interest

SIGIL *n pl.* -S an official seal

SIGLOS *n pl.* -LOI an ancient Persian coin

SIGMA *n pl.* -S a Greek letter SIGMATE *adj*

SIGMOID *n pl.* -S an S-shaped curve in a bodily part

SIGN *v* -ED, -ING, -S to write one's name on

SIGNAGE *n pl.* -S a system of signs in a community

SIGNAL *v* -NALED, -NALING, -NALS or -NALLED, -NALLING, -NALS to notify by a means of communication

SIGNALER *n pl.* -S one that signals

SIGNALLY *adv* notably

SIGNEE *n pl.* -S a signer of a document

SIGNER *n pl.* -S one that signs

SIGNET *v* -ED, -ING, -S to mark with an official seal

SIGNIFY *v* -FIED, -FYING, -FIES to make known

SIGNIOR *n pl.* -GNIORI or -GNIORS signor

SIGNIORY *n pl.* -GNIORIES signory

SIGNOR *n pl.* -GNORI or -GNORS an Italian title of courtesy for a man

SIGNORA *n pl.* -GNORE or -GNORAS an Italian title of courtesy for a married woman

SIGNORE *n pl.* -GNORI signor

SIGNORY *n pl.* -GNORIES seignory

SIGNPOST *v* -ED, -ING, -S to provide with signposts (posts bearing signs)

SIKE *n pl.* -S syke

SIKER *adj* secure

SILAGE *n pl.* -S fodder that has been preserved in a silo

SILANE *n pl.* -S a chemical compound

SILD *n pl.* -S a young herring

SILENCE *v* -LENCED, -LENCING, -LENCES to make silent

SILENCER *n pl.* -S one that silences

SILENI *pl.* of silenus

SILENT *adj* -LENTER, -LENTEST making no sound or noise SILENTLY *adv*

SILENTS *n/pl* silent movies

SILENUS *n pl.* -NI a woodland deity of Greek mythology

SILESIA *n pl.* -S a cotton fabric

SILEX *n pl.* -ES silica

SILICA *n pl.* -S a form of silicon

SILICATE	n pl. -S a chemical salt	**SILVEX**	n pl. -ES an herbicide
SILICIC	adj pertaining to silicon	**SILVICAL**	adj pertaining to silvics
SILICIDE	n pl. -S a silicon compound	**SILVICS**	n/pl the study of forest trees
SILICIFY	v -FIED, -FYING, -FIES to convert into silica	**SIM**	n pl. -S simulation
		SIMA	n pl. -S an igneous rock
SILICIUM	n pl. -S silicon	**SIMAR**	n pl. -S a woman's light jacket or robe
SILICLE	n pl. -S a short, flat silique		
SILICON	n pl. -S a nonmetallic element	**SIMARUBA**	n pl. -S a tropical tree
SILICONE	n pl. -S a silicon compound	**SIMAZINE**	n pl. -S an herbicide
SILICULA	n pl. -LAE a silicle	**SIMIAN**	n pl. -S an ape or monkey
SILIQUA	n pl. -QUAE silique	**SIMILAR**	adj being like but not completely identical to
SILIQUE	n pl. -LIQUES a type of seed vessel		
		SIMILE	n pl. -S a figure of speech
SILK	v -ED, -ING, -S to cover with silk (a soft, lustrous fabric)	**SIMIOID**	adj simious
		SIMIOUS	adj pertaining to simians
SILKEN	adj made of silk	**SIMITAR**	n pl. -S scimitar
SILKIER	comparative of silky	**SIMLIN**	n pl. -S cymling
SILKIEST	superlative of silky	**SIMMER**	v -ED, -ING, -S to cook below or just at the boiling point
SILKILY	adv in a silky manner		
SILKLIKE	adj resembling silk	**SIMNEL**	n pl. -S a crisp bread
SILKWEED	n pl. -S milkweed	**SIMOLEON**	n pl. -S a dollar
SILKWORM	n pl. -S a caterpillar that spins a cocoon of silk fibers	**SIMONIAC**	n pl. -S one who practices simony
SILKY	adj SILKIER, SILKIEST resembling silk	**SIMONIES**	pl. of simony
		SIMONIST	n pl. -S a simoniac
SILKY	n pl. SILKIES a glossy-coated terrier	**SIMONIZE**	v -NIZED, -NIZING, -NIZES to polish with wax
SILL	n pl. -S the horizontal piece that bears the upright portion of a frame	**SIMONY**	n pl. -NIES the buying or selling of a church office
		SIMOOM	n pl. -S a hot, dry desert wind
SILLABUB	n pl. -S an alcoholic beverage or dessert	**SIMOON**	n pl. -S simoom
		SIMP	n pl. -S a foolish person
SILLER	n pl. -S silver	**SIMPER**	v -ED, -ING, -S to smile in a silly manner
SILLIBUB	n pl. -S sillabub		
SILLY	adj -LIER, -LIEST showing a lack of good sense SILLILY adv	**SIMPERER**	n pl. -S one that simpers
		SIMPLE	adj SIMPLER, SIMPLEST not complex or complicated
SILLY	n pl. -LIES a silly person		
SILO	v -ED, -ING, -S to store in a silo (a tall, cylindrical structure)	**SIMPLE**	n pl. -S something that is simple
SILOXANE	n pl. -S a chemical compound	**SIMPLEX**	n pl. -PLEXES, -PLICES, or -PLICIA a simple word
SILT	v -ED, -ING, -S to fill with silt (a sedimentary material)		
		SIMPLIFY	v -FIED, -FYING, -FIES to make simple
SILTY	adj SILTIER, SILTIEST full of silt		
		SIMPLISM	n pl. -S the tendency to oversimplify an issue or problem
SILURID	n pl. -S any of a family of catfishes		
SILUROID	n pl. -S a silurid	**SIMPLIST**	n pl. -S a person given to simplism
SILVA	n pl. -VAS or -VAE sylva		
SILVAN	n pl. -S sylvan	**SIMPLY**	adv in a simple manner
SILVER	v -ED, -ING, -S to cover with silver (a metallic element)	**SIMULANT**	n pl. -S one that simulates
		SIMULAR	n pl. -S a simulant
SILVERER	n pl. -S one that silvers	**SIMULATE**	v -LATED, -LATING, -LATES to take on the appearance of
SILVERLY	adv with a silvery appearance		
SILVERN	adj silvery	**SIN**	v SINNED, SINNING, SINS to commit a sin (an offense against religious or moral law)
SILVERY	adj resembling silver		

SINAPISM *n* pl. -S a pasty mixture applied to an irritated part of the body

SINCE *adv* from then until now

SINCERE *adj* -CERER, -CEREST free from hypocrisy or falseness

SINCIPUT *n* pl. -CIPUTS or -CIPITA the forehead

SINE *n* pl. -S a trigonometric function of an angle

SINECURE *n* pl. -S an office or position requiring little or no work

SINEW *v* -ED, -ING, -S to strengthen

SINEWY *adj* lean and muscular

SINFONIA *n* pl. -NIE a symphony

SINFUL *adj* marked by sin **SINFULLY** *adv*

SING *v* SANG, SUNG, SINGING, SINGS to utter with musical inflections of the voice **SINGABLE** *adj*

SINGE *v* SINGED, SINGEING, SINGES to burn slightly

SINGER *n* pl. -S one that sings

SINGLE *v* -GLED, -GLING, -GLES to select from a group

SINGLET *n* pl. -S a man's undershirt or jersey

SINGLY *adv* without the company of others

SINGSONG *n* pl. -S monotonous cadence in speaking or reading

SINGULAR *n* pl. -S a word form that denotes one person or thing

SINH *n* pl. -S a hyperbolic function of an angle

SINICIZE *v* -CIZED, -CIZING, -CIZES to modify by Chinese influence

SINISTER *adj* threatening or portending evil

SINK *v* SANK, SUNK or SUNKEN, SINKING, SINKS to move to a lower level **SINKABLE** *adj*

SINKAGE *n* pl. -S the act, process, or degree of sinking

SINKER *n* pl. -S one that sinks

SINKHOLE *n* pl. -S a natural depression in a land surface

SINLESS *adj* free from sin

SINNED past tense of sin

SINNER *n* pl. -S one that sins

SINNING present participle of sin

SINOLOGY *n* pl. -GIES the study of the Chinese

SINOPIA *n* pl. -PIAS or -PIE a red pigment

SINSYNE *adv* since

SINTER *v* -ED, -ING, -S to make cohesive by the combined action of heat and pressure

SINUATE *v* -ATED, -ATING, -ATES to curve in and out

SINUOUS *adj* characterized by curves, bends, or turns

SINUS *n* pl. -ES a cranial cavity

SINUSOID *n* pl. -S a mathematical curve

SIP *v* SIPPED, SIPPING, SIPS to drink in small quantities

SIPE *v* SIPED, SIPING, SIPES to seep

SIPHON *v* -ED, -ING, -S to draw off through a siphon (a type of tube)

SIPHONAL *adj* of or pertaining to a siphon

SIPHONIC *adj* siphonal

SIPING present participle of sipe

SIPPED past tense of sip

SIPPER *n* pl. -S one that sips

SIPPET *n* pl. -S a small piece of bread soaked in gravy

SIPPING present participle of sip

SIR *n* pl. -S a respectful form of address used to a man

SIRDAR *n* pl. -S a person of rank in India

SIRE *v* SIRED, SIRING, SIRES to beget

SIREE *n* pl. -S sirree

SIREN *n* pl. -S a device that produces a penetrating warning sound

SIRENIAN *n* pl. -S any of an order of aquatic mammals

SIRING present participle of sire

SIRLOIN *n* pl. -S a cut of beef

SIROCCO *n* pl. -COS a hot, dry wind

SIRRA *n* pl. -S sirrah

SIRRAH *n* pl. -S a form of address used to inferiors

SIRREE *n* pl. -S sir

SIRUP *n* pl. -S syrup **SIRUPY** *adj*

SIRVENTE *n* pl. -S a satirical medieval song or poem

SIS *n* pl. SISES sister

SISAL *n* pl. -S a strong fiber used for rope

SISKIN *n* pl. -S a Eurasian finch

SISSY *n* pl. -SIES an effeminate man or boy

SISSY *adj* SISSIER, SISSIEST sissyish

SISSYISH *adj* resembling a sissy

SISTER v -ED, -ING, -S to treat like a sister (a female sibling)

SISTERLY adj of or resembling a sister

SISTROID adj included between the convex sides of two intersecting curves

SISTRUM n pl. -TRUMS or -TRA an ancient Egyptian percussion instrument

SIT v SAT, SAT or SITTEN, SITTING, SITS to rest on the buttocks

SITAR n pl. -S a lute of India

SITARIST n pl. -S one who plays the sitar

SITCOM n pl. -S a television comedy series with continuing characters

SITE v SITED, SITING, SITES to place in position for operation

SITH adv since

SITHENCE adv since

SITHENS adv since

SITING present participle of site

SITOLOGY n pl. -GIES the science of nutrition and diet

SITTEN a past participle of sit

SITTER n pl. -S one that sits

SITTING n pl. -S a meeting or session

SITUATE v -ATED, -ATING, -ATES to place in a certain position

SITUP n pl. -S an exercise in which one moves from a lying to a sitting position

SITUS n pl. -TUSES a position or location

SITZMARK n pl. -S a mark left in the snow by a skier who has fallen backward

SIVER n pl. -S a sewer

SIX n pl. -ES a number

SIXFOLD adj being six times as great as

SIXMO n pl. -MOS a paper size

SIXPENCE n pl. -S a British coin worth six pennies

SIXPENNY adj worth sixpence

SIXTE n pl. -S a fencing parry

SIXTEEN n pl. -S a number

SIXTH n pl. -S one of six equal parts

SIXTHLY adv in the sixth place

SIXTIETH n pl. -S one of sixty equal parts

SIXTY n pl. -TIES a number

SIXTYISH adj being about sixty years old

SIZABLE adj of considerable size SIZABLY adv

SIZAR n pl. -S a British student who receives financial assistance from his college

SIZE v SIZED, SIZING, SIZES to arrange according to size (physical proportions)

SIZEABLE adj sizable SIZEABLY adv

SIZER n pl. -S sizar

SIZIER comparative of sizy

SIZIEST superlative of sizy

SIZINESS n pl. -ES the quality or state of being sizy

SIZING n pl. -S a substance used as a glaze or filler for porous materials

SIZY adj SIZIER, SIZIEST viscid

SIZZLE v -ZLED, -ZLING, -ZLES to burn or fry with a hissing sound

SIZZLER n pl. -S a very hot day

SJAMBOK v -ED, -ING, -S to strike with a whip used in South Africa

SKA n pl. -S a popular music of Jamaica

SKAG n pl. -S heroin

SKALD n pl. -S an ancient Scandinavian poet SKALDIC adj

SKAT n pl. -S a card game

SKATE v SKATED, SKATING, SKATES to glide over ice or the ground on skates (shoes fitted with runners or wheels)

SKATER n pl. -S one that skates

SKATING n pl. -S the sport of gliding on skates

SKATOL n pl. -S skatole

SKATOLE n pl. -S a chemical compound

SKEAN n pl. -S a type of dagger

SKEANE n pl. -S a length of yarn wound in a loose coil

SKEE v SKEED, SKEEING, SKEES to ski

SKEEN n pl. -S skean

SKEET n pl. -S the sport of shooting at clay pigeons hurled in the air by spring traps

SKEETER n pl. -S a skeet shooter

SKEG n pl. -S a timber that connects the keel and sternpost of a ship

SKEIGH adj proud

SKEIN v -ED, -ING, -S to wind into long, loose coils

SKELETON n pl. -S the supporting or protective framework of a human or animal body **SKELETAL** adj

SKELLUM n pl. -S a rascal

SKELM n pl. -S skellum

SKELP v SKELPED or SKELPIT, SKELPING, SKELPS to slap

SKELTER v -ED, -ING, -S to scurry

SKENE n pl. -S skean

SKEP n pl. -S a beehive

SKEPSIS n pl. -SISES the attitude or outlook of a skeptic

SKEPTIC n pl. -S a person who doubts generally accepted ideas

SKERRY n pl. -RIES a small, rocky island

SKETCH v -ED, -ING, -ES to make a rough, hasty drawing of

SKETCHER n pl. -S one that sketches

SKETCHY adj SKETCHIER, SKETCHIEST lacking in completeness or clearness

SKEW v -ED, -ING, -S to turn aside

SKEWBACK n pl. -S a sloping surface against which the end of an arch rests

SKEWBALD n pl. -S a horse having patches of brown and white

SKEWER v -ED, -ING, -S to pierce with a long pin, as meat

SKEWNESS n pl. -ES lack of symmetry

SKI v -ED, -ING, -S to travel on skis (long, narrow strips of wood or metal)

SKIABLE adj capable of being skied over

SKIAGRAM n pl. -S a picture made up of shadows or outlines

SKIBOB n pl. -S a vehicle used for traveling over snow

SKID v SKIDDED, SKIDDING, SKIDS to slide sideways as a result of a loss of traction

SKIDDER n pl. -S one that skids

SKIDDOO v -ED, -ING, -S to go away

SKIDDY adj -DIER, -DIEST likely to cause skidding

SKIDOO v -ED, -ING, -S to skiddoo

SKIDWAY n pl. -WAYS a platform on which logs are piled for loading or sawing

SKIED past tense of ski and sky

SKIER n pl. -S one that skis

SKIES present 3d person sing. of sky

SKIEY adj skyey

SKIFF n pl. -S a small, open boat

SKIFFLE v -FLED, -FLING, -FLES to play a particular style of music

SKIING n pl. -S the sport of traveling on skis

SKIJORER n pl. -S a skier who is drawn over snow by a horse or vehicle

SKILFUL adj skillful

SKILL n pl. -S the ability to do something well **SKILLED** adj

SKILLESS adj having no skill

SKILLET n pl. -S a frying pan

SKILLFUL adj having skill

SKILLING n pl. -S a former coin of Scandinavian countries

SKIM v SKIMMED, SKIMMING, SKIMS to remove floating matter from the surface of

SKIMMER n pl. -S one that skims

SKIMMING n pl. -S something that is skimmed from a liquid

SKIMP v -ED, -ING, -S to scrimp

SKIMPY adj SKIMPIER, SKIMPIEST scanty **SKIMPILY** adv

SKIN v SKINNED, SKINNING, SKINS to strip or deprive of skin (the membranous tissue covering the body of an animal)

SKINFUL n pl. -S as much as a skin container can hold

SKINHEAD n pl. -S one whose hair is cut very short

SKINK v -ED, -ING, -S to pour out or serve, as liquor

SKINKER n pl. -S one that skinks

SKINLESS adj having no skin

SKINLIKE adj resembling skin

SKINNED past tense of skin

SKINNER n pl. -S one that skins

SKINNING present participle of skin

SKINNY adj -NIER, -NIEST very thin

SKINT adj having no money

SKIORING n pl. -S a form of skiing

SKIP v SKIPPED, SKIPPING, SKIPS to move with light springing steps

SKIPJACK n pl. -S a marine fish

SKIPLANE n pl. -S an airplane designed to take off from or land on snow

SKIPPED past tense of skip

SKIPPER v -ED, -ING, -S to act as master or captain of

SKIPPET *n pl.* -S a small box for protecting an official seal

SKIPPING present participle of skip

SKIRL *v* -ED, -ING, -S to produce a shrill sound

SKIRMISH *v* -ED, -ING, -ES to engage in a minor battle

SKIRR *v* -ED, -ING, -S to move rapidly

SKIRRET *n pl.* -S an Asian herb

SKIRT *v* -ED, -ING, -S to go or pass around

SKIRTER *n pl.* -S one that skirts

SKIRTING *n pl.* -S a board at the base of a wall

SKIT *n pl.* -S a short dramatic scene

SKITE *v* SKITED, SKITING, SKITES to move away quickly

SKITTER *v* -ED, -ING, -S to move lightly or rapidly along a surface

SKITTERY *adj* -TERIER, -TERIEST skittish

SKITTISH *adj* easily frightened

SKITTLE *n pl.* -S a wooden pin used in a bowling game

SKIVE *v* SKIVED, SKIVING, SKIVES to pare

SKIVER *n pl.* -S one that skives

SKIVVY *v* -VIED, -VYING, -VIES to work as a female servant

SKIWEAR *n pl.* SKIWEAR clothing suitable for wear while skiing

SKLENT *v* -ED, -ING, -S to slant

SKOAL *v* -ED, -ING, -S to drink to the health of

SKOOKUM *adj* excellent

SKOSH *n pl.* -ES a small amount

SKREEGH *v* -ED, -ING, -S to screech

SKREIGH *v* -ED, -ING, -S to screech

SKUA *n pl.* -S a predatory seabird

SKULK *v* -ED, -ING, -S to move about stealthily

SKULKER *n pl.* -S one that skulks

SKULL *n pl.* -S the framework of the head **SKULLED** *adj*

SKULLCAP *n pl.* -S a close-fitting cap

SKUNK *v* -ED, -ING, -S to defeat overwhelmingly

SKY *v* SKIED or SKYED, SKYING, SKIES to hit or throw toward the sky (the upper atmosphere)

SKYBORNE *adj* airborne

SKYBOX *n pl.* -ES an enclosure of seats situated high in a stadium

SKYCAP *n pl.* -S a porter at an airport

SKYDIVE *v* -DIVED or -DOVE, -DIVING, -DIVES to parachute from an airplane for sport

SKYDIVER *n pl.* -S one that skydives

SKYEY *adj* resembling the sky

SKYHOOK *n pl.* -S a hook conceived as being suspended from the sky

SKYJACK *v* -ED, -ING, -S to hijack an airplane

SKYLARK *v* -ED, -ING, -S to frolic

SKYLIGHT *n pl.* -S a window in a roof or ceiling

SKYLINE *n pl.* -S the horizon

SKYLIT *adj* having a skylight

SKYMAN *n pl.* -MEN an aviator

SKYPHOS *n pl.* -PHOI a drinking vessel used in ancient Greece

SKYSAIL *n pl.* -S a type of sail

SKYWALK *n pl.* -S an elevated walkway between two buildings

SKYWARD *adv* toward the sky

SKYWARDS *adv* skyward

SKYWAY *n pl.* -WAYS an elevated highway

SKYWRITE *v* -WROTE, -WRITTEN, -WRITING, -WRITES to write in the sky by releasing a visible vapor from an airplane

SLAB *v* SLABBED, SLABBING, SLABS to cover with slabs (broad, flat pieces of solid material)

SLABBER *v* -ED, -ING, -S to slobber

SLABBERY *adj* slobbery

SLABBING present participle of slab

SLABLIKE *adj* resembling a slab

SLACK *adj* SLACKER, SLACKEST not tight or taut

SLACK *v* -ED, -ING, -S to slacken

SLACKEN *v* -ED, -ING, -S to make less tight or taut

SLACKER *n pl.* -S a shirker

SLACKLY *adv* in a slack manner

SLAG *v* SLAGGED, SLAGGING, SLAGS to convert into slag (the fused residue of a smelted ore)

SLAGGY *adj* -GIER, -GIEST resembling slag

SLAIN past participle of slay

SLAINTE *interj* — used to toast one's health

SLAKE v SLAKED, SLAKING, SLAKES to quench SLAKABLE adj

SLAKER n pl. -S one that slakes

SLALOM v -ED, -ING, -S to ski in a zigzag course

SLAM v SLAMMED, SLAMMING, SLAMS to shut forcibly and noisily

SLAMMER n pl. -S a jail

SLANDER v -ED, -ING, -S to defame

SLANG v -ED, -ING, -S to use slang (extremely informal or vulgar language)

SLANGY adj SLANGIER, SLANGIEST being or containing slang SLANGILY adv

SLANK a past tense of slink

SLANT v -ED, -ING, -S to deviate from the horizontal or vertical

SLANTY adj deviating from the horizontal or vertical

SLAP v SLAPPED, SLAPPING, SLAPS to strike with the open hand

SLAPDASH n pl. -ES careless work

SLAPJACK n pl. -S a pancake

SLAPPED past tense of slap

SLAPPER n pl. -S one that slaps

SLAPPING present participle of slap

SLASH v -ED, -ING, -ES to cut with violent sweeping strokes

SLASHER n pl. -S one that slashes

SLASHING n pl. -S the act of one that slashes

SLAT v SLATTED, SLATTING, SLATS to provide with slats (narrow strips of wood or metal)

SLATCH n pl. -ES a calm between breaking waves

SLATE v SLATED, SLATING, SLATES to cover with slate (a roofing material)

SLATER n pl. -S one that slates

SLATEY adj SLATIER, SLATIEST slaty

SLATHER v -ED, -ING, -S to spread thickly

SLATIER comparative of slaty

SLATIEST superlative of slaty

SLATING n pl. -S the act of one that slates

SLATTED past tense of slat

SLATTERN n pl. -S a slovenly woman

SLATTING n pl. -S material for making slats

SLATY adj SLATIER, SLATIEST resembling slate

SLAVE v SLAVED, SLAVING, SLAVES to work like a slave (one who is owned by another)

SLAVER v -ED, -ING, -S to drool

SLAVERER n pl. -S one that slavers

SLAVERY n pl. -ERIES ownership of one person by another

SLAVEY n pl. -EYS a female servant

SLAVING present participle of slave

SLAVISH adj pertaining to or characteristic of a slave

SLAW n pl. -S coleslaw

SLAY v SLEW, SLAIN, SLAYING, SLAYS to kill violently

SLAY v SLAYED, SLAIN, SLAYING, SLAYS to amuse overwhelmingly

SLAYER n pl. -S one that slays

SLEAVE v SLEAVED, SLEAVING, SLEAVES to separate into filaments

SLEAZE n pl. -S a sleazy quality

SLEAZO adj sleazy

SLEAZY adj SLEAZIER, SLEAZIEST shoddy SLEAZILY adv

SLED v SLEDDED, SLEDDING, SLEDS to convey on a sled (a vehicle for carrying people or loads over snow or ice)

SLEDDER n pl. -S one that sleds

SLEDDING n pl. -S the act of one that sleds

SLEDGE v SLEDGED, SLEDGING, SLEDGES to convey on a type of sled

SLEEK adj SLEEKER, SLEEKEST smooth and glossy

SLEEK v -ED, -ING, -S to make sleek

SLEEKEN v -ED, -ING, -S to sleek

SLEEKIER comparative of sleeky

SLEEKIEST superlative of sleeky

SLEEKIT adj sleek

SLEEKLY adv in a sleek manner

SLEEKY adj SLEEKIER, SLEEKIEST sleek

SLEEP v SLEPT, SLEEPING, SLEEPS to be in a natural, periodic state of rest

SLEEPER n pl. -S one that sleeps

SLEEPING n pl. -S the act of one that sleeps

SLEEPY adj SLEEPIER, SLEEPIEST ready or inclined to sleep SLEEPILY adv

SLEET	v -ED, -ING, -S to shower sleet (frozen rain)
SLEETY	adj SLEETIER, SLEETIEST resembling sleet
SLEEVE	v SLEEVED, SLEEVING, SLEEVES to furnish with a sleeve (the part of a garment covering the arm)
SLEIGH	v -ED, -ING, -S to ride in a sled
SLEIGHER	n pl. -S one that sleighs
SLEIGHT	n pl. -S deftness
SLENDER	adj -DERER, -DEREST thin
SLEPT	past tense of sleep
SLEUTH	v -ED, -ING, -S to act as a detective
SLEW	v -ED, -ING, -S to slue
SLICE	v SLICED, SLICING, SLICES to cut into thin, flat pieces
SLICER	n pl. -S one that slices
SLICK	adj SLICKER, SLICKEST smooth and slippery
SLICK	v -ED, -ING, -S to make slick
SLICKER	n pl. -S an oilskin raincoat
SLICKLY	adv in a slick manner
SLIDE	v SLID, SLIDDEN, SLIDING, SLIDES to move smoothly along a surface SLIDABLE adj
SLIDER	n pl. -S one that slides
SLIDEWAY	n pl. -WAYS a route along which something slides
SLIDING	present participle of slide
SLIER	a comparative of sly
SLIEST	a superlative of sly
SLIGHT	adj SLIGHTER, SLIGHTEST small in size or amount SLIGHTLY adv
SLIGHT	v -ED, -ING, -S to treat with disregard
SLILY	adv in a sly manner
SLIM	adj SLIMMER, SLIMMEST slender
SLIM	v SLIMMED, SLIMMING, SLIMS to make slim
SLIME	v SLIMED, SLIMING, SLIMES to cover with slime (viscous mud)
SLIMIER	comparative of slimy
SLIMIEST	superlative of slimy
SLIMILY	adv in a slimy manner
SLIMING	present participle of slime
SLIMLY	adv in a slim manner
SLIMMED	past tense of slim
SLIMMER	n pl. -S a dieter
SLIMMEST	superlative of slim
SLIMMING	present participle of slim

SLIMNESS	n pl. -ES the state of being slim
SLIMPSY	adj -SIER, -SIEST slimsy
SLIMSY	adj -SIER, -SIEST flimsy
SLIMY	adj SLIMIER, SLIMIEST resembling slime
SLING	v SLUNG, SLINGING, SLINGS to throw with a sudden motion
SLINGER	n pl. -S one that slings
SLINK	v SLUNK or SLANK or SLINKED, SLINKING, SLINKS to move stealthily
SLINKY	adj SLINKIER, SLINKIEST stealthy SLINKILY adv
SLIP	v SLIPPED or SLIPT, SLIPPING, SLIPS to slide suddenly and accidentally
SLIPCASE	n pl. -S a protective box for a book
SLIPE	v SLIPED, SLIPING, SLIPES to peel
SLIPFORM	v -ED, -ING, -S to construct with the use of a mold in which concrete is placed to set
SLIPKNOT	n pl. -S a type of knot
SLIPLESS	adj free from errors
SLIPOUT	n pl. -S an insert in a newspaper
SLIPOVER	n pl. -S a pullover
SLIPPAGE	n pl. -S a falling off from a standard or level
SLIPPED	a past tense of slip
SLIPPER	n pl. -S a light, low shoe
SLIPPERY	adj -PERIER, -PERIEST causing or tending to cause slipping
SLIPPING	present participle of slip
SLIPPY	adj -PIER, -PIEST slippery
SLIPSHOD	adj carelessly done or made
SLIPSLOP	n pl. -S watery food
SLIPSOLE	n pl. -S a thin insole
SLIPT	a past tense of slip
SLIPUP	n pl. -S a mistake
SLIPWARE	n pl. -S a type of pottery
SLIPWAY	n pl. -WAYS an area sloping toward the water in a shipyard
SLIT	v SLITTED, SLITTING, SLITS to make a slit (a long, narrow cut) in
SLITHER	v -ED, -ING, -S to slide from side to side
SLITHERY	adj slippery
SLITLESS	adj having no slits
SLITTED	past tense of slit
SLITTER	n pl. -S one that slits

SLITTING present participle of slit

SLIVER v -ED, -ING, -S to cut into long, thin pieces

SLIVERER n pl. -S one that slivers

SLIVOVIC n pl. -ES a plum brandy

SLOB n pl. -S a slovenly or boorish person

SLOBBER v -ED, -ING, -S to drool

SLOBBERY adj slobbering

SLOBBISH adj resembling a slob

SLOBBY adj SLOBBIER, SLOBBIEST characteristic of a slob

SLOE n pl. -S a plumlike fruit

SLOG v SLOGGED, SLOGGING, SLOGS to plod

SLOGAN n pl. -S a motto adopted by a group

SLOGGER n pl. -S one that slogs

SLOGGING present participle of slog

SLOID n pl. -S sloyd

SLOJD n pl. -S sloyd

SLOOP n pl. -S a type of sailing vessel

SLOP v SLOPPED, SLOPPING, SLOPS to spill or splash

SLOPE v SLOPED, SLOPING, SLOPES to slant

SLOPER n pl. -S one that slopes

SLOPPED past tense of slop

SLOPPING present participle of slop

SLOPPY adj -PIER, -PIEST messy SLOPPILY adv

SLOPWORK n pl. -S the manufacture of cheap clothing

SLOSH v -ED, -ING, -ES to move with a splashing motion

SLOSHY adj SLOSHIER, SLOSHIEST slushy

SLOT v SLOTTED, SLOTTING, SLOTS to cut a long, narrow opening in

SLOTBACK n pl. -S a type of football player

SLOTH n pl. -S a slow-moving arboreal mammal

SLOTHFUL adj sluggish

SLOTTED past tense of slot

SLOTTING present participle of slot

SLOUCH v -ED, -ING, -ES to sit, stand, or move with a drooping posture

SLOUCHER n pl. -S one that slouches

SLOUCHY adj SLOUCHIER, SLOUCHIEST slouching

SLOUGH v -ED, -ING, -S to cast off

SLOUGHY adj SLOUGHIER, SLOUGHIEST miry

SLOVEN n pl. -S a slovenly person

SLOVENLY adj -LIER, -LIEST habitually untidy or unclean

SLOW adj SLOWER, SLOWEST moving with little speed

SLOW v -ED, -ING, -S to lessen the speed of

SLOWDOWN n pl. -S a lessening of pace

SLOWISH adj somewhat slow

SLOWLY adv in a slow manner

SLOWNESS n pl. -ES the state of being slow

SLOWPOKE n pl. -S a slow individual

SLOWWORM n pl. -S a European lizard having no legs

SLOYD n pl. -S a Swedish system of manual training

SLUB v SLUBBED, SLUBBING, SLUBS to draw out and twist slightly

SLUBBER v -ED, -ING, -S to stain or dirty

SLUBBING n pl. -S a slightly twisted roll of textile fibers

SLUDGE n pl. -S a muddy deposit

SLUDGY adj SLUDGIER, SLUDGIEST covered with sludge

SLUE v SLUED, SLUING, SLUES to cause to move sideways

SLUFF v -ED, -ING, -S to discard a card or cards

SLUG v SLUGGED, SLUGGING, SLUGS to strike heavily

SLUGABED n pl. -S one inclined to stay in bed out of laziness

SLUGFEST n pl. -S a vigorous fight

SLUGGARD n pl. -S an habitually lazy person

SLUGGED past tense of slug

SLUGGER n pl. -S one that slugs

SLUGGING present participle of slug

SLUGGISH adj displaying little movement or activity

SLUICE v SLUICED, SLUICING, SLUICES to wash with a sudden flow of water

SLUICY adj falling in streams

SLUING present participle of slue

SLUM v SLUMMED, SLUMMING, SLUMS to visit slums (squalid urban areas)

SLUMBER v -ED, -ING, -S to sleep

SLUMBERY adj sleepy

SLUMGUM n pl. -S the residue remaining after honey is extracted from a honeycomb

SLUMISM n pl. -S the prevalence of slums

SLUMLORD n pl. -S a landlord of slum property

SLUMMED past tense of slum

SLUMMER n pl. -S one that slums

SLUMMING present participle of slum

SLUMMY adj -MIER, -MIEST resembling a slum

SLUMP v -ED, -ING, -S to fall or sink suddenly

SLUNG past tense of sling

SLUNK a past tense of slink

SLUR v SLURRED, SLURRING, SLURS to pass over lightly or carelessly

SLURB n pl. -S a poorly planned suburban area **SLURBAN** adj

SLURP v -ED, -ING, -S to eat or drink noisily

SLURRED past tense of slur

SLURRING present participle of slur

SLURRY v -RIED, -RYING, -RIES to convert into a type of watery mixture

SLUSH v -ED, -ING, -ES to splash with slush (partly melted snow)

SLUSHY adj SLUSHIER, SLUSHIEST resembling slush **SLUSHILY** adv

SLUT n pl. -S a slovenly woman **SLUTTISH** adj

SLUTTY adj SLUTTIER, SLUTTIEST characteristic of a slut

SLY adj SLIER, SLIEST or SLYER, SLYEST crafty **SLYLY** adv

SLYBOOTS n pl. SLYBOOTS a sly person

SLYNESS n pl. -ES the quality or state of being sly

SLYPE n pl. -S a narrow passage in an English cathedral

SMACK v -ED, -ING, -S to strike sharply

SMACKER n pl. -S one that smacks

SMALL adj SMALLER, SMALLEST of limited size or quantity

SMALL n pl. -S a small part

SMALLAGE n pl. -S a wild celery

SMALLISH adj somewhat small

SMALLPOX n pl. -ES a virus disease

SMALT n pl. -S a blue pigment

SMALTI a pl. of smalto

SMALTINE n pl. -S smaltite

SMALTITE n pl. -S a mineral

SMALTO n pl. -TOS or -TI colored glass used in mosaics

SMARAGD n pl. -S an emerald

SMARAGDE n pl. -S smaragd

SMARM n pl. -S trite sentimentality

SMARMY adj SMARMIER, SMARMIEST marked by excessive flattery **SMARMILY** adv

SMART v -ED, -ING, -S to cause a sharp, stinging pain

SMART adj SMARTER, SMARTEST characterized by mental acuity

SMARTASS n pl. -ES a smarty

SMARTEN v -ED, -ING, -S to improve in appearance

SMARTIE n pl. -S a smarty

SMARTLY adv in a smart manner

SMARTY n pl. SMARTIES an obnoxiously conceited person

SMASH v -ED, -ING, -ES to shatter violently

SMASHER n pl. -S one that smashes

SMASHUP n pl. -S a collision of motor vehicles

SMATTER v -ED, -ING, -S to speak with little knowledge

SMAZE n pl. -S an atmospheric mixture of smoke and haze

SMEAR v -ED, -ING, -S to spread with a sticky, greasy, or dirty substance

SMEARER n pl. -S one that smears

SMEARY adj SMEARIER, SMEARIEST smeared

SMECTIC adj pertaining to a phase of a liquid crystal

SMECTITE n pl. -S a clayey mineral

SMEDDUM n pl. -S ground malt powder

SMEEK v -ED, -ING, -S to smoke

SMEGMA n pl. -S sebum

SMELL v SMELLED or SMELT, SMELLING, SMELLS to perceive by means of the olfactory nerves

SMELLER n pl. -S one that smells

SMELLY adj SMELLIER, SMELLIEST having an unpleasant odor

SMELT v -ED, -ING, -S to melt or fuse, as ores

SMELTER n pl. -S one that smelts

SMELTERY n pl. -ERIES a place for smelting

SMERK v -ED, -ING, -S to smirk

SMEW n pl. -S a Eurasian duck

SMIDGE n pl. -S a smidgen

SMIDGEN n pl. -S a very small amount

SMIDGEON n pl. -S smidgen

SMIDGIN n pl. -S smidgen

SMILAX *n* pl. -ES a twining plant

SMILE *v* SMILED, SMILING, SMILES to upturn the corners of the mouth in pleasure

SMILER *n* pl. -S one that smiles

SMILEY *adj* exhibiting a smile (a facial expression)

SMIRCH *v* -ED, -ING, -ES to soil

SMIRK *v* -ED, -ING, -S to smile in an affected or smug manner

SMIRKER *n* pl. -S one that smirks

SMIRKY *adj* SMIRKIER, SMIRKIEST smirking

SMITE *v* SMOTE, SMIT or SMITTEN, SMITING, SMITES to strike heavily

SMITER *n* pl. -S one that smites

SMITH *n* pl. -S a worker in metals

SMITHERS *n/pl* small fragments

SMITHERY *n* pl. -ERIES the trade of a smith

SMITHY *n* pl. SMITHIES the workshop of a smith

SMITING present participle of smite

SMITTEN a past participle of smite

SMOCK *v* -ED, -ING, -S to furnish with a smock (a loose outer garment)

SMOCKING *n* pl. -S a type of embroidery

SMOG *n* pl. -S an atmospheric mixture of smoke and fog **SMOGLESS** *adj*

SMOGGY *adj* -GIER, -GIEST filled with smog

SMOKE *v* SMOKED, SMOKING, SMOKES to emit smoke (the gaseous product of burning materials) **SMOKABLE** *adj*

SMOKEPOT *n* pl. -S a container for giving off smoke

SMOKER *n* pl. -S one that smokes

SMOKEY *adj* SMOKIER, SMOKIEST smoky

SMOKING present participle of smoke

SMOKY *adj* SMOKIER, SMOKIEST filled with smoke **SMOKILY** *adv*

SMOLDER *v* -ED, -ING, -S to burn with no flame

SMOLT *n* pl. -S a young salmon

SMOOCH *v* -ED, -ING, -ES to kiss

SMOOCHY *adj* smudgy

SMOOTH *adj* SMOOTHER, SMOOTHEST having a surface that is free from irregularities

SMOOTH *v* -ED, -ING, -S or -ES to make smooth

SMOOTHEN *v* -ED, -ING, -S to smooth

SMOOTHER *n* pl. -S one that smooths

SMOOTHIE *n* pl. -S a person with polished manners

SMOOTHLY *adv* in a smooth manner

SMOOTHY *n* pl. SMOOTHIES smoothie

SMOTE past tense of smite

SMOTHER *v* -ED, -ING, -S to prevent from breathing

SMOTHERY *adj* tending to smother

SMOULDER *v* -ED, -ING, -S to smolder

SMUDGE *v* SMUDGED, SMUDGING, SMUDGES to smear or dirty

SMUDGY *adj* SMUDGIER, SMUDGIEST smudged **SMUDGILY** *adv*

SMUG *adj* SMUGGER, SMUGGEST highly self-satisfied

SMUGGLE *v* -GLED, -GLING, -GLES to import or export illicitly

SMUGGLER *n* pl. -S one that smuggles

SMUGLY *adv* in a smug manner

SMUGNESS *n* pl. -ES the quality or state of being smug

SMUT *v* SMUTTED, SMUTTING, SMUTS to soil

SMUTCH *v* -ED, -ING, -ES to smudge

SMUTCHY *adj* SMUTCHIER, SMUTCHIEST smudgy

SMUTTED past tense of smut

SMUTTING present participle of smut

SMUTTY *adj* -TIER, -TIEST obscene **SMUTTILY** *adv*

SNACK *v* -ED, -ING, -S to eat a light meal

SNAFFLE *v* -FLED, -FLING, -FLES to obtain by devious means

SNAFU *v* -ED, -ING, -S to bring into a state of confusion

SNAG *v* SNAGGED, SNAGGING, SNAGS to catch on a snag (a jagged protuberance)

SNAGGY *adj* -GIER, -GIEST full of snags

SNAGLIKE *adj* resembling a snag

SNAIL *v* -ED, -ING, -S to move slowly

SNAKE *v* SNAKED, SNAKING, SNAKES to move like a snake (a limbless reptile)

SNAKEBIT *adj* unlucky

SNAKEY *adj* SNAKIER, SNAKIEST snaky

SNAKY *adj* SNAKIER, SNAKIEST resembling a snake **SNAKILY** *adv*

SNAP *v* SNAPPED, SNAPPING, SNAPS to make a sharp cracking sound

SNAPBACK *n pl.* -S a sudden rebound or recovery

SNAPLESS *adj* lacking a snap (a type of fastening device)

SNAPPED past tense of snap

SNAPPER *n pl.* -S one that snaps

SNAPPIER comparative of snappy

SNAPPIEST superlative of snappy

SNAPPILY *adv* in a snappy manner

SNAPPING present participle of snap

SNAPPISH *adj* tending to speak in an impatient or irritable manner

SNAPPY *adj* -PIER, -PIEST snappish

SNAPSHOT *v* -SHOTTED, -SHOTTING, -SHOTS to photograph informally and quickly

SNAPWEED *n pl.* -S a flowering plant

SNARE *v* SNARED, SNARING, SNARES to trap

SNARER *n pl.* -S one that snares

SNARK *n pl.* -S an imaginary animal

SNARKY *adj* SNARKIER, SNARKIEST snappish

SNARL *v* -ED, -ING, -S to growl viciously

SNARLER *n pl.* -S one that snarls

SNARLY *adj* SNARLIER, SNARLIEST tangled

SNASH *n pl.* -ES abusive language

SNATCH *v* -ED, -ING, -ES to seize suddenly

SNATCHER *n pl.* -S one that snatches

SNATCHY *adj* SNATCHIER, SNATCHIEST occurring irregularly

SNATH *n pl.* -S the handle of a scythe

SNATHE *n pl.* -S snath

SNAW *v* -ED, -ING, -S to snow

SNAZZY *adj* -ZIER, -ZIEST very stylish

SNEAK *v* SNEAKED or SNUCK, SNEAKING, SNEAKS to move stealthily

SNEAKER *n pl.* -S one that sneaks

SNEAKY *adj* SNEAKIER, SNEAKIEST deceitful **SNEAKILY** *adv*

SNEAP *v* -ED, -ING, -S to chide

SNECK *n pl.* -S a latch

SNED *v* SNEDDED, SNEDDING, SNEDS to prune

SNEER *v* -ED, -ING, -S to curl the lip in contempt

SNEERER *n pl.* -S one that sneers

SNEERFUL *adj* given to sneering

SNEESH *n pl.* -ES snuff

SNEEZE *v* SNEEZED, SNEEZING, SNEEZES to make a sudden, involuntary expiration of breath

SNEEZER *n pl.* -S one that sneezes

SNEEZY *adj* SNEEZIER, SNEEZIEST tending to sneeze

SNELL *v* -ED, -ING, -S to attach a short line to a fishhook

SNELL *adj* SNELLER, SNELLEST keen

SNIB *v* SNIBBED, SNIBBING, SNIBS to latch

SNICK *v* -ED, -ING, -S to nick

SNICKER *v* -ED, -ING, -S to utter a partly stifled laugh

SNICKERY *adj* tending to snicker

SNIDE *adj* SNIDER, SNIDEST maliciously derogatory **SNIDELY** *adv*

SNIFF *v* -ED, -ING, -S to inhale audibly through the nose

SNIFFER *n pl.* -S one that sniffs

SNIFFIER comparative of sniffy

SNIFFIEST superlative of sniffy

SNIFFILY *adv* in a sniffy manner

SNIFFISH *adj* haughty

SNIFFLE *v* -FLED, -FLING, -FLES to sniff repeatedly

SNIFFLER *n pl.* -S one that sniffles

SNIFFY *adj* -FIER, -FIEST sniffish

SNIFTER *n pl.* -S a pear-shaped liquor glass

SNIGGER *v* -ED, -ING, -S to snicker

SNIGGLE *v* -GLED, -GLING, -GLES to fish for eels

SNIGGLER *n pl.* -S one that sniggles

SNIP *v* SNIPPED, SNIPPING, SNIPS to cut with a short, quick stroke

SNIPE *v* SNIPED, SNIPING, SNIPES to shoot at individuals from a concealed place

SNIPER *n pl.* -S one that snipes

SNIPPED past tense of snip

SNIPPER *n pl.* -S one that snips

SNIPPET *n pl.* -S a small piece snipped off

SNIPPETY *adj* -PETIER, -PETIEST snippy

SNIPPING present participle of snip

SNIPPY *adj* -PIER, -PIEST snappish SNIPPILY *adv*

SNIT *n pl.* -S a state of agitation

SNITCH *v* -ED, -ING, -ES to tattle

SNITCHER *n pl.* -S one that snitches

SNIVEL *v* -ELED, -ELING, -ELS or -ELLED, -ELLING, -ELS to cry or whine with sniffling

SNIVELER *n pl.* -S one that snivels

SNOB *n pl.* -S one who tends to avoid or rebuff those regarded as inferior

SNOBBERY *n pl.* -BERIES snobbish behavior

SNOBBIER comparative of snobby

SNOBBIEST superlative of snobby

SNOBBILY *adv* in a snobby manner

SNOBBISH *adj* characteristic of a snob

SNOBBISM *n pl.* -S snobbery

SNOBBY *adj* -BIER, -BIEST snobbish

SNOG *v* SNOGGED, SNOGGING, SNOGS to kiss

SNOOD *v* -ED, -ING, -S to secure with a snood (a net or fabric cap for the hair)

SNOOK *v* -ED, -ING, -S to sniff

SNOOKER *v* -ED, -ING, -S to trick

SNOOL *v* -ED, -ING, -S to yield meekly

SNOOP *v* -ED, -ING, -S to pry about

SNOOPER *n pl.* -S one that snoops

SNOOPY *adj* SNOOPIER, SNOOPIEST given to snooping SNOOPILY *adv*

SNOOT *v* -ED, -ING, -S to treat with disdain

SNOOTY *adj* SNOOTIER, SNOOTIEST snobbish SNOOTILY *adv*

SNOOZE *v* SNOOZED, SNOOZING, SNOOZES to sleep lightly

SNOOZER *n pl.* -S one that snoozes

SNOOZLE *v* -ZLED, -ZLING, -ZLES to nuzzle

SNOOZY *adj* SNOOZIER, SNOOZIEST drowsy

SNORE *v* SNORED, SNORING, SNORES to breathe loudly while sleeping

SNORER *n pl.* -S one that snores

SNORKEL *v* -ED, -ING, -S to swim underwater with a type of breathing device

SNORT *v* -ED, -ING, -S to exhale noisily through the nostrils

SNORTER *n pl.* -S one that snorts

SNOT *n pl.* -S nasal mucus

SNOTTY *adj* -TIER, -TIEST arrogant SNOTTILY *adv*

SNOUT *v* -ED, -ING, -S to provide with a nozzle

SNOUTISH *adj* snouty

SNOUTY *adj* SNOUTIER, SNOUTIEST resembling a long, projecting nose

SNOW *v* -ED, -ING, -S to fall as snow (precipitation in the form of ice crystals)

SNOWBALL *v* -ED, -ING, -S to increase at a rapidly accelerating rate

SNOWBANK *n pl.* -S a mound of snow

SNOWBELL *n pl.* -S a flowering shrub

SNOWBELT *n pl.* -S a region that receives an appreciable amount of snow each year

SNOWBIRD *n pl.* -S a small bird

SNOWBUSH *n pl.* -ES a flowering shrub

SNOWCAP *n pl.* -S a covering of snow

SNOWDROP *n pl.* -S a European herb

SNOWFALL *n pl.* -S a fall of snow

SNOWIER comparative of snowy

SNOWIEST superlative of snowy

SNOWILY *adv* in a snowy manner

SNOWLAND *n pl.* -S an area marked by a great amount of snow

SNOWLESS *adj* having no snow

SNOWLIKE *adj* resembling snow

SNOWMAN *n pl.* -MEN a figure of a person that is made of snow

SNOWMELT *n pl.* -S water produced by the melting of snow

SNOWMOLD *n pl.* -S a fungus disease of grasses near the edge of melting snow

SNOWPACK *n pl.* -S an accumulation of packed snow

SNOWPLOW *v* -ED, -ING, -S to execute a type of skiing maneuver

SNOWSHED *n pl.* -S a structure built to provide protection against snow

SNOWSHOE *v* -SHOED, -SHOEING, -SHOES to walk on snowshoes (oval frames that allow a person to walk on deep snow)

SNOWSUIT *n pl.* -S a child's garment for winter wear

SNOWY *adj* SNOWIER, SNOWIEST abounding in snow

SNUB *v* SNUBBED, SNUBBING, SNUBS to treat with contempt or neglect

SNUBBER *n pl.* -S one that snubs
SNUBBY *adj* -BIER, -BIEST blunt
SNUBNESS *n pl.* -ES bluntness
SNUCK a past tense of sneak
SNUFF *v* -ED, -ING, -S to use or inhale snuff (powdered tobacco)
SNUFFBOX *n pl.* -ES a box for holding snuff
SNUFFER *n pl.* -S one that snuffs
SNUFFIER comparative of snuffy
SNUFFIEST superlative of snuffy
SNUFFILY *adv* in a snuffy manner
SNUFFLE *v* -FLED, -FLING, -FLES to sniffle
SNUFFLER *n pl.* -S one that snuffles
SNUFFLY *adj* -FLIER, -FLIEST tending to snuffle
SNUFFY *adj* SNUFFIER, SNUFFIEST dingy
SNUG *adj* SNUGGER, SNUGGEST warmly comfortable
SNUG *v* SNUGGED, SNUGGING, SNUGS to make snug
SNUGGERY *n pl.* -GERIES a snug place
SNUGGEST superlative of snug
SNUGGIES *n/pl* women's long underwear
SNUGGING present participle of snug
SNUGGLE *v* -GLED, -GLING, -GLES to lie or press closely
SNUGLY *adv* in a snug manner
SNUGNESS *n pl.* -ES the quality or state of being snug
SNYE *n pl.* -S a side channel in a river or creek
SO *n pl.* SOS sol
SOAK *v* -ED, -ING, -S to saturate thoroughly in liquid
SOAKAGE *n pl.* -S the act of soaking
SOAKER *n pl.* -S one that soaks
SOAP *v* -ED, -ING, -S to treat with soap (a cleansing agent)
SOAPBARK *n pl.* -S a tropical tree
SOAPBOX *n pl.* -ES a box for soap
SOAPER *n pl.* -S a serial melodrama on radio or television
SOAPIER comparative of soapy
SOAPIEST superlative of soapy
SOAPILY *adv* in a soapy manner
SOAPLESS *adj* having no soap
SOAPLIKE *adj* resembling soap
SOAPSUDS *n/pl* suds (soapy water)
SOAPWORT *n pl.* -S a perennial herb
SOAPY *adj* SOAPIER, SOAPIEST containing or resembling soap

SOAR *v* -ED, -ING, -S to fly at a great height
SOARER *n pl.* -S one that soars
SOARING *n pl.* -S the sport of flying in a heavier-than-air craft without power
SOAVE *n pl.* -S an Italian wine
SOB *v* SOBBED, SOBBING, SOBS to cry with a convulsive catching of the breath
SOBBER *n pl.* -S one that sobs
SOBEIT *conj* provided that
SOBER *adj* SOBERER, SOBEREST having control of one's faculties
SOBER *v* -ED, -ING, -S to make sober
SOBERIZE *v* -IZED, -IZING, -IZES to sober
SOBERLY *adv* in a sober manner
SOBFUL *adj* given to sobbing
SOBRIETY *n pl.* -ETIES the quality or state of being sober
SOCAGE *n pl.* -S a form of feudal land tenure
SOCAGER *n pl.* -S a tenant by socage
SOCCAGE *n pl.* -S socage
SOCCER *n pl.* -S a type of ball game
SOCIABLE *n pl.* -S a social
SOCIABLY *adv* in a friendly manner
SOCIAL *n pl.* -S a friendly gathering
SOCIALLY *adv* with respect to society
SOCIETY *n pl.* -ETIES an organized group of persons **SOCIETAL** *adj*
SOCK *n pl.* SOCKS or SOX a knitted or woven covering for the foot
SOCK *v* -ED, -ING, -S to strike forcefully
SOCKET *v* -ED, -ING, -S to furnish with a socket (an opening for receiving something)
SOCKEYE *n pl.* -S a food fish
SOCKLESS *adj* having no socks
SOCKMAN *n pl.* -MEN socman
SOCKO *adj* strikingly impressive
SOCLE *n pl.* -S a block used as a base for a column or pedestal
SOCMAN *n pl.* -MEN a socager
SOD *v* SODDED, SODDING, SODS to cover with sod (turf)
SODA *n pl.* -S a type of chemical compound **SODALESS** *adj*
SODALIST *n pl.* -S a member of a sodality
SODALITE *n pl.* -S a mineral
SODALITY *n pl.* -TIES a society

SODAMIDE *n pl.* -S a chemical compound

SODDED past tense of sod

SODDEN *v* -ED, -ING, -S to make soggy

SODDENLY *adv* in a soggy manner

SODDING present participle of sod

SODDY *n pl.* -DIES a house built of sod

SODIUM *n pl.* -S a metallic element
SODIC *adj*

SODOM *n pl.* -S a place notorious for vice and corruption

SODOMIST *n pl.* -S a sodomite

SODOMITE *n pl.* -S one who practices sodomy

SODOMIZE *v* -IZED, -IZING, -IZES to engage in sodomy with

SODOMY *n pl.* -OMIES unnatural copulation

SOEVER *adv* at all

SOFA *n pl.* -S a long, upholstered seat

SOFAR *n pl.* -S a system for locating underwater explosions

SOFFIT *n pl.* -S the underside of an architectural structure

SOFT *adj* SOFTER, SOFTEST yielding readily to pressure

SOFT *n pl.* -S a soft object or part

SOFTA *n pl.* -S a Muslim theological student

SOFTBACK *n pl.* -S a book bound in a flexible paper cover

SOFTBALL *n pl.* -S a type of ball

SOFTEN *v* -ED, -ING, -S to make soft

SOFTENER *n pl.* -S one that softens

SOFTHEAD *n pl.* -S a foolish person

SOFTIE *n pl.* -S softy

SOFTIES pl. of softy

SOFTISH *adj* somewhat soft

SOFTLY *adv* in a soft manner

SOFTNESS *n pl.* -ES the quality or state of being soft

SOFTWARE *n pl.* -S written or printed data used in computer operations

SOFTWOOD *n pl.* -S the soft wood of various trees

SOFTY *n pl.* SOFTIES a sentimental person

SOGGED *adj* soggy

SOGGY *adj* -GIER, -GIEST heavy with moisture SOGGILY *adv*

SOIGNE *adj* carefully done

SOIGNEE *adj* soigne

SOIL *v* -ED, -ING, -S to make dirty

SOILAGE *n pl.* -S green crops for feeding animals

SOILLESS *adj* carried on without soil (finely divided rock mixed with organic matter)

SOILURE *n pl.* -S a stain or smudge

SOIREE *n pl.* -S an evening party

SOJA *n pl.* -S the soybean

SOJOURN *v* -ED, -ING, -S to stay temporarily

SOKE *n pl.* -S a feudal right to administer justice within a certain territory

SOKEMAN *n pl.* -MEN socman

SOKOL *n pl.* -S an international group promoting physical fitness

SOL *n pl.* -S the fifth tone of the diatonic musical scale

SOLA a pl. of solum

SOLACE *v* -LACED, -LACING, -LACES to console

SOLACER *n pl.* -S one that solaces

SOLAN *n pl.* -S a gannet

SOLAND *n pl.* -S solan

SOLANDER *n pl.* -S a protective box for library materials

SOLANIN *n pl.* -S solanine

SOLANINE *n pl.* -S a poisonous alkaloid

SOLANO *n pl.* -NOS a strong, hot wind

SOLANUM *n pl.* -S any of a genus of herbs and shrubs

SOLAR *adj* pertaining to the sun

SOLARIA a pl. of solarium

SOLARISE *v* -ISED, -ISING, -ISES to solarize

SOLARISM *n pl.* -S an interpretation of folk tales as concepts of the nature of the sun

SOLARIUM *n pl.* -IA or -IUMS a room exposed to the sun

SOLARIZE *v* -IZED, -IZING, -IZES to expose to sunlight

SOLATE *v* -ATED, -ATING, -ATES to change to a fluid colloidal system

SOLATION *n pl.* -S the act of solating

SOLATIUM *n pl.* -TIA a compensation given for damage to the feelings

SOLD past tense of sell

SOLDAN *n pl.* -S a Muslim ruler

SOLDER *v* -ED, -ING, -S to join closely together

SOLDERER *n pl.* -S one that solders

SOLDI pl. of soldo

SOLDIER *v* -ED, -ING, -S to perform military service

SOLDIERY *n* pl. -DIERIES the military profession

SOLDO *n* pl. -DI a former coin of Italy

SOLE *v* SOLED, SOLING, SOLES to furnish with a sole (the bottom surface of a shoe or boot)

SOLECISE *v* -CISED, -CISING, -CISES to solecize

SOLECISM *n* pl. -S an ungrammatical combination of words in a sentence

SOLECIST *n* pl. -S one who solecizes

SOLECIZE *v* -CIZED, -CIZING, -CIZES to use solecisms

SOLED past tense of sole

SOLEI pl. of soleus

SOLELESS *adj* having no sole

SOLELY *adv* singly

SOLEMN *adj* -EMNER, -EMNEST serious **SOLEMNLY** *adv*

SOLENESS *n* pl. -ES the state of being the only one

SOLENOID *n* pl. -S a type of electric coil

SOLERET *n* pl. -S solleret

SOLEUS *n* pl. -LEI a leg muscle

SOLFEGE *n* pl. -S a type of singing exercise

SOLFEGGI *n/pl* solfeges

SOLGEL *adj* involving some changes in the state of a colloidal system

SOLI a pl. of solo

SOLICIT *v* -ED, -ING, -S to ask for earnestly

SOLID *adj* -IDER, -IDEST having definite shape and volume

SOLID *n* pl. -S a solid substance

SOLIDAGO *n* pl. -GOS a flowering plant

SOLIDARY *adj* united

SOLIDI pl. of solidus

SOLIDIFY *v* -FIED, -FYING, -FIES to make solid

SOLIDITY *n* pl. -TIES the quality or state of being solid

SOLIDLY *adv* in a solid manner

SOLIDUS *n* pl. -DI a coin of ancient Rome

SOLING present participle of sole

SOLION *n* pl. -S an electronic detecting and amplifying device

SOLIQUID *n* pl. -S a fluid colloidal system

SOLITARY *n* pl. -TARIES one who lives alone

SOLITON *n* pl. -S a solitary wave in physics

SOLITUDE *n* pl. -S the state of being alone

SOLLERET *n* pl. -S a sabaton

SOLO *n* pl. -LOS or -LI a musical composition for a single voice or instrument

SOLO *v* -ED, -ING, -S to perform alone

SOLOIST *n* pl. -S one that performs a solo

SOLON *n* pl. -S a wise lawgiver

SOLONETS *n* pl. -ES solonetz

SOLONETZ *n* pl. -ES a type of soil

SOLSTICE *n* pl. -S the time of the year when the sun is at its greatest distance from the celestial equator

SOLUBLE *n* pl. -S something that is soluble (capable of being dissolved)

SOLUBLY *adv* in a soluble manner

SOLUM *n* pl. -LA or -LUMS a soil layer

SOLUS *adj* alone

SOLUTE *n* pl. -S a dissolved substance

SOLUTION *n* pl. -S a homogeneous liquid mixture

SOLVABLE *adj* capable of being solved

SOLVATE *v* -VATED, -VATING, -VATES to convert into a type of ion

SOLVE *v* SOLVED, SOLVING, SOLVES to find the answer or explanation for

SOLVENCY *n* pl. -CIES the ability to pay all debts

SOLVENT *n* pl. -S a substance capable of dissolving others

SOLVER *n* pl. -S one that solves

SOLVING present participle of solve

SOMA *n* pl. -MATA or -MAS the body of an organism **SOMATIC** *adj*

SOMBER *adj* gloomy **SOMBERLY** *adv*

SOMBRE *adj* somber **SOMBRELY** *adv*

SOMBRERO *n* pl. -ROS a broad-brimmed hat

SOMBROUS *adj* somber

SOME *adj* being an unspecified number or part

SOMEBODY *n* pl. -BODIES an important person

SOMEDAY *adv* at some future time

SOMEDEAL *adv* to some degree

SOMEHOW *adv* by some means

SOMEONE *n* pl. -S a somebody

SOMERSET *v* -SETED, -SETING, -SETS or -SETTED, -SETTING, -SETS to roll the body in a complete circle, head over heels

SOMETIME *adv* at some future time

SOMEWAY *adv* somehow

SOMEWAYS *adv* someway

SOMEWHAT *n pl.* -S an unspecified number or part

SOMEWHEN *adv* sometime

SOMEWISE *adv* somehow

SOMITE *n pl.* -S a longitudinal segment of the body of some animals **SOMITAL, SOMITIC** *adj*

SON *n pl.* -S a male child

SONANCE *n pl.* -S sound

SONANT *n pl.* -S a sound uttered with vibration of the vocal cords **SONANTAL, SONANTIC** *adj*

SONAR *n pl.* -S an underwater locating device

SONARMAN *n pl.* -MEN a person who operates sonar equipment

SONATA *n pl.* -S a type of musical composition

SONATINA *n pl.* -TINAS or -TINE a short sonata

SONDE *n pl.* -S a device for observing atmospheric phenomena

SONDER *n pl.* -S a class of small yachts

SONE *n pl.* -S a unit of loudness

SONG *n pl.* -S a musical composition written or adapted for singing

SONGBIRD *n pl.* -S a bird that utters a musical call

SONGBOOK *n pl.* -S a book of songs

SONGFEST *n pl.* -S an informal gathering for group singing

SONGFUL *adj* melodious

SONGLESS *adj* incapable of singing

SONGLIKE *adj* resembling a song

SONGSTER *n pl.* -S a singer

SONHOOD *n pl.* -S the state of being a son

SONIC *adj* pertaining to sound

SONICATE *v* -CATED, -CATING, -CATES to disrupt with sound waves

SONICS *n/pl* the science dealing with the practical applications of sound

SONLESS *adj* having no son

SONLIKE *adj* resembling a son

SONLY *adj* pertaining to a son

SONNET *v* -NETED, -NETING, -NETS or -NETTED, -NETTING, -NETS to compose a sonnet (a type of poem)

SONNY *n pl.* -NIES a small boy

SONOBUOY *n pl.* -BUOYS a buoy that detects and transmits underwater sounds

SONOGRAM *n pl.* -S an image produced by ultrasound

SONORANT *n pl.* -S a type of voiced sound

SONORITY *n pl.* -TIES the quality or state of being sonorous

SONOROUS *adj* characterized by a full and loud sound

SONOVOX *n pl.* -ES a sound effects device

SONSHIP *n pl.* -S the state of being a son

SONSIE *adj* -SIER, -SIEST sonsy

SONSY *adj* -SIER, -SIEST comely

SOOCHONG *n pl.* -S souchong

SOOEY *interj* — used in calling pigs

SOOK *n pl.* -S souk

SOON *adv* SOONER, SOONEST in the near future

SOONER *n pl.* -S one who settles on government land before it is officially opened for settlement

SOOT *v* -ED, -ING, -S to cover with soot (a black substance produced by combustion)

SOOTH *adj* SOOTHER, SOOTHEST true

SOOTH *n pl.* -S truth

SOOTHE *v* SOOTHED, SOOTHING, SOOTHES to restore to a quiet or normal state

SOOTHER *n pl.* -S one that soothes

SOOTHLY *adv* in truth

SOOTHSAY *v* -SAID, -SAYING, -SAYS to predict

SOOTY *adj* SOOTIER, SOOTIEST covered with soot **SOOTILY** *adv*

SOP *v* SOPPED, SOPPING, SOPS to dip or soak in a liquid

SOPH *n pl.* -S a sophomore

SOPHIES pl. of sophy

SOPHISM *n pl.* -S a plausible but fallacious argument

SOPHIST *n pl.* -S one that uses sophisms

SOPHY *n pl.* -PHIES a ruler of Persia

SOPITE *v* -PITED, -PITING, -PITES to put to sleep

SOPOR *n pl.* -S an abnormally deep sleep

SOPPED past tense of sop

SOPPING *adj* very wet

SOPPY *adj* -PIER, -PIEST very wet

SOPRANO *n* pl. -NOS or -NI the highest singing voice

SORA *n* pl. -S a marsh bird

SORB *v* -ED, -ING, -S to take up and hold by absorption or adsorption **SORBABLE** *adj*

SORBATE *n* pl. -S a sorbed substance

SORBENT *n* pl. -S a substance that sorbs

SORBET *n* pl. -S sherbet

SORBIC *adj* pertaining to a type of fruit

SORBITOL *n* pl. -S a chemical compound

SORBOSE *n* pl. -S a type of sugar

SORCERER *n* pl. -S one who practices sorcery

SORCERY *n* pl. -CERIES alleged use of supernatural powers

SORD *n* pl. -S a flight of mallards

SORDID *adj* filthy **SORDIDLY** *adv*

SORDINE *n* pl. -S a device used to muffle the tone of a musical instrument

SORDINO *n* pl. -NI sordine

SORDOR *n* pl. -S a sordid state

SORE *adj* SORER, SOREST painfully sensitive to the touch

SORE *n* pl. -S a sore area on the body

SOREHEAD *n* pl. -S a person who is easily angered or offended

SOREL *n* pl. -S a sorrel

SORELY *adv* in a sore manner

SORENESS *n* pl. -ES the quality or state of being sore

SORER comparative of sore

SOREST superlative of sore

SORGHO *n* pl. -GHOS sorgo

SORGHUM *n* pl. -S a cereal grass

SORGO *n* pl. -GOS a variety of sorghum

SORI pl. of sorus

SORICINE *adj* belonging to the shrew family of mammals

SORING *n* pl. -S the practice of making a horse's front feet sore to force high stepping

SORITES *n* pl. SORITES a type of argument used in logic **SORITIC** *adj*

SORN *v* -ED, -ING, -S to force oneself on others for food and lodging

SORNER *n* pl. -S one that sorns

SOROCHE *n* pl. -S mountain sickness

SORORAL *adj* sisterly

SORORATE *n* pl. -S the marriage of a man usually with his deceased wife's sister

SORORITY *n* pl. -TIES a social club for women

SOROSIS *n* pl. -ROSES or -ROSISES a women's club or society

SORPTION *n* pl. -S the act or process of sorbing **SORPTIVE** *adj*

SORREL *n* pl. -S a reddish brown color

SORRIER comparative of sorry

SORRIEST superlative of sorry

SORRILY *adv* in a sorry manner

SORROW *v* -ED, -ING, -S to grieve

SORROWER *n* pl. -S one that sorrows

SORRY *adj* -RIER, -RIEST feeling grief or penitence

SORT *v* -ED, -ING, -S to arrange according to kind, class, or size **SORTABLE** *adj* **SORTABLY** *adv*

SORTER *n* pl. -S one that sorts

SORTIE *v* -TIED, -TIEING, -TIES to attack suddenly from a defensive position

SORUS *n* pl. -RI a cluster of plant reproductive bodies

SOT *n* pl. -S an habitual drunkard

SOTH *n* pl. -S sooth

SOTOL *n* pl. -S a flowering plant

SOTTED *adj* besotted

SOTTISH *adj* resembling a sot

SOU *n* pl. -S a former French coin

SOUARI *n* pl. -S a tropical tree

SOUBISE *n* pl. -S a sauce of onions and butter

SOUCAR *n* pl. -S a Hindu banker

SOUCHONG *n* pl. -S a Chinese tea

SOUDAN *n* pl. -S soldan

SOUFFLE *n* pl. -S a light, baked dish

SOUFFLED *adj* made puffy by beating and baking

SOUGH *v* -ED, -ING, -S to make a moaning or sighing sound

SOUGHT past tense of seek

SOUK *n* pl. -S a marketplace in northern Africa and the Middle East

SOUL *n* pl. -S the spiritual aspect of human beings **SOULED, SOULLESS, SOULLIKE** *adj*

SOULFUL *adj* full of emotion

SOUND *adj* SOUNDER, SOUNDEST being in good health or condition

SOUND v -ED, -ING, -S to measure the depth of water

SOUNDBOX n pl. -ES a resonant cavity in a musical instrument

SOUNDER n pl. -S one that sounds

SOUNDING n pl. -S a sampling or test of opinions

SOUNDLY adv in a sound manner

SOUNDMAN n pl. -MEN a person who controls the quality of sound being recorded

SOUP v -ED, -ING, -S to increase the power or efficiency of

SOUPCON n pl. -S a minute amount

SOUPY adj SOUPIER, SOUPIEST foggy

SOUR adj SOURER, SOUREST sharp or biting to the taste

SOUR v -ED, -ING, -S to make or become sour

SOURBALL n pl. -S a sour candy

SOURCE v SOURCED, SOURCING, SOURCES to obtain from a point of origin

SOURDINE n pl. -S sordine

SOURISH adj somewhat sour

SOURLY adv in a sour manner

SOURNESS n pl. -ES the quality or state of being sour

SOURPUSS n pl. -ES a grouchy person

SOURSOP n pl. -S a tropical tree

SOURWOOD n pl. -S a flowering tree

SOUSE v SOUSED, SOUSING, SOUSES to immerse

SOUTACHE n pl. -S a flat, narrow braid

SOUTANE n pl. -S a cassock

SOUTER n pl. -S a shoemaker

SOUTH v -ED, -ING, -S to move toward the south (a cardinal point of the compass)

SOUTHER n pl. -S a wind or storm from the south

SOUTHERN n pl. -S a person living in the south

SOUTHING n pl. -S movement toward the south

SOUTHPAW n pl. -S a left-handed person

SOUTHRON n pl. -S a southern

SOUVENIR n pl. -S a memento

SOUVLAKI n pl. -S a Greek shish kebab

SOVIET n pl. -S a legislative body in a Communist country

SOVKHOZ n pl. -KHOZES or -KHOZY a state-owned farm in the Soviet Union

SOVRAN n pl. -S a monarch

SOVRANLY adv supremely

SOVRANTY n pl. -TIES a monarchy

SOW v SOWED, SOWN, SOWING, SOWS to scatter over land for growth, as seed **SOWABLE** adj

SOWANS n pl. SOWANS sowens

SOWAR n pl. -S a mounted native soldier in India

SOWBELLY n pl. -LIES pork cured in salt

SOWBREAD n pl. -S a flowering plant

SOWCAR n pl. -S soucar

SOWENS n pl. SOWENS porridge made from oat husks

SOWER n pl. -S one that sows

SOWN past participle of sow

SOX a pl. of sock

SOY n pl. SOYS the soybean

SOYA n pl. -S soy

SOYBEAN n pl. -S the seed of a cultivated Asian herb

SOYMILK n pl. -S a milk substitute made from soybeans

SOYUZ n pl. -ES a Soviet manned spacecraft

SOZIN n pl. -S a type of protein

SOZINE n pl. -S sozin

SOZZLED adj drunk

SPA n pl. -S a mineral spring

SPACE v SPACED, SPACING, SPACES to set some distance apart

SPACEMAN n pl. -MEN an astronaut

SPACER n pl. -S one that spaces

SPACEY adj SPACIER, SPACIEST weird in behavior

SPACIAL adj spatial

SPACING n pl. -S the distance between any two objects

SPACIOUS adj vast or ample in extent

SPACKLE v -LED, -LING, -LES to fill cracks or holes in a surface with paste

SPACY adj SPACIER, SPACIEST spacey

SPADE v SPADED, SPADING, SPADES to take up with a spade (a digging implement)

SPADEFUL n pl. -S as much as a spade can hold

SPADER n pl. -S one that spades

SPADICES pl. of spadix

SPADILLE n pl. -S the highest trump in certain card games

SPADING present participle of spade

SPADIX *n pl.* -DICES or -DIXES a flower cluster

SPADO *n pl.* -DONES a castrated man or animal

SPAE *v* SPAED, SPAEING, SPAES to foretell

SPAEING *n pl.* -S the act of foretelling

SPAETZLE *n/pl* tiny dumplings

SPAGYRIC *n pl.* -S a person skilled in alchemy

SPAHEE *n pl.* -S spahi

SPAHI *n pl.* -S a Turkish cavalryman

SPAIL *n pl.* -S spale

SPAIT *n pl.* -S spate

SPAKE a past tense of speak

SPALE *n pl.* -S a splinter or chip

SPALL *v* -ED, -ING, -S to break up into fragments

SPALLER *n pl.* -S one that spalls

SPALPEEN *n pl.* -S a rascal

SPAN *v* SPANNED, SPANNING, SPANS to extend over or across

SPANCEL *v* -CELED, -CELING, -CELS or -CELLED, -CELLING, -CELS to bind or fetter with a rope

SPANDEX *n pl.* -ES a synthetic elastic fiber

SPANDREL *n pl.* -S a space between two adjoining arches

SPANDRIL *n pl.* -S spandrel

SPANG *adv* directly

SPANGLE *v* -GLED, -GLING, -GLES to adorn with spangles (bits of sparkling metal)

SPANGLY *adj* -GLIER, -GLIEST covered with spangles

SPANIEL *n pl.* -S a dog with silky hair

SPANK *v* -ED, -ING, -S to slap on the buttocks

SPANKER *n pl.* -S one that spanks

SPANKING *n pl.* -S the act of one that spanks

SPANLESS *adj* having no extent

SPANNED past tense of span

SPANNER *n pl.* -S one that spans

SPANNING present participle of span

SPANWORM *n pl.* -S an inchworm

SPAR *v* SPARRED, SPARRING, SPARS to provide with spars (stout poles used to support rigging)

SPARABLE *n pl.* -S a type of nail

SPARE *v* SPARED, SPARING, SPARES to refrain from punishing, harming, or destroying

SPARE *adj* SPARER, SPAREST meager **SPARELY** *adv*

SPARER *n pl.* -S one that spares

SPARERIB *n pl.* -S a cut of pork

SPAREST *adj* superlative of spare

SPARGE *v* -SPARGED, SPARGING, SPARGES to sprinkle

SPARGER *n pl.* -S one that sparges

SPARID *n pl.* -S any of a family of marine fishes

SPARING present participle of spare

SPARK *v* -ED, -ING, -S to give off sparks (small fiery particles)

SPARKER *n pl.* -S something that sparks

SPARKIER comparative of sparky

SPARKIEST superlative of sparky

SPARKILY *adv* in a lively manner

SPARKISH *adj* jaunty

SPARKLE *v* -KLED, -KLING, -KLES to give off or reflect flashes of light

SPARKLER *n pl.* -S something that sparkles

SPARKLY *adj* -KLIER, -KLIEST tending to sparkle

SPARKY *adj* SPARKIER, SPARKIEST lively

SPARLIKE *adj* resembling a spar

SPARLING *n pl.* -S a young herring

SPAROID *n pl.* -S a sparid

SPARRED past tense of spar

SPARRIER comparative of sparry

SPARRIEST superlative of sparry

SPARRING present participle of spar

SPARROW *n pl.* -S a small bird

SPARRY *adj* -RIER, -RIEST resembling spar (a lustrous mineral)

SPARSE *adj* SPARSER, SPARSEST thinly distributed **SPARSELY** *adv*

SPARSITY *n pl.* -TIES the quality or state of being sparse

SPARTAN *adj* avoiding luxury and comfort

SPASM *n pl.* -S an abnormal, involuntary muscular contraction

SPASTIC *n pl.* -S one suffering from spastic paralysis (a paralysis with muscle spasms)

SPAT *v* SPATTED, SPATTING, SPATS to strike lightly

SPATE *n pl.* -S a freshet

SPATHE n pl. -S a leaflike organ of certain plants **SPATHAL, SPATHED, SPATHOSE** adj

SPATHIC adj sparry

SPATIAL adj of or pertaining to space

SPATTED past tense of spat

SPATTER v -ED, -ING, -S to scatter in drops

SPATTING present participle of spat

SPATULA n pl. -S a mixing implement **SPATULAR** adj

SPATZLE n/pl spaetzle

SPAVIE n pl. -S spavin **SPAVIET** adj

SPAVIN n pl. -S a disease of horses **SPAVINED** adj

SPAWN v -ED, -ING, -S to deposit eggs

SPAWNER n pl. -S one that spawns

SPAY v -ED, -ING, -S to remove the ovaries of

SPAZ n pl. **SPAZZES** a clumsy, foolish, or incompetent person

SPEAK v **SPOKE** or **SPAKE, SPOKEN, SPEAKING, SPEAKS** to utter words

SPEAKER n pl. -S one that speaks

SPEAKING n pl. -S a speech or discourse

SPEAN v -ED, -ING, -S to wean

SPEAR v -ED, -ING, -S to pierce with a spear (a long, pointed weapon)

SPEARER n pl. -S one that spears

SPEARGUN n pl. -S a gun that shoots a spear

SPEARMAN n pl. -MEN a person armed with a spear

SPEC v **SPECCED, SPECCING, SPECS** to write specifications for

SPECIAL adj -CIALER, -CIALEST of a distinct or particular kind or character

SPECIAL n pl. -S a special person or thing

SPECIATE v -ATED, -ATING, -ATES to undergo a type of evolutionary process

SPECIE n pl. -S coined money

SPECIFIC n pl. -S a remedy intended for a particular disease

SPECIFY v -FIED, -FYING, -FIES to state in detail

SPECIMEN n pl. -S a typical example

SPECIOUS adj having a false look of truth or authenticity

SPECK v -ED, -ING, -S to mark with small spots

SPECKLE v -LED, -LING, -LES to speck

SPECS n/pl eyeglasses

SPECTATE v -TATED, -TATING, -TATES to attend and view

SPECTER n pl. -S a visible disembodied spirit

SPECTRA a pl. of spectrum

SPECTRAL adj resembling a specter

SPECTRE n pl. -S specter

SPECTRUM n pl. -TRA or -TRUMS an array of the components of a light wave

SPECULUM n pl. -LA or -LUMS a medical instrument **SPECULAR** adj

SPEECH n pl. -ES the faculty or act of speaking

SPEED v **SPED** or **SPEEDED, SPEEDING, SPEEDS** to move swiftly

SPEEDER n pl. -S one that speeds

SPEEDIER comparative of speedy

SPEEDIEST superlative of speedy

SPEEDILY adv in a speedy manner

SPEEDING n pl. -S the act of driving faster than the law allows

SPEEDO n pl. **SPEEDOS** a speedometer

SPEEDUP n pl. -S an acceleration of production without an increase in pay

SPEEDWAY n pl. -WAYS a road designed for rapid travel

SPEEDY adj **SPEEDIER, SPEEDIEST** swift

SPEEL v -ED, -ING, -S to climb

SPEER v -ED, -ING, -S to inquire

SPEERING n pl. -S inquiry

SPEIL v -ED, -ING, -S to speel

SPEIR v -ED, -ING, -S to speer

SPEISE n pl. -S speiss

SPEISS n pl. -ES a metallic mixture obtained in smelting certain ores

SPELAEAN adj spelean

SPELEAN adj living in caves

SPELL v **SPELLED** or **SPELT, SPELLING, SPELLS** to name or write the letters of in order

SPELLER n pl. -S one that spells words

SPELLING n pl. -S a sequence of letters composing a word

SPELT n pl. -S a variety of wheat

SPELTER n pl. -S zinc in the form of ingots

SPELTZ *n pl.* -ES spelt

SPELUNK *v* -ED, -ING, -S to explore caves

SPENCE *n pl.* -S a pantry

SPENCER *n pl.* -S a trysail

SPEND *v* SPENT, SPENDING, SPENDS to pay out

SPENDER *n pl.* -S one that spends

SPENSE *n pl.* -S spence

SPENT past tense of spend

SPERM *n pl.* -S a male gamete SPERMIC *adj*

SPERMARY *n pl.* -RIES an organ in which sperms are formed

SPERMINE *n pl.* -S a chemical compound

SPERMOUS *adj* resembling or made up of sperms

SPEW *v* -ED, -ING, -S to vomit

SPEWER *n pl.* -S one that spews

SPHAGNUM *n pl.* -S a grayish moss

SPHENE *n pl.* -S a mineral

SPHENIC *adj* shaped like a wedge

SPHENOID *n pl.* -S a bone of the skull

SPHERAL *adj* of, pertaining to, or having the form of a sphere

SPHERE *v* SPHERED, SPHERING, SPHERES to form into a sphere (a type of geometric solid)

SPHERIC *adj* spheral

SPHERICS *n/pl* the geometry of figures on the surface of a sphere

SPHERIER comparative of sphery

SPHERIEST superlative of sphery

SPHERING present participle of sphere

SPHEROID *n pl.* -S a type of geometric solid

SPHERULE *n pl.* -S a small sphere

SPHERY *adj* SPHERIER, SPHERIEST resembling a sphere

SPHINGES a *pl.* of sphinx

SPHINGID *n pl.* -S the hawkmoth

SPHINX *n pl.* -ES SPHINXES or SPHINGES a monster in Egyptian mythology

SPHYGMUS *n pl.* -ES the pulse SPHYGMIC *adj*

SPICA *n pl.* -CAE or -CAS an ear of grain SPICATE, SPICATED *adj*

SPICCATO *n pl.* -TOS a method of playing a stringed instrument

SPICE *v* SPICED, SPICING, SPICES to season with a spice (an aromatic vegetable substance)

SPICER *n pl.* -S one that spices

SPICERY *n pl.* -ERIES a spicy quality

SPICEY *adj* SPICIER, SPICIEST spicy

SPICIER comparative of spicy

SPICIEST superlative of spicy

SPICILY *adv* in a spicy manner

SPICING present participle of spice

SPICULA *n pl.* -LAE spicule SPICULAR *adj*

SPICULE *n pl.* -S a needlelike structure

SPICULUM *n pl.* -LA spicule

SPICY *adj* SPICIER, SPICIEST containing spices

SPIDER *n pl.* -S a type of arachnid

SPIDERY *adj* -DERIER, -DERIEST resembling a spider

SPIED past tense of spy

SPIEGEL *n pl.* -S a type of cast iron

SPIEL *v* -ED, -ING, -S to talk at length

SPIELER *n pl.* -S one that spiels

SPIER *v* -ED, -ING, -S to speer

SPIES present 3d person sing. of spy

SPIFF *v* -ED, -ING, -S to make spiffy

SPIFFING *adj* spiffy

SPIFFY *adj* -FIER, -FIEST stylish SPIFFILY *adv*

SPIGOT *n pl.* -S a faucet

SPIKE *v* SPIKED, SPIKING, SPIKES to fasten with a spike (a long, thick nail)

SPIKELET *n pl.* -S a type of flower cluster

SPIKER *n pl.* -S one that spikes

SPIKEY *adj* SPIKIER, SPIKIEST spiky

SPIKING present participle of spike

SPIKY *adj* SPIKIER, SPIKIEST resembling a spike SPIKILY *adv*

SPILE *v* SPILED, SPILING, SPILES to stop up with a wooden plug

SPILIKIN *n pl.* -S a strip of wood used in a game

SPILING *n pl.* -S a piling

SPILL *v* SPILLED or SPILT, SPILLING, SPILLS to cause to run out of a container

SPILLAGE *n pl.* -S something that is spilled

SPILLER *n pl.* -S one that spills

SPILLWAY *n pl.* -WAYS a channel for surplus water in a reservoir

SPILT a past tense of spill

SPILTH *n pl.* -S spillage

SPIN *v* SPUN, SPINNING, SPINS to draw out and twist into threads

SPINACH *n* pl. -ES a cultivated herb
SPINACHY *adj*

SPINAGE *n* pl. -S spinach

SPINAL *n* pl. -S an injection of an
anesthetic into the spinal cord

SPINALLY *adv* with respect to the spine

SPINATE *adj* bearing thorns

SPINDLE *v* -DLED, -DLING, -DLES to
impale on a slender rod

SPINDLER *n* pl. -S one that spindles

SPINDLY *adj* -DLIER, -DLIEST long and
slender

SPINE *n* pl. -S the vertebral column
SPINED *adj*

SPINEL *n* pl. -S a mineral

SPINELLE *n* pl. -S spinel

SPINET *n* pl. -S a small piano

SPINIER comparative of spiny

SPINIEST superlative of spiny

SPINIFEX *n* pl. -ES an Australian grass

SPINLESS *adj* having no rotation

SPINNER *n* pl. -S one that spins

SPINNERY *n* pl. -NERIES a spinning mill

SPINNEY *n* pl. -NEYS a thicket

SPINNING *n* pl. -S the act of one that
spins

SPINNY *n* pl. -NIES spinney

SPINOFF *n* pl. -S a new application or
incidental result

SPINOR *n* pl. -S a type of mathematical
vector

SPINOSE *adj* spiny

SPINOUS *adj* spiny

SPINOUT *n* pl. -S a rotational skid by an
automobile

SPINSTER *n* pl. -S an unmarried woman
who is past the usual age for
marrying

SPINTO *n* pl. -TOS a singing voice that
is lyric and dramatic

SPINULA *n* pl. -LAE spinule

SPINULE *n* pl. -S a small thorn

SPINY *adj* SPINIER, SPINIEST
bearing or covered with thorns

SPIRACLE *n* pl. -S an orifice through
which breathing occurs

SPIRAEA *n* pl. -S spirea

SPIRAL *v* -RALED, -RALING, -RALS
or -RALLED, -RALLING,
-RALS to move like a spiral (a
type of plane curve)

SPIRALLY *adv* in a spiral manner

SPIRANT *n* pl. -S a speech sound
produced by the forcing of
breath through a narrow
passage

SPIRE *v* SPIRED, SPIRING, SPIRES
to rise in a tapering manner

SPIREA *n* pl. -S a flowering shrub

SPIREM *n* pl. -S spireme

SPIREME *n* pl. -S a filament forming part
of a cell nucleus during mitosis

SPIRIER comparative of spiry

SPIRIEST superlative of spiry

SPIRILLA *n/pl* spirally twisted, aerobic
bacteria

SPIRING present participle of spire

SPIRIT *v* -ED, -ING, -S to carry off
secretly

SPIROID *adj* resembling a spiral

SPIRT *v* -ED, -ING, -S to spurt

SPIRULA *n* pl. -LAE or -LAS a spiral-
shelled mollusk

SPIRY *adj* SPIRIER, SPIRIEST tall,
slender, and tapering

SPIT *v* SPITTED, SPITTING,
SPITS to impale on a spit (a
pointed rod on which meat is
turned)

SPITAL *n* pl. -S a hospital

SPITBALL *n* pl. -S a type of pitch in
baseball

SPITE *v* SPITED, SPITING, SPITES
to treat with malice

SPITEFUL *adj* -FULLER, -FULLEST
malicious

SPITFIRE *n* pl. -S a quick-tempered
person

SPITING present participle of spite

SPITTED past tense of spit

SPITTER *n* pl. -S a spitball

SPITTING present participle of spit

SPITTLE *n* pl. -S saliva

SPITTOON *n* pl. -S a receptacle for saliva

SPITZ *n* pl. -ES a dog having a
heavy coat

SPIV *n* pl. -S a petty criminal

SPLAKE *n* pl. -S a freshwater fish

SPLASH *v* -ED, -ING, -ES to scatter a
liquid about

SPLASHER *n* pl. -S one that splashes

SPLASHY *adj* SPLASHIER,
SPLASHIEST showy

SPLAT *v* SPLATTED, SPLATTING,
SPLATS to flatten on impact

SPLATTER *v* -ED, -ING, -S to spatter

SPLAY *v* -ED, -ING, -S to spread out

SPLEEN *n* pl. -S a ductless organ of
the body

SPLEENY *adj* SPLEENIER,
SPLEENIEST peevish

SPLENDID *adj* -DIDER, -DIDEST magnificent

SPLENDOR *n pl.* -S magnificence

SPLENIA *pl.* of splenium

SPLENIAL *adj* pertaining to the splenius

SPLENIC *adj* pertaining to the spleen

SPLENIUM *n pl.* -NIA a surgical bandage

SPLENIUS *n pl.* -NII a muscle of the neck

SPLENT *n pl.* -S a splint

SPLICE *v* SPLICED, SPLICING, SPLICES to join at the ends

SPLICER *n pl.* -S one that splices

SPLIFF *n pl.* -S a marijuana cigarette

SPLINE *v* SPLINED, SPLINING, SPLINES to provide with a spline (a key that connects two rotating mechanical parts)

SPLINT *v* -ED, -ING, -S to brace with a splint (a thin piece of wood)

SPLINTER *v* -ED, -ING, -S to split into sharp, slender pieces

SPLIT *v* SPLIT, SPLITTING, SPLITS to separate lengthwise

SPLITTER *n pl.* -S one that splits

SPLODGE *v* SPLODGED, SPLODGING, SPLODGES to splotch

SPLORE *n pl.* -S a carousal

SPLOSH *v* -ED, -ING, -ES to splash

SPLOTCH *v* -ED, -ING, -ES to mark with large, irregular spots

SPLOTCHY *adj* SPLOTCHIER, SPLOTCHIEST splotched

SPLURGE *v* SPLURGED, SPLURGING, SPLURGES to spend money lavishly

SPLURGER *n pl.* -S one that splurges

SPLURGY *adj* SPLURGIER, SPLURGIEST tending to splurge

SPLUTTER *v* -ED, -ING, -S to speak rapidly and confusedly

SPODE *n pl.* -S a fine china

SPOIL *v* SPOILED or SPOILT, SPOILING, SPOILS to impair the value or quality of

SPOILAGE *n pl.* -S something that is spoiled or wasted

SPOILER *n pl.* -S one that spoils

SPOILT a past tense of spoil

SPOKE *v* SPOKED, SPOKING, SPOKES to provide with spokes (rods that support the rim of a wheel)

SPOKEN past participle of speak

SPOLIATE *v* -ATED, -ATING, -ATES to plunder

SPONDAIC *n pl.* -S a spondee

SPONDEE *n pl.* -S a type of metrical foot

SPONGE *v* SPONGED, SPONGING, SPONGES to wipe with a sponge (a mass of absorbent material)

SPONGER *n pl.* -S one that sponges

SPONGIER comparative of spongy

SPONGIEST superlative of spongy

SPONGILY *adv* in a spongy manner

SPONGIN *n pl.* -S a fibrous material

SPONGING present participle of sponge

SPONGY *adj* SPONGIER, SPONGIEST resembling a sponge

SPONSAL *adj* pertaining to marriage

SPONSION *n pl.* -S the act of sponsoring

SPONSON *n pl.* -S a projection from the side of a ship

SPONSOR *v* -ED, -ING, -S to make oneself responsible for

SPONTOON *n pl.* -S a spear-like weapon

SPOOF *v* -ED, -ING, -S to ridicule in fun

SPOOFER *n pl.* -S one that spoofs

SPOOFERY *n pl.* -ERIES good-natured ridicule

SPOOFY *adj* humorously satiric

SPOOK *v* -ED, -ING, -S to scare

SPOOKERY *n pl.* -ERIES something spooky

SPOOKISH *adj* spooky

SPOOKY *adj* SPOOKIER, SPOOKIEST scary **SPOOKILY** *adv*

SPOOL *v* -ED, -ING, -S to wind on a small cylinder

SPOOLING *n pl.* -S the temporary storage of data for later output

SPOON *v* -ED, -ING, -S to take up with a spoon (a type of eating utensil)

SPOONEY *adj* SPOONIER, SPOONIEST spoony

SPOONEY *n pl.* -EYS a spoony

SPOONFUL *n pl.* SPOONFULS or SPOONSFUL as much as a spoon can hold

SPOONIER comparative of spooney

SPOONIES *pl.* of spoony

SPOONIEST superlative of spooney

SPOONSFUL a *pl.* of spoonful

SPOONY *adj* SPOONIER, SPOONIEST overly sentimental **SPOONILY** *adv*

SPOONY *n pl.* SPOONIES a spoony person

SPOOR *v* -ED, -ING, -S to track

SPORADIC adj occurring at irregular intervals

SPORAL adj of, pertaining to, or resembling a spore

SPORE v SPORED, SPORING, SPORES to produce spores (asexual, usually single-celled reproductive bodies)

SPOROID adj resembling a spore

SPOROZOA n/pl parasitic one-celled animals

SPORRAN n pl. -S a large purse worn by Scottish Highlanders

SPORT v -ED, -ING, -S to frolic

SPORTER n pl. -S one that sports

SPORTFUL adj sportive

SPORTIF adj sporty

SPORTIVE adj playful

SPORTY adj SPORTIER, SPORTIEST showy SPORTILY adv

SPORULE n pl. -S a small spore SPORULAR adj

SPOT v SPOTTED, SPOTTING, SPOTS to mark with spots (small, roundish discolorations)

SPOTLESS adj perfectly clean

SPOTLIT a past tense of spotlight

SPOTTER n pl. -S one that spots

SPOTTING present participle of spot

SPOTTY adj -TIER, -TIEST marked with spots SPOTTILY adv

SPOUSAL n pl. -S marriage

SPOUSE v SPOUSED, SPOUSING, SPOUSES to marry

SPOUT v -ED, -ING, -S to eject in a rapid stream

SPOUTER n pl. -S one that spouts

SPRADDLE v -DLED, -DLING, -DLES to straddle

SPRAG n pl. -S a device used to prevent a vehicle from rolling backward

SPRAIN v -ED, -ING, -S to weaken by a sudden and violent twisting or wrenching

SPRANG n pl. -S a weaving technique to form an openwork mesh

SPRAT n pl. -S a small herring

SPRATTLE v -TLED, -TLING, -TLES to struggle

SPRAWL v -ED, -ING, -S to stretch out ungracefully

SPRAWLER n pl. -S one that sprawls

SPRAWLY adj SPHAWLIER, SPRAWLIEST tending to sprawl

SPRAY v -ED, -ING, -S to disperse in fine particles

SPRAYER n pl. -S one that sprays

SPREAD v SPREAD, SPREADING, SPREADS to open or expand over a larger area

SPREADER n pl. -S one that spreads

SPREE n pl. -S an unrestrained indulgence in an activity

SPRENT adj sprinkled over

SPRIER a comparative of spry

SPRIEST a superlative of spry

SPRIG v SPRIGGED, SPRIGGING, SPRIGS to fasten with small, thin nails

SPRIGGER n pl. -S one that sprigs

SPRIGGY adj -GIER, -GIEST having small branches

SPRIGHT n pl. -S sprite

SPRING v SPRANG or SPRUNG, SPRINGING, SPRINGS to move upward suddenly and swiftly

SPRINGAL n pl. -S a young man

SPRINGE v SPRINGED, SPRINGEING, SPRINGES to catch with a type of snare

SPRINGER n pl. -S one that springs

SPRINGY adj SPRINGIER, SPRINGIEST resilient

SPRINKLE v -KLED, -KLING, -KLES to scatter drops or particles on

SPRINT v -ED, -ING, -S to run at top speed

SPRINTER n pl. -S one that sprints

SPRIT n pl. -S a ship's spar

SPRITE n pl. -S an elf or fairy

SPRITZ v -ED, -ING, -ES to spray

SPRITZER n pl. -S a beverage of white wine and soda water

SPROCKET n pl. -S a toothlike projection that engages with the links of a chain

SPROUT v -ED, -ING, -S to begin to grow

SPRUCE adj SPRUCER, SPRUCEST neat and trim in appearance SPRUCELY adv

SPRUCE v SPRUCED, SPRUCING, SPRUCES to make spruce

SPRUCY adj SPRUCIER, SPRUCIEST spruce

SPRUE n pl. -S a tropical disease

SPRUG n pl. -S a sparrow

SPRUNG a past tense of spring

SPRY	*adj* SPRYER, SPRYEST or SPRIER, SPRIEST nimble SPRYLY *adv*
SPRYNESS	*n pl.* -ES the quality or state of being spry
SPUD	*v* SPUDDED, SPUDDING, SPUDS to remove with a spade-like tool
SPUDDER	*n pl.* -S a tool for removing bark from trees
SPUE	*v* SPUED, SPUING, SPUES to spew
SPUME	*v* SPUMED, SPUMING, SPUMES to foam
SPUMIER	comparative of spumy
SPUMIEST	superlative of spumy
SPUMING	present participle of spume
SPUMONE	*n pl.* -S an Italian ice cream made of layers of flavors
SPUMONI	*n pl.* -S spumone
SPUMOUS	*adj* spumy
SPUMY	*adj* SPUMIER, SPUMIEST foamy
SPUN	past tense of spin
SPUNK	*v* -ED, -ING, -S to begin to burn
SPUNKIE	*n pl.* -S a light caused by the combustion of marsh gas
SPUNKY	*adj* SPUNKIER, SPUNKIEST plucky SPUNKILY *adv*
SPUR	*v* SPURRED, SPURRING, SPURS to urge on with a spur (a horseman's goad)
SPURGALL	*v* -ED, -ING, -S to injure with a spur
SPURGE	*n pl.* -S a tropical plant
SPURIOUS	*adj* not genuine
SPURN	*v* -ED, -ING, -S to reject with contempt
SPURNER	*n pl.* -S one that spurns
SPURRED	past tense of spur
SPURRER	*n pl.* -S one that spurs
SPURREY	*n pl.* -REYS spurry
SPURRIER	*n pl.* -S one that makes spurs
SPURRING	present participle of spur
SPURRY	*n pl.* -RIES a European weed
SPURT	*v* -ED, -ING, -S to gush forth
SPURTLE	*n pl.* -S a stick for stirring porridge
SPUTA	pl. of sputum
SPUTNIK	*n pl.* -S a Soviet artificial earth satellite
SPUTTER	*v* -ED, -ING, -S to eject particles in short bursts
SPUTUM	*n pl.* -TA saliva

SPY	*v* SPIED, SPYING, SPIES to watch secretly
SPYGLASS	*n pl.* -ES a small telescope
SQUAB	*n pl.* -S a young pigeon
SQUABBLE	*v* -BLED, -BLING, -BLES to quarrel
SQUABBY	*adj* -BIER, -BIEST short and fat
SQUAD	*v* SQUADDED, SQUADDING, SQUADS to form into squads (small organized groups)
SQUADRON	*v* -ED, -ING, -S to arrange in squadrons (units of military organization)
SQUALENE	*n pl.* -S a chemical compound
SQUALID	*adj* -IDER, -IDEST marked by filthiness caused by neglect or poverty
SQUALL	*v* -ED, -ING, -S to cry or scream loudly
SQUALLER	*n pl.* -S one that squalls
SQUALLY	*adj* SQUALLIER, SQUALLIEST gusty
SQUALOR	*n pl.* -S the quality or state of being squalid
SQUAMA	*n pl.* -MAE a scale SQUAMATE, SQUAMOSE, SQUAMOUS *adj*
SQUANDER	*v* -ED, -ING, -S to spend wastefully
SQUARE	*adj* SQUARER, SQUAREST having four equal sides and four right angles; rigidly conventional
SQUARE	*v* SQUARED, SQUARING, SQUARES to make square
SQUARELY	*adv* in a direct manner
SQUARER	*n pl.* -S one that squares
SQUAREST	superlative of square
SQUARING	present participle of square
SQUARISH	*adj* somewhat square
SQUASH	*v* -ED, -ING, -ES to press into a pulp or flat mass
SQUASHER	*n pl.* -S one that squashes
SQUASHY	*adj* SQUASHIER, SQUASHIEST soft and moist
SQUAT	*v* SQUATTED, SQUATTING, SQUATS to sit on one's heels
SQUAT	*adj* SQUATTER, SQUATTEST short and thick SQUATLY *adv*
SQUATTER	*v* -ED, -ING, -S to move through water
SQUATTING	present participle of squat
SQUATTY	*adj* -TIER, -TIEST squat

SQUAWK v -ED, -ING, -S to utter a loud, harsh cry

SQUAWKER n pl. -S one that squawks

SQUEAK v -ED, -ING, -S to make a sharp, high-pitched sound

SQUEAKER n pl. -S one that squeaks

SQUEAKY adj SQUEAKIER, SQUEAKIEST tending to squeak

SQUEAL v -ED, -ING, -S to utter a sharp, shrill cry

SQUEALER n pl. -S one that squeals

SQUEEGEE v -GEED, -GEEING, -GEES to wipe with a squeegee (an implement for removing water from a surface)

SQUEEZE v SQUEEZED, SQUEEZING, SQUEEZES to press hard upon

SQUEEZER n pl. -S one that squeezes

SQUEG v SQUEGGED, SQUEGGING, SQUEGS to oscillate in an irregular manner

SQUELCH v -ED, -ING, -ES to squash

SQUELCHY adj SQUELCHIER, SQUELCHIEST squashy

SQUIB v SQUIBBED, SQUIBBING, SQUIBS to lampoon

SQUID v SQUIDDED, SQUIDDING, SQUIDS to fish for squid (ten-armed marine mollusks)

SQUIFFED adj drunk

SQUIFFY adj -FIER, -FIEST squiffed

SQUIGGLE v -GLED, -GLING, -GLES to wriggle

SQUIGGLY adj -GLIER, -GLIEST wriggly

SQUILGEE v -GEED, -GEEING, -GEES to squeegee

SQUILL n pl. -S a Eurasian herb

SQUILLA n pl. -LAS or -LAE a burrowing crustacean

SQUINCH v -ED, -ING, -ES to squint

SQUINNY v -NIED, -NYING, -NIES to squint

SQUINNY adj -NIER, -NIEST squinty

SQUINT adj SQUINTER, SQUINTEST cross-eyed

SQUINT v -ED, -ING, -S to look with the eyes partly closed

SQUINTER n pl. -S one that squints

SQUINTY adj SQUINTIER, SQUINTIEST marked by squinting

SQUIRE v SQUIRED, SQUIRING, SQUIRES to serve as a squire (an escort)

SQUIREEN n pl. -S an owner of a small estate

SQUIRISH adj of, resembling, or befitting a squire

SQUIRM v -ED, -ING, -S to wriggle

SQUIRMER n pl. -S one that squirms

SQUIRMY adj SQUIRMIER, SQUIRMIEST wriggly

SQUIRREL v -RELED, -RELING, -RELS or -RELLED, -RELLING, -RELS to store up for future use

SQUIRT v -ED, -ING, -S to eject in a thin, swift stream

SQUIRTER n pl. -S one that squirts

SQUISH v -ED, -ING, -ES to squash

SQUISHY adj SQUISHIER, SQUISHIEST squashy

SQUOOSH v -ED, -ING, -ES to squash

SQUOOSHY adj SQUOOSHIER, SQUOOSHIEST squashy

SQUUSH v -ED, -ING, -ES to squash

SRADDHA n pl. -S sradha

SRADHA n pl. -S a Hindu ceremonial offering

SRI n pl. -S mister; sir — used as a Hindu title of respect

STAB v STABBED, STABBING, STABS to pierce with a pointed weapon

STABBER n pl. -S one that stabs

STABILE n pl. -S a stationary abstract sculpture

STABLE adj -BLER, -BLEST resistant to sudden change or position or condition

STABLE v -BLED, -BLING, -BLES to put in a stable (a shelter for domestic animals)

STABLER n pl. -S one that keeps a stable

STABLEST superlative of stable

STABLING n pl. -S accommodation for animals in a stable

STABLISH v -ED, -ING, -ES to establish

STABLY adv in a stable manner

STACCATO n pl. -TOS or -TI a musical passage marked by the short, clear-cut playing of tones

STACK v -ED, -ING, -S to pile

STACKER n pl. -S one that stacks

STACKUP n pl. -S an arrangement of circling airplanes over an airport waiting to land

STACTE n pl. -S a spice used by the ancient Jews in making incense

STADDLE n pl. -S a platform on which hay is stacked

STADE n pl. -S an ancient Greek unit of length

STADIA n pl. -S a method of surveying distances

STADIUM n pl. -S a structure in which athletic events are held

STAFF v -ED, -ING, -S to provide with a staff (a body of assistants)

STAFFER n pl. -S a member of a staff

STAG v STAGGED, STAGGING, STAGS to attend a social function without a female companion

STAGE v STAGED, STAGING, STAGES to produce for public view

STAGEFUL n pl. -S as much or as many as a stage can hold

STAGER n pl. -S an experienced person

STAGEY adj STAGIER, STAGIEST stagy

STAGGARD n pl. -S a full-grown male red deer

STAGGART n pl. -S staggard

STAGGED past tense of stag

STAGGER v -ED, -ING, -S to walk or stand unsteadily

STAGGERY adj unsteady

STAGGIE n pl. -S a colt

STAGGING present participle of stag

STAGGY adj -GIER, -GIEST having the appearance of a mature male

STAGIER comparative of stagey and stagy

STAGIEST superlative of stagey and stagy

STAGILY adv in a stagy manner

STAGING n pl. -S a temporary platform

STAGNANT adj not moving or flowing

STAGNATE v -NATED, -NATING, -NATES to become stagnant

STAGY adj STAGIER, STAGIEST having a theatrical quality

STAID adj STAIDER, STAIDEST sober and sedate STAIDLY adv

STAIG n pl. -S a colt

STAIN v -ED, -ING, -S to discolor or dirty

STAINER n pl. -S one that stains

STAIR n pl. -S a rest for the foot used in going from one level to another

STAIRWAY n pl. -WAYS a flight of stairs

STAITHE n pl. -S a wharf equipped for transferring coal from railroad cars into ships

STAKE v STAKED, STAKING, STAKES to fasten with a stake (a pointed piece of wood or metal)

STAKEOUT n pl. -S a surveillance of an area especially by the police

STALAG n pl. -S a German prisoner-of-war camp

STALE adj STALER, STALEST not fresh STALELY adv

STALE v STALED, STALING, STALES to become stale

STALK v -ED, -ING, -S to pursue stealthily

STALKER n pl. -S one that stalks

STALKY adj STALKIER, STALKIEST long and slender STALKILY adv

STALL v -ED, -ING, -S to stop the progress of

STALLION n pl. -S an uncastrated male horse

STALWART n pl. -S an unwavering partisan

STAMEN n pl. -S the pollen-bearing organ of flowering plants

STAMINA n pl. -S endurance STAMINAL adj

STAMMEL n pl. -S a red color

STAMMER v -ED, -ING, -S to speak with involuntary breaks and pauses

STAMP v -ED, -ING, -S to bring the foot down heavily

STAMPEDE v -PEDED, -PEDING, -PEDES to cause to run away in headlong panic

STAMPER n pl. -S one that stamps

STANCE n pl. -S a manner of standing

STANCH adj STANCHER, STANCHEST staunch

STANCH v -ED, -ING, -ES to stop the flow of blood from

STANCHER n pl. -S one that stanches

STANCHLY adv in a stanch manner

STAND v STOOD, STANDING, STANDS to assume or maintain an upright position

STANDARD n pl. -S an established measure of comparison

STANDBY n pl. -BYS one that can be relied on

STANDEE n pl. -S one who stands because of the lack of seats

STANDER n pl. -S one that stands

STANDING n pl. -S a position or condition in society

STANDISH n pl. -ES a receptacle for pens and ink

STANDOFF n pl. -S a tie or draw, as in a game

STANDOUT n pl. -S one that shows marked superiority

STANDPAT adj resisting or opposing change

STANDUP adj having an upright position

STANE v STANED, STANING, STANES to stone

STANG v -ED, -ING, -S to sting

STANHOPE n pl. -S a light, open carriage

STANINE n pl. -S one of the nine classes into which a set of scores are divided

STANING present participle of stane

STANK n pl. -S a pond

STANNARY n pl. -RIES a tin-mining region

STANNIC adj pertaining to tin

STANNITE n pl. -S an ore of tin

STANNOUS adj pertaining to tin

STANNUM n pl. -S tin

STANZA n pl. -S a division of a poem STANZAED, STANZAIC adj

STAPEDES pl. of stapes

STAPELIA n pl. -S an African plant

STAPES n pl. -PEDES a bone of the middle ear

STAPH n pl. -S any of various spherical bacteria

STAPLE v -PLED, -PLING, -PLES to fasten by means of a U-shaped metal loop

STAPLER n pl. -S a stapling device

STAR v STARRED, STARRING, STARS to shine as a star (a natural luminous body visible in the sky)

STARCH v -ED, -ING, -ES to treat with starch (a solid carbohydrate)

STARCHY adj STARCHIER, STARCHIEST containing starch

STARDOM n pl. -S the status of a preeminent performer

STARDUST n pl. -S a romantic quality

STARE v STARED, STARING, STARES to gaze fixedly

STARER n pl. -S one that stares

STARETS n pl. STARTSY a spiritual adviser in the Eastern Orthodox Church

STARFISH n pl. -ES a star-shaped marine animal

STARGAZE v -GAZED, -GAZING, -GAZES to gaze at the stars

STARING present participle of stare

STARK adj STARKER, STARKEST harsh in appearance STARKLY adv

STARKERS adj naked

STARLESS adj having no stars

STARLET n pl. -S a small star

STARLIKE adj resembling a star

STARLING n pl. -S a European bird

STARLIT adj lighted by the stars

STARNOSE n pl. -S a burrowing mammal

STARRED past tense of star

STARRING present participle of star

STARRY adj -RIER, -RIEST abounding with stars

STARSHIP n pl. -S a spaceship for interstellar travel

START v -ED, -ING, -S to set out

STARTER n pl. -S one that starts

STARTLE v -TLED, -TLING, -TLES to frighten or surprise suddenly

STARTLER n pl. -S one that startles

STARTSY pl. of starets

STARTUP n pl. -S the act of starting something

STARVE v STARVED, STARVING, STARVES to die from lack of food

STARVER n pl. -S one that starves

STARWORT n pl. -S a flowering plant

STASES pl. of stasis

STASH v -ED, -ING, -ES to store in a secret place

STASIMON n pl. -MA a choral ode in ancient Greek drama

STASIS n pl. STASES a stoppage of the normal flow of bodily fluids

STAT n pl. -S a statistic

STATABLE adj capable of being stated

STATAL adj pertaining to a national government

STATANT adj standing with all feet on the ground — used of a heraldic animal

STATE v STATED, STATING, STATES to set forth in words

STATEDLY adv regularly

STATELY adj -LIER, -LIEST dignified

STATER *n* pl. -S one that states

STATIC *n* pl. -S random noise produced in a radio or television receiver STATICAL *adj*

STATICE *n* pl. -S a flowering plant

STATICKY *adj* marked by static

STATING present participle of state

STATION *v* -ED, -ING, -S to assign to a position

STATISM *n* pl. -S a theory of government

STATIST *n* pl. -S an adherent of statism

STATIVE *n* pl. -S a verb that expresses a condition

STATOR *n* pl. -S the part of a machine about which the rotor revolves

STATUARY *n* pl. -ARIES a group of statues

STATUE *n* pl. -S a three-dimensional work of art STATUED *adj*

STATURE *n* pl. -S the natural height of a human or animal body

STATUS *n* pl. -ES relative position

STATUSY *adj* conferring prestige

STATUTE *n* pl. -S a law enacted by the legislative branch of a government

STAUMREL *n* pl. -S a dolt

STAUNCH *adj* STAUNCHER, STAUNCHEST firm and dependable

STAUNCH *v* -ED, -ING, -ES to stanch

STAVE *v* STAVED or STOVE, STAVING, STAVES to drive or thrust away

STAW a past tense of steal

STAY *v* STAYED or STAID, STAYING, STAYS to continue in a place or condition

STAYER *n* pl. -S one that stays

STAYSAIL *n* pl. -S a type of sail

STEAD *v* -ED, -ING, -S to be of advantage to

STEADIED past tense of steady

STEADIER *n* pl. -S one that steadies

STEADIES present 3d person sing. of steady

STEADING *n* pl. -S a small farm

STEADY *adj* STEADIER, STEADIEST firm in position STEADILY *adv*

STEADY *v* STEADIED, STEADYING, STEADIES to make steady

STEAK *n* pl. -S a slice of meat

STEAL *v* STOLE or STAW, STOLEN, STEALING, STEALS to take without right or permission

STEALAGE *n* pl. -S theft

STEALER *n* pl. -S one that steals

STEALING *n* pl. -S the act of one that steals

STEALTH *n* pl. -S stealthy procedure

STEALTHY *adj* STEALTHIER, STEALTHIEST intended to escape observation

STEAM *v* -ED, -ING, -S to expose to steam (water in the form of vapor)

STEAMER *v* -ED, -ING, -S to travel by steamship

STEAMY *adj* STEAMIER, STEAMIEST marked by steam STEAMILY *adv*

STEAPSIN *n* pl. -S an enzyme

STEARATE *n* pl. -S a chemical salt

STEARIN *n* pl. -S the solid portion of a fat STEARIC *adj*

STEARINE *n* pl. -S stearin

STEATITE *n* pl. -S a variety of talc

STEDFAST *adj* staunch

STEED *n* pl. -S a horse

STEEK *v* -ED, -ING, -S to shut

STEEL *v* -ED, -ING, -S to cover with steel (a tough iron alloy)

STEELIE *n* pl. -S a steel playing marble

STEELY *adj* STEELIER, STEELIEST resembling steel

STEENBOK *n* pl. -S an African antelope

STEEP *adj* STEEPER, STEEPEST inclined sharply

STEEP *v* -ED, -ING, -S to soak in a liquid

STEEPEN *v* -ED, -ING, -S to make steep

STEEPER *n* pl. -S one that steeps

STEEPISH *adj* somewhat steep

STEEPLE *n* pl. -S a tapering structure on a church tower STEEPLED *adj*

STEEPLY *adv* in a steep manner

STEER *v* -ED, -ING, -S to direct the course of

STEERAGE *n* pl. -S the act of steering

STEERER *n* pl. -S one that steers

STEEVE *v* STEEVED, STEEVING, STEEVES to stow in the hold of a ship

STEEVING *n* pl. -S the angular elevation of a bowsprit from a ship's keel

STEGODON *n* pl. -S an extinct elephant-like mammal

STEIN *n* pl. -S a beer mug

STEINBOK n pl. -S steenbok

STELA n pl. -LAE or -LAI an inscribed slab used as a monument **STELAR, STELENE** adj

STELE n pl. -S the central portion of vascular tissue in a plant stem **STELIC** adj

STELLA n pl. -S a former coin of the United States

STELLAR adj pertaining to the stars

STELLATE adj shaped like a star

STELLIFY v -FIED, -FYING, -FIES to convert into a star

STEM v STEMMED, STEMMING, STEMS to remove stems (ascending axes of a plant) from

STEMLESS adj having no stem

STEMLIKE adj resembling a stem

STEMMA n pl. -MAS or -MATA a scroll recording the genealogy of a family in ancient Rome

STEMMED past tense of stem

STEMMER n pl. -S one that removes stems

STEMMERY n pl. -MERIES a place where tobacco leaves are stripped

STEMMING present participle of stem

STEMMY adj -MIER, -MIEST abounding in stems

STEMSON n pl. -S a supporting timber of a ship

STEMWARE n pl. -S a type of glassware

STENCH n pl. -ES a foul odor

STENCHY adj STENCHIER, STENCHIEST having a stench

STENCIL v -CILED, -CILING, -CILS or -CILLED, -CILLING, -CILS to mark by means of a perforated sheet of material

STENGAH n pl. -S a mixed drink

STENO n pl. STENOS a stenographer

STENOKY n pl. -KIES the ability of an organism to live only under a narrow range of conditions

STENOSED adj affected with stenosis

STENOSIS n pl. -NOSES a narrowing of a bodily passage **STENOTIC** adj

STENTOR n pl. -S a person having a very loud voice

STEP v STEPPED, STEPPING, STEPS to move by lifting the foot and setting it down in another place

STEPDAME n pl. -S a stepmother

STEPLIKE adj resembling a stair

STEPPE n pl. -S a vast treeless plain

STEPPED past tense of step

STEPPER n pl. -S one that steps

STEPPING present participle of step

STEPSON n pl. -S a son of one's spouse by a former marriage

STEPWISE adj marked by a gradual progression

STERE n pl. -S a unit of volume

STEREO v -ED, -ING, -S to make a type of printing plate

STERIC adj pertaining to the spatial relationships of atoms in a molecule

STERICAL adj steric

STERIGMA n pl. -MAS or -MATA a spore-bearing stalk of certain fungi

STERILE adj incapable of producing offspring

STERLET n pl. -S a small sturgeon

STERLING n pl. -S British money

STERN adj STERNER, STERNEST unyielding

STERN n pl. -S the rear part of a ship

STERNA a pl. of sternum

STERNAL adj pertaining to the sternum

STERNITE n pl. -S a somitic sclerite

STERNLY adv in a stern manner

STERNSON n pl. -S a reinforcing post of a ship

STERNUM n pl. -NA or -NUMS a long, flat supporting bone of most vertebrates

STERNWAY n pl. -WAYS the backward movement of a vessel

STEROID n pl. -S a type of chemical compound

STEROL n pl. -S a type of solid alcohol

STERTOR n pl. -S a deep snoring sound

STET v STETTED, STETTING, STETS to cancel a previously made printing correction

STEW v -ED, -ING, -S to cook by boiling slowly

STEWARD v -ED, -ING, -S to manage

STEWBUM n pl. -S a drunken bum

STEWPAN n pl. -S a pan used for stewing

STEY adj steep

STHENIA n pl. -S excessive energy **STHENIC** adj

STIBIAL adj pertaining to stibium

STIBINE n pl. -S a poisonous gas

STIBIUM n pl. -S antimony

STIBNITE n pl. -S an ore of antimony

STICH n pl. -S a line of poetry **STICHIC** adj

STICK	v -ED, -ING, -S to support with slender pieces of wood	**STIME**	n pl. -S a glimpse
STICK	v STUCK, STICKING, STICKS to pierce with a pointed object	**STIMULUS**	n pl. -LI something that causes a response
		STIMY	v -MIED, -MYING, -MIES to stymie
STICKER	n pl. -S an adhesive label		
STICKFUL	n pl. -S an amount of set type	**STING**	v STUNG, STINGING, STINGS to prick painfully
STICKIER	comparative of sticky		
STICKIEST	superlative of sticky	**STINGER**	n pl. -S one that stings
STICKILY	adv in a sticky manner	**STINGIER**	comparative of stingy
STICKIT	adj unsuccessful	**STINGIEST**	superlative of stingy
STICKLE	v -LED, -LING, -LES to argue stubbornly	**STINGILY**	adv in a stingy manner
		STINGO	n pl. -GOS a strong ale or beer
STICKLER	n pl. -S one that stickles		
STICKMAN	n pl. -MEN one who supervises the play at a dice table	**STINGRAY**	n pl. -RAYS a flat-bodied marine fish
		STINGY	adj -GIER, -GIEST unwilling to spend or give
STICKOUT	n pl. -S one that is conspicuous		
		STINK	v STANK or STUNK, STINKING, STINKS to emit a foul odor
STICKPIN	n pl. -S a decorative tiepin		
STICKUM	n pl. -S a substance that causes adhesion		
		STINKARD	n pl. -S a despicable person
STICKUP	n pl. -S a robbery at gunpoint	**STINKBUG**	n pl. -S an insect that emits a foul odor
STICKY	adj STICKIER, STICKIEST tending to adhere		
		STINKER	n pl. -S one that stinks
STICTION	n pl. -S the force required to begin to move a body that is in contact with another body	**STINKIER**	comparative of stinky
		STINKIEST	superlative of stinky
		STINKO	adj drunk
STIED	a past tense of sty	**STINKPOT**	n pl. -S a jar containing foul-smelling combustibles formerly used in warfare
STIES	present 3d person sing. of sty		
STIFF	adj STIFFER, STIFFEST difficult to bend or stretch		
		STINKY	adj STINKIER, STINKIEST emitting a foul odor
STIFF	v -ED, -ING, -S to cheat someone by not paying		
		STINT	v -ED, -ING, -S to limit
STIFFEN	v -ED, -ING, -S to make stiff	**STINTER**	n pl. -S one that stints
STIFFISH	adj somewhat stiff	**STIPE**	n pl. -S a slender supporting part of a plant STIPED adj
STIFFLY	adv in a stiff manner		
STIFLE	v -FLED, -FLING, -FLES to smother	**STIPEL**	n pl. -S a small stipule
		STIPEND	n pl. -S a fixed sum of money paid periodically
STIFLER	n pl. -S one that stifles		
STIGMA	n pl. -MAS or -MATA a mark of disgrace STIGMAL adj	**STIPES**	n pl. STIPITES a stipe
		STIPPLE	v -PLED, -PLING, -PLES to draw, paint, or engrave by means of dots or short touches
STILBENE	n pl. -S a chemical compound		
STILBITE	n pl. -S a mineral		
STILE	n pl. -S a series of steps for passing over a fence or wall	**STIPPLER**	n pl. -S one that stipples
		STIPULE	n pl. -S an appendage at the base of a leaf in certain plants STIPULAR, STIPULED adj
STILETTO	v -ED, -ING, -S or -ES to stab with a stiletto (a short dagger)		
		STIR	v STIRRED, STIRRING, STIRS to pass an implement through in circular motions
STILL	adj STILLER, STILLEST free from sound or motion		
		STIRK	n pl. -S a young cow
STILL	v -ED, -ING, -S to make still	**STIRP**	n pl. -S lineage
STILLMAN	n pl. -MEN one who operates a distillery	**STIRPS**	n pl. STIRPES a family or branch of a family
		STIRRED	past tense of stir
STILLY	adj STILLIER, STILLIEST still	**STIRRER**	n pl. -S one that stirs
STILT	v -ED, -ING, -S to raise on stilts (long, slender poles)		

STIRRING present participle of stir

STIRRUP *n* pl. -S a support for the foot of a horseman

STITCH *v* -ED, -ING, -ES to join by making in-and-out movements with a threaded needle

STITCHER *n* pl. -S one that stitches

STITHY *v* STITHIED, STITHYING, STITHIES to forge on an anvil

STIVER *n* pl. -S a former Dutch coin

STOA *n* pl. STOAE, STOAI, or STOAS an ancient Greek covered walkway

STOAT *n* pl. -S a weasel with a black-tipped tail

STOB *v* STOBBED, STOBBING, STOBS to stab

STOCCADO *n* pl. -DOS a thrust with a rapier

STOCCATA *n* pl. -S stoccado

STOCK *v* -ED, -ING, -S to keep for future sale or use

STOCKADE *v* -ADED, -ADING, -ADES to build a type of protective fence around

STOCKCAR *n* pl. -S a boxcar for carrying livestock

STOCKER *n* pl. -S a young animal suitable for being fattened for market

STOCKIER comparative of stocky

STOCKIEST superlative of stocky

STOCKILY *adv* in a stocky manner

STOCKING *n* pl. -S a knitted or woven covering for the foot and leg

STOCKISH *adj* stupid

STOCKIST *n* pl. -S one who stocks goods

STOCKMAN *n* pl. -MEN one who owns or raises livestock

STOCKPOT *n* pl. -S a pot in which broth is prepared

STOCKY *adj* STOCKIER, STOCKIEST having a short, thick body

STODGE *v* STODGED, STODGING, STODGES to stuff full with food

STODGY *adj* STODGIER, STODGIEST boring **STODGILY** *adv*

STOGEY *n* pl. -GEYS stogy

STOGIE *n* pl. -S stogy

STOGY *n* pl. -GIES a long, slender cigar

STOIC *n* pl. -S one who is indifferent to pleasure or pain **STOICAL** *adj*

STOICISM *n* pl. -S indifference to pleasure or pain

STOKE *v* STOKED, STOKING, STOKES to supply a furnace with fuel

STOKER *n* pl. -S one that stokes

STOKESIA *n* pl. -S a perennial herb

STOKING present participle of stoke

STOLE *n* pl. -S a long-wide scarf **STOLED** *adj*

STOLEN past participle of steal

STOLID *adj* -IDER, -IDEST showing little or no emotion **STOLIDLY** *adv*

STOLLEN *n* pl. -S a sweet bread

STOLON *n* pl. -S a type of plant stem **STOLONIC** *adj*

STOLPORT *n* pl. -S an airport for aircraft needing comparatively short runways

STOMA *n* pl. -MAS or -MATA a minute opening in the epidermis of a plant organ

STOMACH *v* -ED, -ING, -S to tolerate

STOMACHY *adj* paunchy

STOMAL *adj* stomatal

STOMATA a pl. of stoma

STOMATAL *adj* pertaining to a stoma

STOMATE *n* pl. -S a stoma

STOMATIC *adj* pertaining to the mouth

STOMODEA *n/pl* embryonic oral cavities

STOMP *v* -ED, -ING, -S to tread heavily

STOMPER *n* pl. -S one that stomps

STONE *v* STONED, STONING, STONES to pelt with stones (pieces of concreted earthy or mineral matter) **STONABLE** *adj*

STONEFLY *n* pl. -FLIES a winged insect

STONER *n* pl. -S one that stones

STONEY *adj* STONIER, STONIEST stony

STONIER comparative of stony

STONIEST superlative of stony

STONILY *adv* in a stony manner

STONING present participle of stone

STONISH *v* -ED, -ING, -ES to astonish

STONY *adj* STONIER, STONIEST abounding in stones

STOOD past tense of stand

STOOGE *v* STOOGED, STOOGING, STOOGES to act as a comedian's straight man

STOOK v -ED, -ING, -S to stack upright in a field for drying, as bundles of grain

STOOKER n pl. -S one that stooks

STOOL v -ED, -ING, -S to defecate

STOOLIE n pl. -S an informer

STOOP v -ED, -ING, -S to bend the body forward and down

STOOPER n pl. -S one that stoops

STOP v STOPPED or STOPT, STOPPING, STOPS to discontinue the progress or motion of

STOPBANK n pl. -S an embankment along a river

STOPCOCK n pl. -S a type of faucet

STOPE v STOPED, STOPING, STOPES to excavate in layers, as ore

STOPER n pl. -S one that stopes

STOPGAP n pl. -S a temporary substitute

STOPING present participle of stope

STOPOVER n pl. -S a brief stop in the course of a journey

STOPPAGE n pl. -S the act of stopping

STOPPED a past tense of stop

STOPPER v -ED, -ING, -S to plug

STOPPING present participle of stop

STOPPLE v -PLED, -PLING, -PLES to stopper

STOPT a past tense of stop

STORABLE n pl. -S something that can be stored

STORAGE n pl. -S a place for storing

STORAX n pl. -ES a fragrant resin

STORE v STORED, STORING, STORES to put away for future use

STOREY n pl. -REYS a horizontal division of a building STOREYED adj

STORIED past tense of story

STORIES present 3d person sing. of story

STORING present participle of store

STORK n pl. -S a wading bird

STORM v -ED, -ING, -S to blow violently

STORMY adj STORMIER, STORMIEST storming STORMILY adv

STORY v -RIED, -RYING, -RIES to relate as a story (an account of an event or series of events)

STOSS adj facing the direction from which a glacier moves

STOTINKA n pl. -KI a monetary unit of Bulgaria

STOUND v -ED, -ING, -S to ache

STOUP n pl. -S a basin for holy water

STOUR n pl. -S dust

STOURE n pl. -S stour

STOURIE adj stoury

STOURY adj dusty

STOUT adj STOUTER, STOUTEST fat

STOUT n pl. -S a strong, dark ale

STOUTEN v -ED, -ING, -S to make stout

STOUTISH adj somewhat stout

STOUTLY adv in a stout manner

STOVE n pl. -S a heating apparatus

STOVER n pl. -S coarse food for cattle

STOW v -ED, -ING, -S to pack STOWABLE adj

STOWAGE n pl. -S goods in storage

STOWAWAY n pl. -AWAYS one who hides aboard a conveyance to obtain free passage

STOWP n pl. -S stoup

STRADDLE v -DLED, -DLING, -DLES to sit, stand, or walk with the legs wide apart

STRAFE v STRAFED, STRAFING, STRAFES to attack with machine-gun fire from an airplane

STRAFER n pl. -S one that strafes

STRAGGLE v -GLED, -GLING, -GLES to stray

STRAGGLY adj -GLIER, -GLIEST irregularly spread out

STRAIGHT adj STRAIGHTER, STRAIGHTEST extending uniformly in one direction without bends or irregularities

STRAIGHT v -ED, -ING, -S to make straight

STRAIN v -ED, -ING, -S to exert to the utmost

STRAINER n pl. -S a utensil used to separate liquids from solids

STRAIT n pl. -S a narrow waterway connecting two larger bodies of water

STRAIT adj STRAITER, STRAITEST narrow STRAITLY adv

STRAITEN v -ED, -ING, -S to make strait

STRAKE n pl. -S a line of planking extending along a ship's hull STRAKED adj

STRAMASH n pl. -ES an uproar

STRAMONY n pl. -NIES a poisonous weed

STRAND *v* -ED, -ING, -S to leave in an unfavorable situation

STRANDER *n pl.* -S a machine that twists fibers into rope

STRANG *adj* strong

STRANGE *adj* STRANGER, STRANGEST unusual or unfamiliar

STRANGER *v* -ED, -ING, -S to estrange

STRANGLE *v* -GLED, -GLING, -GLES to choke to death

STRAP *v* STRAPPED, STRAPPING, STRAPS to fasten with a strap (a narrow strip of flexible material)

STRAPPER *n pl.* -S one that straps

STRASS *n pl.* -ES a brilliant glass used in making imitation gems

STRATA *n pl.* -S a stratum

STRATAL *adj* pertaining to a stratum

STRATEGY *n pl.* -GIES a plan for obtaining a specific goal

STRATH *n pl.* -S a wide river valley

STRATI *pl.* of stratus

STRATIFY *v* -FIED, -FYING, -FIES to form or arrange in layers

STRATOUS *adj* stratal

STRATUM *n pl.* -TA or -TUMS a layer of material

STRATUS *n pl.* -TI a type of cloud

STRAVAGE *v* -VAGED, -VAGING, -VAGES to stroll

STRAVAIG *v* -ED, -ING, -S to stravage

STRAW *v* -ED, -ING, -S to cover with straw (stalks of threshed grain)

STRAWHAT *adj* pertaining to a summer theater situated in a resort area

STRAWY *adj* STRAWIER, STRAWIEST resembling straw

STRAY *v* -ED, -ING, -S to wander from the proper area or course

STRAYER *n pl.* -S one that strays

STREAK *v* -ED, -ING, -S to cover with streaks (long, narrow marks)

STREAKER *n pl.* -S one that streaks

STREAKY *adj* STREAKIER, STREAKIEST covered with streaks

STREAM *v* -ED, -ING, -S to flow in a steady current

STREAMER *n pl.* -S a long, narrow flag

STREAMY *adj* STREAMIER, STREAMIEST streaming

STREEK *v* -ED, -ING, -S to stretch

STREEKER *n pl.* -S one that streeks

STREEL *v* -ED, -ING, -S to saunter

STREET *n pl.* -S a public thoroughfare

STRENGTH *n pl.* -S capacity for exertion or endurance

STREP *n pl.* -S any of various spherical or oval bacteria

STRESS *v* -ED, -ING, -ES to place emphasis on

STRESSOR *n pl.* -S a type of stimulus

STRETCH *v* -ED, -ING, -ES to draw out or open to full length

STRETCHY *adj* STRETCHIER, STRETCHIEST having a tendency to stretch

STRETTA *n pl.* -TE or -TAS stretto

STRETTO *n pl.* -TI or -TOS a concluding musical passage played at a faster tempo

STREUSEL *n pl.* -S a topping for coffee cakes

STREW *v* STREWED, STREWN, STREWING, STREWS to scatter about

STREWER *n pl.* -S one that strews

STRIA *n pl.* STRIAE a thin groove, stripe, or streak

STRIATE *v* -ATED, -ATING, -ATES to mark with striae

STRICK *n pl.* -S a bunch of flax fibers

STRICKEN *adj* strongly affected or afflicted

STRICKLE *v* -LED, -LING, -LES to shape or smooth with a strickle (an instrument for leveling off grain)

STRICT *adj* STRICTER, STRICTEST kept within narrow and specific limits **STRICTLY** *adv*

STRIDE *v* STRODE, STRIDDEN, STRIDING, STRIDES to walk with long steps

STRIDENT *adj* shrill

STRIDER *n pl.* -S one that strides

STRIDING present participle of stride

STRIDOR *n pl.* -S a strident sound

STRIFE *n pl.* -S bitter conflict or dissension

STRIGIL *n pl.* -S a scraping instrument

STRIGOSE *adj* covered with short, stiff hairs

STRIKE *v* STRUCK or STROOK, STRICKEN or STRUCKEN, STRIKING, STRIKES to come or cause to come into contact with

STRIKER *n* pl. -S one that strikes

STRING *v* STRUNG or STRINGED, STRINGING, STRINGS to provide with strings (slender cords)

STRINGER *n* pl. -S one that strings

STRINGY *adj* STRINGIER, STRINGIEST resembling a string or strings

STRIP *v* STRIPPED or STRIPT, STRIPPING, STRIPS to remove the outer covering from

STRIPE *v* STRIPED, STRIPING, STRIPES to mark with stripes (long, distinct bands)

STRIPER *n* pl. -S a food and game fish

STRIPIER comparative of stripy

STRIPIEST superlative of stripy

STRIPING *n* pl. -S the stripes marked or painted on something

STRIPPED a past tense of strip

STRIPPER *n* pl. -S one that strips

STRIPPING present participle of strip

STRIPT a past tense of strip

STRIPY *adj* STRIPIER, STRIPIEST marked with stripes

STRIVE *v* STROVE or STRIVED, STRIVEN, STRIVING, STRIVES to exert much effort or energy

STRIVER *n* pl. -S one that strives

STROBE *n* pl. -S a device that produces brief, high-intensity flashes of light

STROBIC *adj* spinning

STROBIL *n* pl. -S strobile

STROBILA *n* pl. -LAE the entire body of a tapeworm

STROBILE *n* pl. -S the conical, multiple fruit of certain trees

STROBILI *n/pl* strobiles

STRODE a past tense of stride

STROKE *v* STROKED, STROKING, STROKES to rub gently

STROKER *n* pl. -S one that strokes

STROLL *v* -ED, -ING, -S to walk in a leisurely manner

STROLLER *n* pl. -S one that strolls

STROMA *n* pl. -MATA the substance that forms the framework of an organ or cell **STROMAL** *adj*

STRONG *adj* STRONGER, STRONGEST having great strength **STRONGLY** *adv*

STRONGYL *n* pl. -S a parasitic worm

STRONTIA *n* pl. -S a chemical compound **STRONTIC** *adj*

STROOK a past tense of strike

STROP *v* STROPPED, STROPPING, STROPS to sharpen on a strip of leather

STROPHE *n* pl. -S a part of an ancient Greek choral ode **STROPHIC** *adj*

STROPPER *n* pl. -S one that strops

STROPPY *adj* -PIER, -PIEST unruly

STROUD *n* pl. -S a coarse woolen blanket

STROVE a past tense of strive

STROW *v* STROWED, STROWN, STROWING, STROWS to strew

STROY *v* -ED, -ING, -S to destroy

STROYER *n* pl. -S one that stroys

STRUCK a past tense of strike

STRUCKEN a past participle of strike

STRUDEL *n* pl. -S a type of pastry

STRUGGLE *v* -GLED, -GLING, -GLES to make strenuous efforts against opposition

STRUM *v* STRUMMED, STRUMMING, STRUMS to play a stringed instrument by running the fingers lightly across the strings

STRUMA *n* pl. -MAE or -MAS scrofula

STRUMMER *n* pl. -S one that strums

STRUMMING present participle of strum

STRUMOSE *adj* having a struma

STRUMOUS *adj* having or pertaining to a struma

STRUMPET *n* pl. -S a prostitute

STRUNG a past tense of string

STRUNT *v* -ED, -ING, -S to strut

STRUT *v* STRUTTED, STRUTTING, STRUTS to walk with a pompous air

STRUTTER *n* pl. -S one that struts

STUB *v* STUBBED, STUBBING, STUBS to strike accidentally against a projecting object

STUBBIER comparative of stubby

STUBBIEST superlative of stubby

STUBBILY *adv* in a stubby manner

STUBBING present participle of stub

STUBBLE *n* pl. -S a short, rough growth of beard **STUBBLED** *adj*

STUBBLY *adj* -BLIER, -BLIEST covered with stubble

STUBBORN *adj* unyielding

STUBBY	*adj* -BIER, -BIEST short and thick
STUCCO	*v* -ED, -ING, -ES or -S to coat with a type of plaster
STUCCOER	*n pl.* -S one that stuccoes
STUCK	past tense of stick
STUD	*v* STUDDED, STUDDING, STUDS to set thickly with small projections
STUDBOOK	*n pl.* -S a record of the pedigree of purebred animals
STUDDIE	*n pl.* -S an anvil
STUDDING	*n pl.* -S the framework of a wall
STUDENT	*n pl.* -S a person formally engaged in learning
STUDFISH	*n pl.* -ES a freshwater fish
STUDIED	past tense of study
STUDIER	*n pl.* -S one that studies
STUDIES	present 3d person sing. of study
STUDIO	*n pl.* -DIOS an artist's workroom
STUDIOUS	*adj* given to study
STUDLY	*adj* -LIER, -LIEST muscular and attractive
STUDWORK	*n pl.* -S studding
STUDY	*v* STUDIED, STUDYING, STUDIES to apply the mind to the acquisition of knowledge
STUFF	*v* -ED, -ING, -S to fill or pack tightly
STUFFER	*n pl.* -S one that stuffs
STUFFING	*n pl.* -S material with which something is stuffed
STUFFY	*adj* STUFFIER, STUFFIEST poorly ventilated STUFFILY *adv*
STUIVER	*n pl.* -S stiver
STULL	*n pl.* -S a supporting timber in a mine
STULTIFY	*v* -FIED, -FYING, -FIES to cause to appear absurd
STUM	*v* STUMMED, STUMMING, STUMS to increase the fermentation of by adding grape juice
STUMBLE	*v* -BLED, -BLING, -BLES to miss one's step in walking or running
STUMBLER	*n pl.* -S one that stumbles
STUMMED	past tense of stum
STUMMING	present participle of stum
STUMP	*v* -ED, -ING, -S to baffle
STUMPAGE	*n pl.* -S uncut marketable timber
STUMPER	*n pl.* -S a baffling question
STUMPY	*adj* STUMPIER, STUMPIEST short and thick
STUN	*v* STUNNED, STUNNING, STUNS to render senseless or incapable of action
STUNG	past tense of sting
STUNK	a past tense of stink
STUNNED	past tense of stun
STUNNER	*n pl.* -S one that stuns
STUNNING	*adj* strikingly beautiful or attractive
STUNSAIL	*n pl.* -S a type of sail
STUNT	*v* -ED, -ING, -S to hinder the normal growth of
STUNTMAN	*n pl.* -MEN a person who substitutes for an actor in scenes involving dangerous activities
STUPA	*n pl.* -S a Buddhist shrine
STUPE	*n pl.* -S a medicated cloth to be applied to a wound
STUPEFY	*v* -FIED, -FYING, -FIES to dull the senses of
STUPID	*adj* -PIDER, -PIDEST mentally slow STUPIDLY *adv*
STUPID	*n pl.* -S a stupid person
STUPOR	*n pl.* -S a state of reduced sensibility
STURDY	*adj* -DIER, -DIEST strong and durable STURDILY *adv*
STURDY	*n pl.* -DIES a disease of sheep STURDIED *adj*
STURGEON	*n pl.* -S an edible fish
STURT	*n pl.* -S contention
STUTTER	*v* -ED, -ING, -S to speak with spasmodic repetition
STY	*v* STIED or STYED, STYING, STIES to keep in a pigpen
STYE	*n pl.* -S an inflamed swelling of the eyelid
STYGIAN	*adj* gloomy
STYLAR	*adj* pertaining to a stylus
STYLATE	*adj* bearing a stylet
STYLE	*v* STYLED, STYLING, STYLES to name
STYLER	*n pl.* -S one that styles
STYLET	*n pl.* -S a small, stiff organ or appendage of certain animals
STYLI	a pl. of stylus
STYLING	*n pl.* -S the way in which something is styled
STYLISE	*v* -ISED, -ISING, -ISES to stylize
STYLISER	*n pl.* -S one that stylises
STYLISH	*adj* fashionable

STYLISING	present participle of stylise
STYLIST	n pl. -S one who is a master of a literary or rhetorical style
STYLITE	n pl. -S an early Christian ascetic STYLITIC adj
STYLIZE	v -IZED, -IZING, -IZES to make conventional
STYLIZER	n pl. -S one that stylizes
STYLOID	adj slender and pointed
STYLUS	n pl. -LI or -LUSES a pointed instrument for writing, marking, or engraving
STYMIE	v -MIED, -MIEING, -MIES to thwart
STYMY	v -MIED, -MYING, -MIES to stymie
STYPSIS	n pl. -SISES the use of a styptic
STYPTIC	n pl. -S a substance used to check bleeding
STYRAX	n pl. -ES storax
STYRENE	n pl. -S a liquid hydrocarbon
SUABLE	adj capable of being sued SUABLY adv
SUASION	n pl. -S persuasion SUASIVE, SUASORY adj
SUAVE	adj SUAVER, SUAVEST smoothly affable and polite SUAVELY adv
SUAVITY	n pl. -TIES the state of being suave
SUB	v SUBBED, SUBBING, SUBS to act as a substitute
SUBA	n pl. -S subah
SUBABBOT	n pl. -S a subordinate abbot
SUBACID	adj slightly sour
SUBACRID	adj somewhat acrid
SUBACUTE	adj somewhat acute
SUBADAR	n pl. -S subahdar
SUBADULT	n pl. -S an individual approaching adulthood
SUBAGENT	n pl. -S a subordinate agent
SUBAH	n pl. -S a province of India
SUBAHDAR	n pl. -S a governor of a subah
SUBALAR	adj somewhat alar
SUBAREA	n pl. -S a subdivision of an area
SUBARID	adj somewhat arid
SUBATOM	n pl. -S a component of an atom
SUBAXIAL	adj somewhat axial
SUBBASE	n pl. -S the lowest part of a base
SUBBASIN	n pl. -S a section of an area drained by a river

SUBBASS	n pl. -ES a pedal stop producing the lowest tones of an organ
SUBBED	past tense of sub
SUBBING	n pl. -S a thin coating on the support of a photographic film
SUBBLOCK	n pl. -S a subdivision of a block
SUBBREED	n pl. -S a distinguishable strain within a breed
SUBCASTE	n pl. -S a subdivision of a caste
SUBCAUSE	n pl. -S a subordinate cause
SUBCELL	n pl. -S a subdivision of a cell
SUBCHIEF	n pl. -S a subordinate chief
SUBCLAN	n pl. -S a subdivision of a clan
SUBCLASS	v -ED, -ING, -ES to place in a subdivision of a class
SUBCLERK	n pl. -S a subordinate clerk
SUBCODE	n pl. -S a subdivision of a code
SUBCOOL	v -ED, -ING, -S to cool below the freezing point without solidification
SUBCULT	n pl. -S a subdivision of a cult
SUBCUTIS	n pl. -CUTES or -CUTISES the deeper part of the dermis
SUBDEAN	n pl. -S a subordinate dean
SUBDEB	n pl. -S a girl the year before she becomes a debutante
SUBDEPOT	n pl. -S a military depot that operates under the jurisdiction of another depot
SUBDUAL	n pl. -S the act of subduing
SUBDUCE	v -DUCED, -DUCING, -DUCES to take away
SUBDUCT	v -ED, -ING, -S to subduce
SUBDUE	v -DUED, -DUING, -DUES to bring under control
SUBDUER	n pl. -S one that subdues
SUBDURAL	adj situated under the dura mater
SUBECHO	n pl. -ECHOES an inferior echo
SUBEDIT	v -ED, -ING, -S to act as the assistant editor of
SUBENTRY	n pl. -TRIES an entry made under a more general entry
SUBEPOCH	n pl. -S a subdivision of an epoch
SUBER	n pl. -S phellem
SUBERECT	adj nearly erect
SUBERIC	adj pertaining to cork
SUBERIN	n pl. -S a substance found in cork cells

SUBERISE v -ISED, -ISING, -ISES to suberize

SUBERIZE v -IZED, -IZING, -IZES to convert into cork tissue

SUBEROSE adj corky

SUBEROUS adj suberose

SUBFIELD n pl. -S a subset of a mathematical field that is itself a field

SUBFILE n pl. -S a subdivision of a file

SUBFIX n pl. -ES a distinguishing symbol or letter written below another character

SUBFLOOR n pl. -S a rough floor laid as a base for a finished floor

SUBFLUID adj somewhat fluid

SUBFRAME n pl. -S a frame for the attachment of a finish frame

SUBFUSC adj dark in color

SUBGENRE n pl. -S a subdivision of a genre

SUBGENUS n pl. -GENERA or -GENUSES a subdivision of a genus

SUBGOAL n pl. -S a subordinate goal

SUBGRADE n pl. -S a surface on which a pavement is placed

SUBGRAPH n pl. -S a graph contained within a larger graph

SUBGROUP n pl. -S a distinct group within a group

SUBGUM n pl. -S a Chinese dish of mixed vegetables

SUBHEAD n pl. -S the heading of a subdivision

SUBHUMAN n pl. -S one that is less than human

SUBHUMID adj somewhat humid

SUBIDEA n pl. -S an inferior idea

SUBINDEX n pl. -DEXES or -DICES a subfix

SUBITEM n pl. -S an item that forms a subdivision of a larger topic

SUBITO adv quickly — used as a musical direction

SUBJECT v -ED, -ING, -S to cause to experience

SUBJOIN v -ED, -ING, -S to add at the end

SUBLATE v -LATED, -LATING, -LATES to cancel

SUBLEASE v -LEASED, -LEASING, -LEASES to sublet

SUBLET v -LET, -LETTING, -LETS to rent leased property to another

SUBLEVEL n pl. -S a lower level

SUBLIME adj -LIMER, -LIMEST of elevated or noble quality

SUBLIME v -LIMED, -LIMING, -LIMES to make sublime

SUBLIMER n pl. -S one that sublimes

SUBLIMEST superlative of sublime

SUBLIMING present participle of sublime

SUBLINE n pl. -S an inbred line within a strain

SUBLOT n pl. -S a subdivision of a lot

SUBLUNAR adj pertaining to the earth

SUBMENU n pl. -S a secondary list of options for a computer

SUBMERGE v -MERGED, -MERGING, -MERGES to place below the surface of a liquid

SUBMERSE v -MERSED, -MERSING, -MERSES to submerge

SUBMISS adj inclined to submit

SUBMIT v -MITTED, -MITTING, -MITS to yield to the power of another

SUBNASAL adj situated under the nose

SUBNET n pl. -S a system of interconnections within a communications system

SUBNICHE n pl. -S a subdivision of a habitat

SUBNODAL adj situated under a node

SUBOPTIC adj situated under the eyes

SUBORAL adj situated under the mouth

SUBORDER n pl. -S a category of related families within an order

SUBORN v -ED, -ING, -S to induce to commit perjury

SUBORNER n pl. -S one that suborns

SUBOVAL adj nearly oval

SUBOVATE adj nearly ovate

SUBOXIDE n pl. -S an oxide containing relatively little oxygen

SUBPANEL n pl. -S a subdivision of a panel

SUBPAR adj below par

SUBPART n pl. -S a subdivision of a part

SUBPENA v -ED, -ING, -S to subpoena

SUBPHASE n pl. -S a subdivision of a phase

SUBPHYLA n/pl divisions within a phylum

SUBPLOT n pl. -S a secondary literary plot

SUBPOENA v -ED, -ING, -S to summon with a type of judicial writ

SUBPOLAR adj situated just outside the polar circles

SUBPUBIC adj situated under the pubis

SUBRACE n pl. -S a subdivision of a race

SUBRENT n pl. -S rent from a subtenant

SUBRING *n* pl. -S a subset of a mathematical ring that is itself a ring

SUBRULE *n* pl. -S a subordinate rule

SUBSALE *n* pl. -S a resale of purchased goods

SUBSCALE *n* pl. -S a subdivision of a scale

SUBSEA *adj* situated below the surface of the sea

SUBSECT *n* pl. -S a sect directly derived from another

SUBSENSE *n* pl. -S a subdivision of a sense

SUBSERE *n* pl. -S a type of ecological succession

SUBSERVE *v* -SERVED, -SERVING, -SERVES to serve to promote

SUBSET *n* pl. -S a mathematical set contained within a larger set

SUBSHAFT *n* pl. -S a shaft that is beneath another shaft

SUBSHELL *n* pl. -S one of the orbitals making up an electron shell of an atom

SUBSHRUB *n* pl. -S a low shrub

SUBSIDE *v* -SIDED, -SIDING, -SIDES to sink to a lower or normal level

SUBSIDER *n* pl. -S one that subsides

SUBSIDY *n* pl. -DIES a grant or contribution of money

SUBSIST *v* -ED, -ING, -S to live on

SUBSITE *n* pl. -S a subdivision of a site

SUBSKILL *n* pl. -S a subordinate skill

SUBSOIL *v* -ED, -ING, -S to plow so as to turn up the subsoil (the layer of earth beneath the surface soil)

SUBSOLAR *adj* situated directly beneath the sun

SUBSONIC *adj* moving at a speed less than that of sound

SUBSPACE *n* pl. -S a subset of a mathematical space

SUBSTAGE *n* pl. -S a part of a microscope for supporting accessories

SUBSTATE *n* pl. -S a subdivision of a state

SUBSUME *v* -SUMED, -SUMING, -SUMES to classify within a larger category

SUBTASK *n* pl. -S a subordinate task

SUBTAXON *n* pl. -TAXA or -TAXONS a subdivision of a taxon

SUBTEEN *n* pl. -S a person approaching the teenage years

SUBTEND *v* -ED, -ING, -S to extend under or opposite to

SUBTEST *n* pl. -S a subdivision of a test

SUBTEXT *n* pl. -S written or printed matter under a more general text

SUBTHEME *n* pl. -S a subordinate theme

SUBTILE *adj* -TILER, -TILEST subtle

SUBTILIN *n* pl. -S an antibiotic

SUBTILTY *n* pl. -TIES subtlety

SUBTITLE *v* -TLED, -TLING, -TLES to give a secondary title to

SUBTLE *adj* -TLER, -TLEST so slight as to be difficult to detect **SUBTLY** *adv*

SUBTLETY *n* pl. -TIES the state of being subtle

SUBTONE *n* pl. -S a low or subdued tone

SUBTONIC *n* pl. -S a type of musical tone

SUBTOPIA *n* pl. -S the suburbs of a city

SUBTOPIC *n* pl. -S a secondary topic

SUBTOTAL *v* -TALED, -TALING, -TALS or -TALLED, -TALLING, -TALS to total a portion of

SUBTRACT *v* -ED, -ING, -S to take away

SUBTREND *n* pl. -S a subordinate trend

SUBTRIBE *n* pl. -S a subdivision of a tribe

SUBTUNIC *n* pl. -S a tunic worn under another tunic

SUBTYPE *n* pl. -S a type that is subordinate to or included in another type

SUBULATE *adj* slender and tapering to a point

SUBUNIT *n* pl. -S a unit that is a part of a larger unit

SUBURB *n* pl. -S a residential area adjacent to a city **SUBURBED** *adj*

SUBURBAN *n* pl. -S one who lives in a suburb

SUBURBIA *n* pl. -S the suburbs of a city

SUBVENE *v* -VENED, -VENING, -VENES to arrive or occur as a support or relief

SUBVERT *v* -ED, -ING, -S to destroy completely

SUBVICAR *n* pl. -S a subordinate vicar

SUBVIRAL *adj* pertaining to a part of a virus

SUBVOCAL *adj* mentally formulated as words

SUBWAY *v* -ED, -ING, -S to travel by an underground railroad

SUBWORLD *n* pl. -S a subdivision of a sphere of interest or activity

SUBZERO *adj* registering less than zero

SUBZONE *n pl.* -S a subdivision of a zone

SUCCAH *n pl.* -CAHS or -COTH sukkah

SUCCEED *v* -ED, -ING, -S to accomplish something desired or intended

SUCCESS *n pl.* -ES the attainment of something desired or intended

SUCCINCT *adj* -CINCTER, -CINCTEST clearly expressed in few words

SUCCINIC *adj* pertaining to amber

SUCCINYL *n pl.* -S a univalent radical

SUCCOR *v* -ED, -ING, -S to go to the aid of

SUCCORER *n pl.* -S one that succors

SUCCORY *n pl.* -RIES chicory

SUCCOTH *a pl.* of succah

SUCCOUR *v* -ED, -ING, -S to succor

SUCCUBA *n pl.* -BAE a succubus

SUCCUBUS *n pl.* -BI or -BUSES a female demon

SUCCUMB *v* -ED, -ING, -S to yield to superior force

SUCCUSS *v* -ED, -ING, -ES to shake violently

SUCH *adj* of that kind

SUCHLIKE *adj* of a similar kind

SUCHNESS *n pl.* -ES essential or characteristic quality

SUCK *v* -ED, -ING, -S to draw in by establishing a partial vacuum

SUCKER *v* -ED, -ING, -S to strip of lower shoots or branches

SUCKFISH *n pl.* -ES a remora

SUCKLE *v* -LED, -LING, -LES to give milk to from the breast

SUCKLER *n pl.* -S one that suckles

SUCKLESS *adj* having no juice

SUCKLING *n pl.* -S a young mammal that has not been weaned

SUCRASE *n pl.* -S an enzyme

SUCRE *n pl.* -S a monetary unit of Ecuador

SUCROSE *n pl.* -S a type of sugar

SUCTION *v* -ED, -ING, -S to remove by the process of sucking

SUDARIUM *n pl.* -IA a cloth for wiping the face

SUDARY *n pl.* -RIES sudarium

SUDATION *n pl.* -S excessive sweating

SUDATORY *n pl.* -RIES a hot-air bath for inducing sweating

SUDD *n pl.* -S a floating mass of vegetation

SUDDEN *adj* happening unexpectedly **SUDDENLY** *adv*

SUDDEN *n pl.* -S a sudden occurrence

SUDOR *n pl.* -S sweat **SUDORAL** *adj*

SUDS *v* -ED, -ING, -ES to wash in soapy water

SUDSER *n pl.* -S one that sudses

SUDSLESS *adj* having no suds

SUDSY *adj* SUDSIER, SUDSIEST foamy

SUE *v* SUED, SUING, SUES to institute legal proceedings against

SUEDE *v* SUEDED, SUEDING, SUEDES to finish leather with a soft, napped surface

SUER *n pl.* -S one who sues

SUET *n pl.* -S the hard, fatty tissue around the kidneys of cattle and sheep **SUETY** *adj*

SUFFARI *n pl.* -S a safari

SUFFER *v* -ED, -ING, -S to feel pain or distress

SUFFERER *n pl.* -S one that suffers

SUFFICE *v* -FICED, -FICING, -FICES to be adequate

SUFFICER *n pl.* -S one that suffices

SUFFIX *v* -ED, -ING, -ES to add as a suffix (a form affixed to the end of a root word)

SUFFIXAL *adj* pertaining to or being a suffix

SUFFLATE *v* -FLATED, -FLATING, -FLATES to inflate

SUFFRAGE *n pl.* -S the right to vote

SUFFUSE *v* -FUSED, -FUSING, -FUSES to spread through or over

SUGAR *v* -ED, -ING, -S to cover with sugar (a sweet carbohydrate)

SUGARY *adj* -ARIER, -ARIEST containing or resembling sugar

SUGGEST *v* -ED, -ING, -S to bring or put forward for consideration

SUGH *v* -ED, -ING, -S to sough

SUICIDAL *adj* self-destructive

SUICIDE *v* -CIDED, -CIDING, -CIDES to kill oneself intentionally

SUING *present participle of* sue

SUINT *n pl.* -S a natural grease found in the wool of sheep

SUIT *v* -ED, -ING, -S to be appropriate to

SUITABLE *adj* appropriate **SUITABLY** *adv*

SUITCASE *n pl.* -S a flat, rectangular piece of luggage

SUITE *n pl.* -S a series of things forming a unit

SUITER *n pl.* -S a suitcase holding a specified number of suits (sets of garments)

SUITING *n pl.* -S fabric for making suits

SUITLIKE *adj* resembling a suit

SUITOR *n pl.* -S one that is courting a woman

SUKIYAKI *n pl.* -S a Japanese dish

SUKKAH *n pl.* -KAHS or -KOTH or -KOT a temporary shelter in which meals are eaten during a Jewish festival

SULCATE *adj* having narrow furrows

SULCATED *adj* sulcate

SULCUS *n pl.* -CI a narrow furrow **SULCAL** *adj*

SULDAN *n pl.* -S soldan

SULFA *n pl.* -S a bacteria-inhibiting drug

SULFATE *v* -FATED, -FATING, -FATES to treat with sulfuric acid

SULFID *n pl.* -S sulfide

SULFIDE *n pl.* -S a sulfur compound

SULFINYL *n pl.* -S a bivalent radical

SULFITE *n pl.* -S a chemical salt **SULFITIC** *adj*

SULFO *adj* sulfonic

SULFONE *n pl.* -S a sulfur compound

SULFONIC *adj* containing a certain univalent radical

SULFONYL *n pl.* -S a bivalent radical

SULFUR *v* -ED, -ING, -S to treat with sulfur (a nonmetallic element)

SULFURET *v* -RETED, -RETING, -RETS or -RETTED, -RETTING, -RETS to treat with sulfur

SULFURIC *adj* pertaining to sulfur

SULFURY *adj* resembling sulfur

SULFURYL *n pl.* -S sulfonyl

SULK *v* -ED, -ING, -S to be sulky

SULKER *n pl.* -S one that sulks

SULKY *adj* SULKIER, SULKIEST sullenly aloof or withdrawn **SULKILY** *adv*

SULKY *n pl.* SULKIES a light horse-drawn vehicle

SULLAGE *n pl.* -S sewage

SULLEN *adj* -LENER, -LENEST showing a brooding ill humor or resentment **SULLENLY** *adv*

SULLY *v* -LIED, -LYING, -LIES to soil

SULPHA *n pl.* -S sulfa

SULPHATE *v* -PHATED, -PHATING, -PHATES to sulfate

SULPHID *n pl.* -S sulfide

SULPHIDE *n pl.* -S sulfide

SULPHITE *n pl.* -S sulfite

SULPHONE *n pl.* -S sulfone

SULPHUR *v* -ED, -ING, -S to sulfur

SULPHURY *adj* sulfury

SULTAN *n pl.* -S the ruler of a Muslim country **SULTANIC** *adj*

SULTANA *n pl.* -S a sultan's wife

SULTRY *adj* -TRIER, -TRIEST very hot and humid **SULTRILY** *adv*

SULU *n pl.* -S a Melanesian skirt

SUM *v* SUMMED, SUMMING, SUMS to add into one total

SUMAC *n pl.* -S a flowering tree or shrub

SUMACH *n pl.* -S sumac

SUMLESS *adj* too large for calculation

SUMMA *n pl.* -MAE or -MAS a detailed work on a subject

SUMMABLE *adj* capable of being summed

SUMMAND *n pl.* -S an addend

SUMMARY *n pl.* -RIES a condensation of the substance of a larger work

SUMMATE *v* -MATED, -MATING, -MATES to sum

SUMMED past tense of sum

SUMMER *v* -ED, -ING, -S to pass the summer (the warmest season of the year)

SUMMERLY *adj* summery

SUMMERY *adj* -MERIER, -MERIEST characteristic of summer

SUMMING present participle of sum

SUMMIT *v* -ED, -ING, -S to participate in a highest-level conference

SUMMITAL *adj* pertaining to the highest point

SUMMITRY *n pl.* -RIES the use of conferences between chiefs of state for international negotiation

SUMMON *v* -ED, -ING, -S to order to appear

SUMMONER *n pl.* -S one that summons

SUMMONS *v* -ED, -ING, -ES to summon with a court order

SUMO *n pl.* -MOS a Japanese form of wrestling

SUMP *n pl.* -S a low area serving as a drain or receptacle for liquids

SUMPTER *n pl.* -S a pack animal

SUMPWEED *n pl.* -S a marsh plant

SUN *v* SUNNED, SUNNING, SUNS to expose to the sun (the star around which the earth revolves)

SUNBACK *adj* cut low to expose the back to sunlight

SUNBAKED *adj* baked by the sun

SUNBATH *n pl.* -S an exposure to sunlight

SUNBATHE *v* -BATHED, -BATHING, -BATHES to take a sunbath

SUNBEAM *n pl.* -S a beam of sunlight **SUNBEAMY** *adj*

SUNBELT *n pl.* -S the southern and southwestern states of the U.S.

SUNBIRD *n pl.* -S a tropical bird

SUNBLOCK *n pl.* -S a preparation to protect the skin from the sun's rays

SUNBOW *n pl.* -S an arc of spectral colors formed by the sun shining through a mist

SUNBURN *v* -BURNED or -BURNT, -BURNING, -BURNS to burn or discolor from exposure to the sun

SUNBURST *n pl.* -S a burst of sunlight

SUNCHOKE *n pl.* -S a type of sunflower

SUNDAE *n pl.* -S a dish of ice cream served with a topping

SUNDECK *n pl.* -S a deck that is exposed to the sun

SUNDER *v* -ED, -ING, -S to break apart

SUNDERER *n pl.* -S one that sunders

SUNDEW *n pl.* -S a marsh plant

SUNDIAL *n pl.* -S a type of time-telling device

SUNDOG *n pl.* -S a small rainbow

SUNDOWN *n pl.* -S sunset

SUNDRESS *n pl.* -ES a dress with an abbreviated bodice

SUNDRIES *n/pl* miscellaneous items

SUNDROPS *n pl.* SUNDROPS a flowering plant

SUNDRY *adj* miscellaneous

SUNFAST *adj* resistant to fading by the sun

SUNFISH *n pl.* -ES a marine fish

SUNG past participle of sing

SUNGLASS *n pl.* -ES a lens for concentrating the sun's rays in order to produce heat

SUNGLOW *n pl.* -S a glow in the sky caused by the sun

SUNK a past participle of sink

SUNKEN a past participle of sink

SUNKET *n pl.* -S a tidbit

SUNLAMP *n pl.* -S a lamp that radiates ultraviolet rays

SUNLAND *n pl.* -S an area marked by a great amount of sunshine

SUNLESS *adj* having no sunlight

SUNLIGHT *n pl.* -S the light of the sun

SUNLIKE *adj* resembling the sun

SUNLIT *adj* lighted by the sun

SUNN *n pl.* -S an East Indian shrub

SUNNA *n pl.* -S the body of traditional Muslim law

SUNNAH *n pl.* -S sunna

SUNNED past tense of sun

SUNNING present participle of sun

SUNNY *adj* -NIER, -NIEST filled with sunlight **SUNNILY** *adv*

SUNPORCH *n pl.* -ES a porch that admits much sunlight

SUNPROOF *adj* resistant to damage by sunlight

SUNRISE *n pl.* -S the ascent of the sun above the horizon in the morning

SUNROOF *n pl.* -S an automobile roof having an openable panel

SUNROOM *n pl.* -S a room built to admit a great amount of sunlight

SUNSCALD *n pl.* -S an injury of woody plants caused by the sun

SUNSET *n pl.* -S the descent of the sun below the horizon in the evening

SUNSHADE *n pl.* -S something used as a protection from the sun

SUNSHINE *n pl.* -S the light of the sun **SUNSHINY** *adj*

SUNSPOT *n pl.* -S a dark spot on the surface of the sun

SUNSTONE *n pl.* -S a variety of quartz

SUNSUIT *n pl.* -S an outfit worn for sunbathing

SUNTAN *n pl.* -S a brown color on the skin produced by exposure to the sun

SUNUP *n pl.* -S sunrise

SUNWARD *adv* toward the sun

SUNWARDS *adv* sunward

SUNWISE *adv* from left to right

SUP *v* SUPPED, SUPPING, SUPS to eat supper

SUPE *n pl.* -S an actor without a speaking part

SUPER *v* -ED, -ING, -S to reinforce with a thin cotton mesh, as a book

SUPERADD *v* -ED, -ING, -S to add further

SUPERB adj -PERBER, -PERBEST outstanding SUPERBLY adv

SUPERBAD adj exceedingly bad

SUPERCAR n pl. -S a superior car

SUPERCOP n pl. -S a superior police officer

SUPEREGO n pl. -EGOS a part of the psyche

SUPERFAN n pl. -S an exceedingly devoted enthusiast

SUPERFIX n pl. -ES a recurrent pattern of stress in speech

SUPERHIT n pl. -S something exceedingly successful

SUPERHOT adj exceedingly hot

SUPERIOR n pl. -S one of higher rank, quality, or authority than another

SUPERJET n pl. -S a type of jet airplane

SUPERLIE v -LAY, -LAIN, -LYING, -LIES to lie above

SUPERMAN n pl. -MEN a hypothetical superior man

SUPERMOM n pl. -S a superior mom

SUPERNAL adj pertaining to the sky

SUPERPRO n pl. -PROS a superior professional

SUPERSEX n pl. -ES a type of sterile organism

SUPERSPY n pl. -SPIES a superior spy

SUPERTAX n pl. -ES an additional tax

SUPINATE v -NATED, -NATING, -NATES to turn so that the palm is facing upward

SUPINE n pl. -S a Latin verbal noun

SUPINELY adv in an inactive manner

SUPPED past tense of sup

SUPPER n pl. -S an evening meal

SUPPING present participle of sup

SUPPLANT v -ED, -ING, -S to take the place of

SUPPLE adj -PLER, -PLEST pliant SUPPLELY adv

SUPPLE v -PLED, -PLING, -PLES to make supple

SUPPLIER n pl. -S one that supplies

SUPPLY v -PLIED, -PLYING, -PLIES to furnish with what is needed

SUPPORT v -ED, -ING, -S to hold up or add strength to

SUPPOSAL n pl. -S something supposed

SUPPOSE v -POSED, -POSING, -POSES to assume to be true

SUPPOSER n pl. -S one that supposes

SUPPRESS v -ED, -ING, -ES to put an end to forcibly

SUPRA adv above

SUPREME adj -PREMER, -PREMEST highest in power or authority

SUPREMO n pl. -MOS one who is highest in authority

SUQ n pl. -S souk

SURA n pl. -S a chapter of the Koran

SURAH n pl. -S a silk fabric

SURAL adj pertaining to the calf of the leg

SURBASE n pl. -S a molding or border above the base of a structure SURBASED adj

SURCEASE v -CEASED, -CEASING, -CEASES to cease

SURCOAT n pl. -S an outer coat or cloak

SURD n pl. -S a voiceless speech sound

SURE adj SURER, SUREST free from doubt

SUREFIRE adj sure to meet expectations

SURELY adv certainly

SURENESS n pl. -ES the state of being sure

SURER comparative of sure

SUREST superlative of sure

SURETY n pl. -TIES sureness

SURF v -ED, -ING, -S to ride breaking waves on a long, narrow board SURFABLE adj

SURFACE v -FACED, -FACING, -FACES to apply an outer layer to

SURFACER n pl. -S one that surfaces

SURFBIRD n pl. -S a shore bird

SURFBOAT n pl. -S a strong rowboat

SURFEIT v -ED, -ING, -S to supply to excess

SURFER n pl. -S one that surfs

SURFFISH n pl. -ES a marine fish

SURFIER comparative of surfy

SURFIEST superlative of surfy

SURFING n pl. -S the act or sport of riding the surf (breaking waves)

SURFLIKE adj resembling breaking waves

SURFY adj SURFIER, SURFIEST abounding in breaking waves

SURGE v SURGED, SURGING, SURGES to move in a swelling manner

SURGEON n pl. -S one who practices surgery

SURGER n pl. -S one that surges

SURGERY n pl. -GERIES the treatment of medical problems by operation

SURGICAL *adj* pertaining to surgery

SURGING present participle of surge

SURGY *adj* surging

SURICATE *n pl.* -S a burrowing mammal

SURIMI *n pl.* SURIMI an inexpensive fish product

SURLY *adj* -LIER, -LIEST sullenly rude **SURLILY** *adv*

SURMISE *v* -MISED, -MISING, -MISES to infer with little evidence

SURMISER *n pl.* -S one that surmises

SURMOUNT *v* -ED, -ING, -S to get over or across

SURNAME *v* -NAMED, -NAMING, -NAMES to give a family name to

SURNAMER *n pl.* -S one that surnames

SURPASS *v* -ED, -ING, -ES to go beyond

SURPLICE *n pl.* -S a loose-fitting vestment

SURPLUS *n pl.* -ES an excess

SURPRINT *v* -ED, -ING, -S to print over something already printed

SURPRISE *v* -PRISED, -PRISING, -PRISES to come upon unexpectedly

SURPRIZE *v* -PRIZED, -PRIZING, -PRIZES to surprise

SURRA *n pl.* -S a disease of domestic animals

SURREAL *adj* having dreamlike qualities

SURREY *n pl.* -REYS a light carriage

SURROUND *v* -ED, -ING, -S to extend completely around

SURROYAL *n pl.* -S the topmost prong of a stag's antler

SURTAX *v* -ED, -ING, -ES to assess with an extra tax

SURTOUT *n pl.* -S a close-fitting overcoat

SURVEIL *v* -VEILLED, -VEILLING, -VEILS to watch closely

SURVEY *v* -ED, -ING, -S to determine the boundaries, area, or elevations of by measuring angles and distances

SURVEYOR *n pl.* -S one that surveys land

SURVIVAL *n pl.* -S a living or continuing longer than another person or thing

SURVIVE *v* -VIVED, -VIVING, -VIVES to remain in existence

SURVIVER *n pl.* -S survivor

SURVIVOR *n pl.* -S one that survives

SUSHI *n pl.* -S a dish of cold rice cakes topped with strips of raw fish

SUSLIK *n pl.* -S a Eurasian rodent

SUSPECT *v* -ED, -ING, -S to think guilty on slight evidence

SUSPEND *v* -ED, -ING, -S to cause to stop for a period

SUSPENSE *n pl.* -S a state of mental uncertainty or excitement

SUSPIRE *v* -PIRED, -PIRING, -PIRES to sigh

SUSS *v* -ED, -ING, -ES to figure out

SUSTAIN *v* -ED, -ING, -S to maintain by providing with food and drink

SUSURRUS *n pl.* -ES a soft rustling sound

SUTLER *n pl.* -S one that peddles goods to soldiers

SUTRA *n pl.* -S a Hindu aphorism

SUTTA *n pl.* -S sutra

SUTTEE *n pl.* -S a Hindu widow cremated on her husband's funeral pile to show her devotion to him

SUTURAL *adj* pertaining to the line of junction between two bones

SUTURE *v* -TURED, -TURING, -TURES to unite by sewing

SUZERAIN *n pl.* -S a feudal lord

SVARAJ *n pl.* -ES swaraj

SVEDBERG *n pl.* -S a unit of time

SVELTE *adj* SVELTER, SVELTEST gracefully slender **SVELTELY** *adv*

SWAB *v* SWABBED, SWABBING, SWABS to clean with a large mop

SWABBER *n pl.* -S one that swabs

SWABBIE *n pl.* -S a sailor

SWABBING present participle of swab

SWABBY *n pl.* -BIES swabbie

SWACKED *adj* drunk

SWADDLE *v* -DLED, -DLING, -DLES to wrap in bandages

SWAG *v* SWAGGED, SWAGGING, SWAGS to sway

SWAGE *v* SWAGED, SWAGING, SWAGES to shape with a hammering tool

SWAGER *n pl.* -S one that swages

SWAGGED past tense of swag

SWAGGER *v* -ED, -ING, -S to walk with a pompous air

SWAGGIE *n pl.* -S a swagman

SWAGGING present participle of swag

SWAGING present participle of swage

SWAGMAN *n pl.* -MEN a hobo

SWAIL *n pl.* -S swale

SWAIN *n* pl. -S a country boy
SWAINISH *adj*

SWALE *n* pl. -S a tract of low, marshy ground

SWALLOW *v* -ED, -ING, -S to take through the mouth and esophagus into the stomach

SWAM past tense of swim

SWAMI *n* pl. -S a Hindu religious teacher

SWAMIES pl. of swamy

SWAMP *v* -ED, -ING, -S to inundate

SWAMPER *n* pl. -S one that lives in a swampy area

SWAMPISH *adj* swampy

SWAMPY *adj* SWAMPIER, SWAMPIEST marshy

SWAMY *n* pl. -MIES swami

SWAN *v* SWANNED, SWANNING, SWANS to swear

SWANG a past tense of swing

SWANHERD *n* pl. -S one who tends swans (large aquatic birds)

SWANK *adj* SWANKER, SWANKEST imposingly elegant

SWANK *v* -ED, -ING, -S to swagger

SWANKY *adj* SWANKIER, SWANKIEST swank SWANKILY *adv*

SWANLIKE *adj* resembling a swan

SWANNED past tense of swan

SWANNERY *n* pl. -NERIES a place where swans are raised

SWANNING present participle of swan

SWANPAN *n* pl. -S a Chinese abacus

SWANSKIN *n* pl. -S the skin of a swan

SWAP *v* SWAPPED, SWAPPING, SWAPS to trade

SWAPPER *n* pl. -S one that swaps

SWARAJ *n* pl. -ES self-government in British India

SWARD *v* -ED, -ING, -S to cover with turf

SWARE a past tense of swear

SWARF *n* pl. -S material removed by a cutting tool

SWARM *v* -ED, -ING, -S to move in a large group

SWARMER *n* pl. -S one that swarms

SWART *adj* swarthy

SWARTH *n* pl. -S turf

SWARTHY *adj* -THIER, -THIEST having a dark complexion

SWARTY *adj* swarthy

SWASH *v* -ED, -ING, -ES to swagger

SWASHER *n* pl. -S one that swashes

SWASTICA *n* pl. -S swastika

SWASTIKA *n* pl. -S a geometrical figure used as a symbol or ornament

SWAT *v* SWATTED, SWATTING, SWATS to hit sharply

SWATCH *n* pl. -ES a sample piece of cloth

SWATH *n* pl. -S a row of cut grass or grain

SWATHE *v* SWATHED, SWATHING, SWATHES to wrap in bandages

SWATHER *n* pl. -S one that swathes

SWATTED past tense of swat

SWATTER *n* pl. -S one that swats

SWATTING present participle of swat

SWAY *v* -ED, -ING, -S to move slowly back and forth

SWAYBACK *n* pl. -S an abnormal sagging of the back

SWAYER *n* pl. -S one that sways

SWAYFUL *adj* capable of influencing

SWEAR *v* SWORE or SWARE, SWORN, SWEARING, SWEARS to utter a solemn oath

SWEARER *n* pl. -S one that swears

SWEAT *v* -ED, -ING, -S to perspire

SWEATBOX *n* pl. -ES a small enclosure in which one is made to sweat

SWEATER *n* pl. -S a knitted outer garment

SWEATY *adj* SWEATIER, SWEATIEST covered with perspiration SWEATILY *adv*

SWEDE *n* pl. -S a rutabaga

SWEENY *n* pl. -NIES atrophy of the shoulder muscles in horses

SWEEP *v* SWEPT, SWEEPING, SWEEPS to clear or clean with a brush or broom

SWEEPER *n* pl. -S one that sweeps

SWEEPING *n* pl. -S the act of one that sweeps

SWEEPY *adj* SWEEPIER, SWEEPIEST of wide range or scope

SWEER *adj* lazy

SWEET *adj* SWEETER, SWEETEST pleasing to the taste

SWEET *n* pl. -S something that is sweet

SWEETEN *v* -ED, -ING, -S to make sweet

SWEETIE *n* pl. -S darling

SWEETING *n* pl. -S a sweet apple

SWEETISH *adj* somewhat sweet

SWEETLY *adv* in a sweet manner

SWEETSOP *n* pl. -S a tropical tree

SWELL *v* SWELLED, SWOLLEN, SWELLING, SWELLS to increase in size or volume

SWELL *adj* SWELLER, SWELLEST stylish

SWELLING *n* pl. -S something that is swollen

SWELTER *v* -ED, -ING, -S to suffer from oppressive heat

SWELTRY *adj* -TRIER, -TRIEST oppressively hot

SWEPT past tense of sweep

SWERVE *v* SWERVED, SWERVING, SWERVES to turn aside suddenly from a straight course

SWERVER *n* pl. -S one that swerves

SWEVEN *n* pl. -S a dream or vision

SWIDDEN *n* pl. -S an agricultural plot produced by burning off the vegetative cover

SWIFT *adj* SWIFTER, SWIFTEST moving with a great rate of motion

SWIFT *n* pl. -S a fast-flying bird

SWIFTER *n* pl. -S a rope on a ship

SWIFTLET *n* pl. -S a cave-dwelling swift

SWIFTLY *adv* in a swift manner

SWIG *v* SWIGGED, SWIGGING, SWIGS to drink deeply or rapidly

SWIGGER *n* pl. -S one that swigs

SWILL *v* -ED, -ING, -S to swig

SWILLER *n* pl. -S one that swills

SWIM *v* SWAM, SWUM, SWIMMING, SWIMS to propel oneself in water by natural means

SWIMMER *n* pl. -S one that swims

SWIMMING *n* pl. -S the act of one that swims

SWIMMY *adj* -MIER, -MIEST dizzy SWIMMILY *adv*

SWIMSUIT *n* pl. -S a bathing suit

SWIMWEAR *n* pl. SWIMWEAR clothing suitable for swimming

SWINDLE *v* -DLED, -DLING, -DLES to take money or property from by fraudulent means

SWINDLER *n* pl. -S one that swindles

SWINE *n* pl. SWINE a domestic pig

SWINEPOX *n* pl. -ES a disease of swine

SWING *v* SWUNG, SWINGING, SWINGS to move freely back and forth

SWINGBY *n* pl. -BYS a mission in which a spacecraft uses a planet's gravitational pull for making course changes

SWINGE *v* SWINGED, SWINGEING, SWINGES to flog

SWINGER *n* pl. -S one that swings

SWINGIER comparative of swingy

SWINGIEST superlative of swingy

SWINGING *adj* -INGEST lively and hip

SWINGING *n* pl. -S the practice of swapping sex partners

SWINGLE *v* -GLED, -GLING, -GLES to scutch

SWINGMAN *n* pl. -MEN a basketball player who can play guard or forward

SWINGY *adj* SWINGIER, SWINGIEST marked by swinging

SWINISH *adj* resembling or befitting swine

SWINK *v* -ED, -ING, -S to toil

SWINNEY *n* pl. -NEYS sweeny

SWIPE *v* SWIPED, SWIPING, SWIPES to strike with a sweeping blow

SWIPLE *n* pl. -S a part of a threshing device

SWIPPLE *n* pl. -S swiple

SWIRL *v* -ED, -ING, -S to move with a whirling motion

SWIRLY *adj* SWIRLIER, SWIRLIEST swirling

SWISH *v* -ED, -ING, -ES to move with a prolonged hissing sound

SWISHER *n* pl. -S one that swishes

SWISHY *adj* SWISHIER, SWISHIEST swishing

SWISS *n* pl. -ES a cotton fabric

SWITCH *v* -ED, -ING, -ES to beat with a flexible rod

SWITCHER *n* pl. -S one that switches

SWITH *adv* quickly

SWITHE *adv* swith

SWITHER *v* -ED, -ING, -S to doubt

SWITHLY *adv* swith

SWIVE *v* SWIVED, SWIVING, SWIVES to copulate with

SWIVEL *v* -ELED, -ELING, -ELS or -ELLED, -ELLING, -ELS to turn on a pivoted support

SWIVET *n* pl. -S a state of nervous excitement

SWIVING present participle of swive

SWIZZLE *v* -ZLED, -ZLING, -ZLES to drink excessively

SWIZZLER *n* pl. -S one that swizzles

SWOB	*v* SWOBBED, SWOBBING, SWOBS to swab
SWOBBER	*n pl.* -S swabber
SWOLLEN	past participle of swell
SWOON	*v* -ED, -ING, -S to faint
SWOONER	*n pl.* -S one that swoons
SWOOP	*v* -ED, -ING, -S to make a sudden descent
SWOOPER	*n pl.* -S one that swoops
SWOOSH	*v* -ED, -ING, -ES to move with a rustling sound
SWOP	*v* SWOPPED, SWOPPING, SWOPS to swap
SWORD	*n pl.* -S a weapon having a long blade for cutting or thrusting
SWORDMAN	*n pl.* -MEN one skilled in the use of a sword
SWORE	a past tense of swear
SWORN	past participle of swear
SWOT	*v* SWOTTED, SWOTTING, SWOTS to swat
SWOTTER	*n pl.* -S one that swots
SWOUN	*v* -ED, -ING, -S to swoon
SWOUND	*v* -ED, -ING, -S to swoon
SWUM	past participle of swim
SWUNG	a past tense of swing
SYBARITE	*n pl.* -S a person devoted to pleasure and luxury
SYBO	*n pl.* -BOES the cibol
SYCAMINE	*n pl.* -S the mulberry tree
SYCAMORE	*n pl.* -S a North American tree
SYCE	*n pl.* -S a male servant in India
SYCEE	*n pl.* -S fine uncoined silver formerly used in China as money
SYCOMORE	*n pl.* -S sycamore
SYCONIUM	*n pl.* -NIA a fleshy multiple fruit
SYCOSIS	*n pl.* -COSES an inflammatory disease of the hair follicles
SYENITE	*n pl.* -S an igneous rock SYENITIC *adj*
SYKE	*n pl.* -S a small stream
SYLI	*n pl.* -S a former monetary unit of Guinea
SYLLABI	a pl. of syllabus
SYLLABIC	*n pl.* -S a speech sound of high sonority
SYLLABLE	*v* -BLED, -BLING, -BLES to pronounce syllables (units of spoken language)
SYLLABUB	*n pl.* -S sillabub
SYLLABUS	*n pl.* -BI or -BUSES an outline of a course of study

SYLPH	*n pl.* -S a slender, graceful girl or woman SYLPHIC, SYLPHISH, SYLPHY *adj*
SYLPHID	*n pl.* -S a young sylph
SYLVA	*n pl.* -VAS or -VAE the forest trees of an area
SYLVAN	*n pl.* -S one that lives in a forest
SYLVATIC	*adj* pertaining to a forest
SYLVIN	*n pl.* -S sylvite
SYLVINE	*n pl.* -S sylvite
SYLVITE	*n pl.* -S an ore of potassium
SYMBION	*n pl.* -S symbiont
SYMBIONT	*n pl.* -S an organism living in close association with another
SYMBIOT	*n pl.* -S symbiont
SYMBIOTE	*n pl.* -S symbiont
SYMBOL	*v* -BOLED, -BOLING, -BOLS or -BOLLED, -BOLLING, -BOLS to serve as a symbol (a representation) of
SYMBOLIC	*adj* pertaining to a symbol
SYMMETRY	*n pl.* -TRIES an exact correspondence between the opposite halves of a figure
SYMPATHY	*n pl.* -THIES a feeling of compassion for another's suffering
SYMPATRY	*n pl.* -RIES the state of occupying the same area without loss of identity from interbreeding
SYMPHONY	*n pl.* -NIES an orchestral composition
SYMPODIA	*n/pl* plant stems made up of a series of superposed branches
SYMPOSIA	*n/pl* conferences for the purpose of discussion
SYMPTOM	*n pl.* -S an indication of something
SYN	*adv* syne
SYNAGOG	*n pl.* -S a building for Jewish worship
SYNANON	*n pl.* -S a method of group therapy for drug addicts
SYNAPSE	*v* -APSED, -APSING, -APSES to come together in synapsis
SYNAPSID	*n pl.* -S one of a group of extinct reptiles
SYNAPSIS	*n pl.* -APSES the point at which a nervous impulse passes from one neuron to another SYNAPTIC *adj*
SYNC	*v* -ED, -ING, -S to cause to operate in unison
SYNCARP	*n pl.* -S a fleshy multiple fruit

SYNCARPY *n pl.* -PIES the state of being a syncarp

SYNCH *v* -ED, -ING, -S to sync

SYNCHRO *n pl.* -CHROS a selsyn

SYNCLINE *n pl.* -S a type of rock formation

SYNCOM *n pl.* -S a type of communications satellite

SYNCOPE *n pl.* -S the contraction of a word by omitting one or more sounds from the middle SYNCOPAL, SYNCOPIC *adj*

SYNCYTIA *n/pl* masses of protoplasm resulting from cell fusion

SYNDESIS *n pl.* -DESES or -DESISES synapsis

SYNDET *n pl.* -S a synthetic detergent

SYNDETIC *adj* serving to connect

SYNDIC *n pl.* -S a business agent SYNDICAL *adj*

SYNDROME *n pl.* -S a group of symptoms that characterize a particular disorder

SYNE *adv* since

SYNECTIC *adj* pertaining to a system of problem solving

SYNERGIA *n pl.* -S synergy

SYNERGID *n pl.* -S a cell found in the embryo sac of a seed plant

SYNERGY *n pl.* -GIES combined action SYNERGIC *adj*

SYNESIS *n pl.* -SISES a type of grammatical construction

SYNFUEL *n pl.* -S a fuel derived from fossil fuels

SYNGAMY *n pl.* -MIES the union of two gametes SYNGAMIC *adj*

SYNGAS *n pl.* -GASES or -GASSES a mixture of carbon monoxide and hydrogen used in chemical synthesis

SYNOD *n pl.* -S a church council SYNODAL, SYNODIC *adj*

SYNONYM *n pl.* -S a word having the same meaning as another

SYNONYME *n pl.* -S synonym

SYNONYMY *n pl.* -MIES equivalence of meaning

SYNOPSIS *n pl.* -OPSES a summary SYNOPTIC *adj*

SYNOVIA *n pl.* -S a lubricating fluid secreted by certain membranes SYNOVIAL *adj*

SYNTAGMA *n pl.* -MAS or -MATA a syntactic element

SYNTAX *n pl.* -ES the way in which words are put together to form phrases and sentences

SYNTH *n pl.* -S a synthesizer

SYNTONY *n pl.* -NIES the tuning of transmitters and receivers with each other SYNTONIC *adj*

SYNURA *n pl.* -RAE any of a genus of protozoa

SYPH *n pl.* -S syphilis

SYPHER *v* -ED, -ING, -S to overlap so as to make an even surface, as beveled plank edges

SYPHILIS *n pl.* -LISES a venereal disease

SYPHON *v* -ED, -ING, -S to siphon

SYREN *n pl.* -S siren

SYRINGA *n pl.* -S an ornamental shrub

SYRINGE *v* -RINGED, -RINGING, -RINGES to cleanse or treat with injected fluid

SYRINX *n pl.* -INGES or -INXES the vocal organ of a bird

SYRPHIAN *n pl.* -S syrphid

SYRPHID *n pl.* -S a winged insect

SYRUP *n pl.* -S a thick, sweet liquid SYRUPY *adj*

SYSOP *n pl.* -S the administrator of a computer bulletin board

SYSTEM *n pl.* -S a group of interacting elements forming a unified whole

SYSTEMIC *n pl.* -S a type of pesticide

SYSTOLE *n pl.* -S the normal rhythmic contraction of the heart SYSTOLIC *adj*

SYZYGY *n pl.* -GIES the configuration of the earth, moon, and sun lying in a straight line SYZYGAL, SYZYGIAL *adj*

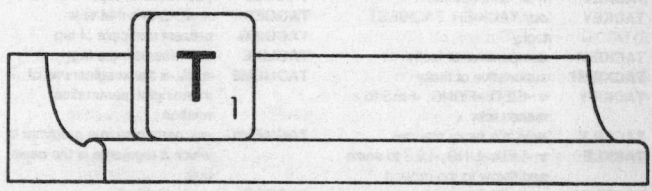

TA	*n pl.* -S an expression of gratitude
TAB	*v* TABBED, TABBING, TABS to name or designate
TABANID	*n pl.* -S a bloodsucking insect
TABARD	*n pl.* -S a sleeveless outer garment TABARDED *adj*
TABARET	*n pl.* -S a silk fabric
TABBED	past tense of tab
TABBIED	past tense of tabby
TABBIES	present 3d person sing. of tabby
TABBING	present participle of tab
TABBIS	*n pl.* -BISES a silk fabric
TABBY	*v* -BIED, -BYING, -BIES to give a wavy appearance to
TABER	*v* -ED, -ING, -S to tabor
TABES	*n pl.* TABES a syphilitic disease
TABETIC	*n pl.* -S one affected with tabes
TABID	*adj* affected with tabes
TABLA	*n pl.* -S a small drum
TABLE	*v* -BLED, -BLING, -BLES to place on a table (a piece of furniture having a flat upper surface)
TABLEAU	*n pl.* -LEAUX or -LEAUS a picture
TABLEFUL	*n pl.* TABLEFULS or TABLESFUL as much as a table can hold
TABLET	*v* -LETED, -LETING, -LETS or -LETTED, -LETTING, -LETS to inscribe on a small, flat surface
TABLETOP	*n pl.* -S the top of a table
TABLING	present participle of table
TABLOID	*n pl.* -S a small newspaper
TABOO	*v* -ED, -ING, -S to exclude from use, approach, or mention
TABOOLEY	*n pl.* -LEYS tabouli
TABOR	*v* -ED, -ING, -S to beat on a small drum
TABORER	*n pl.* -S one that tabors
TABORET	*n pl.* -S a small drum
TABORIN	*n pl.* -S taborine
TABORINE	*n pl.* -S a taboret
TABOULI	*n pl.* -S a Lebanese salad containing bulgur wheat, tomatoes, parsley, onions, and mint
TABOUR	*v* -ED, -ING, -S to tabor
TABOURER	*n pl.* -S taborer
TABOURET	*n pl.* -S taboret
TABU	*v* -ED, -ING, -S to taboo
TABULAR	*adj* of or pertaining to a list
TABULATE	*v* -LATED, -LATING, -LATES to arrange in a list
TABULI	*n pl.* -S tabouli
TABUN	*n pl.* -S a chemical compound
TACE	*n pl.* -S tasse
TACET	*interj* be silent — used as a musical direction
TACH	*n pl.* -S a device for indicating speed of rotation
TACHE	*n pl.* -S a clasp or buckle
TACHINID	*n pl.* -S a grayish fly
TACHISM	*n pl.* -S action painting
TACHISME	*n pl.* -S tachism
TACHIST	*n pl.* -S an action painter
TACHISTE	*n pl.* -S tachist
TACHYON	*n pl.* -S a theoretical subatomic particle
TACIT	*adj* unspoken TACITLY *adv*
TACITURN	*adj* habitually silent

TACK *v* -ED, -ING, -S to fasten with tacks (short, sharp-pointed nails)

TACKER *n pl.* -S one that tacks

TACKET *n pl.* -S a hobnail

TACKEY *adj* TACKIER, TACKIEST tacky

TACKIER comparative of tacky

TACKIEST superlative of tacky

TACKIFY *v* -FIED, -FYING, -FIES to make tacky

TACKILY *adv* in a tacky manner

TACKLE *v* -LED, -LING, -LES to seize and throw to the ground

TACKLER *n pl.* -S one that tackles

TACKLESS *adj* having no tacks

TACKLING *n pl.* -S equipment

TACKY *adj* TACKIER, TACKIEST adhesive

TACNODE *n pl.* -S a point of contact between two curves

TACO *n pl.* -COS a tortilla folded around a filling

TACONITE *n pl.* -S a low-grade iron ore

TACT *n pl.* -S skill in dealing with delicate situations

TACTFUL *adj* having tact

TACTIC *n pl.* -S a maneuver for gaining an objective
TACTICAL *adj*

TACTILE *adj* pertaining to the sense of touch

TACTION *n pl.* -S the act of touching

TACTLESS *adj* lacking tact

TACTUAL *adj* tactile

TAD *n pl.* -S a small boy

TADPOLE *n pl.* -S the aquatic larva of an amphibian

TAE *prep* to

TAEL *n pl.* -S a Chinese unit of weight

TAENIA *n pl.* -NIAE or -NIAS a headband worn in ancient Greece

TAFFAREL *n pl.* -S taffrail

TAFFEREL *n pl.* -S taffrail

TAFFETA *n pl.* -S a lustrous fabric

TAFFIA *n pl.* -S tafia

TAFFRAIL *n pl.* -S a rail around the stern of a ship

TAFFY *n pl.* -FIES a chewy candy

TAFIA *n pl.* -S an inferior rum

TAG *v* TAGGED, TAGGING, TAGS to provide with a tag (an identifying marker)

TAGALONG *n pl.* -S one that follows another

TAGBOARD *n pl.* -S a material for making shipping tags

TAGGED past tense of tag

TAGGER *n pl.* -S one that tags

TAGGING present participle of tag

TAGLIKE *adj* resembling a tag

TAGMEME *n pl.* -S the smallest unit of meaningful grammatical relation

TAGMEMIC *adj* pertaining to a grammar in which a tagmeme is the basic unit

TAGRAG *n pl.* -S riffraff

TAHINI *n pl.* -S a paste of sesame seeds

TAHR *n pl.* -S a goatlike mammal

TAHSIL *n pl.* -S a district in India

TAIGA *n pl.* -S a subarctic evergreen forest

TAIGLACH *n pl.* TAIGLACH teiglach

TAIL *v* -ED, -ING, -S to provide with a tail (a hindmost part)

TAILBACK *n pl.* -S a member of the backfield in some football formations

TAILBONE *n pl.* -S the coccyx

TAILCOAT *n pl.* -S a man's coat

TAILER *n pl.* -S one that secretly follows another

TAILFAN *n pl.* -S a fanlike swimming organ at the rear of some crustaceans

TAILGATE *v* -GATED, -GATING, -GATES to drive dangerously close behind another vehicle

TAILING *n pl.* -S the part of a projecting stone or brick that is inserted into a wall

TAILLAMP *n pl.* -S a light at the rear of a vehicle

TAILLE *n pl.* -S a former French tax

TAILLESS *adj* having no tail

TAILLEUR *n pl.* -S a woman's tailored suit

TAILLIKE *adj* resembling a tail

TAILOR *v* -ED, -ING, -S to fit with clothes

TAILPIPE *n pl.* -S an exhaust pipe

TAILRACE *n pl.* -S a part of a millrace

TAILSKID *n pl.* -S a support on which the tail of an airplane rests

TAILSPIN *n pl.* -S the spiral descent of a stalled airplane

TAILWIND n pl. -S a wind coming from behind a moving vehicle

TAIN n pl. -S a thin plate

TAINT v -ED, -ING, -S to touch or affect slightly with something bad

TAIPAN n pl. -S a venomous snake

TAJ n pl. -ES a tall, conical cap worn in Muslim countries

TAKA n pl. TAKA a monetary unit of Bangladesh

TAKAHE n pl. -S a flightless bird

TAKE v TOOK, TAKEN, TAKING, TAKES to get possession of TAKABLE, TAKEABLE adj

TAKEAWAY adj designating prepared food that is sold for consumption elsewhere

TAKEDOWN n pl. -S an article that can be taken apart easily

TAKEOFF n pl. -S the act of rising in flight

TAKEOUT n pl. -S the act of removing

TAKEOVER n pl. -S the act of assuming control

TAKER n pl. -S one that takes

TAKEUP n pl. -S the act of taking something up

TAKIN n pl. -S a goatlike mammal

TAKING n pl. -S a seizure

TAKINGLY adv in an attractive manner

TALA n pl. -S a traditional rhythmic pattern of music in India

TALAPOIN n pl. -S a small African monkey

TALAR n pl. -S a long cloak

TALARIA n/pl winged sandals worn by various figures of classical mythology

TALC v TALCKED, TALCKING, TALCS or TALCED, TALCING, TALCS to treat with talc (a soft mineral with a soapy texture) TALCKY, TALCOSE, TALCOUS adj

TALCUM n pl. -S a powder made from talc

TALE n pl. -S a story

TALENT n pl. -S a special natural ability TALENTED adj

TALER n pl. -S a former German coin

TALESMAN n pl. -MEN a person summoned to fill a vacancy on a jury

TALEYSIM a pl. of tallith

TALI pl. of talus

TALION n pl. -S a retaliation for a crime

TALIPED n pl. -S a person afflicted with clubfoot

TALIPES n pl. TALIPES clubfoot

TALIPOT n pl. -S a tall palm tree

TALISMAN n pl. -S an object believed to possess magical powers

TALK v -ED, -ING, -S to communicate by speaking

TALKABLE adj able to be talked about

TALKER n pl. -S one that talks

TALKIE n pl. -S a moving picture with synchronized sound

TALKING n pl. -S conversation

TALKY adj TALKIER, TALKIEST tending to talk a great deal

TALL adj TALLER, TALLEST having great height

TALLAGE v -LAGED, -LAGING, -LAGES to tax

TALLAISIM a pl. of tallith

TALLBOY n pl. -BOYS a highboy

TALLIED past tense of tally

TALLIER n pl. -S one that tallies

TALLIES present 3d person sing. of tally

TALLIS n pl. -LISIM tallith

TALLISH adj somewhat tall

TALLIT n pl. -LITIM tallith

TALLITH n pl. TALLITHES, TALLITHIM, TALLITOTH, TALEYSIM, or TALLAISIM a Jewish prayer shawl

TALLNESS n pl. -ES the state of being tall

TALLOL n pl. -S a resinous liquid

TALLOW v -ED, -ING, -S to smear with tallow (a mixture of animal fats)

TALLOWY adj resembling tallow

TALLY v -LIED, -LYING, -LIES to count

TALLYHO v -ED, -ING, -S to make an encouraging shout to hunting hounds

TALLYMAN n pl. -MEN a person who tallies

TALMUDIC adj pertaining to the body of Jewish civil and religious law

TALON n pl. -S a claw of a bird of prey TALONED adj

TALOOKA n pl. -S taluk

TALUK n pl. -S an estate in India

TALUKA n pl. -S taluk

TALUS n pl. -LI a bone of the foot

TALUS n pl. -ES a slope formed by an accumulation of rock debris

TAM *n pl.* -S a tight-fitting Scottish cap

TAMABLE *adj* capable of being tamed

TAMAL *n pl.* -S a tamale

TAMALE *n pl.* -S a Mexican dish

TAMANDU *n pl.* -S tamandua

TAMANDUA *n pl.* -S an arboreal anteater

TAMARACK *n pl.* -S a timber tree

TAMARAO *n pl.* -RAOS tamarau

TAMARAU *n pl.* -S a small buffalo of the Philippines

TAMARI *n pl.* -S a Japanese soy sauce

TAMARIN *n pl.* -S a South American monkey

TAMARIND *n pl.* -S a tropical tree

TAMARISK *n pl.* -S an evergreen shrub

TAMASHA *n pl.* -S a public entertainment in India

TAMBAC *n pl.* -S tombac

TAMBAK *n pl.* -S tombac

TAMBALA *n pl.* -S or MATAMBALA a monetary unit of Malawi

TAMBOUR *v* -ED, -ING, -S to embroider on a round wooden frame

TAMBOURA *n pl.* -S tambura

TAMBUR *n pl.* -S tambura

TAMBURA *n pl.* -S a stringed instrument

TAME *adj* TAMER, TAMEST gentle or docile

TAME *v* TAMED, TAMING, TAMES to make tame

TAMEABLE *adj* tamable

TAMEIN *n pl.* -S a garment worn by Burmese women

TAMELESS *adj* not capable of being tamed

TAMELY *adv* in a tame manner

TAMENESS *n pl.* -ES the state of being tame

TAMER *n pl.* -S one that tames

TAMEST superlative of tame

TAMING present participle of tame

TAMIS *n pl.* -ISES a strainer made of cloth mesh

TAMMIE *n pl.* -S tammy

TAMMY *n pl.* -MIES a fabric of mixed fibers

TAMP *v* -ED, -ING, -S to pack down by tapping

TAMPALA *n pl.* -S an annual herb

TAMPAN *n pl.* -S a biting insect

TAMPER *v* -ED, -ING, -S to interfere in a harmful manner

TAMPERER *n pl.* -S one that tampers

TAMPION *n pl.* -S a plug for the muzzle of a cannon

TAMPON *v* -ED, -ING, -S to plug with a cotton pad

TAN *v* TANNED, TANNING, TANS to convert hide into leather by soaking in chemicals

TAN *adj* TANNER, TANNEST brown from the sun's rays

TANAGER *n pl.* -S a brightly colored bird

TANBARK *n pl.* -S a tree bark used as a source of tannin

TANDEM *n pl.* -S a bicycle built for two

TANDOOR *n pl.* -DOORI a clay oven

TANG *v* -ED, -ING, -S to provide with a pungent flavor

TANGELO *n pl.* -LOS a citrus fruit

TANGENCE *n pl.* -S tangency

TANGENCY *n pl.* -CIES the state of being in immediate physical contact

TANGENT *n pl.* -S a straight line in contact with a curve at one point

TANGIBLE *n pl.* -S something palpable

TANGIBLY *adv* palpably

TANGIER comparative of tangy

TANGIEST superlative of tangy

TANGLE *v* -GLED, -GLING, -GLES to bring together in intricate confusion

TANGLER *n pl.* -S one that tangles

TANGLY *adj* -GLIER, -GLIEST tangled

TANGO *v* -ED, -ING, -S to perform a Latin-American dance

TANGRAM *n pl.* -S a Chinese puzzle

TANGY *adj* TANGIER, TANGIEST pungent

TANIST *n pl.* -S the heir apparent to a Celtic chief

TANISTRY *n pl.* -RIES the system of electing a tanist

TANK *v* -ED, -ING, -S to store in a tank (a container usually for liquids)

TANKA *n pl.* -S a Japanese verse form

TANKAGE *n pl.* -S the capacity of a tank

TANKARD *n pl.* -S a tall drinking vessel

TANKER *n pl.* -S a ship designed to transport liquids

TANKFUL *n pl.* -S the amount a tank can hold

TANKLIKE *adj* resembling a tank

TANKSHIP *n pl.* -S a tanker

TANNABLE *adj* capable of being tanned

TANNAGE *n pl.* -S the process of tanning

TANNATE *n pl.* -S a chemical salt

TANNED past tense of tan

TANNER *n* pl. -S one that tans

TANNERY *n* pl. -NERIES a place where hides are tanned

TANNEST superlative of tan

TANNIC *adj* pertaining to tannin

TANNIN *n* pl. -S a chemical compound used in tanning

TANNING *n* pl. -S the process of converting hides into leather

TANNISH *adj* somewhat tan

TANREC *n* pl. -S tenrec

TANSY *n* pl. -SIES a perennial herb

TANTALUM *n* pl. -S a metallic element **TANTALIC** *adj*

TANTALUS *n* pl. -ES a case for wine bottles

TANTARA *n* pl. -S the sound of a trumpet or horn

TANTIVY *n* pl. -TIVIES a hunting cry

TANTO *adv* so much — used as a musical direction

TANTRA *n* pl. -S one of a class of Hindu religious writings **TANTRIC** *adj*

TANTRUM *n* pl. -S a fit of rage

TANUKI *n* pl. -S a raccoon dog

TANYARD *n* pl. -S the section of a tannery containing the vats

TAO *n* pl. -S the path of virtuous conduct according to a Chinese philosophy

TAP *v* TAPPED, TAPPING, TAPS to strike gently

TAPA *n* pl. -S a cloth made from tree bark

TAPADERA *n* pl. -S a part of a saddle

TAPADERO *n* pl. -ROS tapadera

TAPALO *n* pl. -LOS a scarf worn in Latin-American countries

TAPE *v* TAPED, TAPING, TAPES to fasten with tape (a long, narrow strip or band)

TAPELESS *adj* being without tape

TAPELIKE *adj* resembling tape

TAPELINE *n* pl. -S a tape for measuring distances

TAPER *v* -ED, -ING, -S to become gradually narrower toward one end

TAPERER *n* pl. -S one that carries a candle in a religious procession

TAPESTRY *v* -TRIED, -TRYING, -TRIES to decorate with woven wall hangings

TAPETUM *n* pl. -TA a layer of cells in some plants **TAPETAL** *adj*

TAPEWORM *n* pl. -S a parasitic worm

TAPHOLE *n* pl. -S a hole in a blast furnace

TAPHOUSE *n* pl. -S a tavern

TAPING present participle of tape

TAPIOCA *n* pl. -S a starchy food

TAPIR *n* pl. -S a hoofed mammal

TAPIS *n* pl. -PISES material used for wall hangings and floor coverings

TAPPED past tense of tap

TAPPER *n* pl. -S one that taps

TAPPET *n* pl. -S a sliding rod that causes another part of a mechanism to move

TAPPING *n* pl. -S the process or means by which something is tapped

TAPROOM *n* pl. -S a barroom

TAPROOT *n* pl. -S the main root of a plant

TAPSTER *n* pl. -S one that dispenses liquor in a barroom

TAR *v* TARRED, TARRING, TARS to cover with tar (a black viscous liquid)

TARAMA *n* pl. -S a Greek paste of fish roe, garlic, lemon juice, and olive oil

TARANTAS *n* pl. -ES a Russian carriage

TARBOOSH *n* pl. -ES a cap worn by Muslim men

TARBUSH *n* pl. -ES tarboosh

TARDIER comparative of tardy

TARDIES pl. of tardy

TARDO *adj* slow — used as a musical direction

TARDY *adj* TARDIER, TARDIEST late **TARDILY** *adv*

TARDY *n* pl. -DIES an instance of being late

TARDYON *n* pl. -S a subatomic particle that travels slower than the speed of light

TARE *v* TARED, TARING, TARES to determine the weight of a container holding goods

TARGE *n* pl. -S a small, round shield

TARGET *v* -ED, -ING, -S to make a goal of

TARIFF *v* -ED, -ING, -S to tax imported or exported goods

TARING present participle of tare

TARLATAN *n* pl. -S a cotton fabric

TARLETAN *n* pl. -S tarlatan

TARMAC *n pl.* -S an asphalt road

TARN *n pl.* -S a small mountain lake

TARNAL *adj* damned **TARNALLY** *adv*

TARNISH *v* -ED, -ING, -ES to dull the luster of

TARO *n pl.* -ROS a tropical plant

TAROC *n pl.* -S tarok

TAROK *n pl.* -S a card game

TAROT *n pl.* -S any of a set of playing cards used for fortune-telling

TARP *n pl.* -S a protective canvas covering

TARPAN *n pl.* -S an Asian wild horse

TARPAPER *n pl.* -S a heavy paper coated with tar

TARPON *n pl.* -S a marine game fish

TARRAGON *n pl.* -S a perennial herb

TARRE *v* TARRED, TARRING, TARRES to urge to action

TARRED past tense of tar

TARRIED past tense of tarry

TARRIER *n pl.* -S one that tarries

TARRIES present 3d person sing. of tarry

TARRIEST superlative of tarry

TARRING present participle of tar and tarre

TARRY *v* -RIED, -RYING, -RIES to delay or be slow in acting or doing

TARRY *adj* -RIER, -RIEST resembling tar

TARSAL *n pl.* -S a bone of the foot

TARSI pl. of tarsus

TARSIA *n pl.* -S intarsia

TARSIER *n pl.* -S a nocturnal primate

TARSUS *n pl.* TARSI a part of the foot

TART *adj* TARTER, TARTEST having a sharp, sour taste

TART *v* -ED, -ING, -S to dress up

TARTAN *n pl.* -S a patterned woolen fabric

TARTANA *n pl.* -S a Mediterranean sailing vessel

TARTAR *n pl.* -S a crust on the teeth **TARTARIC** *adj*

TARTISH *adj* somewhat tart

TARTLET *n pl.* -S a small pie

TARTLY *adv* in a tart manner

TARTNESS *n* -ES the state of being tart

TARTRATE *n pl.* -S a chemical salt

TARTUFE *n pl.* -S tartuffe

TARTUFFE *n pl.* -S a hypocrite

TARTY *adj* resembling a prostitute

TARWEED *n pl.* -S a flowering plant

TARZAN *n pl.* -S a person of superior strength and agility

TASK *v* -ED, -ING, -S to assign a job to

TASKWORK *n pl.* -S hard work

TASS *n pl.* -ES a drinking cup

TASSE *n pl.* -S tasset

TASSEL *v* -SELED, -SELING, -SELS or -SELLED, -SELLING, -SELS to adorn with dangling ornaments

TASSET *n pl.* -S a piece of plate armor for the upper thigh

TASSIE *n pl.* -S tass

TASTE *v* TASTED, TASTING, TASTES to perceive the flavor of by taking into the mouth **TASTABLE** *adj*

TASTEFUL *adj* tasty

TASTER *n pl.* -S one that tastes

TASTING present participle of taste

TASTY *adj* TASTIER, TASTIEST pleasant to the taste **TASTILY** *adv*

TAT *v* TATTED, TATTING, TATS to make tatting

TATAMI *n pl.* -S straw matting used as a floor covering

TATAR *n pl.* -S a ferocious person

TATE *n pl.* -S a tuft of hair

TATER *n pl.* -S a potato

TATOUAY *n pl.* -AYS a South American armadillo

TATTED past tense of tat

TATTER *v* -ED, -ING, -S to become torn and worn

TATTIE *n pl.* -S a potato

TATTIER comparative of tatty

TATTIEST superlative of tatty

TATTILY *adv* in a tatty manner

TATTING *n pl.* -S delicate handmade lace

TATTLE *v* -TLED, -TLING, -TLES to reveal the activities of another

TATTLER *n pl.* -S one that tattles

TATTOO *v* -ED, -ING, -S to mark the skin with indelible pigments

TATTOOER *n pl.* -S one that tattoos

TATTY *adj* -TIER, -TIEST shabby

TAU *n pl.* -S a Greek letter

TAUGHT past tense of teach

TAUNT *v* -ED, -ING, -S to challenge or reproach sarcastically

TAUNTER *n pl.* -S one that taunts

TAUPE *n pl.* -S a dark gray color

TAURINE *n pl.* -S a chemical compound

TAUT *adj* TAUTER, TAUTEST fully stretched, so as not to be slack

TAUT v -ED, -ING, -S to tangle

TAUTAUG n pl. -S tautog

TAUTEN v -ED, -ING, -S to make taut

TAUTLY adv in a taut manner

TAUTNESS n pl. -ES the state of being taut

TAUTOG n pl. -S a marine fish

TAUTOMER n pl. -S a type of chemical compound

TAUTONYM n pl. -S a type of taxonomic designation

TAV n pl. -S a Hebrew letter

TAVERN n pl. -S a place where liquor is sold to be drunk on the premises

TAVERNA n pl. -S a cafe in Greece

TAVERNER n pl. -S one that runs a tavern

TAW v -ED, -ING, -S to convert into white leather by the application of minerals

TAWDRY adj -DRIER, -DRIEST gaudy **TAWDRILY** adv

TAWDRY n pl. -DRIES gaudy finery

TAWER n pl. -S one that taws

TAWIE adj docile

TAWNEY n pl. -NEYS tawny

TAWNY adj -NIER, -NIEST light brown **TAWNILY** adv

TAWNY n pl. -NIES a light brown color

TAWPIE n pl. -S a foolish young person

TAWSE v TAWSED, TAWSING, TAWSES to flog

TAX v -ED, -ING, -ES to place a tax (a charge imposed by authority for public purposes) on

TAXA a pl. of taxon

TAXABLE adj subject to tax **TAXABLY** adv

TAXABLE n pl. -S a taxable item

TAXATION n pl. -S the process of taxing

TAXEME n pl. -S a minimum grammatical feature of selection **TAXEMIC** adj

TAXER n pl. -S one that taxes

TAXI v TAXIED, TAXIING or TAXYING, TAXIS or TAXIES to travel in a taxicab

TAXICAB n pl. -S an automobile for hire

TAXIMAN n pl. -MEN the operator of a taxicab

TAXINGLY adv in an onerous manner

TAXITE n pl. -S a volcanic rock **TAXITIC** adj

TAXIWAY n pl. -WAYS a paved strip at an airport

TAXLESS adj free from taxation

TAXMAN n pl. -MEN one who collects taxes

TAXON n pl. TAXA or TAXONS a unit of scientific classification

TAXONOMY n pl. -MIES the study of scientific classification

TAXPAID adj paid for by taxes

TAXPAYER n pl. -S one that pays taxes

TAXUS n pl. TAXUS an evergreen tree or shrub

TAXWISE adj pertaining to taxes

TAXYING a present participle of taxi

TAZZA n pl. -ZAS or -ZE an ornamental bowl

TEA n pl. -S a beverage made by infusing dried leaves in boiling water

TEABERRY n pl. -RIES a North American shrub

TEABOARD n pl. -S a tray for serving tea

TEABOWL n pl. -S a teacup having no handle

TEABOX n pl. -ES a box for tea leaves

TEACAKE n pl. -S a small cake served with tea

TEACART n pl. -S a wheeled table used in serving tea

TEACH v TAUGHT, TEACHING, TEACHES to impart knowledge or skill to

TEACHER n pl. -S one that teaches

TEACHING n pl. -S a doctrine

TEACUP n pl. -S a cup in which tea is served

TEAHOUSE n pl. -S a public establishment serving tea

TEAK n pl. -S an East Indian tree

TEAKWOOD n pl. -S the wood of the teak

TEAL n pl. -S a river duck

TEALIKE adj resembling tea

TEAM v -ED, -ING, -S to form a team (a group of persons associated in a joint action)

TEAMAKER n pl. -S one that makes tea

TEAMMATE n pl. -S a member of the same team

TEAMSTER n pl. -S a truck driver

TEAMWORK n pl. -S cooperative effort to achieve a common goal

TEAPOT n pl. -S a vessel used in making and serving tea

TEAPOY n pl. -POYS a small table used in serving tea

TEAR v -ED, -ING, -S to emit tears (drops of saline liquid secreted by a gland of the eye)

TEAR v TORE, TORN, TEARING, TEARS to pull apart or into pieces **TEARABLE** adj

TEARAWAY n pl. -AWAYS a rebellious person

TEARDOWN n pl. -S the process of disassembling

TEARDROP n pl. -S a tear

TEARER n pl. -S one that tears or rips

TEARFUL adj full of tears

TEARGAS v -GASSED, -GASSING, -GASES or -GASSES to subject to a gas that irritates the eyes

TEARIER comparative of teary

TEARIEST superlative of teary

TEARILY adv in a teary manner

TEARLESS adj being without tears

TEAROOM n pl. -S a restaurant serving tea

TEARY adj TEARIER, TEARIEST tearful

TEASE v TEASED, TEASING, TEASES to make fun of

TEASEL v -SELED, -SELING, -SELS or -SELLED, -SELLING, -SELS to raise a soft surface on fabric with a bristly flower head

TEASELER n pl. -S one that teasels

TEASER n pl. -S one that teases

TEASHOP n pl. -S a tearoom

TEASING present participle of tease

TEASPOON n pl. -S a small spoon

TEAT n pl. -S a mammary gland **TEATED** adj

TEATIME n pl. -S the customary time for tea

TEAWARE n pl. -S a tea service

TEAZEL v -ZELED, -ZELING, -ZELS or -ZELLED, -ZELLING, -ZELS to teasel

TEAZLE v -ZLED, -ZLING, -ZLES to teasel

TECHED adj crazy

TECHIE n pl. -S a technician

TECHNIC n pl. -S technique

TECHY adj TECHIER, TECHIEST tetchy **TECHILY** adv

TECTA pl. of tectum

TECTAL adj pertaining to a tectum

TECTITE n pl. -S a tektite

TECTONIC adj pertaining to construction

TECTRIX n pl. -TRICES a small feather of a bird's wing

TECTUM n pl. -TA a bodily structure resembling or serving as a roof

TED v TEDDED, TEDDING, TEDS to spread for drying

TEDDER n pl. -S one that teds

TEDDY n pl. -DIES a woman's undergarment

TEDIOUS adj causing weariness

TEDIUM n pl. -S the state of being tedious

TEE v TEED, TEEING, TEES to place a golf ball on a small peg

TEEL n pl. -S sesame

TEEM v -ED, -ING, -S to be full to overflowing

TEEMER n pl. -S one that teems

TEEN n pl. -S a teenager

TEENAGE adj pertaining to teenagers

TEENAGED adj teenage

TEENAGER n pl. -S a person between the ages of thirteen and nineteen

TEENER n pl. -S a teenager

TEENFUL adj filled with grief

TEENIER comparative of teeny

TEENIEST superlative of teeny

TEENSY adj -SIER, -SIEST tiny

TEENTSY adj -SIER, -SIEST tiny

TEENY adj -NIER, -NIEST tiny

TEENYBOP adj pertaining to a young teenager

TEEPEE n pl. -S tepee

TEETER v -ED, -ING, -S to move unsteadily

TEETH pl. of tooth

TEETHE v TEETHED, TEETHING, TEETHES to cut teeth

TEETHER n pl. -S an object for a baby to bite on during teething

TEETHING n pl. -S the first growth of teeth

TEETOTAL v -TALED, -TALING, -TALS or -TALLED, -TALLING, -TALS to abstain completely from alcoholic beverages

TEETOTUM n pl. -S a spinning toy

TEFF n pl. -S a cereal grass

TEFILLIN n/pl the phylacteries worn by Jews

TEG n pl. -S a yearling sheep

TEGMEN n pl. -MINA a covering

TEGMENTA n/pl anatomical coverings

TEGMINAL adj pertaining to a tegmen

TEGUA n pl. -S a type of moccasin

TEGULAR adj resembling a tile

TEGUMEN *n pl.* -MINA tegmen

TEGUMENT *n pl.* -S a covering

TEIGLACH *n pl.* TEIGLACH a confection consisting of balls of dough boiled in honey

TEIID *n pl.* -S a tropical American lizard

TEIND *n pl.* -S a tithe

TEKTITE *n pl.* -S a glassy body believed to be of meteoritic origin TEKTITIC *adj*

TEL *n pl.* -S an ancient mound in the Middle East

TELA *n pl.* -LAE an anatomical tissue

TELAMON *n pl.* -ES a male figure used as a supporting column

TELE *n pl.* -S a television set

TELECAST *v* -ED, -ING, -S to broadcast by television

TELEDU *n pl.* -S a carnivorous mammal

TELEFILM *n pl.* -S a motion picture made for television

TELEGA *n pl.* -S a Russian wagon

TELEGONY *n pl.* -NIES the supposed influence of a previous sire on the offspring of later matings of the mother with other males

TELEGRAM *v* -GRAMMED, -GRAMMING, -GRAMS to send a message by telegraph

TELEMAN *n pl.* -MEN a naval officer

TELEMARK *n pl.* -S a type of turn in skiing

TELEOST *n pl.* -S a bony fish

TELEPATH *n pl.* -S one who can communicate with another by some means other than the senses

TELEPLAY *n pl.* -PLAYS a play written for television

TELEPORT *v* -ED, -ING, -S to transport by a process that involves no physical means

TELERAN *n pl.* -S a system of air navigation

TELESIS *n pl.* TELESES planned progress

TELESTIC *n pl.* -S a type of acrostic

TELETEXT *n pl.* -S a communications system in which printed matter is telecast to subscribers

TELETHON *n pl.* -S a fund-raising television program

TELEVIEW *v* -ED, -ING, -S to observe by means of television

TELEVISE *v* -VISED, -VISING, -VISES to broadcast by television (an electronic system of transmitting images and sound)

TELEX *v* -ED, -ING, -ES to send a message by a type of telegraphic system

TELFER *v* -ED, -ING, -S to telpher

TELFORD *n pl.* -S a road made of stones

TELIA *pl.* of telium

TELIAL *adj* pertaining to a telium

TELIC *adj* directed toward a goal

TELIUM *n pl.* -LIA a sorus on the host plant of a rust fungus

TELL *v* TOLD, TELLING, TELLS to give a detailed account of TELLABLE *adj*

TELLER *n pl.* -S a bank employee who receives and pays out money

TELLIES *a pl.* of telly

TELLTALE *n pl.* -S a tattler

TELLURIC *adj* pertaining to the earth

TELLY *n pl.* -LIES or -LYS a television set

TELOME *n pl.* -S a structural unit of a vascular plant TELOMIC *adj*

TELOMERE *n pl.* -S the natural end of a chromosome

TELOS *n pl.* TELOI an ultimate end

TELPHER *v* -ED, -ING, -S to transport by a system of aerial cable cars

TELSON *n pl.* -S the terminal segment of an arthropod TELSONIC *adj*

TEMBLOR *n pl.* -S or -ES an earthquake

TEMERITY *n pl.* -TIES foolish boldness

TEMP *v* -ED, -ING, -S to work as a temporary employee

TEMPEH *n pl.* -S an Asian food

TEMPER *v* -ED, -ING, -S to dilute or soften by adding something

TEMPERA *n pl.* -S a technique of painting

TEMPERER *n pl.* -S one that tempers

TEMPEST *v* -ED, -ING, -S to agitate violently

TEMPI *a pl.* of tempo

TEMPLAR *n pl.* -S a lawyer or student of law in London

TEMPLATE *n pl.* -S a pattern used as a guide in making something

TEMPLE *n pl.* -S a house of worship TEMPLED *adj*

TEMPLET *n pl.* -S template

TEMPO *n pl.* -PI or -POS the rate of speed of a musical piece

TEMPORAL *n pl.* -S a bone of the skull

TEMPT	v -ED, -ING, -S to entice to commit an unwise or immoral act	**TENNIST**	n pl. -S a tennis player
TEMPTER	n pl. -S one that tempts	**TENON**	v -ED, -ING, -S to unite by means of a tenon (a projection on the end of a piece of wood)
TEMPURA	n pl. -S a Japanese dish		
TEN	n pl. -S a number	**TENONER**	n pl. -S one that tenons
TENABLE	adj capable of being held TENABLY adv	**TENOR**	n pl. -S a high male singing voice
TENACE	n pl. -S a combination of two high cards in some card games	**TENORIST**	n pl. -S one who sings tenor or plays a tenor instrument
		TENORITE	n pl. -S a mineral
TENACITY	n pl. -TIES perseverance or persistence	**TENOTOMY**	n pl. -MIES the surgical division of a tendon
TENACULA	n/pl hooked surgical instruments	**TENOUR**	n pl. -S tenor
		TENPENCE	n pl. -S the sum of ten pennies
TENAIL	n pl. -S tenaille		
TENAILLE	n pl. -S an outer defense	**TENPENNY**	adj worth tenpence
TENANCY	n pl. -CIES the temporary occupancy of something that belongs to another	**TENPIN**	n pl. -S a bowling pin
		TENREC	n pl. -S a mammal that feeds on insects
TENANT	v -ED, -ING, -S to inhabit		
TENANTRY	n pl. -RIES tenancy	**TENSE**	adj TENSER, TENSEST taut TENSELY adv
TENCH	n pl. -ES a freshwater fish		
TEND	v -ED, -ING, -S to be disposed or inclined	**TENSE**	v TENSED, TENSING, TENSES to make tense
TENDANCE	n pl. -S watchful care	**TENSIBLE**	adj capable of being stretched TENSIBLY adv
TENDENCE	n pl. -S tendance		
TENDENCY	n pl. -CIES an inclination to act or think in a particular way	**TENSILE**	adj tensible
		TENSING	present participle of tense
TENDER	adj -DERER, -DEREST soft or delicate	**TENSION**	v -ED, -ING, -S to make tense
		TENSITY	n pl. -TIES the state of being tense
TENDER	v -ED, -ING, -S to present for acceptance		
		TENSIVE	adj causing tensity
TENDERER	n pl. -S one that tenders	**TENSOR**	n pl. -S a muscle that stretches a body part
TENDERLY	adv in a tender manner		
TENDON	n pl. -S a band of tough, fibrous tissue	**TENT**	v -ED, -ING, -S to live in a tent (a type of portable shelter)
TENDRIL	n pl. -S a leafless organ of climbing plants	**TENTACLE**	n pl. -S an elongated, flexible appendage of some animals
		TENTAGE	n pl. -S a supply of tents
TENEBRAE	n/pl a religious service	**TENTER**	v -ED, -ING, -S to stretch on a type of frame
TENEMENT	n pl. -S an apartment house		
TENESMUS	n pl. -ES an urgent but ineffectual effort to defecate or urinate TENESMIC adj	**TENTH**	n pl. -S one of ten equal parts
		TENTHLY	adv in the tenth place
		TENTIE	adj TENTIER, TENTIEST tenty
TENET	n pl. -S a principle, belief, or doctrine held to be true		
		TENTIER	comparative of tenty
TENFOLD	n pl. -S an amount ten times as great as a given unit	**TENTIEST**	superlative of tenty
		TENTLESS	adj having no tent
TENIA	n pl. -NIAE or -NIAS a tapeworm	**TENTLIKE**	adj resembling a tent
		TENTY	adj TENTIER, TENTIEST watchful
TENIASIS	n pl. -SISES infestation with tapeworms		
		TENUIS	n pl. -UES a voiceless phonetic stop
TENNER	n pl. -S a ten-dollar bill		
TENNIES	n/pl low-cut sneakers	**TENUITY**	n pl. -ITIES lack of substance or strength
TENNIS	n pl. -NISES an outdoor ball game		
		TENUOUS	adj having little substance or strength

TENURE n pl. -S the holding of something TENURED, TENURIAL adj

TENUTO n pl. -TI or -TOS a musical note or chord held longer than its normal duration

TEOCALLI n pl. -S an Aztec temple

TEOPAN n pl. -S a teocalli

TEOSINTE n pl. -S an annual grass

TEPA n pl. -S a chemical compound

TEPAL n pl. -S a division of a perianth

TEPEE n pl. -S a conical tent of some North American Indians

TEPEFY v -FIED, -FYING, -FIES to make tepid

TEPHRA n pl. -S solid material ejected from a volcano

TEPHRITE n pl. -S a volcanic rock

TEPID adj moderately warm TEPIDLY adv

TEPIDITY n pl. -TIES the state of being tepid

TEPOY n pl. -POYS teapoy

TEQUILA n pl. -S a Mexican liquor

TERAI n pl. -S a sun hat with a wide brim

TERAOHM n pl. -S one trillion ohms

TERAPH n pl. -APHIM an image of a Semitic household god

TERATISM n pl. -S a malformed fetus TERATOID adj

TERATOMA n pl. -MAS or -MATA a type of tumor

TERAWATT n pl. -S one trillion watts

TERBIA n pl. -S an oxide of terbium

TERBIUM n pl. -S a metallic element TERBIC adj

TERCE n pl. -S tierce

TERCEL n pl. -S a male falcon

TERCELET n pl. -S tercel

TERCET n pl. -S a group of three lines of verse

TEREBENE n pl. -S a mixture of terpenes

TEREBIC adj pertaining to an acid derived from oil of turpentine

TEREDO n pl. -DOS or -DINES a bivalve mollusk

TEREFAH adj tref

TERETE adj cylindrical and slightly tapering

TERGA pl. of tergum

TERGAL adj pertaining to a tergum

TERGITE n pl. -S a tergum

TERGUM n pl. -GA a back part of a segment of an arthropod

TERIYAKI n pl. -S a Japanese food

TERM v -ED, -ING, -S to give a name to

TERMER n pl. -S a prisoner serving a specified sentence

TERMINAL n pl. -S an end or extremity

TERMINUS n pl. -NI or -NUSES a terminal

TERMITE n pl. -S an insect resembling an ant TERMITIC adj

TERMLESS adj having no limits

TERMLY adv periodically

TERMOR n pl. -S one that holds land for a certain number of years

TERMTIME n pl. -S the time when a school or court is in session

TERN n pl. -S a seabird

TERNARY n pl. -RIES a group of three

TERNATE adj arranged in groups of three

TERNE n pl. -S an alloy of lead and tin

TERNION n pl. -S a group of three

TERPENE n pl. -S a chemical compound TERPENIC adj

TERPINOL n pl. -S a fragrant liquid

TERRA n pl. -RAE earth; land

TERRACE v -RACED, -RACING, -RACES to provide with a terrace (a raised embankment)

TERRAIN n pl. -S a tract of land

TERRANE n pl. -S a rock formation

TERRAPIN n pl. -S a North American tortoise

TERRARIA n/pl glass enclosures for plants or small animals

TERRAS n pl. -ES trass

TERRAZZO n pl. -ZOS a mosaic flooring

TERREEN n pl. -S terrine

TERRELLA n pl. -S a spherical magnet

TERRENE n pl. -S a land area

TERRET n pl. -S a metal ring on a harness

TERRIBLE adj very bad TERRIBLY adv

TERRIER n pl. -S a small, active dog

TERRIES pl. of terry

TERRIFIC adj very good; fine

TERRIFY v -FIED, -FYING, -FIES to fill with terror

TERRINE n pl. -S an earthenware jar

TERRIT n pl. -S terret

TERROR n pl. -S intense fear

TERRY n pl. -RIES an absorbent fabric

TERSE adj TERSER, TERSEST succinct TERSELY adv

TERTIAL n pl. -S a flight feather of a bird's wing

TERTIAN n pl. -S a recurrent fever

TERTIARY *n pl.* -ARIES a tertial

TESLA *n pl.* -S a unit of magnetic induction

TESSERA *n pl.* -SERAE a small square used in mosaic work

TEST *v* -ED, -ING, -S to subject to an examination **TESTABLE** *adj*

TESTA *n pl.* -TAE the hard outer coating of a seed

TESTACY *n pl.* -CIES the state of being testate

TESTATE *n pl.* -S a testator

TESTATOR *n pl.* -S one that makes a will

TESTEE *n pl.* -S one that is tested

TESTER *n pl.* -S one that tests

TESTES *pl. of* testis

TESTICLE *n pl.* -S a testis

TESTIER *comparative of* testy

TESTIEST *superlative of* testy

TESTIFY *v* -FIED, -FYING, -FIES to make a declaration of truth under oath

TESTILY *adv* in a testy manner

TESTIS *n pl.* TESTES a male reproductive gland

TESTON *n pl.* -S a former French coin

TESTOON *n pl.* -S teston

TESTUDO *n pl.* -DINES or -DOS a portable screen used as a shield by the ancient Romans

TESTY *adj* TESTIER, TESTIEST irritable

TET *n pl.* -S teth

TETANAL *adj* pertaining to tetanus

TETANIC *n pl.* -S a drug capable of causing convulsions

TETANIES *pl. of* tetany

TETANISE *v* -NISED, -NISING, -NISES to tetanize

TETANIZE *v* -NIZED, -NIZING, -NIZES to affect with convulsions

TETANUS *n pl.* -ES an infectious disease **TETANOID** *adj*

TETANY *n pl.* -NIES a condition marked by painful muscular spasms

TETCHED *adj* crazy

TETCHY *adj* TETCHIER, TETCHIEST irritable **TETCHILY** *adv*

TETH *n pl.* -S a Hebrew letter

TETHER *v* -ED, -ING, -S to fasten to a fixed object with a rope

TETOTUM *n pl.* -S teetotum

TETRA *n pl.* -S a tropical fish

TETRACID *n pl.* -S a type of acid

TETRAD *n pl.* -S a group of four **TETRADIC** *adj*

TETRAGON *n pl.* -S a four-sided polygon

TETRAMER *n pl.* -S a type of polymer

TETRAPOD *n pl.* -S a four-footed animal

TETRARCH *n pl.* -S one of four joint rulers

TETRODE *n pl.* -S a type of electron tube

TETROXID *n pl.* -S a type of oxide

TETRYL *n pl.* -S a chemical compound

TETTER *n pl.* -S a skin disease

TEUCH *adj* teugh

TEUGH *adj* tough **TEUGHLY** *adv*

TEW *v* -ED, -ING, -S to work hard

TEXAS *n pl.* -ES the uppermost structure on a steamboat

TEXT *n pl.* -S the main body of a written or printed work

TEXTBOOK *n pl.* -S a book used in the study of a subject

TEXTILE *n pl.* -S a woven fabric

TEXTLESS *adj* having no text

TEXTUAL *adj* pertaining to a text

TEXTUARY *n pl.* -ARIES a specialist in the study of the Scriptures

TEXTURAL *adj* pertaining to the surface characteristics of something

TEXTURE *v* -TURED, -TURING, -TURES to make by weaving

THACK *v* -ED, -ING, -S to thatch

THAE *adj* these; those

THAIRM *n pl.* -S tharm

THALAMUS *n pl.* -MI a part of the brain **THALAMIC** *adj*

THALER *n pl.* -S taler

THALLIUM *n pl.* -S a metallic element **THALLIC, THALLOUS** *adj*

THALLUS *n pl.* -LI or -LUSES a plant body without true root, stem, or leaf **THALLOID** *adj*

THAN *conj* — used to introduce the second element of a comparison

THANAGE *n pl.* -S the land held by a thane

THANATOS *n pl.* -ES an instinctual desire for death

THANE *n pl.* -S a man holding land by military service in Anglo-Saxon England

THANK *v* -ED, -ING, -S to express gratitude to

THANKER *n pl.* -S one that thanks

THANKFUL *adj* -FULLER, -FULLEST feeling gratitude

THARM *n pl.* -S the belly

THAT *pron* pl. THOSE the one indicated

THATAWAY *adv* in that direction

THATCH *v* -ED, -ING, -ES to cover with thatch (plant stalks or foliage)

THATCHER *n* pl. -S one that thatches

THATCHY *adj* THATCHIER, THATCHIEST resembling thatch

THAW *v* -ED, -ING, -S to melt

THAWER *n* pl. -S one that thaws

THAWLESS *adj* never thawing

THE *definite article* — used to specify or make particular

THEARCHY *n* pl. -CHIES rule by a god

THEATER *n* pl. -S a building for dramatic presentations THEATRIC *adj*

THEATRE *n* pl. -S theater

THEBAINE *n* pl. -S a poisonous alkaloid

THEBE *n* pl. THEBE a monetary unit of Botswana

THECA *n* pl. -CAE a protective anatomical covering THECAL, THECATE *adj*

THEE *pron* the objective case of the pronoun thou

THEELIN *n* pl. -S estrone

THEELOL *n* pl. -S estriol

THEFT *n* pl. -S the act of stealing

THEGN *n* pl. -S thane THEGNLY *adj*

THEIN *n* pl. -S theine

THEINE *n* pl. -S caffeine

THEIR *pron* a possessive form of the pronoun they

THEIRS *pron* a possessive form of the pronoun they

THEISM *n* pl. -S belief in the existence of a god

THEIST *n* pl. -S one who believes in the existence of a god THEISTIC *adj*

THELITIS *n* pl. -TISES inflammation of the nipple

THEM *pron* the objective case of the pronoun they

THEMATIC *n* pl. -S a stamp collected according to its subject

THEME *v* THEMED, THEMING, THEMES to plan something according to a central subject

THEN *n* pl. -S that time

THENAGE *n* pl. -S thanage

THENAL *adj* pertaining to the palm of the hand

THENAR *n* pl. -S the palm of the hand

THENCE *adv* from that place

THEOCRAT *n* pl. -S a person who rules as a representative of a god

THEODICY *n* pl. -CIES a defense of God's goodness in respect to the existence of evil

THEOGONY *n* pl. -NIES an account of the origin of the gods

THEOLOG *n* pl. -S a student of theology

THEOLOGY *n* pl. -GIES the study of religion

THEONOMY *n* pl. -MIES rule by a god

THEORBO *n* pl. -BOS a stringed musical instrument

THEOREM *n* pl. -S a proposition that is demonstrably true or is assumed to be so

THEORIES pl. of theory

THEORISE *v* -RISED, -RISING, -RISES to theorize

THEORIST *n* pl. -S one that theorizes

THEORIZE *v* -RIZED, -RIZING, -RIZES to form theories

THEORY *n* pl. -RIES a group of propositions used to explain a class of phenomena

THERAPY *n* pl. -PIES the treatment of illness or disability

THERE *n* pl. -S that place

THEREAT *adv* at that place or time

THEREBY *adv* by that means

THEREFOR *adv* for that

THEREIN *adv* in that place

THEREMIN *n* pl. -S a musical instrument

THEREOF *adv* of that

THEREON *adv* on that

THERETO *adv* to that

THERIAC *n* pl. -S molasses

THERIACA *n* pl. -S theriac

THERM *n* pl. -S a unit of quantity of heat

THERMAE *n/pl* hot springs

THERMAL *n* pl. -S a rising mass of warm air

THERME *n* pl. -S therm

THERMEL *n* pl. -S a device for temperature measurement

THERMIC *adj* pertaining to heat

THERMION *n* pl. -S an ion emitted by a heated body

THERMITE *n* pl. -S a metallic mixture that produces intense heat when ignited

THERMOS *n* pl. -ES a container used to keep liquids either hot or cold

THEROID *adj* resembling a beast

THEROPOD *n* pl. -S a carnivorous dinosaur

THESAURI n/pl dictionaries of synonyms and antonyms

THESE pl. of this

THESIS n pl. THESES a proposition put forward for discussion

THESPIAN n pl. -S an actor or actress

THETA n pl. -S a Greek letter

THETIC adj arbitrary

THETICAL adj thetic

THEURGY n pl. -GIES divine intervention in human affairs **THEURGIC** adj

THEW n pl. -S a well-developed muscle

THEWLESS adj weak

THEWY adj THEWIER, THEWIEST brawny

THEY pron the 3d person pl. pronoun in the nominative case

THIAMIN n pl. -S thiamine

THIAMINE n pl. -S a B vitamin

THIAZIDE n pl. -S a drug used to treat high blood pressure

THIAZIN n pl. -S thiazine

THIAZINE n pl. -S a chemical compound

THIAZOL n pl. -S thiazole

THIAZOLE n pl. -S a chemical compound

THICK adj THICKER, THICKEST having relatively great extent from one surface to its opposite

THICK n pl. -S the thickest part

THICKEN v -ED, -ING, -S to make thick

THICKET n pl. -S a dense growth of shrubs or small trees **THICKETY** adj

THICKISH adj somewhat thick

THICKLY adv in a thick manner

THICKSET n pl. -S a thicket

THIEF n pl. THIEVES one that steals

THIEVE v THIEVED, THIEVING, THIEVES to steal

THIEVERY n pl. -ERIES the act or practice of stealing

THIEVES pl. of thief

THIEVING present participle of thieve

THIEVISH adj given to stealing

THIGH n pl. -S a part of the leg **THIGHED** adj

THILL n pl. -S a shaft of a vehicle

THIMBLE n pl. -S a cap used to protect the fingertip during sewing

THIN adj THINNER, THINNEST having relatively little density or thickness

THIN v THINNED, THINNING, THINS to make thin

THINCLAD n pl. -S a runner on a track team

THINDOWN n pl. -S a lessening in the number of atomic particles and cosmic rays passing through the earth's atmosphere

THINE pron a possessive form of the pronoun thou

THING n pl. -S an inanimate object

THINK v THOUGHT, THINKING, THINKS to formulate in the mind

THINKER n pl. -S one that thinks

THINKING n pl. -S an opinion or judgment

THINLY adv in a thin manner

THINNED past tense of thin

THINNER n pl. -S one that thins

THINNESS n pl. -ES the quality or state of being thin

THINNEST superlative of thin

THINNING present participle of thin

THINNISH adj somewhat thin

THIO adj containing sulfur

THIOL n pl. -S a sulfur compound **THIOLIC** adj

THIONATE n pl. -S a chemical salt

THIONIC adj pertaining to sulfur

THIONIN n pl. -S a violet dye

THIONINE n pl. -S thionin

THIONYL n pl. -S sulfinyl

THIOPHEN n pl. -S a chemical compound

THIOTEPA n pl. -S a chemical compound

THIOUREA n pl. -S a chemical compound

THIR pron these

THIRAM n pl. -S a chemical compound

THIRD n pl. -S one of three equal parts

THIRDLY adv in the third place

THIRL v -ED, -ING, -S to thrill

THIRLAGE n pl. -S an obligation requiring feudal tenants to grind grain at a certain mill

THIRST v -ED, -ING, -S to feel a desire or need to drink

THIRSTER n pl. -S one that thirsts

THIRSTY adj THIRSTIER, THIRSTIEST feeling a desire or need to drink

THIRTEEN n pl. -S a number

THIRTY n pl. -TIES a number

THIS pron pl. THESE the person or thing just mentioned

THISTLE n pl. -S a prickly plant

THISTLY	adj -TLIER, -TLIEST prickly
THITHER	adv in that direction
THO	conj though
THOLE	v THOLED, THOLING, THOLES to endure
THOLEPIN	n pl. -S a pin that serves as an oarlock
THOLOS	n pl. -LOI a circular, underground tomb
THONG	n pl. -S a narrow strip of leather used for binding THONGED adj
THORAX	n pl. -RACES or -RAXES the part of the body between the neck and the abdomen THORACAL, THORACIC adj
THORIA	n pl. -S an oxide of thorium
THORIC	adj pertaining to thorium
THORITE	n pl. -S a thorium ore
THORIUM	n pl. -S a metallic element
THORN	v -ED, -ING, -S to prick with a thorn (a sharp, rigid projection on a plant)
THORNY	adj THORNIER, THORNIEST full of thorns THORNILY adv
THORO	adj thorough
THORON	n pl. -S a radioactive isotope of radon
THOROUGH	adj THOROUGHER, THOROUGHEST complete in all respects
THORP	n pl. -S a small village
THORPE	n pl. -S thorp
THOSE	pl. of that
THOU	v -ED, -ING, -S to address as "thou" (the 2d person sing. pronoun in the nominative case)
THOUGH	conj despite the fact that
THOUGHT	n pl. -S a product of thinking
THOUSAND	n pl. -S a number
THOWLESS	adj listless
THRALDOM	n pl. -S servitude
THRALL	v -ED, -ING, -S to enslave
THRASH	v -ED, -ING, -ES to beat
THRASHER	n pl. -S one that thrashes
THRAVE	n pl. -S a unit of measure for grain
THRAW	v -ED, -ING, -S to twist
THRAWART	adj stubborn
THRAWN	adj twisted THRAWNLY adv
THREAD	v -ED, -ING, -S to pass a thread (a very slender cord) through
THREADER	n pl. -S one that threads
THREADY	adj THREADIER, THREADIEST resembling a thread
THREAP	v -ED, -ING, -S to dispute
THREAPER	n pl. -S one that threaps
THREAT	v -ED, -ING, -S to threaten
THREATEN	v -ED, -ING, -S to be a source of danger to
THREE	n pl. -S a number
THREEP	v -ED, -ING, -S to threap
THRENODE	n pl. -S a threnody
THRENODY	n pl. -DIES a song of lamentation
THRESH	v -ED, -ING, -ES to separate the grain or seeds from a plant mechanically
THRESHER	n pl. -S one that threshes
THREW	past tense of throw
THRICE	adv three times
THRIFT	n pl. -S care and wisdom in the management of one's resources
THRIFTY	adj THRIFTIER, THRIFTIEST displaying thrift
THRILL	v -ED, -ING, -S to excite greatly
THRILLER	n pl. -S one that thrills
THRIP	n pl. -S a British coin
THRIVE	v THROVE or THRIVED, THRIVEN, THRIVING, THRIVES to grow vigorously
THRIVER	n pl. -S one that thrives
THRO	prep through
THROAT	v -ED, -ING, -S to utter in a hoarse voice
THROATY	adj THROATIER, THROATIEST hoarse
THROB	v THROBBED, THROBBING, THROBS to pulsate
THROBBER	n pl. -S one that throbs
THROE	n pl. -S a violent spasm of pain
THROMBIN	n pl. -S an enzyme
THROMBUS	n pl. -BI a clot occluding a blood vessel
THRONE	v THRONED, THRONING, THRONES to place on a throne (a royal chair)
THRONG	v -ED, -ING, -S to crowd into
THROSTLE	n pl. -S a songbird
THROTTLE	v -TLED, -TLING, -TLES to strangle
THROUGH	prep by way of
THROVE	a past tense of thrive

THROW v THREW, THROWN, THROWING, THROWS to propel through the air with a movement of the arm

THROWER n pl. -S one that throws

THRU prep through

THRUM v THRUMMED, THRUMMING, THRUMS to play a stringed instrument idly or monotonously

THRUMMER n pl. -S one that thrums

THRUMMY adj -MIER, -MIEST shaggy

THRUPUT n pl. -S the amount of raw material processed within a given time

THRUSH n pl. -ES a songbird

THRUST v -ED, -ING, -S to push forcibly

THRUSTER n pl. -S one that thrusts

THRUSTOR n pl. -S thruster

THRUWAY n pl. -WAYS an express highway

THUD v THUDDED, THUDDING, THUDS to make a dull, heavy sound

THUG n pl. -S a brutal ruffian or assassin

THUGGEE n pl. -S thuggery in India

THUGGERY n pl. -GERIES thuggish behavior

THUGGISH adj characteristic of a thug

THUJA n pl. -S an evergreen tree or shrub

THULIA n pl. -S an oxide of thulium

THULIUM n pl. -S a metallic element

THUMB v -ED, -ING, -S to leaf through with the thumb (the short, thick digit of the human hand)

THUMBKIN n pl. -S a screw that is turned by the thumb and fingers

THUMBNUT n pl. -S a nut that is turned by the thumb and fingers

THUMP v -ED, -ING, -S to strike so as to make a dull, heavy sound

THUMPER n pl. -S one that thumps

THUNDER v -ED, -ING, -S to produce a loud, resounding sound

THUNDERY adj accompanied with thunder

THUNK v -ED, -ING, -S to make a sudden, muffled sound

THURIBLE n pl. -S a censer

THURIFER n pl. -S one who carries a thurible in a religious ceremony

THURL n pl. -S the hip joint in cattle

THUS adv in this manner

THUSLY adv thus

THUYA n pl. -S thuja

THWACK v -ED, -ING, -S to strike with something flat

THWACKER n pl. -S one that thwacks

THWART v -ED, -ING, -S to prevent the accomplishment of

THWARTER n pl. -S one that thwarts

THWARTLY adv athwart

THY pron a possessive form of the pronoun thou

THYME n pl. -S an aromatic herb

THYMEY adj THYMIER, THYMIEST thymy

THYMI a pl. of thymus

THYMIC adj pertaining to thyme

THYMIER comparative of thymey and thymy

THYMIEST superlative of thymey and thymy

THYMINE n pl. -S a chemical compound

THYMOL n pl. -S a chemical compound

THYMOSIN n pl. -S a hormone secreted by the thymus

THYMUS n pl. -MI or -MUSES a glandular structure in the body

THYMY adj THYMIER, THYMIEST abounding in thyme

THYREOID adj pertaining to the thyroid

THYROID n pl. -S an endocrine gland

THYROXIN n pl. -S an amino acid

THYRSE n pl. -S thyrsus

THYRSUS n pl. -SI a type of flower cluster THYRSOID adj

THYSELF pron yourself

TI n pl. -S the seventh tone of the diatonic musical scale

TIARA n pl. -S a jeweled headpiece worn by women TIARAED adj

TIBIA n pl. -IAE or -IAS a bone of the leg TIBIAL adj

TIC n pl. -S an involuntary muscular contraction

TICAL n pl. -S a former Thai unit of weight

TICK v -ED, -ING, -S to make a recurrent clicking sound

TICKER n pl. -S one that ticks

TICKET v -ED, -ING, -S to attach a tag to

TICKING n pl. -S a strong cotton fabric

TICKLE v -LED, -LING, -LES to touch lightly so as to produce a tingling sensation

TICKLER n pl. -S one that tickles

TICKLISH adj sensitive to tickling

TICKSEED n pl. -S a flowering plant

TICKTACK v -ED, -ING, -S to ticktock

TICKTOCK v -ED, -ING, -S to make the ticking sound of a clock

TICTAC v -TACKED, -TACKING, -TACS to ticktack

TICTOC v -TOCKED, -TOCKING, -TOCS to ticktock

TIDAL adj pertaining to the tides TIDALLY adv

TIDBIT n pl. -S a choice bit of food

TIDDLER n pl. -S a small fish

TIDDLY adj slightly drunk

TIDE v TIDED, TIDING, TIDES to flow like the tide (the rise and fall of the ocean's waters)

TIDELAND n pl. -S land alternately covered and uncovered by the tide

TIDELESS adj lacking a tide

TIDELIKE adj resembling a tide

TIDEMARK n pl. -S a mark showing the highest or lowest point of a tide

TIDERIP n pl. -S a riptide

TIDEWAY n pl. -WAYS a tidal channel

TIDIED past tense of tidy

TIDIER n pl. -S one that tidies

TIDIES present 3d person sing. of tidy

TIDIEST superlative of tidy

TIDILY adv in a tidy manner

TIDINESS n pl. -ES the state of being tidy

TIDING n pl. -S a piece of news

TIDY adj -DIER, -DIEST neat and orderly

TIDY v -DIED, -DYING, -DIES to make tidy

TIDYTIPS n pl. TIDYTIPS an annual herb

TIE v TIED, TYING or TIEING, TIES to fasten with a cord or rope

TIEBACK n pl. -S a loop for holding a curtain back to one side

TIECLASP n pl. -S a clasp for securing a necktie

TIED past tense of tie

TIELESS adj having no necktie

TIEPIN n pl. -S a pin for securing a necktie

TIER v -ED, -ING, -S to arrange in tiers (rows placed one above another)

TIERCE n pl. -S one of seven canonical daily periods for prayer and devotion

TIERCED adj divided into three equal parts

TIERCEL n pl. -S tercel

TIFF v -ED, -ING, -S to have a petty quarrel

TIFFANY n pl. -NIES a thin, mesh fabric

TIFFIN v -ED, -ING, -S to lunch

TIGER n pl. -S a large feline mammal

TIGEREYE n pl. -S a gemstone

TIGERISH adj resembling a tiger

TIGHT adj TIGHTER, TIGHTEST firmly or closely fixed in place TIGHTLY adv

TIGHTEN v -ED, -ING, -S to make tight

TIGHTS n/pl a close-fitting garment

TIGHTWAD n pl. -S a miser

TIGLON n pl. -S the offspring of a male tiger and a female lion

TIGON n pl. -S tiglon

TIGRESS n pl. -ES a female tiger

TIGRISH adj tigerish

TIKE n pl. -S tyke

TIKI n pl. -S a wood or stone image of a Polynesian god

TIL n pl. -S the sesame plant

TILAK n pl. -S a mark worn on the forehead by Hindus

TILAPIA n pl. -S an African fish

TILBURY n pl. -BURIES a carriage having two wheels

TILDE n pl. -S a mark placed over a letter to indicate its sound

TILE v TILED, TILING, TILES to cover with tiles (thin slabs of baked clay)

TILEFISH n pl. -ES a marine food fish

TILELIKE adj resembling a tile

TILER n pl. -S one that tiles

TILING n pl. -S a surface of tiles

TILL v -ED, -ING, -S to prepare land for crops by plowing TILLABLE adj

TILLAGE n pl. -S cultivated land

TILLER v -ED, -ING, -S to put forth stems from a root

TILLITE n pl. -S rock made up of consolidated clay, sand, gravel, and boulders

TILT v -ED, -ING, -S to cause to slant TILTABLE adj

TILTER n pl. -S one that tilts

TILTH n pl. -S tillage

TILTYARD n pl. -S an area for jousting contests

TIMARAU n pl. -S tamarau

TIMBAL n pl. -S a large drum

TIMBALE *n pl.* -S a pastry shell shaped like a drum

TIMBER *v* -ED, -ING, -S to furnish with timber (wood used as a building material)

TIMBRE *n pl.* -S the quality given to a sound by its overtones **TIMBRAL** *adj*

TIMBREL *n pl.* -S a percussion instrument

TIME *v* TIMED, TIMING, TIMES to determine the speed or duration of

TIMECARD *n pl.* -S a card for recording an employee's times of arrival and departure

TIMELESS *adj* having no beginning or end

TIMELINE *n pl.* -S a schedule of events

TIMELY *adj* -LIER, -LIEST occurring at the right moment

TIMEOUS *adj* timely

TIMEOUT *n pl.* -S a brief suspension of activity

TIMER *n pl.* -S one that times

TIMEWORK *n pl.* -S work paid for by the hour or by the day

TIMEWORN *adj* showing the effects of long use or wear

TIMID *adj* -IDER, -IDEST lacking courage or self-confidence **TIMIDLY** *adv*

TIMIDITY *n pl.* -TIES the quality of being timid

TIMING *n pl.* -S the selection of the proper moment for doing something

TIMOLOL *n pl.* -S a drug used to treat glaucoma

TIMOROUS *adj* fearful

TIMOTHY *n pl.* -THIES a European grass

TIMPANO *n pl.* -NI a kettledrum

TIMPANUM *n pl.* -NA or -NUMS tympanum

TIN *v* TINNED, TINNING, TINS to coat with tin (a metallic element)

TINAMOU *n pl.* -S a South American game bird

TINCAL *n pl.* -S crude borax

TINCT *v* -ED, -ING, -S to tinge

TINCTURE *v* -TURED, -TURING, -TURES to tinge

TINDER *n pl.* -S readily combustible material **TINDERY** *adj*

TINE *v* TINED, TINING, TINES to lose

TINEA *n pl.* -S a fungous skin disease **TINEAL** *adj*

TINEID *n pl.* -S one of a family of moths

TINFOIL *n pl.* -S a thin metal sheeting

TINFUL *n pl.* -S as much as a tin container can hold

TING *v* -ED, -ING, -S to emit a high-pitched metallic sound

TINGE *v* TINGED, TINGEING or TINGING, TINGES to apply a trace of color to

TINGLE *v* -GLED, -GLING, -GLES to cause a prickly, stinging sensation

TINGLER *n pl.* -S one that tingles

TINGLY *adj* -GLIER, -GLIEST tingling

TINHORN *n pl.* -S a showily pretentious person

TINIER comparative of tiny

TINIEST superlative of tiny

TINILY *adv* in a tiny manner

TININESS *n pl.* -ES the quality of being tiny

TINING present participle of tine

TINKER *v* -ED, -ING, -S to repair in an unskilled or experimental manner

TINKERER *n pl.* -S one that tinkers

TINKLE *v* -KLED, -KLING, -KLES to make slight, sharp, metallic sounds

TINKLER *n pl.* -S one that tinkles

TINKLING *n pl.* -S the sound made by something that tinkles

TINKLY *adj* -KLIER, -KLIEST producing a tinkling sound

TINLIKE *adj* resembling tin

TINMAN *n pl.* -MEN a tinsmith

TINNED past tense of tin

TINNER *n pl.* -S a tin miner

TINNIER comparative of tinny

TINNIEST superlative of tinny

TINNILY *adv* in a tinny manner

TINNING present participle of tin

TINNITUS *n pl.* -ES a ringing sound in the ears

TINNY *adj* -NIER, -NIEST of or resembling tin

TINPLATE *n pl.* -S thin sheet iron coated with tin

TINSEL _v_ -SELED, -SELING, -SELS or -SELLED, -SELLING, -SELS to give a showy or gaudy appearance to
TINSELLY _adj_ cheaply gaudy
TINSMITH _n pl._ -S one who works with tin
TINSTONE _n pl._ -S a tin ore
TINT _v_ -ED, -ING, -S to color slightly or delicately
TINTER _n pl._ -S one that tints
TINTING _n pl._ -S the process of one that tints
TINTLESS _adj_ lacking color
TINTYPE _n pl._ -S a kind of photograph
TINWARE _n pl._ -S articles made of tinplate
TINWORK _n pl._ -S something made of tin
TINY _adj_ TINIER, TINIEST very small
TIP _v_ TIPPED, TIPPING, TIPS to tilt
TIPCART _n pl._ -S a type of cart
TIPCAT _n pl._ -S a game resembling baseball
TIPI _n pl._ -S tepee
TIPLESS _adj_ having no point or extremity
TIPOFF _n pl._ -S a hint or warning
TIPPABLE _adj_ capable of being tipped
TIPPED past tense of tip
TIPPER _n pl._ -S one that tips
TIPPET _n pl._ -S a covering for the shoulders
TIPPIER comparative of tippy
TIPPIEST superlative of tippy
TIPPING present participle of tip
TIPPLE _v_ -PLED, -PLING, -PLES to drink alcoholic beverages
TIPPLER _n pl._ -S one that tipples
TIPPY _adj_ -PIER, -PIEST unsteady
TIPPYTOE _v_ -TOED, -TOEING, -TOES to tiptoe
TIPSIER comparative of tipsy
TIPSIEST superlative of tipsy
TIPSILY _adv_ in a tipsy manner
TIPSTAFF _n pl._ -STAFFS or -STAVES an attendant in a court of law
TIPSTER _n pl._ -S one that sells information to gamblers
TIPSTOCK _n pl._ -S a part of a gun
TIPSY _adj_ -SIER, -SIEST slightly drunk
TIPTOE _v_ -TOED, -TOEING, -TOES to walk on the tips of one's toes
TIPTOP _n pl._ -S the highest point

TIRADE _n pl._ -S a long, vehement speech
TIRAMISU _n pl._ -S a dessert made with ladyfingers, mascarpone, chocolate, and espresso
TIRE _v_ TIRED, TIRING, TIRES to grow tired
TIRED _adj_ TIREDER, TIREDEST sapped of strength **TIREDLY** _adv_
TIRELESS _adj_ seemingly incapable of tiring
TIRESOME _adj_ tedious
TIRING present participle of tire
TIRL _v_ -ED, -ING, -S to make a vibrating sound
TIRO _n pl._ -ROS tyro
TIRRIVEE _n pl._ -S a tantrum
TISANE _h pl._ -S a ptisan
TISSUAL _adj_ pertaining to tissue
TISSUE _v_ -SUED, -SUING, -SUES to weave into tissue (a fine sheer fabric)
TISSUEY _adj_ resembling tissue
TISSULAR _adj_ affecting an organism's tissue (structural material)
TIT _n pl._ -S a small bird
TITAN _n pl._ -S a person of great size
TITANATE _n pl._ -S a chemical salt
TITANESS _n pl._ -ES a female titan
TITANIA _n pl._ -S a mineral
TITANIC _adj_ of great size
TITANISM _n pl._ -S revolt against social conventions
TITANITE _n pl._ -S a mineral
TITANIUM _n pl._ -S a metallic element
TITANOUS _adj_ pertaining to titanium
TITBIT _n pl._ -S tidbit
TITER _n pl._ -S the strength of a chemical solution
TITFER _n pl._ -S a hat
TITHABLE _adj_ subject to the payment of tithes
TITHE _v_ TITHED, TITHING, TITHES to pay a tithe (a small tax)
TITHER _n pl._ -S one that tithes
TITHING _n pl._ -S the act of levying tithes
TITHONIA _n pl._ -S a tall herb
TITI _n pl._ -S an evergreen shrub or tree
TITIAN _n pl._ -S a reddish brown color
TITIVATE _v_ -VATED, -VATING, -VATES to dress smartly
TITLARK _n pl._ -S a songbird

TITLE	v -TLED, -TLING, -TLES to furnish with a title (a distinctive appellation)
TITLIST	n pl. -S a sports champion
TITMAN	n pl. -MEN the smallest of a litter of pigs
TITMOUSE	n pl. -MICE a small bird
TITRABLE	adj capable of being titrated
TITRANT	n pl. -S the reagent used in titration
TITRATE	v -TRATED, -TRATING, -TRATES to determine the strength of a solution by adding a reagent until a desired reaction occurs
TITRATOR	n pl. -S one that titrates
TITRE	n pl. -S titer
TITTER	v -ED, -ING, -S to utter a restrained, nervous laugh
TITTERER	n pl. -S one that titters
TITTIE	n pl. -S a sister
TITTIES	pl. of titty
TITTLE	n pl. -S a very small mark in writing or printing
TITTUP	v -TUPED, -TUPING, -TUPS or -TUPPED, -TUPPING, -TUPS to move in a lively manner
TITTUPPY	adj shaky; unsteady
TITTY	n pl. -TIES a teat
TITULAR	n pl. -S one who holds a title
TITULARY	n pl. -LARIES a titular
TIVY	adv with great speed
TIZZY	n pl. -ZIES a state of nervous confusion
TMESIS	n pl. TMESES the separation of the parts of a compound word by an intervening word or words
TO	prep in the direction of
TOAD	n pl. -S a tailless, jumping amphibian
TOADFISH	n pl. -ES a marine fish
TOADFLAX	n pl. -ES a perennial herb
TOADIED	past tense of toady
TOADIES	present 3d person sing. of toady
TOADISH	adj resembling a toad
TOADLESS	adj having no toads
TOADLIKE	adj resembling a toad
TOADY	v TOADIED, TOADYING, TOADIES to engage in servile flattering
TOADYISH	adj characteristic of one that toadies
TOADYISM	n pl. -S toadyish behavior

TOAST	v -ED, -ING, -S to brown by exposure to heat
TOASTER	n pl. -S a device for toasting
TOASTY	adj TOASTIER, TOASTIEST comfortably warm
TOBACCO	n pl. -COS or -COES an annual herb cultivated for its leaves
TOBOGGAN	v -ED, -ING, -S to ride on a long, narrow sled
TOBY	n pl. -BIES a type of drinking mug
TOCCATA	n pl. -TAS or -TE a musical composition usually for an organ
TOCHER	v -ED, -ING, -S to give a dowry to
TOCOLOGY	n pl. -GIES the branch of medicine dealing with childbirth
TOCSIN	n pl. -S an alarm sounded on a bell
TOD	n pl. -S a British unit of weight
TODAY	n pl. -DAYS the present day
TODDIES	pl. of toddy
TODDLE	v -DLED, -DLING, -DLES to walk unsteadily
TODDLER	n pl. -S one that toddles
TODDY	n pl. -DIES an alcoholic beverage
TODY	n pl. -DIES a West Indian bird
TOE	v TOED, TOEING, TOES to touch with the toe (one of the terminal members of the foot)
TOEA	n pl. TOEA a monetary unit of Papua New Guinea
TOECAP	n pl. -S a covering for the tip of a shoe or boot
TOEHOLD	n pl. -S a space that supports the toes in climbing
TOELESS	adj having no toes
TOELIKE	adj resembling a toe
TOENAIL	v -ED, -ING, -S to fasten with obliquely driven nails
TOEPIECE	n pl. -S a piece of a shoe designed to cover the toes
TOEPLATE	n pl. -S a metal tab attached to the tip of a shoe
TOESHOE	n pl. -S a dance slipper without a heel
TOFF	n pl. -S a dandy
TOFFEE	n pl. -S a chewy candy
TOFFY	n pl. -FIES toffee
TOFT	n pl. -S a hillock
TOFU	n pl. -S a soft Oriental cheese made from soybean milk

TOG	*v* TOGGED, TOGGING, TOGS to clothe
TOGA	*n pl.* -GAS or -GAE an outer garment worn in ancient Rome TOGAED *adj*
TOGATE	*adj* pertaining to ancient Rome
TOGATED	*adj* wearing a toga
TOGETHER	*adv* into a union or relationship
TOGGED	past tense of tog
TOGGERY	*n pl.* -GERIES clothing
TOGGING	present participle of tog
TOGGLE	*v* -GLED, -GLING, -GLES to fasten with a type of pin or short rod
TOGGLER	*n pl.* -S one that toggles
TOGUE	*n pl.* -S a freshwater fish
TOIL	*v* -ED, -ING, -S to work strenuously
TOILE	*n pl.* -S a sheer linen fabric
TOILER	*n pl.* -S one that toils
TOILET	*v* -ED, -ING, -S to dress and groom oneself
TOILETRY	*n pl.* -TRIES an article used in dressing and grooming oneself
TOILETTE	*n pl.* -S the act of dressing and grooming oneself
TOILFUL	*adj* toilsome
TOILSOME	*adj* demanding much exertion
TOILWORN	*adj* worn by toil
TOIT	*v* -ED, -ING, -S to saunter
TOKAMAK	*n pl.* -S a doughnut-shaped nuclear reactor
TOKAY	*n pl.* -KAYS a Malaysian gecko
TOKE	*v* TOKED, TOKING, TOKES to take a puff on a marijuana cigarette
TOKEN	*v* -ED, -ING, -S to serve as a sign of
TOKENISM	*n pl.* -S the policy of making only a superficial effort
TOKER	*n pl.* -S one that tokes
TOKING	present participle of toke
TOKOLOGY	*n pl.* -GIES tocology
TOKOMAK	*n pl.* -S tokamak
TOKONOMA	*n pl.* -S a small alcove in a Japanese house
TOLA	*n pl.* -S a unit of weight used in India
TOLAN	*n pl.* -S a chemical compound
TOLANE	*n pl.* -S tolan
TOLBOOTH	*n pl.* -S a prison
TOLD	past tense of tell
TOLE	*v* TOLED, TOLING, TOLES to allure

TOLEDO	*n pl.* -DOS a finely tempered sword
TOLERANT	*adj* inclined to tolerate
TOLERATE	*v* -ATED, -ATING, -ATES to allow without active opposition
TOLIDIN	*n pl.* -S tolidine
TOLIDINE	*n pl.* -S a chemical compound
TOLING	present participle of tole
TOLL	*v* -ED, -ING, -S to collect or impose a toll (a fixed charge for a service or privilege)
TOLLAGE	*n pl.* -S a toll
TOLLBAR	*n pl.* -S a tollgate
TOLLER	*n pl.* -S a collector of tolls
TOLLGATE	*n pl.* -S a gate where a toll is collected
TOLLMAN	*n pl.* -MEN a toller
TOLLWAY	*n pl.* -WAYS a road on which tolls are collected
TOLU	*n pl.* -S a fragrant resin
TOLUATE	*n pl.* -S a chemical salt
TOLUENE	*n pl.* -S a flammable liquid
TOLUIC	*adj* pertaining to any of four isomeric acids derived from toluene
TOLUID	*n pl.* -S toluide
TOLUIDE	*n pl.* -S an amide
TOLUIDIN	*n pl.* -S an amine
TOLUOL	*n pl.* -S toluene
TOLUOLE	*n pl.* -S toluol
TOLUYL	*n pl.* -S a univalent chemical radical
TOLYL	*n pl.* -S a univalent chemical radical
TOM	*n pl.* -S the male of various animals
TOMAHAWK	*v* -ED, -ING, -S to strike with a light ax
TOMALLEY	*n pl.* -LEYS the liver of a lobster
TOMAN	*n pl.* -S a coin of Iran
TOMATO	*n pl.* -TOES the fleshy, edible fruit of a perennial plant TOMATOEY *adj*
TOMB	*v* -ED, -ING, -S to place in a tomb (a burial vault or chamber)
TOMBAC	*n pl.* -S an alloy of copper and zinc
TOMBACK	*n pl.* -S tombac
TOMBAK	*n pl.* -S tombac
TOMBAL	*adj* pertaining to a tomb
TOMBLESS	*adj* having no tomb
TOMBLIKE	*adj* resembling a tomb
TOMBOLA	*n pl.* -S a gambling game

TOMBOLO n pl. -LOS a sandbar connecting an island to the mainland

TOMBOY n pl. -BOYS a girl who prefers boyish activities

TOMCAT v -CATTED, -CATTING, -CATS to engage in sexually promiscuous behavior — used of a male

TOMCOD n pl. -S a marine fish

TOME n pl. -S a large book

TOMENTUM n pl. -TA a network of small blood vessels

TOMFOOL n pl. -S a foolish person

TOMMED past tense of tom

TOMMING present participle of tom

TOMMY n pl. -MIES a loaf of bread

TOMMYROT n pl. -S nonsense

TOMOGRAM n pl. -S a photograph made with X rays

TOMORROW n pl. -S the day following today

TOMPION n pl. -S tampion

TOMTIT n pl. -S a small bird

TON n pl. -S a unit of weight

TONAL adj pertaining to tone **TONALLY** adv

TONALITY n pl. -TIES a system of tones

TONDO n pl. -DI or -DOS a circular painting

TONE v TONED, TONING, TONES to give a particular tone (a sound of definite pitch and vibration) to

TONEARM n pl. -S the pivoted part of a record player that holds the needle

TONELESS adj lacking in tone

TONEME n pl. -S a tonal unit of speech **TONEMIC** adj

TONER n pl. -S one that tones

TONETICS n/pl the phonetic study of tone in language **TONETIC** adj

TONETTE n pl. -S a simple flute

TONEY adj TONIER, TONIEST tony

TONG v -ED, -ING, -S to lift with a type of grasping device

TONGA n pl. -S a light cart used in India

TONGER n pl. -S one that tongs

TONGMAN n pl. -MEN a member of a Chinese secret society

TONGUE v TONGUED, TONGUING, TONGUES to touch with the tongue (an organ of the mouth)

TONGUING n pl. -S the use of the tongue in articulating notes on a wind instrument

TONIC n pl. -S something that invigorates or refreshes

TONICITY n pl. -TIES normal, healthy bodily condition

TONIER comparative of tony

TONIEST superlative of tony

TONIGHT n pl. -S the present night

TONING present participle of tone

TONISH adj stylish **TONISHLY** adv

TONLET n pl. -S a skirt of plate armor

TONNAGE n pl. -S total weight in tons

TONNE n pl. -S a unit of weight

TONNEAU n pl. -NEAUS or -NEAUX the rear seating compartment of an automobile

TONNER n pl. -S an object having a specified tonnage

TONNISH adj tonish

TONSIL n pl. -S a lymphoid organ **TONSILAR** adj

TONSURE v -SURED, -SURING, -SURES to shave the head of

TONTINE n pl. -S a form of collective life insurance

TONUS n pl. -ES a normal state of tension in muscle tissue

TONY adj TONIER, TONIEST stylish

TOO adv in addition

TOOK past tense of take

TOOL v -ED, -ING, -S to form or finish with a tool (an implement used in manual work)

TOOLBOX n pl. -ES a box for tools

TOOLER n pl. -S one that tools

TOOLHEAD n pl. -S a part of a machine

TOOLING n pl. -S ornamentation done with tools

TOOLLESS adj having no tools

TOOLROOM n pl. -S a room where tools are stored

TOOLSHED n pl. -S a building where tools are stored

TOOM adj empty

TOON n pl. -S an East Indian tree

TOOT v -ED, -ING, -S to sound a horn or whistle in short blasts

TOOTER n pl. -S one that toots

TOOTH n pl. TEETH one of the hard structures attached in a row to each jaw

TOOTH v -ED, -ING, -S to furnish with toothlike projections

TOOTHY *adj* TOOTHIER, TOOTHIEST having or showing prominent teeth **TOOTHILY** *adv*

TOOTLE *v* -TLED, -TLING, -TLES to toot softly or repeatedly

TOOTLER *n pl.* -S one that tootles

TOOTS *n pl.* -ES a woman or girl — usually used as a form of address

TOOTSIE *n pl.* -S tootsy

TOOTSY *n pl.* -SIES a foot

TOP *v* TOPPED, TOPPING, TOPS to cut off the top (the highest part, point, or surface) of

TOPAZ *n pl.* -ES a mineral **TOPAZINE** *adj*

TOPCOAT *n pl.* -S a lightweight overcoat

TOPCROSS *n pl.* -ES a cross between a purebred male and inferior female stock

TOPE *v* TOPED, TOPING, TOPES to drink liquor to excess

TOPEE *n pl.* -S topi

TOPER *n pl.* -S one that topes

TOPFUL *adj* topfull

TOPFULL *adj* full to the top

TOPH *n pl.* -S tufa

TOPHE *n pl.* -S tufa

TOPHUS *n pl.* -PHI a deposit of urates in the tissue around a joint

TOPI *n pl.* -S a sun helmet

TOPIARY *n pl.* -ARIES the art of trimming shrubs into shapes

TOPIC *n pl.* -S a subject of discourse **TOPICAL** *adj*

TOPING present participle of tope

TOPKICK *n pl.* -S a first sergeant

TOPKNOT *n pl.* -S an ornament for the hair

TOPLESS *adj* having no top

TOPLINE *n pl.* -S the outline of the top of an animal's body

TOPLOFTY *adj* -LOFTIER, -LOFTIEST haughty

TOPMAST *n pl.* -S a mast of a ship

TOPMOST *adj* highest

TOPNOTCH *adj* excellent

TOPOI pl. of topos

TOPOLOGY *n pl.* -GIES a branch of mathematics

TOPONYM *n pl.* -S the name of a place

TOPONYMY *n pl.* -MIES the study of toponyms

TOPOS *n pl.* -POI a stock rhetorical theme

TOPOTYPE *n pl.* -S a specimen selected from a locality typical of a species

TOPPED past tense of top

TOPPER *n pl.* -S one that tops

TOPPING *n pl.* -S something that forms a top

TOPPLE *v* -PLED, -PLING, -PLES to fall forward

TOPSAIL *n pl.* -S a sail of a ship

TOPSIDE *n pl.* -S the upper portion of a ship

TOPSIDER *n pl.* -S one who is at the highest level of authority

TOPSOIL *v* -ED, -ING, -S to remove the surface layer of soil from

TOPSPIN *n pl.* -S a forward spin imparted to a ball

TOPSTONE *n pl.* -S the stone at the top of a structure

TOPWORK *v* -ED, -ING, -S to graft scions of another variety of plant on the main branches of

TOQUE *n pl.* -S a close-fitting woman's hat

TOQUET *n pl.* -S toque

TOR *n pl.* -S a high, craggy hill

TORA *n pl.* -S torah

TORAH *n pl.* -RAHS, -ROTH, or -ROT a law or precept

TORC *n pl.* -S a metal collar or necklace

TORCH *v* -ED, -ING, -ES to set on fire

TORCHERE *n pl.* -S a type of electric lamp

TORCHIER *n pl.* -S torchere

TORCHON *n pl.* -S a coarse lace

TORCHY *adj* TORCHIER, TORCHIEST characteristic of a torch song

TORE *n pl.* -S a torus

TOREADOR *n pl.* -S a bullfighter

TORERO *n pl.* -ROS a bullfighter

TOREUTIC *adj* pertaining to a type of metalwork

TORI pl. of torus

TORIC *adj* pertaining to a torus

TORIES pl. of tory

TORII *n pl.* TORII the gateway of a Japanese temple

TORMENT *v* -ED, -ING, -S to inflict with great bodily or mental suffering

TORN past participle of tear

TORNADO *n pl.* -DOES or -DOS a violent windstorm **TORNADIC** *adj*

TORNILLO *n pl.* -LOS a flowering shrub

TORO *n pl.* -ROS a bull

TOROID n pl. -S a type of geometric surface **TOROIDAL** adj

TOROSE adj cylindrical and swollen at intervals

TOROSITY n pl. -TIES the quality or state of being torose

TOROT a pl. of torah

TOROTH a pl. of torah

TOROUS adj torose

TORPEDO v -ED, -ING, -ES or -S to damage or sink with an underwater missile

TORPID n pl. -S a racing boat

TORPIDLY adv in a sluggish manner

TORPOR n pl. -S mental or physical inactivity

TORQUATE adj having a torques

TORQUE v TORQUED, TORQUING, TORQUES to cause to twist

TORQUER n pl. -S one that torques

TORQUES n pl. -QUESES a band of feathers, hair, or coloration around the neck

TORQUING present participle of torque

TORR n pl. TORR a unit of pressure

TORREFY v -FIED, -FYING, -FIES to subject to intense heat

TORRENT n pl. -S a rapid stream of water

TORRID adj -RIDER, -RIDEST extremely hot **TORRIDLY** adv

TORRIFY v -FIED, -FYING, -FIES to torrefy

TORSADE n pl. -S a twisted cord

TORSE n pl. -S a wreath of twisted silks

TORSI a pl. of torso

TORSION n pl. -S the act of twisting

TORSK n pl. -S a marine food fish

TORSO n pl. -SI or -SOS the trunk of the human body

TORT n pl. -S a civil wrong

TORTE n pl. TORTEN or TORTES a rich cake

TORTILE adj twisted; coiled

TORTILLA n pl. -S a round, flat cake of unleavened cornmeal

TORTIOUS adj of the nature of a tort

TORTOISE n pl. -S any of an order of reptiles having the body enclosed in a bony shell

TORTONI n pl. -S a type of ice cream

TORTRIX n pl. -ES a small moth

TORTUOUS adj marked by repeated turns or bends

TORTURE v -TURED, -TURING, -TURES to subject to severe physical pain

TORTURER n pl. -S one that tortures

TORULA n pl. -LAE or -LAS a type of fungus

TORUS n pl. -RI a large convex molding

TORY n pl. -RIES a political conservative

TOSH n pl. -ES nonsense

TOSS v TOSSED or TOST, TOSSING, TOSSES to throw lightly

TOSSER n pl. -S one that tosses

TOSSPOT n pl. -S a drunkard

TOSSUP n pl. -S an even choice or chance

TOST a past tense of toss

TOSTADA n pl. -S a tortilla fried in deep fat

TOSTADO n pl. -DOS tostada

TOT v TOTTED, TOTTING, TOTS to total

TOTABLE adj capable of being toted

TOTAL v -TALED, -TALING, -TALS or -TALLED, -TALLING, -TALS to ascertain the entire amount of

TOTALISE v -ISED, -ISING, -ISES to totalize

TOTALISM n pl. -S centralized control by an autocratic authority

TOTALIST n pl. -S one who tends to regard things as a unified whole

TOTALITY n pl. -TIES the quality or state of being complete

TOTALIZE v -IZED, -IZING, -IZES to make complete

TOTALLED a past tense of total

TOTALLING a present participle of total

TOTALLY adv completely

TOTE v TOTED, TOTING, TOTES to carry by hand

TOTEM n pl. -S a natural object serving as the emblem of a family or clan **TOTEMIC** adj

TOTEMISM n pl. -S a system of tribal division according to totems

TOTEMIST n pl. -S a specialist in totemism

TOTEMITE n pl. -S a totemist

TOTER n pl. -S one that totes

TOTHER pron the other

TOTING present participle of tote

TOTTED past tense of tot

TOTTER *v* -ED, -ING, -S to walk unsteadily

TOTTERER *n pl.* -S one that totters

TOTTERY *adj* shaky

TOTTING present participle of tot

TOUCAN *n pl.* -S a tropical bird

TOUCH *v* -ED, -ING, -ES to be in or come into contact with

TOUCHE *interj* — used to acknowledge a hit in fencing

TOUCHER *n pl.* -S one that touches

TOUCHUP *n pl.* -S an act of finishing by adding minor improvements

TOUCHY *adj* TOUCHIER, TOUCHIEST overly sensitive TOUCHILY *adv*

TOUGH *adj* TOUGHER, TOUGHEST strong and resilient

TOUGH *v* -ED, -ING, -S to endure hardship

TOUGHEN *v* -ED, -ING, -S to make tough

TOUGHIE *n pl.* -S a tough

TOUGHIES pl. of toughy

TOUGHISH *adj* somewhat tough

TOUGHLY *adv* in a tough manner

TOUGHY *n pl.* TOUGHIES toughie

TOUPEE *n pl.* -S a wig for a bald spot

TOUR *v* -ED, -ING, -S to travel from place to place

TOURACO *n pl.* -COS an African bird

TOURER *n pl.* -S a large, open automobile

TOURING *n pl.* -S cross-country skiing for pleasure

TOURISM *n pl.* -S the practice of touring for pleasure

TOURIST *n pl.* -S one who tours for pleasure TOURISTY *adj*

TOURNEY *v* -ED, -ING, -S to compete in a tournament

TOUSE *v* TOUSED, TOUSING, TOUSES to tousle

TOUSLE *v* -SLED, -SLING, -SLES to dishevel

TOUT *v* -ED, -ING, -S to solicit brazenly

TOUTER *n pl.* -S one that touts

TOUZLE *v* -ZLED, -ZLING, -ZLES to tousle

TOVARICH *n pl.* -ES comrade

TOVARISH *n pl.* -ES tovarich

TOW *v* -ED, -ING, -S to pull by means of a rope or chain

TOWAGE *n pl.* -S the price paid for towing

TOWARD *prep* in the direction of

TOWARDLY *adj* favorable

TOWARDS *prep* toward

TOWAWAY *n pl.* -AWAYS the act of towing away a vehicle

TOWBOAT *n pl.* -S a tugboat

TOWEL *v* -ELED, -ELING, -ELS or -ELLED, -ELLING, -ELS to wipe with a towel (an absorbent cloth)

TOWELING *n pl.* -S material used for towels

TOWER *v* -ED, -ING, -S to rise to a great height

TOWERY *adj* -ERIER, -ERIEST very tall

TOWHEAD *n pl.* -S a head of light blond hair

TOWHEE *n pl.* -S a common finch

TOWIE *n pl.* -S a form of contract bridge for three players

TOWLINE *n pl.* -S a line used in towing

TOWMOND *n pl.* -S a year

TOWMONT *n pl.* -S towmond

TOWN *n pl.* -S a center of population smaller than a city

TOWNEE *n pl.* -S a townsman

TOWNFOLK *n/pl* the inhabitants of a town

TOWNHOME *n pl.* -S one of a series of contiguous houses of two or three stories

TOWNIE *n pl.* -S a nonstudent who lives in a college town

TOWNIES pl. of towny

TOWNISH *adj* characteristic of a town

TOWNLESS *adj* having no towns

TOWNLET *n pl.* -S a small town

TOWNSHIP *n pl.* -S an administrative division of a county

TOWNSMAN *n pl.* -MEN a resident of a town

TOWNWEAR *n pl.* TOWNWEAR apparel that is suitable for wear in the city

TOWNY *n pl.* TOWNIES townie

TOWPATH *n pl.* -S a path along a river that is used by animals towing boats

TOWROPE *n pl.* -S a rope used in towing

TOWY *adj* resembling coarse hemp or flax fiber

TOXAEMIA *n pl.* -S toxemia TOXAEMIC *adj*

TOXEMIA *n pl.* -S the condition of having toxins in the blood TOXEMIC *adj*

TOXIC *n pl.* -S a poisonous substance

TOXICAL *adj* toxic

TOXICANT n pl. -S a poisonous substance

TOXICITY n pl. -TIES the quality of being poisonous

TOXIN n pl. -S a poisonous substance

TOXINE n pl. -S toxin

TOXOID n pl. -S a type of toxin

TOY v -ED, -ING, -S to amuse oneself as if with a toy (a child's plaything)

TOYER n pl. -S one that toys

TOYISH adj frivolous

TOYLESS adj having no toy

TOYLIKE adj resembling a toy

TOYO n pl. -YOS a smooth straw used in making hats

TOYON n pl. -S an ornamental evergreen shrub

TOYSHOP n pl. -S a shop where toys are sold

TRABEATE adj constructed with horizontal beams

TRACE v TRACED, TRACING, TRACES to follow the course of

TRACER n pl. -S one that traces

TRACERY n pl. -ERIES ornamental work of interlaced lines

TRACHEA n pl. -CHEAE or -CHEAS the passage for conveying air to the lungs TRACHEAL adj

TRACHEID n pl. -S a long, tubular plant cell

TRACHLE v -LED, -LING, -LES to draggle

TRACHOMA n pl. -S a disease of the eye

TRACHYTE n pl. -S a light-colored igneous rock

TRACING n pl. -S something that is traced

TRACK v -ED, -ING, -S to follow the marks left by an animal, a person, or a vehicle

TRACKAGE n pl. -S the track system of a railroad

TRACKER n pl. -S one that tracks

TRACKING n pl. -S the placement of students within a curriculum

TRACKMAN n pl. -MEN a railroad worker

TRACKWAY n pl. -WAYS a trodden path

TRACT n pl. -S an expanse of land

TRACTATE n pl. -S a treatise

TRACTILE adj capable of being drawn out in length

TRACTION n pl. -S the act of pulling or drawing over a surface TRACTIVE adj

TRACTOR n pl. -S a motor vehicle used in farming

TRAD adj traditional

TRADE v TRADED, TRADING, TRADES to give in exchange for another commodity TRADABLE adj

TRADEOFF n pl. -S a giving up of one thing in return for another

TRADER n pl. -S one that trades

TRADITOR n pl. -ES a traitor among the early Christians

TRADUCE v -DUCED, -DUCING, -DUCES to defame

TRADUCER n pl. -S one that traduces

TRAFFIC v -FICKED, -FICKING, -FICS to engage in buying and selling

TRAGEDY n pl. -DIES a disastrous event

TRAGI pl. of tragus

TRAGIC n pl. -S the element of a drama that produces tragedy

TRAGICAL adj of the nature of a tragedy

TRAGOPAN n pl. -S an Asian pheasant

TRAGUS n pl. -GI a part of the external opening of the ear

TRAIK v -ED, -ING, -S to trudge

TRAIL v -ED, -ING, -S to drag along a surface

TRAILER v -ED, -ING, -S to transport by means of a trailer (a vehicle drawn by another)

TRAIN v -ED, -ING, -S to instruct systematically

TRAINEE n pl. -S a person receiving training

TRAINER n pl. -S one that trains

TRAINFUL n pl. -S as much as a railroad train can hold

TRAINING n pl. -S systematic instruction

TRAINMAN n pl. -MEN a railroad employee

TRAINWAY n pl. -WAYS a railway

TRAIPSE v TRAIPSED, TRAIPSING, TRAIPSES to walk about in an idle or aimless manner

TRAIT n pl. -S a distinguishing characteristic

TRAITOR n pl. -S one who betrays another

TRAJECT v -ED, -ING, -S to transmit

TRAM v TRAMMED, TRAMMING, TRAMS to convey in a tramcar

TRAMCAR n pl. -S a streetcar

TRAMEL *v* -ELED, -ELING, -ELS or -ELLED, -ELLING, -ELS to trammel

TRAMELL *v* -ED, -ING, -S to trammel

TRAMLESS *adj* having no tramcar

TRAMLINE *n pl.* -S a streetcar line

TRAMMED past tense of tram

TRAMMEL *v* -MELED, -MELING, -MELS or -MELLED, -MELLING, -MELS to hinder

TRAMMING present participle of tram

TRAMP *v* -ED, -ING, -S to walk with a firm, heavy step

TRAMPER *n pl.* -S one that tramps

TRAMPISH *adj* resembling a vagabond

TRAMPLE *v* -PLED, -PLING, -PLES to tread on heavily

TRAMPLER *n pl.* -S one that tramples

TRAMROAD *n pl.* -S a railway in a mine

TRAMWAY *n pl.* -WAYS a tramline

TRANCE *v* TRANCED, TRANCING, TRANCES to put into a trance (a semiconscious state)

TRANCHE *n pl.* -S a portion

TRANGAM *n pl.* -S a gewgaw

TRANK *n pl.* -S a drug that tranquilizes

TRANQ *n pl.* -S trank

TRANQUIL *adj* -QUILER, -QUILEST or -QUILLER, -QUILLEST free from disturbance

TRANS *adj* characterized by the arrangement of different atoms on opposite sides of the molecule

TRANSACT *v* -ED, -ING, -S to carry out

TRANSECT *v* -ED, -ING, -S to cut across

TRANSEPT *n pl.* -S a major transverse part of the body of a church

TRANSFER *v* -FERRED, -FERRING, -FERS to convey from one source to another

TRANSFIX *v* -FIXED or -FIXT, -FIXING, -FIXES to impale

TRANSHIP *v* -SHIPPED, -SHIPPING, -SHIPS to transfer from one conveyance to another

TRANSIT *v* -ED, -ING, -S to pass across or through

TRANSMIT *v* -MITTED, -MITTING, -MITS to send from one place or person to another

TRANSOM *n pl.* -S a small window above a door or another window

TRANSUDE *v* -SUDED, -SUDING, -SUDES to pass through a membrane

TRAP *v* TRAPPED or TRAPT, TRAPPING, TRAPS to catch in a trap (a device for capturing and holding animals)

TRAPAN *v* -PANNED, -PANNING, -PANS to trepan

TRAPBALL *n pl.* -S a type of ball game

TRAPDOOR *n pl.* -S a lifting or sliding door covering an opening

TRAPES *v* -ED, -ING, -ES to traipse

TRAPEZE *n pl.* -S a gymnastic apparatus

TRAPEZIA *n/pl* four-sided polygons having no parallel sides

TRAPLIKE *adj* resembling a trap

TRAPLINE *n pl.* -S a series of traps

TRAPNEST *v* -ED, -ING, -S to determine the productivity of hens with a type of nest

TRAPPEAN *adj* pertaining to traprock

TRAPPED a past tense of trap

TRAPPER *n pl.* -S one that traps

TRAPPING *n pl.* -S a covering for a horse

TRAPPOSE *adj* trappean

TRAPPOUS *adj* trappean

TRAPROCK *n pl.* -S an igneous rock

TRAPT a past tense of trap

TRAPUNTO *n pl.* -TOS a decorative quilted design

TRASH *v* -ED, -ING, -ES to free from trash (worthless or waste matter)

TRASHMAN *n pl.* -MEN a person who removes trash

TRASHY *adj* TRASHIER, TRASHIEST resembling trash **TRASHILY** *adv*

TRASS *n pl.* -ES a volcanic rock

TRAUCHLE *v* -LED, -LING, -LES to trachle

TRAUMA *n pl.* -MAS or -MATA a severe emotional shock

TRAVAIL *v* -ED, -ING, -S to toil

TRAVE *n pl.* -S a frame for confining a horse

TRAVEL *v* -ELED, -ELING, -ELS or -ELLED, -ELLING, -ELS to go from one place to another

TRAVELER *n pl.* -S one that travels

TRAVELOG *n pl.* -S a lecture or film on traveling

TRAVERSE *v* -VERSED, -VERSING, -VERSES to pass across or through

TRAVESTY *v* -TIED, -TYING, -TIES to parody

TRAVOIS *n pl.* -ES a type of sled

TRAVOISE *n pl.* -S travois

TRAWL v -ED, -ING, -S to fish by dragging a net along the sea bottom

TRAWLER n pl. -S a boat used for trawling

TRAWLEY n pl. -LEYS a small truck or car for conveying material

TRAWLNET n pl. -S the large net used in trawling

TRAY n pl. TRAYS a flat, shallow receptacle

TRAYFUL n pl. -S as much as a tray will hold

TREACLE n pl. -S molasses **TREACLY** adj

TREAD v TROD, TRODE, or TREADED, TRODDEN, TREADING, TREADS to walk on, over, or along

TREADER n pl. -S one that treads

TREADLE v -LED, -LING, -LES to work a foot lever

TREADLER n pl. -S one that treadles

TREASON n pl. -S violation of allegiance toward one's country

TREASURE v -URED, -URING, -URES to value highly

TREASURY n pl. -URIES a place where funds are received, kept, and disbursed

TREAT v -ED, -ING, -S to behave in a particular way toward

TREATER n pl. -S one that treats

TREATISE n pl. -S a formal and systematic written account of a subject

TREATY n pl. -TIES a formal agreement between two or more nations

TREBLE v -BLED, -BLING, -BLES to triple

TREBLY adv triply

TRECENTO n pl. -TOS the fourteenth century

TREDDLE v -DLED, -DLING, -DLES to treadle

TREE v TREED, TREEING, TREES to drive up a tree (a tall, woody plant)

TREELAWN n pl. -S the strip of lawn between the street and the sidewalk

TREELESS adj having no tree

TREELIKE adj resembling a tree

TREEN n pl. -S an article made from wood

TREENAIL n pl. -S a wooden peg used for fastening timbers

TREETOP n pl. -S the top of a tree

TREF adj unfit for use according to Jewish law

TREFAH adj tref

TREFOIL n pl. -S a plant having ternate leaves

TREHALA n pl. -S a sweet, edible substance forming the pupal case of certain weevils

TREK v TREKKED, TREKKING, TREKS to make a slow or arduous journey

TREKKER n pl. -S one that treks

TRELLIS v -ED, -ING, -ES to provide with a trellis (a frame used as a support for climbing plants)

TREMBLE v -BLED, -BLING, -BLES to shake involuntarily

TREMBLER n pl. -S one that trembles

TREMBLY adj -BLIER, -BLIEST marked by trembling

TREMOLO n pl. -LOS a vibrating musical effect

TREMOR n pl. -S a shaking movement

TRENAIL n pl. -S treenail

TRENCH v -ED, -ING, -ES to dig a long, narrow excavation in the ground

TRENCHER n pl. -S a wooden platter for serving food

TREND v -ED, -ING, -S to take a particular course

TRENDY adj TRENDIER, TRENDIEST very fashionable **TRENDILY** adv

TRENDY n pl. TRENDIES a trendy person

TREPAN v -PANNED, -PANNING, -PANS to trephine

TREPANG n pl. -S a marine animal

TREPHINE v -PHINED, -PHINING, -PHINES to operate on with a surgical saw

TREPID adj timorous

TRESPASS v -ED, -ING, -ES to enter upon the land of another unlawfully

TRESS n pl. -ES a long lock of hair **TRESSED** adj

TRESSEL n pl. -S trestle

TRESSIER comparative of tressy

TRESSIEST superlative of tressy

TRESSOUR n pl. -S tressure

TRESSURE n pl. -S a type of heraldic design

TRESSY adj TRESSIER, TRESSIEST abounding in tresses

TRESTLE n pl. -S a framework for supporting a bridge

TRET n pl. -S an allowance formerly paid to purchasers for waste incurred in transit

TREVET n pl. -S trivet

TREWS n/pl close-fitting tartan trousers

TREY n pl. TREYS a three in cards, dice, or dominoes

TRIABLE adj subject to judicial examination

TRIAC n pl. -S an electronic device used to control power

TRIACID n pl. -S a type of acid

TRIAD n pl. -S a group of three

TRIADIC n pl. -S a member of a triad

TRIADISM n pl. -S the quality or state of being a triad

TRIAGE v -AGED, -AGING, -AGES to practice a system of treating disaster victims

TRIAL n pl. -S a judicial examination

TRIANGLE n pl. -S a polygon having three sides

TRIARCHY n pl. -CHIES government by three persons

TRIAXIAL adj having three axes

TRIAZIN n pl. -S triazine

TRIAZINE n pl. -S a chemical compound

TRIAZOLE n pl. -S a chemical compound

TRIBADE n pl. -S a lesbian TRIBADIC adj

TRIBAL adj pertaining to a tribe TRIBALLY adv

TRIBASIC adj having three replaceable hydrogen atoms

TRIBE n pl. -S a group of people sharing a common ancestry, language, and culture

TRIBRACH n pl. -S a type of metrical foot

TRIBUNAL n pl. -S a court of justice

TRIBUNE n pl. -S a defender of the rights of the people

TRIBUTE n pl. -S something given to show respect, gratitude, or admiration

TRICE v TRICED, TRICING, TRICES to haul up with a rope

TRICEPS n pl. -ES an arm muscle

TRICHINA n pl. -NAE or -NAS a parasitic worm

TRICHITE n pl. -S a minute mineral body found in volcanic rocks

TRICHOID adj hairlike

TRICHOME n pl. -S a hairlike outgrowth

TRICING present participle of trice

TRICK v -ED, -ING, -S to deceive

TRICKER n pl. -S one that tricks

TRICKERY n pl. -ERIES deception

TRICKIE adj TRICKIER, TRICKIEST tricky

TRICKIER comparative of tricky

TRICKIEST superlative of tricky

TRICKILY adv in a tricky manner

TRICKISH adj tricky

TRICKLE v -LED, -LING, -LES to flow or fall in drops

TRICKLY adj -LIER, -LIEST marked by trickling

TRICKSY adj -SIER, -SIEST mischievous

TRICKY adj TRICKIER, TRICKIEST characterized by deception

TRICLAD n pl. -S an aquatic flatworm

TRICOLOR n pl. -S a flag having three colors

TRICORN n pl. -S a hat with the brim turned up on three sides

TRICORNE n pl. -S tricorn

TRICOT n pl. -S a knitted fabric

TRICTRAC n pl. -S a form of backgammon

TRICYCLE n pl. -S a vehicle having three wheels

TRIDENT n pl. -S a spear having three prongs

TRIDUUM n pl. -S a period of three days of prayer

TRIED past tense of try

TRIENE n pl. -S a type of chemical compound

TRIENNIA n/pl periods of three years

TRIENS n pl. -ENTES a coin of ancient Rome

TRIER n pl. -S one that tries

TRIES present 3d person sing. of try

TRIETHYL adj containing three ethyl groups

TRIFECTA n pl. -S a system of betting

TRIFID adj divided into three parts

TRIFLE v -FLED, -FLING, -FLES to waste time

TRIFLER n pl. -S one that trifles

TRIFLING n pl. -S a waste of time

TRIFOCAL n pl. -S a type of lens

TRIFOLD adj having three parts

TRIFORIA n/pl galleries in a church

TRIFORM	*adj* having three forms	TRIMOTOR	*n pl.* -S an airplane powered by three engines
TRIG •	*adj* TRIGGER, TRIGGEST neat	TRINAL	*adj* having three parts
TRIG	*v* TRIGGED, TRIGGING, TRIGS to make trig	TRINARY	*adj* consisting of three parts
		TRINDLE	*v* -DLED, -DLING, -DLES to trundle
TRIGGER	*v* -ED, -ING, -S to actuate		
TRIGGEST	superlative of trig	TRINE	*v* TRINED, TRINING, TRINES to place in a particular astrological position
TRIGGING	present participle of trig		
TRIGLY	*adv* in a trig manner		
TRIGLYPH	*n pl.* -S an architectural ornament	TRINITY	*n pl.* -TIES a group of three
		TRINKET	*v* -ED, -ING, -S to deal secretly
TRIGNESS	*n pl.* -ES the quality or state of being trig		
		TRINKUMS	*n/pl* small ornaments
TRIGO	*n pl.* -GOS wheat	TRINODAL	*adj* having three nodes
TRIGON	*n pl.* -S an ancient stringed instrument	TRIO	*n pl.* TRIOS a group of three
		TRIODE	*n pl.* -S a type of electron tube
TRIGONAL	*adj* shaped like a triangle	TRIOL	*n pl.* -S a type of chemical compound
TRIGRAM	*n pl.* -S a cluster of three successive letters		
		TRIOLET	*n pl.* -S a short poem of fixed form
TRIGRAPH	*n pl.* -S a group of three letters representing one sound		
		TRIOSE	*n pl.* -S a simple sugar
TRIHEDRA	*n/pl* figures having three plane surfaces meeting at a point	TRIOXID	*n pl.* -S trioxide
		TRIOXIDE	*n pl.* -S a type of oxide
TRIJET	*n pl.* -S an airplane powered by three jet engines	TRIP	*v* TRIPPED, TRIPPING, TRIPS to stumble
TRIKE	*n pl.* -S a tricycle	TRIPACK	*n pl.* -S a type of film pack
TRILBY	*n pl.* -BIES a soft felt hat	TRIPART	*adj* divided into three parts
TRILL	*v* -ED, -ING, -S to sing or play with a vibrating effect	TRIPE	*n pl.* -S a part of the stomach of a ruminant that is used as food
TRILLER	*n pl.* -S one that trills		
TRILLION	*n pl.* -S a number	TRIPEDAL	*adj* having three feet
TRILLIUM	*n pl.* -S a flowering plant	TRIPHASE	*adj* having three phases
TRILOBAL	*adj* trilobed	TRIPLANE	*n pl.* -S a type of airplane
TRILOBED	*adj* having three lobes	TRIPLE	*v* -PLED, -PLING, -PLES to make three times as great
TRILOGY	*n pl.* -GIES a group of three related literary works		
		TRIPLET	*n pl.* -S a group of three of one kind
TRIM	*adj* TRIMMER, TRIMMEST neat and orderly		
		TRIPLEX	*n pl.* -ES an apartment having three floors
TRIM	*v* TRIMMED, TRIMMING, TRIMS to make trim by cutting		
		TRIPLING	present participle of triple
TRIMARAN	*n pl.* -S a sailing vessel	TRIPLITE	*n pl.* -S a mineral
TRIMER	*n pl.* -S a type of chemical compound **TRIMERIC** *adj*	TRIPLOID	*n pl.* -S a cell having a chromosome number that is three times the basic number
TRIMETER	*n pl.* -S a verse of three metrical feet		
		TRIPLY	*adv* in a triple degree, manner, or number
TRIMLY	*adv* in a trim manner		
TRIMMED	past tense of trim	TRIPOD	*n pl.* -S a stand having three legs **TRIPODAL, TRIPODIC** *adj*
TRIMMER	*n pl.* -S one that trims		
TRIMMEST	superlative of trim		
TRIMMING	*n pl.* -S something added as a decoration	TRIPODY	*n pl.* -DIES a verse of three metrical feet
TRIMNESS	*n pl.* -ES the state of being trim	TRIPOLI	*n pl.* -S a soft, friable rock
		TRIPOS	*n pl.* -ES a tripod
TRIMORPH	*n pl.* -S a substance existing in three forms	TRIPPED	past tense of trip
		TRIPPER	*n pl.* -S one that trips

TRIPPET n pl. -S a part of a mechanism designed to strike another part

TRIPPING n pl. -S the act of one that trips

TRIPPY adj -PIER, -PIEST suggesting a trip on psychedelic drugs

TRIPTANE n pl. -S a chemical compound

TRIPTYCA n pl. -S a triptych

TRIPTYCH n pl. -S an ancient writing tablet

TRIPWIRE n pl. -S a low-placed hidden wire that sets off an alarm or a trap

TRIREME n pl. -S an ancient Greek or Roman warship

TRISCELE n pl. -S triskele

TRISECT v -ED, -ING, -S to divide into three equal parts

TRISEME n pl. -S a type of metrical foot **TRISEMIC** adj

TRISHAW n pl. -S a pedicab

TRISKELE n pl. -S a figure consisting of three branches radiating from a center

TRISMUS n pl. -ES lockjaw **TRISMIC** adj

TRISOME n pl. -S an organism having one chromosome in addition to the usual diploid number

TRISOMIC n pl. -S a trisome

TRISOMY n pl. -MIES the condition of being a trisome

TRISTATE adj pertaining to an area made up of three adjoining states

TRISTE adj sad

TRISTEZA n pl. -S a disease of citrus trees

TRISTFUL adj sad

TRISTICH n pl. -S a stanza of three lines

TRITE adj TRITER, TRITEST used so often as to be made commonplace **TRITELY** adv

TRITHING n pl. -S an administrative division in England

TRITICUM n pl. -S a cereal grass

TRITIUM n pl. -S an isotope of hydrogen

TRITOMA n pl. -S an African herb

TRITON n pl. -S a marine mollusk

TRITONE n pl. -S a musical interval of three whole tones

TRIUMPH v -ED, -ING, -S to be victorious

TRIUMVIR n pl. -VIRS or -VIRI one of a ruling body of three in ancient Rome.

TRIUNE n pl. -S a trinity

TRIUNITY n pl. -TIES a trinity

TRIVALVE n pl. -S a type of shell

TRIVET n pl. -S a small stand having three legs

TRIVIA n/pl insignificant matters

TRIVIAL adj insignificant

TRIVIUM n pl. -IA a group of studies in medieval schools

TROAK v -ED, -ING, -S to troke

TROCAR n pl. -S a surgical instrument

TROCHAIC n pl. -S a trochee

TROCHAL adj shaped like a wheel

TROCHAR n pl. -S trocar

TROCHE n pl. -S a medicated lozenge

TROCHEE n pl. -S a type of metrical foot

TROCHIL n pl. -S an African bird

TROCHILI n/pl trochils

TROCHLEA n pl. -LEAE or -LEAS an anatomical structure resembling a pulley

TROCHOID n pl. -S a type of geometric curve

TROCK v -ED, -ING, -S to troke

TROD a past tense of tread

TRODDEN past participle of tread

TRODE a past tense of tread

TROFFER n pl. -S a fixture for fluorescent lighting

TROGON n pl. -S a tropical bird

TROIKA n pl. -S a Russian carriage

TROILISM n pl. -S sexual relations involving three persons

TROILITE n pl. -S a mineral

TROILUS n pl. -ES a large butterfly

TROIS n pl. TROIS the number three

TROKE v TROKED, TROKING, TROKES to exchange

TROLAND n pl. -S a unit of measurement of retinal response to light

TROLL v -ED, -ING, -S to fish with a slowly trailing line

TROLLER n pl. -S one that trolls

TROLLEY v -ED, -ING, -S to convey by streetcar

TROLLIED past tense of trolly

TROLLIES present 3d person sing. of trolly

TROLLING n pl. -S the act of one that trolls

TROLLOP n pl. -S a prostitute **TROLLOPY** adj

TROLLY v -LIED, -LYING, -LIES to trolley

TROMBONE n pl. -S a brass wind instrument

TROMMEL *n* pl. -S a screen used for sifting rock, ore, or coal

TROMP *v* -ED, -ING, -S to tramp

TROMPE *n* pl. -S a device used for supplying air to a furnace

TRONA *n* pl. -S a mineral

TRONE *n* pl. -S a weighing device

TROOP *v* -ED, -ING, -S to move or gather in crowds

TROOPER *n* pl. -S a cavalryman

TROOPIAL *n* pl. -S troupial

TROOZ *n/pl* trews

TROP *adv* too much

TROPE *n* pl. -S the figurative use of a word

TROPHIC *adj* pertaining to nutrition

TROPHY *v* -PHIED, -PHYING, -PHIES to honor with a trophy (a symbol of victory)

TROPIC *n* pl. -S either of two circles of the celestial sphere on each side of the equator **TROPICAL** *adj*

TROPIN *n* pl. -S tropine

TROPINE *n* pl. -S a poisonous alkaloid

TROPISM *n* pl. -S the involuntary response of an organism to an external stimulus

TROPONIN *n* pl. -S a protein of muscle

TROT *v* TROTTED, TROTTING, TROTS to go at a gait between a walk and a run

TROTH *v* -ED, -ING, -S to betroth

TROTLINE *n* pl. -S a strong fishing line

TROTTED past tense of trot

TROTTER *n* pl. -S a horse that trots

TROTTING present participle of trot

TROTYL *n* pl. -S an explosive

TROUBLE *v* -BLED, -BLING, -BLES to distress

TROUBLER *n* pl. -S one that troubles

TROUGH *n* pl. -S a long, narrow receptacle

TROUNCE *v* TROUNCED, TROUNCING, TROUNCES to beat severely

TROUNCER *n* pl. -S one that trounces

TROUPE *v* TROUPED, TROUPING, TROUPES to tour with a theatrical company

TROUPER *n* pl. -S a member of a theatrical company

TROUPIAL *n* pl. -S a tropical bird

TROUPING present participle of troupe

TROUSER *adj* pertaining to trousers

TROUSERS *n/pl* a garment for the lower part of the body

TROUT *n* pl. -S a freshwater fish

TROUTY *adj* TROUTIER, TROUTIEST abounding in trout

TROUVERE *n* pl. -S a medieval poet

TROUVEUR *n* pl. -S trouvere

TROVE *n* pl. -S a valuable discovery

TROVER *n* pl. -S a type of legal action

TROW *v* -ED, -ING, -S to suppose

TROWEL *v* -ELED, -ELING, -ELS or -ELLED, -ELLING, -ELS to smooth with a trowel (a hand tool having a flat blade)

TROWELER *n* pl. -S one that trowels

TROWSERS *n/pl* trousers

TROWTH *n* pl. -S truth

TROY *n* pl. TROYS a system of weights

TRUANCY *n* pl. -CIES an act of truanting

TRUANT *v* -ED, -ING, -S to stay out of school without permission

TRUANTRY *n* pl. -RIES truancy

TRUCE *v* TRUCED, TRUCING, TRUCES to suspend hostilities by mutual agreement

TRUCK *v* -ED, -ING, -S to transport by truck (an automotive vehicle designed to carry loads)

TRUCKAGE *n* pl. -S transportation of goods by trucks

TRUCKER *n* pl. -S a truck driver

TRUCKFUL *n* pl. -S as much as a truck can hold

TRUCKING *n* pl. -S truckage

TRUCKLE *v* -LED, -LING, -LES to yield weakly

TRUCKLER *n* pl. -S one that truckles

TRUCKMAN *n* pl. -MEN a trucker

TRUDGE *v* TRUDGED, TRUDGING, TRUDGES to walk tiredly

TRUDGEN *n* pl. -S a swimming stroke

TRUDGEON *n* pl. -S trudgen

TRUDGER *n* pl. -S one that trudges

TRUDGING present participle of trudge

TRUE *adj* TRUER, TRUEST consistent with fact or reality

TRUE *v* TRUED, TRUING or TRUEING, TRUES to bring to conformity with a standard or requirement

TRUEBLUE *n* pl. -S a person of unwavering loyalty

TRUEBORN *adj* genuinely such by birth

TRUEBRED *adj* designating an animal of unmixed stock

TRUED past tense of true

TRUELOVE *n* pl. -S a sweetheart

TRUENESS *n pl.* -ES the quality or state of being true

TRUER comparative of true

TRUEST superlative of true

TRUFFE *n pl.* -S truffle

TRUFFLE *n pl.* -S an edible fungus **TRUFFLED** *adj*

TRUG *n pl.* -S a gardener's basket

TRUING a present participle of true

TRUISM *n pl.* -S an obvious truth **TRUISTIC** *adj*

TRULL *n pl.* -S a prostitute

TRULY *adv* in conformity with fact or reality

TRUMEAU *n pl.* -MEAUX a column supporting part of a doorway

TRUMP *v* -ED, -ING, -S to outdo

TRUMPERY *n pl.* -ERIES worthless finery

TRUMPET *v* -ED, -ING, -S to sound on a trumpet (a brass wind instrument)

TRUNCATE *v* -CATED, -CATING, -CATES to shorten by cutting off a part

TRUNDLE *v* -DLED, -DLING, -DLES to propel by causing to rotate

TRUNDLER *n pl.* -S one that trundles

TRUNK *n pl.* -S the main stem of a tree **TRUNKED** *adj*

TRUNKFUL *n pl.* -S as much as a trunk (a storage box) can hold

TRUNNEL *n pl.* -S treenail

TRUNNION *n pl.* -S a pin or pivot on which something can be rotated

TRUSS *v* -ED, -ING, -ES to secure tightly

TRUSSER *n pl.* -S one that trusses

TRUSSING *n pl.* -S the framework of a structure

TRUST *v* -ED, -ING, -S to place confidence in

TRUSTEE *v* -TEED, -TEEING, -TEES to commit to the care of an administrator

TRUSTER *n pl.* -S one that trusts

TRUSTFUL *adj* inclined to trust

TRUSTOR *n pl.* -S one that trustees his property

TRUSTY *adj* TRUSTIER, TRUSTIEST worthy of trust **TRUSTILY** *adv*

TRUSTY *n pl.* TRUSTIES one worthy of trust

TRUTH *n pl.* -S conformity to fact or reality

TRUTHFUL *adj* telling the truth

TRY *v* TRIED, TRYING, TRIES to attempt

TRYINGLY *adv* in a distressing manner

TRYMA *n pl.* -MATA a type of nut

TRYOUT *n pl.* -S a test of ability

TRYPSIN *n pl.* -S an enzyme **TRYPTIC** *adj*

TRYSAIL *n pl.* -S a type of sail

TRYST *v* -ED, -ING, -S to agree to meet

TRYSTE *n pl.* -S a market

TRYSTER *n pl.* -S one that trysts

TRYWORKS *n/pl* a type of furnace

TSADE *n pl.* -S sade

TSADI *n pl.* -S sade

TSAR *n pl.* -S czar

TSARDOM *n pl.* -S czardom

TSAREVNA *n pl.* -S czarevna

TSARINA *n pl.* -S czarina

TSARISM *n pl.* -S czarism

TSARIST *n pl.* -S czarist

TSARITZA *n pl.* -S czaritza

TSETSE *n pl.* -S an African fly

TSIMMES *n pl.* TSIMMES tzimmes

TSK *v* -ED, -ING, -S to utter an exclamation of annoyance

TSKTSK *v* -ED, -ING, -S to tsk

TSOORIS *n pl.* TSOORIS tsuris

TSORES *n pl.* TSORES tsuris

TSORIS *n pl.* TSORIS tsuris

TSORRISS *n pl.* TSORRISS tsuris

TSUBA *n pl.* TSUBA a part of a Japanese sword

TSUNAMI *n pl.* -S a very large ocean wave **TSUNAMIC** *adj*

TSURIS *n pl.* TSURIS a series of misfortunes

TUATARA *n pl.* -S a large reptile

TUATERA *n pl.* -S tuatara

TUB *v* TUBBED, TUBBING, TUBS to wash in a tub (a round, open vessel)

TUBA *n pl.* -BAS or -BAE a brass wind instrument

TUBAIST *n pl.* -S a tuba player

TUBAL *adj* pertaining to a tube

TUBATE *adj* tubular

TUBBABLE *adj* suitable for washing in a tub

TUBBED past tense of tub

TUBBER *n pl.* -S one that tubs

TUBBING present participle of tub

TUBBY *adj* -BIER, -BIEST short and fat

TUBE *v* TUBED, TUBING, TUBES to provide with a tube (a long, hollow cylinder)

TUBELESS *adj* having no tube

TUBELIKE	*adj* resembling a tube	**TUGHRIK**	*n* pl. -S tugrik
TUBENOSE	*n* pl. -S a bird having tubular nostrils	**TUGLESS**	*adj* being without a rope or chain with which to pull
TUBER	*n* pl. -S a thick underground stem	**TUGRIK**	*n* pl. -S a monetary unit of Mongolia
TUBERCLE	*n* pl. -S a small, rounded swelling	**TUI**	*n* pl. -S a bird of New Zealand
TUBEROID	*adj* pertaining to a tuber	**TUILLE**	*n* pl. -S a tasset
TUBEROSE	*n* pl. -S a Mexican herb	**TUITION**	*n* pl. -S a fee for instruction
TUBEROUS	*adj* pertaining to a tuber	**TULADI**	*n* pl. -S a freshwater fish
TUBEWORK	*n* pl. -S tubing	**TULE**	*n* pl. -S a tall marsh plant
TUBFUL	*n* pl. -S as much as a tub will hold	**TULIP**	*n* pl. -S a flowering plant
TUBIFEX	*n* pl. -ES an aquatic worm	**TULLE**	*n* pl. -S a silk material
TUBIFORM	*adj* tubular	**TULLIBEE**	*n* pl. -S a freshwater fish
TUBING	*n* pl. -S material in the form of a tube	**TUMBLE**	*v* -BLED, -BLING, -BLES to fall or roll end over end
TUBIST	*n* pl. -S a tubaist		
TUBLIKE	*adj* resembling a tub	**TUMBLER**	*n* pl. -S one that tumbles
TUBULAR	*adj* shaped like a tube	**TUMBLING**	*n* pl. -S the sport of gymnastics
TUBULATE	*v* -LATED, -LATING, -LATES to form into a tube	**TUMBREL**	*n* pl. -S a type of cart
		TUMBRIL	*n* pl. -S tumbrel
TUBULE	*n* pl. -S a small tube	**TUMEFY**	*v* -FIED, -FYING, -FIES to swell
TUBULIN	*n* pl. -S a protein that polymerizes to form tiny tubules	**TUMID**	*adj* swollen **TUMIDLY** *adv*
		TUMIDITY	*n* pl. -TIES the quality or state of being tumid
TUBULOSE	*adj* tubular		
TUBULOUS	*adj* tubular	**TUMMLER**	*n* pl. -S an entertainer who encourages audience participation
TUBULURE	*n* pl. -S a short tubular opening		
		TUMMY	*n* pl. -MIES the stomach
TUCHUN	*n* pl. -S a Chinese military governor	**TUMOR**	*n* pl. -S an abnormal swelling **TUMORAL, TUMOROUS** *adj*
TUCK	*v* -ED, -ING, -S to fold under	**TUMOUR**	*n* pl. -S tumor
TUCKAHOE	*n* pl. -S the edible root of certain arums	**TUMP**	*v* -ED, -ING, -S to tip or turn over
TUCKER	*v* -ED, -ING, -S to weary	**TUMPLINE**	*n* pl. -S a strap for supporting a load on the back
TUCKET	*n* pl. -S a trumpet fanfare		
TUCKSHOP	*n* pl. -S a confectioner's shop	**TUMULAR**	*adj* having the form of a mound
TUFA	*n* pl. -S a porous limestone		
TUFF	*n* pl. -S a volcanic rock	**TUMULI**	*a* pl. of tumulus
TUFFET	*n* pl. -S a clump of grass	**TUMULOSE**	*adj* full of mounds
TUFOLI	*n* pl. TUFOLI a large macaroni shell	**TUMULOUS**	*adj* tumulose
		TUMULT	*n* pl. -S an uproar
TUFT	*v* -ED, -ING, -S to form into tufts (clusters of flexible outgrowths attached at the base)	**TUMULUS**	*n* pl. -LI or -LUSES a mound over a grave
		TUN	*v* TUNNED, TUNNING, TUNS to store in a large cask
TUFTER	*n* pl. -S one that tufts		
TUFTY	*adj* TUFTIER, TUFTIEST abounding in tufts **TUFTILY** *adv*	**TUNA**	*n* pl. -S a marine food fish
		TUNABLE	*adj* capable of being tuned **TUNABLY** *adv*
TUG	*v* TUGGED, TUGGING, TUGS to pull with force		
		TUNDISH	*n* pl. -ES a receptacle for molten metal
TUGBOAT	*n* pl. -S a boat built for towing		
TUGGER	*n* pl. -S one that tugs	**TUNDRA**	*n* pl. -S a level, treeless expanse of arctic land
TUGGING	present participle of tug	**TUNE**	*v* TUNED, TUNING, TUNES to put into the proper pitch
		TUNEABLE	*adj* tunable **TUNEABLY** *adv*

TUNEFUL	adj melodious	**TURF**	n pl. TURFS or TURVES a surface layer of earth bound by grass and its roots
TUNELESS	adj not tuneful		
TUNER	n -S one that tunes		
TUNEUP	n pl. -S an adjustment to insure efficient operation	**TURF**	v -ED, -ING, -S to cover with turf
TUNG	n pl. -S a Chinese tree	**TURFIER**	comparative of turfy
TUNGSTEN	n pl. -S a metallic element **TUNGSTIC** adj	**TURFIEST**	superlative of turfy
		TURFLESS	adj having no turf
TUNIC	n pl. -S a loose-fitting garment	**TURFLIKE**	adj resembling turf
TUNICA	n pl. -CAE an enveloping membrane or layer of body tissue	**TURFMAN**	n pl. -MEN a person who is devoted to horse racing
		TURFSKI	n pl. -S a type of ski
TUNICATE	n pl. -S a small marine animal	**TURFY**	adj TURFIER, TURFIEST covered with turf
TUNICLE	n pl. -S a type of vestment		
TUNING	present participle of tune	**TURGENCY**	n pl. -CIES turgor
TUNNAGE	n pl. -S tonnage	**TURGENT**	adj turgid
TUNNED	past tense of tun	**TURGID**	adj swollen **TURGIDLY** adv
TUNNEL	v -NELED, -NELING, -NELS or -NELLED, -NELLING, -NELS to dig a tunnel (an underground passageway)	**TURGITE**	n pl. -S an iron ore
		TURGOR	n pl. -S the quality or state of being turgid
		TURISTA	n pl. -S intestinal sickness affecting a tourist in a foreign country
TUNNELER	n pl. -S one that tunnels		
TUNNING	present participle of tun		
TUNNY	n pl. -NIES a tuna	**TURK**	n pl. -S one who eagerly advocates change
TUP	v TUPPED, TUPPING, TUPS to copulate with a ewe		
		TURKEY	n pl. -KEYS a large American bird
TUPELO	n pl. -LOS a softwood tree		
TUPIK	n pl. -S an Eskimo tent	**TURKOIS**	n pl. -ES turquois
TUPPED	past tense of tup	**TURMERIC**	n pl. -S an East Indian herb
TUPPENCE	n pl. -S twopence	**TURMOIL**	v -ED, -ING, -S to throw into an uproar
TUPPENNY	adj twopenny		
TUPPING	present participle of tup	**TURN**	v -ED, -ING, -S to rotate **TURNABLE** adj
TUQUE	n pl. -S a knitted woolen cap		
TURACO	n pl. -COS touraco	**TURNCOAT**	n pl. -S a traitor
TURACOU	n pl. -S touraco	**TURNDOWN**	n pl. -S a rejection
TURBAN	n pl. -S a head covering worn by Muslims **TURBANED** adj	**TURNER**	n pl. -S one that turns
		TURNERY	n pl. -ERIES the process of shaping articles on a lathe
TURBARY	n pl. -RIES a place where peat can be dug	**TURNHALL**	n pl. -S a building where gymnasts practice
TURBETH	n pl. -S turpeth		
TURBID	adj thick or opaque with roiled sediment **TURBIDLY** adv	**TURNING**	n pl. -S a rotation about an axis
TURBINAL	n pl. -S a bone of the nasal passage	**TURNIP**	n pl. -S an edible plant root
		TURNKEY	n pl. -KEYS a person who has charge of a prison's keys
TURBINE	n pl. -S a type of engine		
TURBIT	n pl. -S a domestic pigeon	**TURNOFF**	n pl. -S a road that branches off from a larger one
TURBITH	n pl. -S turpeth		
TURBO	n pl. -BOS a turbine	**TURNOUT**	n pl. -S an assemblage of people
TURBOCAR	n pl. -S an auto powered by a gas turbine		
		TURNOVER	n pl. -S an upset or overthrow
TURBOFAN	n pl. -S a type of jet engine	**TURNPIKE**	n pl. -S a highway on which tolls are collected
TURBOJET	n pl. -S a type of jet engine		
TURBOT	n pl. -S a European flatfish	**TURNSOLE**	n pl. -S a plant that turns with the sun
TURDINE	adj belonging to a large family of singing birds		
		TURNSPIT	n pl. -S one that turns a roasting spit
TUREEN	n pl. -S a large, deep bowl		

TURNUP n pl. -S a part of a garment that is turned up

TURPETH n pl. -S a medicinal plant root

TURPS n pl. TURPS turpentine

TURQUOIS n pl. -ES a greenish blue gem

TURRET n pl. -S a small tower **TURRETED** adj

TURRICAL adj resembling a turret

TURTLE v -TLED, -TLING, -TLES to catch turtles (tortoises)

TURTLER n pl. -S one that turtles

TURTLING n pl. -S the act of one that turtles

TURVES a pl. of turf

TUSCHE n pl. -S a liquid used in lithography

TUSH v -ED, -ING, -ES to tusk

TUSHIE n pl. -S the buttocks

TUSHY n pl. TUSHIES tushie

TUSK v -ED, -ING, -S to gore with a tusk (a long, pointed tooth extending outside of the mouth)

TUSKER n pl. -S an animal with tusks

TUSKLESS adj having no tusk

TUSKLIKE adj resembling a tusk

TUSSAH n pl. -S an Asian silkworm

TUSSAL adj pertaining to a cough

TUSSAR n pl. -S tussah

TUSSEH n pl. -S tussah

TUSSER n pl. -S tussah

TUSSIS n pl. -SISES a cough **TUSSIVE** adj

TUSSLE v -SLED, -SLING, -SLES to struggle

TUSSOCK n pl. -S a clump of grass **TUSSOCKY** adj

TUSSOR n pl. -S tussah

TUSSORE n pl. -S tussah

TUSSUCK n pl. -S tussock

TUSSUR n pl. -S tussah

TUT v TUTTED, TUTTING, TUTS to utter an exclamation of impatience

TUTEE n pl. -S one who is being tutored

TUTELAGE n pl. -S the act of tutoring

TUTELAR n pl. -S a tutelary

TUTELARY n pl. -LARIES one who has the power to protect

TUTOR v -ED, -ING, -S to instruct privately

TUTORAGE n pl. -S tutelage

TUTORESS n pl. -ES a female who tutors

TUTORIAL n pl. -S a session of tutoring

TUTOYER v -TOYERED or -TOYED, -TOYERING, -TOYERS to address familiarly

TUTTED past tense of tut

TUTTI n pl. -S a musical passage performed by all the performers

TUTTING present participle of tut

TUTTY n pl. -TIES an impure zinc oxide

TUTU n pl. -S a short ballet skirt

TUX n pl. -ES a tuxedo

TUXEDO n pl. -DOES or -DOS a man's semiformal dinner coat **TUXEDOED** adj

TUYER n pl. -S tuyere

TUYERE n pl. -S a pipe through which air is forced into a blast furnace

TWA n pl. -S two

TWADDLE v -DLED, -DLING, -DLES to talk foolishly

TWADDLER n pl. -S one that twaddles

TWAE n pl. -S two

TWAIN n pl. -S a set of two

TWANG v -ED, -ING, -S to make a sharp, vibrating sound

TWANGER n pl. -S one that twangs

TWANGIER comparative of twangy

TWANGIEST superlative of twangy

TWANGLE v -GLED, -GLING, -GLES to twang

TWANGLER n pl. -S one that twangles

TWANGY adj TWANGIER, TWANGIEST twanging

TWANKY n pl. -KIES a variety of green tea

TWASOME n pl. -S twosome

TWATTLE v -TLED, -TLING, -TLES to twaddle

TWEAK v -ED, -ING, -S to pinch and twist sharply

TWEAKY adj TWEAKIER, TWEAKIEST twitchy

TWEE adj affectedly cute or dainty

TWEED n pl. -S a coarse woolen fabric

TWEEDLE v -DLED, -DLING, -DLES to perform casually on a musical instrument

TWEEDY adj TWEEDIER, TWEEDIEST resembling tweed

TWEEN prep between

TWEENY n pl. TWEENIES a housemaid

TWEET v -ED, -ING, -S to chirp

TWEETER n pl. -S a loudspeaker designed to reproduce high-pitched sounds

TWEEZE v TWEEZED, TWEEZING, TWEEZES to pluck with a tweezer

TWEEZER n pl. -S a pincerlike tool

TWELFTH n pl. -S the number twelve in a series

TWELVE n pl. -S a number

TWELVEMO n pl. -MOS a page size

TWENTY n pl. -TIES a number

TWERP n pl. -S a small, impudent person

TWIBIL n pl. -S a battle-ax with two cutting edges

TWIBILL n pl. -S twibil

TWICE adv two times

TWIDDLE v -DLED, -DLING, -DLES to play idly with something

TWIDDLER n pl. -S one that twiddles

TWIDDLY adj -DLIER, -DLIEST having many turns

TWIER n pl. -S tuyere

TWIG v TWIGGED, TWIGGING, TWIGS to observe

TWIGGEN adj made of twigs (small branches)

TWIGGY adj -GIER, -GIEST twiglike

TWIGLESS adj having no twigs

TWIGLIKE adj resembling a twig

TWILIGHT n pl. -S the early evening light

TWILIT adj lighted by twilight

TWILL v -ED, -ING, -S to weave so as to produce a diagonal pattern

TWILLING n pl. -S a twilled fabric

TWIN v TWINNED, TWINNING, TWINS to bring together in close association

TWINBORN adj born at the same birth

TWINE v TWINED, TWINING, TWINES to twist together

TWINER n pl. -S one that twines

TWINGE v TWINGED, TWINGING or TWINGEING, TWINGES to affect with a sharp pain

TWINIER comparative of twiny

TWINIEST superlative of twiny

TWINIGHT adj pertaining to a baseball doubleheader that begins in the late afternoon

TWINING present participle of twine

TWINJET n pl. -S an aircraft with two jet engines

TWINKLE v -KLED, -KLING, -KLES to shine with a flickering or sparkling light

TWINKLER n pl. -S one that twinkles

TWINKLY adj twinkling

TWINNED past tense of twin

TWINNING n pl. -S the bearing of two children at the same birth

TWINSET n pl. -S a matching pair of sweaters to be worn together

TWINSHIP n pl. -S close similarity or association

TWINY adj TWINIER, TWINIEST resembling twine (a strong string)

TWIRL v -ED, -ING, -S to rotate rapidly

TWIRLER n pl. -S one that twirls

TWIRLY adj TWIRLIER, TWIRLIEST curved

TWIRP n pl. -S twerp

TWIST v -ED, -ING, -S to combine by winding together

TWISTER n pl. -S one that twists

TWISTING n pl. -S a form of trickery used in selling life insurance

TWISTY adj TWISTIER, TWISTIEST full of curves

TWIT v TWITTED, TWITTING, TWITS to ridicule

TWITCH v -ED, -ING, -ES to move or pull with a sudden motion

TWITCHER n pl. -S one that twitches

TWITCHY adj TWITCHIER, TWITCHIEST fidgety

TWITTED past tense of twit

TWITTER v -ED, -ING, -S to utter a succession of chirping sounds

TWITTERY adj nervously agitated

TWITTING present participle of twit

TWIXT prep between

TWO n pl. TWOS a number

TWOFER n pl. -S something sold at the rate of two for the price of one

TWOFOLD n pl. -S an amount twice as great as a given unit

TWOPENCE n pl. -S a British coin worth two pennies

TWOPENNY adj worth twopence

TWOSOME n pl. -S a group of two

TWYER n pl. -S tuyere

TYCOON n pl. -S a wealthy and powerful business person

TYE n pl. -S a chain on a ship

TYEE n pl. -S a food fish

TYER n pl. -S one that ties

TYING a present participle of tie

TYKE n pl. -S a small child

TYLOSIN n pl. -S an antibiotic

TYMBAL n pl. -S timbal

TYMPAN n pl. -S a drum

TYMPANA a pl. of tympanum

TYMPANAL adj tympanic

TYMPANIC adj pertaining to the tympanum

TYMPANO n pl. -NI timpano

TYMPANUM n pl. -NA or -NUMS the middle ear

TYMPANY n pl. -NIES a swelling of the abdomen

TYNE v TYNED, TYNING, TYNES to tine

TYPAL adj typical

TYPE v TYPED, TYPING, TYPES to write with a typewriter
TYPABLE, TYPEABLE adj

TYPEBAR n pl. -S a part of a typewriter

TYPECASE n pl. -S a tray for holding printing type

TYPECAST v -CAST, -CASTING, -CASTS to cast in an acting role befitting one's own nature

TYPED past tense of type

TYPEFACE n pl. -S the face of printing type

TYPESET v -SET, -SETTING, -SETS to set in type

TYPEY adj TYPIER, TYPIEST typy

TYPHOID n pl. -S an infectious disease

TYPHON n pl. -S a type of signal horn

TYPHOON n pl. -S a tropical hurricane
TYPHONIC adj

TYPHOSE adj pertaining to typhoid

TYPHUS n pl. -ES an infectious disease
TYPHOUS adj

TYPIC adj typical

TYPICAL adj having the nature of a representative specimen

TYPIER comparative of typey and typy

TYPIEST superlative of typey and typy

TYPIFIER n pl. -S one that typifies

TYPIFY v -FIED, -FYING, -FIES to serve as a typical example of

TYPING present participle of type

TYPIST n pl. -S one who types

TYPO n pl. -POS a typographical error

TYPOLOGY n pl. -GIES the study of classification according to common characteristics

TYPP n pl. -S a unit of yarn size

TYPY adj TYPIER, TYPIEST characterized by strict conformance to the characteristics of a group

TYRAMINE n pl. -S a chemical compound

TYRANNIC adj characteristic of a tyrant

TYRANNY n pl. -NIES the rule of a tyrant

TYRANT n pl. -S an absolute ruler

TYRE v TYRED, TYRING, TYRES to furnish with a covering for a wheel

TYRO n pl. -ROS a beginner
TYRONIC adj

TYROSINE n pl. -S an amino acid

TYTHE v TYTHED, TYTHING, TYTHES to tithe

TZADDIK n pl. -DIKIM zaddik

TZAR n pl. -S czar

TZARDOM n pl. -S czardom

TZAREVNA n pl. -S czarevna

TZARINA n pl. -S czarina

TZARISM n pl. -S czarism

TZARIST n pl. -S czarist

TZARITZA n pl. -S czaritza

TZETZE n pl. -S tsetse

TZIGANE n pl. -S a gypsy

TZIMMES n pl. TZIMMES a vegetable stew

TZITZIS n/pl zizith

TZITZIT n/pl zizith

TZITZITH n/pl zizith

TZURIS n pl. TZURIS tsuris

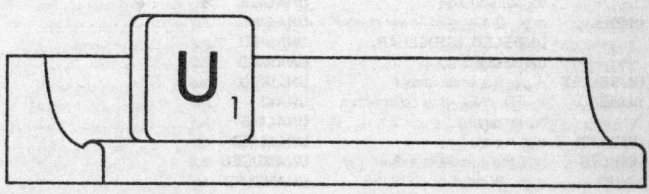

UBIETY   *n pl.* -ETIES the state of having a definite location

UBIQUE   *adv* everywhere

UBIQUITY   *n pl.* -TIES the state of being everywhere at the same time

UDDER   *n pl.* -S a mammary gland

UDO   *n pl.* UDOS a Japanese herb

UDOMETER   *n pl.* -S a rain gauge

UDOMETRY   *n pl.* -TRIES the measurement of rain

UFOLOGY   *n pl.* -GIES the study of unidentified flying objects

UGH   *n pl.* -S the sound of a cough or grunt

UGLIER   comparative of ugly

UGLIES   pl. of ugly

UGLIEST   superlative of ugly

UGLIFIER   *n pl.* -S one that uglifies

UGLIFY   *v* -FIED, -FYING, -FIES to make ugly

UGLINESS   *n pl.* -ES the state of being ugly

UGLY   *adj* -LIER, -LIEST displeasing to the sight **UGLILY** *adv*

UGLY   *n pl.* -LIES one that is ugly

UGSOME   *adj* disgusting

UH   *interj* — used to express hesitation

UHLAN   *n pl.* -S one of a body of Prussian cavalry

UINTAITE   *n pl.* -S a variety of asphalt

UKASE   *n pl.* -S an edict

UKE   *n pl.* -S ukelele

UKELELE   *n pl.* -S ukulele

UKULELE   *n pl.* -S a small guitar-like instrument

ULAMA   *n pl.* -S ulema

ULAN   *n pl.* -S uhlan

ULCER   *v* -ED, -ING, -S to affect with an ulcer (a type of lesion)

ULCERATE   *v* -ATED, -ATING, -ATES to ulcer

ULCEROUS   *adj* being or affected with an ulcer

ULEMA   *n pl.* -S a Muslim scholar

ULEXITE   *n pl.* -S a mineral

ULLAGE   *n pl.* -S the unfilled part of a cask **ULLAGED** *adj*

ULNA   *n pl.* -NAE or -NAS a bone of the forearm **ULNAR** *adj*

ULNAD   *adv* toward the ulna

ULPAN   *n pl.* -PANIM a school in Israel for teaching Hebrew

ULSTER   *n pl.* -S a long, loose overcoat

ULTERIOR   *adj* more remote

ULTIMA   *n pl.* -S the last syllable of a word

ULTIMACY   *n pl.* -CIES an ultimate

ULTIMATA   *n/pl* final proposals

ULTIMATE   *v* -MATED, -MATING, -MATES to come to an end

ULTIMO   *adj* of or occurring in the preceding month

ULTRA   *n pl.* -S an ultraist

ULTRADRY   *adj* extremely dry

ULTRAHIP   *adj* extremely hip

ULTRAHOT   *adj* extremely hot

ULTRAISM   *n pl.* -S advocacy of extreme measures

ULTRAIST   *n pl.* -S an advocate of extreme measures

ULTRALOW   *adj* extremely low

ULTRARED   *n pl.* -S infrared

ULU   *n pl.* -S an Eskimo knife

ULULANT   *adj* howling

ULULATE   *v* -LATED, -LATING, -LATES to howl

ULVA n pl. -S an edible seaweed

UM interj — used to indicate hesitation

UMANGITE n pl. -S a mineral consisting of copper selenide

UMBEL n pl. -S a type of flower cluster **UMBELED, UMBELLAR, UMBELLED** adj

UMBELLET n pl. -S a small umbel

UMBER v -ED, -ING, -S to color with a brown pigment

UMBILICI n/pl navels

UMBLES n/pl the entrails of a deer

UMBO n pl. -BONES or -BOS the rounded elevation at the center of a shield **UMBONAL, UMBONATE, UMBONIC** adj

UMBRA n pl. -BRAE or -BRAS a dark area **UMBRAL** adj

UMBRAGE n pl. -S resentment

UMBRELLA v -ED, -ING, -S to provide with an umbrella (a portable cover for protection from rain or sun)

UMBRETTE n pl. -S a wading bird

UMIAC n pl. -S umiak

UMIACK n pl. -S umiak

UMIAK n pl. -S an open Eskimo boat

UMIAQ n pl. -S umiak

UMLAUT v -ED, -ING, -S to modify a vowel sound by partial assimilation to a succeeding sound

UMM interj um

UMP v -ED, -ING, -S to umpire

UMPIRAGE n pl. -S the function of an umpire

UMPIRE v -PIRED, -PIRING, -PIRES to act as umpire (a person appointed to rule on the plays in a game)

UMPTEEN adj indefinitely numerous

UMTEENTH adj being the last in an indefinitely numerous series

UN pron pl. -S one

Following is a list of self-explanatory adjectives and adverbs containing the prefix UN- (not):

UNABATED adj
UNABLE adj
UNABUSED adj
UNACTED adj

UNADULT adj
UNAFRAID adj
UNAGED adj
UNAGEING adj
UNAGILE adj
UNAGING adj
UNAIDED adj
UNAIMED adj
UNAIRED adj
UNAKIN adj
UNALIKE adj
UNALLIED adj
UNAMUSED adj
UNANELED adj
UNAPT adj
UNAPTLY adv
UNARGUED adj
UNARTFUL adj
UNASKED adj
UNATONED adj
UNAVOWED adj
UNAWAKED adj
UNAWARE adj
UNAWED adj
UNBACKED adj
UNBAKED adj
UNBANNED adj
UNBARBED adj
UNBASED adj
UNBATHED adj
UNBEATEN adj
UNBENIGN adj
UNBIASED adj
UNBILLED adj
UNBITTED adj
UNBITTEN adj
UNBITTER adj
UNBLAMED adj
UNBLEST adj
UNBLOODY adj
UNBONED adj
UNBORN adj
UNBOUGHT adj
UNBOUNCY adj
UNBOWED adj
UNBRED adj
UNBRIGHT adj
UNBROKE adj
UNBROKEN adj
UNBULKY adj
UNBURIED adj
UNBURNED adj
UNBURNT adj
UNBUSTED adj
UNBUSY adj

UNCALLED	adj		UNENDED	adj
UNCANDID	adj		UNENDING	adj
UNCARING	adj		UNENVIED	adj
UNCASHED	adj		UNERASED	adj
UNCASKED	adj		UNEROTIC	adj
UNCATCHY	adj		UNERRING	adj
UNCAUGHT	adj		UNEVADED	adj
UNCAUSED	adj		UNEVEN	adj -EVENER, -EVENEST
UNCHARY	adj		UNEVENLY	adv
UNCHASTE	adj		UNEXOTIC	adj
UNCHEWED	adj		UNEXPERT	adj
UNCHIC	adj		UNFADED	adj
UNCHICLY	adv		UNFADING	adj
UNCHOSEN	adj		UNFAIR	adj -FAIRER, -FAIREST
UNCIVIL	adj		UNFAIRLY	adv
UNCLEAN	adj -CLEANER, -CLEANEST		UNFAKED	adj
UNCLEAR	adj -CLEARER, -CLEAREST		UNFALLEN	adj
UNCLOYED	adj		UNFAMOUS	adj
UNCOATED	adj		UNFANCY	adj
UNCODED	adj		UNFAZED	adj
UNCOINED	adj		UNFEARED	adj
UNCOMBED	adj		UNFED	adj
UNCOMELY	adj		UNFELT	adj
UNCOMIC	adj		UNFILIAL	adj
UNCOMMON	adj -MONER, -MONEST		UNFILLED	adj
UNCOOKED	adj		UNFILMED	adj
UNCOOL	adj		UNFIRED	adj
UNCOOLED	adj		UNFISHED	adj
UNCOUTH	adj		UNFLASHY	adj
UNCOY	adj		UNFLEXED	adj
UNCRAZY	adj		UNFOILED	adj
UNCUFFED	adj		UNFOND	adj
UNCURED	adj		UNFORCED	adj
UNCURSED	adj		UNFORGED	adj
UNCUT	adj		UNFORKED	adj
UNCUTE	adj		UNFORMED	adj
UNDAMPED	adj		UNFOUGHT	adj
UNDARING	adj		UNFOUND	adj
UNDATED	adj		UNFRAMED	adj
UNDECKED	adj		UNFUNDED	adj
UNDENIED	adj		UNFUNNY	adj
UNDEVOUT	adj		UNFUSED	adj
UNDIMMED	adj		UNFUSSY	adj
UNDOABLE	adj		UNGALLED	adj
UNDOCILE	adj		UNGENIAL	adj
UNDOTTED	adj		UNGENTLE	adj
UNDREAMT	adj		UNGENTLY	adv
UNDRIED	adj		UNGIFTED	adj
UNDUBBED	adj		UNGLAZED	adj
UNDULLED	adj		UNGOWNED	adj
UNDYED	adj		UNGRACED	adj
UNEAGER	adj		UNGRADED	adj
UNEARNED	adj		UNGREEDY	adj
UNEATEN	adj		UNGROUND	adj
UNEDIBLE	adj		UNGUIDED	adj
UNEDITED	adj		UNHAILED	adj

UNHALVED adj
UNHAPPY adj -PIER, -PIEST
UNHARMED adj
UNHASTY adj
UNHEALED adj
UNHEARD adj
UNHEATED adj
UNHEDGED adj
UNHEEDED adj
UNHELPED adj
UNHEROIC adj
UNHEWN adj
UNHIP adj
UNHIRED adj
UNHOLILY adv
UNHOLY adj -LIER, -LIEST
UNHUMAN adj
UNHUNG adj
UNHURT adj
UNIDEAL adj
UNIMBUED adj
UNIRONED adj
UNISSUED adj
UNJADED adj
UNJOINED adj
UNJOYFUL adj
UNJUDGED adj
UNJUST adj
UNJUSTLY adv
UNKEPT adj
UNKIND adj -KINDER, -KINDEST
UNKINDLY adv -LIER, -LIEST
UNKINGLY adj
UNKISSED adj
UNKOSHER adj
UNLAWFUL adj
UNLEASED adj
UNLED adj
UNLETHAL adj
UNLETTED adj
UNLEVIED adj
UNLICKED adj
UNLIKE adj
UNLIKELY adj -LIER, -LIEST
UNLINED adj
UNLISTED adj
UNLIT adj
UNLIVELY adj
UNLOBED adj
UNLOVED adj
UNLOVELY adj -LIER, -LIEST
UNLOVING adj
UNLUCKY adj -LUCKIER, -LUCKIEST
UNMACHO adj
UNMANFUL adj
UNMANLY adj

UNMAPPED adj
UNMARKED adj
UNMARRED adj
UNMATED adj
UNMATTED adj
UNMEANT adj
UNMELLOW adj
UNMELTED adj
UNMENDED adj
UNMERRY adj
UNMET adj
UNMILLED adj
UNMINED adj
UNMIXED adj
UNMIXT adj
UNMODISH adj
UNMOLTEN adj
UNMOVED adj
UNMOVING adj
UNMOWN adj
UNNAMED adj
UNNEEDED adj
UNNOISY adj
UNNOTED adj
UNOILED adj
UNOPEN adj
UNOPENED adj
UNORNATE adj
UNOWNED adj
UNPAID adj
UNPAIRED adj
UNPARTED adj
UNPAVED adj
UNPAYING adj
UNPEELED adj
UNPITIED adj
UNPLACED adj
UNPLAYED adj
UNPLIANT adj
UNPLOWED adj
UNPOETIC adj
UNPOISED adj
UNPOLITE adj
UNPOLLED adj
UNPOSED adj
UNPOSTED adj
UNPOTTED adj
UNPRETTY adj
UNPRICED adj
UNPRIMED adj
UNPRIZED adj
UNPROBED adj
UNPROVED adj
UNPROVEN adj
UNPRUNED adj
UNPURE adj

UNPURGED	adj	
UNQUIET	adj	-ETER, -ETEST
UNRAISED	adj	
UNRAKED	adj	
UNRANKED	adj	
UNRATED	adj	
UNRAZED	adj	
UNREAD	adj	
UNREADY	adj	-READIER, -READIEST
UNREAL	adj	
UNREALLY	adv	
UNRENTED	adj	
UNREPAID	adj	
UNRESTED	adj	
UNRHYMED	adj	
UNRIFLED	adj	
UNRIMED	adj	
UNRINSED	adj	
UNRISEN	adj	
UNROPED	adj	
UNROUGH	adj	
UNRULED	adj	
UNRUSHED	adj	
UNRUSTED	adj	
UNSAFE	adj	
UNSAFELY	adv	
UNSALTED	adj	
UNSATED	adj	
UNSAVED	adj	
UNSAVORY	adj	
UNSAWED	adj	
UNSAWN	adj	
UNSCALED	adj	
UNSEARED	adj	
UNSEEDED	adj	
UNSEEING	adj	
UNSEEMLY	adj	-LIER, -LIEST
UNSEEN	adj	
UNSEIZED	adj	
UNSENT	adj	
UNSERVED	adj	
UNSEXUAL	adj	
UNSEXY	adj	
UNSHADED	adj	
UNSHAKEN	adj	
UNSHAMED	adj	
UNSHAPED	adj	
UNSHAPEN	adj	
UNSHARED	adj	
UNSHARP	adj	
UNSHAVED	adj	
UNSHAVEN	adj	
UNSHED	adj	
UNSHOD	adj	
UNSHORN	adj	
UNSHOWY	adj	

UNSHRUNK	adj	
UNSHUT	adj	
UNSIFTED	adj	
UNSIGNED	adj	
UNSILENT	adj	
UNSINFUL	adj	
UNSIZED	adj	
UNSLAKED	adj	
UNSLICED	adj	
UNSMART	adj	
UNSMOKED	adj	
UNSOAKED	adj	
UNSOBER	adj	
UNSOCIAL	adj	
UNSOILED	adj	
UNSOLD	adj	
UNSOLID	adj	
UNSOLVED	adj	
UNSORTED	adj	
UNSOUGHT	adj	
UNSOUND	adj	-SOUNDER, -SOUNDEST
UNSOURED	adj	
UNSOWED	adj	
UNSOWN	adj	
UNSPENT	adj	
UNSPILT	adj	
UNSPLIT	adj	
UNSPOILT	adj	
UNSPRUNG	adj	
UNSPUN	adj	
UNSTABLE	adj	-BLER, -BLEST
UNSTABLY	adv	
UNSTEADY	adj	-STEADIER, -STEADIEST
UNSTONED	adj	
UNSTUFFY	adj	
UNSTUNG	adj	
UNSUBTLE	adj	
UNSUBTLY	adv	
UNSUITED	adj	
UNSUNG	adj	
UNSUNK	adj	
UNSURE	adj	
UNSURELY	adv	
UNSWAYED	adj	
UNSWEPT	adj	
UNTAGGED	adj	
UNTAKEN	adj	
UNTAME	adj	
UNTAMED	adj	
UNTANNED	adj	
UNTAPPED	adj	
UNTASTED	adj	
UNTAXED	adj	
UNTENDED	adj	
UNTESTED	adj	
UNTHAWED	adj	

UNTIDILY	adv	UNWIFELY	adj
UNTIDY	adj -DIER, -DIEST	UNWILLED	adj
UNTILLED	adj	UNWISE	adj -WISER, -WISEST
UNTILTED	adj	UNWISELY	adv
UNTIMELY	adj -LIER, -LIEST	UNWON	adj
UNTINGED	adj	UNWOODED	adj
UNTIPPED	adj	UNWOOED	adj
UNTIRED	adj	UNWORKED	adj
UNTIRING	adj	UNWORN	adj
UNTITLED	adj	UNWORTHY	adj -THIER, -THIEST
UNTOLD	adj	UNWRUNG	adj
UNTORN	adj	UNYOUNG	adj
UNTRACED	adj	UNZONED	adj
UNTRENDY	adj		
UNTRIED	adj		
UNTRUE	adj -TRUER, -TRUEST		
UNTRULY	adv		
UNTRUSTY	adj		
UNTUFTED	adj	UNAI	n pl. -S unau
UNTURNED	adj	UNAKITE	n pl. -S an igneous rock
UNUNITED	adj	UNANCHOR	v -ED, -ING, -S to loosen from
UNURGED	adj		an anchor
UNUSABLE	adj	UNARM	v -ED, -ING, -S to disarm
UNUSED	adj	UNARY	adj consisting of a single
UNUSUAL	adj		element
UNVALUED	adj	UNAU	n pl. -S a two-toed sloth
UNVARIED	adj	UNAWARES	adv without warning
UNVEINED	adj	UNBAN	v -BANNED, -BANNING,
UNVERSED	adj		-BANS to remove a prohibition
UNVEXED	adj		against
UNVEXT	adj	UNBAR	v -BARRED, -BARRING,
UNVIABLE	adj		-BARS to remove a bar from
UNVOCAL	adj	UNBATED	adj unabated
UNWALLED	adj	UNBE	v to cease to have being —
UNWANING	adj		UNBE is the only accepted
UNWANTED	adj		form of this verb; it cannot be
UNWARIER	comparative of unwary		conjugated
UNWARIEST	superlative of unwary	UNBEAR	v -BEARED, -BEARING,
UNWARILY	adv		-BEARS to free from the
UNWARMED	adj		pressure of a rein
UNWARNED	adj	UNBELIEF	n pl. -S lack of belief
UNWARPED	adj	UNBELT	v -ED, -ING, -S to remove the
UNWARY	adj -WARIER, -WARIEST		belt of
UNWASTED	adj	UNBEND	v -BENT or -BENDED,
UNWAXED	adj		-BENDING, -BENDS to make
UNWEANED	adj		or allow to become straight
UNWEARY	adj	UNBID	adj unbidden
UNWED	adj	UNBIDDEN	adj not invited
UNWEDDED	adj	UNBIND	v -BOUND, -BINDING,
UNWEEDED	adj		-BINDS to free from bindings
UNWELDED	adj	UNBLOCK	v -ED, -ING, -S to free from
UNWELL	adj		being blocked
UNWEPT	adj	UNBODIED	adj having no body
UNWETTED	adj	UNBOLT	v -ED, -ING, -S to open by
UNWHITE	adj		withdrawing a bolt (a metal
UNWIELDY	adj -WIELDIER, -WIELDIEST		bar)

UNBONNET *v* -ED, -ING, -S to uncover the head

UNBOSOM *v* -ED, -ING, -S to reveal

UNBOUND past tense of unbind

UNBOX *v* -ED, -ING, -ES to remove from a box

UNBRACE *v* -BRACED, -BRACING, -BRACES to free from braces

UNBRAID *v* -ED, -ING, -S to separate the strands of

UNBRAKE *v* -BRAKED, -BRAKING, -BRAKES to release a brake

UNBREECH *v* -ED, -ING, -ES to remove the breeches of

UNBRIDLE *v* -DLED, -DLING, -DLES to set loose

UNBUCKLE *v* -LED, -LING, -LES to loosen a buckle

UNBUILD *v* -BUILT, -BUILDING, -BUILDS to demolish

UNBUNDLE *v* -DLED, -DLING, -DLES to price separately

UNBURDEN *v* -ED, -ING, -S to free from a burden

UNBUTTON *v* -ED, -ING, -S to unfasten the buttons of

UNCAGE *v* -CAGED, -CAGING, -CAGES to release from a cage

UNCAKE *v* -CAKED, -CAKING, -CAKES to break up a cake (a block of compacted matter)

UNCANNY *adj* -NIER, -NIEST strange and inexplicable

UNCAP *v* -CAPPED, -CAPPING, -CAPS to remove the cap from

UNCASE *v* -CASED, -CASING, -CASES to remove from a case

UNCHAIN *v* -ED, -ING, -S to free by removing a chain

UNCHANCY *adj* unlucky

UNCHARGE *v* -CHARGED, -CHARGING, -CHARGES to acquit

UNCHOKE *v* -CHOKED, -CHOKING, -CHOKES to free from obstruction

UNCHURCH *v* -ED, -ING, -ES to expel from a church

UNCI pl. of uncus

UNCIA *n* pl. -CIAE a coin of ancient Rome

UNCIAL *n* pl. -S a style of writing

UNCIALLY *adv* in the uncial style

UNCIFORM *n* pl. -S a bone of the wrist

UNCINAL *adj* uncinate

UNCINATE *adj* bent at the end like a hook

UNCINUS *n* pl. -NI an uncinate structure

UNCLAD a past tense of unclothe

UNCLAMP *v* -ED, -ING, -S to free from a clamp

UNCLASP *v* -ED, -ING, -S to free from a clasp

UNCLE *n* pl. -S the brother of one's father or mother

UNCLENCH *v* -ED, -ING, -ES to open from a clenched position

UNCLINCH *v* -ED, -ING, -ES to unclench

UNCLIP *v* -CLIPPED, -CLIPPING, -CLIPS to remove a clip (a fastening device) from

UNCLOAK *v* -ED, -ING, -S to remove a cloak from

UNCLOG *v* -CLOGGED, -CLOGGING, -CLOGS to free from a difficulty or obstruction

UNCLOSE *v* -CLOSED, -CLOSING, -CLOSES to open

UNCLOTHE *v* -CLOTHED or -CLAD, -CLOTHING, -CLOTHES to divest of clothing

UNCLOUD *v* -ED, -ING, -S to free from clouds

UNCO *n* pl. -COS a stranger

UNCOCK *v* -ED, -ING, -S to remove from a cocked position

UNCOFFIN *v* -ED, -ING, -S to remove from a coffin

UNCOIL *v* -ED, -ING, -S to release from a coiled position

UNCORK *v* -ED, -ING, -S to draw the cork

UNCOUPLE *v* -PLED, -PLING, -PLES to disconnect

UNCOVER *v* -ED, -ING, -S to remove the covering from

UNCRATE *v* -CRATED, -CRATING, -CRATES to remove from a crate

UNCREATE *v* -ATED, -ATING, -ATES to deprive of existence

UNCROSS *v* -ED, -ING, -ES to change from a crossed position

UNCROWN *v* -ED, -ING, -S to deprive of a crown

UNCTION *n* pl. -S the act of anointing

UNCTUOUS *adj* greasy

UNCUFF *v* -ED, -ING, -S to remove handcuffs from

UNCURB *v* -ED, -ING, -S to remove restraints from

UNCURL *v* -ED, -ING, -S to straighten the curls of

UNCUS n pl. -CI a hook-shaped anatomical part

UNDE adj wavy

UNDEAD n pl. UNDEAD a vampire

UNDEE adj unde

UNDER prep in a lower position than

UNDERACT v -ED, -ING, -S to act subtly and with restraint

UNDERAGE n pl. -S a shortage

UNDERARM n pl. -S the armpit

UNDERATE past tense of undereat

UNDERBID v -BID, -BIDDING, -BIDS to bid lower than

UNDERBUD v -BUDDED, -BUDDING, -BUDS to bud from beneath

UNDERBUY v -BOUGHT, -BUYING, -BUYS to buy at a lower price than

UNDERCUT v -CUT, -CUTTING, -CUTS to cut under

UNDERDO v -DID, -DONE, -DOING, -DOES to do insufficiently

UNDERDOG n pl. -S one who is expected to lose

UNDEREAT v -ATE, -EATEN, -EATING, -EATS to eat an insufficient amount

UNDERFED adj fed an insufficient amount

UNDERFUR n pl. -S the thick, soft fur beneath the outer coat of certain mammals

UNDERGO v -WENT, -GONE, -GOING, -GOES to be subjected to

UNDERGOD n pl. -S a lesser god

UNDERJAW n pl. -S the lower jaw

UNDERLAID past tense of underlay

UNDERLAIN past participle of underlie

UNDERLAP v -LAPPED, -LAPPING, -LAPS to extend partly under

UNDERLAY v -LAID, -LAYING, -LAYS to place under

UNDERLET v -LET, -LETTING, -LETS to lease at less than the usual value

UNDERLIE v -LAY, -LAIN, -LYING, -LIES to lie under

UNDERLIP n pl. -S the lower lip

UNDERLIT adj lacking adequate light

UNDERLYING present participle of underlie

UNDERPAY v -PAID, -PAYING, -PAYS to pay less than is deserved

UNDERPIN v -PINNED, -PINNING, -PINS to support from below

UNDERRUN v -RAN, -RUNNING, -RUNS to pass or extend under

UNDERSEA adv beneath the surface of the sea

UNDERSET n pl. -S a current below the surface of the ocean

UNDERTAX v -ED, -ING, -ES to tax less than the usual amount

UNDERTOW n pl. -S the seaward pull of receding waves breaking on a shore

UNDERWAY adv in progress

UNDERWENT past tense of undergo

UNDID past tense of undo

UNDIES n/pl underwear

UNDINE n pl. -S a female water spirit

UNDO v -DID, -DONE, -DOING, -DOES to bring to ruin

UNDOCK v -ED, -ING, -S to move away from a dock

UNDOER n pl. -S one that undoes

UNDOING n pl. -S a cause of ruin

UNDONE past participle of undo

UNDOUBLE v -BLED, -BLING, -BLES to unfold

UNDRAPE v -DRAPED, -DRAPING, -DRAPES to strip of drapery

UNDRAW v -DREW, -DRAWN, -DRAWING, -DRAWS to draw open

UNDRESS v -DRESSED or -DREST, -DRESSING, -DRESSES to remove one's clothing

UNDRUNK adj not swallowed

UNDUE adj exceeding what is appropriate or normal

UNDULANT adj undulating

UNDULAR adj undulating

UNDULATE v -LATED, -LATING, -LATES to move with a wavelike motion

UNDULY adv in an undue manner

UNDY adj unde

UNDYING adj not subject to death

UNEARTH v -ED, -ING, -S to dig up

UNEASE n pl. -S mental or physical discomfort

UNEASY adj -EASIER, -EASIEST marked by mental or physical discomfort UNEASILY adv

UNEQUAL n pl. -S one that is not equal to another

UNFAITH n pl. -S lack of faith

UNFASTEN v -ED, -ING, -S to release from fastenings

UNFENCE v -FENCED, -FENCING, -FENCES to remove a fence from

UNFETTER v -ED, -ING, -S to free from fetters

UNFIT v -FITTED, -FITTING, -FITS to make unsuitable

UNFITLY adv in an unsuitable manner

UNFIX v -FIXED or -FIXT, -FIXING, -FIXES to unfasten

UNFOLD v -ED, -ING, -S to open something that is folded

UNFOLDER n pl. -S one that unfolds

UNFORGOT adj not forgotten

UNFREE v -FREED, -FREEING, -FREES to deprive of freedom

UNFREEZE v -FROZE, -FROZEN, -FREEZING, -FREEZES to cause to thaw

UNFROCK v -ED, -ING, -S to divest of ecclesiastical authority

UNFURL v -ED, -ING, -S to unroll

UNGAINLY adj -LIER, -LIEST awkward

UNGIRD v -GIRDED or -GIRT, -GIRDING, -GIRDS to remove a belt from

UNGLOVE v -GLOVED, -GLOVING, -GLOVES to uncover by removing a glove

UNGLUE v -GLUED, -GLUING, -GLUES to disjoin

UNGODLY adj -LIER, -LIEST impious

UNGOT adj ungotten

UNGOTTEN adj not obtained

UNGUAL adj pertaining to an unguis

UNGUARD v -ED, -ING, -S to leave unprotected

UNGUENT n pl. -S an ointment

UNGUENTA n/pl ointments

UNGUIS n pl. -GUES a nail, claw, or hoof

UNGULA n pl. -LAE an unguis **UNGULAR** adj

UNGULATE n pl. -S a hoofed mammal

UNHAIR v -ED, -ING, -S to remove the hair from

UNHALLOW v -ED, -ING, -S to profane

UNHAND v -ED, -ING, -S to remove the hand from

UNHANDY adj -HANDIER, -HANDIEST difficult to handle

UNHANG v -HUNG or -HANGED, -HANGING, -HANGS to detach from a hanging support

UNHAT v -HATTED, -HATTING, -HATS to remove one's hat

UNHELM v -ED, -ING, -S to remove the helmet of

UNHINGE v -HINGED, -HINGING, -HINGES to remove from hinges

UNHITCH v -ED, -ING, -ES to free from being hitched

UNHOOD v -ED, -ING, -S to remove a hood from

UNHOOK v -ED, -ING, -S to remove from a hook

UNHOPED adj not hoped for or expected

UNHORSE v -HORSED, -HORSING, -HORSES to cause to fall from a horse

UNHOUSE v -HOUSED, -HOUSING, -HOUSES to deprive of a protective shelter

UNHUSK v -ED, -ING, -S to remove the husk from

UNIALGAL adj pertaining to a single algal cell

UNIAXIAL adj having one axis

UNICOLOR adj of one color

UNICORN n pl. -S a mythical horselike creature

UNICYCLE n pl. -S a one-wheeled vehicle

UNIDEAED adj lacking ideas

UNIFACE n pl. -S a coin having a design on only one side

UNIFIC adj unifying

UNIFIED past tense of unify

UNIFIER n pl. -S one that unifies

UNIFIES present 3d person sing. of unify

UNIFILAR adj having only one thread, wire, or fiber

UNIFORM adj -FORMER, -FORMEST unchanging

UNIFORM v -ED, -ING, -S to make uniform

UNIFY v -FIED, -FYING, -FIES to make into a coherent whole

UNILOBED adj having one lobe

UNION n pl. -S a number of persons, parties, or political entities united for a common purpose

UNIONISE v -ISED, -ISING, -ISES to unionize

UNIONISM n pl. -S the principle of forming a union

UNIONIST n pl. -S an advocate of unionism

UNIONIZE v -IZED, -IZING, -IZES to form into a union

UNIPOD n pl. -S a one-legged support

UNIPOLAR adj showing only one kind of polarity

UNIQUE *adj* UNIQUER, UNIQUEST existing as the only one of its kind; very unusual **UNIQUELY** *adv*

UNIQUE *n* pl. -S something that is unique

UNISEX *n* pl. -ES the condition of not being distinguishable as to sex

UNISON *n* pl. -S complete agreement **UNISONAL** *adj*

UNIT *n* pl. -S a specific quantity used as a standard of measurement

UNITAGE *n* pl. -S amount in units

UNITARD *n* pl. -S a leotard that also covers the legs

UNITARY *adj* pertaining to a unit

UNITE *v* UNITED, UNITING, UNITES to bring together so as to form a whole **UNITEDLY** *adv*

UNITER *n* pl. -S one that unites

UNITIES pl. of unity

UNITING present participle of unite

UNITIVE *adj* serving to unite

UNITIZE *v* -IZED, -IZING, -IZES to divide into units

UNITIZER *n* pl. -S one that unitizes

UNITRUST *n* pl. -S a type of annuity trust

UNITY *n* pl. -TIES the state of being one single entity

UNIVALVE *n* pl. -S a mollusk having a single shell

UNIVERSE *n* pl. -S the totality of all existing things

UNIVOCAL *n* pl. -S a word having only one meaning

UNJOINT *v* -ED, -ING, -S to separate at a juncture

UNKEMPT *adj* untidy

UNKEND *adj* unkenned

UNKENNED *adj* not known or recognized

UNKENNEL *v* -NELED, -NELING, -NELS or -NELLED, -NELLING, -NELS to release from a kennel

UNKENT *adj* unkenned

UNKINK *v* -ED, -ING, -S to remove curls from

UNKNIT *v* -KNITTED, -KNITTING, -KNITS to unravel

UNKNOT *v* -KNOTTED, -KNOTTING, -KNOTS to undo a knot in

UNKNOWN *n* pl. -S one that is not known

UNLACE *v* -LACED, -LACING, -LACES to unfasten the laces of

UNLADE *v* -LADED, -LADEN, -LADING, -LADES to unload

UNLAID past tense of unlay

UNLASH *v* -ED, -ING, -ES to untie the lashing (a type of binding) of

UNLATCH *v* -ED, -ING, -ES to open by lifting the latch (a fastening device)

UNLAY *v* -LAID, -LAYING, -LAYS to untwist

UNLEAD *v* -ED, -ING, -S to remove the lead from

UNLEARN *v* -LEARNED or -LEARNT, -LEARNING, -LEARNS to put out of one's knowledge or memory

UNLEASH *v* -ED, -ING, -ES to free from a leash

UNLESS *conj* except on the condition that

UNLET *adj* not rented

UNLEVEL *v* -ELED, -ELING, -ELS or -ELLED, -ELLING, -ELS to make uneven

UNLIMBER *v* -ED, -ING, -S to prepare for action

UNLINK *v* -ED, -ING, -S to unfasten the links (connecting devices) of

UNLIVE *v* -LIVED, -LIVING, -LIVES to live so as to make amends for

UNLOAD *v* -ED, -ING, -S to remove the load or cargo from

UNLOADER *n* pl. -S one that unloads

UNLOCK *v* -ED, -ING, -S to unfasten the lock of

UNLOOSE *v* -LOOSED, -LOOSING, -LOOSES to set free

UNLOOSEN *v* -ED, -ING, -S to unloose

UNMAKE *v* -MADE, -MAKING, -MAKES to destroy

UNMAKER *n* pl. -S one that unmakes

UNMAN *v* -MANNED, -MANNING, -MANS to deprive of courage

UNMASK *v* -ED, -ING, -S to remove a mask from

UNMASKER *n* pl. -S one that unmasks

UNMEET *adj* improper **UNMEETLY** *adv*

UNMESH *v* -ED, -ING, -ES to disentangle

UNMEW *v* -ED, -ING, -S to set free

UNMINGLE *v* -GLED, -GLING, -GLES to separate things that are mixed

UNMITER *v* -ED, -ING, -S to depose from the rank of bishop

UNMITRE v -TRED, -TRING, -TRES to unmiter

UNMIX v -MIXED or -MIXT, -MIXING, -MIXES to separate from a mixture

UNMOLD v -ED, -ING, -S to remove from a mold

UNMOOR v -ED, -ING, -S to release from moorings

UNMORAL adj amoral

UNMUFFLE v -FLED, -FLING, -FLES to free from something that muffles

UNMUZZLE v -ZLED, -ZLING, -ZLES to remove a muzzle from

UNNAIL v -ED, -ING, -S to remove the nails from

UNNERVE v -NERVED, -NERVING, -NERVES to deprive of courage

UNPACK v -ED, -ING, -S to remove the contents of

UNPACKER n pl. -S one that unpacks

UNPAGED adj having no page numbers

UNPEG v -PEGGED, -PEGGING, -PEGS to remove the pegs from

UNPEN v -PENNED or -PENT, -PENNING, -PENS to release from confinement

UNPEOPLE v -PLED, -PLING, -PLES to remove people from

UNPERSON n pl. -S one who is removed completely from recognition

UNPICK v -ED, -ING, -S to remove the stitches from

UNPILE v -PILED, -PILING, -PILES to take or disentangle from a pile

UNPIN v -PINNED, -PINNING, -PINS to remove the pins from

UNPLAIT v -ED, -ING, -S to undo the plaits of

UNPLUG v -PLUGGED, -PLUGGING, -PLUGS to take a plug out of

UNPUCKER v -ED, -ING, -S to remove the wrinkles from

UNPUZZLE v -ZLED, -ZLING, -ZLES to work out the obscured meaning of

UNQUIET n pl. -S a state of unrest

UNQUOTE v -QUOTED, -QUOTING, -QUOTES to close a quotation

UNRAVEL v -ELED, -ELING, -ELS or -ELLED, -ELLING, -ELS to separate the threads of

UNREASON v -ED, -ING, -S to disrupt the sanity of

UNREEL v -ED, -ING, -S to unwind from a reel

UNREELER n pl. -S one that unreels

UNREEVE v -REEVED or -ROVE, -ROVEN, -REEVING, -REEVES to withdraw a rope from an opening

UNRENT adj not torn

UNREPAIR n pl. -S lack of repair

UNREST n pl. -S a disturbed or uneasy state

UNRIDDLE v -DLED, -DLING, -DLES to solve

UNRIG v -RIGGED, -RIGGING, -RIGS to divest of rigging

UNRIP v -RIPPED, -RIPPING, -RIPS to rip open

UNRIPE adj -RIPER, -RIPEST not ripe **UNRIPELY** adv

UNROBE v -ROBED, -ROBING, -ROBES to undress

UNROLL v -ED, -ING, -S to open something that is rolled up

UNROOF v -ED, -ING, -S to strip off the roof of

UNROOT v -ED, -ING, -S to uproot

UNROUND v -ED, -ING, -S to articulate without rounding the lips

UNROVE a past tense of unreeve

UNROVEN a past participle of unreeve

UNRULY adj -LIER, -LIEST difficult to control

UNSADDLE v -DLED, -DLING, -DLES to remove the saddle from

UNSAFETY n pl. -TIES lack of safety

UNSAY v -SAID, -SAYING, -SAYS to retract something said

UNSCREW v -ED, -ING, -S to remove the screws from

UNSEAL v -ED, -ING, -S to remove the seal of

UNSEAM v -ED, -ING, -S to open the seams of

UNSEAT v -ED, -ING, -S to remove from a seat

UNSET v -SET, -SETTING, -SETS to unsettle

UNSETTLE v -TLED, -TLING, -TLES to make unstable

UNSEW v -SEWED, -SEWN, -SEWING, -SEWS to undo the sewing of

UNSEX v -ED, -ING, -ES to deprive of sexual power

UNSHELL v -ED, -ING, -S to remove the shell from

UNSHIFT v -ED, -ING, -S to release the shift key on a typewriter

UNSHIP v -SHIPPED, -SHIPPING, -SHIPS to unload from a ship

UNSICKER adj unreliable

UNSIGHT v -ED, -ING, -S to prevent from seeing

UNSLING v -SLUNG, -SLINGING, -SLINGS to remove from a slung position

UNSNAP v -SNAPPED, -SNAPPING, -SNAPS to undo the snaps of

UNSNARL v -ED, -ING, -S to untangle

UNSOLDER v -ED, -ING, -S to separate

UNSONCY adj unsonsie

UNSONSIE adj unlucky

UNSONSY adj unsonsie

UNSPEAK v -SPOKE, -SPOKEN, -SPEAKING, -SPEAKS to unsay

UNSPHERE v -SPHERED, -SPHERING, -SPHERES to remove from a sphere

UNSTACK v -ED, -ING, -S to remove from a stack

UNSTATE v -STATED, -STATING, -STATES to deprive of status

UNSTAYED adj not secured with ropes or wires

UNSTEADY v -STEADIED, -STEADYING, -STEADIES to make unsteady

UNSTEEL v -ED, -ING, -S to make soft

UNSTEP v -STEPPED, -STEPPING, -STEPS to remove from a socket

UNSTICK v -STUCK, -STICKING, -STICKS to disjoin

UNSTITCH v -ED, -ING, -ES to remove the stitches from

UNSTOP v -STOPPED, -STOPPING, -STOPS to remove a stopper from

UNSTRAP v -STRAPPED, -STRAPPING, -STRAPS to remove a strap from

UNSTRESS n pl. -ES a syllable having relatively weak stress

UNSTRING v -STRUNG, -STRINGING, -STRINGS to remove from a string

UNSTUCK past tense of unstick

UNSWATHE v -SWATHED, -SWATHING, -SWATHES to unbind

UNSWEAR v -SWORE, -SWORN, -SWEARING, -SWEARS to retract something sworn

UNTACK v -ED, -ING, -S to remove a tack from

UNTANGLE v -GLED, -GLING, -GLES to free from tangles

UNTEACH v -TAUGHT, -TEACHING, -TEACHES to cause to unlearn something

UNTENTED adj not probed or attended to

UNTETHER v -ED, -ING, -S to free from a tether

UNTHINK v -THOUGHT, -THINKING, -THINKS to dismiss from the mind

UNTHREAD v -ED, -ING, -S to remove the thread from

UNTHRONE v -THRONED, -THRONING, -THRONES to remove from a throne

UNTIDY v -DIED, -DYING, -DIES to make untidy

UNTIE v -TIED, -TYING, -TIES to free from something that ties

UNTIL prep up to the time of

UNTO prep to

UNTOWARD adj unruly

UNTREAD v -TROD, -TRODDEN, -TREADING, -TREADS to retrace

UNTRIM v -TRIMMED, -TRIMMING, -TRIMS to strip of trimming

UNTRUSS v -ED, -ING, -ES to free from a truss

UNTRUTH n pl. -S something that is untrue

UNTUCK v -ED, -ING, -S to release from being tucked up

UNTUNE v -TUNED, -TUNING, -TUNES to put out of tune

UNTWINE v -TWINED, -TWINING, -TWINES to separate the twisted or tangled parts of

UNTWIST v -ED, -ING, -S to untwine

UNTYING present participle of untie

UNVEIL v -ED, -ING, -S to remove a covering from

UNVOICE v -VOICED, -VOICING, -VOICES to deprive of voice or vocal quality

UNWASHED n pl. -S an ignorant or underprivileged group

UNWEAVE v -WOVE, -WOVEN, -WEAVING, -WEAVES to undo something woven

UNWEIGHT v -ED, -ING, -S to reduce the weight of

UNWIND v -WOUND, -WINDING, -WINDS to reverse the winding of

UNWINDER n pl. -S one that unwinds

UNWISDOM n pl. -S lack of wisdom

UNWISH v -ED, -ING, -ES to cease to wish for

UNWIT v -WITTED, -WITTING, -WITS to make insane

UNWONTED adj unusual

UNWORTHY n pl. -THIES an unworthy person

UNWOUND past tense of unwind

UNWOVE past tense of unweave

UNWOVEN past participle of unweave

UNWRAP v -WRAPPED, -WRAPPING, -WRAPS to remove the wrapping from

UNYEANED adj unborn

UNYOKE v -YOKED, -YOKING, -YOKES to free from a yoke

UNZIP v -ZIPPED, -ZIPPING, -ZIPS to open the zipper of

UP v UPPED, UPPING, UPS to raise

UPAS n pl. -ES an Asian tree

UPBEAR v -BORE, -BORNE, -BEARING, -BEARS to raise aloft

UPBEARER n pl. -S one that upbears

UPBEAT n pl. -S an unaccented beat in a musical measure

UPBIND v -BOUND, -BINDING, -BINDS to bind completely

UPBOIL v -ED, -ING, -S to boil up

UPBORE past tense of upbear

UPBORNE past participle of upbear

UPBOUND past tense of upbind

UPBOW n pl. -S a type of stroke in playing a bowed instrument

UPBRAID v -ED, -ING, -S to reproach severely

UPBUILD v -BUILT, -BUILDING, -BUILDS to build up

UPBY adv upbye

UPBYE adv a little farther on

UPCAST v -CAST, -CASTING, -CASTS to cast up

UPCHUCK v -ED, -ING, -S to vomit

UPCLIMB v -ED, -ING, -S to climb up

UPCOAST adv up the coast

UPCOIL v -ED, -ING, -S to coil up

UPCOMING adj about to happen or appear

UPCURL v -ED, -ING, -S to curl up

UPCURVE v -CURVED, -CURVING, -CURVES to curve upward

UPDART v -ED, -ING, -S to dart up

UPDATE v -DATED, -DATING, -DATES to bring up to date

UPDATER n pl. -S one that updates

UPDIVE v -DIVED or -DOVE, -DIVING, -DIVES to spring upward

UPDO n pl. -DOS an upswept hairdo

UPDRAFT n pl. -S an upward movement of air

UPDRY v -DRIED, -DRYING, -DRIES to dry completely

UPEND v -ED, -ING, -S to set or stand on end

UPFIELD adv into the part of the field toward which the offensive team is going

UPFLING v -FLUNG, -FLINGING, -FLINGS to fling up

UPFLOW v -ED, -ING, -S to flow up

UPFOLD v -ED, -ING, -S to fold up

UPFRONT adj honest; candid

UPGATHER v -ED, -ING, -S to gather up

UPGAZE v -GAZED, -GAZING, -GAZES to gaze up

UPGIRD v -GIRDED or -GIRT, -GIRDING, -GIRDS to gird completely

UPGOING adj going up

UPGRADE v -GRADED, -GRADING, -GRADES to raise to a higher grade or standard

UPGROW v -GREW, -GROWN, -GROWING, -GROWS to grow up

UPGROWTH n pl. -S the process of growing up

UPHEAP v -ED, -ING, -S to heap up

UPHEAVAL n pl. -S the act of upheaving

UPHEAVE v -HEAVED or -HOVE, -HEAVING, -HEAVES to heave up

UPHEAVER n pl. -S one that upheaves

UPHELD past tense of uphold

UPHILL n pl. -S an upward slope

UPHOARD v -ED, -ING, -S to hoard up

UPHOLD v -HELD, -HOLDING, -HOLDS to hold aloft

UPHOLDER n pl. -S one that upholds

UPHOVE a past tense of upheave

UPHROE n pl. -S euphroe

UPKEEP n pl. -S the cost of maintaining something in good condition

UPLAND n pl. -S the higher land of a region

UPLANDER *n pl.* -S an inhabitant of an upland

UPLEAP *v* -LEAPED or -LEAPT, -LEAPING, -LEAPS to leap up

UPLIFT *v* -ED, -ING, -S to lift up

UPLIFTER *n pl.* -S one that uplifts

UPLIGHT *v* -LIGHTED or -LIT, -LIGHTING, -LIGHTS to light to a higher degree

UPLINK *n pl.* -S a communications channel to a spacecraft

UPLOAD *v* -ED, -ING, -S to transfer information from a small computer to a larger computer

UPMARKET *adj* upscale

UPMOST *adj* highest

UPO *prep* upon

UPON *prep* on

UPPED past tense of up

UPPER *n pl.* -S the part of a boot or shoe above the sole

UPPERCUT *v* -CUT, -CUTTING, -CUTS to strike an upward blow

UPPILE *v* -PILED, -PILING, -PILES to pile up

UPPING *n pl.* -S the process of marking young swans for identification purposes

UPPISH *adj* uppity UPPISHLY *adv*

UPPITY *adj* tending to be snobbish and arrogant

UPPROP *v* -PROPPED, -PROPPING, -PROPS to prop up

UPRAISE *v* -RAISED, -RAISING, -RAISES to raise up

UPRAISER *n pl.* -S one that upraises

UPRATE *v* -RATED, -RATING, -RATES to improve the power output of an engine

UPREACH *v* -ED, -ING, -ES to reach up

UPREAR *v* -ED, -ING, -S to upraise

UPRIGHT *v* -ED, -ING, -S to make vertical

UPRISE *v* -ROSE, -RISEN, -RISING, -RISES to rise up

UPRISER *n pl.* -S one that uprises

UPRISING *n pl.* -S a revolt

UPRIVER *n pl.* -S an area lying toward the source of a river

UPROAR *n pl.* -S a state of noisy excitement and confusion

UPROOT *v* -ED, -ING, -S to pull up by the roots

UPROOTAL *n pl.* -S the act of uprooting

UPROOTER *n pl.* -S one that uproots

UPROSE past tense of uprise

UPROUSE *v* -ROUSED, -ROUSING, -ROUSES to rouse up

UPRUSH *v* -ED, -ING, -ES to rush up

UPSCALE *v* -SCALLED, -SCALING, -SCALES to make appealing to affluent consumers

UPSEND *v* -SENT, -SENDING, -SENDS to send upward

UPSET *v* -SET, -SETTING, -SETS to overturn

UPSETTER *n pl.* -S one that upsets

UPSHIFT *v* -ED, -ING, -S to shift an automotive vehicle into a higher gear

UPSHOOT *v* -SHOT, -SHOOTING, -SHOOTS to shoot upward

UPSHOT *n pl.* -S the final result

UPSIDE *n pl.* -S a positive aspect

UPSILON *n pl.* -S a Greek letter

UPSOAR *v* -ED, -ING, -S to soar upward

UPSPRING *v* -SPRANG or -SPRUNG, -SPRINGING, -SPRINGS to spring up

UPSTAGE *v* -STAGED, -STAGING, -STAGES to outdo theatrically

UPSTAIR *adj* pertaining to an upper floor

UPSTAIRS *adv* up the stairs

UPSTAND *v* -STOOD, -STANDING, -STANDS to stand up on one's feet

UPSTARE *v* -STARED, -STARING, -STARES to stare upward

UPSTART *v* -ED, -ING, -S to spring up suddenly

UPSTATE *n pl.* -S the northern region of a state

UPSTATER *n pl.* -S an inhabitant of an upstate region

UPSTEP *v* -STEPPED, -STEPPING, -STEPS to step up

UPSTIR *v* -STIRRED, -STIRRING, -STIRS to stir up

UPSTOOD past tense of upstand

UPSTREAM *adv* toward the source of a stream

UPSTROKE *n pl.* -S an upward stroke

UPSURGE *v* -SURGED, -SURGING, -SURGES to surge up

UPSWEEP *v* -SWEPT, -SWEEPING, -SWEEPS to sweep upward

UPSWELL *v* -SWELLED, -SWOLLEN, -SWELLING, -SWELLS to swell up

UPSWING *v* -SWUNG, -SWINGING, -SWINGS to swing upward

UPTAKE *n* pl. -S an upward ventilating shaft

UPTEAR *v* -TORE, -TORN, -TEARING, -TEARS to tear out by the roots

UPTHROW *v* -THREW, -THROWN, -THROWING, -THROWS to throw upward

UPTHRUST *v* -THRUST, -THRUSTING, -THRUSTS to thrust up

UPTICK *n* pl. -S an increase or rise

UPTIGHT *adj* nervous

UPTILT *v* -ED, -ING, -S to tilt upward

UPTIME *n* pl. -S the time during which machinery is functioning

UPTORE past tense of uptear

UPTORN past participle of uptear

UPTOSS *v* -ED, -ING, -ES to toss upward

UPTOWN *n* pl. -S the upper part of a city

UPTOWNER *n* pl. -S one that lives uptown

UPTREND *n* pl. -S a tendency upward or toward growth

UPTURN *v* -ED, -ING, -S to turn up or over

UPWAFT *v* -ED, -ING, -S to waft upward

UPWARD *adv* toward a higher place or position **UPWARDLY** *adv*

UPWARDS *adv* upward

UPWELL *v* -ED, -ING, -S to well up

UPWIND *n* pl. -S a wind that blows against one's course

URACIL *n* pl. -S a chemical compound

URAEMIA *n* pl. -S uremia **URAEMIC** *adj*

URAEUS *n* pl. URAEI or URAEUSES the figure of the sacred serpent on the headdress of ancient Egyptian rulers

URALITE *n* pl. -S a mineral **URALITIC** *adj*

URANIA *n* pl. -S uranium dioxide

URANIC *adj* pertaining to uranium

URANIDE *n* pl. -S uranium

URANISM *n* pl. -S homosexuality

URANITE *n* pl. -S a mineral **URANITIC** *adj*

URANIUM *n* pl. -S a radioactive element

URANOUS *adj* pertaining to uranium

URANYL *n* pl. -S a bivalent radical **URANYLIC** *adj*

URARE *n* pl. -S curare

URARI *n* pl. -S curare

URASE *n* pl. -S urease

URATE *n* pl. -S a chemical salt **URATIC** *adj*

URB *n* pl. -S an urban area

URBAN *adj* pertaining to a city

URBANE *adj* -BANER, -BANEST refined and elegant **URBANELY** *adv*

URBANISE *v* -ISED, -ISING, -ISES to urbanize

URBANISM *n* pl. -S the lifestyle of city dwellers

URBANIST *n* pl. -S a specialist in city planning

URBANITE *n* pl. -S one who lives in a city

URBANITY *n* pl. -TIES the quality of being urbane

URBANIZE *v* -IZED, -IZING, -IZES to cause to take on urban characteristics

URBIA *n* pl. -S cities collectively

URCHIN *n* pl. -S a mischievous boy

URD *n* pl. -S an annual bean grown in India

UREA *n* pl. -S a chemical compound **UREAL** *adj*

UREASE *n* pl. -S an enzyme

UREDIA pl. of uredium

UREDIAL *adj* pertaining to a uredium

UREDINIA *n/pl* uredia

UREDIUM *n* pl. -DIA a spore-producing organ of certain fungi

UREDO *n* pl. -DOS a skin irritation

UREIC *adj* pertaining to urea

UREIDE *n* pl. -S a chemical compound

UREMIA *n* pl. -S an abnormal condition of the blood **UREMIC** *adj*

URETER *n* pl. -S the duct that conveys urine from the kidney to the bladder **URETERAL, URETERIC** *adj*

URETHAN *n* pl. -S urethane

URETHANE *n* pl. -S a chemical compound

URETHRA *n* pl. -THRAE or -THRAS the duct through which urine is discharged from the bladder **URETHRAL** *adj*

URETIC *adj* pertaining to urine

URGE *v* URGED, URGING, URGES to force forward

URGENCY *n* pl. -CIES the quality of being urgent

URGENT *adj* requiring immediate attention **URGENTLY** *adv*

URGER *n* pl. -S one that urges

URGING present participle of urge

URGINGLY *adv* in an urging manner

URIAL *n* pl. -S a wild Asian sheep

URIC *adj* pertaining to urine

URIDINE *n* pl. -S a chemical compound

URINAL *n* pl. -S a fixture used for urinating

URINARY *n* pl. -NARIES a urinal

URINATE *v* -NATED, -NATING, -NATES to discharge urine

URINE *n* pl. -S a liquid containing body wastes

URINEMIA *n* pl. -S uremia **URINEMIC** *adj*

URINOSE *adj* pertaining to urine

URINOUS *adj* pertaining to urine

URN *n* pl. -S a type of vase **URNLIKE** *adj*

UROCHORD *n* pl. -S a rodlike structure in certain lower vertebrates

URODELE *n* pl. -S a type of amphibian

UROLITH *n* pl. -S a concretion in the urinary tract

UROLOGY *n* pl. -GIES the branch of medicine dealing with the urinary tract **UROLOGIC** *adj*

UROPOD *n* pl. -S an abdominal limb of an arthropod **UROPODAL** *adj*

UROPYGIA *n/pl* the humps from which birds' tail feathers grow

UROSCOPY *n* pl. -PIES analysis of the urine as a means of diagnosis

UROSTYLE *n* pl. -S a part of the vertebral column of frogs and toads

URSA *n* pl. -SAE a female bear

URSIFORM *adj* having the form of a bear

URSINE *adj* pertaining to a bear

URTEXT *n* pl. -S the original text

URTICANT *n* pl. -S an urticating substance

URTICATE *v* -CATED, -CATING, -CATES to cause itching or stinging

URUS *n* pl. -ES an extinct European ox

URUSHIOL *n* pl. -S a toxic liquid

US *pron* the objective case of the pronoun we

USABLE *adj* capable of being used **USABLY** *adv*

USAGE *n* pl. -S a firmly established and generally accepted practice or procedure

USANCE *n* pl. -S usage

USAUNCE *n* pl. -S usance

USE *v* USED, USING, USES to put into service

USEABLE *adj* usable **USEABLY** *adv*

USEFUL *adj* serving a purpose **USEFULLY** *adv*

USELESS *adj* serving no purpose

USER *n* pl. -S one that uses

USHER *v* -ED, -ING, -S to conduct to a place

USING present participle of use

USNEA *n* pl. -S any of a genus of lichens

USQUABAE *n* pl. -S usquebae

USQUE *n* pl. -S usquebae

USQUEBAE *n* pl. -S whiskey

USTULATE *adj* scorched

USUAL *n* pl. -S something that is usual (ordinary)

USUALLY *adv* ordinarily

USUFRUCT *n* pl. -S the legal right to use another's property so long as it is not damaged or altered

USURER *n* pl. -S one that practices usury

USURIES pl. of usury

USURIOUS *adj* practicing usury

USURP *v* -ED, -ING, -S to seize and hold without legal authority

USURPER *n* pl. -S one that usurps

USURY *n* pl. -RIES the lending of money at an exorbitant interest rate

UT *n* pl. -S the musical tone C in the French solmization system now replaced by do

UTA *n* pl. -S any of a genus of large lizards

UTENSIL *n* pl. -S a useful implement

UTERUS *n* pl. UTERI or UTERUSES an organ of female mammals **UTERINE** *adj*

UTILE *adj* useful

UTILIDOR *n* pl. -S an insulated system of pipes for use in arctic regions

UTILISE *v* -LISED, -LISING, -LISES to utilize

UTILISER *n* pl. -S utilizer

UTILITY *n* pl. -TIES the quality of being useful

UTILIZE *v* -LIZED, -LIZING, -LIZES to make use of

UTILIZER *n* pl. -S one that utilizes

UTMOST *n* pl. -S the greatest degree or amount

UTOPIA *n* pl. -S a place of ideal perfection

UTOPIAN *n* pl. -S one who believes in the perfectibility of human society

UTOPISM *n* pl. -S the body of ideals or principles of a utopian

UTOPIST *n* pl. -S a utopian

UTRICLE *n* pl. -S a saclike cavity in the inner ear

UTRICULI *n/pl* utricles

UTTER *v* -ED, -ING, -S to give audible expression to

UTTERER *n* pl. -S one that utters

UTTERLY *adv* totally

UVEA *n* pl. -S a layer of the eye **UVEAL** *adj*

UVEITIS *n* pl. -ITISES inflammation of the uvea **UVEITIC** *adj*

UVEOUS *adj* pertaining to the uvea

UVULA *n* pl. -LAE or -LAS the pendent, fleshy portion of the soft palate

UVULAR *n* pl. -S a uvularly produced sound

UVULARLY *adv* with the use of the uvula

UVULITIS *n* pl. -TISES inflammation of the uvula

UXORIAL *adj* pertaining to a wife

UXORIOUS *adj* excessively submissive or devoted to one's wife

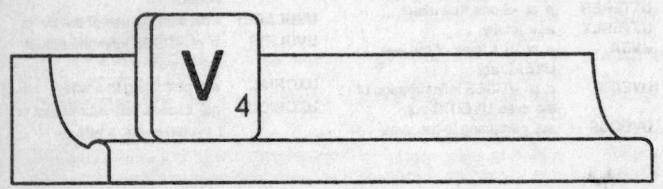

VAC *n pl.* -S a vacuum cleaner

VACANCY *n pl.* -CIES the quality or state of being vacant

VACANT *adj* empty **VACANTLY** *adv*

VACATE *v* -CATED, -CATING, -CATES to make vacant

VACATION *v* -ED, -ING, -S to take a vacation (a period of time devoted to rest and relaxation)

VACCINA *n pl.* -S vaccinia

VACCINE *n pl.* -S a preparation given to produce immunity to a specific disease **VACCINAL** *adj*

VACCINEE *n pl.* -S one that is vaccinated

VACCINIA *n pl.* -S cowpox

VACUA a *pl.* of vacuum

VACUITY *n pl.* -ITIES an empty space

VACUOLE *n pl.* -S a small cavity in organic tissue **VACUOLAR** *adj*

VACUOUS *adj* empty

VACUUM *n pl.* VACUUMS or VACUA a space entirely devoid of matter

VACUUM *v* -ED, -ING, -S to use a device that cleans by suction

VADOSE *adj* located above the permanent groundwater level

VAGABOND *v* -ED, -ING, -S to live like a vagabond (a vagrant)

VAGAL *adj* pertaining to the vagus nerve **VAGALLY** *adv*

VAGARY *n pl.* -RIES a whim

VAGI *pl.* of vagus

VAGILE *adj* free to move about

VAGILITY *n pl.* -TIES freedom of movement

VAGINA *n pl.* -NAE or -NAS the passage leading from the uterus to the vulva **VAGINAL** *adj*

VAGINATE *adj* enclosed in a sheath

VAGOTOMY *n pl.* -MIES surgical division of the vagus nerve

VAGRANCY *n pl.* -CIES the state of being a vagrant

VAGRANT *n pl.* -S a wanderer with no apparent means of support

VAGROM *adj* wandering

VAGUE *adj* VAGUER, VAGUEST not clearly expressed or understood **VAGUELY** *adv*

VAGUS *n pl.* -GI a cranial nerve

VAHINE *n pl.* -S wahine

VAIL *v* -ED, -ING, -S to lower

VAIN *adj* VAINER, VAINEST filled with undue admiration for oneself **VAINLY** *adv*

VAINNESS *n pl.* -ES the quality or state of being vain

VAIR *n pl.* -S a fur used for lining and trimming medieval garments

VAKEEL *n pl.* -S a native lawyer in India

VAKIL *n pl.* -S vakeel

VALANCE *v* -LANCED, -LANCING, -LANCES to furnish with a short drapery

VALE *n pl.* -S a valley

VALENCE *n pl.* -S the degree of combining power of an element or radical

VALENCIA *n pl.* -S a woven fabric

VALENCY *n pl.* -CIES valence

VALERATE *n pl.* -S a chemical salt

VALERIAN *n pl.* -S a perennial herb **VALERIC** *adj*

VALET *v* -ED, -ING, -S to act as a personal servant to

VALGUS *n* pl. -ES the position of a joint that is abnormally turned outward **VALGOID** *adj*

VALIANCE *n* pl. -S valor

VALIANCY *n* pl. -CIES valor

VALIANT *n* pl. -S a courageous person

VALID *adj* based on evidence that can be supported

VALIDATE *v* -DATED, -DATING, -DATES to give legal force to

VALIDITY *n* pl. -TIES the quality or state of being valid

VALIDLY *adv* in a valid manner

VALINE *n* pl. -S an amino acid

VALISE *n* pl. -S a small piece of hand luggage

VALKYR *n* pl. -S valkyrie

VALKYRIE *n* pl. -S a maiden in Norse mythology

VALLATE *adj* bordered by a raised edge

VALLEY *n* pl. -LEYS a depression of the earth's surface

VALONIA *n* pl. -S a substance obtained from dried acorn cups and used in tanning and dyeing

VALOR *n* pl. -S courage

VALORISE *v* -ISED, -ISING, -ISES to valorize

VALORIZE *v* -IZED, -IZING, -IZES to establish and maintain the price of by governmental action

VALOROUS *adj* courageous

VALOUR *n* pl. -S valor

VALSE *n* pl. -S a concert waltz

VALUABLE *n* pl. -S a possession of value

VALUABLY *adv* with value

VALUATE *v* -ATED, -ATING, -ATES to appraise

VALUATOR *n* pl. -S one that valuates

VALUE *v* -UED, -UING, -UES to estimate the value (the quality that renders a thing useful or desirable) of

VALUER *n* pl. -S one who values

VALUTA *n* pl. -S the agreed or exchange value of a currency

VALVAL *adj* resembling or pertaining to a valve

VALVAR *adj* valval

VALVATE *adj* having valves or parts resembling valves

VALVE *v* VALVED, VALVING, VALVES to provide with a valve (a device for controlling the flow of a liquid or gas)

VALVELET *n* pl. -S a small valve

VALVULA *n* pl. -LAE valvule

VALVULAR *adj* pertaining to a valve

VALVULE *n* pl. -S a small valve

VAMBRACE *n* pl. -S a piece of armor for the forearm

VAMOOSE *v* -MOOSED, -MOOSING, -MOOSES to leave quickly

VAMOSE *v* -MOSED, -MOSING, -MOSES to vamoose

VAMP *v* -ED, -ING, -S to repair or patch

VAMPER *n* pl. -S one that vamps

VAMPIRE *n* pl. -S a reanimated corpse believed to feed on sleeping persons' blood **VAMPIRIC** *adj*

VAMPISH *adj* seductive

VAN *v* VANNED, VANNING, VANS to transport in a van (a type of motor vehicle)

VANADATE *n* pl. -S a chemical salt

VANADIUM *n* pl. -S a metallic element **VANADIC, VANADOUS** *adj*

VANDA *n* pl. -S a tropical orchid

VANDAL *n* pl. -S one who willfully destroys or defaces property **VANDALIC** *adj*

VANDYKE *n* pl. -S a short, pointed beard **VANDYKED** *adj*

VANE *n* pl. -S a device for showing the direction of the wind **VANED** *adj*

VANG *n* pl. -S a rope on a ship

VANGUARD *n* pl. -S the forefront of a movement

VANILLA *n* pl. -S a flavoring extract **VANILLIC** *adj*

VANILLIN *n* pl. -S a chemical compound used in flavoring

VANISH *v* -ED, -ING, -ES to disappear

VANISHER *n* pl. -S one that vanishes

VANITORY *n* pl. -RIES a combined dressing table and basin

VANITY *n* pl. -TIES inflated pride in oneself **VANITIED** *adj*

VANMAN *n* pl. -MEN a person who drives a van

VANNED past tense of van

VANNER *n* pl. -S a person who owns a van

VANNING present participle of van

VANPOOL *n* pl. -S an arrangement whereby several commuters travel in one van

VANQUISH *v* -ED, -ING, -ES to defeat in battle

VANTAGE n pl. -S superiority over a competitor

VANWARD adv toward the front

VAPID adj insipid VAPIDLY adv

VAPIDITY n pl. -TIES the quality or state of being vapid

VAPOR v -ED, -ING, -S to emit vapor (visible floating moisture)

VAPORER n pl. -S one that vapors

VAPORING n pl. -S boastful talk

VAPORISE v -ISED, -ISING, -ISES to vaporize

VAPORISH adj resembling vapor

VAPORIZE v -IZED, -IZING, -IZES to convert into vapor

VAPOROUS adj vaporish

VAPORY adj vaporish

VAPOUR v -ED, -ING, -S to vapor

VAPOURER n pl. -S vaporer

VAPOURY adj vapory

VAQUERO n pl. -ROS a cowboy

VAR n pl. -S a unit of reactive power

VARA n pl. -S a Spanish unit of length

VARACTOR n pl. -S a capacitor with variable capacitance

VARIA n/pl a collection of various literary works

VARIABLE n pl. -S something that varies

VARIABLY adv in a varying manner

VARIANCE n pl. -S a license to perform an act contrary to the usual rule

VARIANT n pl. -S a variable

VARIATE v -ATED, -ATING, -ATES to vary

VARICES pl. of varix

VARICOSE adj abnormally swollen or dilated

VARIED past tense of vary

VARIEDLY adv in a varied manner

VARIER n pl. -S one that varies

VARIES present 3d person sing. of vary

VARIETAL n pl. -S a wine designated by the variety of grape

VARIETY n pl. -ETIES something differing from others of the same general kind

VARIFORM adj having various forms

VARIOLA n pl. -S smallpox VARIOLAR adj

VARIOLE n pl. -S a foveola

VARIORUM n pl. -S an edition containing various versions of a text

VARIOUS adj of diverse kinds

VARISTOR n pl. -S a type of electrical resistor

VARIX n pl. VARICES a varicose vein

VARLET n pl. -S a knave

VARLETRY n pl. -RIES a group of common people

VARMENT n pl. -S varmint

VARMINT n pl. -S an animal considered to be a pest

VARNA n pl. -S any of the four main Hindu social classes

VARNISH v -ED, -ING, -ES to give a glossy appearance to

VARNISHY adj glossy

VAROOM v -ED, -ING, -S to vroom

VARSITY n pl. -TIES the principal team representing a university, college, or school in any activity

VARUS n pl. -ES a malformation of a bone or joint

VARVE n pl. -S a deposit of sedimentary material VARVED adj

VARY v VARIED, VARYING, VARIES to become or make different

VAS n pl. VASA an anatomical duct VASAL adj

VASCULAR adj pertaining to ducts that convey body fluids

VASCULUM n pl. -LA or -LUMS a box used to hold plant specimens

VASE n pl. -S a rounded, decorative container VASELIKE adj

VASIFORM adj having the form of a vase

VASOTOMY n pl. -MIES a surgical cutting of the vas deferens

VASSAL n pl. -S a person granted the use of land by a feudal lord in return for homage and allegiance

VAST adj VASTER, VASTEST of great extent or size

VAST n pl. -S a vast space

VASTIER comparative of vasty

VASTIEST superlative of vasty

VASTITY n pl. -TIES vastness

VASTLY adv to a vast extent or degree

VASTNESS n pl. -ES the quality or state of being vast

VASTY adj VASTIER, VASTIEST vast

VAT v VATTED, VATTING, VATS to put into a vat (a large container for holding liquids)

VATFUL   n pl. -S as much as a vat can hold

VATIC   adj pertaining to a prophet

VATICAL   adj vatic

VATICIDE   n pl. -S the killing of a prophet

VATTED   past tense of vat

VATTING   present participle of vat

VATU   n pl. -S a monetary unit of Vanuatu

VAU   n pl. -S vav

VAULT   v -ED, -ING, -S to provide with a vault (an arched ceiling)

VAULTER   n pl. -S one that leaps

VAULTING   n pl. -S the structure forming a vault

VAULTY   adj VAULTIER, VAULTIEST resembling a vault

VAUNT   v -ED, -ING, -S to brag

VAUNTER   n pl. -S one that vaunts

VAUNTFUL   adj boastful

VAUNTIE   adj boastful

VAUNTY   adj vauntie

VAV   n pl. -S a Hebrew letter

VAVASOR   n pl. -S a high-ranking vassal

VAVASOUR   n pl. -S vavasor

VAVASSOR   n pl. -S vavasor

VAW   n pl. -S vav

VAWARD   n pl. -S the foremost part

VAWNTIE   adj vaunty

VEAL   v -ED, -ING, -S to kill and prepare a calf for food

VEALER   n pl. -S a calf raised for food

VEALY   adj VEALIER, VEALIEST immature

VECTOR   v -ED, -ING, -S to guide in flight by means of radioed directions

VEDALIA   n pl. -S an Australian ladybug

VEDETTE   n pl. -S a small boat used for scouting

VEE   n pl. -S the letter V

VEEJAY   n pl. -JAYS an announcer on a program of music videos

VEENA   n pl. -S vina

VEEP   n pl. -S a vice president

VEEPEE   n pl. -S veep

VEER   v -ED, -ING, -S to change direction

VEERY   n pl. -RIES a songbird

VEG   n pl. VEG a vegetable

VEGAN   n pl. -S one that eats only plant products

VEGANISM   n pl. -S the practice of eating only plant products

VEGETAL   adj pertaining to plants

VEGETANT   adj characteristic of plant life

VEGETATE   v -TATED, -TATING, -TATES to grow in the manner of a plant

VEGETE   adj healthy

VEGETIST   n pl. -S one that eats only plant products

VEGETIVE   adj growing or capable of growing

VEGGIE   n pl. -S a vegetable

VEGIE   n pl. -S veggie

VEHEMENT   adj ardent

VEHICLE   n pl. -S a device used as a means of conveyance

VEIL   v -ED, -ING, -S to provide with a veil (a piece of sheer fabric worn over the face)

VEILEDLY   adv in a disguised manner

VEILER   n pl. -S one that veils

VEILING   n pl. -S a veil

VEILLIKE   adj resembling a veil

VEIN   v -ED, -ING, -S to fill with veins (tubular blood vessels)

VEINAL   adj of or pertaining to the veins

VEINER   n pl. -S a tool used in wood carving

VEINIER   comparative of veiny

VEINIEST   superlative of veiny

VEINING   n pl. -S a network of veins

VEINLESS   adj having no veins

VEINLET   n pl. -S a small vein

VEINLIKE   adj resembling a vein

VEINULE   n pl. -S venule

VEINULET   n pl. -S venule

VEINY   adj VEINIER, VEINIEST full of veins

VELA   pl. of velum

VELAMEN   n pl. -MINA a velum

VELAR   n pl. -S a kind of speech sound

VELARIUM   n pl. -IA an awning over an ancient Roman theater

VELARIZE   v -IZED, -IZING, -IZES to pronounce with the back of the tongue touching the soft palate

VELATE   adj having a velum

VELD   n pl. -S veldt

VELDT   n pl. -S a grassland of southern Africa

VELIGER   n pl. -S a larval stage of certain mollusks

VELITES   n/pl foot soldiers of ancient Rome

VELLEITY   n pl. -ITIES a very low degree of desire

VELLUM   n pl. -S a fine parchment

VELOCE adv rapidly — used as a musical direction

VELOCITY n pl. -TIES rapidity of motion

VELOUR n pl. -S a fabric resembling velvet

VELOUTE n pl. -S a type of sauce

VELUM n pl. -LA a thin membranous covering or partition

VELURE v -LURED, -LURING, -LURES to smooth with a velvet or silk pad, as a hat

VELVERET n pl. -S a fabric resembling velvet

VELVET n pl. -S a soft, smooth fabric **VELVETED, VELVETY** adj

VENA n pl. -NAE a vein

VENAL adj open to bribery **VENALLY** adv

VENALITY n pl. -TIES the quality or state of being venal

VENATIC adj pertaining to hunting

VENATION n pl. -S an arrangement of veins

VEND v -ED, -ING, -S to sell **VENDABLE** adj

VENDACE n pl. -S a European fish

VENDEE n pl. -S a buyer

VENDER n pl. -S vendor

VENDETTA n pl. -S a feud between two families

VENDEUSE n pl. -S a saleswoman

VENDIBLE n pl. -S a salable article

VENDIBLY adv salably

VENDOR n pl. -S a seller

VENDUE n pl. -S a public sale

VENEER v -ED, -ING, -S to overlay with thin layers of material

VENEERER n pl. -S one that veneers

VENENATE v -NATED, -NATING, -NATES to poison

VENENOSE adj poisonous

VENERATE v -ATED, -ATING, -ATES to revere

VENEREAL adj involving the genital organs

VENERY n pl. -ERIES sexual intercourse

VENETIAN n pl. -S a flexible window screen

VENGE v VENGED, VENGING, VENGES to avenge

VENGEFUL adj seeking to avenge

VENIAL adj easily excused or forgiven **VENIALLY** adv

VENIN n pl. -S a toxin found in snake venom

VENINE n pl. -S venin

VENIRE n pl. -S a type of judicial writ

VENISON n pl. -S the edible flesh of a deer

VENOGRAM n pl. -S a roentgenogram of a vein

VENOM v -ED, -ING, -S to inject with venom (a poisonous secretion of certain animals)

VENOMER n pl. -S one that venoms

VENOMOUS adj poisonous

VENOSE adj venous

VENOSITY n pl. -TIES the quality or state of being venous

VENOUS adj full of veins **VENOUSLY** adv

VENT v -ED, -ING, -S to provide with a vent (an opening for the escape of gas or liquid)

VENTAGE n pl. -S a small opening

VENTAIL n pl. -S the adjustable front of a medieval helmet

VENTER n pl. -S the abdomen

VENTLESS adj having no vent

VENTRAL n pl. -S a fin located on the underside of a fish

VENTURE v -TURED, -TURING, -TURES to risk

VENTURER n pl. -S one that ventures

VENTURI n pl. -S a device for measuring the flow of a fluid

VENTURING present participle of venture

VENUE n pl. -S the locale of an event

VENULE n pl. -S a small vein **VENULAR, VENULOSE, VENULOUS** adj

VERA adj very

VERACITY n pl. -TIES conformity to truth

VERANDA n pl. -S a type of porch

VERANDAH n pl. -S veranda

VERATRIA n pl. -S veratrin

VERATRIN n pl. -S a poisonous mixture of alkaloids

VERATRUM n pl. -S a poisonous herb

VERB n pl. -S a word used to express an act, occurrence, or mode of being

VERBAL n pl. -S a word derived from a verb

VERBALLY adv in a spoken manner

VERBATIM adv word for word

VERBENA n pl. -S a flowering plant

VERBIAGE n pl. -S an excess of words

VERBID n pl. -S a verbal

VERBIFY v -FIED, -FYING, -FIES to use as a verb

VERBILE *n pl.* -S one whose mental imagery consists of words

VERBLESS *adj* lacking a verb

VERBOSE *adj* wordy

VERBOTEN *adj* forbidden

VERDANCY *n pl.* -CIES the quality or state of being verdant

VERDANT *adj* green with vegetation

VERDERER *n pl.* -S an officer in charge of the royal forests of England

VERDEROR *n pl.* -S verderer

VERDICT *n pl.* -S the decision of a jury at the end of a legal proceeding

VERDIN *n pl.* -S a small bird

VERDITER *n pl.* -S a blue or green pigment

VERDURE *n pl.* -S green vegetation
VERDURED *adj*

VERECUND *adj* shy

VERGE *v* VERGED, VERGING, VERGES to come near

VERGENCE *n pl.* -S a movement of one eye in relation to the other

VERGER *n pl.* -S a church official

VERGING present participle of verge

VERGLAS *n pl.* -ES a thin coating of ice on rock

VERIDIC *adj* truthful

VERIER comparative of very

VERIEST superlative of very

VERIFIER *n pl.* -S one that verifies

VERIFY *v* -FIED, -FYING, -FIES to prove to be true

VERILY *adv* in truth

VERISM *n pl.* -S realism in art or literature

VERISMO *n pl.* -MOS verism

VERIST *n pl.* -S one who practices verism **VERISTIC** *adj*

VERITAS *n pl.* -TATES truth

VERITE *n pl.* -S the technique of filming so as to convey candid realism

VERITY *n pl.* -TIES truth

VERJUICE *n pl.* -S the juice of sour or unripe fruit

VERMEIL *n pl.* -S a red color

VERMES *pl.* of vermis

VERMIAN *adj* pertaining to worms

VERMIN *n pl.* VERMIN small, common, harmful, or objectionable animals

VERMIS *n pl.* -MES a part of the brain

VERMOULU *adj* eaten by worms

VERMOUTH *n pl.* -S a liqueur

VERMUTH *n pl.* -S vermouth

VERNACLE *n pl.* -S vernicle

VERNAL *adj* pertaining to spring
VERNALLY *adv*

VERNICLE *n pl.* -S veronica

VERNIER *n pl.* -S an auxiliary scale used with a main scale to obtain fine measurements

VERNIX *n pl.* -ES a fatty substance covering the skin of a fetus

VERONICA *n pl.* -S a handkerchief bearing the image of Christ's face

VERRUCA *n pl.* -CAE a wart

VERSAL *adj* entire

VERSANT *n pl.* -S the slope of a mountain or mountain chain

VERSE *v* VERSED, VERSING, VERSES to versify

VERSEMAN *n pl.* -MEN one who versifies

VERSER *n pl.* -S a verseman

VERSET *n pl.* -S a versicle

VERSICLE *n pl.* -S a short line of metrical writing

VERSIFY *v* -FIED, -FYING, -FIES to change from prose into metrical form

VERSINE *n pl.* -S a trigonometric function of an angle

VERSING present participle of verse

VERSION *n pl.* -S an account or description from a particular point of view

VERSO *n pl.* -SOS a left-hand page of a book

VERST *n pl.* -S a Russian measure of distance

VERSTE *n pl.* -S verst

VERSUS *prep* against

VERT *n pl.* -S the heraldic color green

VERTEBRA *n pl.* -BRAE or -BRAS any of the bones or segments forming the spinal column

VERTEX *n pl.* -TEXES or -TICES the highest point of something

VERTICAL *n pl.* -S something that is vertical (extending up and down)

VERTICIL *n pl.* -S a circular arrangement, as of flowers or leaves, about a point on an axis

VERTIGO n pl. -GOES, -GOS, or -GINES a disordered state in which the individual or his surroundings seem to whirl dizzily

VERTU n pl. -S virtu

VERVAIN n pl. -S a flowering plant

VERVE n pl. -S vivacity

VERVET n pl. -S an African monkey

VERY adj VERIER, VERIEST absolute

VESICA n pl. -CAE a bladder **VESICAL** adj

VESICANT n pl. -S a chemical warfare agent that induces blistering

VESICATE v -CATED, -CATING, -CATES to blister

VESICLE n pl. -S a small bladder

VESICULA n pl. -LAE a vesicle

VESPER n pl. -S an evening service, prayer, or song

VESPERAL n pl. -S a covering for an altar cloth

VESPIARY n pl. -ARIES a nest of wasps

VESPID n pl. -S a wasp

VESPINE adj pertaining to wasps

VESSEL n pl. -S a craft for traveling on water **VESSELED** adj

VEST v -ED, -ING, -S to place in the control of

VESTA n pl. -S a short friction match

VESTAL n pl. -S a chaste woman

VESTALLY adv chastely

VESTEE n pl. -S a garment worn under a woman's jacket or blouse

VESTIARY n pl. -ARIES a dressing room

VESTIGE n pl. -S a visible sign of something that is no longer in existence

VESTIGIA n/pl vestiges

VESTING n pl. -S the right of an employee to share in and withdraw from a pension fund without penalty

VESTLESS adj being without a vest

VESTLIKE adj resembling a vest (a short, sleeveless garment)

VESTMENT n pl. -S one of the ceremonial garments of the clergy

VESTRY n pl. -TRIES a room in which vestments are kept **VESTRAL** adj

VESTURAL adj pertaining to clothing

VESTURE v -TURED, -TURING, -TURES to clothe

VESUVIAN n pl. -S a mineral

VET v VETTED, VETTING, VETS to treat animals medically

VETCH n pl. -ES a climbing plant

VETERAN n pl. -S a former member of the armed forces

VETIVER n pl. -S an Asian grass

VETIVERT n pl. -S the essential oil of the vetiver

VETO v -ED, -ING, -ES to forbid or prevent authoritatively

VETOER n pl. -S one that vetoes

VETTED past tense of vet

VETTING present participle of vet

VEX v VEXED or VEXT, VEXING, VEXES to annoy

VEXATION n pl. -S a cause of trouble

VEXEDLY adv in a vexed manner

VEXER n pl. -S one that vexes

VEXIL n pl. -S vexillum

VEXILLUM n pl. -LA the web or vane of a feather **VEXILLAR** adj

VEXINGLY adv in a vexing manner

VEXT a past tense of vex

VIA prep by way of

VIABLE adj capable of living **VIABLY** adv

VIADUCT n pl. -S a type of bridge

VIAL v VIALED, VIALING, VIALS or VIALLED, VIALLING, VIALS to put in a vial (a small container for liquids)

VIAND n pl. -S an article of food

VIATIC adj pertaining to traveling

VIATICAL adj viatic

VIATICUM n pl. -CA or -CUMS an allowance for traveling expenses

VIATOR n pl. -ES or -S a traveler

VIBE n pl. -S a vibration

VIBIST n pl. -S one who plays the vibraphone

VIBRANCE n pl. -S vibrancy

VIBRANCY n pl. -CIES the quality or state of being vibrant

VIBRANT n pl. -S a sonant

VIBRATE v -BRATED, -BRATING, -BRATES to move back and forth rapidly

VIBRATO n pl. -TOS a tremulous or pulsating musical effect

VIBRATOR n pl. -S something that vibrates

VIBRIO n pl. -RIOS any of a genus or bacteria shaped like a comma **VIBRIOID** adj

VIBRION n pl. -S vibrio

VIBRISSA *n pl.* -SAE one of the stiff hairs growing about the mouth of certain mammals

VIBRONIC *adj* pertaining to changes in molecular energy states resulting from vibrational energy

VIBURNUM *n pl.* -S a flowering shrub

VICAR *n pl.* -S a church official

VICARAGE *n pl.* -S the office of a vicar

VICARATE *n pl.* -S vicarage

VICARIAL *adj* pertaining to a vicar

VICARLY *adj* vicarial

VICE *v* VICED, VICING, VICES to vise

VICELESS *adj* having no immoral habits

VICENARY *adj* pertaining to the number twenty

VICEROY *n pl.* -ROYS one who rules as the representative of a sovereign

VICHY *n pl.* -CHIES a type of mineral water

VICINAGE *n pl.* -S vicinity

VICINAL *adj* nearby

VICING present participle of vice

VICINITY *n pl.* -TIES the region near or about a place

VICIOUS *adj* dangerously aggressive

VICOMTE *n pl.* -S a French nobleman

VICTIM *n pl.* -S one who suffers from a destructive or injurious action

VICTOR *n pl.* -S one who defeats an adversary

VICTORIA *n pl.* -S a light carriage

VICTORY *n pl.* -RIES a successful outcome in a contest or struggle

VICTRESS *n pl.* -ES a female victor

VICTUAL *v* -UALED, -UALING, -UALS or -UALLED, -UALLING, -UALS to provide with food

VICUGNA *n pl.* -S vicuna

VICUNA *n pl.* -S a ruminant mammal

VIDE *v* see — used to direct a reader to another item; VIDE is the only form of this verb; it cannot be conjugated

VIDEO *n pl.* -EOS television

VIDEOTEX *n pl.* -ES an electronic system for transmitting data to a subscriber's video screen

VIDETTE *n pl.* -S vedette

VIDICON *n pl.* -S a type of television camera tube

VIDUITY *n pl.* -ITIES the quality or state of being a widow

VIE *v* VIED, VYING, VIES to strive for superiority

VIER *n pl.* -S one that vies

VIEW *v* -ED, -ING, -S to look at VIEWABLE *adj*

VIEWDATA *n pl.* VIEWDATA a videotex

VIEWER *n pl.* -S one that views

VIEWIER comparative of viewy

VIEWIEST superlative of viewy

VIEWING *n pl.* -S an act of seeing, watching, or looking

VIEWLESS *adj* having no opinions

VIEWY *adj* VIEWIER, VIEWIEST showy

VIG *n pl.* -S a vigorish

VIGA *n pl.* -S a ceiling beam in Spanish architecture

VIGIL *n pl.* -S a period of watchfulness maintained during normal sleeping hours

VIGILANT *adj* watchful

VIGNERON *n pl.* -S a winegrower

VIGNETTE *v* -GNETTED, -GNETTING, -GNETTES to describe briefly

VIGOR *n pl.* -S active strength or force

VIGORISH *n pl.* -ES a charge paid to a bookie on a bet

VIGOROSO *adv* with emphasis and spirit — used as a musical direction

VIGOROUS *adj* full of vigor

VIGOUR *n pl.* -S vigor

VIKING *n pl.* -S a Scandinavian pirate

VILAYET *n pl.* -S an administrative division of Turkey

VILE *adj* VILER, VILEST physically repulsive VILELY *adv*

VILENESS *n pl.* -ES the state of being vile

VILIFIER *n pl.* -S one that vilifies

VILIFY *v* -FIED, -FYING, -FIES to defame

VILIPEND *v* -ED, -ING, -S to vilify

VILL *n pl.* -S a village

VILLA *n pl.* -LAE or -LAS an agricultural estate of ancient Rome

VILLADOM *n pl.* -S the world constituted by suburban residences and their occupants

VILLAGE *n pl.* -S a small community in a rural area

VILLAGER *n pl.* -S one who lives in a village

VILLAIN *n pl.* -S a cruelly malicious person

VILLAINY *n pl.* -LAINIES conduct characteristic of a villain

VILLATIC *adj* rural

VILLEIN *n pl.* -S a type of serf

VILLUS *n pl.* -LI one of the hairlike projections found on certain membranes VILLOSE, VILLOUS *adj*

VIM *n pl.* -S energy

VIMEN *n pl.* -MINA a long, flexible branch of a plant VIMINAL *adj*

VINA *n pl.* -S a stringed instrument of India

VINAL *n pl.* -S a synthetic textile fiber

VINASSE *n pl.* -S a residue left after the distillation of liquor

VINCA *n pl.* -S a flowering plant

VINCIBLE *adj* capable of being conquered VINCIBLY *adv*

VINCULUM *n pl.* -LA or -LUMS a unifying bond

VINDALOO *n pl.* -LOOS a curried dish made with meat, garlic, and wine

VINE *v* VINED, VINING, VINES to grow like a vine (a climbing plant)

VINEAL *adj* vinous

VINEGAR *n pl.* -S a sour liquid used as a condiment or preservative VINEGARY *adj*

VINERY *n pl.* -ERIES a place in which grapevines are grown

VINEYARD *n pl.* -S an area planted with grapevines

VINIC *adj* derived from wine

VINIER comparative of viny

VINIEST superlative of viny

VINIFERA *n pl.* -S a European grape

VINIFY *v* -FIED, -FYING, -FIES to convert into wine by fermentation

VINING present participle of vine

VINO *n pl.* -NOS wine

VINOSITY *n pl.* -TIES the character of a wine

VINOUS *adj* pertaining to wine VINOUSLY *adv*

VINTAGE *n pl.* -S a season's yield of wine from a vineyard

VINTAGER *n pl.* -S one that harvests wine grapes

VINTNER *n pl.* -S a wine merchant

VINY *adj* VINIER, VINIEST covered with vines

VINYL *n pl.* -S a type of plastic VINYLIC *adj*

VIOL *n pl.* -S a stringed instrument

VIOLA *n pl.* -S a stringed instrument

VIOLABLE *adj* capable of being violated VIOLABLY *adv*

VIOLATE *v* -LATED, -LATING, -LATES to break or disregard the terms or requirements of

VIOLATER *n pl.* -S violator

VIOLATOR *n pl.* -S one that violates

VIOLENCE *n pl.* -S violent action

VIOLENT *adj* marked by intense physical force or roughness

VIOLET *n pl.* -S a flowering plant

VIOLIN *n pl.* -S a stringed instrument

VIOLIST *n pl.* -S one who plays the viol or viola

VIOLONE *n pl.* -S a stringed instrument

VIOMYCIN *n pl.* -S an antibiotic

VIPER *n pl.* -S a venomous snake VIPERINE, VIPERISH, VIPEROUS *adj*

VIRAGO *n pl.* -GOES or -GOS a noisy, domineering woman

VIRAL *adj* pertaining to or caused by a virus VIRALLY *adv*

VIRELAI *n pl.* -S virelay

VIRELAY *n pl.* -LAYS a medieval French verse form

VIREMIA *n pl.* -S the presence of a virus in the blood VIREMIC *adj*

VIREO *n pl.* -EOS a small bird

VIRES *pl.* of vis

VIRGA *n pl.* -S wisps of precipitation evaporating before reaching ground

VIRGATE *n pl.* -S an early English measure of land area

VIRGIN *n pl.* -S a person who has never had sexual intercourse

VIRGINAL *n pl.* -S a musical instrument

VIRGULE *n pl.* -S a diagonal printing mark used to separate alternatives

VIRICIDE *n pl.* -S a substance that destroys viruses

VIRID *adj* verdant

VIRIDIAN *n pl.* -S a bluish-green pigment

VIRIDITY *n pl.* -TIES verdancy

VIRILE *adj* having masculine vigor VIRILELY *adv*

VIRILISM *n* pl. -S the development of male secondary sex characteristics in a female

VIRILITY *n* pl. -TIES the quality or state of being virile

VIRION *n* pl. -S a virus particle

VIRL *n* pl. -S a metal ring or cap put around a shaft to prevent splitting

VIROID *n* pl. -S a viruslike plant pathogen

VIROLOGY *n* pl. -GIES the study of viruses

VIROSIS *n* pl. -ROSES infection with a virus

VIRTU *n* pl. -S a love or taste for the fine arts

VIRTUAL *adj* having the effect but not the actual form of what is specified

VIRTUE *n* pl. -S moral excellence

VIRTUOSA *n* pl. -SAS or -SE a female virtuoso

VIRTUOSO *n* pl. -SOS or -SI a highly skilled artistic performer

VIRTUOUS *adj* characterized by virtue

VIRUCIDE *n* pl. -S viricide

VIRULENT *adj* extremely poisonous

VIRUS *n* pl. -ES any of a class of submicroscopic pathogens

VIS *n* pl. VIRES force or power

VISA *v* -ED, -ING, -S to put an official endorsement on, as a passport

VISAGE *n* pl. -S the face or facial expression of a person **VISAGED** *adj*

VISARD *n* pl. -S vizard

VISCACHA *n* pl. -S a burrowing rodent

VISCERA pl. of viscus

VISCERAL *adj* pertaining to the internal organs

VISCID *adj* thick and adhesive **VISCIDLY** *adv*

VISCOID *adj* somewhat viscid

VISCOSE *n* pl. -S a viscous solution

VISCOUNT *n* pl. -S a British nobleman

VISCOUS *adj* having relatively high resistance to flow

VISCUS *n* pl. -CERA an internal organ

VISE *v* VISED, VISING, VISES to hold in a vise (a clamping device)

VISE *v* VISEED, VISEING, VISES to visa

VISELIKE *adj* resembling a vise

VISIBLE *adj* capable of being seen **VISIBLY** *adv*

VISING present participle of vise

VISION *v* -ED, -ING, -S to imagine

VISIONAL *adj* imaginary

VISIT *v* -ED, -ING, -S to go or come to see someone or something

VISITANT *n* pl. -S a visitor

VISITER *n* pl. -S a visitor

VISITOR *n* pl. -S one that visits

VISIVE *adj* visible

VISOR *v* -ED, -ING, -S to provide with a visor (a projecting brim)

VISTA *n* pl. -S a distant view **VISTAED** *adj*

VISUAL *n* pl. -S something that illustrates by pictures or diagrams

VISUALLY *adv* with regard to the sense of sight

VITA *n* pl. -TAE a brief, autobiographical sketch

VITAL *adj* necessary to life

VITALISE *v* -ISED, -ISING, -ISES to vitalize

VITALISM *n* pl. -S a philosophical doctrine

VITALIST *n* pl. -S an advocate of vitalism

VITALITY *n* pl. -TIES exuberant physical strength or mental vigor

VITALIZE *v* -IZED, -IZING, -IZES to give life to .

VITALLY *adv* in a vital manner

VITALS *n/pl* vital organs

VITAMER *n* pl. -S a type of chemical compound

VITAMIN *n* pl. -S any of various organic substances essential to proper nutrition

VITAMINE *n* pl. -S vitamin

VITELLIN *n* pl. -S a protein found in egg yolk

VITELLUS *n* pl. -ES the yolk of an egg

VITESSE *n* pl. -S speed

VITIATE *v* -ATED, -ATING, -ATES to impair the value or quality of **VITIABLE** *adj*

VITIATOR *n* pl. -S one that vitiates

VITILIGO *n* pl. -GOS a skin disease

VITRAIN *n* pl. -S the material in the vitreous layers of banded bituminous coal

VITREOUS *n* pl. -ES the clear jelly that fills the eyeball

VITRIC *adj* pertaining to glass

VITRICS *n/pl* the art of making or decorating glass articles

VITRIFY *v* -FIED, -FYING, -FIES to convert into glass

VITRINE *n* pl. -S a glass showcase for art objects

VITRIOL *v* -OLED, -OLING, -OLS or -OLLED, -OLLING, -OLS to treat with sulfuric acid

VITTA *n* pl. -TAE a streak or band of color **VITTATE** *adj*

VITTLE *v* -TLED, -TLING, -TLES to victual

VITULINE *adj* pertaining to a calf

VIVA *n* pl. -S a shout or cry used to express approval

VIVACE *n* pl. -S a musical passage played in a brisk spirited manner

VIVACITY *n* pl. -TIES the quality or state of being lively

VIVARIUM *n* pl. -IA or -IUMS a place for raising and keeping live animals

VIVARY *n* pl. -RIES vivarium

VIVE *interj* — used as an exclamation of approval

VIVERRID *n* pl. -S any of a family of small carnivorous mammals

VIVERS *n/pl* food

VIVID *adj* -IDER, -IDEST strikingly bright or intense **VIVIDLY** *adv*

VIVIFIC *adj* vivifying

VIVIFIER *n* pl. -S one that vivifies

VIVIFY *v* -FIED, -FYING, -FIES to give life to

VIVIPARA *n/pl* animals that bring forth living young

VIVISECT *v* -ED, -ING, -S to dissect the living body of

VIXEN *n* pl. -S a shrewish woman **VIXENISH, VIXENLY** *adj*

VIZARD *n* pl. -S a mask **VIZARDED** *adj*

VIZCACHA *n* pl. -S viscacha

VIZIER *n* pl. -S a high official in some Muslim countries

VIZIR *n* pl. -S vizier **VIZIRIAL** *adj*

VIZIRATE *n* pl. -S the office of a vizir

VIZOR *v* -ED, -ING, -S to visor

VIZSLA *n* pl. -S a Hungarian breed of dog

VOCABLE *n* pl. -S a word

VOCABLY *adv* in a manner that may be voiced aloud

VOCAL *n* pl. -S a sound produced with the voice

VOCALIC *n* pl. -S a vowel sound

VOCALISE *v* -ISED, -ISING, -ISES to vocalize

VOCALISM *n* pl. -S the act of vocalizing

VOCALIST *n* pl. -S a singer

VOCALITY *n* pl. -TIES possession or exercise of vocal powers

VOCALIZE *v* -IZED, -IZING, -IZES to produce with the voice

VOCALLY *adv* with the voice

VOCATION *n* pl. -S the work in which a person is regularly employed

VOCATIVE *n* pl. -S a grammatical case used in some languages

VOCES pl. of vox

VOCODER *n* pl. -S an electronic device used in transmitting speech signals

VODKA *n* pl. -S a liquor

VODOUN *n* pl. -S vodun

VODUN *n* pl. -S a primitive religion of the West Indies

VOE *n* pl. -S a small bay, creek, or inlet

VOGIE *adj* vain

VOGUE *v* VOGUED, VOGUING or VOGUEING, VOGUES to imitate poses of fashion models

VOGUISH *adj* fashionable

VOICE *v* VOICED, VOICING, VOICES to express or utter

VOICEFUL *adj* sonorous

VOICER *n* pl. -S one that voices

VOICING present participle of voice

VOID *v* -ED, -ING, -S to make void (of no legal force or effect) **VOIDABLE** *adj*

VOIDANCE *n* pl. -S the act or process of voiding

VOIDER *n* pl. -S one that voids

VOIDNESS *n* pl. -ES the quality or state of being void

VOILA *interj* — used to call attention to something

VOILE *n* pl. -S a sheer fabric

VOLANT *adj* flying or capable of flying

VOLANTE *adj* moving with light rapidity — used as a musical direction

VOLAR *adj* pertaining to flight

VOLATILE *n* pl. -S a winged creature

VOLCANIC *n* pl. -S a rock produced by a volcano

VOLCANO *n* pl. -NOES or -NOS an opening in the earth's crust through which molten rock and gases are ejected

VOLE *v* VOLED, VOLING, VOLES to win all the tricks in a card game

VOLERY *n* pl. -ERIES a large birdcage

VOLITANT *adj* volant

VOLITION *n* pl. -S the power of choosing or determining

VOLITIVE *adj* pertaining to volition

VOLLEY *v* -ED, -ING, -S to return a tennis ball before it touches the ground

VOLLEYER *n* pl. -S one that volleys

VOLOST *n* pl. -S an administrative district in Russia

VOLPLANE *v* -PLANED, -PLANING, -PLANES to glide in an airplane

VOLT *n* pl. -S a unit of electromotive force

VOLTA *n* pl. -TE a turning

VOLTAGE *n* pl. -S electromotive force expressed in volts

VOLTAISM *n* pl. -S electricity produced by chemical action **VOLTAIC** *adj*

VOLTE *n* pl. -S a fencing movement

VOLTI *interj* — used to direct musicians to turn the page

VOLUBLE *adj* talkative **VOLUBLY** *adv*

VOLUME *v* -UMED, -UMING, -UMES to send or give out in large quantities

VOLUTE *n* pl. -S a spiral architectural ornament **VOLUTED** *adj*

VOLUTIN *n* pl. -S a granular substance that is common in microorganisms

VOLUTION *n* pl. -S a spiral

VOLVA *n* pl. -S a membranous sac that encloses certain immature mushrooms **VOLVATE** *adj*

VOLVOX *n* pl. -ES any of a genus of freshwater protozoa

VOLVULUS *n* pl. -LI or -LUSES a twisting of the intestine that causes obstruction

VOMER *n* pl. -S a bone of the skull **VOMERINE** *adj*

VOMICA *n* pl. -CAE a cavity in the body containing pus

VOMIT *v* -ED, -ING, -S to eject the contents of the stomach through the mouth

VOMITER *n* pl. -S one that vomits

VOMITIVE *n* pl. -S an emetic

VOMITO *n* pl. -TOS the black vomit of yellow fever

VOMITORY *n* pl. -RIES an emetic

VOMITOUS *adj* pertaining to vomiting

VOMITUS *n* pl. -ES vomited matter

VOODOO *v* -ED, -ING, -S to hex

VORACITY *n* pl. -TIES the quality or state of being ravenous

VORLAGE *n* pl. -S a position in skiing

VORTEX *n* pl. -TEXES or -TICES a whirling mass of fluid **VORTICAL** *adj*

VOTABLE *adj* capable of being voted on

VOTARESS *n* pl. -ES a female votary

VOTARIST *n* pl. -S a votary

VOTARY *n* pl. -RIES a person who is bound by religious vows

VOTE *v* VOTED, VOTING, VOTES to cast a vote (a formal expression of will or opinion)

VOTEABLE *adj* votable

VOTELESS *adj* having no vote

VOTER *n* pl. -S one that votes

VOTING present participle of vote

VOTIVE *adj* performed in fulfillment of a vow **VOTIVELY** *adv*

VOTRESS *n* pl. -ES votaress

VOUCH *v* -ED, -ING, -ES to give one's personal assurance or guarantee

VOUCHEE *n* pl. -S one for whom another vouches

VOUCHER *v* -ED, -ING, -S to establish the authenticity of

VOUSSOIR *n* pl. -S a wedge-shaped building stone

VOUVRAY *n* pl. -VRAYS a French white wine

VOW *v* -ED, -ING, -S to make a vow (a solemn promise)

VOWEL *n* pl. -S a type of speech sound

VOWELIZE *v* -IZED, -IZING, -IZES to provide with symbols used to indicate vowels

VOWER *n* pl. -S one that vows

VOWLESS *adj* having made no vow

VOX *n* pl. VOCES voice

VOYAGE *v* -AGED, -AGING, -AGES to travel

VOYAGER *n* pl. -S one that voyages

VOYAGEUR n pl. -S a person employed by a fur company to transport goods between distant stations

VOYEUR n pl. -S one who is sexually gratified by looking at sexual objects or acts

VROOM v -ED, -ING, -S to run an engine at high speed

VROUW n pl. -S a Dutch woman

VROW n pl. -S vrouw

VUG n pl. -S a small cavity in a rock or lode

VUGG n pl. -S vug

VUGGY adj -GIER, -GIEST abounding in vugs

VUGH n pl. -S vug

VULCANIC adj pertaining to a volcano

VULGAR adj -GARER, -GAREST crude **VULGARLY** adv

VULGAR n pl. -S a common person

VULGATE n pl. -S the common speech of a people

VULGO adv commonly

VULGUS n pl. -ES an exercise in Latin formerly required of pupils in some English public schools

VULPINE adj pertaining to a fox

VULTURE n pl. -S a bird of prey

VULVA n pl. -VAE or -VAS the external genital organs of a female **VULVAL, VULVAR, VULVATE** adj

VULVITIS n pl. -TISES inflammation of the vulva

VYING present participle of vie

VYINGLY adv in a vying manner

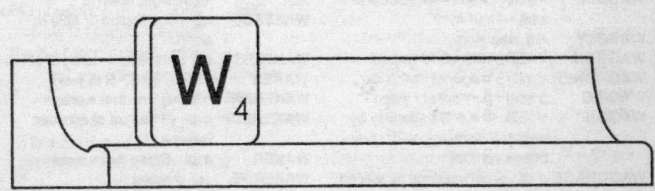

WAB	n pl. -S a web	**WADMEL**	n pl. -S wadmal
WABBLE	v -BLED, -BLING, -BLES to wobble	**WADMOL**	n pl. -S wadmal
		WADMOLL	n pl. -S wadmal
WABBLER	n pl. -S one that wabbles	**WADSET**	v -SETTED, -SETTING, -SETS to mortgage
WABBLY	adj -BLIER, -BLIEST wobbly		
WACK	n pl. -S a wacky person	**WADY**	n pl. -DIES wadi
WACKE	n pl. -S a type of basaltic rock	**WAE**	n pl. -S woe
WACKO	n pl. WACKOS a person who is wacky	**WAEFUL**	adj woeful
		WAENESS	n pl. -ES woeness
WACKY	adj WACKIER, WACKIEST very irrational **WACKILY** adv	**WAESUCK**	interj waesucks
		WAESUCKS	interj — used to express pity
WAD	v WADDED, WADDING, WADS to form into a wad (a small mass of soft material)	**WAFER**	v -ED, -ING, -S to seal with an adhesive disk
		WAFERY	adj resembling a wafer (a thin, crisp biscuit)
WADABLE	adj wadeable		
WADDER	n pl. -S one that wads	**WAFF**	v -ED, -ING, -S to wave
WADDIE	n pl. -S a cowboy	**WAFFIE**	n pl. -S a vagabond
WADDIED	past tense of waddy	**WAFFLE**	v -FLED, -FLING, -FLES to talk vaguely or indecisively
WADDIES	present 3d person sing. of waddy		
		WAFFLER	n pl. -S one that waffles
WADDING	n pl. -S a wad	**WAFFLING**	n pl. -S an indecisive statement or position
WADDLE	v -DLED, -DLING, -DLES to walk with short, swaying steps		
		WAFT	v -ED, -ING, -S to carry lightly over air or water
WADDLER	n pl. -S one that waddles		
WADDLY	adj having or being a waddling gait	**WAFTAGE**	n pl. -S the act of wafting
		WAFTER	n pl. -S one that wafts
WADDY	v -DIED, -DYING, -DIES to strike with a thick club	**WAFTURE**	n pl. -S waftage
		WAG	v WAGGED, WAGGING, WAGS to move briskly up and down or to and fro
WADE	v WADED, WADING, WADES to walk through water		
WADEABLE	adj capable of being passed through by wading	**WAGE**	v WAGED, WAGING, WAGES to engage in or carry on
WADER	n pl. -S one that wades		
WADI	n pl. -S the bed of a usually dry watercourse	**WAGELESS**	adj unpaid
		WAGER	v -ED, -ING, -S to risk on an uncertain outcome
WADIES	pl. of wady		
WADING	present participle of wade	**WAGERER**	n pl. -S one that wagers
WADMAAL	n pl. -S wadmal	**WAGGED**	past tense of wag
WADMAL	n pl. -S a thick woolen fabric	**WAGGER**	n pl. -S one that wags

WAGGERY *n pl.* -GERIES waggish behavior

WAGGING present participle of wag

WAGGISH *adj* playfully humorous

WAGGLE *v* -GLED, -GLING, -GLES to wag

WAGGLY *adj* waggling

WAGGON *v* -ED, -ING, -S to wagon

WAGGONER *n pl.* -S wagoner

WAGING present participle of wage

WAGON *v* -ED, -ING, -S to convey by wagon (a four-wheeled, horse-drawn vehicle)

WAGONAGE *n pl.* -S conveyance by wagon

WAGONER *n pl.* -S one who drives a wagon

WAGSOME *adj* waggish

WAGTAIL *n pl.* -S a songbird

WAHCONDA *n pl.* -S a wakanda

WAHINE *n pl.* -S a Hawaiian woman

WAHOO *n pl.* -HOOS a flowering shrub

WAIF *v* -ED, -ING, -S to throw away

WAIFLIKE *adj* resembling a waif (a homeless child)

WAIL *v* -ED, -ING, -S to utter a long, mournful cry

WAILER *n pl.* -S one that wails

WAILFUL *adj* mournful

WAILSOME *adj* wailful

WAIN *n pl.* -S a large, open wagon

WAINSCOT *v* -SCOTED, -SCOTING, -SCOTS or -SCOTTED, -SCOTTING, -SCOTS to line the walls of with wooden paneling

WAIR *v* -ED, -ING, -S to spend

WAIST *n pl.* -S the part of the body between the ribs and the hips **WAISTED** *adj*

WAISTER *n pl.* -S a seaman stationed in the middle section of a ship

WAISTING *n pl.* -S a type of dressmaking material

WAIT *v* -ED, -ING, -S to stay in expectation of

WAITER *n pl.* -S one who serves food in a restaurant

WAITING *n pl.* -S the act of one who waits

WAITRESS *v* -ED, -ING, -ES to work as a female server in a restaurant

WAIVE *v* WAIVED, WAIVING, WAIVES to give up intentionally

WAIVER *n pl.* -S the act of waiving something

WAKANDA *n pl.* -S a supernatural force in Sioux beliefs

WAKE *v* WAKED or WOKE, WOKEN, WAKING, WAKES to rouse from sleep

WAKEFUL *adj* not sleeping or able to sleep

WAKELESS *adj* unbroken — used of sleep

WAKEN *v* -ED, -ING, -S to wake

WAKENER *n pl.* -S one that wakens

WAKENING *n pl.* -S the act of one that wakens

WAKER *n pl.* -S one that wakes

WAKERIFE *adj* wakeful

WAKIKI *n pl.* -S shell money of the South Sea Islands

WAKING present participle of wake

WALE *v* WALED, WALING, WALES to mark with welts

WALER *n pl.* -S an Australian-bred saddle horse

WALIES pl. of waly

WALING present participle of wale

WALK *v* -ED, -ING, -S to advance on foot **WALKABLE** *adj*

WALKAWAY *n pl.* -AWAYS an easy victory

WALKER *n pl.* -S one that walks

WALKING *n pl.* -S the act of one that walks

WALKOUT *n pl.* -S a strike by workers

WALKOVER *n pl.* -S a walkaway

WALKUP *n pl.* -S an apartment house having no elevator

WALKWAY *n pl.* -WAYS a passage for walking

WALKYRIE *n pl.* -S valkyrie

WALL *v* -ED, -ING, -S to provide with a wall (an upright structure built to enclose an area)

WALLA *n pl.* -S wallah

WALLABY *n pl.* -BIES a small kangaroo

WALLAH *n pl.* -S a person engaged in a particular occupation or activity

WALLAROO *n pl.* -ROOS a large kangaroo

WALLET *n pl.* -S a flat folding case

WALLEYE *n pl.* -S an eye having a white cornea **WALLEYED** *adj*

WALLIE *n pl.* -S a valet

WALLIES pl. of wally

WALLOP *v* -ED, -ING, -S to beat soundly

WALLOPER *n pl.* -S one that wallops

WALLOW *v* -ED, -ING, -S to roll about

WALLOWER *n pl.* -S one that wallows

WALLY *n pl.* -LIES waly

WALNUT *n pl.* -S an edible nut

WALRUS n pl. -ES a marine mammal

WALTZ v -ED, -ING, -ES to perform a ballroom dance

WALTZER n pl. -S one that waltzes

WALY n pl. WALIES something visually pleasing

WAMBLE v -BLED, -BLING, -BLES to move unsteadily

WAMBLY adj -BLIER, -BLIEST unsteady

WAME n pl. -S the belly

WAMEFOU n pl. -S a bellyful

WAMEFUL n pl. -S wamefou

WAMMUS n pl. -ES wamus

WAMPISH v -ED, -ING, -ES to throw about

WAMPUM n pl. -S a form of currency formerly used by North American Indians

WAMPUS n pl. -ES wamus

WAMUS n pl. -ES a heavy outer jacket

WAN adj WANNER, WANNEST unnaturally pale

WAN v WANNED, WANNING, WANS to become wan

WAND n pl. -S a slender rod

WANDER v -ED, -ING, -S to move about with no destination or purpose

WANDERER n pl. -S one that wanders

WANDEROO n pl. -ROOS an Asian monkey

WANDLE adj supple

WANE v WANED, WANING, WANES to decrease in size or extent

WANEY adj WANIER, WANIEST wany

WANGAN n pl. -S wanigan

WANGLE v -GLED, -GLING, -GLES to obtain or accomplish by contrivance

WANGLER n pl. -S one that wangles

WANGUN n pl. -S wanigan

WANIER comparative of waney and wany

WANIEST superlative of waney and wany

WANIGAN n pl. -S a supply chest used in a logging camp

WANING present participle of wane

WANION n pl. -S vengeance

WANLY adv in a wan manner

WANNED past tense of wan

WANNER comparative of wan

WANNESS n pl. -ES the quality of being wan

WANNEST superlative of wan

WANNIGAN n pl. -S wanigan

WANNING present participle of wan

WANT v -ED, -ING, -S to have a desire for

WANTAGE n pl. -S something that is lacking

WANTER n pl. -S one that wants

WANTON v -ED, -ING, -S to behave immorally

WANTONER n pl. -S one that wantons

WANTONLY adv immorally

WANY adj WANIER, WANIEST waning in some parts

WAP v WAPPED, WAPPING, WAPS to wrap

WAPITI n pl. -S a large deer

WAR v WARRED, WARRING, WARS to engage in war (a state of open, armed conflict)

WARBLE v -BLED, -BLING, -BLES to sing with melodic embellishments

WARBLER n pl. -S one that warbles

WARCRAFT n pl. -S the art of war

WARD v -ED, -ING, -S to turn aside

WARDEN n pl. -S the chief officer of a prison

WARDENRY n pl. -RIES the office of a warden

WARDER n pl. -S a person who guards something

WARDRESS n pl. -ES a female warden

WARDROBE n pl. -S a collection of garments

WARDROOM n pl. -S a dining area for officers on a warship

WARDSHIP n pl. -S the state of being under a guardian

WARE v WARED, WARING, WARES to beware of

WAREROOM n pl. -S a room in which goods are displayed for sale

WARFARE n pl. -S the act of engaging in war

WARFARIN n pl. -S a chemical compound

WARHEAD n pl. -S the front part of a missile containing the explosive

WARHORSE n pl. -S a musical or dramatic work that has been performed to excess

WARIER comparative of wary

WARIEST superlative of wary

WARILY adv in a wary manner

WARINESS n pl. -ES the state of being wary

WARING present participle of ware

WARISON n pl. -S a call to attack

WARK v -ED, -ING, -S to endure pain

WARLESS adj free from war

WARLIKE	adj disposed to engage in war
WARLOCK	n pl. -S a sorcerer
WARLORD	n pl. -S a military leader of a warlike nation
WARM	adj WARMER, WARMEST moderately hot
WARM	v -ED, -ING, -S to make warm
WARMAKER	n pl. -S one that wars
WARMER	n pl. -S one that warms
WARMISH	adj somewhat warm
WARMLY	adv in a warm manner
WARMNESS	n pl. -ES the state of being warm
WARMOUTH	n pl. -S a freshwater fish
WARMTH	n pl. -S warmness
WARMUP	n pl. -S a preparatory exercise or procedure
WARN	v -ED, -ING, -S to make aware of impending or possible danger
WARNER	n pl. -S one that warns
WARNING	n pl. -S something that warns
WARP	v -ED, -ING, -S to turn or twist out of shape
WARPAGE	n pl. -S the act of warping
WARPATH	n pl. -S the route taken by attacking American Indians
WARPER	n pl. -S one that warps
WARPLANE	n pl. -S an airplane armed for combat
WARPOWER	n pl. -S the power to make war
WARPWISE	adv in a vertical direction
WARRAGAL	n pl. -S warrigal
WARRANT	v -ED, -ING, -S to give authority to
WARRANTY	n pl. -TIES the act of warranting
WARRED	past tense of war
WARREN	n pl. -S a place where rabbits live and breed
WARRENER	n pl. -S the keeper of a warren
WARRIGAL	n pl. -S a dingo
WARRING	present participle of war
WARRIOR	n pl. -S one engaged or experienced in warfare
WARSAW	n pl. -S a marine fish
WARSHIP	n pl. -S a ship armed for combat
WARSLE	v -SLED, -SLING, -SLES to wrestle
WARSLER	n pl. -S a wrestler
WARSTLE	v -TLED, -TLING, -TLES to wrestle
WARSTLER	n pl. -S a wrestler

WART	n pl. -S a protuberance on the skin WARTED adj
WARTHOG	n pl. -S an African wild hog
WARTIER	comparative of warty
WARTIEST	superlative of warty
WARTIME	n pl. -S a time of war
WARTLESS	adj having no warts
WARTLIKE	adj resembling a wart
WARTY	adj WARTIER, WARTIEST covered with warts
WARWORK	n pl. -S work done during a war
WARWORN	adj showing the effects of war
WARY	adj WARIER, WARIEST watchful
WAS	1st and 3d person sing. past indicative of be
WASABI	n pl. -S a pungent herb
WASH	v -ED, -ING, -ES to cleanse by immersing in or applying a liquid
WASHABLE	n pl. -S something that can be washed without damage
WASHBOWL	n pl. -S a bowl used for washing oneself
WASHDAY	n pl. -DAYS a day set aside for washing clothes
WASHER	n pl. -S one that washes
WASHIER	comparative of washy
WASHIEST	superlative of washy
WASHING	n pl. -S articles washed or to be washed
WASHOUT	n pl. -S an erosion of earth by the action of water
WASHRAG	n pl. -S a small cloth used for washing oneself
WASHROOM	n pl. -S a lavatory
WASHTUB	n pl. -S a tub used for washing clothes
WASHUP	n pl. -S the act of washing clean
WASHY	adj WASHIER, WASHIEST overly diluted
WASP	n pl. -S a stinging insect WASPISH, WASPLIKE adj
WASPY	adj WASPIER, WASPIEST resembling a wasp WASPILY adv
WASSAIL	v -ED, -ING, -S to drink to the health of
WAST	n pl. -S west
WASTABLE	adj capable of being wasted
WASTAGE	n pl. -S something that is wasted
WASTE	v WASTED, WASTING, WASTES to use thoughtlessly

WASTEFUL adj tending to waste
WASTELOT n pl. -S a vacant lot
WASTER n pl. -S one that wastes
WASTERIE n pl. -S wastry
WASTERY n pl. -RIES wastry
WASTEWAY n pl. -WAYS a channel for excess water
WASTING present participle of waste
WASTREL n pl. -S one that wastes
WASTRIE n pl. -S wastry
WASTRY n pl. -RIES reckless extravagance
WAT adj WATTER, WATTEST wet
WAT n pl. -S a hare
WATAP n pl. -S a thread made from the roots of various trees
WATAPE n pl. -S watap
WATCH v -ED, -ING, -ES to observe carefully
WATCHCRY n pl. -CRIES a password
WATCHDOG v -DOGGED, -DOGGING, -DOGS to act as a guardian for
WATCHER n pl. -S one that watches
WATCHEYE n pl. -S a walleye
WATCHFUL adj closely observant or alert
WATCHMAN n pl. -MEN a man employed to stand guard
WATCHOUT n pl. -S the act of looking out for something
WATER v -ED, -ING, -S to sprinkle with water (a transparent, odorless, tasteless liquid)
WATERAGE n pl. -S the conveyance of goods by water
WATERBED n pl. -S a bed whose mattress is a plastic bag filled with water
WATERDOG n pl. -S a large salamander
WATERER n pl. -S one that waters
WATERIER comparative of watery
WATERIEST superlative of watery
WATERILY adv in a watery manner
WATERING n pl. -S the act of one that waters
WATERISH adj watery
WATERLOG v -LOGGED, -LOGGING, -LOGS to soak with water
WATERLOO n pl. -LOOS a decisive defeat
WATERMAN n pl. -MEN a boatman
WATERWAY n pl. -WAYS a navigable body of water
WATERY adj -TERIER, -TERIEST containing water
WATT n pl. -S a unit of power
WATTAGE n pl. -S an amount of power in terms of watts
WATTAPE n pl. -S watap

WATTER comparative of wat
WATTEST superlative of wat
WATTHOUR n pl. -S a unit of energy
WATTLE v -TLED, -TLING, -TLES to weave into a network
WATTLESS adj denoting a type of electric current
WAUCHT v -ED, -ING, -S to waught
WAUGH adj damp
WAUGHT v -ED, -ING, -S to drink deeply
WAUK v -ED, -ING, -S to wake
WAUL v -ED, -ING, -S to cry like a cat
WAUR adj worse
WAVE v WAVED, WAVING, WAVES to move freely back and forth or up and down
WAVEBAND n pl. -S a range of radio frequencies
WAVEFORM n pl. -S a type of mathematical graph
WAVELESS adj having no waves (moving ridges on the surface of a liquid)
WAVELET n pl. -S a small wave
WAVELIKE adj resembling a wave
WAVEOFF n pl. -S the act of denying landing permission to an approaching aircraft
WAVER v -ED, -ING, -S to move back and forth
WAVERER n pl. -S one that wavers
WAVERY adj wavering
WAVEY n pl. -VEYS the snow goose
WAVIER comparative of wavy
WAVIES pl. of wavy
WAVIEST superlative of wavy
WAVILY adv in a wavy manner
WAVINESS n pl. -ES the state of being wavy
WAVING present participle of wave
WAVY adj WAVIER, WAVIEST having waves
WAVY n pl. -VIES wavey
WAW n pl. -S vav
WAWL v -ED, -ING, -S to waul
WAX v -ED, -ING, -ES to coat with wax (a natural, heat-sensitive substance)
WAXBERRY n pl. -RIES a berry with a waxy coating
WAXBILL n pl. -S a tropical bird
WAXEN adj covered with wax
WAXER n pl. -S one that waxes
WAXIER comparative of waxy
WAXIEST superlative of waxy

WAXILY	adv in a waxy manner
WAXINESS	n pl. -ES the quality of being waxy
WAXING	n pl. -S the act of one that waxes
WAXLIKE	adj resembling wax
WAXPLANT	n pl. -S a tropical plant
WAXWEED	n pl. -S an annual herb
WAXWING	n pl. -S a type of passerine bird
WAXWORK	n pl. -S an effigy made of wax
WAXWORM	n pl. -S a moth that infests beehives
WAXY	adj WAXIER, WAXIEST resembling wax
WAY	n pl. WAYS a method of doing something
WAYBILL	n pl. -S a list of goods relative to a shipment
WAYFARER	n pl. -S a traveler
WAYGOING	n pl. -S the act of leaving
WAYLAY	v -LAID, -LAYING, -LAYS to ambush
WAYLAYER	n pl. -S one that waylays
WAYLESS	adj having no road or path
WAYSIDE	n pl. -S the side of a road
WAYWARD	adj willful
WAYWORN	adj fatigued by travel
WE	pron 1st person pl. pronoun in the nominative case
WEAK	adj WEAKER, WEAKEST lacking strength
WEAKEN	v -ED, -ING, -S to make weak
WEAKENER	n pl. -S one that weakens
WEAKFISH	n pl. -ES a marine fish
WEAKISH	adj somewhat weak
WEAKLING	n pl. -S a weak person
WEAKLY	adj -LIER, -LIEST weak and sickly
WEAKNESS	n pl. -ES the state of being weak
WEAKSIDE	n pl. -S the side of a basketball court with fewer players
WEAL	n pl. -S a welt
WEALD	n pl. -S a woodland
WEALTH	n pl. -S a great quantity of valuable material
WEALTHY	adj WEALTHIER, WEALTHIEST having wealth
WEAN	v -ED, -ING, -S to withhold mother's milk from and substitute other nourishment
WEANER	n pl. -S one that weans
WEANLING	n pl. -S a recently weaned child or animal

WEAPON	v -ED, -ING, -S to supply with a weapon (an instrument used in combat)
WEAPONRY	n pl. -RIES an aggregate of weapons
WEAR	v WORE, WORN, WEARING, WEARS to have on one's person
WEARABLE	n pl. -S a garment
WEARER	n pl. -S one that wears something
WEARIED	past tense of weary
WEARIER	comparative of weary
WEARIES	present 3d person sing. of weary
WEARIEST	superlative of weary
WEARIFUL	adj tiresome
WEARISH	adj tasteless
WEARY	adj -RIER, -RIEST tired **WEARILY** adv
WEARY	v -RIED, -RYING, -RIES to make or become weary
WEASAND	n pl. -S the throat
WEASEL	v -SELED, -SELING, -SELS or -SELLED, -SELLING, -SELS to act evasively
WEASELLY	adj resembling a weasel (a small carnivorous mammal)
WEASELY	adj weaselly
WEASON	n pl. -S weasand
WEATHER	v -ED, -ING, -S to expose to atmospheric conditions
WEAVE	v WOVE or WEAVED, WOVEN, WEAVING, WEAVES to form by interlacing threads
WEAVER	n pl. -S one that weaves
WEAZAND	n pl. -S weasand
WEB	v WEBBED, WEBBING, WEBS to provide with a web (an interlaced fabric or structure)
WEBBING	n pl. -S a woven strip of fiber
WEBBY	adj -BIER, -BIEST weblike
WEBER	n pl. -S a unit of magnetic flux
WEBFED	adj designed to print a continuous roll of paper
WEBFOOT	n pl. -FEET a foot having the toes joined by a membrane
WEBLESS	adj having no webs
WEBLIKE	adj resembling a web
WEBSTER	n pl. -S a weaver
WEBWORK	n pl. -S a weblike pattern or structure
WEBWORM	n pl. -S a web-spinning caterpillar

WECHT n pl. -S weight

WED v WEDDED, WEDDING, WEDS to marry

WEDDER n pl. -S one that weds

WEDDING n pl. -S a marriage ceremony

WEDEL v -ED, -ING, -S to perform a wedeln

WEDELN n pl. -S a skiing technique

WEDGE v WEDGED, WEDGING, WEDGES to force apart with a wedge (a tapering piece of wood or metal)

WEDGIE n pl. -S a type of woman's shoe

WEDGY adj WEDGIER, WEDGIEST resembling a wedge

WEDLOCK n pl. -S the state of being married

WEE adj WEER, WEEST very small

WEE n pl. -S a short time

WEED v -ED, -ING, -S to remove weeds (undesirable plants)

WEEDER n pl. -S one that weeds

WEEDIER comparative of weedy

WEEDIEST superlative of weedy

WEEDILY adv in a weedy manner

WEEDLESS adj having no weeds

WEEDLIKE adj resembling a weed

WEEDY adj WEEDIER, WEEDIEST resembling a weed

WEEK n pl. -S a period of seven days

WEEKDAY n pl. -DAYS any day of the week except Sunday

WEEKEND v -ED, -ING, -S to spend the weekend (the end of the week)

WEEKLONG adj continuing for a week

WEEKLY n pl. -LIES a publication issued once a week

WEEL adj well

WEEN v -ED, -ING, -S to suppose

WEENIE n pl. -S a wiener

WEENSY adj -SIER, -SIEST tiny

WEENY adj -NIER, -NIEST tiny

WEEP v WEPT, WEEPING, WEEPS to express sorrow by shedding tears

WEEPER n pl. -S one that weeps

WEEPIE n pl. -S a very maudlin movie

WEEPING n pl. -S the act of one that weeps

WEEPY adj WEEPIER, WEEPIEST tending to weep

WEER comparative of wee

WEEST superlative of wee

WEET v -ED, -ING, -S to know

WEEVER n pl. -S a marine fish

WEEVIL n pl. -S a small beetle

WEEVILED, WEEVILLY, WEEVILY adj

WEEWEE v -WEED, -WEEING, -WEES to urinate

WEFT n pl. -S a woven fabric or garment

WEFTWISE adv in a horizontal direction

WEIGELA n pl. -S a flowering shrub

WEIGELIA n pl. -S weigela

WEIGH v -ED, -ING, -S to determine the weight of

WEIGHER n pl. -S one that weighs

WEIGHMAN n pl. -MEN one whose occupation is weighing goods

WEIGHT v -ED, -ING, -S to add weight (heaviness) to

WEIGHTER n pl. -S one that weights

WEIGHTY adj WEIGHTIER, WEIGHTIEST having great weight

WEINER n pl. -S wiener

WEIR n pl. -S a fence placed in a stream to catch fish

WEIRD adj WEIRDER, WEIRDEST mysteriously strange

WEIRD n pl. -S destiny

WEIRDIE n pl. -S a very strange person

WEIRDIES pl. of weirdy

WEIRDLY adv in a weird manner

WEIRDO n pl. WEIRDOES or WEIRDOS a weirdie

WEIRDY n pl. WEIRDIES weirdie

WEKA n pl. -S a flightless bird

WELCH v -ED, -ING, -ES to welsh

WELCHER n pl. -S one that welshes

WELCOME v -COMED, -COMING, -COMES to greet cordially

WELCOMER n pl. -S one that welcomes

WELD v -ED, -ING, -S to join by applying heat **WELDABLE** adj

WELDER n pl. -S one that welds

WELDLESS adj having no welded joints

WELDMENT n pl. -S a unit composed of welded pieces

WELDOR n pl. -S welder

WELFARE n pl. -S general well-being

WELKIN n pl. -S the sky

WELL v -ED, -ING, -S to rise to the surface and flow forth

WELLADAY n pl. -DAYS wellaway

WELLAWAY n pl. -WAYS an expression of sorrow

WELLBORN adj of good birth or ancestry

WELLCURB n pl. -S the stone ring around a well (a hole dug in the ground to obtain water)

WELLDOER n pl. -S a doer of good deeds

WELLHEAD n pl. -S the source of a spring or stream

WELLHOLE n pl. -S the shaft of a well

WELLIE n pl. -S a Wellington boot

WELLIES pl. of welly

WELLNESS n pl. -ES the state of being healthy

WELLSITE n pl. -S a mineral

WELLY n pl. -LIES wellie

WELSH v -ED, -ING, -ES to fail to pay a debt

WELSHER n pl. -S one that welshes

WELT v -ED, -ING, -S to mark with welts (ridges or lumps raised on the skin)

WELTER v -ED, -ING, -S to roll about

WELTING n pl. -S a cord or strip used to reinforce a seam

WEN n pl. -S a benign tumor of the skin

WENCH v -ED, -ING, -ES to consort with prostitutes

WENCHER n pl. -S one that wenches

WEND v -ED, -ING, -S to proceed along

WENDIGO n pl. -GOS windigo

WENNISH adj wenny

WENNY adj -NIER, -NIEST resembling a wen

WENT past tense of go

WEPT past tense of weep

WERE a pl. and 2d person sing. past indicative, and past subjunctive of be

WEREGILD n pl. -S wergeld

WEREWOLF n pl. -WOLVES a person capable of assuming the form of a wolf

WERGELD n pl. -S a price paid for the taking of a man's life in Anglo-Saxon law

WERGELT n pl. -S wergeld

WERGILD n pl. -S wergeld

WERT a 2d person sing. past tense of be

WERWOLF n pl. -WOLVES werewolf

WESKIT n pl. -S a vest

WESSAND n pl. -S a weasand

WEST n pl. -S a cardinal point of the compass

WESTER v -ED, -ING, -S to move toward the west

WESTERLY n pl. -LIES a wind from the west

WESTERN n pl. -S one who lives in the west

WESTING n pl. -S a shifting west

WESTMOST adj farthest west

WESTWARD n pl. -S a direction toward the west

WET adj WETTER, WETTEST covered or saturated with a liquid

WET v WETTED, WETTING, WETS to make wet

WETHER n pl. -S a gelded male sheep

WETLAND n pl. -S land containing much soil moisture

WETLY adv in a wet manner

WETNESS n pl. -ES the state of being wet

WETPROOF adj waterproof

WETTABLE adj capable of being wetted

WETTED past tense of wet

WETTER n pl. -S one that wets

WETTEST superlative of wet

WETTING n pl. -S a liquid used in moistening something

WETTISH adj somewhat wet

WHA pron who

WHACK v -ED, -ING, -S to strike sharply

WHACKER n pl. -S one that whacks

WHACKO n pl. WHACKOS wacko

WHACKY adj WHACKIER, WHACKIEST wacky

WHALE v WHALED, WHALING, WHALES to engage in the hunting of whales (large marine mammals)

WHALEMAN n pl. -MEN a whaler

WHALER n pl. -S a person engaged in whaling

WHALING n pl. -S the industry of hunting and processing whales

WHAM v WHAMMED, WHAMMING, WHAMS to hit with a loud impact

WHAMMO interj — used to indicate a startling event

WHAMMY n pl. -MIES a supernatural spell bringing bad luck

WHAMO interj whammo

WHANG v -ED, -ING, -S to beat with a whip

WHANGEE n pl. -S an Asian grass

WHAP v WHAPPED, WHAPPING, WHAPS to whop

WHAPPER	n pl. -S whopper
WHARF	v -ED, -ING, -S to moor to a wharf (a docking place for vessels)
WHARFAGE	n pl. -S the use of a wharf
WHARVE	n pl. -S a round piece of wood used in spinning thread
WHAT	n pl. -S the true nature of something
WHATEVER	adj being what or who it may be
WHATNESS	n pl. -ES the true nature of something
WHATNOT	n pl. -S an ornamental set of shelves
WHATSIS	n pl. -SISES whatsit
WHATSIT	n pl. -S something whose name is unknown or forgotten
WHAUP	n pl. -S a European bird
WHEAL	n pl. -S a welt
WHEAT	n pl. -S a cereal grass
WHEATEAR	n pl. -S a small bird of northern regions
WHEATEN	n pl. -S a pale yellowish color
WHEE	interj — used to express delight
WHEEDLE	v -DLED, -DLING, -DLES to attempt to persuade by flattery
WHEEDLER	n pl. -S one that wheedles
WHEEL	v -ED, -ING, -S to convey on wheels (circular frames designed to turn on an axis)
WHEELER	n pl. -S one that wheels
WHEELIE	n pl. -S a maneuver made on a wheeled vehicle
WHEELING	n pl. -S the condition of a road for vehicles
WHEELMAN	n pl. -MEN a helmsman
WHEEN	n pl. -S a fairly large amount
WHEEP	v -ED, -ING, -S to wheeple
WHEEPLE	v -PLED, -PLING, -PLES to give forth a prolonged whistle
WHEEZE	v WHEEZED, WHEEZING, WHEEZES to breathe with a whistling sound
WHEEZER	n pl. -S one that wheezes
WHEEZY	adj WHEEZIER, WHEEZIEST characterized by wheezing WHEEZILY adv
WHELK	n pl. -S a pustule
WHELKY	adj WHELKIER, WHELKIEST marked with whelks
WHELM	v -ED, -ING, -S to cover with water
WHELP	v -ED, -ING, -S to give birth to

WHEN	n pl. -S the time in which something is done or occurs
WHENAS	conj at which time
WHENCE	adv from what place
WHENEVER	adv at whatever time
WHERE	n pl. -S the place at or in which something is located or occurs
WHEREAS	n pl. -ES an introductory statement of a formal document
WHEREAT	adv at what
WHEREBY	adv by what
WHEREIN	adv in what
WHEREOF	adv of what
WHEREON	adv on what
WHERETO	adv to what
WHEREVER	adv in or to whatever place
WHERRY	v -RIED, -RYING, -RIES to transport in a light rowboat
WHERVE	n pl. -S wharve
WHET	v WHETTED, WHETTING, WHETS to sharpen by friction
WHETHER	conj if it be the case that
WHETTER	n pl. -S one that whets
WHETTING	present participle of whet
WHEW	n pl. -S a whistling sound
WHEY	n pl. WHEYS the watery part of milk WHEYEY, WHEYISH adj
WHEYFACE	n pl. -S a pale, sallow face
WHEYLIKE	adj resembling whey
WHICH	pron what particular one or ones
WHICKER	v -ED, -ING, -S to whinny
WHID	v WHIDDED, WHIDDING, WHIDS to move rapidly and quietly
WHIDAH	n pl. -S whydah
WHIFF	v -ED, -ING, -S to blow or convey with slight gusts of air
WHIFFER	n pl. -S one that whiffs
WHIFFET	n pl. -S an insignificant person
WHIFFLE	v -FLED, -FLING, -FLES to move or think erratically
WHIFFLER	n pl. -S one that whiffles
WHIG	n pl. -S one who interprets history as a continuing victory of progress over reactionary forces
WHILE	v WHILED, WHILING, WHILES to cause to pass pleasantly
WHILOM	adv formerly
WHILST	conj during the time that
WHIM	n pl. -S an impulsive idea

WHIMBREL *n* pl. -S a shore bird

WHIMPER *v* -ED, -ING, -S to cry with plaintive, broken sounds

WHIMSEY *n* pl. -SEYS whimsy

WHIMSY *n* pl. -SIES a whim
WHIMSIED *adj*

WHIN *n* pl. -S furze

WHINCHAT *n* pl. -S a songbird

WHINE *v* WHINED, WHINING, WHINES to utter a plaintive, high-pitched sound

WHINER *n* pl. -S one that whines

WHINEY *adj* WHINIER, WHINIEST whiny

WHINGE *v* WHINGED, WHINGEING or WHINGING, WHINGES to whine

WHINIER comparative of whiny

WHINIEST superlative of whiny

WHINING present participle of whine

WHINNY *v* -NIED, -NYING, -NIES to neigh in a low or gentle manner

WHINNY *adj* -NIER, -NIEST abounding in whin

WHINY *adj* WHINIER, WHINIEST tending to whine

WHIP *v* WHIPPED or WHIPT, WHIPPING, WHIPS to strike with a whip (an instrument for administering corporal punishment)

WHIPCORD *n* pl. -S a strong, twisted cord

WHIPLASH *n* pl. -ES the lash of a whip

WHIPLIKE *adj* resembling a whip

WHIPPED a past tense of whip

WHIPPER *n* pl. -S one that whips

WHIPPET *n* pl. -S a small, swift dog

WHIPPIER comparative of whippy

WHIPPIEST superlative of whippy

WHIPPING *n* pl. -S material used to whip

WHIPPY *adj* -PIER, -PIEST pertaining to or resembling a whip

WHIPRAY *n* pl. -RAYS a stingray

WHIPSAW *v* -SAWED, -SAWN, -SAWING, -SAWS to cut with a narrow, tapering saw

WHIPT a past tense of whip

WHIPTAIL *n* pl. -S a lizard having a long, slender tail

WHIPWORM *n* pl. -S a parasitic worm

WHIR *v* WHIRRED, WHIRRING, WHIRS to move with a buzzing sound

WHIRL *v* -ED, -ING, -S to revolve rapidly

WHIRLER *n* pl. -S one that whirls

WHIRLY *adj* WHIRLIER, WHIRLIEST marked by a whirling motion

WHIRLY *n* pl. WHIRLIES a small tornado

WHIRR *v* -ED, -ING, -S to whir

WHIRRED past tense of whir

WHIRRING present participle of whir

WHIRRY *v* -RIED, -RYING, -RIES to hurry

WHISH *v* -ED, -ING, -ES to move with a hissing sound

WHISHT *v* -ED, -ING, -S to hush

WHISK *v* -ED, -ING, -S to move briskly

WHISKER *n* pl. -S a hair on a man's face
WHISKERY *adj*

WHISKEY *n* pl. -KEYS a liquor

WHISKY *n* pl. -KIES whiskey

WHISPER *v* -ED, -ING, -S to speak softly

WHISPERY *adj* resembling a whisper

WHIST *v* -ED, -ING, -S to hush

WHISTLE *v* -TLED, -TLING, -TLES to make a shrill, clear musical sound

WHISTLER *n* pl. -S one that whistles

WHIT *n* pl. -S a particle

WHITE *adj* WHITER, WHITEST of the color of pure snow

WHITE *v* WHITED, WHITING, WHITES to whiten

WHITECAP *n* pl. -S a wave with a crest of foam

WHITEFLY *n* pl. -FLIES a small whitish insect

WHITELY *adv* in a white manner

WHITEN *v* -ED, -ING, -S to make white

WHITENER *n* pl. -S one that whitens

WHITEOUT *n* pl. -S an arctic weather condition

WHITER comparative of white

WHITEST superlative of white

WHITEY *adj* whity

WHITHER *adv* to what place

WHITIER comparative of whity

WHITIEST superlative of whity

WHITING *n* pl. -S a marine food fish

WHITISH *adj* somewhat white

WHITLOW *n* pl. -S an inflammation of the finger or toe

WHITRACK *n* pl. -S a weasel

WHITTER *n* pl. -S a large draft of liquor

WHITTLE *v* -TLED, -TLING, -TLES to cut or shave bits from

WHITTLER *n* pl. -S one that whittles

WHITTRET *n* pl. -S a weasel

WHITY _adj_ WHITIER, WHITIEST whitish

WHIZ _v_ WHIZZED, WHIZZING, WHIZZES to move with a buzzing or hissing sound

WHIZBANG _n pl._ -S a type of explosive shell

WHIZZ _v_ -ED, -ING, -ES to whiz

WHIZZED past tense of whiz

WHIZZER _n pl._ -S one that whizzes

WHIZZES present 3d person sing. of whiz

WHIZZING present participle of whiz

WHO _pron_ what or which person or persons

WHOA _interj_ — used to command an animal to stop

WHODUNIT _n pl._ -S a mystery story

WHOEVER _pron_ whatever person

WHOLE _n pl._ -S all the parts or elements entering into and making up a thing

WHOLISM _n pl._ -S holism

WHOLLY _adv_ totally

WHOM _pron_ the objective case of who

WHOMEVER _pron_ the objective case of whoever

WHOMP _v_ -ED, -ING, -S to defeat decisively

WHOMSO _pron_ the objective case of whoso

WHOOF _v_ -ED, -ING, -S to make a deep snorting sound

WHOOP _v_ -ED, -ING, -S to utter loud cries

WHOOPEE _n pl._ -S boisterous fun

WHOOPER _n pl._ -S one that whoops

WHOOPLA _n pl._ -S a noisy commotion

WHOOSH _v_ -ED, -ING, -ES to move with a hissing sound

WHOOSIS _n pl._ -SISES an object or person whose name is not known

WHOP _v_ WHOPPED, WHOPPING, WHOPS to strike forcibly

WHOPPER _n pl._ -S something unusually large

WHORE _v_ WHORED, WHORING, WHORES to consort with prostitutes

WHOREDOM _n pl._ -S prostitution

WHORESON _n pl._ -S a bastard

WHORING present participle of whore

WHORISH _adj_ lewd

WHORL _n pl._ -S a circular arrangement of similar parts WHORLED _adj_

WHORT _n pl._ -S an edible berry

WHORTLE _n pl._ -S whort

WHOSE _pron_ the possessive case of who

WHOSEVER _pron_ the possessive case of whoever

WHOSIS _n pl._ -SISES whoosis

WHOSO _pron_ whoever

WHUMP _v_ -ED, -ING, -S to thump

WHY _n pl._ WHYS the reason or cause of something

WHYDAH _n pl._ -S an African bird

WICH _n pl._ -ES wych

WICK _n pl._ -S a bundle of loosely twisted fibers in a candle or oil lamp

WICKAPE _n pl._ -S wicopy

WICKED _adj_ -EDER, -EDEST evil WICKEDLY _adv_

WICKER _n pl._ -S a slender, pliant twig or branch

WICKET _n pl._ -S a small door or gate

WICKING _n pl._ -S material for wicks

WICKIUP _n pl._ -S an American Indian hut

WICKYUP _n pl._ -S wickiup

WICOPY _n pl._ -PIES a flowering shrub

WIDDER _n pl._ -S a widow

WIDDIE _n pl._ -S widdy

WIDDLE _v_ -DLED, -DLING, -DLES to wriggle

WIDDY _n pl._ -DIES a hangman's noose

WIDE _adj_ WIDER, WIDEST having great extent from side to side WIDELY _adv_

WIDE _n pl._ -S a type of bowled ball in cricket

WIDEBAND _adj_ operating over a wide band of frequencies

WIDEN _v_ -ED, -ING, -S to make wide or wider

WIDENER _n pl._ -S one that widens

WIDENESS _n pl._ -ES the state of being wide

WIDEOUT _n pl._ -S a receiver in football

WIDER comparative of wide

WIDEST superlative of wide

WIDGEON _n pl._ -S a river duck

WIDGET _n pl._ -S a gadget

WIDISH _adj_ somewhat wide

WIDOW _v_ -ED, -ING, -S to deprive of a husband

WIDOWER _n pl._ -S a man whose wife has died and who has not remarried

WIDTH *n* pl. -S extent from side to side

WIDTHWAY *adv* from side to side

WIELD *v* -ED, -ING, -S to handle or use effectively

WIELDER *n* pl. -S one that wields

WIELDY *adj* WIELDIER, WIELDIEST easily wielded

WIENER *n* pl. -S a frankfurter

WIENIE *n* pl. -S a wiener

WIFE *n* pl. WIVES a woman married to a man

WIFE *v* WIFED, WIFING, WIFES to wive

WIFEDOM *n* pl. -S the status or function of a wife

WIFEHOOD *n* pl. -S the state of being wife

WIFELESS *adj* having no wife

WIFELIKE *adj* wifely

WIFELY *adj* -LIER, -LIEST of or befitting a wife

WIFING present participle of wife

WIFTY *adj* -TIER, -TIEST ditsy

WIG *v* WIGGED, WIGGING, WIGS to provide with a wig (an artificial covering of hair for the head)

WIGAN *n* pl. -S a stiff fabric

WIGEON *n* pl. -S widgeon

WIGGED past tense of wig

WIGGERY *n* pl. -GERIES a wig

WIGGIER comparative of wiggy

WIGGIEST superlative of wiggy

WIGGING *n* pl. -S a scolding

WIGGLE *v* -GLED, -GLING, -GLES to move with short, quick movements from side to side

WIGGLER *n* pl. -S one that wiggles

WIGGLY *adj* -GLIER, -GLIEST tending to wiggle

WIGGY *adj* -GIER, -GIEST crazy

WIGHT *n* pl. -S a living being

WIGLESS *adj* having no wig

WIGLET *n* pl. -S a small wig

WIGLIKE *adj* resembling a wig

WIGMAKER *n* pl. -S one that makes wigs

WIGWAG *v* -WAGGED, -WAGGING, -WAGS to move back and forth

WIGWAM *n* pl. -S an American Indian dwelling

WIKIUP *n* pl. -S wickiup

WILCO *interj* — used to indicate that a message received will be complied with

WILD *adj* WILDER, WILDEST living in a natural state

WILD *n* pl. -S an uninhabited or uncultivated area

WILDCAT *v* -CATTED, -CATTING, -CATS to search for oil in an area of doubtful productivity

WILDER *v* -ED, -ING, -S to bewilder

WILDFIRE *n* pl. -S a raging, destructive fire

WILDFOWL *n* pl. -S a wild game bird

WILDING *n* pl. -S a wild plant or animal

WILDISH *adj* somewhat wild

WILDLAND *n* pl. -S uncultivated land

WILDLIFE *n* pl. WILDLIFE wild animals and vegetation

WILDLING *n* pl. -S a wilding

WILDLY *adv* in a wild manner

WILDNESS *n* pl. -ES the state of being wild

WILDWOOD *n* pl. -S natural forest land

WILE *v* WILED, WILING, WILES to entice

WILFUL *adj* willful **WILFULLY** *adv*

WILIER comparative of wily

WILIEST superlative of wily

WILILY *adv* in a wily manner

WILINESS *n* pl. -ES the quality of being wily

WILING present participle of wile

WILL *v* -ED, -ING, -S to decide upon **WILLABLE** *adj*

WILL *v* past sing. 2d person WOULD, WOULDEST, or WOULDST — used as an auxiliary followed by a simple infinitive to express futurity, inclination, likelihood, or requirement

WILLER *n* pl. -S one that wills

WILLET *n* pl. -S a shore bird

WILLFUL *adj* bent on having one's own way

WILLIED past tense of willy

WILLIES present 3d person sing. of willy

WILLING *adj* -INGER, -INGEST inclined or favorably disposed in mind

WILLIWAU *n* pl. -S williwaw

WILLIWAW *n* pl. -S a violent gust of cold wind

WILLOW *v* -ED, -ING, -S to clean textile fibers with a certain machine

WILLOWER *n* pl. -S one that willows

WILLOWY *adj* -LOWIER, -LOWIEST pliant

WILLY v -LIED, -LYING, -LIES to willow

WILLYARD adj willful

WILLYART adj willyard

WILLYWAW n pl. -S williwaw

WILT v -ED, -ING, -S to become limp

WILY adj WILIER, WILIEST crafty

WIMBLE v -BLED, -BLING, -BLES to bore with a hand tool

WIMP n pl. -S a weak or ineffectual person

WIMPISH adj wimpy

WIMPLE v -PLED, -PLING, -PLES to pleat

WIMPY adj WIMPIER, WIMPIEST weak, ineffectual

WIN v WON or WAN, WINNING, WINS to be victorious

WIN v WINNED, WINNING, WINS to winnow

WINCE v WINCED, WINCING, WINCES to flinch

WINCER n pl. -S one that winces

WINCEY n pl. -CEYS a type of fabric

WINCH v -ED, -ING, -ES to raise with a winch (a hoisting machine)

WINCHER n pl. -S one that winches

WINCING present participle of wince

WIND v WOUND or WINDED, WINDING, WINDS to pass around an object or fixed center **WINDABLE** adj

WINDAGE n pl. -S the effect of the wind (air in natural motion) on a projectile

WINDBAG n pl. -S a talkative person

WINDBURN v -BURNED or -BURNT, -BURNING, -BURNS to be affected with skin irritation caused by exposure to the wind

WINDER n pl. -S one that winds

WINDFALL n pl. -S a sudden and unexpected gain

WINDFLAW n pl. -S a gust of wind

WINDGALL n pl. -S a swelling on a horse's leg

WINDIER comparative of windy

WINDIEST superlative of windy

WINDIGO n pl. -GOS an evil demon in Algonquian mythology

WINDILY adv in a windy manner

WINDING n pl. -S material wound about an object

WINDLASS v -ED, -ING, -ES to raise with a windlass (a hoisting machine)

WINDLE v -DLED, -DLING, -DLES to wind

WINDLESS adj being without wind

WINDLING n pl. -S a bundle of straw

WINDMILL v -ED, -ING, -S to rotate solely under the force of a passing airstream

WINDOW v -ED, -ING, -S to provide with a window (an opening in a wall to admit light and air)

WINDPIPE n pl. -S the trachea

WINDROW v -ED, -ING, -S to arrange in long rows, as hay or grain

WINDSOCK n pl. -S a device used to indicate wind direction

WINDSURF v -ED, -ING, -S to sail on a sailboard

WINDUP n pl. -S a conclusion

WINDWARD n pl. -S the direction from which the wind blows

WINDWAY n pl. -WAYS a passage for air

WINDY adj WINDIER, WINDIEST marked by strong wind

WINE v WINED, WINING, WINES to provide with wine (the fermented juice of the grape)

WINELESS adj having no wine

WINERY n pl. -ERIES an establishment for making wine

WINESHOP n pl. -S a shop where wine is sold

WINESKIN n pl. -S a goatskin bag for holding wine

WINESOP n pl. -S a food sopped in wine

WINEY adj WINIER, WINIEST winy

WING v -ED, -ING, -S to travel by means of wings (organs of flight)

WINGBACK n pl. -S a certain player in football

WINGBOW n pl. -S a mark on the wing of a domestic fowl

WINGDING n pl. -S a lively party

WINGEDLY adv swiftly

WINGER n pl. -S a certain player in soccer

WINGIER comparative of wingy

WINGIEST superlative of wingy

WINGLESS adj having no wings

WINGLET n pl. -S a small wing

WINGLIKE adj resembling a wing

WINGMAN n pl. -MEN a pilot behind the leader of a flying formation

WINGOVER	*n* pl. -S a flight maneuver
WINGSPAN	*n* pl. -S the distance from the tip of one of a pair of wings to that of the other
WINGTIP	*n* pl. -S a type of man's shoe
WINGY	*adj* WINGIER, WINGIEST swift
WINIER	comparative of winey and winy
WINIEST	superlative of winey and winy
WINING	present participle of wine
WINISH	*adj* winy
WINK	*v* -ED, -ING, -S to close and open one eye quickly
WINKER	*n* pl. -S one who winks
WINKLE	*v* -KLED, -KLING, -KLES to displace, extract, or evict from a position
WINLESS	*adj* having no wins
WINNABLE	*adj* able to be won
WINNED	past tense of win (to winnow)
WINNER	*n* pl. -S one that wins
WINNING	*n* pl. -S money won in a game or competition
WINNOCK	*n* pl. -S a window
WINNOW	*v* -ED, -ING, -S to free grain from impurities
WINNOWER	*n* pl. -S one that winnows
WINO	*n* pl. WINOES or WINOS one who is habitually drunk on wine
WINSOME	*adj* -SOMER, -SOMEST charming
WINTER	*v* -ED, -ING, -S to pass the winter (the coldest season of the year)
WINTERER	*n* pl. -S one that winters
WINTERLY	*adj* wintry
WINTERY	*adj* -TERIER, -TERIEST wintry
WINTLE	*v* -TLED, -TLING, -TLES to stagger
WINTRY	*adj* -TRIER, -TRIEST characteristic of winter **WINTRILY** *adv*
WINY	*adj* WINIER, WINIEST having the taste or qualities of wine
WINZE	*n* pl. -S a steeply inclined mine shaft
WIPE	*v* WIPED, WIPING, WIPES to rub lightly in order to clean or dry
WIPEOUT	*n* pl. -S a fall from a surfboard
WIPER	*n* pl. -S one that wipes
WIPING	present participle of wipe

WIRE	*v* WIRED, WIRING, WIRES to fasten with wire (a slender rod, strand, or thread of ductile metal) **WIRABLE** *adj*
WIREDRAW	*v* -DREW, -DRAWN, -DRAWING, -DRAWS to draw into wire
WIREHAIR	*n* pl. -S a dog having a wiry coat
WIRELESS	*v* -ED, -ING, -ES to radio
WIRELIKE	*adj* resembling wire
WIREMAN	*n* pl. -MEN one who makes or works with wire
WIRER	*n* pl. -S one that wires
WIRETAP	*v* -TAPPED, -TAPPING, -TAPS to intercept messages by means of a concealed monitoring device
WIREWAY	*n* pl. -WAYS a tube for protecting electric wires
WIREWORK	*n* pl. -S an article made of wire
WIREWORM	*n* pl. -S a wirelike worm
WIRIER	comparative of wiry
WIRIEST	superlative of wiry
WIRILY	*adv* in a wiry manner
WIRINESS	*n* pl. -ES the quality of being wiry
WIRING	*n* pl. -S a system of electric wires
WIRRA	*interj* — used to express sorrow
WIRY	*adj* WIRIER, WIRIEST resembling wire
WIS	*v* past tense WIST to know — WIS and WIST are the only accepted forms of this verb; it cannot be conjugated further
WISDOM	*n* pl. -S the power of true and right discernment
WISE	*v* WISED, WISING, WISES to become aware or informed
WISE	*adj* WISER, WISEST having wisdom
WISEACRE	*n* pl. -S a pretentiously wise person
WISEASS	*n* pl. -ES a wiseacre
WISED	past tense of wise
WISELY	*adv* -LIER, -LIEST in a wise manner
WISENESS	*n* pl. -ES wisdom
WISENT	*n* pl. -S a European bison
WISER	comparative of wise
WISEST	superlative of wise
WISH	*v* -ED, -ING, -ES to feel an impulse toward attainment or possession of something

WISHA	*interj* — used to express surprise	**WITHOUT**	*n* pl. -S an exterior place or area
WISHBONE	*n* pl. -S a forked bone in front of a bird's breastbone	**WITHY**	*n* pl. WITHIES a flexible twig
WISHER	*n* pl. -S one that wishes	**WITHY**	*adj* WITHIER, WITHIEST flexible and tough
WISHFUL	*adj* desirous	**WITING**	present participle of wit and wite
WISHLESS	*adj* not wishful		
WISING	present participle of wise	**WITLESS**	*adj* lacking intelligence
WISP	*v* -ED, -ING, -S to twist into a wisp (a small bunch or bundle)	**WITLING**	*n* pl. -S one who considers himself witty
WISPIER	comparative of wispy	**WITLOOF**	*n* pl. -S chicory
WISPIEST	superlative of wispy	**WITNESS**	*v* -ED, -ING, -ES to see or know by personal experience
WISPILY	*adv* in a wispy manner	**WITNEY**	*n* pl. -NEYS a heavy woolen fabric
WISPISH	*adj* wispy		
WISPLIKE	*adj* wispy	**WITTED**	*adj* having intelligence
WISPY	*adj* WISPIER, WISPIEST resembling a wisp	**WITTIER**	comparative of witty
		WITTIEST	superlative of witty
WISS	*v* -ED, -ING, -ES to wish	**WITTILY**	*adv* in a witty manner
WIST	*v* -ED, -ING, -S to know	**WITTING**	*n* pl. -S knowledge
WISTARIA	*n* pl. -S wisteria	**WITTOL**	*n* pl. -S a man who tolerates his wife's infidelity
WISTERIA	*n* pl. -S a flowering shrub		
WISTFUL	*adj* yearning	**WITTY**	*adj* -TIER, -TIEST humorously clever
WIT	*n* pl. -S intelligence		
WIT	*v* WIST, WITING or WITTING, present sing. 1st person WOT, 2d WOST, 3d WOT, present pl. WITE to know	**WIVE**	*v* WIVED, WIVING, WIVES to marry a woman
		WIVER	*n* pl. -S wivern
WITAN	*n/pl* the members of a national council in Anglo-Saxon England	**WIVERN**	*n* pl. -S a two-legged dragon
		WIVES	pl. of wife
		WIVING	present participle of wive
WITCH	*v* -ED, -ING, -ES to bewitch	**WIZ**	*n* pl. -ES a very clever or skillful person
WITCHERY	*n* pl. -ERIES sorcery		
WITCHING	*n* pl. -S sorcery	**WIZARD**	*n* pl. -S a sorcerer **WIZARDLY** *adj*
WITCHY	*adj* WITCHIER, WITCHIEST malicious		
		WIZARDRY	*n* pl. -RIES sorcery
WITE	*v* WITED, WITING, WITES to blame	**WIZEN**	*v* -ED, -ING, -S to shrivel
		WIZZEN	*n* pl. -S weasand
WITH	*prep* in the company of	**WO**	*n* pl. WOS woe
WITHAL	*adv* in addition	**WOAD**	*n* pl. -S a blue dye **WOADED** *adj*
WITHDRAW	*v* -DREW, -DRAWN, -DRAWING, -DRAWS to move back or away		
		WOADWAX	*n* pl. -ES an ornamental shrub
WITHE	*v* WITHED, WITHING, WITHES to bind with flexible twigs	**WOALD**	*n* pl. -S a yellow pigment
		WOBBLE	*v* -BLED, -BLING, -BLES to move unsteadily
WITHER	*v* -ED, -ING, -S to dry up and wilt		
		WOBBLER	*n* pl. -S one that wobbles
WITHERER	*n* pl. -S one that withers	**WOBBLY**	*adj* -BLIER, -BLIEST unsteady
WITHHOLD	*v* -HELD, -HOLDING, -HOLDS to hold back	**WOBBLY**	*n* pl. -BLIES a member of the Industrial Workers of the World
WITHIER	comparative of withy	**WOBEGONE**	*adj* affected with woe
WITHIES	pl. of withy	**WODGE**	*n* pl. -S a chunk of something
WITHIEST	superlative of withy	**WOE**	*n* pl. -S tremendous grief
WITHIN	*n* pl. -S an interior place or area	**WOEFUL**	*adj* -FULLER, -FULLEST full of woe **WOEFULLY** *adv*
		WOENESS	*n* pl. -ES sadness
		WOESOME	*adj* woeful
WITHING	present participle of withe	**WOFUL**	*adj* woeful **WOFULLY** *adv*

WOK	n pl. -S a cooking utensil
WOKE	a past tense of wake
WOKEN	a past participle of wake
WOLD	n pl. -S an elevated tract of open land
WOLF	n pl. WOLVES a carnivorous mammal
WOLF	v -ED, -ING, -S to devour voraciously
WOLFER	n pl. -S one who hunts wolves
WOLFFISH	n pl. -ES a marine fish
WOLFISH	adj wolflike
WOLFLIKE	adj resembling a wolf
WOLFRAM	n pl. -S tungsten
WOLVER	n pl. -S wolfer
WOLVES	pl. of wolf
WOMAN	n pl. WOMEN an adult human female
WOMAN	v -ED, -ING, -S to play the part of a woman
WOMANISE	v -ISED, -ISING, -ISES to womanize
WOMANISH	adj characteristic of a woman
WOMANIZE	v -IZED, -IZING, -IZES to make effeminate
WOMANLY	adj -LIER, -LIEST having the qualities of a woman
WOMB	n pl. -S the uterus **WOMBED** adj
WOMBAT	n pl. -S a nocturnal mammal
WOMBY	adj WOMBIER, WOMBIEST hollow
WOMEN	pl. of woman
WOMERA	n pl. -S a device used to propel spears
WOMMERA	n pl. -S womera
WON	v WONNED, WONNING, WONS to dwell
WONDER	v -ED, -ING, -S to have a feeling of curiosity or doubt
WONDERER	n pl. -S one that wonders
WONDROUS	adj marvelous
WONK	n pl. -S an overly studious student
WONKY	adj -KIER, -KIEST unsteady
WONNED	past tense of won
WONNER	n pl. -S a prodigy
WONNING	present participle of won
WONT	v -ED, -ING, -S to make accustomed to
WONTEDLY	adv in a usual manner
WONTON	n pl. -S a pork-filled dumpling used in Chinese cooking
WOO	v -ED, -ING, -S to seek the affection of

WOOD	v -ED, -ING, -S to furnish with wood (the hard, fibrous substance beneath the bark of a tree or shrub)
WOODBIN	n pl. -S a bin for holding firewood
WOODBIND	n pl. -S woodbine
WOODBINE	n pl. -S a European shrub
WOODBOX	n pl. -ES a woodbin
WOODCHAT	n pl. -S a European shrike
WOODCOCK	n pl. -S a game bird
WOODCUT	n pl. -S an engraved block of wood
WOODEN	adj -ENER, -ENEST resembling wood in stiffness **WOODENLY** adv
WOODHEN	n pl. -S the weka
WOODIE	n pl. -S woody
WOODIER	comparative of woody
WOODIES	pl. of woody
WOODIEST	superlative of woody
WOODLAND	n pl. -S land covered with trees
WOODLARK	n pl. -S a songbird
WOODLESS	adj having no wood
WOODLORE	n pl. -S knowledge of the forest
WOODLOT	n pl. -S an area restricted to the growing of forest trees
WOODMAN	n pl. -MEN woodsman
WOODNOTE	n pl. -S a song or call of a forest bird
WOODPILE	n pl. -S a pile of wood
WOODRUFF	n pl. -S an aromatic herb
WOODSHED	v -SHEDDED, -SHEDDING, -SHEDS to practice on a musical instrument
WOODSIA	n pl. -S a small fern
WOODSMAN	n pl. -MEN one who works or lives in the forest
WOODSY	adj WOODSIER, WOODSIEST suggestive of a forest
WOODWAX	n pl. -ES woadwax
WOODWIND	n pl. -S a musical wind instrument
WOODWORK	n pl. -S work made of wood
WOODWORM	n pl. -S a wood-boring worm
WOODY	adj WOODIER, WOODIEST containing or resembling wood
WOODY	n pl. WOODIES a wood-paneled station wagon
WOOER	n pl. -S one that woos
WOOF	v -ED, -ING, -S to utter a gruff barking sound

WOOFER *n pl.* -S a loudspeaker designed to reproduce low-pitched sounds

WOOINGLY *adv* attractively

WOOL *n pl.* -S the dense, soft hair forming the coat of certain mammals

WOOLED *adj* having wool of a specified kind

WOOLEN *n pl.* -S a fabric made of wool

WOOLER *n pl.* -S a domestic animal raised for its wool

WOOLFELL *n pl.* -S woolskin

WOOLHAT *n pl.* -S one who works a small farm

WOOLIE *n pl.* -S a woolly

WOOLIER comparative of wooly

WOOLIES pl. of wooly

WOOLIEST superlative of wooly

WOOLLED *adj* wooled

WOOLLEN *n pl.* -S woolen

WOOLLIER comparative of woolly

WOOLLIES pl. of woolly

WOOLLIKE *adj* resembling wool

WOOLLY *adj* -LIER, -LIEST consisting of or resembling wool
  WOOLLILY *adv*

WOOLLY *n pl.* -LIES a garment made of wool

WOOLMAN *n pl.* -MEN a dealer in wool

WOOLPACK *n pl.* -S a bag for packing a bale of wool

WOOLSACK *n pl.* -S a sack of wool

WOOLSHED *n pl.* -S a building in which sheep are sheared

WOOLSKIN *n pl.* -S a sheepskin with the wool still on it

WOOLWORK *n pl.* -S needlework

WOOLY *adj* WOOLIER, WOOLIEST woolly

WOOLY *n pl.* WOOLIES a woolly

WOOMERA *n pl.* -S womera

WOOPS *v* -ED, -ING, -ES to vomit

WOORALI *n pl.* -S curare

WOORARI *n pl.* -S curare

WOOSH *v* -ED, -ING, -ES to whoosh

WOOZY *adj* -ZIER, -ZIEST dazed
  WOOZILY *adv*

WORD *v* -ED, -ING, -S to express in words (speech sounds that communicate meaning)

WORDAGE *n pl.* -S the number of words used

WORDBOOK *n pl.* -S a dictionary

WORDIER comparative of wordy

WORDIEST superlative of wordy

WORDILY *adv* in a wordy manner

WORDING *n pl.* -S the act or style of expressing in words

WORDLESS *adj* being without words

WORDPLAY *n pl.* -PLAYS a witty exchange of words

WORDY *adj* WORDIER, WORDIEST using many or too many words

WORE past tense of wear

WORK *v* WORKED or WROUGHT, WORKING, WORKS to exert one's powers of body or mind for some purpose

WORKABLE *adj* capable of being done

WORKADAY *adj* everyday

WORKBAG *n pl.* -S a bag for holding work instruments and materials

WORKBOAT *n pl.* -S a boat used for commercial purposes

WORKBOOK *n pl.* -S an exercise book for a student

WORKBOX *n pl.* -ES a box for holding work instruments and materials

WORKDAY *n pl.* -DAYS a day on which work is done

WORKER *n pl.* -S one that works

WORKFARE *n pl.* -S a welfare program that requires recipients to perform public-service work

WORKFOLK *n/pl* manual laborers

WORKING *n pl.* -S a mining excavation

WORKLESS *adj* unemployed

WORKLOAD *n pl.* -S the amount of work assigned to an employee

WORKMAN *n pl.* -MEN a male worker

WORKMATE *n pl.* -S a fellow worker

WORKOUT *n pl.* -S a period of physical exercise

WORKROOM *n pl.* -S a room in which work is done

WORKSHOP *n pl.* -S a workroom

WORKUP *n pl.* -S an intensive diagnostic study

WORKWEEK *n pl.* -S the number of hours worked in a week

WORLD *n pl.* -S the earth and all its inhabitants

WORLDLY *adj* -LIER, -LIEST pertaining to the world

WORM *v* -ED, -ING, -S to rid of worms (small, limbless invertebrates)

WORMER *n pl.* -S one that worms

WORMHOLE *n pl.* -S a hole made by a burrowing worm

WORMIER comparative of wormy

WORMIEST superlative of wormy
WORMIL n pl. -S a lump in the skin of an animal's back
WORMISH adj wormlike
WORMLIKE adj resembling a worm
WORMROOT n pl. -S pinkroot
WORMSEED n pl. -S a tropical plant
WORMWOOD n pl. -S a European herb
WORMY adj WORMIER, WORMIEST infested with worms
WORN adj affected by wear or use
WORNNESS n pl. -ES the state of being worn
WORRIED past tense of worry
WORRIER n pl. -S one that worries
WORRIT v -ED, -ING, -S to worry
WORRY v -RIED, -RYING, -RIES to feel anxious and uneasy about something
WORSE n pl. -S something that is worse (bad in a greater degree)
WORSEN v -ED, -ING, -S to make or become worse
WORSER adj worse
WORSET n pl. -S worsted
WORSHIP v -SHIPED, -SHIPING, -SHIPS or -SHIPPED, -SHIPPING, -SHIPS to honor and love as a divine being
WORST v -ED, -ING, -S to defeat
WORSTED n pl. -S a woolen yarn
WORT n pl. -S a plant, herb, or vegetable
WORTH v -ED, -ING, -S to befall
WORTHFUL adj worthy
WORTHY adj -THIER, -THIEST having value or merit WORTHILY adv
WORTHY n pl. -THIES a worthy person
WOST a present 2d person sing. of wit
WOT v WOTTED, WOTTING, WOTS to know
WOULD past tense of will
WOULDEST a 2d person sing. past tense of will
WOULDST a 2d person sing. past tense of will
WOUND v -ED, -ING, -S to inflict an injury upon
WOVE a past tense of weave
WOVEN n pl. -S a woven fabric
WOW v -ED, -ING, -S to excite to enthusiastic approval
WOWSER n pl. -S a puritanical person
WRACK v -ED, -ING, -S to wreck

WRACKFUL adj destructive
WRAITH n pl. -S a ghost
WRANG n pl. -S a wrong
WRANGLE v -GLED, -GLING, -GLES to argue noisily
WRANGLER n pl. -S one that wrangles
WRAP v WRAPPED or WRAPT, WRAPPING, WRAPS to enclose in something wound or folded about
WRAPPER n pl. -S one that wraps
WRAPPING n pl. -S the material in which something is wrapped
WRAPT a past tense of wrap
WRASSE n pl. -S a marine fish
WRASSLE v -SLED, -SLING, -SLES to wrastle
WRASTLE v -TLED, -TLING, -TLES to wrestle
WRATH v -ED, -ING, -S to make wrathful
WRATHFUL adj extremely angry
WRATHY adj WRATHIER, WRATHIEST wrathful WRATHILY adv
WREAK v -ED, -ING, -S to inflict
WREAKER n pl. -S one that wreaks
WREATH n pl. -S a band of flowers WREATHY adj
WREATHE v WREATHED, WREATHEN, WREATHING, WREATHES to shape into a wreath
WRECK v -ED, -ING, -S to cause the ruin of
WRECKAGE n pl. -S the act of wrecking
WRECKER n pl. -S one that wrecks
WRECKFUL adj destructive
WRECKING n pl. -S the occupation of salvaging wrecked objects
WREN n pl. -S a small songbird
WRENCH v -ED, -ING, -ES to twist suddenly and forcibly
WREST v -ED, -ING, -S to take away by force
WRESTER n pl. -S one that wrests
WRESTLE v -TLED, -TLING, -TLES to engage in a type of hand-to-hand contest
WRESTLER n pl. -S one that wrestles
WRETCH n pl. -ES a wretched person
WRETCHED adj -EDER, -EDEST extremely unhappy
WRICK v -ED, -ING, -S to wrench
WRIED past tense of wry
WRIER a comparative of wry
WRIES present 3d person sing. of wry
WRIEST a superlative of wry

WRIGGLE *v* -GLED, -GLING, -GLES to turn or twist in a sinuous manner

WRIGGLER *n pl.* -S one that wriggles

WRIGGLY *adj* -GLIER, -GLIEST wriggling

WRIGHT *n pl.* -S one who constructs or creates

WRING *v* WRUNG or WRINGED, WRINGING, WRINGS to twist so as to compress

WRINGER *n pl.* -S one that wrings

WRINKLE *v* -KLED, -KLING, -KLES to make wrinkles (small ridges or furrows) in

WRINKLY *adj* -KLIER, -KLIEST having wrinkles

WRIST *n pl.* -S the junction between the hand and forearm

WRISTLET *n pl.* -S a band worn around the wrist

WRISTY *adj* WRISTIER, WRISTIEST using much wrist action

WRIT *n pl.* -S a written legal order

WRITE *v* WROTE, WRITTEN, WRITING, WRITES to form characters or symbols on a surface with an instrument **WRITABLE** *adj*

WRITER *n pl.* -S one that writes

WRITERLY *adj* characteristic of a writer

WRITHE *v* WRITHED, WRITHING, WRITHES to squirm or twist in pain

WRITHEN *adj* twisted

WRITHER *n pl.* -S one that writhes

WRITHING present participle of writhe

WRITING *n pl.* -S a written composition

WRITTEN past participle of write

WRONG *adj* WRONGER, WRONGEST not according to what is right, proper, or correct

WRONG *v* -ED, -ING, -S to treat injuriously or unjustly

WRONGER *n pl.* -S one that wrongs

WRONGFUL *adj* wrong

WRONGLY *adv* in a wrong manner

WROTE past tense of write

WROTH *adj* very angry

WROTHFUL *adj* wroth

WROUGHT a past tense of work

WRUNG a past tense of wring

WRY *adj* WRIER, WRIEST or WRYER, WRYEST contorted **WRYLY** *adv*

WRY *v* WRIED, WRYING, WRIES to contort

WRYNECK *n pl.* -S a European bird

WRYNESS *n pl.* -ES the state of being wry

WUD *adj* insane

WURST *n pl.* -S sausage

WURZEL *n pl.* -S a variety of beet

WUSS *n pl.* -ES a wimp

WUSSY *n pl.* -SIES a wuss

WUSSY *adj* WUSSIER, WUSSIEST wimpy

WUTHER *v* -ED, -ING, -S to blow with a dull roaring sound

WYCH *n pl.* -ES a European elm

WYE *n pl.* -S the letter Y

WYLE *v* WYLED, WYLING, WYLES to beguile

WYN *n pl.* -S wynn

WYND *n pl.* -S a narrow street

WYNN *n pl.* -S the rune for W

WYTE *v* WYTED, WYTING, WYTES to wite

WYVERN *n pl.* -S wivern

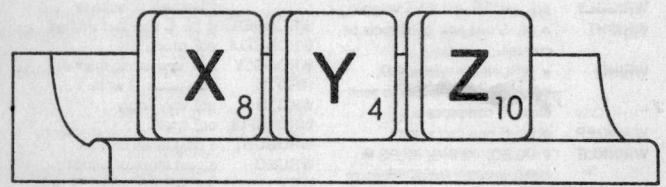

XANTHAN *n* pl. -S a gum produced by bacterial fermentation

XANTHATE *n* pl. -S a chemical salt

XANTHEIN *n* pl. -S the water-soluble part of the coloring matter in yellow flowers

XANTHENE *n* pl. -S a chemical compound

XANTHIC *adj* tending to have a yellow color

XANTHIN *n* pl. -S a yellow pigment

XANTHINE *n* pl. -S a chemical compound

XANTHOMA *n* pl. -MAS or -MATA a skin disease

XANTHONE *n* pl. -S a chemical compound

XANTHOUS *adj* yellow

XEBEC *n* pl. -S a Mediterranean sailing vessel

XENIA *n* pl. -S the effect of pollen on certain plant structures **XENIAL** *adj*

XENIC *adj* pertaining to a type of culture medium

XENOGAMY *n* pl. -MIES the transfer of pollen from one plant to another

XENOGENY *n* pl. -NIES the supposed production of offspring totally different from the parent

XENOLITH *n* pl. -S a rock fragment included in another rock

XENON *n* pl. -S a gaseous element

XERARCH *adj* developing in a dry area

XERIC *adj* requiring only a small amount of moisture

XEROSERE *n* pl. -S a dry-land sere

XEROSIS *n* pl. -ROSES abnormal dryness of a body part or tissue **XEROTIC** *adj*

XEROX *v* -ED, -ING, -ES to copy on a xerographic copier

XERUS *n* pl. -ES an African ground squirrel

XI *n* pl. -S a Greek letter

XIPHOID *n* pl. -S a part of the sternum

XU *n* pl. XU a monetary unit of Vietnam

XYLAN *n* pl. -S a substance found in cell walls of plants

XYLEM *n* pl. -S a complex plant tissue

XYLENE *n* pl. -S a flammable hydrocarbon

XYLIDIN *n* pl. -S xylidine

XYLIDINE *n* pl. -S a chemical compound

XYLITOL *n* pl. -S an alcohol

XYLOCARP *n* pl. -S a hard, woody fruit

XYLOID *adj* resembling wood

XYLOL *n* pl. -S xylene

XYLOSE *n* pl. -S a type of sugar

XYLOTOMY *n* pl. -MIES the preparation of sections of wood for microscopic examination

XYLYL *n* pl. -S a univalent radical

XYST *n* pl. -S xystus

XYSTER *n* pl. -S a surgical instrument for scraping bones

XYSTOS *n* pl. -TOI xystus

XYSTUS *n* pl. -TI a roofed area where athletes trained in ancient Greece

YA *pron* you

YABBER *v* -ED, -ING, -S to jabber

YACHT *v* -ED, -ING, -S to sail in a yacht (a vessel used for pleasure cruising or racing)

YACHTER *n* pl. -S one who sails a yacht

YACHTING *n* pl. -S the sport of sailing in yachts

YACHTMAN *n pl.* -MEN a yachter

YACK *v* -ED, -ING, -S to yak

YAFF *v* -ED, -ING, -S to bark

YAGER *n pl.* -S jaeger

YAGI *n pl.* -S a type of shortwave antenna

YAH *interj* — used as an exclamation of disgust

YAHOO *n pl.* -HOOS a coarse, uncouth person

YAHOOISM *n pl.* -S coarse, uncouth behavior

YAHRZEIT *n pl.* -S an anniversary of the death of a family member observed by Jews

YAIRD *n pl.* -S a garden

YAK *v* YAKKED, YAKKING, YAKS to chatter

YAKITORI *n pl.* -S marinated chicken pieces on skewers

YAKKER *n pl.* -S one that yaks

YALD *adj* yauld

YAM *n pl.* -S a plant having an edible root

YAMALKA *n pl.* -S yarmulke

YAMEN *n pl.* -S the residence of a Chinese public official

YAMMER *v* -ED, -ING, -S to whine or complain peevishly

YAMMERER *n pl.* -S one that yammers

YAMULKA *n pl.* -S yarmulke

YAMUN *n pl.* -S yamen

YANG *n pl.* -S the masculine active principle in Chinese cosmology

YANK *v* -ED, -ING, -S to pull suddenly

YANQUI *n pl.* -S a United States citizen

YANTRA *n pl.* -S a geometrical diagram used in meditation

YAP *v* YAPPED, YAPPING, YAPS to bark shrilly

YAPOCK *n pl.* -S an aquatic mammal

YAPOK *n pl.* -S yapock

YAPON *n pl.* -S yaupon

YAPPED past tense of yap

YAPPER *n pl.* -S one that yaps

YAPPING present participle of yap

YAR *adj* yare

YARD *v* -ED, -ING, -S to put in a yard (a tract of ground adjacent to a building)

YARDAGE *n pl.* -S the use of an enclosure for livestock at a railroad station

YARDARM *n pl.* -S either end of a ship's spar

YARDBIRD *n pl.* -S an army recruit

YARDLAND *n pl.* -S an old English unit of land measure

YARDMAN *n pl.* -MEN a man employed to do outdoor work

YARDWAND *n pl.* -S a measuring stick

YARDWORK *n pl.* -S the work of caring for a lawn

YARE *adj* YARER, YAREST nimble YARELY *adv*

YARMELKE *n pl.* -S yarmulke

YARMULKE *n pl.* -S a skullcap worn by Jewish males

YARN *v* -ED, -ING, -S to tell a long story

YARNER *n pl.* -S one that yarns

YARROW *n pl.* -S a perennial herb

YASHMAC *n pl.* -S yashmak

YASHMAK *n pl.* -S a veil worn by Muslim women

YASMAK *n pl.* -S yashmak

YATAGAN *n pl.* -S yataghan

YATAGHAN *n pl.* -S a Turkish sword

YATTER *v* -ED, -ING, -S to talk idly

YAUD *n pl.* -S an old mare

YAULD *adj* vigorous

YAUP *v* -ED, -ING, -S to yawp

YAUPER *n pl.* -S one that yaups

YAUPON *n pl.* -S an evergreen shrub

YAUTIA *n pl.* -S a tropical plant

YAW *v* -ED, -ING, -S to deviate from an intended course

YAWL *v* -ED, -ING, -S to yowl

YAWMETER *n pl.* -S an instrument in an aircraft

YAWN *v* -ED, -ING, -S to open the mouth wide with a deep inhalation of air

YAWNER *n pl.* -S one that yawns

YAWP *v* -ED, -ING, -S to utter a loud, harsh cry

YAWPER *n pl.* -S one that yawps

YAWPING *n pl.* -S a loud, harsh cry

YAY *n pl.* YAYS yea

YCLEPED *adj* yclept

YCLEPT *adj* called; named

YE *pron* you

YEA *n pl.* -S an affirmative vote

YEAH *adv* yes

YEALING *n pl.* -S a person of the same age

YEAN *v* -ED, -ING, -S to bear young

YEANLING *n pl.* -S the young of a sheep or goat

YEAR *n pl.* -S a period of time consisting of 365 or 366 days

YEARBOOK *n pl.* -S a book published each year by a graduating class

YEAREND *n pl.* -S the end of a year

YEARLIES *pl.* of yearly

YEARLING *n pl.* -S an animal past its first year and not yet two years old

YEARLONG *adj* lasting through a year

YEARLY *n pl.* -LIES a publication appearing once a year

YEARN *v* -ED, -ING, -S to have a strong or deep desire

YEARNER *n pl.* -S one that yearns

YEARNING *n pl.* -S a strong or deep desire

YEASAYER *n pl.* -S one that affirms something

YEAST *v* -ED, -ING, -S to foam

YEASTY *adj* YEASTIER, YEASTIEST foamy YEASTILY *adv*

YECCH *n pl.* -S something disgusting

YECH *n pl.* -S yecch

YECHY *adj* disgusting

YEELIN *n pl.* -S yealing

YEGG *n pl.* -S a burglar

YEGGMAN *n pl.* -MEN a yegg

YEH *adv* yeah

YELD *adj* not giving milk

YELK *n pl.* -S yolk

YELL *v* -ED, -ING, -S to cry out loudly

YELLER *n pl.* -S one that yells

YELLOW *adj* -LOWER, -LOWEST of a bright color like that of ripe lemons YELLOWLY *adv*

YELLOW *v* -ED, -ING, -S to make or become yellow

YELLOWY *adj* somewhat yellow

YELP *v* -ED, -ING, -S to utter a sharp, shrill cry

YELPER *n pl.* -S one that yelps

YEN *v* YENNED, YENNING, YENS to yearn

YENTA *n pl.* -S a gossipy woman

YENTE *n pl.* -S yenta

YEOMAN *n pl.* -MEN an independent farmer YEOMANLY *adj*

YEOMANRY *n pl.* -RIES the collective body of yeomen

YEP *adv* yes

YERBA *n pl.* -S a South American beverage resembling tea

YERK *v* -ED, -ING, -S to beat vigorously

YES *v* YESSED, YESSING, YESSES or YESES to give an affirmative reply to

YESHIVA *n pl.* -VAS, -VOT, or -VOTH an orthodox Jewish school

YESHIVAH *n pl.* -S yeshiva

YESSED past tense of yes

YESSES a 3d person sing. of yes

YESSING present participle of yes

YESTER *adj* pertaining to yesterday

YESTERN *adj* yester

YESTREEN *n pl.* -S the previous evening

YET *adv* up to now

YETI *n pl.* -S the abominable snowman

YETT *n pl.* -S a gate

YEUK *v* -ED, -ING, -S to itch

YEUKY *adj* itchy

YEW *n pl.* -S an evergreen tree or shrub

YIELD *v* -ED, -ING, -S to give up

YIELDER *n pl.* -S one that yields

YIKES *interj* — used to express fear or pain

YILL *n pl.* -S ale

YIN *n pl.* -S the feminine passive principle in Chinese cosmology

YINCE *adv* once

YIP *v* YIPPED, YIPPING, YIPS to yelp

YIPE *interj* — used to express fear or surprise

YIPES *interj* yipe

YIPPED past tense of yip

YIPPEE *interj* — used to express joy

YIPPIE *n pl.* -S a politically radical hippie

YIPPING present participle of yip

YIRD *n pl.* -S earth

YIRR *v* -ED, -ING, -S to snarl

YIRTH *n pl.* -S yird

YLEM *n pl.* -S hypothetical matter from which the elements are derived

YO *interj* — used to call attention or to express affirmation

YOB *n pl.* -S a hooligan

YOBBO *n pl.* -BOS or -BOES a yob

YOCK *v* -ED, -ING, -S to laugh boisterously

YOD *n pl.* -S a Hebrew letter

YODEL *v* -DELED, -DELING, -DELS or -DELLED, -DELLING, -DELS to sing with a fluctuating voice

YODELER *n pl.* -S one that yodels

YODELLER *n pl.* -S yodeler

YODELLING a present participle of yodel

YODH	*n* pl. -S yod
YODLE	*v* -DLED, -DLING, -DLES to yodel
YODLER	*n* pl. -S yodeler
YOGA	*n* pl. -S a Hindu philosophy involving mental and physical disciplines
YOGEE	*n* pl. -S yogi
YOGH	*n* pl. -S a Middle English letter
YOGHOURT	*n* pl. -S yogurt
YOGHURT	*n* pl. -S yogurt
YOGI	*n* pl. -S a person who practices yoga
YOGIC	*adj* pertaining to yoga
YOGIN	*n* pl. -S yogi
YOGINI	*n* pl. -S a female yogi
YOGURT	*n* pl. -S a food made from milk
YOICKS	*interj* — used to encourage hunting hounds
YOK	*n* pl. -S a boisterous laugh
YOKE	*v* YOKED, YOKING, YOKES to fit with a yoke (a wooden frame for joining together draft animals)
YOKEL	*n* pl. -S a naive or gullible rustic
YOKELESS	*adj* having no yoke
YOKELISH	*adj* resembling a yokel
YOKEMATE	*n* pl. -S a companion in work
YOKING	present participle of yoke
YOKOZUNA	*n* pl. -S a champion sumo wrestler
YOLK	*n* pl. -S the yellow portion of an egg YOLKED *adj*
YOLKY	*adj* YOLKIER, YOLKIEST resembling a yolk
YOM	*n* pl. YOMIM day
YON	*adv* yonder
YOND	*adv* yonder
YONDER	*adv* over there
YONI	*n* pl. -S a symbol for the vulva in Hindu religion YONIC *adj*
YONKER	*n* pl. -S younker
YORE	*n* pl. -S time past
YOU	*pron* the 2d person sing. or pl. pronoun
YOUNG	*adj* YOUNGER, YOUNGEST being in the early period of life or growth
YOUNG	*n* pl. -S offspring
YOUNGER	*n* pl. -S an inferior in age
YOUNGISH	*adj* somewhat young
YOUNKER	*n* pl. -S a young gentleman
YOUPON	*n* pl. -S yaupon
YOUR	*adj* a possessive form of the pronoun you

YOURN	*pron* yours
YOURS	*pron* a possessive form of the pronoun you
YOURSELF	*pron* pl. -SELVES a form of the 2d person pronoun
YOUSE	*pron* you
YOUTH	*n* pl. -S a young person
YOUTHEN	*v* -ED, -ING, -S to make youthful
YOUTHFUL	*adj* young
YOW	*v* -ED, -ING, -S to yowl
YOWE	*n* pl. -S a ewe
YOWIE	*n* pl. -S a small ewe
YOWL	*v* -ED, -ING, -S to utter a loud, long, mournful cry
YOWLER	*n* pl. -S one that yowls
YPERITE	*n* pl. -S a poisonous gas
YTTERBIA	*n* pl. -S a chemical compound YTTERBIC *adj*
YTTRIA	*n* pl. -S a chemical compound
YTTRIUM	*n* pl. -S a metallic element YTTRIC *adj*
YUAN	*n* pl. -S a monetary unit of China
YUCA	*n* pl. -S a tropical plant
YUCCA	*n* pl. -S a tropical plant
YUCCH	*interj* — used to express disgust
YUCH	*interj* yucch
YUCK	*v* -ED, -ING, -S to yuk
YUCKY	*adj* YUCKIER, YUCKIEST disgusting
YUGA	*n* pl. -S an age of time in Hinduism
YUK	*v* YUKKED, YUKKING, YUKS to laugh loudly
YULAN	*n* pl. -S a Chinese tree
YULE	*n* pl. -S Christmas time
YULETIDE	*n* pl. -S yule
YUM	*interj* — used to express pleasurable satisfaction
YUMMY	*adj* -MIER, -MIEST delicious
YUMMY	*n* pl. -MIES something delicious
YUP	*n* pl. -S a yuppie
YUPON	*n* pl. -S yaupon
YUPPIE	*n* pl. -S a young professional person working in a city
YURT	*n* pl. YURTA or YURTS a portable tent
YWIS	*adv* iwis
ZABAIONE	*n* pl. -S a dessert resembling custard
ZABAJONE	*n* pl. -S zabaione
ZACATON	*n* pl. -S a Mexican grass

ZADDICK n pl. -DIKIM zaddik
ZADDIK n pl. -DIKIM a virtuous person by Jewish religious standards
ZAFFAR n pl. -S zaffer
ZAFFER n pl. -S a blue ceramic coloring
ZAFFIR n pl. -S zaffer
ZAFFRE n pl. -S zaffer
ZAFTIG adj full-bosomed
ZAG v ZAGGED, ZAGGING, ZAGS to turn sharply
ZAIBATSU n pl. ZAIBATSU a powerful family combine in Japan
ZAIKAI n pl. -S the business community of Japan
ZAIRE n pl. -S a monetary unit of Zaire
ZAMARRA n pl. -S a sheepskin coat
ZAMARRO n pl. -ROS zamarra
ZAMIA n pl. -S a tropical plant
ZAMINDAR n pl. -S a tax collector in precolonial India
ZANANA n pl. -S zenana
ZANDER n pl. -S a freshwater fish
ZANIER comparative of zany
ZANIES pl. of zany
ZANINESS n pl. -ES the quality or state of being zany
ZANY adj ZANIER, ZANIEST ludicrously comical **ZANILY** adv
ZANY n pl. -NIES a zany person
ZANYISH adj somewhat zany
ZANZA n pl. -S an African musical instrument
ZAP v ZAPPED, ZAPPING, ZAPS to kill or destroy instantaneously
ZAPATEO n pl. -TEOS a Spanish dance
ZAPPER n pl. -S a device that zaps
ZAPPY adj -PIER, -PIEST zippy
ZAPTIAH n pl. -S a Turkish policeman
ZAPTIEH n pl. -S zaptiah
ZARATITE n pl. -S a chemical compound
ZAREBA n pl. -S an improvised stockade
ZAREEBA n pl. -S zareba
ZARF n pl. -S a metal holder for a coffee cup
ZARIBA n pl. -S zareba
ZARZUELA n pl. -S a Spanish operetta
ZASTRUGA n pl. -GI sastruga
ZAX n pl. -ES a tool for cutting roof slates
ZAYIN n pl. -S a Hebrew letter

ZAZEN n pl. -S meditation in Zen Buddhism
ZEAL n pl. -S enthusiastic devotion
ZEALOT n pl. -S one who is zealous
ZEALOTRY n pl. -RIES excessive zeal
ZEALOUS adj filled with zeal
ZEATIN n pl. -S a chemical compound found in maize
ZEBEC n pl. -S xebec
ZEBECK n pl. -S xebec
ZEBRA n pl. -S an African mammal that is related to the horse **ZEBRAIC** adj
ZEBRASS n pl. -ES the offspring of a zebra and an ass
ZEBRINE adj pertaining to a zebra
ZEBROID adj zebrine
ZEBU n pl. -S an Asian ox
ZECCHIN n pl. -S zecchino
ZECCHINO n pl. -NI or -NOS a former gold coin of Italy
ZECHIN n pl. -S zecchino
ZED n pl. -S the letter Z
ZEDOARY n pl. -ARIES the medicinal root of a tropical plant
ZEE n pl. -S the letter Z
ZEIN n pl. -S a simple protein
ZEK n pl. -S an inmate in a Soviet labor camp
ZELKOVA n pl. -S a Japanese tree
ZEMINDAR n pl. -S zamindar
ZEMSTVO n pl. -VOS or -VA an elective council in czarist Russia
ZENAIDA n pl. -S a wild dove
ZENANA n pl. -S the section of a house in India reserved for women
ZENITH n pl. -S the highest point **ZENITHAL** adj
ZEOLITE n pl. -S a mineral **ZEOLITIC** adj
ZEPHYR n pl. -S a gentle breeze
ZEPPELIN n pl. -S a long, rigid airship
ZERK n pl. -S a grease fitting
ZERO v -ED, -ING, -ES or -S to aim at the exact center of a target
ZEROTH adj being numbered zero in a series
ZEST v -ED, -ING, -S to fill with zest (invigorating excitement)
ZESTER n pl. -S a utensil for peeling citrus rind
ZESTFUL adj full of zest
ZESTLESS adj lacking zest
ZESTY adj ZESTIER, ZESTIEST marked by zest
ZETA n pl. -S a Greek letter

ZEUGMA *n pl.* -S the use of a word to modify or govern two or more words, while applying to each in a different sense

ZIBELINE *n pl.* -S a soft fabric

ZIBET *n pl.* -S an Asian civet

ZIBETH *n pl.* -S zibet

ZIG *v* ZIGGED, ZIGGING, ZIGS to turn sharply

ZIGGURAT *n pl.* -S an ancient Babylonian temple tower

ZIGZAG *v* -ZAGGED, -ZAGGING, -ZAGS to proceed on a course marked by sharp turns

ZIKKURAT *n pl.* -S ziggurat

ZIKURAT *n pl.* -S ziggurat

ZILCH *n pl.* -ES nothing

ZILL *n pl.* -S one of a pair of finger cymbals

ZILLAH *n pl.* -S an administrative district in India

ZILLION *n pl.* -S an indeterminately large number

ZIN *n pl.* -S a dry red wine

ZINC *v* ZINCED, ZINCING, ZINCS or ZINCKED, ZINCKING, ZINCS to coat with zinc (a metallic element)

ZINCATE *n pl.* -S a chemical salt

ZINCIC *adj* pertaining to zinc

ZINCIFY *v* -FIED, -FYING, -FIES to coat with zinc

ZINCITE *n pl.* -S an ore of zinc

ZINCKED a past tense of zinc

ZINCKING a present participle of zinc

ZINCKY *adj* resembling zinc

ZINCOID *adj* zincic

ZINCOUS *adj* zincic

ZINCY *adj* zincky

ZINEB *n pl.* -S an insecticide

ZING *v* -ED, -ING, -S to move with a high-pitched humming sound

ZINGANO *n pl.* -NI zingaro

ZINGARA *n pl.* -RE a female gypsy

ZINGARO *n pl.* -RI a gypsy

ZINGER *n pl.* -S a pointed witty retort or remark

ZINGY *adj* ZINGIER, ZINGIEST enjoyably exciting

ZINKIFY *v* -FIED, -FYING, -FIES to zincify

ZINKY *adj* zincky

ZINNIA *n pl.* -S a tropical plant

ZIP *v* ZIPPED, ZIPPING, ZIPS to move with speed and vigor

ZIPLESS *adj* lacking vigor or energy

ZIPPER *v* -ED, -ING, -S to fasten with a zipper (a fastener consisting of two rows of interlocking teeth)

ZIPPING present participle of zip

ZIPPY *adj* -PIER, -PIEST full of energy

ZIRAM *n pl.* -S a chemical salt

ZIRCON *n pl.* -S a mineral

ZIRCONIA *n pl.* -S a chemical compound

ZIRCONIC *adj* pertaining to a certain metallic element

ZIT *n pl.* -S a pimple

ZITHER *n pl.* -S a stringed instrument

ZITHERN *n pl.* -S zither

ZITI *n pl.* -S a tubular pasta

ZIZIT *n/pl* zizith

ZIZITH *n/pl* the tassels on the four corners of a Jewish prayer shawl

ZIZZLE *v* -ZLED, -ZLING, -ZLES to sizzle

ZLOTY *n pl.* ZLOTYS, ZLOTE, ZLOTIES, or ZLOTYCH a monetary unit of Poland

ZOA a *pl.* of zoon

ZOARIUM *n pl.* -IA a colony of bryozoans ZOARIAL *adj*

ZODIAC *n pl.* -S an imaginary belt encircling the celestial sphere ZODIACAL *adj*

ZOEA *n pl.* ZOEAE or ZOEAS a larval form of certain crustaceans ZOEAL *adj*

ZOECIUM *n pl.* -CIA zooecium

ZOFTIG *adj* zaftig

ZOIC *adj* pertaining to animals or animal life

ZOISITE *n pl.* -S a mineral

ZOMBI *n pl.* -S a zombie

ZOMBIE *n pl.* -S a will-less human capable only of automatic movement

ZOMBIFY *v* -FIED, -FYING, -FIES to turn into a zombie

ZOMBIISM *n pl.* -S the system of beliefs connected with a West African snake god

ZONAL *adj* pertaining to a zone ZONALLY *adv*

ZONARY *adj* zonal

ZONATE *adj* arranged in zones

ZONATED *adj* zonate

ZONATION *n pl.* -S arrangement in zones

ZONE v ZONED, ZONING, ZONES to arrange in zones (areas distinguished from other adjacent areas)

ZONELESS adj having no zone or belt

ZONER n pl. -S one that zones

ZONETIME n pl. -S standard time used at sea

ZONING present participle of zone

ZONK v -ED, -ING, -S to stupefy

ZONULA n pl. -LAE or -LAS zonule

ZONULE n pl. -S a small zone ZONULAR adj

ZOO n pl. ZOOS a place where animals are kept for public exhibition

ZOOCHORE n pl. -S a plant dispersed by animals

ZOOECIUM n pl. -CIA a sac secreted and lived in by an aquatic organism

ZOOGENIC adj caused by animals or their activities

ZOOGLEA n pl. -GLEAE or -GLEAS a jellylike mass of bacteria ZOOGLEAL adj

ZOOGLOEA n pl. -GLOEAE or -GLOEAS zooglea

ZOOID n pl. -S an organic cell or body capable of independent movement ZOOIDAL adj

ZOOKS interj — used as a mild oath

ZOOLATER n pl. -S one that worships animals

ZOOLATRY n pl. -TRIES the worship of animals

ZOOLOGY n pl. -GIES the science that deals with animals ZOOLOGIC adj

ZOOM v -ED, -ING, -S to move with a loud humming sound

ZOOMANIA n pl. -S an excessive interest in animals

ZOOMETRY n pl. -TRIES the measurement of animals or animal parts

ZOOMORPH n pl. -S something in the form of an animal

ZOON n pl. ZOA or ZOONS the whole product of one fertilized egg ZOONAL adj

ZOONOSIS n pl. -NOSES a disease that can be transmitted from animals to man ZOONOTIC adj

ZOOPHILE n pl. -S a lover of animals

ZOOPHILY n pl. -LIES a love of animals

ZOOPHOBE n pl. -S one who fears or hates animals

ZOOPHYTE n pl. -S an invertebrate animal

ZOOSPERM n pl. -S the male fertilizing element of an animal

ZOOSPORE n pl. -S a type of spore

ZOOTOMY n pl. -MIES the dissection of animals ZOOTOMIC adj

ZOOTY adj ZOOTIER, ZOOTIEST flashy in manner or style

ZORI n pl. ZORI or ZORIS a type of sandal

ZORIL n pl. -S a small African mammal

ZORILLA n pl. -S zoril

ZORILLE n pl. -S zoril

ZORILLO n pl. -LOS zoril

ZOSTER n pl. -S a virus disease

ZOUAVE n pl. -S a French infantryman

ZOUNDS interj — used as a mild oath

ZOWIE interj — used to express surprise or pleasure

ZOYSIA n pl. -S a perennial grass

ZUCCHINI n pl. -S a vegetable

ZWIEBACK n pl. -S a sweetened bread

ZYDECO n pl. -COS popular music of southern Louisiana

ZYGOID adj pertaining to a zygote

ZYGOMA n pl. -MAS or -MATA the cheekbone

ZYGOSIS n pl. -GOSES the union of two gametes ZYGOSE adj

ZYGOSITY n pl. -TIES the makeup of a particular zygote

ZYGOTE n pl. -S a cell formed by the union of two gametes ZYGOTIC adj

ZYGOTENE n pl. -S a stage in meiosis

ZYMASE n pl. -S an enzyme

ZYME n pl. -S an enzyme

ZYMOGEN n pl. -S a substance that develops into an enzyme when suitably activated

ZYMOGENE n pl. -S zymogen

ZYMOGRAM n pl. -S a record of separated proteins after electrophoresis

ZYMOLOGY n pl. -GIES the science of fermentation

ZYMOSAN n pl. -S an insoluble fraction of yeast cell walls

ZYMOSIS n pl. -MOSES fermentation ZYMOTIC adj

ZYMURGY n pl. -GIES a branch of chemistry dealing with fermentation

ZYZZYVA n pl. -S a tropical weevil